STRATEGIC HUMAN RESOURCE MANAGEMENT

SECOND EDITION

STRATEGIC HUMAN RESOURCE MANAGEMENT

WILLIAM P. ANTHONY
PAMELA L. PERREWÉ
K. MICHELE KACMAR
Florida State University

THE DRYDEN PRESS
Harcourt Brace College Publishers

Fort Worth   Philadelphia   San Diego   New York   Orlando   Austin   San Antonio
Toronto   Montreal   London   Sydney   Tokyo

Acquisitions Editor   **RUTH ROMINGER**
Developmental Editor   **DONA HIGHTOWER**
Project Editor   **MICHELE TOMIAK**
Production Manager   **EDDIE DAWSON**
Art and Design Supervisor   **BRIAN SALISBURY**
Permissions Editor   **ADELE KRAUSE**
Executive Product Manager   **LISÉ JOHNSON**
Marketing Coordinator   **SAM STUBBLEFIELD**

Copyeditor   **JANOEL LOWE**
Proofreader   **ROBERTA KIRCHHOFF**
Indexer   **EDWIN DURBIN**

Compositor   **GRAPHIC WORLD INC.**
Text Type   **10/12 TIMES ROMAN**

ABOUT THE COVER

We believe the image of an archer poised to hit the mark reflects today's need for a strategic aim in the direction an organization wants to go and how human resource management can play an integral part in that journey. Managers and HRM professionals must use their skills to manage human resources in a way that leads to organizational success through strategic planning, implementation, and evaluation. As the authors write in Chapter 1, "A change in strategy will determine the direction of each function within the organization, including the human resource management function."

Address for Editorial Correspondence
The Dryden Press, 301 Commerce Street, Suite 3700, Fort Worth, TX 76102

Address for Orders
The Dryden Press, 6277 Sea Harbor Drive, Orlando, FL 32887-6777
1-800-782-4479, or 1-800-433-0001 (in Florida)

ISBN: 0-03-012887-0

Library of Congress Catalog Number: 95-067703

Printed in the United States of America

5 6 7 8 9 0 1 2 3 4   048   9 8 7 6 5 4 3 2 1

The Dryden Press
Harcourt Brace College Publishers

To Roz, Cathie, and Sarah
To Frank, Erin, Jenny, Stephen, and Matthew
To Chuck

THE DRYDEN PRESS SERIES IN MANAGEMENT

Anthony, Perrewé, and Kacmar
Strategic Human Resource Management
Second Edition

Bartlett
Cases in Strategic Management for Business

Bereman and Lengnick-Hall, Mark
Compensation Decision Making: A Computer-Based Approach

Bourgeois
Strategic Management: From Concept to Implementation

Bracker, Montanari, and Morgan
Cases in Strategic Management

Brechner
Contemporary Mathematics for Business and Consumers

Calvasina and Barton
Chopstick Company: A Business Simulation

Costin
Readings in Total Quality Management

Costin
Managing in the Global Economy: The European Union

Costin
Management Development and Training: A TQM Approach

Czinkota, Ronkainen, and Moffett
International Business
Fourth Edition

Czinkota, Ronkainen, Moffett, and Moynihan
Global Business

Daft
Management
Third Edition

Daft
Understanding Management

Dessler
Managing Organizations in an Era of Change

Foegen
Business Plan Guidebook
Revised Edition

Gatewood and Feild
Human Resource Selection
Third Edition

Gold
Exploring Organizational Behavior: Readings, Cases, Experiences

Greenhaus Callanan
Career Management
Second Edition

Harris and DeSimone
Human Resource Development

Higgins and Vincze
Strategic Management: Text and Cases
Fifth Edition

Hills, Bergmann, and Scarpello
Compensation Decision Making
Second Edition

Hodgetts
Modern Human Relations at Work
Sixth Edition

Hodgetts and Kroeck
Personnel and Human Resource Management

Hodgetts and Kuratko
Effective Small Business Management
Fifth Edition

Holley and Jennings
The Labor Relations Process
Fifth Edition

Jauch and Coltrin
The Managerial Experience: Cases and Exercises
Sixth Edition

Kindler and Ginsburg
Strategic & Interpersonal Skill Building

Kirkpatrick and Lewis
Effective Supervision: Preparing for the 21st Century

Kuehl and Lambing
Small Business: Planning and Management
Third Edition

Kuratko and Hodgetts
Entrepreneurship: A Contemporary Approach
Third Edition

Kuratko and Welsch
Entrepreneurial Strategy: Text and Cases

Lengnick-Hall, Cynthia, and Hartman
Experiencing Quality

Lewis
Io Enterprises Simulation

Long and Arnold
The Power of Environmental Partnerships

McMullen and Long
Developing New Ventures: The Entrepreneurial Option

Matsuura
International Business: A New Era

Montanari, Morgan, and Bracker
Strategic Management: A Choice Approach

Morgan
Managing for Success

Northcraft and Neale
Organizational Behavior: A Management Challenge
Second Edition

Penderghast
Entrepreneurial Simulation Program

Ryan, Eckert, and Ray
Small Business: An Entrepreneur's Plan
Fourth Edition

Sandburg
Career Design Software

Vecchio
Organizational Behavior
Third Edition

Walton
Corporate Encounters: Law, Ethics, and the Business Environment

Zikmund
Business Research Methods
Fourth Edition

THE HARCOURT BRACE COLLEGE OUTLINE SERIES

Pentico
Management Science

Pierson
Introduction to Business Information Systems

Sigband
Business Communication

PREFACE

Few of you who read this textbook will actually become human resource managers in organizations, but most of you will (at some point in your career) manage a group of people. Also, some of you will be in a position to influence your organization's human resource policy significantly, even if you are not in your firm's human resource department. Of course, no matter where you are in the organization, you will be affected by your organization's human resource policy simply because you are a member of that organization.

The bulk of this textbook examines the formulation and implementation of human resource policy at the *strategic* level. In other words, we are most concerned with the major aspects of how an organization deals with its people—how it acquires them, utilizes them, rewards them, and separates them. We are concerned with the interplay of the human resource department and line managers as strategic decisions are made and implemented on human resource acquisition and use in organizations. We are also concerned with how strategic human resource decisions interplay with the overall strategic decisions an organization makes.

The book examines typical functions in human resources such as recruitment, selection, training, rewarding (wage and salary analysis), and so on, but it does so from a strategic perspective. Specifically, it explores how these functions integrate with the overall strategy of the firm in order for the firm to become more effective and efficient—in short, more competitive.

IMPROVEMENTS TO THE SECOND EDITION

- A **marginal glossary** has been added to increase understanding and comprehension of key strategic human resource management (HRM) concepts.
- Updated or entirely **new cases** at the beginning and end of each chapter and at the end of the book. More human resource material is built into each case, especially those at the end of the book.
- **Ethics** is integrated into each chapter, both within the chapter and in the "Focus on Ethics and Social Responsibility" boxes.
- **Internationalization** is also integrated within each chapter and the "Focus on International Issues" and "HR Challenge" boxes.

- **Emphasis on small business** has also been added by including small business examples and cases.
- The most **current information** on the following concepts has been added: NAFTA and GATT, change and diversity, information systems, total quality management, the new national health-care plan and the way it relates to companies, workplace violence, discrimination in the workplace, leadership, improving productivity, outsourcing, managing an OSHA inspection, the virtual organization, and cross training.

FEATURES

The textbook relies heavily on actual case examples of human resource strategies and practices of organizations. Not only are these examples used liberally in each chapter, each chapter also begins and ends with an actual case of an organization's strategies. The last part of the textbook is devoted to a compendium of comprehensive cases showing how specific companies integrate their human resource strategy with their overall corporate strategy. The cases are integral to this textbook and make the study of strategy come alive. In this edition, many new cases have been added, and all remaining cases have been significantly updated.

Part of the method of strategic analysis is case problem solving. The cases used throughout and at the end of the book have the most value when you try to analyze the situations and suggest courses of action. By applying the concepts discussed in the textbook to case analyses, you will see their relevance in actual organizational situations.

The cases used throughout this book ask you to identify current and potential problems and issues and to formulate strategies for their resolution. This requires that you take a problem- or issue-solving approach to *apply* material in this text. The cases revolve around real organizations you will most likely recognize. They have real human resource problems and challenges. You will need to be both reactive and proactive in examining these cases. Some companies that are included have readily apparent current human resource problems needing immediate solutions. We included other companies because their cases demonstrate good examples of typical human resource policy: They may have few obvious human resource problems at the moment, but problems could be developing on the horizon.

The cases at the end of each chapter are relatively short and are followed by a few questions to guide you in analyzing the cases, using the material covered in the chapter. In reviewing these cases, you will see very few "hard" right or wrong answers to the questions. Be concerned with examining both the overall strategies as well as the human resource strategies involved in each case. Try to determine how well each type of strategy is working and whether the human resource strategy seems to be meshing well with both overall strategy and other functional strategies. Ask yourself what you could do if you were in a position to change things. The cases at the end of the book are comprehensive and require you to integrate the material covered throughout the text in order to analyze them successfully.

The textbook contains several examples in each chapter of primary issues currently confronting human resource strategists. "Focus On" boxes provide insight into the ways companies and their human resource departments deal with international concerns, ethical concerns, and management of today's culturally diverse workforce. "HR Challenge" boxes offer insight into the ways different organizations deal with the challenges presented to them on a day-to-day basis.

Another special feature of the book is its use of management applications. For example, to highlight how any manager, human resource or otherwise, can have an impact on the practices of the human resource function, the summaries at the end of each chapter are provided in the form of "Management Guidelines." These guidelines summarize the key ideas presented in the chapter, but they are restated in the form of guidelines or admonitions for management action.

PLAN OF THE BOOK

As shown in the accompanying figure, the textbook is organized into six parts. Part One examines the concept of organizational strategy and how it relates to an organization's human resources. We begin in Chapter 1 by examining the strategic approach to human resource management. An overview of the strategic approach, a historical perspective of human resource management, and a discussion of how these two concepts can be integrated are provided. In Chapter 2 we examine the global and external environments of the organization and their impact on corporate and human resource strategy.

The formulation of corporate and human resource strategies is the subject of Chapter 3. The strategy formulation process is discussed, along with an examination of specific types of strategies.

Part Two focuses on the ways organizations acquire and place people. Legal issues such as equal employment, sexual harassment, and managing a diverse workforce are covered in Chapter 4. Chapter 5 discusses job analysis in light of determining job requirements. Chapter 6 focuses on the human resource planning, staffing, and information functions. It deals with planning for the appropriate number and type of employees needed by the organization. Chapter 7 then examines how to obtain these employees through strategic recruiting and selection methods.

Next we move to Part Three, "Strategies for Maximizing Human Resource Productivity." Assuming that the employees have been hired and placed, we are now interested in maximizing their productivity. First, Chapter 8 looks at job design. Then Chapter 9 looks at socialization and training and development methods. Chapter 10 takes a look at how performance appraisal can be used to develop employees and make them more productive. Providing fair and equitable monetary and other rewards that encourage desired performance is the subject of Chapter 11. Chapter 12 examines Total Quality Management and productivity improvement.

In Part Four we examine ways of maintaining human resources in the organization. We begin in Chapter 13 by discussing various benefit programs available today for organizations. Chapter 14 looks at health, safety, and stress in today's organizations. Ethics, employee rights, and employer responsibilities are the subject of Chapter 15. Dealing with troubled employees, a major issue today for many organizations, is a major focus of this chapter. Chapter 16 examines unions and collective bargaining.

In Part Five, Chapter 17 focuses on strategies for restructuring or retrenching organizations. Particular emphasis is placed on layoff and termination strategies.

The book concludes with Part Six, a series of comprehensive cases that explain a variety of strategic human resource issues of actual organizations. The emphasis is on applying the ideas learned throughout the book in examining real-world organizational issues.

SUPPORT MATERIALS

The Dryden Press will provide complimentary supplements or supplement packages to those adopters qualified under our adoption policy. Please contact your sales representative to learn how you may qualify. If as

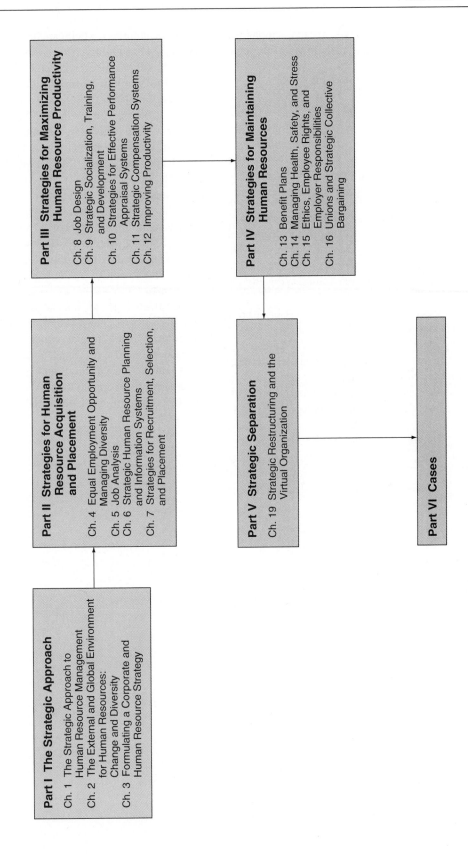

Part I The Strategic Approach

Ch. 1 The Strategic Approach to Human Resource Management
Ch. 2 The External and Global Environment for Human Resources: Change and Diversity
Ch. 3 Formulating a Corporate and Human Resource Strategy

Part II Strategies for Human Resource Acquisition and Placement

Ch. 4 Equal Employment Opportunity and Managing Diversity
Ch. 5 Job Analysis
Ch. 6 Strategic Human Resource Planning and Information Systems
Ch. 7 Strategies for Recruitment, Selection, and Placement

Part III Strategies for Maximizing Human Resource Productivity

Ch. 8 Job Design
Ch. 9 Strategic Socialization, Training, and Development
Ch. 10 Strategies for Effective Performance Appraisal Systems
Ch. 11 Strategic Compensation Systems
Ch. 12 Improving Productivity

Part IV Strategies for Maintaining Human Resources

Ch. 13 Benefit Plans
Ch. 14 Managing Health, Safety, and Stress
Ch. 15 Ethics, Employee Rights, and Employer Responsibilities
Ch. 16 Unions and Strategic Collective Bargaining

Part V Strategic Separation

Ch. 19 Strategic Restructuring and the Virtual Organization

Part VI Cases

an adopter or potential user you receive supplements you do not need, please return them to your sales representative or send them to:

Attn: Returns Department
Troy Warehouse
465 South Lincoln Drive
Troy, MO 63379

ACKNOWLEDGMENTS

We would like to thank all those individuals who were involved in the first edition of this book as well as the following individuals who assisted in the second edition: Robert Bennett, Dr. Dawn Carlson, Dr. Don Daake, Maribel Estrada, Charles Fornaciari, Fred Schmidt, Dr. Matt Valle, Angela Young, and Kelly Zollars.

We are especially grateful to the professors who reviewed the manuscript throughout its various stages for the first and second editions: Matthew M. Amano, Oregon State University; Brendan D. Bannister, Northeastern University; Nathan Bennett, Louisiana State University; Linda Bleicken, Georgia Southern University; David E. Bowen, Arizona State University West; Anthony F. Campagna, Ohio State University; Gerald E. Calvasina, University of North Carolina–Charlotte; Stephen J. Carroll, University of Maryland, College Park; Jeffrey G. Covin, Georgia Institute of Technology; Joseph H. Culver, University of Texas at Austin; Karen J. Cummings, Michigan State University; Dan R. Dalton, Indiana University; Thomas G. Gutteridge, Southern Illinois University at Carbondale; Ken Jennings, University of North Florida; Thomas H. Jerdee, University of North Carolina at Chapel Hill; Vicki S. Kaman, Colorado State University; Matthew C. Lane, Portland State University; Elaine Lemay, Colorado State University; Robert C. Liden, University of Illinois at Chicago; Marjorie L. McInerney, Marshall University; Michael T. Quinn, California State University, Long Beach; Marcus Hart Sandver, Ohio State University; Sid Siegel, Drexel University; Scott A. Snell, Pennsylvania State University; David Tansik, University of Arizona; Mark A. Wesolowski, Miami University; Donna Wiley, California State University–Hayward; and Arthur Yeung, San Francisco State University.

Our thanks go to our acquisitions editor, Ruth Rominger; developmental editor, Dona Hightower; project editor, Michele Tomiak; production manager, Eddie Dawson; text and art designer, Brian Salisbury; permissions editor, Adele Krause; and others who helped in the process. Even though we have been aided greatly by this help, any errors of commission or omission rest with us.

WPA
PLP
KMK
Tallahassee, Florida

CONTENTS

PART FIVE
Strategic Separation   631

PART SIX
Cases   679

PART ONE
THE STRATEGIC APPROACH

CHAPTER 1

THE STRATEGIC APPROACH TO HUMAN RESOURCE MANAGEMENT

The environment within which an organization operates is dynamic. External and internal forces are constantly changing the rules of the game, and the organization must amend or adopt new strategies to remain competitive. A change in strategy will determine the direction of each function within the organization, including the human resource management function. This chapter examines the definition of strategy and explores the history and practice of human resources management. The major goals are to lay the foundation for the way these two concepts interrelate and to demonstrate that in today's complex business environment, a strategic approach to human resources management is a necessity.

CHAPTER OBJECTIVES

As a result of studying this chapter, you should be able to

1. Define the concept of strategy and explain the basics of the strategy formulation process.
2. Distinguish the strategic approach to human resources from the traditional functional approach.
3. Explain the relationship of decision making to the strategy formulation process.
4. Understand the decision-making process in organizations and the reasons that human resources management should be an integral part of the process.
5. Explain the environment–organization link and the strategic approach.
6. Explain the relationship of human resource strategy with overall organizational strategy and functional strategy.
7. Understand the history and evolution of the field of human resources.

GM SHRINKS AND REBOUNDS

On April 22, 1988, General Motors Corporation announced a strategic retreat that significantly shrank the largest industrial company in the world for the first time in its 80-year history. GM placed itself on a corporate crash diet in an effort to shed both factories and workers in order to stop its falling net income. It made a similar announcement on December 18, 1991, when it reported plans to close 21 of its plants and eliminate 74,000 jobs in four years, 9,000 of which would be white-collar positions. By 1995, this downsizing was having positive results.

GM once claimed almost 50 percent of the U.S. auto market. By 1992 that share had fallen to 33 percent (see Exhibit 1.1), largely due to the increased sales of imports, Fords, and Chryslers. To match its sales, it reduced car production capacity. Unlike the past, when plant closings and employee layoffs were a regular part of the business cycle, these changes are not temporary. Rather, they represent a major downsizing that resulted in a considerable restructuring of the firm.

The downsizing or retrenchment began in 1988 and is expected to continue through 1995. During this period, nearly every Japanese automaker is expected to open a new full-scale plant in the United States. While GM eventually hopes to regain its market share, the move indicates that the company anticipates an overcapacity in the North American car market, at least in the foreseeable future.

In December 1992, General Motors was in the midst of this continuing corporate trauma of historic proportions. It had 44 percent of the U.S. car-making capacity, but sales had dropped to 32 percent of the market.[1] To bring the two figures into line, the company planned to close 23 additional plants, cutting at least 74,000 jobs (50,000 hourly and 24,000 salaried workers). It had to carry out a formidable internal restructuring while fending off increasing competition at home, a downturn in foreign car markets, and pressure from the United Auto Workers (UAW).

GM's plants were badly underutilized, running at close to 65 percent of capacity in 1993. Part of the solution lay in condensing the operations by 1994 from three plants running short schedules to two plants running full schedules and eventually eliminating $150 million a year in labor costs plus the cost of one of the plant's operations and equipment.[2]

Although GM's former chairman, Roger Smith, had previously maintained that the carmaker's market-share drop was temporary, GM's strategic retreat suggested that it shared the belief Ford Motor Company held in 1981 when it went through a similar retrenchment to adjust to a lower market share.

The company set a goal for 1995 to operate at close to 100 percent of its capacity with all plants running two shifts a day, five days a week. As of this writing, however, this goal appears unattainable. GM has not been at the 100 percent level since spring 1984. In the 1985–1988 period, the company varied its strategy from producing all the cars it could to running several plants below capacity for periods of time. In between, the company offered deep discounting with low financing and cash-back offers to clear its oversupply of cars. In addition, GM missed its third quarter 1992 production quota by 95,000 vehicles because of widespread problems in its factories. Working with a mandate from senior management, GM simplified the structure of the company's North American Operations, slashed the corporate staff, pared product offerings, and began a sell-off of the company's parts operations.

EXHIBIT 1.1

GM's Total Profit and Market Share: Annual Unit Sales as a Percentage of U.S. New Car Market

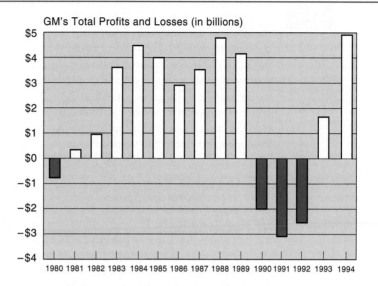

GM's Total Profits and Losses (in billions)

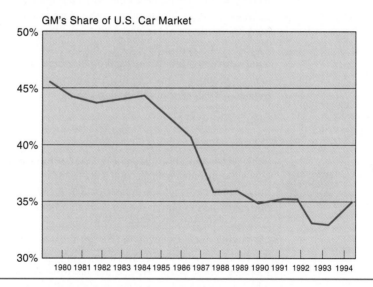

GM's Share of U.S. Car Market

Many have blamed Roger Smith for the lack of vision that resulted in the lagging GM market share and inconsistent production strategy. They believe that GM should have taken steps to downsize years earlier when it became apparent that imports would maintain a strong, permanent share of the market instead of continually denying their existence. Some even argue that the proposed cuts are not enough to make GM fully cost competitive in the global industry.

The possibility of closing plants is a very sensitive subject for employees and the UAW, especially because the fall 1987 labor agreement was sold to its members based on increased job security. The head of the UAW GM department believed the strategy to close plants was a "loser."

By mid-1995, morale at GM's 36 assembly plants was said to be at an all-time low due to poor year-end bonuses and concerns about job security.

GM followed a similar entrenchment strategy in Europe during the mid-1980s. This resulted in a profit of $1.88 billion in 1987 over a loss of $568 million in 1986 in European operations. It appears that the retrenchment in North America has produced a similar badly needed financial reversal. In the first quarter of 1995, GM made $1.1 billion in profits, continuing the trend started in late 1993. 1995 profits were attributed to higher volume, improved productivity, and continued cost cutting.[3]

By gearing its capacity to the low end of the business cycle, GM is following a similar retrenchment strategy instituted earlier by Ford. Since Ford permanently reduced capacity in 1981, it has run plants overtime, added third shifts, or increased production efficiencies to meet increased demand.

HUMAN RESOURCE CHANGES

Even with its revised cost-cutting plan, General Motors Corporation (jointly with the UAW) has contributed $805 million to educate, train, and retrain its working and laid-off employees. This is a new way of doing business for GM. In the past, managers competed fiercely with one another, concentrating on their individual departments while ignoring the difficulties blue-collar workers and other departments might be having. But this is all changing. With the realization that personnel, not technology, is its most important commodity with regard to the bottom line, the company is working hard to replace its old image with one of teamwork and unity. GM is striving for a winning team spirit in hope that this will lead to better productivity, an improved competitive position in the marketplace, and, eventually, higher profits, more jobs, and job security. Consequently, GM hopes ultimately to recapture what it once owned—50 percent of the market share.

SATURN

One of GM's brightest hopes for recapturing its markets share is its newest division. GM's Saturn facility in Spring Hill, Tennessee, has a specific competitive goal: to build better cars than the Japanese. Saturn, estimated to have cost $3.5 billion to bring on line, is taking aim at the imports and plans to sell over 80 percent of its cars to customers who had intended to buy an import. Because fewer than 5 percent of the car-buying market knew what Saturn is all about, Saturn officials say that generating awareness was the first objective in its early advertising; they planned to do this by focusing on the people behind the car. Most of Saturn's workforce, 20 percent of which is composed of women, was recruited and screened from UAW locals in 38 states and has given up future options to ever work at another GM division. The workers have a shop-floor average salary of $34,000, with 20 percent of that dependent on company profits, productivity, and car quality. In addition, each worker is eligible for a bonus for beating targeted production goals.

Saturn is breaking ground in four new areas: (1) as a partnership between management and the UAW; (2) through its franchise agreements with dealers giving them rights to establish multiple outlets over larger-than-average territories; (3) as an integrated manufacturing complex; and (4) through its emphasis on teamwork, both internally with Saturn's employees and externally with Saturn's suppliers.

Saturn sales opened weak across the country with fewer than 100,000 cars sold in 1991. Despite production restraints, Saturn sold 170,495 cars in the 1992 model year that ended September 30, 1992, a 236 percent increase over its first-year sales in

1991, for a 2.1 percent share of the U.S. car market.[4] In the first eight months of 1992, Saturn sold almost 130,000 cars—three times as many as it did in the same period of 1991. It hopes to produce 360,000 a year by the end of 1995.[5] By 1998, GM expects to introduce a new model every 29 days.[6]

DEVELOPING ACCOUNTABILITY IN THE WORKER

Change of this magnitude will require a skilled, flexible workforce. GM hopes to help employees acquire the new skills, knowledge, and abilities needed for product improvement through education, training, and retraining programs. Approximately 10 percent of former laid-off workers (5,000) have been retrained and placed in new jobs with other companies. Almost all currently employed workers went through some type of program at their local GM plant. GM is making this possible by allowing employees to attend classes on a regular basis during company time. However, as illustrated in this case, such sobering times as these in GM's recent past call for employees to account for how they contribute to company performance. Top managers at GM and at other organizations now view humans as a strategic resource and, like it or not, are compelled to insist on their active contribution to future success.

Despite the low morale in 1995 noted earlier, worker accountability programs appeared to succeed by mid-1995 in propelling GM's quality ratings ahead of both Ford Motor Company and Chrysler Corporation.[7]

General Motors had to make some tough strategic choices that were harmful in some respects to certain segments of the organization. GM's chosen strategy of retrenchment has proven largely successful and, once again, the corporate giant is charting excellent performance. This case suggests, however, that a strategic decision impacts the multiple functions of the corporation, even at the lowest levels. The functional area of human resources was most dramatically impacted because GM had to increase the number of workers transferred to other plants, slow the rate of hiring, reduce overtime pay, increase the numbers of terminations and layoffs, improve training and retraining efforts, and insist on accountability and contribution to measurable performance standards. Though these changes seemed harsh and dire at the time, the case notes that retrenchment has bolstered GM's chances for long-term future success.

STRATEGIC CHOICES

When managers, such as those at GM, are faced with deciding which corporate strategy they should embark upon, they must make several decisions. The following is only a partial list of some of the strategic choices managers face.

1. Routinely managers must evaluate where they are. They must decide if they should remain with the strategy they have selected and implemented or if they need a new strategy.
2. To make this decision, managers must know exactly what has and hasn't changed since the current strategic approach was implemented. For example, has the economy changed dramatically in any way that may influence whether or not the selected strategy will continue to be effective?
3. If any changes are suggested, it is important that managers understand the ripple effects these changes may have on other functions. For example, if a growth strategy

is selected, will the human resources unit be able to provide the qualified personnel needed to develop this strategy?

4. Finally, managers should try to evaluate the current approach and what any changes to this approach might have on what their competitors do. For example, if GM offers a low financing rate, is Chrysler or Ford in a position to offer an even lower rate, thereby making GM's offer unattractive?

THE STRATEGIC APPROACH

Chances are that you have encountered, or soon will encounter, the strategic approach in your course of studies. It is used in marketing, finance, and information systems courses and serves as the heart of the capstone course in most business programs: the policy course. Not until recently, however, has it been widely used as an approach to human resource/personnel management.

Even though you will not likely become a personnel manager in a firm, you will very likely manage human resources if the position you take gives you some authority over other employees. Even if this does not happen, you will be affected by the human resource decisions made in your firm. You will also have the occasion to ask the human resource unit for advice on hiring, pay increases, discipline, discharge, and other personnel-related issues.

STRATEGY DEFINED

A strategy is a way of doing something. It is a game plan for action. It usually includes the formulation of a goal and a set of action plans for accomplishment. It implies consideration of the competitive forces at work in managing an organization and the impact of the outside environment on organization actions.

While managers have probably managed strategically for many years, the strategic approach is relatively new to management literature. The concept of strategy has its roots in military literature, particularly that developed by the Chinese strategist Sun Tzu.[8] However, Alfred Chandler's work, *Strategy and Structure,* as well as the development of management by objectives (MBO), set the stage for the present-day popularity of the strategic focus in business and management books.[9]

Management by objectives (MBO) has been popular in business writings since the mid-1950s when it first was used by Peter Drucker in his classic *The Practice of Management.*[10] MBO essentially involves three steps: setting a mission or purpose, setting goals or objectives, and determining action plans to achieve the goals or objectives.

The strategic focus accepts these three basic ideas of MBO but goes beyond them by giving explicit recognition to both the outside and competitive environments. The actions and reactions of competition are the heart of the modern approach to strategy. Two popular works of Michael Porter, *Competitive Strategy* and *Competitive Advantage,* no doubt have enhanced this competitive focus.[11] These two books examine how strategy can be used to obtain competitive advantage and have been widely read and referred to by people in both academic institutions and businesses.

For our purpose, we define **strategy** as *the formulation of organizational missions, goals and objectives, as well as action plans for achievement, that explicitly recognize the competition and the impact of outside environmental forces.*

Before we can clearly see how strategy formulation impacts the human resource function of an organization, we must first understand what human resources in an organization is all about. The following section provides a brief overview of the duties that are in-

STRATEGY
The formulation of organizational missions, goals, and objectives, as well as action plans for achievement, that explicitly recognize the competition and the impact of outside environmental forces.

volved in human resources management, a historical look at the field of human resources, and an explanation of the popular functional approach to human resource management.

AN OVERVIEW OF HUMAN RESOURCE MANAGEMENT[12]

THE TASKS OF HUMAN RESOURCE MANAGEMENT

What sort of activities are included under the province of human resource management? As you will see, this text approaches human resource management as a fairly broad strategic duty performed by all managers rather than as a more narrowly defined, purely "staff" role played by professional HR managers. In simple terms, however, we can think of human resource management as a variety of tasks associated with acquiring, training, developing, motivating, organizing, and maintaining the human employees of the firm. Given our understanding of strategy, we might add that these tasks should be performed in a way that helps the company deal effectively with any environmental forces and ensures the company's long-term achievement of its goals and objectives.

Human resource managers and academics have debated for some time the point at which human resource management ends and other functional management begins. In 1989, the American Society for Training and Development (ASTD) determined the activities that professionals typically considered to be HR roles.[13] Among those roles listed were personnel selection and staffing, human resource planning, organization and job design, career development, organization development, training and development, research and information, labor relations, employee assistance and support, and compensation and benefits administration. Much of this textbook is dedicated to the discussion of these duties and how each should be performed within a strategic framework. In today's complex business environment, strategy formulation and implementation may be the most important duties performed by managers. Later in this chapter, we discuss how this important function is performed, but first let's review how the HR function developed into the multifaceted set of tasks defined by the ASTD's survey.

THE DEVELOPMENT OF HUMAN RESOURCE MANAGEMENT

THE CRAFT SYSTEM

People who worked during the 1600s to 1700s were guided by a craft system. Under this system, the production of goods and services was generated by small groups of workers in relatively small workplaces, usually in a home. The work was customized and supervised by a master craftsman. Each master craftsman had several apprentices and journeymen who actually performed the work. When the craftsman retired, the most senior journeyman normally replaced him or her. There was no confusion about career paths and no disputes over wages. This system held for more than 200 years.

As demand for products increased, the craft system could not keep up. Craftsmen had to hire more and more journeymen and apprentices, and the small workplace became more like a small factory. At the same time, machines were being introduced that could be used to help produce high-quality products much faster than could experienced craftsmen. These changes helped usher in the Industrial Revolution.

SCIENTIFIC MANAGEMENT

In the early 1900s, many changes occurred in the workplace. Machines and factory methods that increased production were introduced. However, with this increased production came several problems. Since the machines required several people to operate them, the number of workers increased dramatically. This forced managers to develop rules, regulations, and procedures to control the workers. Some of the regulations required an increase in job specialization, which led to boring, monotonous jobs. Specialization also allowed managers the ability to replace quickly and economically any worker who demanded too much or caused a problem. One of the most significant developments that arose during this time was a process called *scientific management.*

The premise of scientific management is that there is one best way to do a job. This one best way will be the cheapest, fastest, and most efficient way to perform the task. The process may not be the safest or the most humane, but it will allow the company to make the most profit. Frederick Taylor, the father of scientific management, spent his career collecting data and analyzing the specific motions required to perform various jobs. He then broke the job into specific tasks and refined the motions needed to complete them until the tasks could be refined no more. He then selected, trained, and closely monitored workers who performed the tasks. Those workers who were successful (that is, those who followed the orders of management exactly and by doing so significantly increased their production) earned a great deal of money. Those who were not successful were terminated.

Although scientific management did prove to be an effective management tool that increased the productivity of workers, it was criticized for treating the worker as a tool, and not as a person. To compensate for this tendency to depersonalize the work environment, welfare secretaries were hired. People in these positions oversaw programs for the welfare of the employees, such as the installation of libraries and recreational facilities, financial assistance programs, and medical and health programs. The welfare programs were the forerunner of modern-day benefit packages, and the welfare secretary position was the forerunner of the current-day human resource manager.

HUMAN RELATIONS

The next significant step in the development of human resources occurred in the late 1920s and early 1930s: the Hawthorne studies. Elton Mayo and Fritz Roethlisberger were asked by Western Electric to determine what could be done to increase the productivity of workers at the Hawthorne Works plant in Chicago. While the researchers were specifically examining the effect that lighting had on productivity, their results really had nothing to do with lighting. What they concluded was that the human interaction and attention paid to the workers by the researchers caused their productivity to increase. This finding was the first one to indicate that the social factors in a work environment could have a significant effect on the productivity of workers.

Fueled by the findings of the Hawthorne studies, further research on social factors and how individuals respond to them was undertaken. Results from these studies indicated that the needs of employees must be understood and acted upon by management in order for a worker to be satisfied and productive. Communication between the worker and his or her superior was stressed as was the need for a more participative workplace atmosphere. More often than not, however, these tactics did little to increase a worker's productivity. The idea that a happy worker is a productive worker failed to be proven, and many of the concepts were modified or abandoned. It is interesting to note that the focus of the human relations era is now the backbone of more recent employee involvement programs that have been found to increase the productivity of workers and increase the profits of companies that adopt them.

BEHAVIORAL SCIENCE

Expanding on the human relations school of thought of including academic findings from various other disciplines such as psychology, political science, sociology, and biology, the behavioral science era was born. Behavioral science focuses more on the total organization and less on the individual. It examines how the workplace affects the individual worker and how the individual worker affects the workplace. Many believe that the modern-day fields of organizational behavior (OB), the study of employee behavior in the organization; organizational development (OD), the process of changing employee and organizational attitudes and beliefs; and human resource management (HRM) grew out of the behavioral science era.

THE HUMAN RESOURCE FUNCTION

As noted, in the early years companies set up welfare secretaries whose job was to keep track of employees' welfare. Through the years, the welfare secretaries' job encompassed more and more duties. As laws were passed that restricted the rights of employers and employees, the welfare secretaries were required to stay informed and determine what impact those laws would have on the organization. The employees in these positions also were required to keep files about employees, maintain payroll systems, and counsel employees. As more and more tasks were delegated to the welfare secretaries, offshoots began to form. One group of welfare secretaries took responsibility for payroll duties, setting wages, and determining raises. A second group focused on hiring and training workers, and yet another concentrated on working with the union to negotiate an acceptable contract. Each of these offshoots eventually became a function of the human resources unit.

So the human resources functional unit has evolved and is now responsible for a large, complex array of duties related not only to the company and the employees but also to the government and other entities from the external environment. What do these units look like today? What do companies want from their HR professionals? Exhibit 1.2 gives us some insight into the answers to these questions. A recent ad in *The Wall Street Journal* demonstrates the enormous importance of the human resources function to a company's fortunes. The ad was placed by a Florida company looking for a vice-president of human resources. The requirements cited by the company point to

EXHIBIT 1.2   **The Requirements for HR Professionals Today**

Vice-President
Human Resources

Florida-based services business of Fortune 500 company is seeking experienced, business-oriented, HR professional to lead the growth and development of the organization as a key member of the management team.

Responsibilities include managing all aspects of Human Resources function for a large, multilocation operation.

We require a Bachelor's degree in Business (MBA or MA preferred), along with 10-15 years of progressively responsible experience in compensation, labor relations, recruitment/staffing, employee benefits, and organization development. Experience should include working in a TQM and teaming environment. Strong communication and leadership skills a must.

Please send your resume with salary history.

SOURCE: Adapted from an advertisement in *The Wall Street Journal.*

the central importance of the position. First, the chief personnel officer of this company, and of most larger companies, is given the title of vice-president. The leader of the human resources function is a key member of senior management and probably plays a large part in setting corporate strategy and making major decisions. Additional evidence of the position's lofty status and responsibility relates to the requirement of 10 to 15 years of "progressively responsible experience." The list of responsibilities includes all of the human resources functions, thus making the job a highly diversified, comprehensive management position. In fact, the recruiters seem to be looking for someone with many of the same qualities and characteristics of today's chief executive officer (CEO). The ad requests someone with extensive experience in working in team settings, strong communication abilities, and highly developed leadership skills. The welfare secretary of old would certainly be surprised at the evolution of this position!

THE STRATEGIC APPROACH TO HUMAN RESOURCE MANAGEMENT

The strategic approach to human resource management applies the concept of strategy to managing a firm's human resources. This approach has six key elements as shown in Exhibit 1.3. Let's look at each of these.

RECOGNITION OF THE IMPACT OF THE OUTSIDE ENVIRONMENT

The outside environment presents a set of opportunities and threats to the organization in the form of laws, economic conditions, social and demographic changes, domestic and international political forces, technology, and so on. Strategic human resource strategy explicitly recognizes the threats and opportunities in each area and attempts to capitalize on the opportunities while minimizing or deflecting the effect of threats. For example, GM's strategic decision to open its Saturn plant in Spring Hill, Tennessee, was made only after serious consideration of the potential threat posed by the lack of experienced, qualified technical workers in the area. Top managers, working in close cooperation with human resources experts, had to determine that the company's internal ability to recruit, train, and transfer valuable employees would be strong enough to offset this potential external threat. Decision makers in this situation were also faced with the question of labor availability in the years to come. In other words, success could be achieved only if managers developed ways to deal with the external environment.

EXHIBIT 1.3	**Characteristics of a Strategic Approach to Human Resource Management**

HUMAN RESOURCE STRATEGY

- Explicitly recognizes the impact of the outside environment.
- Explicitly recognizes the impact of competition and the dynamics of the labor market.
- Has a long-range focus (three to five years).
- Focuses on the issue of choice and decision making.
- Considers all personnel, not just hourly or operational employees.
- Is integrated with overall corporate strategy and functional strategies.

RECOGNITION OF THE IMPACT OF COMPETITION AND THE DYNAMICS OF THE LABOR MARKET

Employers compete for employees just as they do for customers. The forces of competition in attracting, rewarding, and using employees has a major effect on corporate human resource strategy. Forces play out in both local, regional, and national labor markets. The joint GM–Toyota venture, New United Motors Manufacturing, Inc. (NUMMI), through its construction of a plant in Fremont, California, had a major effect on and was very much affected by the local labor market in its area. Labor market dynamics of wage rates, unemployment rates, working conditions, benefit levels, minimum wage legislation, and competitor reputation all have an impact on and are affected by strategic human resource decisions.

LONG-RANGE FOCUS

A strategic focus tends to set the long-range direction of a company's human resource style and basic approach. Strategy can be changed but it is not always easy. It depends on the inertia, flexibility, and management philosophy of the firm. The intent, however, is to develop a consistent strategy to guide the firm into its future. Sometimes the word vision is used to capture this idea.

CHOICE AND DECISION-MAKING FOCUS

Strategy implies choosing among alternatives. It implies making major decisions about human resources—decisions that commit the organization's resources toward a particular direction. For example, when Ford established its management-labor worker participation program in the mid-1980s, it did so because of a major decision to increase employee involvement. Of course, the fact that Nissan, Toyota, and other Japanese automakers had successfully used such programs for years probably served as part of the impetus to follow suit. Ford's strategy of employee involvement, based on its "Quality Is Job 1" campaign, was adopted because of a perceived need to resolve issues or prevent new ones from forming—specifically, to improve product quality.

In other words, strategy has a problem-solving or problem-preventing focus. Strategy concentrates on the question, "What should the organization do and why?" This action orientation requires that decisions be made and carried out.

CONSIDERATION OF ALL PERSONNEL

A strategic approach to human resources is concerned with *all* of the firm's employees, not just its hourly or operational personnel. Traditionally, human resource management focuses on hourly employees, with most clerical exempt employees also included. However, as the province of human resource management has broadened, the focus today, at least from a strategic perspective, is on all employees—from top-level management to unskilled operative workers. Consequently, we are just as much concerned with executive pay and benefit plans as we are with hourly wages. We are just as interested in top management's wage and benefit package as we are that of hourly union members in the plant. We want to examine management development and training as well as hourly skill training programs.

INTEGRATION WITH CORPORATE STRATEGY

The particular human resource strategy adopted by a firm should be integrated with the firm's corporate strategy. In other words, corporate strategy should drive human resource strategy. Tom Kelley, former chairman of the American Society of Personnel Administrators' Board of Directors (now the Society of Human Resource Management), remarked that human resource managers "are involved in the strategic planning of global issues, rather than the day-to-day personnel transactions of the previous personnel administrators . . . [and] along with that strategic planning process, it is imperative that the Human Resource Professional establish goals and objectives that support the corporate goals."[14]

If corporate strategy is to grow and dominate a market, such as Apple Computer's strategy in the early 1980s or Intel's in the 1990s, then human resource strategy should focus on the rapid acquisition and placement of employees. If retrenchment is the strategy, as was shown in the GM case at the beginning of the chapter, then no or low hiring plus layoff and termination of employees is the strategy. Exhibit 1.4 summarizes some key overall strategies and the associated human resource applications that demonstrate this concept.

SYNERGY
The extra benefit or value realized when resources have been combined and coordinated effectively.

ECONOMIES OF SCOPE
The concept of synergy that makes the combined whole of the company (or companies) more valuable than the sum of its parts.

The key idea behind overall strategic management is to coordinate all of the company's resources, including human resources, in such a way that everything a company does contributes to carrying out its strategy. If all the resources are integrated within an overall, appropriate strategy, additional value to the company is generated by the effective combination of integrated forces. There is no counterproductivity, and everything works together in the firm's chosen direction. Excellent coordination and combination of functions often result in a very special phenomenon known as **synergy,** the extra benefit or value realized when resources have been combined and coordinated effectively. This concept, often referred to as **economies of scope,** makes the combined whole of the company (or companies) more valuable than the sum of its parts. It is a true benefit of good strategic management of resources.

EXHIBIT 1.4	**Examples of Organizational Strategies and Associated Human Resource Strategies**

CORPORATE STRATEGY	EXAMPLE	HUMAN RESOURCE STRATEGIES
Retrenchment (cost reduction)	GM	Layoffs, Wage Reduction, Productivity Increases, Job Redesign, Renegotiated Labor Agreements
Growth	Intel	Aggressive Recruiting and Hiring, Rapidly Rising Wages, Job Creation, Expanding Training and Development
Renewal	Chrysler	Managed Turnover, Selective Layoff, Organizational Development, Transfer/Replacement, Productivity Increases, Employee Involvement
Niche Focus	Kentucky Fried Chicken	Specialized Job Creation, Elimination of Other Jobs, Specialized Training and Development
Acquisition	GE	Selective Layoffs, Transfers/Placement, Job Combinations, Orientation and Training, Managing Cultural Transitions

DIFFERENCES FROM TYPICAL FUNCTIONAL APPROACH TO PERSONNEL

The strategic management approach to human resources and the typical functional approach differ in many ways. As Leonard Schlesinger states, human resource management needs to get out of the "people business" and into the business of people.[15] In other words, human resource managers and other human resource professionals need to be full players on the management team.

Exhibit 1.5 enumerates the major differences between the strategic human resource approach and the traditional personnel management approach along six dimensions: planning, authority, scope, decision making, integration, and coordination. Basically, *the strategic human resource approach is involved in strategic planning and decision making and coordinates all human resource functions for all employees.* The approach vests more authority in the chief human resource officer in the organization. It also views the human resource function as an *integral part* of all corporate functions: marketing, production, finance, legal, and so on. The strategic human resource approach accepts the vice-president of human resources as an integral part of the management team. Exhibit 1.6 (on page 16) shows a typical organization chart that includes human resources in the top level of management and, by doing so, provides the human resource vice-president with the same authority as the other functional vice-presidents. Remember also our job announcement for a human resources vice-president on page 11. This person is an integral part of the overall strategy of the firm.

EXHIBIT 1.5 **Difference between Strategic Human Resource Approach and Traditional Personnel Approach**

DIMENSIONS	STRATEGIC HUMAN RESOURCE APPROACH	TRADITIONAL PERSONNEL MANAGEMENT APPROACH
Planning and Strategy Formulation	Participates in formulating overall organizational strategic plan and aligning human resource functions with company strategy	Is involved in operational planning only
Authority	Has high status and authority for top personnel officer (e.g., vice-president for Human Resources)	Has medium status and authority (e.g., personnel director)
Scope	Is concerned with all managers and employees	Is concerned primarily with hourly, operational, and clerical employees
Decision Making	Is involved in making strategic decisions	Makes operational decisions only
Integration	Is fully integrated with other organizational functions: marketing, finance, legal, production	Has moderate to small integration with other organizational functions
Coordination	Coordinates all human resource activities (e.g., training, recruitment, staffing, Equal Employment Opportunity)	Does not coordinate all human resource functions

EXHIBIT 1.6 **Departmental Structure for Human Resources**

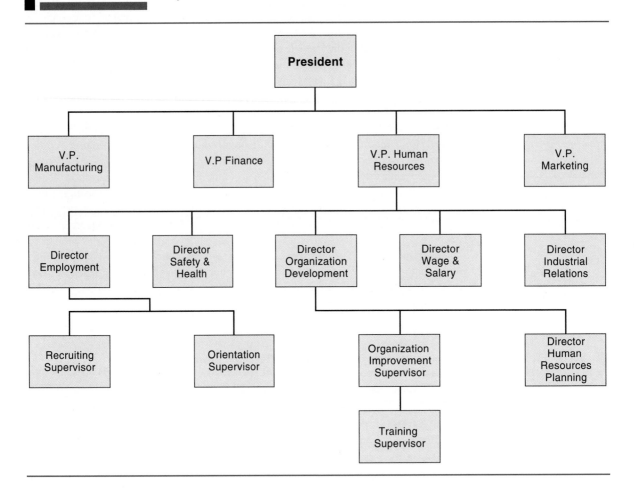

For the vice-president of human resources to have any significant impact on the corporation, however, he or she must be able to do several things. First, he or she must know when to delegate responsibility and when to remain involved. If a project warrants the top person's input, then the vice-president should remain involved. If the project does not warrant it, the project should be delegated to a knowledgeable subordinate who is instructed to keep the vice-president informed. Second, the vice-president must have the respect of his or her peers because it is through these people that things will get done. Keeping the relationships well oiled will help to make the wheels turn when necessary. To make sensible policy decisions, a vice-president must have a good idea of how employees at all levels in the organization think. If a policy decision will be unpopular with the majority of the workers, it will not be a good policy. However, there is no way to know the popularity of a policy without knowing how others think and feel. Finally, a vice-president must have a good rapport with the CEO. To build this needed rapport, the vice-president should become immersed in the business, understand the financial ramifications of the human resource policies, and try to be objective when dealing with the CEO. By practicing these fundamentals, the vice-president of human resources can have a significant impact on the organization.[16]

ALL MANAGERS ARE HUMAN RESOURCE MANAGERS

The strategic human resource management approach views all managers as human resource managers. Human resource management issues are not simply the province of the human resources unit. Rather, all managers must take responsibility for efficient and effective utilization of their subordinates. By the same token, human resource managers, because they are in a *staff* position, must view their role as essentially supportive of *operating (line)* managers. That is, they should see their role as advising, helping, and providing expert guidance to line managers on human resource issues. In essence, human resource professionals should view the people whom they advise as customers and themselves as service representatives.[17]

As environmental changes confront organizations with increasingly more complex people issues, they can, in turn, affect the bottom line—profits or survival of the organization. Keeping abreast of these issues requires a broader understanding of human resource management and an increased time commitment for the line manager away from the particular business function. The human resource department, therefore, is a watchful eye that frees up the line managers across the organization by helping with the people-related business issues and working with the line managers to respond to the issues.[18] Although this relationship can lead to staff-line conflict, such conflict is not necessarily all bad if it results in full discussion of key human resource issues and better role clarification of the parties involved.

A feeling of interdependence between line and staff managers should be generated over time. Human resource managers expect line managers to become very knowledgeable about HR issues. Line managers believe that it is equally important for human resource managers to become knowledgeable about the interworkings of the business. This seems fairly obvious, but many HR managers are not adequately familiar with the company's products, markets, and finances. It is difficult for an unfamiliar HR staff manager to work closely with a line manager in a situation in which expert knowledge of the company is necessary. The human resources staff and other departments should cultivate mutual trust as quickly as possible. The support of other areas is critical as line departments must be willing to give new ideas and new perspectives a try. The success of the HR department and its services is also highly dependent on the support and endorsement of all top management and this too should be sought and cultivated as quickly as possible.

ENVIRONMENT-ORGANIZATION LINK AND THE STRATEGIC APPROACH

As we have indicated, the strategic approach explicitly recognizes the impact of the outside environment on both the firm and the formulation of human resource strategy. Chapter 2 discusses the outside environment and its impact in more depth. However, at this point we are interested in the impact on strategy formulation from a broad conceptual view.

The outside environment presents a set of *opportunities* and *threats* to the firm. In formulating strategy, the firm seeks to take advantage of the opportunities while minimizing or deflecting the threats. What might be a threat to one firm can be an opportunity

KFC Finds Success Where Others Have Failed—In China

After 18 months of tough negotiations, Kentucky Fried Chicken opened its first restaurant in Beijing, China in 1988. While KFC has dubbed its venture an instant success and touts sales of nearly $3,000 a day, other fast-food competitors are not so sure the success will continue. Research findings of both Burger King and McDonald's indicate that the vital ingredients for fast-food success—high-quality supplies, a disciplined labor force, and receptive consumers—may not be available in China.

Daniel Ng, managing director of McDonald's Restaurants in Hong Kong, said that he has been talking with Chinese authorities about the possibility of entering the East Asia fast-food market for the past 10 years. He concedes that, while being the first to break into a new marketplace is good, he would rather be sure that it is done right, even if it means being last.

Officials at Burger King hold a similar attitude. Their preliminary research study conducted two years prior to the KFC opening indicated that a full-blown feasibility study was ill advised at this point in time. The main problems they foresaw were the difficulty of procuring supplies and the uncertainty that there would be enough interested customers to ensure a strong return on their investment.

Since 1988, however, Pizza Hut, McDonald's, and Burger King have all opened in China and are enjoying moderate success.

SOURCE: Adapted from Brian Caplan, "Kentucky Hatches Its Chickens in Beijing," *Asian Business,* February 1988, p. 17.

to another. The oil shocks of the 1970s and 1980s threatened oil-fired electrical utilities but provided a great opportunity for coal producers and shippers.

ENVIRONMENTAL SCANNING

SCANNING
The gathering of information about environmental issues on a regular basis and interpreting them in light of the organization's business.

The firm learns of its environment through a **scanning** process. This refers to the gathering of information about environmental issues on a regular basis and interpreting them in light of the organization's business. Scanning is the first step to strategic planning and strategy formulation. A scan and a forecast are developed and serve as the basis for the plan.

Competitive and market analysis is also important to strategy formulation. When the steel industry finally decided to restructure during the severe recession of the 1980s, it chose this strategy of restructuring largely because of the severe competition from Japanese and German steel makers. Japan and Germany had rebuilt their steel-making facilities (largely with U.S. dollars) after World War II. This technology was more efficient than that in place in the United States. Consequently, during the early 1980s, U.S. steel plants were closed in Pennsylvania, West Virginia, and other industrial areas. Many people lost good-paying jobs and have been unable to find work paying a comparable wage. People who travel the Monongahela and Eastern Ohio River valleys still see rusted hulks of former steel plants sitting idle and vacant fields where other plants once stood. Much steel-making capacity has been lost to foreign producers.

SUSTAINABLE COMPETITIVE ADVANTAGE
A differential advantage a particular organization can achieve over its competition.

A firm tries to achieve a **sustainable competitive advantage** by analyzing competition.[19] This advantage is a long-term distinctive competence that sets one company apart from the competition. It answers the question, "Why would someone buy our service or product over someone else's?" This advantage can be based on any number of factors: price, cost, service, quality, image, reliability, convenience, safety, or any combination of the above. For example, Mercedes-Benz has a sustainable competitive advantage in reliability and image over many other automobiles.

HR CHALLENGE

Human Resources at America's Most Admired Companies

Every year *Fortune* Magazine asks experts in various fields to rate businesses to determine which are most admired. The categories on which they are judged are quality of management, quality of products or services, innovativeness, long-term investment values, financial soundness, and the ability to attract, develop, and keep talented people.

From 1986 to 1992, Merck, a pharmaceutical giant, won top honors. Interestingly enough, much of the success of the firm can be traced back to the human resource functions. For example, promotions and salaries for senior managers at Merck are based on how many people that person recruited and trained. Merck emphasizes the basic human resource functions of finding the best person, getting that person into the right job, and providing him or her with the skills and tools needed to succeed. These functions are just as important to the company as are the functions of the researchers who develop new chemicals for the firm to sell.

Merck works hard to preserve its reputation. The CEO, Roy Vagelos, visits six to eight college campuses each year. During these visits, he talks with both the medical schools and the business schools about new drugs and the wonderful opportunities at Merck. These talks do not go unnoticed. Over the past several years, Merck has been able to lure top scientific talent away from the faculties of Harvard, MIT, and Yale. Once hired, these researchers are provided with plenty of reasons to stay at Merck. Research and development money is made available to Merck's scientists in large amounts. In 1991, approximately 12 percent of sales (about $1 billion) was funneled back into the labs. In return for this treatment, the researchers are asked to keep the marketable drugs coming. And they do.

Merck has found that its key to being number one is in the way it recruits, trains, develops, and supports its human resources. If it can keep its employees happy, it can maintain its reputation. If it can maintain its reputation, it will continue to be rated the number one corporation in America.

SOURCE: Adapted from Kate Ballen, "America's Most Admired Companies," *Fortune*, February 10, 1992, pp. 40–72; and Susan Caminiti, "The Payoff from a Good Reputation," *Fortune*, February 10, 1992, pp. 73–77.

Besides competition the market also brings an industry structure. The industry structure involves a number of factors: growth rates, concentration ratio (the number of firms that have a large percentage of the market), substitute products or services in related industries, technology, change, and so on.

CRITICAL SUCCESS FACTORS
The keys to sucess in a particular industry.

A key aspect in industry analysis is determining **critical success factors** or keys to success. These are what it takes to be successful in that industry. For example, to be successful in fast foods, a firm must have convenient locations, quick service, a consistent standard of product quality, store cleanliness, mass advertising, high volume, and low margins. Firms such as McDonald's, Wendy's, Kentucky Fried Chicken, Burger King, Hardees, and other fast-food chains are successful because they have largely acquired these characteristics.

Success factors for other industries are different. For example, for department stores, success factors are magnet mall locations, wide variety or choice of merchandise, good service, good- to high-quality merchandise, and a liberal customer return policy, among others. The point is that a firm must know the critical success factors of its industry and formulate a strategy that allows it to meet these factors.

The human resource strategy is based on overall corporate strategy and needs to be consistent with it. A department store emphasizing friendly, competent service to customers must hire, train, and reward employees so that such services are efficiently and effectively provided.

Finally, technology has a major impact on strategy formulation and on human resource strategy in particular. The technology available in the environment plus that actually adopted by an organization has a profound effect on job design decisions, that, in turn, affect many other human resource decisions such as pay, training, work assignment, leadership, and so on. Think of the technology employed by an automobile manufacturer on the assembly line. The configuration of machines, movement, and technical expertise caused by the kind of technology employed creates a set of constraints within which human resource decisions must be made. To change these constraints, the technology must be changed. For example, robotics technology is being substituted for people using hand tools in a repetitive manner.

INTEGRATING HUMAN RESOURCE STRATEGY WITH CORPORATE AND FUNCTIONAL STRATEGIES

GM's corporate strategy of retrenchment and revitalization that we examined in the case at the beginning of this chapter will drive human resource, marketing, operations (production), finance, and other functional policies. GM appears to be resigning itself to a 32 percent market share, at least in the foreseeable future, because it has permanently closed eleven plants instead of using temporary layoffs, the traditional way of dealing with sale falloffs in the auto industry. Thus, GM's overall corporate retrenchment strategy will have profound effects on its functional strategies, including its human resource strategy. GM has specifically recognized these linkages in the way it established and operates its Saturn Division. Exhibit 1.7 shows how GM's Saturn project has been used to link corporate strategies to business strategies and finally to human resource strategies.

CORPORATE STRATEGY DRIVES FUNCTIONAL STRATEGIES

As Exhibit 1.8 exemplifies, corporate strategy should drive functional strategy. In other words, a firm determines its overall strategy and then sets functional strategy to carry it out. For example, GM's retrenchment strategy has caused downsizing in human resource management, consolidation in production and operations, cutbacks or at least very moderate growth in marketing (including advertising expenditures), restructuring and consolidation in finance, restructuring of engineering, and so on. GM's major functions will be affected in a substantial way by the retrenchment strategy.

Also note that in Exhibit 1.8 functional strategy can impact corporate strategy in that a firm must consider existing functional strategy when setting corporate strategy. For example, the existing human resource strategy and capabilities are a major factor to consider in formulating corporate strategy.

Also, various functional strategies must be integrated with one another. It would be inconsistent for GM to adopt a high-growth human resource strategy while scaling back production and operations. Nor would high investment in new plants and equipment be an appropriate financial strategy for retrenchment. Marketing strategy must be focused at an anticipated 35 percent market share instead of the 50 percent to which GM has traditionally been accustomed.

The implication for human resource managers is that they must be acutely aware of overall corporate strategy and how human resource strategy dovetails with it. More-

EXHIBIT 1.7　**Example of Corporate, Business, and Human Resource Management Strategy Interrelationship**

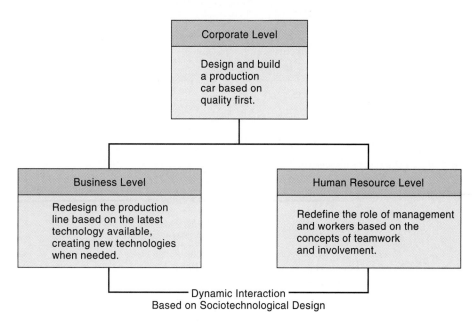

General Motors Saturn Project

over, they need to be aware of functional strategies and attempt to integrate human resource strategy with them. This awareness argues for participation in the strategy formulation process at both the corporate and functional levels as discussed previously in this chapter.

EXHIBIT 1.8　**Corporate Strategy Drives Functional Strategies**

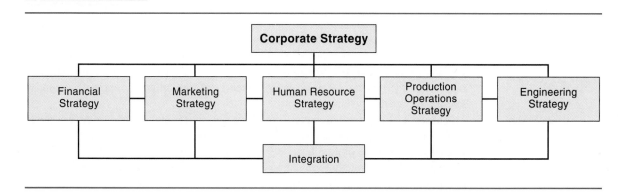

 **EXHIBIT 1.9**   **Organizational Human Resource Strategy**

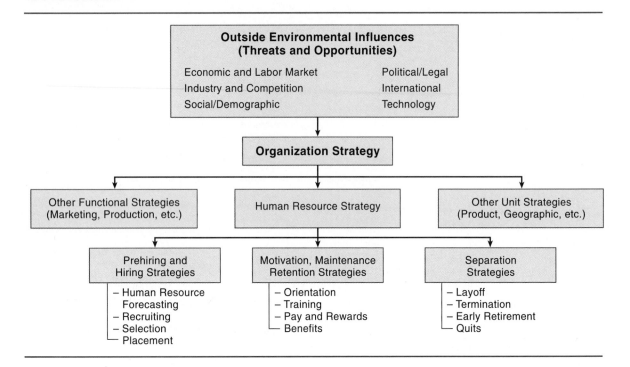

A summary model of organizational strategy and its relationship to human resource strategies is presented in Exhibit 1.9. Notice the substrategies that make up overall human resource strategy. Substrategies are developed for prehiring and hiring, motivation, retraining and retention, and separating human resources. Exhibit 1.9 shows the substrategies for each of these areas.

STRATEGY FORMULATION, DECISION MAKING, AND PROBLEM SOLVING

The strategy formulation process is not a neat and clean process. It advances in fits and starts and is subject to much revision and ad hoc interpretation. It approximates the "garbage can theory" of decision making in that there is much post hoc attribution or explanation of why certain actions were carried out.[20] Sometimes action drives strategy rather than the reverse. Decision makers then justify a particular course of action by looking for a strategy that supports it.

Thus, strategic formulation is a *dynamic* process.[21] It is evolutionary in nature and is subject to change as outside environmental conditions, competition, or internal conditions change. This flexibility in strategy formulation and implementation is essential to the process. Since strategy formulation deals with the future (for example, what we will do in the future, how, and why) and since no one can predict the future with certainty,

LOGICAL INCREMENTALISM
Measured change or reaction to a particular event.
REACTION
An approach to strategy formulation or decision making wherein an organization reacts to threats "after the fact."
PROACTION
An approach to strategy formulation or decision making wherein strategies are formed in anticipation of problems.

INTENDED STRATEGY
The strategy formulated during the planning period.
REALIZED STRATEGY
The "actual" strategy the organization follows.

the process must be kept flexible. The firm must be able to respond to changes as they occur—*in spite of* the plans.

The ability of a large corporation such as Ford Motor Company to completely change and refocus strategy in the early 1980s to the "Quality Is Job 1" campaign shows how Ford was able to meet new threats in both domestic (Chrysler) and foreign competition as well as weather the unexpected fuel price shocks of the late 1970s and early 1980s.

This ability to redirect strategy formulation is sometimes called **logical incrementalism.**[22] This concept refers to the additional measured change or reaction to a particular event. Actions appear to be taken in a step-by-step fashion without the appearance of an overall plan. For example, a particular environmental pressure (such as a new unexpected law) or a competitive threat (such as an unanticipated price cut) could cause a firm to take a calculated course of action that was not originally planned as part of the strategy. A series of these actions might make it appear that the strategy is simply one of **reaction** rather than **proaction,** that is, the company is reacting to the latest threat. In other words, "the squeaky wheel gets the grease."

While the reactive label might be appropriate if every course of action a firm undertook was in response to a threat, it certainly would not be appropriate if the firm followed a well-formulated strategy but was able to modify it as conditions changed. In this case, the firm would be proactive—establishing plans and strategy ahead of time—but flexible. Yet the line between flexibility in strategy and a reactive mode sometimes can be a thin one.

Another way to view this phenomenon is to make a distinction between **intended strategy** and **realized strategy.** The intended strategy is the strategy that is formulated during the planning period. The realized strategy is that which the organization actually follows. Often the realized strategy is different from the intended strategy because unanticipated forces affect the intended strategy or because of implementation problems, the strategy is modified.

A RELIANCE ON DECISIONS

Each of the various components of the strategy process is really nothing more than a series of decisions. In the traditional model of strategic management, once an understanding of the environment has been developed, the company's strategy makers must formulate, implement, and evaluate/control the strategic thrust of the company. These actions call for different but interrelated decisions. For example, after McDonald's decided to add breakfast to its operation and had formulated its breakfast strategy, a whole series of implementation decisions had to be made, including what to serve, how to prepare the food, and how to handle the need for new employees. After implementation, McDonald's management had to make adjustments to the menu and to operations as part of its evaluation and control of the strategy.

As a matter of fact, the essence of strategy is decision making. Many questions must be answered. What should the company do and why? How does the company respond to the competition? What new products and markets should the company be developing? How much does the company want or need to grow? When dealing with the human resources strategy, more specific questions must be asked. What must the company's workforce look like in the future? Does the company's training program really fit its needs? What sort of pay and incentive plan should be developed? Should more employees be hired or laid off? Most managers are flooded with questions such as these and often wonder what is the best way to solve the problems and answer the questions.

A VARIETY OF APPROACHES TO DECISION MAKING

Some decisions are proactive and some are reactive. Many are made without the benefit of complete knowledge and information. In fact, in an ever-changing, turbulent business environment, it is often not in the best interest of top managers to act completely rationally, that is, to carefully and completely analyze every piece of relevant information. It is interesting to note that decision makers once believed that careful, rational decisions were the only acceptable option; however, reality proved this approach to be virtually impossible. To take its place, a number of alternative models of decision making have been developed over the years to better reflect reality. Today, for example, practitioners and theorists alike agree that in many cases *decisions must evolve.* The correct strategy may not be realized until outside environmental forces converge in such a way to point out the right "road" to take. Strategies must sometimes be followed because of commitments over time or political constraints. Many times, strategies must be selected and decisions made based on a hunch or a feeling because adequate time for information gathering and analysis is not available. We base many of our personal decisions on intangible factors that "we can't put our finger on." Many factors cannot be quantified, measured, and weighed, so these nonrational techniques must be employed.[23]

SATISFICE
Making decisions that strike an appropriate balance or compromise among all the demands of those who have a stake in the decision.

BOUNDED RATIONALITY
The recognition in decision making that too much information exists to know and process it all when considering alternatives.

In a classical theory of subrational decision making, Herbert Simon argued that firms cannot always maximize and as a result, they **"satisfice."** Satisficing means making decisions that strike an appropriate balance or compromise among all the demands of those who have a stake in the decision. The results of the decision may reasonably satisfy stockholders, employees, managers, government regulations, and other stakeholders but may not completely satisfy any one group.[24] Firms satisfice instead of maximize for several reasons. First, there is simply too much information to know and process in order to maximize. The assumptions of full and perfect knowledge often made by economists are not normally realistic. As Simon put it, managers operate under **bounded rationality.** The second reason for satisficing decisions is that there are many stakeholders other than the owners and stockholders. Maximization of profit or wealth primarily benefits ownerships but the demands of other stakeholder groups also must be considered. See Exhibit 1.10 for a more complete comparison of rational versus more realistic, qualitative, decisions.

EXHIBIT 1.10 **Characteristics of the Rational and Realistic (Qualitative) Models of Decision Making**

Rational Model	Realistic (Qualitative) Model
Clear definition of problem	Problems often unclear
Extensive gathering of needed information	Incomplete information for decisions
Factors judged using cost-benefit analysis	Intangible factors often important
Quantitative or "number-crunching" based-decisions	Emotional, intuitive or "gut" decision making
Organization benefit maximization/cost minimization decisions	Satisficing, or compromise decisions due to incomplete information and demands of stakeholders
Careful analysis and monitoring of decision	Use of retrospective reconstruction to justify decisions

THE GARBAGE CAN MODEL OF DECISION MAKING

GARBAGE CAN MODEL OF DECISION MAKING
Method of decision making based on the reconstructive interpretation of historical events. Past events are given new meanings in light of a current situation.

A particularly interesting theory of realistic decision making is the *garbage can model*. The **garbage can model of decision making**[25] is based on the reconstructive interpretation of historical events. Past events are given new meanings in light of the present situation. After the fact, once a decision has been made and played out, people have a tendency to highlight facts that justify having made the decision. These facts are carefully interpreted and attributions of cause are given in a manner that reinforces one's view of the decision. This retrospective reconstruction of data is a human tendency that is often quite healthy to one's ego or to the company's morale or culture. On the other hand, such distortion of reality can be quite dysfunctional to the person or organization. Researchers believe that this human tendency is caused by the need to protect the ego.

For example, one of your authors purchased a GM diesel automobile in 1981. In retrospect, it was not a good decision since the car had many repair needs and was virtually worthless after a few years. When questioned about the choice of the car, the owner waded through a garbage can of possible reasons and attributions for the choice. The purpose of this search through the garbage can was to find and use legitimate, acceptable reasons for the choice. All of the advantages and none of the disadvantages were reiterated. The fact that many other purchasers were fooled was stressed. The author was not the only one who supposedly made a mistake.

The garbage can model is used to justify good and bad decisions. The model, like other qualitative theories of decision making, is complex but seems to more accurately reflect the actual decision process and other human cognitions (thoughts) and behavior. The more realistic, qualitative theories of decision making certainly raise the issue of how people interpret and use information in making decisions, which, once understood, helps to explain the role that human resources plays in strategic decision making.

INTEGRATING HUMAN RESOURCES IN STRATEGIC DECISIONS

People in organizations make decisions. Even in automatic decisions, such as an automatic cutoff in a launch sequence for a space rocket, someone programmed a computer to shut down the firing sequence if certain data were present or not present. Automatic or programmed decisions are ultimately people driven, even though in some cases tracing back the sequence to the place where human involvement occurred can be complex.

In this section we examine the human resource impact of decisions from four perspectives. First, we look at the issue of the substitutability of capital for labor. Second, we look at the impact of strategic decisions on human resources in general in the organization. Third, we examine the political forces at work in human resources. Finally, we examine the role of the human resources unit in strategic decision making.

CAPITAL VERSUS LABOR

From a strategic and economic perspective, the underlying decision an organization must make regarding its human resources is its capital/labor ratio. Each organization must decide to what extent it will substitute capital for labor and vice versa. In other words, an organization must decide to what extent it will fill its jobs by substituting machines for people.

Since the Industrial Revolution, organizations have substituted capital for labor by using machine power to replace human power. Generally, this has led to higher levels of productivity and lower per unit costs of production. The back hoe replaced the ditch digger; the automatic glass-blowing machine replaced hand blowers; the high-speed printing press replaced the hand press, and so on. Mass production—changeable parts and specialized machines performing the same function over and over again to produce huge quantities—has allowed for tremendous increases in productivity.

Today the same capital and labor decision is being made in factories, offices, and mines around the country, only today it involves substituting smart machines—computers—for other machines and labor.[26] Personal computers replace electric typewriters and calculators in offices; automated management and control systems replace people-controlled machines in paper and steel plants; robots replace welders on automobile assembly lines; automated answering devices replace receptionists who answer telephones and guide people to the right extension; automatic teller machines replace tellers at banks; optical scanners read prices off grocery items, replacing clerks who ring up the price—the list goes on and on.

Organizations invest in these smart machines because, in general, they do the job more cheaply and efficiently than people do. But these changes do not come without both monetary and human costs. Some people who are laid off may never get a job again. Those who do find work may find much lower-paying jobs. Other people enter retraining programs to learn new skills to operate the smart machines. Still others must move and relocate to cities in parts of the country offering suitable employment. Finally, others may become alienated and drop out of society as a form of rebellion against technology.

This technological change brings dislocations, which are the costs of substituting capital for labor. Society as a whole rather than individual firms largely bears these costs, so firms often do not consider them when making a technological decision to automate a job or process. In fact, some firms often have no choice. In order to remain competitive from a cost basis in worldwide markets they *must* automate, and they do. We saw this during the 1980s in the steel, rubber, auto, and a host of other major industries, and we will likely continue to see it as other industries including financial services, insurance, and even housing become globalized.

The extensive job design consequences of substituting capital for labor by incorporating more technology into jobs is fully explored in later chapters.

STRATEGIC DECISION IMPACT ON PEOPLE IN THE ORGANIZATION

In our discussion above it is obvious that automating jobs has a significant impact on human resources. However, many important or strategic decisions are often considered non–human resource decisions. In other words, restructuring a loan package from lenders is usually considered only a financial decision. A decision to develop a new product is usually looked at from research and development, marketing, engineering, design, and production perspectives. A decision to change a company name or logo is usually a public relations decision.

Yet all of these decisions have a human resource dimension. First, people make the decision. People who make strategic decisions in an organization constitute what is called the **dominant coalition.** The dominant coalition almost always includes top management, but it also often includes people with technical expertise in an area under consideration. More and more frequently, top-level human resource managers are included in the dominant coalition. For example, a computer and information systems specialist in the organization may have a significant role to play in making a decision to purchase a new information management system. The same is true of a design engineer in new product development.

DOMINANT COALITION
Group of individuals in the organization who make strategic decisions.

PARTICIPATION
The level of involvement in the decision-making process among managers and employees.

QUALITY CIRCLES
Groups of employees who meet to recommend ways to improve production and quality.

So the composition of the dominant coalition may change, depending on the strategic decision under consideration. The extent to which people further down in the organization have input to membership in the dominant coalition is a major factor in determining the extent of **participation** in the decision process. In general, many organizations have tried to involve their managers and employees more in the decision process and thereby increase their input. However, this involvement is usually in routine or operating decisions rather than strategic decisions. The theory behind employee involvement is that by giving lower-level managers and employees more of a role to play in decisions, they will have a greater commitment to the decision output.

Japanese auto companies exemplify this policy through their **quality circles,** which are groups of employees who meet to recommend ways to improve production and quality. The Motorola Participative Management Program and Florida Power and Light's Quality Improvement Program (which won Japan's prestigious Deming Award in 1989) are patterned after the Japanese participative model.

Involving people throughout the organization in decisions provides an opportunity to consider the human resource impact of the decision. People who eventually have to carry out the strategic decision made by the dominant coalition may be in the best position to provide input and advice on what must be done to make the decision work.

For example, a plant-closing decision that would involve transfer, retraining, and severance rights for employees certainly would involve the union, if one were present. If no union were present, employees still might be involved through transition committees. Steel companies have used transition committees, even to the extent of allowing the employees to buy the plant, as was done with Wierton Steel in West Virginia.

So obtaining input throughout the organization by using participative management and involvement techniques is a popular way to expose the human resource implications of strategic decisions. Of course, this is best done with decisions that very much affect human resources compared to those that do not. Exhibit 1.11 lists samples of decisions that tend to have a direct impact on human resources and those that have little or no direct effect.

POLITICAL INFLUENCES IN HUMAN RESOURCE MANAGEMENT

The strategic perspective of human resource management looks at the long-term implications of human resource decisions and integrates the human resource strategy with the organization's overall strategy. In keeping with the discussion on the dominant coalition, the members in the organization influence the human resource information system. They influence not only who will be hired and promoted but also the criteria used in hiring and job evaluation decisions. Not all behavior is political, but it becomes political when it attempts to manage or control the meanings, norms, and behavior of employees in an organization.

Political influence, like any other behavior in organizations, does not operate in a vacuum. People answer for their actions. This accountability to others can have a substantial impact on their behavior, including political influence behavior. Politics is not "bad" per se; it is a fact of life in most organizations.

Managers may hire employees based on political influence. Although, at the time, they may say that the person hired "fit" better in the organization, the definition of "fit" may be a political one based on whom the managers think they can influence or control. If they hire enough employees who fit their mold, then they can create a powerful political base in the organization. This may not be the best situation for the organization, and the consequences of such behavior will soon become apparent.

ROLE OF THE HUMAN RESOURCE UNIT IN STRATEGIC DECISIONS

When a strategic decision has a major impact on human resources, such as those decisions listed at the top of Exhibit 1.11, the human resource unit should play a major role in the decision. Human resource professionals are in the best position to advise and otherwise influence the decision process. To become true business partners, human resource managers must focus their attention on issues that are of concern to the company's chief executive.

Traditionally, the human resource unit has *not* been part of the dominant coalition. Largely this is because of the staff or advisory role that human resources plays. However, even though the role of human resources is still largely advisory, the *level* of human resource units has been elevated as explained in Chapter 2. Today companies have vice-presidents of human resources both at the corporate and divisional level. This enhances their membership in the dominant coalition. Yet because human resources is essentially staff oriented, the models of influence on decisions tend to fall along the continuum of staff involvement in decision making. Exhibit 1.12 summarizes this continuum and we discuss it below.

LEVELS OF STAFF INVOLVEMENT IN DECISIONS

The organization's human resource unit can have anywhere from a minimal to a maximum role to play in strategic decisions. At the far left of the continuum, the human resource unit simply provides raw data and information to the dominant coalition. For example, if a company were considering closing a plant, the human resource unit would simply provide the decision makers with information on the number of people affected, severance costs, early retirement costs, and so on, with no analysis.

In the next position to the right, the human resource unit would analyze the data. Graphs and trends might be developed. Interpretive paragraphs would be written and implications would be spelled out regarding the plant closing.

EXHIBIT 1.11

Examples of Strategic Decisions That Have Major and Minor Impacts on Human Resources

EXAMPLES OF STRATEGIC DECISIONS THAT TEND TO HAVE A DIRECT HUMAN RESOURCE IMPACT

Plant Location	Job Design/Redesign
Plant Closing	Production Technology
Wage Cutting	Supervisory Style
Restructuring	Organization Culture Changes
Collective Bargaining	Market Expansion/Retrenchment
Automation	

EXAMPLES OF STRATEGIC DECISIONS THAT TEND TO HAVE INDIRECT HUMAN RESOURCE IMPACT

Loan/Portfolio Restructuring	Public Relations Campaign
Stock Issuance	Changes in Accounting
Logo/Name Change	Methods
Product Feature Change	

In the middle position, the staff role of human resources is carried a step further. Here specific recommendations as to what the company should do with respect to the human resource issues raised in the closing would be developed but would be unranked. In other words, human resources would simply lay out the options with the associated costs and benefits of each option, but the decision makers would choose the option. In the plant-closing example, human resources might detail the costs and benefits of retraining, transfer, outplacement, early retirement, layoff, and severance programs.

In the fourth position to the right, human resources ranks the options as to what they would recommend and why. Finally, in the fifth option, human resources provides the rank order and makes an admonition—no decision could be made without first hearing and considering the options recommended by human resources. The principle of compulsory staff advice forces line decision makers at least to consider staff advice before making the decision, even if they decide not to take it. This gives human resources its strongest staff authority in influencing strategic decisions.

Of course, remember that we are discussing strategic decisions that have a major human resource impact. In those decisions that are strictly human resource decisions— such as how to best administer a pay plan or how to set up a human resource division— human resources exercises line authority over those employed in the unit. The vice-president of human resources (or whatever the head human resource person is called) has line authority to manage the unit.

POSSIBLE LINE AUTHORITY IN STRATEGIC DECISIONS

Taking the plant-closing example a step further, suppose the human resource unit were given not just a staff role to play in making a plant-closing decision but a line role. In other words, the human resource unit would share in the line authority for the plant-closing decision. The human resource vice-president's "vote" would carry as much weight as the manufacturing vice-president's vote. Here, the authority of the human

EXHIBIT 1.12   **Continuum of Staff Involvement for Human Resources Unit in Strategic Decisions Affecting Human Resources**

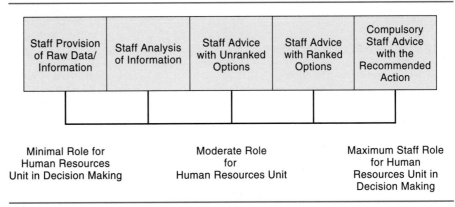

resource unit is no longer staff but has become line. This is rare in strategic decision making but does happen occasionally. However, with increasing authority and responsibility being given to the human resource unit, direct line authority over strategic decisions will likely become more common.

MANAGEMENT GUIDELINES

Based on the material covered in this chapter, we can provide the following management guidelines.

1. Corporate strategy should be determined first, and then human resource strategy should be developed. The human resource strategy that is developed should be consistent with the corporate strategy.
2. Human resource strategy should be consistent with other functional strategies, such as finance, marketing, and engineering.
3. The strategy formulation process should remain flexible and readily adaptable to change.
4. Human resource managers, particularly those at the top of the organization, should be involved in the strategy formulation process.
5. Human resource strategy should consider all human resources in the organization, not just hourly or operative employees.
6. The outside environment and competition should be explicitly considered in formulating both overall organizations and human resource strategy.
7. Decision making is the essence of the strategy process and managers should understand that decision making involves aspects of qualitative (subrational) and quantitative (rational) behavior and justification.
8. The better and more accurately that managers make sense of the organization's internal and external environment, the better their decisions will be.
9. Human resources should be the major unit used to scan and monitor the environment for human resource and labor market issues.
10. Human resources should project both intended and unintended consequences of decisions as they might affect human resources.

QUESTIONS FOR REVIEW

1. What is meant by the term *strategy*?
2. What is meant by a strategic approach to human resources?
3. How does the strategic approach to human resources differ from the functional approach?
4. What role does the outside environment and competition have in formulating organizational strategy?
5. Why should human resource strategy be consistent with both organizational strategy and functional strategy?
6. What roles do problem solving and decision making play in strategy formulation?
7. How has the field of human resources changed over the past 200 years? Why?
8. How does the rational approach to decision making differ from the qualitative approach?
9. Why are managers compelled to satisfice rather than maximize?
10. What is the garbage can model of decision making?
11. What is the role of the human resource unit in making strategic decisions?
12. Should human resources exercise more line authority in strategic decision making? Why or why not?

CASE

RIGHT ASSOCIATES SUCCEEDS BY MANAGING CHANGE*

Right Associates has become an international leader in human resources and management consulting by assisting companies and their employees to manage the one constant in business today—change.

At the same time, effectively dealing with change is driving the company's own success. Right has launched fast-track growth by broadening its scope from outplacement services to consulting on the full range of restructuring issues.

ENTREPRENEURIAL BEGINNINGS

Four experienced outplacement and career management consultants—entrepreneurs Frank P. Louchheim, Larry A. Evans, Robert A. Fish, and C. Boardman Thompson—founded Right Associates in 1980 in Philadelphia. In 1982, they expanded the company dramatically to serve a major client with locations throughout the United States. To meet that need, Right opened additional offices and entered into an affiliate agreement with several qualified existing firms, creating a national network of 12 Right Associates offices.

That expansion introduced Right to new markets and opened the door for continuing growth. By 1986, Right had 36 offices in North America with total revenues of $18 million. To expand further in both North America and Western Europe, the company completed an initial public offering in 1986.

Today Right Associates is the largest publicly traded organization in the industry with more than 115 offices in North America, Europe, and Australia. There are nine offices in the Florida/Caribbean division alone.

Right Associates has served more than 80 percent of the Fortune 500 and thousands of other companies and has helped more than one million individuals make successful career transitions. In 1991, *Businessweek* named Right "one of the top 100 small businesses in the United States." *Forbes* magazine in November 1993 named Right to its annual tally of The Best Small Companies in the World.

"Several factors account for Right Associates' rapid growth," said Thomas H. Shea, managing principal of the Florida/Caribbean Division. "We emphasize professional training and development for consulting staff, and we've streamlined administrative processes to ensure responsive service. Equally important, Right Associates tailors its services precisely to each client's specific situation and needs."

EXPANDING SERVICE FOCUS

Beginning with the first wave of downsizing and restructuring in the mid-1980s, Right began expanding its focus to become

*This case was prepared by Tom Shea of Right Associates

business's "partner in managing change." Today, Right Associates consults with companies on restructuring and organizational change issues and with their employees at every level, in managing career transitions.

Programs initiated by Right include the customized Key Executive Service for departing CEOs and other senior-level managers. A lead consultant directing a team of internal/external consultants works with the key executive in determining the right path such as an entrepreneurial venture, reemployment, or retirement. The team also assists in developing strategy and positioning and provides a "resource bridge" to reach the goal as quickly as possible. Support services may include those such as personal financial consulting, contract and legal advice, communications/image consulting, and research data base assistance.

Another program Right has developed is Spouse Employment Assistance. In the past, corporations provided job search assistance for the spouse of a transferee or new recruit on an informal, as-needed basis. Today, with more than half of America's married couples committed to two careers, a more focused approach is necessary. In addition, the "trailing spouse" is no longer typically a female clerical worker; a male or female executive is just as likely.

Right's program thoroughly prepares spouses for the job search with career goal development, an individualized action plan and job development assistance, such as tapping local networks that can lead to interviews and opportunities. Right uses its JobBank℠ and Career Search™ technology to support the effort. JobBank, for example, is a private database listing middle management through key executive positions available in specific markets and nationwide.

MANAGING THE HUMAN SIDE OF CHANGE

These specific programs and support services are elements of Right Associates' mission to help corporations manage the human resource issues resulting from reengineering, acquisitions, mergers, and relocations. Services are provided in three basic areas: restructuring planning and implementation, transition management, and recommitment.

In counseling a company facing a major restructuring, for example, Right works closely with the in-house human resources department to develop a customized program. Services include assistance in planning the corporation realignment and career transition support for outplaced key executives and employees at all levels. Right also offers an organizational renewal program for remaining workers taking on new responsibilities and a recommitment program to energize the company after the transition.

Along with helping companies manage change, Right counsels its employees. For example, Individual and Group Career Transition Support prepares employees for reemployment with services such as career decision consulting, assessment of potential, development of self-marketing materials, and effectiveness coaching.

Right's track record underlines the effectiveness of its change management programs. The company's market share has increased in every year of operation, and presently stands at 15 percent. In 1993, sales were up a record 149 percent and revenues topped $105 million.

QUESTIONS FOR DISCUSSION

1. What are the challenges faced by this company when the downsizing effort no longer is a popular human resource strategy?
2. What conflicts do you see between a company of this type and a firm's human resources department?
3. What do you recommend Right do at this time to prepare for the future?

ADDITIONAL READINGS

Anthony, William P. *Practical Strategic Planning: A Guide and Manual for Line Managers,* Westport, CT: Quorum Books, 1985.

Devanna, Mary Anne, Charles Fombrun, Noel Tichy, and E. Kirby Warren. "Strategic Planning and Human Resource Management," *Human Resource Management* 21, Spring 1982, pp. 11 + .

Dolliver, Mark. "Volkswagen's Latest: Point Gets Lost in the Translation." *Adweek's Marketing Week.* February 12, 1990, p. 63.

Fossum, John A., and Donald F. Parker. "Building State-of-the-Art Human Resource Strategies." *Human Resource Management* 22, Spring/Summer 1983, pp. 97 + .

Gwynne, S. C. "The Right Stuff." *Time.* October 29, 1990, pp. 74–84.

Hax, Arnoldo C. "A New Competitive Weapon: The Human Resource Strategy." *Training and Development Journal* 39, no. 5, May 1985, pp. 76–82.

Kelley, Tom. 1989 chairman of the American Society of Personnel Administrators' Board of Directors (now the Society of Human Resource Management), in an interview by John T. Adams III, "Strategic Partnerships in HRM." *Personnel Administrator.* January 1989, pp. 76–82.

Kravtiz, Dennis. *The Human Resources Revolution.* 1988, San Francisco, CA: Jossey-Bass.

Linkow, Peter. "Human Resource Development at the Roots of Corporate Strategy." *Training and Development Journal* 39, no. 5, May 1985, pp. 85–87.

McLellan, R., and G. Kelly. "Business Policy Formulation: Understanding the Process." *Journal of General Management* 6, no. 1, Autumn 1980, pp. 38–47.

Mahoney, Thomas A., and John R. Deckop. "Evolution of Concept and Practice in Personnel Administration/Human Resource Management." *Journal of Management* 12, no. 2, Summer 1986, pp. 223–241.

Miller, Edwin, L., Schan Beechler, Bhal Bhatt, and Roghi Nath. "The Relationship between the Global Strategic Planning Process and the Human Resource Management Function." *Human Resource Planning* 9, no. 1, 1986, pp. 9–23.

Ohmae, Kenichi. *The Mind of the Strategist.* New York: Penguin Books, 1983.

Peters, Thomas J., and Robert H. Waterman. *In Search of Excellence: Lessons from America's Best-Run Companies.* New York: Harper and Row, 1982.

Porter, Michael E. *Competitive Strategy: Techniques for Analyzing Industries and Competitors.* New York: The Free Press, 1980.

Quinn, James Brian, Henry Mintzberg, and Robert M. James. *The Strategy Process.* Englewood Cliffs, NJ: Prentice Hall, 1988.

Schmid, Hillel. "Managing the Environment: Strategies for Executives in Human Services Organizations." *Human Systems Management* 6, 1986, pp. 307–315.

Serafin, Raymond. "VW Pronounces Ad Shift." *Advertising Age.* February 5, 1990, p. 16.

Stertz, Bradley A. "Volkswagen Tries for a Little Mystique." *The Wall Street Journal.* February 7, 1990, p. B6.

Thompson, Arthur A., Jr., and A. J. Strickland Ill. *Strategic Formulation and Implementation: The Tasks of the General Manager.* 3rd ed. Plano, TX: Business Publications, Inc., 1986.

Thompson, Arthur A., Jr., and A. J. Strickland III. *Strategic Management: Concepts and Cases.* 5th ed. Plano, TX: Business Publications, Inc., 1991.

Thompson, Arthur A., Jr., A. J. Strickland III, and William E. Fulmer. *Readings in Strategic Management.* 2nd ed. Plano, TX: Business Publications, Inc., 1987.

Walker, James W., and Gregory Moorehead. "CEOs: What They Want from HRM." *Personnel Administration.* December 1987, pp. 50–59.

Woodruff, David. "Audi Finally Gets Some Traction." *Business Week.* October 15, 1990, pp. 78–79.

NOTES

1. "General Motors Finds Its Best Salesman Yet," *Economist,* December 12, 1992, pp. 79–80.

2. Kathleen Kerwin, "Can Jack Smith Fix GM?" *Businessweek,* November 1, 1993, pp. 126–131.

3. Alex Taylor III, "GM: Some Gain, Much Pain," *Fortune,* May 29, 1995, p. 80.

4. Raymond Serafin, "The Saturn Story," *Advertising Age,* November 16, 1992, pp. 1, 13, 16.

5. "The Car Industry: On Another Planet," *Economist,* October 17, 1992, pp. S9–S13.

6. Alex Taylor III, "GM: Some Gain, Much Pain," *Fortune,* May 29, 1995, p. 84.

7. Neal Templin, "GM Overtakes Ford as No. 1 in Quality Among Domestic Car Firms, Study Says," *The Wall Street Journal,* May 25, 1995, p. A4.

8. See Lionel Giles, ed. and trans., *Sun Tzu on the Art of War* (London: Luzae, 1910).

9. Alfred O. Chandler, Jr., *Strategy and Structure* (Cambridge, MA: MIT Press, 1962).

10. Peter Drucker, *The Practice of Management* (New York: Harper & Row, 1955).

11. Michael Porter, *Competitive Strategy* (New York: The Free Press, 1980); and Michael Porter, *Competitive Advantage* (New York: The Free Press, 1985).

12. This section is based on the following sources: W. F. Cascio, *Managing Human Resources* (New York: McGraw Hill, 1992); M. R. Carrell, F. E. Kuzmits, and N. F. Elbert *Personnel/Human Resource Management* (New York: Macmillian, 1992); W. B. Werther and K. Davis, *Human Resources and Personnel Management* (New York: McGraw Hill, 1989); and A. W. Sherman and G. W. Bohlander, *Managing Human Resources* (Cincinnati: South-Western, 1992).

13. American Society for Training and Development, *Models for Excellence* (Alexandria, VA: ASTD, 1989).

14. Tom Kelley, 1989 chairman of the American Society of Personnel Administrators' Board of Directors (now the Society of Human Resource Management) in an interview by John T. Adams III, "Strategic Partnerships in HRM," *Personnel Administrator,* January 1989, pp. 76–82.

15. Leonard A. Schlesinger, "The Normative Underpinnings of Human Resource Strategy," *Human Resource Management* 22, Spring/Summer 1983, pp. 83–96.

16. Robert Berra, "What It Takes to Succeed at the Top," *HRMagazine,* October 1991, pp. 34–37.

17. Peter Rosik, "Building a Customer-Oriented Department," *HRMagazine,* October 1991, pp. 64–66.

18. Randall S. Schuler, "Repositioning the Human Resource Function: Transformation or Demise?" *The Executive* 4, no. 3, August 1990, pp. 49–60.

19. Porter, *Competitive Advantage.* This concept is very similar to the concept of "differential advantage" used in marketing or "economic or comparative advantage" used in economics.

20. Michael D. Cohen, James C. March, and Johan P. Olsen, "A Garbage Can Model of Organizational Choice," *Administrative Science Quarterly* 17, no. 1, March 1972, pp. 1–25.

21. K. Michele Kacmor and Gerald R. Ferris, "Politics at Work: Sharpening the Focus of Political Behavior in Organizations," *Business Horizons,* July–August, 1993, pp. 70–74.

22. James Brian Quinn, *Strategies for Change: Logical Incrementalism* (Homewood, IL: Richard D. Irwin, 1980).

23. Daniel J. Isenberg, "The Structure and Process of Understanding: Implication for Managerial Action," in *The Thinking Organization: Dynamics of Organizational Social Cognition,* ed. H.P. Sims and D.A. Gioia, (San Francisco: Jossey-Bass, 1986); Roy Rowan, *The Intuitive Manager* (Boston: Brown, 1986); and Amanda Bennett, "We've Got a Hunch Intuition Is 'In,'" *The Wall Street Journal,* October 4, 1990, p. B1.

24. Herbert A. Simon, *Administrative Behavior,* 2nd ed. (New York: McMillan, 1957), pp. xxv–xxvi.

25. Much of this discussion is based on Michael Cohen, James C. March, and Johan P. Olsen, "A Garbage Can Model of Organizational Choice," *Administrative Sciences Quarterly,* March 1972, pp. 1–25; and Charles Perrow, *Complex Organizations,* 3rd ed. (New York: Random House, 1986).

CHAPTER 2

THE EXTERNAL AND GLOBAL ENVIRONMENT FOR HUMAN RESOURCES: CHANGE AND DIVERSITY

The environment within which an organization operates has a profound impact on the organization's success. In today's changing, global community, the firm faces many challenges not faced before. The company's ability to adopt or amend strategies to compensate for or take advantage of such changes will dictate its success and even survival. In this chapter we separate the external environment into areas that influence the company's strategy and operations and that could potentially be a major concern for human resource management. We pay special attention to the emerging global community in which modern firms operate and the implications of this environment to the company and its human resource management efforts.

CHAPTER OBJECTIVES

After reading this chapter, you should be able to
1. Describe the components of an organization's external and global environments.
2. Explain how an organization knows or learns of these environments and their components.
3. Describe how these environments impact the firm directly and indirectly.
4. Describe the various basic positions an organization can establish with respect to its environment.
5. Understand that the environment must now be considered global, incorporating influential elements from around the world.

MA BELL HAS LEARNED THE COMPETITION GAME[1]

"AT&T is no sunset company!" Chairman Robert E. Allen boasted to shareholders of the communication giant at the company's annual meeting in Atlanta in April 1994. Allen remarked that the worldwide information industry should be worth $1 trillion in the next few years and that he fully anticipates that American Telephone & Telegraph Company (AT&T) will lead the way toward that impressive mark. In fact, analysts predict that AT&T is on the verge of good performance, but the battle "back" has been difficult.

In late 1983, a federal antitrust suit forced AT&T to divest itself of three-fourths of its $150 billion in assets. The trend toward competition, which had been developing in trucking, airline, and other industries since the late 1970s, hit the communications industry, and AT&T in particular, full force. New rules to the ball game were being written. The breakup led to greater flexibility in the regulation of AT&T proper. No longer would monopoly power and government regulation provide a safe harbor for AT&T. The environment was being radically restructured. In other words, times were changing.

In fact, most business experts agree that never before has a company been "shaken up" by an external environmental force as severely as was AT&T. The company was forced to change its basic way of doing business. In other words, AT&T's internal operations had been totally reshaped by a force from the external environment.

Meeting this drastic change in the environment has been a major challenge for AT&T. As a regulated utility, costs, not efficiency, drove its profits. Higher costs just expanded the base in which its regulated rate of return was calculated. This automatically boosted earnings. Competition changed all this. First, AT&T had to spin off its regional phone companies—the so-called baby bells—which now operate independently. In fact, AT&T now competes with the seven regional companies in short long-distance services. The company also lost its monopoly in the long-distance market as satellite technology opened this market to a host of competitive long-distance companies: Microtel, U.S. Sprint, and MCI, among others. In addition, resellers who buy long-distance time on AT&T lines at wholesale prices, and then resell it to customers have emerged. No longer could AT&T count on an assured income stream from long-distance and regional telephone services. It had to aggressively compete in the marketplace.

COMPETITIVE STRATEGY

AT&T's first task was to remove some of the "excess baggage" associated with giant non-competitive organizations. Costs were cut by eliminating 27,000 jobs plus another 48,000 through layoffs and retirements. This amounted to approximately 20 percent of the workforce. Some work was shifted overseas. For example, residential phones are now made in Singapore. The number of models in AT&T's phone line was cut from 54 to 12. Domestic plants were automated. Sales personnel at its retail telephone stores were put on a commission basis. In short, during the restructuring of the early 1980s, the company adopted many of the same cost-cutting tactics used by nonregulated companies.

AT&T desperately wants to remain a leader and "bell-wether" in the communications industry. At this time, AT&T is following a competitive strategy based on exploiting its creative knowledge, financial resources, and marketing power. AT&T has been forced, however, to rebuild its organization and reorient its human resources to instill the sense of creativity and competitiveness. AT&T has had to change its overall personality or culture. This is certainly a hard thing to do, but the competitive environment dictated by the government regulators forced the AT&T staff to change its style. For example, never before had the employees been exposed to the pressure of creating new products and services. Never before had employees been expected to beat competitors in the race for radically new ideas and solutions to human problems. AT&T had always been able to sell itself because it was the "only game in town." The regulatory action had drastically changed the workplace for AT&T's employees. AT&T's viability as a firm, however, rested on the abilities of its employees to adapt.

Employees did develop new products, especially computers suited to AT&T's particular needs. After all, the company believed that its Private Branch Exchange (PBX) and switching systems were, in fact, computers. Company leaders believed that the marriage of telephones and computers was the key union for success in the communications and "information management" industry of tomorrow. The company purchased the once-mighty National Cash Register and struck joint ventures with such well-knowns as Olivetti, NEC Corporation, and Mitsubishi Electric to develop advanced hardware and components that would aid the compatibility of telephones and computers. This portion of AT&T's business, known as Global Information Solutions, has not performed well thus far, but company leaders remain optimistic. In the meantime, AT&T has noted the potential importance of cellular technology in the communications industry of the future. In 1994, AT&T received government approval for a $12.6 billion merger with McCaw Cellular, Inc. This would make AT&T a leader in the cellular industry, a business that analysts agree will be of great importance in communications over the next several years.

AT&T also adopted an aggressive marketing campaign. No longer would AT&T wait for customers to discover it. It began to share its vision for the future of communications and began to illustrate to customers that AT&T was committed to innovation and leadership. In recent television commercials, a spokesman tells viewers about the day in the future when driver's licenses will be renewed at ATMs, groceries will be checked a full cart at a time, and faxes could be sent from virtually anywhere. The spokesman vows to the audience that AT&T, an old familiar friend, will lead the way in developing these technologies.

AT&T responded forcefully to the advertising by MCI and Sprint designed to "win away" loyal AT&T customers. AT&T developed creative television, radio, and newspaper ads suggesting that savings associated with switching to the "upstarts" were not substantial. In addition, the advertisements emphasized the superior service and product quality offered by AT&T. The company also developed valuable package plans and discount programs, such as the TRUE campaign, which posed a major threat to the relatively smaller competitors. In 1994, it appeared that these programs were working. AT&T's core business, long-distance and other telephone operations, is prospering and smooth sailing is predicted for at least the near future. Also, AT&T has recently strengthened its position in overseas long distance and has entered the financial services industry. The company now offers leasing services and a credit card that can also be used as a calling card. All of these businesses boasted robust gains early in 1994.

In recent years, AT&T has created many new sales and marketing positions. The employees used to staff these posts were not hired from outside the firm but were transferred from other departments. This was only a small part of AT&T's innovative restructuring plan. While seeking to increase productivity, the company retrained many of its employees to work in sales and marketing positions. The downside of this large retraining project is that because many of these jobs required voluntary transfers on the part of the employees, employees who did not take the newly created posts were reassigned or terminated. Even though the firm did not force resignations, it did try to reduce nonrevenue-producing staff positions and to streamline overhead costs.

However frugal AT&T has become, it is continuing its generous pension, insurance, health-care plans, and others benefits. As of 1994, it was still providing a noncontributory-defined pension benefit plan covering substantially all management and nonmanagement employees. Nonmanagement employee benefits are based on a nonpay-related plan, and the benefits for management employees are based on a career-average pay plan.

Like current employees, AT&T's retirees are also being cared for. The company's provided-benefit plan includes health-care and life insurance. In 1994 the company paid the annual insurance premiums, which amounted to $336 each, for approximately 127,000 retired employees.

MORALE

Though it is apparent that AT&T's aggressive new strategy depends heavily on human resources, all of this change has had an adverse effect on many employees who had grown up in the traditional AT&T culture. Under regulation, loyalty, commitment, and longevity were rewarded in a sort of "cradle to grave" management philosophy. The company took care of its employees as long as they went along with the status quo. Innovation, challenge, and new ideas were not rewarded.

Therefore, this change has been particularly difficult for long-time employees brought up in the old system. Many could not adjust and took early retirement, quit, or transferred to the baby bells. Others were fired. Some managed to stay on the job by biding their time until early retirement.

Fortunately, AT&T has been considered one of the most innovative companies in labor relations. Early in the restructuring period, top company managers met with leaders of the company's two unions every few months for so-called common interest forums. Financial figures and improvements in products and services were discussed. In 1985, this meeting process almost collapsed. However, by 1987 it had been revived. Progress has been made in improving the layoff process through crisis counseling, retraining, and transfer. While labor relations have not completely healed, they are improving, as is employee morale.

The AT&T case demonstrates the dramatic effect a change in a firm's external environment can have on its overall and human resource strategies. Deregulation changed the rules dramatically, virtually overnight. Employees and managers hired and schooled in one set of rules had to learn an entirely new set. Whereas loyalty and stability were once the primary employee attributes rewarded, innovation and change became the new desirable attributes. Reward systems had to change, socialization and training processes were modified, and performance appraisal now emphasized newly determined employee actions. The uncertainty caused by these changes hurt morale and further affected the company's deteriorating relationship with the unions. Yet, as the case indicates, AT&T is making a sound comeback. It is competing aggressively in both its old markets of long-distance service and telecommunications equipment and in its new markets of computer technology, international telecommunications, and financial services.

STRATEGIC CHOICES

An organization makes strategic decisions in dealing with its environment. These decisions serve to link the organization with its environment and to establish the basic direction of the organization, as is shown in Exhibit 2.1. A firm can establish several basic strategic postures with the environment. Four postures, which follow the Miles and Snow topology,[2] are outlined below.

DEFENDERS

Organizations that focus on a narrow line of products and strongly defend their position in the market.

PROSPECTORS

Organizations that are always looking for new market opportunities and aggressively seek to develop both new products and new markets.

ANALYZERS

Organizations that have one product in a stable market and one in a changing market.

REACTORS

Organizations that see major changes in their environments but have difficulty adapting quickly enough to meet the changes.

1. An organization can adopt a defender strategy. **Defenders** focus on a narrow line of products and strongly defend their position in the market against anyone—competitors, government, and so on. Traditional cigarette companies prior to diversification, such as Liggett and Myers, used this strategy.
2. A firm can become a prospector. **Prospectors** always are looking for new market opportunities and aggressively seek to develop both new products and new markets. IBM fits this strategy well, as does the new AT&T.
3. A firm can adopt an analyzer posture. **Analyzers** have a split personality. They have one product in a stable market and one in a changing market. In the stable market they operate routinely; in the rapidly changing market they closely watch their competitors and then adapt as best they can. The Schering-Plough Corporation uses this strategy. Known for producing mostly "me-too" drugs (copies of drugs already on the market), the company has one stable product, the antibiotic Garamycin, that has been the mainstay of its prescription drug line. As the company watched its competitors advance in the biotech field, it embarked on a crash program to develop the drug Interferon.
4. Finally, a firm can become a reactor. **Reactors** see major changes in their environment but have difficulty changing quickly enough to meet these changes. Bethlehem Steel and other major steel companies have this strategy primarily because of fixed capital investment, size, and a high wage structure. Changing fast enough to meet foreign competition in steel is a continuing challenge for domestic steel companies.

Adopting any of these strategic profiles will impact human resources. Defenders want aggressively trained specialists in the industry in order to produce and market

EXHIBIT 2.1   **Strategic Decisions Link the Organization with the Environment**

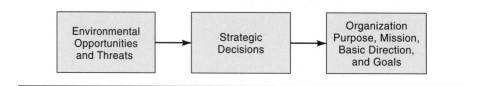

their narrow line of products. Prospectors want aggressive entrepreneurial types of people who are willing to take risks to develop new products and markets. Analyzers value both stability and innovation in employees, depending on which unit the employees worked. Finally, reactors want employees who are less resistant to change and able to help the organization move along its chosen path.

Now that we have examined the basic strategic choices an organization makes in dealing with the environment, we can now examine the environmental components that impact overall strategy and human resource strategy formulation.

COMPONENTS OF THE EXTERNAL ENVIRONMENT

As Exhibit 2.2 illustrates, the external environment is multifaceted and complex. It has many factors, or elements, that can have a major impact upon the long-term success of a company. We can generally divide these elements into two broad environmental types, the societal environment and the task environment.

The societal environment involves the varying trends and general forces that do not relate directly to the company but could have an impact eventually or indirectly on the

EXHIBIT 2.2　　**External Environment: Societal and Task Environment Forces**

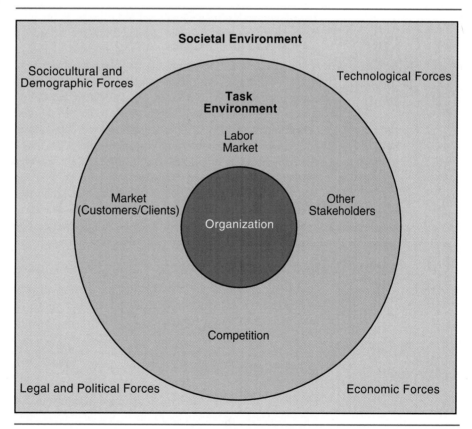

Source: Adapted from Thomas Wheelen and David Hunger, *Strategic Management and Business Policy,* 4th ed., Reading, MA: Addison-Wesley, 1992, p. 14.

company.[3] Within the societal environment, we typically refer to four general forces: economic forces, technological forces, legal and political forces, and sociocultural and demographic forces. These forces indirectly impact the success of a particular company through their effect on the task environment over time.

The task environment includes those elements that directly influence the operations and strategy of the company. These elements are also affected by the operations of the company.[4] We will consider the task environment elements that follow: the labor market, competition, the market (customers and clients), and other stakeholders such as the government and special interest groups. The task environment elements are in direct contact with the company and are influenced by elements from the societal environment. For example, it became a societal goal and a trend in the 1960s to ensure equal employment opportunity for all Americans. The government soon passed laws prohibiting discrimination of any kind. The labor market was impacted by these regulations. In turn, almost every U.S. business has been impacted by the laws mandating equality and nondiscrimination in employment practices.

Let's turn our attention now toward a better description and understanding of the societal forces and then to the more directly influential task environment forces. The first societal forces we examine are the economic forces. Then we look at additional societal forces of technology, law and politics, and finally sociocultural and demographic.

ECONOMIC FORCES

The economy sets the general level of business. Economic forces can be thought of as mechanisms that "set the tone" or determine the attitudes of all who participate in the conduct of business. These forces regulate the exchange of resources such as money, labor, and information. Often the implications of economic trends are hard to determine. For example, one might suspect a high level of inflation to deflate the value of a given wage dollar. This deflation can cause a variety of human reactions. For example, employees might demand higher wages to absorb the decrease in purchasing power. Others might seek to work longer hours or to find additional employment. Inflation might make many products unaffordable. Labor itself may become unaffordable. All of these implications could potentially impact the success of the company. While the government gathers many statistical measures of the economy, the three that we are most interested in are the gross national product, inflation, and real disposable income. Although other measures are also important (for example, leading indicators, lagging indicators, and so on), we focus on these three because they provide good basic descriptions of overall economic activity.

GROSS NATIONAL PRODUCT

Gross national product (GNP) is a total measure of all goods and services produced in a country for a period of time, usually one quarter or one year. It gives a broad measure of overall economic performance. Exhibit 2.3 shows the U.S. GNP for 1982 through 1994. Even though GNP has had its ups and downs during periods of prosperity and recession, it has grown from $3,200 billion to $6,700 billion over the last 11 years.

INFLATION

Inflation measures the increase in the price of products and services. There are various ways to measure inflation, for example, the GNP deflator, the producer price index, and the wholesale price index, but the most popular measure of inflation is the consumer price index (CPI). Exhibit 2.4 shows the CPI for the 1983–1994 period. The index health-care and other professions while laid-off factory workers have had to take low-paying jobs in service, restaurant, and retail organizations.

TECHNOLOGICAL FORCES

Technological forces are the next societal force we examine. These forces have a major influence on the formulation of overall and human resource strategy. Technology is the art and science of the production and distribution of goods and services.[5] Technological advances can be reflected in the product itself or in the processes used to design, manufacture, and distribute the product or service. Technology also has a substantial impact on the design of jobs in an organization—a critical human resource issue. It also has a major impact on the demand for products and services produced by companies.

The most significant technological advance over the last 25 years affecting employment has been the revolution in information handling brought on by the computer, including the personal computer. The computer has allowed much quicker access to and processing of information and has upgraded job requirements for most clerical and staff assistant jobs. In *In the Age of the Smart Machine,* Shoshana Zuboff argues that the effects of the computer have yet to be felt since work itself will change completely as information becomes more readily available right at the workstation.[6] Computers have also spawned robotics, the use of computer-controlled machines, in such diverse areas as welding in auto assembly and forming in steel production. For example, at the Chicago Heights Ford stamping plant, robotic welders and other automated computer-controlled processes reduced the labor force by one-half, from over 1,400 people to about 700 employees, over the 1981–1988 period. Robotics has led to the development of **artificial intelligence**—the use of computers to simulate the knowledge and thinking patterns of experts.

ARTIFICIAL INTELLIGENCE
The use of computers to simulate the knowledge and thinking patterns of experts.

SUPERCONDUCTIVITY
Transmitting electricity at almost zero resistance.

GENETIC ENGINEERING
Artificially changing the DNA molecule in genes to alter biological characteristics.

FIBEROPTICS
The transmission of data, voice, pictures, or other types of information along a light beam (laser).

Other significant technological advances include superconductivity, genetic engineering, fiberoptics, and microelectronics. **Superconductivity** refers to transmitting electricity at almost zero resistance. This will revolutionize electrical transmission from power lines to electrical circuitry in computers. **Genetic engineering** refers to artificially changing the DNA molecule in genes to change biological characteristics. **Fiberoptics** allows the transmission of data, voices, pictures, or other types of information along a beam (laser) light. Finally, microelectronics will result in even smaller computers, new artificial organs, and many other developments in electronics for which space is a limitation.

Technology is changing rapidly, and monitoring as well as predicting this change is a strategic challenge for all organizations. Developing new products that are not obsolete before they hit the market requires systematic attention to this sector of the external environment. Today, U.S. companies find themselves competing with the advanced minds of scientists and innovators from both here in the United States and abroad.

LEGAL AND POLITICAL FORCES

The legal and political forces impact each of the elements in the task environment. In fact, probably no other sector of the external environment has had a greater impact on human resource management than the changes in the legal environment over the past 60 years. Legislation has been passed covering virtually every aspect of the employment relationship from hiring to firing. Exhibit 2.7 (on page 44) lists the significant court cases, and Exhibit 2.8 (on pages 45 and 46) provides a summary of the legislation

EXHIBIT 2.7   **Major Court Cases Related to Human Resources**

Case	Year
Griggs v. *Duke Power* Strengthened 1964 Civil Rights Act by requiring companies to prove that selection procedures do not discriminate.	1971
Albemarle Paper v. *Moody* "Tests" must be valid predictors of performance; burden of proof falls on employer.	1975
Washington v. *Davis* Tests are not illegal, even if they cause "adverse" impact, as long as they are job related.	1976
Kaiser Aluminum v. *Weber* "Reverse discrimination" (favoring blacks over whites) in affirmative action is *not* illegal, at least when a company and union voluntarily agreed to an affirmative action plan for training.	1979
Texas Department of Community Affairs v. *Burdine* Burden of proof in sex discrimination rests first with employee that application was made and then rejected, then with employer to prove nondiscrimination.	1981
Ford Motor Company v. *EEOC* Employer may cut off liability for back pay in discrimination penalty if job reinstatement is offered.	1982
Arizona Governing Committee v. *Norris* Deferred compensation can discriminate against women if they receive lower monthly benefits, despite equal contributions. Gender cannot be used to predict longevity.	1983
Memphis Fire Fighters, Local v. *Stotts* A bona fide seniority system takes precedence over affirmative action in a layoff.	1984
Wards Care v. *Atonio* Substantially weakened disparate impact standard of *Griggs* v. *Duke Power.* Plaintiff must shoulder the burden of *disproving* an employer's assertion that a practice adopted and administered by the employer itself is a legitimate one. Cannot just cite statistics to "prove" discrimination.	1989
Martin v. *Wilks* White men could challenge a court-approved affirmative action plan.	1989
Patterson v. *McClean* Plaintiff cannot sue under the 1866 Civil Rights Act for discrimination in employment.	1989

for this 60-year period. However, we do not discuss these laws in this chapter. Rather, we will deal with each law and significant court case as we review key issues in human resource management in the following chapters.

The legal environment provides a complex web of rules that very much constrains and specifies what can be done legally in human resource management. These laws developed because of abuses in the labor market: misuse of child labor, sexual harassment, lack of protection against injury or layoff for old age and disability, and systematic discrimination of groups, resulting in extreme poverty. We sometimes forget the abuses that spawned the plethora of laws related to employment and human resources; these laws are summarized in Exhibit 2.8.

EXHIBIT 2.8   **Major Laws Related to Human Resources**

Act	Year
EQUAL EMPLOYMENT OPPORTUNITY	
Equal Pay Act	**1963**
Requires equal pay for men and women performing substantially the same work.	
Title VII, Civil Rights Act	**1964**
Prohibits discrimination in employment on basis of race, religion, color, sex, or national origin.	
Executive Orders 11246 and 11375	**1965/1967**
Requires federal contractors and subcontractors to eliminate employment discrimination and prior discrimination through affirmative action.	
Age Discrimination in Employment Act (as amended)	**1967/1978**
Prohibits discrimination against persons ages 40–70, and restricts mandatory retirement requirements, except where age is a "bona fide occupational qualification."	
Executive Order 11478	**1969**
Prohibits discrimination in the Postal Service and in the various government agencies on the basis of race, color, religion, sex, national origin, handicap, or age.	
Vocational Rehabilitation Act, Rehabilitation Act of 1974	**1973/1974**
Prohibits employers with federal contracts over $2,500 from discriminating against handicapped individuals.	
Vietnam Veterans Readjustment Act	**1974**
Prohibits discrimination against Vietnam-era veterans by federal contractors and the U.S. government and requires affirmative action.	
Pregnancy Discrimination Act	**1978**
Prohibits discrimination against women affected by pregnancy, childbirth, or related medical conditions. Requires that they be treated as all other employees for employment-related purposes, including benefits.	
Americans with Disabilities Act	**1990**
Makes it illegal to discriminate against individuals with disabilities in employment, public accommodation, public services, transportation, and telecommunications.	
Civil Rights Act	**1991**
Focuses on establishing an employer's responsibility for justifying hiring practices that seem to adversely affect people because of their race, color, religion, sex, or national origin.	
WAGE AND HOUR	
Davis-Bacon Act	**1931**
Sets pay at prevailing wage for federal construction projects over $2,000.	
Fair Labor Standards Act	**1936**
Sets minimum wage and overtime payment regulations.	
Walsh-Healey Act	**1936**
Sets pay at prevailing wage for federal supply contracts over $10,000.	

continued

EXHIBIT 2.8   *continued*

Act	Year
HEALTH AND BENEFITS	
Workers' Compensation Laws	**Early 1900s**
Provides compensation for job related injuries.	
Social Security Act	**1935**
Establishes old age and survivors' insurance and retirement income. Establishes unemployment insurance system.	
Occupational Safety and Health Act (OSHA)	**1970**
Establishes comprehensive safety and health guidelines.	
Early Retirement Income Security Act (ERISA)	**1974**
Regulates pension funds to ensure that employees actually get money when they retire.	
The Family and Medical Leave Act	**1993**
Allows employees time off from work (up to 12 weeks) to take care of family members or oneself with the assurance of an equivalent position on return to work.	
Projected Healthcare Reform Act	**1996 (estimated)**
Will change, to some degree, the means by which employee healthcare costs are paid. Could possibly compel employers to provide a substantial portion of employee healthcare costs.	
PROTECTION	
Consumer Credit Protection Act	**1968**
Limits and restricts the amount of wages that can be garnished.	
Federal Privacy Act	**1974**
Provides protection for federal employee records and other information.	
TRAINING	
Job Training Partnership Act	**1983**
Establishes a system of federal funding for training programs with business (superceded MTDA and CETA).	
LABOR LAW	
Wagner Act (National Labor Relations Act)	**1935**
Essentially legalized unions.	
Taft-Hartley (Labor-Management Relations Act)	**1947**
Specified illegal actions of unions; enhanced power of employers.	
Landrum-Griffin (Labor-Management Reporting and Disclosure Act)	**1959**
Provided protections for union members; restricted union actions toward members.	
IMMIGRATION	
Immigration Reform and Control Act	**1986**
Makes hiring of illegal immigrants illegal; imposes major record-keeping requirements to document employees.	

Because of the complexity of the law and the frequency of changing interpretations due to court cases and administrative rule making, wise managers rely on legal advice from an attorney when questions arise. In this textbook we cover the basics that most managers should be familiar with, but our intent is not to train managers to be attorneys in employment law.

The political aspect of this sector refers to the political processes and mood of the nation, which has ebbed and flowed from conservative to liberal throughout its history. In recent history, the relatively liberal presidential years of Kennedy/Johnson in the 1960s were followed by the conservative years of Nixon, Ford, and Reagan in the 1970s, 1980s, and 1990s. Even the Carter administration is viewed as having been somewhat conservative.

Under the more conservative political climate, especially under Reagan in the 1980s, the enforcement of antitrust laws were not as stringent as they had been previously. Hence, the 1980s saw many takeovers and mergers—a favorite corporate strategy of that decade. The 1990s has seen a less conservative climate and a tightening of antitrust enforcement.

Political trends are closely related to sociocultural and demographic trends in that politics is largely shaped by the character and mood of the people of a society. This is the next sector we will examine.

SOCIOCULTURAL AND DEMOGRAPHIC FORCES

This sector of the environment refers to social and demographic characteristics that make up a society. It includes the society's cultural values, norms, and institutions as well as its physical characteristics of age, sex, and geographic breakdowns. Lifestyle issues are also part of this sector. These forces relate to the ways people think and react, relate to one another, and live their lives. Obviously, these sociocultural and demographic characteristics impact business in general and particular businesses through elements in the task environment such as customers and the labor force. For example, the increased number of working mothers in U.S. society has increased the concern about and demand for quality day-care facilities for young children.

In general, the U.S. population is becoming older and more urban. The most significant population trend of this century has been the baby boom generation born after World War II. As this group ages, the median age of the population will age and lifestyles will change. In 1970, the median age was 28.0. By 1990 it was 32.8, and it is projected to be 37.3 by 2030.

Exhibit 2.9 shows the projected growth of the top 20 major population areas from 1987 to 2005. The most rapidly growing areas are in the Sunbelt from California through Texas to Florida.

Total U.S. population is expected to increase to 260,000,000 by 1995 from 239,000,000 in 1985. Overall population growth and regional migration have an overall impact on strategy formulation. Labor force composition is driven by population characteristics: age and geographic distribution, growth, and so on. These factors very much affect corporate and human resource strategy.

For example, many companies have moved operations and headquarters to the Sunbelt. A growing labor force, low interest in unions, space, lower taxes, better climate, and lower wage rates have been factors in this movement. The movement feeds on itself. As companies move, so do people. Many families left the rust bowl sections in the upper Midwest and Northeast to find jobs in California, Texas, Florida, Arizona, North Carolina, and other Sunbelt states. However, this trend may be changing.[7]

EXHIBIT 2.9	Projected Growth for Top 20 Metropolitan Areas by Total Increase

	Population*		Change 1987– 2005	Percentage Point Change
	1987	2005		
Los Angeles–Long Beach, CA	8,225.1	10,230.3	2,005.3	24.4%
Anaheim–Santa Ana, CA	2,255.5	4,141.0	1,885.5	83.6
Dallas, TX	2,397.7	3,827.2	1,429.4	59.6
Atlanta, GA	2,556.0	3,848.6	1,292.6	50.6
Oakland, CA	1,994.3	3,101.1	1,106.8	55.5
Tampa–St. Petersburg– Clearwater, FL	1,960.4	3,036.4	1,076.0	54.9
Phoenix, AZ	1,864.5	2,839.2	974.6	52.3
San Jose, CA	1,454.4	2,351.4	897.0	61.7
Denver, CO	1,693.9	2,529.5	835.5	49.3
Sacramento, CA	1,317.5	2,149.9	832.4	63.2
Washington, D.C.–MD–VA	3,541.0	4,367.6	826.6	23.3
San Diego, CA	2,196.5	3,011.9	815.4	37.1
Orlando, FL	919.1	1,712.4	793.3	86.3
Fort Lauderdale–Hollywood– Pompano Beach, FL	1,185.3	1,948.7	763.4	64.4
Nassau–Suffolk, NY	2,703.6	3,416.1	712.6	26.4
San Francisco, CA	1,587.4	2,254.1	666.7	42.0
Houston, TX	3,316.7	3,974.8	658.2	19.8
Minneapolis–St. Paul, MN–WI	2,307.7	2,922.1	614.4	26.6
West Palm Beach–Boca Raton– Delray Beach, FL	786.7	1,377.2	590.4	75.0
Riverside–San Bernardino, CA	2,017.6	2,592.2	574.5	28.5

*In thousands

TASK ENVIRONMENT FORCES

LABOR MARKET

The nature of the labor market, including its members' abilities, attitudes, knowledge level, preferred scheduling, and special needs and demands, is determined by all of the elements of the societal environment. Today, we are seeing special demographic and economic changes that are especially important in shaping the nature of the workforce today and in the next few years. We pay special attention to these changes in this section.

The labor market is a very important factor in determining human resource strategy. The labor market is the configuration of individuals working or available for employment in a particular geographic region—either a nation, region, state, or local area. Four key measures of the labor market will be examined: unemployment rate, education levels, occupation levels, and the age and sex mix.

█ EXHIBIT 2.10   **Unemployment Rates in the United States, 1985–1992**

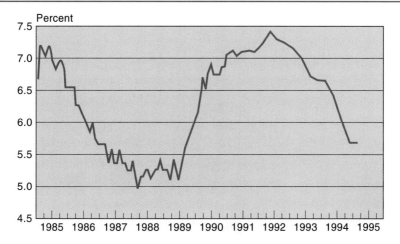

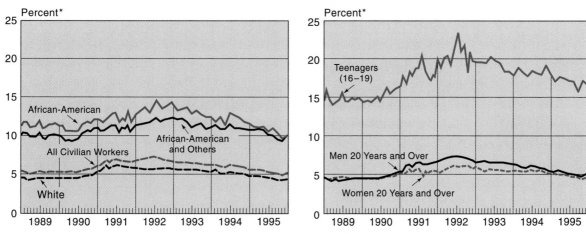

*Seasonally adjusted

SOURCE: *Economic Indicators.* Washington, D.C.: United States Government Printing Office, April 1995.

UNEMPLOYMENT RATE

The unemployment rate measures the number or percentage of people looking for work but unable to find it. It does not measure people not working but *not* looking for work as being unemployed (homemakers, retirees, and students, for example). These people are simply considered as being "out of the labor force."[8]

Exhibit 2.10 shows that during the second half of the 1980s and early 1990s the unemployment rate varied from a high of about 7.4 percent to a low of less than 5 percent. Note also in Exhibit 2.10 that the rate for African-Americans has been about twice that of white people and that the rate for teenagers has been three times as high as the general rule. Of course, during periods of low unemployment, it is often difficult to attract employees.[9]

EDUCATION LEVELS

The education level of the U.S. labor force is shown in Exhibit 2.11 (on page 50). Workers with college degrees earn about twice that of those with a high school education.

■ **EXHIBIT 2.11** **Education Levels of the U.S. Labor Force**

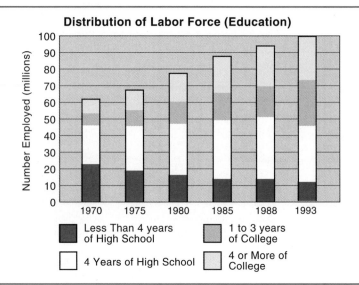

Source: United States Department of Labor, Bureau of Labor Statistics.

OCCUPATIONAL LEVELS

The U.S. labor force now includes more white-collar and professional and less blue-collar and laborer jobs than in the past (see Exhibit 2.12 on page 51). Notice also the increase in employment in the service industries shown in Exhibit 2.13 (on page 51). With respect to specific occupations, throughout the 1990s it is expected that the largest single job percentage climb will be for paralegals. With respect to an occupational field, health care will grow the most, followed by entry-level computer and customer service jobs.[10]

AGE AND SEX MIX

As Exhibit 2.14 (on page 52) shows, the labor force is more female and older than in the past. Almost 60 percent of women are now in the labor force compared to 80 percent of men. Male rates are declining while female rates are increasing. In the 35- to 44-year age group of women, the participation rate is over 70 percent. Exhibit 2.14 shows the projected age and sex composition of the labor force in 1995 and beyond.

LABOR FORCE 2000: WHAT WILL IT LOOK LIKE?

The baby boomer generation—those people born between 1946 and 1964—produced millions of new participants in the workforce. This large and comparatively homogenous group of workers made business employment decisions less complex. Now the baby boomers are reaching middle age, and businesses must adapt to the changes in the workforce to remain competitive in the 1990s and beyond.

One of the greatest challenges that businesses face is the fact that the baby boomers are not having children of their own, or are postponing having children until their late 30s and early 40s. As a result, many businesses will have trouble filling entry-level positions due to the declining number of new workers. However, demographers have an eye on California. It seems that California is a proven bellwether of national legislative change, and this may translate into population changes as well. If this is true, there could be a rise in the number of births. Currently, one of every six births in the United

EXHIBIT 2.12   **Employment by Occupational Group**

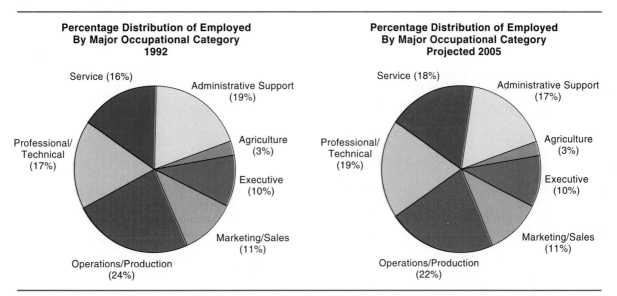

Percentage Distribution of Employed By Major Occupational Category 1992

Percentage Distribution of Employed By Major Occupational Category Projected 2005

SOURCE: *The World Almanac and Book of Facts* 1995. New Jersey: Funk & Wagnells.

States occurs in California. While the state still faces a shortage of people in the 15- to 24-year-old range, it appears that there will be an ample supply of workers in 20 years.[11]

This problem of filling entry-level positions is made worse due to the fact that jobs are demanding more technical skills. The time when a worker could survive with a high school diploma is rapidly coming to an end. More and more businesses are requiring

EXHIBIT 2.13   **Service-Producing Employment Surges in the U.S. Labor Force**

Employees in Three Major Sectors 1950–1988 (000 omitted)

SOURCE: United States Department of Labor, Bureau of Labor Statistics.

EXHIBIT 2.14   **Age, Sex, and Race of the Labor Force Projected to 1995 and Beyond**

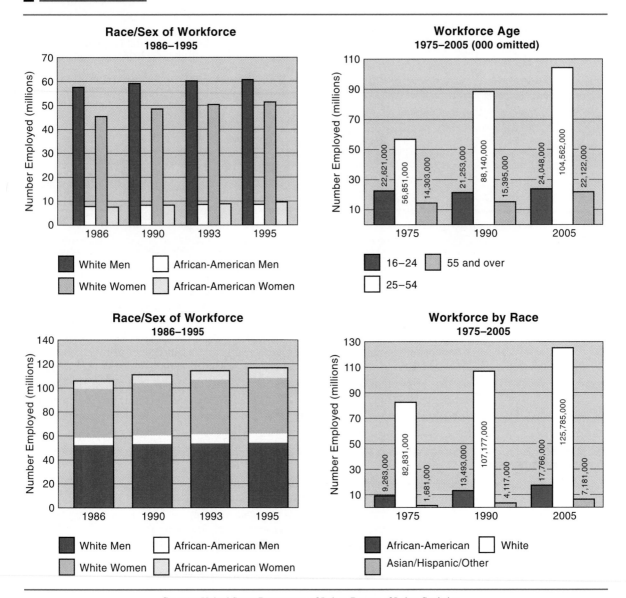

SOURCE: United States Department of Labor, Bureau of Labor Statistics.

that their employees have writing, mathematical, computer, and other advanced skills to be able to work in today's more complex business environment.[12] Businesses are already having a difficult time filling technical positions (such as computer technicians), skilled/craft positions (such as mechanics and carpenters), and even basic unskilled labor positions.[13] This problem is made even worse by the fact that an increasing number of students are dropping out of school each year. The high school graduation rate for the United States is about 71 percent. The lowest level is found in the Southeast where only 67 percent of the high school students receive degrees.[14] Businesses are now in the position of having to pay higher wages for a smaller work pool and investing additional money in job training programs.

FOCUS ON CULTURAL DIVERSITY

Help for Teenage Unemployment

Alex Perez lives on New York City's lower east side. Because he is unemployed, he looks for work, but only sometimes. Most of the time he "hangs out" with some of the more than 100,000 teenagers like himself. Alex is unskilled and does not have a high school diploma. These two factors make both him and potential employers unsure of what he can do.

Alex is not alone. Only one in five teenagers in New York City has a job or is looking for one. Other metropolitan areas face a similar situation. In Philadelphia, Chicago, and Detroit, fewer than 40 percent of the teenagers are in the labor force. These numbers are even higher for African-American and Hispanic youths.

Reasons for this problem are many. Some say that as an increasing number of laid-off white-collar workers enter the workforce, the skill requirements grow. Others suggest that the types of industry that are prevalent in these areas of the country are not conducive to part-time jobs. Discrimination also has been cited as a cause of high teenage unemployment.

Whatever the reason, solutions must be found. In New York, youth counselors are working with teenagers to help them understand the job search process and to motivate them to continue to look. Sometimes these interventions work. For example, Asalmah Muhammad, an 18-year-old from Brooklyn, found a job with Mitsui through the Summer Jobs Program. The first time she had ever seen a Japanese person was during her interview. She admits that without the program, she would have never even thought of applying at Mitsui.

SOURCE: Adapted from Paul Duke, Jr., "Urban Teen-Agers, Who Often Live Isolated from the World of Work, Shun the Job Market," *The Wall Street Journal*, August 14, 1991, p. A10.

The aging of the baby boomers has created another problem. The workforce that was once predominantly white, male, and middle class is reflecting more diversity. The 1960s and 1970s saw the entry of more women into the workplace. Many today are waiting until they reach their thirties and forties before they have their first children.[15] Businesses must cope with maternity leaves, flexible work schedules, and single mothers. The labor force participation rate for women with children under three rose to 54.5 percent in the fourth quarter of 1991.[16]

The 1980s began the great wave of minority entries into the workforce. The Americans with Disabilities Act and other factors have urged and inspired physically and mentally challenged individuals to participate more in the workforce. This trend, which is expected to last well into the 21st century, also presents difficulties for businesses. Only 15 percent of the new employees in the workforce through the year 2000 will be white males. The rest will be women, African-Americans, Hispanics, Asians, and other ethnic groups.[17] *Nation's Business* describes the challenge this way:

> Little by little, senior executives and management experts across America are recognizing that these vast demographic shifts demand a new way of running things—an approach often called **"managing diversity."** This means recognizing that diversity is already a fact of life, learning to understand "culturally different" workers and creating an environment in which they will flourish.[18]

MANAGING DIVERSITY
Learning to understand cultural and other differences among workers and creating an environment in which they will be productive.

The increasing number of foreigners settling in the United States is a factor in the impact of cultural diversity on the workplace. In October 1991, a new law went into effect that raised the number of legal immigrants entering the United States annually to 700,000. Not only do these new Americans make the workplace more culturally diverse, but they also tend to lower the education level. Approximately 36 percent of the male immigrants in 1988 lacked a high school education, more than double the rate for American males.[19]

All of these changing demographic patterns affect the way firms operate. Old methods and traditions are rapidly becoming obsolete. Business managers must be aware of and adapt to these trends if they wish to succeed in the coming years.

Managers must also consider the very real possibility that the company's products or services could be produced overseas. The trend toward globalization has compelled many managers to learn to deal with distinctly different cultures, norms, practices, and attitudes. The human resources directors of large multinational companies must become well versed in the differing customs and beliefs among various cultures including such factors as motivation, leadership, interpersonal and interfirm competition, creativity and innovation, daily habits and hygiene, and commitment to the organization. Globalization and diversity should continue to be the key challenge that managers face as we approach the turn of the century.

COMPETITION

The strategies and practices of competitors have a major direct impact on strategy formulation. If a company discovers that its competitor pays higher wages for similar jobs, the company must decide to match or exceed those wage rates if it expects to attract and retain a productive workforce.

Other strategies of competitors can set the overall level of business for a particular firm. For example, even though Apple Computer has experienced tremendous growth since its founding, it faced major competition when IBM entered the personal computer market in the mid-1980s. IBM is a formidable competitor and initially had an adverse effect on Apple. Apple hired John Scully from PepsiCo as its CEO to design a new corporate and marketing strategy and has rebounded nicely. During the late 1980s and early 1990s, Apple prospered while IBM suffered declines and cutbacks.

Competitive factors have always been a major force in strategy formulation, but they took on renewed importance during the early 1980s when the United States experienced its worst recession since the depression of the 1930s. Michael Porter's book, *Competitive*

EXHIBIT 2.15   **Porter's Forces of Competition Model**

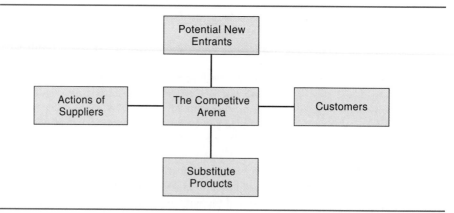

Source: Adapted from Michael E. Porter, "How Competitive Forces Shape Strategy," *Harvard Business Review* Vol. 57, No. 2 (March–April 1979), p. 141.

The Midwest on the Rise Again

Watch out "Coasties" and "Southerners," the "Midwesterners" are on the rise. In the 1980s, people left the Midwest and headed for either the coasts or the South. What they left behind, they thought, was the "Rust Belt," outdated factories and shrinking rural communities. But now, when the coasts and the South are reporting declines in financial services, computer and defense spending, and real estate values, the Midwest is moving forward. While most of its success can be attributed to its diversified manufacturing base, which has begun to expand due to a surge in exports, all areas look good. In fact, even the farmers look for a good year.

A quick comparison of statistics will help to prove the point. While retail sales on the coasts were down, they were up in the Midwest. Unemployment on the coasts was up while it fell in the Midwest. The price of single-family housing sank on both coasts in 1990; in the Midwest, defined as the 13-state region from Ohio to Nebraska, it rose 4 percent. However, even with the

rise in house prices in the Midwest, they are still extremely affordable. For example, the median house price in Peoria, Illinois, during the first quarter of 1991 was $48,400, which is about $7,000 less than a 1991 Cadillac Allante.

These positive statistics are wooing back Midwesterners who left during the 1980s. The chamber of commerce in Omaha, Nebraska, reported a record number of inquiries about moving to the area. The unemployment rate of 2.9 percent probably fueled the inquiries. But Indiana and Wisconsin have also seen an increase in the number of people returning after short stays on the coasts. Most of the returning cite Midwestern values and living pace as the reason for their return. Whatever the reason, the Midwest is on the rise again.

SOURCE: Adapted from Robert Rose and Alex Kotlowitz, "Midwest's Revenge: Once the 'Rust Belt,' Heartland Fares Better than Coastal States," *The Wall Street Journal,* July 30, 1991, p. A1+

Strategy, set the tune for the new competitiveness.[20] He presents a model for analyzing the competitive environment, which is shown in Exhibit 2.15. Note that this model considers all relevant aspects of competition from specific competitive actions to substitute products. Essentially, Porter's model indicates that four major factors determine the competitive arena for an individual firm. These are (1) the potential new entrants into the marketplace, (2) the firm's customers, (3) the actions of various suppliers, and (4) the availability of substitutes for the firm's products. Each of these forces interacts with the others in a dynamic fashion to establish a certain level and type of competition.

For example, the competitive arena of the auto industry is much different than that for the restaurant industry because each of the four major forces at work are so different. Compared with the restaurant industry, the auto industry has few substitute products, few potential new entrants, a rather limited set of suppliers, and customers who make infrequent purchases.

We will revisit the issue of competition in Chapter 3, Formulating a Corporate Strategy, since it has such profound effects on a company. We will also explain how overall corporate strategy formulation affects human resource strategy. However, at this time we can summarize the competitive arena by noting two major trends. First, competition has become global in many markets, especially consumer electronics and computers, steel, and automobiles. No longer can U.S. firms ignore the strong competition that comes from other countries, especially Germany, Japan, Taiwan, and Korea. Second, U.S. firms experienced a major acquisition binge during the 1980s as we have previously indicated. This series of acquisitions and mergers involved both foreign firms and domestic firms and has served to consolidate the power of many into the hands of a few in many domestic industry sectors. The strategy of acquisition and takeover has been a consistent one during the 1980s and has caused firms to design both offensive and defensive competitive takeover strategies. In particular, the *hostile* takeover has been troublesome for many firms. We will examine this in the next chapter also.

MARKET (CUSTOMER/CLIENTS)

Another major sector of the task environment that affects strategy formulation is the market. There is no question that the market and industry characteristics drive much of the corporate strategy. This environmental sector is closely related to competition since competitive forces interplay within specific markets. But the sector goes beyond competition. For example, the market itself presents a set of challenges for a firm, and the firm must know the answers to these questions, among others, concerning the market:

1. Who exactly is the customer?
2. Do we have several distinct customer groups?
3. How shall we define our market(s)?
4. What industry and market characteristics must we be aware of?
5. How are our market and customers changing?
6. What does it take to be successful in our market(s)?
7. What wage and employment patterns exist in our market(s)?

Developing precise, accurate answers to these questions is critical for successful strategy formulation.

OTHER STAKEHOLDERS

Individuals or groups who have a stake in the outcomes generated by the company's operation both impact those operations and are impacted by them. These stakeholders, such as creditors, local organizations, labor unions, government organizations, and trade associations, may express their specific expectations about how the company should operate.

For example, special interest groups may protest an organization's employment practices or hiring practices. Members of a community may expect a local organization to become actively involved in local charity events and activities for its residents. The government may enforce regulation to ensure that the organization meets governmental expectations concerning the company's contributions to society and to its community. These stakeholder groups are always "in tune" with societal forces and are quite adept at applying pressure to organizations to get the things they expect. Many experts claim that we now live in an increasingly fragmented society with individuals identifying more with certain groups than with society as a whole. It is not difficult to see that the proliferation of groups, with their own distinct agenda of expectations, will lead to increased pressure on organizations to provide certain things in response.

So we see that the four societal forces and four task environment elements present much information for the organization—almost too much information to be handled in an efficient way. How does an organization get a grip on this formidable environment? How does it *know* this environment? How does it decide what it needs to know and what it can safely ignore? In short, how can an organization manage the information presented to it by the environment? These issues are addressed in the Knowing the Environment section, later in this chapter.

GLOBAL BUSINESS ENVIRONMENT

The global business environment has changed dramatically since the end of World War II in 1945. The United States became the world's economic superpower as a result of the war, which destroyed the economies of Great Britain, France, Italy, Germany, and Japan. These nations had to rely on U.S. aid to rebuild. However, these nations began to reassert their industrial might and challenged the U.S. economic supremacy during the 1970s. Traditional U.S. products, such as electronics, steel, automobiles, and heavy machinery, faced stiff foreign competition. The 1980s produced more competition with the rise of newly industrialized countries, such as South Korea, Singapore, and Taiwan.[21] Recent moves by China to improve its industrialization status pose a particularly interesting threat (or opportunity) due to the immense size of the Chinese population and economy.

Some of the most sweeping changes have occurred and continue to occur in the new Commonwealth of Independent States (the former Soviet Union). Maps become out of date overnight as yet another republic announces its freedom. As these new republics acquire their independence, they are beginning to realize that they will not be able to become economically stable on their own. Foreign investment and joint ventures have already begun. AT&T sold a digital switching system directly to the Armenian government, bypassing Moscow for the first time, and Chevron and Amoco are both attempting to gain access to the huge Tenghiz oil field. Some firms are waiting until Russia and the republics establish an effective credit and banking infrastructure at the republic level so that the ruble, which cannot be converted into dollars, can regain some value. It is important that these firms not wait too long, because the window of opportunity may be smaller than first imagined.[22]

The changes that occurred over the past few years have resulted in an increasingly complex global business environment and vastly expanded markets. Not only are foreign firms building plants and doing business in the United States, but U.S. firms are operating overseas as well. For example, U.S. computer giant IBM earned over $5 billion in profits on overseas revenues of $44.4 billion in 1994. This represented 58 percent of the company's total revenues and 75 percent of its profits for the year.[23] General Motors, Ford, Chrysler, Xerox, Texaco, and Mobil all have international subsidiaries big enough to be included in the list of the 500 largest corporations outside the United States.[24] *Fortune* magazine now provides a ranking of the top 500 global firms as well as its Fortune 500 list. Clearly, organizations now compete in a global economy.[25]

Japan has even surpassed the United States in the market value of its firms. As shown in Exhibit 2.16, the 15 largest industrial firms in the world in terms of market value in 1993 included 9 Japanese firms, 5 U.S. firms, and 1 European firm.[26] The United States is no longer the only market in the world.

There has been some debate in recent years as to how U.S. workers currently compare with foreign workers in such things as productivity and costs. Critics of U.S. workers have found that foreign workers are less costly and more productive.[27] Pessimists have called Americans lazy, unskilled, and even greedy. Many companies have moved their manufacturing operations to countries where manual, low-wage labor is extremely cheap. For example, a 1993 report notes that compensation in Mexico averaged about 15 percent of the wages paid in the United States. Wages in Hong Kong, Korea, Singapore, and Taiwan were between 24 percent and 32 percent of the U.S. wage.[28]

These figures do not, however, tell the whole story. Other data provide a more favorable image of the average U.S. worker. First, when Americans are compared with

EXHIBIT 2.16   **The Fifteen Largest Public Companies in the World by Market Value as of June 30, 1993 (in millions of U.S. dollars)**

THE WORLD'S 15 LARGEST PUBLIC COMPANIES

Ranked by market value as of June 30, 1993, as determined by Morgan Stanley Capital International Perspective (In millions of U.S. dollars; financial data at Dec. 31, 1992, exchange rates; percentage change based on home currency)

Rank 1993	Rank 1992	Company (Country)	Market Value	Fiscal 1992 Sales	Percent Change From 1991	Fiscal 1992 Profit	Percent Change From 1991
1	3	NT&T (Japan)	$127,287	$ 61,565	2%	$1,590	− 12%
2	7	AT&T (U.S.)	84,409	64,900	45	3,850	640
3	2	Exxon Corp. (U.S.)	82,127	117,000	1	4,800	− 14
4	5	General Electric (U.S.)	81,907	57,073	4	4,305	8
5	1	Royal Dutch/Shell (Netherlands/U.K.)	81,606	83,031	− 5	4,623	27
6	17	Mitsubishi Bank (Japan)	73,237	469,734	− 4	530	− 25
7	16	Sumitomo Bank (Japan)	67,195	583,937	− 2	199	− 82
8	25	Industrial Bank of Japan (Japan)	65,662	419,376	9	388	− 30
9	24	Dai-Ichi Kangyo Bank (Japan)	64,688	561,957	− 1	445	− 44
10	22	Fuji Bank (Japan)	64,134	572,919	8	549	− 37
11	29	Sanwa Bank (Japan)	61,225	559,922	− 4	899	− 11
12	6	Wal-Mart Stores (U.S.)	60,331	55,483	27	1,995	24
13	10	Coca-Cola Co. (U.S.)	56,191	13,074	13	1,905	18
14	11	Toyota Motor (Japan)	53,546	96,200	3	2,253	− 45
15	32	Sakura Bank (Japan)	51,130	508,495	− 10	546	− 29

SOURCE: *The Wall Street Journal,* September 24, 1993, p. R26.

Japanese and European workers (see Exhibit 2.17), U.S. workers do not seem quite so expensive.[29] In fact, when one considers that U.S. productivity is among the highest in the world, higher costs for workers may not seem so problematic. According to a pair of 1992 reports,[30] U.S. workers are more productive in most types of labor than are foreigners. For example, in the expansive service industries such as food service, retailing, banking, telecommunications, and travel, U.S. workers rank at or near the top in productivity, which is simply the amount of goods or services produced per hour of work. Even in heavy industrial production such as chemicals, metals, and heavy equipment manufacturing, U.S. workers rank favorably compared to those in Germany and Japan. The reports attribute this production to management prowess at organizing tasks and managing their completion. The reports also give credit for production improvements to the highly competitive markets found in the United States and the relatively high level of skill necessary for success in these markets. The workers in other countries are demanding higher and higher wages. In fact, U.S. wages are growing relatively slowly compared to those in other industrialized countries.

The 1990s proved the importance of the international sector, which has been more significant in the 1990s and will continue to be as the world economy develops further. This expansion of the international sector presents new *opportunities* for firms, but it

EXHIBIT 2.17   **Japan is No. 1 (in Labor Costs)**

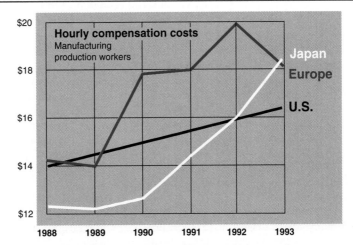

The ever mightier yen has made Japanese factory workers more expensive than Americans and even Europeans.

SOURCE: "Economic Intelligence," *Fortune,* September 19, 1994, p. 32.

also presents new *threats.* As a result, each firm must consider many issues when deciding whether to operate in the global business environment.

CAUSES OF INCREASED GLOBAL BUSINESS

Why do firms choose to operate overseas? As our preceding discussion noted, one of the most common reasons is the desire to *reduce costs.* By locating plants abroad, firms can be closer to their supply of raw materials. This step eliminates the need for expensive transportation, insurance, and administration costs. The availability of inexpensive labor abroad also reduces costs. Labor costs in the United States are affected by more than minimum wage and overtime laws and labor contracts. Taxes, such as social security, unemployment, and worker's compensation, and employee perquisites add to labor costs. In contrast, many nations do not have or enforce wage laws, and labor unions and perquisites are often small or nonexistent. As a result, firms can significantly reduce their labor costs by establishing plants overseas. Finally, costs can be reduced by building semifinished goods abroad. By producing most of an item abroad, especially labor-intensive products, firms can drive costs below domestic costs. To prosper, global firms must invest wherever opportunity is the greatest, whether that means the United States, Mexico, South Korea, or Japan.[31]

Firms will choose to locate abroad due to *less government regulation* in other countries. Two of the most common factors are pollution controls and safety requirements placed on firms. Plant emission controls, OSHA requirements, waste disposal, and many other pollution and safety laws increase the costs of doing business in the United States. These requirements may not exist or are waived in other countries, especially in those that are trying to attract new business.

Locating abroad can enable firms to be closer to their product markets. This cuts transportation costs and helps firms to learn the unique characteristics of each market.

FOCUS ON INTERNATIONAL ISSUES

The Exportation of Clerical Jobs

In a small Irish town of 3,000, where unemployment averages nearly 20 percent, Cigna Corporation, an insurance company from Connecticut, has hired 120 young Irish workers to process medical claims flown in daily from the United States. The pay for these workers averages about $11,000 a year. Across town, at McGraw-Hill Data Services—Ireland, 40 women working full-time and a dozen part-time workers maintain the worldwide circulation files for McGraw-Hill, Inc., magazines by a direct link to McGraw-Hill's mainframe computers in Highstown, New Jersey.

These two examples are just that: examples of a trend. U.S. businesses are moving "back office" jobs overseas where the wages are cheaper, people speak English, and the state-of-the-art telecommunications facilities allow instantaneous links to U.S. companies' host computers. The most popular locations for these back offices are Barbados, Jamaica, the Philippines, Singapore, and Ireland. The jobs in these offices can range from simple accounting, medical transcriptions, and telemarketing, to technical support for high-technology products.

But don't blame it all on U.S. companies. Many have been lured to Ireland. To increase its attractiveness to foreign companies, Ireland took many steps. The country invested $3.5 billion to upgrade its telecommunications network with both satellite technology and fiber-optic cables. It supplied tax breaks, employment grants, training grants, construction grants, and promised a 10 percent tax rate until the year 2010.

Once there, the businesses find qualified employees and very little turnover. With an over 20 percent unemployment rate, people hold on to jobs with all their might. With virtually no turnover, there is increased pressure on management to select high-quality employees the first time. Also, because the employees value their jobs, accuracy is extremely high. The only drawback on the personnel side is that workers want to leave when the work day is over and overtime is not an option.

SOURCE: Adapted from Bernard Wysocki, Jr., "Overseas Calling: American Firms Send Office Work Abroad to Use Cheap Labor," *The Wall Street Journal,* August 14, 1991, p. A1+.

Such was the case for BMW, which has located a new plant in South Carolina. Locating near the expansive U.S. market was an important factor in its decision to make the move. Other elements BMW considered included the perceived quality of the U.S. workforce and tax and other incentives. Tax and utility benefits offered to the German automaker, along with the strength of the German currency, make the South Carolina plant approximately 20% less expensive than the company's Bavarian plants.[32] See the case at the end of the chapter for more on German companies locating in the Carolinas.

The international sector can provide access to growth opportunities that are not available at home. Several U.S. banks and stockbrokerages operate subsidiaries in Tokyo, Japan, to be near the world's largest securities market, which is nearly three times larger than the New York Stock Exchange. So far the results have been mixed. U.S. competitors such as Chase, Citicorp, and Security Pacific have lost money. On the other hand, Salomon Brothers, Morgan Stanley, and Goldman Sachs have made money. As John Wadsworth of Morgan Stanley's Tokyo office states, "The opportunities here are huge."[33]

Firms also locate facilities abroad to take advantage of labor force quantity and quality. It is not difficult to find areas where the people want to work and where the local government wants foreign firms to be there to put its people to work. While the labor quantity may be abundant, there can also be problems with quality. Some nations, such as South Korea, have an educated and skilled workforce. In other nations some workers, such as farmers migrating to the cities, often lack the basic skills needed for jobs in factories.[34]

Many firms will locate facilities overseas to *avoid or reduce trade and tariff barrier problems.* Japanese automobile manufacturers have been abiding by a self-imposed export quota to the United States since the mid-1980s to avoid potential tariff problems with the U.S. government. This quota does not apply to Japanese cars built in the United States, however. As a result, more and more Toyotas, Hondas, Mazdas, and Nissans are being built in Georgetown, Kentucky; Marysville, Ohio; Flat Rock, Michigan; and Smyrna, Tennessee.[35] In 1994 Japanese firms built almost 20 percent of the cars made in the United States, compared to less than 8 percent in 1980.

In fact, a number of countries have made great efforts recently to establish agreements that limit such tariffs and trade barriers. For example, most of Western Europe is currently considered a free economic trade area, or economic community, with very few tariffs and other restrictions applying to trade across these borders. Some effort has also been made to establish a unified currency to aid in the free trade among the various European participants. In 1993, an interesting debate in the U.S. Congress preceded ratification of the North American Free Trade Agreement (NAFTA), which would effectively eliminate many of the problematic trade restrictions hindering trade among the three major North American countries, United States, Canada, and Mexico. Many of the issues discussed above, such as wage differentials across countries (i.e., United States and Mexico) and disparate requirements by the various governments concerning environmental protection, were at the center of the debate on this agreement.

A more far-reaching agreement, known as the General Agreement on Tariffs and Trade (GATT), was approved in 1995. This agreement will eliminate even more of the hindrances to free trade worldwide.

Improved transportation and communication systems, at least with developed countries, have helped increase the number of firms doing business abroad. Markets that were physically inaccessible 20 or 30 years ago are now open as new technologies such as satellites, computers, facsimile machines, container shipping, and air freight are available. Inducements provided by countries to encourage companies to relocate or start an operation overseas have also led to increased international business. Nations are willing to provide these inducements, often in the form of tax breaks or cheap loans for new plants, to obtain the jobs and foreign exchange created by new business activity.[36]

IMPORTANT GLOBAL BUSINESS ARENAS

PACIFIC RIM

In their book *Megatrends 2000,* John Naisbitt and Patricia Aburdene devote an entire chapter to "The Rise of the Pacific Rim." Leveraging both massive labor pools and technology-driven economies, the countries of the Pacific Rim are experiencing the fastest period of economic expansion in history. They are growing at a rate that is five times the growth rate during the Industrial Revolution.[37] The current economy-building phase of the Pacific Rim development is being led by Japan. Japan is injecting money and developmental decision making into the area and is trying to coordinate the emerging economies. In its view, Japan's Ministry of International Trade and Industry sees that "Indonesia will pay special attention to textiles, forest products, and plastics. . . . Thailand will focus on furniture, toys, and die cast molds . . . and Malaysia will concentrate on sneakers, copiers, and television picture tubes."[38]

The "diamond in the rough," however, might be the world giant China. A recent U.S. Commerce Department study noted that China's total annual imports are expected to grow by slightly less than $500 billion by 2010. There is little doubt that the absolutely huge population and newly expressed desire to open relations with the world will lead

FOCUS ON CULTURAL DIVERSITY

Twin Cities across the Border

Some people are confused by all the talk about free-trade agreements with Mexico. These people live on the border towns between Mexico and the United States. The people who live in towns such as Laredo, Texas, and Nuevo Laredo, Mexico, view their towns as twin cities, much like Minneapolis and St. Paul. Nearly everyone living in Laredo is related to someone living in Nuevo Laredo. Over 95 percent of the people living in "Los Dos Laredos" are of Hispanic origin.

However, the connection between the two cities is based on more than just blood. The years of cross-border shopping has changed the face of Laredo. It is geared to the Mexican consumer. So closely are the two communities tied that in 1982 when the peso was devalued, 800 stores in Laredo went bust. Many merchants in Laredo live and die by the dollar-peso exchange rate.

What makes "Los Dos Laredos" and other border towns different from other American towns? Plenty. On average, residents of border towns are younger, poorer, and more likely to come from a large family than other Americans. The average age for women in border towns is 28 while the national average is 34 and men in border towns average 25 years of age while nationwide the average is 31. Border-town residents rank low in disposable income in the United States. Laredo residents had an average income of $13,800 in 1988 as compared to $27,000 in Dallas. Finally, about 10 percent of border town families have six members or more. The national average for family size is 2.6.

Laredo and other border towns do not view these differences as a problem. Instead, the stores view them as a marketing segment. Local grocery stores, instead of stocking rack after rack of microwavable dinners, offer family-size boxes of detergent and 50-pound sacks of rice. Another difference between other Americans and border town residents that affects marketing is a strong brand loyalty. This loyalty is fueled by the deep family orientation held by border-town residents.

SOURCE: Adapted from Blayne Cutler, "Welcome to Border-land," *American Demographics,* February 1991, pp. 44–57.

China into a very active role in world trade. Alan Murray of *The Wall Street Journal* notes that China is the most dynamic economy in the world. The Chinese economy, concludes Murray, has the potential to contribute more to the U.S. growth and living standards over the next two decades than any other nation.[39]

The vast majority of the Pacific Rim's human resources are unskilled and semiskilled workers. These workers are being trained and used in factory settings at a fraction of the cost the rest of the world would demand. Malaysia's director of the Industrial Development Authority explained that in Malaysia over 200,000 young people are leaving school each year, which means that to break even and keep at or below the current unemployment rate of 7.9 percent, at least 200,000 new jobs need to be created each year.[40]

The Pacific Rim is an emerging area for new investment and development. The validity of some analysts' perception of the Pacific Rim as being the world's next economic empire, however, is debatable when compared to the potential for the European Community.

EUROPEAN COMMUNITY (EC)

The year 1992 marked the largest deregulation of any demographic entity ever. The removal of most of Europe's internal trade barriers is a great step forward for the economies of European countries, aligning them to effectively compete with Japan and the United States. When all of the trade mechanisms are in place, organizations will be better able to react to changes in consumer needs and desires, the result being more competition and more choices for the consumer. Although there still remains powerful resistance from the big industries in Europe, including automobiles, agriculture, and airlines, the vision has been set since 1986 and there is no turning back.[41]

Already, investors have flocked to the region to get an edge on the future. Some have moved because their competitors have; others have moved because of fears of a protectionist atmosphere aimed at protecting the EC from foreign dumping.[42] Unlike the Pacific Rim, the European Community's industrial base is more established as is its consumer base. This means that *both industrial* and *consumer* industries have more choices for profit in the EC than currently exist in the Pacific Rim.

The *continued* transition of the EC into a unified economy means that firms will be forced to compete in an open market without internal barriers. For human resource management, this means that organizations will begin to rely more heavily on recruiting people with specific skills, such as a knowledge of the politics and tax and labor laws of newly targeted countries, and the bi- or trilingual professionals needed to anchor the ventures.

MEXICO

Boasting low labor costs and a large population, Mexico is fertile ground for investment. Trade between the United States and Mexico was approximately $50 billion a year in 1990, up from $29.7 billion in 1986. NAFTA, which we mentioned earlier, could pave the way to greatly expanded investment in Mexico. An almost immediate impact of the trade agreement would be the stabilization of Mexico's high inflation—the very factor most foreign investors are wary of.

Other environmental concerns in Mexico include its dilapidated infrastructure. Mexico has already begun reconstruction on some of its infrastructure, swapping debt for equity with foreign investors who then help in the rebuilding. The phone company, which was government owned and notorious for poor service, has been privatized and has begun to be modernized. The mail service has been given a new life with the entrance of Federal Express. Road construction has also been turned over to private industry. The new roads are toll roads, which are run by the construction company until the costs for building the roads and a reasonable profit are collected. After that, they will be turned over to the government.[43]

Mexico's former president, Carlos Salinas de Gortari, had come a long way in allowing stronger employment of Mexico's human resources by attracting outside investors. Since the mid-1980s, he had privatized more than three-quarters of Mexico's state-owned companies, and the revenue from these sales, which is estimated at $4 billion, will go toward reducing the national debt. He sent some prominent business and labor leaders to jail for corrupt practices and started a campaign against tax evasion.[44] *Maquiladoras,* U.S.–owned assembly plants, which are host to nearly half a million Mexican workers at the border of Mexico and the United States, are growing at roughly 15 percent per year.[45] This is evidence of foreign (U.S.) investors taking advantage of Mexico's cheap labor. Mexico's economic volatility, however, still remains to be tamed and for those organizations willing to take the risks associated with Mexico's current environment, the long-term consequences of lowered labor costs are attractive.

WAYS GLOBAL BUSINESS OPERATIONS DIFFER FROM DOMESTIC BUSINESS OPERATIONS

Global business operations differ from domestic operations in several ways. Culture is often a key issue in these differences. Each nation has its own custom-value orientations, and problems can easily develop in the global environment. Selecting a manager for an overseas assignment is becoming increasingly difficult. High failure rates from poorly matched past assignments have increased costs. Thus, selecting an expatriate is an important human resource function in today's global businesses.[46] Some managers view an international assignment as a career risk. If the post to which you are assigned is cut or does not work out, you may lose your job.[47] The humorous problems Michael Keaton's character faced as an American union leader working in a Japanese-managed automobile factory in the movie *Gung-Ho* highlights the real differences that often exist between two cultures. The Japanese custom of strong worker loyalties to their companies contrasts sharply with the sometimes volatile labor-management relationship exemplified by the "Big Three" U.S. automobile manufacturers and the United Auto Workers union.[48] However, things are changing. The younger Japanese generation, those age 20 to 39 years, seem to want different things than their parents do. They are no longer willing to put their employers' needs and desires ahead of their own. They want two-day weekends and diversions unlike those enjoyed by their parents. Some Japanese firms have realized that their employees are different than they used to be and that the company must change to meet the needs of the younger generation. For example, NEC put together a task force of 100 young employees to draft a new corporate vision for the 21st century.[49]

 The political environment also differs from nation to nation and this creates both opportunities and risks for international business. We mentioned earlier the huge potential of the Chinese economy. Many U.S. firms started doing business in China as part of the government's drive to build its economy. U.S. products manufactured in China include trucks, chemicals, processed foods, appliances, and apparel. But the student protest in Tiananmen Square and the Chinese government's reaction have forced foreign firms to reexamine their presence in the country.[50] More recently, China's lack of respect for U.S. copyrights and patents led to heated debates and nearly an all-out trade war between the two countries. However, just before the U.S. deadline, an agreement was reached. China promised to outlaw theft of software and agreed to protect patents of agricultural chemicals and pharmaceuticals. In return, Washington decided to lighten its view of trading with China. In general, the relationship now between the U.S. and China is becoming more positive.[51]

 Businesses must also face other political risks. The Iranian revolution of Ayatollah Khomeini not only caused the overthrow of the Shah of Iran but also resulted in the nationalization of U.S. business assets. Khomeini made the United States a scapegoat for many of Iran's problems, and his solutions included the nationalization of assets, the taking of U.S. hostages, and the economic isolation of Iran from the Western world.[52]

Issues such as bribery also take on international significance. In the United States, bribing a public official is illegal. In many nations, however, bribery is an expected part of doing business with the government. The problem becomes worse when cultural clashes occur. It is still a violation of U.S. law for a U.S. firm to commit bribery, even if the recipient of the bribe is the member of a foreign government. How does a firm compete abroad if it isn't allowed to play by the rules of the host nation?

 The global legal environment also differs from the domestic environment. Many firms operate with a mix of expatriate managers and local employees. Laws about responsibility for corporate actions are often more severe in other countries than in the United States. In Venezuela, top executives can be imprisoned without bail if their firms are accused of violating Venezuelan law. Venezuelan officials issued over 45 arrest warrants in 1989 to executives of firms suspected of being involved in a foreign exchange scandal. As a result, many foreign managers fled the country to avoid prosecution for acts that would have been the responsibility of lower-level employees in the United States. In the U.S., they would not have been jailed; rather, subordinates who committed the crime would have been. The fact that the expatriates held higher-level positions in Venezuela was thought to be the reason why the government went after them.

The infrastructure of each nation also varies considerably. The state of road, telephone, water, sewage, and other systems may range from modern to nonexistent. All these systems affect a firm's ability to operate in the global environment. If an operation such as a steel plant requires massive amounts of power, the region must be able to supply power to the plant or it must have adequate roads for transporting fuel to it. If the local government is unwilling or unable to provide these services, the firm must measure the worth of building the necessary systems itself.

 Business practices also differ in the global environment. What's acceptable in France may not be acceptable in Honduras. These differences may be as small as the standard hours of business or as large as what makes a contract. In many nations a handshake may be as binding as a legal contract in the eyes of a local businessperson. At best, a failure to realize these differences causes hard feelings. At worst, it may wind up costing a firm a lot of money.

 Firms also face a variety of financial and currency problems that must not be ignored. Exchange rate problems occur when one type of currency is exchanged for another at a time when the exchange rate is unfavorable. A profit in one currency can be a loss in another at the time of exchange. Many other problems also exist. There may be no hard currency in the country; that is, it cannot be exchanged. Inflation in foreign countries is more volatile than in the United States and can present a real problem. In addition, firms can be robbed by piracy schemes and other infringements via the relatively prevalent black market. Some nations are unreasonable in their requirements of the foreign company. They may expect large tax payments or further investment. Accounting laws may differ from country to country, resulting in confusion. Finally, certain moral issues such as playing on friendships or favoring relatives over others can cloud the business decisions of managers.

Whatever differences exist, if the firm is organized and managed correctly, it will be able to face any global problem. The following six principles can be used to make a firm's strategy come alive and prosper in a global economy.

1. Build a fluid, dynamic organization so that it is relatively easy to respond to changes and opportunities as they arise. This means that both people and structure must be adaptable.
2. Create mechanisms to respond to revolutionary change instead of routine change.
3. Keep specialization to a minimum and stress interchangeability.
4. Draft the best players, regardless of their expertise. If you hire the best players, they can learn whatever you need and will be instrumental in helping to achieve number 3 above.
5. Develop from within, but stimulate from outside. Because you are hiring the best players, there is no reason to fill positions from outside. However, it is also suggested that new ideas be infused into the organization by hiring consultants or temporary workers.
6. Encourage everyone to take full responsibility for everything. Encourage managers to develop their workers' talents. Encourage workers to make decisions and follow through.[54]

KNOWING THE ENVIRONMENT

For most organizations, the environment is an ambiguous mass of information. Of course, not everything in the external environment is of equal importance for the organization. Information in some sectors deserves closer monitoring than information in other sectors. How does an organization decide this issue? To answer, we examine two closely related concepts: the *enacted environment* and the *domain* and *domain consensus.*

ENACTED ENVIRONMENT

Karl Weick explains that an organization does not and cannot conceivably know everything there is to know in the external environment.[55] Rather, the organization *creates* its own environment out of the external environment. This is called *enactment.* Enactment means that the organization creates a relevant environment for itself by aggressively scoping, narrowing, and scanning the external environment. In effect, the organization creates the environment to which it reacts; it does not react to the entire environment. The difference between creating the environment and reacting to it is a fine but important difference. In effect, the top managers in the organization state, "This is our environment, given what we are trying to accomplish. We will be concerned with these aspects and will ignore, at least temporarily, other aspects of the environment." Organizations then give meaning to the environment based on what they determine to be important for their proper functioning.

An enacted environment implies a *proactive* approach in dealing with the environment. The organization takes an active and aggressive role in actually defining its environment. On the other hand, a *reactive* approach implies that the organization is not aggressive, but merely reacts to its environment. It does not define its environment but instead allows important factors in the environment to define it. The organization reacts to the crisis of the moment.

Unfortunately, an organization may so narrowly define its environment through the enactment process that it neglects to consider important forces that may affect it. For example, very few organizations monitored the Oil Producing Exporting Countries (OPEC) in the early 1970s and were caught completely off guard by its oil embargo and rapid energy price rise in 1973 and 1974. From that point, of course, OPEC actions have been monitored.

 GM and other domestic auto manufacturers initially believed overseas competition from Nissan, Toyota, Mitsubishi, Mazda, and other Japanese auto manufacturers would not be a formidable force on a long-term basis and only casually monitored these competitors' actions. They were more concerned with monitoring each others' actions. On the other hand, Japanese automakers were intent on studying U.S. automakers. To get a closer look, many Japanese automakers entered into joint ventures with domestic U.S. automakers. Eventually, the U.S. automakers realized that they were teaching the Japanese in a few short years what it took them decades to learn.[56]

Of course, the 1970s and 1980s clearly established the competitive staying power and force of these Japanese auto manufacturers. Many other automobile manufacturers are trying to imitate their production techniques in the hope of imitating their success. Adam Opel AG built a new car plant in Eisenach, Germany. The goal was to have people think they had entered a Toyota plant, not an Opel plant. The concepts and processes that were implemented were foreign to the workforce; however, this is the way of the future. This project reflects the increasing globalization of the auto industry. A Canadian president of the firm is working for a German subsidiary of a U.S. carmaker (GM) implementing Japanese systems.[57]

DOMAIN AND DOMAIN CONSENSUS

DOMAIN CONSENSUS

The agreement among those individuals who have a vested interest in the organization to the environment the organization stakes out for itself.

STAKEHOLDERS

Those individuals who have a vested interest or claim on the operations or output of the organization.

The domain is that part of the environment the organization *stakes out* for itself. The organization formally states that a certain part of the environment is its *territory,* both literally and figuratively. The domain consists of the (1) range of products offered, (2) population served, and (3) services rendered.[58] The organization focuses its efforts on these three areas while giving less attention to the other areas.

Domain consensus forms when those who have a vested interest in the organization agree to its domain. Those with a vested interest are sometimes called **stakeholders.** For example, stakeholders of UAL, Inc. (formerly Allegis), the parent company of United Airlines, include top management, stockholders, employees, customers, suppliers, and lenders. When these groups reach a general consensus as to what UAL's domain is, domain consensus forms. Consensus sometimes is difficult to form, such as in the electric utility industry in the 1980s when investors, management, and communities could not agree on the use of nuclear generation. At best, consensus forms on a relative basis and is subject to wide shifts over time.

When domain consensus does not form, conflicts can arise as to which parts of the external environment should be monitored. This conflict causes confusion and backbiting when the company is blindsided by an unexpected occurrence from a poorly monitored sector. The Steelworkers Union faulted management at U.S. Steel for not closely monitoring and anticipating the foreign steel invasion of the 1970s. The argument was that management at U.S. Steel had become lax in aggressively anticipating the foreign threat, thus causing the demise of the big steel maker in that industry.[59]

ENVIRONMENTAL SCANNING

ENVIRONMENTAL SCANNING

The process of examining the external environment to determine trends and projections of factors that will affect the organization.

As discussed in Chapter 1, **environmental scanning** is the process of examining the external environment to determine trends and projections of factors that will affect the organization.[60] It is closely related to the strategic planning process and serves as the basis for the forecast on which the plan is built. Assumptions about the future are derived from the plan.

The scan focuses primarily as the organization's enacted environment. The task environment is scanned the most; elements outside the task environment are not ignored, but they receive less attention. Scanning is done to prevent information overload for decision makers. Scanning should focus on providing relevant information for planning and decision making.

The primary environmental areas that should be scanned for human resource management planning and decision making are the labor market, legal environment, and technological environment. This does not mean that other elements, such as the international environment, should be ignored; it does mean that the three sectors identified tend to have a major impact on human resource decisions. Of course, if a firm has overseas operations, these three environmental sectors in other countries of operation need to be examined.

Exhibit 2.18 summarizes these concepts of domain, domain consensus, and enactment. Notice that the enactment and scanning process result in a narrowing or focusing of the external environment.

THE ROLE OF HUMAN RESOURCES IN ENVIRONMENTAL SCANNING

Human resources is in the best position of any unit in the organization to scan the environment for human resources and labor market issues. As Exhibit 2.18 shows, human resources can help the organization to obtain environmental information and feed it to

EXHIBIT 2.18 **Organizations Enact and Limit the Environment**

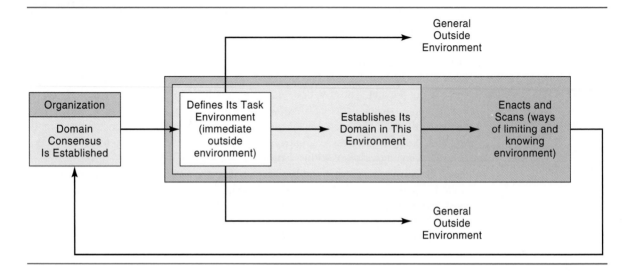

BOUNDARY SPANNING
The process of scanning the environment in an effort to link the organization to its environment.

key decision makers. In fact, human resources may play a major role in making the decision as explained above. Human resources also has the responsibility of obtaining internal organizational information for consideration by strategic decision makers.

Notice that the human resource unit plays a **boundary-spanning** role in that it helps to link the organization to its environment through scanning the environment. We will expand on this linking role when we discuss recruiting and selection as well as termination, retirement, and layoff—other linking processes—in subsequent chapters.

ENVIRONMENTAL SUMMARY

We can see that the environment presents a multitude of important but ambiguous information to a firm. Yet for effective strategy formulation, a firm must monitor the relevant portions of each environmental sector: the economy, the labor market, technology, the social and demographics market, competitors, and the legal/political sectors. Organizations do this through a process of enactment that involves scoping and scanning tactics to reduce the relevant parts of the environment to manageable proportions. In doing this, the organization attempts to establish the set of environmental threats and opportunities presented to it by the environment.

In the next chapter, we see how the organization uses these environmental threats to formulate basic organization and resultant human resource strategies.

MANAGEMENT GUIDELINES

The information presented in this chapter can be used to generate several guidelines relevant to managers. These guidelines are presented below.

1. The external and global environments are very important to an organization and must be monitored.

Continued

2. Organizations monitor and "scan" the environment through a process of enactment and scoping to make the available information manageable.
3. Societal forces influence task environment elements, which influence the firm's operations and strategy.
4. Organizations use this environmental information to formulate overall and basic human resource strategies.
5. Organizations have several choices in designing a basic posture with regard to the environment, from prospector to reactor.
6. The basic strategy an organization chooses has profound *impact* on the resultant human resource strategy.
7. Anticipating environmental trends requires a proactive management approach in strategy formulation.
8. Major issues that must be dealt with include the facts that companies operate in a global environment, today's workforce is constantly changing and is diverse, and the rate of technological change is rapid.

QUESTIONS FOR REVIEW

1. Why should an organization be interested in its external environment?

2. What are the basic forces of the societal environments? What are the key elements of the task environment?

3. What profound changes are likely to occur in the labor market sector and how will this affect human resource management issues?

4. How is the global environment changing?

5. Why does globalization make management difficult? What changes are occurring in the technological environment and what are the implications for human resource management?

6. How does an organization scope or limit its external environment for monitoring purposes?

7. What are the basic choices of an organization as to the basic posture it takes with respect to its external environment?

8. What are the environmental changes faced by AT&T as described in the case at the beginning of this chapter and how have these changes affected basic AT&T strategy?

9. How have these changes affected the human resource strategy of AT&T?

10. Can a large company such as AT&T ever really completely know its environment? Would it be easier for a smaller company, such as a locally owned restaurant in your community, to know its environment? Discuss your answers.

11. Has AT&T performed well in dealing with these changes?

12. Many have written that the external environment changes very rapidly, often in unpredictable ways. Do you agree? Why or why not? Assuming that the environment does change in unpredictable ways, what relevance does this have for both (1) attempting to take a proactive approach and (2) strategy formulation?

13. Why is it important to consider both direct and indirect (eventual) environmental influences?

CASE

FOR GERMANS, "NOTHIN' (MUCH) COULD BE FINER"[61]

German companies are becoming increasingly aware that southern U.S. states, especially the Carolinas, have a great deal to offer international enterprises. In recent years, many German companies have expanded their operations in the United States and searched for an appropriate location. A large number have chosen the Carolinas.

So what is the result when the cool, calculating, sophisticated Germans come to the warmth of the U.S. South? It is far

from a marriage made in heaven; the two cultures have needed time to get used to each other. Corey Lutynski had her doubts about the German alliances when her boss at Baker Corp., a German-owned forklift maker, threw his stapler into her office to have it filled. A German manager at Baker was alarmed one morning when a large portion of the workforce failed to show up. He later learned that, of course, it was the first day of hunting season.

At first, the U.S. workers were offended when the Germans, attempting to conserve heat, kept their office doors closed. Workers cite the importance of warm, personal relationships at work as opposed to the seemingly aloof style implied by a closed door and the lack of friendly conversation.

A real point of contention has been the disparity in pay and benefits. German workers are some of the highest-paid individuals in the world. In addition, they receive benefits, such as vacations of six or more weeks, that U.S. workers find excessive. One secretary complained that the German bosses were never in their office, making it difficult for the U.S. workers.

DESPITE THE GROWING PAINS, BENEFITS ABOUND

More than 200 German companies have $4 billion worth of industrial sites in the two-state area known as the Carolinas. What has attracted such companies? One key factor seems to be the reception offered by the Carolina trade representatives. The states, especially South Carolina, are more than willing to offer incentives to cover such things as tax expenses, land development costs, and infrastructure improvements.

The Germans are thrilled about the high-quality state technical and vocational school systems. In general, they are happy about the qualifications of the workers available. The Germans proclaim that costs are low: wages are cheap, especially while the German currency is strong against the U.S. dollar. One German plant, BMW, professes that it considers preserving the image of prestige and precision very important, but it also wants to control costs and appeal to a large segment of the U.S. automobile market. To BMW, South Carolina was the logical choice.

The Germans also claim that the easy-going, likable Southerners are malleable. They tolerate many management practices that many other Americans would find obnoxious, and most Southerners want no part of a union. The Germans call the Carolinians friendly and loyal. The Carolinians appreciate the high-tech training, high wages, and good working conditions.

The Carolinians also are reaping some nice rewards. Primarily, the Germans are helping in the state's transition from a primarily agrarian economy to a more high-tech industrial-based economy. A huge amount of money is flowing into and throughout the state. The tax base has expanded, and the money can be used to improve such things as highways and schools.

HUMAN RESOURCE ISSUES

The German expansion into the Carolinas involves many elements related to global business management in general and human resource management in particular. When cultures collide like this, there is a need for accommodation. Both parties in this case have been asked to accept some negatives in order to enjoy the positives that have been delineated. German managers dealing with the Carolinian workers face new challenges, not unlike U.S. managers sent overseas. To deal with the issues important to management and to the workforce, the Germans and the Americans have been forced to forge an understanding of each other's goals and ways of thinking.

A second key element relates to the global business environment that compelled the large German companies to locate in the Carolinas. They considered numerous issues dealing with shipping costs, U.S. market potential, currency fluctuations and the competitive nature of the local labor market relative to that in other countries prior to making their decision to locate in South Carolina. To the Germans, the key human resource factors of skill, wages, training and availability were a key part of their global decision process.

QUESTIONS

1. What were the strategic issues related to the workforce that the Germans likely considered before deciding to locate in the Carolinas? Why are these issues important?

2. Why do you suspect that German and U.S. workers have different beliefs, attitudes, and behaviors about work? What were the root causes of the minor differences noted in the case?

3. Do you foresee any potential management problems in the future? If so, what are they, what caused them, and how can they be solved (or avoided)?

ADDITIONAL READINGS

Bacas, Harry. "Desperately Seeking Workers." *Nation's Business.* February 1988, pp. 16–17, 20–23.

Bacon, Kenneth H. "Population and Power Preparing for Change." *The Wall Street Journal.* June 6, 1988, pp. 1, 5.

Badaracco, Joseph. *The Knowledge Link.* Cambridge, MA: Harvard Business School Press, 1991.

Baker, Stephen. "Now Mexico Looks Like a Fiesta for Investors." *Business Week.* August 28, 1989, pp. 42–43.

Bernstein, Aaron. "America's Income Gap: The Closer You Look, the Worse It Gets." *Business Week.* April 17, 1989, pp. 78–79.

Bogue, Marcus C., and Elwood S. Buffa. *Corporate Strategic Analysis.* New York: Free Press, 1986.

Borrus, Amy, and John Carey. "An Open Door the U.S. Isn't Using." *Business Week.* May 15, 1989, pp. 59–62.

Borrus, Amy, Dinah Lee, Victoria English, and Blanca Riemer. "Who's the Biggest of Them All?" *Business Week.* July 17, 1989, pp. 139–177.

Boyett, Joseph, and Harry Conn. *Workplace 2000: The Revolution Reshaping American Business.* New York: Penguin, 1991.

Bradshaw, Thorton F., Daniel F. Burton, Jr., Richard N. Cooper, and Robert D. Hormats. *America's New Competitors.* New York: Harper & Row, 1989.

Brauchli, Marcus W. "Trading in Tokyo." *The Wall Street Journal.* August 16, 1989, pp. A1-6, A8-1.

Carlson, Rose, and Eugene Carlson. "Made in Michigan." *The Wall Street Journal.* August 11, 1988, pp. 1–6, 17–1.

Carson, Carol S. "GNP: An Overview of Source Data and Estimating Methods." *Survey of Current Business* 67 (1987), pp. 103–126.

Carter, Susan, John Rossanto, Frank J. Comes, and John Templeman.

"Why the Ayatollah is Whipping Up a New Wave of Fanaticism." *Business Week.* March 6, 1989, p. 47.

Coates, Joseph, Jennifer Jarratt, and John Mahaffie. *Future Work.* San Francisco: Jossey-Bass, 1990.

Cooper, James C., and Kathleen Madigan. "As the Expansion Faces Bigger Bills." *Business Week.* April 24, 1989, p. 21.

Daft, Richard L., Juhani Sormunen, and Don Parks. "Chief Executive Scanning, Environmental Characteristics and Company Performance: An Empirical Study," *Strategic Management Journal.* March/April 1988, pp. 123–140.

de Cordoba, Jose. "Wanted in Caracas." *The Wall Street Journal.* August 24, 1989, pp. A1-1, A6-1.

Dess, Gregory G., and Donald W. Beard, "Dimensions of Organizational Task Environments." *Administrative Science Quarterly* 29 (1984), pp. 52–73.

Dowling, Peter, and Randall Schuler. *International Dimensions of Human Resource Management.* Boston: PWS Kent, 1990.

Dreyfuss, Joel. "Reinventing IBM." *Fortune,* August 21, 1989, p. 38.

Dwyer, Paula, Laura Jereski, Zachary Schiller, and Dinah Lee. "The Raging Battle over 'Intellectual Property.' " *Business Week.* May 22, 1989, p. 88.

Egelhoff, William G. *Organizing the Multinational Enterprise.* New York: Harper & Row, 1989.

Ellig, Bruce R. "Employee Resource Planning and Issues of the 1980's." *Personnel* 63, no. 2. February 1986, pp. 24–30.

Fahey, Liam, and William R. King. "Environmental Scanning for Corporate Planning." *Business Horizons.* August 1977, p. 63.

Fernandez, John. *Managing a Diverse Workforce.* New York: Lexington Books, 1991.

Finney, Martha I. "The ASPA Labor Shortage Survey." *Personnel Administrator.* February 1989, pp. 35–42.

Frumkin, Norman. *Tracking America's Economy.* Armonk, NY: M. E. Sharpe, 1988.

Fuller, Graham. *The Democracy Trap: Perils of the Post-Cold War World.* Novato, CA: Dutton, 1991.

Fullerton, H. N., Jr. "Labor Force Projections: 1986–2000," *Monthly Labor Review* 110 (1987), pp. 19–29.

Fyock, Catherine. *America's Work Force Is Coming of Age.* New York: Lexington Books, 1990.

Gamota, George, and Wendy Frieman. *Gaining Ground.* New York: Harper & Row, 1989.

Glasgall, William, Dori Jones Yang, Dinah Lee, Joe Weber, and Amy Borrus. "Has Beijing Burned Its Bridges with Business?" *Business Week.* June 19, 1989, pp. 32–33.

Gleckman, Howard. "Mike Dukakis Has His Own Industrial Policy—But Will It Work?" *Business Week.* March 28, 1988, p. 37.

Goldenberg, Susan. *Hands across the Ocean: Managing Joint Ventures with a Spotlight on China and Japan.* Novato, CA: Dutton, 1988.

Gross, Neil, "IBM Clones a Strategy from the Clonemakers." *Business Week.* August 21, 1989, p. 42.

Guenther, Robert, and Michael R. Sesit, "U.S. Banks Are Losing Business to Japanese at Home and Abroad." *The Wall Street Journal.* October 12, 1989, p. A12.

Harrison, Roger, "Strategies for a New Age." *Human Resource Management* 22. Fall 1983, pp. 209+.

Hawkins, Chuck. "Is Paul Stern Tough Enough to Toughen Up Northern Telecom?" *Business Week.* August 14, 1989, pp. 84–85.

Health, Robert L., and Associates. *Strategic Issues Management: How Organizations Influence and Respond to Public Interests and Policies.* San Francisco: Jossey-Bass, 1988.

Holloway, Thomas M., and Richard W. Peach. "Demographics for the 1990's," *Mortgage Banking.* March 1988, pp. 60–72.

Jamieson, David, and Julie O'Mara. *Managing Workforce 2000.* San Francisco; Jossey-Bass, 1991.

Johnson, Chalmers, Laura D'Andrea Tyson, and John Zysman, eds. *Politics and Productivity.* Cambridge, MA: Ballinger, 1989.

Kelly, Rita Mae. *The Gendered Economy.* Newbury Park, CA: Sage, 1991.

Koberg, Christine S. "Resource Scarcity, Environmental Uncertainty, and Adaptive Organizational Behavior." *Academy of Management Journal* 30, no. 4. December 1987, pp. 798–812.

Knouse, Stephen, Paul Rosenfeld, and Amy Culbertson. *Hispanics and Work.* Newbury Park, CA: Sage, 1992.

Kraar, Louis. "Japan's Gung-Ho U.S. Car Plants." *Fortune.* January 30, 1989, pp. 98–108.

____. "Korea, Tomorrow's Powerhouse," *Fortune.* August 15, 1988, pp. 75–81.

Kuhn, Susan E., and David J. Morrow. "The Fortune International 500 Directory." *Fortune.* July 31, 1989, pp. 291–318.

Langley, Monica. "America First." *The Wall Street Journal.* May 16, 1988, pp. A1-6, A8-1.

Lee, James R., and David Walters. *International Trade in Construction, Design and Engineering Services.* New York: Harper & Row, 1989.

Licht, Walter. "How the Workplace Has Changed in 75 Years." *Monthly Labor Review.* February 1988, pp. 19–25.

Lindroth, Joan. "How to Beat the Coming Labor Shortage." *Personnel Journal* 61:4. April 1982, pp. 268–272.

Maidment, Fred. "American Economy Suffers from Lack of Educated and Trained Work Force." *The Atlanta Journal and Constitution.* December 28, 1987, p. 9.

Main, Jeremy. "Business Schools Get a Global Vision." *Fortune.* July 17, 1989, pp. 78–86.

Maremont, Mark. "British Telecom Is Getting Less British All the Time." *Business Week.* August 14, 1989, p. 62.

Mendenhall, Mark, and Gary Oddou. *Readings and Cases in International Human Resource Management.* Boston: PWS Kent, 1990.

Mercer, David. *Managing the External Environment.* Newbury Park, CA: Sage, 1992.

Moffett, Matt. "Back in Business." *The Wall Street Journal.* July 26, 1989, pp. A1-1, A8-4.

Naisbitt, John, and Patricia Aburdene. *Megatrends 2000: Ten New Directions for the 1990's.* New York: Morrow, 1990.

Nakarmi, Laxmi, Larry Armstrong, and William J. Holstein, "Korea." *Business Week.* September 5, 1988, pp. 44–50.

Negandhi, Anant, and Arun Savara. *International Strategic Management.* New York: Lexington Books, 1989.

Nelton, Sharon. "Meet Your New Work Force." *Nation's Business.* July 1988, pp. 14–21.

Noyelle, Thierry J., and Anna B. Dutka. *International Trade in Business Services.* New York: Harper & Row, 1989.

Ohmae, Kenichi. *Triad Power: The Coming Shape of Global Competition.* New York: Free Press, 1985.

Oriorne, George S. "Human Resource Strategies for the 80's." *Training* 22, no. 1. January 1985, pp. 47–50.

Osterman, Paul. *Employment Futures.* New York: Oxford University Press, 1988.

Porter, Michael. *The Competitive Advantage of Nations.* New York: Free Press, 1990.

Prescott, John E. "Environments as Moderators of the Relationship between Strategy and Performance." *Academy of Management Journal* 29, no. 2. June 1986, p. 329.

Punnett, Betty J., and David Ricks. *International Business.* Boston: PWS-Kent, 1992.

Redman, Christopher. "Charging Ahead." *Time.* September 18, 1989, pp. 40–45.

Reed, Stanley. "When the Dust Settles, Iran May Be Facing West." *Business Week.* June 19, 1989, p. 50.

Schiller, Zachary, Ted Holden, and Mark Maremont. "P&G Goes Global by Acting Like a Local." *Business Week.* August 28, 1989, p. 58.

Schmid, Hillel, "Managing the Environment: Strategies for Executives in Human Service Organizations." *Human Systems Management* 6 (1986), pp. 307–315.

Sekaran, Uma, and Frederick Leong. *Womanpower.* Newbury Park, CA: Sage, 1991.

Singleton, Loy A. *Global Impact.* New York: Harper & Row, 1989.

Solis, Dianna. "For Many Employers, Immigration Law Is Still Puzzling and a Burden to Follow," *The Wall Street Journal.* June 27, 1988, p. 15.

Solomon, Charlene Marmer. "The Corporate Response to Work-Force Diversity." *Personnel Journal.* August 1989.

Steers, Richard M., Yoo Keum Shin, and Gerardo Ungson. *The Chaebol.* New York: Harper & Row, 1989.

Tatsuno, Sheridan M. *Created in Japan.* New York: Harper & Row, 1989.

Thiederman, Sondra. *Bridging Cultural Barriers for Corporate Success.* New York: Lexington Books, 1990.

Treece, James B., and John Hoerr. "Shaking Up Detroit." *Business Week.* August 14, 1989, pp. 74–80.

Wessel, David. "Census Bureau Study Finds Shift in Fertility Patterns." *The Wall Street Journal.* June 26, 1989, p. B1–4.

Winter, Ralph E. "Costs Increase as Labor Supply Dries Up." *The Wall Street Journal.* March 10, 1989, p. A2-2.

Woodruff, David. "Detroit's Big Worry for the 1990's: The Greenhouse Effect." *Business Week.* September 4, 1989, pp. 103–107.

Worthy, Ford S. "The Perils of Getting Tough on Korea." *Fortune.* June 5, 1989, pp. 263–268.

Yang, Dori Jones, Dinah Lee, William J. Holstein, and Maria Shao. "China: The Great Leap Backward." *Business Week.* June 19, 1989, pp. 28–32.

NOTES

1. *AT&T 1986 Annual Report,* February 7, 1987, pp. 3, 23, 24; John Keller, Geoff Lewis, Todd Mason, Russell Mitchell, and Thane Peterson, "AT&T—The Making of a Comeback," *Business Week,* January 18, 1988, pp. 56–62; Jeffrey A. Tannenbaum, "AT&T to Cut Hiring, Change Jobs of Workers," *The Wall Street Journal,* July 22, 1989, p. 3; "AT&T to Transfer up to 1,500 of Staff to Sales Organization," *The Wall Street Journal,* July 25, 1989, p. 9; Bernard Wysocki, Jr., "Cross-Border Alliances Become Favorite Way to Crack New Markets," *The Wall Street Journal,* March 26, 1990, p. A1+; John J. Keller, "AT&T Earnings Rose Strongly in First Quarter," *The Wall Street Journal,* April 21, 1994, p. A4; and Carol Kennedy, "The Transformation of AT&T," *Long Range Planning,* June 1989, pp. 10–17.

2. Raymond E. Miles and Charles C. Snow, *Organization Strategy, Structure, and Process* (New York: McGraw-Hill, 1978), pp. 29–30.

3. These definitions are based on the discussion by Thomas Wheelen and David Hunger, *Strategic Management and Business Policy,* 4th ed. (Reading, MA: Addison-Wesley, 1992), pp. 92–98.

4. Ibid.

5. B. J. Hodge and William P. Anthony, *Organization Theory,* 3rd ed. (Boston: Allyn and Bacon, 1988), p. 428.

6. Shoshana Zuboff, *In the Age of the Smart Machine: The Future of Work and Power* (New York: Basic, 1988).

7. Robert Rose and Alex Kotolowitz, "Midwest's Revenge: Once the 'Rust-Belt,' Heartland Fares Better than Coastal States," *The Wall Street Journal,* July 30, 1991, p. A1+.

8. There is some evidence that the unemployment rate actually undercounts unemployment because of the discouraged worker hypothesis. Some people who actually want to work may have given up looking. These people are not counted as unemployed.

9. It should be noted that during the Great Depression of the 1930s the unemployment rate reached 25 percent on several occasions.

10. Albert Karr, "Health Care Jobs," *The Wall Street Journal,* June 19, 1990, p. A1.

11. "California," *HRMagazine,* April 1991, p. 41.

12. "Investing in GEMS: Global Employees, Mobile and Skilled," *HRMagazine,* January 1991, p. 37.

13. Martha I. Finney, "The ASPA Labor Shortage Survey," *Personnel Administrator,* February 1989, pp. 36–42.

14. Martha Brannigan, "Work Force Skills Lag in the Southeast, Despite Reforms," *The Wall Street Journal,* February 18, 1992, p. A1.

15. David Wessel, "Census Bureau Study Finds Shift in Fertility Patterns," *The Wall Street Journal,* June 26, 1989, p. B1.

16. Sue Schellenbarger, "Women with Children Increase in Work Force," *The Wall Street Journal,* February 12, 1992, p. B1.

17. Sharon Nelton, "Meet Your New Work Force," *Nation's Business,* July 1988, pp. 14–21.

18. Ibid., pp. 14–15.

19. "More Skilled Workers Coming to the U.S.," *Fortune,* September 9, 1991, p. 14.

20. Michael Porter, *Competitive Strategy: Techniques for Analyzing Industries and Competitors* (New York: Free Press, 1980).

21. Ford S. Worthy, "The Perils of Getting Tough on Korea," *Fortune,* June 5, 1989, pp. 263–268.

22. Paul Hofheinz, "Let's Do Business," *Fortune,* September 23, 1991, pp. 62–68.

23. Joel Dreyfuss, "Reinventing IBM," *Fortune,* August 21, 1989, p. 38.

24. Susan E. Kuhn and David J. Morrow, "The Fortune International 500 Directory," *Fortune,* July 31, 1989, pp. 291–318.

25. Nicholas Fasciano, "The Fortune Global 500," *Fortune,* July 29, 1991, pp. 237–280.

26. "The World's 100 Largest Public Companies," *The Wall Street Journal,* September 24, 1993, p. R26.

27. Dana Milbank, "U.S. Productivity Gains Cut Costs, Close Gap with Low-Wage Overseas Firms," *The Wall Street Journal,* December 23, 1992, p. A1.

28. Christopher Conte, "Closing the Gap," *The Wall Street Journal,* March 30, 1993, p. A1.

29. Amity Shlaes, "Anywhere but Germany," *The Wall Street Journal,* January 22, 1993, p. A10.

30. David Wessel, "U.S. Workers Excel in Productivity Poll," *The Wall Street Journal,* October 13, 1992, p. A2; and Thomas Stewart, "U.S. Productivity: First but Fading," *Fortune,* October 19, 1992, pp. 54–59.

31. Emily Thornton, Thomas Martin, and Cindy Kano, "What Now for the U.S. and Japan," *Fortune,* February 10, 1992, pp. 80–95.

32. Robert Keatley, "Luxury Auto Makers Consider Mexico: Its Low Cost Labor vs. Image Perception," *The Wall Street Journal,* November 27, 1992, p. A6.

33. Marcus W. Brauchli, "Trading in Tokyo," *The Wall Street Journal,* August 16, 1989, pp. A1;6.

34. Louis Kraar, "Korea, Tomorrow's Powerhouse," *Fortune,* August 15, 1988, pp. 75–81; and Laxmi Nakarmi, Larry Armstrong, and William J. Holstein, "Korea," *Business Week,* September 5, 1988, pp. 44–50.

35. Thomas O'Boyle, "New Neighbor: To Georgetown, KY, Toyota Plant Seems a Blessing and a Curse," *The Wall Street Journal,* November 26, 1991, p. A1+.

36. Ford Worthy, "Getting in on the Ground Floor," *Fortune,* 1990 Special Edition, pp. 63–67.

37. John Naisbitt and Patricia Aburdene, *Megatrends 2000: Ten New Directions for the 1990's* (New York: Morrow, 1990).

38. Bernard Wysocki, Jr., "In Asia, The Japanese Hope to 'Coordinate' What Nations Produce," *The Wall Street Journal,* August 20, 1990, p. A1.

39. Alan Murray, "China Trade Dilemma: New Thinking Needed," *The Wall Street Journal,* March 14, 1994, p. A1.

40. Wysocki, op cit.

41. Shawn Tully, "Europe Hits the Brakes on 1992," *Fortune,* December 17, 1990, pp. 133–140.

42. Heinz Weihrich, "Europe 1992: What the Future May Hold," *Academy of Management Executive* 4, 1990, pp. 7–18.

43. Nancy Perry, "What's Powering Mexico's Success?" *Fortune,* February 10, 1992, pp. 109–115.

44. Ibid.

45. Stephen Baker, David Woodruff, Bill Javetski, "Along the Border, Free Trade Is Becoming a Fact of Life," *Business Week,* June 18, 1990, pp. 41–42.

46. Gilbert Fuchsberg, "The Costs of Overseas Assignments Climb, Firms Select Expatriates More Carefully," *The Wall Street Journal,* January 9, 1992, p. B1+.

47. "Risky Opportunity," *HRMagazine,* June 1990, p. 26.

48. Louis Kraar, "Japan's Gung-Ho U.S. Car Plants," *Fortune,* January 30, 1989, pp. 98–108; and Joseph White, Gregory Patterson, and Paul Ingrassia, "American Auto Makers Need Overhaul to Match the Japanese," *The Wall Street Journal,* January 10, 1992, pp. A1, A4.

49. Emily Thornton, "50 Fateful Years from Enemy to Friend to __?" *Fortune,* December 16, 1991, pp. 126–134.

50. Dori Jones Yang, Dinah Lee, William J. Holstein, and Maria Shao, "China: The Great Leap Backward," *Business Week,* June 19, 1989, pp. 28–32; and William Glasgall, Dori Jones Yang, Dinah Lee, Joe Weber, and Amy Borrus, "Has Beijing Burned Its Bridges with Business?" *Business Week,* June 19, 1989, pp. 32–33.

51. Pete Engardio and Laurence Zuckerman, "Yankee Traders Breathe a Sigh of Relief," *Business Week,* February 3, 1992, pp. 39–42.

52. Susan Carter, John Rossanto, Frank J. Comes, and John Templeman, "Why the Ayatollah Is Whipping Up a New Wave of Fanaticism," *Business Week,* March 6, 1989, p. 47; and Stanley Reed, "When the Dust Settles, Iran May Be Facing West," *Business Week,* June 19, 1989, p. 50.

53. Jose de Cordoba, "Wanted in Caracas," *The Wall Street Journal,* August 24, 1989, p. A1.

54. John Dupuy, "Learning to Manage World-Class Strategy," *Management Review,* October 1991, pp. 40–44.

55. Karl Weick, *The Social Psychology of Organizing* (Reading, MA: Addison-Wesley, 1969).

56. Brian Dumaine, "The Best Management Books of 1991," *Fortune,* January 27, 1992, pp. 113–114.

57. Timothy Aeppel, "Opel Designs Car Plant on Japanese Lines," *The Wall Street Journal,* January 21, 1992, p. A16.

58. Sol Levine and Paul E. White, "Exchange as a Conceptual Framework for the Study of Interorganizational Relationships," *Administrative Science Quarterly* 5, March 1961, pp. 683–701.

59. Stephen S. Cohen and John Zysman, *Manufacturing Matters: The Myth of the Post Industrial Economy* (New York: Basic Books, 1987).

60. Liam Fahey and William R. King, "Environmental Scanning for Corporate Planning," *Business Horizons,* August 1977, p. 63.

61. Robert Keatley, "Luxury Auto Makers Consider Mexico: Its Low Cost Labor vs. Image Perception," *The Wall Street Journal,* November 27, 1992, p. A6; and Michael J. McCarthy, "Why German Firms Choose the Carolinas to Build U.S. Plants," *The Wall Street Journal,* May 4, 1993, p. A1.

CHAPTER 3

FORMULATING A CORPORATE AND HUMAN RESOURCE STRATEGY

When a company makes decisions about such issues as the market in which it will compete, how it can ensure continued growth over the next several years, and ways in which it can better utilize its human resources, it is formulating corporate strategy. To formulate strategies, managers try to find a way for their organizations to best fit into the environment in which they function. To do this, they must understand the current environment as well as predict any changes that may occur to that environment, all the while being sure that they understand their customers' needs and desires. Obviously, formulating corporate strategy is a difficult and time-consuming process. This chapter explains how managers go about this process. It also considers the various human resource strategies and how this important functional strategy contributes to a company's overall success.

CHAPTER OBJECTIVES

After studying this chapter, you should be able to

1. Describe the strategy formulation process.
2. List and define at least 10 generic strategies.
3. Differentiate between business level and corporate strategies.
4. Explain the role of the personnel/human resources department in strategy formulation.
5. Understand the importance of functional strategies, especially human resource strategy.
6. Understand how human resource strategy contributes to overall strategy success.
7. Understand the importance of the human resource audit.
8. Explain the contingency approach or situational approach to strategy formulation.

SOUTHWEST AIRLINES—FLYING HIGH WITH KELLEHER[1]

For a little while, it looked as if the major players in the U.S. airline industry had finally struck a crippling blow to the one competitor who had made them all "pea green with envy." In one announcement after another in the spring and summer of 1994, several travel agencies unveiled their plans to stop using the services of Southwest Airlines. These moves represented a threat to Southwest, with the worst possibility being that many customers of travel agencies nationwide would have limited access to its flights. The reason for the action cited by most of the travel agencies was the fact that Southwest refused to pay their pricy booking fees. Officials at Southwest defended their refusal to pay for several reasons. First, paying such premiums would affect Southwest's overall strategy of offering value prices and quality service. Southwest also refused to pay because its competition owned most of the travel agencies. Southwest was determined not to back down, vowing to beat the competition by doing what no one else seemed to be doing: providing efficient and pleasing service at a very reasonable price. This new threat changed the game a bit, but it certainly did not change Southwest's underlying strategy of efficiency, good service, and low price that had proven very successful.

In response to this action by travel agencies, Southwest chairman Herb Kelleher took an action that exemplifies company strategy. The savvy, bright, and witty head of the nation's highest-rated and most admired airline published a personal letter to customers in numerous publications including *The Wall Street Journal.* The letter basically stated that Southwest had never bowed to the pressure of competition and that this latest ploy by the competition would be treated no differently. Southwest would work hard, as always, to make things "right" for the customer. Kelleher reported to customers that Southwest was working to make ticket purchase as easy as possible. He noted that negotiations were continuing with the major travel agencies but in the meantime, Southwest was developing a number of ways that customers could purchase tickets, such as by calling a toll-free number. He was enthusiastic and reassuring. Considering the prevailing reputation of the company and of Kelleher, it appeared that Southwest would not be hampered by this competitive move.

INNOVATION AND WIT IN A SERIOUS BUSINESS

Why was Kelleher so confident that customers would take his letter seriously? To put it simply, customers seem to enjoy dealing with Southwest. They have described traveling with Southwest as a refreshing adventure, mainly because of its employees and their commitment to the customer and to the company. Southwest is a nontraditional airline. It outperforms the competition consistently by doing a number of things considered radical and innovative when first introduced but that the industry quickly imitates.

Southwest is a domestic airline specializing in linking large and medium-sized cities throughout the Southwest, South, and Midwest. This short-haul airline (average flight is of less than 375 miles) offers services that are very good but not fancy. For instance, because Southwest offers mainly short-haul flights, it does not serve an in-flight meal, resulting in a savings for the customer. Its low fares attract many customers, for example businesspeople, who choose to fly rather than drive. Their fares are shockingly low (averaging less than $100). These low fares result in flights that are almost always full.

To keep fares so low, Southwest has become very efficient in its operations. Planes arrive just minutes before boarding and are back in the air very quickly, 15 to 20 minutes versus the industry average of 60 minutes. Southwest gets high mileage out of each plane every day. Each plane makes 10 flights per day, more than twice the industry average. Southwest saves big money by making more flights with fewer planes and fewer employees than do other airlines. Southwest planes, all 737s (another cost-cutting ploy) fly the less-crowded "second airports" such as Love Field in Dallas and Midway Airport in Chicago. Luggage is routed correctly and is waiting for customers at the baggage claim on arrival.

PEOPLE MAKE THE DIFFERENCE

An especially notable difference between Southwest and other airlines relates to human resources. Most analysts say that the people at Southwest make the difference. Its flight attendants and pilots are very pleasant, even witty.

Kelleher is an imaginative, engaging, and witty person. He is a free spirit who enjoys talking to employees about how to solve company problems. One airline analyst remarked that "Herb," as he is known by even the lowest-level employees, is the kind of manager who will stay out late with a mechanic in a bar to find out what the company's problems are. He jokes with colleagues and employees. He encourages a light attitude about work and about helping customers in every way possible. Employees identify closely with him and work extra hard to keep Southwest ahead of the competition in pleasing customers. Obviously, labor relations are excellent due to Herb's hands-on approach.

A STRATEGIC HUMAN RESOURCE MATTER

The strategy of offering highly efficient and superb service would be very difficult to pull off without an excellent human resource strategy. Kelleher attracts witty, professional individuals and demands a great deal of them. Employees say that working for Herb is great fun. Flight attendants, for example, go out of their way to amuse and entertain passengers by adding humor to such otherwise mundane activities as the safety lecture and the beverage service. One flight attendant asked passengers to "pass the plastic cups to the center aisle so they could be washed out and used for the next flight." Another flight attendant told passengers, "Those of you who wish to smoke are invited out to our lounge on the wing, where the feature film will be *Gone with the Wind*." Southwest is committed to winning passengers away from its competitors. Attendants invite customers on arrival at a destination, which almost always occurs on time, to "choose Southwest next time." Most passengers do.

The bond between employees and the company is close. Employees know that the company's success depends on their performance. Everyone focuses on efficiency and is committed to improvement. In return for this commitment, the employee gets good pay and a great job. One analyst reports that at most airlines, managers say that people are the most important resource, but only at Southwest is that fact proven day after day. Employees are the key to Southwest's superior efficiency and customer satisfaction. Southwest is a unique company because of an almost unbelievable employee commitment to success. What's interesting is that employees are more than happy to perform so well for the company.

Southwest recognizes the importance of employees and is spending time and money to ensure quality recruitment, training, compensation, motivation, and labor relations. The dividends are paying off. Southwest has lower turnover, higher employee satisfaction and commitment, and a higher ratio of passengers per employee and operates more aircraft per employee than any other airline.

As Kelleher put it in his published letter, "Southwest has survived many challenges during its 23-year history." Under Kelleher's leadership, Southwest will likely suffer little from this threat by travel agencies. Southwest has always succeeded, and, with such a well-run company, one must believe that many of Southwest's thousands of customers would forgo the inconvenience related to making reservations in order to get such a great value.

This case describes a company that has been very successful by providing a high-quality, valuable service to customers. It is evident, however, that a company cannot just go out and provide such services without the key resources and the means to manage them. This case shows that a company's human resource strategy and practices contribute largely to its overall success. Efficiency, professionalism, humor and quality service characterize most Southwest employees, and company leaders attribute success to the overall pride they exhibit. Southwest's human resource strategy reflects the efforts of managers to maintain this "mix." Southwest's continued success certainly depends on it.

STRATEGIC CHOICES

When formulating a corporate strategy, managers must consider several strategic choices. To make the appropriate choice, the following should be addressed:

1. Choosing the strategy that the company should adopt to maintain or improve its position in the marketplace.
2. Ensuring continued sales growth and maintenance of its workforce to avoid retrenchment and layoff.
3. Adapting to its ever-changing environment.
4. Collecting the information it needs to understand and influence its environment.
5. Determining whether to change operating environments. If so, to which one? Why?

THE STRATEGY FORMULATION PROCESS

STRATEGY
The basic way an organization operates and competes.

Organizations devise and adopt **strategies** to compete and survive. Often particular strategies are not clearly articulated but can be inferred from the organization's actions. When this is the case, it is possible for the strategies to fail because all of the parties involved may not understand the strategy. Further, misunderstanding can lead to non-compliance, which can cause the strategy to fail.[2] Sometimes strategies are clearly articulated, but the organization's actions are not consistent with the strategy. Nevertheless, a strategy exists when there is a pattern, either articulated or suggested through action. Without a pattern, there is no strategy.[3]

The strategy formulation process is not neat and clean, nor should it be. Even though it should be systematic, strategy must remain *flexible*. This requirement for flexibility contributes to the messy appearance of the strategy formation process—revisions are made as conditions change, new ideas are incorporated, and ineffective actions are discontinued.

One example of flexibility in strategy formulation was Pillsbury's changes in Burger King's management and promotional campaign in 1988. At that time, Burger King's advertisements focused on the theme, "We do it like you'd do it." However, this approach was not working as evidenced by falling sales. New leadership was selected and a new strategy was adopted for the nineties. Even though the 1986–1987 strategy had been carefully formulated, it was changed because Pillsbury's management did not believe it was working as it should. This flexibility and change, while necessary, can be confusing when trying to determine exactly what an organization's strategy is.

A second factor that makes understanding the strategy formulation process difficult is *secrecy*. Many firms, particularly those in highly competitive markets, do not want to make their strategy public because they do not want competition to use their knowledge of it to their advantage. For this reason, Southwest Airline's strategy described at the beginning of this chapter is no doubt more complex than that related by the articles on which the case was based.

Yet, even though it is often difficult to determine the precise strategy of a firm, a strategy exists, no matter how ill formed or ambiguous it might be.

STRATEGIC PLANNING

STRATEGIC PLANNING

Forming a strategy and deciding how to achieve it.

The basis of strategy formulation is usually the strategic planning process. **Strategic planning** *is the systematic determination of strategic goals and the strategies to obtain them.* Many organizations formulate strategy through a series of strategic planning retreats—usually off-site meetings of key executives where plans are made and strategies formulated. For example, Clay Electric Cooperative in Florida holds an annual strategic planning retreat each summer in St. Augustine, Florida. At this retreat, the previous year's strategic plan, strategies, and goals are reviewed and new ones are set for the coming year and beyond.

Strategic plans are generally *long-term (three to five years or more) plans* that involve major decisions and the commitment of large amounts of organizational resources to key goals. While there are several models of strategic planning, each usually involves a series of analytical steps, such as those presented in Exhibit 3.1. Note that the model begins with broad consideration of environmental factors and ends with specific operational steps. We will briefly examine each step in the process.[4]

ENVIRONMENTAL SCAN

The first step in developing a strategic plan is to examine the outside environment surrounding the organization. The idea is to do a point-in-time analysis of significant aspects of the outside environment as they affect the organization, as was discussed in Chapter 2. Participants in the planning process should scan the societal and task environmental forces.

ENVIRONMENTAL FORECAST

This step involves predicting how the environment is changing. Trends are explored and new issues of impact are identified. Implications for the future of the organization are explored. We also discussed this step in Chapter 2.

CUSTOMER/MARKET/COMPETITOR ANALYSIS

Establishing a sharper understanding of why the organization exists (such as to serve a market) is the next step in the planning process. Emphasis is placed on analyzing how

EXHIBIT 3.1   **The Strategic Planning Process**

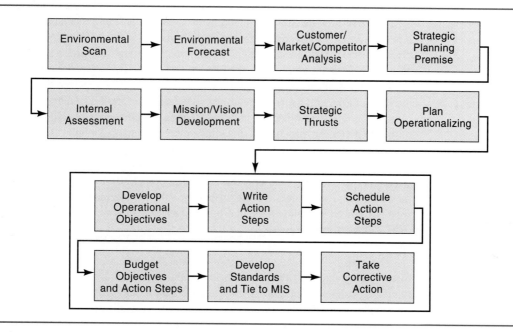

the market is changing and developing a profile of the customer of tomorrow. An organization's competitors are also examined here. For example, Southwest Airlines attempts to understand the changing needs of the short-haul airline commuter.

STRATEGIC PLANNING PREMISES

The organization develops strategic planning premises that reflect key assumptions about the future. The premises are based on the forecast and serve as the basis for developing the strategic plan.

INTERNAL ASSESSMENT

In this step, management attempts to determine the strengths and weaknesses of the organization as it currently exists in order to establish a planning base. The internal assessment and environmental analysis identify the firm's strengths, weaknesses, opportunities, and threats (SWOT). A well-conceived strategy emphasizes strengths and minimizes weaknesses in an effort to exploit opportunities and avoid threats.

MISSION/VISION DEVELOPMENT

MISSION
Basic purpose of the organization.

VISION
Statement of what the organization will be like in the future.

This step in the planning process outlines the role and **mission** of the organization in view of the environment it faces and the resources it has or can reasonably expect to obtain. The mission provides the ultimate rationale for the organization's existence and gives the organization identity. The **vision,** which may be incorporated as part of the mission or be a separate statement, describes what the organization will look like at some point in the future.

STRATEGIC THRUSTS

These are the three or four *major strategies* or key goals on which the organization plans to focus its efforts in the next three to five years. They reflect the mission and forecast.

PLAN OPERATIONALIZATION

The way to implement the strategic plan, from the development of operational objectives through the process of taking corrective action, is reflected in this step. Even though we present the strategic planning process in this step-by-step process, in reality it is not this simple. Even though it is best to proceed in the order suggested here, most organizations revisit previous steps as they move through the process. This is a good policy check, and it emphasizes the need to make the planning process flexible.

The factors of this process are presented in Exhibit 3.2. Note that the environment, the competition, and internal strengths and weaknesses are the elements of the strategy formulation process. When formulating strategy, organizations should try to capitalize on their strengths while taking advantage of environmental opportunities in order to beat their competition. Strategy also is formulated to protect the organization from environmental threats and to overcome internal weaknesses. For example, Southwest is attempting to overcome the new threat of old competition by reminding customers of their excellent experiences on Southwest—an inherent strength of the company. Southwest has vowed to maintain its quality service and overcome the threat.

FUTURE ORIENTATION

Strategy formulation is an attempt to anchor the organization to some position in the future. This future orientation is a key concept to strategy formulation. Decisions are made today to formulate strategy that will place the organization at a particular position at a particular point in the future. Every organization attempts to create a desirable future for itself.

For example, the German companies discussed in Chapter 2's ending case were well aware of the fact that future success would depend on a close relationship with the enormous U.S. auto market. The German companies determined that future success depends on using high-quality workers to manufacture cars in the United States at a moderate to low cost. The companies have decided that the workers available in the Carolinas as well as other human resource opportunities have the potential to help the companies reach their goals.

EXHIBIT 3.2   **Key Factors in Strategy Formulation**

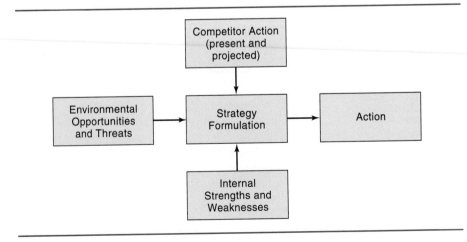

Strategy is goal oriented, and goals exist in the future. In strategy formulation, organizations learn from the past—they learn from their mistakes—but they cannot change the past. "We should have done this" or "We should have done that" has relevance only so far as it specifies what the company should do now.

EVOLUTIONARY PROCESS

The strategy formulation process is evolutionary in nature. It evolves over time as conditions change. Sometimes, however, this process is more revolutionary than evolutionary. When Lee Iacocca became the CEO of Chrysler, strategy changed quickly and abruptly. When an organization faces an immediate danger or crisis, quick change in strategy is needed. Even though such rapid change in strategy does occur, organizational inertia works against it.

ORGANIZATIONAL INERTIA

The tendency of an organization to stay in its present form or on its present path.

Inertia is the tendency of an organization to stay on its present course or in its present form. The stronger the inertia, the less likely change will occur. **Organizational inertia** serves to anchor the organization and is the principal reason that strategy formulation is evolutionary rather than revolutionary most of the time.

Factors that enhance inertia include organizational culture, tradition, competitive forces, size, and the ability to standardize routines. However, sometimes inertia can be overcome by sudden changes or disturbances. For example, the space shuttle *Challenger* disaster forced Morton-Thoikol, the booster contractor, as well as NASA, to undertake major changes in management and operational procedures to prevent such a disaster from occurring again.

PHILOSOPHICAL AND ETHICAL DIMENSIONS

Strategy is heavily laden with the personal philosophies and codes of ethics of key decision makers in an organization. Of course, this is clearly seen in family-run organizations, even large ones such as Ford Motor Company in the 1920s. Henry Ford *was* Ford Motor and his philosophy and ethical values dominated the company.

Yet, even in large organizations where the power is diffused, the philosophy and ethical values of decision makers shape the strategy. For years, General Motors has been known as a company that widely distributes decision authority for strategy formulation among members of its executive committee. The personal values and ethics of individuals on this committee come into play in decisions involving product safety, design, fuel economy, dealer relations, customer warranties, labor costs, and so on. For example, in the initial discussion about the installation of passive restraint systems in autos (air bags), some believed that such installation was sound from a moral standpoint, even though the official position of GM was not to install them on all makes and models automatically. This position contrasted with that of Chrysler, which ran a personal pledge from Lee Iacocca in *The Wall Street Journal* advertisements to install such systems in every car and truck Chrysler makes. Such a competitive action may have caused GM to change its position on the issue. It certainly has won Chrysler wide approval and has boosted sales.

STAKEHOLDER ANALYSIS

STAKEHOLDERS

Constituent groups who have a stake in the organization's operations.

Another major influence on the formulation of strategy comes from **stakeholders.** Stakeholders are groups of people who have a major interest in or claim on the operations or output of the organization.[5] They are also referred to as constituent groups. While the specific stakeholder groups for a particular organization are unique to that organization, Exhibit 3.3 shows examples of stakeholder groups in an organization and Exhibit 3.4 shows some of the stakeholder groups for a human resource unit.

Notice that some of an organization's stakeholders are actual members of the organization: employees, managers, and boards of directors (except for outside board members). However, notice the range of outside groups that can affect the formulation of an organization's strategy—unions, suppliers, dealers, and government regulatory agencies. Each of these groups lays claims to part of the organization's output. Employees want more wages and job security; stockholders want more dividends and higher stock prices; customers want quality products and services at the lowest possible price.

Obviously, an organization cannot possibly satisfy all of these groups completely. Therefore, it bargains, negotiates, and compromises. No group receives maximum returns on its claims from the organization; rather the organization tries to at least minimally satisfy each group.

Of course, the claims of some groups sometimes become stronger than others. The Teamsters Union pushes strongly for a wage increase. Ford's dealers argue for better financing terms. A public interest group from a small midwestern community storms a corporation's headquarters to protest the local plant's relocation to Mexico. A corporate raider tries to buy enough stock to take control of a company. In each of these situations, the organization must decide what its basic position will be and how this position will affect the organization now and in the future.

EXHIBIT 3.3   **Example Stakeholder Groups of an Organization**

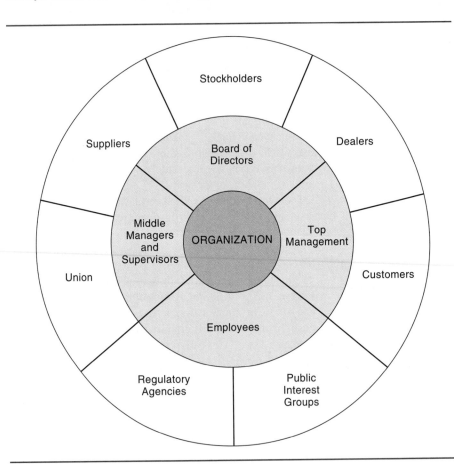

SOCIETAL FORCES

As we noted in Chapter 2, a powerful influence on policy formulation comes from the *societal forces* at work in the environment, in which the organization exists. Social forces are the broad trends in the economy, politics, and culture of a society. These ebb and flow with time. As we noted in Chapter 2, these general forces can be sociocultural, political and legal, economic, or technological in nature. For example, in the political area, the liberalism of the Kennedy and Johnson administrations gave way to the conservatism of the Reagan administration as the political mood of the country shifted.

Sometimes these shifts are dramatic, as occurred with both the civil rights movement in the United States and the cultural revolution in the People's Republic of China in the 1960s and the Khomeini revolution in Iran in the late 1970s. Other times, they are less dramatic but just as powerful, such as the increasing participation of women in career-oriented jobs that began in the 1960s in the United States. Today, many business and political discussions and decisions are dominated by the fact that the population of the

EXHIBIT 3.4   **Example Stakeholder Groups of the Human Resource Subunit**

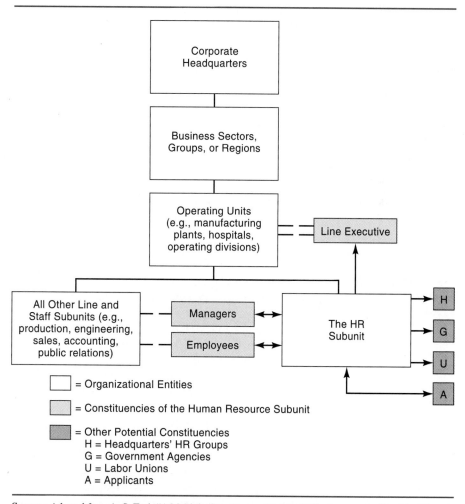

SOURCE: Adapted from A. S. Tsui, "A Multiple-Constituency Model of Effectiveness: An Empirical Examination at the Human Resouce Subunit Level," *Administrative Science Quarterly* 35 (1990), pp. 458–483.

United States, especially in Sunbelt states such as Florida, is aging rapidly. Many new companies and innovative services will capitalize on this change in U.S. society.

The point is that underlying societal forces heavily affect strategy formulation in individual organizations. Of course, this occurs in the strategy formulation process of many organizations. For example, when performing an environmental scan, strategists attempt both to discern and forecast these trends and to position their organization to capitalize on them. This is why John Naisbitt's books *Megatrends* and *Megatrends 2000* were such top sellers for so long during the 1980s and 1990s. Many decision makers are hungry for information that expands on and predicts trends.[6] Of course, not everyone agrees with these trends and some have been severely criticized.[7]

TYPES OF STRATEGIES

GENERIC STRATEGIES
Basic strategies that any organization can use.

It is impossible to list completely all of the strategies available to an organization, but it is possible to identify a core set of **generic strategies.** These are distinctly identifiable, basic strategies that an organization may choose to follow. The appropriateness of each strategy for a particular organization is situational in that it depends on the environment, market, social forces, mission, and internal strengths and weaknesses faced by a particular organization. Moreover, the selection of the strategy has a profound impact on human resource strategy. In fact, as we have indicated and will discuss further in this chapter, human resource strategy should also affect the formation of corporate strategy.

Two primary levels of generic strategy are discussed: corporate or organizationwide strategies and business or industry-level strategies. It is important to note that in a single-product company operating in one line of business or industry, there is virtually no difference between corporatewide and business-level strategies. Exhibit 3.5 summarizes the types of strategies found at each level. We will briefly examine each one.

GENERIC CORPORATE-LEVEL STRATEGIES

These strategies are adopted and followed by the organization as a whole. They fall into four main categories: (1) growth, (2) stability, (3) defensive, and (4) combination.

GROWTH STRATEGIES

CONCENTRATION GROWTH STRATEGY
An organization's plans to focus its growth on a single product or on a group of closely related products.

Most organizations wish to grow. As a matter of fact, a study of 358 *Fortune* companies by William Glueck indicated that 54.2 percent pursue a growth strategy.[8] A **concentration growth strategy** means that the organization plans to focus its growth on a single product or group of closely related products, as is the situation with Coors Breweries, which has a very narrow line of brewery products compared to the vast number of different products from Anheuser-Busch.

A growth strategy can be pursued in three ways. First, the existing market can be developed by expanding market share or moving into new geographic regions. Second, the product can be slightly changed or developed. Perhaps a new or closely aligned product can be added (such as the introduction of Coors Light to the Coors line). Third, a concentration growth strategy can be achieved through horizontal integration. Here, another product in the same business is added, usually through buying an organization, as when Dr. Pepper bought Canada Dry in 1982.

The James River Corporation, a Virginia paper goods manufacturer, is aggressively pursuing a growth strategy using these methods. First, the company is attempting to expand its market share by pushing its product in the northeastern states. Second, it is de-

| **EXHIBIT 3.5** | **Generic Corporate- and Business-Level Strategies** |

I. Generic corporate-level strategies
   A. Growth strategies
     1. Concentration
      a. Market development
      b. Product development
      c. Horizontal integration
     2. Vertical integration
      a. Backward integration
      b. Forward integration
     3. Diversification
      a. Concentric diversification
      b. Conglomerate diversification
     4. Implementation of growth strategy
      a. Internal growth
      b. Acquisition
      c. Merger
      d. Joint venture

   B. Stability strategy
     1. Neutral
     2. Harvest (milk the investment)
   C. Defensive (retrenchment) strategies
     1. Turnaround
     2. Divestiture
     3. Liquidation
     4. Bankruptcy
     5. Captive
   D. Combination strategies
II. Generic business-level strategies
   A. Overall cost leadership
   B. Product/service differentiation
   C. Market segment focus
   D. Preemptive strategies

SOURCE: Reprinted by permission from p. 254 of *Organizaion Theory,* third edition, by B. J. Hodge and William P. Anthony; copyright © 1988 by Allyn & Bacon, Inc. All Rights Reserved.

VERTICAL INTEGRATION STRATEGY
A plan to achieve growth by acquiring other firms in the marketing or distribution chain.

DIVERSIFICATION
Moving into products or services different from current ones.

INTERNAL GROWTH
Implementing a growth strategy by expanding current market share with current products.

ACQUISITION
Implementing a growth strategy by buying another company while retaining the buyer's company name.

MERGER
Implementing a growth strategy by joining two companies to form a new company and adopting a new name.

JOINT VENTURE
Implementing a growth strategy by working together with another company on a specific project.

veloping a host of new paper products, such as coated paper plates, that it hopes will win a large share of the $500 million per year paper plate market. Third, through the process of horizontal integration, it has purchased other paper goods companies, such as Connecticut's Dixie Northern.[9]

Vertical integration strategy is another way to achieve growth. Here, the organization can either acquire its suppliers (backward integration) or acquire its distributors (forward integration); some organizations do both. Miller Brewing has purchased its own aluminum can manufacturing facilities in addition to acquiring some of its distribution channels.

The third way growth can occur is through **diversification.** Diversification occurs when an organization moves into products or services that are clearly different from its current businesses. Diversification has two forms. Concentric diversification occurs when related but clearly differentiated products or services are developed or obtained. Coca-Cola's purchase of Minute Maid is an excellent example. Conglomerate diversification occurs when the firm diversifies into an area totally unrelated to the product or service. Bic's development of the disposable safety razor resulted in a product totally unrelated to its pen business.

The implementation of growth strategies can be accomplished through four basic methods: internal growth, acquisition, merger, and joint venture. **Internal growth** occurs when current market share for current products is expanded (for example, GM sells more Chevrolets relative to competitive brands). An **acquisition** occurs when one company buys another and absorbs it but keeps its own name; a **merger** occurs when two companies join to form a new company and adopt a new name. A **joint venture** occurs when two or more companies work together for a specific project, such as oil exploration and drilling; they pool their resources and take a risk for a specific endeavor.

HR CHALLENGE

Megatrends

John Naisbitt and Patricia Aburdene lead an organization dedicated to identifying very large social, economic, political, and technological changes in our society. According to Naisbitt and Aburdene, *megatrends,* or the large societal shifts taking place, form the context for life. Indeed, megatrends will likely impact career and job decisions, travel, investments, place of residence, and business decisions. The organization finds these megatrends by systematically analyzing the media over time. Staff members scan newspaper, television, radio, and other media reports. According to Naisbitt, one can begin to see patterns emerging in what the media covers versus what it does not. The concerns and directions of society are soon apparent. In the early 1980s, Naisbitt introduced us to *Megatrends,* 10 trends for the 1980s. In 1990, Naisbitt and Aburdene revealed the 10 Megatrends for the 1990s and beyond in *Megatrends 2000.* In *Megatrends,* Naisbitt correctly noted the shift in the United States from an industrial society to an information society, a new emphasis on networking, the continued move to the Sunbelt, and the move to a world economy. The following are the shifts that Naisbitt and Aburdene described in *Megatrends 2000.*

1. **The Booming World Economy:** The economic forces of the world are surging across national borders, resulting in more democracy, more freedom, more trade, more opportunity, and greater prosperity.
2. **Renaissance in the Arts:** In the final years before the millennium there will be a fundamental . . . shift in leisure time and spending priorities. . . . the arts will gradually replace sports as society's primary leisure activity.
3. **The Emergence of Free Market Socialism:** The world is undergoing a profound shift from

economies run by governments to economies run by markets.
4. **Global Lifestyles and Cultural Nationalism:** The world is becoming more cosmopolitan, and we are all influencing each other.
5. **Privatization of the Welfare State:** Globally the key to transforming socialism and the welfare state is . . . privatization of state enterprise and private stock ownership.
6. **The Rise of the Pacific Rim:** Today the Pacific Rim is undergoing the fastest period of economic expansion in world history.
7. **Decade of Women in Leadership:** After two decades of quietly preparing, gaining experience, and being frustrated with the male establishment, women in business are on the verge of revolutionary change.
8. **The Age of Biology:** We are shifting from the models and metaphors of physics to the models and metaphors of biology to help us understand today's . . . opportunities. . . . *Biology* as a metaphor suggests: information intensive, micro, inner-directed, adaptive, holistic.
9. **Return to Religion:** At the dawn of the third millenium there are unmistakable signs of a worldwide multidenominational religious revival.
10. **Triumph of the Individual:** The great unifying theme at the conclusion of the 20th century is the triumph of the individual. The triumph of the individual signals the demise of the collective.

SOURCE: John Naisbitt and Patricia Aburdene, *Megatrends 2000: Ten New Directions for the 1990s* (New York: Morrow, 1990).

STABILITY STRATEGIES

HARVEST STRATEGY
A plan to get money out of a unit before disposing of it.

As opposed to growth strategies, stability strategies attempt to maintain the status quo. The two basic stability strategies are neutral and harvest. Neutral strategies are do-nothing approaches. The organization just keeps doing what it always has done without a growth goal in mind. A **harvest strategy,** sometimes called *milk-the-investment* strategy, represents an end-game strategy identified by Kathryn Harrigan in *Strategies for a*

Declining Business.[10] The idea is to retrieve the value of earlier investments because the firm intends to sell its assets and get out of the business.

DEFENSIVE STRATEGIES

RETRENCHMENT STRATEGIES
Plans to cut back or downsize.

TURNAROUND STRATEGIES
Plans to reverse a negative trend in performance back up to desired levels.

DIVESTITURE
A defensive strategy wherein an organization sells or divests itself of a business or part of a business.

LIQUIDATION
A defensive strategy that occurs when an organization is either sold or dissolved.

CAPTIVE
A defensive stategy wherein an organization allows another organization to manage it in return for promising to buy a certain amount of the captive's products or services.

A third set of corporate-level strategies involves actions taken to reverse a negative situation or overcome a crisis or problem. These are often called defensive or **retrenchment strategies.** An organization can adopt five basic defensive strategies. **Turnaround strategies** are designed to reverse a negative trend in performance, such as falling profits or increasing costs. Layoffs, wage cuts, expense account reduction, and advertising cuts are forms of turnaround strategies. LTV Steel, for example, postponed paying $180 million in pension fund contributions to cut costs.[11] Later, the company declared bankruptcy and could not pay bonuses to employees who had taken early retirement. They since have re-organized and are now a profitable firm.

A second type of defensive strategy is **divestiture.** This occurs when an organization sells or divests itself of a business or part of a business, as ITT did with many of its operations during the mid-1980s. In a **liquidation,** the organization is either sold or dissolved. DeLorean Motor Company, which was dissolved a number of years ago, and Walter E. Heller Corporation, a financial investment company that was sold to Fuji Bank of Japan in 1984, are good examples of liquidations.

Since the Bankruptcy Reform Act of 1978, bankruptcy has been used as a defensive strategy. Chapter 11 (in Title 11 of the United States Code), which involves a reorganization, is the device most used to rehabilitate corporate debtors who are having financial difficulties; it can be a way to escape a heavy debt load, contracted high wages, or even legal claims. Continental Airlines used Chapter 11 to negate its labor contracts with its unions; Manville Corporation used this method to avoid high legal costs caused by asbestos claims.

The final defensive strategy is to become a **captive** of another organization. This situation occurs when an organization allows another organization to manage it in return for promising to buy a certain amount of the captive's products or services. This strategy often occurs between a small- to medium-sized supplier and a major manufacturer or retailer.

COMBINATION STRATEGIES

The last major set of generic corporate-level strategies occurs when an organization simultaneously uses different strategies for different units. Next to growth strategies, combination strategies are most commonly used. Large diversified corporations, for example, are using combination strategies when they acquire new companies while selling others. They carve out market segments, develop new products, acquire suppliers and distributors, and so on. General Motors' recent actions, which involved dropping and adding models while acquiring Hughes Aircraft and EDS, are a good example of using a combination strategy.

GENERIC BUSINESS-LEVEL STRATEGIES

An organization employs business-level strategies for one of its particular product or service lines. This type of plan tends to be less generic than corporate-level strategies because it must be tailored to fit the unique circumstances of each organization. However, four basic strategy types are often used to classify business-level strategies: (1) overall cost leadership, (2) product/service differentiation, (3) market segment focus, and (4) preemptive strategies.

OVERALL COST LEADERSHIP

This strategy allows an organization to cut its prices by producing a product or service at less expense than the competition does. An organization achieves this strategy through extensive experience, cheap labor, size (economies of scale), reduced overhead, or more efficient technology. By providing less expensive goods and services, an organization can either sell at a lower price than its competition, garner a larger share of the market, or maintain its price and achieve a higher profit margin.

PRODUCT/SERVICE DIFFERENTIATION

An organization uses this strategy to create a perception in the market of the uniqueness of its product or service. A brand image, such as Bud Light beer or Polo sportswear, a quality image, such as that associated with Mercedes or Rolls Royce, or customer service, such as IBM offers, are but three ways to achieve this differentiation. Differentiation relies on convincing customers that the product or service is so unique that the customer should buy it.

MARKET SEGMENT FOCUS

This strategy attempts to carve out a part of the market and focus organizational efforts on serving it. The market segment selected for focus may be chosen on the basis of a demographic factor, such as age, income, family size, or geographic region. The idea is to achieve a competitive advantage within a narrowly focused market segment rather than to appeal to a broad market. The strategies of a high-fashion men's clothing store and Porsche automobiles are examples of market segmentation strategy. These products are aimed at a specific market segment.

PREEMPTIVE STRATEGIES

PREEMPTIVE STRATEGY
A plan to be first with a strategy before others adopt it.

Preemptive strategies are undertaken to disrupt the normal operations in an industry or product line by being first with a new product or process. A **preemptive strategy** essentially rewrites the rules of the game to compete in the industry. Such preemptive strategies may occur because of new product developments, as happened when Xerox became the first company in the office copier market, or they may occur when an unsegmented market is segmented, as happened when Miller Brewing developed the first low-calorie beer, Miller Lite. This type of strategy also could affect costs, as was the case when People Express Airlines was built around the concept of low price and discount air fares.

In each of these examples, the organization developed an innovative product or tactic that caught the competition off guard. Hence, the competition had to scramble to remain viable.

TWO KEY STRATEGIES FOR HUMAN RESOURCE MANAGEMENT

Two gross generic categories of strategy seem to have had the greatest impact on human resource management in recent years. Following a review of the literature, Cynthia Fisher classified strategies into two categories:[12]

1. Growth–prospector–high-tech entrepreneurial strategies.
2. Mature–defender–cost efficiency strategies.

Firms in the growth mode require creative, innovative, and risk-taking behavior from employees. Mature-defender firms need just the opposite kind of behavior—repetitive, predictable, and carefully specified.

Human resource management strategies under each mode are substantially different in terms of function. Human resource management units in growth firms typically

---

HR CHALLENGE

Examples of the Two Key Strategies for HRM

**Growth–Prospector–High-Tech
Entrepreneurial Strategy**

Apple Computer began in a California garage in 1975.
Its employment grew very rapidly from 2,000 in 1980
to 6,700 in 1989. Creativity was the key ingredient
desired in employees, who were recruited at all levels
in the company. Hours and dress were very flexible. In
the early years, the style of management reflected the
creative entrepreneurial whims of its youthful founders:
brilliant college dropouts Steve Wozniak, 23, and Steve
Jobs, 19. Their freewheeling style led to an organization
described as "camp run amok." In March 1977, Apple
introduced its Apple II aimed primarily at the home and
school markets.

   Along with growth and success came the realization
that the business market was the potential source of
expansion. As sales in the company grew, new
employees, opportunities, and problems were presented
to the "entrepreneurial" staff. The Apple II was rushed
to the market in 1980 without adequate quality control,
and the product failed miserably. The introduction of
the Apple III in 1981 unfortunately coincided with
IBM's entry into the market with the PC. Apple did
score a success with the IIe in 1983, but the Lisa model
met with considerable market resistance because of its
price. It became clear that Apple needed to retain its
creative spirit but at the same time react to the turbulent
market environment. In the summer of 1981, Apple
began an intensive search for a new CEO. In April
1983, John Scully from Pepsi-Cola was hired as CEO.
Scully brought a new sense of professionalism,
marketing expertise, and organizational skills. The more
formalized structure led to conflicts and disagreements
with the founders. In January 1985, Wozniak removed
himself as a major decision maker. In April 1985, the
Apple board of directors removed Steve Jobs from his
Macintosh position and eventually from the entire
company.

   Scully's human resource management challenge was
to retain Apple's innovative spirit but in a more
business-like atmosphere that could support an ever-
growing market. He has reorganized Apple into four
internal operating divisions: Apple Products, Apple
USA, Apple Europe, and Apple Pacific. According to
Scully, one of the primary reasons for the company's
reorganization is the preservation of the employees'
independent spirit, innovation, and passion to build
great products. The human resource management
decision to reorganize into the four divisions distributed
leadership of the company. This fatter organizational
structure allows Apple to react more quickly to
technological and market changes.

Mature–Defender–Cost Efficiency Strategy

More often than not, firms that have adopted this
strategy have been around for some time. A good
example is the Campbell Soup Company. In the fall of
1989, Campbell closed four U.S. plants, consolidated
operations overseas, and eliminated about 2,800 jobs.
Its original plant in Camden, New Jersey, was among
those closed. During 1989 its plants ran at only about
60 percent of its capacity. These closings were in
addition to several plants closed in 1988. Workers
affected by the closings were given at least six-months
notice and severance benefits.

   The company president and CEO indicated that the
restructuring and plant consolidations were part of "an
ongoing effort to slim down" and become a more
efficient global competitor.

   The company also retrofitted many of its older
plants with new technology and is studying prototype
plans for a major technological breakthrough involving
sophisticated computer applications. The firm
acknowledged that the restructuring will cause a
massive change in job design structure and skills
needed. Training programs will need to be redesigned.

SOURCE: Charles W. L. Hill and Gareth R. Jones, *Strategic
Management,* 2nd ed. (Boston: Houghton Mifflin, 1992), pp.
87–89; 176–179.

---

recruit at all levels from the external labor market in order to obtain enough employees
at all skill levels to meet growth needs. They tend to assess people based on the results
they achieve rather than the process they employ or their personal traits. They also tend
to look to the long term for success and usually do not pursue innovative efforts that
fail. Performance incentives serve as the basis for compensation; when bonuses and
profit-sharing and stock options are common, base salaries are modest.[13]

Mature–defender–cost competitors follow opposite personnel actions.[14] They tend to recruit primarily at the entry level and promote from within. They emphasize doing things the right way in assessing performance and focus on quantifiable short-term results. Compensation is based on hierarchical wage structures determined by job evaluation. Length of service, loyalty, and other traits are rewarded rather than performance. Financial incentives may be present but tend to be available only to few select employee groups.

ROLE OF THE MARKET AND COMPETITION IN STRATEGY FORMULATION

Probably no other factor has had such a major influence on strategy formulation and human resource strategy during the 1980s as *competitive analysis.* Even though we briefly discussed this in Chapters 1 and 2, it is useful to review it at this point to see its impact on strategy formulation.

The essential action that an organization attempts to achieve with respect to its competitors is a **sustainable competitive advantage (SCA).**[15] Although this idea has been around for a long time, it took on new meaning and urgency in the 1980s as U.S. corporations attempted to become more competitive in a global economy.

SUSTAINABLE COMPETITIVE ADVANTAGE (SCA)
Achieving something different and important from the competition and being able to maintain this difference (i.e., differential advantage).

Basically, a sustainable competitive advantage is an advantage that differentiates a particular organization from its competition and that allows it to achieve success. It may be low cost, such as the inexpensive Hyundai in the automotive market; it may be brand loyalty, such as that enjoyed by Coke. In fact, it could be just about anything an organization can come up with to differentiate itself from its competition: speed, friendliness, reliability, image or prestige, convenience, and so on. What matters is that the organization can make the customer believe that such a differential advantage exists and that the organization can sustain this advantage over time.

COMPETITIVE ANALYSIS[16]

In performing a competitive analysis, the market, industry, competition, and the internal organization are examined. To do this, several additional levels of analysis must be performed. Exhibit 3.6 presents some factors to consider.

The questions listed in Exhibit 3.6 are not easy to answer, but they must be answered to establish and maintain a sustainable competitive advantage. This advantage may be a package of product/service attributes as opposed to any one attribute. People buy BMWs for prestige, reliability, and resale value. People fly Southwest Airlines because of its low cost and personable employees.

COST-CUTTING COMPETITIVE STRATEGY

As we previously stated, the mature–defender–cost efficiency strategy was common during the 1980s when many organizations attempted to become more competitive by cutting costs. This strategy had a significant effect on human resources in individual organizations that adopted it in at least three major ways: their wages or rate of increase slowed significantly; a significant number of employees were cut or their rate of promotion slowed, especially for higher-paid and staff employees; and production was shifted to lower-wage labor markets, such as the southern United States or developing countries. Sometimes these actions were taken at the initiative of the company;

EXHIBIT 3.6   **Some Factors to Consider in Performing a Competitive Strategy Analysis**

MARKET

1. What is the market? Who now purchases the product/service and why?
2. What is the potential market? Who *could* purchase the product/service?
3. How fast is the market growing?
4. Can product/service usage be increased or has saturation been achieved?

INDUSTRY

1. Within what industry does the market exist? How narrowly should the industry be defined (e.g., transportation industry vs. railroad industry; energy industry vs. oil industry)?
2. What barriers to entry and exit exist in the industry?
3. Who dominates the industry and why?
4. What substitute products exist for industry products?
5. What is the growth stage of the industry (e.g., emerging, rapid, mature, declining)?
6. What are the critical success factors to be successful in the industry?

COMPETITION

1. Who are the major competitors? What are their descriptive profiles (e.g., size, location, product features)?
2. What does each competitor do well? What does each do poorly?
3. What gaps exist in the market? What service or product features not now being provided could be?
4. Can this service or product be provided profitably? How do we know this?

INTERNAL ORGANIZATION

1. What are our strengths and weaknesses?
2. What are our unique attributes relative to the competition?
3. How can we capitalize on these attributes?
4. Do we have or can we obtain additional resources to capitalize on these attributes or to develop new ones?
5. Can we be profitable relying on these attributes?
6. How can we sustain this differential over time? How is present competition likely to change? How is new competition likely to change?
7. Can we convince the customer that we do indeed have something better to offer? How many do we have to convince to remain profitable (e.g., what must be our market share)?

sometimes they occurred as a result of a takeover or merger. Regardless, when an organization adopts a competitive strategy that emphasizes cost cutting, the decision has a profound impact on human resource strategies in all phases of human resource activity: hiring, placement, promotion, pay, layoff, outplacement, retraining, retirement, and so on. The effects and implications of this cost-cutting strategy on human resources are so significant that they will be explored throughout this book.

   The popularity of cost-cutting strategies reflects the attempt of corporations to reach a more competitive level on a global basis. Competing with imports produced by foreign manufacturers in lower-wage countries required U.S. corporations to find ways to cut costs to remain competitive. Human resource costs, of course, were not the only ones attacked. Inventory cost and availability were scrutinized as a result of the just-in-time approach to inventory. Just-in-time inventory reflects efforts to shift the carrying costs of inventories to suppliers. Relocation and new plant construction costs could be cut without jeopardizing a firm's competitiveness. This concern with cost cutting will likely pervade human resource and other strategies throughout the 1990s as global competition becomes even more intense.

CUSTOMER PERSPECTIVE

In addition to understanding the industrial and market forces at work in formulating a sustainable competitive advantage, it is very important to look at the firm's product or service from the eyes of the customer.[17] What the firm believes to be its competitive advantage does not matter if it is not what the customer wants. Henry Ford was initially successful by competing on the basis of price. He was known to declare that the customer could have any color Ford he or she wanted, as long as it was black. This strategy worked until customers wanted style and color. GM quickly became dominant in the market by offering these attributes as a competitive advantage while Ford stuck to price.

Understanding the customer and what the customer expects and looks for in the product is at the heart of determining a sustainable competitive advantage. This calls for customer and consumer research and the incorporation of these findings into new product/service development as well as into the firm's advertising and promotional campaign. The sustainable competitive advantage must be communicated to the customer and amplified in his or her mind if the product/service is to be successful. It does IBM no good to justify the price of its OS/2 PC operating system on the basis of quality if price is the customer's primary consideration.

QUALITY

TOTAL QUALITY MANAGEMENT (TQM)
A systematic way to get all managers and employees involved in improving quality and meeting customer expectations.

EMPOWERMENT
Giving employees the power and authority to make decisions in order to satisfy the customer.

In recent years, many U.S. managers have attempted to implement **total quality management (TQM)** in their companies. We can loosely define TQM as a program that asks a company's human resources to become totally involved in eliminating company waste and improving product quality and customer satisfaction.[18] The goals of TQM workers are pleasing the customer, producing quality work with no reprocessing or recalls, and constantly improving the company.

To get workers to achieve these high goals, managers must empower their employees. **Empowerment** means that workers are given the authority and the know-how to actively solve problems themselves and, as a result, employees assume ownership of their products' quality and become committed to improvement. To perform at this level, workers must be trained thoroughly. TQM focuses on holistic, strategic improvement. Workers traditionally have been concerned with only a small portion of the production process, but under the TQM system, they work in teams to manage and improve the system as a whole. TQM workers must have a broad understanding of the company and its products or services. Employees must, of course, communicate with each other and with management more than they did in the past. In a TQM program, employees and managers must experience a sense of interdependence and have mutual respect for each other. Teamwork is the key to success, and recognition and reward are heaped on individuals and teams who contribute to the company's improvement and success. We talk about TQM in some detail later in the book, but it is important now to think of it as a strategic initiative that relies heavily on the commitment of human resources to quality in every aspect of the company's operations.[19]

TQM is an approach to utilizing human resources in developing a competitive advantage relative to customers. In the next section, we continue to explore the role that human resources plays in developing and sustaining a competitive advantage as it formulates and seeks to achieve its overall strategy.

ROLE OF HUMAN RESOURCES IN STRATEGY FORMULATION

Up to this point, we have argued that overall corporate strategy should drive functional, including human resource, strategies. That is, a company should first decide what it as a whole needs to do to achieve a strategic competitive advantage and then formulate specific strategies for each functional area—marketing, finance, operations/productions, human resources—to carry it out. We have stated that in formulating overall strategy, the company should consider various aspects of each functional strategy. It needs to assess how well it is performing in each functional area.

Thus, in reality, the formulation of corporate strategy is really interactive with the formulation of functional strategy. In other words, by considering its capabilities in each functional area, the company is actually using its existing functional strategy and capabilities to help shape its future corporate strategy.

This interactive effect is an important notion, particularly with respect to human resource strategy. Lengnick-Hall and Lengnick-Hall argue in "Strategic Human Resource Management" that "reciprocal interdependence between a firm's business strategy and its human resources strategy underlies the proposed approach to the strategic management of human resources."[20] Their conceptual diagram, shown in Exhibit 3.7, depicts this reciprocal interdependence. Notice that the formation of corporate competitive advantage not only influences but also is influenced by human resource strategy. Certainly, economic conditions, industry structure, the labor market, and other factors depicted in the exhibit must be considered in light of the interactive effect of competitive strategy and human resource strategy.

EXHIBIT 3.7   **Reciprocal Interdependence of Corporate Strategy and Human Resource Strategy**

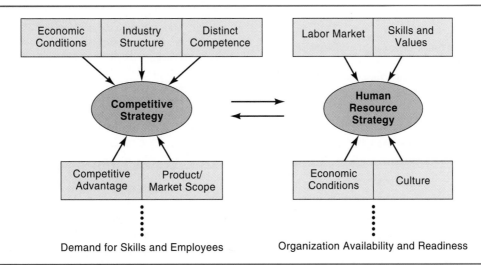

SOURCE: Reprinted by permission from Cynthia A. Lengnick-Hall and Mark L. Lengnick-Hall, "Strategic Human Resources Management: A Review of the Literature and a Proposed Typology," *Academy of Management Review,* Vol. 13, No. 3 (July 1988), p. 467.

<hr>

HR CHALLENGE

Super-Lube's Sustainable Competitive Advantage

Super-Lube 10 Minute Oil Change is a Tallahassee, Florida, based corporation involved in the quick oil change business. This market is relatively new and offers drive-in, drive-out convenience in oil changes and lubrication. Over one hundred separate firms operate in this market; Jiffy-Lube is the largest. With 51 stations, Super-Lube ranked as the number one independent lube facility in the market nationally in 1994.

Quick-Lube Industry

The quick-lube industry began in the late 1970s in the upper Midwest. Its primary offering is convenience, since the customer does not have to leave the car for a long period of time for servicing. The primary services provided are oil changes and lubrications, although some companies also provide free tire fills, tune-ups, and brake checks.

The quick-lube industry has grown rapidly because of the demise of full-service gas stations and the rise of self-service brought on by the oil crisis. The social trend toward greater convenience also has been a major reason for the success of the industry. It is estimated that one-third of the oil change business is now handled by quick-lube type stations, one-third by garages, service stations, and auto dealers, and one-third by do-it-yourselfers. Analysts believe the quick-lube sector will grow rapidly to perhaps two-thirds of the market by 1996.

Super-Lube

The strategy of Super-Lube can be explained as follows: to be absolutely the best fast oil change facility in the market areas served *and* to gain a position of clear market dominance therein. Strategic priorities follow:

1. Complete customer satisfaction through friendly, competent, and courteous service.

2. Highest consistent standards of performance.
3. High level of employee job satisfaction and opportunity for advancement.
4. Comparatively high return to stockholders within a three-year period.

Since its founding in 1983, the company has emphasized fast, competent, courteous service as its key trademark. It prides itself on clean, attractive stations that will make both male and female customers feel comfortable.

Human resources have always played a key role in overall corporate strategy. Bright, helpful, courteous people are hired at substantially above minimum wage. Employees are thoroughly trained in the Super-Lube way—from both technical and customer relations standpoints. Within six months, employees are placed on a merit bonus system that supplements their pay.

The company projects growth to 61 stations by 1997. All stations and land are company owned; none are franchised. Total sales were about $10 million in 1993 with net operating revenue about $1.2 million.

Company founder and president, John Lewis, attributes the bulk of the company's success to the outstanding employees it has been able to attract and hold. The company has a very good reputation in the entire industry with respect to employee competence and courtesy.

Super-Lube shows how a firm was able to use its human resources to help it achieve a strategic competitive advantage in the marketplace. The overall corporate strategy of dominance in a limited number of markets was achieved by being the first in these markets and then using well-trained, polite employees to obtain and keep customer loyalty.

SOURCE: Adapted from "Special Stockholders' Meeting Report," Super-Lube 10 Minute Oil Change (Tallahassee, Fla., 1994), p. 1.

Human resource strategy is now considered to be closely allied or linked to overall corporate strategy; the two go hand-in-hand. Robert Sibson notes in his recent book 16 critical human resource areas that should reflect any strategic plan. He devotes an entire chapter to each area, including organizational restructuring, educational level of the workforce, and managing cultural diversity.[21] This link is seen in practice as well as in theory. *HRMagazine* reported the findings of a 1992 survey of human resources professionals. The results indicated that human resource professionals are extremely concerned with strategic, long-term issues that reflect the concerns of top strategic managers. Among the issues dominating the agendas of human resource professionals are improving overall quality, controlling costs associated with employees, and improving overall productivity of workers.[22] At the very least, we must recognize that human resources integrally affect the overall strategy of a company, and, therefore, overall strategy must incorporate human resources considerations.

The importance of human resources to overall strategy is reflected in Super-Lube's success. From Super-Lube's very beginning, a major ingredient in forming its overall corporate strategy was a human resource strategy that stressed competent and courteous employees. This, plus a limited geographic focus, enabled Super-Lube to achieve success in the highly competitive quick-lube market.

Other examples of the link between human resource and overall strategies exist. Ford's "Quality Is Job 1" strategy would have had little chance of success had the company not explicitly considered both present and future human resource capability and strategy when formulating its quality strategy. 3M's strategy of innovation depends heavily on programs for innovation instituted with employees. Without innovative employees, the program would not work. The same is true of Florida Power and Light's (FP&L) Quality Improvement Program. The heart of this program rests with employee Quality Improvement Groups. FP&L spent much money and effort in forming, guiding, and training these groups during the 1980s.

A NEW ROLE FOR HUMAN RESOURCES

We see that human resources plays an expanded role under the strategic human resource approach. No longer is human resource strategy simply personnel management strategy with operative employees driven by overall corporate strategy. In short, no longer is personnel management simply left out of the strategic competitive arena. As Michael Porter argues in *Competitive Advantage,* human resource management can help a firm achieve a competitive advantage.[23] By involving human resource considerations when overall strategy is formulated, human resources can help achieve a strategic advantage. This is true for Super-Lube, as well as other firms that have fully integrated human resource considerations in strategy formulation.

In fact, managers are increasingly recognizing human resource management as one of the key considerations for ensuring overall success of the company's strategy. For example, many new training programs for human resource managers are taking a strategic perspective. One sales brochure informed managers that they must somehow utilize the human resource function as the company's source of competitive advantage. The same program talks of making sure that human resources provide the key competencies necessary for the company's chosen strategy. David Calfee, a management consultant, notes that the critical skills, capabilities, and efforts required of human resources should be reflected in a company's mission statement, the primary statement of its strategic goals. He notes that all employees should "live" the mission statement as they perform even their most mundane duties.[24] Human resource management is generally seen as a way to connect a company's upper-level strategic decisions to the lower-level, day-to-day tasks of all employees. An article in *The Wall Street Journal* reports a computer program that allows managers to set overall company goals. The program then helps each manager formulate goals for his or her department and each employee in an effort to help the company achieve its overall strategy. The program also helps managers to evaluate each employee's performance in meeting the set goal.[25]

One of the most dramatic documentations of the impact of human resources on overall strategy and success was provided by the U.S. Department of Energy Secretary

Hazel O'Leary in a recent address to several hundred HR professionals.[26] O'Leary told the professionals that, for the first time, the large government agency she heads was looking at how jobs were being done and how job performance led to agency success. She reported that her agency was ensuring that all jobs are woven together to meet the goals of the agency. She notes that past efforts of energy secretaries were concerned with allocating and spending budgeted funds rather than the current approach of determining how each job in the agency and the person in that position contribute to the agency's quality. O'Leary concluded that incorporating human resource elements (specifically diversity, quality, and leadership) can lead to the overall success of an organization.

Is there any proof that human resource management and strategy can help a company achieve its overall strategy? A recent award-winning study by Mark Huselid discovered that a well-formulated human resource strategy and extensive management of human resources led to improved company performance in a number of ways. First, Huselid learned that extensive human resource management improves the quality and performance of employees. Improved quality and performance increase overall company success and achievement of company strategies. Huselid's most important findings were that proper human resource planning and management lead to improved employee performance and to improved company performance.[27]

Unfortunately, however, in the 1980s, many companies that focused on human resource strategy issues when forming corporate strategy looked at the issue simply from a cost-cutting perspective. We saw this strategy manifested in the policies of Ford, GM, and Kodak—in short, almost all major older U.S. firms have tried to reduce labor costs to become more competitive.

Because of this cost-cutting strategy, many employees have lost jobs, taken early retirement, or suffered wage cuts. While such actions are often necessary, organizations do not always provide needed transition assistance. Employee assistance, such as severance pay, outplacement (that is, helping a person find a new job), and retraining could cushion the effect of cost-cutting strategies on labor.

LINE VERSUS STAFF CONFLICT

STAFF-LINE CONFLICT
Disagreements and jealousy between operating managers/units and staff/support managers and units.

Human resource managers have long suffered from the **staff-line conflict** that tends to arise in many organizations. We review six aspects of this issue and see how this conflict affects the strategic role for human resources.

First, it is important to remember that all managers are human resource managers. That is, all managers have subordinates on whom they rely to carry out work.

Second, the functions of hiring, training, placing, paying, and otherwise dealing with the workforce must be performed by somebody in the organization. If a human resource unit does not exist, then line managers must perform all of these actions themselves. For example, when Southwest Airlines was first formed, line managers made all personnel decisions. As the company grew, a human resource department was added and personnel decisions became its responsibility.

Third, human resource units are set up as specialized departments to help line managers in their role as human resource managers. In other words, human resource units help line managers carry out the human resource functions of hiring, paying, and so on. As Southwest Airlines grew, many of these personnel functions were transferred from line managers to the human resource staff.

Fourth, in some organizations, human resource units are given wide latitude to do some of the hiring, benefit determination, training, and so on. In these organizations, the human resource unit may be criticized for "taking on too much" or "taking too much authority away from line managers."

Fifth, in many organizations, human resource units serve as police units. They enforce the myriad of laws in human resources that a company must abide by: wage and hour, social security, discrimination, benefits, and safety and health policies, for example. These units also are often given the job of enforcing company human resource policy. This results in the human resource unit telling line managers what they can and cannot do according to the law or corporate policy. At Southwest, Kelleher's introduction of a policy manual involved more than just writing the policy; it also required a means to enforce them. This responsibility falls on both the line and staff managers. This division of responsibility can sometimes cause line-staff conflict because goals and objectives can differ between departments.

Finally, because human resource units do not have primary authority to produce or market a product or service but line managers do, line managers often view human resource people as "out of touch" with the real world. Line managers must meet production and sales quotas and deadlines. They see themselves "on the firing line," or "in the trenches." To them, human resources has none of these deadlines and pressures. Instead, they often see human resource specialists as people who throw roadblocks or hindrances in their way or as people who have the luxury of sitting back in their offices dreaming up new rules and regulations to thwart efficient operations.

This raises the issue of the *credibility* of the human resource unit. Unfortunately in some organizations, employees in human resource units are often viewed as people who could not cut it in a line position. While this problem is not as serious as it once was because the human resource function has become more professionalized, it can be a problem in some organizations and must be addressed.

All of these factors cause line-staff conflict and credibility issues. This conflict and credibility gap can be so serious as to prevent human resources from playing an important role in strategy formulation. Therefore, conflict must be reduced and credibility enhanced if the human resources function is to be fully involved in strategy formulation. What can be done? Let us examine some courses of action.[28]

ENHANCING CREDIBILITY AND REDUCING STAFF-LINE CONFLICT

Exhibit 3.8 notes a number of actions that a company can take to reduce line-staff conflict and enhance the credibility of the human resource unit. First, it should ensure that people who staff the human resource unit are competent, well trained, and experienced in the various human resource functions.

Second, the human resource unit's role should be clearly spelled out in corporate policy vis-à-vis line manager roles. Who has responsibility of what and when needs to be determined, put in writing, and shared among line managers and the human resource unit. Both line managers and human resource professionals should play a role in determining this responsibility.

Third, human resource people should view their role as supporting line staff. The human resource unit exists to help line managers do a better job as human resource managers. Even though the human resource unit must enforce human resource laws and policies, it essentially exists to help line managers and keep them out of trouble.

Fourth, the human resource unit and line managers should work together in formulating human resource policies, programs, and actions. For example, at Clay Electric Cooperative in Florida, even though the human resource unit was given the primary responsibility to come up with a new performance appraisal system, it did so by work-

EXHIBIT 3.8   **Some Ways to Enhance the Human Resource Unit's Credibility and Reduce Line-Staff Conflict**

1. Hire only competent, well trained, and experienced people for the human resource unit.

2. Clearly spell out human resource responsibilities in relation to line management responsibilities.

3. Have human resource staff members view their roles as supportive to line staff members.

4. Have human resource and line staff members work together in forming personnel policies.

5. Ensure that human resource staff members have firsthand contact and experience with line operations.

6. Ensure that managers remember the important role that human resource plays in reducing burdensome tasks.

ing with line managers every step of the way. At each step the work of the human resource unit was "bounced off" of the line managers in group sessions, and their suggestions were incorporated into modified versions of the system.

Fifth, the human resource unit should practice "managing by wandering around" as Peters and Austin call it in *A Passion for Excellence.*[29] In other words, human resource people should get out of their offices and out to where the work is done—the factory, office, mine, or field. Human resource isolation from line work can be a serious cause of poor credibility and staff-line conflict. In fact, because of this, many companies, including Procter & Gamble, IBM, and GE, do not place people in human resource positions until they have had line experience and training.

Sixth, line managers need to understand the important and significant role that the human resource unit plays in today's environment. It takes many burdensome chores away from line managers, which actually makes their jobs much easier. Line managers sometimes forget this fact.

Line-staff conflict can seldom be completely eliminated. These points noted here should serve to enhance the human resource unit's credibility and reduce line-staff conflict, thereby opening the door for greater participation of human resource professionals in the strategy formulation process.

Let us turn our attention now to the human resource audit, a program that is helpful in ensuring that the operations of the human resource function meet the needs of the company. The human resource audit is an excellent means to ensure that this function is viewed in terms beyond just costs and benefits. The human resource audit is very important in creating an appropriate linkage between human resources strategy and overall corporate strategy.

HUMAN RESOURCE AUDIT

Human resource units have been concerned with their effectiveness and efficiency for some time. For example, a survey of human resource departments by the Bureau of National Affairs (BNA) shows that human resource staff ratios to 100 employees have dropped slightly from 1.1 to 1.0 from 1990 to 1994 as shown in Exhibit 3.9. However, total human resource expenditures continued to increase approximately 5.5 percent per year from 1990 to 1994 while human resource expenditures per employee remained at about $700 from 1990 to 1994, although they did increase to $863 in 1991.[30]

One way human resource staffs assess their effectiveness and efficiency is through human resource research and human resource audits. Human resource research is one of the primary means by which the human resource department assists the organization in meeting the ever-increasing demand for high productivity in today's competitive marketplace. Human resource research involves evaluating the department's effectiveness in serving the organization's human resource needs. It helps the organization analyze its human resource practices and policies and to determine whether changes and improvements are necessary.[31] One of the key tools for conducting such research is the **human resource audit.** Its main function is to help decision makers understand what is happening with various activities, such as recruitment, hiring, separation, and training.

HUMAN RESOURCE AUDIT
A study of the human resource unit to determine its effectivness and efficiency.

WHY DO AN AUDIT?

A human resource audit often is conducted when management perceives that certain programs or activities are not meeting the goals set for them or have other problems.[32] Another reason for the audit is to determine what programs or positions to eliminate when a firm decides to downsize. Programs or activities identified as the least effective are targeted for elimination. For the audit to be effective, the firm must determine what

▌EXHIBIT 3.9   Human Resources Department Staffing and Expenditures, 1990–1994

Human Resources Department Staffing and Expenditures, 1990–1994

HR Staff Ratios
Median HR Staff per 100 Employees

1.1 1.0 1.1 1.0 1.0
1990 1991 1992 1993 1994

Change in Total HR Expenditures
Median Change, in Percent*

6.2% 5.4% 6.3% 5.0% 5.2%
1990 1991 1992 1993 1994

HR Expenditures per Employee
Median Cost per Employee†

$697 $863 $804 $696 $710
1990 1991 1992 1993 1994

*Median percentage difference between HR budget for current year and actual expenditures in previous year.
†Figures for 1990–1993 based on actual HR costs in each year. The 1994 figure is based on 1994 HR budgets.

SOURCE: Bureau of National Affairs, *Bulletin to Management,* June 30, 1994, p. 1.

HR CHALLENGE

Exactly How Do Businesses Evaluate Their HR Departments?

A recent study by researchers at the University of Iowa indicated that approximately one-third of the businesses in their survey seldom or never conduct evaluations of their human resource departments. Another one-third said that they conduct human resource reviews at least annually, while the final one-third fell somewhere in the middle.

The two most frequently cited reasons for not evaluating the human resource function were difficulty in conducting a scientific evaluation and difficulty in quantifying human resource's return on investment.

However, this did not seem to stop the one-third of the respondents who frequently evaluate their human resource departments. When asked what type of evaluation is performed, they indicated a more judgmental and qualitative process is used rather than a quantitative or scientific one. Further, when asked who

performs the evaluation, the majority of the respondents indicated that the human resource function evaluates itself.

The results of this study indicate that human resource departments are clearly not being evaluated properly. Further, the true value of the human resource function to the organization is not being made clear. Even in organizations in which evaluations are performed, the informally gathered information by the people in the department will not hold much weight. Before human resource departments can be judged on their merit, procedures must exist for determining how well they perform.

SOURCE: Adapted from Margaret Cashman and James McElroy, "Evaluating the HR Function," *HRMagazine,* January 1991, pp. 70–73.

it seeks to achieve by performing it.[33] This will help determine who is to perform the audit and the methods to be used in conducting it.

PERFORMING THE AUDIT

The choice of who will conduct the audit must be made carefully. In-house staff, who are most familiar with the organization, may be selected, but their knowledge may perpetuate past errors and misconceptions. A third-party human resource consultant may be employed. The advantage of having an outsider perform the audit must be weighed against the possibility that the consultant may miss some subtleties of the organization's system or may bring a preconceived set of solutions to the project. An organization's lawyers are able to advise on the legality of programs but lack the expertise to evaluate their effectiveness. The firm must decide which of these options best meets its needs.

The human resource audit involves collecting data. A number of methods, such as employee observation, surveys, questionnaires, and computer data reviews, are employed in the process. These techniques are used to gather information and compare it to some expected or predicted outcome. For example, the audits can compare rates or ratios such as turnover, attendance, or training and development against past firm or industry levels of performance. Surveys can measure morale and job satisfaction or wages and salaries. All of these factors serve as broad measures of the success of underlying personnel and organizational functions. For example, poor attendance and tardiness rates may indicate poor morale, an overly permissive sick-pay policy, lack of line supervisor discipline, or even a poorly laid-out plant that prevents employees from returning from breaks on time. Exhibit 3.10 provides additional examples. The technique

EXHIBIT 3.10   **Human Resource Audit Measurements and Their Organization's Underlying Indicators**

RATE	PERSONNEL FUNCTIONS TO EXAMINE
Turnover Rate	Salary and benefits package
• Quit rate	Supervisory practices
• Termination rate	Job design
• Layoff rate	Retirement plan
• Retention rate	
• Retirement rate	
• Length of service rate	
Job Attendance Rate	Exit interviews
• Absence rate	Discipline
• Tardiness rate	Convenience of lunchroom and rest room
	Sick-pay policy
Overtime Rate	Employee planning and scheduling
	Shortage of staff
	Selection and training process
Position Vacancy Rate	Recruitment and selection process
	Salary and benefit package
	Company image in community
Error/Scrap Rate	Recruitment selection and placement
	Training and development
	Job satisfaction
Training Development Rate	Recruitment and selection
	Training and development
Grievance Rate	Supervisory practices
	Job dissatisfaction

used depends on the information sought. Surveys are an excellent way to measure effects on large groups; interviews and observations can be used for a more comprehensive analysis of smaller groups. Information obtained may be compared against information from outside sources or internal research.

However the information is gathered, the main purpose of the human resource audit is to evaluate the effectiveness of the organization's human resource function, and the information should reflect this. It should show both the department's strengths and weaknesses and provide management with a clear picture of the department's role in the organization. The audit also should allow management to evaluate the human resource department's broad role in helping the organization meet its strategic goals and objectives.

RESULTS OF THE AUDIT

The information gathered during the audit may indicate that a specific program or activity is in fact meeting its goals, in which case no further action is necessary. Or the audit may produce unanticipated results. For example, an audit to examine employee turnover for the past year might indicate that turnover was within reasonable limits. An unexpected result of the audit could be the indication that the firm's reward and compensation plan has contributed to decreased turnover.

CONTINGENCY FOR SITUATIONAL APPROACH TO STRATEGY

Our discussion of formulating corporate strategy concludes with a review of the situational nature of strategy formulation. Basically, this idea states that what might be good for one firm may not be good for another. The formulation of a proper strategy for a particular firm is firm specific. Thus, the strategy is contingent upon specific aspects of the firm. The proper strategy is determined by its unique internal characteristics and its specific environmental opportunities and threats. This is true of firms in the same industry—what is right for Ford may not be right for GM and vice versa.

However, the situational or contingency approach does not mean that firms should ignore what other firms are doing. In fact, in the case of their competitors, firms need to consider explicitly the strategies of the competition in formulating their own strategy. A firm can examine its competitors, see what they are doing, and make judgments as to whether its situation is similar enough to allow it to use a comparable or modified version of competitors' strategy.

Sometimes strategies roll like waves across the business landscape. In these cases, a particular strategy catches on with many firms. As pointed out several places in this book, merger and acquisition and cost-cutting were very popular strategies in the 1980s. In the area of human resources, two popular strategies have been cutting labor cost and involving human resource. Even though it is tempting to jump uncritically on the bandwagon with wholesale adoption of a popular strategy, each firm should carefully examine the strategy and its own situation to determine if the strategy is, in fact, right for it.

To a large extent, this decision to adopt a popular strategy depends on two key factors: (1) how well a firm monitors what goes on around it and (2) the firm's philosophy with respect to strategy innovation. We examined the first factor when we discussed scanning and knowing the environment in Chapter 2. We will now address the philosophy of strategy innovation.

PHILOSOPHY OF STRATEGY INNOVATION

Companies that wish to be "firstest with the mostest," Peter Drucker's term in "Entrepreneurial Strategies," design their own strategies that fit their own circumstances.[34] They do not follow or copy others. They are risk takers and want to be the first ones out with the new strategy, new product, new feature, or new service. They want to be first to enter a new market. For them strategy formulation is completely situational because there is no one to copy. Apple Computer is an example of a firm with this strategy.

At the other extreme are the followers. Seldom do they develop a new strategy. They have a low tolerance for risk. They want to go with the tried and true. They closely watch others, see what works, and adopt it in their own firm. For them strategy formulation is less situational than it is with the innovators, although they often adjust an existing strategy to fit their own circumstances. Makers of IBM compatible personal computers, such as Standard Computer, follow this strategy.

The strategy innovators have the opportunity to experience huge successes as a result of hitting the market first, as did Apple with the Apple II. But they also can experience failure as did People Express with cut-rate pricing and "jack-of-all-trades" job assignments for employees. (People Express filed for bankruptcy and was absorbed by Texas Air in the mid-1980s.)

A number of factors affect the degree of innovation in strategy formulation. Exhibit 3.11 lists some of these factors. Regardless of the degree of innovation, strategy should

EXHIBIT 3.11   **Factors That Affect the Likelihood That a Firm Is Innovative**

THE DYNAMICS OF THE MARKET AND COMPETITION

The more dynamic the market, the likelihood that innovation will occur increases.

THE AMOUNT AND EXTENT OF GOVERNMENT REGULATION

The more government regulation is exerted, the likelihood that innovation will occur decreases.

THE PERSONAL PHILOSOPHY OF TOP MANAGEMENT

The more conservative the philosophy, the likelihood that innovation will occur decreases.

PREVIOUS EXPERIENCE WITH INNOVATION

Previous positive experience with innovation will foster more innovation. However, some firms who successfully innovated in the past tend to stick with these innovations beyond their usefulness in the market. Consider, for example, GM's overreliance on standard styling and car components across division lines. Initially successful in the early 1980s, this policy became dysfunctional in the late 1980s as Chevrolet, Pontiac, Buick, Oldsmobile, and Cadillac became less differentiated in the customer's mind.

THE COST OF INNOVATION

When costs of innovation are high, there is less likelihood of significant innovation. Witness the reluctance of U.S. steel producers to adopt the new technology used by Japanese and German steel producers.

AGE OF THE FIRM

Often it is a new company, not an existing company in the industry, which comes up with a new product. Apple, not IBM, invented the PC. Xerox, not mimeograph machine makers, invented electrostatic copying. The quick-lube market was developed by new firms, not the existing oil companies, gas station dealers, or auto dealers.

be situational for it to be successful. It is likely more situational with more innovative firms, however, than it is with less innovative ones. The less innovative ones borrow successful existing strategy and use it as best they can.

MANAGEMENT GUIDELINES

We can summarize the key points of this chapter with the following guidelines:

1. Strategy formulation is not a neat and clean process. It moves in "fits and starts" with much backtracking and revision. It is evolutionary in nature more often than it is revolutionary.
2. Strategy and the process of formulating it must be flexible and adaptable.
3. Much strategy formulation occurs in the strategic planning process, especially in the environmental scan and internal assessment.
4. The market, especially competition, plays a very important role in the formation of strategy and the firm's sustainable competitive advantage.

Continued

5. Total quality management allows human resources to meet major company goals.
6. Even though corporate strategy should drive functional strategy, human resource units play an interactive role with respect to overall corporate strategy formulation.
7. Human resources is becoming a key consideration in overall strategy formulation.
8. For human resources to maximize its role in strategy formulation, it must reduce the line-staff conflict and credibility gap that may exist between it and line managers.
9. The human resource audit can be seen as a key in collecting important human resources information and ensuring that the human resource function is meeting the needs of the overall strategy.
10. All strategy is situational. The proper strategy for a particular firm depends on the unique situation it faces. What works for one firm may not work for another.

QUESTIONS FOR REVIEW

1. Describe the strategy formulation process and the role strategic planning plays in the process. Specifically, what is the role of the environmental scan and the internal assessment (SWOT)?
2. Why should strategy be flexible and adaptive in nature?
3. What are generic strategies? List and explain six of them.
4. How do line-of-business and corporate strategies differ? Give examples of each.
5. What role do the market and competition play in strategy formulation? Specifically, what is a sustainable competitive advantage and why is this idea important?
6. What are the ways a firm can obtain or achieve a sustainable competitive advantage?
7. We have stated that corporate strategy should drive functional and human resource strategy. We also have stated

that the formation of corporate and human resource strategy is interactive in nature. Do you see an apparent contradiction in these two statements? Explain your answer.
8. What is the line-staff conflict and credibility gap that often exists between the human resource unit and line managers? What causes this conflict?
9. How can line-staff conflict and the credibility gap between line managers and the human resource unit be reduced? Why must it be reduced?
10. What do we mean when we say that strategy formation is situational or contingent in nature? Why is this important to understand?
11. What role does a firm's posture on innovation play in strategy formulation?

CASE

FARMERS EXCHANGE BANK—HUMAN RESOURCES AND STRATEGY AT A SMALL BANK

When times get tough, companies are often forced to change their strategy to one of retrenchment or "turnaround." We see this happening in large and small companies alike. For example, in the banking industry, giant BankAmerica (with more than $100 billion in assets) performed an incredible turnaround in the mid- and late 1980s when its management or-

chestrated a series of cost-cutting measures and admonished employees to be as efficient as possible. Now the company is highly profitable again and is performing well.

The situation is not much different for Farmers Exchange Bank, a small bank in rural Louisville, Alabama. It has been in existence for 36 years and has assets of just over $35 million.

The bank has been family run for all of its 36 years and until recently was managed almost solely by three individuals: chairman and CEO Robert H. Bennett, Jr.; his father and bank founder, Robert H. Bennett; and his mother, Lenoree S. Bennett. The bank has fewer than 30 employees with very little formal structure between the CEO and the first-line employees. In recent years, Farmers Exchange Bank has experienced what might be called growing pains. To cure these pains, Farmers Exchange Bank altered its strategy somewhat, and the focus of human resource management has changed in turn.

GROWTH BY "TREATING PEOPLE RIGHT"

Farmers Exchange Bank was founded on the principle of "doing whatever it takes to befriend the customer." Bank employees were empowered to "treat people right" and make sure that the customer was happy. The bank staff, especially the Bennetts, built close, personal relationships with customers, many of whom recognize that the bank and the Bennetts helped them get their start in life. Customers were charged reasonable prices and could expect close, personal attention when they entered the bank with even the most insignificant business. Tellers and loan officers knew many, if not most, customers and dealt with them on a personal basis. This philosophy was sound and contributed to a successful entrepreneurial venture in the early years of the bank.

This philosophy is one factor in the bank's growth in recent years. Customers of other banks in nearby communities began to recognize the value of banking with Farmers Exchange Bank. In the past 10 years the Bennetts implemented a growth strategy to capitalize on the bank's reputation for personal service. In reality, the company did nothing differently but encouraged new business through word-of-mouth advertising and offering additional services to meet the needs of new customers. The employees were the reason for success, because the primary emphasis continued to be the bank's customer orientation. When new customers came into the bank, they were there to stay. The bank posted extremely high growth and excellent earnings throughout the late 1980s and early 1990s. The elder Bennett died in 1991, but the growth continued as it became evident that Robert H. Bennett, Jr. would continue to subscribe to the bank's customer-oriented philosophy.

The younger Bennett continued to push for growth by emphasizing to customers that the bank wanted to be a good neighbor. In 1992 he realized that large numbers of the bank's new customers were coming from a neighboring community where residents were especially disgruntled about the service provided by the two banks there. In late 1992 Bennett opened Farmers Exchange Bank's first branch office in that community, and its success was immediate. The branch office grew rapidly, almost doubling management projections for growth and profit. In late 1993, Bennett observed that almost every commercial account in the small community utilized Farmers Exchange Bank's services almost exclusively. In total, the bank's assets increased about 450 percent in the decade between 1984 and 1994.

A FEW PROBLEMS

A number of factors, however, combined to result in several serious problems for the highly successful bank. The rapid growth resulted in the need for new employees, but meeting this need quickly with qualified people was difficult. Employees recognized the importance of giving customers their complete attention. As a result of attempting to provide personal service to an increasing number of customers, details were often overlooked on such things as commercial loans, agricultural and real estate loans, and bank investments. New procedures were not put into place to ensure that all the details were in order. Loan officers were often smothered by requests for financing. New and old customers requested loans, CDs, and checking accounts. In many cases, the history of loan applicants was not adequately investigated and necessary supporting documentation often was completed hastily if at all.

During this time, employees did not sufficiently keep Bennett up to date on the overall health of the bank. In a number of ways, the growth made Bennett feel that he no longer controlled the bank's operations as he once had. No real departmentalization existed, so delegation of duties was problematic.

The growth problems were exacerbated by a large number of regulatory changes brought on by the savings and loan disaster and other societal and economic trends of the 1980s and 1990s. The regulations of the FDIC and other government agencies seriously impacted community banks. New and different reports and new policies and procedures were required. These new requirements placed strains on a bank having troubles resulting from its rapid growth.

A number of economic factors also presented real problems for local businesses and, consequently, for the bank. A number of small businesses were forced to make cutbacks. Droughts and changing government policy caused unforeseen difficulties for farmers, who represented a large portion of the bank's customer base. As a result, the economic health of the rural area deteriorated somewhat during the early 1990s.

A NEW STRATEGY

As expected, the combination of rapid growth and new and increased government regulations began to cause problems for the bank. In early 1993 the number of past due accounts and delinquent loans increased. Loan charge-offs (uncollectable loans) were up during 1993 and 1994. A record number of loans characterized by management as "poor performers" negatively affected the bank's profitability and health ratings. Overdrafts increased during much of 1993. Most important, earnings decreased during 1993 due to loan problems. In 1994 the bank continued to make a profit, although earnings dropped. Capitalization, a very important indicator of a bank's health, was down because earnings did not sufficiently keep pace with growth. Growth had been rapid but began to show signs of slowing.

Bennett recognized the problems the bank was experiencing and decided to revise its strategy somewhat. The revised strategy continues to emphasize the personal approach to customers but to slow growth in some areas. He realized that the size of the staff was inadequate to implement the strategy. For example, the current staff members were unable to provide personal service while following procedures completely and correctly. He also recognized that staff members needed training in areas related to regulatory compliance, loan portfolio management, credit analysis, and collection.

Bennett took several steps to solve major problems that existed in the loan department. He initiated a strategy of retrenchment concerning the bank's loan policy; new loan customers are no longer sought. Bennett hired four new staff members so that all documentation relating to loans can be kept up to date and standard procedures can be followed. Loan applicants' financial history and credit history are adequately investigated and loan officers now have more time to monitor accounts and to take necessary action when they become delinquent.

Overall, the bank's strategy emphasizes following procedures and processes in an orderly manner, correcting existing problems, and preparing adequately for future growth. No longer are growth and market development major parts of the strategy. Maintaining current size and offering personal service are current strategy. It will be interesting to see how the bank fares in the next few years with this revised strategy.

QUESTIONS

1. Why did a positive thing such as growth eventually present problems to Farmers Exchange Bank? What could have been done to avoid these problems?

2. At what point did Bennett not adequately foresee the implications of his growth strategy? What should have been done when growth came so rapidly?

3. Do you believe that Bennett adequately changed the company's strategy to remedy the problems discussed? What are the main concerns he is addressing? What are the main concerns he is not addressing?

4. What overall strategy and human resource strategy would you follow under these conditions? Do you think Farmers Exchange Bank has a viable future?

ADDITIONAL READINGS

Allio, R. J. *The Practical Strategist.* New York: Harper & Row, 1988.

Baird, L., I. Meshoulam, and G. DeGive. "Meshing Human Resources Planning with Strategic Business Planning: A Model Approach." *Personnel* 60(5) (1983), pp. 14–25.

Buller, P. F., and N. K. Napier. "Strategy and Human Resource Management Integration in Fast Growth versus Other Mid-sized Firms." Paper presented at the 1990 Academy of Management Meeting. San Francisco, 1990.

Carroll, G. R., and D. Vogel. *Organizational Approaches to Strategy.* New York: Harper & Row, 1988.

Cheek, L. M. "Cost Effectiveness Comes from the Personnel Function." *Harvard Business Review* 51(3) (1973), pp. 96–105.

Child, J. "Organization Structure, Environment, and Performance: The Role of Strategic Choice." *Sociology* 6 (1972), pp. 2–22.

Cooper, A. C., and D. Schendel. "Strategic Responses to Technological Threats." *Business Horizons* 19(1) (1976), pp. 1–9.

DeSanto, J. F. "Work Force Planning and Corporate Strategy." *Personnel Administrator* 28(10) (1983), pp. 33–42.

Deutch, A. "How Employee Retention Strategies Can Aid Productivity." *Journal of Business Strategy* 2(4) (1982), pp. 106–109.

Dimick, D. E., and V. V. Murray. "Correlates of Substantive Policy Decisions in Organizations: The Case of Human Resource Management." *Academy of Management Journal* 21 (1978), pp. 611–623.

Dyer, L. "Bringing Human Resources into the Strategy Formulation Process." *Human Resource Management* 22(3) (1983), pp. 257–271.

Dyer, L. "Strategic Human Resources Management and Planning." In *Research in Personnel and Human Resources Management,* ed. K. M. Rowland and G. R. Ferris. Greenwich, CT: JAI Press, 1985, pp. 1–30.

Dyer, L. "Studying Human Resource Strategy: An Approach and an Agenda." *Industrial Relations* 23(2) (1984), pp. 156–169.

Evans, Alastair J. "Britain and the United States: A Comparison of Human Resource Strategies." *Personnel Journal* 61(9) (September 1982), pp. 656–662.

Finkelstein, S., and D. Hambrick. "Top-Management Team Tenure and Organizational Outcomes: The Moderating Role of Managerial Discretion." *Administrative Science Quarterly* 35 (1990), pp. 484–503.

Flamholtz, E. "A Model for Human Resource Valuation: A Stochastic Process with Service Rewards." *Accounting Review* 46(2) (1971), pp. 253–267.

Fombrun, C. "Environmental Trends Create New Pressures on Human Resources." *Journal of Business Strategy* 3(1) (1982), pp. 61–69.

Foltz, Roy. "Senior Management Views the Human Resource Function." *Personnel Administrator* 27(9), (September 1984), pp. 37–50.

Frantzreb, R. B., L. T. Landau, and D. P. Lundberg. "The Valuation of Human Resources." *Business Horizons* 20(3) (1977), pp. 73–80.

Galbraith, J. R., and R. J. Kazanjian. *Strategy Implementation: Structure, System and Process.* 2nd ed. St. Paul: West, 1986.

Galosy, J. R. "Meshing Human Resources Planning with Strategic Business Planning: One Company's Experience." *Personnel* 60(5) (1983), pp. 26–35.

Gilbert, D. R., Jr., E. Hartman, J. J. Muriel, and R. E. Freeman. *A Logic for Strategy.* New York: Harper & Row, 1988.

Green, Robert, and Russell G. Roberts. "Strategic Integration of Compensation and Benefits." *Personnel Administrator* 28(5) (May 1983), pp. 79–83.

Guth, W., and I. MacMillan. "Strategy Implementation versus Middle Management Self-Interest." *Strategic Management Journal* 7 (1986), pp. 313–327.

Harvey, L. J. "Effective Planning for Human Resource Development." *Personnel Administrator* 28(10) (1983), pp. 45–52.

Hayes, R. H., and S. C. Wheelwright. "The Dynamics of Process-Product Life Cycles." *Harvard Business Review* 57(2) (1979), pp. 127–136.

Hofer, C. W., and D. Schendel. *Strategy Formulation: Analytical Concepts.* St. Paul: West, 1978.

Hrebiniak, L. G., and W. F. Joyce. *Implementing Strategy.* New York: Macmillan, 1984.

Kerr, J., and E. Jackofsky. "Aligning Managers to Strategies: Management Development versus Selection." *Academy of Management Review* 10 (1989), pp. 157–170.

Krackhardt, D. "Assessing the Political Landscape: Structure, Cognition, and Power in Organizations." *Administrative Science Quarterly* 35 (1990), pp. 342–369.

Lawrence, P. *Executive Summary—The History of Resource Management in America.* Human Resource Management Future Conference, Harvard Business School, May 9–11, 1984.

Lengnick-Hall, C., and M. Lengnick-Hall. "Strategic Human Resource Management: A Review of the Literature and a Proposed Typology." *Academy of Management Review* 13 (1988), pp. 454–470.

Lengnick-Hall, C. A., and R. R. McDaniel, Jr. "Scanning Policies, Structure and Adaptability in Human Service Systems." *American Business Review* 2(1) (1984), pp. 12–23.

Lenz, R. T. "Determinants of Organizational Performance: An Interdisciplinary Review." *Strategic Management Journal* 2(2) (1981), pp. 131–154.

Leontiades, M. "Choosing the Right Manager to Fit the Strategy." *Journal of Business Strategy* 2(2) (1982), pp. 58–69.

Lieberman, M., L. Lau, and M. Williams. "Firm-Level Productivity and Management Influence: A Comparison of U.S. and Japanese Automobile Producers." *Management Science* 36 (1990), pp. 1193–1215.

Lindblom, C. "The Science of Muddling Through." *Public Administration Review* 19 (1959), pp. 79–88.

Lindroth, J. "How to Beat the Coming Labor Shortage." *Personnel Journal* 61(4) (1982), pp. 268–272.

MacMillan, I. C., and P. E. Jones. *Strategy Formulation: Power and Politics.* 2nd ed. St. Paul: West, 1986.

MacMillan, I. C., and R. S. Schuler. "Gaining a Competitive Edge through Human Resources." *Personnel* 62(4) (1985), pp. 24–29.

Maier, H. "Innovation, Efficiency, and the Quantitative and Qualitative Demand for Human Resources." *Technological Forecasting and Social Change* 21 (1982), pp. 15–31.

Miles, R., C. C. Snow, A. D. Meyer, and H. J. Coleman, Jr. "Organization Strategy, Structure, and Process." *Academy of Management Review* 3 (1978), pp. 546–662.

Mintzberg, H. "Strategy Formation: Schools of Thought." In *Perspectives on Strategic Management,* ed. J. Fredrickson. New York: Harper & Row, 1990, pp. 105–235.

Olian, J. D., and S. L. Rynes. "Organizational Staffing: Integrating Practice with Strategy." *Industrial Relations* 23(2) (1984), pp. 170–183.

Perry, L. T. "Least-Cost Alternatives to Layoffs in Declining Industries." *Organizational Dynamics* 14(4) (1986), pp. 48–61.

Pitts, R. A., and C. C. Snow. *Strategies for Competitive Success.* New York: Wiley, 1986.

Porter, M. E. *Competitive Strategy.* New York: Free Press, 1980.

Porter, M. E. *Competitive Advantage.* New York: Free Press, 1985.

Reed, R., and R. DeFillippi. "Causal Ambiguity, Barriers to Imitation, and Sustainable Competitive Advantage." *Academy of Management Review* 15 (1990), pp. 88–102.

Rumelt, R. P. *Strategy, Structure and Economic Performance in Large American Industrial Corporations.* Boston: Harvard Graduate School of Business Administration, 1974.

Schuler, R. S., and I. C. MacMillan. "Gaining Competitive Advantage through Human Resource Management Practices." *Human Resource Management* 23(3) (1984), pp. 241–256.

Schuler, R. S., and S. E. Jackson. "Linking Competitive Strategies with Human Resource Management Practices." *Academy of Management Executive* 1 (1987), pp. 207–219.

Schultheiss, E. E. *Optimizing The Organization.* New York: Harper & Row, 1988.

Scott, B. R. *Stages of Corporate Development–Part 1* (Case No. 9-371-294). Boston: Intercollegiate Case Clearinghouse, 1971.

Smith, E. C. "Strategic Business Planning and Human Resources: Part I." *Personnel Journal* 61(8), (1982a), pp. 606–610.

_____. "Strategic Business Planning and Human Resources: Part II." *Personnel Journal* 61(9), (1982b), pp. 680–682.

"Strategic Planning: Hedging Future Shock." *Personnel Administrator,* December 1987, pp. 73–80.

Stumpf, S. A., and N. M. Hanrahan. "Designing Organizational Career Management Practices to Fit the Strategic Management Objectives." In *Readings in Personnel and Human Resource Management,* eds. R. S. Schuler and S. A. Youngblood, 2nd ed. St. Paul: West, 1984, pp. 326–348.

Sweet, J. "How Manpower Development Can Support Your Strategic Plan." *Journal of Business Strategy* 3(1) (1982), pp. 77–81.

Szilagyi, A., and D. Schweiger. "Matching Managers to Strategies: A Review and Suggested Framework." *Academy of Management Review* 9 (1984), pp. 626–637.

Tichy, N. M., C. J. Fombrun, and M. A. Devanna. "Strategic Human Resource Management." *Sloan Management Review* 23(2) (1982), pp. 47–61.

Tsui, A. S. "A Multiple-Constituency Model of Effectiveness: An Empirical Examination at the Human Resource Subunit Level." *Administrative Science Quarterly* 35 (1990), pp. 458–483.

Wagel, W. H., and H. Z. Levine. "Surveying the Past. Planning the Future." *Personnel.* June 1989, pp. 25–44.

Walton, R. E. *From Control to Commitment: Transforming Work Force Management in the United States.* Harvard Business School's 75th Anniversary Colloquium on Technology and Productivity, 1984.

Wils, T., and L. Dyer. *Relating Business Strategy to Human Resource Strategy: Some Preliminary Evidence.* Paper presented at the meeting of the Academy of Management. Boston, August 1984.

NOTES

1. Kenneth Labich, "Is Herb Kelleher America's Best CEO?" *Fortune,* May 2, 1994, pp. 44–52; "A Letter to Those Who Appreciate Southwest Airline's Low Fares," Southwest Airlines advertisement, *The Wall Street Journal,* May 4, 1994, p. B12; and Bridget O'Brian, "Giant Reservation System to Dump Southwest," *The Wall Street Journal,* April 22, 1994, p. B1.

2. Selwyn Feinstein, "Best Laid Plans," *The Wall Street Journal,* May 1, 1990, p. A1.

3. R. E. Miles, C. C. Snow, A. D. Meyer, and H. J. Coleman, Jr., "Organizational Strategy, Structure, and Process," *Academy of Management Review* 3, 1978, pp. 546–662.

4. For more detail, see William P. Anthony, *Practical Strategic Planning: A Guide for Line Managers* (Westport, CT: Greenwood Press, 1985), chs. 1 and 2.

5. R. E. Freeman, *Strategic Management: A Stakeholder Approach* (Boston: Pitman, 1984).

6. John Naisbett, *Megatrends: Ten New Directions for Transforming Our Lives* (New York: Warner, 1982); and John Naisbett and Patricia Aburdene, *Megatrends 2000: Ten New Directions for the 1990s,* (New York: Morrow, 1990).

7. Emily Yoffe, "Naisbett's Clip Joint: The Selling of Content Analysis and Megatrends," *Harpers,* September 1983, pp. 16 +.

8. William F. Glueck, *Business Policy and Strategic Management,* 3rd ed. (New York: McGraw-Hill, 1980), p. 290.

9. Kimberly Carpenter and John P. Tarpey, "A Southern Paper Maker's Yankee Campaign," *Business Week,* October 14, 1985, pp. 77–82.

10. Kathryn R. Harrigan, *Strategies for Declining Business* (Lexington, MA: D. C. Heath, 1980).

11. William C. Symands, "It's Every Man for Himself in the Steel Business," *Business Week,* June 3, 1985, p. 76.

12. Cynthia D. Fisher, "Current and Recurrent Challenges in HRM" *Journal of Management* 15(2) June 1989, pp. 157–180.

13. Ibid., p. 158.

14. Ibid., p. 159.

15. Michael Porter, *Competitive Advantage* (New York: Free Press, 1985), pp. 11, 515; and Kevin P. Coyne, "Sustainable Competitive Advantage—What It Is, What It Isn't," *Business Horizons,* January–February 1986, pp. 54–56.

16. This section is based on M. E. Porter, *Competitive Strategy* (New York: Free Press, 1980); and M. E. Porter, *Competitive Advantage* (New York: Free Press, 1985).

17. Kevin Coyne, "Sustainable Competitive Advantage," *Business Horizons,* January–February 1986, p. 55.

18. Paul Walley and Emil Kowalski, "The Role of Training in Total Quality Implementation," *Journal of European Industrial Training* 16(3), 1992, pp. 25–31.

19. David E. Bowen and Edward E. Lawler III, "Total Quality-Oriented Human Resources Management," *Organizational Dynamics* 20(4), 1992, pp. 29–41.

20. Cynthia A. Lengnick-Hall and Mark L. Lengnick-Hall, "Strategic Human Resources Management: A Review of the Literature and a Proposed Typology," *Academy of Management Review* 13(3), July 1988, pp. 466–467.

21. Robert E. Sibson, *Strategic Planning for Human Resource Management* (New York: AMACOM Books, 1992).

22. Ceel Pasternak, "Benefits," *HRMagazine,* August 1992, p. 27.

23. Michael Porter, *Competitive Advantage.* New York: Free Press, 1985.

24. David L. Calfee, "Get Your Mission Statement Working," *Management Review,* January 1993, pp. 54–57.

25. Walter S. Mossberg, "Personnel Technology: PC Program Lets Machines Help Bosses Manage People," *The Wall Street Journal,* December 24, 1992, p. 7.

26. Bill Leonard, "U.S. Energy Secretary O'Leary Uses an HR Approach," *HRNews,* October 1993, p. A9.

27. Mark A. Huselid, "Documenting HR's Effect on Company Performance," *HRMagazine,* January 1994, pp. 79–84.

28. See also James A. McCambridge and Vicki S. Kaman, "Programs That Strengthen Relations," *HRMagazine,* May 1992, pp. 75–78.

29. Tom Peters and Nancy Austin, *A Passion for Excellence* (New York: Random House, 1985), p. 11.

30. Bureau of National Affairs, *Bulletin to Management,* June 30, 1994, p.1.

31. Robert L. Mathis and John H. Jackson, *Personnel/Human Resource Management,* 5th ed. (St. Paul, Minn.: West, 1988), p. 599.

32. Johnathan A. Seagal and Mary A. Quinn, "How to Audit Your HR Programs," *Personnel Administrator,* May 1989, pp. 67–70.

33. Ibid., p. 67.

34. Peter Drucker, "Entrepreneurial Strategies," in *Innovation and Entrepreneurship* (New York: Harper & Row, 1985).

PART TWO
STRATEGIES FOR HUMAN RESOURCE ACQUISITION AND PLACEMENT

CHAPTER 4

EQUAL EMPLOYMENT OPPORTUNITY AND MANAGING DIVERSITY

This chapter examines the role of equal employment opportunities and managing a diverse workforce. Specific laws prohibiting employment discrimination based on sex, race, national origin, age, religion, disabilities and health-related issues (including AIDS), and status as a Vietnam veteran are covered. Affirmative action programs, the issue of "equal pay for equal work," and the Equal Pay Act are covered as is the controversial topic of comparable worth. Finally, the issue of managing a diverse workforce is addressed.

CHAPTER OBJECTIVES

As a result of studying this chapter, you should be able to

1. Discuss the strategic choices available to firms regarding equal employment opportunities.
2. Understand the meaning of Title VII of the Civil Rights Act and the procedures the Equal Employment Opportunity Commission follows in investigating claims and trying cases filed under Title VII, and how cases are tried and investigated by the EEOC.
3. Describe the regulations that prohibit employment discrimination because of sex, race, national origin, age, religion, handicaps and health-related issues (including AIDS), or status as a Vietnam veteran.
4. Discuss recent Equal Employment Opportunity (EEO) case law.
5. Describe the components for strengthening or establishing affirmative action programs.
6. Discuss the Equal Pay Act of 1963 and some of the controversies surrounding comparable worth.
7. Understand the issues regarding managing a diverse workforce and the importance of having a diverse workforce.
8. Discuss strategic EEO guidelines for managers.

C A S E

ACCOUNTING FIRM HELD ACCOUNTABLE UNDER TITLE VII[1]

In May 1989, the Supreme Court ruled that Price Waterhouse, one of the Big 8 accounting firms, violated Title VII of the 1964 Civil Rights Act. Ann B. Hopkins, a senior manager at Price Waterhouse, was nominated for partnership in the firm in August 1982, and the partners decided in early 1983 to deny her a partnership. Hopkins was the only woman among 88 candidates being considered, and she had brought $34 to $44 million worth of business to the firm, more than any other candidate. When Hopkins was not renominated for partnership in 1984, she left the firm and filed suit, charging that sexual stereotyping was the reason she had been rejected.

TOO AGGRESSIVE

At the time Hopkins was denied partnership in the firm, the Price Waterhouse evaluations described her as "macho, harsh, and aggressive," speculating that she "may have overcompensated for being a woman." A male supporter in the firm advised her to "walk more femininely, talk more femininely, dress more femininely, wear makeup, have her hair styled, and wear jewelry."

All of the comments in the evaluations made by the Price Waterhouse partners dealt with Hopkins' "interpersonal skills"; her aggressive behavior was derided as "unladylike." Hopkins believed she was denied promotion because her superiors believed she acted too much like a man.

BURDEN OF PROOF

Price Waterhouse attorneys argued that sexual stereotypes were not unlawful unless they were a decisive factor in partnership determinations. They argued that Hopkins' poor interpersonal skills constituted a nondiscriminatory reason for the denial of partnership. Price Waterhouse further contended that Hopkins bore the burden of refuting its explanation by proving that the business reasons were not the "true reasons" for the decision and that her sex was the motivating factor.

Hopkins' attorneys argued that the use of sex-based stereotypes violated Title VII and that women should not have to prove that discriminatory action was the sole reason for the employment decision. In this case, the Supreme Court was called upon to decide whether or not "stereotyping" was the basis for the denial of partnership status and if this constituted unlawful discrimination.

THE SUPREME COURT RULING

The Supreme Court ruled that when there is direct evidence of both lawful and unlawful motives for an employment action, the burden is on the employer to establish that the discriminatory reasons were not determinative and that it would have made the same decision based on the purely nondiscriminatory factors. Supreme Court Justice William Brennan stated, "We are beyond the day when an employer could evaluate employees by assuming or insisting that they matched the stereotype associated with their group." He further stated, "An employer who objects to aggressiveness in women but whose positions require this trait places women in an intolerable and impermissible Catch-22; out of a job if they behave aggressively and out of a job if they don't. Title VII lifts women out of the bind."

On May 14, 1990, Price Waterhouse was ordered to make Hopkins a partner as of 1983 and award her back pay and full seniority. Based upon Hopkins' earnings, the back pay award was approximately $250,000. Price Waterhouse was also responsible for the cost of Hopkins' attorney and all court costs.

The Court's ruling in *Price Waterhouse* v. *Hopkins* is significant for at least two reasons. First, it recognizes "sexual stereotyping" as a discriminatory element in evaluations. Second, it shifts the burden of proof to the employer when direct evidence suggests that sex played a substantial role in a challenged decision.

The basic premise of unlawful discrimination is that an employer should not be able to make employment decisions, such as promoting, hiring, discharging, compensating, training, and so on, based on the applicant's or employee's age, race, sex, national origin, or religion. The term *protected group* is used to describe the people who are protected under the particular antidiscrimination law. It is commonly believed that only minorities and females, for example, are protected groups and males are not, but the term *protected group* can include Caucasians and males in certain circumstances.

The concept of equal opportunity is an ideal basic to the free enterprise system. The positive growth of any economy results from nurturing and using the ability of all persons to the fullest extent. Merit, not irrelevant factors such as race, sex, or religion, is the most important consideration in our society. Under a meritorious system, the best performers and competitors should be rewarded.

This concept means that all persons have an equal opportunity to demonstrate their merit. Unfortunately, a substantial number of employers have discriminated against certain classes of individuals based on characteristics such as gender or race. As a result, the government passed laws to end discrimination that prevented members of society from having an equal chance at available employment and the training and experience necessary to pursue all employment opportunities.

STRATEGIC CHOICES

An organization has a number of important strategic choices to make regarding equal employment opportunities (EEO). These choices are outlined below:

1. The organization can choose to be proactive or reactive in its strategy toward equal employment opportunities.
2. The organization can choose the breadth of its focus.
3. The organization can decide on the depth of its EEO plan.
4. The organization can choose the *degree of tie* between its EEO plan and the overall strategic plan of the firm.
5. The organization can decide on the degree of *formality* in its approach to EEO.

STRATEGIC CHOICES FOR EEO

PROACTIVE OR REACTIVE

An organization can decide to plan carefully and anticipate any potential discriminatory practices. This means examining new *and* existing employment policies to ensure equal opportunities. In addition, proactive organizations can develop equal opportunity programs, including affirmative action programs, to ensure that any discriminatory practices are eliminated. Affirmative action programs will be discussed later in this chapter. Some organizations, however, are more reactive to EEO and minimally satisfy only those regulations required by law and demanded by the courts.

BREADTH

An organization can choose a narrow focus by meeting EEO regulations in hiring and promotion decisions only. However, organizations can choose a broader scope by ensuring equal opportunities in areas such as training, rewarding, and so on. Although organizations are required by law to ensure fair and equal treatment in all areas of employment, many organizations fall short of this requirement.

DEPTH

The organization can choose to have an EEO plan that mostly involves only a few employees (for example, the heads of the human resource department) in its management and enforcement. On the other hand, it can involve all organizational personnel in an effort to promote *commitment* to nondiscriminatory practices throughout the organization.

TIE WITH STRATEGY

The organization's EEO policies can be tied loosely, if at all, to the firm's overall strategic plan. Conversely, the EEO policies can be fully integrated with the strategic plan of the organization. Integration of the firm's EEO policies and its overall strategic plan can best occur by fully integrating the two through strategic human resource planning, as discussed in Chapter 6.

FORMALITY

Finally, the organization can choose to have a rather informal plan that depends on the knowledge of its managers or personnel staff regarding EEO regulations. On the other hand, the organization can have a formalized plan that is clearly defined in written policy and supported by documentation and data.

EMPLOYMENT DISCRIMINATION[2]

Discrimination can be defined as the process of responding to a person differently based on that person's individual differences. This is often the goal for human resource managers. These managers make selection decisions by discriminating among the applicants. For example, when six applicants apply for one job, one has to be selected. As long as decisions of this type are based on the abilities of the applicants, discrimination is legal. Discrimination becomes illegal, however, when the differences used to separate individuals are nonjob-related characteristics such as gender, race, national origin, or handicap. This chapter discusses *illegal* discrimination acts defined by Title VII of the Civil Rights Act of 1964. Exhibit 4.1 is one firm's stated philosophy and policy regarding employment decisions.

TITLE VII OF THE CIVIL RIGHTS ACT

Title VII of the Civil Rights Act of 1964 prohibits discrimination against any individual based upon race, color, religion, sex, age, or national origin in any employment

EXHIBIT 4.1   **An Insurance Company's Employment Philosophy and Policy**

1. We have an obligation to our policyholders to determine realistically our needs for employees and to select the best qualified available personnel to handle the insurance business.

2. We shall hire, promote, compensate, and provide terms, conditions, and privileges of employment solely on the basis of the companies' personnel requirements and each individual's qualifications.

3. In fulfilling our obligations, we will not practice, tolerate, or condone discrimination because of race, color, religion, sex, national origin, age, or handicap.

4. We shall comply at all times with the letter and the spirit of all national, state, and local laws pertaining to employment.

5. Just as we will not discriminate against prospective employees because of race, color, religion, sex, national origin, age, or handicap, we will not terminate any competent person to make room for another on the basis of any of these reasons.

condition (for example, training and hiring). Title VII was amended in 1972 to strengthen its enforcement and to expand its coverage to include government employees, educational institutions, and private employers of more than 15 persons. Title VII was amended again in 1978, making it illegal to discriminate because of pregnancy, childbirth, or related conditions.

Finally, the Civil Rights Act of 1991 was enacted. The need for this new act was precipitated in part by the 1989 Supreme Court rulings on discrimination in the workplace. In 1989 the Supreme Court in *Wards Cove* v. *Antonio* set new limits in the area of civil rights by reexamining laws against job discrimination. The significance of the Supreme Court's decisions on civil rights is best understood when compared with earlier decisions on fair employment legislation. In one of the landmark employment cases, *Griggs* v. *Duke Power Company,* the Court ruled in 1971 that companies must be able to prove that their selection procedures do not discriminate unfairly. In essence, the *Griggs* v. *Duke Power Company* case involved promotion and transfer policies requiring employees to have a high school diploma and to obtain satisfactory scores on two aptitude tests. One of these tests, the Wonderlic Intelligence Test, failed African-Americans at a higher rate than Caucasians. In addition, fewer African-Americans had high school diplomas than Caucasians. Passing the aptitude test and having a high school diploma were not judged to be job-related requirements. The Court held that when plaintiffs demonstrate that otherwise neutral employment practices disproportionately and adversely affect minorities and women, they have demonstrated that a Title VII violation exists. To avoid this violation, employers had to demonstrate that (1) the plaintiff's statistics were wrong or (2) the practices at issue were dictated by business necessity.

According to civil rights activists, the Court (1) put limits on the abilities of individuals to bring employment discrimination suits (*Wards Cove* v. *Antonio*), (2) allowed challenges to affirmative action programs that had been in effect for years (*Martin* v. *Wilks* and *Lorance* v. *AT&T*), and (3) decided that federal governmental laws do not cover racial harassment in the workplace (*Patterson* v. *McLean*). According to civil rights leader Ralph G. Neas, overturning the *Wards Cove* v. *Antonio* decision was the number one legislative priority of the civil rights community during 1990 (see Exhibit 4.2 for more information on these controversial Supreme Court decisions).[3]

The Civil Rights Act of 1991 was, for the most part, in response to the U.S. Supreme Court decisions in 1989. The new civil rights law makes it easier for certain workers to

| **EXHIBIT 4.2** | **Summary of EEO Case Laws that Preceded the Civil Rights Act of 1991** |

WARDS COVE V. ANTONIO (1989)

Wards Cove involved two salmon-packing companies in the Northwest. Each firm hired only minority workers (Eskimos and Filipinos) for the lower-paid, unskilled packing jobs during the salmon season. Other more skilled jobs (e.g., engineers or mechanics), which were not seasonal, were given only to nonminority workers. Because of the statistical differences between the representation of minorities in the skilled jobs, the plaintiffs sued, claiming discrimination. The Supreme Court ruled against previous decisions and said that statistical disparity does not establish a prima facie case. The results of this case limited the ability of employees to bring employment discrimination suits by shifting the burden of proof to the employee.

MARTIN V. WILKS (1989)

In this case, the National Association for the Advancement of Colored People (NAACP) sued the city of Birmingham, Alabama, because the city was not hiring minority firefighters. To avoid litigation, the city entered into a consent agreement to hold a certain number of positions open for minority candidates. The Caucasian firefighters objected to the agreement but did not take part in developing it. Later, the Caucasian firefighters challenged the agreement under Title VII and the 14th Amendment. The Supreme Court ruled in favor of the Caucasian firefighters and said that they had not been given adequate opportunity to participate in making the agreement that violated their rights. This decision opened the door for reverse discrimination challenges to affirmative action plans that have been in place for years.

LORANCE V. AT&T (1989)

AT&T's seniority system was changed from companywide to departmentwide. In other words, a person's seniority did not go with him or her after a transfer but started over. Union men favored the change, but the women opposed it. A few years later when layoffs occurred, the women filed a suit claiming the departmentwide seniority system discriminated against them. The Supreme Court ruled that the 300-day filing deadline from the time of the act in question had long passed and dismissed the case. This decision limited the ability of employees to challenge past changes that may have a future discriminatory impact.

PATTERSON V. MCLEAN (1978)

The plaintiff, an African American, filed a racial harassment case against the McLean Credit Union because she had not received a promotion or raise while employed there. Further, she was told "blacks work slower than whites" and thus had grounds for a discrimination suit. The Supreme Court ruled that the section under which she filed (Section 1981 of the 1991 Civil Rights Act) was not appropriate because it dealt only with making and enforcing contracts and her situation did not fall under this section. This decision narrowed the view of Section 1981 by not covering racial harassment in the workplace.

CITY OF RICHMOND V. CROSON COMPANY (1989)

The city of Richmond had set aside 30 percent of its contractual work for minority business enterprises since the city was 50 percent African-American and historically less than 1 percent of the contracts had been awarded to local African-American companies. Croson, an African-American, was denied a city contract even though he was the only bidder. He sued and the lower courts decided in his favor. However, the Supreme Court ruled against him. This decision made preferential treatment (i.e., Affirmative Action plans) for minority groups discriminated against in the past unprotected by law.

sue their employers over alleged job discrimination. The law creates new, but limited, rights for women and the disabled to collect money damages that already are available to racial minorities. In addition, the act provides for compensatory and punitive damages for victims of intentional discrimination. Jury trials may be requested. Further, the new law applies to on-the-job problems as well as hiring issues.[4] Exhibit 4.3 summarizes the major provisions of the 1991 Civil Rights Act. Interestingly, one very important unsettled issue is whether the legislation is retroactive and thus applies to conduct that occurred prior to November 1991 when it was enacted. If the act is determined to be retroactive, those who have actions pending may be entitled to seek the act's expanded remedies, such as compensatory and punitive damages and a jury trial.[5]

WHAT IS DISCRIMINATION

Discrimination in employment decisions is usually manifested in one of three ways: (1) disparate treatment, (2) adverse impact, and (3) present effects of past discrimination.[6]

DISPARATE TREATMENT

DISPARATE TREATMENT
Using different standards for different applicants or employees.

A manager who intentionally treats an applicant or employee differently because of race, color, religion, national origin, sex, or age is guilty of **disparate treatment.** One example of disparate treatment is rejecting Asian applicants because of the concern that one or more might be an illegal alien. Another case of disparate treatment is applying a rule against applicants or employees of a protected group. For example, an organizational rule that allows men to marry but prohibits women from marrying treats women differently from men and violates Title VII. Finally, disparate treatment can arise from sexual, racial, religious, or national-origin harassment. For example, managers violate the law if they make sexual advances or demands as a condition for employment or promotion.

ADVERSE IMPACT

ADVERSE IMPACT
The effect of using one set of standards that result in a disproportionate number of minorities being treated unfairly.

Seemingly neutral qualifications for employment or promotions have been found to have an **adverse impact** on some minority groups. That is, selection and promotion tests that screen out minority candidates adversely impact them and are discriminatory. It has been found that some job qualifications thought to be necessary for effective performance in organizations are not actually needed and have an adverse impact on members of minority groups, women, or older workers. For example, requirements of minimum height or weight can have adverse impact on women, as well as some ethnic groups. Some employment tests tend to eliminate certain minority groups disproportionately, yet have a questionable relationship to job performance.

The *Uniform Guidelines on Employee Selection Procedures,* developed by the Equal Employment Opportunity Commission (EEOC), the Department of Labor, the Department of Justice, and the U.S. Civil Service Commission, provides guidance on ways to develop selection systems that avoid having an adverse impact and therefore do not violate Title VII. One of the recommendations included in this document is the Four-Fifths rule. In essence, this rule states that the selection rate of any minority group should be at least 80 percent (i.e., four-fifths) of the group with the highest selection ratio. A selection ratio is simply the number of applicants selected divided by the number of applicants who applied. Exhibit 4.4 provides an example of how to apply the Four-Fifths rule.

PAST DISCRIMINATION

The third way employers have been guilty of discrimination is by perpetuating the effects of past discriminatory policies. For example, a policy of hiring persons who are referred

EXHIBIT 4.3   **Major Provisions of the 1991 Civil Rights Act**

- *Damages and Jury Trials:* Provides for compensatory and punitive damages for victims of intentional discrimination suing under Title VII, the Age Discrimination Act (ADA), or federal employment sections of the Rehabilitation Act. The combined amount of compensatory and punitive damages depends on the size of the employer, with caps ranging from $50,000 to $300,000. Jury trials may be requested by any party seeking compensatory or punitive damages.
- *"Race Norming" of Employment Tests:* Prohibits adjustments in test scores, use of different cutoff scores, or other amendments to employment-related tests based on race, color, religion, sex, or national origin.
- *Expanded Coverage under Section 1981:* Amends interpretation of language in Supreme Court decision in *Patterson* v. *McLean,* regarding the right "to make and enforce contracts." Prior to this decision, Section 1981 was applied to race discrimination in all aspects of the employment contract, that is, hiring, duration of employment, and contract termination. After the *Patterson* decision, Section 1981 applied to hiring only. The Civil Rights Act of 1991 restores the pre-*Patterson* interpretation specifying that the term "make and enforce" contracts includes all benefits, privileges, terms, and conditions of the employment relationship. This is significant since there are no caps on awards for compensatory and punitive damages under Section 1981.
- *Mixed Motive Cases:* Reverses *Price Waterhouse* v. *Hopkins,* in which the Supreme Court held that an employer could avoid liability for discrimination by showing that it would have made the same employment decision in the absence of discrimination. Under the new act, this rule is changed by providing that an illegal employment practice has occurred if discrimination was a motivating factor, even though other factors also motivated the employment decision. In such cases, plaintiffs may recover declaratory and injunctive relief, attorneys fees, and costs.
- *Disparate Impact:* Reverses the Supreme Court decision of *Wards Cove* v. *Antonio,* which stated that plaintiffs injured by disparate impact discrimination had to prove that the challenged practices were not significantly related to legitimate business objectives. Under the 1991 act, an employer must demonstrate that a challenged practice is job-related and consistent with "business necessity" after the plaintiff has shown that the employment practice caused a disparate impact. Once the employer has met its burden, the plaintiff must prove that an alternative practice exists having less of a disparate impact and that the employer refused to adopt it. If the employer can prove that its employment practice does not cause disparate impact, it is not required to show the practice is required by business necessity.
- *Extraterritorial Employment:* Defines *employee* in both Title VII and the ADA to include U.S. citizens employed abroad and provides exemptions for otherwise unlawful employment actions if compliance violates laws of the foreign country where the employee works. Additionally, the 1991 act creates a presumption that violations of Title VII by foreign corporations controlled by a U.S. employer are violations by the U.S. employer itself.
- *Glass Ceiling:* The Glass Ceiling Commission was established to study barriers to advancement of minorities and women in the workforce and to recommend means of overcoming those barriers. Also establishes the National Award for diversity and excellence in executive management.

Source: Adapted from L.Z. Lorber, "Legal Report: The Civil Rights Act of 1991," *Society for Human Resource Management,* Spring 1992; and M. Kobata, "The Civil Rights Act of 1991," *Personnel Journal,* March 1992, p. 48.

by current employees before hiring other applicants may appear to be a nondiscriminatory policy. However, if the workforce is Caucasian because of discrimination in the past, the use of an employee referral policy in hiring may tend to perpetuate the Caucasian workforce because new recruits might come primarily from the Caucasian community.

Seniority systems have been challenged because of their perpetuation of past discrimination practices. However, if a seniority system was not developed out of an intent

EXHIBIT 4.4   **Example of the Four-Fifths Rule**

A company hired 193 of the 344 Caucasian applicants who applied, 40 of the 49 Hispanic applicants, 110 of the 209 African-American applicants, and 62 of the 89 Asians who applied. The selection ratio for each group follows:

- Caucasian applicants: 193/344 = 56 percent.
- Hispanic applicants: 40/49 = 82 percent.
- African-American applicants: 110/209 = 53 percent.
- Asian applicants: 62/89 = 70 percent.

The most favorably treated group in terms of selection ratio in this example is the Hispanics with a selection ratio of 82 percent.

To avoid discriminating against the Caucasian, African-American, and Asian applicants, each of the other groups must have a selection ratio of at least 80 percent of 82 percent, or 66 percent. Since their selection ratios were less than 66 percent, both Caucasian and African-American applicants were discriminated against by the hiring plan used by this firm but Asians and Hispanics were not.

to discriminate, it is not unlawful, even though it may result in restrictions of employment opportunities. For example, if women were not hired into an organization until recently, a promotion system based on seniority would have an unequal impact on female employees. The promotion system in this case would be considered nondiscriminatory (if it were developed without the intent of being discriminatory) because it applies equally to all groups.

EQUAL EMPLOYMENT OPPORTUNITY COMMISSION

The Equal Employment Opportunity Commission (EEOC) enforces compliance with Title VII, the Equal Pay Act (discussed later in the chapter), the Pregnancy Discrimination Act, the Age Discrimination Act, the Rehabilitation Act, and the Americans with Disabilities Act. The EEOC has the authority to process, investigate, and conciliate grievances alleging discrimination. *Conciliation* is the process of trying to reach an out-of-court settlement.

Any charge filed against an organization must be made within 180 days of the discriminatory act. When there is a state or local agency with the authority to handle discrimination, the charging party must file the complaint with the agency. An individual dissatisfied with the decision has 30 days after the state or local ruling to file with the federal EEOC. The EEOC then conducts an investigation to determine if reasonable cause exists that discrimination occurred. The charging party is interviewed and counseled on EEOC procedures. If reasonable cause is believed to exist, the EEOC attempts to conciliate the dispute. If reasonable cause is not found, the case is dismissed.

After a charge is filed, the employer is notified within 10 days and a fact-finding conference is held subsequently. The charging party and the employer present evidence to an EEOC specialist (conciliator). The EEOC specialist tries to work out a satisfactory settlement with both sides. If the EEOC is unable to conciliate the charge, it will be considered by EEOC attorneys for a possible lawsuit to be filed in federal district court. However, if the EEOC decides not to file a lawsuit, a "right to sue letter" is issued permitting the charging party to take the case to court. However, this suit must be filed within 300 days of the discriminatory act taking place. The only exception to the 300 day rule is in the case of a change in a seniority system that will eventually lead to intentional discrimination. (Exhibit 4.5 presents the EEOC complaint processing system.)

In discrimination court cases, the burden of proof begins with the plaintiff. The plaintiff must prove to the judge that discriminatory acts took place. If the plaintiff is able to do this, a prima facie case of discrimination has been established. If the plaintiff is unable to do so, the case is dismissed. If a prima facie case is established, the burden of proof switches to the defendant, who must present arguments to rebut the charges and offer a legal reason for its actions. If successful, the burden of proof shifts once again to the plaintiff, who has one final chance to discredit the defendant's case. The type of evidence needed to establish a prima facie case and the defense of the firm differs with the type of discrimination being charged. Exhibit 4.6 outlines the evidence required for each. This information is discussed in the following sections.

ADVERSE IMPACT

Court cases relating to adverse impact require that the plaintiff demonstrate statistically that the practices used by a firm affect various groups differently. The Four-Fifths rule

EXHIBIT 4.5   **EEOC Complaint Processing System**

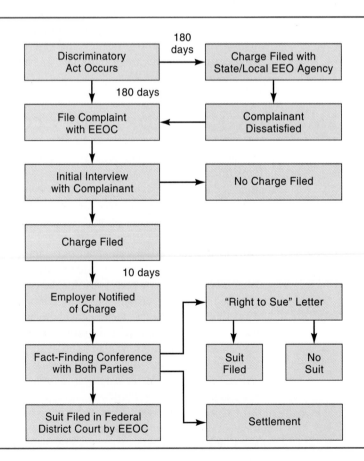

■ **EXHIBIT 4.6**   **Evidence Presented in Title VII Discrimination Suits**

ADVERSE IMPACT

- **Plaintiff** must demonstrate statistically that the practice in question affects various groups differently.
- **Defendant** can use either business necessity, bona fide occupational qualification, or validation data to rebut the charges.
- **Plaintiff** must show that an alternative practice can be used and that the alternative practice results in less adverse impact.

DISPARATE TREATMENT

- **Plaintiff** must demonstrate that (1) he or she belongs to a minority, (2) he or she applied for and was qualified for the job, (3) he or she was rejected for the job, and (4) that the job remained open.
- **Defendant** must show job-based reasons for the action taken.
- **Plaintiff** must prove that the reasons given are a pretense and the true reason for the decision was prejudice.

is an example of one type of statistic that can be used to establish a prima facie case. This statistical demonstration is often accomplished by comparing the percentage of minorities in the firm to the percentage of minorities represented in the relevant labor market. The relevant labor market refers to all individuals who qualify for the job. Often the relevant labor market is limited in geographic scope. For example, it is highly unlikely that an individual would commute more than 100 miles one way for a job that pays $5 an hour. Hence, the relevant labor market for such a position may be limited to the population in a 100-mile radius of the firm. However, if the position is chief of medicine at the city hospital, then the relevant labor market expands geographically to encompass virtually the whole world because it is likely that an individual will move a great distance to take this type of job.

Once the plaintiff has established a case, the defendant can use one of three options to rebut the charges: business necessity, bona fide occupational qualification (BFOQ), or validation data. Each of these defenses is a legal exception to discrimination. When a firm claims a business necessity, it is arguing that hiring people other than those it has selected will jeopardize the safety of customers or other employees. The firm must show that if the selection procedures were not used, the risk to customers or current employees greatly increases. In the past it has not been enough for the firm to say that not using the procedures in question would result in a substantial cost or loss to the firm. That is, the Court has not defined business necessity in economic terms.

When claiming a BFOQ defense, a company must prove that no person from a protected class could adequately perform the job. This type of defense has been used mainly in gender or religious discrimination cases. For example, the shower room attendant at the YWCA should be a woman; no man qualifies for this position. The preference of the customer is not a BFOQ. That is to say, firms that hire only men because their clients prefer to work with men could not claim a BFOQ defense. However, genuineness or authenticity has been upheld in the courts as a BFOQ. This allows a director to hire a woman to play the female lead in a play or a dance troop to hire only Polynesians for the Tahiti Fire Dance portion of their show. The hiring practices of Hooters, a national restaurant chain notorious for its scantily clad waitresses, would also fall under this exception. Patricia Casey, a lawyer for Hooters, which is currently facing a class-action discrimination suit on behalf of all men who have been denied a waitress position at Hooters, says that the "Hooter-girl" is an essential component to the marketing goals of the restaurant. She goes on to note that there is nothing illegal about passing over a man for the job because only women can meet the BFOQ for the job.[7] However, not all firms have been successful using this defense. When Johnson Controls tried to ban women of child-bearing age from working in areas that could lead to birth defects, it used BFOQ. In *UAW* v. *Johnson Controls* (1991), Johnson Controls argued that a BFOQ of being a man was necessary to protect job holders from having children with birth defects. The Supreme Court ruled that BFOQs are limited to policies that directly relate to the worker's ability to do the job.

The final defense a firm can claim is validation evidence. To use this defense, a firm must have performed a validation study in which the results clearly link the requirements for the job to the procedure in question. For example, if the firm is being sued because it uses a selection test that has a higher pass rate for whites than for minorities, the firm must prove that the skills measured by the test are essential to adequate job performance. Hence, any person failing the test would not be able to adequately perform the job and should not be hired.

DISPARATE TREATMENT

As in an adverse impact case, the plaintiff claiming disparate treatment must begin by establishing a prima facie case. The requirement for establishing a prima facie case in a disparate treatment case was spelled out in the 1973 *McDonnell-Douglas* v. *Green* case. Hence, the requirement is often referred to as the *McDonnell-Douglas Rule*. Specifically, this rule requires that the plaintiff prove four things: (1) that he or she belongs to a minority, (2) that he or she applied and was qualified for the job, (3) that he or she was rejected for the job, and (4) that the job remained open. These four steps taken together show that the firm *intentionally* discriminated and thereby establish a prima facie case.

The defendant must deny the allegations. To do this, it must provide clear and specific job-related reasons for its actions. In the case that set the precedent (i.e., *McDonnell-Douglas* v. *Green*), Green argued that his layoff was racially motivated. McDonnell-Douglas defended its actions by saying that Green had been rejected from the job because he had participated in a protest and took illegal actions against the company. The court accepted this defense.

If the court accepts the defendant's case, the plaintiff can rebut the reasoning. To do this the plaintiff must show that what the defense offered was simply a "pretext" and the real reason for the firm's actions was discrimination. This could be done by showing evidence that when the position was eventually filled, nonminority applicants with very similar qualifications were hired over minority applicants. In the *McDonnell-Douglas* case, Green could have rebutted McDonnell-Douglas's claims if he could have shown that the rehire practices McDonnell-Douglas used to fill his vacant position favored nonminority applicants or that McDonnell-Douglas had a general practice of discriminatory practices against minority applicants.

TYPES OF DISCRIMINATION

SEX DISCRIMINATION

Title VII of the Civil Rights Act of 1964 prohibits discrimination because of the gender of a person. This law has been amended to include pregnancy discrimination and sexual harassment. This section covers all three areas.

When the sex of an employee or job applicant is one of the factors on which an employment decision is based, the decision is most likely unlawful. The use of height or weight requirements may be challenged and found to be discriminatory if the requirements eliminate a significantly larger number of women than men. Other types of sex discrimination include refusing employment to a woman based on the assumption that parenthood might cause her to be absent more than a male employee. Sex stereotyping can also result in unlawful sex discrimination. For example, if a male manager evaluates the performance of a female subordinate more critically because she demonstrates stereotypically masculine characteristics (for example, assertiveness), he is guilty of sex discrimination. The opening case to this chapter provides another example. The Supreme Court ruled that the use of sex-based stereotypes for employment decisions violated Title VII.

Even though sex-based stereotypes should not be considered when hiring workers, they still exist in the workplace and often hinder women's chances for promotion and raises. The most damaging stereotyping is that women have lower career commitment than men do. If a woman is in her child-bearing years, managers look at her and ask themselves whether they should invest in her knowing she might leave. More than likely the answer is no, even if the woman cannot or chooses not to have children. A second damaging stereotype is that women are too emotional to handle management positions. When men blow up, they are considered to have a good reason; when women do it, they are considered to be emotional. Finally, women are either too aggressive or not aggressive enough. Those who are too aggressive are considered shrews; those who are not aggressive enough are not considered management material.[8]

While overt discrimination may be waning in corporate America, covert, subtle discrimination is on the rise. Deborah Flick, a diversity trainer, equates subtle sexism to water torture, one drip at a time. Even though it is hard to detect, it can be devastating to a woman and her career.

Modern-day sexism takes many forms. Exclusion is one example. Women are left out of decision making, important meetings, and business trips. The results of exclusion are lawsuits, adverse impact on women's careers, and the loss of important contributions by women.[9]

Sexual discrimination lawsuits are on the rise on Wall Street. One Wall Street firm, Kidder, Peabody & Co., has had more than its share of suits. According to interviews with 15 women who are former Kidder employees, ranging from entry-level associates to managing director, top executives froze them out of top jobs, limited their pay, and verbally harassed them. At least four women have filed sex-discrimination complaints with the New York Stock Exchange, the National Association of Securities Dealers, and the EEOC. Kidder's chief executive, Michael Carpenter, denies any wrongdoing. Instead he explains that he has personally initiated meetings with senior women, has put women on seven of the operating committees that run the firm, and has begun hiring more women.[10]

Women are making headway in some of the last male bastions. For example, Shannon Faulkner won her court case and was allowed to attend The Citadel. However, pending an appeal of the Court's decision, she can only enroll as a "day student," which means she cannot live on campus or wear a cadet uniform. Prior to her admittance, The Citadel had been an all-male institution for 151 years. Even the armed services are changing their rules toward women. Les Aspin, the former secretary of defense, lifted key restrictions that barred women from certain military tasks simply because they were considered dangerous. He explained that "expanding roles for women in the military is right, and it's smart."[11]

Interestingly, homosexuals are not covered under Title VII. Although some states and local governments prohibit discrimination against homosexuals, it is not prohibited by federal EEO laws. As of 1990, only Wisconsin and Massachusetts had outlawed discrimination on the basis of sexual orientation in public accommodation, housing, credit, and employment.

SEXUAL HARASSMENT

Sexual harassment is also a violation of Title VII of the Civil Rights Act. The highly publicized hearings regarding sexual harassment charges made by the law professor, Anita Hill, against the then Supreme Court nominee Clarence Thomas made the issue of sexual harassment more salient.[12] Essentially, sexual harassment means unwelcome verbal or physical conduct from others of a sexual nature. According to the EEOC guidelines, behavior becomes sexual harassment when

1. Submission to sexual conduct is made either explicitly or implicitly a term or condition of an individual's employment.
2. An individual's submission to or rejection of sexual conduct is used as the basis for employment decisions affecting that individual.
3. Unwelcome conduct unreasonably interferes with an individual's work performance or creates an intimidating, hostile, or offensive work environment.[13]

The first two items illustrate *quid pro quo* (literally, "something for something") harassment, the third illustrates hostile environment sexual harassment. Each will be discussed.

Quid pro quo harassment occurs when unwelcome sexual advances or requests for sexual favors are made explicitly or implicitly as a condition for employment. For example, if a manager tells a job applicant that, in terms of hiring, "It would be beneficial for you to go out on a date with me," this would constitute *quid pro quo* sexual harassment. The rules for establishing a prima facie *quid pro quo* case were established in the *Barnes* v. *Costle* (1977) ruling. The District of Columbia circuit court suggested that two criteria are needed to establish such a case: disparate treatment of women versus men and a tangible employment consequence.[14] The disparate treatment requirement is needed to show that only women are being harassed. If, however, a bisexual manager was equally harassing both men and women, there would be no case. In *Barnes*, the court found that she was harassed because she was a woman and that men in her office were not being and were not likely to be harassed, thus indicating disparate treatment.[15]

One well-known example of a *quid pro quo* court case is *Bundy* v. *Jackson*.[16] The plaintiff in the case was Sandra Bundy, who held the position of personnel clerk with the District of Columbia Department of Corrections. Jackson, the defendant, made repeated sexual advances toward her. Jackson began as her peer but was later promoted to the director of the agency. Bundy indicated that two other supervisors, Aurthur Burton and James Gainey, also made sexual advances toward her. When she complained to their boss, Lawrence Swain, he asked her to begin a sexual relationship with him. When she was passed over for promotion, she was told the reason was that her work was not adequate. However, since she had never been told that her work was unsatisfactory, she sued on the grounds of discrimination. The U.S. court of appeals found that Bundy had been discriminated against due to her sex and extended the definition of discrimination to include sexual harassment.

Hostile environment sexual harassment involves unwelcome conduct that interferes with the employee's job performance or creates an offensive working environment. This type of discrimination was first recognized in the 1986 Supreme Court case of

Meritor Savings Bank v. *Vinson.*[17] The employer argued that if no tangible losses in terms of compensation or the job itself occurred and that there was no stipulation that sexual conduct was the only way to retain the job, Title VII did not hold. That is, the only type of sexual harassment covered by Title VII is *quid pro quo*. Because *quid pro quo* harassment could not be proved in the *Meritor* case, lower courts found that the bank was not liable. However, the U.S. Supreme Court had a different interpretation. It held that hostile environment sexual harassment, as defined in the EEOC guidelines, was unlawful. It further found that any activities that create an abusive working environment are unlawful sexual harassment.

Every employee has the right to work in a work environment free of discriminatory intimidation or insult. Photographs and posters of nude women in the workplace and verbal or written obscenities can be defined as creating a sexually hostile environment. Recently, a number of female employees of Stroh's Brewery in St. Paul, Minnesota, claimed they had been sexually harassed. What is unique is that the women charged that Stroh's advertising campaigns contributed to the alleged workplace harassment. The suit asked Stroh to stop using women as sexual objects and specifically asked that the series of television advertisements featuring the Swedish Bikini Team be discontinued. Although Stroh agreed to discontinue the advertisements, the company denied allegations of sexual harassment and argued against the connection between the advertisements and workplace behavior.[18]

An employer should take all necessary steps to prevent sexual harassment in the workplace. Some guidelines to prevent harassment include developing a written policy prohibiting sexual harassment, informing managers and employees of the policy, informing managers and employees of appropriate action to take if they are harassed, promptly investigating any complaints, and taking appropriate action against the offender (see Exhibit 4.7). Even if the employer has a policy against sexual harassment, the employer can still be held liable for the actions of managers, employees, and even customers and vendors if the employer *knew* or *should have known* about the occurrence and failed to take appropriate action. The best defense against sexual harassment claims is to have a well-designed grievance procedure and to encourage employees to speak up.[19] Exhibit 4.8 presents a company's policy on sexual harassment. A policy statement should be consistent with the firm's grievance procedure, and be specific and objective.[20]

Companies need strong sexual harassment policies for a variety of important reasons. First, the monetary awards for plaintiffs winning harassment cases have increased significantly in recent years. In 1993 about 1,500 people, mostly women, won $25.2 million from employers. The year prior, 1,340 people won $12.7 million.[21] Second, the costs for such cases can be reduced if the firm has a plan in place and moves quickly when violations are reported. For example, a court recently found that Electrospace

EXHIBIT 4.7   **Sample of Guidelines to Prevent Sexual Harassment**

1. Develop a written policy prohibiting sexual harassment.
2. Inform managers and employees of the policy.
3. Inform managers and employees of the appropriate action to take if they are harassed.
4. *Promptly* investigate any complaints.
5. Take appropriate action against the offender.

■ **EXHIBIT 4.8**   **Example of a Company Policy on Sexual Harassment***

---

1. Sexual harassment is a violation of the corporation's EEO policy. Abuse of anyone through sexist slurs or other objectionable conduct is offensive behavior.

2. Management must ensure that a credible program exists for handling sexual harassment problems. If complaints are filed, they should receive prompt consideration without fear of negative consequences.

3. When a supervisor is made aware of an allegation of sexual harassment, the following guidelines should be considered:

   a. Obtain information about the allegation through discussion with the complainant. Ask for and document facts about what was said, what was done, when and where it occurred, and what the complainant believes was the inappropriate behavior. In addition, find out if any other individuals observed the incident, or similar incidents, to the complainant's knowledge. This is an *initial* step. In no case will the supervisor handle the complaint process alone.

   b. If the complaint is from an hourly employee, a request for union representation at any point must be handled as described in the labor agreement.

   c. The immediate supervisor or the department head and the personnel department must be notified *immediately.* When a complaint is raised by, or concerns, an hourly employee, the local labor relations representative is to be advised. When a complaint is raised by or concerns a salaried employee, the personnel director is to be advised.

4. The personnel department will conduct a complete investigation of the complaint for hourly and salaried employees. The investigation is to be handled in a professional and confidential manner.

---

*Policy example is based on General Motor's Corporate policy on sexual harassment.

System Inc. was not responsible because of its quick response to the allegations.[22] Finally, sexual harassment can happen anywhere. One study shows that 90 percent of Fortune 500 companies have dealt with sexual harassment complaints. More than one-third of these companies have been sued at least once, and about one-quarter have been sued over and over again. All of this litigation costs the average large corporation $6.7 million a year, or an average of $200,000 for each complaint investigated.[23]

Not all employees are able to take their case to court, however. In the securities industry, the path taken to report a harassment incident is through the firm's internal grievance procedures. This may seem to be a reasonable solution, but it apparently does not work well. The case of Helen Walters is an example. She filed a complaint against her boss for calling her a "hooker," a "bitch," brandishing a riding crop in front of her, and leaving condoms on her desk. In any court of law, she could clearly establish a prima facie case of hostile environment. However, she lost her grievance even though her boss readily admitted to all of the acts of which he was accused. The problem lies in the grievance panel members. The three-person panel is appointed and paid by the industry organization such as the New York Stock Exchange. Nearly 90 percent of the panel members are men, roughly half are retired, and their average age is 60. According to Marilyn Stringer, a former Paine Weber sales assistant, asking arbitrators with this type of profile to judge a sexual harassment case is like asking the "brother of the fox who raided the hen house." Unlike Ms. Walters, Ms. Stringer won her grievance, but her award was only $300, a far cry from the average settlement won in court cases.[24]

Although 9 of 10 sexual harassment cases filed are by women, the number of cases filed by men is on the rise. In 1993 the number of cases filed by men (1,070) more than doubled from 1992 (490). It may be harder for a man to file a claim, but the devastation sexual harassment has on his life is the same as that for a woman. An example is the case of David Papa, who ran a Domino's Pizza store. His regional supervisor, Beth Carrier, made continued detailed lewd comments and advances toward him. One week after he asked her to stop, Papa was fired. Domino's denies all charges, but the EEOC says Papa has a case.[25]

One of the most celebrated cases of a man suing a woman for sexual harassment is *Gutierrez* v. *Martinez.* In May 1993, a Los Angeles court awarded Sabino Gutierrez $1.017 million in damages in the suit he had brought against Cal-Spa and its chief financial officer, Maria Martinez. Reports indicated that the jury did not believe either party, but they apparently liked Gutierrez more than Martinez. She was described as being a cold, hard, ice princess. As the story goes, Martinez befriended Gutierrez when he first began working at Cal-Spa. At that time he could not speak English and could not read or write. She mentored him, and he rose from an hourly employee to a production supervisor overseeing a staff of nearly 70 with a salary of about $45,000 a year. However, when he announced that he was engaged, Gutierrez claims that Martinez demolished his office, threw away his personal things, and demoted him in retaliation. Martinez says that she was the one being harassed. She claims that Gutierrez made a sexual advance toward her the month his first child was born. She also claims that he would not attend a company function because he could not stand to see her with her husband. The truth of what happened may never be known, but people who worked with them and knew both sides say the truth resides somewhere between their stories.[26]

What the court requires as proof of sexual harassment changes continually. The Supreme Court recently held in *Harris* v. *Forklift Systems* that an individual does not have to have a nervous breakdown to qualify as suffering from the effects of harassment. Instead, an abusive work environment, even if it does not seriously affect the worker's psychological well-being, can detract from his or her ability to perform the job and should be considered hostile.[27] However, for every court ruling that moves the plight of sexual harassment forward, one that moves it backward can be found. For example, in the case of *Burns* v. *McGregor Electric Industries,* the court ruled that even though the sexual advances Ms. Burns faced from her boss were unwelcome and not solicited, they were not offensive to her because of her personal history, her appearance on the stand, her manner of dress, the location of her tattoo, and the fact that she had appeared nude in a magazine.[28]

PREGNANCY DISCRIMINATION

Under the Pregnancy Discrimination Act of 1978, a female employee or job applicant may not be treated differently from a male because of her pregnancy or capacity to become pregnant. Essentially, a woman is protected against being fired or refused a promotion or not hired because she is pregnant or has had an abortion. As long as they can still work, pregnant employees cannot be forced to quit or go on leave. Some states have variations of a parental leave law that enable both parents to take time off from work to care for their newborn child. However, only a few states require the employer to guarantee the same job to the employee upon return.

Special problems arise when an organization manufactures or uses products or processes that may be harmful to female reproductivity or the unborn child. Interestingly, a policy that excludes women from the workplace because of reproductive or fetal hazards may violate Title VII, even if it can be justified by scientific evidence.

Immigration Act Compliance

With the continuing influx of immigrants into the United States workforce, the need for proper identification and work authorization forms has become a primary concern to American businesses. Headlines alert the public to the problems of not only hiring illegal aliens but also discriminating against immigrants as well. In 1986, the Immigration Reform and Control Act was established to clarify the hiring process of immigrants and curb employment discrimination by providing clear, concrete guidelines for employers to follow in the hiring process.

It is important that employers be aware of the dynamics of the act and remember it when hiring immigrants. Employment decisions should *not* be based upon national origin, citizenship status, foreign appearance, name, or accent but on an employee's qualifications. Any decision based on these attributes may be construed as discriminatory, resulting in a host of legal headaches.

According to the act, employers are required to complete an I-9 verification form within three business days of the hire. This necessitates the documentation of not only the employee's identity but of work authorization as well. The following is a list of documents that can establish both identity and work authorization. The employer should be careful not to ask for "more" or "better" proof from one group of individuals than from another because this, too, may be viewed as discriminatory.

The following documents establish identity and work authorization:

1. U.S. Passport.
2. Certificate of U.S. citizenship.
3. U.S. Citizen ID Card.
4. Certificate of Naturalization.
5. Alien Registration Card with photograph.
6. Unexpired foreign passport with attached employment authorization.
7. Temporary Resident Card with attached employment authorization.

Finally, employers should *never* knowingly hire illegal aliens. The legal ramifications of this type of employment practice are serious and far outweigh any perceived benefits. By using these guidelines to comply with the Immigration Act's requirements, the employer will ease the hiring process and reduce any threat of discrimination.

SOURCE: Contributed by Donald Levine, Esq., Levine & Ginsburg Ltd., Chicago, IL.

Although the number of EEOC filings for alleged pregnancy-related discrimination has declined since a high in 1987, the numbers rose in 1992 and 1993. In 1993 pregnancy-based filings rose 2.7 percent to 3,543, and in 1992 filings increased 11 percent over those in 1991. Filings may be on the increase because juries have been granting plaintiffs lucrative awards. For example, Lana Ambruster, a former claims adjuster for California Casualty Management Company, was awarded $2.7 million, including $1.5 million in punitive damages. She claimed that her boss threatened to fire her if she came back from her honeymoon pregnant. Two months later, when she told him she was expecting a child, he placed her on written probation. She was fired two months later. California Casualty said that she was fired for performance reasons and had been warned about her poor performance. The firm also mentioned that the allegedly discriminatory remarks by Ms. Ambruster's boss were taken lightly by the other employees.[29]

RACE DISCRIMINATION AND HARASSMENT

Race discrimination means that employment decisions are based on an employee's race or color. Charges of race discrimination remain the most common type of EEO complaint. Under Title VII, employers have a responsibility to maintain a bias-free work environment and correct any discriminatory situations. As with sexual harassment, it is unlawful to engage in racial harassment. Racial harassment includes making racial and ethnic slurs or jokes directed at minority employees or in the presence of minority employees. In addition, it is unlawful to address minority employees by their first name if nonminority employees are addressed by titles such as "Mr." or "Ms." The failure of a nonminority employee to train a minority employee properly is also considered a form of racial harassment.

Almost any factor can be used to determine whether minorities have been treated differently from nonminority employees. For example, performance ratings, average salaries, records of termination, and employee training opportunities are ways in which minority groups can be compared with nonminority groups. Thus, it is important for managers to maintain accurate records of all employment decisions.

The restaurant industry has been hard hit with race-bias allegations over the past few years. Three major chain restaurants, Shoney's, Wendy's, and Denny's have been targets of race-bias filings with the EEOC. Shoney's trouble started in the small town of Marianna, Florida. Henry and Billie Elliott, comanagers of a Captain D's Seafood restaurant, which is owned by the parent company Shoney's, were fired because they refused to practice immoral, illegal policies. For example, they were instructed by their area manager to "find more attractive white girls" to hire and to cut the hours of the African-American workers to force them to quit so Caucasians could be hired to replace them. After the Elliotts promoted two African-American employees, the area manager demoted the two African-American employees and fired the Elliotts. Upon being fired, the Florida couple sued. The court found for the Elliotts and ordered Shoney's to distribute $105 million in damages and back pay over the next five years to approximately 10,000 African-American workers who had worked for Shoney's or had been denied employment during the last seven years.[30]

Several former employees of Wendy's International have filed a discrimination suit alleging that the company imposed a "lighten up" policy to reduce the number of African-Americans working in mostly Caucasian Southeast neighborhoods. The suit also claims that the firm limited the advancement potential of African-American managers.[31] The suit seeks damages for employees who were discriminated against and for managers who say they were penalized for not engaging in discriminatory acts.

Unlike Shoney's and Wendy's, Denny's was sued by customers who claimed to have been discriminated against. The charges included the fact that African-Americans were required to prepay their meals as well as pay cover charges in some Denny's in California. The suit also noted that Denny's promotional offer of providing customers a free birthday meal was not offered to African-American customers. Finally, the suit claims that managers used a racial coding system in which the term *blackout* meant that too many African-American customers were in the restaurant. The lawyer for Denny's explained that the "late-night" policies such as prepayment and cover charges were installed to address "security problems."[32]

Racial discrimination is not confined to the restaurant industry. Brooks Brothers, an apparel retailer, recently settled a lawsuit alleging discrimination in hiring. Brooks Brothers was accused of using a policy in which nonminority applicants are told that a job is open but minority applicants are told that it is closed. This discrimination was identified by finding "testers" to apply for advertised openings. Testers are equally qualified individuals who differ only with respect to race and/or gender. In the case of Brooks Brothers, the nonminority testers were told the job was still open, while the minority testers were informed that the job had been filled. Critics argue that testing is not perfect and should not be used to prove discrimination. Supporters of the system say it is one of the few ways subtle discrimination can be shown.[33]

NATIONAL ORIGIN DISCRIMINATION AND HARASSMENT

Employment discrimination based on national origin affects members of all national groups and groups of persons of common ancestry or heritage. National origin discrimination differs from race or color discrimination because other factors besides skin color or obvious race identification may be the basis for discrimination. For example, an employee's or job applicant's Cajun accent or manner of speaking cannot be part of the employment decision. Similar to race discrimination and harassment, the employer is responsible for the conduct of its employees regarding ethnic slurs and other harassing comments or actions.

The EEOC reported that national origin discrimination claims have increased 30 percent in the past five years. In 1989 only 10,736 claims were filed but in 1993 that figure had jumped to 14,035. The increase has been attributed to the nationwide job insecurity and downsizing that has been occurring as well as the increase in immigration to this country. According to William Ho-Gonzales, who heads the Office of Special Counsel (OSC) for Immigration Related Unfair Employment Practices, many people fear that "foreigners" are coming to take away the few jobs left for Americans. The OSC investigates national origin discrimination charges in businesses with 4 to 14 employees; the EEOC handles those with more than 14.[34]

Some of the discrimination claims investigated by the EEOC have been based on the way applicants sound on the phone. For example, Hollis Nurse, a Trinidad-born American, called a bank in California about the teller positions that had been advertised on two different occasions. He was told that all positions had been filled. However, when his friend who spoke flawless English called on the same day, he was told that the positions were still available. Nurse filed a suit with the EEOC alleging that the bank discriminated on the basis of national origin.[35]

The chances that Nurse will win a settlement are good. In a similar suit, Cambodian-American Planna K. Xieng alleged that the bank he worked for overlooked him for a promotion because of his accent. The bank felt that he did not have good enough English skills to calm irate customers.[36] The court awarded Xieng $389,000 in damages.

Many cases are not making it to the courts, however. Instead, employers have been settling cases without admitting liability. A Filipino nurse from Pomona, California, challenged a hospital's "English-only" policy as being discriminatory against bilingual workers. The hosptial paid an undisclosed amount but admitted no guilt to settle the case.[37]

AGE DISCRIMINATION AND HARASSMENT

The Age Discrimination in Employment Act (ADEA) of 1967 protects employees 40 years of age and older from discrimination based on their age. In general, an employer cannot force an employee to retire after turning 70. In addition, an employer generally cannot refuse to hire or promote an individual because he or she is 70 or older. Unlike Title VII, ADEA allows victims of age discrimination or harassment to have their case heard before a jury. In the fall of 1990, President George Bush signed into law the Older Workers Benefit Protection Act. This law was enacted to include employee-benefit programs under the coverage of the ADEA.[38]

Employers have a duty under the law to maintain a work environment free from age discrimination and harassment just as they do to provide an environment free of sexual discrimination and harassment. A preference for employees who will remain on the job for a long time might be considered unlawful if it excludes older workers. An employer must demonstrate a bona fide occupational qualification if challenged on eliminating individuals from certain positions because of age.

Double Damages for Age Discrimination

In *Brown* v. *M&M Mars* (1989), the U.S. Court of Appeals for the 7th Circuit ruled that to receive double back pay damages under the federal Age Discrimination and Employment Act (ADEA), a plaintiff does not need to prove that the employer's conduct was "outrageous," only that the employer knew or demonstrated reckless disregard for the discrimination laws regarding older workers. Brown had been a supervisor since 1978 and was discharged in 1983 for not handling a production problem properly. Rejecting the company's position that the discharge was based upon performance, the jury found that age was a determining factor. The 7th Circuit confirmed the jury's finding that the company's articulated reasons for discharging Brown were a cover-up and that there was sufficient circumstantial evidence to support the jury's award of double damages.

SOURCE: *Resource: Legal Report,* Society for Human Resource Management, October 1989, p. 15.

Subjective hiring or promotion decisions should be examined carefully. For example, qualities such as "energetic" might be viewed as not applying to older workers. In addition, cost-cutting is not a legitimate reason for firing older workers and replacing them with younger and equally qualified employees merely because the older employee earns more money, although this is often done through early retirement programs. For example, an employer may make an exceptionally good offer to a group of older employees to encourage retirement. This is legal as long as it is made to all employees over a specific age in an occupational class and if no one is compelled to retire. Finally, some organizations have been requiring their employees to sign "waivers" that forfeit the employee's right to file an age discrimination claim. According to a 1989 survey by the U.S. General Accounting Office, approximately 25 to 30 percent of major corporations required their employees to waive their rights to file a claim of age discrimination in order to participate in the organization's early retirement incentive program. The practice of having employees sign waivers has come under fire and recent legislation has been introduced to restrict the use of age discrimination waivers.[39]

As with most other types of discrimination-related cases, the number of age discrimination cases reported to the EEOC has increased. EEOC data suggest an increase of 14 percent from 1993 to 1994. A number of reasons have been offered to explain this; the most common one is corporate restructuring. When jobs are cut, people over 40 often can be replaced by less expensive, younger workers. However, the people in the over 40 group have a hard time finding another job and often file discrimination cases to ease the financial burden.[40] And for good reason. Successful age-bias claims have resulted in average awards of $302,914 as compared to $255,734 for sex discrimination, $176,578 for race discrimination, and $151,421 for disability discrimination. It appears that juries can visualize themselves as old and therefore can relate to the plaintiff. Another reason for the large sums is that the jury has the ability to provide double back pay if an organization's wrongful conduct is found to be willful.[41] This was the outcome for Walter Biggins, who was fired at the age of 62 just weeks prior to his pension vesting. The jury awarded him $419,000 in damages and then doubled it because the jury believed that Hazen Paper Company had willfully violated the Age Discrimination in Employment Act (ADEA).[42]

In 1992 the ADEA was extended to cover retired workers as well. The EEOC filed suit against a plumbers and pipefitters union on behalf of the retired workers who were

---

HR CHALLENGE

Sixtysomething

Much of America is mentally trapped in stereotyping people over 60 years old as being worn out, having slow minds, and longing for retirement. Despite the fact that federal laws are against mandatory retirement, our culture seems to push employees toward leaving organizations early. In 1950 about half of all men at the age of 65 were still working; today only 15 percent still work and the median retirement age has dropped to 61. A recent survey by the American Association of Retired Persons (AARP) shows that as many as 40 percent of retired people would prefer to return to the workforce.

America is facing an era of labor shortages. With the number of 18- to 44-year-olds expected to drop by 1.6 million over the next decade, the country will need its older workers as never before. Progressive corporations are already moving in these directions. One-third of the reservations staff at Days Inn are considered "older workers." McDonald's actively recruits older employees, offering them flexible working hours and training them in a "McMasters" program. Sears,

Roebuck, and Co. has expanded its part-time staff, relying primarily on older workers. Finally, Polaroid (among other companies) offers "retirement rehearsals," allowing its employees to try out a short-term leave before retirement; if the change is too dramatic and the employee is unhappy, the job is still there.

Public leaders are needed to help spread the practice of utilizing older workers. Warren Buffett has built an investment empire by paying close attention to both his companies and employees. When asked about leaving a woman in charge of one of his companies after her 94th birthday, he said, "She is clearly gathering speed and may well reach her full potential in another 5 or 10 years. Therefore, I've persuaded the Board to scrap our mandatory-retirement-at-100 policy . . . My God, good managers are so scarce I can't afford the luxury of letting them go just because they've added a year to their age."

SOURCE: Adapted from David R. Gergen, "Sixtysomething," *U.S. News & World Report,* April 16, 1990.

---

trying to get work through the local union. The union refused to let retired workers sign up for work unless they forfeited their retirement benefits. The court ruled that the policy discourages retired employees from seeking to return to the workforce and frustrates the ADEA's goal of promoting employment opportunities for older workers.[43]

To avoid the risk of age-based lawsuits, firms can and must take action. To begin, they must analyze their recruitment strategies. They must ensure that brochures and other information distributed to potential employees pictures older workers. They must develop messages that attract mature workers. Firms must ensure that their recruitment activities target the mature audience. For example, some firms offer an "unretirement" party and invite individuals interested in rejoining the workforce to attend. Organizations should advertise in sections of the newspaper other than the classifieds. The American Association for Retired Persons (AARP) can help firms locate retired employees who want to work. Hiring older workers is only one step, perhaps the easiest, in avoiding age-based discrimination suits. If older workers do not feel welcome, they will not remain. To create a positive environment for them, sensitivity training programs should be offered to employees to make them aware of the advantages older workers bring to the workplace. It is also important to offer flexible schedules or a variety of hours, especially as older workers ease out of retirement. These actions may seem to represent a big investment, but the benefits of hiring older workers will far outweigh the costs in just a short time.[44]

RELIGIOUS DISCRIMINATION

Title VII of the Civil Rights Act prohibits employment discrimination on the basis of religion, including all aspects of religious practice and beliefs. Discrimination occurs

FOCUS ON CULTURAL DIVERSITY

Using Peyote: Religious Discrimination?

Discriminating against a job applicant because he uses peyote, a mescaline hallucinogen derived from a cactus, as part of his religion was determined a violation of Title VII of the Civil Rights Act. In *Toledo* v. *Nobel-Sysco, Inc.* (1989), the plaintiff applied for a truck driving job with Nobel, a restaurant supply business. The job required driving on mountain roads and working on weekends. When the plaintiff applied for the job, he was told that he was qualified, provided he had not used drugs during the last two years (a policy specified in Nobel's employment advertisements). The plaintiff informed the company that he had used peyote twice in the past six months as part of his religion with the Native American Church. The Native American Church believes that peyote heals and helps its practitioners communicate with God. When he was rejected, the plaintiff filed a claim alleging religious discrimination. Although peyote is legal for use in religious services, the company was concerned with liability should the driver have an accident. Experts agreed that an individual

should not drive a truck for at least 24 hours after using peyote.

During the hearings, Nobel offered the following to the plaintiff: reinstatement with $500 in back pay, a limit of two peyote ceremonies per year, a requirement that he give one week's notice prior to taking part in a ceremony, and permission to take time off after each ceremony. The plaintiff refused all offers.

The Tenth Circuit reversed an earlier trial court's decision and ruled that a settlement made during the course of an administrative proceeding is *not* a reasonable attempt to accommodate. Since Nobel had made no attempt to accommodate the plaintiff until a discrimination charge was filed, the plaintiff had no obligation to cooperate with the employer. The court found that Nobel would not experience undue hardship in accommodating the plaintiff.

SOURCE: Adapted from *HR News,* Society for Human Resource Management, February 1990, p. A9; and *The Florida Law Weekly, Federal,* vol. 4, no. 12, April 20, 1990, pp. S254–S255.

when an employee is forced to choose between giving up an employment opportunity or a fundamental belief or practice. The most common problem occurs when an employee asks the manager to accommodate a religious need and there is a scheduling conflict that must be resolved (for example, conflict might arise if management asks a Seventh Day Adventist to work on Saturdays).

When religious conflicts arise, the employer must make every effort to reasonably accommodate the employee. Reasonable accommodations include the use of voluntary substitutes, flexible work scheduling, transfers to other departments, or changes in job assignments or training methods. Agnostics and atheists are also protected from religious discrimination. For example, an atheist cannot be forced to attend meetings that include prayer. Employers who can demonstrate that they are unable to reasonably accommodate an employee's or job applicant's religious practice or beliefs without undue hardship on the company are not engaging in religious discrimination.

In October 1993, the EEOC defined religious harassment as conduct that "denigrates" or shows "hostility or aversion" toward someone because of his or her religion. This conduct must create an offensive work environment and interfere with performance or employment opportunities. Although most people would view the EEOC's guidelines as fair, they are currently being challenged. Interestingly, the challenge is coming from religious conservatives. They argue that they may not be able to hold morning prayers, pray before meals, or hold lunchtime Bible studies if someone in the organization finds it "offensive" and sues. The pressure in the debate was strong enough to push more than 100 members of Congress to support a House resolution calling for EEOC to withdraw the guidelines. EEOC would rather explain how the existing law is designed to protect everyone's rights than change its guidelines.[45]

HANDICAP DISCRIMINATION

The Rehabilitation Act of 1973 prohibits all federal contractors from discriminating against persons with physical or mental handicaps and requires them to take affirmative action to employ job applicants or employees with such handicaps.[46] The Acquired Immune Deficiency Syndrome (AIDS) is now classified as a form of handicap; thus, this disease is covered under the Rehabilitation Act. Although most handicaps are readily detectable, some are not. The law covers both types. In addition, the law covers cases in which an employee does not have a handicap but is perceived as having one. Managers should not assume that a particular employee is not capable of performing certain types of jobs. Instead, the manager should allow the employee to decide whether he or she can perform a specific job. Although the Rehabilitation Act applies only to companies with a federal government contract or subcontract, many states have laws that cover all employers.

Handicapped individuals are protected under law if they are handicapped but are qualified and able to perform the job. Employers are required to make *reasonable accommodations* for handicapped employees. Often, accommodation involves no more than common sense and does not need to be expensive to be effective. Wheelchair users need space for their chairs entering and leaving a building as well as in work areas. Local building codes state the amount of space required. Wheelchair ramps, wide doorways, and accessible restrooms are all necessary to accommodate handicapped workers in wheelchairs. Specially designed workstations in which desks or worktables can be raised and lowered mechanically can help the handicapped worker to feel more comfortable and perform effectively.

A variety of devices is available for telephones to amplify hearing and speech for hearing-impaired employees. Individuals with severe hearing loss can use more elaborate telecommunication devices. Individuals with vision impairments can be accommodated in various ways. For example, raising lettering or Braille symbols on signs and elevator buttons can be extremely helpful. Agencies dealing with specific disabilities, such as state commissions for the blind and visually impaired, and state and local rehabilitation facilities are sources of assistance in providing successful accommodations.

The law does not extend to alcohol or drug abusers.[47] However, it is recommended that a company encourage any employee with an alcohol or drug abuse problem to seek professional help (such as through an Employee Assistance Program) prior to any disciplinary measures or discharge. In addition, the law does not extend to employees who have currently contagious diseases or infections and who, because of this disease, would be a direct health or safety threat to others. AIDS cases do not fall under this category because research has shown that AIDS cannot be transmitted through casual contact. Employers should not wait until they are confronted with an AIDS case before developing a comprehensive AIDS policy. Policies and educational programs need to be implemented before a crisis situation occurs. Medical evidence showing that AIDS cannot be contracted through casual contact will not appear genuine to employees if the evidence is presented to them *after* a coworker is known to have AIDS.

AMERICANS WITH DISABILITIES ACT

The Americans with Disabilities Act (ADA) of 1990 prohibits discrimination against individuals with disabilities. Under the ADA, the term *disability* is defined as it is in Title V of the Rehabilitation Act of 1973; however, the ADA is *not* limited to federal grantees or contractors.[48] The ADA has been described as "revolutionary" because of the scope of protection it provides to individuals with disabilities. The ultimate goal is the integration of persons with disabilities into all segments of society.[49]

The ADA is made up of five sections.[50] Title I (employment) makes it illegal to discriminate against a qualified individual with a disability and imposes an obligation for employers to make reasonable accommodations for the disabled. The ADA covers physical and mental impairments such as visual, speech, and hearing impairments, cerebral palsy, epilepsy, multiple sclerosis, AIDS, cancer, heart disease, mental retardation, and emotional illness.[51] The ADA prohibits most preemployment health questions. Although a user of illegal drugs is not protected under the ADA, a rehabilitated drug user or someone who is participating in a supervised rehabilitation program is protected.

Title II (public service) makes it illegal for state or local governments to discriminate against qualified disabled persons in the provision of public services and includes requirements regarding the accessibility of public transportation for individuals with disabilities. Title III of the ADA (public accommodation) makes it illegal for public accommodations (such as restaurants, retail stores, or places of recreation) to discriminate against individuals with disabilities in the provision of goods, benefits, services, facilities, privileges, advantages, or accommodations. In addition, Title III requires existing public accommodation to be made accessible.

Title IV of the ADA (telecommunications) requires all common carriers in interstate communication to ensure that telecommunications systems are available to individuals with hearing and speech impairments and to provide reasonable technological accommodations. Title V (miscellaneous) is a more general "catch-all" provision that relates ADA to other laws. Among the provisions, retaliation against individuals who exercise their rights under the act is made illegal.

As of October 31, 1993, 17,355 ADA violation charges had been filed with the EEOC. Of those, 2,822 "right to sue" letters were issued and 122 case filings were found. In 1994 charges were filed at a rate of more than 1,500 a month. Based on these data, projected filings per year total 18,000. The people filing the claims are not applicants seeking jobs but current employees. For example, injured workers make 30 percent of all ADA charges. Nearly 50 percent of the filings relate to disabilities with the biggest single disability category being "other," meaning that the charging party does not have any of the 35 types of impairments identified by the EEOC. The next largest category is back impairments, which account for almost 20 percent of all ADA charges. Mental illness accounted for an additional 10 percent of the claims. Claims for persons with disabilities intended to be covered by legislation (e.g., persons who use wheelchairs, walk with crutches, carry a white cane, use a guide dog, and suffer from epilepsy or cerebral palsy, etc.) make up only 4 percent of the claims.[52]

Reasonable accommodation violations represent 23 percent of the claims filed. According to the EEOC, an employer is required to use a four-step method to identify reasonable accommodation. First, the employer should determine the purpose of the job and the essential functions required in performing the job. Next, the employer should consult with the individual with the disability and determine his or her physical and mental abilities and his or her precise limitations. Third, in the discussions with the individual with the disability, the employer should try to identify possible accommodations and the effectiveness of each in helping that person perform the essential functions of the job. Finally, the employer should consider the preferences of the individual with the disability and then select the accommodation that best serves the needs of that individual and the employer. The employer is free to choose among effective accommodations and may choose the one that is less expensive or easier to provide.[53]

Employers have been quick to settle ADA claims out of court. Few companies want to face a sympathetic jury with a disabled plaintiff sitting in front of them. If an organization loses a court case, it can be responsible for $300,000 in compensatory and

HR CHALLENGE

Rx for AIDS in the Workplace

The prescription for dealing with Acquired Immune Deficiency Syndrome (AIDS) in the workplace continues to be education. Through the efforts of government agencies, employers, and local groups, most members of the population now realize that AIDS cannot be spread by the casual contact that is encountered in the workplace. The incidence of AIDS among health-care professionals dealing with AIDS patients has remained remarkably low. In fact, many people have not yet had to deal with a co-worker, a family member, or a friend who has tested HIV positive and progressed through the disease process.

The situation will surely change during the 1990s. Even the conservative estimate of the Centers for Disease Control (which calculated that 800,000 to 1.3 million Americans were infected with the AIDS virus by 1990) indicates that it is likely that employees in large organizations will know one or more persons infected with the AIDS virus. The need for the dissemination of accurate information about all aspects of AIDS will thus be critically important in the years to come. Assistance programs will be dealing with more and more employees infected with the AIDS virus. Education will be the method by which human resource managers deal with the guilt, anger, fear, and concern of employees.

The courts have consistently ruled that AIDS sufferers are covered by existing handicap laws; therefore, discrimination against employees testing positive for AIDS is illegal. It is imperative for employers to ensure that these employees' rights are maintained and that confidentiality is a requirement.

The following guidelines developed by the Citizens' Commission on AIDS for New York City should form the basis for the development of policies that deal with AIDS in the workplace. Similar guidelines have been developed by other cities, including Boston, San Francisco, Chicago, Philadelphia, and Miami.

- Employees with AIDS or HIV infection are entitled to the same rights and opportunities as people with other serious or life-threatening illnesses.
- Employment policies must comply with laws and regulations.
- Employment policies should be based on scientific and epidemiological evidence that people with AIDS or HIV infection do not pose a risk of transmission of the virus to co-workers through ordinary contact.
- The highest levels of management and union leadership should unequivocally endorse nondiscriminatory employment policies and educational programs about AIDS.
- Employers and unions should communicate their support of these policies to workers in simple, clear, and unambiguous terms.
- Employers should provide employees with sensitive, accurate, and up-to-date education about risk reduction in their personal lives.
- Employers have a duty to protect the confidentiality of employees' medical information.
- To prevent work disruption and the rejection by co-workers of an employee with AIDS or HIV infection, employers and unions should undertake education for all employees before such an incident occurs and as needed thereafter.
- Employers should not require HIV screening as part of general preemployment or workplace physical examination.
- In those occupational settings where there may be a potential risk of exposure to HIV, employers should provide training and equipment for infection control procedures.

Source: Adapted from J. Wieser, S. Fuller, M. Shriver, and D. Oelhafen, "Rx for AIDS in the Workplace," *Human Resource Management Today,* Spring/Summer 1990.

punitive damages plus back pay and attorney fees. If a firm settles, costs may be only $20,000. But when the number of ADA cases is multiplied by the 18,000 claims filed, the costs begin to accumulate quickly.[54]

Those cases that have made it to court provide good examples of what employers should not do. For example, in *EEOC* v. *AIC Security Investigation, LTD.,* the EEOC represented a senior executive with terminal brain cancer who was fired by his employers despite the fact that he could still perform his job. The complainant, Charles Wessel, was fired three days after the ADA took effect. According to his employer,

Wessel's health problems were interfering with his job performance. However, no record of counseling, reprimands, or other evidence to document his poor performance were ever provided. The company claimed that Wessel was absent 25 percent of the time during 1992 for cancer treatment and that he therefore could not adequately perform his job. The court disagreed, noting that a number of Mr. Wessel's tasks could be performed over the phone whether the phone be in his car, home, or office. Where the work is done is immaterial as long as it is done. The jury awarded Wessel $572,000 in back pay and damages. The judge later reduced this amount to $222,000, which is the cap on damages allowed by the 1991 Civil Rights Act. It appears that the company's attitude toward Mr. Wessel, who was forced to seek employment during the remaining few months of his life, made an expensive impression on the jury.[55]

The first civil penalty imposed under the ADA was a $20,000 fine. It was levied against a Denver business with more than 100 parking lots and garages that allegedly failed to provide handicapped-accessible spaces. In addition to the $20,000 penalty, the firm was required to provide over 400 handicapped-accessible parking spaces. This decision showed a significant shift in attitude from a warning and announcement approach to an enforcement approach. The Department of Justice, which imposed the penalty, says that businesses should have been aware of the ADA by the time of this action and should have already taken corrective action regarding potential violations. With this type of warning shot fired, other firms will likely take notice.[56]

AFFIRMATIVE ACTION[57]

Similarities exist between the legal concepts of "discrimination" and "affirmative action"; however, there are important differences. Equal Employment Opportunity laws are designed to rid the workplace of current and future discriminatory acts. Affirmative action is designed to remedy past discrimination by requiring employers to hire and promote minorities and females based on the number of *qualified* minorities and females in the relevant labor market.

WHO IS REQUIRED TO DEVELOP AFFIRMATIVE ACTION PROGRAMS?

According to the Executive Orders 11246, 11375, and 11478, federal contractors and subcontractors are required to develop, implement, and maintain a written affirmative action program (AAP). Specifically, companies with at least 50 employees and a $50,000 contract or subcontract with the federal government (or with another company doing business with the federal government) are usually compelled to develop, implement, and maintain a written AAP on an annual basis. If a company does not meet these criteria, it is not required to comply. For example, a company with 5,000 people and a $5,000 contract with the federal government is not required to comply with AAP regulations. However, companies found guilty of discrimination may be required to have an AAP.

Court decisions have made a distinction between *voluntary* and *required* AAP. Many employers have developed an affirmative action program on a volunteer basis. That is, they realize that having a diverse workforce is a wise policy and take steps to locate and hire qualified minority applicants. If an AAP is voluntary, the employer is not required to adhere to the goals of the plan. However, if a plan is required, an employer has been ordered by the court to have an AAP and is obligated to adhere to the goals of the plan.

HOW AFFIRMATIVE ACTION WORKS

According to Seligman in "How Equal Opportunity Turned into Employment Quotas,"[58] affirmative action operates on four levels. The first level is *pure nondiscrimination* and embodies a willingness to treat all races and both sexes the same in employment decisions. Many critics find the approach insensitive to the deleterious effects of past discrimination because this level of affirmative action may not significantly increase minority and female employment in nonstereotyped positions.

The second level of affirmative action hires and/or promotes employees entirely based on merit. However, this level includes a concerted effort to expand the number of minority and female applicants and employees (such as minority-focused recruiting efforts).

The third and fourth levels of affirmative action programs use *preferential hiring* and *quota systems,* respectively. Preferential hiring means that the company systematically favors minorities and females in hiring and promotion decisions. Use of the quota system includes preferential hiring and advocates a specific number of minorities and females that should be hired and/or promoted in the organization.

REVERSE DISCRIMINATION

Critics of preferential hiring and the use of quota systems have argued that this can lead to reverse discrimination against white males. *Reverse discrimination* occurs when an equally or more qualified nonminority, usually a Caucasian male, is not hired or promoted in favor of a racial or sexual minority group member. For example, in *City of Richmond* v. *Croson Company* (1989), the Supreme Court addressed the problem of reverse discrimination. The Richmond City Council adopted the Minority Business Utilization Plan, which required prime contractors (to whom the city awards construction contracts) to set aside 30 percent of the dollar amount of the contract for minority business enterprises. The Court held that the minority contractor set-aside requirement denied equal protection because it discriminated on the basis of race. Essentially, the Supreme Court recognized that preferential treatment for "protected classes" can have a discriminatory effect against other groups, who may be in the actual majority of the population.[59]

Chrysler was found guilty of reverse discrimination in 1993. Mary Hand Frost, a Caucasian woman from Oklahoma, sought a Dodge dealership in Edmond, Oklahoma, under Chrysler's Marketing Investment Program. Under the terms of this program, Chrysler pays dealers to operate and manage its dealerships with the understanding that the dealer can buy out Chrysler's interests. Candidates for the program can either be graduates of Chrysler's Minority Dealer Development Program or have business experience that qualifies them for the position. According to Ms. Frost's claim, she approached a Chrysler zone representative about the dealership and was informed that she was the most qualified applicant, having spent 14 years selling new and used cars and was more or less assured of getting the assignment. Chrysler denied her application and the dealership was run by an interim manager until an African-American candidate was found. The judge noted that "the evidence in the case strongly suggested that Chrysler's affirmative action program was a mere pretext for rejecting the application of the plaintiff, a white female," and granted a summary judgment against Chrysler. The Court decided against Chrysler for three reasons: The firm failed to demonstrate that there was "conspicuous" racial imbalance that it was trying to correct, the firm did not recruit from other racial minorities, and the program should have been temporary.[60]

It is important that employers realize that nothing about affirmative action requires companies to recruit, hire, or promote employees not qualified to do the job under question. Affirmative action means that employers should make every effort to place minorities and females in jobs in which these groups are underutilized. However, various Supreme Court cases illustrate how difficult it is to determine when gender and race are actually being used as selection criteria. In the case of *United Steelworkers* v. *Weber* (1979), Brian Weber issued a Title VII challenge to the voluntary AA program of Kaiser Aluminum. His case centered on being denied entrance into an in-house skilled trades training class in favor of African-American employees who had less seniority than he did. Kaiser selected the African-American workers over Weber because Kaiser had reserved 50 percent of the training slots for minority workers in an effort to correct past discrimination (i.e., the company implemented a voluntary Affirmative Action Plan). The district court and the U.S. Court of Appeals for the Fifth Circuit Court agreed with Weber. However, the Supreme Court overturned the ruling in a 5–2 vote. The five justices (Brennan, Blackmun, Marshall, Stewart, and White) indicated that the plan did not absolutely bar advancements of whites, nor were white workers discharged and replaced with African-American workers. Further, the plan was temporary and designed to balance racial imbalance or correct a past wrong. In essence, affirmative action plans that caused reverse discrimination were allowed. In a second court case, *Johnson* v. *Transportation Agency* (1987), gender was the focus. Specifically, Paul Johnson, a male who had applied to an open craft position, was one of seven finalists. Also among the finalists was Diane Joyce. Johnson was rated slightly higher than Joyce and was recommended by three supervisors for the open position. However, the director, with input from the affirmative action officer whom Joyce had petitioned, ordered his subordinate to select any of the seven candidates. When he selected Joyce, Johnson sued. The district court agreed with Johnson, but the Ninth Circuit Court reversed the decision, and the Supreme Court upheld the reversal in a 6–3 decision. The ruling was based on the fact that the affirmative action plan did not set aside specific jobs for minorities. Instead, it authorized the consideration of ethnicity or gender as a factor when evaluating qualifications for a job in which members of such groups were historically poorly represented. The three judges who dissented where White, Scalia, and Rehnquist. This was a reversal for White from the *Weber* case. White's rationale for changing his vote in this case was because gender, not race, was the key focus. He stated, "My understanding of *Weber* was, and is, the employer's plan did not violate Title VII because it was designed to remedy the intentional and systematic exclusion of blacks. . . . That is how I understood 'traditional segregated jobs'. . . . The Court now interprets it to mean nothing more than a manifest imbalance between one identifiable group and another in an employer's labor force." He then stated that for the written record, he would henceforth vote in favor of overturning the *Weber* ruling. While the decisions in both cases are consistent (the plaintiffs lost), there is some belief that such an outcome may not continue. With the current composition of the Supreme Court, the *Weber* case, if reopened, could be overturned.[61]

ESTABLISHING AFFIRMATIVE ACTION PROGRAMS

Many employers face penalties for violation of equal employment opportunity and affirmative action regulations. The development of a comprehensive affirmative action program is an important step in avoiding expensive litigation. Elements of an effective program, shown in Exhibit 4.9 include underutilization and availability analyses, the examination of current job specifications and descriptions, the development of goals and timetables, effective recruiting, and the development of a comprehensive inventory of existing employee skills. Each of these is described below.

Components of an Effective Affirmative Action Program

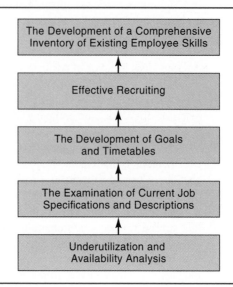

UNDERUTILIZATION AND AVAILABILITY ANALYSES

An underutilization analysis examines the number of protected group members (for example, minorities) employed and the types of jobs they hold in an organization. An availability analysis examines the number of protected group members who are available to work in the relevant labor market. The firm should determine where minorities and women are clustered, excluded, or underutilized based on reasonable expectations from the labor market. An availability analysis can be developed with data from a state labor department or the U.S. Census Bureau. The availability analysis is the basis for determining whether underutilization is occurring within a company.

EXAMINATION OF CURRENT JOB SPECIFICATIONS AND DESCRIPTIONS

Employers should examine the current job specifications and descriptions in their company to ensure their accuracy. The firm should establish prescribed qualifications and wage scales based on the actual job to ensure that barriers to minorities and women are not present. Irrelevant qualifications or qualifications that exceed the requirements of the job have been the cause of many lawsuits.

DEVELOPMENT OF GOALS AND TIMETABLES

Employers should correct underutilization of minorities and women by establishing measurable and realistic hiring and promoting goals. In addition, employers should develop realistic timetables by which these goals are to be actualized. The firm's goals should remedy exclusion and/or underutilization of protected groups in specified jobs.

EFFECTIVE RECRUITING

Employers can actively recruit minorities and women to fill positions that have been found to exclude or underutilize minorities and women. Systematic recordkeeping should describe the flow of minorities and women seeking employment and promotions. Job application forms should not contain information about race or sex.

INVENTORY OF EXISTING EMPLOYEE SKILLS

A comprehensive skills inventory of current employees can help to establish a baseline for training and development programs. Employers can learn the skill level of the firm's employees, which is important for identifying qualified employees to fill higher-level positions. Employers also can use this information to create training and development programs for all employees, including minorities and women. General Motors, for example, has spent millions of dollars to provide a variety of educational programs for minorities and women.

LEGAL ISSUES IN COMPENSATION

THE EQUAL PAY ACT OF 1963

The Equal Pay Act (EPA) requires that men and women who work for the same organization be paid the same for work that is equal in skill (such as experience or training), effort (mental or physical effort), responsibility (the degree of accountability), and working conditions (the physical surroundings and hazards).[62] This act was passed as an amendment to an earlier compensation law called the Fair Labor Standards Act of 1938. Essentially, the Fair Labor Standards Act applies to employees engaged in interstate commerce.[63] The Equal Pay Act also forbids wage discrimination on the basis of sex but extends coverage to employees in executive, administrative, professional, and outside sales force categories, as well as employees in most state and local governments, hospitals, and schools. Pay discrimination against minorities and women is also covered under Title VII.

The Equal Pay Act of 1963 was designed to close the salary gap between men and women. However, 30 years after it was passed, the gap still existed. In 1993 women made 70 cents to every dollar made by a man. The pay gap between men and women actually has widened nine times since the law was passed. Further, the narrowing of the pay gap has resulted primarily from falling wages for men, not rising wages for women. Specifically, median hourly wages for women were $8.42 in 1992, up only 31 cents from 1979. During this same period, median hourly wages for men fell $1.84 to $11.03. Experts argue that wages will not approach equality in the near future because the EEOC is not doing much to enforce the law. It filed only 2 suits in 1992, which was down from 6 the previous year and from 79 in 1980. According to the EEOC, people prefer to file under Title VII gender discrimination because the EPA has a two-year time limit.[64]

Some people believe that the wage gap should not be closed because women are less qualified than their male counterparts. However, research appears not to support this claim. Dr. Peter Hammerschmidt, an economist at Eckerd College in St. Petersburg, Florida, analyzed the pay and credentials of 194 corporate managers randomly selected from 800 participants who enrolled in a leadership course at Eckerd in recent years. He found that the men he studied earned approximately 18 percent more than women.[65]

Another reason that the pay gap has not narrowed in recent years is that discussing one's salary in the work place is taboo. Hence, underpaid women and overpaid men do not know each other's pay rate. Women find out in subtle ways, however. For example, when her counterparts were purchasing boats and homes that Marcia Rafter could not afford, she began to wonder why. Even though she was rated number 1 or 2 every

FOCUS ON INTERNATIONAL ISSUES

Danish Women Begin to Sing "I've Been Working on the Railroad"

The government-owned Danske Statsbaner (DSB), the Danish state rail system, has implemented an aggressive policy to place women on the management fast track. For example, one woman, Birthe Oestergaard Peterson, went from working the switch signals on the night shift to heading the team that plans Denmark's train schedules. DSB's plans include training programs to give women the skills needed to become engineers. It offers seminars for female workers such as one on "Is Management for Me?" DSB also has instituted a confidence-building job development program for secretaries. To attract women, DSB offers 24-hour daycare. Recruiters and managers have been told to look for qualified women, and male managers were placed in discussion groups with women to help break down the stereotypes each held.

Since it began its program six years ago, DSB has increased the proportion of female workers from 11 percent to 18 percent. This number is predicted to reach 20 percent by 1996. Even more exciting is the fact that the number of female executives has increased from 1 percent to 10 percent, front-line managers from 2 percent to 12 percent, and female train conductors from virtually zero to 40 percent.

Even with these advances, DSB has a long way to go. It still has no female board members, and only one

woman is at the highest management level. "There is still a glass ceiling," reports Tore Haakomsson, the personnel lawyer for DSB. He also noted that there is still gross pay inequity between men and women at DSB and that the company cannot find enough women to recruit. To overcome this problem, it has initiated its own training programs. For example, it now has a class of 37 women learning metalworking skills so they can become locomotive engineers.

Some argue that the firm is going too far. One woman declined a job offer when she found that she was the only female applicant out of 50. She realized that getting a job just because she was a woman was not good for the company or for her. Other women feel differently. One of the first women to break into top management, Anne-Lise Bach Soerensen, has seen both her responsibility and salary double. She is now taking business trips out of the country and actively helping the women in positions below her rise through the ranks. Recognizing the potential in one of her assistants, she enrolled her in the management training program.

SOURCE: Dana Milbank, "Danish Women Given Inside Track on the Rail," *The Wall Street Journal,* May 16, 1994, p. A1+.

quarter, she was told that as a single woman, she did not need as much money as did men who had families. This policy of basing salary on need is not limited to women. Men, especially when their wives work, and particularly if they have no children, also are being told that their need is not as great as some of their co-workers. This policy may be a factor in the decrease in wages for men.[66]

Pay differentials between equal jobs can be justified, however, when they are based on a seniority system, a merit system, a system based on measuring earnings by quality or quantity of production, or any factor other than sex. Under the Equal Pay Act, employers must correct any pay inequities by raising the pay of lower-paid employees, not by lowering the pay of higher-paid employees.

COMPARABLE WORTH

Comparable worth means that jobs requiring comparable knowledge, skills, and abilities should be paid similar amounts. Comparable worth and the Equal Pay Act (EPA) differ in that EPA requires equal pay for male and female employees who perform work that is substantially equal. Comparable worth means employers are required to provide equal pay for work of *equal value*. For example, a 1980 court case examined whether nurses (a predominantly female job) should be paid the same as tree trimmers (a predominantly male job).[67]

The issue of comparable worth was developed primarily as an answer to the persistent wage gap between men and women employees. On average, women's earnings are approximately 70 percent of men's earnings. Comparable worth advocates that employees who work on "comparable" jobs (even though the actual job duties may differ) should be paid equally. Rather than comparing jobs based on job duties, proponents of comparable worth advocate comparing jobs based on four factors: (1) knowledge and skill level, (2) effort, (3) responsibility, and (4) working conditions.

The most publicized comparable worth case occurred in the state of Washington. The state was sued by the American Federation of State, County, and Municipal Employees (AFSCME). The union alleged that women who worked for the state of Washington were experiencing pay discrimination. The state's job evaluation plan placed many of the jobs traditionally held by women at a higher level than those held by men, but the wage rates were less than those for jobs traditionally held by men. Although the discrimination charges were upheld in U.S. District Court, the U.S. Supreme Court ultimately ruled against the women claiming comparable worth. However, following the decision, the state of Washington and the AFSCME reached a settlement in which the state paid $41.4 million on pay equity adjustments from April 1986 through June 1987 to employees such as nurses, library technicians, and clerk typists. Supplemental pay increases brought the total to $482 million by 1992.[68]

One of the biggest problems facing comparable worth advocates is the cost of replacing the supply-and-demand market with a government-run job evaluation system. Closing the earnings gap between men and women has been estimated as costing $320 billion a year.[69] In addition, some have argued that a more effective solution would be to encourage women to enter nontraditional occupations and provide them with equal access to education, training, and employment, rather than raise the price of labor for specific jobs.[70]

CURRENT STRATEGIC ISSUES IN EQUAL EMPLOYMENT OPPORTUNITY

THE GLASS CEILING

The term *glass ceiling* refers to the often subtle attitudes and prejudices that create barriers that block women and minorities from climbing the corporate ladder[71] or, in some cases, even moving laterally.[72] Glass ceilings have recently begun to receive a great deal of attention because of the Department of Labor's investigation into these invisible barriers. After reviewing a study done in September 1990 by researchers at the University of California, Los Angeles, in conjunction with Korn/Ferry International, the Department of Labor announced plans to begin investigating and removing glass ceilings in large government contractors.

The UCLA/Korn/Ferry study revealed that women and minorities hold less than 5 percent of the senior management positions among the Fortune 500 companies surveyed.[73] This represents an increase of only 2 percent in the last 10 years for women and minority representation in executive positions.[74] Given that women and minorities represent over 50 percent of the workforce, these facts have caught the attention of officials at the Department of Labor.[75] As can be seen in Exhibit 4.10, the leading occupations for women have not really changed much over the last 100 years.

■ **EXHIBIT 4.10**   **Top Ten Positions Occupied by Women—Have You Really "Come a Long Way, Baby"?**

RANK	1990	1940	1890
1	Secretary	Servant	Servant
2	Cashier	Stenographer, secretary	Agricultural laborer
3	Bookkeeper	Teacher	Dressmaker
4	Registered nurse	Clerical worker	Teacher
5	Nursing aide, orderly	Sales worker	Farmer, planter
6	Elementary school teacher	Factory worker (apparel)	Laundress
7	Waitress	Bookkeeper, accountant, cashier	Seamstress
8	Sales worker	Waitress	Cotton-mill operative
9	Child-care worker	Housekeeper	Housekeeper, steward
10	Cook	Nurse	Clerk, cashier

SOURCE: *Fortune,* September 23, 1991, p. 9.

In a study that tracked the career paths of male and female MBAs, evidence of glass-ceiling effects was discovered. Over the time of the study, females received on average the same number of promotions as men; however, they experienced lower salary increases, fewer managerial promotions, and lower hierarchical levels as compared to men of similar background and experience.[76]

Pursuant to the discovery of glass-ceiling effects, investigations were begun to find out why women and minorities cannot penetrate the invisible barriers, other than as a result of overt and covert discrimination. An 18-month study by the Department of Labor in 1990–1991 reveals that, in many cases, women and minorities were not given critical training early on that would have made promotions possible. In addition, women and minorities were often passed over for the higher visibility projects that would have allowed them to prove themselves. Finally, Caucasian males were found to mentor and help other Caucasian males. Given that very few top management positions are occupied by women and minorities, less mentoring seems to be occurring with the groups who need it the most.[77] Mentoring has been found to be related to organizational advancement.[78] Mentors provide critical thinking, share inside information, lend social support, and serve as a buffer between the organization and the mentored employee. Women who have been mentored have been found to advance more rapidly than those without mentors.[79] However, women are less likely to develop a mentoring relationship than men.[80] Since mentoring appears to be a factor in organizational success, encouraging it may help to crack glass-ceiling barriers.

Managers should be aware of the possible glass ceiling within their organization. The following guidelines can help to encourage women and minority promotions into higher-level positions.

1. Formal Training. If promotions depend on critical and specialized skills, it is important that training opportunities are offered to all employees.
2. Networking. Encourage women and minorities to communicate and exchange information and ideas about the job (that is, to engage in networking). In addition, managers can bridge various "networks," including Caucasian male networks, by arranging for representatives from different networks to meet and discuss job-related issues. Of course, it is also important to discourage Caucasian males from networking in private clubs where women and minorities are officially excluded.

3. Mentoring. *Mentoring* refers to an informal relationship between top managers and newer, lower-level employees that helps the newer employees to gain status and be promoted. Mentors often achieve these results by explaining the corporate culture, providing strategic advice, suggesting career moves, and supporting these employees for promotion. As mentioned earlier, the Department of Labor found that some Caucasian male managers tend to mentor other Caucasian males. One way to overcome this tendency is to create a more formalized mentoring program and pair top managers with women and minorities.

4. Diversity Training. Top managers may need to have some diversity training in order to understand gender and cultural differences. For example, diversity training programs have shown why women make decisions differently than men. This will be discussed in more detail in the next section.

Breaking the subtle barriers of the glass ceiling will require the efforts of human resource professionals.[81] The human resource professional should not only make sure that discrimination does not exist but also make sure companies make a good faith effort to allow women and minorities to advance. Continuing to maintain glass ceilings will not go unnoticed for long, and the cost of "fixing" their ill effects may be a major cost to organizations in the future. Exhibit 4.11 outlines the estimated cost of the glass ceiling to one firm.

MANAGING WORKPLACE DIVERSITY

Today's workforce is becoming increasingly diverse. Although affirmative action has done much to open doors for women, minorities, and older employees, the retention and advancement of a diverse workforce will require dramatic changes in corporate culture and human resource policies.[82] For example, the concept of treating everyone equally is now being replaced by emphasizing individualism. The corporate culture will have to consider the ethnic, cultural, educational, and gender differences that now represent today's workforce. New human resource policies will have to reflect the unique needs of individuals rather than focusing on only one "mold" for all employees.[83]

The goal of managing a diverse workforce is to create a culture in which each employee has the opportunity to make a full contribution to the organization and to advance on the basis of excellent performance.[84] Although more minority workers are being hired, as shown in Exhibit 4.12, this is not enough to ensure a diverse workforce. Whether minorities remain in the organization and thrive seems to depend on how well they adapt to the culture in which they work.[85] Some cultures are more accepting, and hence, more successful at managing diversity. Lawrence Otis Graham recently published the book *The Best Companies for Minorities,* which recognized the 85 best companies among the Fortune 1000 for hiring minority members. This book indicates that although the workplace is becoming a more hospitable place for minority workers, there is still room for improvement. Graham's goal was to list the top 100, but he found only 85 worth citing.[86] One of the many statistics listed in the book is a ranking of firms with minorities in management positions. Topping the list is Levi Strauss with 36 percent followed by Turner Broadcasting with 26 percent. Other firms such as Coors and Corning made the list even though their numbers were not impressive but because they supported minority causes and had strong diversity programs underway.

As Graham's book notes, some firms are managing diversity well but others are not and are losing minority employees. In one study, researchers found that six factors kept

EXHIBIT 4.11	**Costs of the Glass Ceiling**

By auditing the practices of firms, one can determine the costs resulting from the presence of a glass ceiling. The following are the estimated costs of gender bias, excluding sexual harassment, at a Fortune 500 utility company. The results are based on time and training wasted, reduced productivity, underutilization of human potential, and turnover.

Coaching and Mentoring
  Women report an increase of nearly 94 percent in their professional effectiveness as a direct result of mentoring. Given that 10 percent of women at this firm were already in a successful mentoring relationship, 90 percent are only contributing half of what they are capable of. If only 25 percent of these women were provided effective mentors, the value added would be $ 9,562,320

Disparate Treatment
  This firm provides merit pay raises for employees having the specific qualities it values. For example, individuals who are rated as promotable receive higher pay raises than those not rated as promotable. However, even though 25 percent of the women were rated as promotable and only 16 percent of the men were, 29 percent of the women earned merit money for the ratings while 31 percent of the men did. The cost of these promotable women leaving for a job that will actually promote them as well as the cost of their decreased loyalty and commitment would be   1,107,138

Transfers and Promotions
  Women managers at this Fortune 500 firm filed 33 percent more applications before receiving a promotion or transfer than did men in comparable positions. Thus, the cost to the firm in excess effort expended by women is   45,329

Turnover among Women
  To replace the women managers it lost will cost approximately 93 percent of the salary of the woman who left. For women in management, this came out to be   1,561,190
  For nonmanagement women, this figure was   3,000,000

Total $15,275,977

Source: Adapted from Peggy Stuart, "What Does the Glass Ceiling Cost You?" *Personnel Journal,* November 1992, pp. 70–80.

minority employees from remaining with a firm: (1) how frequently they had to fight stereotypes, (2) the level of discrimination and harassment in the workplace, (3) how excluded and isolated the minority employees felt, (4) how employee-friendly policies were, (5) whether career development was available, and (6) how closely minority employees' values aligned with those of the organization. One woman noted that the day she arrived at her new job, she saw buyers yelling, cursing, and threatening sales representatives. Among the words uttered were racial and sexist slurs. It took only one day before she was back actively seeking employment.[87] It is difficult to keep minority employees in this situation.

Other firms, and even cities, have found ways to overcome these turnover factors. For example, Talladega, Alabama, has been dubbed the "user-friendly" city for disabled

EXHIBIT 4.12   Percentage of Minority Hiring Rates

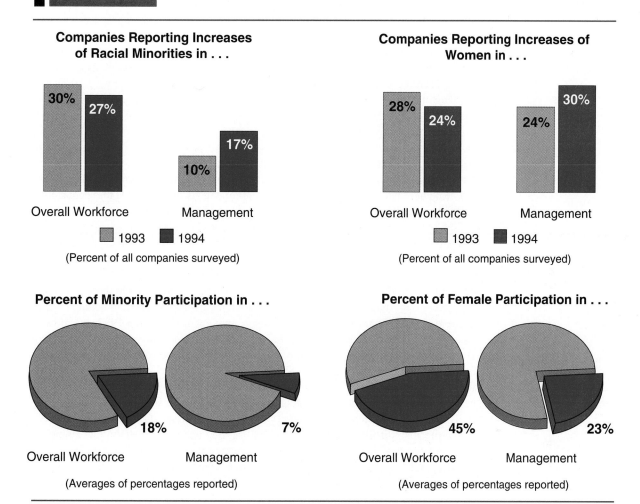

Companies Reporting Increases of Racial Minorities in . . .

30% 27%   10% 17%

Overall Workforce   Management

☐ 1993   ■ 1994

(Percent of all companies surveyed)

Companies Reporting Increases of Women in . . .

28% 24%   24% 30%

Overall Workforce   Management

☐ 1993   ■ 1994

(Percent of all companies surveyed)

Percent of Minority Participation in . . .

18%   7%

Overall Workforce   Management

(Averages of percentages reported)

Percent of Female Participation in . . .

45%   23%

Overall Workforce   Management

(Averages of percentages reported)

SOURCE: Olsten Corporation

people, and for good reasons.[88] Talladega is custom fitted to citizens with disabilities. Its crosswalks announce the name of the street as well as when it is safe to cross. Bank statements are printed in braille as are menus at local restaurants, even at McDonald's. Even pizza delivery people can use American Sign Language to communicate with the customer upon delivery. One reason for the disabled-accepting culture is the fact that the Alabama Institute for the Deaf and Blind is located here. It did not take long for the community to realize that it could be prosperous if it accepted its large contingent of disabled people. However, the term *disabled* no longer fits the citizens of Talladega because they do so much: hold jobs, raise families, and support the community. Distinctions between disabled and nondisabled have disappeared. Diversity is the norm.

As the citizens of Talladega found, embracing diversity is good business. According to a survey performed by a Chicago-based investment management firm, diversity pays off greatly. The survey found that the 20 percent of companies rated highest for hiring women and minorities outperformed the stock market by 2.4 percentage points from

1988 to 1992. The companies cited as the worst 20 percent with respect to hiring women and minorities trailed the market by 8 percentage points. One reason given for the discrepancy was the fact that firms with poor employment records faced stricter regulations, lower productivity, and more litigation.[89]

The idea of managing a diverse workforce is relatively new to human resource professionals. It is so new that many people are still struggling with the concept, its definition, and its usefulness. There is a great deal of resistance to diversity in the workplace. The growing attention paid to diversity has led to a growing alienation of Caucasian males within many organizations.[90] Caucasian males are feeling the pinch of job insecurity due to downsizing. They see themselves as the first to be placed on the chopping block in the name of diversity. According to Thomas Kochman, a professor at the University of Illinois at Chicago, "Race and gender have become factors for white men, much the way they always have been for other groups. White males are like the firstborn in the family, the ones who have had the best love of both parents and never quite forgave the second child for being born. What they are dealing with is a sense of entitlements."[91]

The second child the Caucasian males are resentful of appears to be more like a set of sextuplets. Specifically, managers named six different groups as having minority status including women, older workers, disabled workers, workers for whom English is a second language, African-Americans, and gay and lesbian workers.[92] Individuals who belong to more than one of these groups are even more highly sought than those from only one group. Judge Deborah Batts is one individual who can claim to belong to three of these groups. Confirmed as a federal judge in New York in June 1994, Judge Batts has an impressive resume. She graduated from Radcliffe and Harvard, practiced law for six years in private practice, served five years as a federal prosecutor, and taught law at Fordham University for 10 years. She is a woman who also is an African-American who is openly gay. She does not want to be known as the "gay judge," but gay activists believe that her appointment will do a great deal for their cause.[93]

There is some evidence that diversity management is working. According to Cal Atwood, president of ERIQ, a Houston-based firm that undertook a study to examine the effects of diversity in the workplace, "The results of the survey show once people start working together and getting acquainted, barriers come down and performance matters more than race and gender."[94] However, not all the barriers have fallen, at least according to one former employee of Boeing. "John Doe" recently lost his court case alleging discrimination. His complaint was that he was not allowed to use the women's restroom even though he was dressing as a woman prior to his sex change operation. The court ruled that Boeing did not discriminate because "gender dysphoria," or discomfort with one's sex, is not a true handicap. Interestingly, Boeing has had 18 employees ask about the policy, indicating that they plan to have sex change operations.[95]

MANAGEMENT GUIDELINES

Title VII suits based on alleged violations of the law prohibiting discrimination in employment and executive orders requiring affirmative action have been litigated for three decades. Penalties for EEO violations not only include monetary sanctions against organizations but also public embarrassment and the possible loss of consumer loyalty. Thus, it is imperative that organizations develop and implement a comprehensive plan to ensure equity in employment decisions.

Continued

Components of an effective affirmative action program were discussed earlier in the chapter. The following strategic guidelines will help to ensure the success of affirmative action programs and equal employment opportunity policies and help develop and support a diverse workforce:[96]

1. All levels of management, including top management, should be committed to the entire program. If employees perceive a lack of commitment from management, they may become less willing to try to make the program work and suspect of management's motives for implementing EEO policies or AAPs.

2. Every employee should understand fully the organization's policy on equal employment. Managers and employees need to be aware of both their obligations and their rights.

3. The organization should appoint an equal employment opportunity officer with the following responsibilities:
   A. The handling of all contracts with and approval of information submitted to government agencies.
   B. The coordination of the organization's EEO programs.
   C. The interpretation of EEO laws, regulations, statutes, and executive orders with the assistance of the organization's legal counsel.
   D. The dissemination of information to all employees regarding the organization's EEO policies and guidelines.

4. Top management, including EEO officers, should ensure that the organization recruits, selects, trains, transfers, promotes, lays off, and compensates employees on the basis of ability and other meritorious qualifications without discrimination because of sex, race, color, religion, age, national origin, or ancestry.

5. Top management should ensure that the organization does not discriminate against any qualified job applicant or employee because of a mental or physical handicap or status as a disabled or Vietnam-era veteran.

6. Managers should act to *remedy any deficiencies* in the firm's equal employment opportunity and affirmative action programs. This includes evaluating the utilization of minorities, females, physically or mentally handicapped individuals, and disabled or Vietnam-era veterans.

7. Managers should consider *establishing results-oriented goals* and timetables to eliminate the underutilization of minorities and females throughout the organization. If quotas or goals are used, this does not mean that the organization should hire unqualified applicants or promote unqualified employees. Quotas and goals should be developed subject to the availability of qualified minority and female applicants.

8. Managers should be careful *not to limit, segregate, or classify employees* in any way that would tend to deprive them of employment opportunities or adversely affect any employee's status because of sex, race, color, religion, national origin, or ancestry.

9. Managers should ensure that the organization *does not use sexual or racial stereotyping* in any oral or written description of an applicant or employee. In addition, managers must eliminate any sexism or racism, whether conscious or otherwise, in any evaluation process.

QUESTIONS FOR REVIEW

1. What are the important strategic choices managers should make regarding equal employment opportunities?
2. Discuss Title VII of the Civil Rights Act. What does this act prohibit? Be specific.
3. What is a bona fide occupational qualification (BFOQ)? Give an example of a BFOQ.
4. The chapter covered three ways to demonstrate discrimination in employment decisions. What are those?
5. What is the difference between sex discrimination and sexual harassment?
6. What is the difference between race discrimination and national origin discrimination?
7. Has recent EEO case law affected civil rights? If so, how?
8. What is the difference between equal employment opportunity laws and affirmative action?
9. What is reverse discrimination? Give an example.
10. What are the components of an effective affirmative action program?
11. What is the difference between the Equal Pay Act and comparable worth?
12. Do you believe implementing comparable worth laws and guidelines would have a positive or negative impact on the workforce? Do you believe comparable worth is realistic?
13. What are ways to manage diversity?

CASE

AN EXAMPLE OF SUBTLE AND NOT-SO-SUBTLE DISCRIMINATION

The following is an excerpt from an essay written by an employee of a Fortune 500 company that was undertaking an initiative to diversify its workforce. All of the incidents reported are actual situations encountered by the author of the essay. This particular essay was written by an African-American, but the same feelings and problems experienced by this individual also are experienced by virtually every individual who falls into a protected class. The following is a cover letter from the area director attached to the employee's essay. The director circulated these items to all managers in his area of the company in an effort to help others understand what minority members face every day.

Dear Senior Managers,

As we advanced our careers, many of us were challenged directly or indirectly by the culture of our organization. The very culture that adds stability and meaning to the organization often times gets in the way of our aspirations and goals. We have either learned to address these barriers or have been supported along the way to cope or to take action. Thus, we have moved ahead in the organization.

For some of our employees, the ability and opportunity to resolve incongruities in behavior and practices is not an easy task. The support systems needed to help address these issues are not available. This becomes a daily struggle—a painful experience that drains their energy and robs them of enthusiasm. For our business,

these conditions thwart our ability to put the full talent and skills of all our employees to work for us.

The attached essay was written by one of our black employees who, over the years, has directly experienced the pain of some of our inexpedient practices and behaviors. It is a compelling case study of the impact that our decisions and behavior have on employees who feel or are, in fact, excluded.

The plight of this essay's author is intolerable. We cannot afford to have these types of conditions at this company. Please send your diversity representative your reactions and, most important, your comments and recommendations on the concerns raised.

The essay:

Throughout this essay, I will attempt to illustrate the development of the corporate African American by discussing personal events encountered during my five years in this company. I intend, through an analysis of my own personal experiences, to show the reader the types of obstacles placed before corporate blacks and the impact these obstacles/events have on their development. Simply, I hope to sensitize the reader to the cumulative effect of the daily racial incidents many corporate African Americans confront. I caution the reader not to dismiss the following incidents as a comedy of mishandlings unique to me alone, because to do so would mitigate the value of the message. The fact is, similar incidents as those described below infest the lives of most corporate African Americans.

In June 1988, I began working for this company. I brought along the enthusiasm and dreams that every fresh graduated new entrant into the workforce brings. I could hardly wait to find my desk and dive in. I ached to impress someone; to show all the right people that I was ready to begin my journey to the top. Of course I understood I would have to pay my "dues" along the way, but I was willing (after all that's what I'd been doing in college all these years!).

The first six months were almost perfect. The learning was interesting and stimulating and a bond of friendship had grown between myself and other new employees starting the same day as I (referred to as my cohorts). We attended training together by day, and hung out together by night. Other employees were supportive also. Especially the black ones. They seemed supportive, but lifeless—at least professionally. By lifeless, I mean they did not seem to expect much from the company. I sensed that the battle to survive preempted the battle to progress, but mine would not falter. So long as I concentrated on my performance, I could not be denied.

For the next few months, work was wonderful. April 1989 was the first performance review session for which my cohorts and I were eligible. The possible ratings included an "E" for excellent, an "H" for above average and an "S" for satisfactory performance. Anyone below an "S" was on the way out the door. I received an "H." At first I was disappointed because I thought I deserved an "E," but at lunch that day, my cohorts and I discussed the ratings we each received, and I realized that many received "S"s and none received "E"s. I still thought I deserved an "E," but I felt a little better.

On May 5, 1989, while sitting in my cubicle, I was approached by a white co-worker and asked if I listened to "nigger music." Right out of the blue, this person walked into my space and the first thing out of his mouth was this question. I reported the incident to management, and they investigated. Within a few days, the co-worker was demoted, and I was assured that this was a "Single Isolated Incident" (SII).

In October of 1989, a special promotion window was declared to promote any deserving grade 7 employees (which included me and my cohorts) to a grade 8. The morning the promotions were to be announced, my desk phone rang off the hook. Each phone call was

from one of my cohorts informing me that their boss first asked them into his office and sat them down to announce the promotion. I must have peeked over the walls of my cubicle 100 times before my boss finally arrived to invite me to his office. As I faced him in his office, I tried to contain my smile, but I am sure I had a pretty stupid looking smirk on my face. However, as my boss began to speak, that stupid smirk was drowned in confusion. My boss informed me that there were just not enough promotions in our area for me to receive one. However, he reassured me that I would be eligible next year.

I could not believe my ears. I knew for a fact that some of those joy filled phone calls were from individuals who received lower ratings than mine. How in the hell could they get promoted and not me? By the way, not one of the phone calls was from an African American. I was so upset that I requested a meeting with my boss's boss. We met the next day. After explaining my case, he explained his position. He told me he knew how I felt, but that there were just more promotions available in other areas. He told me it was a "Single Isolated Incident" and to not let it upset me.

I looked forward to April 1990 because that was the next promotion period. I recall my supervisor approaching my work space and inviting me to his office. This was it. The moment I had been waiting for. I entered his office and awaited his words. After extending my new promotion to grade 8, he sat back and waited for my grin and thank you. We were both surprised by my reaction. I was appalled. I was just given a promotion that was six months overdue and I was suppose to jump for joy? I thanked him for the promotion and shook his hand and retreated back to my area to think. Soon, one of my friends called to tell me he had been promoted to a 9. The call was from a white man who had the same performance ratings I did.

April arrived again and I was somewhat unsure about my promotional prognosis. I knew I had an above average year, but was not sure when to expect a 9. Once again I was called into my boss' office for the news. I was not given a promotion, but my raise was relatively high. Over the next few days I learned that most of my cohorts received their promotions to 9 even though my performance ratings were higher than theirs. I began to think that the old cliche—a black person must do more to get equal—may be right. I decided to get equal.

In January 1992 I enrolled in an evening MBA program. I looked up the corporate ladder and concluded that an MBA would insure positive treatment. I was pleasantly surprised to find other company employees also enrolled in the program. I began to study and socialize with a group of five or six folks who had served similar time at the company. While I was the only African American in the group, this was not surprising to me.

I announced my plans for graduate school to my immediate supervisor first. I am not sure what I expected to be his reply, but I knew it would be positive. He surprised me by saying that I needed to realize that an MBA would not change the way the company looked at me. I would hear this statement many more times from other employees and other managers.

I attended classes two nights a week from 6 p.m. to 9 p.m. It was difficult finding adequate time to study, so in addition to studying at home, I would find an empty conference room at work and study there during lunch. During the week of midterms and finals, I would also keep my books at my desk and sneak a peek whenever possible. I often had to quickly shove my books aside or cover them when my project leader or boss came by. Sometimes I was not quick enough and would be reprimanded for studying on the job. I never thought to question their position because, after all, it was company time. I would simply put my books away and find something else to do.

One afternoon I got together with my study group to prepare for an exam. What I learned from that study session has affected my relationship with the company profoundly. As we began to talk, I heard stories of the grand support each received from their respective supervisors. Each was given unrecorded afternoons and even days off to study and were able to study at their desks when they needed to. They were given company computers to support their schoolwork and other allowances. I believe this incident marked the beginning of the "absenteeism effect." Simply, as a work environment becomes increasingly unsupportive and oftentimes blatantly exclusionary, the resulting stress and frustration will attack the physical and mental health of the target. The relief is found in less exposure to the cause...the workplace.

One afternoon in January of 1993, I was standing at the fax machine faxing three pages of notes for a classmate from another company. My boss happened into the fax room and noticed I was faxing schoolwork. He called me to his office and informed me that company resources are not be used for school. He asked me if I wanted to go to school or work. I replied that I did not believe the two were mutually exclusive; he disagreed.

Because his stance about my MBA made me wonder if he may do something to make them mutually exclu-

sive, I decided to go to HR for an impartial audience. In January of 1993 I arranged to meet my HR representative. For more than an hour I voiced my concerns with regard to my lack of support with school and various other issues. I was assured that my issues would be handled in a way that would not jeopardize my future.

The result of my actions was a meeting with my boss and his boss. They sat on one side of the table and I sat on the other. Unbelievably, no member of HR attended. They made their disappointment in my going outside the department evident. While I was able to voice some of my concerns, I spent most of the meeting apologizing for my actions. At the conclusion of the meeting my boss did apologize for his statement and informed me that "it was out of line." However, his apology sounded like a statement for the record, not an apology. He also pledged to support my school efforts. To his credit, he has improved. In fact, I can even use the fax now.

It is my impression that HR identified the potentially discriminating actions of my management and asked that they be discontinued, resulting in an apology and support of my schooling. However, it was not apparent that any attempt was made to address the discriminatory thinking of my management. Clearly, no firm can control the thoughts and feelings of its agents; however, the actions of these agents can certainly be managed. Until there are true consequences for the discriminatory actions of the agents, the more than occasional "mistake and apologize" incident will continue to thrive.

I have come to realize that the impulse to solely address the particular racial act, as opposed to the root of the act, is not limited to HR. In fact, throughout this essay, I am only highlighting a very small fraction of the SIIs that I have personally encountered. I have limited my report to events which would be documented by myself and others. This documentation will most likely be necessary because I expect the reaction to this essay will be one of defensive reflex. Much like the HR reaction above, the impulse will be to first dispute the facts, and those that cannot be disputed, explained.

SIIs are certainly not limited to such personal experiences as described above. In fact, it might be said that many of the most damaging SIIs afflicting the African American workforce are delivered by single thunderous blows, affecting the entire black community at once. I have heard countless discussions among my white co-workers professing their contempt for having to "pay for the crimes" they themselves did not commit. It became obvious that to many of them, my presence served only as a reminder of what they thought they had to give up. The SIIs that result from this dilemma are difficult to articulate because of their abstract intangible nature. Perhaps this will help you understand:

> Have you ever worked with someone who obviously resented your presence but was forced to work with you anyway? Or with someone who considers you a personal threat to his/her security? If you have not, I assure you the contempt and fear is [sic] felt, even through smiles and handshakes. Now consider an environment where the person described above is the norm instead of the exception. Every encounter attacks your self-esteem.

It is not my intention to focus the attention of the reader on the details of my personal SIIs. It is my intention to sensitize the reader to the existence and frequency of racially motivated SIIs and bare [sic] out the effect on its victims. Clearly, most people, regardless of color or gender, can identify the blatant act of racism but few recognize the cumulative effect of many small hidden acts. Even with regard to the small SIIs the reflect [sic] is to view each one individually. This prospective tends to make the victim of the individual SII seem irrational in his/her reaction. For example, consider yourself to be the target of a series of single words, each shouted individually at one hour intervals. At the delivery of the final word, you (the target) come to understand the insulting nature of the entire sentence, and react. To the casual observer who happened to witness only the delivery of the single final word, your reaction will appear irrational. "Why are you getting so upset over a word?" Until the existence of the not-so-blatant daily racial blows suffered by most African American employees is acknowledged, and the cumulative effect of these daily reminders is understood and respected, the recovery period cannot begin and the true value of diversity will never be realized.

QUESTIONS

1. What are some of the ways in which the not-so-blatant discrimination felt by this employee impacted the success of the organization?

2. How do you feel about the statement that HR deals with the problem, not the cause of the problem. How could HR actually deal with the cause?

3. Can you describe a situation in which you felt not-so-blatantly discriminated against? What was the outcome of the situation?

4. What suggestions do you have for this company for implementing a diversity plan that will be effective?

5. Do you think the employee who wrote this essay was simply overreacting? Why or why not?

ADDITIONAL READINGS

Albert, Rory Judd, and Neal S. Schelberg. "Benefit Plans Redefined under ADEA." *Pension World* 25, iss. 10 (1989), pp. 45–48.

Banta, William, F. *AIDS in the Workplace: Legal Questions and Practical Answers.* Lexington, MA: Lexington Books, 1988.

Cohen, Murray E., and Cynthia Fryer Cohen. "Comparable Worth and Compensation: Complexities and Controversies in the United States." *Equal Opportunities International* (UK) 6, iss. 2 (1987), pp. 7–10.

Creighton, Helen. "Age Discrimination." *Nursing Management* 20, iss. 2 (1989), pp. 21–22.

Dennis, Helen. *Fourteen Steps in Managing an Aging Workforce.* Lexington, MA: Lexington Books, 1988.

Gaines, Sally. "State Farm Settles Sex Bias Case." *Chicago Tribune.* January 20, 1988, p. 1.

Hale, Noreen. *The Older Worker: Effective Strategies for Management and Human Resource Development.* San Francisco: Jossey-Base Publishers, 1990.

Hall, Francine S., and Elizabeth L. Hall. "The ADA: Going Beyond the Law," *Academy of Management Executive.* 8(1)(1994), pp. 17–32.

Israel, David, and Stephen Beiser. "Immune from the ADEA." *Personnel Administrator* 34, iss. 11 (1989), p. 102.

Jolly, James P., and James G. Frierson. "Playing It Safe." *Personnel Administrator* 34, iss. 6 (1989), pp. 44–50.

Knowles, Robert G. "Women Sue State Farm over Status." *National Underwriter (Life/Health/Financial Services)* 93, no. 27. July 3, 1989, p. 1.

LaVan, Helen, Marsha Katz, Maura S. Malloy, and Peter Stonebraker. "Comparable Worth: A Comparison of Litigated Cases in the Public and Private Sectors." *Public Personnel Management* 16, iss. 3 (1987), pp. 281–293.

Lewis, Chad T. "Assessing the Validity of Job Evaluation." *Public Personnel Management* 18, iss. 1 (1989), pp. 45–53.

McCann, Nancy Dodd, and Thomas A. McGinn. *Harassed: 100 Women Define Inappropriate Behavior in the Workplace.* Homewood, IL: Business One Irwin, 1992.

Mamorsky, Jeffrey D. "Supreme Court Permits Age-Based Benefit Distinctions in Plans." *Journal of Compensation & Benefits* 5, iss. 3 (1989), pp. 175–177.

Matusewitch, Eric. "Retirement: An Executive Decision?" *Personnel Journal* 68, iss. 7 (1989), pp. 86–89.

Miceli, Marcia P., John Blackburn, and Stephen Mangum. "Employers' Pay Practices and Potential Responses to 'Comparable Worth' Litigation: An Identification of Research Issues." *Journal of Business Ethics* (Netherlands) 7, iss. 5 (1988), pp. 347–358.

Mulcahy, Colleen. "State Farm Settles Major Sex Bias Case." *National Underwriter (Life/Health/Financial Services)* 92, no. 5. February 1, 1988, p. 6.

Powell, Gary N. "Male/Female Work Roles—What Kind of Future?" *Personnel* 66, iss. 7 (1989), pp. 47–50.

_____.*Gender and Diversity in the Workplace.* Newbury Park, CA: Sage, 1994.

Schroeder, Patricia, and Constance Horner. "Comparable Worth: A

Wrong Turn; Point-Counterpoint." *Bureaucrat* 16, iss. 4 (1987/1988), pp. 4–9.

Shearer, Robert A. "Paramour Claims under Title VII: Liability for Co-Worker/Employer Sexual Relationships." *Employee Relations Law Journal* 15, iss. 1 (1989), pp. 57–66.

Stacy, Donald R. "Avoid Double Dipping without Incurring an ADEA Violation." *Compensation & Benefits Review* 21, iss. 6 (1989), pp. 48–57.

"State Farm Faces a $100 Million Bias Suit." *The New York Times* June 24, 1989, p. 24.

"State Farm Is Cited in Texas Suit Charging Hiring Discrimination." *The Wall Street Journal.* June 23, 1989, p. B12.

Susser, Peter A., and David H. Jett. "In a Recently Published Notice, the EEOC Has Set Forth Its View of Sexual Harassment after Vinson." *Employment Relations Today* 16, iss. 1 (1989), pp. 81–87.

Turner, Ronald. *The Past and Future of Affirmative Action: A Guide and Analysis for Human Resource Professionals and Corporate Counsel.* Westport, CT: Quorum Books, 1990.

NOTES

1. Ginger C. Reed, "Employers' New Burden of Proof in Discrimination Cases," *Employment Relations Today* 16, no. 2, Summer 1989, pp. 111–113; Andrea Sachs, "A Slap at Sex Stereotypes," *Time,* May 15, 1989, p. 66; Deborah L. Jacobs, "Smile When You Say That, Partner," *MS,* January to February 1989, p. 137; "Court Rules on 'Sex Stereotyping,'" *Monthly Labor Review* 112, July 1989, p. 45; "Myth America in the Workplace," *U.S. News & World Report,* May 15, 1989, p. 14; "High Court Rules in PW Bias Case," *Journal of Accountancy* 168, no. 1, July 1989, p. 16; D. Israel and P. Sweeney, "Supreme Court Allows Relief for Female Plaintiff," *HRNews Legal Report,* August 1990.

2. The discrimination discussion that follows is based on the *Equal Employment Opportunity Manual for Managers and Supervisors.* A publication of the American Society for Personnel Administration and Commerce Clearing House, Inc. (1989).

3. Tim Smart, "This Civil Rights Bill May Fly—If It Stays Light Enough," *Business Week,* February 5, 1990, p. 35.

4. P. M. Barrett, "Some Specifics about the New Law," *The Wall Street Journal,* November 4, 1991, p. B1.

5. B. Murphy, W. Barlow, and D. Hatch, "Retroactivity of the Civil Rights Act of 1991 Unsettled," *Personnel Journal,* March 1992, p. 24; and C. Naidoff, "Understanding the Civil Rights Act of 1991," *Management Review,* April 1992, pp. 58–59.

6. D. P. Twomey, *A Concise Guide to Employment Law* (Cincinnati; South-Western, 1986).

7. "Great Moments in Civil Rights," *Fortune,* February 7, 1994, p. 162.

8. Patricia Hamilton, "Running in Place," *D&B Reports,* March/April 1993, pp. 24–26.

9. Carol Kleinman, "How Women Can Deal with Today's Underground Sexism," *Tallahassee Democrat,* March 30, 1994, p. 18D.

10. Leah Nathans Spiro, "The Angry Voices at Kidder," *Business Week,* February 1, 1993, pp. 60–63.

11. "Aspin Seeking to Open More Combat Jobs to Women," *Panama City News Herald,* January 14, 1994, p. B2; and "Shannon Faulkner," *People Weekly,* December 26, 1994, pp. 58–59.

12. For discussions of the hearings, see *Time,* October 21, 1991; and *U.S. News & World Report,* October 21, 1991.

13. Section 1604.1 of the EEOC Guidelines based on the Civil Rights Act of 1964, Title VII.

14. Arthur Gutman, *EEO Law and Personnel Practices* (Newbury Park, CA: Sage, 1993).

15. Junda Woo, "Harassing Both Sexes Equally Isn't Excuse," *The Wall Street Journal,* June 16, 1994, p. B5.

16. *Bundy* v. *Jackson,* 641 F.2d 934, 24 FEP 1155 (D.C. Cir., 1981).

17. *Meritor Savings Bank* v. *Vinson,* 477 U.S. 57 (1986).

18. C. Kleiman, "Sexual Harassment Suit Claims Ads Affect Workplace Behavior," *Tallahassee Democrat,* March 1992, p. 24D.

19. S. J. Garvin, "Employer Liability for Sexual Harassment," *HRMagazine,* June 1991, pp. 101–108.

20. M. Lengnick-Hall, "Checking Out Sexual Harassment Claims," *HRMagazine,* March 1992, pp. 77–81.

21. Asra Nomani, "Labor Letter," *The Wall Street Journal,* May 24, 1994, p. A1.

22. Garwood, McKenna, and McKenna, "EEO," *The Counsellor* (Orlando, FL, February 28, 1994).

23. Anne Fisher, "Sexual Harassment: What to Do," *Fortune,* August 23, 1993, pp. 84–88.

24. Margaret A. Jacobs, "Riding Crop and Slurs: How Wall Street Dealt with a Sex-Bias Case," *The Wall Street Journal,* June 9, 1994, p. A1+.

25. Sarah Cohen, "More Men Claiming Sexual Harassment," *Tampa Tribune,* January 24, 1994, p. 1+.

26. Elizabeth Kadetsky, "The Million Dollar Man," *Working Woman,* October 1993, p. 46+.

27. Kellyanne Fitzpatrick, "What to Expect from Plaintiff Jones and Defendant Clinton," *The Wall Street Journal,* May 11, 1994, p. A15.

28. "Women and Work," *Employment Relations Bulletin,* January 1993, p. 2.

29. Sue Shellenbarger, "As More Pregnant Women Work, Bias Complaints Rise," *The Wall Street Journal,* December 6, 1993, p. B1+.

30. Brett Pulley, "Culture of Racial Bias at Shoney's Underlies Chairman's Departure," *The Wall Street Journal,* December 21, 1992, p. A1+; "Shoney's Settles EEO Dispute," *HRNews,* March 1993, p. A3; and Jan Pudlow, "Marianna Couple's Stand Was a Victory for Thousands," *Tallahassee Democrat,* February 7, 1993, p. A1+.

31. Gabriella Stern, "Wendy's is Accused of Racial Bias in Suit by Ex-Workers," *The Wall Street Journal,* April 15, 1994, p. B7.

32. Benjamin Holden, "Parent of Denny's Restaurants Signs Bias-Case Decree," *The Wall Street Journal,* March 26, 1993, p. A5.

33. Ron Suskind, "Brooks Brothers Settles Job-Bias Suit: Inquiry Used Controversial 'Tests,'" *The Wall Street Journal,* April 21, 1993, p. B7; and James P. Scanlan, "Measuring Hiring Discrimination," *Labor Law Journal,* July 1993, pp. 387–394.

34. Mary Ann Barton, "National Origin Discrimination Claims Rising," *HRNews,* December 1993, p. 5.

35. Catherine Yang, "In Any Language It's Unfair," *Business Week,* June 21, 1993, pp. 110–111.

36. Ibid.

37. Ibid.

38. D. Israel and G. McConnell, "New Law Protects Older Workers," *HRMagazine,* March 1991, pp. 77–79.

39. *Resource: Legal Report,* Society for Human Resource Management, October 1989, p. 7.

40. Sue Shellenbarger and Carol Hymowitz, "As Population Ages, Older Workers Clash with Younger Bosses," *The Wall Street Journal,* June 13, 1994, p. A1+.

41. Milo Geyelin, "Age-Bias Cases Found to Bring Big Jury Awards," *The Wall Street Journal,"* December 17, 1993, p. B1+.

42. "Supreme Court Says Years of Service Not a 'Proxy for Age' in Bias Case," *Business & Legal Reports,* 0888-6228/93, p. 3.

43. "Age Bias Law Covers Retired Workers," *HRNews,* February 1993, p. A19.

44. Catherine Fyock, "Finding the Gold in the Graying of America," *HRMagazine,* February 1994, pp. 74–76.

45. Richard Schmitt, "EECO May Pit Church vs. State at Work," *The Wall Street Journal,* June 8, 1994, p. B8.

46. E. J. Conry, G. R. Ferrera, and K. H. Fox, *The Legal Environment of Business,* 2nd ed. (Boston: Allyn and Bacon, 1990).

47. Ibid.

48. P. A. Morrissey, "How Is Disability Defined?" *HRNews,* January 1991, p. 6.

49. R. Pimentel and M. Litito, "Shining Light on ADA," *HRMagazine,* February 1992, pp. 47–49.

50. The following section is based on D. Gold and B. Unger, "ADA Prohibits Most Preemployment Health Questions," *HRNews,* March 1992, p. A5; and W.F. Casio and J. W. Walker, *HRM Update* (New York: McGraw-Hill, 1992).

51. S. R. Meisinger, "The Americans with Disabilities Act: Begin Preparing Now," *HR Legal Report,* Winter 1991, pp. 1–12.

52. Christopher Bell, "What the First ADA Cases Tell Us," *HR Legal Report,* Winter 1994, pp. 4–6.

53. Neville Tompkins, "Tools that Help Performance on the Job," *HRMagazine,* April 1993, pp. 84–91.

54. Bell, "What the First ADA Cases Tell Us."

55. Ibid.

56. Garwood, McKenna, and McKenna, "EEO," p. 1.

57. This discussion was based largely upon the *Equal Employment Opportunity Manual.*

58. D. Seligman, "How Equal Opportunity Turned into Employment Quotas," *Fortune,* March 1973, p. 162.

59. Conry et al., *The Legal Environment of Business.*

60. Arlena Sawyers, "Chrysler Found Guilty of Reverse Discrimination," *Automotive News,* June 21, 1993; and Harry N. Tuchman, "Will an Employer That Voluntarily Implements an Affirmative Action Program be Subjected to Possible Liability under Title VII of the Civil Rights Act of 1964?" *Employment Relations Today,* Spring 1994, vol. 21, p. 111.

61. Gutman, *EEO Law and Personnel Practices.*

62. U.S. Department of Labor, *Equal Pay for Equal Work under the Fair Labor Standards Act* (Washington, DC: Interpretive Bulletin, August 31, 1971).

63. U.S. Department of Labor, *Employment Relations under the Fair Labor Standards Act* (Washington, DC: Employment Standards Administration, Wage and Hour Division, revised May 1980, reprinted August 1985).

64. Joan Rigdon, "Three Decades after the Equal Pay Act, Women's Wages Remain Far from Parity," *The Wall Street Journal,* June 9, 1993, p. B1+.

65. Ibid.

66. Ibid.

67. *Lemons* v. *City and County of Denver 1980,* 620 F.2d 228.

68. *AFSCME* v. *State of Washington,* 770 F.2d 1401 (Ninth Circuit, 1985) as adapted from Reichenberg, "Pay Equity in Review," pp. 220–221.

69. "Twenty Questions of Comparable Worth," The Equal Employment Advisory Council, 1984. Reprinted in *Personnel Administrator* 30, April 1985, p. 65.

70. Julie M. Buchanan, "Comparable Worth: Where Is It Headed?" *Human Resources: Journal of the International Association for Personnel Women* 2, Summer 1985, p. 12.

71. S. B. Garland, "Throwing Stones at the 'Glass Ceiling,'" *Business Week,* August 19, 1991, p. 29.

72. J. Lopez, "Study Says Women Face Glass Walls as Well as Ceiling," *The Wall Street Journal,* March 3, 1993, p. B1.

73. C. M. Dominguez, "A Crack in the Glass Ceiling," *HRMagazine,* December 1990, pp. 65–66.

74. Ibid.

75. Garland, "Throwing Stones at the 'Glass Ceiling.'"

76. T. H. Cox and C. V. Harquail, "Career Paths and Career Success in the Early Career Stages of Male and Female MBAs," *Journal of Vocational Behavior* 39(1), 1991, pp. 54–75.

77. Garland, "Throwing Stones at the 'Glass Ceiling.'"

78. K. E. Kram, "Phases of the Mentor Relationship," *Academy of Management Journal* 26(4), 1983, pp. 608–625.

79. B. R. Ragins, "Barriers to Mentoring: The Female Manager's Dilemma," *Human Relations* 42(1), 1989, pp. 1–22.

80. Ibid.

81. Overman, "HR Urged to Strike Blow against Glass Ceiling," *HRNews* 10, September 1991, p. 1+.

82. B. Rosen and K. Lovelace, "Piecing Together the Diversity Puzzle," *HRMagazine,* June 1991, pp. 71–84.

83. L. Bayots, "Launching Successful Diversity Initiatives," *HRMagazine,* March 1992, pp. 91–97.

84. B. Rosen and K. Lovelace, "Fitting Square Pegs into Round Holes," *HRMagazine,* January 1994, pp. 86–93.

85. "Diversity Training Is a Culture Change, Not Just Training," *1993 SHRM/CCH Survey,* May 26, 1993, p. 1.

86. Leon Wynter, "Corporate America's Best Bets for Minorities," *The Wall Street Journal,* December 22, 1993, p. B1.

87. Rosen and Lovelace, "Fitting Square Pegs into Round Holes."

88. Tony Horwitz, "Talladega, Alabama, Is a User-Friendly City for Disabled People," *The Wall Street Journal,* February 14, 1994, p. A1.

89. Christopher Conte, "Equal Opportunity Pays," *The Wall Street Journal,* May 4, 1993, p. A1.

90. Michele Gordon and Ann Therese Palmer, "White, Male, and Worried," *Business Week,* January 31, 1994, pp. 50–56.

91. Ibid.

92. "Diversity Management Is a Culture Change, Not Just Training."

93. Frances McMorris, "Judge Brings New Look to Federal Bench," *The Wall Street Journal,"* September 13, 1994, p. B16.

94. Leon Rubis, "Survey Shows Encouraging Progress on Diversity, Employee Involvement," *HRNews,* March 1994, p. 2.

95. Kevin Salwen, "Transsexual Employees," *The Wall Street Journal,* April 13, 1993, p. A1.

96. These "Management Guidelines" were based largely on the work of Walter Manley, Esq., unpublished manuscript (1989) and on the content of the chapter.

CHAPTER 5

JOB ANALYSIS

Before an individual can be hired to perform a job, the requirements of that job must be identified. Before the level of pay for a job can be established, the knowledge, skills, and abilities (KSAs) required to perform the job must be determined. *Knowledge* is defined as the degree to which a job holder is required to know specific technical material. *Skill* is defined as adequate performance on tasks requiring the use of tools, equipment, and machinery. Finally, *abilities* refer to the physical and mental capacities needed to perform tasks not requiring the use of tools, equipment, or machinery. Similarly, before the performance of an employee can be evaluated, what the employee should be doing must be identified. Therefore, before any of these human resource functions can be performed, there must be a thorough understanding of the domain of the job. To do this, human resource professionals use a job analysis, which is a means of collecting information about various aspects of a job. Results from a job analysis serve as the foundation for many of the human resource functions including selection, compensation, and performance evaluation.

CHAPTER OBJECTIVES

As a result of studying this chapter, you should be able to
1. Discuss the strategic choices regarding job analysis that are available to organizations.
2. Define job analysis.
3. Describe the steps involved in a typical job analysis.
4. Be familiar with various methods of conducting a job analysis.
5. Discuss how job descriptions and job specifications can be developed from the results of a job analysis.
6. Understand the many ways that the results of a job analysis can be used in other functions of human resource management.
7. Discuss the relationship between organizational strategy, the subsequent emphasis on certain human resource activities, and the job analysis methods appropriate for specific human resource activities.

WHIRLPOOL'S USE OF JOB ANALYSIS

When you hear the name Whirlpool, you naturally think of home appliances. Over the past 80-plus years, Whirlpool has developed a national and international reputation for producing quality appliances. Whirlpool claims to be the largest home appliance manufacturer and marketer in the world. The brand names of the products sold include Whirlpool, KitchenAid, Roper, and Estate. Whirlpool also produces the appliances sold by Sears under its store brand, Kenmore.[1]

There is a constant need for replacement parts for Whirlpool products. The Whirlpool division that provides these parts is located in the small town of La Porte, Indiana, approximately two hours east of Chicago.

The parts distribution warehouse in La Porte receives orders from retail customers, appliance stores that sell Whirlpool products, and Sears. Each of the orders is entered into a computer file and held until the end of the day. At the end of each day, a computer program develops the orders into processing schedules; the employees at the warehouse, working three shifts, are assigned to fill those orders. Whirlpool guarantees its customers 72-hour turnaround from the time the order is processed.

MANUAL PARTS DISTRIBUTION SYSTEM

Until 1994 the locating, picking, packing, and shipping activities at the warehouse were parts of a manual system. Essentially, the orders were printed on 3 × 6 inch cards called *pick tickets*. At the beginning of each shift, a worker was assigned a deck of pick tickets to process. Each ticket directed the employee to a certain location in the warehouse and informed him or her how many parts to pick. The employee then stapled the pick ticket to the part and delivered the part to the appropriate packing station. Upon arrival at the packing station, a packer surveyed the items to be packed, selected a box of suitable size, and packed the parts in any way that he or she felt was appropriate. Finally, these boxes were delivered to the dock and packed in trucks to be shipped to the awaiting customer. The trucks were packed in the order in which the boxes arrived at the docks and in a way that most efficiently utilized the space available. Both of these contingencies were determined by the person at the dock as the boxes arrived.

AUTOMATED PARTS DISTRIBUTION SYSTEM

In an effort to become more efficient as well as productive, Whirlpool decided to automate each of these warehouse functions using a variety of computerized systems linked together via a central computer system. Obviously, this decision would change the way in which every job in the warehouse was performed. Virtually all of the redesigned jobs would require some computer expertise. For example, pickers, under the automated system, would be directed by handheld computers programmed to plot the most efficient pick paths instead of allowing the pickers to determine the order in which the parts were picked. Packers would be required to use a computer terminal set up at their packing station that told them which size box to select, which parts to place in the box, and in what order. Finally, the packed boxes would travel on a computerized conveyor belt and arrive at the appropriate dock in the order in which they were to be packed onto the truck.

Along with these major production changes, in order to be more flexible, Whirlpool also wanted to cross-train as many of the employees as possible on each of the new automated jobs. Whirlpool realized, however, that before any training began, it needed to ensure that its current workforce possessed the knowledge, skills, and abilities (KSAs) required by the new automated jobs. To accomplish this goal, a job analysis was performed.

JOB ANALYSIS

The first step in Whirlpool's job analysis was to determine the KSAs required by the current jobs. To do this, the Common-Metric Questionnaire by Psychological Corporation was administered to three employees in each position in the warehouse. Multiple respondents from the same position were used so that the information gathered could be cross-checked. The results from the job analysis were used to ascertain the level and variety of KSAs that warehouse employees used on a daily basis. Results indicated that the physical requirements of the current job (i.e., lifting, pulling, pushing, walking) were much more extensive than the mental requirements (i.e., decision making, mathematical requirements).

Next, because the warehouse had not been automated yet, a substitute location had to be used to collect data about the KSAs that would be required by the redesigned jobs. The parts distribution warehouse for Radio Shack in Dallas, Texas, was used for this purpose. This facility was already using equipment similar to what Whirlpool planned to install. Some differences in the equipment and its functioning existed, but the basic KSAs required were similar enough to be useful. Therefore, the Common-Metric Questionnaire was administered to several employees at the Radio Shack location, and the data gathered were used to determine the KSAs required by the automated jobs. Results from this analysis indicated that the physical requirements did not exceed the mental requirements. Instead, the physical requirements of the redesigned jobs were much less than those under Whirlpool's current manual system, but the mental requirements were often higher. For example, in many of the picking jobs under the automated system, the parts came to the picker instead of the picker going to the part. Hence, the number of physical movements under the automated system decreased. However, it was still necessary to verify that the part that arrived was the appropriate part and that the correct number of parts was available. If either or both of these could not be verified the picker had to use the computer to correct the problem, thus increasing the mental requirements of the job.

COMPARISON OF REQUIREMENTS: PREVIOUS AND REDESIGNED JOBS

The results of the job analysis at the two locations were then compared to determine whether any KSAs required by the automated system were not currently being used in the manual system. Based on this analysis, a needs assessment test was developed. This test focused on the KSAs found to be required from the Radio Shack analysis and was administered to each Whirlpool warehouse employee. The results from this test indicated that only a handful of employees lacked the KSAs required to perform the automated jobs. Prior to beginning the automation training, Whirlpool offered classes (e.g., a refresher course on numerical problem solving) free of charge to the employees who lacked the specific knowledge, skills, and abilities required by the job.

Because the human resource manager at the Whirlpool plant realized that even *planned* changes can cause major problems (e.g., employee resentment) in the future, he made a proactive strategic decision to try to prevent possible problems. A thorough job analysis of the current manual and of proposed automated jobs allowed Whirlpool to pinpoint differences in skills, knowledge, and abilities. The company then set up pretraining for the employees who lacked the KSAs required by the new job requirements prior to their participation in the actual automation training. This allowed the conversion to the newly automated jobs to proceed smoothly and effectively.

This case presents typical changes that many companies have faced as they have integrated computers into the workforce. Think how different a secretary's job is today compared with what it was just a few years ago, before personal computers sat on every secretary's desk.

The computer has had a revolutionary effect on jobs. Many jobs in factories, offices, and mines have been totally redesigned because of the computer. Paper making, steel manufacturing, rubber and glass manufacturing, and many other processes are all very different than they were even five years ago because of computers. The activities performed by employees no longer include packing, pulling, lifting, and walking. Instead they consist of sitting at a terminal or computer console and pushing buttons. As more and more computerized changes occur in the workplace, companies must be sure to update the requirements for jobs. To do this, any job that changes due to computers, or for any other reason, should be analyzed. The purpose of this chapter is to describe how this analysis should be performed.

STRATEGIC CHOICES

Because the results of a job analysis can be applied to many aspects of human resource management, even making the decision to perform a job analysis is a strategic decision in itself. However, several other strategic considerations about job analysis should be mentioned.

1. Managers must decide the extent to which employees can participate in the job analysis process. Involving employees in the job analysis process may be wise for a number of reasons. First, if workers are asked to participate in the process, they feel more ownership for the results and accept them more easily. Further, employees trust the results more because they know they took part in developing them. However, a disadvantage of employee involvement in the job analysis process is that employees may try to inflate the importance of their job. Therefore, it is important to use more than one job incumbent in the job analysis process so that information gathered about the requirements can be double-checked for accuracy.

2. A second strategic decision about performing a job analysis is to determine how detailed it must be. Should the results of the job analysis be extremely specific, such as how long it should take to perform each task, or should they just highlight the major components of the job? The answer to these questions depends on the use of the job analysis results. If a company wants to determine the salary of an individual performing the job, the major components might be sufficient. However, if the results are to be used to determine the type of training that should be offered to individuals recently hired to fill a position, more specific results are needed.

3. When a job analysis should be conducted is another strategic decision managers must make. It may be useful to conduct a job analysis when a job has changed in any major way (e.g., new equipment or procedures are introduced) or when a job is added. Also, if a department, division, or organization is restructured, the jobs impacted by the restructuring should be analyzed.[2] Another indication that it is time to conduct a job analysis is when the turnover rate for a job is higher than the organization's average rate. This may indicate that the job is extremely difficult and that modifications to it may be warranted.

4. Finally, managers must decide whether to use a traditional or future-oriented job analysis. Traditional job analysis methods are used to collect information about how the job is currently being performed. However, if an organization is changing rapidly due to constant growth or technological changes, a more future-oriented approach to job analysis may be desired. To reorient traditional job analysis approaches to have a future perspective, managers need to predict changes that should occur in the industry during a specific time period and determine how jobs will probably need to be performed in the future.[3]

THE COMPONENTS OF A JOB

ELEMENT
The smallest practical unit into which any work activity can be subdivided.

TASK
An identifiable unit of work activity that is produced through the application of a composite of methods, procedures, and techniques.

DUTY
Several distinct tasks that are performed by an individual to complete a work activity for which he or she is responsible.

POSITION
The combination of all the duties required of one person performing a job.

JOB
A group of positions that are similar enough in their job elements, tasks, and duties to be covered by the same job analysis.

A variety of activities is involved in performing any job in an organization. Sometimes the activities of two different jobs are extremely similar and other times they are very different. For example, customer service representatives are required to answer phone calls from customers who have problems or complaints and to direct them to the person or area that can solve the problem. Similarly, receptionists and secretaries often serve this same function. However, receptionists and secretaries also may be required to open mail and screen calls, functions that customer service representatives may not be required to perform.

To truly understand a specific job and to be able to make comparisons among or between jobs, anyone analyzing a job should know that it can be broken down into several components and arranged into a hierarchy of the work activities. This hierarchy is depicted in Exhibit 5.1. As the exhibit illustrates, the lowest level component is an **element.** An element can be defined as the smallest practical unit into which any work activity can be subdivided.[4] An example of a job element for a payroll manager is signing the paychecks each pay period. When several elements are combined to produce a predetermined output, an employee has completed a **task.** A task is an identifiable unit of work activity that is produced through the application of a composite of methods, procedures, and techniques.[5] A task for a payroll manager might be preparing the required forms to have the checks cut each pay period.

The next step in the hierarchy of work activities is a **duty,** which can be defined as several distinct tasks that are performed by an individual to complete a work activity for which he or she is responsible. One of the duties of a payroll manager is to process the payroll each pay period. This involves performing all of the elements (e.g., signing the checks) and tasks (e.g., ordering the checks to be printed) required to fulfill this responsibility. The combination of all of the duties required of one person in performing a job is referred to as a **position.** Each person in the organization holds a position. The position of payroll manager could include ensuring the integrity of the data used to compute the amount of pay, verifying the accuracy of the deductions required by the local, state, and federal governments, and physically processing the weekly payroll.

The next level in the hierarchy is a **job.** A job is a group of positions that are similar enough with respect to their job elements, tasks, and duties to be covered by the

Hierarchy of Work Activities

Job Family: Human Resource Professional

Occupation: Compensation Specialist

Job: Payroll Manager

Position: Compensation Policy Administrator

Duty: Payroll Processing

Task: Preparing Forms

Element: Signing Paychecks

OCCUPATION
Jobs that are combined across organizations based upon the skills, effort, and responsibilities required by the jobs.

JOB FAMILY
A category in which similar occupations are grouped together.

same job description. More than one person in an organization can hold the same job. For example, several employees in an organization may perform the job of night-shift supervisor. With respect to our payroll example, the job is payroll manager.

An **occupation** is a combination of jobs across organizations based upon the skills, effort, and responsibilities required by the jobs. For example, our payroll manager may be called a *benefits coordinator* in another organization, even though he or she performs the same job elements, tasks, and duties. These two jobs could be grouped together under the occupation of compensation specialist. Finally, similar occupations can be grouped together into a **job family.**[6] Compensation specialists can be combined with other occupations in the field of human resources (e.g., staffing specialists) and placed into the job family of human resource professional.

JOB ANALYSIS

JOB ANALYSIS
Collecting data about the jobs performed in an organization.

Simply stated, a **job analysis** involves collecting data about the jobs performed in an organization. However, this definition is probably too simplistic when all of the different types of information that must be collected are considered. For example, the data collected should clearly describe *exactly* what is required to perform a specific job. This should include the knowledge, skills, and abilities that the incumbent must possess, as well as any machinery or tools that must be used to perform the job. Further, where the job is completed must be considered. For example, is the environment dangerous, hot, or isolated? Exhibit 5.2 provides a more complete list of the types of information that should be collected when performing a job analysis.

EXHIBIT 5.2   **Types of Information to be Collected by a Job Analysis**

WORK ACTIVITIES

- Job-oriented activities (description of the work activities performed, expressed in "job" terms, usually indicating what is accomplished, such as galvanizing, weaving, cleaning, and so on; sometimes such activity descriptions also indicate how, why, and when a worker performs an activity; usually the activities are those involving active human participation, but in certain instances they may characterize machine or system functions).
- Work activities/processes.
- Procedures used.
- Activity records (such as films).
- Personal accountability/responsibility.

WORKER-ORIENTED ACTIVITIES

- Human behaviors performed in work (such as sensing, decision making, performing physical actions, or communicating).
- Elemental motions (such as those used in time and motion studies).
- Personal job demands (human expenditures involved in work, such as energy expenditure).

MACHINES, TOOLS, EQUIPMENT AND WORK AIDS USED

- Computers (hardware and software).
- Safety equipment (goggles and gloves).
- Office tools (phone, fax, and books).

JOB-RELATED TANGIBLES AND INTANGIBLES

- Materials processed.
- Products made.
- Knowledge dealt with or applied (such as law or chemistry).
- Services rendered (such as laundering or repairing).

WORK PERFORMANCE

- Work measurement (that is, time taken).
- Work standards.
- Error analysis.
- Other aspects.

JOB CONTEXT

- Physical working conditions.
- Work schedule.
- Organized context.
- Social context.
- Incentives (financial and nonfinancial).

PERSONAL REQUIREMENTS

- Job-related knowledge and/or skills (such as education, training, or work experience required).
- Personal attributes (such as aptitudes, physical characteristics, personality, interests required).

SOURCE: Adapted from J. McCormick, "Job and Task Analysis," in *Handbook of Industrial and Organizational Psychology* (Chicago: Rand McNally College Publishing Company, 1976), pp. 652–653.

Because such a variety of information must be collected when conducting a job analysis, the exact procedures followed will vary from organization to organization and according to the purpose of the analysis. However, there is a series of steps that all job analyses should include. These steps are listed in Exhibit 5.3 and are discussed in the sections that follow.

STEP 1—DETERMINE THE PURPOSE FOR CONDUCTING A JOB ANALYSIS

The first decision human resource managers typically make is the purpose for conducting a job analysis. Has the company been experiencing rapid growth or downsizing and, thus, found the need to add to, delete from, or change the current job in any way? Has a merger taken place? Are employee salaries equitable?[7] The purpose for conducting a job analysis should be explicit and tied to the overall strategy of the firm in order to increase the likelihood of a successful job analysis.

STEP 2—IDENTIFY THE JOBS TO BE ANALYZED

The second task managers typically undertake is deciding which jobs need to be analyzed. If a formal job analysis has never been performed, then this task is easy—analyze *all* of the jobs. If, however, the organization has undergone any changes that have affected only certain jobs or new jobs have been added, then managers must pinpoint the exact jobs to be analyzed. Also, existing jobs that have a high turnover rate may

EXHIBIT 5.3   **Steps in Conducting a Job Analysis**

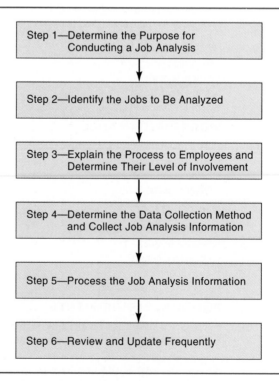

Step 1—Determine the Purpose for
Conducting a Job Analysis

Step 2—Identify the Jobs to Be Analyzed

Step 3—Explain the Process to Employees and
Determine Their Level of Involvement

Step 4—Determine the Data Collection Method
and Collect Job Analysis Information

Step 5—Process the Job Analysis Information

Step 6—Review and Update Frequently

benefit from a job analysis. The turnover rate may indicate that the job has grown too complex and may need to be modified.

STEP 3—EXPLAIN THE PROCESS TO EMPLOYEES AND DETERMINE THEIR LEVEL OF INVOLVEMENT

The purpose of conducting a job analysis should not be kept from the employees and managers. They should be informed of who will be conducting the analysis, why the job analysis is needed, whom to contact if they have questions or concerns, the schedule or timetable of events, and their role in the job analysis. Too often employees are uncertain about these issues and begin to feel that their jobs are being threatened. To reduce any anxiety employees may be experiencing, communication is of the utmost importance. If anxieties and uncertainties exist among employees, accurate job analysis information will be difficult to obtain. Another means of reducing anxiety and adding validity to the process is to form a committee (elected by the employees) to represent various jobs and to verify that the job analysis information gathered is accurate. These elected committee members can also help answer questions and concerns employees may have.

STEP 4—DETERMINE THE DATA COLLECTION METHOD AND COLLECT JOB ANALYSIS INFORMATION

The fourth step consists of actually collecting the job analysis information. Managers must decide which method or combination of methods will be used and how to collect the information. Once this has been determined, managers must make sure that the information collected is complete. If additional information is required for purposes of clarification, it is best to go back immediately and gather it while the job analysis issues are still salient to employees.

STEP 5—PROCESS THE JOB ANALYSIS INFORMATION

Once the job analysis information has been collected, it is important to place it into a form that will be useful to managers and human resource departments. One way to do this is to develop a specialized form on which the job analysis results can be printed. Using a form for reporting the results serves several purposes. First, it can be used as a step to verify that all required information has been collected. If during the transfer process a blank on the form cannot be completed, it becomes obvious that more data must be collected. Also, a standardized reporting format makes it easy for a manager to compare several different jobs to a specific criterion of interest. All he or she has to do is focus on the fields on the form that are of concern and compare them across the different jobs analyzed.

STEP 6—REVIEW AND UPDATE FREQUENTLY

The final step is actually an ongoing phenomenon. Given that organizations are dynamic, jobs seldom go unchanged for very long. Managers and personnel specialists need to review job descriptions and specifications frequently. The job analysis process can be time consuming and costly. Thus, it is to the organization's advantage to update information on all jobs rather than repeating the entire process in a few years. If no major changes have occurred within the organization, then a complete review of all jobs should be performed every three years.[8] Obviously, more frequent reviews are necessary if organizational changes occur.

JOB ANALYSIS DATA COLLECTION METHODS

Because the information needed to be collected about a job varies depending upon the purposes to be served by the organization, a number of methods can be used to collect job analysis information. Managers should consider using a number of different methods of data collection because it is unlikely that any one method will provide all the necessary information needed for a job analysis. The use of multiple methods to collect job analysis data provides a means of cross-checking the accuracy of the data collected. The information collected from incumbents may not be completely accurate for a variety of reasons. First, incumbents may not recall all of the components of their jobs during an interview because performance of the same job for an extended period of time often causes it to become rote. Employees may try to inflate the importance of their jobs in order to appear more valuable to the organization to ensure job security or to seek a salary increase. Also, people mold the jobs they do to fit themselves. Therefore, conflicting responses may be obtained from people performing the same job. Finally, none of these responses may describe the performance of a job exactly the way the company would like it to be performed. Three of the most popular forms of data collection include (1) observation of tasks and behaviors of the jobholders, (2) interviews, and (3) questionnaires and checklists. These are summarized in Exhibit 5.4 and are discussed in the following sections.

OBSERVATION

Jobholders are observed performing their work. Observation may be continuous or intermittent based on work sampling (observing only a sampling of tasks performed). For many jobs, observation may be of limited usefulness because the job does not consist of physically active tasks. For example, observing a bookkeeper reviewing reports or filling out forms may not lead to very valuable information about the job. Thus, observation is most useful when the job is composed of physically active tasks, such as those performed by an assembler on an automobile production line or a receptionist handling phone calls and visitors. However, even with more active jobs, observation does not always reveal vital information, such as the importance or difficulty of the tasks. Given the limitations of using observation as the only data collection method for job analysis, it is helpful to incorporate additional methods for obtaining job analysis information. Observation is most helpful to managers or job analysts as a means to gain a general familiarity with the job.

CRITICAL INCIDENT METHOD
One job analysis method that uses observation of "critical" incidents.

One specific job analysis method that uses observation is the **critical incident method.** To use this method, incumbents, supervisors, or other "experts" are asked to recall incidents that they witnessed (i.e., observed) that they consider critical to a successful job performance.

This approach focuses on the things a worker does (incidents) that distinguish that person as an effective or ineffective employee. To be considered *critical,* an incident must occur in a situation in which the intent of the act seems clear to the observer and its consequences leave little doubt about the effects. The data collection process results in a mass of incidents descriptive of effective and ineffective job behaviors in critical situations. In addition, they describe behaviors that reflect outstanding versus poor

EXHIBIT 5.4   **Popular Analysis Data Collection Methods**

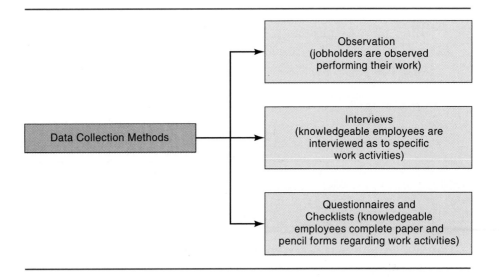

performance on the job. These incident descriptions are examined and put into job dimension categories that characterize particular facets of job performance.

INTERVIEWING

Employees knowledgeable about a particular job (for example, jobholders, supervisors, or individuals who have worked on the job before) are interviewed as to the specific work activities that the job comprises. Usually a structured interview form is used to record information. Exhibit 5.5 is a sample structured interview form used to collect data.

Interviewing can be a rather time consuming and, thus, a costly method of data collection. For example, if a company has 25 jobs and two people are interviewed for each job for 30 minutes, the time involved in the interview process alone is a minimum of 25 hours not counting the interviewer's time. Managerial and professional jobs are more complicated and may require between one and two hours of interviewing. There are also costs involved in training interviewers to perform the job analysis interviews. Given the time-consuming nature of interviews, managers and job analysts might prefer to use the interview as a means to answer specific queries generated from observations and questionnaires.

QUESTIONNAIRES AND CHECKLISTS

The use of questionnaires and checklists is most efficient when a large number of employees are involved or when a number of widely dispersed employees are to be questioned about their jobs. The questionnaire allows for a relatively quick and inexpensive way to collect information about the job. At least one employee knowledgeable about the job should complete the questionnaire. If possible, it is often desirable to have two or even three people complete the questionnaire for purposes of verification. Additional data collection is often necessary if some questions need clarifying or some information

EXHIBIT 5.5

Job Analysis Structured Interview Form

Name _____ Age _____

Date _____ Length of Time with Company _____

Present Job Title and Grade _____

                    Section or   Supervisor's

Dept. _____ Group _____ Name _____

1. Purpose of Job: _____

_____

_____

_____

_____

2. Describe major duties of your job: _____

_____

_____

_____

_____

3. Other, less important job duties: _____

_____

_____

_____

_____

4. Machines or equipment used:	Continually	Frequently	Occasionally
_____	_____	_____	_____
_____	_____	_____	_____
_____	_____	_____	_____

====== **HR CHALLENGE** ======

High-Tech Questionnaires

The use of written questionnaires to collect data about a job is popular because it is a relatively low-cost way to gather data from a large number of people. However, today's surveys can be improved by using computers to collect the data. PC–based job analysis surveys offer a variety of advantages over written surveys. For example, employees who use computers in their work find PC-based surveys interesting and novel and may be more inclined to respond to a computerized survey than to a written one.

The computer technology also can be used when administering the surveys. For example, if the survey must be administered during a specific time frame, reminders can be sent via electronic mail to the respondents to increase the response rate. Further, the questionnaires can be entered onto and removed from the computer system at a precise time to ensure that respondents had no extra time to complete them. This also eliminates the problem of having surveys returned after all the data have been entered and analyzed.

SOURCE: Adapted from William E. Wymer and Jeanne M. Carsten, "Alternative Ways to Gather Opinion" *HRMagazine,* April 1992, pp. 71–78.

is missing. Follow-up observations and interviews are not uncommon if a questionnaire or checklist is chosen as the primary means for collecting the job analysis information.

Questionnaires and checklists provide the employee with a simplified method for providing important information. The difficulty arises in constructing a structured questionnaire. It must be extremely detailed and comprehensive so that valuable information is not missed. Obviously, management must decide whether the benefits of a simplified method of data collection outweigh the costs of its construction. Strategically, managers would most likely favor methods of data collection that do not require much work up front if the content of jobs changes frequently. However, another option might be to adopt an existing structured questionnaire. Exhibit 5.6 lists a variety of prefabricated job analysis questionnaires and checklists that can be used to perform a job analysis. Each of these is briefly discussed in the following sections.

JOB-ELEMENT METHOD

JOB-ELEMENT METHOD
A method of job analysis that yields worker-oriented information.

The Civil Service has used the **job-element method** to identify the worker characteristics associated with effective performance. People familiar with the job identify the knowledge, skills, abilities, and personal traits (job elements) needed to perform the job. As Exhibit 5.7 illustrates, each of these job elements is rated on four scales: barely acceptable (number of employees who have this element), superior (number of superior employees who have this element), trouble likely (probability of trouble occurring if an employee does not have the element), and practical (practicality of expecting to find people with the element). The job-element method helps the human resource manager decide whether the element is a characteristic workers must have before beginning the job or whether it is an element likely to require training.

ABILITY REQUIREMENT SCALES

ABILITY REQUIREMENT SCALES
A method of job analysis that focuses on worker characteristics rather than on job characteristics.

The **Ability Requirement Scales** focus on worker characteristics rather than job characteristics. Unlike the job-element method, however, the scales in this technique yield standardized information. Tasks are described, contrasted, and compared in terms of the abilities that a given task requires of the performer. These abilities are relatively enduring traits of the employee performing the task. An assumption is made that each task requires specific abilities for effective performance. Tasks requiring similar abilities are placed in the same category.

EXHIBIT 5.6   **Prefabricated Job Analysis Questionnaires and Checklists**

JOB-ELEMENT METHOD (JEM)

Developed by Dr. Ernest Primoff; establishes selection standards and validates selection tests for jobs in the federal government.

ABILITY REQUIREMENT SCALES (ARS)

Developed by Edwin Fleishman; lists 50 physical and nonphysical abilities that may be necessary for performing a job.

COMPREHENSIVE OCCUPATIONAL DATA ANALYSIS PROGRAM (CODAP)

Includes task checklists for 216 of the 240 Air Force specialties.

POSITION ANALYSIS QUESTIONNAIRE (PAQ)

Developed by Ernest J. McCormick and his colleagues; consists of 194 elements that are grouped within six major divisions and 28 sections.

MANAGEMENT POSITION DESCRIPTION QUESTIONNAIRE (MPDQ)

Developed by Walter W. Tornow and Patrick R. Pinto; includes 208 items that describe a manager's job.

FUNCTIONAL JOB ANALYSIS (FJA)

Developed by Sidney Fine; produces information about what a worker does and how a task is performed.

COMMON-METRIC QUESTIONNAIRE (CMQ)

Developed by Robert J. Harvey; is comprehensive enough to be used with any job found in any organization.

EXHIBIT 5.7   **Job-Element Instruments**

Rater's Name and Grade

Job Rated: Title and Grade

Element	Barely acceptable workers 2 All have 1 Some have 0 Almost none have	To pick out superior worker 2 Very important 1 Valuable 0 Does not differentiate	Trouble likely if not considered 2 Much trouble 1 Some trouble 0 Safe to ignore	Practicality demanding this element 2 All openings 1 Some openings 0 Almost no openings
Ability to add 2-digit numbers	2	0	2	2
Can cook hamburgers	0	1	1	0
Can scrub floors, etc.	1	1	1	2

Abilities are listed under perceptual-motor, physical performance, and cognitive domains. Behaviorally anchored scales define the abilities to be rated. Specifically, a set of behaviorally anchored scales measures how much each of 37 abilities is needed to perform the job. For example, the ability *verbal comprehension* has behavioral anchors that range from "understanding a comic book" to "understanding in its entirety a mortgage contract for a new home."

COMPREHENSIVE OCCUPATIONAL DATA ANALYSIS PROGRAM

The **Comprehensive Occupational Data Analysis Program (CODAP)** is a structured job analysis questionnaire consisting of a list of tasks relevant to some occupational area. This instrument uses job "experts" (individuals familiar with the content of the jobs) to create a list of tasks and then rate each task according to the relative amount of time spent on it. Because the list of tasks involved in the performance of a job is likely to differ across jobs, task inventories must be developed separately for each occupational area. These ratings are entered into a computer (CODAP is a computer program that summarizes job analysis ratings), analyzed, and converted into job dimensions. The Air Force has used task inventories successfully for years to monitor the changes that occur in jobs as a result of technological or personal changes.

POSITION ANALYSIS QUESTIONNAIRE

The **Position Analysis Questionnaire (PAQ)** contains 194 job elements. Employees familiar with a particular job rate it on the 194 descriptors by judging the degree to which an element (or descriptor) is present. These elements are grouped into six general categories.[9] Exhibit 5.8 describes the categories and gives examples of rating scales used to collect information and rate jobs. The PAQ has been thoroughly researched and enables a statistical comparison of the dimensions of jobs in an organization to be made. Responses to the PAQ can be sent to PAQ Services in Logan, Utah, for scoring. This analysis provides an estimate of worker attributes predictive of success in a particular job. In addition, this analysis provides a comparison of a specific job with other job classifications. The use of the PAQ is not as widespread as one might believe because above average reading skills are necessary to use it.

MANAGEMENT POSITION DESCRIPTION QUESTIONNAIRE

An instrument similar to the PAQ has been developed to describe managerial jobs. The **Management Position Description Questionnaire (MPDQ)** developed the 13 factors shown in Exhibit 5.9 that may be used to describe managerial jobs. These factors resulted from a 208-item questionnaire completed by 434 managers.

FUNCTIONAL JOB ANALYSIS

Functional job analysis (FJA) is an instrument that examines the functions of a job in relation to three classifications: data, people, and things. Within each of these classifications are degrees or levels with corresponding numbers (see Exhibit 5.10 on page 174). The lower the number, the more the job is involved with that particular function.

COMMON-METRIC QUESTIONNAIRE

The **Common-Metric Questionnaire (CMQ)** is one of the newest job analysis packages available for sale. Designed to be useful for any job in any organization, the CMQ is completed by the job expert (i.e., incumbent, supervisor, or job analyst), but some sections require a job analysis administrator to complete. The CMQ is divided into five sections with between 41 and 80 questions in each section. The respondent reads each

---

COMPREHENSIVE OCCUPATIONAL DATA ANALYSIS PROGRAM (CODAP)
A structured job analysis questionnaire consisting of a list of tasks relevant to some occupational area.

POSITION ANALYSIS QUESTIONNAIRE (PAQ)
A questionnaire that contains 194 job elements an employee rates by judging the degree to which an element is present.

MANAGEMENT POSITION DESCRIPTION QUESTIONNAIRE (MPDQ)
Thirteen factors used to describe managerial jobs.

FUNCTIONAL JOB ANALYSIS (FJA)
A method of job analysis in which the functions of a job can be examined in relation to three classifications: data, people, and things.

COMMON-METRIC QUESTIONNAIRE (CMQ)
One of the newest job analysis packages available, designed to be completed by the job expert and a job analysis administrator.

EXHIBIT 5.8   **Position Analysis Questionnaire (PAQ)**

ORGANIZATION OF THE PAQ

The job elements in the PAQ are organized in six divisions as follows (examples of two job elements from each division are included):

1. *Information input.* (Where and how does the worker get the information he or she uses in performing his or her job?)
   Examples: Use of written materials
   Near-visual differentiation
2. *Mental processes.* (What reasoning, decision-making, planning, and information-processing activities are involved in performing the job?)
   Examples: Level of reasoning in problem solving
   Coding/decoding
3. *Work output.* (What physical activities does the worker perform and what tools or devices does he or she use?)
   Examples: Using keyboard devices
   Assembling/disassembling
4. *Relationships with other persons.* (What relationships with other people are required in performing the job?)
   Examples: Instruction
   Contact with public, customers
5. *Job context.* (In what physical or social contexts is the work performed?)
   Examples: High temperature
   Interpersonal conflict situations
6. *Other job characteristics.* (What activities, conditions, or characteristics other than those described above are relevant to the job?)

RATING SCALES USED WITH THE PAQ

There is a provision for rating each job on each job element. Six types of rating scales are used:

LETTER IDENTIFICATION	TYPE OF RATING SCALE
U	Extent of Use
I	Importance to the Job
T	Amount of Time
P	Possibility of Occurrence
A	Applicability
S	Special Code (used in the case of a few specific job elements)

A specific rating scale is designated to be used with each job element, in particular the scale considered most appropriate to the content of the element. All but the "A" (Applicability) scale are 6-point scales, and "0" (which is coded as "N") is for "Does not apply," as illustrated below:

RATING	IMPORTANCE TO THE JOB
N	Does not apply
1	Very minor (importance)
2	Low
3	Average
4	High
5	Extreme

SOURCE: Reprinted by permission from Ernest J. McCormick, *Job Analysis: Methods and Applications,* copyright ©1979 AMACOM. All Rights Reserved.

EXHIBIT 5.9

Management Position Description Questionnaire (MPDQ) Factors

1. *Product, Marketing, and Financial Strategy Planning:* Indicates long-range thinking and planning. The incumbent's concerns are broad and oriented toward the future. They may include such areas as long-range business potential, organizational objectives, company solvency, business activities the company should engage in, and new idea evaluation.

2. *Coordination of Other Organization Units and Personnel:* The incumbent coordinates the efforts of others over whom he or she exercises no direct control, handles conflicts or disagreements when necessary, and works in an environment where he or she must cut across existing organizational boundaries.

3. *Internal Business Control:* The incumbent exercises business controls, that is, reviews and controls the allocation of human and other resources. Activities and concerns are in the areas of assignments of supervisory responsibility, expense control, cost reduction, setting performance goals, preparation and review of budgets, protection of the company's monies and properties, and employee relations practices.

4. *Products and Services Responsibility:* Activities and concerns of the incumbent in technical areas related to products, services, and their marketability. Specifically included are the planning, scheduling, and monitoring of products and services delivery along with keeping track of their quality and costs. The incumbent is concerned with promises that are difficult to meet, anticipates new or changed demands for the products and services, and closely maintains the progress of specific projects.

5. *Public and Customer Relations:* A general responsibility for the reputation of the company's products and services. The incumbent is concerned with promoting the company's products and services, the goodwill of the company in the community, and general public relations. The position involves firsthand contact with the customer, frequent contact and negotiation with representatives from other organizations, and understanding the needs of customers.

6. *Advanced Consulting:* The incumbent is asked to apply technical expertise to special problems, issues, questions, or policies. The incumbent should have an understanding of advanced principles, theories, and concepts in more than one required field. He or she is often asked to apply highly advanced techniques and methods to address issues and questions, which very few people in the company can do.

7. *Autonomy of Action:* The incumbent has a considerable amount of discretion in the handling of a job, engaging in activities that are not closely supervised or controlled, and making decisions that are often not subject to review. The incumbent may have to handle unique problems, know how to ask key questions even on subject matters with which he or she is not intimately familiar, and engage in free-wheeling or unstructured thinking to deal with problems that are themselves abstract or unstructured.

8. *Approval of Financial Commitments:* The incumbent has the authority to approve large financial commitments and obligate the company. The incumbent may make final and, for the most part, irreversible decisions, negotiate with representatives from other organizations, and make many important decisions on almost a daily basis.

9. *Staff Service:* The incumbent renders various staff services to supervisors. Such activities can include fact gathering, data acquisition and compilation, and record keeping.

10. *Supervision:* The incumbent plans, organizes, and controls the work of others. The activities require face-to-face contact with subordinates on almost a daily basis. The concerns revolve around getting work done efficiently through the effective utilization of people.

11. *Complexity and Stress:* The incumbent has to operate under pressure. This may include activities of handling information under time pressure to meet deadlines, frequently taking risks, and interfering with personal or family life.

12. *Advanced Financial Responsibility:* Activities and responsibilities concerned with the preservation of assets, making investment decisions, and other large-scale financial decisions that affect the company's performance.

13. *Broad Personnel Responsibility:* The incumbent has broad responsibility for the management of human resources and the policies affecting them.

SOURCE: Adapted from W. W. Tornow and P. R. Pinto, "The Development of a Managerial Job Taxonomy: A System for Describing, Classifying and Evaluating Executive Positions," *Journal of Applied Psychology* (1976), pp. 61, 410–418.

█ **EXHIBIT 5.10**   **Functional Job Analysis Classifications**

DATA		PEOPLE		THINGS	
0	Synthesizing	0	Mentoring	0	Setting Up
1	Coordinating	1	Negotiating	1	Precision Working
2	Analyzing	2	Instructing	2	Operating–Controlling
3	Compiling	3	Supervising	3	Driving–Operating
4	Computing	4	Diverting	4	Manipulating
5	Copying	5	Persuading	5	Tending
6	Comparing	6	Speaking–Signaling	6	Feeding–Offbearing
		7	Serving	7	Handling
		8	Taking Instructions–Helping		

SOURCE: United States Department of Labor, *Dictionary of Occupational Titles,* fourth edition (Washington, DC: United States Government Printing Office, 1977), p. xviii.

question and determines whether it is applicable to his or her job. If it is not, it is simply skipped. If it is applicable, then various other questions pertaining to that one item also must be answered. Because the questionnaire is designed to cover every possible job in an organization, some (many) of the items may be irrelevant to the position being analyzed. However, the respondent must first read each item to determine whether it is relevant. Thus, a great deal of time may be required to complete the entire list of questions.

JOB ANALYSIS DATA OUTPUT

JOB DESCRIPTION
Description of the duties, responsibilities, working conditions, and activities of a particular job.

The data collected from the job analysis can be used for a variety of purposes. One of the most important is in writing job descriptions and job specifications. **Job descriptions** describe the duties, responsibilities, working conditions, and activities of a particular job. **Job specifications** describe employee qualifications, such as experience, knowledge, skills, or abilities, that are required to perform the job.

JOB DESCRIPTION

JOB SPECIFICATION
Description of employee qualifications, such as experience, knowledge, skills, or abilities, that are required to perform a particular job.

DICTIONARY OF OCCUPATIONAL TITLES (DOT)
A valuable source for locating standardized job descriptions, published by the U.S. Department of Labor and providing information on more than 12,000 occupations.

Job descriptions vary in terms of the level of detail provided. However, several components are present in virtually every job description. For example, the title of the job is always provided. It is important that the title be descriptive of the job so that people reading it immediately understand what the job entails. Some type of summary that describes the work performed in the job and the worker requirements also are extremely important to include in the job description.

One valuable source for locating standardized job descriptions is the ***Dictionary of Occupational Titles (DOT)***. The U.S. Department of Labor publishes the *DOT*, which provides information on over 12,000 occupations. The job description for a personnel manager from the *DOT* is presented in Exhibit 5.11.

The numbers next to the job title (166.117-018) are important if you want to utilize the information in the *DOT*. The first three numbers (166) represent the occupational code, title, and industry, respectively. The next three numbers (117) represent the degree to which a typical human resource manager is involved with data, people, and things, respectively. The final three numbers indicate the alphabetical order of job titles within the same occupational grouping that have the same involvement over data, people, and things. The *DOT* job descriptions are endorsed by the federal government.

EXHIBIT 5.11   **Job Title and Description from *Dictionary of Occupational Titles***

166.117-018 MANAGER, PERSONNEL (PROFESS. & KIN.)

Plans and carries out policies relating to all phases of personnel activity. Recruits, interviews, and selects employees to fill vacant positions. Plans and conducts new employee orientation to foster positive attitude toward company goals. Keeps record of insurance coverage, pension plan, and personnel transactions, such as hires, promotions, transfers, and terminations. Investigates accidents and prepares reports for insurance carrier. Conducts wage survey within labor market to determine competitive wage rate. Prepares budget of personnel operations. Meets with shop stewards and supervisors to resolve grievances. Writes separation notices for employees separating with cause and conducts exit interviews to determine reasons behind separations. Prepares reports and recommends procedures to reduce absenteeism and turnover. Contracts with outside suppliers to provide employee services, such as canteen, transportation, or relocation service. May keep records of hired employee characteristics for governmental reporting purposes. May negotiate collective bargaining agreement with BUSINESS REPRESENTATION LABOR UNION (profess. & kin.)

SOURCE: United States Department of Labor, *Dictionary of Occupational Titles,* fourth edition (Washington, DC: United States Government Printing Office, 1977), p. 98.

Managers can adapt the standardized job descriptions from the *DOT* to the specific jobs within their firm. The *DOT* is particularly useful when a large number of jobs needs to be analyzed. Rather than "starting from scratch," managers can use the *DOT* as a guide. The *DOT* may also prove invaluable to managers who are not human resource specialists.

JOB SPECIFICATION

The personal qualifications an employee must possess in order to perform the duties and responsibilities depicted in the job description are contained in the job specifications. Typically, job specifications detail the knowledge, skills, and abilities relevant to a job including the education, experience, specialized training, personal traits, and manual dexterity required. A sample job specification is provided in Exhibit 5.12. At times, an organization may also include the physical demands the job places upon an employee.[10] The physical demands of a job might include the amount of walking, standing, reaching, or lifting that is required of the employee. In addition, the condition of

EXHIBIT 5.12   **Job Specification**

Department: Executive President's Office	*Job Title:* Executive Secretary
Reports to: President	

Required Knowledge, Skills, and Abilities:
1. Knowledge of office routines and procedures.
2. Knowledge of the executive secretarial field.
3. Skill in the operation of computerized office equipment.
4. Skill in typing, filing, answering the telephone, and composing routine letters and reports.
5. Ability to act as a liaison between company officials, board members, customer executives, and state and federal government officials when president is out of town.
6. Ability to plan and prioritize work.

HR CHALLENGE

Computerized Job Descriptions

Writing job descriptions does not have to be a tedious process. Instead, human resource managers can purchase software that virtually writes the job descriptions for them. Because of the demands placed on firms by the Americans with Disabilities Act of 1991 (ADA), complete job descriptions are vital. Further, job descriptions are a prime defense tool in discrimination cases filed under ADA.

No software package can be purchased that will completely write job descriptions for a company, but some can eliminate 70 percent of the work required to develop them. For example, the *Dictionary of Occupational Titles (DOT)* is available on a database. Any job description imaginable can simply be retrieved from the database and altered to fit the specific needs of the company. For small companies, the *DOT* may be far too large to be useful. Instead, these organizations can purchase other, less extensive, packages that focus more directly on the specific needs of the firm.

Source: Adapted from Michael Cronin, "Choosing Job-Description Software" *INC,* February 1993, p. 30.

the physical work environment and the hazards employees may encounter may also be included among the physical demands of a job.

The job specification is important for a number of reasons. First, certain jobs have qualifications required by law. For example, airline pilots, attorneys, and medical doctors all need to be licensed. Another type of job specification is based on professional tradition. For example, university professors must usually hold a Ph.D or equivalent degree if they are going to be in a tenure-track position. Whether having a Ph.D or its equivalent is important for teaching and research is still debatable and has not been empirically verified beyond question. Finally, job specifications might involve establishing certain standards or criteria that are deemed necessary for successful performance. This depends primarily, however, upon the judgment of the employer.

For example, secretarial and clerical workers may be required to demonstrate typing speeds in excess of 100 to 120 words per minute. Management positions may be available only to those applicants with at least three to five years of experience in a similar position. It is important to remember, however, that these job specifications must be directly linked to the job description. Specifically, job specifications must be job relevant.

The Americans with Disabilities Act of 1991 (ADA) has had a significant impact on the development of job descriptions and job specifications. ADA prohibits employers from discriminating against qualified individuals with disabilities. Specifically, a qualified individual with a disability refers to someone who can, with or without "reasonable accommodation," perform the "essential functions" of the job. Reasonable accommodation refers to any accommodation that does not impose an undue hardship on the business. These can include lowering counters and knobs, installing ramps, or providing interpreters. The essential functions of a job are the fundamental job duties required of the position as determined by the employer. The essential job duties traditionally are identified by a job analysis and then are documented in the job description and the job specifications; this may no longer be sufficient, however. A job analysis simply describes how the job is currently performed. ADA may now require that the job analysis data be used to produce job descriptions and job specifications that also illustrate how the job might be performed with reasonable accommodations.

USES OF JOB ANALYSIS DATA

Once the job analysis has been conducted, the data can be applied to a variety of human resource functions. Exhibit 5.13 describes the traditional ways in which the results from a job analysis can be used; the following sections describe them in more detail.

JOB EVALUATION

The information gathered during a job analysis is used primarily as input for the organization's job evaluation system. The job evaluation determines the worth of a particular job to the organization. This information is primarily used to determine the pay for the job. Thus, employees should be paid more for working on more difficult jobs. Job analysis information is instrumental in determining which jobs contain more difficult tasks, duties, and responsibilities. This is discussed further in Chapter 11 on compensation systems.

RECRUITMENT, SELECTION, AND PLACEMENT

A good job analysis should provide information useful in planning for recruitment, selection, and placement. Managers will be better able to plan for the staffing of their organizations if they understand the skills needed and the types of jobs that will most likely open up in the future. Further, selecting an individual for a job requires a thorough understanding of the type of work to be done and the qualifications necessary to perform the work. Selecting individuals to fill positions is effective only if there is a clear and accurate understanding of what the job entails. Job analysis information is also useful for detecting unnecessary job requirements. For example, a manager for a manufacturing plant may be able to hold recruiting and salary costs down if the job analysis reveals that it is not necessary for first-line supervisors to have a college degree. Finally, placing employees into jobs by means of promotions and transfers is made easier if the details of what the job entails are known and the qualifications necessary to do the job are well understood.

LABOR AND HUMAN RESOURCE RELATIONS

Information generated from the job analysis can help both labor and management understand what should be expected from each job incumbent and how much employees should

EXHIBIT 5.13   **Traditional Uses of Job Analysis Information**

	Programs for Salary Rated	Programs for Hourly Rated
Job Evaluation	98%	95%
Recruitment, Selection, and Placement	95	92
Labor and Human Resource Relations	83	79
Utilizing Human Resources	72	67
Training and Development	61	63

SOURCE: "Job Analysis: National Survey Findings," by Jean L. Jones, Jr. and Thomas A. Decoths, copyright May 1974. Reprinted with the permission of *Personnel Journal,* Costa Mesa, California. All Rights Reserved.

be compensated for performing a particular job. Obviously, the information generated from the job analysis is most beneficial if it is clearly communicated to both employees and management. This communication can help alleviate perceived inequities among employees. For example, many employees would like to know why their jobs do not pay as well as other jobs. Much of the controversy about comparable worth revolves around this issue. Comparable worth will be discussed in more detail in Chapter 11.

UTILIZING HUMAN RESOURCES

All managers would like to utilize their employees optimally. However, performance appraisals often reveal that many employees are not performing even adequately. Job analysis information can help both employees and managers pinpoint the root of the problem. By comparing what the employee is *supposed* to be doing with what the employee is *actually* doing, supervisors can determine whether the employee is performing adequately and, if not, what areas need improvement. Sharing this information with the employee can be enlightening for both parties. Employees may not have realized what was expected of them and what their work role entailed. Thus, job analysis information can help clear up any uncertainties employees might have regarding their work performance and work role.

TRAINING AND DEVELOPMENT

Job analysis information can also be useful for training and development needs. By clearly depicting what the job entails and what qualifications are necessary to do the job, managers should be able to discover any qualification deficiencies. Most deficiencies are probably best remedied by training or retraining employees. In addition to identifying training needs, job analysis information is helpful in career development. Specifically, managers will be able to tell employees what *will be* expected if the employee desires a transfer or promotion. This information can help employees prepare for career advancement.

ORGANIZATION STRATEGY AND JOB ANALYSIS

All of the job analysis methods discussed in this chapter are viable alternatives for the human resource manager. Unfortunately, many methods are chosen simply because the human resource manager is familiar with it. Only a few researchers have discussed job analysis as an activity that can enhance the strategy of an organization. Given that job analysis provides managers with clear descriptions and specifications about jobs, it is possible to determine which jobs are the most critical for a particular organizational strategy or objective. For example, if management decides to downsize an organization, the information provided by the job analysis should prove invaluable once a company decides which jobs to retain, change, or eliminate. Similarly, an organization with a growth strategy can use this information to identify the areas that need expansion or development.[11]

As discussed in Chapter 2, Miles and Snow developed a strategy typology of organizations. *Defenders* have narrow and relatively stable product-market domains, *prospectors* continually search for product and market opportunities, and *analyzers* operate in two types of product-market domains—one relatively stable and the other changing. These strategies affect the emphasis and the nature of many human resource activities. We will examine five specific human resource activities; the selection process, performance appraisals, job evaluations, career planning, and human resource planning. The purpose of discussing other human resource issues in the job analysis chapter is twofold. First, the following discussion is designed to integrate strategy with some of the major *uses* of job analysis. Second, the discussion should enable the reader to better understand many of the complexities and interrelationships between a job analysis and traditional human resource activities. The following discussion is based primarily on the work by Miles and Snow and by Wright and Wexley.[12]

SELECTION

Selection tests can be categorized as either achievement tests or aptitude tests. Achievement tests demonstrate whether an applicant can perform the job at the time of testing. These tests often involve having applicants perform samples of work using actual job tasks. In order to develop reliable and valid work sample tests, specific information about the job is needed. Thus, the best job analysis methods are critical incident technique or Comprehensive Occupational Data Analysis (CODAP). Aptitude tests, on the other hand, attempt to measure an applicant's potential or ability to learn. Information about the actual job may not be as relevant as information about the worker. Thus, information needed to develop an aptitude test may be obtained with the Position Analysis Questionnaire, the Management Position Description Questionnaire, Functional Job Analysis, Job-Element Method, or Ability Requirement Scales.

The strategy adopted by an organization can affect whether to utilize an achievement test or an aptitude test for selection purposes. If an organization adopts a defender strategy, its emphasis is on building human resources. Little recruiting is done above the entry level, and training programs are usually formal and extensive. Because the focus is on skill building, aptitude tests may be preferred. Aptitude tests can be used to identify employees who have the potential to learn from training. However, an organization with a defender strategy may want to use an achievement test to determine whether an applicant has the initial skills needed for selection or promotion.

An organization with a prospector strategy emphasizes acquiring human resources. Rather than "making" qualified employees through training, the focus is on "buying" already qualified personnel. Recruiting is sophisticated, and training is usually informal and limited. Because the focus is on skill identification and acquisition, achievement tests would most likely be preferred.

Finally, an organization with an analyzer strategy emphasizes allocating human resources. Training programs are usually formal and extensive. The focus is on skill building, so identifying applicants' potential to learn is important. Thus, aptitude tests would be the preferred method of selection. Exhibit 5.14 summarizes the relationship between a firm's organizational strategy and its preferred selection test.

PERFORMANCE APPRAISAL

Performance appraisal techniques measure employee traits, behaviors, or results. The trait approach (rating employees on traits such as temperament) has been criticized due to its subjectivity and because many trait appraisals have not been developed with the use of a thorough job analysis. However, the trait approach can be a useful measure if done correctly. Since trait approaches require position-specific information about the worker, the Job-Element Method would be a good choice.

EXHIBIT 5.14 **The Relationship between Organizational Strategy and Types of Selection Tests**

Organizational Strategy	Preferred Selection Test
Defender (building human resources) ⟶	Aptitude
Prospector (acquiring human resources) ⟶	Achievement
Analyzer (allocating human resources) ⟶	Aptitude

Behaviorally oriented appraisal systems (such as Behaviorally Anchored Rating Scales) measure employees' actual job-oriented behaviors. Results-oriented appraisals measure the outcomes or the products generated by employees. Management-by-objectives is often the basis for results-oriented appraisals. Since both types of appraisal systems require position-specific information about the work, the critical incident technique and the CODAP are often viewed as the best choices.

An organization's strategy can affect the choice of performance appraisal systems. Organizations with a defender or analyzer strategy use process-oriented procedures when examining performance. Process-oriented procedures are based on critical incidents or production targets. These organizations emphasize the identification of training needs. Thus, a behaviorally oriented appraisal system would most likely be preferred by organizations with these strategies.

Organizations with a prospector strategy use results-oriented procedures (such as profit targets). These organizations focus on the identification of staffing needs. Since the concern is with the ultimate result, results-oriented systems are often the logical choice. Exhibit 5.15 summarizes the relationship between organizational strategy and the preferred performance appraisal system.

JOB EVALUATION

Job evaluation is concerned with comparing different jobs across work-related factors (that is, skill, effort, responsibility, and working conditions) to determine the relative (dollar) worth of, and placement in, a hierarchy for each job. Given that the focus

EXHIBIT 5.15 **The Relationship between Organizational Strategy and Performance Appraisal Systems**

Organizational Strategy	Performance Appraisal System
Defender (identification of training needs) ⟶	Behaviorally Oriented System
Prospector (identification of staffing needs) ⟶	Results-Oriented System
Analyzer (identification of training needs) ⟶	Behaviorally Oriented System

is on comparing jobs, standardized job analysis methods are usually recommended. In addition, since information on both the worker and the job is needed, instruments such as the Position Analysis Questionnaire, the Management Position Description Questionnaire, and Functional Job Analysis are most effective for this purpose.

An organization's strategy can affect the importance of conducting a job evaluation. An organization with a prospector strategy focuses on acquiring or "buying" human resources. Since the concern is with attracting qualified employees, competitive salaries are extremely important. Thus, organizations with a prospector strategy would, most likely, be interested in conducting frequent job evaluations to ensure both internal equity (fair salaries within the company) and external equity (fair salaries between companies).

Organizations with a defender strategy focus on building human resources from the entry level. Since recruiting above the entry level is not a priority, job evaluations may not be viewed as a major concern. However, if turnover in the organization is high (often due to low pay), a complete job evaluation may be needed.

Organizations with an analyzer strategy focus on allocating human resources but are still concerned with some higher-level recruiting. Similar to prospectors, organizations with an analyzer strategy would want to have job evaluations conducted; however, the emphasis probably would not be as strong as that placed on job evaluations in prospecting organizations. Exhibit 5.16 summarizes the relationship between the organizational strategy and the importance of conducting a job evaluation.

CAREER PLANNING

Career planning involves identifying and comparing employees' current abilities with those required for a specific job. Strategies are devised to develop any skills or abilities employees lack. Since standardized information about the worker is needed, the Ability Requirements Scales, the Position Analysis Questionnaire, the Management Position Description Questionnaire, and Functional Job Analysis are all viable options.

Career planning is most likely to be salient in organizations that have a defender strategy or an analyzer strategy. Defenders and analyzers focus on formal and extensive training and skill building; thus, career planning is emphasized. Since prospectors are more likely to "buy" needed personnel through sophisticated recruiting techniques, career planning is of less concern than to others. However, attracting qualified personnel may require some career-planning activities. Most individuals are not interested in working for organizations that offer little or no career advancement opportunities.

EXHIBIT 5.16   **The Relationship between Organizational Strategy and the Importance of Conducting a Job Evaluation**

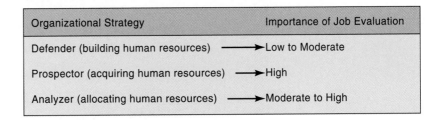

Organizational Strategy	Importance of Job Evaluation
Defender (building human resources)	Low to Moderate
Prospector (acquiring human resources)	High
Analyzer (allocating human resources)	Moderate to High

Exhibit 5.17 summarizes the relationship between career planning and the strategy of the organization.

HUMAN RESOURCE PLANNING

Human resource planning calls for an analysis of personnel needs in a dynamic environment and the development of activities that aid an organization's adaptation to change. These activities can include any of the aforementioned personnel functions. Since the analytic phase requires standardized information about the worker and the job, the Position Analysis Questionnaire or the Management Position Description Questionnaire are the recommended job analysis methods.

Human resource planning should be a concern for all organizations, regardless of their specific strategy. However, prospectors (and, to a lesser extent, analyzers) are in changing markets; thus, human resource planning may be critical for survival. Since defenders have more predictable markets, these organizations may be less concerned with extensive human resource planning. Exhibit 5.18 summarizes the relationship between human resource planning and organizational strategy.

In summary, the strategy of an organization can have a direct impact on many human resource activities. These activities, as Wright and Wexley argue, should be considered when choosing a job analysis method. However, regardless of the specific method chosen, certain guidelines should be followed for an effective job analysis.

EXHIBIT 5.17   **The Relationship between Organizational Strategy and the Importance of Career Planning**

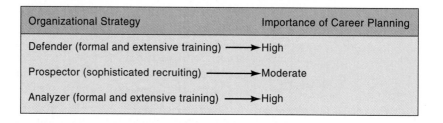

Organizational Strategy	Importance of Career Planning
Defender (formal and extensive training) ⟶	High
Prospector (sophisticated recruiting) ⟶	Moderate
Analyzer (formal and extensive training) ⟶	High

EXHIBIT 5.18   **The Relationship between Organizational Strategy and Human Resource Planning**

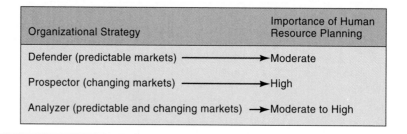

Organizational Strategy	Importance of Human Resource Planning
Defender (predictable markets) ⟶	Moderate
Prospector (changing markets) ⟶	High
Analyzer (predictable and changing markets) ⟶	Moderate to High

MANAGEMENT GUIDELINES

The following strategic guidelines should be examined when deciding whether to conduct a job analysis.

1. The reasons for conducting a job analysis should be clearly specified (such as establishing wage rates or recruiting) to help ensure that all relevant information is examined.
2. The primary purpose for conducting a job analysis should serve as input for the types of information collected (for example, work activities, machines and tools used, or job context).
3. The purpose for the job analysis, the types of information required, the time and cost constraints, the extent of employee involvement, and the level of detail desired should be specified before choosing one or more of the available methods of data collection.
4. The strategy of an organization can influence which human resource activities will be emphasized. In turn, certain human resource activities (such as selection or performance appraisal) may require different job analysis methods.
5. Managers should follow or include the following steps when conducting a job analysis:
   A. Determine the purpose for the job analysis.
   B. Identify the jobs to be analyzed.
   C. Determine the data collection method.
   D. Explain the process to employees and involve them.
   E. Collect job analysis information.
   F. Process the job analysis information.
   G. Review and update frequently.
6. The job analysis should be designed so that job descriptions and job specifications can be derived easily.
7. Managers should communicate all relevant information to employees concerning the job analysis to prevent unnecessary uncertainty and anxiety.
8. If major organizational changes have taken place, managers should consider conducting a job analysis.
9. If major organizational changes are anticipated, managers should consider conducting a more future-oriented job analysis.

QUESTIONS FOR REVIEW

1. Why should managers conduct a job analysis? What purpose does it serve?
2. What are the advantages and disadvantages of using each of the described data collection methods?
3. What are the steps in the job analysis process?
4. What are the pros and cons of involving employees in the job analysis process?
5. What is a future-oriented job analysis? When would you want to use it?
6. What are job descriptions and job specifications? What is their relationship to the job analysis?
7. How often should a job analysis be conducted?
8. What are the various methods of job analysis?
9. Under what conditions should each of these job analysis methods be used?

JOB ANALYSIS AS A MEANS OF REVAMPING TRAINING FOR THE GAS INDUSTRY IN THE NETHERLANDS[13]

As the environment in which a business operates changes, so must the business. One industry that experienced tremendous changes in recent years is the gas industry in the Netherlands. Specifically, the distribution processes used by the gas industry were changed so drastically by new technologies that the training programs that were in place to teach gas technicians their jobs became obsolete. In an effort to keep pace with the changes, the gas industry commissioned a group of researchers to develop new training programs. To accomplish this goal, job analysis was used.

The job analysis project was designed around four major questions that needed to be answered:

1. What tasks and subtasks must be performed by specific employees in the gas and energy distribution industry?
2. What knowledge, skills, and abilities (KSAs) are required by these tasks and subtasks?
3. What changes will the tasks outlined go through in the near future?
4. Are there any significant differences between the tasks performed by the gas side of the industry as compared to the energy side?

To answer these questions, a model based on a general job analysis approach was developed. At the heart of this model is an activity, the smallest unit of analysis, which is conceived of as an action directed at the realization of a task. A task, the next level in the hierarchy, is a prescribed activity. Coherent sets of tasks define a job. Jobs can be described in job descriptions, and related jobs can be combined into job families. A job profile is a graph that depicts the relative importance of the tasks accomplished by the employees within a job. The KSAs required by a job can be outlined and presented in a KSA profile. One or more KSA profiles can be used to determine the curriculum required in a course. Courses can be combined to form modules. Each module is oriented toward a specific learning goal and is linked directly to the performance of a task. How well the task is performed after training can be evaluated and compared to a prescribed standard. Once again, all of these components are based on and determined by a job analysis.

Several data collection formats were used to perform the job analysis. First, job experts were interviewed. Qualitative data also were collected by studying documents about jobs, tasks, and the KSAs provided by the gas and energy companies involved. Mailed questionnaires were also used to collect more quantitative data. Each firm involved also was asked to nominate a key informant who could be contacted to fill in the data gaps when needed. The data were collected in a three-stage process.

STAGE 1

Interviews were held with each of the key informants to collect data about the structure of the organization, human resource management policies and procedures, jobs and tasks, education levels of the employees, career patterns available for the workers, and the training policies of the firm. The results from the interviews were used to develop the first part of the questionnaire sent out in Stage 2, and written job descriptions provided by the informant were content analyzed and edited to form the second part of the questionnaire. Finally, the training documents available were analyzed to develop the third (i.e., learning goals and course content) and fourth (i.e., inventory of available courses) sections of the survey.

STAGE 2

Due to the large number of specific tasks and subtasks identified, the second part of the survey had to be tailored to one of three different job families: logistics, support, and administrative staff; gas-technical specialists, inspection, service, and public relations; and managers, assistants to the managers, and supervisors of technical personnel. However, parts 1, 3, and 4 of the survey were identical for each job analyzed.

STAGE 3

The final stage was a conference that included the informants, the course instructors, and key members of the training staffs for each of the firms involved. The preliminary results of the interviews and surveys were presented. The conference attendees were encouraged to modify the proposed course content and procedures to better meet their individual needs.

The end results of the job analysis process were two courses designed to allow the workers to be fully competent in their jobs. The courses were based on learning goals that stressed the KSAs needed to perform the jobs in question. Further, the courses incorporated as much of the existing information and training methods as possible to make the transition process easier for the employees.

QUESTIONS

1. How did the job analysts go about answering the four major questions that prompted this study?
2. What exactly is a KSA profile and how was it used? How could this profile be used in the other human resource

functions, such as selection, compensation, or performance appraisal, that use job analysis as a basis?

3. Using a job you are familiar with, define an activity, a task, a job, and a job profile. For what purposes can these items be used?

4. Although a variety of means of collecting the job analysis data was used in this case, which ones discussed in the text

were not applied? Describe how they could have been utilized.

5. This case indicates that a variety of firms that normally competed with one another banned together to develop industrywide courses. What is another industry that could benefit from this type of project?

ADDITIONAL READINGS

Ash, R. A., and S. L. Edgell. "A Note on the Readability of the Position Analysis Questionnaire (PAQ)." *Journal of Applied Psychology* 60 (1975), pp. 765–766.

Cain, P. S., and B. F. Green. "Reliabilities of Selected Ratings Available from the *Dictionary of Occupational Titles.*" *Journal of Applied Psychology* 68 (1983), pp. 155–165.

Conley, P. R., and P. R. Sackett. "Effects of Using High- versus Low-Performing Job Incumbents as Sources of Job-Analysis Information." *Journal of Applied Psychology* 72 (1987), pp. 434–437.

DiNisi, A. S., E. T. Cornelius III, and A. G. Blencoe. "Further Investigation of Common Knowledge Effects on Job Analysis Ratings." *Journal of Applied Psychology* 72 (1987), pp. 262–268.

Dowell, B. E., and K. N. Wexley. "Development of a Work Behavior Taxonomy for First-Line Supervisors." *Journal of Applied Psychology* 63 (1978), pp. 563–572.

Friedman, L., and R. J. Harvey. "Can Raters with Reduced Job Descriptive Information Provide Accurate Position Analysis Questionnaire (PAQ) Ratings?" *Personnel Psychology* 39 (1986), pp. 779–789.

Gael, Sidney. *Job Analysis: A Guide to Assessing Work Activities.* San Francisco, CA: Jossey-Bass, 1983.

Harvey, Robert J., Lee Friedman, Milton D. Hakel, and Edwin T. Cornelius III. "Dimensionality of the Job Element Inventory. A Simplified Worker-Oriented Job Analysis Questionnaire." *Journal of Applied Psychology* 73, no. 4 (1988), pp. 639–646.

Harvey, Robert J., and Susana R. Lozada-Larsen. "Influence of Amount of Job Descriptive Information on Job Analysis Rating Accuracy." *Journal of Applied Psychology* 73, no. 3 (1988), pp. 457–461.

Hunt, Allen H., and Timothy L. Hunt. *Human Resource Implications of Robotics.* (Kalamazoo, MI: W. E. Upjohn Institute for Employment Research, 1982).

Levine, E. L., R. A. Ash, and N. Bennett. "Exploratory Comparative Study of Four Job Analysis Methods." *Journal of Applied Psychology* 65 (1980), pp 524–535.

Levine, E. L., R. A. Ash, H. Hall, and F. Sistrunk. "Evaluation of Job Analysis Methods by Experienced Job Analysts." *Academy of Management Journal* 26, no. 2 (1983), pp. 339–348.

McCormick, E. J., P. R. Jeanneret, and R. C. Mecham. "A Study of Job Characteristics and Job Dimensions as Based on the Position Analysis Questionnaire (PAQ)." *Journal of Applied Psychology* 56 (1982), pp. 347–368.

McGregor, Douglas. *Human Side of Enterprise.* (New York: McGraw-Hill, 1960).

Miller, A. R., D. J. Treiman, P. S. Cain, and P. A. Roos, eds. *Work, Jobs, and Occupations: A Critical Review of the Dictionary of Occupational Titles.* (Washington, DC: National Academy Press, 1980).

Mullins, Wayman C., and Wilson W. Kimbrough. "Group Composition as a Determinant of Job Analysis Outcomes." *Journal of Applied Psychology* 73, no. 4 (1988), pp. 657–664.

Tornow, W. W., and P. R. Pinto. "The Development of a Managerial Taxonomy: A System for Describing, Classifying, and Evaluating Executive Positions." *Journal of Applied Psychology* 61 (1976), pp. 410–418.

NOTES

1. Gary Hoover, Alta Campbell, and Patrick Spain, *Hoover's Handbook of American Business* (Austin, TX: The Reference Press, 1992), p. 568.

2. "HR's Role in the Reengineering Process," *Personnel Journal,* December 1993, p. 48H.

3. William J. Rothwell and N. C. Kazanas, *Strategic Human Resource Development* (Englewood Cliffs, NJ: Prentice-Hall, 1989), p. 140.

4. Richard Henderson, *Compensation Management* (Englewood Cliffs, NJ: Prentice-Hall), p. 106.

5. H. L. Ammerman, *Performance Content for Job Training* (Columbus, OH: Center for Vocational Education, Ohio State University, 1977), p. 21.

6. "Managers Make Pay Decisions through Job Families," *Personnel Journal,* June 1993, p. 64D.

7. Paul Dorf, "Classify Jobs Properly to Avoid Overtime Trap," *HRMagazine,* April 1994, pp. 29–30.

8. Robert L. Mathis and John H. Jackson, *Personnel/Human Resource Management* (St. Paul: West, 1985), p. 177.

9. Ernest J. McCormick, *Job Analysis: Methods and Applications* (New York: AMACOM, 1979), pp. 144–145.

10. Kristen Shingleton, "Job Audits as Interviews: Define Physical Requirements," *HR Focus* 69(7), July 1992, p. 11.

11. J. E. Butler, G. R. Ferris, and N. K. Napier, *Strategy and Human Resources Management* (Cincinnati, OH: South-Western, 1991).

12. R. Miles and C. Snow, "Designing Strategic Human Resources Systems," *Organizational Dynamics* 13, Summer 1984, pp. 36–52; and Patrick M. Wright and Kenneth N. Wexley, "How to Choose the Kind of Job Analysis You Really Need," *Personnel* 62, May 1985, pp. 51–55.

13. J. M. van der Veen and A. M. Versloot, "A Research-Based Model for Job Analysis," *Journal of European Industrial Training* 17 (1993), pp. 15–23.

CHAPTER 6

STRATEGIC HUMAN RESOURCE PLANNING AND INFORMATION SYSTEMS

Human resource planning is a vital link between strategic planning and human resource management. Human resource planning is the process of making decisions in hiring and staffing for the organization. Planning and staffing involve job design, recruitment, screening, compensation, training, promotion, and work policies. In this chapter, we present factors found within the organization and throughout its environment that influence human resource planning. We also offer guidelines for managing and analyzing human resource planning requirements.

CHAPTER OBJECTIVES

As a result of studying this chapter, you should be able to
1. Define strategic human resource planning.
2. Explain the critical link between strategic management and strategic human resource planning.
3. Identify and explain the external and internal factors that affect a human resource plan.
4. Identify and explain the steps in constructing a human resource plan.
5. Explain the relationship of strategic human resource planning to the staffing function.
6. Discuss human resource costing in organizations.
7. Explain the importance of human resource information systems (HRIS) to organizations.

HOW A COMPUTER KEEPS MRS. FIELDS FROM LOSING HER COOKIES[1]

Computers have made the workplace more efficient. Even in the "low-tech" cookie business, operations can be programmed to smooth the production flow as well as schedule personnel. Mrs. Fields Cookies is a good example of how to utilize technology in human resource management.

The real Mrs. Fields is Debra Fields, who started the company with her husband Randy, a former systems programmer for IBM. Together they have built a corporation that includes their original company and others, such as La Petite Boulangerie and Retail Operations Intelligence (ROI) Systems. The ROI division sells its expertise to other companies.

From its beginning in 1977, the couple's enterprise has grown substantially. Success in their own business and competition from other businesses led them into other markets and other industries.

The company's strategy was typical of the trends of the 1980s. Increased competition from other cookie companies and from substitutes, such as specialty confectionery companies, caused problems. In 1988, problems from the "combination stores" concept hurt business. Analysts said that the company had made strategic mistakes. The Fields hoped to recoup through diversification and globalization. By 1990, the company was selected by NutraSweet's Desserve Foods Division for a joint marketing effort, the first time NutraSweet had made such a move with another company.

HOW A COOKIE COMPANY CAN USE COMPUTERS

Paul Quinn heads up ROI, Mrs. Fields' management information systems. He directs the efforts of Mrs. Fields' diversified divisions and markets the systems to over 600 other locations.

One of the features of the ROI system is that it has several components, called *modules*, which handle most of the day-to-day operations in human resource management. Among the modules already up and running are the daily production planner and components that focus on interviewing, setting personnel schedules, and skill testing. One benefit of a computerized human resource information system is that it standardizes routine tasks, such as interviewing prospective employees. A further benefit is that it can customize the standard employment questionnaire based on the individual responses that the applicant has given.

For example, suppose Jane Dough is looking for a part-time job at Mrs. Fields Cookies to help pay expenses while she is in school. She would be instructed to sit at a computer terminal and answer the series of questions that appear on the screen. The questions take about 15 minutes to answer. Some are true/false, others are multiple choice. So far, this could be done with a printed form. However, the computer is programmed to ask additional questions based on Jane's answers. If she says she is interested in temporary work, the computer asks how long she would plan to stay with the company. The follow-up question is similar to one that a store manager might ask in conducting an interview. Not all store managers are able to keep current with legislation affecting employment recruiting practices. The computerized system is updated to make certain that only legal language is used in the interviewing process. The computer package also is programmed to catch discrepancies, such as overlapping dates in previous employment.

After Jane has finished answering the questions, the computer tabulates a score on her responses based on minimum qualifications the company has set. This score provides information to help the manager decide whether or not to hire Jane. However, although the computer program is a part of the human resource information system, it is not there to replace the human resource decision-making system. That job is still handled by people.

Suppose Jane is hired and after working for a couple of months in the baking operations wants to work at the front counter because that position pays more. She must pass the skills test before being considered for the change. The skill training module works like the interviewing module. It asks questions about tasks and gives correct responses and a final score so that Jane can get instant feedback on her skill level. A "help text" explains why an answer was right or wrong, and the test then becomes a tutor. If Jane doesn't pass, she can retake the test immediately or get further training before trying again. Jane isn't the only one who benefits from this system. The human resource staff at the company's headquarters feed her responses into a database. If several sources show the same problem, then the program is checked for wording errors. If there is no problem there, then the human resource staff looks at the training techniques, materials, or workforce skill levels for problems. Again, this system is designed to provide information to the people who are responsible for the company's human resources.

MORE USES FOR COMPUTERS

In addition to hiring and training, the human resource information system (HRIS) is used by Mrs. Fields Cookies to schedule personnel for production. Information is fed into the computer on a number of employees, their preferred or available hours, and anticipated traffic in the store. Even breaks are programmed so that each outlet operates at peak efficiency. The system then schedules personnel on an hourly basis. If Jane calls in sick, the labor scheduler module quickly formulates an alternate schedule and alerts the manager.

While Mrs. Fields is a leader in HRIS management, it is not alone. Over 2,000 human resource information systems were in operation at the beginning of the 1990s, with more systems coming on line, according to Dianne and Peter Kirrane, consultants who specialize in expert systems. Older systems using paper forms can make timely information virtually impossible. Today, companies like Arthur Andersen specialize in designing systems to provide the human resource manager with vital information in seconds.

Despite intense competition, Mrs. Fields tries to keep her cookie business healthy. Part of her strategy is the human resource information system used by the company to speed the flow of information from the source to where it is needed throughout the corporation.

Strategic human resource planning is the key link between a firm's strategic plan and its overall human resource management function as shown in Exhibit 6.1. The strategic human resource plan is a projection of how the firm plans to acquire and utilize its human resources. It affects and is affected by the firm's overall strategic plan, and it serves as the basis for overall human resource management.

EXHIBIT 6.1 **Strategic Human Resource Planning Serves as the Key Link between the Overall Strategic Plan and Human Resource Management**

| Overall Strategic Plan | ←→ | Strategic Human Resource Planning | ←→ | Human Resource Management |

Now we begin to look at how organizations fill the jobs. How do they decide how many people they need? How do they determine the skill/ability mix of these people? What should be the mix of hiring from the outside versus promoting from within? How are vacancies estimated? Would the company benefit from a computerized human resource management information system?

STRATEGIC CHOICES

The key choices in strategic human resource planning can and must be made along several key dimensions.[2] These dimensions reflect the degree to which an organization engages in planning per se. Each dimension represents a choice a firm makes when committing to any type of planning activity. First, the organization can choose to be *proactive* or *reactive* in human resource planning. That is, it can decide to carefully anticipate needs and systematically plan to fill them far in advance, or it can simply react to needs as they arise. Of course, careful planning to fill human resource needs better helps to ensure that the organization obtains the right number of employees with the proper skills and abilities at the time they are needed.

The second decision the organization makes determines its *breadth.* Essentially, the organization can choose a narrow focus by planning in only one or two human resource areas, such as recruitment or selection, or it can choose a broad focus by planning in all human resource areas including training, rewarding, and so on. This continuum is depicted in Exhibit 6.2.

The third choice involves the *formality* of the plan. The organization can choose to have a rather informal plan that is mostly in the heads of its managers and personnel

EXHIBIT 6.2 **The Breadth of Focus in Human Resource Planning Can Be Narrow or Broad**

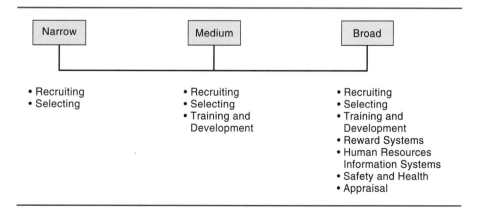

Narrow	Medium	Broad
• Recruiting • Selecting	• Recruiting • Selecting • Training and Development	• Recruiting • Selecting • Training and Development • Reward Systems • Human Resources Information Systems • Safety and Health • Appraisal

staff, or it can have a *formalized* plan that is clearly spelled out in writing backed up by supporting documentation and data. Including a computerized human resource management information system (HRIS) in an organization is one way to help formalize the process.

The fourth choice involves the *degree of tie* the human resource plan has with the strategic plan. The plan can be *loosely tied,* if at all, to the firm's strategic plan, or it can be *fully integrated* with the strategic plan. As we have indicated, integration of the strategic plan and strategic human resource management can best occur by fully integrating the two through strategic human resource planning.

Finally, the fifth choice in the human resource plan involves *flexibility*—the ability of the plan to anticipate and deal with contingencies. As we have indicated, organizations do not like high levels of uncertainty. They reduce this uncertainty by planning, which includes forecasting and predicting possible future conditions and events. Human resource planning can contain many contingencies, which reflect differing scenarios and thereby ensure that the plan is flexible and adaptable, or it can be fairly set and geared to one scenario, thereby requiring much time and effort to obtain change—assuming it can be changed at all.

Exhibit 6.3 summarizes these five major choices faced by organizations in strategic human resource planning. Organizations often tend to be to the left or to the right on all continua rather than to the left on some and to the right on others, although there are exceptions. A firm could be at one end of the extreme on some plan characteristics and

EXHIBIT 6.3   **Continual Strategic Choices in Human Resource Planning**

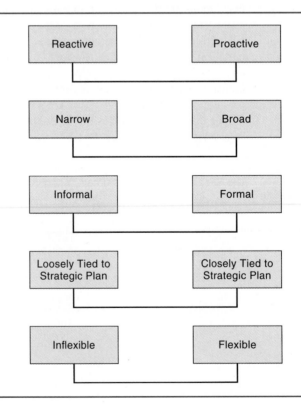

at the other end on other characteristics. Contrast, for example, the human resource planning done by Apple Computer during the first two years of its existence with that done under CEO John Scully. Apple's rapid growth in a short period of time occurred haphazardly with little real human resource planning. Under Scully, formalized flexible plans were developed and fully integrated with the company's overall strategic plan; yet these were often reactive because of the firm's growth cycles in the mid-1980s[3].

ORGANIZATIONAL GROWTH CYCLES AND PLANNING

The stage of an organization's growth can have an important effect on the human resource planning adopted by the organization.[4] Small organizations just starting out in the embryonic stage often do little human resource planning. What planning that is done is often informal and reactive in nature. (Professors often receive calls from small organizations in their communities with job openings. When asked, "When do you need the person?" the reply often is, "Yesterday!") Many young firms do not recruit for replacements until *after* the positions become vacant. Little real anticipatory recruiting and hiring is done.

As the organization enters the second stage, rapid growth, the need for planning becomes more apparent. Human resource forecasting becomes a necessary addition. Internal development of people also begins to receive attention in order to keep up with growth.

A mature firm experiences less flexibility and variability. Growth has slowed and the organization tends to become set in its ways. The workforce ages as few younger people are hired. Planning becomes more formalized and less flexible and innovative. Concerns with retirement, mid-career plateauing, and possible retrenchment dominate planning.

Finally, in the aging or declining stage, human resource planning takes a different focus. Planning is done for layoff, retrenchment, and retirement, and since decisions are often made after serious financial and sales shocks are experienced by the organization, planning is often reactive in nature. In some cyclical industries such as autos, however, layoffs can be and are planned well in advance. Only if the organization attempts *renewal* and renaissance (rebirth) will strategic human resource planning focus on growth again.

In the next section, we examine the overall framework and nature of human resource planning.

THE NATURE OF HUMAN RESOURCE PLANNING

Human resource planning is the process of making decisions regarding the acquisition and utilization of human resources. As such, it is part of the strategic decision-making process. The human resource plan focuses on an analysis of the organization's objectives and the plan for acquiring resources to meet those objectives. The organization's objectives and the resource acquisition process are analyzed in terms of the role that human resources plays in achieving organizational goals.

Human resource planning is the sum total of the plan formulated for the recruiting, screening, compensation, training, job structure, promotion, and work rules of an organization's human resources. It is a process designed to translate the corporate plans and objectives into future quantitative and qualitative employment requirements, together with plans to fulfill those requirements over both the shorter and longer terms, through human resource utilization, human resource development, employment and recruiting, and the use of information systems.[5]

This definition emphasizes structuring plans to carry out what are considered to be the traditional personnel management functions of hiring, training, compensation, and promotion. Thus, even though the primary focus of human resource planning is on obtaining people to fill jobs, human resource planning is a pervasive function in that it involves planning for the operation of other areas of human resource management as well.

ECONOMIC FORCES

Human resource planning is influenced by national employment and economic policy planning. National economic policy planning sets the stage for national policy in training and education and the level of economic activity through monetary and fiscal policy. Congress and various federal agencies, such as the Department of Labor, particularly the Employment and Training Administration, and certain agencies within the Department of Health and Human Services and the Department of Education, play a major role. Laws are passed to encourage certain types of training or the hiring of certain groups. For example, the Jobs Training Partnership Act encourages private sector hiring of disadvantaged groups.

Economic and human resource policy at the national level changes as the priorities of a particular Congress or administration change. For example, under Presidents Kennedy and Johnson, a great deal of effort and funds were spent to develop plans to deal with specific employment problems. Those administrations established programs for remedial education and skill training, mobility benefits, equal employment opportunity, and labor market information system. Most of these programs in this period were directed at improving the employment relationship of minorities and disadvantaged groups in keeping with the philosophy of the New Frontier of the Kennedy administration and the Great Society of the Johnson administration.

However, during the Nixon and Ford administrations, human resource priorities changed. These administrations increased the emphasis on improving the employment situation of veterans and in improving the already existing federal offices, such as the federal-state divisions of employment, to help all levels of employment. The emphasis on programs for the disadvantaged and minorities was reduced.

The Nixon administration also decentralized the national human resource planning effort by establishing regional offices throughout the nation and, through the revenue sharing program, by asking each state to handle its employment planning function. The responsibility for national human resource planning has shifted from a centralized federal government in Washington to decentralized regional offices and individual state governments.

The Carter administration continued this decentralized approach to human resource planning but sought to increase the scope and funding of programs for the disadvantaged and minorities. The Reagan and Bush administrations reduced the emphasis on the federal government's role in human resource planning and provided incentives for private industry to take over more of the planning and training function. Reagan also instituted the "block grant" concept for the states as opposed to previous grants by category for human resource utilization. This plan gave states more flexibility in using human resource funds. Under this plan, money is allocated to state and local governments as a block or whole, not by program or funding category. This allows the states to allocate funds to priority programs with a minimum of federal red tape.[6]

National economic and human resource policy plays a major underlying role in a firm's human resource planning. For example, when federal programs were established to improve the employment opportunities for the unskilled, disadvantaged, and unemployed, all individual organizations were asked to commit extra efforts for recruiting, training, and employing these individuals.

Often federal programs stimulate an organization to increase human resource planning efforts. Federal laws and court interpretations of those laws dealing with equal employment opportunity and affirmative action often make it necessary for many organizations to review their human resource planning process. As noted previously, the thrust of affirmative action planning involves the development of an organizational plan to recruit, train, and employ more members of minorities and women than the organization presently employs. As organizations review the number of employees presently employed in various positions and develop plans to replace these employees to ensure that minorities are being recruited, they usually end up making a comprehensive review of their total human resource planning system.

THE LABOR MARKET

To a great extent, organizations view the labor market as a pool of skills and abilities that will be tapped as the need arises. For most job requirements, employees with appropriate skills and abilities are readily available. From time to time, organizations experience shortages of people with certain skills or find that the wage level is so high that they cannot "afford" to hire the type of people needed to fill the available jobs. For example, for many years employers faced a shortage of people with computer expertise. The relationship between the organization's job requirements and the available pool of skills and abilities is typically viewed by managers as a sequential process whereby the organization first establishes the best job structure in terms of job content and task assignments, determines each job's worth in the production process (job evaluation), and then proceeds to hire and develop human resources that match these requirements. Often things do not work out so smoothly for a firm because the labor market is not perfect and is constantly changing. Shortages and surpluses of skill areas develop and workers are laid off permanently as plants close. Auto workers must move from Detroit to Ohio, Tennessee, Kentucky, and California if they want to continue working in the auto industry.

Economists typically indicate four main determinants of the labor supply:

1. The size, age, sex, and educational composition of the population.
2. The demand for goods and services in the economy.
3. The nature of production technology.
4. The labor force participation rates (people working or looking for work) of major subgroups (for example, women).

DIVERSITY AND THE LABOR MARKET

Effective human resource planning must include the diverse workforce. In 1987, the Hudson Institute released a study entitled "Workforce 2000: Work and Workers for the Twenty-first Century." The study projects that by the year 2000, only 15 percent of the people entering the workforce will be American-born white males, compared with 47 percent in 1987. To plan effectively, companies should stress that managing diversity is more than affirmative action or being sensitive to gender, race, culture, and age differences. Managers should use the diverse workforce as a competitive weapon to help the organization capitalize on its talent pool and compete in the global marketplace.[7]

SKILL CHANGES AND PERSONNEL SHORTAGES

Changes in the labor market have led to skill shortages as well as areas of oversupply. When the human resource educational/skill mix differs significantly from the skills required by employers, personnel shortages develop. Employers have jobs open but cannot find people with the skills needed. Many people who want jobs are not hired because they do not have the skills demanded. This mismatch between job skill requirements and the skills of the labor force plagued the U.S. economy during the 1970s and 1980s and can have serious negative impact on the economy of a society. For example, employment rates in traditional industries such as steel, automobiles, and rubber, have declined as demand and technology in these areas change; yet severe personnel shortages are occurring in such high-tech areas as computers, information processing, and genetic engineering. In many cases, rust-belt jobs in traditional industries in the Midwest have moved to Sunbelt jobs in information systems and services.

This human resource dislocation in part drives inflation, since employers bid up the wage rate for the few qualified workers in the high-demand fields. The wage rates of computer-trained auto mechanics, for example, soared in the late 1980s. At the same time, relative wage rates tumbled in the old-line industries. The federal government has reacted to this situation by encouraging employers to improve the computer-related skills of employees by developing training programs. These programs are embodied in the Jobs Training Partnership Act, a joint federal-private business action that provides the skills necessary for many entry-level jobs in high-tech industries and various federally funded vocational and technical education programs at two-year technical schools.

Because of the types of skills needed by employers in the 1990s will likely be much more sophisticated than they were in the 1970s and 1980s, this will, most likely, increase the educational attainment level of workers. For example, various new engineering, computer, and medical technical jobs require much higher skills than previously required. Even the automotive mechanic of the 1990s will be more highly skilled than his or her counterpart in the 1980s because of the more sophisticated design of automobile computers, engines, and related systems and because of the tremendous variety in automotive models within a given manufacturer's line.

Thus, any human resource plan must assess the human resource educational/skill level of the labor market from which it draws, predict future changes in this mix, assess the effect of federal human resource programs, and then plan recruiting, training, and job design systems that take maximum advantage of the forecasted educational/skill mix. Human resource management units perform a boundary spanning or scanning role when assessing labor market characteristics. Recognizing that the labor market and federal legislation and activities related to it have a major impact on any company's individual human resource plan, now we look at a model or procedure for constructing a human resource plan.

MODEL FOR HUMAN RESOURCE PLANNING

Exhibit 6.4 shows an overall model or procedure for constructing a human resource plan. We will examine each step in the model.

DETERMINE GROWTH/RETRENCHMENT OBJECTIVES

Notice the impact that outside factors in the environment, as well as market opportunities and the personal values of strategic managers, have in formulating an organization's growth objectives. Growth/retrenchment objectives drive the human resource

EXHIBIT 6.4   **A Model for Constructing a Human Resource Plan**

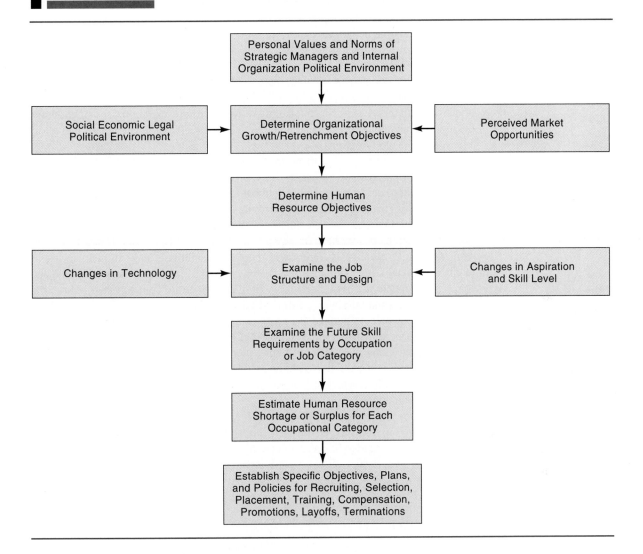

plan. If an organization decides to scale back, retrench, or restructure, people will be let go. We saw this often in the 1980s. Eastern Airlines, Ford, General Motors, Beatrice, and AT&T, among others, went through major retrenchments. Even very successful companies, such as IBM, experienced periods of retrenchment in the late 1980s.

If a company grows rapidly, with little retrenchment, such as Apple or American Express did in the 1980s, employment expands. Growth objectives are a key part of an organization's overall strategic plan. Almost all strategic plans deal with the size the company wishes to be in the future. For example, under Jack Welch, General Electric decided that it wants to be either number one or two in every industry it enters or it will either not enter it or will exit if already in it.[8] This is a key factor of GE's strategic plan. *Managed growth* is a popular phrase today because companies can grow too fast; two excellent examples are People Express and Air Florida. Both companies grew faster than their internal operations could handle, and both died. There are costs to growth.

Growth/retrenchment objectives may be expressed in terms of sales, market share, asset size, return on investment, development of new products and services or selling off product lines, and development of new markets or abandonment of markets.

Human resource departments need to align the strategic human resource plan with the firm's growth/retrenchment strategy. A growth-oriented strategy needs to be supported by a human resource strategy of aggressive recruiting, hiring, and training. Many of the high-tech companies, such as Apple, NeXT, and Microsoft, were ill-prepared for their rapid growth and either could not find qualified personnel or had to pay premium prices to fulfill their needs. Since it is not always clear how fast a company might grow, the top executive team needs to be prepared with a set of contingency plans that allow a reasonable range of options.

In contrast to fast-growing firms are those facing retrenchment and declining markets. Here, human resource planning must deal with hard and unpleasant issues. The firm may want to act in a guarded way to avoid alerting suppliers, customers, and employees of an impending cutback. It is important, though, that the strategic plan address these issues to minimize damage and make the best of a difficult situation. During the mid-1980s, companies in the farm equipment business, such as John Deere and Company, faced massive layoffs. Deere was more successful than most in maintaining its public image and critical human resources by proactive planning and executing the cutbacks in a humane and thoughtful way. By 1988–1989 the company had returned to high levels of profitability with a trimmed but efficient workforce.

Years of downsizing thinned the ranks of Deere employees, including white-collar supervisors. Deere managers realized that they had to rely more on blue-collar talent and have spent many resources in training these workers. Training classes include robotics as well as cost-reduction techniques. The results have been very favorable; employees are not only receptive to improving efficiency but also are happy to be part of the decision making.[9]

Divestitures and mergers provide a challenge for the human resource department. Merging two or more firms may involve cutbacks or at least reassignment. Conflicting corporate cultures need to be meshed, and this needs to be part of the strategic plan. Divestiture involves issues such as staff reconfiguration, reassignments, and layoffs. Union contracts and other labor agreements may need to be considered. Careful negotiations and agreements with the acquiring company need to be planned for and executed.

A product differentiation or divisionalization will require a decentralized approach in human resource issues. Hiring, recruiting, and training can often better be handled at the local level. Companywide standards, though, may be set at the corporate level.

A company may decide to fill a particular niche based on cost/price segmentation. A low-cost producer could require a human resource strategy that involves wage cuts, efficiency improvements, and perhaps staff reductions. At times companies are forced into this position by a competitor. Iowa Beef Processors, through its tough, some would say antiunion posture, forced other traditional high labor/cost producers, such as Hormel, to attempt wage cuts at its operations. The result was a bitter strike.

On the other hand, a company may choose to pursue a luxury, high-quality niche. Special training, recruitment of highly skilled personnel, and a unique compensation plan will be of particular importance. Exhibit 6.5 summarizes the firm strategy—human resource strategy connection.

The objectives that companies set are usually expressed in terms of a time frame or **planning horizon**—the length of time over which the objectives and the plan for accomplishing them will occur.

PLANNING HORIZON
The time frame estimated to accomplish organizational objectives.

EXHIBIT 6.5   **Firm Strategy—Human Resource Strategy Relationship**

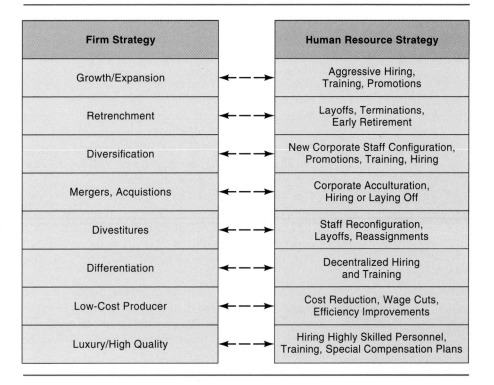

Firm Strategy		Human Resource Strategy
Growth/Expansion	←---→	Aggressive Hiring, Training, Promotions
Retrenchment	←---→	Layoffs, Terminations, Early Retirement
Diversification	←---→	New Corporate Staff Configuration, Promotions, Training, Hiring
Mergers, Acquistions	←---→	Corporate Acculturation, Hiring or Laying Off
Divestitures	←---→	Staff Reconfiguration, Layoffs, Reassignments
Differentiation	←---→	Decentralized Hiring and Training
Low-Cost Producer	←---→	Cost Reduction, Wage Cuts, Efficiency Improvements
Luxury/High Quality	←---→	Hiring Highly Skilled Personnel, Training, Special Compensation Plans

The planning horizon for growth in many organizations seldom exceeds 15 years and is often expressed in terms of short-range, intermediate-range, and long-range periods. General Electric is widely known for preparing long-range forecasts for products needed in the next century. Auto companies, such as Ford, General Motors, and Chrysler also emphasize long-range objectives. As a rule of thumb, *short-range* is defined as a horizon of 1 year or less, *intermediate-range* as 2 to 4 years, and *long-range* as 5 to 15 years. Often the long-range objectives are quite general, and the intermediate and short-range objectives are much more specific. This specificity is especially true of short-range or **operational objectives**.

OPERATIONAL OBJECTIVES

Day-to-day short-term objectives.

Retrenchment objectives typically have a short time frame—often one year or less—since cutbacks cannot necessarily be easily predicted and often come unexpectedly.

Human resource professionals often play a role in helping to form growth/retrenchment objectives if the firm has adopted a strategic human resource approach. They can provide advice on how internal staffing needs will likely change as well as the likely availability of people with necessary skills.

DETERMINE HUMAN RESOURCE OBJECTIVES

Once the organization's objectives are specified, communicated, and understood by all affected, the personnel or human resource unit should *specify its objectives with regard to human resource utilization in the organization.* In developing these objectives, specific policies need to be formulated to address the following questions:

1. Shall we attempt to fill positions from within or by hiring individuals from the labor market?
2. Can we meet our commitments to affirmative action and equal employment opportunity?
3. How do our training and development objectives interface with our human resource planning objectives?
4. What union constraints do we face in human resource planning, and what policies should we develop to effectively handle these constraints?
5. What is our policy toward providing everyone in the organization with a meaningful, challenging job (job enrichment)? Will we continue to have some boring, routine jobs, or should we eliminate them?
6. Can some positions and jobs be eliminated so that we can become more competitive?[10]
7. To what extent can we automate production and operations, and what shall we do about those displaced?
8. How do we ensure that we have a continuously adaptive and flexible workforce?

These are not easy questions to answer, but they go to the heart of human resource planning. Imagine a large company such as Federal Express or IBM facing these questions. With far-flung growing domestic and international operations, developing an overall human resource plan that systematically answers these questions is essential for managed growth.

Exhibit 6.6 shows some actual human resource objectives for organizations. Notice the variety of specific human resource areas addressed: promotion, staffing, training and development, career development, employment levels, pay, and so on. A large firm with a well-developed human resource plan, such as Campbell's or American Express, has a large number of human resource objectives spelled out at the corporate level and each division has a list of its own subobjectives. These continue down to the unit level as shown in Exhibit 6.7. Taking the objectives to this level is what makes them opera-

EXHIBIT 6.6   **Example of Human Resource Objectives**

1. To develop and implement a pay for performance system by January 1, 1995 (large bank).
2. To achieve the staffing plans for the 1994–1996 period (information services company).
3. To reduce employment levels in current manufacturing operations by 10 percent per year from 1993–1995 (plastics manufacturer).
4. To implement a career development plan for all employees by July 1, 1994 (state agency).
5. To ensure that all supervisors receive 60 hours of classroom training prior to appointment of supervision by July 1, 1995 (utility).
6. To establish a computerized human resource skills inventory of all employees by April 1, 1993 (credit union).
7. To reduce employee turnover 33 percent by January 1, 1994 (convenience store chain).
8. To develop and implement an aggressive program to hire older employees by September 1, 1996 (fast-food chain).
9. To achieve a 60/40 inside/outside mix for promotion during the next three years (large restaurant chain).

EXHIBIT 6.7   **Integration of Human Resource Objectives**

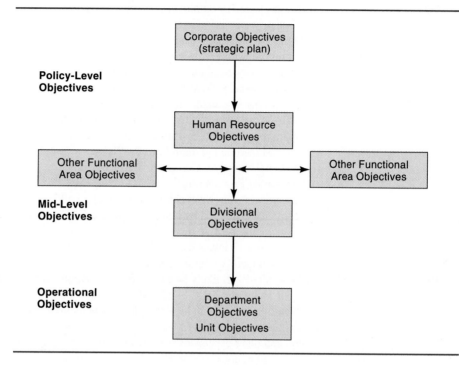

Policy-Level
Objectives

Corporate Objectives
(strategic plan)

Human Resource
Objectives

Other Functional
Area Objectives

Other Functional
Area Objectives

Mid-Level
Objectives

Divisional
Objectives

Operational
Objectives

Department
Objectives
Unit Objectives

tional. If the objectives are never taken to the unit level of specificity, they will never be achieved. Translating the objective to the unit level ("the trenches") is required for implementation.

Notice also that human resource objectives should be integrated with other functional area objectives. For example, training and development objectives should be geared toward and integrated with production, sales, and skill needs. Staffing needs should be coordinated with forecasted growth in sales, and so on. This kind of integration is not always easy to achieve but is necessary. Having human resources play the role of full partner in the strategic planning process will help to ensure better integration among functional areas.

EXAMINE JOB DESIGN AND STRUCTURE

An important step in strategic human resource management is the design of jobs. It is also an important step in human resource planning. Companies should not take the particular configuration of jobs that exist at a particular point in time as unchangeable; in fact, during the 1980s many changes in job design and structure occurred. Think of how much the robotic welding process used in auto assembly differs from the hand welding of earlier times.

Computer-assisted design/computer-assisted manufacturing (CAD/CAM), an infant industry, is already having a major effect on employment in some industries. For example, computer-assisted design can greatly increase the work output of designers, such as design engineers in the auto industry, leading to a reduced workforce with a very high increase in productivity for the remaining designers. Estimates show that CAD/CAM can improve productivity in an operation by 300 percent.[11]

ROBOTICS

The use of computer-assisted machines to accomplish work tasks.

QUALITY CIRCLES AND QUALITY IMPROVEMENT PROGRAMS

Groups of employees who meet to recommend ways to improve production and quality.

PARTICIPATIVE MANAGEMENT PROGRAMS

A decision-making process that involves managers as well as employees.

The same effects can be experienced in the manufacturing end of the operation. Computer-assisted manufacturing can greatly increase output per employee while reducing the need for employees. **Robotics**—the use of computer-assisted machines to accomplish work tasks, such as welding, cutting, and so on—is an essential part of CAM, and we are likely to see a greater usage of robots in many disagreeable and dirty jobs and in jobs that require very close tolerances.

We have only begun to feel the effects of CAD/CAM. Sales for the CAD/CAM industry were about $700 million in 1981 and grew to $4 billion by 1986. CAD/CAM can be used in any organization to design, draft, and print out specifications of products. CAD/CAM can also use this information to generate instructions for the numerical control equipment needed to make these products. Some of the companies now using CAD/CAM include the main Pratt & Whitney jet engine plant of United Technologies, International Harvester Company, Merck & Company, General Motors, Nissan Motors, and Koltanbar Engineering.

This very significant technological change will have a major impact on human resource plans developed by companies where CAD/CAM can be used. Most human resource planning is of an incremental nature from year to year. But CAD/CAM is likely to cause major changes in the human resource plan. Not only will fewer engineers, designers, and factory operators be needed in these companies, but the skill requirements for those hired will likely be changed. For example, people who can work with, as well as repair and maintain, CAD/CAM will be needed.

Therefore, examining jobs in light of new technological change will likely result in a reconfiguration of jobs in the organization. This will greatly impact staffing, training, hiring, and other aspects of the overall human resource plan.

A second major factor to be examined in this step involves the aspirations and skill levels of employees. This issue deals with the motivation levels, work ethic, expectations, and job skills employees bring to a job. For years, the trend has been that employees want jobs that are challenging, responsible, and that provide opportunities for advancement and involvement—jobs that require higher skills. Company efforts at involvement and participation through various programs such as **quality circles and quality improvement programs** or **participative management programs** rest on the fundamental belief that employees want an enriched job experience that involves their minds as well as their hands. Motorola, Florida Power and Light, Ford, and Nissan are all companies that have heavily invested in programs of this nature, as we have pointed out elsewhere in this book. The changing nature of employee aspirations, expectations, and skills will cause companies to redefine and restructure jobs to some extent to reflect these changes.

The final issue to discuss in terms of technology and human resource planning is the shortages of trained personnel for engineering-, computer-, and other high-tech–related occupations. Our analysis in Chapter 2 shows that, from a macro perspective, a tremendous growth in employment openings in these occupations is forecasted. These data also show the projected shortage of people to fill these occupations. From an employer's micro perspective, this means that it will be increasingly more difficult for organizations to attract and keep people with engineering, computer, and high-tech skills.

Another disturbing phenomenon related to this issue is the "eating your own seed corn" dilemma. Personnel shortages in engineering and computer occupations have caused many firms to hire university faculty members from engineering and computer information programs at salaries greatly in excess of the university salary. This, of course, leads to further shortages in the production of college-educated engineers and computer information specialists for the future.

ESTIMATE FUTURE SKILL REQUIREMENTS BY OCCUPATION OR JOB CATEGORY

Once the new job structure and design are determined, the next step is to examine the skills required in each job category. As noted above, job structure changes due to technology or other reasons cause skill changes. Computers in cars require different skills for mechanics. Robot welders in auto assembly changed the skill mix in auto factories. Word processors and personal computers changed the skill requirements for secretaries. For example, one convenience store chain restructured district manager jobs by changing information analysis and reporting requirements and requiring that computers with modems be used.

Occupational skills change over time. Therefore, it is important at this stage that an organization have a complete, current listing of all occupational categories in the organization with explanatory job descriptions that specify the duties, skills, and qualifications required for each job. Such a **skills bank** should be computerized and easily accessed for promotion and training purposes. Estimations of how these skills will change need to be built into the human resource plan.

SKILLS BANK
A list of job descriptions specifying the duties, skills, and qualifications for each job.

For example, during the late 1980s, a large wholesaler in the auto industry in the southeastern United States made a decision that each manager and clerical employee should have a personal computer on his or her desk. This necessitated a massive training program to ensure that all clerical and managerial employees were computer literate so that the PCs would actually be used. The training need was forecast well before the computers were ordered so that a training program could be established and funded, ready to be implemented once the computers were ordered. Key people were sent to off-site training programs so that they could learn to use computers and then train other employees once the computers arrived.

Forecasting future skill needs and preparing to fill those needs today is a critical feature of the strategic approach to human resource planning.

ESTIMATE HUMAN RESOURCE SHORTAGES OR SURPLUSES FOR EACH OCCUPATIONAL CATEGORY

This takes us to the fifth step in the human resource planning model. The human resource shortage or surplus should be estimated for each occupational and job category. Decisions should be made about what to do to deal with estimated surpluses or shortages in view of the organization's human resource utilization objectives. Exhibit 6.8 presents a procedure that is useful in estimating a given surplus or shortage for a particular occupation or job category. Note that this procedure ties in consideration of human resource objectives in filling jobs from within via internal promotions and organizational growth objectives.

If a surplus is predicted for an occupational category, the human resource plan needs to consider whether these individuals will be discharged, temporarily laid off, transferred, or provided with a cash bonus for quitting, severance pay, or given early retirement. These decisions are probably determined by the organization's overall human resource objectives for training and development.

If a shortage is predicted, the organization must hire from the outside labor market if it expects to fill the resulting job vacancies. This decision may cause the organization to review its human resource objectives with regard to hiring from the outside market vis-à-vis other objectives. For example, if the organization finds that it has to pay a higher than expected wage to attract new people, it may decide to make do with fewer people and either schedule more overtime or subcontract out some of the work. In fact, many organizations do this at least on a temporary basis. Computer and software companies commonly used this practice in the mid-1980s. Of course, most construction

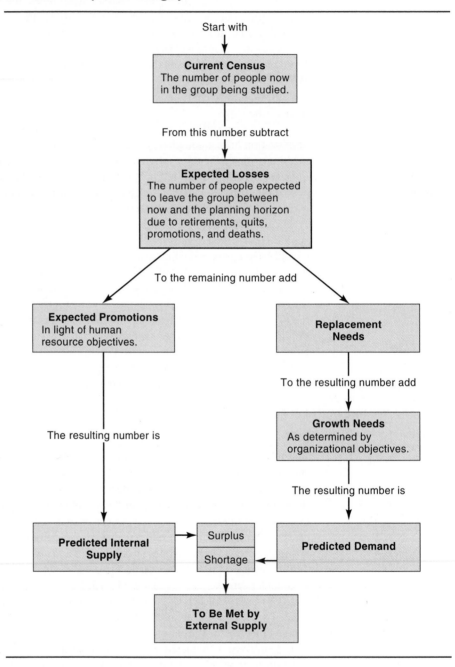

contractors do this as a matter of course, as do most state departments of transportation for road maintenance and construction. Subcontracting and the use of overtime is especially desirable if the shortage is reviewed as temporary (six months or less).

TRANSITION MATRIX (MARKOV ANALYSIS)

The changes or movements of human resources within an organization are called the *flows* of employees. One method of mathematically determining and depicting the flows of people in an organization is through use of Markov Analysis using a "transition matrix."[12] A simple example will help explain how this works. Assume that an organization had 100 Clerk Is and 50 Clerk IIs in 1995. As of 1997, only 80 percent of the original 100 Clerk Is may have remained in that position, and only 60 percent of the original 50 Clerk IIs may still be employed by the organization as Clerk IIs. The transition matrix shows this flow:

	1997	
1995	**Clerk I**	**Clerk II**
CLERK I	80%(s)	
CLERK II		60%(s)

(s) = stayed

Suppose that the following conditions actually existed as of 1997. Ten of the Clerk Is were promoted to Clerk II, 10 of the Clerk Is left the organization, 15 of the Clerk IIs left the organization, and 5 were demoted to Clerk I. This flow analysis would appear as follows:

	1997			
1995	**Clerk I**	**Clerk II**	**Left Organization**	**Total**
CLERK I	80% stayed	10% promoted	10%	100%
CLERK II	10% demoted	60% stayed	30%	100%

This information could then be integrated into the human resource plan to chart a trend. These percentages are then used as indicators of the probability of transition in each category to project future supply movement. The staffing level in each category at the beginning of a planning period is multiplied by the transition probabilities within each category. Then the columns are summed to yield the future labor supply within job categories.

The analysis is somewhat complex and appears to be used mostly by large firms. Weyerhaeuser, Eaton, and Corning have reported using it with mixed results.[13] Clearly more research and refinement are needed. However, we are likely to see more widespread use as computer software is refined to make Markov Analysis easier to use.

COMPUTER SIMULATION

Computer simulation of future staffing needs and levels is becoming more common as software such as Lotus 1-2-3 becomes available. Disney World uses a computer model to predict its employment levels by job category. This model is especially useful when seasonal factors affect employment.

Since forecasting contains an inherent amount of uncertainty, this technique and others are limited in their usefulness and application by the reliability and validity of the input data. The identification of key variables believed to affect future trends is very important. But selection of these key variables is not enough to ensure success. They must be measured accurately. The data must also be received in a timely fashion because old data are not as useful as new data. Organizations generally rely on past educational and job experience to predict future performance.

However, establishing valid criteria for this type of forecasting is difficult to do, much more difficult than using historical data or future requirements as a means of setting overall organizational objectives.[14] For example, if an organization wished to determine how many workers would be needed in a specific department in five years, a computer model (a representation of reality) might be utilized. Critical variables would have to be selected. These might include anticipated technological changes, outside labor force changes, required skills, absenteeism and turnover rates, past growth rates within the department, and so on. The model would then give the organization an estimated number of workers.

The firm could obtain not only a single estimate but also, through manipulation or modification of the variables, estimates under varying situations and conditions. For example, Disney develops and runs various alternative future scenarios. How many employees would be needed if the quit rate doubled in certain jobs? How many would be needed if visitor growth rate to the park fell by 25 percent? Forecasting varying scenarios and using the model to manipulate various data under each scenario makes computer simulation an extremely useful tool in human resource planning.

LINEAR PROGRAMMING

Another technique to plan and forecast changes in employment by job level is linear programming. Linear programming, a method used to determine the optimal way of allocating scarce resources among competing demands, has been used by Lilien and Rao to describe the movements of people through the organization.[15] It is a quantitative method of analysis technique used for maximizing an objective function, expressed in the form of a mathematical equation (for example, MAX $z = \$10x + \$30y$), subject to some particular set of constraints, also expressed in mathematical notation (for example, $4x + 6y < 12$; $8x + 4y < 16$). There are several ways to solve linear programming problems, ranging from a graphic method for less complicated problems to computer utilization for more detailed or complex problems.

Linear programming has proven beneficial in areas such as aggregate planning, distribution, product mix decisions, and scheduling. Parsons used a combination of a matrix and demand analysis in allocating personnel.[16] Drandell worked along similar lines using exponential smoothing and regression analysis.[17] The U.S. Office of Personnel Management has used each of these in its personnel planning operations in the federal government.[18] Imagine the difficulty of planning to fill job vacancies and respond to job growth in an organization as large as the U.S. government! Much of this work is decentralized in each agency, but centralized coordination and planning assistance are provided by the Office of Personnel Management. With over two million employees, human resource planning would be impossible for the federal government without these sophisticated models.

DELPHI TECHNIQUES

Another technique used in planning and forecasting and recently used in human resource planning is the Delphi technique.[19] In the Delphi technique, a panel of experts arrives at a consensus of opinion about growth and scenarios. These experts come from numerous related fields, and they fill out a detailed questionnaire concerning the issue to be addressed. They also supply their own personal opinions on the issue. Later these experts receive a summary of the responses. If their opinion differs from the summary, they are asked to reconsider their original viewpoint. If they still hold the same opinion thereafter, they are asked to explain their stance. This process is repeated, usually three or four times, until a consensus prediction is reached. One important aspect of the Delphi technique lies in its anonymity. This helps to avoid "groupthink" and reduce conflict among the panel members.

Delphi processes can be used to derive overall trends in changing job demands. For example, the Florida Association of Independent Insurance Agents used the process to speculate on changing job demands and characteristics in the offices of independent insurance agents. The Delphi technique developed scenarios of highly automated insurance offices using computers and word processors to handle recordkeeping, billing, and claims payments. These scenarios were "played out" to forecast changing needs in terms of skills and numbers of office employees, including the agent.

SUMMARY OF FORECASTING SURPLUSES/SHORTAGES AND CHANGING SKILL NEEDS

All of these techniques must be clearly integrated with the needs of line managers, who help supply the necessary data and help make decisions. Plans must be monitored and evaluated to ensure that they are meeting objectives. If necessary, plans must be redesigned as input data or forecasts change. Human resource planning is a dynamic process rather than a static event. In this regard, the human resource plan responds to changes in the organization's goals and its environment, as well as internal desires for work levels and line manager desires.

ESTABLISH SPECIFIC OBJECTIVES FOR HUMAN RESOURCE FUNCTIONS

The final step in human resource planning is to establish specific objectives for each human resource function. Specific objectives should be established for everything from recruiting to terminating.

The overall human resource plan should drive the specific operational objectives established for each human resource function as shown in Exhibit 6.9. These then

EXHIBIT 6.9   **Specific Operational Objectives**

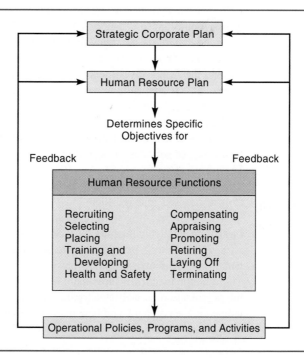

determine specific operational policies, programs, and activities developed to meet objectives. Both specific functional objectives and operating programs are integrated with the overall human resource plan by means of a feedback loop. If realistic objectives and program activities cannot be set or met under the human resource plan, the plan should be modified. As Exhibit 6.9 indicates, the entire resource plan is integrated with the organization's overall strategic plan. The next sections will examine human resource costing and human resource information systems as they relate to human resource planning.

HUMAN RESOURCE COSTING

Making human resource planning decisions because "it's the right thing to do" or because it will "make employees happy" is increasingly a less acceptable reason to justify policy. Today, organizations want to know how human resource policy affects the bottom line. Some of the more common costing measures include HRMex, or the human resource department's expenses as a percent of company operating expense. Human resource managers are increasingly being asked to justify decisions and programs on a cost-benefit basis. They are being held accountable in a financial sense for policy and procedure. They are being asked time and time again, "Are our programs and policies worth it? Are our decisions producing the desired results?"

No doubt cost-competitive factors and restructuring efforts have exacerbated this demand for accountability. But so has the traditional human resource defense of its programs, which has emphasized less tangible benefits such as good morale and job satisfaction. Line managers today want to know how these benefits contribute to the bottom line.

HUMAN RESOURCE ACCOUNTING

When asked to name their most important resource, many managers will respond "our people." When asked to put a value on its human resources, most managers say they cannot or that their people are invaluable. Yet valuing human resources has been a subject of inquiry since the late 1960s. The R. G. Barry Corporation of Columbus, Ohio, made the first major attempt to put a value on their human resources.[20] This model uses historical costs (actual expenses for recruiting, training, development, and so on) to determine the firm's investments in its employees and thus the asset value for the employee. This is a traditional way for accountants to value any resource, such as a building.[21] The asset value of the human resource staff can also be computed by calculating the human resource expenditure per employee. This calculation includes the cost of all human resource activities and staff divided by the number of employees covered by human resource services. In 1988, the average per capita expenditure per employee was $629. This value rose to $654 in 1989 and to $730 in 1990.[22]

 Some companies are moving further with human resource accounting by attempting to measure and manage their most valuable asset—intellectual capital or employee knowledge. According to several progressive companies, promoting, managing, and measuring intellectual capital is a critical step in human resource planning.[23] Scandia AFS, a Scandinavia-based insurance firm, recently included a description of the important nonfinancial measures that contribute to the company's success in its annual report. These nonfinancial measures included processes for development and renewal within the organization as well as corporate culture characteristics such as the proportion of women in the company and how many supervisors were from countries other than Sweden. According to Leif Edvinsson, director of intellectual capital at AFS, the issue is not to measure only financial capital but to have a more balanced measurement system that will ultimately create financial capital. The knowledge of individual workers (human capital) and its relationship to the knowledge of the organization (structural capital) is what is meant by *intellectual capital*. The process of extracting knowledge from employees is, in essence, creating structural capital.

Asset value, replacement costs, present value of future earnings, and value to the organization have also been used to place a value on a firm's human resources. However, a major limitation to all of these approaches is that they focus on inputs and outputs. In other words, they do not relate a firm's investment in people with the output the people produce.[24]

Newer approaches attempt to put a dollar value on the behavioral outcomes produced by working in an organization. Costs are determined for such behaviors as absenteeism, turnover, and poor job performance. This method measures the economic consequences of employee behavior, not the value of the individual.

COSTING EMPLOYEE BEHAVIORS

The costing approach may be more useful today when compared with the human resource accounting approach.[25] Financial quantification of a set of common behavior and performance outcomes use standard cost accounting procedures applied to employee behavior. To do this, cost elements associated with each behavior must be identified and their separate and independent dollar values computed.

For example, look at costing labor turnover. High turnover can be a very expensive proposition for any organization. To compute turnover costs, dollar figures must be attached to separation costs, replacement costs (including recruiting and hiring), and training and orientation costs. In addition, there is an opportunity cost of having the job unfilled for a period of time or filled with a less than fully trained person. The opportunity cost is the forgone productivity because the job was not filled or because it was filled with a new, less well-trained employee.

FAST-FOOD EXAMPLE

A firm may put up with high turnover if it believes that the costs of curing the problem are higher than turnover costs themselves. Look at a typical fast-food operation such as McDonald's, for example. Suppose that a McDonald's franchise experiences a 100 percent annual average turnover rate, about the national average for fast-food stores. In calculating the costs of this turnover, the costs of people leaving (separation), hiring, training, and forgone productivity would be compared with the costs of reducing the turnover. Assume for a moment that the costs of reducing turnover to say 25 percent result in the following:

1. Increasing wages by $1 per hour.
2. Implementing career tracks and promotion routes for all employees.
3. Increasing the benefits package.
4. Allowing employees a more flexible work schedule.

Also assume that when calculating these costs, the franchise determines that they far outweigh the turnover costs. In this case, the franchise may put up with 100 percent turnover as the less costly alternative.

Of course, in estimating the costs of these four steps, errors may be made since costs are estimated or projected, *not* actual. Also, it may be possible to reduce turnover by doing only step 1 or steps 1 and 2. In other words, an **incremental approach** could be used to see if a step affects the turnover rate. This would be less costly than attempting all four steps at once.

UTILITY THEORY

UTILITY THEORY
An area of decision making that provides a framework for selecting the decision alternative that provides maximum payment.

Through trial-and-error experience, a firm may develop fairly accurate costs of various behaviors. It may be possible to provide a reasonably accurate estimate of resultant benefits. Yet since choices are involved, the decision should be to select the option that provides the maximum payment or *utility*. The study of this area of decision making is called **utility theory**.[26] Utility theory provides a framework for making decisions that requires decision makers to state goals clearly, specify outcomes of the decision options, and attach differing values or utilities to each outcome. Probabilities for the outcome of each decision also can be specified. This information is used to construct a payoff table or matrix.

Returning to the McDonald's franchise turnover example, we can see how utility theory might work. The object is to cut turnover. Four possible steps were identified. If we assign a dollar value to the effect of each alternative—the amount it will save in turnover—plus the probability that it will occur, we then have the following payoff matrix:

	Effect		Payout Probability		(Costs Saved)
Payoff, Option 1 (Raise wages)	$5,000	×	.60	=	$3,000
Payoff, Option 2 (Career tracks)	3,000	×	.20	=	600
Payoff, Option 3 (Benefits package)	2,000	×	.10	=	200
Payoff, Option 4 (Flexible hours)	1,500	×	.10	=	150

Clearly, in this example, we will get our highest probable payout by raising wages (Option 1). The effect of this option is that we will reduce turnover costs by $3,000 ($5,000 estimated cost reduction × .60 probability of occurrence).

The final step is to compare the cost of this option to the cost of the other options to compute a cost/benefit ratio for each. This can be computed as follows:

Option	Annual Cost	Annual Payout (Benefit)	Cost/Benefit Ratio
1	$10,000	$3,000	.30
2	5,000	600	.12
3	4,000	200	.05
4	3,000	150	.05

Using these hypothetical figures, Option 1 would be chosen: it costs the most ($10,000) but has the highest payout relative to cost, giving it the highest cost/benefit ratio of .30.

Of course, this example is hypothetical. Actual figures of a problem of this type would differ because of individual firm circumstances. Furthermore, probabilities, even though based on experience and judgment, are still somewhat subjective. Nevertheless, this affords a much more rigorous analysis of decision options than typical seat-of-the-pants decision making that so often characterizes human resource decisions.

From a strategic standpoint, human resource costing and utility analysis offer much opportunity for the human resource professional. Far more sophisticated models using predictors, criterion cutoffs, and sophisticated mathematical notation are available in the literature. These models, coupled with computer manipulation and software packages, make it possible for even the most minimally skilled novice to incorporate quantitative cost analysis in human resource decisions. The emphasis on controlling human resource costs will likely spur more reliance on these quantitative techniques throughout the 1990s; however, they are unlikely to completely replace qualitative decision making discussed at the beginning of the chapter. Judgment will always play a role in human resource decision making.

Now we will examine human resource information systems as a way to track key information about human resources. Making good human resource decisions implies that we have a solid information set on which to base our decisions. We cannot cost human resource decisions if we do not have a cost database available.

HUMAN RESOURCE INFORMATION SYSTEMS

The basis for good human resource decisions is good human resource information. Human resource information should be provided to both human resource and line managers in such a way to facilitate decision making. This concept is known as a decision-support system (DSS). A decision support system places information for decision making literally at the fingertips of decision makers. Using personal computers or terminals, human resource and line managers can call up information as needed for recruiting, promoting, paying, or developing decisions.

A human resource information system (HRIS) is made up of numerous elements. Each element must function properly if the system is going to benefit the organization. Basically, a **system** is a set of activities that takes *inputs* (an application for employment in the finance department, for example), *transforms* them into useful items (a hiring approval from the personnel department), and then *outputs* the new items to where they can be used (sends the approval to the finance department). Most systems also have some form of *control* mechanism (the finance department sends back a completed new employee report) that enables supervisors to manage the operation of the system.[27]

Systems may be found on a departmental level, a plant level, or even an organization level. In short, a system is any activity that involves inputs, transformations, outputs, and feedbacks, and one system may be a subsystem—or a part—of another system. The HRIS is usually a part of the organization's larger management information system (MIS), which would include accounting, production, and marketing functions, to name just a few. The special function of HRIS is to gather, collect, and help analyze the data necessary for the human resources department to do its jobs properly. The opening case on Mrs. Fields Cookies is an example of how the HRIS works.

What distinguishes a manual system from an HRIS is the use of computers or information technology. A big advantage of an information technology-based HRIS is that it can provide many more DSS functions than a manually based system can. For the rest of the chapter, we will assume that an HRIS represents a computer-based system unless otherwise noted. With this in mind, we will examine the components of an HRIS in more depth.

INPUTS

The inputs of an HRIS resemble that of a manually based system. Employee information, company policies and procedures, and other personnel-related information must

==

HR CHALLENGE

An HRIS for New York City

In order to become more efficient, New York City's Department of Personnel installed an automated online HRIS system called PRISE (Personnel Reporting and Information System for Employees). The department is responsible for providing numerous services to the city's 60 agencies and more than 200,000 employees. These services include auditing and controlling each agency's personnel activities, such as hiring, transferring, and promoting. Before the installation of PRISE in late 1984, most of the city's personnel system was based on a traditional manual system of cards and folders. The city often experienced backlogs of 15 days or more under the old system, and it was almost impossible to tell exactly where a transaction was in the system. As a

result, it was almost impossible to locate the file or to determine where any delays in processing had occurred.

The new system not only eliminated these problems but provided other advantages as well. Backup files and records are now automatically generated and personnel employees spend more time solving problems and providing assistance as opposed to filling out forms. PRISE has helped the New York City's Department of Personnel reduce errors, eliminate backlogs, and provide more useful answers to inquiries for managers.

SOURCE: Adapted from Stephen Rosenberg, "Flexibility in Installing Large Scale HRIS: New York City's Experience," *Personnel Administrator,* December 1985, pp. 39–46.

==

be entered into the system in order to be used. This information is usually entered from documents (such as an application form on an insurance report) into a computer terminal or a personal computer connected to a mainframe computer. Information can be typed in, digitally read—or scanned—from documents, loaded into the system from other computers, or retrieved from other machines connected to the computer (for example, a time clock linked to the computer).

A computerized HRIS is superior to manual systems in many respects. Since much of the information is automatically entered into the system, errors are less likely to occur. Also, the HRIS's ability to connect to other computers exposes it to data that would otherwise be too difficult or costly to obtain. For example, the U.S. government and several private organizations maintain databases—or lists of information on certain topics—that can be accessed by computers. If the human resource manager of a New York–based firm realized that its Georgia plant would be needing a new entry-level chemical engineer within six months, he or she could connect into a database that would report the number of persons graduating from college with a bachelor's degree in chemical engineering in the Southeast during the past year and their average starting salaries. Another advantage of an automated HRIS is backlog reduction. A well-designed HRIS will allow for more efficient input operation than a manual system could provide.

TRANSFORMATIONS

This portion of the system is most closely associated with the actual computer. It also usually includes the software, or the written instructions that tell the computer what to do, how to do it and when to do it. Computers and software for human resource information systems range from simple and inexpensive to complex and expensive. Many small firms can establish a functional HRIS to meet their needs with a personal computer and standard database and spreadsheet programs. Large multinational firms may need to use a mainframe computer running sophisticated custom-designed programs to meet their needs. Whichever route taken (or possibly something in between), each firm has an HRIS.

During the transformation stage, the input information is changed into something more useful to the organization. In information systems the computer and the software usually perform the transformation (input hours worked by an employee transformed into a calculation of gross pay, taxes, other deductions, and net pay, for example). We highlight this stage by continuing with the example of the New York firm needing a chemical engineer in Georgia. The manager's database inquiry may have provided the following information:

Number of chemical engineering graduates last year: 1,216.

Number of graduates in the Southeast: 432.

Number of chemical engineering graduates hired: 1,114.

Number of graduates hired in the Southeast: 516.

Average annual starting salary of chemical engineering graduates: $32,400.

Average annual starting salary in the Southeast: $34,800.

At this point, the information does not have any meaning for the manager. It is just a set of numbers that may or may not be significant for the firm. But suppose that the following information was in the computer concerning the new position:

Minimum budgeted annual salary: $22,000.

Maximum budgeted annual salary: $28,000.

The system would compare the salary information against the budgeted funds and be ready to produce a report on the situation. The report would indicate that the demand for chemical engineers in the Southeast is high and that the average annual starting salary is higher than the firm is currently willing to pay. This comparison of information constitutes the transformation process of the example. Of course, transformations can take many forms, whether it is the generation of a report, the calculation of a paycheck, or another function. Essentially, then, the transformation process changes the input into a new form that is more usable by the organization.

Again, the HRIS has several advantages over the manual system. The first advantage is speed and efficiency. The comparison of the database report to the budget may have taken days or weeks to perform with several employee hours involved in looking up and comparing the data. Another advantage is that many operations could be performed that would not have been—or could not have been—done in the past. The enormous power of a computer system may allow for activities such as a weekly comparison of absenteeism rates and worker productivity that would have been too expensive in the past.

OUTPUTS

The next element of the HRIS is the actual use of the newly processed material. In the above example, the output is the production of the report on the chemical engineer for the human resource manager, or the printing of the paycheck for the employee. These are new items whose distinct use has been created by the transformation. The information technology used in the output stage varies. It may involve material produced by printers, terminal screens, or any number of other devices. A well-designed HRIS will begin to show its worth as a DSS during this stage. The report on the potential problem in hiring a new chemical engineer for the Georgia plant alerts the manager to the fact that action must be taken or a decision made under the current guidelines. It should be noted that a decision support system does not make the decision for the manager but provides high-quality information necessary to make a good decision. For information to be of high-quality, it must meet the following five criteria:

Accurate. The information must correctly reflect what it reports. A 100 percent accuracy rate is not always needed; for example, less accuracy is needed when measuring employee age trends than in reporting EEO compliance.

Significant and relevant. The information provided must be usable, and to be usable, information must be available in a timely manner.

Comprehensive. Information should provide a complete picture of the problem and possibly offer alternative solutions.

Readable and visual impact. Information must be easily understandable; it should not be in lists or tables when it can be in graphs and charts.

Consistent in format. The same information should not come in several different forms when one standard is possible.[28]

These elements, if present, will help to ensure the usefulness of a firm's HRIS. But the question remains, For what do firms typically use their HRIS? The next section on feedback will examine this issue.

FEEDBACK

Feedback represents the managerial control element of a system. The feedback element helps to ensure that the outputs are the ones that the system seeks to achieve. Most human resource information systems report information on numerous human resource activities. The following brief list gives some of the more common HRIS functions and what is typically included within each function:

Wages and salaries: Company pay structure, planned raises, and wage histories.

Benefits: Company benefit packages, data on benefits used/accumulated.

EEO compliance: Information on minority hiring, recruitment, and advancement.

Labor relations: Labor contract data, grievance information, and worker seniority lists.

Training and development: Information on various training programs, employees who have received training, and planned training and development activities.

Health and safety: Information on company accidents and the individuals involved, costs of accidents, and other data required by government and insurance reports.

Management succession/career planning: Information on skills, specialties, accomplishments, and possible promotions.

HR planning: Projections of future needs.

Staffing: Job assignments and possible employee specialties.

HR data management: Basic employee information such as wages, social security numbers, and job titles.

Monitoring and reporting HR policy: A DSS component, helps organizations compare actual HR performance to desired HR performance.

General organizational data: Organization structure, management levels, and special functions information.

Demographics: Information about worker availability, education, ages.

External databases: Information on other companies or economic trends.[29]

This list is not comprehensive. Some firms' human resource information systems will have all this information and more. Other firms will only need part of this list to meet their needs. Now that we know what an HRIS is and what it does, we will examine how it can be used as a tool for corporate strategy.

TYING AN HRIS TO CORPORATE STRATEGY

When used properly, an HRIS can be a valuable tool for strategic planning and implementation. HRIS information should help decision makers better understand how human resource management can be a valuable competitive tool. It can be used to monitor morale, efficiency, and labor costs. It can be used to plan for the future human resource needs of the firm or to anticipate changes in the competitive environment. Its use is limited only by the extent to which the organization uses it to make strategic human resource decisions. Many firms are beginning to realize the value of using human resources to gain a strategic advantage—or a unique skill or competence that other firms do not have. This trend is likely to continue in the 1990s and beyond as firms attempt to cope with the challenges that lie ahead.

TYPES OF HRISs

As mentioned earlier, an HRIS can be as small as a single personal computer or as large as one or more mainframe computers connected to each other. Depending on the firm's structure and philosophy of management concerning centralization of resources and decisions, an HRIS can be configured in one of several different ways. The most typical types of HRIS configurations are concentrated, distributed, and independent, or a hybrid combination of the first three.[30] Their features are summarized in Exhibit 6.10.

A *concentrated* HRIS places all control and accountability in one centralized location. This placement gives management the greatest degree of control over the system and reduces costs but limits the flexibility of persons who need to use or to access the system's information.

A *distributed* HRIS features both a central facility and multiple other sites connected to the facility and/or each other. This feature still allows for a great deal of management control over the operation and design of the system while providing some flexibility for its users.

Next, an *independent* system features multiple systems that may or may not be connected to each other. This system provides the greatest amount of flexibility to individual users who can design systems to fit their specific needs. Management control is often minimal, and this can result in increased costs due to different users "reinventing the wheel," or creating a new system function that may already exist somewhere else in the organization.

A final HRIS design configuration is the *hybrid* approach. Many firms have found it useful to have certain elements of their HRIS centralized while allowing other functions to be left to the discretion of individual users. In certain circumstances, hybrid systems

■ **EXHIBIT 6.10**   **Features of Various HRIS Design Configurations**

CONCENTRATED

Centralized computer facility

Strong management control

Reduced costs

Limited user flexibility and access

DISTRIBUTED

Central facility with other sites connected

Strong management control

Increased user flexibility and access

INDEPENDENT

Multiple systems

Minimal management control

High user access and flexibility

High costs and redundancy of functions

HYBRID

A mix of system designs

Allows for centralization of certain functions and decentralization of others

Level of management control varies

Flexibility levels vary

Higher costs than other configurations

---

can be designed to provide the right mix of centralization-control and decentralization-autonomy within an organization, but the drawbacks to hybrid systems are that they tend to be very expensive since many different functions must be supported.

Once an organization has decided on the capabilities and configuration of its HRIS, it needs to ensure that its users actually know how to use and do use the system. This is the subject of the next section.

MAKING AN HRIS WORK

Ensuring that an HRIS works for an organization involves two key issues: (1) training users and (2) tying strategies and decisions.

Just as it is the role of a human resource department to provide training to members of an organization in certain areas, the department also must make sure that its employees and other users are properly trained to use the HRIS. Training often includes introducing users to new terms and familiarizing them with the capabilities of the system. Commercial systems developers often provide training to organizations. If the system is developed in-house, then the training function may fall to the department that created the system.

The second step in making an HRIS work is tying strategies and decisions. Even if users know how to use the system, it will not serve the organization if they cannot perceive any benefits from its use. As a result, a firm should make sure that the system serves necessary functions and provides information that will aid decision makers in achieving organization goals and strategies. If management believes that the HRIS is not being used effectively, an HRIS audit can be conducted. This entails examining company-specific reasons for having an HRIS, for gathering the data included, for the procedures used to access the data, for the reports it provides, and many other functional characteristics. Misuse, underuse, and potential use all are uncovered.[31]

PRIVACY AND THE HRIS

The final issue we will discuss concerning human resource information systems relates to the privacy of the information it contains. A prime reason for an organization to install an HRIS is to make it easier to find information. This ease of accessing information also has a downside: it is easier for unauthorized individuals to obtain private information (both company and personnel information) or for system users to accidentally disclose private information. Some laws exist that provide penalties for illegally obtaining certain kinds of employee information, but this does not always stop it from happening. An employee whose employer has accidentally divulged her performance appraisal history (when only her salary history was supposed to be released) to a bank loan division will not be any less upset if it was an accident. Organizations should make every attempt to provide safeguards against revealing private information—whether illegally or accidentally obtained. Protections such as system passwords, restricting access to confidential information on a need-to-know basis, and physically locking up files at the end of each day is just the first step in protecting the organization's reputation, its competitive position, and its legal liability.[32] Other issues that need to be considered include carefully defining and limiting user authorization, verifying that a user is actually the person authorized to use the system, encoding the data if it is transmitted and when it is stored, and using audit trails that provide a clear picture of who accessed what and when. By incorporating some or all of these ideas, the HRIS system should be secure.[33]

SUMMARY OF HUMAN RESOURCE INFORMATION SYSTEMS

In summary, it can be seen that a human resource information system serves a number of functions within an organization. An HRIS can help to reduce errors, increase efficiency, and reduce costs for an organization. As a decision support system, it can provide valuable information to decision makers and alert them to potential future problems or opportunities. The HRIS can be used as a strategic tool to help firms better plan and prepare for the future and reduce costs. The HRIS configuration also will reflect the organization's attitude about how human resource decisions are made, whether the HRIS is distributed, centralized, or independent. Of course, for an HRIS to be effective, users must be properly trained to use it, and it must be used by those whom it is intended to serve. Finally, a computer-based HRIS raises concerns about the privacy of information that it contains. Proper care must be taken to restrict access to the system to those individuals who have a legitimate need for its information.

MANAGEMENT GUIDELINES

So we see that human resource planning is an important and fundamental aspect to strategic human resource management. Such planning helps to establish a *proactive* approach to human resource management and to integrate human resources with corporate-level strategic planning. Furthermore, it helps to ensure that specific objectives, programs, policies, and activities of each human resource function are fully integrated.

While human resource planning is not easy—especially in large organizations—the use of computer models and other mathematical techniques helps to make it a more manageable process. The following management guidelines should be observed during the human resource planning process.

1. The human resource plan should be fully integrated with the overall organizational strategic plan, especially the firm's growth objectives.
2. Outside influences of economic conditions, technology, the labor market, and so on should be given adequate consideration when developing the human resource plan.
3. Changes in job design should be explicitly recognized in the plan; the plan should not assume that the structure of jobs in the future will be the same as that today.
4. The plan should explicitly realize that staffing levels should be based on increasing productivity in order for the firm to remain cost competitive. Just because a job becomes vacant does not mean that it should automatically be filled. Perhaps it should be eliminated or combined with another job.
5. Estimating future shortages or surpluses by job or skill category should use computer techniques and quantitative models as appropriate in order to better manage the process.
6. The specific operational objectives of each functional area in personnel should be integrated with the overall human resource plan.
7. Specific personnel programs, policies, and activities should be integrated with the specific functional objectives.
8. The human resource plan should involve significant line management input at all points in the process.
9. The human resource plan should be kept flexible and adaptable so it can change as conditions change.
10. From a strategic perspective, human resource costing should offer opportunities for the human resource professional.
11. Human resource information systems should be used as a decision support system and should alert managers to problems and/or opportunities.

QUESTIONS FOR REVIEW

1. What is a strategic human resource plan? Why is it important?
2. What impact do outside forces have on the strategic human resource plan (for example, labor market, technology, economic conditions, and so on)?
3. Why should the human resource plan be integrated with the overall organizational strategic plan? How can this integration be achieved?
4. Outline an overall model or procedure for developing a strategic human resource plan.
5. What are some quantitative techniques for estimating a surplus or shortage in a job category or occupation? Define each technique you list.
6. Why is it important to use the computer and quantitative techniques in human resource planning?

7. How can specific human resource functional objectives be linked with the human resource plan? Why is this linkage important?

8. Why should specific human resource programs, policies, and activities be linked with human resource objectives?

9. Why should a human resource plan be kept flexible?

10. Why should line managers be involved in helping to formulate a human resource plan?

11. What is human resource costing? How is human resource costing a strategic activity?

12. What is the primary purpose of a human resource information system? Discuss the typical HRIS functions and configurations.

CASE

POLAROID—HARD LANDING[34]

The day after Thanksgiving in 1948, a new camera went on sale at a Boston department store. Worried that it wouldn't sell well, nervous officials of the small company that made it cut the price from $95 to $89.75 at the last minute. They thought the 56 cameras they had produced might be gone by Christmas. The cameras sold out that day.

After struggling more than a decade, Polaroid Corporation, run by a young scientist named Edwin H. Land, had a big winner. Its instant camera developed photos on the spot, in 60 seconds. It was a technological marvel, and it captivated America.

As Polaroid's laboratories made one breakthrough after another in the 1950s and 1960s, the company grew rapidly. By the early 1970s, its stock was one of the highest highfliers, selling at more than 100 times annual earnings. Polaroid was more than just another success story; it was an icon to American ingenuity. Land exhorted his employees, "Do not undertake a program unless the goal is manifestly important and achievement is nearly impossible."

A BRIGHT BEGINNING

Polaroid was Land's life mission. By all accounts a genius, he quit Harvard University in 1932, one semester before graduating, to start a research lab. The name of the company, Polaroid, comes from the company's first product, the "polaroid filter", so named because its cellul*oid* filter *polar*ized light. Land developed his polarizing process, a feat which had long eluded scientists, by aligning microscopic crystals in a specific pattern on the celluloid, thus sharply reducing glare when light passed through it.

This discovery was put to use in the making of sunglasses and car headlights, and the revenues from these modest applications provided Land and his new company with money to support other research. Some critics believed that the company, in its early days, resembled a research project run by a group of graduate students.

During World War II, Polaroid survived on military work. It was also during this time that inspiration visited itself upon Polaroid and Edwin Land. While he was taking photos in 1943, Land's three-year-old daughter asked why she couldn't see the pictures right away. Land must have realized at that moment that the future looked very bright, indeed.

PERFECT TIMING

The instant camera took several years to develop and, ironically, didn't use Land's polarizing invention, but rather technologies from Polaroid's labs. But it was the right product at the right time. Americans were just becoming addicted to instant gratification. The baby boom had begun, and proud parents wanted to photograph their growing families. So what if instant cameras and film cost more? Postwar America was increasingly affluent.

Under Land, a savvy showman, Polaroid embraced live television to sell cameras. Entertainers such as Steve Allen took photos in front of the audience. "The essence of TV is dramatization. We had viewers holding their breath. Would it work? Every now and then, it didn't, but that was OK," says Joseph Daly, an executive at DDB Needham Worldwide ad agency, which had the Polaroid account for 30 years. "Never was a product more suited for TV."

It was a period of intense excitement. Many Polaroid employees worked six days a week and loved every minute. "It wouldn't be unusual to work around the clock a few days in a row. Nobody got too tired because it was exciting. We'd sleep on a lab table or office desk or on the floor," recalls Richard Young, a former executive who joined the company in the early 1950s as assistant research director. Polaroid hands held Land in awe, and for good reason. Land's 533 patents are second only to Thomas Edison's 1,093.

Polaroid sold its one millionth camera in 1956 and went public the next year. In 1960, sales hit $99.4 million; in 1970, they hit $444 million.

CROWNING ACHIEVEMENT

In 1972 came Land's crowning achievement: the pocket-sized SX-70 camera. He was featured on the covers of *Life* magazine

("A genius and his magic camera") and *Time* ("Here comes those great new cameras"). His Polaroid stock was valued at more than $700 million.

The SX-70 scored a great sales success, but Polaroid's stock plummeted because the huge expense of developing the camera held down profit growth. Adding to the pressure, Kodak ended Polaroid's monopoly by entering the instant-camera market in 1976. Polaroid promptly sued, charging patent infringement, but the case would not be decided in its favor until 1985.

Then came Land's greatest flop: Polavision instant movies, which were introduced in 1977. The camera cost too much at $700, didn't have sound, and took only 2 ½ minutes of film at a time. Land had the right idea, but the wrong technology. The Japanese had something better: video recorders, whose hours-long tapes could be reused and played back on a TV set.

Even worse, another Japanese product, klutz-proof 35mm cameras, took America by storm in the late 1970s and early 1980s. One-hour photo shops made instant cameras moot. From a high of $9.4 million in 1978, Polaroid's instant-camera sales plunged to $3.5 million in 1985. Also during those years, the company profits fared just as badly, skidding from a record $118.4 million on sales of $1.38 billion to $36.9 million on sales of $1.30 billion.

THE DOWNHILL SLIDE

In the late 1970s, things started to go wrong for Polaroid. The market matured while Polaroid stagnated. Its visionary founder lost his vision, and in 1982, Land retired from the company. Newer, better gadgets captured the public's fancy. In 1988 the company became a takeover target. Shamrock Holdings, Inc., a television and radio concern owned by the Roy E. Disney family, tried to buy Polaroid for $2.28 billion.

Polaroid's history is, in some ways, the latest twist in the decline of American industry. But unlike the auto and steel producers, Polaroid isn't an old-line manufacturer. It is one of the earliest postwar high-tech pioneers, a nonunion company lauded for enlightened employee relations. However, its heady growth has given way to hard times for similar reasons. In becoming big, the company became lethargic. The Japanese have emerged as industry innovators, in Polaroid's case, indirectly, with 35mm cameras and video cameras. Instead of adding jobs, Polaroid is cutting them.

MISSING CREATIVE SPARK

Worse yet, the company has lost its creative spark. "Polaroid hasn't had a breakthrough product for years," says Peter Wensberg, a former Polaroid executive. Despite lavish spending on research, efforts to diversify have been half-hearted, at best. "The problem for so many big companies is that they don't have an encore," says Thomas V. DiBacco, a professor of business history at American University. "No company can stay very long in a staid position. A lot of firms several

decades old, what do they do after they achieve success? It's one of the biggest dilemmas, trying to find the next stage."

Some other companies have had trouble finding the next stage. The sales of Avon Products, Inc., have languished in recent times. Its door-to-door sales strategy has faltered because more and more women work outside the home. Nike, Inc., stubbed its toe when smaller competitors managed to sell athletic shoes as fashion items.

IGNORING THE OUTSIDE WORLD

Polaroid's management was too inbred to notice that the world was changing, critics say. "Here's a company that had a field to itself for a long, long time. Many executives spent their entire careers on internal problems and technology. Some didn't consider it important to take a close look at the outside world," says Murray Swindell, a former marketing executive and one of many officials who departed in frustration in the early 1980s.

"Polaroid has been very myopic," comments Alex Henderson, an analyst at Prudential Securities Research. He says Polaroid's executives have failed to commercialize the good technology in its laboratories. "They limited their definition of what markets they're in. . . . It's the 'not invented here' syndrome," he adds. He suggests that Polaroid's imaging technology might be valuable in developing products for the computer publishing and medical-diagnostics markets, but only if the company enters joint ventures with companies offering expertise in those areas. "There's a lot of value in the Polaroid name," Swindell says. "There are any number of products we could have marketed . . . but we couldn't get Land's attention. He preferred to stick to instant photography."

The focus on basic research and development, and not on the exploitation of technology and markets, may be due, in great part, to the philosophy of Polaroid's founder, director of research, and chairman of the board, Edwin Land. Annual meetings contained little by way of sales figures and profit estimates. They were more like a show and tell for Land. He would use the meetings as an opportunity to showcase some of the more interesting developments of the various research teams. Many of these inventions and prospective products never reached production. And Polaroid is still characterized by many as a company that holds too tight a grip on its patents.

DIVERSIFICATION (GROWTH) OR RETRENCHMENT

The company now finds itself in a strategic bind with no easy way out. Some analysts and former executives think that the company should try to diversify, while others think that it should stick close to its instant photography line.

Diversification may help bolster losses suffered due to weak sales in Polaroid's principal photography business. Instant photography may have lost its magic, despite the introduction in 1986 of an improved, third-generation camera (Polaroid Spectra). Instant camera sales have slumped, while sales of 35mm cameras have increased dramatically. The 35mms "have automatic everything: auto focus, auto load, auto rewind, auto zoom," says Jack Crunkleton, the general manager of Camera Shop, Inc., an Eastern chain. "Affluent people still count on 35mm for better quality pictures. It will be hard for Polaroid to get back to the growth days."

Only recently has Polaroid entered the conventional film market, and this represents a major break from the notion that instant photography was the only photography worth pursuing. Polaroid itself argues that instant photography isn't just a quaint gimmick of the past, and it is working on a next-generation system that combines electronics with the use of heat to develop film. The technology could be used to make photographic prints of images stored electronically and initially viewed on computer or TV screens. "Instant imaging will become the dominant form (of photography), surpassing conventional film. . . . We do not want to be just 'that other form of imaging'; we want to be No. 1," a spokesperson says. But that won't be easy. "Japanese expertise in the imaging area will really put a lot of pressure on a company like Polaroid," says Young, the former executive.

Polaroid's chairman, president, and chief executive officer, I. MacAllister Booth, has decided to concentrate more fully on implementing Polaroid's core business strategy "through a more focused, aggressive approach to our markets and a streamlining of our operations." Manufacturing facilities will be consolidated, emerging markets in China, India, and Southeast Asia will be explored, product development will focus on speeding more profitable wares to market, and employees will be shifted to new jobs. And most likely, employment cuts will occur.

EMPLOYMENT CUTS

In 1988, Polaroid went through a major downsizing, eliminating 8,500 jobs. In the first quarter of 1995, Polaroid again announced that it would cut its workforce, this time by 5 percent, or 600 workers. Interestingly, in the midst of downsizing, Polaroid was rated one of the best 100 companies to work for. This may be due in great part to the progressive human resources practices of the company, which include a basic skills training program called Technology Readiness (TR), skill-based pay systems for workers, and an aggressive human resource staff training program. Only time will tell whether these adjustments can bring back some of the old magic to a company which, at times, must have seemed like a magical place in which to work.

QUESTIONS

1. What has been Polaroid's overall growth strategy? How has this affected its human resource planning and strategy?
2. Whose fault is it when employment falls as it has at Polaroid? What responsibility, if any, do operative employees have?
3. Why would employees work virtually around the clock as they did in the early days of Polaroid?
4. How does Polaroid's human resource plan in the 1950s, 1960s, and 1970s compare with its plan for the 1980s and 1990s? How do cutbacks and retrenchment change a human resource plan? Could these cuts have been avoided? If so, how?
5. What other companies do you know of that failed to mature to other growth stages with new products after the initial product played out? What causes this to happen?

ADDITIONAL READINGS

Anthony, William P. "Get to Know Your Employees: The Human Resource Information Systems." *Personnel Journal,* (April 1977), pp. 179–183.

Baker, C. Richard. "Personnel and Organization Structures Factors in Planning." *Managerial Planning,* (May–June 1977), pp. 26–28.

Bartholomew, David J., and Andrew F. Forbes. *Statistical Techniques for Manpower Planning.* New York: Wiley, 1979.

Branch, P., and E. Mansfield. "Firm's Forecasts of Engineering Employment." *Management Science* 28, February 1982, pp. 156–160.

Burack, E. H. "Corporate Business and Human Resource Planning Practices: Strategic Issues and Concerns." *Organization Dynamics* 15, Summer 1986, pp. 73–87.

Burack, E. H. "Human Resource Planning and Labor Market Information—Need for Change, Now." *Public Personnel Management* 7, September 1978, pp. 279–286.

Burack, E. H. *Planning for Human Resources.* Lake Forest, IL: Brace-Park Press, 1989.

Burack, E. H., and N. J. Mathys. *Human Resource Planning.* 2nd ed. Lake Forest, IL: Brace-Park Press, 1987.

Burack, Elmer. *Creative Human Resource Planning and Applications.* Englewood Cliffs, NJ: Prentice-Hall, 1988.

Butensky, C. F., and O. Harari. "Models vs. Reality. An Analysis of Twelve Human Resource Planning Systems." *Human Resource Planning* 6, no. 1 (1983), pp. 11–25.

Cascio, W., ed. *Human Resource Planning, Employment and Placement.* Washington D.C.: The Bureau of National Affairs, 1989.

Clark, Harry L., and Dona R. Thurston. *Planning Your Staffing Needs: A Handbook for Personnel Workers.* U.S. Civil Service Commission. Bureau of Policies and Standards (order through Superintendent of Documents). Washington D.C.: U.S. Government Printing Office, 1977, p. 360.

Courtney, R. S. "A Human Resource Plan That Helps Management and Employees Prepare for the Future." *Personnel* 63, no. 5 (May 1986), pp. 32–40.

Deckhard, N. S., and K. W. Lessey. "A Model for Understanding Management Manpower: Forecasting and Planning." *Personnel Journal* 54 (1975), pp. 169–173+.

Dill, W. R., D. P. Gavar, and W. C. Weber. "Models and Modeling for Manpower Planning." *Management Science* 13 (1966), pp. B142–B167.

Drandell, M. "A Composite Forecasting Methodology for Manpower Planning Using Objective and Subjective Criteria." *Academy of Management Journal* 18 (1975), pp. 510–519.

Gatewood, R. D., and B. W. Rockmore. "Combining Organizational Manpower and Career Development Needs: An Operational Human Resource Planning Model." *Human Resource Planning* 9, no. 3 (1986), pp. 81–96.

Gehrman, D. B. "Objective Based Human Resource Planning." *Personnel Journal* 60 (December 1981), pp. 942–946.

Greer, Charles R., and Daniel Armstrong. "Human Resource Forecasting and Planning: A State of the Art Investigation." *Human Resource Planning* 3, no. 2 (April 1980), pp. 67–78.

Henderson, J. C., et al. "Integrated Approach for Manpower Planning in the Service Sector." *Omega* 10, no. 1 (1982), pp. 61–73.

Hill, A. W. "Strategic Human Resource Planning: How to Succeed." *Management Review* 75 (November 1986), pp. 79–80.

Hollmann, R. W. "Strategic Planning." *Personnel Administrator,* March 1989, pp. 97–100.

Hopkins, D. S. P. "Models for Affirmative Action Planning and Evaluation." *Management Science* 26 (October 1980), pp. 994–1006.

Kanter, Rosabeth M. "Frontiers for Strategic Human Resource Planning and Management." *Human Resource Management* 22 (Spring/Summer 1983), pp. 9–21.

Kerr, Clark, and Paul D. Staudohan, eds. *Economics of Labor in Industrial Society.* San Francisco: Jossey-Bass, 1986.

Klein, E. "Determinants of Manpower Utilization and Availability." *International Labour Review* 122 (March-April 1983), pp. 183–195.

McAvoy R., and D. M. Hubsch. "Manpower Planning and Corporate Objectives: Two Points of View." *Management Review* 70 (August 1981), pp. 55–59.

Manzini, A. O., and J. D. Gridley. "Human Resource Planning for Mergers and Acquisitions: Preparing for the 'People Issues' That Can Prevent Merger Synergies." *Human Resource Planning* 9, no. 2 (1986), pp. 51–57.

Miller, E. L., S. Beechler, B. Bhatt, and R. Nath. "The Relationship between the Global Strategic Planning Process and the Human Resource Management Function." *Human Resource Planning* 9, no. 2 (1986), pp. 9–29.

Mirengoff, Wm. *CETA, Accomplishments, Problems, Solutions: A Report by the Bureau of Social Science Research, Inc.* Kalamazoo, MI: W. E. Upjohn Institute for Employment Research, 1982.

Morlock, J. "Impact and Implications of Changing Federal Manpower Policy on the Administration and Implementation of Social Manpower Programs." *Labor Law Journal* 32 (August 1981), pp. 514–518.

Morrison, M. H. "The Aging of the US Population: Human Resource Implications." *Monthly Labor Review* 106 (May 1983), pp 13–19.

Muczyk, J. P. "Comprehensive Manpower Planning." *Managerial Planning* 30 (November/December 1981), pp. 36–41.

Niehaus, Richard. *Computer-Assisted Human Resources Planning.* New York: Wiley, 1979.

Niehaus, R. J., ed. *Strategic Human Resource Applications.* The Philadelphia Conference proceedings. 1987.

Nkomo, S. M. "Human Resource Planning and Organizational Performance: On Exploratory Analysis." *Strategic Management Journal* 8 (1987), pp. 387–392.

Nkomo, S. M. "The Theory and Practice of HR Planning: The Gap Still Remains." *Personnel Administrator* 31 (August 1986), pp. 71–84.

Rothwell, W. J., and Kazanas, H. C. *Strategic Human Resources Planning and Management.* Englewood Cliffs, NJ: Prentice-Hall, 1989.

Rush, I. C. "Strategic Planning for Human Resources." *Business Quarterly* 46 (Summer 1981), pp. 40–43.

Russ, C. F., Jr. "Manpower Planning Systems." *Personnel Journal* 61 (January 1982), pp. 40–45.

Scarborough, N., and T. W. Zimmerer. "Human Resources Forecasting: Why and Where to Begin." *Personnel Administration* 27 (May 1982), pp. 55–61.

Smith, W. J., and F. A. Zeller. "Impact of Federal Manpower Policy and Programs on the Employment and Earnings Experiences of Special Problem Groups of the Unemployed: A Critical Historical Overview." *Labor Law Journal* 32 (August 1981), pp. 518–528.

Strauss, J. S., and E. H. Burack. "The Human Resource Planning Professional: A Challenge in Change." *Human Resource Planning* 6, no. 1 (1983), pp. 1–9.

Subramaniam, S. "Engineering Manpower Planning in an Airline." *Long Range Planning,* August 1977, pp. 56–60.

Sylvia, Robert A. "TOSS: An Aerospace System That's GO for Manpower Planning." *Personnel,* January-February 1977, pp. 56–64.

Thomsen, D. J. "Keeping Track of Managers in a Large Corporation." *Personnel* 53 (November 1976), pp. 23–30.

Ulrich, David. "Human Resources Planning as a Competitive Edge." *Human Resource Planning* 9, no. 2 (1986), pp. 41–50.

Valliant, Richard, and George Milkovich. "Comparison of Semi-Markov and Markov Models in a Personnel Forecasting Application." *Decision Sciences,* April 1977, pp. 465–477.

Zanakis, S. H., and M. W. Maret. "Markovian Goal Programming Approach to Aggregate Manpower Planning." *Journal of the Operational Research Society* 32 (January 1981), pp. 55–63.

NOTES

1. Greg Matusky, "Rebirth! Businesses Find New Life as Franchises," *Success,* Volume 40, September, 1993, pp. 64–71; Buck Brown, "How the Cookie Crumbled at Mrs. Fields: Company Seeks to Revive Itself by Diversifying," *The Wall Street Journal,* January 26, 1989, p. B1; "Mrs. Fields Inc.," *The Wall Street Journal,* February 15, 1989, p. B10; Dianne E. Kirrane and Peter R. Kirrane, "Managing by Expert Systems," *HRMagazine,* March 1990, pp. 37–39; and Richard Koenig, "NutraSweet Allies with Mrs. Fields for Diet Food Line," *The Wall Street Journal,* September 19, 1990, p. B6.

2. Charles Barwick, "Eight Ways to Assess Succession Plans," *HRMagazine,* May 1993, pp. 109–114.

3. Brenton R. Schlender, "Shedding His Shyness, John Scully Promotes Apple—and Himself," *The Wall Street Journal,* August 18, 1988, pp. 1, 8.

4. Eddie Smith, "Strategic Business Planning and Human Resources: Part I," *Personnel Journal* 61, no. 8, August 1982, pp. 606–610.

5. Elmer H. Burach, "Corporate Business and Human Resources Planning Practices: Strategic Issues and Concerns," *Organization Dynamics* 15, Summer 1986, pp. 73–87.

6. Richard P. Nathan, "Clearing Up the Confusion over Block Grants," *The Wall Street Journal,* November 3, 1981, p. 3.

7. Michele Galen and Ann Therese Palmer, "Taking Adversity out of Diversity," *Business Week,* January 31, 1994, pp. 54–55.

8. Russell Mitchell and Judith Dobrzynski, "Jack Welch: How Good a Manager?" *Business Week,* December 14, 1987, pp. 92–103.

9. Kevin Kelly, "The New Soul of John Deere," *Business Week,* January 31, 1994, pp. 64–66.

10. Thomas M. Hunt and George Stalk, "Working Better and Faster with Fewer People," *The Wall Street Journal,* May 15, 1987, p. 14.

11. Robert J. Koyma, "Low Cost CAD/CAM Units: Major Growth Area?" *Management Information Systems Weekly,* June 3, 1981, p. 4.

12. K. M. Rowland and M. G. Sovereign, "Markov Chain Analysis of Internal Manpower Supply," *Industrial Relations* 9, 1969, pp. 88–89.

13. P. F. Buller and W. R. Maki, "A Case History of a Manpower Planning Model," *Human Resource Planning* 4, 1981, pp. 129–138; and J. A. Hooper and R. F. Catalanello, "R. F. Markov Analysis Applied to Forecasting Technical Personnel," *Human Resource Planning* 4, 1981, pp. 41–45.

14. William P. Anthony, "Get To Know Your Employee—The Human Resource Information System," *Personnel Journal,* April 1977, pp. 179–183, 202.

15. Gorg L. Lilian and Ambar G. Rao, "A Model for Manpower Management," *Management Science* 21, no. 12, 1975, pp. 1447–1457.

16. James A. Parsons, "Manpower Allocation to Meet Cyclic Requirements," *Journal Systems Management* 27, no. 6, 1976, pp. 26–27.

17. Milton Drandell, "A Composite Forecasting Methodology for Manpower Planning Utilizing Objective and Subjective Criteria," *Academy of Management Journal* 18, no. 3, 1975, pp. 510–519.

18. G. A. Keenay, R. W. Morgan, and K. H. Ray, "An Analytical Model for Company Manpower Planning," *Operational Research Quarterly* 28, no. 4, 1977, pp. 983–995.

19. Andre L. Nelberq, Andrew H. Van de Ven, and David H. Gustafson, *Group Techniques for Program Planning: A Guide to Nominal Group and Delphi Processes* (Glenview, IL: Scott-Foresman, 1975).

20. R. C. Woodruff, Jr., "Human Resource Accounting," *Canadian Chartered Accountant* 97, 1970, pp. 156–161.

21. R. L. Brummet, E. Flamhol, and W. Pyle, "Human Resource Accounting—A Challenge for Accountants," *Accounting Review* 43, 1968, pp. 217–224.

22. "The Personnel/Human Resources Department: 1989–1990," *SHRM-BNA Survey #54,* June 28, 1990, p. 10 (Washington, DC: Bureau of National Affairs).

23. Linda Thornburg, "Accounting for Knowledge," *HRMagazine,* October 1994, pp. 50–56; Stephanie Losee, "Your Company's Most Valuable Asset: Intellectual Capital," *Fortune,* October 3, 1994, pp. 68–74.

24. Wayne F. Cascio, *Costing Human Resources: The Financial Impact of Behavior in Organizations,* 2nd ed. (Boston: PWS-Kent, 1987), p. 5.

25. Ibid., p. 6.

26. Ibid., pp. 147–170.

27. Sandra E. O'Connell, "Planning and Setting Up a New HRIS: Part 1," *HRMagazine,* February 1994, pp. 36–40; Robert W. Zmud, *Information Systems in Organizations* (Glenview, IL: Scott-Foresman, 1983), pp. 65–67.

28. Kirk J. Anderson, "Putting the 'I' in HRIS," *Personnel,* September 1988, pp. 12–24.

29. Michael L. Jenkins and Gayle Lloyd, "How Corporate Philosophy and Strategy Shape the Use of HR Information Systems," *Personnel*, May 1985, p. 29; and Alfred J. Walker, "New Technologies in Human Resource Planning," *Human Resource Planning,* November 4, 1986, pp. 149–151.

30. Robert D. Marceluk, "Accountability and Control of Human Resource Information," *Personnel Administrator,* July 1985, pp. 24–26.

31. Joe Pasqualetto, "New Competencies Define the HRIS Manager's Future Role," *Personnel Journal,* January 1993, pp. 91–99; Joanne Wisniewski, "The Needs-Based HRIS Audit," *HRMagazine,* September 1991, pp. 61–64.

32. Helen LaVan, Nicholas J. Mathys, and Wayne Hockwarter, "Insecurity in Numbers," *Computers in Personnel,* Spring 1989, pp. 51–53.

33. Lynn Adams, "Securing Your HRIS in a Microcomputer Environment," *HRMagazine,* February 1992, pp. 56–61.

34. Richard L. Bunning, "Models for Skill-Based Pay Plans," *HRMagazine,* February 1992, pp. 62–64; Barbara Carton, "Polaroid to Cut Work Force by up to 5%, Take Charge; Operating Loss Is Likely," *The Wall Street Journal,* February 6, 1995, p. 7A; Marilyn W. Daudelin, "HR Development at Polaroid," *Personnel Journal,* February 1991, pp. 56–63; Mary Ann Castronovo Fusco, "Employment Relations Programs," *Employment Relations Today,* Spring 1989, pp. 89–92; Ronald Grover, "Maybe I'll Raid You—And Maybe I Won't," *Business Week,* September 5, 1988, p. 25; K. H. Hammonds, "Why Polaroid Must Remake Itself Instantly," *Business Week,* September 19, 1988, pp. 66–72; Lawrence Ingrossio, "How Polaroid Went from Highest Flier to Takeover Target," *The Wall Street Journal,* August 12, 1988, pp. 1, 16; and Lawrence Ingrossio, "Kodak's Motion Denied by Judge in Polaroid Case," *The Wall Street Journal,* August 12, 1988, p. 16.

CHAPTER 7

STRATEGIES FOR RECRUITMENT, SELECTION, AND PLACEMENT

Recruiting and selecting the right employees have always been a challenge for managers. Current economic and demographic factors of the labor force will undoubtedly increase the challenges managers face. During the next decade, the overall growth in the workforce will slow down as fewer young people enter the workforce and the employees already working begin to grow older. Approximately 83 percent of new entrants into the labor force will be minorities, immigrants, and women.[1] The diversity among workers will call for new strategies and approaches to recruitment and selection. In addition, jobs will require increasingly skilled workers. This chapter examines recruiting and selection strategies for the 1990s.

CHAPTER OBJECTIVES

After studying this chapter, you should be able to
1. Discuss the recruiting methods available to organizations.
2. Understand the selection process organizations use to choose future employees.
3. Explain strategies for effective recruitment and selection.
4. Discuss how an organization's strategy can affect its recruitment and selection process.
5. Explain how an organization should select staff to support implementation of its strategy.

CASE

XEROX MANAGES WORKER DIVERSITY[2]

With the rapidly shifting demographic makeup of the workforce, U.S. corporations are facing an ever increasing diversity of workers. By the year 2000, only 32 percent of the workers entering the labor force will be Caucasian non-Hispanics, a drop from 44 percent of the workforce in 1986. The biggest growth will be seen in the number of women entering the workforce (51 percent), followed by Hispanics, the fastest growing minority, which will have a 15 percent growth rate. Blacks will account for 13 percent of all new entering employees, while Asian and other minorities are expected to account for 6 percent of all new workers by the end of the century.

ENCOURAGING AND PROMOTING MINORITIES

The Xerox corporation has acknowledged the shifting makeup of its workforce and believes that the proper management of worker diversity will become a necessity in the future. David Kearns, CEO of Xerox, states that "we have to manage diversity right now and much more so in the future. American business will not be able to survive if we do not have a large diverse workforce because those are the demographics." Kearns goes on to state, "If you fail to include women and minorities, you've restricted yourself from a major part of the labor pool, which economically doesn't make sense. Beyond that, one of the major advantages you get out of having women and minorities in business is that they bring in a whole new set of ideas. Right now, American business needs new ideas and thought if we're going to compete on a worldwide basis."

Xerox has supported its beliefs by encouraging and promoting minorities into fast-track management positions. While the average percentage of minorities in managerial positions across U.S. firms was 9 percent in 1989 (based on figures from the Equal Employment Opportunity Commission), 16 percent of Xerox managers are minorities. Xerox also exceeded the industry average of 12 percent by filling 18 percent of its professional positions with minorities.

TRAINING IS KEY TO SUCCESS

Simply recruiting and hiring a diverse workforce does not guarantee success. The key to Xerox's success comes from the implementation of training programs that foster support and cooperation among minorities. "You can't just hire large numbers of women and minorities and think it'll work," Kearns cautions. "You need a process to identify the right experiences people will need to move ahead. You need to have training programs for your managers that talk about managing diversity. What are the issues of managing minorities and women, because there are things that are different."

Xerox began to encourage the development and management of diversity during the 1970s when the managers of Xerox's affirmative action program looked at the careers of 10 top executives to determine which key position helped them the most in their careers. The result of the study showed that the pivotal position for success was the first-level sales manager. The managers of the affirmative action program also discovered that all 500 first-level sales manager positions were held by Caucasian employees.

ENCOURAGING AFFIRMATIVE ACTION

Xerox started to encourage affirmative action by basing 20 percent of a manager's performance review on the manager's success with human resource management, which included affirmative action. The performance program has met with some resistance from Caucasian managers. As Theodore Payne, Xerox's affirmative action manager, states, "There are some . . . who just could not adjust."

To avoid upsetting the informal structures already established, Xerox did not try to dismantle the Caucasian male "old boy" network within Xerox; instead, the company encouraged the growth of networking. The minority caucuses met on their own to develop advancement strategies. A major change sought and won by the caucuses was to allow the posting of "stepping stone" job openings, which was a major breakthrough since a number of major U.S. corporations still refuse to implement this policy.

By selecting the best people from all minority groups, Xerox believes that it is better prepared than most other U.S. firms to compete in an ever increasing global market. As a top marketing executive at Xerox states, "We'd like to be able to stand up and say that we've done that [beaten international competition] as a multicultural company . . . I think that will serve as a beacon for the rest of American industry."

STRATEGIC CHOICES

Diversity is only one of many issues currently facing U.S. corporations as they attempt to recruit, select, and place the best individuals in available jobs. Other issues include locating qualified workers, developing selection procedures that treat all applicants equally, and using temporary or part-time workers to help manage costs. Because all of these issues should be considered when managers develop their recruitment, selection, and placement plans, managers have to make a number of choices regarding their recruiting and selection strategies. These strategies are outlined below:

1. An organization can make a strategic choice to *focus recruiting efforts on minorities and women.*
2. Organizations can choose to "*make*" or "*buy*" their employees (that is, hire less skilled workers or hire skilled workers and professionals).
3. Organizations make strategic decisions regarding the *budget allocated* for recruiting and selecting employees.
4. An organization can make a strategic choice to explore *untapped labor sources.*
5. Organizations make strategic decisions regarding the *technological sophistication* of their recruiting and selection devices.
6. An organization can choose the extent to which *internal versus external recruiting methods* are used (that is, recruiting within the organization or outside the organization).

RECRUITING EFFORTS FOCUSED ON MINORITIES AND WOMEN

The changing demographics of the workforce will undoubtedly affect recruiting and selection efforts in the current decade. Organizations can choose to recruit minorities and women actively as Xerox did, or maintain the status quo. Managers are acknowledging that a different set of incentives will be needed to hire and train future employees. Women will represent the largest percentage of new workers. Given that many of these women will have caretaker responsibilities for their children or elderly relatives, flexible work schedules, job sharing, and child-care facilities and/or support will be crucial to them. Managers need to recognize that if it is acceptable for male executives to take time off from work to golf, it also should be acceptable for women to take time off to attend parent-child conferences at school. Even though the activities engaged in differ, the benefit to the individual worker should be the same.[3] Many employers are already implementing programs designed to attract and retain women. Recently, an agreement with the National Treasury Employees Union (NTEU) has made it possible for the Internal Revenue Service to offer affordable, on-site child care at eight IRS offices. According to Greg Denier, the NTEU director of research, employee response has been "overwhelmingly favorable."[4]

Minorities and immigrants are also getting more attention from company recruiters. Traditionally, these groups have not received the level of education and training necessary to enter technical fields. Mentoring programs and internships allow employers to sponsor students through college with the possibility of hiring them. In addition, employers are providing training to minority and immigrant workers to develop an educated workforce that will remain on the job. Aetna Life & Casualty offers courses on basic writing skills and job-specific training. Thus far, 40 of the 41 recruits are still working at Aetna.[5] Finally, some firms are recruiting minorities even when no openings exist. Because it is often difficult to locate the right minority candidate when a job opening does exist, having a premade list of qualified applicants will reduce the pressure felt by recruiters when an opening does occur.[6]

MAKE OR BUY DECISION

Organizations can make a strategic decision to hire less-skilled labor and invest in training and educational programs, or they can recruit and hire skilled labor and professionals. Essentially, this is the "make" (hire less-skilled workers) or "buy" (hire skilled workers and professionals) decision. Managers who recruit only skilled labor and professionals can expect to pay considerably more for these employees.

The advantage to hiring skilled labor and professionals is that they possess the necessary skills to begin working immediately and require little training. However, the amount of money it might take to attract skilled labor and professionals may outweigh the benefits. In addition, many organizations may prefer to conduct their own training programs to ensure some measure of standardization. For example, IBM has an elaborate training program designed to promote not only skill acquisition but also socialization and commitment to the organization.

BUDGET

In 1988, a survey of 4,000 U.S. companies conducted by the Professional Employment Research Council (PERC) revealed that only 35 percent of the companies responding measured the cost of hiring an employee. In 1989, that figure fell to 33 percent.[7] If most firms do not attempt to determine their hiring costs, they are not in a position to control these costs rationally. Organizations can make a strategic decision to control hiring costs only after determining the approximate cost per hire. Information on employee recruitment, selection, orientation, and start-up (such as training) costs is imperative if managers choose to develop and manage cost-effective programs. The costs associated with employee replacement in organizations should also be figured into the cost per hire.

HR CHALLENGE

Keeping the Competitive Edge

James McElwain is vice-president for personnel resources and education for NCR and the winner of the 1989 American Society of Personnel Administrators Award of Professional Excellence for Human Resource Management. McElwain argues that "NCR is in a highly competitive industry. We need to keep a competitive edge and I believe that people differences give us that competitive edge. Having top people and productive people working for NCR is an advantage . . . We have to seek a competitive advantage in the people we hire."

One of the programs at NCR, called project 6K, is designed to improve the way that NCR hires new employees. The goal is to use standardized procedures to recruit the best college students for entry-level positions. Project 6K has a numerical system for

colleges and universities. Schools are given a rating between one (the highest rating) and four (the lowest rating). In the number one category, students with a grade point average of 3.2 or higher are selected. At a school ranked in the number four category, only students with grade point averages of 3.4 or higher are considered. McElwain is quick to point out that even schools rated number four are still very good schools.

The jobs available at NCR are generally entry-level positions. As jobs become open, NCR promotes from within. McElwain emphasizes that NCR's Project 6K strategy is to hire the very best entry-level employees, retain them, and promote from within.

SOURCE: Adapted from B. Leonard, "High-Winning Game Plan," *Personnel Administrator,* September 1989, pp. 58–62.

The process of recruiting can be very expensive. According to a survey by the Employment Management Association, the cost of hiring a salaried employee in 1990 was between $4,000 and $4,500. However, when this figure includes relocation costs, processing time, agency fee payments, and other costs, it can rise to over $27,000.[8] Even though these costs seem high, they are only about 10 percent of what Japanese firms pay to hire a new college graduate.[9] The $40,000 price tag per candidate seems worth it to Japanese firms because once hired, the individual will more than likely stay until he or she retires 30 years later.

Organizations with very low turnover and growth may be less concerned about cost-effective hiring due to the infrequency of hiring. However, organizations that experience high turnover would be very concerned about controlling these hiring costs.

Finally, managers must consider geographical factors when budgeting for recruiting and selection. Some areas may have a severe shortage of workers, an intense competition for qualified applicants, or a high cost of living that necessitates more extensive recruiting methods, more incentives (such as benefits), and a higher salary to attract qualified workers.

UNTAPPED LABOR SOURCES

Organizations can make a strategic decision to tap into less traditional labor pools. Three labor sources receiving the attention of recruiters recently are the handicapped, the homeless, and welfare recipients. Handicapped workers, also called *physically challenged* workers, have not been pursued seriously as potential hires by many organizations. However, the fact that 68 percent of handicapped persons are employable and *want* to work, coupled with the limited number of applicants for entry-level, low skilled jobs, has made recruiters aware of this valuable employee resource.[10] Although special accommodations are often needed (see Chapter 4 on equal employment opportunity), handicapped workers offer organizations a plethora of knowledge, skills, and abilities.

HR CHALLENGE

From Welfare to Work Force

Many Americans erroneously assume that welfare recipients simply do not want to work. We can open any newspaper to the classified advertisement section and locate numerous ads placed by companies searching for workers. It would seem that anyone on welfare wanting a job should simply answer some of those countless ads. If this were the case, however, the American Works Company, located in Hartford, Connecticut, and New York City would be out of business.

American Works has been extremely successful tapping into a labor force typically ignored by the business world. By exclusively recruiting and training welfare recipients for entry-level positions, American Works gets people off of welfare and into the workplace, saves the taxpayers money, and provides hiring employers with a valuable tax credit. If the social benefits of helping welfare recipients find jobs were included, American Works' profits would be even greater.

The crucial element in the American Works' approach to finding jobs for those on welfare who want to work is its focus on assimilating the worker into the system. American Works teaches basic interviewing and job skills, as well as proper English. It also acts as mediator between the applicant and employer during a four-month trial period while the employee is adjusting to the new job. Roughly 70 percent of the employees trained by American Works are retained by the companies and almost 90 percent stay in the job past the first year. Overall, companies are pleased with their new employees, stating that compared to other applicants, they are better prepared to accept responsibility, and are more motivated and ready to work.

Chrysalis, a Los Angeles–based assistance agency, extends this service to the homeless. By offering full-service help that includes job search training, interview rehearsals, hygiene items, haircuts, interviewing clothes, and a place to receive mail and phone calls, Chrysalis has helped more than 400 homeless people find jobs. The officials at Chrysalis use statistics to show how effective their services are. For example, it spends $350 per client to help him or her find work. Welfare would pay the same person $343 a month for *not* finding a job. For every 100 people Chrysalis places, they will earn $1,152,000 rather than costing the taxpayers $411,600.

SOURCES: Adapted from "From Welfare to Work Force," *HRMagazine,* July 1991, pp. 36–38; "Homeless + Employment = Ex-Homeless," *Management Review,* June 1993, p. 7.

Another labor source that has been left untapped is the homeless. Although still in experimental stages, Days Inns successfully placed numerous homeless people into jobs. Homeless workers are offered a hotel room for a small fee, along with wages. Days Inns hopes to fill more vacant positions and offer homeless individuals a new beginning.[11] Finally, using recruiting efforts to target welfare recipients may be beneficial for the organization as well as society in general.

TECHNOLOGICAL SOPHISTICATION

Organizations make strategic decisions regarding the methods used in recruiting and hiring. Often these decisions are influenced by available technology. The proliferation of computers has made it possible for employers to scan national and international applicant qualifications. Computerized resume scanning and tracking systems have made finding the right person for the job much easier. Although each is unique, these systems share common features. First, clerks scan resumes into the system. These clerks are also responsible for verifying the accuracy of the scanning process and for requesting a computer-generated "thank you letter" to each applicant. When managers need an employee, they provide a recruiter with the requirements of the job and the recruiter searches the database using keywords. If the pool is too small, requirements are relaxed; if it is too large, requirements are tightened (e.g., number of years experience could be decreased or increased). Use of such systems has many advantages. Companies can reduce their

HR CHALLENGE

Recruiting a CEO for Ben & Jerry's

Instead of using the normal channels of recruitment, Ben and Jerry, the founders of Ben & Jerry's Homemade, Inc., decided to run a contest. To enter, contestants were asked to send in an essay of 100 words entitled "Why I Would be a Great CEO for Ben & Jerry's" and a lid from their favorite flavor of Ben and Jerry's ice cream to the following address:

Yo! I'm Your CEO
c/o Ben & Jerry's
Box 240
Waterbury, VT 05676

Responses were plentiful (more than 23,000 by the end of the second month) and as creative as the campaign. For example, one woman sent her essay in a shoe and noted that she was trying to get her foot in the door. Another man sent in a Superman cape and kryptonite rocks with an explanation that he had been downsized from a major metropolitan newspaper and

was in search of a job. Yet another suggested a few new flavors for Ben and Jerry to consider: Pasture Pleasure and Utter Delight.

Such a recruiting stunt reflects the culture at Ben and Jerry's. The founders do what they want, what they feel is right, and they do it well. For example, they support ecological efforts by donating a portion of their sales on Rain Forest Crunch to the Save the Rain Forest campaign, and they promote peace on earth by selling Peace Pops. Obviously, one major quality that the winner of the contest will have to possess is the ability to fit into and continue this culture. Perhaps it will be Rogert Staub, who sent in an 8 foot × 4 foot postcard with a picture of a Holstein cow (Ben & Jerry's logo) painted on one side and his essay on the other. The stamp cost him $62.

SOURCES: Adapted from Ellen Neuborne, "Ben & Jerry's Job Contest Kicks Off," *The Wall Street Journal,* June 15, 1994, p. 2B; Larry A. Strauss, "Ben & Jerry's Contestants Come in All Flavors," *The Wall Street Journal,* August 29, 1994, p. 5B.

---

reliance on recruitment agencies by generating their own applicant pools. Assessing resumes by computer is more efficient and faster than manual assessment, so it speeds the hiring process. Finally, unsolicited resumes are no longer viewed as a source of irritation but as a valuable resource.[12] Although impersonal, computers have given employers and job applicants a wide scope of options in the initial screening stage. For example, some firms have implemented an on-line application system. When an applicant arrives at the company for an interview or simply walks in to inquire about openings, he or she is asked to complete a computer application. The application program greets the applicant and one by one feeds questions to him or her. Once all of the questions have been answered, a copy of the application is printed for the applicant to sign. The benefits of such a system are obvious. First, the form is easy to read and all sections are completed. Next, since the information is already in the computer, it can be used by various other human resource systems such as resume scanning systems or skills databases. However, because the system does require some degree of computer literacy on the part of the applicant, it may not be appropriate for every position or every applicant.[13]

Job applicants have begun sending videotapes of themselves to companies (and colleges) in hope of gaining access. Videotaping enables the job applicant to contact a number of organizations without the time and expense of travel. Managers are able to conduct an initial screening of applicants based on the videotapes. Some organizations have developed their own videotapes as a recruiting device.

Finally, the newest method of recruiting, "telerecruiting," has become increasingly popular. Telerecruiting allows the screening process to be done by telephone. Large organizations have begun to form telerecruiting departments, which screen job applicants, and put their resume information on a computer.[14] This procedure has enabled managers to interview and hire new employees more quickly. Employers who do not have the staff or budget to develop a telerecruiting department can get assistance from outside services that do the telerecruiting for them.

INTERNAL VERSUS EXTERNAL RECRUITING METHODS

Internal recruiting methods include posting position openings, distributing memos within the organization, and searching organizational databases for a match between the skills required to perform the job and the skills held by current employees. This method of recruiting looks to internal sources to fill positions and encourages promotions from within. External recruiting methods include advertising position openings in newspapers and magazines and looking to external sources to fill positions. Whether managers choose internal or external methods depends on the degree to which the organization's strategy encourages promotions and transfers from within the organization. Recruiting from within can lead to job satisfaction and motivation if employees see new career opportunities available. In addition, filling positions with existing employees ensures, to a large extent, that these employees are socialized as to the organization's culture or "personality." However, external recruiting helps to bring new ideas and approaches to the organization. In the university system, faculty positions are almost always filled by using external recruiting methods and sources. In academia, new ideas and approaches are encouraged; thus, Ph.D students rarely become part of the faculty at the school where they receive their degree.

RECRUITING METHODS

Most job openings are filled with people from within the organization, and entry-level positions are the most likely to be filled by external sources.[15] Methods of internal recruiting include job posting, skills inventories, job bidding, and referrals. Methods of external recruiting include school and college recruiting, advertising, and using employment agencies and executive search firms. The advantages and disadvantages of internal versus external recruitment are depicted in Exhibit 7.1. Each of these methods will be discussed in the following section.

EXHIBIT 7.1   **Internal versus External Recruitment: Advantages and Disadvantages**

INTERNAL RECRUITMENT

Advantages	Disadvantages
1. Employees familiar with the organization.	1. Political infighting for promotions.
2. Lower recruiting and training costs.	2. Inbreeding.
3. Increase morale and motivation of employees.	3. Morale problem for those not promoted.
4. Probability of success due to better assessment of abilities and skills.	

EXTERNAL RECRUITMENT

Advantages	Disadvantages
1. New ideas and approaches.	1. Lack of "fit" between employee and organization.
2. "Clean slate" regarding company-specific experiences from which to build.	2. Lowered morale and commitment of employees.
3. Level of knowledge and skill not available in current organization.	3. Increased adjustment period.

INTERNAL RECRUITING

JOB POSTING

Many positions can be filled as a result of posting the job opening on bulletin boards or announcing the opening in the company newsletter. A job posting procedure enables employees to strive for a better position within the company. Notices of position openings should include all important information about the job (for example, brief job description, the education or training required, the salary, and whether it is full- or part-time). An example of a job posting document used in a hospital is provided in Exhibit 7.2.

Some firms have turned to computers to make their job-posting efforts more fruitful. For example, when Household International (HI) restructured itself from three core businesses (consumer finance, banking, and insurance) to 10 distinct business entities, it wanted to transfer employees laterally across and within businesses as well as promote from within. To accomplish this, HI developed an electronic job-posting system based on a skills inventory database. All employees who wish to participate complete questionnaires about themselves, which include items concerning relocation willingness and preferences as well as training and educational backgrounds. They then select 3 skills from a list of 60 that best represent their functional skills. When a position needs to be filled, human resource managers search the database for a match between the skills of the individuals in the database and the skills required for the job. Employees who are found to possess the needed skills are then contacted to see whether they are interested in the position. However, an employee does not have to sit back and wait to be approached. Instead, he or she can use the computer software to peruse the available openings at HI throughout the United States. If an opening looks attractive, the employee sends an electronic application to the appropriate contact.[16]

Although posting jobs can be an efficient method of recruiting, a number of problems have been associated with it. For example, job posting can lead to conflict if an employee perceives he or she is more qualified for the job than his or her peer who is hired. In addition, having employees compete for jobs can put a supervisor in a very stressful situation. A supervisor might have to decide among three very qualified employees—all of whom would do a good job.

SKILLS INVENTORIES

Another internal recruiting method is the use of skills inventories. Essentially, a skills inventory includes a list of employee names, their education, training, present position, work experience, relevant job skills and abilities, and other qualifications. The organization can search through the company skill inventory to identify potential candidates for the position opening. This was the foundation on which HI built its job-posting computer system discussed above.

JOB BIDDING

When a union is present, the labor-management agreement usually includes job-bidding procedures. These procedures typically specify that all jobs covered by the agreement must be filled by qualified applicants from within the bargaining unit. Those interested in the vacancy "bid" for the job by applying if they are qualified. The position is filled by the individual with the highest seniority from among the qualified applicants. In some cases, applicants take competitive examinations and the position is filled by the highest-scoring applicant. In either case, only those currently employed are permitted

EXHIBIT 7.2   **Job Posting for a Large Hospital**

CLERICAL/NONTECHNICAL POSITIONS

- *Medical Transcriptionist*—Medical records; FT; 8:30–5:00 M–F; high school education or equivalent required; completion of an approved vocational training program for medical transcriptionist; two years experience in an acute care setting as transcriptionist may be substitute in lieu of training program; at least two years prior experience in a hospital or physician's office required.
- *Accounting Technician*—FT; two years of college in a business-related area is required; experience may substitute for the education requirement; experience in mathematics, accounting, and/or bookkeeping is required.
- *Production Manager*—FT; Food and Nutrition Services Dept.; high school education or equivalent required; at least five years health-care food service experience required; certified dietary manager preferred.
- *Food Service Aide*—PRN; high school education or equivalent required; food service experience desired but not necessary.
- *Chemical Dependency Tech*—addiction recovery center; PRN; high school education or equivalent required; trained in CPR and working knowledge of chemical dependency.
- *Environmental Services Tech I, II*—PRN; high school education or equivalent required; housekeeping experience in a health-care setting preferred but not required; flexible schedule.

PROFESSIONAL/TECHNICAL POSITIONS

- *Business Manager—addiction recovery center*—FT; high school education or equivalent required, BS preferred; one year of experience; WordPerfect skills.
- *Staff Physical Therapist*—PRN; requires B.S. degree in physical therapy; must be a graduate of an accredited school of physical therapy; one year of experience preferred; must be a registered therapist with a Florida license; BLS certified.
- *Physical Therapy Assistant*—FT; A.A. degree as a physical therapy assistant from an accredited school of physical therapy; one year of experience preferred.
- *Aerobics Instructor*—PT; must have senior class certification.
- *CT Staff Technologist*—PRN; graduate of an AMA-accredited school of radiological technology; previous hospital experience preferred, but not mandatory; current registration with American Registry of Radiologic Technology; current licensure with the Florida Department of Radiation Safety.

NURSING POSITIONS

REGISTERED NURSE

- *Family Nurse Practitioner*—FT; 4P–12A, family practitioner experience required.
- *Med/Tele*—FT; 12:30P–9P (one year exp. required); FT; 7A–7P.
- *ER*–PRN.
- *ICU*—FT; 7P–7A.
- *Surgical Unit*—Charge nurse FT; 3P–11P; staff RN 3P–11P.
- *ARC*—PRN; 2 yrs. addiction recovery exp. required.
- *Case Manager*—FT; BSN required and 1 year MID management experience.
- *Family Center*—FT; 7P–7A

LICENSED PRACTICAL NURSE

- *Med/Tele*—FT; 7A–7P.
- *Surgical/ARC*—FT; 3P–11P, PT; 3P–11P, PT; 7A–3P.

to apply. This has the effect, especially among blue-collar and other unionized jobs, of filling only entry-level positions from external sources.

Using a job-bidding system is normally very easy. The negotiated contract specifically outlines how the procedure is to work by designating who is qualified to bid, how often bids can be made, and how the bid is to be processed once submitted. However, a job-bidding system can present difficulties. For example, when one division of Whirlpool completely changed the way its jobs were performed by introducing computers, every single job had to be bid for because all of the old jobs were eliminated. The workers had one week to analyze job descriptions of the new jobs and bid on their top three choices. Once the bids were in, the head supervisor and his assistant analyzed the bids, trying to match the workers to the jobs following the formula outlined in the contract. This process took two days. Once completed, the job assignments were posted for inspection by the employees. Many workers found that they had been assigned a job for which they had not even bid because co-workers with higher seniority had filled all of the jobs they had requested. Hence, these employees immediately submitted new bids for different jobs, causing the process to begin all over again.

REFERRALS

An excellent source of information is the current employee who may know someone who would be qualified and interested in the open position. To entice employees to suggest candidates, some companies offer a referral bonus. An employee who recommends someone who is hired receives a small bonus, usually between $100 and $1,000. Obviously, this source of information is very low cost, yet it can yield a number of good prospects because normally only individuals who are happy in their jobs recommend their company to their friends and family. Further, because people tend to associate with people like themselves, if the employee fits in well in the organization, chances are his or her referrals will too. However, managers should be aware that when the organization does not have a representative number of minorities, referrals have been considered a violation of Title VII of the Civil Rights Act.[17]

EXTERNAL RECRUITING

SCHOOL AND COLLEGE RECRUITING

Recruiting at high schools or vocational schools is often the strategic approach adopted by organizations with position openings at the entry level or in internal training programs. Recruiting at the college level serves as a major source for acquiring managerial, professional, and technical skills.[18] College recruiting can be expensive, so human resource managers should be certain that a college degree is needed for successful performance in the position openings. In general, professionals (such as engineers and human resource managers) are recruited nationally while more technical or lower-level jobs are recruited regionally or locally.

Large organizations (such as IBM) often have recruiters all over the country (and sometimes outside of the country) searching for qualified candidates. Smaller organizations usually recruit locally or regionally. One of the most important decisions that human resource managers must make is from which schools and colleges to recruit. Many organizations make a strategic decision to recruit from certain schools or colleges exclusively. The rationale for limiting the number (besides time and money) includes recruiting from only prestigious schools to enhance the reputation of the organization, from schools to which the organization makes financial donations, or from schools from which previous hires have performed effectively. Over the past few years, college placement figures have dropped. Instead of adding people to the payroll, organizations have been downsizing. However, this trend may be changing. According to a survey performed by the College Placement Council, 57 percent of the 245 employers surveyed planned to hire more college graduates in 1994 than in 1993. The overall increase was projected to be 5.9 percent, which equates to 80 new hires per employer rather than the 76 reported in 1993.[19] Some of these additional positions appear to be coming from small businesses, generally in the service sector. In an effort to place more students, college placement centers have been courting small businesses. By implementing low-cost alternatives, such as job fairs, videoconferencing, and resume booklets, to the normal college recruitment practices, small businesses have begun turning to college campuses when they seek to increase their ranks.[20]

ADVERTISING

Advertising job openings in newspapers, magazines, newsletters, and other media sources (such as radio) is a relatively inexpensive recruiting mechanism. *The Wall Street Journal,* for example, has a large section devoted to managerial and professional openings. Advertising is useful for filling open positions quickly. However, advertising does not usually target a specific audience. For example, McDonald's often includes an abbreviated application blank on every paper placemat. These placemats are given to customers when they pick up their food order. McDonald's views every customer as a potential employee! The cost of screening candidates may preclude the use of media sources for most jobs other than entry level. The effectiveness of media advertising for position openings should be examined periodically. Evaluating the success or failure of recruiting efforts by counting the number of qualified candidates is *not* a recommended method. For example, it is far more expensive and time consuming to screen 100 applicants and find five qualified candidates than to screen 15 applicants and find five qualified candidates.[21] However, when developing advertisements for open positions, steps can be taken to increase their effectiveness.

Clearly written, specifically defined advertisements will attract qualified applicants, dissuade unqualified ones from applying, and make the recruiting process more efficient. But what exactly should be included in an employment advertisement? Obviously, the answer depends on the job. For example, the ad may require applicants to submit salary history, which can be used to determine whether the salary for the current opening will be attractive to the applicant. A more useful and practical way to attract only those who will be satisfied with the salary offered is to include in the advertisement an anticipated starting salary range with a disclaimer stating that actual salary will depend upon the candidate's experience and credentials.

Other items that should be included in the ad are a closing date so that the applicant and the organization will know when the application period ends. The ad also should list three to five key requirements for the job. It is imperative from a legal perspective that the qualities listed are essential for successful job performance. It is also important to request in the ad that applicants submit a traditional resume with a cover letter specifically responding to each requirement for the job. The traditional resume makes comparing applicants easier, and the cover letter gives the company information about how well the applicant writes and analyzes information. Also, the ad should note the way applications are to be made, especially to discourage phone applications. Information in the ad should indicate what type of response, if any, applicants will receive in response to their submission.[22] Including some or all of these suggestions in employment advertisements should make them more effective for the organization.

PUBLIC EMPLOYMENT AGENCIES

All states provide employment services to job seekers and employers. An effort has been undertaken in recent years to improve the image and the services provided by the public employment service. Traditionally, employers and job seekers believed that the public employment system was useful only for filling blue-collar, unskilled jobs. In part, this resulted from the association that the public employment system has with the payment of unemployment compensation. Another problem with the service has been its preoccupation with filling placement goals or quotas at the expense of effective screening of candidates for jobs. Individuals without proper qualifications were sometimes sent to particular jobs simply because the service was attempting to meet its referral and placement quotas. However, the service has been used successfully by employers even though it has been focused on unskilled or low-skilled jobs.

PRIVATE EMPLOYMENT AGENCIES

Private employment agencies vary considerably in size and effectiveness as good sources of employees and must be chosen carefully by employers and job seekers alike. For a fee, these agencies conduct the preliminary applicant screening for the organization. Agencies usually charge the job seeker a fee if he or she is hired by an employer through the agency. The employer may agree to pay all, part, or none of this fee. Regardless, the fee is usually based upon some multiple of the employee's salary. Unfortunately, some agencies are more concerned with placing employees quickly than in effecting a good match between the employee and the organization. Human resource managers can reduce problems if they supply the employment agency with a detailed description of the position to be filled. Similar to that in a well-written employment advertisement, relevant information about the job should include a job title, job description, the education level needed, special training or skills required, and pay ranges.

EXECUTIVE SEARCH FIRMS

Some employment agencies focus their efforts on seeking quality management-level employees. An executive search is characterized by aggressive action on the part of consultants and management who actively pursue the optimal candidate. The search seeks to identify those whose careers are on track with their current employers and those who are not actually looking for another job but who would be interested in considering another opportunity. Recently, some companies have decided to not limit this type of recruiting activity to executives. Recruiting for any position within the organization can be done by sending out "scouts" to look for good employees who are not necessarily looking for another job.[23]

While most recruiting activities focus on selecting from those who apply, search activities focus on selecting from among candidates who have to be found. Since search activities are often directed at candidates from companies with competitive products or services, the industry backgrounds of those identified are usually closely related to the industry of the organization conducting the search.[24]

Because it is often difficult to locate professional applicants at higher levels in the organization, the recruiting process may have to take a different approach. It is important to make sure that the applicant believes his or her best interests are kept in mind as well as those of the company. Attention should be paid to the candidate's home life by showing interest in and helping the spouse/family become knowledgeable about the company and its location.[25]

Companies frequently use a variety of internal and external recruiting strategies to locate and hire their workers. Although one technique may work well for some organizations, the same technique may prove ineffective for others. Some techniques may mesh well with the organization's competitive strategy, but others do not. Exhibit 7.3 provides a graphical summary of the effectiveness of many of the recruiting strategies just described. As this exhibit notes, not all methods are used for all jobs, and the effectiveness of the methods varies greatly across job categories.

By integrating both internal and external recruiting techniques, a company can develop an overall recruiting plan that is specifically tailored to support its overall strat-

EXHIBIT 7.3   **Effectiveness of Recruiting Sources by Job Category**

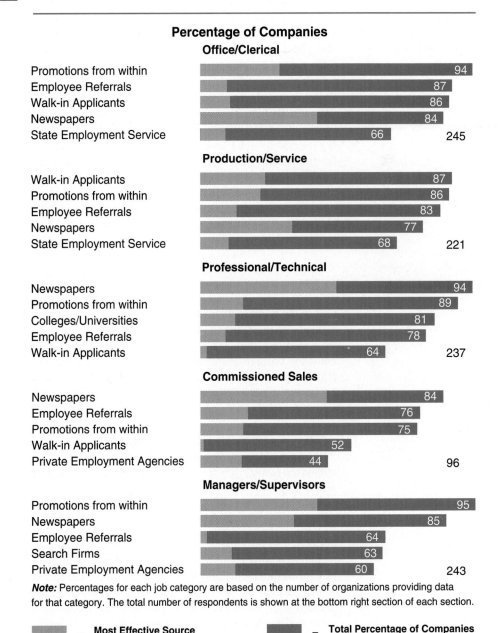

Percentage of Companies
Office/Clerical

Source	Value
Promotions from within	94
Employee Referrals	87
Walk-in Applicants	86
Newspapers	84
State Employment Service	66

245

Production/Service

Walk-in Applicants	87
Promotions from within	86
Employee Referrals	83
Newspapers	77
State Employment Service	68

221

Professional/Technical

Newspapers	94
Promotions from within	89
Colleges/Universities	81
Employee Referrals	78
Walk-in Applicants	64

237

Commissioned Sales

Newspapers	84
Employee Referrals	76
Promotions from within	75
Walk-in Applicants	52
Private Employment Agencies	44

96

Managers/Supervisors

Promotions from within	95
Newspapers	85
Employee Referrals	64
Search Firms	63
Private Employment Agencies	60

243

Note: Percentages for each job category are based on the number of organizations providing data for that category. The total number of respondents is shown at the bottom right section of each section.

☐ = **Most Effective Source for Job Category**   ■ = **Total Percentage of Companies Using This Technique**

SOURCE: *HRMagazine,* February 1993, p. 57.

egy and result in the selection of highly qualified applicants. Exhibit 7.4 is an illustrative description of one possible recruitment plan. Plans such as this one are needed for a variety of reasons. First, to ensure productivity, a fully staffed workforce is needed. When employees are asked to do too much for too long, both morale and productivity can sag. Also, more than one applicant must be recruited to fill one position. In fact, it may take hundreds of applicants to fill one position, depending upon the position. Exactly how many recruits are needed can be determined from past recruitment efforts. Specifically, a yield ratio can be developed for each position to be filled. A **yield ratio** is the number of candidates who pass a particular recruitment hurdle divided by the number who attempted the hurdle. For example, we would calculate a ratio for each step outlined in Exhibit 7.4 in the recruiting process in which a decision about an applicant was made. One set of possible yield ratios is provided in Exhibit 7.4 in parentheses after each decision point in the diagram. Specifically, 20 internal candidates of 1,000 possible (20/1,000) were found by the human resource department and passed on to the hiring department. It selected 3 of these 20 to interview and 1 of the 3 (or zero of these 3) to offer a job. On the external side of the diagram, 10 of 250 applicants were passed on to the hiring department, with 4 receiving interviews and 1 or none receiving an offer. This scenario, while fictitious, is not far from reality. The overall point is that a large applicant pool may be required to hire even one person for the job and hence prior planning must be done. Finally, it is important to keep in mind that this plan should mesh with and support the organization's overall strategic plan. For example, if the organization makes the strategic decision to promote only from within, then a detailed internal recruitment plan should be developed.

YIELD RATIO
Percentage of candidates passed on to the next step in the selection process.

RETAINING EMPLOYEES

One of the primary roles of a recruiting effort is to attract a number of qualified applicants; however, retaining those employees selected is also an important issue. Too often a recruiter attempts to "sell" the organization to the candidate and subsequently inflates the positive characteristics of the organization while minimizing any negative features. This is often termed the *flypaper* approach, which assumes that if an organization can attract people, these new employees will "stick" with the organization. One survey found that job candidates can be enticed to join a company if offered a large enough salary, but another survey revealed that retaining those same employees requires strong leadership skills among top management.[26]

Along with strong leadership, two other programs that can help a firm increase retention are realistic job previews (RJPs) and career development opportunities. Both are discussed below.

REALISTIC JOB PREVIEWS

Many human resource managers, as well as organizational researchers, believe that if recruiters portray an accurate and balanced picture of the organization, the number of candidates hired remaining with the organization will increase (even though fewer may actually accept the job offer).[27] This happens primarily because new employees' expectations are more likely to be met. If a new employee has unrealistic expectations about the organization, any unmet expectations could cause the person to become a disgruntled worker. The process of giving recruits a more accurate picture of the job and the organization, including the negative aspects, is called a *realistic job preview*.

EXHIBIT 7.4   **Possible Organizational Recruiting Plan**

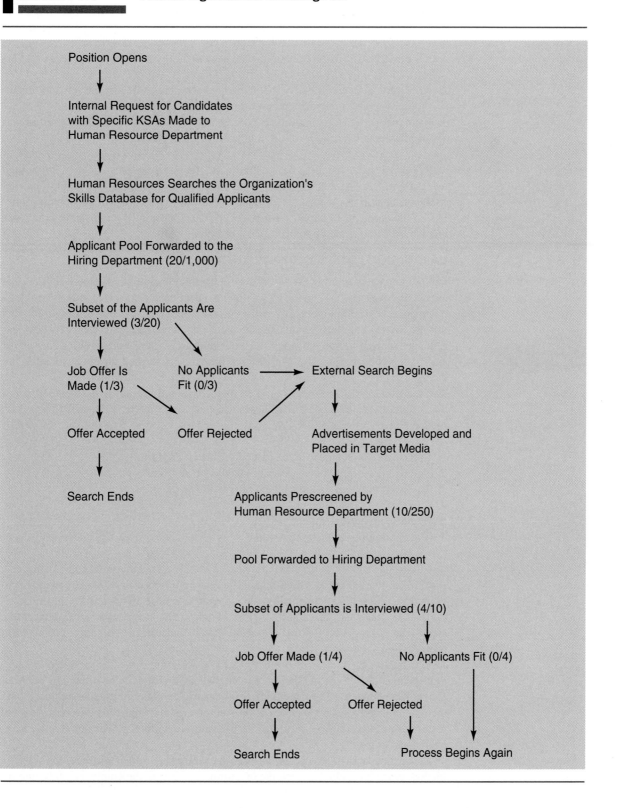

Some studies have demonstrated that realistic job previews (RJP) can reduce turnover, lower expectations about the job, and increase job satisfaction and organizational commitment for the following reasons:[28]

1. RJPs may provide a "vaccination" of expectations against the negative aspects of organizational life by lowering the expectations of new hires.
2. RJPs may facilitate effective matching between applicants and the job and organization by giving more accurate information.
3. RJPs may increase commitment because the choice to join the organization was made without external pressure or coercion.

RJPs have been found to be most effective for organizations experiencing a high level of turnover or for entry-level jobs in which the job applicant may not have an accurate perception of (1) what the job entails or (2) the expectations of the organization.[29] Due to the problems of slightly reduced acceptance rates, RJPs are most feasible when there is an abundance of applicants for a position.

CAREER DEVELOPMENT OPPORTUNITIES

College graduates entering the workforce for the first time, or "first careerists," are clear about their expectations and are less willing to adapt their values and work styles to accommodate their employers. Given the shrinking entry-level labor force and the fact that 19 out of 20 college graduates who enter the labor force over the 1986–2000 period are expected to find jobs requiring college degrees, the labor conditions are on the side of the college graduate.[30] In general, first careerists want coaching, training, rewards, and quick promotions. Information gathered from in-depth interviews with college graduates and representatives of 20 major corporations revealed a clear pattern of desires and expectations.[31] The following factors entice the first careerist to stay with the job and the company:

1. Immediate involvement in the essential work of the firm.
2. The ability to apply newly learned knowledge and skills.
3. The opportunity to understand the big picture of the firm.
4. Rapid career development.
5. Rapid salary advancement.
6. The opportunity to learn new skills.

Companies are responding to these needs by offering a variety of programs for new employees. For example, Allied-Signal, Inc., has implemented a new orientation program designed to give new employees an opportunity to learn about how the organization works and what its values are. In addition, many companies are implementing sophisticated programs for first careerists that include career planning, management training, and mentoring.

One factor that should be considered prior to selection is the "fit" between the individual career objectives and the career path that can realistically be offered by the firm. Career plateauing, which refers to the point in a career where future hierarchical movement is unlikely,[32] has become a real problem in organizations today. Downsizing and restructuring have severely restricted the potential for vertical movement in many managerial career paths.

Career plateauing can lead to, among other things, poor performance, job dissatisfaction, or the individual leaving the organization.[33] It is in the employer's best interest to either select those employees whose personal career goals match viable career paths within the company or to inform the employees up front, during the RJP, about the alternate methods the organization might use to foster continued growth in the employee. Such methods include present job (in-place) development, cross-functional rotational moves, specialization within a function (or discipline or specialty), and lateral moves within a specific geographic location.[34]

ALTERNATIVES TO RECRUITMENT

Another strategic decision businesses can make is to *not* recruit. Instead, they can rely on contingent workers. Contingent workers include temporary employees, part-time workers, leased employees, freelancers, and independent professional contractors.[35] Temporary workers are employees hired on an as-needed basis. The need could be for a specific project (e.g., opening a new restaurant) or for a specific time (e.g., seasonal workers). Part-time workers are those who are employed on a continuing basis but who work less than full-time, normally less than 35 hours a week. Organizations can lease employees in the same way as they lease cars. Just as an organization would not own a leased car, it would not employ a leased employee. Instead, it would pay the firm who does employ the worker (own the car) a leasing fee. This fee is generally more than the worker would earn in base salary if working for the leasing firm, but the leasing firm is not responsible for paying benefits, which often makes the fee less than would be paid if the employee were hired directly. Freelancers are individuals who have a specific knowledge, skill, or ability that organizations need. These individuals offer to apply their talent to a specific problem for a variety of companies. Freelancers are paid for the product they produce and sometimes for expenses incurred while developing the product. Many consultants and writers work in this fashion. Finally, an independent contractor is an individual who works for one company but receives few, if any, benefits. Real-estate agents are generally considered to be independent contractors. The working arrangement for each type of contingent worker is unique, but some similarities exist. First, the organization that uses contingent workers makes no long-term commitment to them. Instead, it negotiates a contract for a specific length of time or for a specific project. Upon completing the contract, the employment relationship ends. Second, the organization pays virtually no benefits to the contingent workers. Instead, the individual—an independent contractor or a freelancer—or the temporary or leasing firm is responsible for benefits. For these reasons and many others, the use of contingent workers has increased rapidly over the past several years. Exhibit 7.5 reports the increase in the employment of both temporary workers and leased employees. Each of these alternatives to recruiting is described in detail below.

TEMPORARY WORKERS

Temporary workers are generally contracted through a temporary employment agency. There are over 7,000 U.S. temporary agencies with the largest, Manpower, employing over 600,000 employees, making it the nation's largest private employer.[36] When contacted, a temporary agency immediately sends the contracting firm fully qualified employees and bills the firm for their wages. The temporary agency is responsible for these employees, who are on its payroll. Temporary agencies were used in the past mainly when extra secretarial support was needed, but this has changed. More and more frequently, organizations are turning to temporary agencies to help staff managerial positions while a search is underway or to provide an employee for a project that has a definite ending date.[37] The most important benefit of temporary employees is decreased

EXHIBIT 7.5   Increase in Temporary and Leased Workers

Temporary Help Employment (number of average daily employees)

	(in 1,000's)	(in millions)
1991 (annual)	1,149.6	$20,456.0
1992 1st quarter	1,160.3	5,462.0
1992 *2nd quarter*	*1,246.2*	*6,070.0*
1992 3rd quarter	1,431.8	6,159.0
1992 4th quarter	1,556.1	6,849.0
1992 (annual)	1,348.6	24,900.0
1993 1st quarter	1,480.1	6,467.0
1993 *2nd quarter*	*1,601.9*	*6,877.0*

Quick Growth
Number of Employees within Employee-Leasing Operations (in millions)

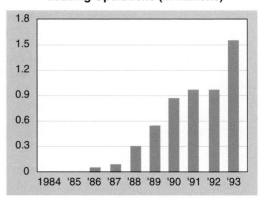

SOURCES: Adapted from Stephanie Overman, "Hiring Bakers by the Dozen," *HRMagazine,* February 1994, p. 56; Timothy L. O'Brien, "Rise in Employee Leasing Spurs Scan," *The Wall Street Journal,* March 22, 1994, p. B1.

cost. All recruitment costs are eliminated, as are the costs of benefits for these employees and outplacement or severance costs.

LEASED WORKERS

Under a leasing agreement, a firm terminates a group of employees who are then hired by a leasing agency, which leases them back to the original organization. This may seem to be an unusual way to staff an organization, but it is growing in popularity as Exhibit 7.5 indicates. An organization that leases employees is responsible only for giving them a place to work and work to do, as well as supervising them. Training costs, benefits, health insurance, and all of the other human resource administration costs are the responsibility of the leasing agency, not the organization. This type of arrangement has been the salvation of small businesses. With only a few employees, most small businesses could not qualify for competitively priced health-care plans. However, by pooling several small businesses into one leasing agency, more affordable rates can be negotiated.[38] Although it may seem to be a win-win situation, there is a negative side to employee leasing. The FBI and the Department of Labor have been investigating leasing agencies. Some are accused of embezzling large sums of money from benefit plans. Further, it appears that as many as 500,000 leased workers who believe they have health-care coverage may not.[39] Despite the potential for problems, employee leasing can be a viable option for an organization.

RECRUITING AND THE LEGAL ENVIRONMENT

Recruiting and hiring employees must be done within the legal environment of the organization. To avoid problems in the early stages of the hiring process, preemployment application forms should not ask questions that later could be used in recruitment materials to unfairly discriminate against a candidate. Specifically, job applicants and screening interviews should never include questions referring to the candidate's gender, religion, or race. Employers need to obtain a certain amount of information from the job candidate, but, as Exhibit 7.6 indicates, there is a correct and an incorrect way to ask these questions.

Affirmative action principles should also be observed in the recruiting process. For example, it is recommended that minorities be used in the recruiting process and minority leaders contacted for possible employment candidates. Using the phrase "an equal opportunity employer" is important, but this alone is not enough to fulfill the goals of affirmative action. Since affirmative action plans include goals for increasing the number of minorities and women holding certain jobs, the organization's recruiting efforts should be directed toward meeting these goals. Many organizations make an effort to recruit from predominately female and/or black colleges. For example, the Xerox case in this chapter demonstrates how making a strategic decision to recruit, hire, and train minorities can help meet the affirmative action goals of the corporation while achieving a diverse workforce. Affirmative action was discussed in more detail in Chapter 4.

EVALUATING RECRUITING METHODS

Given the importance of recruiting to the organization, the methods used in recruiting should be evaluated periodically. One of the most important reasons to evaluate recruiting methods is to determine the costs versus the benefits of various methods. When recruiting methods do not attract enough applicants, many organizations respond by raising starting salaries. Although some job applicants may be enticed by money, this may not be the most cost-effective method of recruiting. Further, employees within the organization may perceive inequity if new employees are brought in at a similar or even higher salary.

EXHIBIT 7.6   **Asking the Right Questions**

NATIONAL ORIGIN

Unacceptable

Are you a U.S. citizen?

What is your birthplace and the birthplace of your spouse (or relatives)?

Acceptable

Are you lawfully employable full-time in the United States by citizenship or by obtaining the proper authorization?

What languages do you speak, read, and write fluently? (Ask only if job related.)

AGE

Unacceptable

How old are you?

What is your date of birth?

Acceptable

Are you over the age of 18?

continued

EXHIBIT 7.6

continued

Asking the Right Questions

MARITAL AND FAMILY STATUS

Unacceptable

Are you married?

How many children do you have?

What are your child-care arrangements?

Acceptable

Will you be able and willing to travel as required by the job?

Are you willing to relocate if necessary?

ORGANIZATIONS

Unacceptable

To what clubs or social organizations do you belong?

Acceptable

What professional, trade groups, or organizations do you consider relevant to your job?

PHYSICAL CONDITION

Unacceptable

Do you have any handicaps or disabilities?

What is your medical history?

Have you had any recent or past illnesses or operations? If so, please list the type and date of the illness.

When was your last physical exam?

Have you ever filed a claim for workers' compensation?

Acceptable

Do you have any disabilities that could limit your ability to perform the job for which you applied?

Are there any jobs or types of jobs for which you should not be considered because of a disability or health condition?

ARREST/CONVICTION RECORD

Unacceptable

Have you ever been arrested?

Acceptable

Have you ever been convicted of a crime? (It is recommended that questions ask only about a specific crime or crimes that may be reasonably related to performing the job in question.)

MILITARY (APPROPRIATE ONLY IF JOB RELATED)

Unacceptable

Have you served in the U.S. armed forces? If so, what type of discharge did you receive?

Acceptable

In what branch of the U.S. Armed Forces did you serve?

What type of education or training did you receive in the military?

SOURCE: Adapted from B. Leonard, "Right Questions on Applications Avoid Trouble," *HRNews*, February 1990, pp. B9, B15.

Recruiting costs include factors such as the cost of advertising, the salaries and travel expenses of recruiters, travel expenses of potential job applicants, and recruiting agency fees. These costs must be weighed against factors such as the proportion of acceptances to offers. At a minimum, organizations should compare the length of time applicants from each recruiting source *stay* with the organization with the cost of *hiring* from a particular source. The effectiveness of recruiting methods varies among organizations and even jobs within the same organization.

THE SELECTION PROCESS

SELECTION
Choosing an individual from a pool of recruited applicants.

Selection is the process of choosing individuals who have the necessary qualifications to perform a particular job well. Organizations differ as to the complexity of their selection systems. Some organizations make a strategic decision to fill positions quickly and inexpensively by scanning application forms and hiring individuals based on this information alone. Other organizations, however, make a strategic decision to choose the best person possible by having an elaborate and sometimes costly selection system. These systems may require potential employees to fill out application forms and provide information for a background check, take a number of job-related tests, and perform well through a series of interviews. Most organizations have more than one selection process. Exhibit 7.7 presents an overview of the selection process. Each element in this process will be discussed.

APPLICATION BLANKS AND RESUMES

The initial screening of potential employees is usually done by examining resumes and/or having the applicant fill out an application blank. Items that should be requested on an application include general biographical information; an extensive employment history including most recent jobs, employers' names, addresses, dates of employment, positions held, and reason for leaving; personal references; and the applicant's signature showing consent for the employer to investigate all of the information provided. An incomplete application should automatically disqualify a candidate.[40] Much of the information gathered on application blanks is objective so that the human resource manager can verify it. Verification of information on an application is becoming increasingly important to avoid claims of negligent hiring. An employer is guilty of **negligent hiring** if he or she failed to perform a thorough background check on an employee whose infliction of harm on a customer or third party could have been predicted by the employing firm. For example, a carpet cleaning company was found to be guilty of negligent hiring and was ordered to pay $1 million to the parents of two University of Florida students who were strangled by an employee who was in their apartment to clean the carpet. A thorough background check would have revealed that the employee was a bad risk because he had been arrested on drug charges, had violently resisted arrest, and had been fired from two previous jobs.[41] Another important reason for verifying information provided on application blanks is that job applicants are increasingly lying about the degrees they have earned. In 1994, one application-checking firm found that 1 in 12 applicants checked lied about a college degree. Sometimes applicants slip up when doing this. For example, one applicant boasted that he had played varsity football at the University of Colorado's main campus in Denver. However, the University of Colorado's main campus is in Boulder.[42]

NEGLIGENT HIRING
A finding that an employer is responsible for using poor selection procedures after an employee inflicts harm on a customer or other third party.

Once the application has been verified, it can be numerically scored to make it more comparable to others. The process of quantifying an application is called *weighting an*

EXHIBIT 7.7   **The Selection Process**

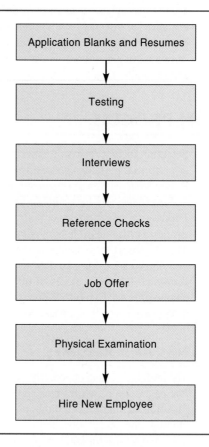

WEIGHTED APPLICATION BLANK (WAB)
An application in which numeric "weights" are assigned to important questions in order to create a numeric score.

application. The use of a **weighted application blank (WAB)** involves placing a value or score for the items on the application that have been found to predict successful job performance. Applicants receive points according to the information they report on the form and can then be ranked based on their total points.

Although weighted application blanks have been found to be predictive of future performance,[43] the time and cost of developing an effective system are often prohibitive.

Resumes are often used instead of application blanks. Job applicants develop their own resumes, which should include essentially standard information. Managers sometimes ask for both a resume and an application blank, since the resume contains only the information the applicant is willing to voluntarily share. Interestingly, studies have estimated that between 20 percent and 50 percent of the information reported in resumes is false or inflated.[44] Thus, caution must be taken if this is a primary selection tool. Because the resume represents the individual, it is imperative that it contain no errors. Exhibit 7.8 provides some examples of bloopers that personnel expert Robert Half has collected over the past 40 years.

Although an applicant may believe that his or her resume is the way to get a foot in the door, this is probably not the case. According to James Challenger, president of a Chicago outplacement agency, the odds that an unsolicited resume will result in employment are very poor because employers have been inundated with resumes from

EXHIBIT 7.8 **Resume Bloopers**

Please disregard the attached resume, it is terribly out of date.

Here are my qualifications for you to overlook.

My intensity and focus are at inordinately high levels, and my ability to complete projects on time is unspeakable.

I am an outstanding worker; flexible 24 hours a day, seven days a week, 365 days a year.

In my past position I set up entire offices including furniture, lighting, computers, filing cabinets and office procedures. I also have a flair for floral arrangements and catering.

I hold a B.A. in Loberal Arts.

I have expertise in dealing with customers' conflicts that arouse.

I seek challenges that test my mind and body, since the two are usually inseparable.

I am good at checking out customers.

I will not accept employment in foreign countries, including New York and California.

My compensation should be at least equal to my age.

I have an extensive background in public accounting. I can also stand on my head.

Flunked the CPA exam with high grades.

There is acuracy in all phases of my work.

Thank you for your consideration and I hope to hear from you shorty.

SOURCE: Robert Half, *Finding, Hiring, and Keeping the Best Employees*" (New York: Wiley & Sons, 1993).

laid-off workers seeking jobs. When a hiring decision must be made, the decision maker normally turns to people he or she knows rather than to a pile of unsolicited resumes.[45]

RELIABILITY AND VALIDITY IN TESTING

Selection testing is a means of obtaining standardized information from potential employees. Standardization means that the test contains the same content for each applicant and is administered and scored in the same way for everyone. Using tests as a selection device is useful only when the tests are reliable and valid.

RELIABILITY

RELIABILITY
Proof that a selection method consistently produces a similar score.

Test **reliability** means that the test is consistent in its measurement. For a test to be consistent in its measurement it must be free from error. That is, the more error in the measurement, the less reliable it will be. However, every measure has some error in it. If a person steps on a digital scale five times in a row, chances are that the weight reported will not be the same in each instance. It may read 155, 157 twice, 156, and 155. Although the reading of the scale changed over these five times, the actual or true weight did not. The variation in the readings was due to error in the measurement of the weight.

This example illustrates that every measurement is composed of two parts: *true score* and *error*. This error can be systematic. *Systematic error* occurs when the measure is incorrect by the same amount each time it is used. For example, if an oven always heats to 340 degrees when it is set for 350 degrees, the 10 degree difference is systematic error. It is always present, and it is always the same. The error in measurement can also be *random*. This type of error is not consistent. The weight example used above is an example of random error. The measure fluctuated up and down, but not always by the same amount.

Error can be introduced into a measurement in many ways. Let's looks at some of the possible sources in a selection test. For example, the person taking the test may make errors as a result of being worried, anxious, bored, or fatigued and by not working to his or her full potential (i.e., not producing his or her true score). The test itself could introduce error if two tests were developed that were designed to be equivalent but were not because one contained items that were not appropriate or were extremely difficult. Also, the environment in which the measure is being made—a room that is extremely hot or extremely cold—could cause error.

Before ways to measure reliability can be presented, we must first discuss correlation coefficients because this statistic is often used to calculate the reliability of a measure. Essentially, a correlation coefficient is a numerical index that represents the degree of relationship between two variables. A correlation coefficient indicates the direction as well as the strength of a relationship. Correlations vary from -1.00 to $+1.00$. A negative correlation means that as one variable increases, the other variable decreases (for example, as employee satisfaction increases, intentions to quit decrease). Conversely, a positive correlation means that both variables move in the same way (as employee satisfaction increases, intentions to remain with the organization increase). The strength of the relationship is determined by the magnitude of the correlation. The closer the correlation comes to 1.00 (or -1.00), the stronger the relationship. A zero correlation indicates no relationship between two variables. Exhibit 7.9 illustrates the concept of a correlation coefficient and Exhibit 7.10 presents a variety of scatterplots and the resulting correlation coefficients.

METHODS FOR ESTIMATING RELIABILITY

The reliability of a scale or test can be estimated in a variety of ways. Five different types will be discussed here: test-retest, parallel forms, split-half, interrater, and internal consistency. The estimate of reliability for the first four methods is a correlation coefficient. It is suggested that a correlation of .80 or higher indicates good reliability. The final method uses a coefficient alpha, which represents the average correlation of each item on the test with each other item. This value also should be .80 or higher.

Test-Retest Method   As the name implies, this method of estimating reliability requires a test to be given twice. Specifically, a group of people complete the test. This same group of people takes the same test at a later date. The scores on the two tests are correlated to produce the reliability estimate. The resulting coefficient is often referred to as the **coefficient of stability.** The idea behind this method is that if the test or measure is stable (i.e., reliable), the scores on each administration should be similar and hence correlated. It is important that the two administration times be far enough apart that the respondents will not remember their answers on the first test and simply repeat them. However, it is also important to note that if the administrations are too far apart, the individuals may have changed in some way (e.g., completed a class) that will also change their answers.

COEFFICIENT OF STABILITY
A measure of how reliable a selection test is over time.

Split-Half Method   The split-half method of estimating reliability splits the results from one administration of the test into two equal halves and correlates the results from the two halves. This is often accomplished by correlating the odd items with the even ones. This method is based on the notion that if the questions within the scale are similar enough to one another (i.e., reliable), the correlations between them should be

EXHIBIT 7.9   **Correlation Coefficient**

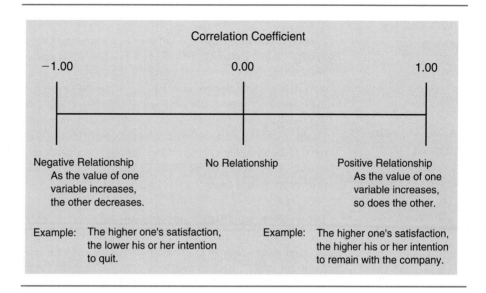

Correlation Coefficient

−1.00   0.00   1.00

Negative Relationship   No Relationship   Positive Relationship
   As the value of one   As the value of one
   variable increases,   variable increases,
   the other decreases.   so does the other.

Example: The higher one's satisfaction,   Example: The higher one's satisfaction,
          the lower his or her intention   the higher his or her intention
          to quit.   to remain with the company.

EXHIBIT 7.10   **Examples of Scatterplots and the Resulting Correlation Coefficient**

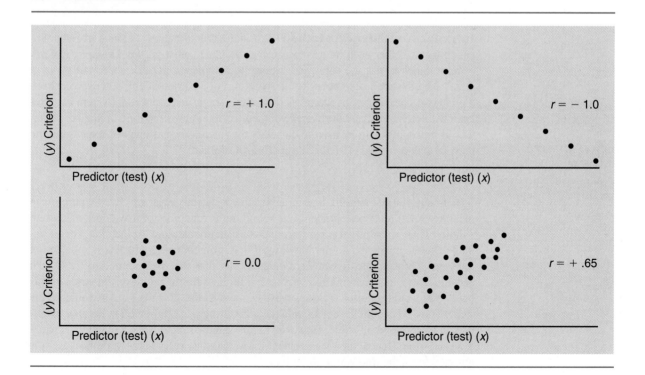

high. It is important that each half be representative of the test's content and format. For example, if the test has two different types of question formats (e.g., multiple choice and true false), an equal number of each should be included in each half.

Parallel Tests Method   To use the parallel tests method of estimating reliability, two equivalent forms of the same test must be generated. The two tests do not have to be identical, but they should cover the same material and be equal in length and difficulty. These two tests are either given to the same group at the same time, or as with the test-retest method, the same group completes one form at one time and a second form at a different time. In either case, the scores from the two tests are correlated. The resulting correlation is referred to as the **coefficient of equivalence.** In other words, if the correlation is high (greater than .80), the two forms are seen to be equivalent to one another. Obviously, the difficulty in using this method arises in developing two tests that are truly equivalent.

COEFFICIENT OF EQUIVALENCE
A measure of how similarly two measures tap the same construct.

Interrater Method   Interrater reliability refers to the agreement between two raters who use the same measure to evaluate a candidate. This type of reliability is often used in interview settings. Essentially, two different interviewers interview the same applicant using the same interview format. After the interview, each interviewer rates the applicant on a scale. The ratings from the two different interviewers are correlated to determine the agreement rate between them. This correlation is the interrater reliability coefficient. Interrater reliability may be low for many reasons. For example, the interviewers may not receive the same response from the applicant to the same question. Further, each interviewer may weigh the information he or she receives differently. Finally, the questions asked may differ for a number of reasons. Hence, low interrater reliability coefficients may mean that the interview procedure is faulty or that it was not followed correctly.

Internal Consistency Method   An internal consistency estimate of reliability determines whether each item is measuring the same construct. For example, if items were designed to test the applicant's ability to complete a balance sheet, but some of them asked the applicant about the interworkings of a particular computer spreadsheet, the internal consistency of the test would not be high. In essence, each item is correlated with each other, and the average of these correlations is reported. A number of statistical procedures can be used to calculate the internal consistency of a measure; the most frequently used is Cronbach's **coefficient alpha.**[46]

COEFFICIENT ALPHA
A measure of the internal consistency of a test.

VALIDITY

Specifically, if a test is valid, it accurately and consistently measures what it purports to measure. A test must be reliable if it is valid but the reliability of a test does not ensure validity. Thus, a test might accurately and consistently measure "something," but if human resource managers do not know what that "something" is, the test is reliable but not valid. For example, if you were given a ruler that was marked incorrectly (1 inch actually was 2 inches long) and were asked to measure the width of the cover of this book, you would report 4 inches. Likewise, anyone else given this ruler would do the same. Thus, we would have a reliable measure of the width of the book because everyone reported the same value. However, is this value correct? No. The book is actually 8 inches wide. Hence, the measurement made with this ruler is not valid because it is not measuring the true width of the book.

There are many different ways to assess validity. In the sections that follow, four different types of validity will be discussed: content, construct, criterion related (i.e., concurrent and predictive), and face validity.

Content Validity   Every test developed seeks to measure some underlying concept. For example, a typing test could measure someone's knowledge of typing rules. Further, there is a pool of questions that, if asked, would help to determine whether a person understands these rules. This pool could include questions concerning how many type lines are on a page or how many blank lines are needed in triple-spaced material. However, the pool would not include items about banking procedures or cooking instructions. This pool of questions is often referred to as the **content domain.** Thus, if every question on the measure is drawn from the content domain for that concept, the test has content validity. The more questions on the test from outside the domain, the lower the content validity.

It is also important to note that the concept being measured (e.g., typing knowledge) must also be relevant to a particular job. A good job analysis can help the human resource manager determine whether the specific knowledge, skill, or ability measured by a test is needed for adequate performance of the job. Content validation also must demonstrate that the items, questions, or problems required to be completed by the applicant are representative (from the domain) of the types of situations and problems the applicant would encounter on the job.[47] For example, suppose a typing test focused mainly on centering and headings, but the job required the applicant only to do this sort of typing once a year. Although the test was composed of items from the content domain of typing, it was not composed of situations that were relevant to the job. Hence, the content validity of this test as a selection tool for this job would be low.

To determine content validity, a panel of experts who know the specific skills, knowledge, and abilities required to successfully perform the job in question can be used. To verify the content validity of a test, each expert is asked to rate each item on the test as not necessary on the job (0), useful on the job (1), or essential to the job (2). These ratings are then combined to compute a content validity ratio (CVR) for each item and a content validity index (CVI) for the overall test. The combination procedure used to create a CVR is

$$\text{CVR} = \frac{N_e - N/2}{N/2}$$

where

N_e = the number of panel members who give the item a rating of essential to the job (2)

N = total number of panel members

The closer the CVR is to 1.00, the more the experts believe that the test item covers a concept that is essential to the job in question. A CVR of 0.00 means that there is lack of agreement among the panel members. Human resource managers can compare the CVR values for a variety of items on the same test to determine whether any need to be deleted. The CVI is simply an average of the CVRs for the items in the test that were retained. Likewise, the CVI for different tests can be compared to determine which test is the best measure of the job in question.[48] Exhibit 7.11 provides an example of how this procedure works.

One specific type of content validity is known as **face validity.** Essentially, a measure has face validity if the people required to take it view the items on the test as job related. In other words, on the face of it, the test appears to be tapping the skills, knowl-

CONTENT DOMAIN
All questions possible on a specific topic.

FACE VALIDITY
How well the questions appear to tap the construct of interest.

EXHIBIT 7.11   **Example of Using Experts to Determine Content Validity**

Experts' Rating*

Test Item	1	2	3	4
1	0	0	1	1
2	2	2	2	2
3	2	1	1	1
4	2	2	0	0
5	2	2	2	2
6	2	0	1	2
7	2	2	2	1
8	2	2	2	0
9	2	1	1	0
10	2	2	2	2

$CVR_{item1} = (0 - 2)/2 = -1.0$ delete item
$CVR_{item2} = (4 - 2)/2 = 1.0$ retain item
$CVR_{item3} = (1 - 2)/2 = -0.5$ delete item
$CVR_{item4} = (2 - 2)/2 = 0.0$ delete item
$CVR_{item5} = (4 - 2)/2 = 1.0$ retain item
$CVR_{item6} = (2 - 2)/2 = 0.0$ delete item
$CVR_{item7} = (3 - 2)/2 = 0.5$ retain item
$CVR_{item8} = (3 - 2)/2 = 0.5$ retain item
$CVR_{item9} = (1 - 2)/2 = -0.5$ delete item
$CVR_{item10} = (4 - 2)/2 = 1.0$ retain item
CVI for retained items $(1.0 + 1.0 + 0.5 + 0.5 + 1.0)/5 = .80$
* 0 = not necessary on the job
  1 = useful on the job
  2 = essential to the job

$$CVR = \frac{N_e - N/2}{N/2}$$

Ne = the number of panel members who give the item a rating of essential to the job (i.e., 2).
  N = total number of experts
CVI = average of CVRs

edge, and abilities required by the job. Face validity also is determined by experts, usually test takers. At the end of the test, questions that ask whether the items were appropriate for or related to the job might be included to gather information about the face validity of the measure.

Construct Validity A *construct* is any characteristic that a human resource manager seeks to measure for selection purposes. For example, creativity, anxiety, motivation, and intelligence are all constructs. A test is said to have construct validity when the scores obtained from it can be accurately interpreted as measuring the construct intended to be measured, that is, whether a scale developed to measure motivation did indeed measure motivation. However, determining just how well a scale measures the identified construct is not easy, especially when the construct is an abstract one such as creativity. Hence, no one study can determine construct validity. Instead, a series of studies must be used. For example, the construct of interest, its components, and the way the job behavior relates to it must be defined. The degree to which the measure developed to evaluate this construct compares to other measures that are reported to measure the same thing must be determined. In addition, two groups that should possess very different levels of the construct under investigation should be identified and the results from the administration of the test to these two groups compared.

Criterion-Related Validity   Human resource managers use criterion-related validity to determine how well a test predicts an outcome. In simple terms, it is a correlation between a predictor (resume, application form, test results, letter of reference, and so on) and a criterion measure (performance appraisal instrument, performance ratings on some dimension, and so on). The higher the correlation, the better the test (predictor) predicts the outcome (criterion). The two ways to perform a criterion-related validity study are concurrent and predictive.

Performing a concurrent validity study is fairly easy. It entails developing a test or measure to use in future selection decisions. This test is then given to a group of employees who are currently employed in the organization. At or about the same time that the test is administered, performance data about these individuals are collected. The performance data and the test results are then correlated. The idea behind this validation technique is that those who score high on the test should also be the ones who have a good performance evaluation rating *if* the test is valid. Therefore, a high correlation indicates that the test should be able to select qualified employees in the future.

There are limitations to this type of validity study. First, the employees currently doing the job will have more knowledge about the job than job applicants. Hence, the question arises as to whether these two groups really are comparable. Also, everyone currently performing the job knows how to do it. Hence, no one should score poorly on the test unless the test is not related to the job. Therefore, the scores will be clustered with very little variance. When a distribution of scores contains little variance, restriction of range has occurred. Restriction of range occurs when all of the scores are grouped together, rather than distributed over the possible range of scores. If these scores are plotted, the scores are all clustered together, similar to the third example in Exhibit 7.10. The correlation for scores such as these will be low because the relationship depicted is not linear. This may lead human resource managers to assume that the test does not measure job-relevant factors when in reality it does.[49]

The goal behind predictive validity is to gather the data about the test from the same population that will take it. In other words, to overcome the problem found in concurrent validity that the test takers (i.e., incumbent workers) have more knowledge than the applicants, actual applicants are used to validate the test in predictive validity. Specifically, a test is developed and is given to persons applying for the job. However, the scores on this test are *not* used to select the applicants; some other means are used. Approximately six months later, the performance measures of the individuals hired are collected. The tests taken when these individuals applied for the job are then correlated with the performance ratings. The higher the correlation, the more predictive the test.

Some problems are associated with predictive validity. For example, if only a few people are hired each year, it may take years to gather enough tests to compare to the performance ratings. Consequently, only the largest companies may be able to utilize this technique. A long period of time must be invested in determining validity, and it is possible that the results may indicate that the tool is a poor predictor.

TYPES OF SELECTION TESTS

A number of selection tests have been developed to aid the human resource manager in hiring employees. The following section covers mental ability tests, work sample tests, trainability tests, personality and interest inventories, and honesty tests as selection devices. Large organizations may have a psychologist on staff who is responsible for administering and evaluating selection tests.

MENTAL ABILITY TESTS

Paper and pencil tests have been developed by psychologists and are used by organizations to measure mental ability and aptitude. Ability and aptitude tests examine a variety of traits, such as general intelligence, an understanding of spatial relationships, numerical skills, reasoning, and comprehension.

One firm that has used pencil and paper tests to its advantage is BBC Engineering. Pencil and paper ability tests were designed to replace the initial interview. Once prepared, trial tests were administered to volunteers who worked at BBC. Concurrent validity results indicated that strong job performance correlated with high tests scores. Now, the recruitment staff sends applicants a "self-selection guide" full of information about the job, including sample items from the tests. With the implementation of the new system, the quality of the candidates has improved. BBC attributes this to the fact that unqualified workers self-select themselves out of the pool.[50]

WORK SAMPLES

Also called performance tests, work sample tests measure the ability to *do* something rather than the ability to *know* something.[51] These tests may measure motor skills or verbal skills. Motor skills include physically manipulating various types of job-related equipment. Verbal skills include problem-solving and language skills. Work sample tests should test the *important* aspects of the job. Since job applicants are actually performing a small portion of the job, it is difficult to "fake" one's ability on these tests.

One of the most effective ways to design work sample tests is by using the results of a job analysis. Because the results of a job analysis indicate which tasks are most critical and which are required for successful completion of the task, it is easy to determine which activities need to be represented on the tests. Provided that the materials are not too costly, requiring work samples that parallel what is actually done on the job can be an excellent way to locate only the most qualified applicants. Some examples of work sample tests include reading a blueprint for errors, correctly identifying the order in which 30 subcontractors work on a project from start to finish, locating construction errors in a building, and developing a daily schedule that matches the skills employees who are to work that day possess with the jobs that need to be accomplished.[52]

TRAINABILITY TESTS

For jobs in which training is necessary due to (1) the skill level of the job applicants or (2) the changing nature of the job, trainability tests are useful. Essentially, the goal is to determine the trainability of the candidate. In the first step of the process, the trainer demonstrates how to perform a particular task. Then the job applicant is asked to perform the task while the trainer helps to coach him or her through the process several times. Finally, the candidate is expected to perform the task independently. The trainer carefully monitors the performance, recording any errors, to determine the overall trainability of the job applicant.

Both work sample tests and trainability tests have been shown to have high to moderate success predicting job performance.[53] Many managers, as well as job applicants, prefer these types of tests over the cognitive ability or aptitude tests because of their face validity (that is, the tests are *perceived* to be valid measures of future work performance by applicants and managers). Essentially, job applicants are more readily able

---

Exactly What Are Personality Inventories?

Personality inventories attempt to discern general personality characteristics by asking applicants questions. Although there are numerous types, in general, personality inventories are designed to identify applicants' personality traits or expected behavior in order to assess their fitness for employment.

Personality inventories can be administered in several ways. One means is to have applicants read the questions and complete a computer-readable answer sheet by filling in the circles that correspond to their responses with a number 2 pencil. The answer sheets are either sent to the test developer for grading or graded by the employer using a grading system purchased from the test creator. Another alternative is to have the test creator telephone the applicants and read them questions. Respondents indicate their answers by pressing certain keys on the telephone keypad. A more personalized option is to have the applicant participate in a face-to-face interview with a psychologist who asks the questions.

Because the focus of questions found on personality inventories is on personal beliefs, some of the questions may be intrusive and illegal. For example, questions that refer to religious affiliation or practices may cause disparate treatment in that employers may use answers provided to decide not to hire an individual. Questions that may fall into this category include the following:

- Do you ever argue a point with an older person whom you respect?
- Do you feel marriage is essential to your present or future happiness?
- Do you tend to be radical in your political, religious, or social beliefs?
- Would you like to be a church worker?
- Would you like to be a priest, minister, or rabbi?
- Would you like to read the Bible as a way of having fun?

Another problem that employers may face when using personality inventories as a selection device is invasion of privacy. This is exactly what happened in the Target case. Some questions that may invade an applicant's privacy include the following:

- I am fascinated by fire.
- I feel sure there is only one true religion.
- I would like to be a florist.
- My sex life is satisfactory.
- I am very strongly attracted to members of my own sex.
- Evil spirits possess me sometimes.

SOURCE: Adapted from Daniel P. O'Meara, "Personality Tests Raise Questions of Legality and Effectiveness," *HRMagazine*, January 1994, pp. 97–100.

---

to understand why they are suited or not suited for a particular job by actually performing the job or a portion of it.

PERSONALITY AND GENERAL INTEREST INVENTORIES

Personality and general interest inventories are tests that have no "correct" or "incorrect" answers. Interest tests are used to measure an individual's work and career orientations. Personality tests focus on identifying traits or typical behaviors of individuals and are used to measure a variety of traits including aggression, self-esteem, and Type A behavior. Although personality tests can be costly, they can help human resource managers determine individual characteristics not obtained from a resume, thus increasing the likelihood of finding a good "fit" between the job position and the employee. Most human resource managers and psychologists caution, however, that personality and general tests are not usually predictive of performance on the job and should not be used as selection devices. Nevertheless, some evidence exists in support of the use of personality inventories as a selection device.[54]

A serious criticism of personality inventories is their tendency to be invasive in that they seek to "uncover revealing data about a person's psyche."[55] Companies that use this type of preemployment test must therefore ensure that the information they seek and the way they use this information are relevant to the job in order to prevent lawsuits by rejected applicants. The legal challenges to written preemployment tests, in particular personality inventories, could result in legislation restricting their use,[56] especially after the well-publicized *Soroka* vs. *Dayton Hudson Corporation* case in which Target stores were sued for using a personality inventory to select security guards for their stores. Target admitted no wrongdoing, but it did settle the case for $2 million, a costly sum for not doing anything wrong.

HONESTY TESTS

In an attempt to identify employees who do not have a propensity to steal, firms may rely on honesty tests as a selection tool. Until 1988, the best way to assess an applicant's honesty was by performing a polygraph test. A polygraph, or lie detector, measures an individual's respiration, blood pressure, and perspiration while the individual answers a series of questions. Changes from the baseline for any of these indicators may mean the person is lying. However, in 1988 President Reagan approved new legislation that disallowed polygraph testing for preemployment screening of applicants.[57]

The more current way in which honesty is measured is via a paper and pencil test. Research has shown that thieves will give themselves away when asked direct questions about their honesty.[58] Specifically, thieves believe that everybody steals. Hence, if they indicate that they do not steal, their test results indicate that they are lying. So, they admit to stealing. Further, they suspect that their employers know they are stealing and openly admit to their crimes, even though they may tone down the actual severity of their transgressions. In other words, it is difficult for thieves to fake honesty. For this reason, honesty tests can be good predictors of applicants with the propensity to steal.

THE INTERVIEW

Most organizations, regardless of size, use interviewing as a selection method. Interestingly, interviews have been criticized for being unreliable sources of information due to perceptual and judgment errors on the part of the interviewer.[59] For example, interviewers often form a first impression of the job applicant based on information obtained on the application blank or the first two minutes of the interview. Initial impressions are often resistant to change, even though they are made with little objective information. Interviewers may base subsequent questions and judge the candidate's responses on these first impressions in an attempt to confirm their beliefs about the candidate.

HALO EFFECT
Rating someone high or low on a number of characteristics simply because he or she possesses one characteristic.

Another type of perceptual error is called the **halo effect.** In this case, one characteristic or behavior of the job applicant (positive or negative) overrides all or most other characteristics. For example, if an applicant comes to the interview dressed very professionally, the interviewer might unconsciously evaluate other characteristics (such as dependability or knowledge of the business field) as also being of a professional nature.

CONTRAST EFFECT
Evaluating an applicant as higher or lower based solely on the perceived quality of previous applicants.

Contrast effects have also been found to distort interviewers' judgments about job applicants. Contrast effects occur when the interviewer evaluates a job applicant by comparing this person to previous job applicants. For example, an average applicant might be judged as excellent if prior applicants were of very poor quality. Similarly, this same person might be evaluated lower if he or she follows a high-quality applicant.

Other perceptual errors that can distort an interviewer's evaluation include stereotyping, leniency, strictness, and central tendency errors. These perceptual errors are discussed in detail in Chapter 10 on performance evaluations.

To Tell the Truth

NEWSFLASH: American employees steal $40 billion worth of goods and services from businesses every year! Such an astounding figure was estimated by the U.S. Chamber of Commerce and works out to $7,125 a minute in thefts, which is 10 times the cost of the nation's street crime. It is no wonder that U.S. employers are grasping at any tools that might assist them in policing dishonest employees. The methods employers choose to screen applicants may be dependent upon factors outside of their control, however.

What "guns" are available to help employers screen applicants and fight the crimes committed by employees inside organizations? The 1988 Employee Polygraph Protection Act declared preemployment screening by polygraph illegal in most cases (the government can still use polygraph testing). Credit checks have proven to be unreliable predictors of honesty. Although helpful, background and reference checks are proving to be less and less valuable to employers since the applicants' former employers are less willing to provide information beyond verifying when the candidate was employed. One obvious reason that companies are hesitant about providing information about a former employee is the fear of the potential legal ramifications.

One tool employers may use to screen dishonest applicants is the paper-and-pencil assessment instrument known as an *integrity* or *honesty test.* Although honesty tests certainly have their share of critics, the American Psychological Association (APA) recently released a report stating that the preponderance of the evidence supports the idea that some of the tests can help predict which prospective employees may be undependable or steal. The question has been raised, however, whether the users of these tests even understand how to interpret what the scores mean. The APA report recommends better training for employers who use and interpret the exams and proposes that the tests not be used as a primary or sole means for assessing an applicant's qualifications. Although an earlier report released by Congressional Office of Technology Assessment raised questions about the reliability of honesty tests, the APA report may serve to reduce those concerns. At any rate, the debate about whether honesty tests should be used as a preemployment screening device is certainly not over.

SOURCES: Adapted from R. Zemke, "Do Honesty Tests Tell the Truth?" *Training,* October 1990, pp. 75–81; and G. Fuchsberg, "Prominent Psychologists Group Gives Qualified Support to Integrity Tests," *The Wall Street Journal,* March 7, 1991, p. A6.

Establishing a system for conducting an interview can improve the reliability and validity of interview assessments.[60] The following guidelines should be followed when establishing a system for interviewing:

1. Determine the job requirements through a formal job analysis.
2. Focus on only those knowledge requirements, skills, abilities, and other characteristics necessary to perform the job well.
3. Develop interview questions based on the information gathered in the job analysis.
4. Conduct the interview in a relaxed setting. Try to put the job applicant at ease by giving general information about the company and asking simple questions.
5. Evaluate each candidate according to his or her relevant job knowledge, skills, and abilities.

In addition to these guidelines, human resource managers must choose which *type* of interview to conduct. Interviews can be classified into three general categories: structured, semistructured, and unstructured. The following sections describe each of these categories. In addition, stress interviews are discussed.

STRUCTURED

When conducting a structured interview, the interviewer asks questions from a prepared list and does not deviate from this list except for some follow-up questions. During the interview, the interviewer records his or her thoughts and reactions on a standard organizational form. When different interviewers reach the same or very similar conclusions about a given candidate, the interrater reliability is high. Generally, structured interviews result in a high interrater reliability and can be helpful if gathering precisely the same information from each candidate is very important. In addition, structured interviews help to ensure that all necessary information is obtained. Unfortunately, this type of interview is very restrictive; thus, important and relevant information about the candidate may never be discussed. This approach can also be frustrating to job candidates who are not allowed to elaborate on or qualify their responses.

BEHAVIORAL DESCRIPTION INTERVIEW
Asking applicants questions about how they performed in the past in order to predict how they will perform in the future.

Two common types of structured interviews are the behavioral description interview and the situational interview. The **behavioral description interview** was developed by Tom Janz based on the notion that the best predictor of future performance is past performance.[61] When using this type of interview, applicants are asked to give specific examples of how they performed their job duties in the past or how they handled a specific problem in the past. Their initial responses are followed by probing questions designed to garner even more information about exactly *how* the individual acted in a past situation. The types of activities focused on are ones that will most likely be part of the job. To determine what these activities might be, job analysis results can be used.

Hershey Foods uses the behavioral description type of structured interview. Candidates are asked what they would do to resolve a real-life work problem. They are given a work situation and asked how they would respond if actually confronted with this situation.[62] By using behavioral description interviews, John T. Phillips, director of Training and Development at S.C. Johnson & Son, Inc., hopes to discover whether the job applicant will "fit" with the company. A job candidate might be told, "Give me a specific example of a time you had to reprimand an employee and tell me what action you took. In addition, what were the results of your reprimand?"[63] Note the specific nature of the question rather than a general one: "How would you reprimand an employee?" Another firm that implemented this type of interview system surveyed all of the above average workers in the organization to determine what characteristics they all shared that made them successful. Then, the firm designed specific questions to elicit information about whether applicants possessed these qualities. A guideline about specific behaviors to look for in candidate's answers was developed and used to train interviewers. Currently, every applicant who applies to this firm must take part in a behavioral description interview.

However, these interviews are not always kind to the applicant. Applicants are generally not prepared for questions such as, "Tell me about a time in the past when you had to get someone to do something for you. How did you go about it?" This could be followed up with questions such as "How did the person react to your actions?" or "How did it turn out?" Because the applicant is not expecting such a question, he or she may have to sit quietly and think about an example that fits the situation. A silence of only 30 seconds feels like 5 minutes, and the applicant may begin to fill the quiet by talking about an example that does not fit. Hence, in this type of interview, applicants who think well on their feet generally succeed. However, if this is not a characteristic needed in the job, this type of interview may not be the appropriate one.

SITUATIONAL INTERVIEW
A type of interview in which interviewees are asked to describe how they might act in a given situation.

The second type of structured interview is the **situational interview,** which was developed by Gary Latham and his associates.[64] To create this type of interview, job experts develop questions that focus on situations that might arise in the actual job. For example, an applicant for a teller position might be asked to describe how he or she would act if an irate customer came to his or her window. The job experts also develop above average, average, and below average responses to which interviewers can refer to judge the quality of an answer. Finally, situational interviews usually are conducted with a panel of interviewers, each of whom independently rates the applicant. These ratings are then averaged to produce an overall rating for the applicant. This type of interview is kinder to the applicant because a past example does not have to be provided. However, this same kindness is a potential problem for this type of interview procedure. Specifically, an applicant may respond in the manner that he or she thinks will get the job, not necessarily in the way he or she would actually act.

SEMISTRUCTURED

In a semistructured interview, only the major questions are prepared in advance and are recorded on a standardized form. This type of interview involves some planning on the part of the interviewer but allows for some flexibility regarding exactly what and how questions are asked. Although the interrater reliability of the information is not as high as with the structured interview, the information obtained may be richer and possibly more relevant. In essence, this approach to interviewing allows the interviewer to ask the key questions without imposing unnecessary restrictions on the interviewee. Interviewers go into the interview knowing what they hope to learn from a candidate and then ask questions to elicit this information. One way this is accomplished is by asking the candidate a very broad question and then getting more and more specific with follow-up questions. For example, an interviewer might ask a college applicant to talk about a class he or she recently completed. Based on the information provided by the candidate, many different paths could be taken in follow-up questions. One possibility would be to focus on a group project that was required. Another would be to ask the applicant to summarize the one main point that he or she remembered from the class. Whichever approach is taken, it is selected to provide the most job-relevant information about the applicant as possible. Once this approach is exhausted, a new general question is posed and the process is repeated.

UNSTRUCTURED

The unstructured interview involves little or no planning on the part of the interviewer. Due to a lack of planning, the interviews tend to vary greatly between interviewees and also between interviewers. In addition, important job-related issues may be left unexplored. Unstructured interviews have low interrater reliability and seldom yield valid or useful information. Thus, unstructured interviews are not recommended as a selection device.

STRESS

The stress interview attempts to create anxiety in the job candidates and to put pressure on them to see how they perform under these conditions. The interviewer usually behaves aggressively and at times insults the candidate. Managers who have used this approach justify it by arguing that, if hired, the job candidate would be placed in a stressful position. This type of interview can help the human resource manager evaluate how a job candidate might react under stress. Of course, this type of interview often creates a negative image of the interviewer and the company, thus, the job candidate may decide to look elsewhere. Because they may cause a firm to lose an excellent job candidate, stress interviews are not common. If a position is inherently stressful and the organization would like to ascertain the candidate's stress management skills, this can be assessed by asking an applicant to recall a time when he or she dealt with a stressful situation, such as an irate customer. Simulating a stressful work experience is another viable technique.[65]

One company that has successfully used stress interviews is Dataflex.[66] Rick Rose, CEO of Dataflex, says that to be a successful sales associate for the company, an employee needs four qualities. These include (1) confidence in his or her own abilities, (2) a willingness to take calculated risks, (3) a great sense of humor, and (4) nimble thinking, or the ability when put on the spot to take the available information and formulate the best possible response instantly. To make sure that applicants have these qualities, Rose uses the stress interview technique. It begins with a phone conversation with the applicant in which his administrative assistant tells the applicant that he or she is not the type of employee the firm is looking for. Those who hang up lose; those who argue with her proceed to the next step, an interview with Rose.

In the first interview, Rose says he is deliberately confrontational. He criticizes applicants, puts them on the spot, and challenges them. This is all done in an effort to see what they would be like when confronted by a customer. If they are too sensitive, they will not do well. If the responses are rote interview responses, not truthful answers, the applicants fail. For example, Rose tells a candidate who says that he or she is in sales to help people, to become a nurse. After five minutes or so, Rose tells the applicant that he or she is not very impressive (even when he or she is). This is done to get the applicant to sell himself or herself to Rose, demonstrating the strength of his or her sales potential. After several other negative activities, Rose sends the candidates on their way and waits for them to call back. Those who do not call do not get the job; those who do get a second interview.

The second interview is with the current sales staff. Each candidate spends 15 minutes or so with each member of the sales staff. These interviews are much like the one with Rose.

Currently, Dataflex has fewer sales associates than when Rose joined the company; current sales associates write $90 to $100 million of sales compared to $5 million of sales written when there were more associates. This stress interview tactic weeds out the squeamish and the uncommitted and seems to work for Dataflex.

IMPROVING THE INTERVIEW

A company can take a variety of steps to improve the quality of its interviews. For example, it is important that the negative as well as positive aspects of the job are mentioned.[67] The interview is usually thought of as a means of selling the company, but if only positive information is presented, the hopes and expectations of applicants may be unrealistically high. When this occurs, turnover rises and satisfaction plummets. Another improvement involves revamping the interview system to make sure that it can identify the type of people the firm wants to hire.[68] Because the demographic makeup of the workforce is changing so rapidly, the interview procedures organizations use may also need to change. Taking a closer look to ensure that the interview procedures are gender and race neutral is a wise organizational decision.

Drexelbrook Engineering took steps to improve its screening interview.[69] First, the applicant is asked to complete an application form while seated at a table where information about the company is available. Whether or not the applicant looks at the material is noted. Next, the interviewer studies the application to determine whether any information has been omitted, and why the applicant left (or wishes to leave) the last (current) place of employment. The interviewer then engages the applicant in verbal interaction to judge his or her verbal expression and appearance. The interviewer is instructed to explore the applicant's needs. If he or she is currently unemployed, when can he or she start? If currently employed, what does he or she do in the present job? Next the interviewer talks about the company and the job to be filled. Finally, the applicant is asked what he or she wants to know. The type of questions asked are noted. The interview ends on a friendly note with a specific promise of when the applicant will hear from the company. Although this may not seem like a great deal of information, it is more than adequate to determine whether to consider the applicant. Because this system collects more than just information about the verbal qualities of the applicant, the hiring decisions made have improved since the system was implemented.

REFERENCE CHECKING

Most organizations ask an applicant for a list of references that includes previous supervisors or co-workers. Because the employee generates the list of references, these individuals will most likely present a positive image of the applicant. Letters of recommendation are also considered a type of reference. Again, these letters are usually solicited by the applicant, so many employers do not consider these as a good selection device by themselves. Studies have found, however, that if the letter contains specific behavioral examples, the applicant is viewed more favorably.[70]

Another reason that references can be overly positive is that many organizations are afraid to provide accurate appraisals of their former or present employees for fear of lawsuits.[71] Instead, they simply provide dates of employment as references. However, this is not as safe as one might imagine. Following this policy also can open a firm to litigation. For example, negligent hiring can occur due to the acceptance of a weak reference. As previously discussed, an employer can be held liable if an employee causes injury to a third party (customer, co-worker, and so on) and it is proven that the employer failed to adequately check the employee's background. Employers have a duty to find out if an employee is unfit. Charges of negligent referrals can be lodged by a third party or an employer against another employer for giving a reference that either misstated or omitted facts about the individual. Further, under the compelled self-publication doctrine, an employer can be held liable for defamation, even if it provides only dates of services, if a former employee is compelled to report to his or her prospective employer the reason for termination. The increase of cases involving these issues indicates that potential employers believe that they have the right to accurate information and that former employers have a duty to report it. Providing anything else is a risky proposition.

A firm can take several steps to use reference checking to its advantage.[72] First, the organization must decide, usually through a thorough job analysis, what key qualities are needed for the job. Reference checkers should ask questions designed to elicit information that will tell whether the applicant possesses these qualities. Some of these qualities might be a person's commitment to project completion (i.e., getting things done) or ability to predict needs before they arise (i.e., to plan). Giving the reference two alternatives helps to identify strengths and weaknesses. For example, asking whether the individual prefers to work with people or with technical equipment elicits specific information. If you are looking for the one they do not mention, you have revealed a weakness.

PHYSICAL EXAMINATION

Many organizations require a complete physical examination prior to hiring to ensure that the candidate is physically able to perform the job. For example, airline pilots are required by law to undergo an extensive physical examination. Physical examinations can also be useful for placement purposes. Individuals with lung or breathing problems may be best placed into jobs void of any smoke, dust, or fumes. In addition, a good physical examination should document any physical problems to avoid the possibility of worker compensation claims being filed against the company for a preexisting condition.

Physical examinations can also include drug and alcohol testing. Employers are reluctant to hire individuals who abuse drugs or alcohol, partially because of the higher absenteeism and turnover rates among these employees. In addition, employees do not work to their full potential and are more susceptible to accidents when they are under the influence of drugs or alcohol. Although many employees find substance abuse testing programs in violation of their privacy, local, state, and federal regulations have not provided a standard and definitive set of guidelines for testing.

Acquired Immune Deficiency Syndrome (AIDS) testing has become a very controversial topic for businesses.[73] In general, most medical specialists believe that AIDS testing in organizations is unnecessary because the disease cannot be contracted from AIDS patients under normal working conditions. Although AIDS testing is not part of a routine physical examination, some cities, such as San Francisco, have adopted city ordinances prohibiting discrimination on the basis of AIDS. Discrimination issues regarding the acquired immune deficiency syndrome were discussed in Chapter 4.

Many large companies choose to employ an in-house physician to perform physical examinations. A company physician has the advantage of knowing the physical demands and hazards for jobs and may be better able to help make knowledgeable decisions about hiring or placement. Obviously, the cost of an in-house physician may be prohibitive for many organizations. Exhibit 7.12 summarizes many of the selection methods discussed here and the frequency with which organizations use them.

JOB OFFER AND HIRING

The final steps in the selection process are making the job offer and hiring the candidate. When employers extend a job offer to a candidate, it usually describes the types

EXHIBIT 7.12   Selection Techniques and the Frequency of Usage

Technique	Percentage of Firms Reporting Use
Application forms	87%
Medical examinations	50
Mental ability	31
Ability tests	78
Drug tests	26
Honesty tests	7
Reference checking	96
Weighted application forms	11
Interviews	94
Personality inventory	17
Lie detector tests	5

Sources: A.M. Ryan and P. Sackett, "A Survey of Individual Assessment Practices by I/O Psychologists," *Personnel Psychology,* 40, 1987, pp. 455–488; Bureau of National Affairs, *1988-89 Survey of Fortune 500 Companies,* Washington DC; I.T. Robertson and P.J. Makin, "Management Selection in Britain: A Survey and Critique," *Journal of Occupational Psychology* 59, pp. 45–57.

HR CHALLENGE

Selecting Expatriates

As more and more organizations expand internationally, selecting the appropriate expatriate for these new international jobs becomes an important consideration. Recent reports indicate that between 40 and 70 percent of all expatriate placements do not serve their allotted appointment. Reasons for early returns vary, but the most common are the spouse's inability to adjust, the employee's inability to adjust, the employee's lack of personal and or emotional maturity, and other family problems. There are two ways to combat these problems: develop better procedures to select expatriates and provide support for the whole family.

With respect to the improving selection procedures, several suggestions can be made. Research has found that three qualities—self-orientation, other orientation, and perceptual orientation—are needed for an expatriate to succeed in an international placement. *Self-orientation* means that the individual has good mental health, high self-esteem, and self-confidence. *Other orientation* means that the individual can get along well with others, has strong language skills, and understands nonverbal language. Finally, *perceptual*

orientation means that the individual has the ability to understand why foreigners act as they do and can accept these actions. To ensure that the expatriate selected possesses these qualities, the selection procedure should incorporate selection techniques that measure them.

Support for the entire family can be provided in a variety of ways. First, before they leave the country, family members can be enrolled in culture and language classes. This will help them to better understand what to expect on arrival. Also, cultural counselors should be available on arrival. These counselors provide services that include helping to secure a place to live, registering with the authorities, shopping, or assisting with any other problems that arise during the move. Incorporating one or both of these suggestions should help to increase the expatriate's length of stay.

SOURCES: Bill Leonard, "Guardian Angels Help Overseas Employees," *HRMagazine,* April 1994, pp. 59–60; Marvina Shilling, "Avoid Expatriate Shock," *HRMagazine,* July 1993, pp. 58–63.

of duties and responsibilities the new employee will be expected to perform. The employer usually discusses salary (although this is often established well before the actual hiring occurs), benefits, promotions, vacation time, sick leave, employee assistance programs, and other policies of the organization. Although many of these were probably discussed during recruitment, it is always wise to keep important organizational policies and strategies salient to the employee. Finally, important documents are completed and signed (such as the employment contract and benefit forms), and the new employee begins his or her new job and new role as a member of the organization.

MANAGERIAL SELECTION DEVICES

ASSESSMENT CENTERS
Processes in which applicants are asked to perform a variety of job-related tasks and then judged on their perfomances.

Selection devices for managers can differ from nonmanagerial employee selection. In general, selection devices for managers should assess numerous skills and abilities because of the wide range of skills needed for successful performance. **Assessment centers** (which can last from one day to one week) were developed to tap these numerous managerial skills by collecting work sample information. An assessment center is not a place but a process. In this process, trained professional evaluators, called *assessors,* observe, record and evaluate how a candidate performs in simulated job situations.[74] Generally, a variety of tasks is required to be completed by the assessees. Some of the most common ones include (1) in-basket techniques, in which the job candidate must decide how to organize numerous letters and memorandums by priority and ask for more information, delegate, or make a decision regarding them, (2) leaderless group discussions, in which the candidate engages in a typical simulated meeting, (3) role-playing, in which the candidate interacts with other "managers" or "subordinates," and (4) speech making. Each potential manager is assessed by several raters to increase the reliability of the hiring or promotion decision. Assessment centers have been found to be a valid means of assessing managerial potential,[75] but they are extremely costly; thus, they are usually used for upper-level or top managerial positions.

However, one firm, Mercury Communications in England, has found that assessment centers can be used for front-line staff selection as well. In a two-year period, Mercury had to select 1,000 customer service representatives. When hiring such large numbers, turnover can be a problem. Unless the person hired can do the job well, fit well in the organization, and like the job, he or she will quit, usually very quickly. To avoid this problem, Mercury decided to design an assessment center to select telecommunications customer assistants. The perfect applicant would have active listening skills, customer sensitivity, and the ability to cope in a pressurized environment. To locate individuals with these skills, the assessment center requires applicants to participate in simulated exercises with customers, a criteria-based interview, a keyboard skills test, and psychometric tests. From the initial pool of 1,600 applicants, 350 were sent through the assessment center. Of these, 127 were hired. The process resulted in about 18 hires per week. Mercury says by 1995 it hopes to have filled 1,300 full and part-time positions.[76]

Although the validity of assessment centers tends to be high, some problems recently have been identified with this selection device. For example, some researchers have found that assessment centers can produce hostile or defensive reactions among some candidates.[77] Also, assessment center formats have been found to cause a high level of anxiety in some applicants. Further, the "audience effect" may be detrimental to the performance of some individuals. That is, some participants may not perform as well as they are capable of because the assessors constantly watch them.[78] Hence, when using assessment centers it is important to keep in mind that these problems could prevent the identification of qualified applicants.

CONSEQUENCES OF NOT HIRING AN APPLICANT

FALSE NEGATIVE SELECTION DECISION
Rejecting a qualified applicant.

Not hiring certain individuals can have numerous consequences. As depicted in Exhibit 7.13 both personal and societal outcomes are affected by rejecting an individual who should have been selected, that is, making a **false negative selection decision,** or by correctly rejecting an applicant who should not have been selected. Using the model in Exhibit 7.13, let's examine what might happen to a qualified individual who was rejected. At one extreme, the applicant could attribute the rejection to his or her lack of ability, which could lower his or her level of self-esteem and motivation to seek employment, resulting in a decision to abandon the job search. This scenario has possible detrimental outcomes for society as a whole. For example, this person's talent and ability are wasted and the firm must continue to expend resources to locate a qualified applicant. However, if this applicant understood that the rejection was due to a decision error, he or she might feel inequitably treated but continue to seek the same type of employment. The odds are in his or her favor that such a decision error will not occur again and that he or she will secure an appropriate job.

If the decision not to hire the person was correct, and the applicant realized that a correctable deficiency prevented his or her selection, the applicant might seek to correct this deficiency. After completing the developmental activities, the applicant's next attempt to locate a similar job should have a higher probability of success. Another op-

■ **EXHIBIT 7.13**   **The Consequences of Rejecting an Applicant**

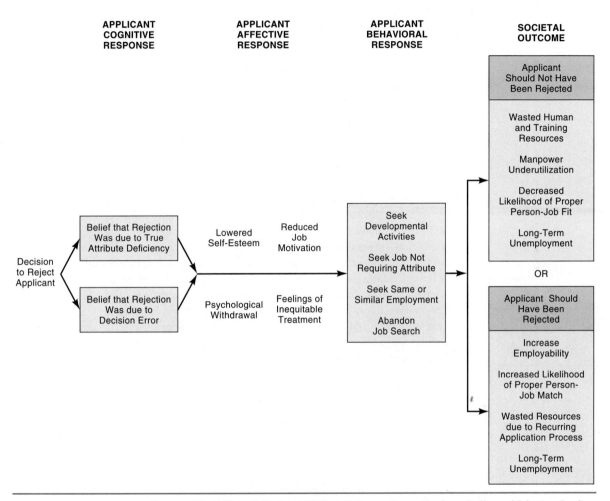

SOURCE: Adapted from G. Dreher and P. Sackett, *Perspectives on Employee Staffing and Selection: Readings and Commentary* (Homewood, IL: Irwin, 1983).

tion is for the individual to realize that the rejection was due to a deficiency and to seek employment in a different area that better matches his or her current qualifications. Both of these cases have very positive societal outcomes; the organization hires a person who possesses the job skills required and the applicant obtains a job he or she feels confident doing. Thus, both the individual and the organization win.

STRATEGIES FOR EFFECTIVE RECRUITING AND SELECTION

The organization's strategy can affect the recruiting and selection process. The following section is based on Miles and Snow's strategy typology discussed in previous chapters, namely, defenders, prospectors, and analyzers.[79] In general, organizations with different strategies should recruit different types of individuals for employment.[80]

Organizations with a defender strategy have narrow and relatively stable product-market domains. As a result of their narrow focus, these types of organizations seldom make major changes in their technology, structure, or methods of operation. They devote most of their attention to improving efficiency. Defenders emphasize "making" employees rather than "buying" highly trained or educated employees. Thus, little recruiting is done above the entry level and selection is based on weeding out undesirable or unqualified applicants. Defenders emphasize training their employees and usually have formal and extensive training programs. Thus, defenders might choose to use trainability tests or to give intelligence or aptitude tests to identify those individuals most likely to learn from training. Finally, defenders will usually seek out people with backgrounds in finance or production, given their narrow and stable market.[81]

Organizations with a prospector strategy search for product and market opportunities and experiment with responses to emerging environmental trends. Often, these types of organizations create change and uncertainty to which competing organizations must respond. Prospectors emphasize "buying" their employees rather than "making" employees through elaborate training programs. Recruiting methods are sophisticated at all levels of the hierarchy and efforts are focused on identifying appropriate skills and acquiring qualified individuals. Given the emphasis on "buying" employees, training programs are limited. Thus, prospectors might prefer to use work sample tests as a selection device. Finally, because prospectors seek to exploit new product and market domains, they often look for individuals with basic marketing or engineering research skills.[82]

Organizations with an analyzer strategy operate in two types of product-market domains, one relatively stable and the other changing. In stable areas, these organizations operate routinely and efficiently. However, in their more innovative areas, managers watch the competition carefully for new ideas and quickly respond or adapt to those that appear to be the most promising. Analyzers use a mix of recruiting and selection approaches and emphasize both "make" and "buy" strategies. Training programs are usually formal and extensive, although little recruitment is done outside the organization. Analyzers might prefer to use a variety of selection devices given their emphasis on both "make" and "buy" strategies. Given that analyzers operate in mixed markets, they look for individuals with abilities in applied research, marketing, and production.[83]

The organizational strategy not only affects a firm's recruiting approaches and selection criteria but also affects which attitudes and personality traits are seen as the best match or "fit" between the applicant and the organization.[84] For example, employees with a need for risk taking and a high tolerance for change and ambiguity would be well suited in an organization with a prospector strategy. Conversely, an employee with a need for structure and a low tolerance for change and ambiguity might be better suited in an organization with a defender strategy.[85]

Managers must not only be sure that the selection criteria are job related but also should consider whether the criteria are consistent with the strategies and culture of the organization. The relationships between strategy and recruiting and between selection and training are still somewhat speculative. These relationships assume that staffing decisions are (1) consistent with one another and (2) consistent with the strategy of the firm.[86] Thus, these relationships should be viewed only as a general guide for managers.

STRATEGIC STAFFING TO SUPPORT STRATEGY IMPLEMENTATION

The focus of this chapter so far has been on identifying the key aspects of recruiting and selection that are necessary for an employer to find the right people. Although accurate and comprehensive techniques are critical to effective acquisition, they represent only part of the process that organizations must consider. Taking a broader perspective, human resource professionals recognize that proper staffing is critical to the implementation of the strategic plan of the firm. After all, employees should enhance and facilitate the firm's strategy, not complicate it.

Strategic staffing involves three groups of activities: (1) the acquisition of personnel, (2) the orientation and socialization of new employees, and (3) the movement of employees into the proper positions within the organization.[87] This section focuses on how staffing will enhance strategic implementation via the three activities mentioned above.

ACQUISITION OF EMPLOYEES

Generally speaking, the role of acquisition in strategic implementation refers to getting the right people in key places.[88] Once there, they can maximize their contribution to the organization's goals. Acquiring people with the right skill mix and characteristics for any given position is the crux of human resource management. One major trend in employee acquisition is the use of contingent personnel.

As organizations focus on cost-cutting strategies, the use of contingent personnel as opposed to permanent employees receives more consideration from top management. Contingent personnel refers to those employees hired from temporary employment agencies, leased from employee leasing companies, or, obtained through independent contracting to perform specific tasks.[89] As previously discussed, the costs of maintaining the employee on the payroll system and completing the paperwork involved to be in compliance with federal employee regulations are greatly reduced, and to some extent eliminated, if contingent personnel are utilized. Thus, the organization can realize sizable savings in administrative human resource costs through the use of contingent personnel. Additionally, the use of contingent personnel can be increased or decreased to coincide with the changes in business conditions without severely penalizing the organization.[90] Contingent personnel may be obtained through the use of temporary employees, employee leasing, and independent contracting, and is a strategic decision that all firms must contemplate.

SOCIALIZATION AND ORIENTATION

The socialization and orientation of a new employee can be critical to the employee's acceptance of his or her new role and subsequent performance. Although socialization and orientation will be discussed in detail in Chapter 9, the emphasis here is on indoctrinating new employees to the strategic goals and objectives of the company at the outset. This process ensures that employee commitment will be increased and that the new employee's reasons for joining and staying with the company will be reaffirmed.[91]

MOVEMENT OF EMPLOYEES

The last aspect of strategic staffing involves the movement of employees into positions that best utilize their specific skills and abilities. Typically, we think of promotion as the movement in organizations that fulfills this role and achieves objectives. As hierarchical movement in the company becomes less likely due to downsizing, restructuring, or career plateauing, lateral moves and sometimes demotion become necessary movements.[92] If this process is managed properly, however, these movements can be positive and need not represent a de facto "career end."

Promotion can motivate and challenge employees, allowing them to grow intellectually while making an even greater contribution to the overall corporate goals. Unfortunately, most companies do not have an endless career tract for every employee, and for those in nonmanagerial or technical positions, the upward movement is almost nonexistent. Nevertheless, a few companies are creating technical and nonmanagerial career tracts for those who do not desire a managerial role in the company.[93] These alternative movements coincide with managerial tract movements in terms of recognition and compensation, creating incentive for employees in these areas to further their careers and continue to grow. The dual career-path choice is not for all firms, however, because it tends to be more costly than traditional movement systems.[94]

Lateral moves are increasingly being used as a way to broaden employee skills and present continued challenge. Learning a new job or a new aspect of the business is beneficial to both the employee and the company and should not be overlooked as a viable method for achieving corporate goals.[95] Especially important to firms pursuing an international expansion strategy, lateral transfers of U.S. managers to foreign operations can be critical to the success or failure of the global expansion.[96] It is the creation of this broad perspective and the familiarity with several aspects of the firm's business that is often critical to formulating and implementing successful strategic plans.

Demotion is the final movement that must be considered in organizations. Although it is often viewed as a "dirty word," demotion is sometimes inevitable because of mergers and downsizing.[97] In the face of layoffs and cuts in the workforce, many employees may gladly accept a decrease in responsibility and authority in order to stay employed. Although demotion need not always be a result of disciplinary action, this is often the case, and many organizations simply will not consider it as a career movement to enhance strategy.[98] Demotion often results in employee dissatisfaction, poor subsequent performance, and eventually, turnover.[99] All of these effects are costly to the organization and should be minimized as much as possible.

Strategic staffing can and should be used to enhance and facilitate the strategic plan of the organization. Any implementation of an organizational goal or objective should include an analysis of the types and extent of staffing changes necessary. This allows the strategic plan to be carried out in the most efficient, timely manner.

MANAGEMENT GUIDELINES

Decisions regarding recruitment and selection are crucial for effective organizational performance. The following management guidelines should be helpful when making these decisions.

1. Managers should consider recruiting minorities, females, handicapped, and older workers as the workforce demographics change.
2. Managers can often improve employee satisfaction and commitment and lower turnover costs by promoting from within the company when feasible.
3. Realistic job previews can provide employees with accurate expectations and, as a result, the organization may benefit from higher employee satisfaction and lower turnover.
4. Career development should usually be part of any training program for new hires.

Continued

> 5. Preemployment forms should be free of questions that could be perceived as discriminating.
> 6. Affirmative action principles, if observed in the recruiting and selection process, can help to develop a more diverse workforce.
> 7. Measurement reliability and validity should always be considered in the recruiting and selection process.
> 8. The specific recruiting and selection methods should be consistent with the strategic thrust of the firm.

QUESTIONS FOR REVIEW

1. What types of strategic choices do managers have when deciding on recruiting and selection efforts?
2. What is the purpose of a realistic job preview?
3. What are the alternatives to recruiting?
4. What is negligent hiring? How can it be avoided?
5. Why should selection measures be reliable and valid? What does this mean?
6. How does the strategy of the firm affect the recruiting and selection process?
7. What is a correlation coefficient?

CASE

HIRING THE EDUCATED—A NEW APPROACH TO STAFFING THE AUTOMOBILE FACTORY[100]

Working in a factory is often a tedious, boring, and relentless job. Because of these job characteristics, highly educated workers have not been considered appropriate candidates for such work. Placing educated people in a monotonous job without any possibility for advancement was thought to be a good recipe for turnover. However, this theory is being reconsidered. Both Ford and Chrysler are looking for better educated employees to staff their automobile lines. The reason? Things are changing.

First, old plants where cars were made by hand by skilled craftsmen are virtually nonexistent. In their place stand high-tech factories. Training the workers who staffed the old plants to run the new ones has been a nightmare. In one specific example, training hours reached 1 million because of the poor skills of the workers, the vast majority of whom had not even finished high school. By selecting educated employees, a firm's training costs should decline.

Second, team-based management is becoming a necessity. Three years ago, Chrysler had 1 salaried worker for every 25 hourly workers. That figure has now dropped to 1 to 48. Because there are not enough supervisors, workers will have to supervise themselves. Educated workers have more potential to do this than workers who have not finished high school.

Third, the nature of the work is changing. When a line worker notices a problem in production, he or she can stop the line, inform the authorities, and help to find a way to fix it. Performing these tasks will require better educated workers.

Fourth, competition is changing. All of the auto manufacturers have entered the global market, and they need qualified workers to help them succeed. To compete, Ford and Chrysler have begun to use the manufacturing techniques developed by their foreign competitors. However, these competitors select from among the best and brightest graduates from technical schools to employ in their plants. To compete, Ford and Chrysler will have to recruit better educated employees too.

But what educated worker would want this type of job? Plenty of them. With job opportunities so tight for college graduates, jobs that once were considered beneath them are now viewed as plum. Jeffrey Pancheshan holds an MBA from the University of Windsor; he earned his degree to find a good job. The best job he found was working in a Chrysler car plant in Windsor. He is not alone. Twenty-six percent of the workers hired at the Windsor plant in December 1993 were college graduates. This is quite a change from the situation three short years ago, when 10 percent of the workforce had so much trouble reading and writing English that the union and the company had to institute a remedial education plan for the workers.

The current flood of highly qualified applicants is a very different situation for auto manufacturers than they previously experienced. Twenty and 30 years ago, Ford had trouble getting enough people to show up for work to keep its lines running. Recently, it had 110,000 applicants for 1,300 positions. While this may sound like an enviable position, designing a selection system to weigh each applicant's qualifications was no easy process.

To accomplish this task, Ford designed a selection system that incorporated a number of tests and procedures. Specifically, each applicant was given a test that lasted three and one-half hours. The test included working math problems, including the use of fractions and percentages; reading technical material and answering questions about it; performing a variety of dexterity tests; and demonstrating the ability to work as a team. Applicants who scored in the top half of the group and who had solid work histories were then interviewed by at least two employees who were responsible for selecting the most promising prospects. Then each applicant had to pass a drug test and a physical exam to ensure they have adequate physical ability to perform the job.

What type of employee does a selection system like this choose? About one-third attended college, and 4 percent have college degrees. Ninety-seven percent have high school diplomas. Some have completed trade school, and many are military veterans. The average age is higher than the past, nearly 30 years as compared to 17 to 18 years when high school dropouts were hired.

But what about turnover? Can a highly educated person be placed in a dead-end, boring job and be expected to stay? This question will only be answered with time. Both Ford and Chrysler recognize the potential for problems and realize that keeping these employees will be a challenge. But they also acknowledge that it takes a different person to build today's cars than it did to build them for these new workers' fathers.

QUESTIONS

1. What do you think Ford's overall strategic perspective is? How well does its new selection system support this strategy?

2. What steps are included in Ford's selection procedure? According to the chapter, what other techniques could it incorporate?

3. Are there any other factors that are causing the auto companies to alter their selection procedures and look for more educated employees?

4. How do you think this scenario will play out? Will the educated workers leave? Will they stay?

5. What type of work will the high school dropouts and immigrants who used to be selected to work in these car plants now be doing?

ADDITIONAL READINGS

Bies, Robert J., and Debra L. Shapiro. "Voice and Justification: Their Influence on Procedural Fairness Judgements." *Academy of Management* 31 (September 1988), pp. 676–685.

Buck, David N. "Staffing Internal Audit Departments in the Year 2000." *Internal Auditor* 47 (April 1990), pp. 24–30.

Cosentino, Chuck, John Allen, and Richard Wellins. "Choosing the Right People." *HRMagazine* 35 (March 1990), pp. 66–70.

Cowan, Robert A. "Sacred Cows—Roadblock to Professional Staffing?" *Manufacturing Systems* 8 (March 1990), pp. 58–61.

Dossin, Milton N., and Nancie L. Merritt. "Sign-On Bonu$e$ Score for Recruiters." *HRMagazine* 35 (March 1990), pp. 42–43.

Dreyfuss, Joel. "Get Ready for the New Work Force." *Fortune* 121 (April 23, 1990), pp. 165–181.

Elliott, Brian. "Astride the Demographic Time-Bomb." *Accountancy* (United Kingdom) 105. (March 1990), pp. 110, 112.

Greenbury, Linda. "What Do I Want to Do?" *Women in Management Review* (United Kingdom) 3 (1988), pp. 202–206.

Harrison, Sheila S., and Geraldine D. Jones. "Star Search: The Black Enterprise Executive Recruiter Directory." *Black Enterprise* 20 (April 1990), pp. 74–82.

Herman, Roger E. "The Competitive Environment." *Security Management* 34 (April 1990), pp. 107–110.

Hildenbrandt, Herbert W., and Jinuyin Liu. "Chinese Women Managers: A Comparison with Their U.S. and Asian Counterparts." *Human Resource Management* 27 (Fall 1989), pp. 291–314.

Kaman, Vicki S., and Cynthia Bentson. "Roleplay Simulations for Employee Selection: Design and Implementation." *Public Personnel Management* 17 (Spring 1988), pp. 1–8.

Kleinschrod, Walter A. "Temporary Help Complete Your Personnel Picture." *Today's Office* 24 (January 1990), pp. 28–40.

Koch, Jennifer. "Apple Ads Target Intellect." *Personnel Journal* 69 (March 1990), pp. 107–114.

Landes, Jennifer. "GAMC Report: Agent Referrals Produce Agents." *National Underwriter* 94 (March 26, 1990), pp. 3, 22.

Lee, Paula Munier. "The Employee Equation: A New System for Solving Your Business's 'People Problems.'" *Small Business Reports* 15 (April 1990), pp. 61–71.

Licht, Walter. "How the Workplace Has Changed in 75 Years." *Monthly Labor Review* 111 (February 1988), pp. 19–25.

McQuaid, Maureen, and Daren Winkler. "Using PMTs in Handicapped Workshops." *MTM Journal of Methods-Time Measurement* 13 (1987), pp. 50–58.

Marx, Jonathon. "Organizational Recruitment as a Two-Stage Process: A Comparative Analysis of Detroit and Yokohama." *Work & Occupations* 15 (August 1988), pp. 276–293.

Matte, Harry. "Cheese Plant Closing Opens New Doors." *Personnel Administrator* 33 (January 1988), pp. 52–56.

Packer, Arnold. "Skills Shortage Looms: We Can Handle It." *HRMagazine* 35 (April 1990), pp. 38–42.

Rhodes, David W. "Shootout in the Classroom." *Journal of Business Strategy* 11 (March–April 1990), pp. 50–52.

Samorodov, Aleksandr. "Coping with the Employment Effects of Restructuring in Eastern Europe." *International Labour Review* 128 (1989), pp. 357–371.

Schnorbus, Paula. "The Confidence Game." *Marketing & Media Decisions* 23 (May 1988), pp. 133–148.

Smith, Charles. "Cosmic Disturbance: Political Scandal Hits Operations of Japan's Recruit Group." *Far Eastern Economic Review* (Hong Kong) 143 (March 30, 1989), pp. 44–45.

Sonnerfield, Jeffrey A., and Maury A. Peiperl. "Staffing Policy as a Strategic Response: A Typology of Career Systems." *Academy of Management Review* 13 (October 1988), pp. 588–600.

Stanton, Michael. "Cooperative Education: Working towards Your Future." *Occupational Outlook Quarterly* 32 (Fall 1988), pp. 22–29.

Suppos, Dean A. "What Accident Histories Can Tell You." *Business & Health* 7 (March 1989), pp. 43–44.

Sweeney, Dennis C., Dean Haller, and Frederick Sale, Jr. "Individually Controlled Career Counseling." *Training & Development Journal* 41 (August 1987), pp. 58–61.

Tobias, Lester L. "Selecting for Excellence: How to Hire the Best." *Non Profit World* 8 (March–April 1990), pp. 23–25.

Zhou, Songnian. "A Trace-Drive Simulation Study of Dynamic Load Balancing." *IEEE Transactions on Software Engineering* 14 (September 1988), pp. 1327–1341.

NOTES

1. E. Blacharczyk, "Recruiters Challenged by Economy, Shortages, Unskilled," *HR News,* February 1990, p. B1.

2. Ibid; J. Braham, "No, You Don't Manage Everyone the Same," *Industry Week,* February 6, 1989, p. 29; and L. E. Wynter and J. Solomon, "A New Push to Break the 'Glass Ceiling,'" *The Wall Street Journal,* November 15, 1989, p. B1.

3. "Diversity-Friendly Practices Are Key to Survival" *HRNews,* March 1993, p A15.

4. E. Blacharczyk, "Recruiters Challenged."

5. Ibid., p. B4.

6. "Finding the Candidate before Panic Sets In," *The Wall Street Journal,* December 23, 1993, p. B1.

7. J. Jarrell, "A Wider Vision Needed to Control Hiring Costs," *HR News,* February 1990, p. B2.

8. "Survey Report: Hiring Costs Decreased in 1990," *HRFocus,* November 1991, p. 6; Margaret Magnus, "Is Your Recruitment All It Can Be?" *Personnel Journal,* February 1987, pp. 54–63.

9. "For Your Information," *Personnel Journal,* May 1991, p. 16.

10. E. Blacharczyk, "Recruiters Challenged," p. B4.

11. Ibid.

12. Larry Stevens, "Resume Scanning Simplifies Tracking," *Personnel Journal,* April 1993, pp. 77–79.

13. Lyn Murphy, "Streamline the Application Process," *HRMagazine,* July 1993, pp. 35–38.

14. B. Leonard, "High-Winning Game Plan," *Personnel Administrator,* September 1989, pp. 58–62.

15. B. Schneider and N. Schmitt, *Staffing Organizations,* 2nd ed. (Glenview, IL: Scott, Foresman, 1986).

16. Sharon M. Tarrant, "Setting up an Electronic Job-posting System," *Training and Development,* January 1994, pp. 39–42.

17. R. Mathis and J. Jackson, *Personnel/Human Resource Management,* 5th ed. (St. Paul: West, 1988).

18. A. E. Marshall, "Recruiting Alumni on College Campuses," *Personnel Journal,* April 1982, pp. 264–266.

19. "Good News for College Graduates," *Tallahassee Democrat,* February 16, 1994, p. 19.

20. R. G. Blumenthal, "Entrepreneurs Vying for Graduates the Giants Recruit," *The Wall Street Journal,* February 4, 1994, p. B1.

21. C. Edwards, "Aggressive Recruitment," *Personnel Journal,* January 1986, pp. 40–48.

22. Martin Asdorian, Jr., "Drowning in Resumes," *HRMagazine,* September 1992, pp. 59–62.

23. E. E. Spragins, "Hiring Without," *Inc.,* February 1992, pp. 80–87.

24. J. B. Spangenberg, "Executive Search: A Misunderstood Resource," *HRNews,* February 1990, p. B6.

25. "Clever Recruiting," *Executive Edge,* May 1993, p. 3.

26. Kevin Salwen, "Money Gets 'Em," *The Wall Street Journal,* April 12, 1994, p. A1.

27. B. M. Meglino, A. S. DeNisi, S. A. Youngblood, and K. J. Williams, "Efforts of Realistic Job Previews: A Comparison Using an Enhancement and a Reduction Preview," *Journal of Applied Psychology,* May 1988, pp. 259–266.

28. J. P. Wanous, *Organizational Entry: Recruitment, Selection, and Socialization of Newcomers* (Reading, MA: Addison-Wesley, 1980).

29. R. Riley, B. Brown, M Blood, and C. MaLatesta, "The Effects of Realistic Previews: A Study and Discussion of the Literature," *Personnel Psychology,* Winter 1981, pp. 823–834.

30. M. Manter and J. Benjamin, "How to Hold on to First Careerists," *Personnel Administrator,* September 1989, pp. 43–48.

31. Ibid.

32. T. P. Ference, J. A. F. Stoner, and E. K. Warren, "Managing the Career Plateau," *Academy of Management Review* 2, 1977, pp. 602–612.

33. Pricilla M. Elsass and David A. Ralston, "Individual Responses to the Stress of Career Plateauing," *Journal of Management* 15, 1989, pp. 35–47.

34. Douglas T. Hall and Judith Richter, "Career Gridlock: Baby Boomers Hit the Wall," *Academy of Management Executive* 4, 1990, pp. 7–22.

35. Ann Crittenden, "Temporary Solutions," *Working Woman,* February 1994, pp. 32–35+.

36. Jaclyn Fierman, "The Contingency Work Force," *Fortune,* January 24, 1994, pp. 30–36.

37. Marcie Schorr Hirsch, "When a Key Person Leaves," *Working Woman,* June 1994, pp. 20–23.

38. Timothy L. O'Brien, "Rise in Employee Leasing Spurs Scams," *The Wall Street Journal,* March 22, 1994, p. B1.

39. Ibid.

40. "Suggested Hiring Procedures," *Risk Management,* October 1992, p. 58.

41. "Company Liable in Slayings," *Tallahassee Democrat,* March 13, 1994, p. 4C.

42. "Did I say Harvard? I Meant Hartford," *Tallahassee Democrat,* February 16, 1994, p. B2.

43. J. Hunter and R. Hunter, "Validity and Utility of Alternative Predictors of Job Performance," *Psychological Bulletin* 96, 1984, pp. 72–98.

44. J. Andrew, "Resume Liars Are Abundant, Experts Assert," *The Wall Street Journal,* April 24, 1981, p. 25; A. Gates, "The Secret Life of Making a Good Hire," *Working Woman,* February 1992, pp. 70–72.

45. Bob Tippee, "The Resume: A Contrary View," *Oil & Gas Journal,* December 6, 1993, p. 13.

46. L. J. Cronbach, "Coefficient Alpha and the Internal Structure of Tests," *Psychometrika* 16, 1951, pp. 297–334.

47. C. H. Lawshe, "Inferences from Personnel Tests and Their Validity," *Journal of Applied Psychology* 70, 1985, pp. 237–238.

48. C. H. Lawshe, "A Quantative Approach to Content Validity," *Personnel Psychology* 28, 1975, pp. 563–575.

49. R. L. Thorndike, *Personnel Selection: Test and Measurement Techniques* (New York: Wiley, 1949).

50. Philip Schofield, "Improving the Candidate Job-Match," *Personnel Management,* February 1993, p. 69.

51. W. Cascio, *Managing Human Resources: Productivity, Quality of Work Life, Profits* (New York: McGraw-Hill, 1989).

52. David D. Robinson, "Content-Oriented Personnel Selection in a Small Business," *Personnel Psychology,* Spring 1981, pp. 77–87.

53. W. Cascio and N. Phillips, "Performance Testing: A Rose among Thorns?" *Personnel Psychology,* Winter 1979, pp. 751–766.

54. D. Day and S. Silverman, "Personality and Job Performance: Evidence of Incremental Validity," *Personnel Psychology,* Spring 1989, pp. 25–36; and R. Helmreich, L. Sawin, and A. Carsrud, "The Honeymoon Effect in Job Performance: Temporal Increases in the Predictive Power of Achievement Motivation," *Journal of Applied Psychology* 71, 1986, pp. 185–188.

55. K. M. Evans and R. Brown, "Reducing Recruitment Risk through Preemployment Testing," *Personnel* 65, September 1988, pp. 55–64.

56. R. Zemke, "Do Honesty Tests Tell the Truth?" *Training* 27, October 1990, pp. 75–81.

57. S. Moss, "Polygraph Protection Act," *Personnel Today* 3, Fall 1988, p. 2.

58. "Searching for Integrity," *Fortune,* March 8, 1993, p. 140.

59. R. Arvey, "The Employment Interview: A Summary and Review of Recent Research," *Personnel Psychology,* Summer 1982, pp. 281–322.

60. B. Felton and S. Lamb, "A Model for Systematic Selection Interviewing," *Personnel* 59, 1982, pp. 40–49.

61. Tom Janz, Lowell Hellervik, and David Gilmore, *Behavior Description Interviewing* (Boston: Allyn and Bacon, 1986).

62. A. Karr, "Creative Interviewing Takes Firmer Hold, and the Job Pinch Worsens," *The Wall Street Journal,* May 8, 1990, p. A1.

63. J. Solomon, "The New Job Interview: Show Thyself," *The Wall Street Journal,* December 4, 1989, p. B1.

64. Gary P. Latham, Lise A. Saari, Elliott D. Pursell, and Michael A. Campion, "The Situational Interview," *Journal of Applied Psychology,* August 1980, pp. 422–427.

65. C. R. Bell and D. Anderson, "Selecting Super Service People," *HRMagazine,* February 1992, pp. 52–54.

66. Richard Rose and Echo Montgomery Garrett, "Guerrilla Interviewing," *Inc.,* December 1992, pp. 145–147.

67. T. L. Brink, "A Discouraging Word Improves Your Interviews," *HRMagazine,* December 1992, pp. 49–52.

68. K. Michele Kacmar, "Look at Who's Talking," *HRMagazine,* February 1993, pp. 56–58.

69. "A Structure for Job Interviews," *HRMNews,* February 10, 1993, pp. 3–4.

70. B. Wonder and K. Keleman, "Increasing the Value of Reference Information," *Personnel Administrator,* March 1984, pp. 98–103.

71. Karen Matthes, "Staying Neutral Doesn't Mean You're Protected," *HRFocus,* April 1993, p. 3.

72. Paul Falcone, "Reference Checking: Revitalizing a Critical Selection Tool," *HRFocus,* December 1992, p. 19.

73. P. Myers and D. Myers, "AIDS: Tackling a Tough Problem through Policy," *Personnel Administrator,* April 1987, pp. 95–108.

74. "Assessment Centers Help Target Employees for Management Selection," *HR Measurements,* January 1993, pp. 1–2.

75. B. Gaugler, D. Rosenthal, G. Thornton, and C. Bentson, "Meta-analyses of Assessment Center Validity," *Journal of Applied Psychology* 72, 1987, pp. 493–511.

76. Mike Thatcher, "'Front-line' Staff Selected by Assessment Center," *Personnel Management,* November 1993, p. 83.

77. P.A. Iles and I.T. Robertson, "The Impact of Personnel Selection Procedures on Candidates," in *Assessment and Selection in Organizations,* ed. P. Herriott, (Chichester: John Wiley, 1989).

78. Clive Fletcher and Claire Kerslake, "Candidate Anxiety Level and Assessment Center Performance," *Journal of Managerial Psychology* 8, 1993, pp. 19–23.

79. R. Miles and C. Snow, *Organization Strategy, Structure and Process* (New York: McGraw-Hill, 1978); and R. Miles and C. Snow, "Designing Strategic Human Resources Systems," *Organizational Dynamics,* 1983, pp. 36–52.

80. J. Olian and S. Rynes, "Organizational Staffing: Integrating Practice with Strategy," *Industrial Relations,* Spring 1984, pp. 170–183.

81. Ibid.

82. Ibid.

83. Ibid.

84. G. Milkovich and W. Glueck, *Personnel—Human Resource Management: A Diagnostic Approach* (Plano, TX: Business Publications, 1985).

85. S. Rynes, H. Heneman III, and D. Schwab, "Individual Reactions to Organizational Recruiting: A Review," *Personnel Psychology,* Autumn 1980, pp. 529–542.

86. Ibid.

87. J. Butler, G. Ferris, N. Napier, *Strategy and Human Resources Management,* South-Western Series in Human Resources Management, (Cincinnati: South-Western, 1991).

88. Ibid.

89. J. Ross, "Effective Ways to Hire Contingent Personnel," *HRMagazine,* February 1991, pp. 52–54.

90. Ibid.

91. Butler et al., *Strategy and Human Resources Management.*

92. Ibid.

93. R. Goddard, "Lateral Moves Enhance Careers," *HRMagazine,* December 1990, pp. 69–74.

94. Ibid.

95. P. Thompson and S. Hammond, "From Career Plateau to Peak Performance," *Executive Excellence* 5, 1988, pp. 14–15.

96. Butler et al., *Strategy and Human Resources Management.*

97. Ibid.

98. J. Kohl and D. Stephens, "Is Demotion a Four-Letter Word?" *Business Horizons* 33, 1990, pp. 74–76.

99. E. Roskies and C. Louis-Guerin, "Job Insecurity in Managers: Antecedents and Consequences," *Journal of Organizational Behavior* 11, 1990, pp. 345–359.

100. Neal Templin, "Dr Goodwrench: The Auto Factories Are Hiring Better-Educated Workers, Including College Grads," *The Wall Street Journal,* March 11, 1994, p. A1+.

CHAPTER 8

JOB DESIGN

How a job is designed has a tremendous impact on the effectiveness of the organization and the quality of work life for employees. Given the importance of job design, it should be tied directly to the strategies and goals of the organization.

Job design can be thought of as a blueprint of tasks required to accomplish a job successfully. Job design and redesign techniques have become more complex due to the downsizing that has plagued many organizations. Essentially, fewer challenging jobs are available and employees are sometimes placed in jobs for which they are clearly overqualified.[1]

CHAPTER OBJECTIVES

As a result of studying this chapter, you should be able to
1. Discuss the various environmental, organizational, and behavioral factors that need to be considered in job design.
2. Discuss early approaches to job design.
3. Describe the various individual and group design options.
4. Discuss the sociotechnical model and the characteristics of autonomous work groups.
5. Describe how the job characteristics model can aid managers in job design or redesign.
6. Discuss the relationship between organizational strategy and job design.
7. List and describe the steps involved in the strategic framework for job redesign.

FEARFUL SKIES AND THE BORED X-RAY OPERATORS[2]

As Americans make plans to fly abroad, many find themselves concerned about terrorism. The airplane explosion over Lockerbie, Scotland, left them with reason for concern. Who can forget how terrorists planted a bomb aboard Pan Am Flight 103 in December 1988, killing 270 people?

In May 1989, the fear of terrorism struck again. One of Iran's most powerful leaders, Hashemi Rafsanjani, suggested that Americans, French, and British be murdered—five for every Palestinian killed by Israelis. "It is not hard to kill Americans or Frenchmen," Rafsanjani said, adding that hijacking planes for hostages was another possibility.

The U.S. government has been trying to respond to these dangerous threats. Because bombs can be hidden and disguised in ordinary items such as radios and laptop computers so that X-rays cannot spot them, the Transportation Department is considering a total ban on such items. However, the fact remains that there are few defenses against sophisticated terrorists. Worse yet, even those procedures that exist can fail through human error, when airport workers are overloaded and overwhelmed by hoards of impatient passengers and mountains of luggage.

The Lockerbie case is sobering. Two Libyans were suspected in the bombing incident, and the United States negotiated with Libya to have them tried in the United States. The two said to be responsible for this were indicted, and investigators now know the bomb was planted inside a radio-cassette recorder hidden in a suitcase.

X-RAY LIMITATIONS

All X-ray machines depend on interpretations by operators, some of whom may be ill trained or poorly motivated. The Transportation Department task force reports that training of U.S. X-ray screeners was described as "perfunctory." The President called for a commission to investigate aviation security measures. The commission recommended numerous changes including new screening technologies, more training, and better coordination of security measures across countries.

To avoid paying high airline wages and flight benefits, U.S. carriers generally hire outside security firms to perform screening. The firms, which often are hired by submitting the lowest bid, pay screeners poorly, sometimes only slightly above the minimum wage. Two contractors interviewed by the task force said fast-food chains were their chief competitors for staff. "The restaurants occasionally paid more . . . , and even if pay were the same, had the advantage because they provide meals as well," the task force said.

Perhaps the biggest problem is the nature of the job itself. "Anyone standing in front of a monitor watching suitcase after suitcase go by is bound over time to become tired and inattentive," the task force stated. At peak periods, it added, screeners are confronted with "long lines of anxious passengers, putting the screening crew under extreme pressure" to rush bags through.

In Europe, government employees usually screen passengers, with U.S. carriers often performing a second screening. But the same problems afflict screeners overseas, of course.

Since the Lockerbie disaster, the U.S. Department of Transportation has ordered U.S. carriers to intensify security procedures on all bags checked in Europe and the Middle East. Federal regulation requires that bags be searched or X-rayed and all must be matched to a passenger on board. But even today, bags checked on most carriers at most airports around the world are neither searched nor X-rayed. They are put, unexamined, on airplanes.

Pan Am charged the Federal Aviation Administration with approving security procedures in Frankfurt that the airline found after the Lockerbie crash were in violation of federal regulations. Pan Am did not match each bag checked with a passenger on board; it simply relied on the X-ray screeners to identify bombs in unmatched bags. Terrorists countered by using unwitting bomb carriers.

For example, an Irish woman passed through London Heathrow security—which was equipped with an X-ray machine—with a suitcase that was packed with a bomb prepared by her Arab boyfriend. The timer was concealed in a calculator, and the bomb was in the bottom of the suitcase. Fortunately, El Al security personnel at the gate discovered the bomb just before the woman boarded.

One of the major problems is with the way an X-ray machine operator's job is designed. The work is so repetitive, it is no wonder that the workers become bored, tired, and inattentive. Given the potential disastrous effects of an inattentive X-ray machine operator, airlines might consider evaluating the current job design. Redesigning the work of airline X-ray personnel to be more interesting and motivating could save lives.

Poor job design is not always associated with life or death consequences; however, in an era of shrinking profits and increased global competition, corporations cannot afford to neglect continuous product and process improvement. Job design and redesign strategies can help companies maintain their competitive edge by making the most efficient use of their resources (human, capital, and technological).

STRATEGIC CHOICES

The decision to initially design or later redesign jobs in an organization should not be made hastily. Managers must consider a number of factors before deciding on a job redesign effort. Any job redesign program should be carefully examined and consistent with the overall strategy of the organization. Environmental, organizational, and behavioral factors should be considered before designing jobs for the first time or redesigning jobs because of a needed change.

ENVIRONMENTAL FACTORS

POLITICAL SYSTEM

All organizations are affected by the political systems in their environment. Organizations must comply with international, national, state, and local laws, regulations, and ordinances if they want to survive. Managers need to be aware of a plethora of laws because virtually every aspect of their organizational operations is affected by legal considerations. In the United States, numerous laws cover wages, hiring practices, benefits, drug testing, and safety standards. These laws can have a direct or indirect impact on the design of the job. For example, safety regulations may directly affect the design of certain jobs. Consider a factory worker who walks between dangerous machinery or moving belts because this is the most efficient path to obtain needed supplies. The Occupational Safety and Health Act (OSHA) would most likely prohibit such behavior. The organization should redesign this job to avoid employee injuries and a fine from OSHA. If a number of jobs required employees to walk through dangerous areas, the organization might need to consider a total redesign effort.

Organization managers must also consider the political systems in other countries. Organizations in the United States are affected by problems such as the grain shortages in the Soviet Union and international terrorism. The opening case to this chapter demonstrates the need for the jobs of airline X-ray operators to be redesigned to better detect terrorist bombs. It is vital that managers consider their political and economic environments in order to design or redesign jobs within the organization.

SOCIAL EXPECTATIONS

The acceptability of a job's design is partially due to societal expectations. Culture, the work ethic, and religion all help to shape societal expectations. For example, uneducated immigrants flocked to America in the early days of the automobile industry. They were willing to accept low-paying jobs that were routine, physically difficult, and demanding of long work days. Often these immigrants were willing to accept this type of job because they had left countries where work was unavailable. Today, however, employees are better educated and expect a higher quality of work life from their jobs. Failure to meet these expectations can lead to low motivation, dissatisfaction, low performance, and high absenteeism and turnover.

ORGANIZATIONAL FACTORS

AUTOMATION

One important decision that managers must make when designing jobs initially or when considering job redesign is whether they want to automate the job and, if so, to what degree. Job redesign through automation has been undertaken by many companies, including companies in the automobile and steel industries, in order to cut labor costs. Reducing labor costs has helped many organizations to achieve or remain competitive in world markets. One strategic choice the firm must make is to decide how much it wants to substitute capital for labor through automation, robotics, and other highly technical innovations. A company can reduce per unit labor costs by increasing automating, thus reducing labor costs. McDonald's is trying out a grill that cooks hamburgers on both sides at once. This new device could eliminate the hamburger flipper. PepsiCo has developed a beverage dispenser that fills cups by computer.[3] General Motors introduced robotics on the assembly line, changing many of the jobs while making others obsolete.

In some instances, more interesting and challenging jobs can be opened for employees in the organization by automating the more repetitive and routine jobs. Automation (for example, word processors or laser printers) has given secretaries more time for new and higher-level duties. Firms are training secretaries as managerial assistants and paraprofessionals. Thus, secretarial skills are broadening, partially due to automation. At Quanex Corporation in Houston, many secretaries take on marketing or personnel responsibilities.[4] However, automation should not be seen as a panacea for job enrichment. Automation often leads to more routine jobs, a decrease in social interaction, displacement, or even the elimination of jobs.[5] Continually performing repetitive and routine jobs, although efficient, can lead to employee boredom, fatigue, tardiness, absenteeism, performance decrements, and ultimately lower productivity. This issue will be explored in greater detail later in the chapter.

TECHNOLOGY

Many managers want to have state-of-the-art equipment in their organization. Often keeping up with the latest developments in the technical field can help keep a company on the "cutting edge." For managers who master the newest in office technologies, the payoff can be more power and greater control.[6] Just as often, however, investing in expensive equipment can serve to be a waste of resources. Investing in a new computer system, for example, may not be cost effective. Not only should the cost of the equipment be a concern, but managers also must consider the costs of any additional training needed to teach employees the new system, any loss of productivity due to training or computer down time during implementation, and how jobs will be affected. For example, some very specific workplace effects attributable to computerization have been identified from the research.[7] The implementation of a computer-aided design system has been found to increase and change communication patterns on the job, increase skill requirements, and increase the formalization of work methods. Interestingly, computer-aided designs have not affected job displacement or wages significantly.

If managers fail to understand and prepare for the revolutionary capabilities of high-technology computer systems, new technology can become as much an expense and inconvenience as a benefit.[8] If the new system changes a number of jobs, additional considerations need to be made. First, are the employees skilled enough to work their newly designed job? Do they want to take on additional (or fewer) responsibilities? Will the time and effort required for training and learning be cost effective? How well can the organization respond to new incentives if jobs are substantially changed?[9] Finally, are the employees committed to the job redesign change and willing to try and make it work? A longitudinal study examined the adjustment of unskilled workers transferring from traditional assembly lines to computer-automated batch production. Results suggest that actual changes to jobs increased employee stress and decreased job satisfaction, organizational commitment, and the perceived quality of work life.[10]

An essential ingredient for a successful job redesign effort is employee training. Ingersoll-Rand, for example, developed a special program designed to help employees cope with plant modernization.[11] Ingersoll-Rand in Athens, Pennsylvania, is the primary manufacturing location for the company's power tool division. Parts of the plant were over 100 years old. To remain competitive, Ingersoll-Rand needed to modernize its machinery. Employees had been operating conventional machine tools (such as cranks, dials, and buttons); however, as a result of the job redesign effort, employees were expected to operate numerically controlled machinery. They had to perform computer setups, interact with this new technology, and integrate these skills with their regular work teams. Essentially, production methods went from the traditional assembly line system to cellular manufacturing. Penn State University's Institute for Research in Training and Development conducted a training program on two levels: basic skills (reading, writing, and arithmetic) and floor skills (the daily skills needed to operate the computerized equipment). The results have exceeded expectations. The training program helped Ingersoll-Rand profit from plant modernization, since computerization has kept costs down and has enabled the company to offer products priced competitively. Just as important, the employee response to the program was extremely favorable: 99 percent of the eligible employees volunteered to participate. In addition, many of these employees have gone beyond the training program and are continuing their education in the classroom. Managers should carefully analyze all aspects of any job redesign program to give it the best chance for success.

CROSS-FUNCTIONAL INTEGRATION

Cross-functional integration is the act of combining several jobs into one. Recently, a number of organizations have begun cross-functional integration in order to cut labor costs and raise productivity. In 1986, National Steel reduced 78 job classifications to 16 by broadening worker responsibilities. The new system requires 20 percent fewer worker-hours. Motorola rewards workers who learn a variety of skills and, as a consequence, has found that its defect rate has dropped by 77 percent.[12] Service firms have been particularly interested in cross-functional integration because of today's tight labor market and tomorrow's expected labor shortage in the service industry. For example, Manor Care, which operates the Sleep Inn hotel chain, is designing its hotels with the flair of an industrial engineer. By simplifying jobs and carefully examining the time it takes to complete them, Manor Care is able to combine jobs and keep its staff size down.[13] A typical 100-bed Sleep Inn employs only 12 full-time employees, 13 percent fewer than the average no-frills hotel. To simplify housekeeping, the nightstands are bolted to the walls so that workers do not need to vacuum around the legs. The closet has no doors to open and shut. The shower is round to prevent dirt from collecting in the corners. These labor-saving devices give housekeepers more time to do additional tasks, such as working with room service or even at the front desk.

The hotel's security system helps the owners keep track of the time it takes a housekeeper to clean a room. The employee inserts a card that tells the front-desk computer where the housekeeper is located and when he or she entered the room, finished cleaning it and exited it. This same computer can bar a guest's access to the room after checkout time and automatically turns off the heat or air-conditioning. Thus, by simplifying jobs, combining jobs, and utilizing technology, Manor Care has been able to cut its labor force and raise wages while remaining competitive.

BEHAVIORAL FACTORS

LABOR POOL SKILL MIX

Before attempting a job design or redesign program, managers should decide whether their employees' skills will match or "fit" the new jobs. Sometimes additional training is all that is necessary. However, on occasion, employees will not have the abilities or education to perform the newly designed jobs. This can lead to dissatisfaction, frustration, and poor performance. If the job design or redesign effort simplifies the work too much, employees may become bored, apathetic, unchallenged, and dissatisfied. These individual factors could lead to poor performance and lower productivity even if the job has been designed to be more efficient.

Unfortunately, most companies cannot afford to train workers to perform the duties required by a job redesign. A significant proportion of the individuals looking for work today lack the necessary skills to read computer manuals, program robotic welders, perform statistical quality control, and the like. Many of the new entrants to the job market will not be qualified for jobs of the future. One expert estimates that "new workers will be qualified for only 40 percent of the new jobs created between 1985 and 2000".[14]

Companies have responded by making jobs less complex and more routine. You may have noticed that the numbers on the registers of fast-food restaurants have been replaced by symbols corresponding to the requested food item. The price of each item,

HR CHALLENGE

Early Job Specialization and Mechanization—A Thing of the Past

As the United States began to evolve into a more industrialized nation, many organizations began to increase in size and complexity. To manage this complexity, organizations began to specialize by breaking the components of the job down into smaller segments and adopting scientific management principles.

The use of specialization and mechanization (the use of machines to perform work) also made it easier to manage the influx of immigrant workers. Many of the immigrant workers had poor communications skills in terms of the English language, and they performed best on jobs that were designed to be performed in a more simple and repetitive manner. This emphasis on specialization led to the development of many highly automated assembly lines and, consequently, created many repetitive and boring jobs.

Job specialization and mechanization may be a thing of the past, however, according to some experts. Many organizations are well along the path toward being "dejobbed." The argument is that the job is an artificial structure and we are losing the need to package work in that way. Today's organizations are rapidly being transformed from a structure composed of specific jobs into a field of more general "work" needing to be completed. According to William Bridges, "When the work that needs doing changes constantly, we cannot afford the inflexibility that the job brings with it."

Organizations need employees who can work well without the cue system of job descriptions. Complex hierarchies are out, and the flattened organizational hierarchy is preferred. Employees and contractors must understand the organization's strategy far better than they do today. The dejobbed worker needs to be much more aware of the organization's vision and values than the job-based worker. Most of today's middle managers will disappear, many returning to "real work," according to William Bridges. Managers will be of two general types: process managers and employee coaches. Process managers will oversee a reengineered process such as product development. Their skills will need to be more performance based. Employee coaches will support and nurture employees, similar to what senior managers do in business today. Bridges recommends getting rid of jobs and redesigning the organization to get the best out of a dejobbed worker. He argues that this challenge will separate the survivors from the extinct.

SOURCES: Adapted from William Bridges, "The End of the Job," *Fortune,* September 19, 1994, pp. 62–74; T. Kochan, H. Katz, and R. McKersie, *The Transformation of American Industrial Relations* (New York: Basic Books, 1986); and P. Taft, "Organized Labor and Technical Change: A Backward Look," in *Adjusting to Technological Change,* G. Somers, E. Cushman, and N. Weignberg, ed. (New York: Harper & Row, 1963).

---

the total price, and the change from the transaction are automatically computed. Some restaurants even have registers that dispense the correct coin change to the customer via a change chute!

DESIGNING JOBS TO FIT THE NEEDS OF EMPLOYEES OR TECHNOLOGY

Designing or redesigning jobs can be made to fit the employees, the existing technology, or a combination of both. Managers must decide which direction they believe is most appropriate for their organization. Designing jobs for people involves an important examination of the wants, needs, and desires of employees. Managers of car and light truck fleets often overlook the needs of their drivers when buying the cars and trucks. Some managers, however, view their drivers as customers, often allowing the drivers a choice of vehicle to use. Patsy Brownson, of Cox Enterprises, Inc., allows her entry-level drivers to pick any four-door sedan under $17,500, which she then purchases for company use. She finds that the drivers seem to be happier with their choice, have pride in their vehicles, and take better care of them.[15] Jobs can be designed to increase the meaningfulness of the work for employees' satisfaction and motivation. The job characteristics model, which addresses the issue, will be discussed later in this chapter. Designing jobs to fit the technology is often a primary concern. For example, organizations that have large amounts of money invested into machinery and equipment (such as the General Motors assembly line) must keep these capital investments in mind if job redesign is considered. Another approach of management to design or redesign is to consider the needs of both the technology and people simultaneously. This is called a *sociotechnical system.* Basically, it involves forming autonomous work groups that recognize the importance of integrating the social system with the technical system. This approach will be explored further later in the chapter. Before examining new approaches to job redesign, early job design efforts will be discussed.

EARLY JOB DESIGN EFFORTS

SCIENTIFIC MANAGEMENT

Frederick Taylor, the father of "scientific management," focused on the efficiency of operations after the turn of the century. Taylor's scientific management principles and general management philosophy emphasized the following components:

1. Specialization (narrow range of tasks per job).
2. Clear and specific job descriptions.
3. Systematic scheduling of work and rest breaks.
4. Close supervision.

Utilizing the scientific management approach, industrial engineers and job analysts focused on specialization in designing jobs so that they would not exceed the abilities of the workers. As a result, most jobs were mechanistic and reduced to extremely simple and repetitive tasks. These tasks lent themselves to time and motion studies and piece rate reward systems. Although efficient, scientific management overlooked the human element when designing the job. Many workers became bored, tired, and dissatisfied with their repetitive jobs. In effect, the personal goals of the employee (growth and challenge) were sacrificed for the goals of the organization (productivity).

HUMAN RELATIONS

In the early 1930s, managers became aware of the need to emphasize employee morale and cooperation. Treating employees as "human beings" as opposed to machines and acknowledging their needs was the emphasis of the human relations movement. Historically, three critical factors gave impetus to this new approach to management: the Great Depression, the labor movement, and the Hawthorne studies.[16] The depression was due to a number of factors including a piling up of business inventories and consumer resistance to rising prices. After the stock market crash, management realized that production was not the only important organizational factor. Marketing, finance, and personnel also needed to be emphasized. Unemployment, a weakening of confidence, and a general discontent made human problems more salient to managers. Human relations became a more significant issue.

The passage of the Wagner Act in 1935 gave employees the right to organize and unionize. The organized labor movement helped make managers aware of the employee concerns. Typical areas of employee concern included fair wages, decent working conditions, and reasonable hours. Although many organizations initially resisted labor interference, organized labor became legal and management (some more willingly than others) began to work with employees to resolve grievances and emphasize employee relations.

The final contributing factor to the human relations movement was a series of studies conducted at the Hawthorne Works of the Western Electric Company outside Chicago. Conducted under the direction of Harvard professor Elton Mayo, the Hawthorne studies demonstrated the importance of group influences in affecting individual behavior and performance. These studies concluded that group norms and standards had a more significant impact on worker output than did money. Together, the Great Depression, the labor movement, and the Hawthorne studies gave impetus to a new organizational emphasis—the human factor. Today, managers are interested in determining how to design jobs to better motivate their employees.

The importance of job design can be seen in the results of a study that surveyed over 56,000 people. Individuals were asked to rate the most important factor in a job. Interesting work was rated as the most important factor in a job over security, pay, advancement opportunities, pleasant co-workers, or a considerate boss. Thus, it appears that the job itself can provide a significant source of motivation for employees.[17]

THE SOCIOTECHNICAL MODEL

The work environment includes both technical and social aspects. These two systems are interrelated and influence each other. The sociotechnical model proposes a fit among the needs of individuals, groups, and technological processes for effective organizational goal attainment. This approach gave impetus to autonomous work groups and work teams, which provide employees with control over the design and management of their work. Volvo and General Foods are two widely publicized companies using a sociotechnical approach (see the "Volvo" Focus on International Issues and the "Autonomous Work Teams" HRChallenge). The sociotechnical approach to job design was started in the 1950s by the Tavistock Institute in London. One of the first studies conducted by this research team examined the effects on productivity of implementing an efficient long-wall method (assembly line) in a coal mine.[18] The intervention experiment failed because management did not consider the problems associated with removing the coal miners from their small autonomous work groups.

JOB REDESIGN APPROACHES

As shown in Exhibit 8.1, a variety of individual and group job design options is available for managers. Job rotation, job enlargement, and job enrichment are among the approaches concerned with designing or redesigning individual tasks. Approaches for designing or redesigning jobs or groups include forming work teams, autonomous work groups, and quality circles.

JOB ROTATION

JOB ROTATION
The systematic movement of workers from one job to another in an attempt to minimize monotony and boredom.

Job rotation does not change the actual job content but it rotates employees from one job to another after a specified period of time. Job rotation often increases the number of employee skills and duties and can add flexibility to the organization. For example, organizations that emphasize specialization and train employees on only one task do not have the flexibility to substitute employees on jobs if someone is absent or abruptly quits. However, training every employee to be a "jack of all trades" is not always advantageous to the organization.

JOB ENLARGEMENT

JOB ENLARGEMENT
An increase in the number of tasks an employee performs.

Job enlargement (horizontal job loading) increases the number of tasks an individual performs, thereby increasing the diversity of a job. Adding more tasks to the job in-

EXHIBIT 8.1   **Individual and Group Job Design Options**

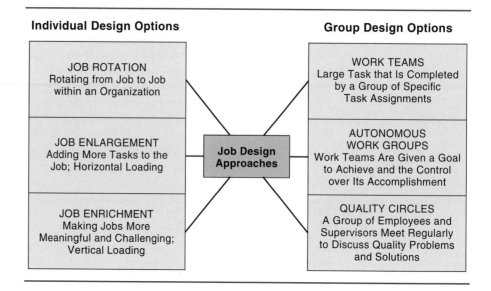

creases variety for the worker. Job enlargement's major shortcoming is that many workers do not perceive enlargement as adding variety but as simply giving them more work to do. Thus, job enlargement can add variety to highly specialized jobs; however, it does little to add meaning and significance to the job.

JOB ENRICHMENT

JOB ENRICHMENT

An increase in the meaningfulness of the work and the responsibilities of an employee.

Job enrichment (vertical job loading) increases the depth of a job by expanding it vertically. Managers must add meaningfulness to the job and allow workers more control over their work if the job is to be perceived as enriched. In addition, workers should receive feedback regarding their performance. The following list illustrates how Travelers Insurance enriched the jobs of its keypunch operators:[19]

1. The random assignment of work was changed so that each operator was responsible for specific accounts.
2. The task of keypunching was expanded to include some planning and control functions.
3. The operators were given direct contact with clients. If a problem arose, the client dealt with the operator—not a supervisor.
4. The operators were given the control to plan their schedules, prioritize their work, and correct their own coding errors.
5. Weekly computer printouts of errors were sent to the operator rather than to the supervisor.

Travelers Insurance found the results of its enrichment program to be outstanding. The changes saved Travelers an estimated $90,000 a year. The quantity and quality of performance increased, errors and absenteeism were reduced, and worker attitudes seemed to improve.

FOCUS ON INTERNATIONAL ISSUES

Volvo

When Pehr Gyllenhammer became the head of Volvo in Sweden, he inherited serious turnover and absenteeism problems. Convinced that the employees wanted more meaningful work, he decided to use the sociotechnical model to redesign the job. Traditionally automobile assembly plants had used an assembly line. Gyllenhammer arranged the technological process to reflect more natural modules of work and formed autonomous work groups to give employees more control over their work and to increase the meaningfulness of their work.

The Volvo assembly plant in Kalmar was totally redesigned in 1974. The autonomous work groups performed work according to general and natural modules, such as modules for the electrical system, brake system, interior, and steering and controls. Employees within these work modules had control over scheduling their work and breaks, inspecting their work, and even electing their own group leader.

The Volvo plants in Uddevalla, Sweden, were also mass-producing the Volvo without using assembly lines. However, Uddevalla went much further than Kalmar. There were six assembly plants with eight teams each. The teams managed themselves by handling scheduling, quality control, hiring, and other duties usually performed by supervisors. Each team worked in one area and assembled four cars every shift. Since workers were trained to handle all assembly jobs, they worked an average of three hours before repeating the same task. Thus, Uddevalla was able to avoid the classic problem associated with assembly lines: boredom, inattention, poor quality, and high absenteeism. Morale seemed high at Uddevalla.

It wasn't an effectiveness problem that prompted Volvo to design its plants using a radically different approach. The country's highly educated, well-trained labor force does not like to work in factories, and many Swedish manufacturers are having trouble attracting and retaining employees. Volvo's conventional assembly-line plants suffer absenteeism rates of 20 percent and almost one-third of its employees turn over annually. Absenteeism at Uddevalla was only 8 percent, although at Kalmar, absenteeism was at 17 percent. Although absenteeism had been reduced, the overall efficiency of the plants had not been systematically examined until recently.

The reported efficiency and productivity at Volvo have not all been favorable. In 1992 Volvo planned to scrap two of its three Swedish car plants in its most drastic downsizing in Volvo's 80-year history. Lennart Jeansson, president of the company's car division, argued that the plant closings and firing of over 2,000 employees were necessary to safeguard Volvo's survival as an independent car maker. As the markets soured and costs increased, the attempts to "humanize" factory work simply became an unaffordable luxury. The three-year-old Uddevalla car plant closed in May 1993 and the Kalmar plant closed on June 2, 1994.

SOURCE: Adapted from S. Moore, "Volvo Planning Two Plant Closings at Swedish Sites," *The Wall Street Journal,* p. A–8, 1992; Volvo Corporation's Annual Report Securities and Exchange Commission, (Washington, D.C.: June, 29, 1993); J. Kapstein, "Volvo's Radical New Plant: 'The Death of the Assembly Line'?" *Business Week,* August 28, 1989, pp. 92–93; and B. Jonsson and A. Lank, "Volvo: A Report on the Workshop on Production Technology and Quality of Working Life," *Human Resources Management,* Winter 1985, p. 463.

WORK TEAMS

WORK TEAM
A group of employees who have been assigned a large task to complete.

The goal of a work team is to implement job enlargement at the group level. To create a **work team,** a group of workers is given a large task to complete and the team members are responsible for deciding on specific task assignments, solving production problems, creating their own schedules and deadlines, and continually improving work activities. The members of the work team can rotate the tasks among members or assign specific tasks to members. The group has a supervisor who oversees the entire operation.[20] The supervisor must concentrate on coaching and training while keeping the team's focus in line with the goals of the entire organization.[21] Construction builders often use work teams to complete a house, for example. Japan Air Lines uses dedicated maintenance crews to service its planes. These work teams, or *kizuki* as they are called at JAL, become intimately familiar with their planes and therefore are able to anticipate problems. A plaque located in the passenger section lists the names of the maintenance team members. The condition of the plane is a source of great pride to the team members.[22]

Research suggests that the success of work teams is primarily due to the workers' awareness of time constraints and deadlines.[23] The case at the end of the chapter shows how much General Motors is now using work teams in production.

A newer concept, team selling, has become popular with a number of large corporations. For example, General Electric Company has teamed over 50 salespeople from nine different businesses to sell equipment to be used on the General Motors Saturn car project. Hewlett-Packard Company and Apple Computer Incorporated have switched to a team-based approach. These particular teams generally consist of a leader, who serves as a source of information and strategist, and a team of workers, which can include specialists from every part of the company. Although a team approach is an efficient way to meet the needs of large, competitive firms, it requires a fundamental redesign of the entire organization. Thus, it is not surprising that a survey of 476 large companies by the U.S. General Accounting Office showed that while 27 percent were using work teams, these teams usually involved fewer than one-fifth of the employees.[24]

Implementing work teams can present problems for the organization. Supervisors and managers often feel that the use of work teams dilutes their power and authority. Further, if the number of team members is too large (over 15), smaller interest groups tend to develop.[25] In order for more teams to be successful, management must consider these problems and monitor the transition process carefully. By keeping the groups small in number and providing clear, explicit roles for the supervisor, the organization can ensure that the opportunity for team success is high.

AUTONOMOUS WORK GROUPS

AUTONOMOUS WORK GROUPS
Work groups that have been assigned complex tasks and the authority to decide the best way to get the job done.

Forming autonomous work groups recognizes the importance of integrating the social system with the technical system. In essence, an **autonomous work group** is responsible for achieving a complex goal and is given a considerable amount of control over work assignments, rest breaks, prioritizing, inspection procedures, and so on. Some autonomous work groups even have the freedom to select their members. Autonomous work groups can be thought of as implementing job enrichment (vertical loading) at the group level. The most widely publicized use of autonomous work groups occurred at the Volvo automobile plant in Sweden discussed earlier.

Monsanto Chemical Company has made some dramatic changes at its fibers plant in Greenwood, South Carolina. Monsanto has instituted its own version of autonomous work groups. The employees in the work groups divide the work and make key decisions themselves. One of the workers said that he knew 20 years ago that he could direct his own job, but nobody wanted to hear what he had to say. This has now changed. Workers are getting involved in decision making and quality control. Using autonomous work groups has enabled Monsanto to use fewer supervisors, which has, subsequently, left more money for employee training. Quality has improved and productivity has increased 47 percent in a four-year period. This program is not without problems, however. By focusing on quality and productivity, employees have become less safety conscious, and injuries have increased. In addition, the reduction in management positions has resulted in few promotions. Nonetheless, the autonomous work group approach will remain. As Jack W. Treece, Greenwood's personnel chief, argued, "Once you give people freedom, you can't take it back."[26]

━━ HR CHALLENGE ━━

Autonomous Work Teams

The General Foods pet food plant in Topeka, Kansas, was designed around the concept of autonomous work groups. Each work group consisted of 7 to 14 members including a group leader. Every group was responsible for deciding members' work tasks, selecting new members, and developing and training new members. The plant was designed to facilitate informal gatherings for better coordination and social interaction by removing unnecessary status symbols such as plush offices or preferential parking spaces. In addition, the company decentralized decision making down to the operating employees rather than keeping it centralized with top management. Decentralization was thought to be motivating and necessary if employees were actually going to be working in autonomous work groups.

The Topeka plant began to show some fairly impressive improvements. Fixed overhead was 33 percent lower than comparable plants, quality rejects were reduced by 92 percent, employee morale was good, the plant's safety record was excellent, and turnover and absenteeism were low. Although General Foods no longer owns the plant, many of these positive characteristics remain. However, top management has attempted to take control of the operations, which has caused numerous problems. Managers are sometimes insecure about letting employees have considerable control over their own work and work-related decisions because they fear a loss of power. Managing autonomous work groups requires different skills than does managing traditional work groups.

Production employees at Marquette Electronics in Milwaukee, Wisconsin, work in autonomous teams and are offered flexible work scheduling comparable to that of office employees. The company expects the employees to work 40 hours per week, but when they do is of no concern as long as quality work is produced. The team concept is a heavily integrated part of the workplace, but Marquette employees are treated as individuals, says Frank Schmidt, manufacturing manager. If necessary, a person can take time off because of a personal or family issue and make up the time on another shift. Marquette Electronics has successfully implemented autonomous work teams without alienating management by heavily integrating the team concept throughout the organization and training management.

Recent research indicates that to receive high performance from autonomous work teams, a number of factors should be considered. For example, employees should agree with team goals, the level of team goals should be high but reachable, employees must be willing to be cross-trained, they should participate in decision making, and they should have a sense of team commitment. To be effective, teams should be self-managed and empowered to organize their work and make decisions.

SOURCE: Adapted from M. Martinez, "Factory Flexibility for Shift Workers," *HRMagazine*, August, 1994, p. 24; B. Dumaine, "The Trouble with Teams," *Fortune*, September 5, 1994, pp. 86–92; K. Scott and A. Townsend, "Teams—Why Some Succeed and Others Fail," *HRMagazine*, August 1994, pp. 62–67; B. Saporito, "The Revolt Against Working Smarter," *Fortune*, July 21, 1986, pp. 58–64; and R. E. Walton, "The Topeka Story: Teaching an Old Dog New Tricks," *The Wharton Magazine*, Spring 1978, pp. 38–46.

MANAGING AUTONOMOUS WORK GROUPS

Autonomous work groups need a manager but not one who attempts to plan, organize, or control the group. These activities are the responsibilities of the members of the work group. Managers of autonomous work groups should carefully monitor any organizational changes that might affect the work group and serve as a liaison between the work group and top management. Unfortunately, most managers do not have the training or skills to act in an advisory, consultative, or liaison role. Thus, it is imperative that all managers of autonomous work groups receive the appropriate training required to perform the broader organizational assignment. In addition, these managers need to be given the power to help develop effective work teams that are consistent with the overall goals of the organization.[27]

QUALITY CIRCLES

QUALITY CIRCLES
Regular meetings of a
group of employees and
supervisors to discuss
quality problems and
solutions.

The concept of a quality circle primarily focuses on maintaining and enhancing the quality of a product. It is a management-employee group effort designed to find and solve production and coordination problems. Although originally developed in the United States and referred to as *quality control circles,* the name has been shortened to quality circles (QCs). Japan has used quality circles extensively, and they have become increasingly popular in the United States.[28] Typically, **quality circles** include a group of 7 to 10 employees and supervisors who meet at regular intervals (usually once a week) to discuss quality control problems and solutions. The Lockheed Missile and Space Company was one of the first U.S. organizations to implement and study the effects of an extensive quality circle program. Results of its program are reported to have saved the company six dollars for every one dollar it spent on the process. In addition, defects in manufacturing declined by two-thirds and job satisfaction among quality circle members increased.[29] The potential for improving individual performance and organizational effectiveness has given impetus to the respect and support that quality circles now receive from many management and union members.[30]

To achieve the potential benefits from a quality circle, management must be committed to the concept and provide good training to the members. Employees must not be allowed to use the meeting time to explore problems with working conditions, environmental issues, or salary and benefit systems. Instead, the focus must be on work-process problems and concerns.[31] In fact, many of the problems found in trying to implement Japan's popular quality circles in the United States are due to misconceptions about their true intent and purpose.[32] However, if the proper focus is attained, quality circles can produce tremendous benefits for almost any U.S. company.

A twist to the concept of quality circles relates to numerous informal methods of job improvement used in U.S. business. Suggestion programs have been set up to allow workers a forum to express their ideas for new innovations. Most companies reward good suggestions by paying the worker a certain percentage of the savings or increased earnings from a successful idea. G.E. holds "town meetings" by department throughout the company that allow workers to examine and challenge all kinds of company practices. In one "work-out session," as they are called, a group from a medical systems division came up with 55 items that could be eliminated or improved. In many cases, it was found that the reasons for performing a procedure were no longer applicable to the present-day task.[33]

STRATEGIC GUIDELINES FOR JOB DESIGN

One of the most comprehensive frameworks for job design is the job characteristics model. It proposes specific characteristics of jobs that can lead to important psychological states. In turn, these psychological states lead to a number of positive personal and work outcomes.[34]

THE JOB CHARACTERISTICS MODEL

As shown in Exhibit 8.2, the job characteristics model recognizes that certain aspects of the job are inherently motivating for most people and that individuals may perceive and respond to the same stimuli differently. Thus, its designers, Hackman and Oldham, proposed that the relationship between core job characteristics and the psychological states is moderated by an individual's growth need strength. Similarly, the relationship between the psychological states and the personal and work outcome is moderated by growth need strength. *Growth need strength* is the need to learn, grow, and be challenged. This means that employees who perceive their jobs as being high on the core

EXHIBIT 8.2   **Hackman-Oldham's Job Characteristics Model**

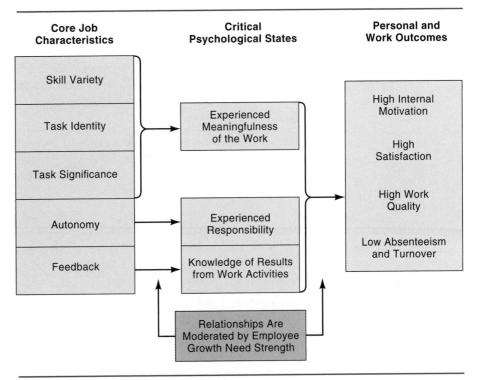

SOURCE: Adapted from J. R. Hackman and G. R. Oldham, "Motivation Through the Design of Work: Test of a Theory," *Organizational Behavior and Human Performance* 16 (1976), pp. 250–279.

job characteristics and who have a high growth need strength, are more likely to experience the psychological state. If employees perceive the psychological states from their work and they have high growth need strength, they are more likely to experience the personal and work outcomes. In essence, this model works best for employees with a need to learn, grow, and be challenged (high growth need strength).

The five core job characteristics are defined in the following terms:

1. *Task identity.* Seeing a whole piece of work. Employees can complete a task from beginning to end with an identifiable outcome.
2. *Task significance.* Importance of the job. The characteristic is determined by the impact the employee's work has on others within or outside the organization.
3. *Skill variety.* The degree to which employees are able to do a number of different tasks using many different skills, abilities, and talents determines the skill variety.
4. *Autonomy.* The degree to which employees have control over their work. This refers to the amount of discretion and independence employees have regarding such things as scheduling, prioritizing, and determining procedures for task completion.
5. *Feedback.* The degree to which the job offers information to employees regarding performance and work outcomes.

The three psychological states are defined in the following terms:

1. *Experienced meaningfulness.* The degree to which employees perceive the work as being meaningful, valuable, and worthwhile.

2. *Responsibility.* The degree to which employees feel accountable and responsible for the outcomes of their work.

3. *Knowledge of results.* The degree to which employees know and understand how well they are performing on the job.

Although the five job characteristics are widely accepted, recent evidence suggests that an expanded set of job characteristics among other modifications may be more predictive of employee attitudes and behaviors.[35] Further, the characteristics of the job should match the abilities and needs of jobholders.[36]

JOB DIAGNOSTIC SURVEY

Hackman and Oldham developed a questionnaire for testing the job characteristics model called the Job Diagnostic Survey.[37] The survey contains measures of the core job characteristics, critical psychological states, personal and work outcomes, and growth need strength. Research results indicate that the job diagnostic survey can discriminate among different jobs.

STRATEGIES FOR MANAGERS

The job characteristics model offers managers strategic guidelines for increasing core job dimensions in the workplace. As depicted in Exhibit 8.3, each strategic guideline affects one or more job characteristics.

EXHIBIT 8.3   **Strategic Guidelines Offered by the Job Characteristics Model**

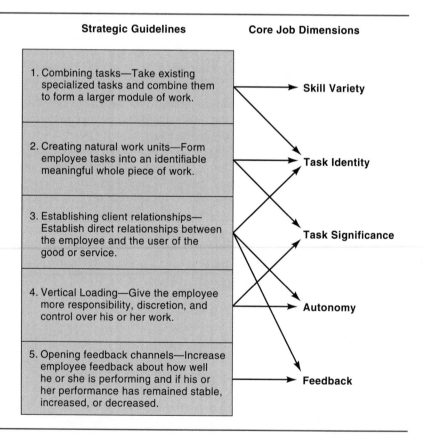

SOURCE: Adapted from J. R. Hackman, G. R. Oldham, R. Janson, and K. A. Purdy, "A New Strategy for Job Enrichment," *California Management Review* (Summer 1975), pp. 57–71.

A recent application of the job characteristics model offers some evidence that use of this model can be useful to improve both employee satisfaction and performance.[38] Sales jobs in a large department store were redesigned in the following manner:

1. *Skill variety.* Salespeople were asked to try to think of and use different selling approaches, new merchandising displays, and new record-keeping methods.
2. *Task identity.* Salespeople were asked to keep a personal record of daily sales in dollars, keep a daily record of the number of sales/customers, and determine a display area that would be theirs and keep it orderly and finished looking.
3. *Task significance.* Salespeople were reoriented to the store objectives, reminded of the importance of their display areas to selling, and told that, to the customers, the salespeople are "the store."
4. *Autonomy.* Salespeople were encouraged to develop and use their own unique sales approaches, select their own breaks, and make suggestions for improvement in any phase of policy or operations.
5. *Feedback.* Salespeople were encouraged to keep personal records of their performance, observe and help each other with selling techniques, and invite supervisor and customer reactions to merchandise, service, and so forth.

The salespeople's effective performance behaviors (conversing with customers, handling returns, and showing merchandise, for example) increased while ineffective performance behaviors (such as socializing with co-workers or leaving their work stations without legitimate reason) decreased. Satisfaction also increased for this group of salespeople. Another group of salespeople who did not receive the intervention (the control group) showed no change in performance. This is an example of how job redesign can be used as a strategic intervention for both employee and organizational benefits.

ORGANIZATIONAL STRATEGY AND ITS RELATIONSHIP WITH JOB DESIGN

An organization's job design should be consistent with its overall strategy. Beginning in the early 1970s, Raymond Miles and Charles Snow examined the competitive strategies of several hundred companies in more than a dozen different industries.[39] Over time, they realized that all of the competitive approaches revolved around a few fundamental business strategies. As discussed in earlier chapters, they observed the *defender* strategy (narrow and relatively stable product market domains), the *prospector* strategy (continual searches for product and market opportunities and experiments with responses to environmental trends), and the *analyzer* strategy (operating in two types of product market domains, one relatively stable and the other changing). Miles and Snow found that successful firms displayed a consistent strategy supported by complementary organizational structures, designs, and management processes. Those firms in which the strategy was poorly aligned with the structure, design, or process of the organization were termed *reactors* and performed less well than the other three types.[40]

Organizations operating under a defender strategy have a limited, stable product line with predictable markets. This type of strategy is consistent with high-volume and low-cost production. Thus, the jobs should be designed with an emphasis on efficiency and process engineering (such as assembly lines). The goal of this type of design is to achieve economies of scale.

Organizations operating under a prospector strategy have a broad, changing product line with changing markets. This type of strategy focuses on being first on the market. The jobs should be designed to emphasize effectiveness and product design. There

---

FOCUS ON INTERNATIONAL ISSUES

Texas Instruments Bets Its Marbles on Chips

During a strategy meeting at Texas Instruments (TI), it was decided that TI should return to making computer chips. According to Jerry R. Junkins, chairman of TI, the projected demand for chips during the 1990s should generate a semiconductor market worth approximately $1 billion. TI is the only U.S. chipmaker that did not abandon this market under the pressure of the Japanese in the early and mid-1980s. Many of the semiconductor industry experts admire TI's new strategy and expect the company to make a strong comeback. However, Junkins is planning TI's future on a volatile and dynamic random access memory business. During the 1990s, the progress of TI will be interesting to watch.

SOURCE: Adapted from J. Bartimo, "TI Bets Most of Its Marbles on Chips," *Business Week,* January 29, 1990, pp. 73–74.

---

should be a low degree of routinization and mechanization (such as can be seen at Hewlett-Packard). The goal of this type of design is flexibility.

Building flexibility into an organization is not often an easy and inexpensive task. For example, Ford Motor Company started a flexible manufacturing plant to build innovative modular engines for the 1990s.[41] Ford is taking a billion-dollar gamble on its modular engine concept. U.S. automobile manufacturers typically design individual factories to build a single engine type. The factories produced the same basic engine for decades. This seemed to work fine when the U.S. automotive industry could count on steady sales and stable markets. However, changing government fuel-economy regulations, intense competition from the Japanese, and changes in consumer tastes have forced many automobile manufacturers to reevaluate their mechanistic factories. Ford's new plant has flexible manufacturing equipment, and the modular design allows for the production of more than a dozen engine sizes and configurations on one line. In addition, this new plant design allows inexpensive, rapid shifts to smaller, lighter engines. Ford and its competitors are a long way from knowing whether this concept will be a success. However, most believe that carmakers will need modular design and flexible manufacturing to remain competitive in a changing and more volatile industry.

Finally, organizations operating under an analyzer strategy have both a stable and a changing product line with predictable and changing markets. The focus is on being second on the market. Although the organization is concerned with high volume and low cost, there is some emphasis on prototypical designs. The analyzer strategy uses a dual technological core—one with a stable and a flexible component. Thus, this strategy lies somewhere between the defender and prospector extremes. The jobs are designed to emphasize process engineering and product or brand management. Texas Instruments is a company that uses an analyzer strategy.[42] Texas Instruments (TI) believes that it can compete in product development by emphasizing uniqueness. In addition, this firm can compete with efficient mass producers. TI prides itself on its ability to shift the organization's structure, design, and management process to match the phases of its product life cycles. Recently, TI has gone back to making computer chips.

WORK FLEXIBILITY: A CURRENT STRATEGIC ISSUE IN JOB DESIGN

The 1980s has been called the *decade of career obsessions.*[43] However, in the 1990s, men and women are trying to create a better balance between work and family. In 1989,

Felice Schwartz wrote a controversial article in the *Harvard Business Review* on women managers and their conflict between career and family. She suggested that businesses needed to adapt to this conflict by introducing flextime, job sharing, and other personnel policies that would add flexibility to work schedules.[44]

The controversy stems from Schwartz's conclusion and recommendation that corporate officials treat women in managerial positions according to whether they are on a *career track* or a *career/family* track, also called the *mommy track*. Critics have been concerned that this could provide companies with a rationale for discrimination against women who have or plan to have children. In other words, the fear is that career tracks would be equated with "fast" tracks and mommy tracks would be equated with "slow" or "dead-end" tracks.[45] Regardless of problems associated with career tracking, organizations are being pressed by employees and society in general to offer more flexible work schedule options for *both* men and women. Another issue involves employees' need to take leaves from their jobs to take care of family responsibilities. Women may need maternity leaves, men may wish to care for young children, and more and more Americans are experiencing the demands of caring for elderly relatives. In response to this issue, LinguiSystems has initiated parental leave, which give employees (father or mother) time off with pay to be with the newborn. The first two weeks are at full pay, the following four weeks are at $150 a week, and the remaining six weeks are unpaid. Insurance benefits are not interrupted during the leave period.[46] In a recent survey, 56 percent of the organizations reported offering some type of flexible scheduling (see Exhibit 8.4).

The most popular options for introducing flexibility into the job are **flextime,** which gives employees some latitude as to when to begin and end their workdays, and part-time employment. **Job sharing,** in which an employee shares his or her job with another employee; **compressed work schedules,** in which employees put in their 40

FLEXTIME
A work schedule that gives workers some control over when they begin and end their workday.

JOB SHARING
A work schedule where two part-time employees share one full-time job.

COMPRESSED WORK SCHEDULES
Work schedules that allow for a 40-hour workweek in fewer than the traditional five days.

EXHIBIT 8.4   The Use of Flexible Work Schedules

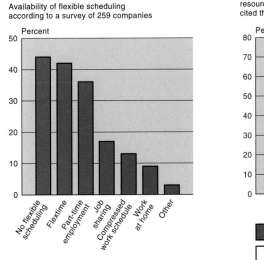

Availability of flexible scheduling according to a survey of 259 companies

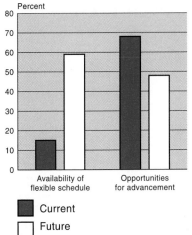

When asked what is highly important for recruitment now and what will grow in the early 1990s, human resource executives at 216 large companies cited the following incentives in these percentages:

Source: Reprinted by permission of *The Wall Street Journal,* ©1990 Dow Jones & Company, Inc. All Rights Reserved Worldwide.

hours in less than a full five-day work week (for example, working 10 hours for four days), and working at home are less popular options but will most likely become more common due to the importance of flexibility in the work place.

TELECOMMUTING
A work method that allows workers to complete their work at home or at another location and communicate with their place of business through electronic media.

Telecommuting is a more recent trend in which employees can work from their home or another location of their choice and communicate through the use of computers, express mail, facsimiles, and improved telephone networks. For example, Charles Lazarus, the chief executive of Toys 'R' Us, has a computerized office in his vacation house on Long Island.[47] His system ties into his company's sophisticated computer system, allowing him to track the sales of all of the company's 20,000 products in any part of the world.

Although women (especially baby boomers in their late thirties and forties) seem to be leading the push for more flexibility in their work schedule, men are also interested in flexible scheduling. In fact, a recent survey by Robert Half International, an executive recruiting firm, determined that more than half of the 500 men polled said they would be willing to cut their salaries as much as 25 percent to have more family or personal time and about 45 percent said they would likely decline a promotion if it meant spending less time with their families.[48]

More and more companies are experimenting with flexible work schedules and finding, for the most part, that workers like the changes and are more productive.[49] However, some worry that telecommuters and other flexible workers will become invisible to the companies they serve and fall off the fast track to success.[50] Some home workers lament the loss of personal space and personal freedoms in their home offices.[51] Some are afraid to go to the bathroom for fear of missing an important phone call! The virtual corporation, a futuristic conglomerate of just-in-time employees, throwaway executives, and temporary workers, is becoming more fact than fiction.[52] This drive for corporate flexibility runs headlong into the belief that competitive advantage relies on a dedicated, motivated workforce. Ultimately, job redesign provides promise for a compromise between the needs of flexibility and the necessity of worker involvement.

Whether managers choose to redesign (or design) a small portion of the organization, a new plant, or the entire firm, a well-integrated job design plan is crucial. The following section discusses the steps involved in implementation.

STRATEGIC FRAMEWORK FOR IMPLEMENTATION

Recognizing the need for job redesign is one of nine steps in an integrative strategic implementation framework designed by Ricky Griffin.[53] The nine steps are summarized in Exhibit 8.5.

RECOGNITION OF THE NEED FOR CHANGE

The first step in strategic job redesign is the recognition that a change is needed. A number of factors in the workplace typically serve as indicators that a change is needed. Employee complaints about their job and a subsequent decline in motivation and performance are often the first signs that the design of the job needs improvement. If managers want to retain and attract good employees, a well-designed, motivating job is imperative.

Another factor that could lead to strategic job redesign is the technology available to an organization. New computer advancements for more efficient production processes often necessitate new work methods. If companies want to stay competitive, they may make a strategic decision to acquire state-of-the-art equipment. New equipment or methods often create the need to redesign some jobs.

EXHIBIT 8.5   **A Strategic Framework for Implementing Job Redesign in Organizations**

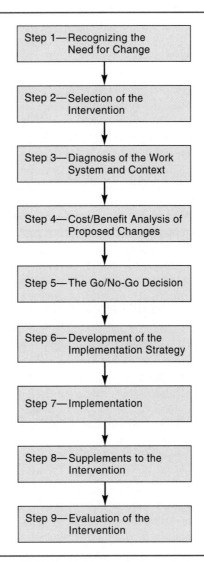

SOURCE: Adapted from R. W. Griffin, *Task Design: An Integrative Approach* (Glenview, IL: Scott, Foresman 1982), p. 208.

SELECTION OF THE INTERVENTION

After determining that a change is needed, managers must decide on the appropriate intervention. Job redesign is only one of the many options available to the human resource manager. For example, the recognition of a drop in employee motivation and performance could be the result of numerous factors—such as poor communication, leadership, or training—not necessarily a poor job design. If, however, employees complain of boring, unchallenging work, job redesign may be the most logical intervention. This step requires managerial experience, intuition, and tacit knowledge to choose the appropriate intervention strategy.

DIAGNOSIS OF THE WORK SYSTEM AND CONTEXT

An in-depth diagnosis of the work system and its context is important after management decides to implement a job redesign program. Human resource managers need to ensure that any job redesign effort is consistent with the existing work system. In *Task Design,* Ricky Griffin described six areas to be examined when diagnosing the work system and context:[54]

1. *Diagnosis of existing jobs.* For example, evaluate using methods such as job analyses and the job diagnostic survey.
2. *Diagnosis of the existing workforce.* For example, compare the current performance, motivation, and satisfaction of employees with the desired level of performance, motivation, and satisfaction.
3. *Diagnosis of technology.* For example, technology may be a constraint because expensive equipment and heavy machinery are necessary.
4. *Diagnosis of organization design.* Categorize the organization as being either mechanistic or organic. Determine the organization culture. Is it accepting of change?
5. *Diagnosis of leader behavior.* The cooperation of the supervisor is crucial in order to reinforce a job redesign effort.
6. *Diagnosis of group and social processes.* The degree of group cohesiveness is crucial if the job redesign effort includes the development of autonomous work groups.

COST/BENEFIT ANALYSIS OF PROPOSED CHANGES

The possible costs of a job redesign intervention must be balanced against potential benefits. Cost to an organization might include new machinery, downtime during the transition, and possible wage increases due to increased employee responsibility and task performance. Benefits from the job redesign effort include an increase in worker motivation, satisfaction, commitment to the organization, and performance and a decrease in absenteeism, turnover, tardiness, errors, and grievances. The goals of a job redesign intervention should be realistic and the benefits should outweigh any costs incurred.

THE GO/NO-GO DECISION

After conducting a cost/benefit analysis, managers should make a decision to "go with" a job redesign intervention or consider other alternatives. It is important for managers to consider both short-term and long-term consequences and determine how this meshes with the overall strategy of the organization. Even after a systematic cost/benefit analysis, managers often believe that they do not have all of the information to make the correct decision. Managers must rely on both quantitative information as well as their expertise and intuition.

DEVELOPMENT OF THE IMPLEMENTATION STRATEGY

Strategy considerations for implementation include (1) who will plan the job redesign intervention, (2) what actual job changes will have to be made, (3) who will be affected by these changes, and (4) when the intervention will take place. These strategic issues should be systematically developed prior to initiating any changes. Some researchers advocate a participative approach using employees, supervisors, and consultants to plan the job redesign intervention.[55] Others, however, advocate participation in some situations and a top-down approach in other situations.[56] The decision for participation will depend on the degree to which employees have important information, see the need to accept the change, and desire to add their input to the plan.

Decisions also have to be made regarding the jobs to be changed, who would be affected by the change, and whether the intervention will be individual based or group based. For example, group-based interventions (such as autonomous work groups) should be used only if there is an obvious benefit over individual-based interventions, due to their added complexity.[57] Finally, the planning group must determine the time frame for implementation. Considerations include how long it will take to purchase new equipment, install it, and train the employees to use it.

IMPLEMENTATION

The actual intervention seldom occurs without unforeseen problems. The best protection against implementation difficulties is to carefully diagnose the work situation, develop a specific strategy, and follow a detailed plan based on the previous steps.

SUPPLEMENTS TO THE INTERVENTION

Supplemental changes are often necessary, particularly regarding contextual factors in the organization. For example, changes in the structure of the organization, workflow patterns, or reward system may be necessary due to the job redesign intervention. For example, if autonomous work groups are formed, the organization cannot continue to pay workers based on individual achievement. Group performance as opposed to individual performance becomes the basis for evaluation. Thus, the organizational reward system should reinforce the job redesign intervention.

EVALUATION OF THE INTERVENTION

The final step determines whether the job redesign intervention was effective. If managers want to see the impact of a change, employee perceptions, performance, and other work-related outcomes need to be measured prior to actual intervention. After the intervention, they should be measured again and compared with the outcomes prior to the intervention. Unfortunately, this step is often not included as part of an organizational job redesign effort, possibly due to additional time and cost constraints. Managers should thoroughly examine the effects of any intervention and evaluate the cost and benefits incurred. This information is invaluable as input for future strategic decisions in the workplace.

MANAGEMENT GUIDELINES

Deciding how to design a job or implement a job redesign program is an important decision for managers. The management guidelines that follow should be considered before making these types of decisions.

1. Human resource managers need to carefully monitor the *interaction* between employees and jobs in their organizations to ensure that a productive relationship is achieved and maintained.
2. Job design or redesign should be undertaken only after careful consideration is given to environmental, organizational, cost, and behavioral factors.
3. After job redesign, managers need to conduct a job analysis to update job descriptions, specifications, and evaluations.

Continued

> 4. The reward system in the organization should reflect the new roles and responsibilities caused by job design or redesign.
> 5. The employees' growth need strength and their desire for job redesign should be given at least as much weight as the costs and technical aspects of efficiency before developing and implementing a job design or redesign program.
> 6. Managers should use a strategic framework for job redesign as a guide throughout the entire job design or redesign program to ensure a systematic and consistent approach.

QUESTIONS FOR REVIEW

1. What are the strategic choices managers should make before considering redesigning jobs?

2. What were some of the problems associated with scientific management?

3. What are the various individual and group job design options?

4. What is the job characteristics model? Explain how growth need strength affects the model.

5. How can a manager increase the core job dimensions for his or her employees? What strategies are available?

6. What is the strategic framework for implementing job redesign? Discuss it and explain the importance of intervention evaluation.

7. Should a job redesign be undertaken if it will improve efficiency even if the employees do not want it? Explain your answer.

8. What are the fundamental premises of the sociotechnical model? What are some advantages to using autonomous work groups?

9. Can employees be trained to work in autonomous work groups if they are unwilling or incapable of doing so? Explain your answer.

10. In what ways could the X-ray jobs discussed in this chapter's opening case be redesigned? How could this be accomplished?

CASE

WE'VE GOT TO MAKE IT[58]

I'm on my way to work on the assembly line in Lansing, Michigan, at General Motors' newest plant, the only one that makes Buick Reattas, priced at $25,000 apiece. It's called a craft center now. Its predecessor, "the old forge plant," was slated for closing—before labor and management struck a deal: Management yielded some say to give labor more responsibility for quality, and labor gave up or combined some jobs to save others. I want to see how—and if—labor/management teams really work.

In good times, there were 2,000 workers at the old factory. By 1984, there were 700. General Motors no longer needed the axles made there; the plant was obsolete. In December 1990, the first Reatta rolled off the line. Now, 675 men and women work there at a base pay of $14.49 an hour. They are full of hope for the Reatta's success—and for their own survival.

But survival requires change. "It's a lot more difficult working *together*," says one worker. "When labor and management used to fight, hell, that was easy. You'd take a position and hold it—win or lose. Now it's compromising all the way through to solve problems."

Bob Thompson, the plant manager, maintains that labor/management teamwork can succeed. Once a month, he puts in a day building cars with union members. "I found that when I put on coveralls and went to work on the floor, some management people didn't even recognize me as a human being," says Thompson. "That really hurt me. It made me think about how the hourly workers must feel about that."

Thompson told his managers to get to know the craftsmen, as the workers are now called, and to listen to them. "Thompson's not afraid of hard work," says one craftsman. "I'd like to see the rest of them management turkeys come down here and work for a day. Half of them probably would quit."

When I had asked Thompson for a chance to work on the assembly line, he said I could, if the union agreed. Then he added, "Just remember you have to build the same high-quality cars that we do." I kept hearing the word "quality" over and over.

I went next to shop committee chairman, Stan Pewoski, with the same request. Pewoski, has been a union officer for 17 years. I told him that I had worked as an auto mechanic, sold car parts, edited a car magazine, and that I write about cars for a living. He told me, "Okay, so long as you don't screw up. Quality is the thing."

"We want to succeed," he says. "When a plant closes, you lose more than jobs. You lose your families, your homes, your style of living. And what other work would we find out there?"

I also asked for—and got—free access to the plant. I can explore on my own.

It's a whisker before seven on a warm morning in Lansing. I'm given a vinyl cover to keep the belt buckle on my jeans from scratching the paint on the new Reattas.

Stan turns me over to his brother, Larry Pewoski, a crafts-man in the final-assembly section. "Watch me build a car, then you build one," says Larry.

In front of us is the shell of a car, parked on four stan-chions. The body has been welded, sanded, and painted. Now, teams of workers will add more than 2,000 components, in-cluding the engine, transmission, and interior, before a Reatta is driven away.

This team approach differs vastly from the assembly line Henry Ford made famous. Under the old process, still used by many factories, every 50 seconds, hour after hour, workers at-tach the same one or two pieces to a constantly moving line of cars. Miss a piece? Too late. The resultant problem—if de-tected by an inspector—will be fixed in a special repair area. That's a big if.

"You sort of plan to fail when you put 30 people in a row with one-way nut drivers," says Bernie Ballesteros, a manager in the trim-and-chassis area. "Say that a screw goes crooked—ZZZT! Well, the gun's got no reverse. What's the guy gonna do—take it out with his teeth?"

Here, most aspects of the old assembly line are gone. Each car sits for 28 minutes as teams install a variety of pieces. The variety reduces boredom. The worker's personal involvement in producing top quality humanizes the process. Ideally, errors are corrected on the spot and costs are cut, since inspectors are no longer needed.

Promptly at 7 A.M., Larry opens the car's right door, held shut by tape (no latch yet). Onto the car's floor he puts pieces of carpet padding, a harness made of dozens of multicolored wires, and a box of screws.

Larry's bearded partner, Rod Zimmerman, wearing a black "Harley Davidson" T-shirt that matches the color of the car,

loads in the gas pedal and the parking brake. He places a pa-per towel over the greasy brake to keep himself and the car clean—his own neat trick.

Soon, Larry carries another harness and some cables to the car. He slips the wires through the firewall as Zimmerman routes them down the door sill. Larry pushes the gear-shifter cable and a vacuum line into the firewall. Zimmerman then fastens them. Many other painstaking processes follow.

At 7:27, Larry punches his code number through the car's identification sheet. He's inspecting the car they've just fin-ished. No short cuts. No wasted motion. No managers in sight.

An "Automatic Guided Vehicle" comes into our bay. It's a self-propelled platform that moves a car to each work station. The team's coordinator, Darwin Maas, walks beside it. "Care-ful—that one there is crazy," Maas says, pointing to the AGV. A still-new computer program isn't perfected yet and some-times the AGVs lose their way. The AGV positions itself un-der the car, lifts it off the stanchions and backs out.

Maas had worked for 22 years at the axle plant. Here, he directs the work, eyes the quality and represents the team at meetings with supervisors.

Another AGV delivers another car. Now it's my turn. The wiring harnesses are heavy. Grab one wrong, and it becomes a squirming octopus. I fumble with black screws and squint in search of black holes in the black car.

This is no place for amateurs. Lose your concentration, and you can cut your fingers on unfinished edges. Make a mistake, and you jeopardize the reputation of the entire team. It's myth that anyone can build a car. Even with coaching and a lot of sweat—physical fitness is a must—I can't finish in the ex-pected 28 minutes. They work harder to recover the time I lose.

At 11:30, the team gets a half-hour for lunch, which today turns into a celebration. The results of the first quality audit are in, showing the initial Reattas to be among the best cars produced by GM. Copies of the excellent rating sheets are taped up in the work stations.

Along a hallway near the assembly area hang color pic-tures of the cars that pulled jobs to Japan—Toyotas, Mazdas, and Nissans—along with their excellent quality ratings.

Later, Maas spots a gap in the undercoating inside a fender. He registers a complaint and soon a worker from the body shop, from which the car came, is fixing the undercoating. "It just takes one vehicle to give you a bad reputation," Maas says. "I'll tell you what: If this plant shuts down, it's going to be be-cause of management, not because of union workers."

Most of the workers were hired right out of high school. There are husbands and wives in this plant, brothers and sis-ters, parents and their offspring. But what happens to high-school grads now? "Let's not kid each other," Stan Pewoski says. "It's going to be a long, long time before we get to new hires, with all the plant closings. My son, Jon, is married, and making auto parts in a nonunion shop in Grand Rapids for about $8 an hour. I've got a daughter, Cindy, who's working as a cook for about $5 an hour."

This break in the old ways heightens the workers' suspicion of outsiders. For example, some of the managers are on loan from Cadillac in Detroit, only 86 miles—and another world—away. These managers are there to help during the plant's start-up. "If they screw up this plant, *they'll* go somewhere else," one worker tells me. "But where can *we* go?"

He's got a point—145,000 hourly workers have vanished from GM payroll nationwide. GM also has eliminated 40,000 white-collar jobs.

After one day on the line, I spend two days wandering on my own, trying to cover all 650,000 square feet of the plant's floor space. Word spreads that Frank Sinatra, Jr., has ordered a dark gunmetal model. "He's got a lot of rich friends—maybe they'll all buy new Reattas," says one worker.

I go to a quality control meeting. Every day, five completed cars are picked at random and scrutinized for defects by about 60 labor and management people in an auditorium built just for this purpose. Thompson comes over. "See that ding in the fender?" he asks me, pointing to a car. I have to shift position several times before finding the dent. "Will a customer ever see that?" he asks. "I don't know—but why take the chance?" The ding will be fixed.

As a car writer, the problems seem minor to me: a grille protrudes slightly; one trunk is hard to close; a brake pedal squeaks. Thompson asks about the redesigned speaker grille. It's a design problem, not an assembly problem, all agree. We're told a new design already has been ordered.

I take a hard look at the Reatta, calculating its chances. The paint is superb. The design turns heads. Fewer than 5,500 will be made this year but every one has a buyer.

At the end of my final day, I watch trucks being loaded with finished cars. I think of Al Martin, and Connie May, who seal the windshield openings. I think of Don Wollenberg, and Steve Nettleton, who install the wiper motor and hood latch. And I think of all the workers whose names I don't know. Assembly quality is only one element of success. But it's an important element, and I'm convinced these cars have been built right. And even though the $25,000 Reatta holds but two people, there are 675 jobs riding on every car.

Although the Reatta was a high quality car, GM's Buick division canceled the car after the 1991 model. Sales on the Reatta were too slow to justify its continuation. In addition, the marketing efforts were inadequate to stimulate widespread interest in this high priced, two-seater car. Interestingly, the Reatta plant is now being used to produce electric cars, expected on the market in the near future.

QUESTIONS

1. Why do some workers argue that working together with management is more difficult than fighting with management?

2. How did job redesign help to keep the plant alive?

3. How does the General Motors Reatta plant use the team approach?

4. Do you believe the team approach would work for other car manufacturers? Why or why not?

5. How has the team approach used by the General Motors Reatta plant affected the quality of the cars produced?

ADDITIONAL READINGS

Adler, S., R. B. Skov, and N. J. Salvemini. "Job Characteristics and Job Satisfaction: When Cause Becomes Consequence." *Organizational Behavior and Human Decision Processes* 35 (1985), pp. 266–278.

Campion, M. A. "Interdisciplinary Approaches to Job Design: A Constructive Replication with Extensions." *Journal of Applied Psychology* 73, no. 3 (1988), pp. 467–481.

Cummings, T. "Self-Regulating Work Groups: A Sociotechnical Synthesis." *Academy of Management Review* 3 (1978), pp. 625–634.

Dunham, R. B., J. L. Pierce, and M. B. Castaneda. "Alternative Work Schedules: Two Field Quasi-Experiments." *Personnel Psychology* 40 (1987), pp. 215–242.

Fein, M. "Job Enrichment: A Reevaluation." *Sloan Management Review,* Winter 1974, pp. 69–88.

Fried, Y., and G. R. Ferris. "The Validity of the Job Characteristics Model: A Review and Meta-Analysis." *Personnel Psychology* 40 (1987), pp. 287–322.

Gerhart, B. "How Important Are Dispositional Factors as Determinants of Job Satisfaction? Implications for Job Design and Other Personnel Programs." *Journal of Applied Psychology* 72 (1987), pp. 366–373.

Gerstein, M. S. *The Technology Connection: Strategy and Change in the Information Age.* Reading, MA: Addison-Wesley OD Series, 1987.

Graen, G. B., T. A. Scandura, and M. R. Graen. "A Field Experimental Test of the Moderating Effects of Growth Need Strength on Productivity." *Journal of Applied Psychology* 71 (1986), pp. 484–491.

Griffin, R. W. "Objective and Social Sources of Information in Task Redesign: A Field Experiment." *Administrative Science Quarterly* 28 (1983), pp. 194–200.

Griffin, R. W., T. S. Bateman, and S. J. Wayne. "Objective and Social Factors as Determinants of Task Perceptions and Responses: An Integrated Perspective and Empirical Investigation." *Academy of Management Journal* 30 (1987), pp. 501–523.

Hackman, J. R., and G. R. Oldham. *Work Redesign.* Reading, MA: Addison-Wesley, 1980.

Idaszak, J. R., and F. Drasgow. "A Revision of the Job Diagnostic Survey: Elimination of a Measurement Artifact." *Journal of Applied Psychology* 72 (1987), pp. 69–74.

Idaszak, Jacqueline R., William P. Bottom, and Fritz Drasgow. "A Test of the Measurement Equivalence of the Revised Job Diagnostic Survey: Past Problems and Current Solutions." *Journal of Applied Psychology* 73, no. 4 (1988), pp. 647-656.

Kulik, Carol T., Greg R. Oldham, and Paul H. Langner. "Measurement of Job Characteristics: Comparison of the Original and the Revised Job Diagnostic Survey." *Journal of Applied Psychology* 73, no. 3 (1988), pp. 462–466.

Loher, B. T., R. A. Noe, N. L. Moeller, and M. P. Fitzgerald. "A Meta-

Analysis of the Relation of Job Characteristics to Job Satisfaction." *Journal of Applied Psychology* 70 (1985), pp. 280–289.

Majchrzak, A. *The Human Side of Factory Automation: Managerial and Human Resource Strategies for Making Automation Succeed.* San Francisco: Jossey-Bass, 1988.

Nemetz, P., and L. Fry. "Flexible Manufacturing Organizations: Implications for Strategy Formulation and Organization Design." *Academy of Management Review* 13 (1988), pp. 627–638.

Olmsted, B., and S. Smith. *Creating a Flexible Workplace: How to Select and Manage Alternative Work Options.* New York: AMACOM Books, 1989.

O'Reilly, C., G. Parlette, and J. Bloom. "Perceptual Measures of Task Characteristics: The Biasing Effects of Differing Frames of References and Job Attitudes." *Academy of Management Journal* 33 (1980), pp. 118–131.

Roberts, K., and W. Glick. "The Job Characteristics Approach to Task Design: A Critical Review." *Journal of Applied Psychology* 66 (1982), pp. 193–217.

Taylor, F. W. *The Principles of Scientific Management.* New York: Harper & Row, 1911.

Unstot, D. D., C. H. Bell, and T. R. Mitchell. "Effects of Job Enrichment and Task Goals on Satisfaction and Productivity Implications for Job Design." *Journal of Applied Psychology* 61 (1976), pp. 379–394.

Van der Zwann, A. H. "The Sociotechnical Systems Approach: A Critical Evaluation." *International Journal of Production Research* 13 (1975), pp. 149–163.

Wall, T. D., N. J. Kemp, P. R. Jackson, and C. W. Clegg. "Outcomes of Autonomous Workgroups: A Long-Term Field Experiment." *Academy of Management Journal* 29 (1986), pp. 280–304.

Zuboff, S. *The Age of the Smart Machine.* New York: Basic Books, 1988.

NOTES

1. R. D. Middlemist and M. A. Hitt, *Organizational Behavior: Managerial Strategies for Performance* (St. Paul, MN: West, 1988), p. 171.

2. William M. Carley, "Fearful Skies: Airline Security Offers Only Weak Protection Against Bombs on Jets," *The Wall Street Journal,* May 10, 1989, pp. 1, 12; "Pan Am Employees Allege FAA Approved Use of Family Security Measures in Europe," *Aviation Week & Space Technology,* April 9, 1990, p. 63; "On The Trial of Terror," *U.S. News and World Report,* November 13, 1989, pp. 44–46; Andrew Blum, "Court Chides Insurers in Pan Am Bomb Case," *The National Law Journal,* November 28, 1994, p. A7; and "Commission Offers Recommendations To Improve Airline, Airport Security," *Aviation Week & Space Technology,* May 21, 1990, p. 125.

3. A. Murray, "Jobs Don't Guarantee a Sound Economy," *The Wall Street Journal,* October 24, 1988, p. 1.

4. A. Karr, "Secretaries Seek More Authority, with Some Success," *The Wall Street Journal,* August 22, 1989, p. 1.

5. O. Shenkar, "Robotics: A Challenge for Occupational Psychology," *Journal of Occupational Psychology,* March 1988, pp. 103–112.

6. J. Dreyfuss, "Catching the Computer Wave," *Fortune,* September 1988, pp. 78–82.

7. A. Majchrzak, T. Chang, W. Barfield, R. Eberts, and G. Salvendy, *Human Aspects of Computer-Aided Design* (Philadelphia: Taylor & Francis, 1987), pp. 160–196.

8. R. Hayes and R. Jaikumar, "Manufacturing's Crisis: New Technologies, Obsolete Organizations," *Harvard Business Review,* September–October, 1988, pp. 77–85.

9. P. Collins, J. Hage, and F. Hull, "Organizational and Technological Predictors of Change in Automaticity," *Academy of Management Journal,* September 1988, pp. 512–543.

10. A. Majchrzak and J. Cotton, "A Longitudinal Study of Adjustment to Technological Change: From Mass to Computer-Automated Batch Production," *Journal of Occupational Psychology,* March 1988, pp. 43–66.

11. J. Sheedy, "Retooling Your Workers Along with Your Machines," *The Wall Street Journal,* July 31, 1989, p. A10.

12. N. Alster, "What Flexible Workers Can Do," *Fortune,* February 13, 1989, pp. 49–52.

13. D. Wessel, "Working Smart: With Labor Scarce, Service Firms Strive to Raise Productivity," *The Wall Street Journal,* June 1, 1989, pp. A1, A12.

14. J. C. Szabo, "Finding the Right Workers," *Nation's Business,* February 1991, p. 19.

15. J. Candler, "Treating Drivers like Customers," *Nation's Business,* December 1993, pp. 56–58.

16. Fred Luthans, *Organizational Behavior,* 6th ed. (New York: McGraw-Hill, 1992), pp. 23–25.

17. Clifford E. Jergensen, "Job Preferences (What Makes a Job Good or Bad?)," *Journal of Applied Psychology,* June 1978, pp. 267–276.

18. E. Trist and K. Banforth, "Social and Psychological Consequences of the Long-Wall Method of Coal-Getting," *Human Relations,* February 1951, pp. 3–38.

19. J. Richard Hackman, Greg R. Oldham, R. Janson, and K. Purdy, "A New Strategy for Job Enrichment," *California Management Review,* Summer 1975, pp. 57–71.

20. B. Dutton, "A Case for Work Teams," *Manufacturing Systems,* July 1991, 9(7), p. 58.

21. Ibid.

22. A. Ramirez, "How Safe Are You in the Air?" *Fortune,* May 22, 1994, pp. 30–34.

23. C. J. Gersick, "Time and Transition in Work Teams: Toward a New Model of Group Development," *Academy of Management Journal,* March 1988, pp. 9–41.

24. E. Ehrlich, J. Hoerr, M. Mondel, D. Castellion, A. Fins, and T. Mason, "The Password Is 'Flexible'," *Business Week,* September 25, 1989, pp. 152-154.

25. G. S. Odiorne, "The New Breed of Supervisor: Leaders in Self-Managed Work Teams," *Supervision* 52(8) (1989), pp. 14-17.

26. J. Ellis, "Monsanto Is Teaching Old Workers New Tricks," *Business Week,* August 21, 1989, p. 67.

27. J. R. Hackman and G. R. Oldham, *Work Redesign* (Reading, MA: Addison-Wesley, 1980); C. Manz and H. Sims, "Leading Workers to Lead Themselves: The External Leadership of Self-Managing Work Teams," *Administrative Science Quarterly,* March 1987, pp. 106–129.

28. P. C. Thompson, *Quality Circles: How to Make Them Work in America* (New York: AMACOM, 1982).

29. R. L. Cole, "Made in Japan—Quality Control Circles," *Across the Board* 16, 1979, pp. 72–78.

30. T. Tang, P. Tollison, and H. Whiteside, "The Effect of Quality Circle Initiation on Motivation to Attend Quality Circle Meetings and on Task Performance," *Personnel Psychology,* Winter 1987, pp. 799–814; and A. Whatley and W. Hoffman, "Quality Circles Earn Union Respect," *Personnel Journal,* December 1987, pp. 89–93.

31. P. F. Koons, "Getting Comfortable with TQM," *Bureaucrat* 20(2), Summer 1991, pp. 35–38.

32. S. Watanabe, "The Japanese Quality Control Circle: Why It Works," *International Labor Review* 130(1), 1991, pp. 57–80.

33. D. K. Denton, "!*#@#! I Hate This Job!" *Business Horizons* 37(1), January–February 1994.

34. J. Richard Hackman and Greg R. Oldham, "Motivation through the Design of Work; Test of a Theory," *Organizational Behavior and Human Performance,* 16, 1976, pp. 250–279.

35. S. J. Zaccaro and E. F. Stone, "Incremental Validity of an Empirically Based Measure of Job Characteristics," *Journal of Applied Psychology,* May 1988, pp. 245–252; Y. Fried and G. Ferris, "The Validity of the Job Characteristics Model: A Review and Meta-Analysis," *Personnel Psychology,* Summer 1987, pp. 287–322.

36. C. T. Kulik, G. R. Oldham, and J. R. Hackman, "Work Design as an Approach to Person-Environment Fit," *Journal of Vocational Behavior,* December 1988, pp. 278–296.

37. J. Richard Hackman and Greg R. Oldham, "Development of the Job Diagnostic Survey," *Journal of Applied Psychology* 60, 1976, pp. 159–170.

38. Fred Luthans, Barbara Kemmerer, Robert Paul, and Lew Taylor, "The Impact of a Job Redesign Intervention on Sales-persons' Observed Performance Behaviors," *Group and Organization Studies,* March 1987, pp. 55–72.

39. R. Miles, C. Snow, A. Meyer, and H. Coleman, Jr., "Organizational Strategy, Structure, and Process," *Academy of Management Review,* July 1978, pp. 546–562.

40. Ibid.; and R. Miles and C. Snow, "Designing Strategic Human Resources Systems," *Organizational Dynamics* 13, Summer 1984, pp. 36–52.

41. D. Woodruff, "A Dozen Motor Factors—Under One Roof," *Business Week,* November 20, 1989, pp. 92–93.

42. R. Miles and C. Snow, "Designing Strategic Human Resources Systems."

43. C. Trost and C. Hymowitz, "Careers Start Giving In to Family Needs," *The Wall Street Journal,* June 18, 1990, pp. B1, B5.

44. C. Trost, "How One Bank is Handling a 'Two Track' Career Plan," *The Wall Street Journal,* March 3, 1989, pp. B1, B8.

45. Women and Work, *Employment Relations Bulletin* 7, no. 8, April 1989.

46. S. Nelton, "A Flexible Style of Management," *Nations' Business,* December 1993.

47. L. Castro, "Managers Declare Independence to Run Businesses from Their Personal Utopias," *The Wall Street Journal,* September 3, 1991, pp. B1, B4.

48. Ibid.

49. S. Shellenbarger, "More Companies Experiment with Workers' Schedules," *The Wall Street Journal,* January 13, 1994. pp. B1, B6.

50. S. Shellenbarger, "I'm Still Here! Home Workers Worry They're Invisible," *The Wall Street Journal,* December 16, 1993. pp. B1, B4.

51. D. Warner, "The Move to Curb Worker Monitoring," *Nations' Business,* December 1993, pp. 37–38.

52. J. Fierman, "The Contingency Workforce," *Fortune,* January 24, 1994, pp. 30–36.

53. Ricky W. Griffin, *Task Design: An Integrative Approach* (Glenview, IL: The Scott, Foresman Series in Management and Organizations, 1982), pp. 207–227.

54. Griffin, *Task Design.*

55. Raymond J. Aldag and Arthur P. Brief, *Task Design and Employee Motivation* (Glenview, IL: Scott, Foresman, 1979).

56. Hackman and Oldham, *Work Redesign.*

57. Ibid.

58. Ken Zino, "We've Got to Make It," *Parade Magazine,* September 4, 1988, pp. 22–25; J. Mitchell, "GM to Discontinue the Buick Reatta, Citing Slow Sales," *The Wall Street Journal,* March 5, 1991, pp. A4, A5; and "Reatta Plant to Produce Electric Cars," *Washington Post,* March 5, 1991, p. P8.

CHAPTER 9

STRATEGIC SOCIALIZATION, TRAINING, AND DEVELOPMENT

It is imperative that organizations socialize their employees into the culture of the organization so that they can become effective, productive members soon after entering them. One of the main ways to do this is through training and development. Both formal and informal methods of orienting new employees can be used, as well as both on-the-job and off-the-job methods of training. Development is a concept that is broader than training, which is tied more closely to the skills and aptitudes of the employee. To explore these topics, we include the important elements of training programs and materials used in the training and development process and indicate how they relate to the human resource strategy of the firm.

CHAPTER OBJECTIVES

As a result of studying this chapter, you should be able to
1. Define *culture* and explain its relationship to the socialization process.
2. Define *socialization* and explain the socialization process.
3. Explain the role training and development play in socialization and in improving performance.
4. List and describe training and development methods.
5. Understand how to evaluate a training program.

CASE

CULTURAL CHANGE AT CIGNA[1]

For legal and competitive reasons, many companies stress hiring minorities. Because the customer base and labor force are changing, it is imperative that an employer's workforce change too. Diversity brings people with varying views and backgrounds to the workplace and allows the employer to take advantage of the full range of skills in the labor market. However, developing a diverse workforce is only half of the battle. Specifically, an employer's workforce may be diverse but upper management may not be. Senior managers at CIGNA, a large insurance company headquartered in Philadelphia, Pennsylvania, have recognized this problem and are taking significant steps to change it. According to Jim Engle, the senior vice president of Claims and Loss Contracts, CIGNA wants to change the environment so that employees can feel as good as possible about the settings in which they work. They want to make sure that everyone knows that CIGNA values all people, and to do that, top management must look different.

THE PLAN

To make these radical changes, CIGNA instituted a three-step process. First, it installed an affirmative action program to hire women and people of color. CIGNA strove to provide those hired with a place where they had an opportunity to fit in and achieve upward mobility. The plan was working, but just bringing in new faces does not change the culture. CIGNA recognized that and moved to phase two.

In this phase, emphasis is on working through the problems and difficulties faced by individual and group behavior associated with race and gender. This means bringing the negative and positive feelings to the surface and dealing with them. The goal is to get past the intellectual response and focus on the gut-level feelings people have for one another. This is not always pleasant, but it is very valuable. CIGNA chose to address this problem by conducting awareness seminars. It hired Elsie Cross, a well-known organization development consultant, to offer these seminars for several divisions at CIGNA. Her goal was to help participants understand how different groups of employees feel. Once this awareness is developed, the need for change becomes clear. The link between diversity and business success is obvious, once awareness is heightened.

The third step is to change the corporate culture. To do this, the company must analyze and evaluate its institutional procedures in terms of their effects on various groups at CIGNA. Policies that are found to hold back minorities and women will be changed. New programs that support the new culture will be woven into the human resource systems, such as recruitment and compensation, at CIGNA.

PUTTING THE CART BEFORE THE HORSE

CIGNA made a few false starts. Wanting to immediately change the culture, it implemented a few pilot programs that were unsuccessful. The company soon learned that phase 2 was the critical step in culture change. Before people could recognize the need for change in the policies and procedures at CIGNA, problems with the current processes had to be raised. Therefore, awareness across the organization needed to be raised.

To accomplish this, CIGNA knew it needed to expand the awareness training experienced by a few of the divisions so that everyone could experience it. A steering committee was designed to find a way to do just that. The committee assembled various groups of employees and asked them how they thought CIGNA felt about them. The responses were eye-opening. These results made the company realize it had a long way to go before the culture would actually change. Engle noted that Cigna is at the beginning of a long journey toward a more inclusive culture. He states, "Exactly where we have to go to get where we want to go is not clear yet, but we want to find better ways to operate the business and better ways to support all employees who work here."

BARRIERS TO THE GOAL

A variety of reasons that would cause the culture change to take a while have been identified. For example, Susan Wood, an assistant vice president at CIGNA Worldwide, says that although senior management knows that a change is needed, it is at a loss as to why this is so or how to do it. She believes that senior management has been so isolated from what those on the front line have had to face that they do not recognize the urgency and need for change. She also thinks that white males have not had the experiences and opportunities to understand what it means to be excluded. According to Wood, women and minorities have moved up by sheer grit, restraining their anger and behaving well while doing so. However, the higher they rise, the more isolated they become. Only recently has she seen a change. She says that CIGNA is now a more open place. Talk about how all systems are affecting minorities is occurring. This is a good sign. Only time will tell whether it can continue and actually become the norm—part of the culture.

Another problem is that the minorities and women who have made it to the top are not willing to help those behind them reach the same level. Many fear being labeled a conspirator against the establishment and ostracized. So the much-needed network that worked so well for the white males falls short for other groups. Other reasons explaining why help from above may not be readily available to minorities, women especially, are that two different generations are vying for the same jobs, and these two generations do not understand each other. Older women without degrees have moved up, slowly, because of their competence. The younger women behind them are moving up because of the degrees they hold. The older women do not like the fact that the younger women expect opportunities just to be given to them and that younger women do not see themselves as responsible for their own advancement. The older women do not like the fact that their experience in getting where they are is neither understood nor appreciated by the younger women.

Loss of power is another reason for slow change. According to Engle, white males are having the hardest time with diversity initiatives. They do not want to say that somebody did something wrong. They do not want to blame themselves for the limiting policies and procedures that were sanctioned for so many years. However, they view diversity as a diminishment of their opportunities. Engle hopes that they will soon view it as a way to value the best from everyone, and that no one has to move backward so someone else can move forward.

SOLUTIONS TO OVERCOME THE BARRIERS

CIGNA has taken a variety of steps to help overcome some of these problems. For example, it held a glass ceiling forum in 1993 in conjunction with the Women's Bureau of the Department of Labor. Women in the insurance industry from all over the United States met at CIGNA's headquarters in Philadelphia. Discussions at the meeting emphasized the barriers women and other minority groups have faced when breaking into upper management. And few would know better. Even though over 70 percent of the people in the insurance industry are women, only a small percentage has made it to the top management slots.

The forum identified several reasons contributing to the glass ceiling. These included the lack of commitment by top management to make a change, the lack of knowledge about how to share power, the fear of diversity, and the unwillingness to set up informal mentoring programs for women and minorities. CIGNA is consciously working to break down these barriers so that phase 3, a change to an inclusive culture, can be achieved.

ON THEIR WAY

There are many indications that the culture change that CIGNA wants will be achieved. Mike Daly, a 40-year-old white male who is a vice president of claims, is one example of the changes occurring. While attending one of the awareness seminars, it became overwhelmingly obvious to him that he had been the creator of a system that excluded people of color. He thought that he was treating others the way he would like to be treated, but in reality he was doing that only with white employees. Although he mentored both males and females, he realized that none of his mentees were black. To rectify the problem, he began reading about and talking to people of color in an effort to find a way to revamp his people-selection processes so that they are truly color blind. It is interesting to note that Daly thinks that a more diverse culture will benefit him as well. He realizes that he will no longer have to be a conformist. He hopes that in 10 years, even he can take a day off to be with his kids and not feel bad about doing so.

An organization's culture is its set of values or shared beliefs, history, tradition, norms, mores, and artifacts that its members hold in common.[2] As the CIGNA case shows, an organization's culture is a powerful force. Human resource policies and procedures that are in sync with the culture may not be in the best interests of the employees. However, changing that culture is extremely difficult. Members of an organization usually value its culture, and they will be slow to change any aspect of it. The way things are done simply becomes accepted and expected. Any deviations from the norm often are not tolerated. When an organization strives to change its culture, as CIGNA is doing, the process is long. However, CIGNA appears to be on its way.

STRATEGIC CHOICES

An organization must make four basic choices with regard to socialization and the development of employees:

1. Does the firm want employees who conform to the organization, or does it want employees who are creative and show innovation?
2. Should the organization develop its human resources ("grow its own"), or should it focus on hiring employees who are already developed ("buy its own")?
3. Should the organization find ways to improve the performance of marginal workers, or should it simply replace them?

4. How well does the organization's culture match the organization's overall strategy? If the match is not good, decisions about what and how to change must be made.

Each of these choices is analyzed in the following sections.

CONFORMITY VERSUS CREATIVITY AND INNOVATION

All organizations want their employees to conform to some extent to prevent an organizational anarchy. Organizations need rules, procedures, and policy to function as an organization. Structural hierarchy and job descriptions spell out job duties, responsibilities, authority, and reporting relationships.

So the issue is not whether to have conformity. Rather, the issue is how much conformity to have. Conformity reduces variation and uncertainty. Uncertainty reduces risk because it enhances predictability. But conformity comes at a price—when there is "too much" conformity, innovation and creativity are stifled. When innovation and creativity among organizational members are stifled, the organization finds it difficult to come up with new ideas, approaches, products, and creative solutions to problems.

So, the issue becomes how to achieve the conformity from organizational members that is needed to function as an organization and, at the same time, to encourage employees to develop their creativity.

Companies such as Nissan and Toyota have solved this problem through the quality circle concept to encourage creativity among employee groups. As noted previously, employees meet periodically to discuss ways to improve both production and quality. 3M uses a form of "intrapreneurship" that encourages employees to actually form mini-companies within it to develop and market new products and ideas.[3] This is how the highly successful Post-It notes and Thinsulate were developed for 3M.

Yet not all firms want creativity from their employees. Even a highly successful company such as Walt Disney World has a very specific dress code. The dress code for Walt Disney World cast members (this is what employees at Disney are called) is laid out clearly in the *Handbook For Cast Members.* A quick look through this handbook illustrates how detailed the guidelines are. For example, two pages are devoted to exactly what constitutes an acceptable and unacceptable sideburn. To the untrained eye, there is virtually no difference between the pictures that illustrate this section. However, cast members are trained to be able to recognize a difference.

Just because a company requires conformity under a rigid culture does not mean that it cannot be successful. It may obtain its creativity and innovation through structured research and development programs and other formal organizational units charged with this responsibility. Still, the amount of socialization used to exact conformity is a key strategic decision for a firm.

DEVELOPING PEOPLE VERSUS HIRING DEVELOPED PEOPLE

The second key decision regarding socialization, training, and development involves the extent to which the firm will train and develop employees versus hiring already well-trained and developed persons. For example, Procter & Gamble exerts a great deal of time and effort in the comprehensive training of new employees, whereas Parker Foods, a much smaller organization based in Colorado, tries to hire people with extensive experience. The same is true of IBM compared to a smaller computer company such as Standard.

Size is often a major factor in this decision. Larger companies often can afford to spend extensive amounts on training and developing new employees; most of the firms that offer training are large Fortune 500 companies that can afford to do so. Both IBM and Procter & Gamble have served as training grounds for hosts of smaller firms in their respective industries. Statistically, however, this accounts for a very small percentage of companies providing training for U.S. workers. Only five-tenths of 1 percent of all the companies in the United States deliver 90 percent of the workplace training.[4] Some critics believe that not nearly enough money is being spent on training the U.S. workforce. Most agree that organizations should be spending at least 5 percent of their funds on training; however, the current figure is closer to 2 percent.[5] Further, some firms spend nothing on training while others concentrate the training they do provide on managers, technical employees, and professionals.[6] When training is provided, it often does not focus on what employers list as the number one deficiency of the U.S. workforce: written communication.[7]

Frequently, a company will hire untrained and inexperienced people for two major reasons. First, they can get them for a fairly low wage rate and, second, they can train the employees in their preferred way of carrying out the job. Many companies hire new college graduates for these reasons while shunning more experienced and expensive employees. Another factor that influences this decision is the firm's policy to promote from within versus hiring from the outside. Firms such as GM and Polaroid have a strong promote-from-within policy and, therefore, tend to hire inexperienced people at entry-level positions in order to provide promotion opportunities. Apple Computer, on the other hand, hires experienced people for higher-level jobs primarily because of the very rapid growth the firm experienced in the 1980s. In fact, Apple hired many people from IBM, a firm known for its thorough training and orientation program. This presents a dilemma for many firms that provide thorough training: they may end up training employees who leave and eventually work for competitors. Some firms known for their sophisticated training programs, such as Electronics Data Systems (EDS), have tried to prevent this from happening by requiring new employees to sign a form indicating that they will repay EDS for their training if they take a job with a competitor during a specified number of years after completing the EDS training program.

So the organization must decide how much time, effort, and money it wishes to invest in a training and development program relative to its position on hiring well-trained and experienced employees. Of course, even those firms that hire well-trained and experienced employees will have at least a minimal training and development program to show employees "how we do it here."

IMPROVING VERSUS REPLACING POOR PERFORMERS

A third key strategic choice in the socialization and development of employees involves how much the firm will invest in an employee to improve subpar performance. Several key issues must be considered: the probability of improving the performance, the cost of improving it, legal considerations, replacement costs, and top management philosophy.

When employees do not perform their jobs to the standards expected in some companies, they are terminated. In other companies, they are coached, counseled, and trained in hopes of improving their performance. With the emphasis on drug and substance abuse rehabilitation and the legal protections prohibiting discriminatory actions (including termination) based on age, sex, race, religion, or disability, companies often seek ways to improve employees' performance instead of terminating them. Employee Assistance

---

HR CHALLENGE

In Search of Talent

Every organization needs good people. Where can they be found? One answer is to look within the organization. Many highly qualified employees are under the noses of their bosses but are never recognized. The following are some techniques that managers have used to locate hidden talent.

1. *Argue with an employee.* If he or she immediately changes his or her opinion to match yours, look elsewhere for the talent you need.
2. *Watch how people clock in and out.* Those who walk with purpose in both directions have more on the ball than those who straggle in and run out.
3. *Watch whom a manager goes to for help in solving a problem.* That employee has the most potential and talent, or he or she wouldn't be asked for an opinion.
4. *Determine who comes up with the solutions, not who finds problems.* Those who solve the problems and

then come to you to explain what they did have talent. Those who simply come in and say there is a problem lack foresight.

5. *Try not to pick a clone.* Just because someone looks and acts like you doesn't make that person the most talented. Look for differences so that your strengths will be different from his or hers.

Once the talent in the ranks has been recognized, do everything in your power to groom these people. Finding a replacement for high-potential, high performers is far more difficult than locating talent in the organization.

SOURCE: Robert McGarvey, "Talent Scout," *USAir Magazine,* April 1993, pp. 68–73.

Programs (EAP) have been developed to help the substance abuser or troubled employee. In addition, many employers fear that termination for poor performance could result in litigation charges of discrimination. Because of this, employers who at one time might have immediately terminated an employee (for drunkenness, for example) now may continue the person's employment but require that the employee enter an EAP.

Thus, today an employer must decide whether additional socialization and training can salvage marginal performance or whether a swift termination policy is more desirable.

STRATEGY AND CULTURE

An organization's strategy and its corporate culture are closely related. The relationship is bidirectional in nature, as shown in Exhibit 9.1. That is, both concepts impact each other. For the corporate strategy to be implemented, the proper culture must be in place. If it is not, cultural change may be necessary. On the other hand, culture can facilitate or limit the very strategies that are even considered.

EXHIBIT 9.1   **The Bidirectional Relationship of Organizational Strategy and Culture**

When Lee Iacocca took over Chrysler, he sought to make the company a trim, flexible, innovative organization. The bloated bureaucracy resisted change and new ideas. Iacocca cut thousands of jobs not only to reduce costs but also to dramatically reverse prevailing cultural values. He was able to bring in managers who shared his vision of the organization. To some degree, the new strategy necessitated a new culture and yet once a new culture was created, new strategies were possible. A similar thing happened at Cray Research, Inc., when John Rollwagan, chairman of Cray, asked the CEO, Marcelo Gumucio, to step down. The bureaucracy at Cray became too much for free-form culture. Rollwagan's reasoning for asking for the chairman's resignation was that the reports and procedures demanded by Gumucio were clashing with the "Cray-style" culture that Rollwagan was nurturing.[8]

The culture of a low-cost mass producer is likely to be quite different than that of a specialized custom-made machine tool company. The mass production operation values conformity, rules, and probably has a clearly defined hierarchy of control. The machine tool company that creates one-of-a-kind products based on customer needs and specifications favors a more team-oriented, flexible environment. Exhibit 9.2 outlines some possible strategy/culture links.

Frequently organizations that attempt to diversify encounter a strategy-culture dilemma. Large conglomerates with diverse businesses may seek only minimal cultural conformity. The conglomerate is viewed primarily as a financial umbrella and gains little by attempting uniformity. The situation is frequently different, however, when two or more companies merge horizontally. Culture clashes are seen as one of the major causes of failure. When Philadelphia's Mellon Bank acquired its rival, Girard, two very different philosophies collided. Mellon insisted that the Girard organization conform. The combined merged organization suffered huge losses. An example of a successful cultural merger was the uniting of Baxter Travenol and American Hospital Supply. Both companies were committed to creating an entirely new organization with a combined culture building on the strengths of both former companies.

Another strategy/culture issue arises when a company, in response to its environment, changes its strategy. Apple Computers started out as a very freewheeling organization in

EXHIBIT 9.2   **Examples of Different Strategy/Culture Environments**

STRATEGY	CULTURE	TRAINING AND DEVELOPMENT EMPHASIS	EXAMPLE
Combination Strategy	Conformity, Rule	Strong Orientation in Company Policies and Practices	General Motors
Market Segment Focus	Flexible Team-Oriented, Creative License	Team Building, Problem Solving	Berg Pipe Company
Growth Oriented	Aggressive, Risk Taking	Assertiveness, Problem Solving	Knowledge Adventure
Neutral	Risk Adverse, Quality	TQM and Policy Orientation	Alcoa
Product/Service Differentiation	Quality-Conscious Elitist	TQM, Craftsmanship	Rolls Royce

FOCUS ON INTERNATIONAL ISSUES

Blending Organizational Cultures: The French Way

In 1988, Hachette, a French magazine empire, purchased Diamandis Communications, a U.S. publishing firm whose magazines included *Woman's Day, Road & Track,* and *Popular Photography,* among others. While critics felt that the acquisition seemed to be a good idea at the time, they later ate their words after the battle of the cultures took place.

The battle seemed to center on the chairman and chief executive of Diamandis Communications, Peter Diamandis. After the acquisition, Diamandis remained in these roles, but he soon found that he was having trouble adjusting to how Hachette did things. Admittedly, Diamandis had trouble taking advice, even from the golf pro he hired to help with his game. This personality shortcoming may have been the source of the majority of the problems that arose.

Hachette officials tended to take away a great deal of the responsibility Diamandis had as they began making the changes to his magazines and altering decisions he had made. At first the changes were confined to decisions about layouts and advertisers, but eventually Hachette dropped Diamandis' favorite magazine, *Memories,* a nostalgia magazine that Hachette felt missed the mark with French readers who did not recognize people such as Ted Williams and Fred Astaire, about whom the stories were written.

While more and more responsibility was taken away from Diamandis, more and more responsibility was given to the French editors. U.S. editors were left out of the decision-making meetings, creating an atmosphere of back stabbing and little trust. U.S. managers began talking in the halls with exaggerated French accents and ignoring their French counterparts. As morale dropped, people including Diamandis, began to leave.

In September 1990, Hachette officials asked Diamandis if he would like to leave the company at the end of his contract. He suggested that he and two of his top officials not wait but leave immediately. The next day, the phones were being answered, "Hachette Magazines." All told, the payroll fell 35 percent in the two years after the merger. An entire floor at Hachette Magazine headquarters had been leased. While expansion was the main reason Hachette purchased Diamandis Communications, that plan had to wait until the corporate culture could be reestablished and the organization became stable again.

SOURCE: Adapted from Patrick Reilly, "Egos, Culture Clash When French Firm Buys U.S. Magazines," *The Wall Street Journal,* February 15, 1991, pp. A1 + .

the garage of two young entrepreneurs, Steve Jobs and Steve Wozinak. In the early days, they encouraged this flexible, nonconformist atmosphere. As the company grew, more controls and discipline were required in order to meet new markets. When the board of directors decided that it could indeed compete with companies such as IBM and Compaq in the business market, they removed Jobs from his position in the company and replaced him with a professional business team headed by John Scully. Scully achieved the goals set forth, but the early culture was a casualty.

One of the criticisms of U.S. "smokestack" industries is that they cannot develop and sustain new strategic positions. U.S. steel companies are a prime example. Their cultures are so entrenched and based on a different economic reality that they seem incapable of effective strategic positions. Starbuck and Hedberg, based on their study of a large Swedish company, believe that the only way to bring about the necessary revolutionary changes is to remove top management and bring in a new team.[9]

Managers need to understand the dynamics of the strategy/culture connection. It is important not only in the successful formulation and implementation of strategy but in filtering what type of strategy is even possible in the first place. Strategic decisions often lead to changing culture. Sometimes it may be necessary to change the culture before it is possible to undertake a certain strategy.

SOCIALIZATION AND CULTURE

SOCIALIZATION

The process of learning how and why things are done in an organization.

Before a new hire can become a productive part of an organization, he or she must learn the culture of the organization, as well as how "things are done." This learning process is often referred to as **socialization.** Some socialization takes place before the individual actually starts to work. For example, individuals develop expectations about what the job will be like through their interactions with company contacts. Upon arrival at work, these expectations will begin to clash with the reality of the job. As long as those around the individual recognize that support and help are needed during this adjustment time, expectations and reality will soon be in sync. Eventually, the employee will begin to feel comfortable with the requirements of his or her job and those with whom he or she must interact to accomplish this job. At this point, the individual has become completely socialized into the organization.

CULTURE AND ACCULTURATION

ACCULTURATION

The process of learning the culture of an organization.

Learning the culture of an organization is an important step in the socialization process. As previously mentioned, the culture of a group or society is a set of values (shared beliefs), history, tradition, norms, mores, and artifacts that the group holds in common.[10] Culture is the cement or glue that holds a society or group together. Generally, culture consists of those items listed in Exhibit 9.3. The process of acquiring the culture of an organization is known as **acculturation.**

Even though culture is represented by art and artifacts, it is rather intangible, hidden, and not easily recognized. Some people refer to the obvious aspects of culture, such as art and artifacts, as being only the tip of the iceberg while much of culture is actually hidden. It is not easy to see an organization's history or tradition. Even certain norms may be difficult to determine, at least for the new organizational member or casual observer. That's why it is up to the organization to acculturate new employees to the organization.

Companies such as IBM, 3M, and Apple take great pride in building and maintaining their desired culture. Not knowing or ignoring an organization's culture can be perilous for any organization member. This is why organizations often spend much time and money instilling their culture in new employees through sometimes long and expensive orientation and training programs. An example is the P&G College of Procter & Gamble. To impress its culture on people as they enter the organization, Procter & Gamble sends all new hires to P&G College for three or four days during their first year.[11]

EXHIBIT 9.3   **Components of Culture**

Values—Basic beliefs; strongly held attitudes about important ideas.

Norms—Accepted standards of behavior.

History and Tradition—The historical or traditional way of doing and thinking about things.

Mores—Customs or rituals that the society believes in and follows.

Myths—Common stories or folklore passed from one generation to another.

Art and Artifacts—Art, symbols, weapons, pottery, and so on that are physical representations of the culture.

ORIENTATION

ORIENTATION
Familiarizing new employees with the rules, policies, and procedures of the organization.

Probably nothing does more to begin the acculturation process in a specific organization than the orientation program. **Orientation** is the process of welcoming new employees, bringing them into the organization, and familiarizing them with its operations and culture. Orientation occurs two ways: formally and informally. The formal orientation is conducted by the organization. Then, informal orientation occurs through daily interactions with fellow employees.

FORMAL ORIENTATION PROGRAMS

FORMAL ORIENTATION
An orientation program sponsored and developed by an organization.

A **formal orientation** program is sponsored and developed by the organization. Its primary purpose is to welcome new employees and acquaint them with the rules, policies, and procedures of the organization. It should be held as soon as possible after a new hire begins the job, usually the first day of work, so that the new employee does not have time to pick up any "bad habits."

In "Where the Training Dollars Go," Chris Lee reports that 76 percent of firms with 50 or more employees have a formal orientation program.[12] Several companies have excellent ones—IBM, Frito-Lay, and Dana Corporation among them. Many of these firms follow the suggestions outlined in Exhibit 9.4 that highlight the way to develop a strong orientation program.

Some firms have overall orientation programs designed for any and all employees, others develop specific orientation programs for one job classification or one unit. Exhibit 9.5 shows the elements of the Quaker Oats orientation program for college graduates in sales. Notice that the Quaker philosophy is an important part of the program. Also note that some sales techniques (presentation skills and promotional materials) are also covered. All new sales hires are put through this three- to six-month orientation before receiving additional sales training.

Barnett Banks offers a full 10 days of orientation. Topics covered include Barnett's history, current strategic plan, financial background, personnel policies, marketing and growth plans, job responsibilities, responsibilites of selected jobs, and administrative matters. After this orientation, employees receive 11 months of additional training.[13]

COMMON COMPONENTS OF AN ORIENTATION

WELCOMING

Orientations frequently begin with an official welcoming of the employee. In small organizations, this should be done by the CEO. In larger organizations, someone from human resources and/or the immediate supervisor should welcome the employee and make him or her feel comfortable and accepted.

MEETING THE BOSS AND FELLOW EMPLOYEES

The employee should be introduced to those with whom he or she will work by either the supervisor or someone from human resources. In some cases, a peer employee or buddy might introduce the new employee to his or her co-workers. These introductions are very important and should not be taken lightly.

EXHIBIT 9.4   **Tips for Building a Strong Orientation Program**

The very first step in welcoming new employees into the organization is the orientation program. However, an ever-increasing number of firms are sending a stale, stagnant message to their employees. To fix this problem, organizations need to focus on updating and revamping their orientation programs. Some suggestions for making needed changes follow.

1. Keep the paperwork portion of the orientation light the first day. Information overload can be a real turnoff for employees. Try to separate the required paperwork into two piles: those forms that must be completed the first day and those that can wait a week or two.

2. Start the orientation with an informal meeting with the new recruit's immediate supervisor. The meeting should be brief, no more than 20 minutes, and it should start on time. This meeting will serve two purposes. First, the employee will see that his or her immediate supervisor is a person with whom he or she can come to with problems and concerns. Second, it shows that the firm and the supervisor stress punctuality.

3. Alternate heavy information such as benefits and insurance forms with short taped or live accounts of the organization with the CEO or other important and not-so-important organizational members. This helps to reassure the new employees that the organization is made up of people, not just forms and rules.

4. Provide the new employees with a glossary of terms unique to the organization. This can be done in a variety of ways. For example, two long-time employees can act out a scene in which the organization's jargon is used and then allow the new employees to guess what the terms stand for. Afterward, the same scene can be acted out by two new employees who have mastered the corporate lingo. Having employees learn the organization language up front is an easy way to help them begin to think like an organization member. This exercise also cuts down on the feelings of being an outsider once the employee begins working.

5. Find a buddy for each new employee. Matching employees with new recruits does not have to focus on the job to be performed. Sometimes it may be useful to match people on a personality basis rather than on a job basis. This allows new employees to build links with employees outside their immediate department, further reinforcing the organization's culture of working together as an organization.

EXHIBIT 9.5   **Elements of Quaker Oats Orientation of College Graduates as Sales Trainees**

Field Training with District Manager
Quaker's Company Philosophy
Presentation Skills
Organization Structure
Use of Sales Promotion Materials, Trade Allowances, and Consumer Events
Administrative Details

- Payroll
- Health insurance
- Leave and vacation policy

- Pension benefits
- Employee benefits
- Forms

SOURCE: Reprinted by permission from *Quaker Sales Careers: Leadership Through Innovation;* copyright © Quaker Oats Company. All Rights Reserved.

HR CHALLENGE

Disney's Orientation Program

One of the most successful orientation programs for U.S. firms is the one developed by the Disney organization. Everyone—all employees hired at all levels—attends Disney University and must pass Traditions I before going for specialized training. Traditions I is an all-day experience in which the Disney philosophy, tradition, and culture are presented.

At Disney, employees are called "cast members" and whenever they work with the public, they are "on stage." Customers are called "guests." Employees are told about all functions and how they relate to the "show." They are reminded of how important their role is in making the show a success. Even ticket takers receive four 8-hour days of instruction in order to learn locations of restrooms, when the parade starts, show schedules, and so on. In other words, they are required to know more than the ticket-taking job; they are also

expected to know other information to make the guest's stay as enjoyable as possible.

Disney emphasizes the "Disney Way" in orientation, training, and follow-up employee evaluations. Because of this emphasis, the company is sometimes criticized for "brainwashing" its employees. The firm requires conformity to the Disney Way, and employees are given little opportunity to express creativity and innovation.

Yet when one examines the success of Disney theme parks, the wide use of part-time and student help, and the critical nature of their jobs in terms of customer contact, a rigid, highly formalized orientation and training program are probably the best. And of course, it's difficult to argue with success.

SOURCE: Adapted from Thomas J. Peters and Robert H. Waterman, Jr., *In Search of Excellence.* (New York: Harper & Row, 1982), p. 168.

COMPLETING PAPERWORK

All essential paperwork should be completed during orientation so that the employee is paid accurately and on time. Various tax and insurance forms as well as time cards, citizenship-resident documentation, and other items need to be properly completed in a timely fashion. There is nothing more aggravating for a new employee than to miss the first paycheck or to be paid improperly because the correct forms were not completed accurately. Someone in the company should be given the responsibility to be the expert on new hires. This person should ensure that all needed forms for new hires are completed promptly and accurately.

REVIEWING THE EMPLOYEE HANDBOOK

One critical step in the orientation program is a review of the employee handbook. Exhibit 9.6 is the table of contents of a typical one. As this table of contents indicates, this handbook contains a vast amount of information. It would be impossible to discuss it all, but at least a brief mention of each section should be made. Sections that need to be covered carefully might include employee benefits and retirement programs and company policies, rules, regulations, and expectations. Some attention also might need to be paid to grievance procedures and disciplinary procedures.

Specific language about the term of employment also should be stated in the handbook, and new employees should be made aware of this passage. Terminology in the handbook should be chosen carefully to avoid **employment-at-will** litigation. In essence, under employment-at-will, the employer or the employee can terminate their relationship for good cause, no cause, or even bad cause without warning because their relationship is based upon an implied contract, not a written one.[14] Employees who believe that they have been dismissed unfairly can file a wrongful discharge lawsuit in the hope of getting their job back, and the odds of winning are on their side. In approximately

EMPLOYMENT-AT-WILL
An employment situation where either the employee or employer can terminate the working relationship for any reason at any time.

EXHIBIT 9.6   **Table of Contents for Employee Manual**

70 percent of these cases, the court has ruled in favor of the employee, costing the employer court costs of up to $250,000, as well as damages that average around $500,000.[15]

Wrongful discharge suits have generally been heard for four different reasons. First, the employee can argue that the employer violated public policy by firing him or her. This line of defense includes dismissing an employee for refusing to perform some illegal, unethical, or unsafe procedure. A second defense is that the employer did not deal with the employee fairly and in good faith. If an employee was fired just before his or her retirement benefits were to begin, the organization could be found not to have acted in good faith. The employer also can be charged with tortuous acts toward an employee; an example of this is an employee seeking a job outside the company whose job search was sabotaged by the company, which then dismissed the employee. The company could be held to be at fault. Finally, if an employer breaches an implied contract, an employee can sue for wrongful discharge. Cases of this type relate to verbal statements made during an interview that elude to or imply a long-term commitment on the part of the employer, and/or statements in the employee handbook that suggest that after a probationary period, employees move to "permanent" status. In just such a case in Michigan, the court ruled in favor of the employee and against Blue Cross and Blue Shield.[16]

INTRODUCING JOB DUTIES AND PERFORMING INITIAL TRAINING

Of course, the job duties were discussed during the hiring interview. However, they should be reviewed as part of the orientation process. The job description, goals (objectives), and employee performance evaluation form and process all should be reviewed. The employee needs to know the following:

What he or she is to do (job description).

What is to be accomplished (job goals or objectives).

How he or she will be evaluated (performance evaluation).

Failure to clearly point out and discuss these items at the time of hiring will likely cause many problems later. The employee needs to also be given initial training as to how the job is done at the particular company with specific follow-up training conducted later.

CONDUCTING A FOLLOW-UP SESSION

Finally, after a period of one to three months, a follow-up session should be held with the employee by either the supervisor or someone in human resources. This may occur at the end of the employee's probationary period. The use of such a session is a good idea to give both the employee and the employer time to assess whether a good choice has been made. Employers should not indicate in the handbook that a recent hire becomes a *permanent employee* once the probationary period ends. In wrongful discharge cases, some courts have ruled that this *implies a contractual obligation.* It is better to state that the employee moves from probationary to "regular" status. A careful review of the employee's performance at the end of the probationary period and a review of the company policies and rules will help ensure that the employee is fitting in properly.

We now examine how the informal orientation process operates in the organization.

INFORMAL ORIENTATION
An orientation that an employee receives from other employees.

INFORMAL ORIENTATION

Informal orientation occurs when new hires receive information about the organization and how to perform their jobs from current employees. Organizations hope that the information passed to new hires from current employees matches the information given during the formal orientation program. The stronger the belief of the employees in the organization's culture, the closer the two types of information will be.

Many companies go to great lengths to ensure a match between information provided formally and informally. For example, Dana Corporation, under the leadership of former Chairman Rene McPherson, emphasized a one-page statement of philosophy, which was communicated to new and existing employees over and over again. This helped to reinforce corporate philosophy with existing employees as well as new ones. This philosophy covers four key points:[17]

1. Face-to-face communication of all performance figures with all employees is critical.
2. Training and the opportunity for development should be provided to all employees.
3. Job security should be provided for all people.
4. Incentive programs based on ideas, suggestions, and hard work should be established as a reward.

A short, simple, straightforward statement, such as the one above, consistently emphasized and communicated, can do much to ensure that the formal orientation strategy for acculturation is reinforced on the job. This is particularly so if the CEO exemplifies the desired culture. CEOs who stressed and exemplified the culture they wanted employees to adopt include John Scully of Apple, Lee Iacocca when at Chrysler, Jack Welch of GE, Rene McPherson when at Dana, and Tom Watson when at IBM. CEOs carry great symbolic power when they exemplify a strategy they desire the firm to implement.

REINFORCING BEHAVIOR

In addition to the exemplary role played by the CEO in reinforcing a desired cultural strategy, the organization should also have systems that reinforce behavior that exemplifies the desired culture. For example, if participation and employee involvement are keystones in a desired organization's culture, then employees and managers who engage in participative behavior should be rewarded for it. These rewards could be in the form of salary increases or incentive pay, promotions, praise, and symbols (such as plaques or certificates). Negative sanctions could be used for those who do not participate in desired activities. These could include the absence of rewards as well as managerial and peer censure in the form of verbal and written comments. At the extreme, it might even involve termination.

The point is this: If the organization wants to maintain a particular culture, it must develop and implement a strategy to this effect. Simply sending new employees to a one-day orientation program will not guarantee that the acculturation process will occur as desired. The informal acculturation process (orientation) must reinforce the formal if the desired strategy is to be successful.

Let's now turn to developmental strategies that organizations use to enhance and improve the performance of their employees. We examine these as training and development strategies and programs.

TRAINING, DEVELOPMENT, AND PERFORMANCE IMPROVEMENT

The goal of training and development programs of all organizations should be to maintain or improve the performance of individuals and, in so doing, that of the organization.

HR CHALLENGE

Career Paths Help Keep Training and Development on Track

As the abundance of baby boomers continues to clog corporate ladders, organizations are making changes. Many firms have implemented dual-career tracks to allow more individuals to climb up the corporate ladder. Generally, one ladder is the management track and the other is a professional track. By installing two tracks, organizations hope to change the idea that moving into management is the only way to "make it to the top."

 To develop these dual-career paths, one firm, British Petroleum Exploration (BPX), assigned teams to develop two truly comparable tracks in terms of responsibility, rewards, and influence for management and for individual contributors. Current paths were scrapped and the teams began developing things as they should be done, not as they were currently done. The result was a dual-career track that employees could jump between and progress up as BPX's needs, abilities, and interests changed. Many other firms, such as ITT, IBM, and NCR, have similar programs.

The benefits of these types of programs are evident. However, there are potential costs as well. For example, even though the ladders are designed to let employees move from one to the other, at some point this becomes impossible. This is especially true for managers who have been away from the technical aspects of the job so long that their skills are obsolete. Also, the organization's compensation costs can increase as employees begin to climb their chosen ladders. Further, organizational costs for implementing and monitoring the system can also be quite high.

However these new career paths are enacted, the human resource unit will have the major responsibility for them. Making sure that all of the human resource professionals understand the process can make the transition period and subsequent operations of the dual tracks much easier.

Source: Adapted from Robert Goddard, "Lateral Moves Enhance Careers," *HRMagazine,* December 1990, pp. 69–74; James McElwain, "Succession Plans Designed to Manage Change," *HRMagazine,* February 1991, pp. 67–71; and Milan Moravec and Robert Tucker, "Transforming Organizations for Good," *HRMagazine,* October 1991, pp. 74–76.

Many organizations spend much time, effort, and money on training and developing their employees, including managers. In some organizations, such as Federal Express, this system is very sophisticated and quite formalized. Federal Express uses a database of 25 interactive videodiscs to train its 35,000 employees. Before a courier ever delivers a package, he or she receives three weeks of training and a customer service agent receives five weeks of training before answering a call.[18] In other organizations, training and development are very informal and unstructured. Whether or not the system is highly structured, a major responsibility of any organization is to *invest* in the education and development of its employees by formulating and implementing a human resource development strategy that includes programs, objectives, and procedures for development programs, on- and off-the-job training, and other learning experiences.

TRAINING AND DEVELOPMENT

TRAINING
Providing an employee with skills that can be used immediately on the job.

DEVELOPMENT
Providing an employee with knowledge that may be used today or at some time in the future.

Training refers to providing instruction to develop skills that can be used immediately on the job. It has a rather narrow focus and should provide skills that will benefit the organization rather quickly. The financial benefits to the organization usually occur quickly. **Development,** on the other hand, has a broader scope. It involves developing knowledge that may be used today or sometime in the future. It may not be focused on either the present or future job but more on meeting the organization's general long-term needs. The payoff is less direct and can be measured only in the long term.[19] Let's consider an example to illustrate the difference.

If an organization taught its managers to use *Lotus 1-2-3* to manage their budgets, that would constitute training. If these same managers took courses in general systems theory and management information systems to help the company to develop into a more efficient, effective organization over the long term, the effort would more properly be labeled as a development activity. Both are obviously important and need emphasis.

The terms *training* and *development* refer to the total structure of on-the-job and off-the-job programs utilized by organizations in developing employee skills and knowledge necessary for proficient job performance and career advancement. **Management development** refers to the training and development programs for supervisors and managers and often excludes programs for professionals (such as engineers, salespeople, and accountants), skilled operative employees (such as draftsmen, tool and die makers, and bookkeepers), and semiskilled and unskilled operatives (such as assembly line workers, packers, and material handlers, unless these individuals are being prepared for supervision or management).

Any meaningful training and development system must be closely integrated with other human resource strategies in the organization if it is to operate most effectively. Organizations that have effectively integrated training and development with other human resource strategies in performance appraisal, promotion, or pay advances recognize the importance of the training function. This integration also helps to ensure that development strategies help support other related personnel strategies.

MANAGEMENT DEVELOPMENT

Training and development programs for supervisors and managers.

TRAINING RESPONSIBILITIES

The major responsibilities for training and development are shared by top management, human resources, the immediate supervisor, and the employee, as shown in Exhibit 9.7. Each is described below.

TOP MANAGEMENT

The commitment of the chief executive officer and top management is critical for effective training to take place throughout the organization. Managers tend to manage as they are managed. Any developmental program that doesn't have the attention, understanding, and commitment from top management will be severely limited in terms of the basic changes it can bring about.

Top management has the responsibility to provide the general policies and procedures required to implement the training program. They need to provide administrative control to ensure that managers and employees comply with the program and give it a conscientious commitment.

Setting the proper culture for encouraging training and development rests with top management. If top management does not do this, establishing the proper climate in the organization will be very difficult.

THE HUMAN RESOURCE DEPARTMENT

The human resource department in the organization performs essentially a staff support function. It *assists* line management in training and development by providing expertise and resources and sponsoring training conferences and programs.

THE IMMEDIATE SUPERVISOR

Each employee's immediate supervisor and those higher on the organizational hierarchy have the direct responsibility to ensure that training and development occur. The

FOCUS ON INTERNATIONAL ISSUES

Becoming the First Woman to Become a Training Manager for a Dutch Firm

Paulette Pellani is a training manager with Philips Electronics Corporation of North America. Pellani recently did what no woman has done before. She took a position as a training manager in Holland. In an effort to internationalize its staff, Philips Gloeilampenfabrieken, the home office of the giant Dutch electronics enterprise, asked Pellani to be the first woman to hold a training manager slot. How could she refuse this once-in-a-lifetime opportunity?

She describes her two-year stint as an investment and a learning experience. She knew that the skills she would gather while living abroad would make her marketable to other firms if her position disappeared while she was overseas. To keep her face familiar, she visited her old office every time she was in town on business.

Pellani admitted that she did have to wrestle with a gender gap problem. For example, she provided a lot of directions for lost guests as well as made more than a dozen copies for people before she realized that she shouldn't. She decided that she would make sure that people understood her position from the beginning. When introduced to someone, she would simply mention that her job was the same as the man who introduced her. Since she was the first and only woman to hold this position, she was not easily forgotten. However, when she learned that her replacement was a Dutch woman, she knew that her services had been appreciated. Now back in the states for a year, she is ready to go again.

SOURCE: Adapted from Cynthia Barnum, "U.S. Training Manager Becomes Expatriate," *HRMagazine,* April 1994, pp. 82–84

EXHIBIT 9.7   **Training and Development Is a Shared Responsibility**

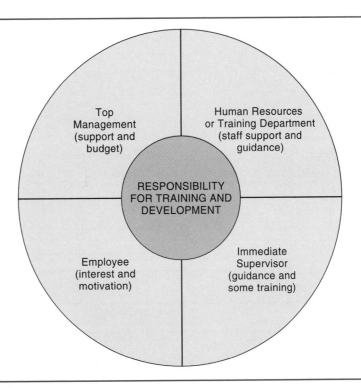

supervisor should encourage employees to develop themselves and should provide time for this to occur. The immediate supervisor, indeed the whole organization, must provide the atmosphere, resources, and encouragement for self-development.

THE EMPLOYEE

Even though human resource professionals and line managers must facilitate and manage the training and development process, the primary responsibility lies with the individual. The employee has the responsibility for demonstrating interest in personal career development relative to the goals of the organization. Finally, each employee should encourage other employees to take advantage of development opportunities.

So we see that the responsibilities for training and development are shared among human resources, top management, the immediate supervisor, and the employee. Let's now look at how companies decide what training and development programs should be offered. The model of the training process is illustrated in Exhibit 9.8.

EXHIBIT 9.8   **Model of the Training Process**

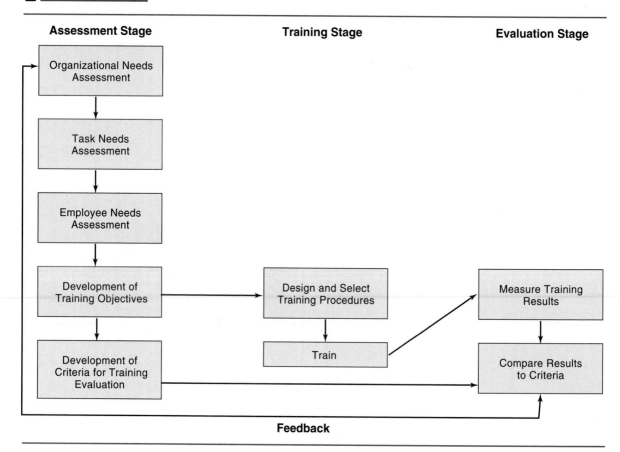

SOURCE: Adapted from I.L. Goldstein, *Training in Organizations: Needs Assessment, Development, and Evaluation* (Monterey, CA: Brooks/Cole, 1986), p. 16.

ASSESSMENT STAGE OF THE TRAINING PROCESS

ASSESSMENT STAGE
The stage of the training process in which training needs are discovered.

Before any training can be done, the need for it must first be analyzed. This is referred to as the **assessment stage** of the training process. In this stage, the training needs of the organization, the job, and the individuals in the organization are examined. Different types of information and different methods of gathering it can be used at each of the levels; Exhibit 9.9 lists some of the most common sources of and methods to obtain these data. For example, virtually every member of the organization can provide some information about what areas need training and what kind of training is needed. An overlap between the responses provided from a variety of sources can identify a need for training. Data about the type of training needed and what group(s) need the training can and should be collected through a variety of methods. Some individuals may be able to voice their opinions in an interview setting; others may prefer to write their responses, especially if they feel they are too busy for a formal interview. Regardless of

EXHIBIT 9.9   **Examples of Sources and Methods for Data Collection for the Needs Assessment Stage of the Model of the Training Process**

Written sources
  Employee files
    Requests for training
    Requests for a job transfer
    Reasons mentioned for leaving the organization
    Accident reports
    Employee complaints
    Performance appraisals
  Job descriptions
  Job specifications
  Job analysis reports
  Records of missed deadlines
  Customer complaints
  Equipment repair requests
  Equipment downtime reports
  Employment tests
Other sources
  Employees
  Customers
  Management
  Consultants
Methods
  Individual interviews
  Group interviews
  Questionnaires
  Focus groups
  Observation
  Examination of written sources
  Job analysis
  Performance appraisals
  Testing

the sources or methods used, data must be collected and analyzed at three different levels. Each of these is described below.

ORGANIZATIONAL NEEDS ASSESSMENT

To perform an organizational needs analysis, one must examine the proposed training projects with respect to the organization's goals, objectives, and strategies. Some things to consider are whether the corporate culture will support the training and development programs that are planned, whether the goals of these training programs align with and support the mission, goals, and strategies of the organization, and whether top management fully supports the proposed training. Further, to be prepared for the future, the goals and strategies the organization has included in its 5- and 10-year plans also must be compared with the proposed training programs to ensure that they develop the skills, knowledge, and abilities required by the workforce to implement the plan.

It is also important to note how the proposed training will impact other areas that may or may not be scheduled for training. Will the new procedures being implemented in one area change the work procedures of employees in units that interact with this area? When all areas are to receive some type of training, an organizational assessment can determine the order in which the areas need to be trained. The expense of the proposed training programs also should be considered when performing an organizational needs assessment. If funding is an issue, prioritizing the training programs might be needed.

TASK NEEDS ASSESSMENT

The goal of the job needs assessment is to isolate the specific requirements of the job in question. Any of the job analysis methods discussed in Chapter 5 can be used for this purpose. For example, incumbents could be interviewed to determine what is actually done on the job, and supervisors could be interviewed to determine what should be done. Task checklists or questionnaires about the job could be distributed to individuals who are knowledgeable about the job such as the trainers, supervisors, or employees holding it. Employees could be observed actually performing their jobs. Written materials also can be examined to determine the requirements of the job.

EMPLOYEE NEEDS ASSESSMENT

The employee needs assessment determines whether a gap exists between the requirements of a job and the skills of the employees who perform it. This is a critical step prior to implementing any major change in procedure as Kash and Karry, a southern grocery store chain, found. After installing a major computerized system in its stocking warehouse, Kash and Karry learned that the majority of its workers could not read English well enough to use the new system. Had an employee needs analysis been performed prior to installing the system, the firm would have realized that the messages on the computer screens either had to be written in Spanish or the workers needed to be trained to read or at least recognize the English messages.

While this step is listed as the final level of needs analysis (i.e., organizational, task, employee), many organizations begin and end their training planning at this level. However, only analyzing employee needs shows a lack of adequate planning on the part of the organization. Organizations' lack of planning for training is evident when the annual training dollars spent are examined. Only 0.5 percent of employers account for 90 percent of the $30 billion spent annually on training.[20] This means that more than 99 percent of firms spend the remaining $3 billion. Obviously, this means that some spend very little or no money on training. Organizations that completely lack training appear to value their employees less than the equipment they purchase because when a major piece of equipment is purchased, a percentage of the cost is set aside for maintenance. Training is maintenance of the work force.[21]

DEVELOPMENT OF TRAINING OBJECTIVES

Before training begins, the objectives of the training program must be identified. They should be written as **behavioral objectives** that include what the outcome of the training is to be (for example, learning a skill), a way to measure the degree to which the training objective has been met, and under what conditions employees can expect to perform the skill. A behavioral objective for a mail sorter might be to sort 50 letters per minute using the conveyor belt system after training.

DEVELOPMENT OF CRITERIA FOR TRAINING EVALUATION

BEHAVIORAL OBJECTIVES
The goals of the training program, including hoped-for outcome, a way of measuring the program's success, and a statement of situations in which an employee could expect to use the skill.

To determine whether the training program achieved its goals, some criteria against which to measure the results must be developed. It is important to use more than one criterion in an effort to determine the overall effect of the training program on the organization. Often the performance level specifically stated in the behavioral objectives is used as one type of criteria. Other criteria might include the reactions of the trainees to the training program, the changes in behavior of the trainees, or even results from test scores. Whatever criteria are developed to judge the training program, they should be consistent with the organization's goals and strategies for the training program.

TRAINING STAGE OF THE TRAINING PROCESS

DESIGN AND SELECT TRAINING PROCEDURES

Training procedures fall into two broad categories: on-the-job training (OJT) and off-the-job training. Any comprehensive training system in an organization utilizes both types of training.

ON-THE-JOB TRAINING (OJT)

At its lowest level, OJT provides a person with the skills to do a minimum level on the job, but it can and should do much more than that. A number of techniques can be employed to provide OJT.

One technique that is frequently used is expanding the job duties, assignments, and responsibilities of an individual both horizontally and vertically in the organization. Opportunities are created for the individual in his or her present job to practice higher-level and diverse skills not normally required in the present job.

JOB ROTATION (CROSS TRAINING)
Temporarily moving employees to various jobs within an organization as a part of training.

Similarly, **job rotation,** also called **cross training,** can be used. This involves moving individuals to various types of jobs within the organization at the same level or next immediate higher level for periods of time. This rotation may be for as short as an hour or two or as long as a year. Many organizations use this approach during the first two or three years of a person's career to familiarize him or her with broad functional operations and processes of the organization. Job rotation is a common occurrence in

FOCUS ON INTERNATIONAL ISSUES

The Costs Can Be High Without the Cross-Cultural Training of Expatriates

While most employees who have been assigned to a foreign post receive training in the functional skills they will need in their new assignments, cross-cultural training may be overlooked. Failure of an expatriate generally occurs because he or she has not been trained to perform those functional skills in ways accepted by a different culture.

Expatriate failures can be costly. It is estimated that each failure costs the company anywhere from $250,000 to $1 million. And the failures are frequent. The failure rate for expatriates in London is 18 percent, Brussels 27 percent, Tokyo 36 percent, and Saudi Arabia 68 percent. These rates can be lowered by training newly assigned expatriates to function in ways acceptable in the culture.

Negotiation Styles

Negotiation styles differ from country to country. For example, Russian negotiators are conflict oriented and attempt to put their counterpart on the defensive. Italians frequently argue trivial points to excess. Asian negotiators use a consensus-oriented style that attempts to include all participants equally. Americans try to win as much as they can for their side even if it means the other side must give up something for this to happen.

On-the-Job Communication

The U.S. communication style used at work is not shared by other cultures. For example, in France it can take business associates over six months to feel comfortable enough to address their business associates by their first names. Also, keeping more than a one-foot distance between yourself and an Arab colleague with whom you are talking is seen as impolite. But stand that close to your Spanish business associates and they would be insulted.

U.S. customs can insult and offend non-U.S. business associates in a host of other ways. For example, asking a French person "Where do you live" or "What do you do" would be equivalent to someone asking you "How much do you make?" Using the phrase "Let's do lunch" with German business counterparts will motivate them to pull out their calendars and begin searching for a mutually agreeable time. Exposing the underside of your foot in the Middle East or the palm of your hand in Africa is a rude and demeaning gesture. Finally, it is nice to bring a small, wrapped gift to the home of a Japanese business associate when invited over. However, do not wrap it in white paper. This is a sign of death.

Offensive actions such as the ones listed above are made by many expatriates in foreign countries for the first time. That is the reason that expatriate training in the culture of the host country is just as important, if not more so, than functional training. Various consulting firms can be used to provide specialized training. Obviously, it is important for expatriates to listen to the voice of experience before they leave. Quick cultural lessons can save the high costs of yet another expatriate failure.

SOURCE: Adapted from Shari Caudron, "Training Ensures Success Overseas," *Personnel Journal,* December 1991, pp. 27–30; Bob Hagerty, "Trainers Help Expatriate Employees Build Bridges to Different Cultures," *The Wall Street Journal,* June 14, 1993, p. B1+.

Japanese companies such as Toyota. However, few U.S. companies use it except on the factory floors. One reason for this is the U.S. culture. Movement in the job is expected to be upward. Lateral movements are hard to sell to employees, especially to managers of other divisions. Because of the pressure on managers to save money and produce more, taking on a rotated employee is not seen as a good business decision since the person can be expected to take six months or longer to become fully productive.[22] Interestingly, two U.S. chemical companies are taking job rotation to a new level. Dow Chemical and Nalco Chemical have swapped employees. Nalco traded Dow an expert in sales and marketing for someone with expertise in environmental and safety operations. Each employee will serve a two-year stint at the competitor's office. By borrowing from each other's strengths, both firms gained the experience they needed without having to hire to get it.[23]

Staff development meetings discuss facets of each individual's job and ways to develop ideas for improving job performance. These meetings may be held away from the job in a "retreat-type" atmosphere.

Another training technique is placing someone in an *"assistant to" position.* This involves having promising employees serve as staff assistants to higher skill level jobs for a specified period of time (often one to three months) to become more familiar with these positions in the organization.

Problem-solving conferences are called to solve a specific problem being experienced by a group or the organization as a whole. It involves brainstorming and other creative means to come up with mutually determined solutions to basic problems.

Mentoring assigns a guide or knowledgeable person higher up in the organization to help a new employee "learn the ropes" of the organization and to provide other advice. Usually a social relationship is developed so that the employee feels that she or he can go to the mentor for advice that cannot be asked of the immediate superior.

Special assignments are special tasks or responsibilities given to an individual for a specified period of time. The assignment may be writing a report; investigating the feasibility for a new project, process, service, or product; preparing a newsletter; or evaluating a company policy or procedure. Whatever the assignment, new skills are learned.

Employees can also attend *in-company training done by company trainers.* These programs can cover such topics as safety, new human resource procedures, new products or services, affirmative action, and technical programs.

A variation of this is *in-company training done by outside consultants.* Recognized experts are brought to the company to conduct training on such topics as goal setting, communications, assessment techniques, safety, and other current topics of importance. They often supplement training done by company trainers. One type of in-house training by external experts that has become popular over the past several years is basic skills training in literacy and writing. With the ever-increasing demand for computer-literate workers, companies are having to address their employees' deficiencies in the three Rs before they can learn advanced computer skills. Collins & Aikman, a Georgia carpet mill, undertook this type of in-house training. When customers started requesting elaborate corporate emblems woven into their carpets and multiple colors in each rug, Collins & Aikman responded by purchasing state-of-the-art computerized equipment. Soon it found, however, that very few employees were capable of reading the instructions required to use the machine. After a thorough analysis, the firm learned that only 8 percent of its current employees had the skills needed, and at least 33 percent had not graduated from high school. To remedy the situation, Collins & Aikman hired an adult education teacher to set up classrooms on the shop floor. Classes are held in reading, writing, science, social studies, and math two days a week on each shift. Some classes are designed to prepare students to take the high school equivalency exam; others are more remedial in nature and are teaching students to read and write. However, this wonderful opportunity is not for everyone. Some workers are too proud or too nervous to take part in the classes. Instead, these workers have asked for demotions to lower-paying jobs that they know they can do without going back to school.[24]

Often one of the most overlooked training methods is the distribution of reading materials. This formal program is created to circulate books, journals, selected articles, new business material, and so on to selected employees. An effective program also includes periodic scheduled meetings to discuss the material. Finally, *apprenticeships* can be used. This refers to training provided by working under an experienced worker or

HR CHALLENGE

Avoiding Lawsuits after Training

Various types of nontraditional training have been used by organizations. For example, wilderness and survival training exercises are used to build team spirit and unite previously disjointed groups. The results are often positive, but this type of training has also produced some extremely negative outcomes: lawsuits. Adventure training exercises can lead to claims of infliction of emotional distress when an employee is humiliated by the inability to perform an assigned survival task; invasion of privacy claims may arise if employees are forced to reveal deep-rooted fears and emotions to fellow employees; false imprisonment claims could result from, for example, placing an employee on a raft in the middle of a raging river and failing to respond to his or her demands to be returned to shore; and, finally, wrongful discharge claims can be made when an employee is fired because he or she refused to participate in or performed poorly during an adventure training program.

To protect themselves from lawsuits, organizations can take several steps. First, they should ensure that participation in such programs is truly voluntary. This means that the employees who elect not to participate must not be evaluated differently than those who do when performance appraisals are made or promotions are offered. Second, the employees' written consent to participate in such programs must be obtained. It is important that the employee understand all aspects of the training program before consenting to participate. Third, alternative types of team-building experiences must be provided for those who choose not to participate. Fourth, an employee who wants to stop during the exercise should have this option. The employee should not be embarrassed or harassed into continuing. Finally, every step of the program should be documented and the job-related goals of the program should be stated.

SOURCE: Adapted from Scott Kexman and Eugene Connors, "Avoid Legal Pitfalls in Nontraditional Training," *HRMagazine,* May 1993, pp. 71–74.

master in a craft. The apprentice works alongside a person skilled in the craft and is taught by that person. This often occurs on the job, and it sometimes is done in off-the-job settings. Apprenticeship programs also often include some classroom work. Craft unions frequently take advantage of apprenticeship training and, in some cases, may be responsible for the entire program. Apprenticeship programs are best known in the skilled crafts, such as masonry, electricity, bricklaying, and carpentry. The University Hospital in Salt Lake City has developed its Multidisciplinary Apprentice Program (MAP) which is designed to recruit and retain a well-trained, professional labor force. Capitalizing on a large pool of relatively untrained workers in need of work, the program targets youth, older workers, ethnic minorities, dislocated workers, and displaced homemakers. A task force composed of a variety of health-care workers teaches the principal classes in nursing, pharmacy, physical therapy, and human resources. The students who master the classroom knowledge move up a job level after passing a certifying exam. At this point, they are assigned to work as an apprentice with someone at the next level. Once the student decides that nursing is a career he or she wants to pursue, he or she may continue training by enrolling in additional courses as preparation for moving to the next level after passing the courses and any required exams. By providing training to workers who need it, the program has a good chance of succeeding.[25]

OFF-THE-JOB TRAINING

An effective training system supplements OJT with various forms of off-the-job training. Most of this type of training is classroom training. Some of the more frequently used types of training include the following:

Outside short courses and seminars. These are specialized courses conducted by educational institutions, professional associations, or private consulting and training firms that last one day to one week. If employees selectively attend programs that complement their career development plan, these courses can be extremely beneficial.

College or university degree and certificate programs. Specialized degree and certification programs are offered as evening and weekend classes by a variety of colleges and universities. Often these are in professional fields such as management, accounting, finance, or law. Many employers have a tuition refund program that reimburses employees for all or part of the tuition and book expense.

Advanced management programs. UCLA, Harvard, MIT, Ohio State, and other well-known universities offer in-residence programs of two weeks to a full year for top management. Often they cover material typically found in an MBA program but at a very accelerated rate.

Correspondence schools. If individuals can practice rigorous self-discipline, home correspondence study can be an excellent self-development tool. However, an employee needs to ensure that the correspondence school with which he or she deals is reputable.

Outside meetings and conferences. Most managers and professionals have opportunities to attend trade and professional conferences and conventions during the year. If participants actually attend the scheduled meetings and workshops at these conferences, they can be excellent learning experiences.

INSTRUCTIONAL TECHNIQUES FOR TRAINING AND DEVELOPMENT

A virtual explosion in training techniques has occurred in the past few years. These new techniques plus the tried-and-true methods give an organization a wide variety of training techniques from which to choose in building an effective program. The following are some of these techniques.

Lecture-discussion. Almost all training programs, particularly outside programs, utilize this technique. Most college classes utilize this technique extensively. It has the advantage of being spontaneous and allows the participants to become involved in exploring concepts and in seeking clarification. It requires a professional training leader with broad expertise in the field and related fields under discussion. The major disadvantage is that this technique is difficult to use with large groups.

Lecture. This method is very useful for large groups. It requires a training leader who is dynamic and who can organize and present material in an effective fashion. For best use, it should be supplemented with additional types of training techniques. Eighty-two percent of firms use the lecture method in their training programs.

Multimedia presentations. Lecture and lecture-discussion work best when a multimedia approach is used. This involves using handouts of materials (such as subject outlines, advanced reading assignments, and cases), films, slides, film strips, videotapes, audio cassettes, overhead projectors, flip charts, and the old stand-by, the chalkboard. The major disadvantage here is that sophisticated equipment can fail at the most inopportune time. Also, the multimedia approach is but one tool for management development. It can't substitute for an effective instructor. Eighty-three percent of companies report using videotapes in training.

Job coaching. The best on-the-job technique is coaching. This involves either the individual's immediate supervisor or a mentor (a person located elsewhere in the organization who can help the employee). The mentor acts as a guide, counselor, friend, and interested party in helping his or her subordinates perform their jobs more effectively and in developing a comprehensive career plan for each subordinate.

Self-paced (programmed). Self-paced learning techniques use programmed texts and exercises to guide students through a step-by-step series of learning experiences. It is a learner-centered method of instruction and seldom, if ever, requires the services of an instructor at the time the training occurs. The technique presents subject matter to the trainees in small steps, which require them to respond and immediately inform them of appropriateness of their responses.

Computer-assisted instruction. Actually, this is a form of multimedia, self-paced instruction learning. Some computer-assisted techniques can be quite sophisticated and expensive. When used as a part of a total educational program, it can be quite effective.

Gaming and role-playing (simulation). This technique gives participants actual practice in applying concepts in an artificial situation. An opportunity to solve a problem is provided, and the participants actually act out the solution. Gaming usually involves some element of competitiveness in which one group tries to outperform other groups. In the hands of a skillful seminar leader, this technique can be an extremely useful training tool since it gives participants actual practice before peers, yet it allows them to make mistakes without having the repercussions such mistakes would have on the job.

Case analysis. Usually combined with role-playing and/or gaming, this technique also gives participants the opportunity to solve an actual or hypothetical problem. If used without gaming or role-playing, it relies very heavily on group discussion without the participants putting themselves in the actual roles of individuals in the case. Cases are used extensively in this book.

TRANSFER OF TRAINING

Probably the greatest criticism leveled at training and development, particularly management development, is the inability of participants in training programs to practice on the job what has been learned in the classroom. For example, many management development programs stress participative leadership styles, humanistic management, and Theory Y assumptions (that is, employees are internally motivated, committed to the organization, seek and accept responsibility, and innovatively solve problems) about people, yet when training participants try to practice these beliefs on the job, they often find that they are thwarted by an autocratic Theory X (that is, employees avoid work and therefore must be controlled and monitored in order to reach organizational goals) organizational culture.[26]

This blockage of the "transfer of training" is a very serious impediment to making training effective. After all, if the organization itself needs to be changed, rather than the behavior of individuals in the organization, training activities in and of themselves may have little effect. The organization's objectives, policies, structure, procedures, methods, and philosophy should be examined so that the organizational context in which the training will be practiced is consistent with the concepts taught to the managers in training and development programs. This approach to training, therefore, calls for training to be part of an organization's overall strategic plan. EDS is currently revamping its entire culture so that the training and development management receives is consistent with the organization functions.[27] Exhibit 9.10 lists the skills most easily transferred back to the job.

■ **EXHIBIT 9.1O**   **The Six Most Transferable Skills**

The skills that companies look for most often when interviewing new employees:

**Public Speaking
Financial Management
People Management
Interviewing
Training
Writing**

SOURCE: *HRMagazine,* November 1992, p. 24.

BLOCKAGE OF THE TRANSFER OF TRAINING

Let's explore the blockage of training issue further, since it is such a key one in development. Trainers and training managers are often admonished to make training "relevant" in order for it to be used by trainees on the job. But what does this mean? Presumably, *relevant* means that the actual training relates directly either to the job held or to a job to which a person may be promoted. That is, the training deals with the specific skills and knowledge that must actually be practiced on the job. For example, supervisors must know how to solve problems on the job so a training program on problem-solving methods and techniques for supervisors is presumably relevant.

But making the training relevant does not always ensure the transfer of training. As we indicated earlier, culture on the job may not reinforce the training learned. The trainee may not actually understand *how* to practice the skill and knowledge back on the job even though it is relevant. For this reason, five factors that encourage the actual use of training on the job should be observed in any program.[28] These factors work in a successive fashion; that is, the addition of each factor to the training program increases the likelihood the training will be practiced on the job. These factors are summarized in Exhibit 9.11.

THEORY

People need to know the theory that underlies the training they are receiving. Discussion of the theory helps people to understand why they are being asked to perform tasks in a certain way.

For example, a training session on problem solving might include a discussion on problem-solving methods and the theory and concepts that underlie each method. If the theory is explained in such a fashion that the trainee can understand it and see its relationship to the problem-solving methods, the chances that he or she will use the problem-solving methods on the job are enhanced. Theory explanation need not be a long and involved academic discourse. It can be kept short and to the point.

DEMONSTRATION

When a demonstration of the concepts and methods being taught occurs, the chances of the participants using the idea on the job increase. Here, the trainees are given the

EXHIBIT 9.11   **Factors That Increase the Likelihood that Training Will Be Used on the Job**

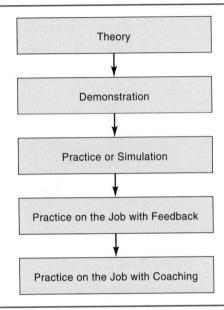

opportunity to actually see how the particular method or technique works. For example, if communication techniques are being taught, participants are more likely to use the techniques if they are able to observe and discuss a demonstration of the techniques during the training session. This makes the concept, theory, and technique "come alive." The participants learn through a *vicarious process.* In other words, they learn by example.

LABORATORY PRACTICE OR SIMULATION

When participants are able to actually practice the desired technique, the transfer of learning to the job increases. Here the participants learn by doing. They are actually given the opportunity to experience the desired method or technique in a simulated setting. This type of learning is enhanced further when feedback and critique are provided to participants by other participants and/or the instructor. They practice the expected behavior or techniques in a classroom or lab setting that they are expected to practice on the job. Of course, this is the type of training used by most computer courses.[29]

A communication training program, for example, would allow the participants to perform mock communication sessions in a role-playing situation. The class and/or instructor would provide feedback and critique the participants at the conclusion of the session.

Practice in a simulated situation allows the participants to experience the expected behavior and the feelings that accompany it. The person sees the problems involved in carrying out the expected action. When the problems are overcome and success is experienced, the trainee has an increased sense of confidence brought about by an actual, although simulated, experience. Of course, if failure is experienced in simulation, and the individual is not able to overcome the failure in a succeeding simulation, there is little likelihood that he or she will try the new technique on the job.

PRACTICE ON THE JOB WITH FEEDBACK

When the individual is given an opportunity to actually try the behavior on the job under some guidance, there is a greater likelihood that the trainee will continue to practice the behavior in his or her job environment. During and after this opportunity, the person is provided with evaluative feedback. This type of training, much like on-the-job training, is the basis for most apprenticeships.

PRACTICE ON THE JOB WITH COACHING

The best way to tie the training and job practice on the job together is to extend the period during which feedback and guidance are provided on the job while the trainee practices the desired behavior. This method differs from the one above in that job coaching continues for a considerable period of time as opposed to a one-time trial on the job with feedback.

Of course, this method requires that someone be available to coach. This could be an immediate supervisor, if he or she is trained in the desired behavior, a training consultant employed by the organization, or a **mentor** located someplace else in the organization who is responsible for guiding various subordinates. If the responsibility falls on the immediate supervisor, the role of the supervisor changes. He or she becomes a coach or catalyst skilled in the behavior desired on the part of subordinates. The manager becomes a teacher as well as a manager.

Obviously, not all managers make good coaches or teachers, and this is a serious limitation. Training on how to coach and teach can be expensive and fruitless if various managers do not accept coaching or instruction as a legitimate part of their role. Yet, if on-the-job coaching is provided for a sustained period after the training, the training is very likely to be used on the job by the trainees.

All managers in an organization from top to supervisory should be training and development oriented. Training and development are essentially line functions. The training staff, should the firm have one, should assist and advise, but the major responsibility rests with line managers.

If a company wants to see young managers grow, it perhaps should not rely solely on mentoring and training courses, but it should also include a little danger. In a survey of 600 professional or managerial men and women at big companies, 60 percent defined developmental experiences as being at risk in a novel or unsupervised environment; only 12 percent cited a relationship with a supervisor or mentor, and just 7 percent named training courses. Examples of risky involvement include asking someone to turn around a business who has never had such experience or sending a computer novice to computerize a unit.[30]

MENTOR
An employee who is responsible for guiding or "coaching" various subordinates as they practice newly learned skills.

EVALUATION STAGE OF TRAINING AND DEVELOPMENT

A variety of approaches is available for evaluating training programs. One of the most widely accepted and used approach was developed by Donald Kirkpatrick.[31] He identified four different forms of evaluation that should be performed for each training program. Each level focuses on a different aspect of the training program. The results taken from all four levels provide a clear picture of the effectiveness of the training program. Let's look at each level in more detail.

REACTION

The reaction of the participants to the training program is the first level of evaluation. Information gathered about the reactions of the trainees should include what they thought about the program in general, the facilities in which the training program took place, the trainers involved, and the content of the program. These reactions are generally gathered through questionnaires distributed to the participants at the conclusion of the program.

LEARNING

The second level evaluates the degree of learning that took place. Specifically, the goal is to determine whether the trainees have mastered the facts, techniques, skills, and processes that were taught during the training program. A variety of tests, such as performance tests or pencil and paper tests, can be administered to determine the level of competency achieved by the trainees. Another approach is to have the trainees demonstrate their level of knowledge through a simulated exercise or through role-playing. Whatever method is used, the testing usually takes place immediately after the training program concludes.

BEHAVIOR

Behavior evaluation of a training program examines whether participants exhibit behavior changes in their jobs. The data used to evaluate the trainees' behavior are usually collected from individuals, such as supervisors or co-workers, who work closely enough with the trainees to evaluate their performance on the job. The more the behaviors taught at the training program are being used by the trainees, the more the training program has successfully transferred training to the work site.

RESULTS

The last level of evaluation is the results level. This phase investigates how the program has impacted the organization. Data collected to evaluate a training program at this level might include cost savings, projected and actual profits, increases in sales, decreases in accidents, improved employee attitudes, lowered turnover and absenteeism, or increases in production. Evaluation at this level should relate directly to the goals of the organization outlined during the initial assessment stages of the training program. If these results match the expectations, the training program can be deemed successful. If they do not match, more specifically if they fail to reach the desired goals, adjustments to the training program need to be made. These adjustments are filtered into the training program beginning at the assessment stage, and the process begins again.

LONGITUDINAL COST-BENEFIT ANALYSIS WITH CONTROL GROUPS

A methodologically superior assessment technique of training effectiveness attempts to determine the measurable benefits from a training program over given time periods measured at periodic intervals (such as three months, six months, and one year). These benefits would be compared to the costs of the program. Ideally, this information would then be compared with a similar group of employees who did not go through the training program. Any differences in the benefits (as measured by improving job performance) of the group who experienced the training program could be at least partially attributable to the training effort.

The following procedures can be used to make a longitudinal evaluation of learning from training programs:

1. Randomly assign employees of a similar occupation or level in the organization to two groups. One group of employees receives the training; the other does not.

2. Administer a pretest to measure the performance and/or knowledge of both groups to determine their present level of performance and/or knowledge.
3. Conduct the training for one group.
4. Accurately assess all costs of the training effort, including those for the instructor, media, facilities, and employee time away from the job.
5. Conduct a posttest measure of performance and/or knowledge of both groups at periodic intervals after the completion of training.
6. Compare the benefits of the program as measured by higher performance and more complete job knowledge with the costs of the program for the trained group.
7. Compare the posttest performance and job knowledge of the trained group with the nontrained or control group.

This procedure can be diagrammed as shown in Exhibit 9.12.

APPLYING THE TRAINING EFFECTIVENESS MODEL: AN EXAMPLE

Even though the longitudinal cost-benefit training effectiveness model is seldom used because it is time consuming and requires denying some people training, it can be an effective way to systematically determine the results of training. This is especially so if accurate performance measures exist for the job on which dollar estimates can be made. Let's look at an example to see how this evaluation model works.

Assume that you are the training director for a business organization that has a number of field salespeople. You have noticed, after receiving a selected number of periodic performance appraisals of these salespeople, that many seem to be having a problem selling a new product that your company has recently developed.

EXHIBIT 9.12 **A Model of the Longitudinal Cost-Benefit Analysis for Training Effectiveness Using a Control Group**

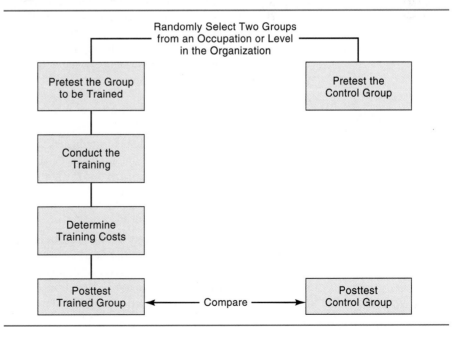

You decide that this problem is significant and that product notices and staff meetings have not helped significantly in reducing the problem. A comprehensive training program is necessary. You realize that even though not all salespeople need the program, many do. Using the following procedure, you set up, conduct, and evaluate the program:

1. Determine the specific training and development needs of the group by examining performance appraisals, assessment center results, conferences with supervisors, and other methods.
2. Design specific performance objectives that the training is to accomplish.
3. Identify the salespeople who need the training.
4. Assign one-half of those identified to a group that will receive the training and the other half to a control group that will not receive the training.
5. Conduct a pretest for both groups on the performance objectives the training is to cover.
6. Design the training program including topics, instructors, media, cases, exercises, handouts, and so on.
7. Conduct the training program for the group to be trained.
8. Assess the total cost of the training program including all instructional and travel costs, loss of time away from job, and so on.
9. Conduct a posttest at periodic intervals for both sales groups on specific performance measures that the training covered.
10. Compare the performance measures of the salespeople who went through the program with those who did not.
11. Compare the benefits, as measured as improvement in performance measures for the trained group, with the costs of the program.

Admittedly, most training directors do not go through such an elaborate procedure. It is costly and often difficult to withhold training from those who may need it. But this procedure will give an organization a much more documented basis on which to assess training effectiveness and plan future programs. Additionally, this information is very useful for presenting a case to top management on the value of training and development for the organization. Then, if the organization should go through a period of economic downturn, a strong case can be made not to drastically cut or eliminate the training budget, as so often happens.

ALTERNATIVE EVALUATION DESIGNS

The difficulties in using a longitudinal cost-benefit analysis often render it impossible to apply. Hence, alternative forms of designs that can be used to evaluate a training program have been presented. Three such designs are presented in Exhibit 9.13 and explained below.

POSTTEST DESIGN

The easiest, but least effective, way to evaluate a training program is to use the posttest design. To apply this design, the trainees are trained and are then tested on what they learned in the training program. This type of design is used to collect reaction or learning results. This method is easy to use and the results are quickly known. However, the results may not be accurate for a number of reasons. First, the skill level of the indi-

EXHIBIT 9.13   **Alternative Designs for Evaluating Training Programs**

Posttest Design

1. Train
2. Test

Pretest/Posttest Design

1. Test
2. Train
3. Test

Multiple Pretest/Multiple Posttest Design

1. Test
2. Test
3. Test
4. Train
5. Test
6. Test
7. Test

viduals prior to training is not known so whether the training program is responsible for the results cannot be determined. Another problem is that how long these results will last cannot be determined. Because the test is administered immediately upon completion of the training program only short-term memory is being tested. It is impossible to know whether these skills will be transferred to the job.

PRETEST/POSTTEST DESIGN

The pretest/posttest design is an extension of the posttest design that addresses the problem of not knowing the ability of the trainees prior to training. To use this design, the trainees are tested both prior to and after the training program. The difference between the pretest and posttest results can be said to be due to the training program. This is an improvement over the posttest design, but it still has some problems. Some participants may have some ability in the subject area of the training program before the program. As you learned in Chapter 7, all measures include error. Hence, the pretest score may not reflect the individual's true ability. Also, as mentioned above, this design does not allow measurement of the level of transfer of training that occurs.

MULTIPLE PRETEST/MULTIPLE POSTTEST DESIGN

In an effort to overcome the weaknesses in both the posttest design and the pretest/posttest design, the multiple pretest/multiple posttest design was developed. This design involves testing trainees multiple times prior to training as well as multiple times after training. Using this design allows the trainer to determine whether improvement occurred prior to training by comparing the results of the multiple pretests as well as whether the training program had a lasting effect by comparing the results of the multiple posttests. This design also provides greater confidence that the changes were actually due to the training program.

MANAGEMENT GUIDELINES

Our focus in this chapter has been on orientation and training as two related key methods to improve performance and productivity in the organization. Although other ways could be used to improve productivity, such as the adoption of new technology and methods, orientation and training are very much linked to these efforts. In other words, orientation and training of employees have very strong roles to play in using and adapting to a new technology and instituting new methods. The following are some management guidelines that can be delineated based on the information presented in this chapter.

1. An effective training program needs to be integrated with a comprehensive development program to reinforce the concepts and practices stressed in training on the job.

2. Effective training also requires a commitment to self-development from all employees, top management support, a comprehensive on-the-job training program supplemented with off-the-job training, and support from first-line supervisors.

3. The responsibilities for effective training and development are shared by the organization's top management, the human resource department, the immediate supervisor, and the employee. The greatest responsibility lies with the employee. The immediate supervisor has the next greatest responsibility in the role as coach and adviser. The human resource department assists line management in training by acting as supportive staff. Top management must give whole-hearted support to the process.

4. Methods for training and, development involve various on-the-job techniques and, as responsibilities are expanded, job rotation, "assistant-to" positions, and other techniques. Programs include outside short courses and seminars, college degree programs, and correspondence courses. An effective training and development program achieves a unique blend of on-the-job and off-the-job methods suitable for the individuals in the particular organization.

5. Instructional techniques have mushroomed over the past few years and include lecture, lecture-discussion, multimedia presentations, job coaching, programmed instruction, case analysis, role-playing, and gaming. Newer techniques involve computer-assisted instruction. A good program utilizes all techniques as appropriate rather than relying on any one technique at the exclusion of others.

6. It is important that an organization choose resources that best meet its needs for training and development.

7. The real success of a training and development program can be assessed ultimately on the basis of the success and health of the organization. However, assessments should be made of specific programs through some longitudinal analysis. The ideal assessment framework involves a cost-benefit analysis of the skill or knowledge a group who has attended a training program compared to a control group not receiving the training.

QUESTIONS FOR REVIEW

1. How can an organization's culture impact its training efforts?
2. What is socialization? Why is it important to an organization?
3. What are the similarities and differences between training and development?
4. What are four different on-the-job training methods? Describe each.
5. If you were asked to design a socialization program for all employees who entered your organization, what would the program be like?
6. How often should an orientation program be updated? Why?
7. What can an organization do to determine which employees need training and what type of training they need?
8. When is it to an organization's advantage to hire employees who need training and when is it advantageous to hire employees who are already trained?
9. What factors influence whether an employee who is a marginal performer is trained or fired?
10. How can an organization ensure that its employees conform? Why is this beneficial? When is it a problem?
11. What are the steps in the training need analysis process? Describe each.
12. How can the organization determine whether its training program is effective?
13. What are the similarities and differences between two of the off-the-job training opportunities described in this chapter?

CASE

DEVELOPMENT—THE FORD EXPERIENCE[32]

"There's nothing glamorous about trying to change an organization—it takes a strong resolution to change, and persistence," said Nancy Badore, program director of the Executive Development Center of Ford Motor Company in Dearborn, Michigan. "You just have to walk down the road, and stick with it. We've been consciously trying to change and to apply the lessons we've learned about change management. We've been sticking with it for about eight years now—and it's every bit as difficult every step of the way.

"We outdistanced the literature early on. We've been fortunate that we've been able to look at many different models and learn from them—and then had to rely on our own experience.

"At Ford, we've gone through three progressive stages of change during the past eight years. Toward the end of each stage, pressure within the organization mounted to create the setting for the next stage of change—and it would have been impossible to grow past each stage if the organization hadn't positively responded to this internal pressure."

STAGE I: QUALITY IMPROVEMENT/PLANT LEVEL

"During the first stage, we focused on how to create and improve quality, and we concentrated at the plant level. We worked with plant managers and union leadership and shared information with employees about business objectives. We were learning to focus our organization on an issue—and quality was the issue.

"After two to three years, it was clear that more people needed to be included in the quality effort—above the plant level—or the progress that had been made at the plant level would be stymied, and people would become frustrated. These pressures created the second stage."

STAGE II: INTERMEDIATE LEVEL

"At the intermediate or division level, changes increased in speed. There was more education involved—much of the learning we did was derived from Japanese management techniques and 'excellent' companies. Study groups and task forces were the primary vehicles we used to introduce change at this level.

"Again it became clear that, for change to continue spreading throughout the organization, the next-highest level of management would need to be involved."

STAGE III: SENIOR-MOST MANAGEMENT LEVEL

"By the time our senior-most management level became involved, we had come to realize an important lesson: that *everyone* must take responsibility for change—that a piece of a problem is in everybody, and everybody has to act and not wait for others to become perfect. At the same time, in taking responsibility for change, each individual must recognize limitations and the need for help from higher levels of management or other parts of the company."

EXECUTIVE DEVELOPMENT

"At the senior level, one task force recognized that the combination of high people skills and high quality could put us at a tremendous competitive advantage. Management began placing great emphasis on encouraging continual challenges and acquiring new skills and perspectives. With this in mind, we set out to create an executive development center. Our senior executive program has been introduced to the top 2,000 managers. The program is being institutionalized, with plans for everyone to come back for another session every couple of years, with revised content.

"Now, we are introducing a second generation of programs, centering on special topics—issues we can beat competition on. These issues include the following:

- We are organized functionally, but we must behave globally.
- We don't have any generalists, like Procter & Gamble. We must define what a generalist manager is here and prepare people for a transition into that role.
- We don't have a product until a car has been assembled—and when producing a very complex product in volume, accountability is difficult to achieve."

QUESTIONS

1. What role does change play in Ford's concept of development? Do you agree with this role? Why or why not?
2. Ford instituted an integrated development program at four levels: plant, intermediate, senior, and executive. How does development at each level relate to each other level? Why is this important in a development program?
3. Critique the three challenges faced by Ford that are listed at the end of the case. Do you see other challenges for Ford besides those listed? If so, what are they?

ADDITIONAL READINGS

Bard, Roy, Chez R. Bell, Leslie Stephen, and Linda Webster. *The Trainer's Professional Development Handbook.* San Francisco: Jossey-Bass, 1987.

Bernold, Thomas, and James Finkelstein, eds. *Computer Assisted Approaches to Training Foundations of Industry's Future.* New York: North-Holland, 1988.

Bresnick, David. *Managing Employment and Training Programs Making JTPA Work.* New York: Human Services Press, 1986.

Brinkeroff, Robert O. *Achieving Results from Training: How to Evaluate Human Resource Development to Strengthen Programs and Increase Impact.* San Francisco: Jossey-Bass, 1987.

Brown, Duane, Linda Brooke, and Associates. *Career Choice and Development.* San Francisco: Jossey-Bass, 1984.

Calvert, Robert, Jr. "Training America: The Numbers Add Up." *Training and Development Journal,* November 1985, pp. 35–37.

Carnivale, Anthony R. "The Learning Enterprise." *Training and Development Journal,* January 1986, pp. 18–26.

Carnivale, Anthony, Leila Gainer, and Ann Meltzer. *Workplace Basics.* San Francisco: Jossey-Bass, 1990.

Carnivale, Anthony, Leila Gainer, and Ann Meltzer. *Workplace Basics Training Manual.* San Francisco: Jossey-Bass, 1990.

Carnivale, Anthony, Leila Gainer, and Ann Schultz. *Training the Technical Work Force.* San Francisco: Jossey-Bass, 1990.

Carnivale, Anthony, Leila Gainer, and Janice Villet. *Training in America: The Organization and the Strategic Role of Training.* San Francisco: Jossey-Bass, 1990.

Casner-Lotto, Jill, and Associates. *Successful Training Strategies: Twenty-Six Innovative Corporate Models.* San Francisco: Jossey-Bass, 1988.

Chalofsky, Neal E., and Carlene Reinhart. *Effective Human Resource Development.* San Francisco: Jossey-Bass, 1988.

Cook, D. R. "Improving Employee Development Programs." *Personnel Administrator* 23, July 1978, pp. 38–40.

Cothran, Tom. "Build or Buy?" *Training,* May 1987, pp. 83–85.

Dayel, Mohammed. "Taking the Mystery Out of Career Development." *Personnel 55,* March–April 1978, pp. 46–53.

Fisher, D. W. "Educational Psychology Involved in On-the-Job Training." *Personnel Journal* 56, October 1977, pp. 16–19.

Fraser, R. F., et al. "System for Determining Training Needs." *Personnel Journal* 57, December 1978, pp. 682–685.

Frost, Peter, Larry Moore, Meryl Louis, Craig Lundberg, and Joanne Martin. *Organizational Culture.* Beverly Hills: Sage, 1985.

Fucini, Joseph, and Suzy Fucini. *Working for the Japanese: Inside Mazda's American Auto Plant.* New York: Free Press, 1990.

Hall, F., and M. Albrecht. "Training for EEO, What Kinds and for Whom?" *Personnel Administrator* 22, October 1977, pp. 25–28.

Harris, P. R. "Cultural Awareness Training for Human Resource Development." *Training and Development Journal* 33, March 1978, pp. 64–74.

Hastings, Robert E. "Career Development: Maximizing Options." *Personnel Administrator* 23, May 1978, pp. 58–61.

Hyman, Jeff. *Training at Work.* New York: Routledge, 1992.

Kilman, Ralph A., Mary J. Saxton, Roy Serpa, and Associates. *Gaining Control of the Corporate Culture.* San Francisco: Jossey-Bass, 1985.

Langford, H. "Need Analysis in the Training Department." *Supervisory Management* 23, August 1978, pp. 18–25.

Leach, John. "Career Management Focusing on Human Resources." *Personnel Administrator* 22, November 1977, pp. 59–66.

Lee, Chris. "Where the Training Dollars Go." *Training,* October 1987, pp. 51–65.

Miner, John B. "The OD-Management Development Conflict." *Business Horizons* 16, no. 6, December 1973, p. 35.

Mirabel, T. E. "Forecasting Future Training Costs." *Training and Development Journal* 32, July 1978, pp. 78–87.

Moore, M.L., and T. Dutton. "Training Needs Analysis: Review and Critique." *Academy of Management Review* 3, July 1978, pp. 532–545.

Morgan, Marilyn, T. Douglas, and Alison Martier. "Career Development Strategies in Industry—Where Are We and Where Should We Be?" *Personnel* 56, March–April 1979, pp. 13–30.

Mumford, Alan. *Gower Handbook of Management Development.* Brookfield, VT: Gower Publishing, 1991.

Murray, Margo, and Marna Owen. *Beyond the Myths and Magic of Mentoring: How to Facilitate an Effective Mentoring Program.* San Francisco: Jossey-Bass, 1991.

Nadler, Leonard, and Garland D. Wiggs. *Managing Human Resource Development.* San Francisco: Jossey-Bass, 1986.

Nadler, Leonard, and Garland D. Wiggs. *Managing Human Resource Development: A Practical Guide.* San Francisco: Jossey-Bass, 1986.

Olson, Lawrence. "Training Trends: The Corporate View." *Training and Development Journal,* September 1986, pp. 32–35.

Oliver, Robert. *Career Unrest: A Source of Creativity.* New York: Columbia Business School, 1982.

Ott, J. Steven. *The Organizational Culture Perspective.* Chicago: Dorsey Press, 1989.

Phillips, Jack J. *Handbook of Training Evaluation and Measurement Methods.* Houston: Gulf Publishing Company, 1987.

Phillips, Jack J. *Recruiting, Training and Retraining New Employees.* San Francisco: Jossey-Bass, 1987.

Prior, John. *Gower Handbook of Training and Development.* Brookfield, VT: Gower Publishing, 1991.

Quick, Thomas. *Training Managers So They Can Really Manage: Confessions of a Frustrated Trainer.* San Francisco: Jossey-Bass, 1991.

Reid, Thomas J. "The Context of Management Development." *Personnel Journal* 53, no. 4, April 1974, pp. 280–287.

Ressler, Ralph. *Career Education: The New Frontier.* Worthington, OH: C. A. Jones, 1973.

Rosow, Jerome M., and Robert Zoger. *Training—The Competitive Edge: Introducing New Technology into the Workplace.* San Francisco: Jossey-Bass, 1988.

Rothwell, William, and Dale Brandenburg. *The Workplace Literacy Primer.* Amherst, MA: HRD Press, 1990.

Saffold, Guy S., III. "Culture, Traits, Strength, and Organizational Performance: Moving Beyond 'Strong' Culture." *Academy of Management Review* 13, no. 4, October 1988, pp. 546–558.

Schein, Edgar H. *Career Dynamics: Matching Individual and Organizational Needs.* Reading, MA: Addison-Wesley, 1980.

Scott, R. K. "Management's Dilemma: To Train or Not to Train People." *Training and Development Journal* 32, February 1978, pp. 3–6.

Swanson, Richard A., and Diane B. Gradric. *Forecasting Financial Benefits of Human Resource Development.* San Francisco: Jossey-Bass, 1988.

Tabbush, V. C. "Investment in Training: A Broader Approach." *Journal of Human Resources* 12, Spring 1977, pp. 252–257.

This, L. "Results-Oriented Training Designs." *Training and Development Journal* 34, June 1980, pp. 14–22.

Timperly, Stuart R. *Personnel Planning and Occupational Choice.* London: Allen and Irwin, 1974.

Wehrenberg, S., and R. Kuhnle. "How Training through Behavior Modeling Works." *Personnel Journal* 59, July 1980, pp. 576–604.

Wellbank, Harry L., Douglas T. Hall, Marilyn A. Morgan, et al. "Planning Job Progression for Effective Career Development and Human Resources Management." *Personnel* 55, March–April 1978, pp. 54–64.

Wiggenhorn, William. "Motorola U: Training Becomes an Education." *Harvard Business Review,* July–August, 1990.

NOTES

1. Linda Thornburg, "Journey toward a More Inclusive Culture," *HRMagazine,* February 1994, pp. 79–86.

2. Edgar H. Schein, *Organizational Culture and Leadership* (San Francisco: Jossey-Bass, 1985).

3. For more explanation of this concept, see Gifford Pinchot, *Intrapreneuring* (New York: Harper & Row, 1985).

4. Bill Leonard, "Study Links Training, Competitive Woes," *HRNews,* July 1991, pp. 1 + .

5. Albert Karr, "Corporate Job Training Expands, but Is It Still Inadequate," *The Wall Street Journal,* June 19, 1990, p. A1.

6. Christopher Conte, "Corporate Commitment to Training Is Inadequate and Uneven, Analysts Say," *The Wall Street Journal,* October 22, 1991, p. A1.

7. Joe Lamoglia, "Study: Training Doesn't Match Skills Needed," *HRNews,* October 1991, p. 3.

8. Russell Mitchell, "Can Cray Reprogram Itself for Creativity?" *Business Week,* August 20, 1990, p. 86.

9. W. Starbuck and B. Hedberg, "Saving an Organization from a Stagnating Environment," in *Strategy + Structure = Performance,* ed. H. Thorelli, (Bloomington: Indiana University Press, 1977), pp. 249–258.

10. Edgar Schein, *Organizational Culture and Leadership.*

11. Zachary Schiller, "Ready, Aim, Market: Combat Training at P&G College," *Business Week,* February 3, 1992, p. 56.

12. Chris Lee, "Where the Training Dollars Go," *Training* (October 1987), p. 64.

13. "Banker Development Program for Management Associates," *Barnett: Extra Effort Does Make the Difference* (Jacksonville, FL: Barnett Banks, 1988).

14. *Payne* v. *Western and Atlantic RA Co.,* 82 Tenn 507, 1884.

15. J. B. Copeland, W. Turque, L. Wright, and D. Shapiro, "The Revenge of the Fired," *Newsweek,* February 16, 1987, pp. 46–47.

16. *Toussaint* v. *Blue Cross/Blue Shield of Michigan,* 408 Mich. (1980).

17. Peters and Waterman, *In Search of Excellence* (NY: Harper & Row, 1982) pp. 248–249.

18. Diane Filipowski, "How Federal Express Makes Your Package Its Most Important," *Personnel Journal,* February 1992, pp. 40–46.

19. David E. Bartz, David R. Schwandt, and Larry W. Hillman, "Differences between 'T' and 'D'," *Personnel Administrator,* June 1989, pp. 164–170.

20. Ronald Henkof, "Companies That Train Best," *Fortune,* March 22, 1993, pp. 62–75.

21. Ibid.

22. Timothy Schellhardt, "Few Employees Give Job Rotation a Whirl," *The Wall Street Journal,* July 22, 1992, p. B1.

23. Kevin Salwen, "Trading Places," *The Wall Street Journal,* April 12, 1994, p. A1.

24. Helene Cooper, "Carpet Firm Sets up an In-house School to Stay Competitive," *The Wall Street Journal,* October 5, 1992, A1+ .

25. Kay Hart, Susan Beck, and William Cesarone, "Apprentice Program Develops Diverse Talent Pool," *HRMagazine,* April 1994, pp. 66–69.

26. Gilda Dangot-Simpkin, "How Come Nothing Changed," *HRMagazine,* November 1991, pp. 66–68.

27. "The Transformation of EDS' Culture," *Open Line* (Dallas: EDS, Spring 1990).

28. These factors and conclusions come from a paper that examined 200 studies covering the effectiveness of training by Bruce Joyce and Beverly Showers, *Training Ourselves to Teach: The Messages of Research* (Palo Alto: Stanford University, 1982).

29. Ralph Ganger, "HRIS Logs on to Strategic Training," *Personnel Journal,* August 1991, pp. 50–55.

30. Jolie Soloman, "Managing," *The Wall Street Journal,* February 17, 1989, p. B1.

31. Donald L. Kirkpatrick, "Four Steps to Measuring Training Effectiveness," *Personnel Administrator,* November 1983, pp. 19–25.

32. *HR Reporter,* Bureau of National Affairs, September 1988, p. 5. Used with permission.

CHAPTER 10

STRATEGIES FOR EFFECTIVE PERFORMANCE APPRAISAL SYSTEMS

Performance appraisals are useful tools not only for evaluating the work of employees but also for developing and motivating employees.[1] Unfortunately, performance appraisals also can be a tremendous source of anxiety and frustration for both the manager and the employee. This is often due to the uncertainties and ambiguities that surround many performance appraisal systems. In general, performance appraisals can be thought of as a means to verify that individuals are meeting performance standards that have been set. Performance appraisals also are a way to help individuals manage their performance. The terms *performance appraisal* and *performance evaluation* are used interchangeably throughout this chapter. The purpose of this chapter is to examine the role of performance appraisals in human resource management and the relationship between performance appraisals and the strategy of the organization.

CHAPTER OBJECTIVES

After completing this chapter, you should be able to

1. Discuss some of the major strategic choices regarding the performance appraisals that are available to organizations.
2. Discuss the process of the performance appraisal.
3. Examine the various methods of performance appraisal, including those based on a standard, human resources comparison system and results-oriented performance appraisals.
4. Identify a number of perceptual errors that can affect the objectivity and validity of the performance appraisal.
5. Discuss the relationship between the strategy of the organization and the performance appraisal process.
6. Examine the requirements for an effective performance appraisal system.

PERFORMANCE MANAGEMENT AT ST. LUKE'S HOSPITAL[2]

One goal of any useful performance appraisal system is to differentiate between high and low performers. This sounds simple, but it is not so easy to implement. Rating scales that tend to lump all employees together in the middle, supervisors who have a difficult time rating a worker poorly, and cultures that reward longevity instead of performance interfere with the goal of differentiation in performance appraisals. One firm that is striving to overcome these problems is St. Luke's Hospital in Fargo, North Dakota. St. Luke's recently dramatically redesigned its performance appraisal process in an effort to identify and reward high-quality performers.

St. Luke's instituted its new performance appraisal system, the Performance Review and Development System (PRDS). Even the title focuses attention on the goals of the system: to make people aware of their performance and to provide guidance to improve that performance. In designing this system, St. Luke's took a strategic approach. That is, it developed the new performance appraisal system to dovetail with its overall strategic plan. Specifically, the hospital was in the midst of redesigning itself so that all service groups in the organization would epitomize St. Luke's corporate commitment to excellence, customer service, and support for one another.

THE STRATEGIC PLAN

St. Luke's strategic efforts were multifaceted. To begin, it changed titles of all employees to *associate*. Hence, there were no longer titles such as physician, nurse, and staff; instead, everyone was an associate. Next, St. Luke's empowered its associates at the customer level. This provided them with the opportunity to serve a customer to the best of their ability and prevented them from hiding behind the phrase "I can't; it's not allowed." In addition, the hospital integrated the organization's needs with those of its associates to foster individual growth and development. Next, decision making was decentralized so that those who were impacted by a decision were included in making it. Finally, the PRDS was developed to include corporate commitments such as quality, customer service, and individual growth in the performance appraisal process and as a means of recognizing and rewarding individuals and teams for high-quality performance.

The actual development of the PRDS was undertaken by a multidisciplinary task force of 16 individuals including hospital managers and a college professor. They began by clarifying the goals of the task force, reviewing current performance appraisal systems, and envisioning the ideal system of performance review and management.

THE PREVIOUS APPRAISAL SYSTEM

The one feature of the previous appraisal system that all members of the task force objected to was the fact that there were two different appraisal forms, one for management and one for nonmanagement. The management format accentuated objectives and contained consistent standards for all management. However, the forms were not individualized to each manager's job description. The system did not mention team objectives, and neither differential weights nor special categories were included to individualize the form. The overall view of the task force and the associates was that the previous management appraisal system was rather subjective.

The appraisal form for nonmanagement positions focused on job-related accountabilities, included specific measures of performance, and incorporated differential weighting schemes. However, it did not include objectives for individuals or teams, nor did it encourage personal growth and development. Training opportunities were not available for nonmanagement associates, although they were for management personnel.

The implementation of the system also had some problems. First, it required each individual to have a performance review yearly, but individuals in some areas had not received a formal appraisal in several years. Because there had been no means to track compliance with the yearly appraisal requirement, it was often ignored. Second, even though there were five rating levels available for use, only three, the highest ones, were ever used. This resulted in inflated ratings and the inability to distinguish between top and average performers.

Based on their analysis of the former system, the task force decided to develop only one performance appraisal system that would be used for all positions in the hospital. Several items were identified as being important to include in the new system, including tying behavioral criteria to corporate commitments and training individuals who would perform the appraisals. A variety of raters also was to be used, including self, peer, customer, and supervisory raters. The rating scale also had to be redesigned, an appeals process was added, and a monitoring system was developed to ensure that the appraisals were completed yearly. Finally, the task force decided to use computers as much as possible in the new evaluation procedures. To achieve these goals, the PRDS system includes three major components: ongoing responsibilities and objectives, shared values, and self-development.

ONGOING RESPONSIBILITIES AND OBJECTIVES

Based on each individual associate's job responsibilities as outlined in the job description, jointly developed ongoing responsibilities were identified by the associate and the appraiser. In addition to the ongoing responsibilities that are always part of the associate's job, both parties agreed to specific objectives that have deadlines and ending dates. Both ongoing responsibilities and the temporary objectives are then assigned a weight totaling 100 percent. The weights can differ with each new appraisal period so that strategic changes needed by the organization can be factored into the appraisal system to keep the objectives of the organization and the individual associates in agreement. This portion of the rating system is worth 60 percent of the total percentage available.

SHARED VALUES

The shared values component of the appraisal system focuses on *how* the job is done, not what is expected. This segment of the PRDS was designed specifically to reflect the firm's corporate commitments to excellence, customers, and support for one another. It is assessed by using 14 items such as "Does this associate meet customer needs in an effective and timely manner?" This evaluates the degree of commitment the individual has in the areas of excellence, customer service, and support for other associates. Responses to the 14 items are solicited from managers, peers, subordinates, and customers to obtain the most accurate assessment possible. The importance of this component of the appraisal process is emphasized by assigning it 40 percent of the total evaluation.

SELF-DEVELOPMENT

This component of the evaluation is not numerically scored as the other two are. However, it is an important part of the total performance appraisal process. Because of the high expectations for each of the associates with respect to quality service, constant self-development is essential. This segment also fits nicely with St. Luke's strategic thrust for continuous quality improvement.

IMPLEMENTATION

In May 1992 all appraisers received training in how to use the PRDS and in July 1992, it was implemented. Since its initiation, several positive outcomes have occurred. First, because the process is interactive, the appraisers no longer are expected to know when each individual is to be appraised. Instead, the associate can and does initiate the appraisal on his or her anniversary date. This means that an individual can no longer go years without receiving feedback about his or her performance. Weighting the shared values component 40 percent of the total has underscored the importance of the organization's commitment to excellence, customer service, and support for one another. This has been a powerful force for change in the culture toward increased customer awareness. Associates have expressed a more positive attitude toward the appraisal system as well as the feedback they receive. No longer do they feel as though they are simply being evaluated on their performance, but that the focus is on their work toward achieving personal and organizational goals. Finally, using a variety of raters such as customers, peers, and the employees themselves has resulted in ratings that associates see as fairer and more informative.

It appears that St. Luke's has developed a successful performance appraisal system that will allow individuals to work toward improving themselves as they advance the hospital's goals. Appraisal systems of the type described in this case are deemed fairer and more accurate by all those involved than the more traditional systems. Organizations can enjoy substantial benefits from appraisals, including the knowledge that the most deserving performers will be identified accurately and rewarded appropriately. Such employee knowledge contributes directly to productivity. Further, well-designed appraisal systems can alleviate some of the negative attitudes both managers and employees frequently hold. How this can be done successfully is the focus of this chapter.

STRATEGIC CHOICES

Managers have a number of strategic choices to make regarding the performance appraisal system. Some of the most important choices are outlined below.

1. Managers should decide on the *objectives* and *purpose for the performance appraisal.* Will the evaluations be for correcting problems, for determining rewards, or for other purposes? Will the evaluations be individual or group based?

2. Managers can choose between *formal and informal procedures* for the performance appraisal. Should the reviews be structured and occur at a specific point in time (formal), or should the manager and the subordinate discuss problems and ways to correct them as they occur (informal)?

3. Performance appraisal formats can emphasize more *objectivity versus subjectivity*. Should managers use their own judgments when evaluating subordinates, or should more concrete factors such as number of units produced and absenteeism be used to evaluate an employee?

4. Managers must decide on the *frequency* of the performance appraisals. Most often, yearly appraisals are performed. However, with new job procedures in which feedback about performance is given monthly, daily, and even hourly, perhaps less frequent formal reviews could be performed. On the other hand, if the job provides no specific feedback about performance, yearly intervals may be too long between appraisals.

5. Managers must decide *who conducts* the performance appraisal. Immediate supervisors are the frequent choice, but, as you will see in this chapter, they are by no means the only choice.

PERFORMANCE APPRAISAL OBJECTIVES

One human resource objective for using performance appraisal systems is to determine who should be promoted, demoted, transferred, or terminated. However, these are not the only human resource functions that are related to performance appraisals. For example, an organization may use the results from a performance appraisal to determine who needs formal training and development opportunities. Further, such opportunities may be used as a reward for individuals whose appraisals were positive. A variety of developmental opportunities that can be used as a reward are presented in Exhibit 10.1.

Performance appraisals also can be used to motivate and improve performance. By showing an individual where his or her strengths lie and pointing out areas that still need improvement, an evaluator can help focus an employee's attention on a course that will produce the most positive benefits. Additionally, reinforcing behaviors that have produced strong positive results should motivate the individual to continue to perform in this manner.

A well-designed performance appraisal system also can encourage individuals to work together as a team. If this is an organization's goal, it must face several challenges in designing and implementing such a system. Obviously, the traditional, individual-focused performance appraisal systems are no longer appropriate. In fact, applying an individual results–based appraisal system to individuals who perform highly interdependent tasks may discourage team efforts. Instead, peer pressure may be enough to motivate team members to perform.[3] Rather than using the supervisor in the evaluation process, self-managed group members can evaluate each other. Because self-managed teams require a unique approach to performance appraisals, the process may need to be redesigned.

FORMAL VERSUS INFORMAL PERFORMANCE APPRAISALS

Formal performance appraisals usually occur at specified time periods once or twice a year. Formal appraisals are most often required by the organization to evaluate employee performance. Informal performance appraisals can occur whenever the supervisor feels communication is needed. For example, if the employee has been consistently

EXHIBIT 10.1 **Available Developmental Opportunities That Can be Used as Rewards for Effective Performance**

On the Job
    One-on-One Supervisor Training
    Job Rotation
    Role-Plays
    Computer-Assisted Instruction
    Programmed Instruction
    Organizational Sponsored Training
    In-Basket Exercises
    Special Projects/Assignments
    Reference Material Review
    Mentoring
Off the Job
    College Courses
    Professional Seminars
    Networking
    Professional Certificate Programs
    Field Trips
    Correspondence Courses
    Research/Writing Assignments
    Benchmarking
    Executive Development Programs

SOURCE: Robert Lucas, "Performance Coaching: Now and for the Future," *HRMagazine,* January 1994, p. 13.

meeting or exceeding standards, an informal performance appraisal may be in order simply to recognize this fact. Discussions can take place in a variety of places in the organization ranging from the manager's office to the cafeteria. Of course, it is always wise to discuss employee performance in private.

Many organizations encourage a combination of both formal and informal appraisals. The formal appraisal is most often used as the primary evaluation. However, the informal appraisal is very helpful for more frequent performance feedback. Informal appraisals should *not* take the place of a formal performance evaluation.

OBJECTIVE VERSUS SUBJECTIVE PERFORMANCE APPRAISALS

Organizations must choose the degree to which performance appraisals are to be objective (evaluating performance against specific standards) versus subjective (evaluating how "well" an employee performs in general). Although at first glance it may seem that objective measures are the best strategic choice for an organization, subjective measures can be helpful when identifying desirable characteristics that are difficult to quantify. For example, objectively measuring communication skills or management potential is an extremely difficult task. The formal performance appraisal should contain both objective and subjective measures of performance.

Standards for performance appraisals should be based on job requirements. Job requirements should include documented performance standards based on a thorough job analysis. A detailed discussion of job descriptions and job analysis was provided in Chapter 5.

============================== **HR CHALLENGE** ==============================

Computerizing Performance Feedback

Giving feedback is never easy. Individuals do not want either to give or to receive negative feedback. Therefore, constructive criticism may come across as an attempt to undermine one's self-esteem instead of the way it was intended. One way to overcome this problem is to use a computer to provide feedback. Because computers are viewed as analytic and not personal, the feedback may be more readily accepted.

One such system is Acumen's *WorkStyles*. It asks a person to rate himself or herself on 176 questions on a scale ranging from "extremely so" to "not at all." After the input procedure, which usually takes between 15 and 30 minutes, the software analyzes the individual's work style on 12 different assessment scales that encompass three orientations: satisfaction, people, or task. The individualized feedback provides a complete picture of how individuals perceive themselves. Also, individuals can use the system any time to better understand how they are doing. The system also can be used to plot one's improvements and to make one more self-aware. One of its best features is that negative feedback is presented in a positive way and, therefore, is more likely to be accepted.

Another computerized feedback system is called *TEAMS 360 Degree Feedback*. The software is

designed to help evaluators collect performance evaluation data from multiple sources such as supervisors, colleagues, direct reports, and customers to provide an all-inclusive view of an individual's behavior. The program also can be used to plot the performance of a group, department, division, or company. Because a variety of raters is used, a "trimmed mean" approach is calculated. In essence, the highest and lowest scores are deleted to provide a more accurate rating of the individual. Another advantage of this system is that the review can be tied directly to the job description of the person being evaluated, thus customizing the review process. With the current emphasis on team environments, the use of multiple raters may become commonplace in the workplace in just a few years. Software such as this package should make changes in the evaluation process easier for organizations.

SOURCE: Adapted from Charlene O'Brien, "Assessment Tool Makes Giving Feedback Easier," *HRMagazine,* May 1994, pp. 99–103; and Debra J. Cohen, "Teams 360 Degree Feedback Offers Varied Ways to Create Feedback Surveys," *HRMagazine,* November 1993, pp. 32–38.

From a strategic view, it is often best for an organization to encourage objectivity in the formal appraisal process (that is, the employee should be rated on behavior rather than attitudes). Not only can this help to alleviate some of the ambiguities for employees and managers (such as determining what an *attitude* really is), but from a legal standpoint, objective measures are easier to defend. Unfortunately, the more objective performance appraisals, such as a behaviorally anchored rating scale discussed later, are often extremely time consuming and expensive to develop. Thus, the organization must weigh the costs and benefits of developing such a format.

FREQUENCY OF PERFORMANCE APPRAISALS

Traditionally, most organizations recommend that performance appraisals be conducted every 6 to 12 months for employees. Interestingly, many employees report that their performance is evaluated much less frequently.[4] Infrequent performance appraisals are most often due to the manager's negative view of the process. It can be stressful for both the employee *and* the manager, especially when employee performance has been below expectations. Thus, the manager may want to avoid this situation.[5] In addition, the manager may view the performance appraisal process as extra work and, thus, burdensome. Regardless of the reasons, managers should be encouraged (possibly through training) to view the process as an opportunity to communicate with his or her employees and as a means to improve performance and to develop employees.

Research has shown that many employees believe performance feedback should be given more frequently than once or twice a year.[6] In fact, over 80 percent of the employees asked rank feedback about their performance as one of their top five priorities, while only 45 percent feel they receive adequate feedback.[7] Interestingly, the employees desire informal rather than formal evaluations. The former can reduce the anxiety connected with formal assessment by minimizing "surprises," concerning behavior identified long before the session but not mentioned. Thus, one strategy that an organization might use is to encourage frequent informal appraisal sessions between managers and employees while limiting the formal and more labor-intensive sessions to one or two every year.

WHO CONDUCTS THE PERFORMANCE APPRAISAL?

Employee evaluations can be performed by a number of individuals or groups. In matrix-type organizations, for example, employees most often have two immediate supervisors and receive ratings from both of them. Having more than one rater can increase the reliability of the performance evaluation. A number of potential sources of performance ratings are discussed in the following sections.

SUPERVISORS

The most common evaluator is the employee's immediate supervisor. It has been estimated that over 90 percent of all performance appraisals are completed *only* by the immediate supervisor.[8] To be able to evaluate the employee effectively, the supervisor should have frequent contact with the employee and be able to obtain the specific information regarding his or her performance. Although it might be assumed that this degree of contact occurs regularly, many supervisors do not actually have much opportunity to observe their employees' behavior. For example, an employee who heads up a branch firm in a different city or even state from the "home office" may have little direct contact with his or her supervisor. Although the supervisor may be able to gather relevant information about this employee, the supervisor may benefit from obtaining information from some of the additional sources described below.

CO-WORKERS

In certain situations co-workers may evaluate their peers' performance. Although co-workers may be somewhat uncomfortable and resistant to evaluating their peers, at least one study has shown that peer evaluations are more stable over time and may be the *most* accurate evaluations of employee performance.[9] An organization may choose to encourage peer evaluations, particularly if the contact between supervisor and employee is limited. Also, if self-managed work teams are used, peer rating is an important component in the performance appraisal system.

EMPLOYEES THEMSELVES

Occasionally, employees are given the opportunity to assess their own performance. Although many are reluctant to engage in self-ratings, this information can be extremely

=== **HR CHALLENGE** ===

Making Co-Worker Reviews Work

With an ever-increasing emphasis being placed on work teams and employee involvement, the use of co-worker evaluations should begin to increase. Many firms have long overlooked this untapped resource. But who besides the person next to you day after day, frequently trained to perform the same job, knows your actual job performance better?

YSI, an instrumentation maker located in Yellow Springs, Ohio, agrees with this philosophy so much that it has instituted a twice-a-year peer review in work centers throughout its production area. YSI employees realize that the feedback they receive from their peers is the most important information they will receive. Their leaders (formally supervisors) will also evaluate their performance, but these ratings hold no more weight than those received from co-workers.

Some employees enjoy giving feedback. For years they tried to tell management about the problems they encountered with other workers, but most of the criticism fell on deaf ears. But no more. Finally, what the workers say means something and usually results in changes.

While the process seems to be working in many cases, one drawback is the employee's disinclination to criticize a co-worker one day and then work effectively with that person the next day. Some workers simply refuse to participate, and others find it impossible to take constructive criticism from fellow workers. However, as YSI found, minor adjustments and some transfers can overcome the majority of the resistance.

SOURCE: Adapted from "Measuring Performance," *Inc.*, October 1991, pp. 161–162.

valuable to the supervisor. Large discrepancies between the supervisor's and employee's evaluation should be reason for concern. Discrepancies often occur due to a lack of communication and performance feedback from the supervisor. For example, if employees hear nothing from their supervisor for months, they might erroneously conclude that they are performing well (or poorly). When a comparison of evaluations indicates a discrepancy, this information can be used to convince the manager to increase the amount of feedback to the employee in the future.

Research has found that employees who are given the opportunity to evaluate themselves have a tendency to inflate their ratings.[10] One study reported that mean self-ratings for a group of workers were at least one standard deviation higher than those of the supervisors. Further, the range of ratings given by the employees for their performance was much smaller than those provided by their supervisors.[11] Interestingly, however, women tend to rate themselves lower than do their supervisors.[12]

Finally, self-evaluations have been found to be extremely helpful when used for employee development purposes.[13] Self-evaluations can encourage discussions about the employee's strengths and weaknesses from both the employee's and supervisor's points of view. In addition, some companies are now encouraging employees to fill out "discussion forms" (see the following HR Challenge box on this topic) so that the supervisor is better able to help the employees in career development. If an organization's strategy is to hire inexperienced workers at a low salary ("make" versus "buy") and to promote from within, self-evaluations and discussion forms are an excellent way to motivate and develop employees.

SUBORDINATES

Subordinates are valuable sources of information when examining the performance of supervisory employees.[14] It is important to encourage subordinates to be candid if the information is to be at all useful. Candor, of course, is most likely to occur when

HR CHALLENGE

Employee Discussion Form

To encourage subordinates to talk about their self-evaluations, organizations have employed the use of discussion forms much like the example shown here.

HANDY-DANDY STORES

Please complete prior to the performance appraisal interview.

Name: _____

Supervisor's Suggested Decision Date: _____

Discussion Date: _____

Present Job Title: _____

Please circle any of the following comments, questions, or ideas you want to talk about during your performance appraisal. For those areas you circle, I would like you to write down any specific thoughts you want to discuss.

1. MY JOB

   A. Responsibilities I'm unclear of:

   B. Things I'd like to do more of:

   C. Things I'd like to do less of:

2. OUR ORGANIZATION

   A. Things I'd like to know more about:

   B. Barriers that keep me from doing a better job:

3. ME

   A. Training and development I'd like to have:

   B. My future in this organization:

   C. Other areas I'm concerned about:

subordinates are guaranteed anonymity and have no fear of reprisal.[15] Information from subordinates is helpful not only for determining how well a manager leads, communicates, plans, delegates, and organizes but also for identifying general problem areas within a department. The use of subordinate input for managerial evaluations can be valuable if the information is gathered in an atmosphere of trust and candor.

COMPUTERS

Computer-aided management involves the use of computers to monitor, supervise, and evaluate employee performance electronically. It has been estimated that by the year 2000, as many as 30 million visual display terminal users might be evaluated and monitored by electronic methods.[16] Monitoring employees by computer is open to serious invasions of privacy issues. Some lawmakers are already attempting to introduce legislation that would limit the use of computer monitoring in organizations.[17] Despite the concerns, computerized appraisals could be a valuable aid to human resource managers. Computer monitoring must include benefits for both the employees and the employers if it is to be effective. Exhibit 10.2 outlines benefits of using computer monitoring of performance.

Computers have an additional use in the appraisal process. When artificial intelligence is used (making computers exhibit intelligent behavior), DuPont and the University of Minnesota built and are testing a multiple-rater appraisal system. The artificial intelligence component can evaluate ratings and determine whether they are reliable. Also, the system can pinpoint problems, such as a particular question that is being misinterpreted or a specific evaluator who is out of line when compared to all other raters. The problems can be relayed back to the evaluator or the group that developed the system for corrections. By using computers in this manner, the evaluation process can become more valid and reliable over time.[18]

EXHIBIT 10.2   **Results of Using Computer Monitoring of Performance**

1. ***Response-Outcome Dependency.*** Computer monitoring indicates to the worker which responses are correct. In turn, this can lead to an increase in the performance of desired behaviors. It also makes undesired behaviors stand out.
2. ***Effective Feedback Vehicle.*** Summary reports from the computer can provide immediate feedback to employees so that they can choose to modify their behavior.
3. ***Constructive Expectations.*** Electronic performance monitoring sets specific standards accompanied by expectations that are incorporated into the daily work routines. Workers have a clear idea of what is expected of them.
4. ***Reduced Unpredictability.*** Computer monitoring allows the employee to track his or her performance throughout the year. Thus, the yearly performance evaluation should be less of a surprise.
5. ***Direct Accountability.*** Performance monitoring by computer is a direct measurement of work, making it difficult for an employee to cover up errors or to blame others. Thus, those employees who are good performers would be the most likely to accept electronic monitoring.
6. ***Better Training Programs.*** Gathering summary information regarding the types of mistakes most commonly made could lead to training programs that precisely target the problems.
7. ***Objective Documentation.*** Electronic monitoring can identify good performers objectively because the computer generates a quantitative appraisal.
8. ***Increased Flexibility.*** Flexibility can occur because "fast" workers will have more control over scheduling of required work. "Slower" workers can be allowed some additional time to complete the tasks if the computer information shows that the worker output is adequate.

SOURCE: Adapted from N. F. Angel, "Evaluating Employees by Computer," *Personnel Administrator,* November 1989, pp. 67–72.

CUSTOMERS

In service organizations, the customer is in a perfect position to provide performance feedback. For example, guests checking out of a hotel are asked frequently to complete a response card about their stay and indicate whether any staff member enhanced the visit. Hampton Inn asks guests to "catch an employee in the act" of making their stay more enjoyable. Any employee who is singled out by a satisfied customer for a job well done earns a Hampton Inn sticker, which the employee can display prominently on his or her name tag. This type of constant evaluation works as a reinforcing mechanism for Hampton Inn's motto: "100 percent satisfaction guaranteed."

THE JOB ITSELF

Finally, employees at all levels in the organization can receive feedback from the job they perform. For example, when a secretary mistakenly presses the wrong button on his or her word processor, a beep sounds. This negative feedback is a reminder that the last behavior was inappropriate. Similarly, workers who are linked by an interdependent work situation—that is, one person cannot perform his or her job without input from someone else—are constantly aware of their level of performance as they realize that others are waiting for them to supply the needed part or information. To use this type of performance feedback successfully, organizations must carefully design the jobs their workers perform.

WHICH AND HOW MANY EVALUATORS SHOULD BE USED?

The organization's choice of type and number of evaluators to use is not easy. The strategy of the firm, the culture within the firm, and purpose of the evaluation must be taken into consideration. For example, if the culture and strategy of an organization emphasize efficiency and one-on-one supervisor-subordinate relationships, the most effective way to evaluate performance might be to have only the input from the immediate supervisor and/or from computer monitoring. On the other hand, if the organization emphasizes development, training, and promotions from within, performance information might be solicited from a variety of sources including supervisors, co-workers, and the employee. Collecting information from a number of different sources can increase the reliability of the performance appraisal and is attracting ever-increasing attention.

The review process known as *360-degree feedback,* in which an individual receives performance feedback from subordinates, peers, supervisors, and even internal and external customers, is the hottest new approach to performance appraisals. According to a survey by Watt, 26 percent of the 897 firms surveyed used some form of 360-degree feedback in their appraisal process.[19] One reason for its use is the realization that the traditional approach to performance appraisals is not adequate with the new emphasis on teamwork, empowerment, and total quality management.[20] Instead, a more flexible system that incorporates feedback from the people the employee most closely works with is more appropriate.[21] However, as with most new techniques, it does present some problems. For example, with so many reviewers involved, conflicting and unclear messages about performance could result. When there are conflicting evaluations, how can the more accurate ones be determined, and when should this be done? Another problem involves the type of format to use to poll different constituencies. Because each party is concerned with different aspects of an individual's performance, one generic form may not be suitable. Also, if multiple forms are used, how can the ratings be compared and combined? Although the 360-degree feedback method presents some problems, the interest generated by this type of appraisal appears to indicate that the advantages outweigh the problems.

PERFORMANCE APPRAISAL PROCESS

Developing and conducting performance appraisals should not be done in isolation. The performance appraisal is closely related to a number of human resource management activities that should be considered. Exhibit 10.3 illustrates some of these relationships which are described below.

JOB ANALYSIS

The performance appraisal should be based on a thorough job analysis. The results of the job analysis can be used to produce a job description, which describes the work to be performed, and job specifications, which outline the requirements necessary to accomplish the job. A discussion of job analysis is presented in Chapter 5. Only when the duties, responsibilities, working conditions, and activities of a job are clearly defined can performance be evaluated.

PERFORMANCE STANDARDS

Performance standards should be derived from the job analysis information. Based on this information, the levels of performance deemed to be acceptable versus those that are unacceptable are developed. In essence, this determines a standard against which to

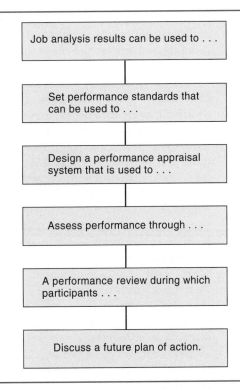

compare employee performance. A good performance standard describes what an employee should have produced or accomplished upon completing a specific activity. It focuses on the results or the degree of accomplishment achieved by the worker. The standard should answer questions such as what, how much, and by when. For example, a performance standard for a sales representative might be to obtain $2,000 worth of new business by the end of the quarter. This standard informs the sales representative what (new business), how much ($2,000), and by when (end of the quarter).

Performance standards should meet several important requirements. First, the standards should be written so that anyone who reads them will recognize the difference between acceptable and unacceptable behavior. In the preceding example, any quarter in which the sales representative did not sign $2,000 worth of new business would be considered unacceptable. Second, the standard should challenge the employee while being realistic. Setting an extremely high standard to motivate employees to perform at their maximum level may backfire. Instead of motivating an individual to work hard to achieve the goal, it might cause employees to give up and not try at all because they believe that achieving the high expectation is impossible. Defining the methods by which the activity is to be accomplished may also be useful. For example, a sales representative who steals customers from other representatives achieves the goal but at the expense of other sales representatives. Therefore, the standard must state clearly what qualifies as an appropriate behavior (obtaining new business). Finally, it is important that a time frame be specified and that the goal be observable and measurable. Simply asking a sales representative to increase customer satisfaction is not enough. Exactly how and when this should be accomplished (e.g., reduce the number of complaint letters received in one quarter by 50 percent) must be stated.

THE PERFORMANCE APPRAISAL SYSTEM

DEFICIENT
Job dimensions that fail to measure all the important aspects of performance.

CONTAMINATION
Evaluation error that occurs when extraneous factors not central to overall successful performance are included in the evaluation of one's job performance.

DISTORTION
Evaluation error that occurs when components of a job are not emphasized in relation to their importance to the job.

RELEVANT
A job dimension that measures only aspects of performance that are truly important in determining job effectiveness.

In general, employees should be evaluated on a number of specific dimensions of job performance. Each of the specific dimensions of job performance used to evaluate an individual's performance should be developed so that it is not deficient, contaminated, distorted, or irrelevant. Job dimensions that fail to measure all of the important aspects of performance would be viewed as **deficient.** When extraneous factors that are not central to overall successful performance are included in the evaluation of one's job performance, **contamination** has occurred. Job dimensions that suffer from **distortion** do not emphasize each component in relation to its importance to the job. Finally, a job dimension that measures only aspects of performance that are truly important in determining job effectiveness would be considered **relevant.** An example that includes each of these elements may be useful in understanding the distinction of each of these concepts. To effectively perform the job of airline reservation agents, a person must be able to effectively use the computerized reservation system, make changes to tickets, reserve tickets, and assign seats. These four components are all relevant to the job. If we rank them from most important to least important and weigh them accordingly, we will have a job dimension that is free from distortion. If we add the dimension of getting along with the other booking agents, we introduce contamination because this component is not absolutely critical to performing the job well. Finally, if we do not include the ability to make seat assignments, the job dimension is deficient because it does not measure all of the important aspects of this job.

Using a single global or overall measure can present difficulties. Global measures are more prone to distortion on the part of the evaluator. The Supreme Court ruling in 1975 regarding *Albemarle Paper Company* v. *Moody* was based on the fact that no specific job dimensions of performance were assessed.[22] Raters were asked to evaluate employees by comparing them to one another based on a single, global rating. The Court found significant racial differences on the criterion (the overall rating), with no objective information to back it.

ASSESSING PERFORMANCE

The actual performance assessment is the determination of the employee's strengths *and* weaknesses. One purpose of a performance appraisal is to improve the employee's performance. As a result, performance weaknesses must be determined. However, it is also important to reinforce existing behavior that is deemed to be strong.

If multiple evaluators are used, assessing performance also includes compiling all evaluations into summary form. If evaluators' assessments are in agreement, high interrater reliability exists and summarizing the ratings is not problematic. However, if there is a substantial amount of disagreement as to the employee's performance, interrater reliability is low. The supervisor must use this information as more of a heuristic device or guide for the final evaluation.

PERFORMANCE REVIEW

The performance review is the actual discussion that transpires between the rater and the ratee regarding the ratee's performance. Research suggests that the performance review should be approximately 60 minutes long and be a mutual discussion.[23] However, employee responses to an employment survey indicated that most performance reviews are relatively short.[24] In fact, most employees reported that their last performance review session lasted less than 15 minutes!

Because the performance review involves two people, the appraiser and the appraisee, the review should entail an exchange of information between these two parties. This information exchange can take many forms. Three of the most common include closed reporting, open reporting, and coaching. Each of these is discussed in the following section.

TYPES OF PERFORMANCE REVIEW

The three types of performance reviews can be viewed as three points on a continuum that measures the degree of involvement of the appraisee. At one extreme of the continuum is the **closed reporting** method. When it is used, the appraisee has very little input into the discussion. Instead, the appraiser reports how the appraisee performed during the time period considered and then attempts to persuade the appraisee to accept this evaluation. In the middle of the continuum is the **open reporting** approach. This method begins as with closed reporting, with the appraiser identifying the strengths and weaknesses of performance, but then the appraiser listens to the reactions of the appraisee. Finally, a **coaching** approach anchors the other end of the continuum. In this type of performance review, the employee evaluates his or her own performance while the appraiser serves as a coach, not a critic.

If employed under the appropriate circumstances, each of these methods can prove useful. For example, the closed reporting method could be used in situations in which the performance appraisal is simply an activity that must be done each year but is not used as a basis for human resource decisions. Likewise, the open reporting method is appropriate when extenuating circumstances may have affected the individual's performance on the job, and the appraisee needs to make the appraiser aware of these issues. Finally, the coaching method can be used when the individual being appraised holds a job that has very few clear-cut standards upon which to base an assessment. One job that might not have clear standards is that of a research scientist. A person in this position could spend several years working on a product before it is actually marketable. During those years working on the project, the scientist is in the best position to know the type of goals he or she can reach and how to describe them.

PROBLEMS RELATED TO PERFORMANCE REVIEWS

Closed reporting, open reporting, and coaching have both strengths and weaknesses. First, both the closed and open reporting approaches can make the person being evaluated defensive. It is human nature to want to defend oneself when weaknesses are identified. Therefore, as soon as they are mentioned, the person being evaluated may "tune out" what is being said and prepare to defend himself or herself.[25] This leads to a second problem, which is trying to accomplish too much in one session. For example, if a pay increase is an outcome of the appraisal process, as soon as it is mentioned, it tends to remain the topic of discussion, and any suggestions for future improvement are ignored. Further, if the feedback given to the appraisee is even partially negative, he or she may not be receptive to suggestions for addressing the problems in the future.[26] Instead, he or she may have a closed mind (sometimes indicated by a defensive posture, such as crossed arms). In these situations, the constructive criticism offered is viewed only as criticism. To avoid this, eliminating the discussion of salary and focusing only on ways to improve performance should help to concentrate on the appraisee's performance.

Another element that can cause an ineffective review is an unprepared appraiser. Nothing upsets an appraisee more than having an appraiser who does not know what he or she has accomplished during the evaluation period. To perform an effective performance review, an appraiser must take the time to carefully review and evaluate the

CLOSED REPORTING
A method of performance review in which the appraisee has very little input into the discussion.

OPEN REPORTING
A method of performance review in which after the reporting is complete, the appraiser listens to the reactions of the appraisee.

COACHING
A method of performance review in which the appraisee evaluates his or her own performance while the appraiser serves as a coach, not a critic.

performance during the time period in question. Only after he or she is familiar with the performance is the appraiser ready to discuss the evaluation.

IMPROVEMENT OF PERFORMANCE REVIEW

The problems outlined above can be improved in a variety of ways. Exhibit 10.4 lists several of these. The one thing that is important to keep in mind is that both the appraiser and the appraisee will be nervous. Giving and receiving performance feedback is often looked at as a negative experience. By following the suggestions listed in Exhibit 10.4, the performance review session can be more helpful and positive for all involved.

The format of the performance review is likely to undergo some significant changes in the future. As organizations move toward a more employee-oriented strategy, the supervisor-subordinate formal appraisal may no longer be effective. Instead, a performance review discussion based on the employee's evaluation of his or her own work for a specified period of time may be more useful. When this format is followed, the manager becomes a counselor instead of an evaluator. This type of review session appears to be more useful and enjoyable for both the evaluator and the employee.[27]

SETTING A PLAN OF ACTION

By this point in the review, the employee should have an accurate idea of his or her performance evaluation. The employee should know his or her strengths and weaknesses.

EXHIBIT 10.4   **Tips for a Successful Performance Review**

- Give the employee fair notice as to when the review is to take place.
- Ask the employee to think about and evaluate his or her own performance prior to the review session.
- Prepare for the review by examining information available about the employee's performance. Seek additional information if needed.
- Begin the session on a positive tone to set the employee at ease and make him or her receptive to the performance review process.
- Explain the format of the performance review session.
- Make the employee aware of the uses of the performance appraisal results (e.g., training and development, salary decisions, promotion decisions).
- If needed, set a second meeting to discuss nonperformance-related issues such as the salary increase, future goals, or developmental suggestions.
- Encourage the employee to participate, especially when his or her appraisal differs from yours.
- Review the standards to which the employee will be compared to remind him or her that the process is not completely subjective.
- Make sure to praise the employee for his or her accomplishments during the evaluation period. Recognize his or her achievements, and indicate where the employee has excelled.
- Highlight, but do not dwell on, areas in which performance did not meet the standards.
- Discuss ways to improve performance in the areas in which the employee was weak or to solve problems that have caused the employee to be less effective than desired.
- Make sure that the employee fully understands the appraisal.
- End the discussion on a positive note.

SOURCE: Adapted from James G. Goodale, "Seven Ways to Improve Performance Appraisals," *HRMagazine,* May 1993, pp. 77–80; Fred A. Schneyer, "Here's How to Write an Effective Employee Evaluation," *Tallahassee Democrat,* January 19, 1994, p. 3D; and "Harnessing the Power of Performance Appraisals," *HRMNews,* February, 1993, pp. 3–4.

Recapping key points and asking the employee to summarize the major issues discussed is usually a good way for the supervisor to ensure joint understanding before ending the performance review.

At this point the supervisor and employee should focus on the future. Job performance objectives should be discussed to establish a plan of action. The employee as well as the supervisor should have input in this process. This is often an appropriate time to explore the employee's career interest and developmental needs. The employee should be aware of the supervisor's expectations in regard to the plan.

Finally, the supervisor reviews the job performance and plan of action developed, and then sets objectives, based at least in part on the plan identified, for the next rating period. This will provide the employee with direction and guidance as to what is expected. The employee needs to understand areas *where* improvement is needed and *how* to strengthen job performance (such as additional training). In closing the discussion, the supervisor may wish to reassure the employee that he or she is interested in the employee's success and should indicate a willingness to talk further at a later date.

Given the importance of the performance evaluation, it is surprising that most supervisors do not receive any training in this area. It has been estimated that over 90 percent of raters receive no training at all in how to conduct a performance appraisal.[28] Comprehensive training programs can help ensure the success of any performance appraisal system and of a system already in place. New evaluators should be trained, and current evaluators' skills can be fine-tuned.

TYPES OF PERFORMANCE APPRAISAL METHODS

A number of different performance appraisal methods or formats are available. Some methods focus more on employee behavior (for example, planning or organizing); others are more results oriented and emphasize the *results* of employee behavior (such as the extent to which an employee reaches goals and objectives). Within the behavioral methods, employees can be evaluated based on an organizational or departmental standard or they can be evaluated relative to others.

BEHAVIORAL PERFORMANCE APPRAISAL METHODS

CHECKLISTS

In its simplest form, the checklist is a list of descriptive statements and/or adjectives describing job-related behavior. If the evaluator perceives the employee as possessing a particular trait, the item is checked. If the evaluator does not perceive the employee as possessing this trait, the item is left blank. Each item listed reflects either a positive or negative quality that an employee could possess. One point is added for every positive item checked, and one point is subtracted for every negative quality checked. Qualities left blank are excluded from the calculations. An example of a checklist is provided in Exhibit 10.5.

WEIGHTED CHECKLIST
A checklist used for performance evaluation that places weighted values on each response; the weighted responses are then summed to provide an overall rating.

WEIGHTED CHECKLISTS

The checklist described above evenly weights each item. When this type of weighting scheme is not appropriate, a **weighted checklist** can be used. This method uses essentially the same format as the one described above. However, after the list has been completed, a weighted value is applied to the responses. The evaluator does not know

EXHIBIT 10.5   **Example of a Checklist Appraisal Form**

Instructions: Read each item below and determine whether the individual you are rating exhibits this quality. If the answer is "yes," place a check in the blank in front of the statement. If the answer is "no," leave the blank empty.

_____ Asks for assistance when encountering problems.

_____ Recognizes others' contributions to his or her production.

_____ Maintains good relations with other workers.

_____ Takes initiative when faced with a new situation.

_____ Requires an excessive amount of instructions when confronted with a new situation.

_____ Can see more than one alternative to a situation.

_____ Continually meets deadlines.

how the items are weighted. The points assigned to the weighted responses are then totaled to provide an overall rating. An example of a weighted checklist is provided in Exhibit 10.6.

GRAPHIC RATING SCALE

One of the most widely used performance evaluation formats is the graphic rating scale. There are many reasons for its widespread use. First, graphic rating scales are easy to use. Evaluators can rate a large number of individuals in a short amount of time. Also, these scales are easy to understand and explain to the ratees. Finally, they are simple to develop and change when needed. The ratings are made using a scale that is divided into several levels, usually 5 to 7, with adjectives such as unsatisfactory and outstanding anchored at the two extremes of the scale (i.e., 1 = unsatisfactory and 5 = outstanding). The evaluator reads the quality to be rated and then determines at what level,

EXHIBIT 10.6   **Example of a Weighted Checklist**

Instructions: Below is a list of qualities upon which you are to rate each employee. If you believe that the employee possesses the quality listed, place a check in the blank in front of the item; otherwise, leave the blank empty.

		*Value**
_____	Is asked for advice by others.	3.0
_____	Follows directions well.	2.0
_____	Does not work well in group settings.	−1.0
_____	Works well without direct supervision.	2.5
_____	Continually misses deadlines.	−2.0
_____	Applies quick fixes to recurring problems.	−1.0
_____	Treats others fairly.	1.0

*These values would not be included on the actual rating form.

if at all, the individual demonstrates it. A graphic rating scale can be used to rate an employee's overall performance, but usually, it rates a number of characteristics such as quality of work and knowledge of the job and then the values on each of the individual characteristics are summed to create an overall rating. An example of a graphic rating scale is provided in Exhibit 10.7. Similar to weighted checklists, certain items on a graphic rating scale can be weighted differentially.[29]

MIXED-STANDARD SCALE

One variation of the graphic rating scale is the mixed-standard scale. Instead of rating a behavior, such as attendance, the evaluator is given three conceptually compatible statements describing that behavior at high, medium, and low levels. These statements are mixed with sets of three statements that describe various other qualities to be rated. The evaluator is asked to rate each individual on each item by indicating whether he or she exhibits "better than" (indicated by a +), "as good as" (indicated by a 0), or "worse than" (indicated by a −) performance on the behavior described in each statement. A special scoring key is used to translate the ratings into a numerical score. The key is based on the ratings within a behavioral category. That is, all three ratings for a category are examined and matched to a pattern in the scoring key. A score is then assigned for that pattern. For example, if an individual was rated "better than" (i.e., +) on each of the three statements designed to determine the behavioral dimension attendance, that individual would earn a 7 for that category. If he or she was rated "worse than" (i.e., −) on all three behaviors, the value assigned would be a 1. Finally, it is important to note that all of the possible patterns are not represented in the scoring key. For instance, the pattern of 0 0 0 is not listed because the ratings given to the moderate and low behaviors

| **EXHIBIT 10.7** | **Examples of Graphic Rating Scales** |

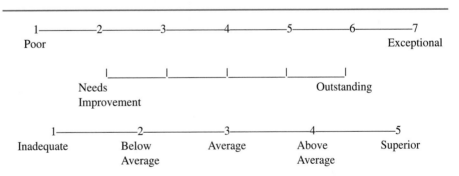

1 = Clearly inadequate performance. Consistently performed below expectations and did not meet a majority of the objectives.
2 = Performance did not meet objectives in several key areas. Results were generally achieved in an unacceptable manner.
3 = Performance met all objectives. Results were achieved in an effective fashion. Represents good, solid performance.
4 = Performance met all objectives and exceeded objectives in several key areas. Results were achieved in a manner that surpassed the generally accepted norms for the position.
5 = Truly exceptional performance. Performance exceeded all objectives. Results were achieved utilizing superior techniques.

have to be higher (or equal to if it is a +) than the rating assigned to the high behavior. That is, if an individual is "as good as" (i.e., 0) on a high behavior, he or she will naturally be "better than" (i.e., +) a moderate example of this same behavior. Exhibit 10.8 provides an example of a mixed-standard appraisal form, including the scoring key. The mixed-standard scale gives a wider range of scores than the simple graphic rating scale.

EXHIBIT 10.8

Example of a Mixed-Standard Assessment Format

Instructions: Read each statement provided. Using the scale below, rate the individual on each statement. Place your response in the blank in front of each item.

Scale

+   This employee's performance is **better than** the behavior described in this statement.

0   This employee's performance is **as good as** the behavior described in this statement.

−   This employee's performance is **worse than** the behavior described in this statement.

_____ **1.** Always at work unless a critical emergency has arisen.

_____ **2.** Always volunteers for difficult assignments.

_____ **3.** Misses work less than twice a month.

_____ **4.** Mistakes are present in virtually all work completed by this individual.

_____ **5.** Requests only assignments he or she has performed in the past.

_____ **6.** While rare, corrections sometimes must be made to work submitted by this individual.

_____ **7.** Will take on challenging assignments if requested to do so.

_____ **8.** Has more than two absences a week.

_____ **9.** Assignments are always accurate.

Note

Statements 1 (high), 3 (moderate), and 8 (low) represent the three levels of absenteeism.
Statements 2 (high), 7 (moderate), and 5 (low) represent the three levels of drive.
Statements 9 (high), 6 (moderate), and 4 (low) represent the three levels of ability.

Scoring Key

Determine the pattern of responses within a behavioral dimension and match that pattern to the matrix below. The score for each pattern is provided at the end of the line.

High	Moderate	Low	Score
+	+	+	7
0	+	+	6
−	+	+	5
−	0	+	4
−	−	+	3
−	−	0	2
−	−	−	1

Statements

FORCED-CHOICE SCALE

The forced-choice scale was designed to increase objectivity and decrease subjectivity in ratings by camouflaging the "best" responses.[30] With many appraisal formats, raters are able to easily locate the positive and negative items and therefore can inflate the score they provided by rating the positive items high and the negative items low. Forced-choice ratings scales make padding ratings more difficult because raters are required to select an item from a pair of items that most closely reflects the individual being rated. Although *both* items are equally positive, only one is important for the job in question. Because the raters cannot tell by reading the items which one is more important, they cannot intentionally inflate their ratings. Exhibit 10.9 illustrates an example of a forced-choice scale for a teacher. The statement with the highest ability to discriminate is worth one point. The other item is worth zero points. Thus, the subject would receive one point if the rater chose item 1 and zero points if the rater chose item 2. One problem with this procedure is the difficulty in developing items that are not related to performance but that appear to be.[31]

CRITICAL INCIDENT METHOD

CRITICAL INCIDENT
An example of a highly effective or highly ineffective performance.

A **critical incident** is a written description of a highly effective or highly ineffective performance. To use the critical incident method to appraise an individual's performance, the evaluator keeps a journal of critical incidents for each individual being evaluated. It is important that the evaluator record the incident as soon as it happens; relying on one's memory at a later date often proves ineffectual. Examples of a highly favorable and highly unfavorable critical incidents recorded for a sales clerk at a large department store chain might read as follows:

> A customer approached a sales clerk and asked for a specific line of clothing. The clerk showed the customer to that section of the store. She then offered to help the customer locate a specific item within the line. After realizing that the store did not have the particular color, style, and size the customer wanted, the clerk called the other stores in the area until she located the item and placed it on hold for the customer.

> Near the end of an evening, a customer approached the cash register where a sales clerk was positioned and requested that the clerk ring up her purchases. The clerk asked the customer to go to a different counter because he had already counted his money drawer and did not want to have to do so again.

EXHIBIT 10.9   **Forced-Choice Rating Scale Example**

Please check the statement that *best* describes the employee:

Statement	Discriminability Index	Favorableness Index
_____ 1. Shows patience with slow learners.	1.72	2.82
_____ 2. Lectures with confidence.	.51	2.75
	Unknown to Evaluator	

Note that the statements are similar in their social desirability but differ in their ability to determine high from low performers (that is, discriminability).

Critical incidents should contain (1) the circumstances that preceded the incident, (2) the setting in which the incident occurred, (3) precisely what the employee did that was effective or ineffective, (4) the consequences of the incident, and (5) the extent to which the consequences were within the employee's control. At the end of the evaluation period, these reports are used to appraise the employee's performance. Although recording employee behavior can help the evaluator remember the range of behavior that occurred during the evaluation period, it is very time consuming and difficult to quantify.

BEHAVIORALLY ANCHORED RATING SCALE (BARS)

BARS is a sophisticated method of evaluating employee performance based on employee *behavior* rather than attitudes or assumptions about motivation or potential. BARS is a numerical scale that is anchored by specific narrative examples of behaviors that range from very negative to very positive descriptions of performance.[32]

BARS is a difficult and time-consuming scale to develop. Each job must be analyzed and a list of critical incidents developed by experts in the job. Once the critical incidents are developed, they are matched to a set of performance dimensions that are then scaled from effective to ineffective performance. Exhibit 10.10 illustrates one aspect of a BARS for a manager. The BARS technique offers a high degree of interrater reliability and objectivity because of its emphasis on behavior. Unfortunately, because of the complexity and expense of setting up the scale, managers should carefully consider the administrative investment before adopting BARS as their performance appraisal technique.

The performance appraisal methods just discussed base the employee's evaluation on some type of standard. The standard may be set at the department or the organization level. The next three performance appraisal methods evaluate the employee's performance relative to that of others in the employee's department. These are called *personnel comparison systems.*

PERSONNEL COMPARISON SYSTEMS

RANKING

ALTERNATIVE RANKING
A ranking approach in which the rater selects the best overall performer, writes the name on a sheet of paper, and crosses the name off the list of ratees. Next, the rater selects the overall worst performer, transfers the name to the bottom of the sheet, and crosses off that name. From the remaining names, the rater chooses alternately the best and worst performers until all employees have been ranked.

The ranking method is used to evaluate an employee on his or her overall performance. To use this method, the evaluator places the employees in a specified group (e.g., all subordinates reporting to a supervisor) in order from the "best" performer to the "worst" performer. In essence, the evaluator simply looks down the list of employees to be rated and selects the individual he or she believes had the best overall performance for the evaluation period. This name is written at the top of a sheet of paper and crossed off the list of names. This process is repeated until all the names have been crossed off the list. Another ranking approach is called **alternative ranking.** Under this method, the rater selects the best overall performer, writes the name on a new sheet of paper, and then crosses the name off the list of ratees. Next, the appraiser selects the overall *worst* performer, crosses off that name, and transfers it to the new list. He or she then selects the best performer from those left on the list. This alternating process continues until all employees have been ranked.

One advantage to the ranking method is that it does not allow the evaluator to rate everyone high. Unfortunately, rank ordering produces ordinal data, thus, the *amount* of difference between employees is unknown. For example, it is impossible to determine if the employee with the second highest ranking is close to the highest performer or if there is a large gap between them.

EXHIBIT 10.10   **Behaviorally Anchored Rating Scale Example**

Position: _____

Job Dimension: _____

Plans work and organizes time carefully so as to maximize resources and meet commitments.	9	
	8	Even though this associate has a report due on another project, he or she would be well prepared for the assigned discussion on your project.
	7	This associate would keep a calendar or schedule on which deadlines and activities are carefully noted, and which would be consulted before making new commitments.
	6	As program chief, this associate would manage arrangements for enlisting resources for a special project reasonably well, but would probably omit one or two details that would have to be handled by improvisation.
Plans and organizes time and effort primarily for large segments of a task. Usually meets commitments, but may overlook what are considered secondary details.	5	This associate would meet a deadline in handing in a report, but the report might be below usual standard if other deadlines occur on the same day the report is due.
	4	This associate's evaluations are likely not to reflect abilities because of overcommitments in other activities.
	3	This associate would plan more by enthusiasm than by timetable and frequently have to work late the night before an assignment is due, although it would be completed on time.
	2	This associate would often be late for meetings, although others in similar circumstances do not seem to find it difficult to be on time.
Appears to do little planning. May perform effectively, despite what seems to be a disorganized approach, although deadlines may be missed.	1	This associate never makes a deadline, even with sufficient notice.

FORCED DISTRIBUTION

This method requires the evaluator to place a certain percentage of employees into each of several categories based on overall performance. For example, 10 percent of the employees must be placed in the "unsatisfactory" category, 15 percent must be placed in the "fair" category, 50 percent must be placed in the "satisfactory or average" category, 15 percent in the "good" category, and 10 percent in the "outstanding" category. Similar to the ranking method, forced distribution forces the evaluator to discriminate between the employees; however, the absolute difference between them is not known. Exhibit 10.11 provides an example of a possible distribution schedule.

PAIRED COMPARISONS

When the paired comparisons method is used, the evaluator compares all possible pairs of subordinates on their overall ability to do the job. From each possible pair of employees, the evalutor selects the employee with the higher overall ability to do the job. The number of comparisons required by the evaluator is based on a simple formula: number of pairs = $[N (N - 1)]/2$ where N is the number of people who will be rated. Thus, 10 subordinates require 45 comparisons $[10 (10 - 1)]/2$.

Due to the subjectivity of evaluating "overall performance," some managers use a number of different job-related dimensions when comparing. If the rater compares all employees on more than one dimension (D), the number of pairs = $D\{[N (N - 1)]/2\}$. Thus, 10 employees compared on only five different job dimensions would result in 225 comparisons $(5[(10 (10 - 1))/2])$. Obviously, this method can become very cumbersome if there are many employees to evaluate or if the evaluation uses a variety of job dimensions.

PROBLEMS WITH PERSONNEL COMPARISON SYSTEMS

At first glance, comparison systems appear easy to implement and use, intuitively appealing, and simple to explain to others. However, these types of appraisal systems have some negative aspects. First, comparison systems are highly subjective. Many rating

EXHIBIT 10.11   **Example of a Forced Distribution Performance Appraisal Method**

Performance	Percentage Distribution
Highest Level Employees who exhibit this level of performance *continually* produce more than is required, before it is due, and the work is of exceptional quality.	No more than 7%
Above Average Level Employees who exhibit this level of performance often produce more than is required, sometimes beat their deadlines, and frequently produce work of above average quality.	No more than 17%
Average Level Employees who exhibit this level of performance produce the work required, meet their deadlines, and produce acceptable work.	No more than 45%
Below Average Level Employees who exhibit this level of performance sometimes fail to produce the work required, often miss their deadlines, and frequently produce work that is unacceptable.	No more than 21%
Lowest Level Employees who exhibit this level of performance *continually* fail to produce assigned work, miss deadlines, and produce work that is unacceptable.	No more than 10%

systems ask the evaluator to make a global judgment about an individual's performance. This is a difficult, if not impossible, task. Further, because individuals are compared to one another, this squelches team spirit and encourages competition. This may be effective for some positions such as sales, but those companies that wish to use a team-based management approach would find it counterproductive to implement an appraisal system based on comparisons.

The ranking and paired comparison methods become difficult to manage when a large number of employees must be evaluated. These systems also become unwieldly when a variety of dimensions is evaluated instead of overall performance. One of the major disadvantages of the forced distribution method is that the performance of the employees to be evaluated may not fit the imposed distribution. Think about this from an exam perspective. Let's say you earned a 97, the *second highest* grade, on the first exam in this class. Let's suppose further that your instructor decided to use the distribution system described in Exhibit 10.11, making the highest level of performance the *A*s and the lowest level of performance the *F*s. Finally, let's say that there are 25 students in your class. Applying the distribution outlined in Exhibit 10.11 to your exam grade would place you in the B range, or the above average level of performance. Because there are 25 students in the class, no more than one person can be in the top level (i.e., $1/25 = .04$, but $2/25 = .08$, which is more than 7 percent). Obviously, you would disagree with this grade assignment. The point is that the performance distribution may not reflect the distribution that is forced upon it.

RESULTS-ORIENTED PERFORMANCE APPRAISAL METHODS

The following two performance appraisal formats are results oriented. Thus, the evaluator is rating the outcomes of the employee's behavior rather than the actual behavior itself.

MANAGEMENT BY OBJECTIVES (MBO)

A frequently used performance appraisal method is management by objectives. Management by objectives (MBO) has been around for over 30 years and is usually credited to Peter Drucker. Drucker was trying to design a systematic approach to setting objectives and performing appraisals by using results that would lead to improved organizational productivity. Recent research findings indicate that MBO does indeed increase productivity. In 68 of 70 studies, productivity gains were reported by organizations that have implemented MBO programs. However, this research also indicated that the degree of productivity increase was directly linked to whether or not top management fully supported the MBO process. In organizations where top management did support MBO, the average productivity gain was 56 percent. However, in organizations where there was no, or limited, top-level management support for the program, productivity gains averaged only 6 percent.[33]

Although there are a number of variations, MBO generally consists of the following steps: setting organizational objectives, setting individual objectives, and appraisal according to results.

Since MBO takes a top-down approach, top management must decide the overall objectives of the organization and the departments. Objectives should always be stated so that they can be measured or quantified. Also, the objectives should include target dates for completion and action plans that discuss the process of achieving these objectives.

After the overall objectives have been set, individual objectives for employees at each level of the organization (for example, upper-level management, then

==

HR CHALLENGE

Tips for Developing a Legally Defensible Performance Appraisal

Based on outcomes of various court cases that centered on the performance appraisal, the following list suggests ways to create a legally defensible performance appraisal system. While reading this list, keep in mind that there is no such thing as a completely safe performance appraisal system.

1. Begin with a job analysis that determines the necessary characteristics for successful job performance.
2. From the job analysis results, determine performance standards.
3. These standards must be communicated and accepted by the employees who will be judged by them.
4. Using the standard as a guideline, develop a rating scheme. The scheme should measure clearly defined individual components of job performance rather than global or undefined measures. The standards and rating scheme should be distributed to all raters.
5. The type of scale selected is not significant from a legal perspective. The courts have not indicated any problems with using simple graphic rating scales or trait ratings. However, when these types of methods are used, it is helpful to avoid abstract trait names

such as loyalty and to anchor the scales with brief, logically consistent tags.
6. Train the raters to use the scale correctly. Focus on how to apply the standards when making decisions. It is important that the raters uniformly apply the standards because in 6 of 10 cases in which the organization lost the court case, the plaintiffs showed the standards were not uniformly applied.
7. Include a mechanism for appealing the rating. The appeal should be directed to upper-level management.
8. Document all appraisals. These are very useful in court cases.
9. Provide a way for poor performers to receive corrective guidance. When the organization made an attempt to help poor performers, the court ruled more favorably toward the organization.

SOURCE: Adapted from Gerald Barrett and Mary Kernan, "Performance Appraisal and Terminations: A Review of Court Decisions Since *Brito* v. *Zia* with Implications for Personnel Practices," *Personnel Psychology* 40, 1987, pp. 489–502; Wayne Cascio and H. John Bernardin, "Implications of Performance Appraisal Litigation for Personnel Decisions," *Personnel Psychology* 34, 1981, pp. 211–226; and David Rosen, "Appraisals Can Make or Break Your Court Case," *Personnel Journal,* November 1992, pp. 113–118.

==

middle-level management, then lower-level management, and finally the employees with no supervisory responsibilities) are set. Employee objectives and the specified period of time for the accomplishment of these objectives are determined jointly by the supervisor and the employee. See Exhibit 10.12 for an illustration of an MBO performance worksheet. The objectives set should be specific, measurable, challenging, and accepted by both parties.

These objectives play an important role in the feedback process and the final evaluation. Specifically, employees should be given periodic feedback on their progress toward their stated goals and objectives. In addition, the final performance appraisal should be based on how well the employee met the objectives set forth. Obviously, situations arise that might require the initial objectives to be modified throughout the year, such as a change in the competition or the economy. Changes in objectives can be made during periodic reviews or feedback sessions. The use of MBO as a performance appraisal technique is popular, partly because of the high level of employee involvement.

WORK PLANNING

Work planning is similar to MBO except that its primary focus is the periodic feedback and review. Less emphasis is given to setting each objective in terms of being measurable. Thus, work planning allows the supervisor latitude for "judgment calls" regarding whether or not the employee met the objective.

EXHIBIT 10.12   **Handy-Dandy Stores Performance Objectives Worksheet**

Directions: This sheet is to be completed at the *beginning* of the appraisal period.

Employee Name: Sam Swanson   Length of Time in Position: 4 years

Employee Number: 189   Date Prepared: 9/1/87, revised 4/1/91

Job Title: District Manager   Department/Region: Lakeland, Florida

Strategic Planning Goals	Results Expected	Time Frame (By When)
1. Reduce turnover 33%	Reduce turnover 33% in all stores	9/1/92
2. Improve store appearance	Paint outside of all stores	4/92
3. Improve store mgr. part.	Send store mgrs. to mgt. dev.	8/1/92
4. Improve communications	Send all mgrs. to comm. training	8/1/92
5. Increase sales	Increase sales by 10% per store	9/1/92
6. Reduce shrink	Reduce shrink losses by 45%	9/1/92

Maintenance/Routine Goals	Results Expected	Time Frame (By When)
1. Monitor costs	Reduce costs by at least 8%	9/1/92
2. Reduce stock outs	Reduce stock out level by 20%	9/1/92
3.		
4.		

Personal Development Goals	Results Expected	Time Frame (By When)
1. Improve communications	Attend communications workshop	9/1/92
2. Improve computer skills	Attend community college course on computers	9/1/91
3. Improve planning ability	Develop written plan for stores; attend planning workshop	9/1/92

Employee Signature   Supervisor Signature

SELECTING A PERFORMANCE APPRAISAL METHOD

In general, there is no one *best* performance appraisal method.[34] However, depending on the situation, certain methods might be better than others. For example, if *objective* performance data are available, then MBO is a good strategy to use. If, however, employees are going to be compared for determining pay increases, promotions, and so on, then some common denominator must be determined to make comparisons among many employees. This usually implies a numerical rating of performance, such as ranking or rating methods rather than MBO or work-planning methods in which employee objectives can vary. Thus, the *purpose* of the performance appraisal is an important consideration when choosing a performance appraisal method.

An increasingly important factor in selecting a performance appraisal method is whether or not the technique is legally defensible. While there is no way to *guarantee* a completely "safe" performance appraisal, managers need to be aware of the outcomes of court cases that made judgments about the performance appraisal process. In general, the important cases suggest, among other things, that the courts do not reject subjective reviews such as those made by the employee's immediate supervisor. Further, the use of objective measures, such as production figures, do not ensure favorable decisions for the organization. In each case, it is up to the court to determine if subjective or objective measures are appropriate for the job in question. It also has been found that techniques used to develop and refine the performance appraisal process, such as training raters and validating the process, have not helped win court cases. While these practices are useful to ensure a quality performance appraisal process, they do not carry much weight in the court's eyes except when these procedures are used to help ensure that the standards are being applied evenly to all employees.[35]

Another consideration to make when choosing an appraisal method is how well it will control the types of rater errors that will most likely be encountered. To better explain this factor, the following section defines and describes typical rater errors or biases that can occur in the performance appraisal process.

PERCEPTUAL ERRORS IN EVALUATION

Performance evaluations can be biased due to a variety of perceptual errors made by raters. Regardless of the performance criterion or the scientific nature of the appraisal method, perceptual error can occur. Typical errors include the halo effect, stereotypes, attributions, recency effects, leniency, strictness, and central tendency. Each of these is examined in the following sections.

HALO EFFECT

The halo effect occurs when the rater allows one trait or characteristic (either positive or negative) of the employee to override a realistic appraisal of other traits or characteristics. For example, if an employee is always on time to work, a supervisor might allow this positive characteristic to influence his or her evaluation of this employee's performance on other dimensions. Thus, this employee might be judged as a good performer—not because of actual performance, but because of the halo effect. The halo effect has been examined extensively in the performance appraisal literature.[36] Some approaches used to control halo effects include using performance appraisal simulations prior to evaluations, and having raters listen to short lectures on the halo effect before rating employees.[37]

Of the different types of performance appraisal methods described in the previous section, several would be more susceptible to halo error than others. For example, any of the scales that request the evaluator to judge the individual on more than one factor, such as checklists and the graphic rating scale, could be subject to halo effect error. The best methods to use to avoid or reduce halo effect error might be the critical incident approach provided that the evaluator collected negative as well as positive incidents. Also, adding a weight, which is unknown by the evaluator, to the factors evaluated may help to alleviate this error. Finally, as with most of these errors, raters can be trained to recognize this bias and to work to overcome it.

STEREOTYPING

Stereotyping occurs when the rater places an employee into a class or category based on one or a few traits or characteristics. For example, an older worker may be stereotyped as being slower, more difficult to train, and unwilling to learn new approaches. Obviously, this perceptual error could negatively affect the overall performance evaluation. Of course, the older worker being evaluated may not fit this stereotype at all and may be quick to pick up new concepts and anxious to participate in new training programs. Some research has indicated that the composition of the group from which the stereotyped employee comes may influence whether or not the stereotype influences the rating. For example, women received lower ratings when the proportion of women in the group of employees was small; however, the stereotype did not lower ratings for African-Americans who came from a group that had more Caucasians than African-Americans. These results suggest that some stereotypes may be stronger than others.[38] Similar to reducing the halo effect, stereotyping may be controlled by offering specialized training to raters and making the problem associated with stereotyping salient. Further, avoiding scales that are not tied to performance standards can help to reduce stereotyping errors.

ATTRIBUTIONS

Another perceptual error that can affect the validity of the performance appraisal involves the attributions the rater makes about employee behavior. Making an attribution means to assign causation for another's behavior.[39] For example, if a supervisor attributes an employee's good performance to external causes, such as luck, holding an easy job, or receiving help from co-workers, then the performance evaluation will not be as positive as if the supervisor had attributed good performance to internal causes, such as effort or ability. Similarly, if the supervisor attributes poor performance to external causes rather than internal causes, the performance evaluation will not be as negative. Frequently, attribution errors can be avoided by using BARS, because this method requires the evaluator to rate the behavior but not judge it.

RECENCY EFFECTS

Recency errors occur when performance is evaluated based on performance information that occurred most recently. Essentially, supervisors rate the employee's most recent behavior. Recency errors are most likely to occur when there is a long period of time between performance evaluations (such as a year). Since recent employee behavior is the most salient to a supervisor, using a method that requires the rater to keep a log of employee performance throughout the year, such as the critical incidents approach, and forcing the rater to review the log before making a rating can help to alleviate this problem.

LENIENCY/STRICTNESS ERRORS

Leniency and strictness errors occur when the rater tends to use one of the extremes of a rating scale. When leniency errors occur, most employees receive very favorable ratings, even though it is not warranted by their performance. Leniency errors can occur for a number of reasons. For example, a supervisor may be uncomfortable confronting particularly aggressive employees with less than favorable evaluations. To avoid conflict, the supervisor might choose to rate everyone high. It is also possible that the supervisor's own performance evaluation is based partially on the performance of his or her work group. Rating everyone favorably gives the impression that the entire work group is very effective.

Strictness errors, which are basically the opposite of leniency errors, occur when the rater erroneously evaluates most employees unfavorably. In this case, supervisors may simply want to appear "tough," or they may have unrealistic expectations of performance. Regardless, most employees are assigned ratings at the lower end of the performance scale.

Both of these errors can be eliminated by using any of the personnel comparison systems discussed previously. For example, the forced distribution method requires that the rater place a certain percentage of the people being evaluated in various categories, from outstanding to below average. By forcing the rater to use all of the categories, both leniency and strictness errors will disappear.

CENTRAL TENDENCY ERRORS

Central tendency errors occur when the rater avoids the extremes of the performance scale and evaluates most employees somewhere near the middle of the scale. This error results in most employees being rated as "average." Leniency, strictness, and central tendency errors limit the ability of the performance appraisal to discriminate between the performance of workers. Thus, employees are grouped together at the low, mid-point, or high end of the scale, and it is virtually impossible to differentiate performance levels among the employees. As with the leniency and strictness errors described above, using a human resources comparison performance appraisal method can help to alleviate this problem.

STRATEGY AND THE PERFORMANCE APPRAISAL PROCESS

The performance appraisal system can be utilized to promote a variety of management goals and objectives. In addition to systematically encouraging high levels of performance, the system is useful in identifying employees with potential, rewarding performance equitably, and determining employees' needs for development. These are all activities that should support the organization's strategic orientation. Although these activities are clearly instrumental in achieving corporate plans and long-term growth, typical appraisal systems in most organizations have been focused on short-run goals.[40]

ORGANIZATIONAL STRATEGY

Strengthening the linkage between the performance appraisal system and the organization's long-term strategic plans can improve organizational effectiveness. By designing a performance appraisal system that matches the organization's strategy, individuals should naturally perform in such a way to support the organization's mission. A clear linkage between the two also can help to build a culture that will further reinforce the organization's strategy. In addition, if the system is designed to help employees manage rather than critique their performances, there is a better chance for both the organization's and individual's goals to be met.[41] The following discussion is based on Miles and Snow's organizational strategy typology.[42] Specifically, the organizational strategies of defender, prospector, and analyzer will be examined as they relate to performance appraisal systems.

As discussed in previous chapters, defenders have a narrow and relatively stable product-market domain. As a result of this narrow focus, these types of organizations seldom need to make major adjustments in their technology, structure, or methods of operation. They devote primary attention to improving the efficiency of their existing operations. Because of the emphasis on skill building within the organization, successful defenders use performance appraisal as a means for identifying training needs. The performance ap-

HR CHALLENGE

Effective Appraisal Systems Produce Effective Organizations

John Strazzanti, general manager and president of Com-Corp Industries, which produces light bulb shields for GM, knew it was time for a change. For years, the company had kept pay under wraps and had rarely given employees raises. When his employees began to react emotionally to never being appraised or promoted, Strazzanti made his move.

He asked for volunteers for a salary committee, which he charged with setting wages in the organization based on salary surveys from the marketplace. He also gathered input about the criteria upon which the employees thought they should be evaluated.

As a result, a new performance appraisal system is administered three times a year. The employees are rated both quantitatively and qualitatively on technical proficiency and professional attitude. Workers are measured against their past performance, goals that they had set for themselves, and industry conditions and standards. If the review determines that a worker needs to improve, he or she can do so by participating in any

of a number of ongoing instructional classes offered by Com-Corp.

Additionally, the new performance appraisal system allows the employees to review the firm. Each employee must submit a detailed review of the company's performance three times a year. They are encouraged to question the methods used and suggest ways to improve. Frequently, the suggestions are acted upon and new procedures are implemented.

The payback for all these changes can be seen in many ways. From a human resource perspective, turnover is low, averaging between 2 and 3 percent. Absenteeism and tardiness also are low at about 2.5 percent. With respect to profits, the company has earned money every year since the program was placed into effect. Finally, in terms of customer satisfaction, General Motors gave Com-Corp one of the highest ratings ever under its Targets for Excellence program for GM suppliers.

SOURCE: Adapted from "The Interactive Employee Review," *Inc.,* November 1991, pp. 73–75.

praisal system is usually more behaviorally oriented as opposed to results oriented and the emphasis is on the *process* (such as critical incidents). Finally, the focus is often on comparing individual or group performance with the previous year's performance.

Organizations with a prospector strategy continually search for different product and market opportunities. In addition, prospectors regularly experiment with potential responses to new and emerging environmental trends. These organizations are often the creators of change. Because of the emphasis on skill identification and acquisition of human resources *outside* of the organization as opposed to skill building within the organization, prospectors often use the performance appraisal as a means of identifying staffing needs. The emphasis is more results oriented (such as management by objectives) rather than process oriented. Finally, the focus is on division and corporate performance evaluations as they compare with other companies during the same evaluation period.

Organizations with an analyzer strategy operate in two types of product-market domains. One domain is stable while the other is changing. In their more innovative areas, managers watch their competitors closely and rapidly adapt to ideas that appear promising. In general, analyzers use cost-efficient technologies for stable products and project or matrix technologies for new products. Analyzers tend to emphasize both skill building and skill acquisition and employ extensive training programs. Thus, analyzers attempt to identify both training needs *and* staffing needs. The performance appraisal system most conducive to an analyzer strategy is one that is more behavioral and process oriented. Performance evaluations are considered at the individual, group, and division level. Finally, successful analyzers have a tendency to examine current performance with past performance within the organization; however, some cross-sectional comparisons (comparisons between companies) do occur.

IDENTIFYING SUCCESSFUL VERSUS UNSUCCESSFUL APPRAISAL SYSTEMS[43]

Performance appraisal systems can fail for a variety of reasons. Exhibit 10.13 illustrates some of the reasons that trouble may occur. The following discussion focuses on diagnosing the problems of an unsuccessful performance appraisal system.

POORLY DEFINED SYSTEMS

A poorly defined system means that something is wrong with the design. For example, the system might lack written documentation to use as a guide. Often poorly defined systems emerge out of "tradition." Another possibility is that the system is defined but not well. The performance appraisal system must be tied directly to clearly stated organizational objectives and strategies. Managers should not have to guess as to the objectives of the organization, the purpose of the performance appraisal, and how these issues tie together.

POORLY COMMUNICATED SYSTEMS

Even a sophisticated appraisal system is doomed to fail if it is not communicated properly to everyone involved. The evaluators and the employees should have similar expectations as to the purpose and the importance of the appraisal system. For example, the employee should know whether the performance appraisal system will consist of periodic reviews of performance aimed at changing work behavior or if it is to be an annual evaluation to determine salary and promotion opportunities.

INAPPROPRIATE SYSTEMS

Some of the most common characteristics of inappropriate systems include measuring inappropriate types of performance (those that are not job related), asking the wrong people to do the evaluating, conducting the performance appraisal discussions too infrequently, and using a rating system that is not suited to the performance being measured. Any of these problems could lead to an ineffective performance appraisal system.

POORLY SUPPORTED SYSTEMS

The performance appraisal system can fail if it is supported only by top management. Even a good appraisal design can fail if the people using it are not committed to its success. Similarly, if the performance appraisal system is accepted and supported by employees, but not by top management, management may not choose to utilize the information gained from the appraisal. Essentially, a successful performance appraisal system should be accepted and supported by all who use it.

UNMONITORED SYSTEMS

If problems with the performance appraisal system go unmonitored, they can become serious over time. For example, suppose that raters are consistently making leniency errors so that everyone receives high ratings. If this problem goes undetected, the perfor-

EXHIBIT 10.13   **Common Problems with Unsuccessful Performance Appraisal Systems**

1. A poorly defined appraisal system
2. A poorly communicated appraisal system
3. An inappropriate appraisal system
4. A poorly supported appraisal system
5. An unmonitored appraisal system

SOURCE: Adapted from C. Lee, "Smoothing Our Appraisal Systems," *HRMagazine,* March 1990, pp. 72–76.

mance appraisal becomes meaningless. Thus, a performance appraisal system, even a good one, can fail if problems are not monitored regularly.

CRITERIA FOR A SUCCESSFUL PERFORMANCE APPRAISAL SYSTEM

Successful performance appraisal systems have a number of common characteristics. The following discussion focuses on the criteria for a successful performance appraisal system, which are listed in Exhibit 10.14.

CLEAR OBJECTIVES

A good performance appraisal should be built around unambiguous objectives. These objectives should cover all levels and areas of the organization and reflect the needs of each. The appraisal system should be clear as to its purpose. Participants should know whether it is being used to determine raises and promotions or to determine development needs. It is important to clearly delineate who should participate in the system. That is, will employees at all levels be involved or will some areas or layers in the organization be excluded? Finally, participants must be aware of what type of information will be collected, how often, and who will have access to this information.

MANAGEMENT AND EMPLOYEE ENDORSEMENT

To be effective, the appraisal system should be supported by the entire workforce. This includes management support for possible expenses such as additional training, employee meetings, appraisal forms and other materials, and staff time. In addition, employees can benefit from involvement in the performance appraisal. For example, many companies encourage employees to do a self-appraisal as a means for discussion. The information solicited by self-appraisals should be consistent with both the organization's objectives and individual goals.

FLEXIBILITY

An organization must design its system with enough flexibility to adapt to any changes that might occur. For example, the appraisal system should be flexible enough to accommodate different management philosophies, employee subcultures, and geographic locations. Sometimes it is necessary to establish different sets of procedures for very different employee groups or locations.

PREDICTABILITY

The timing of the performance appraisal(s) and any other feedback sessions should be predictable. For example, some organizations have an annual performance appraisal close to the hiring anniversary date of the employee. This enables the employee to

---

EXHIBIT 10.14   **Criteria for a Successful Performance Appraisal System**

---

1. Construction reflects clear objectives
2. Endorsement by management and employee
3. Flexibility to adapt
4. Predictable timing of appraisal
5. Performance *dialogue*
6. Appropriate appraisal form
7. Periodic system checks

SOURCE: Adapted from C. Lee, "Smoothing Our Appraisal Systems," *HRMagazine*, March 1990, pp. 72–76.

prepare for the evaluation. Some organizations have two separate performance appraisals each year—one for salary considerations and one to assess employee development needs. Regardless of the number of evaluations, the employee should always have advance knowledge of what to expect in the performance review and when to expect it.

PERFORMANCE DIALOGUE

Performance discussions between the rater and the employee are perhaps the most critical component of a successful performance appraisal system. Performance reviews should not emphasize a "tell-and-sell" approach, in which the rater tells employees how good or bad their performance has been and attempts to convince them to accept this rating. Using a tell-and-sell approach can alienate employees and destroy the possibility of open communication in the future.

Instead, the performance review should emphasize a dialogue between the evaluator and the employee. During the discussion, the employee should be given the opportunity to see all written appraisals of his or her performance, discuss them with the evaluator, and respond to them both verbally and in writing. Some organizations encourage employees to fill out a self-appraisal form to facilitate these dialogues.

APPRAISAL FORM

The importance of an appropriate appraisal form should not be overlooked. Many organizations simply adopt some "standard" form that may or may not be tailored to their goals and objectives. Failure to tailor the appraisal form to the objectives of the organization can lead to ratings based on irrelevant or unimportant issues. It is important that the form contain questions that directly relate to the employee's job in terms the employee can understand.

PERIODIC SYSTEM CHECKS

Systematically evaluating the validity of the performance appraisal system should be a key feature. As previously mentioned, an unmonitored system can create havoc within an organization if problems go undetected. At a minimum, the performance appraisal system is consistent with the strategic objectives of the organization. Validity checks should occur more often if problems have been detected with the system.

MANAGEMENT GUIDELINES

This chapter has examined a number of issues regarding the process and requirements of an effective performance appraisal system. Various methods of performance appraisals have been presented as well as a number of perceptual and system errors that can hinder the success of an appraisal system. The following management guidelines on performance appraisals are offered as an aid to managerial decision making.

1. Performance appraisals should be based on a thorough job analysis that is current regarding both job descriptions and job specifications.
2. Performance standards should be developed from the job analysis as input into the performance appraisal.
3. Performance appraisals should evaluate a number of specific behaviors as opposed to evaluating "overall job performance" using one or a few global measures.

Continued

4. The performance review discussion should be a two-way communication between the evaluator and the employee.
5. The performance appraisal should be used not only as a means of evaluating performance but also as a means of motivating and developing the employee.
6. The *purpose* of the performance appraisal and the *objectives* of the organization must be considered carefully before deciding on a performance appraisal method.
7. Training programs should be implemented to (a) help raters avoid common perceptual errors in evaluations and (b) help raters with their performance review/feedback skills.
8. The link between the performance appraisal system and the organization's long-term strategic plans should be clearly defined.
9. In general, a successful performance appraisal system should be built around clear objectives, have the support of both management and employees, be flexible enough to adapt to organizational changes, and foster open discussions between supervisors and employees.
10. The validity of the performance appraisal system should be examined at regular intervals.

QUESTIONS FOR REVIEW

1. What are some of the major strategic choices that organizations should make prior to implementing a performance appraisal system?
2. Why is a job analysis important to the performance appraisal system design?
3. What are the differences between the behavioral methods and the personnel comparison methods of performance appraisal?
4. What is the purpose of a performance appraisal?
5. What is the relationship between the performance appraisal system and the strategy of the organization?
6. How does the halo effect differ from stereotyping?
7. What are some ways an evaluator can avoid recency effects?
8. How can evaluators avoid leniency, strictness, and central tendency errors in ratings?
9. What are some characteristics of an unsuccessful versus a successful performance appraisal system?

CASE

XEROX REVAMPS PERFORMANCE APPRAISAL SYSTEM[44]

In the mid-1980s Xerox corporation was faced with a problem—its performance appraisal system was not working. Rather than motivating the employees, its system was leaving them discouraged and disgruntled. Xerox recognized this problem and developed a new system to eliminate it.

THE OLD SYSTEM

The original system used by Xerox encompassed seven main principles:

1. The appraisal occurred once a year.
2. It required employees to document their accomplishments.

3. The manager would assess these accomplishments in writing and assign numerical ratings.
4. The appraisal included a summary written appraisal and a rating from 1 (unsatisfactory) to 5 (exceptional).
5. The ratings were on a forced distribution, controlled at the 3 level or below.
6. Merit increases were tied to the summary rating level.
7. Merit increase information and performance appraisals occurred in one session.

This system resulted in inequitable ratings and was cited by employees as a major source of dissatisfaction. In fact, in

1983, the Reprographic Business Group (RBG), Xerox's main copier division, reported that 95 percent of its employees received either a 3 or 4 on their appraisal. Merit raises for people in these two groups only varied by 1 to 2 percent. Essentially, across-the-board raises were being given to all employees, regardless of performance.

THE NEW SYSTEM

Rather than attempting to fix the old appraisal system, Xerox formed a task force to create a new system from scratch. The task force itself was made up of senior human resources executives; however, members of the task force also consulted with councils of employees and a council of middle managers. Together they created a new system, which differed from the old one in many key respects:

1. The absence of a numerical rating system.
2. The presence of a half-year feedback session.
3. The provision for development planning.
4. Prohibition in the appraisal guidelines of the use of subjective assessments of performance.

The new system has three stages, as opposed to the one-step process of the old system. These stages are spread out over the course of the year.

The first stage occurs at the beginning of the year when the manager meets with each employee. Together, they work out a written agreement on the employee's goals, objectives, plans, and tasks for the year. Standards of satisfactory performance are explicitly spelled out in measurable, attainable, and specific terms.

The second stage is a mid-year, mandatory feedback and discussion session between the manager and the employee. Progress toward objectives and performance strengths and weaknesses are discussed, as well as possible means for improving performance in the latter half of the year. Both the manager and the employee sign an "objectives sheet" indicating that the meeting took place.

The third stage in the appraisal process is the formal performance review, which takes place at year's end. Both the manager and the employee prepare a written document, stating how well the employee met the preset performance targets. They then meet and discuss the performance of the employee, resolving any discrepancies between the perceptions of the manager and the employee. This meeting emphasizes feedback and improvement. Efforts are made to stress the positive aspects of the employee's performance as well as the negative. This stage also includes a developmental planning session in which training, education, or development experiences that can help the employee are discussed.

The merit increase discussion takes place in a separate meeting from the performance appraisal, usually a month or two later. The discussion usually centers on the specific reasons for the merit raise amount, such as performance, relationship with peers, and position in salary range. This allows the employee to better see the reasons behind the salary increase amount, as opposed to the summary rank, which tells the employee very little.

A follow-up survey was conducted the year after the implementation of the new appraisal system. Results were as follows:

81 percent better understood work group objectives

84 percent considered the new appraisal fair

72 percent said they understood how their merit raise was determined

70 percent met their personal and work objectives

77 percent considered the system a step in the right direction

In conclusion, it can be clearly seen that the new system is a vast improvement over the previous one. Despite the fact that some of the philosophies, such as the use of self-appraisals, run counter to conventional management practices, the results speak for themselves.

QUESTIONS

1. What type of performance appraisal is central to the new system at Xerox? Which, if any, of the criteria for a successful appraisal system does this new system have?
2. Given the emphasis on employee development, what implications does this have for hiring and promotions?
3. How do you think management feels about the new performance appraisal system? Why?
4. Are there any potential negative aspects of the new performance appraisal system?

ADDITIONAL READINGS

Becker, B. E., and R. L. Cardy. "Influence of Halo Error on Appraisal Effectiveness: A Conceptual and Empirical Reconsideration." *Journal of Applied Psychology* 71 (1986), pp. 662–671.

Borman, W. C., and G. L. Hallam. "Observation Accuracy for Assessors of Work-Sample Performance: Consistency Across Task and Individual-Differences Correlates." *Journal of Applied Psychology* 76 (1991), pp. 11–18.

Borman, W. C., Leonard A. White, E. D. Pulakos, and S. H. Oppler. "Models of Supervisory Job Performance Ratings." *Journal of Applied Psychology* 76 (1991), pp. 863–872.

Campbell, D. J., and C. Lee. "Self-Appraisal in Performance Evaluation: Development versus Education." *Academy of Management Review* 13 (1988), pp. 302–314.

Dorfman, P. W., W. G. Stephan, and J. Loveland. "Performance Appraisal Behaviors: Supervisor Perceptions and Subordinate Reactions." *Personnel Psychology* 39 (1986), pp. 579–597.

Giles, W. F., and K. W. Mossholder. "Employee Reactions to Contextual and Session Components of Performance Appraisal." *Journal of Applied Psychology* 75 (1990), pp. 371–377.

Glen, R. M. "Performance Appraisal: An Unnerving yet Useful Process." *Public Personnel Management* 19 (1990), pp. 1–10.

Greenhaus, J. H., S. Parasuraman, and W. M. Wormley. "Effects of Race on Organizational Experiences, Job Performance Evaluations, and Career Outcomes," *Academy of Management Journal* 33 (1990), pp. 64–86.

Hanges, P. J., E. P. Braverman, and J. R. Rentsch. "Changes in Raters' Perceptions of Subordinates: A Catastrophe Model." *Journal of Applied Psychology* 76 (1991), pp. 878–888.

Harris, M. M., and J. Schaubroeck. "A Meta-Analysis of Self-Supervisor, Self-Peer, and Peer-Supervisor Ratings." *Personnel Psychology* 41 (1988), pp. 43–62.

Hedge, J. W., and M. J. Kavanagh. "Improving the Accuracy of Performance Evaluations: Comparison of Three Methods of Performance Appraiser Training." *Journal of Applied Psychology* 73 (1988), pp. 68–73.

Kamouri, A. L., and W. K. Balzer. "The Effects of Performance Sampling Methods on Frequency Estimation, Probability Estimation, and Evaluation of Performance Information." *Organizational Behavior and Human Decision Processes* 45 (1990), pp. 285–316.

Klimoski, R., and L. Inks. "Accountability Forces in Performance Appraisal." *Organizational Behavior and Human Decision Processes* 45 (1990), pp. 194–208.

Larson, J. R., and C. Callahan. "Performance Monitoring: How It Affects Work Productivity." *Journal of Applied Psychology* 74 (1990), pp. 530–538.

Londao, M., and A. J. Wohlers. "Agreement between Subordinate and Self-Ratings in Upward Feedback." *Personnel Psychology* 43 (1991), pp. 375–390.

Longenecker, C. O., H. P. Sims, and D. A. Gioia. "Behind the Mask: The Politics of Employee Appraisal." *Academy of Management Executive* 1 (1987), pp. 183–193.

Ludeman, Kate. "Customized Skills Assessments." *HRMagazine,* July 1991, pp. 67–85.

Maurer, T. J., and R. A. Alexander. "Contrast Effects in Behavioral Measurement: An Investigation of Alternative Process Explanations." *Journal of Applied Psychology* 76 (1991), pp. 3–10.

McEvoy, G. M., and P. F. Buller. "User Acceptance of Peer Appraisals in an Industrial Setting." *Personnel Psychology* 40 (1987), pp. 785–797.

McEvoy, G. M. "Public Sector Managers' Reactions to Appraisals by Subordinates." *Public Personnel Management* 19 (1990), pp. 201–212.

Meyer, Herbert. "A Solution to the Performance Appraisal Feedback Enigma." *Academy of Management Executive* 5 (1991), pp. 68–76.

Mohrman, A. M., S. M. Resnick-West, and E. E. Lawler. *Designing Performance Appraisal Systems.* San Francisco: Jossey-Bass, 1989.

Nathan, B. R., A. Mohrman, and J. Milliman. "Interpersonal Relations as a Context for the Effects of Appraisal Interviews on Performance and Satisfaction." *Academy of Management Journal* 34 (1991), pp. 352–369.

Nathan, B. R., and N. Tippins. "The Consequences of Halo 'Error' in Performance Ratings: A Field Study of the Moderating Effect of

Halo on Test Validation Results." *Journal of Applied Psychology* 75 (1990), pp. 290–296.

Pulakos, E. D., L. A. White, S. H. Oppler, and W. C. Borman. "Examination of Race and Sex Effects on Performance Ratings." *Journal of Applied Psychology* 74 (1989), pp. 770–780.

Sackett, P. R., and C. L. Z. DuBois, "Rater-Ratee Effects on Performance Evaluation: Challenging Meta-Analytic Conclusions." *Journal of Applied Psychology* 76 (1991), pp. 873–877.

Solomon, R. J. "Developing Job Specific Appraisal Factors in Large Organizations." *Public Personnel Management* 19 (1990), pp. 11–24.

Waldman, D. A., and B. J. Avolio. "Race Effects in Performance Evaluations: Controlling for Ability, Education, and Experience." *Journal of Applied Psychology* 76 (1991), pp. 897–901.

Williams, K. J., T. P. Cafferty, and A. S. DeNisi. "The Effect of Performance Appraisal Salience on Recall and Ratings." *Organizational Behavior and Human Decision Processes* 46 (1990), pp. 217–239.

NOTES

1. D. Waldman, and R. Kenett, "Improve Performance by Appraisals," *HRMagazine,* July 1990, pp. 60–69.

2. L. Fleury, R. Hanson, and J. McCaul, "Review System Supports Customer Focus," *HRMagazine,* January 1994, pp. 66–69.

3. Labor Letter, *The Wall Street Journal,* September 7, 1993, p. A1.

4. J. Laumeyer and T. Beebe, "Employees and Their Appraisal," *Personnel Administrator,* December 1988, pp. 76–80.

5. Robert McGarvey, "But I'm Doing a Great Job," *USAir Magazine,* May 1993, pp. 62–69.

6. H. J. Bernardin, "A Performance Appraisal System," in *Performance Assessment,* ed. R. A. Berk (Baltimore: Johns Hopkins University Press), pp. 277–304.

7. Kate Ludeman, "Customized Skills Assessments," *HRMagazine,* July 1991, pp. 67–85.

8. D. L. DeVries, A. M. Morrison, S. L. Shullman, and M. L. Gerlach, *Performance Appraisal on the Line* (New York: Wiley, 1981).

9. K. Wexley and R. Klimoski, "Performance Appraisal: An Update," in *Research in Personnel and Human Resources Management,* K. Rowland and G. Ferris, ed. (Greenwich, CT: JAI Press, 1984), vol. 2, pp. 35–80.

10. See M. M. Harris and J. Schaubroeck, "A Meta-Analysis of Self-Supervisor, Self-Peer, and Peer-Supervisor Ratings," *Personnel Psychology* 41, 1988, pp. 43–62; and G. C. Thornton, "Psychometric Properties of Self-Appraisals of Job Performance," *Personnel Psychology* 33, 1980, pp. 263–271.

11. C. C. Hoffman, B. R. Nathan, and L. M. Holden, "A Comparison of Validation Criteria: Objective versus Subjective Performance Measures and Self-Versus Supervisor Ratings," *Personnel Psychology* 44, 1991, pp. 601–619.

12. "Gender Gap," *The Wall Street Journal,* July 21, 1992, p. A1.

13. D. Campbell and C. Lee, "Self-Appraisal in Performance Evaluation: Development versus Education," *Academy of Management Review* 13, 1988, pp. 302–314.

14. Albert Karr, "Rating the Boss," *The Wall Street Journal,* July 11, 1991, p. A1; Kate Ludeman, "Upward Feedback Helps Managers

Talk the Talk," *HRMagazine,* May 1993, pp. 85–93; and Harry Gaines, "How Do You Rate?" *Sky,* September 1993, pp. 20–34.

15. J. Segal, "Ignorance Is No Defense," *HRMagazine,* April 1990, pp. 93–94.

16. N. Angel, "Evaluating Employees by Computer," *Personnel Administrator,* November 1989, pp. 67–72.

17. "Is Your Friendly Computer Rating You on the Job?" *U.S. News and World Report,* February 18, 1987, p. 66.

18. Mark Edwards, "Accurate Performance Measurement Tools," *HRMagazine,* June 1991, pp. 95–98.

19. Richard J. Newman, "Job Reviews Go Full Circle," *U.S. News & World Report,* November 1, 1993, pp. 21–22.

20. Robert C. Jones, Steve Quisenberry, and Gary W. Sawyer, "Business Strategy Drives Three-Pronged Assessment System," *HRMagazine,* December 1993, pp. 68–72.

21. Matthew Budman and Berkeley Rice, "The Rating Game," *Across the Board,* February 1994, pp. 35–38.

22. *Albemarle Paper Company* v. *Moody,* 422 U.S. 405, 1975.

23. D. L. Kirkpatrick, "Performance Appraisals, Your Questions Answered," *Training and Development Journal,* 1986, pp. 68–71.

24. Laumeyer and Beebe, "Employees and Their Appraisal."

25. Richard Ringer, David Balkin, and Wayne Boss, "Managing Employee Emotion," *HRMagazine,* May 1993, pp. 140–144.

26. Leon E. Wynter, "Black Managers Reject White Bosses' Criticism," *The Wall Street Journal,* February 2, 1994, p. B1.

27. Herbert Meyer, "A Solution to the Performance Appraisal Feedback Enigma," *Academy of Management Executive* 5, 1991, pp. 68–76.

28. Laumeyer and Beebe, "Employees and Their Appraisal."

29. F. J. Landy and J. L. Farr, "Performance Rating," *Psychological Bulletin,* April 1980, pp. 72–107.

30. F. Blanz and E. E. Ghiselli, "The Mixed Standard Scale: A New Rating System," *Personnel Psychology* 25, 1972, pp. 185–199.

31. D. A. Bownas and H. J. Bernardin, "Suppressing Illusory Halo with Forced-Choice Items," *Journal of Applied Psychology* 76, 1991, pp. 592–594.

32. D. Gold and B. Unger, "Evaluating Employees through Rating Scales," *HRNews,* July 1990, p. 5.

33. R. Rodgers and J. E. Hunter, "Impact of Management by Objectives on Organizational Productivity," *Journal of Applied Psychology* 76, 1991, pp. 322–326.

34. H. J. Bernardin and R. W. Beatty, *Performance Appraisal: Assessing Human Behavior at Work* (Boston: PWS Kent, 1984).

35. G. V. Barrett and M. C. Kernan, "Performance Appraisal and Terminations: A Review of Court Decisions Since Brito v. Zia with Implications for Personnel Practices," *Personnel Psychology* 40, 1987, pp. 489–503.

36. K. R. Murphy and W. K. Balzer, "Systematic Distortions in Memory-Based Behavior Ratings and Performance Evaluations: Consequences for Rating Accuracy," *Journal of Applied Psychology* 70, 1986, pp. 39–44.

37. See, for example, R. Smither, *The Psychology of Work and Human Performance* (New York: Harper & Row, 1988), p. 164.

38. P. R. Sackett, C. L. Z. DuBois, and A. W. Noe, "Tokenism in Performance Evaluation: The Effects of Work Group Representation on Male-Female and White-Black Differences in Performance Ratings," *Journal of Applied Psychology* 76, 1991, pp. 263–267.

39. See, for example, J. H. Harvey and G. Weary, "Current Issues in Attribution Theory and Research," in *Annual Review of Psychology* 35, ed. M. R. Rosenzweig and L. W. Porter, 1984, pp. 427–459; and M. J. Martinko and W. L. Gardner, "The Leader/Member Attribution Process," *Academy of Management Review* 12, 1987, pp. 235–249.

40. Fombrun and Laud, "Strategic Issues in Performance Appraisal: Theory and Practice." in *Current Issues in Personnel Management,* 3rd ed, K. Rowland and G. Ferris, ed. (Boston: Allyn & Bacon, 1986).

41. Clive Fletcher, "Appraisal: An Idea Whose Time Has Gone," *Personnel Management,* September 1993, pp. 34–37.

42. R. Miles and C. Snow, "Designing Strategic Human Resources Systems," *Orgaizational Dynamics,* 1983, pp. 36–52.

43. The following discussion is based on C. Lee, "Smoothing Out Appraisal Systems," *HRMagazine,* March 1990, pp. 72–76.

44. Norman R. Deets and D. Tyler, "How Xerox Improved Its Performance Appraisals," *Personnel Journal,* April 1986, p. 50; Michael F. Wolff, "Appraising Performance at Xerox Corporate R & D," *Research Management,* July–August 1987, p. 8; and Mary Riley and Richard Noland, "Beyond Performance Reviews," *Management Solutions,* October 1987, p. 15.

CHAPTER 11

STRATEGIC COMPENSATION SYSTEMS

Designing and implementing an effective compensation program is a critical human resource activity. It may be difficult to say exactly how much a compensation system can influence an organization, but the creative use of compensation plans can work to maximize human resource productivity and contribute significantly to the achievement of human resource and organizational objectives. A pay system can reinforce an overall corporate objective of increased profitability, focus on both individual and team effort, and emphasize both short-term and long-term strategies. How best to pay people has replaced downsizing as the human resource management challenge of the 1990s.[1]

CHAPTER OBJECTIVES

After you have studied this chapter, you should be able to
1. Describe the various influences on the design and implementation of compensation systems.
2. Discuss the lead, match, and lag pay level policies available to organizations.
3. Explain the concept of pay for performance and the advantages and disadvantages associated with it.
4. Summarize the major issues in communicating salary information.
5. Understand the relationship between motivation and compensation.
6. Differentiate between salary, incentives, commissions, profit-sharing plans, and gain-sharing plans for groups and individuals.
7. Be familiar with a variety of nonfinancial rewards that may be useful when designing compensation systems.

THE ELEVEN-MILLION-DOLLAR MEN[2]

While some retailers may find the going rough these days, Phillips-Van Heusen (PVH) is having its best years ever. PVH, a manufacturer of shirts, sweaters, and casual shoes, attributes its increased sales and earnings before interest and taxes to a deceptively simple incentive plan devised by its chair, Lawrence S. Phillips.

Each of the senior executives, regardless of the size of their operations, will earn $1 million if earnings per share (EPS) grow 35 percent during a four-year period. The first $500,000 is earned in increments when EPS goals are met each year. The second $500,000 is the bonus for making the combined target in the fourth year. Even if they miss their target one year, they can make it up by the last year and still earn the full $1 million.

Alison Bisno, director of research for an investment bank, states, "The incentive compensation program has been critical to the success, evolution, and expanding growth of Phillips-Van Heusen." In fact, the plan demonstrates that money motivates individual performance and it can be used to reinforce a team-oriented culture that focuses management's attention on achieving strategic goals.

Phillips had two goals in implementing this plan. The first goal was to aid refinancing after a successful but costly battle against an unfriendly takeover. The second goal was to help PVH gain a measure of control over its destiny by eliminating "the cyclical swings of its notoriously fickle business."

As retailers moved to limit the number of brands on their shelves or to push store brands, PVH found its merchandise being squeezed off the shelves of department stores and decided to fight back. In response, PVH expanded its wholesale business and created its own retail division, setting up a chain of specialty stores and factory outlets to sell its own products. The potential for competition between PVH's own wholesale and retail divisions had to be minimized. Thus, a major objective of the incentive plan was to foster camaraderie and cooperation between those units.

So far, the plan seems to be working. Soon after its introduction, the senior executives, already close friends, jelled as a team. They began to meet more frequently, talk more openly about operations, and work harder to make each division more profitable. Cooperative efforts multiplied. Salespeople in the sweater and shirt divisions teamed up to sell color-coordinated combinations, boosting sales for both divisions. All groups contributed recommendations for a new chain to upscale mall stores targeted at shoppers who have "outgrown The Gap."

Plan participants easily met their goals for the first year this plan was in operation. The second year, however, was tough on them. Even though the participants outlined and followed a detailed plan, the year was frought with unpredictable events that rendered the plan unsuccessful. For example, the revolt at Tiananmen Square hurt production of sweaters in China, and Hurricane Hugo closed three suppliers in Puerto Rico for two weeks. Last, the Campeau retail empire's financial problems delayed payments for PVH merchandise. Soft sales in the retail division sealed the company's fate, and it failed to reach that year's target.

Mike Culang, sweater division chief, spoke for all when he said, "It will be terribly difficult, but with our mind-set the way it is, if there is a way to make it, we will make it." Also, Phillips is truly satisfied with the results of his plan. "The plan reinforced the religion and put everybody in his own confessional. Now each of these guys is terribly supportive of every other division of this company. You don't find that very often in corporate America."

STRATEGIC CHOICES

The design of an organization's compensation system may have a critical impact on its ability to achieve its strategic goals. For this reason, the reward system's philosophy and objectives must reinforce and reflect the organization's culture, external environment, and business strategy.[3] Among other things, reward systems can influence (1) who is attracted to and who remains with an organization,[4] (2) an employee's motivation level,[5] and (3) the organization's operating costs.[6] Managers must face several strategic choices with respect to the organization's reward system.

1. Management must decide the *importance of external equity* in the organization's compensation system. This decision is manifested in the type of pay policy implemented by the firm. The firm must make the strategic choice as to how much to pay employees with respect to the competition. Is the firm going to pay the highest wages in the market to ensure attracting the most qualified applicants, or is the firm going to match the market salary or even pay less? This strategic choice is one of the most important choices an organization must make. It frequently forms the basis on which the rest of the compensation system is built.

   External equity occurs when an employer pays wage rates that correspond to those prevailing in the external labor markets. Factors that are potentially important to consider when defining the labor market include geography or the location of the organization, the education or technical background required, the industry type, licensing or certification requirements, and the experience required by the job.

   Wage and salary surveys are designed to help the compensation analyst make informed decisions about wage rates that will maintain external equity. An organization can choose to run its own survey or use data collected by others. Creating an in-house survey will result in up-to-date comparisons; however, these surveys can be costly. When designing a wage and salary survey, managers must be concerned about (a) selecting which jobs should be examined, (b) defining relevant labor markets, (c) selecting firms to be surveyed, (d) determining information to be asked, and (e) determining data collection techniques.

   Outside wage and salary surveys use data collected by others to determine external equity. Surveys are available from a variety of sources including the Bureau of Labor Statistics, trade groups, and professional compensation analysts (such as the Hay Group). Although less expensive than creating an in-house survey, using information collected by others may not be as relevant or timely.

2. An additional strategic choice a firm faces is *how closely the compensation plan will be linked to the organization's overall strategic plan.* It is important that the compensation plan reward behavior that will lead to the accomplishment of the organization's overall goals. Rewarding managers for meeting short-term goals at the expense of long-term goals may indicate a reward system that is inconsistent with the organization's overall strategy.

3. With respect to raises, a firm must choose between *merit pay raises (paying for performance)* or *across-the-board raises.* Firms that elect to pay for performance face

the challenge of setting standards of performance against which the employees can be compared. Firms that decide to provide equal raises across the board face the challenge of keeping highly productive workers motivated and committed to the organization.

4. Firms also must choose the *level of pay secrecy* the organization will enforce. Many firms have decided that how much an individual is paid is between the firm and that individual. Employees who violate this agreement may be terminated. Other firms have more open views on pay secrecy and publicly post the salaries of their employees.

5. An organization must also determine its stance on *internal equity* when designing compensation systems. Firms that strive to ensure that the pay structure among different jobs is based on the relative worth of these jobs to the organization have selected a strong internal equity stance. Other firms that determine pay based on the person in the job, not the job itself, may have internal inequity with respect to compensation.

Internal equity is the objective of setting wage rates that conform to the job's internal worth to the employer. A job evaluation is a formal process by which management assigns wage rates to jobs according to some preestablished formula. Most job evaluation techniques employ compensable factors in assessing job worth. A compensable factor provides a basis for defining the internal worth of a job. The most commonly employed compensable factors are (a) skills required by the job, (b) responsibility for people and/or equipment, (c) effort required, and (d) working conditions. Four general types of job evaluations can be seen in Exhibit 11.1. Job evaluation techniques can be differentiated on the basis of (a) whether the job being

EXHIBIT 11.1   **Typology of Job Evaluation Methods**

	Whole Job	Specific Job Factors
Job vs. Job	**Ranking Method**	**Factor Comparison Method**
	Identify the job with the most "worth" to the company. Identify the next job with the most worth. Continue this until all jobs are in a hierarchical order.	Select compensable factors and describe the jobs in terms of these factors. Rank the jobs on each factor. Weight each factor in terms of its relative importance to the organization. Calculate the total points for each job.
Job vs. Standard	**Classification Method**	**Point Method**
	Decide how many grade levels the job value structure is to be broken into (usually varies from 5 to 15) and write generic descriptions at each level. Compare the job descriptions with the description of the grade level. Assign each job to the grade level it most closely matches.	Select compensable factors and develop levels (with points attached) for each factor. Analyze the job in terms of the compensable factors and determine which point level best fits the job. Assign points for each factor for the total points for each job.

evaluated is *compared to other jobs* directly or *against some standard* and (b) whether the comparison is based on the *job as a whole* or on *specific factors* in the job.

6. Finally, managers must decide how to *mix intrinsic rewards* (rewards that come from performing the job) and *extrinsic rewards* (rewards that come from a person outside the job) when developing a compensation system. When monetary rewards are not available or applicable, firms must locate other means by which to reward employees. Managers can make the strategic choice to design jobs so that intrinsic rewards are available to workers.

EXTERNAL ENVIRONMENTAL VARIABLES

When developing and designing a compensation system, organizations must take into consideration the external environment in which they do business. Many external environmental factors impact an organization, but only a few have a direct effect on an organization's reward system. Three of these—the nature of the competition, the nature of the labor market, and governmental regulations—are discussed in the following sections.

NATURE OF THE COMPETITION

The level of competition a firm faces in the product market is an important consideration when designing a compensation system. When an organization has many product competitors, cost control assumes greater significance. Price pressures generally are downward, and increased costs due to salary increases cannot be passed on to customers without risking loss of market share. In this situation, noneconomic rewards (such as promotions, job enrichment, and training and development programs) may assume greater importance in the pay scheme. Few competitors, on the other hand, increase flexibility in the design of the compensation system because wage increases are absorbed into the cost of the product or service.

An example of an industry with few competitors is flight simulation training. Simulflite and FlightSafety International are the only two organizations (outside of individual airline companies) that provide pilots with such training. Because their services have a high level of demand and have no practical product substitutes, they are able to pass on any increase in costs to their customers.

NATURE OF THE LABOR MARKET

A discussion of the impact of the nature of the labor market on designing reward systems focuses on two issues: labor supply and demand and the wage levels that competitors are paying to their employees. When the supply of labor is greater than the demand, the competition among job applicants for a limited number of positions permits companies to pay lower salaries. When demand for labor is greater than the supply, competition for the scarce resource of labor increases, bidding up the cost of labor. Applicants can afford to "shop around" for a company that pays a higher salary when labor is in demand.

This is not the only way that wages paid by competitors in the labor market can influence a company's wages. Some industries or individual organizations pay higher salaries than others as a policy. Certainly, high-tech and research and development industries must attract highly qualified employees. One way to do this is to pay more than other employers in the area. The strategic choice of paying above the market rate is discussed in more detail later in the chapter.

GOVERNMENT REGULATIONS

Specific employment legislation affecting compensation decisions is addressed in Chapter 4, and it is included here again because of its significant organizational impact. Federal legislation affects almost every aspect of the compensation plan. It places a lower limit on wages that can be paid; it affects raise and incentive decisions; it proscribes wage discrimination; and it requires that certain benefits be paid for all employees.

Recent changes in tax legislation have further complicated benefit decisions for many companies and made it very difficult to determine the employment tax status of an organization's workers. For federal employment tax purposes, one set of rules applies to employees, and a completely different set applies to independent contractors. While the costs of misclassifying workers can be very costly, it is extremely difficult to categorize workers with accuracy. For example, an employee may be classified as a statutory employee, an employee whom the Internal Revenue Code specifically classifies as an employee for FICA and FUTA purposes, but as an independent contractor for income tax withholding purposes. This crossover of status makes it important for an organization to categorize the employee for each specific tax purpose rather than in one set category.[7]

A second recent governmental regulation change, the increase of the minimum wage, also has caused some companies problems with respect to compensation. Small businesses, which have had to increase pay rates to comply with the new wage law, have had to cut back on staff to stay in business. The owner of a small motel in Wisconsin noted that the increase in the minimum wage from $3.80 to $4.25 costs her motel about $5,000 a year. Raising room rates to cover this cost will only decrease occupancy rates and thus reduce income even further. Also, if the hotel really had an extra $5,000 to spend, it would much rather invest in new carpeting for the rooms than spend it on labor costs.[8]

The change in the minimum wage law, agreed to by Congress in late 1989, raised the minimum wage from $3.35 to $3.80 in April 1990. A second increase from $3.80 to $4.25 took effect April 1991. The law has a loophole that allows employers to pay a lower "training wage" to new employees for up to six months while they are learning the job.[9] Originally, the minimum wage law was designed to hold the minimum wages paid to unskilled or part-time workers at one half of the average U.S. hourly wage. However, it has not always reached its goal. Although the current hourly rate is still $4.25, Congress is considering raising the minimum wage. The history of the minimum wage is presented in Exhibit 11.2.

INTERNAL ENVIRONMENTAL VARIABLES

Internal as well as external environmental variables are important to organizations when developing compensation systems. Four of the most salient internal variables—corporate strategy, management philosophy, the type of job, and productivity—are examined in the sections that follow.

CORPORATE STRATEGY

The overall corporate strategy provides the direction for the organization. Because its focus is primarily long term, the pay system should be designed to support this focus. One way to accomplish this goal is to tie the compensation system to the developmental stage

EXHIBIT 11.2

The History of Minimum Wage

Date	Minimum Wage	Date	Minimum Wage
October 24, 1938	0.25	May 1, 1974	2.00
October 24, 1939	0.30	January 1, 1975	2.10
October 24, 1945	0.40	January 1, 1976	2.30
January 25, 1950	0.75	January 1, 1978	2.65
March 1, 1956	1.00	January 1, 1979	2.90
September 3, 1961	1.15	January 1, 1980	3.10
September 3, 1963	1.25	January 1, 1981	3.35
February 1, 1967	1.40	April 1, 1990	3.80
February 1, 1968	1.60	April 1, 1991	4.25

of the company. Different combinations of pay are designed to fit with the strategic conditions faced by the firm. As shown in Exhibit 11.3, six organizational stages are possible, ranging from start-up through maturity, decline, and renewal. Each of these cycles requires a different combination of base pay, incentives, and benefits.

For example, a mature organization would have several product lines and strong earnings. The focus of its human resource department would be on cost cutting, consistency of program application, and efficiency. The most effective pay mix would offer a competitive base pay, incentives, and benefits. It is possible that a single organization could have more than one compensation strategy and system. Within an organization, the various subdivisions or units may be in different stages in their life cycle. This would require separate compensation plans for different divisions.

EXHIBIT 11.3

Strategic Pay and the Organization Life Cycle

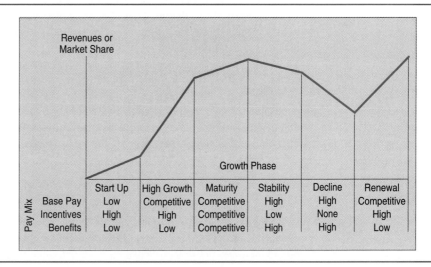

Pay Mix		Start Up	High Growth	Maturity	Stability	Decline	Renewal
	Base Pay	Low	Competitive	Competitive	High	High	Competitive
	Incentives	High	High	Competitive	Low	None	High
	Benefits	Low	Low	Competitive	High	High	Low

SOURCE: George Milkovich and Jerry Newman, *Compensation,* 2nd edition (Homewood, IL: BPI/Irwin, 1987), p. 16.

MANAGEMENT PHILOSOPHY

One component of management philosophy is the value it places on its human resources. This value is reflected in the relationship between management and line employees. Take, for example, this statement of company mission for Herman Miller, Inc., a manufacturer of office furniture. Central to the company's mission is that it attempts to share values, ideals, goals, and have respect for each person. To implement this mission, in 1950, Miller installed a plan that pays every employee a quarterly bonus based on attainment of production goals, employee cost-saving suggestions, customer satisfaction, and the company's return on assets. As you can see, an organization's culture is reflected in its pay system.

THE TYPE OF JOB

Jobs differ in many ways. These differences include the variety of tasks performed, the amount of physical or mental effort, the pleasantness of the working conditions, the degree of autonomy (control over how, when, and what to do), the responsibility for labor, materials, and equipment, and the amount of interaction with others.

Contrast the job of a coal miner with that of a computer analyst. A coal miner's job is mainly physical, involves a limited number of tasks under working conditions that most of us would find unpleasant (working underground, in dangerous conditions, with the potential for health problems in the long run) with little or no control over how, when, or what to do on the job. A computer analyst, on the other hand, uses mainly mental skills, may have a wide variety of tasks (debugging programs, developing and writing computer programs, and systems planning), a climate-controlled, generally pleasant environment with some freedom as to program development and perhaps control over job priorities. It's possible that both of these jobs could exist within a large organization. How can a company develop a system that equitably compensates both types of employees? Their job tasks vary considerably; yet, each is a valuable employee to the organization.

Where the employee performs his or her job may also change the value and compensation associated with the position. For example, in the early 1990s U.S. managers who accepted positions overseas often made more money than their stateside counterparts.[10] A manager who made $100,000 in the United States earned three times that when transferred to London. That same manager would have made close to a million dollars if transferred to Stockholm or Tokyo. Exhibit 11.4 indicates the items that were included in the higher salary.

Today, however, most multinational companies compensate their expatriates according to a fairly rigid formula. Often, that includes paying them their stateside salary, plus allowances for foreign taxes and the higher cost of overseas housing and basic goods and services. Although most companies will tack on a premium of 10–15 percent to a person's salary, these premiums are carefully crafted so that employees do not see their standard of living increase or decrease substantially.

PRODUCTIVITY

Productivity, as you have learned, is simply the ratio of outputs (product or service provided by the company) to inputs (for example, costs in terms of labor, capital, energy, materials, and machinery). Any increase in labor costs decreases productivity unless output increases or other costs decrease. How to minimize the impact of these salary increases on productivity requires careful consideration.

Now that we've examined some of the major external and internal environmental variables that influence compensation decisions, let's turn our attention to a number of

EXHIBIT 11.4	The Price of an Expatriate in London

Item	Cost
Base salary	$100,000
Foreign service bonus	15,000
Good and service differential	21,000
Housing costs	39,000
Relocation allowance	5,000
Air fare to London	2,000
Moving household goods	25,000
Company car	15,000
Schooling costs (2 children)	20,000
Annual home leave for family (4 persons)	4,000
U.K. personal income tax	56,000

Additional costs
   Language/culture training
   Selling home/cars
   Miscellaneous
	20,000

Total	$322,000

SOURCE: Adapted from J. Lublin, "Grappling with the Expatriate Issue," *The Wall Street Journal,* December 11, 1989, p. B1.

strategic options that must be considered. These options include the organization's pay level policy, the mix of extrinsic and intrinsic rewards, pay-for-performance systems, and pay secrecy versus openness.

STRATEGIC COMPENSATION OPTIONS

In developing a pay system, several policy decisions must be made. Three of the most critical are pay level policy, pay structure policy, and types of reward offered.

PAY LEVEL POLICY

PAY LEVEL
The average wage rate paid for a specific group of jobs.

EXTERNAL EQUITY
The degree to which an organization's wages are competitive with those of its competitors.

An organization's **pay level** is simply the average wage rate paid for a specific group of jobs.[11] Pay level is important because it influences both the organization's ability to attract and retain competent employees and its competitive position in the product market. Pay level policy refers to how an organization's pay level compares to its competitors' pay levels. The concept of **external equity,** the degree to which an organization's wages are competitive with those of its competitors, is reflected in a firm's pay level policy.

Basically, three pay level policy options may be chosen: lead, lag, or match.[12] Employers with a lead policy pay higher wages than the average wage paid in the labor market. Employers who choose a lag policy pay lower than average wages, while employers with a match policy "match" the market wage rate.

Why does an organization choose one pay level policy over another? Many factors go into the decision and several are outlined in Exhibit 11.5. However, the basic answer to this question is that the organization chooses the pay level that (1) maximizes its ability to attract and keep qualified employees, (2) is within its ability to pay, and (3) allows it to remain competitive in its product market.

EXHIBIT 11.5 **Environmental Factors Affecting Pay Policy**

Factors in the External Environment	Factors in the Internal Environment
Supply of Labor	Organization Size
Demand for Labor	Characteristics of the Work Force
Geographic Location of Company	Ability to Pay
Economic Conditions	Willingness to Pay
Product Competition	Unionization
Demand for Product	Desired Quality of Employee
Union Influence	Tradition
	Employer Prestige
	Ratio of Labor Costs to Total Costs
	Nature of the Job

Most organizations use a "match" policy. This enables them to recruit and retain a competent (but not superior) workforce, to pay their employees a wage that is perceived as fair, and to keep their labor costs in line with those of their competitors. Organizations who desire to attract the "cream of the crop" and therefore obtain higher product quality, lower turnover, less pay dissatisfaction, and therefore fewer unionization attempts or labor disputes select a lead policy. Firms that can offer employees some benefit (such as the ability to perform a job that is consistent with employees' beliefs and values) other than a high salary or that always face an overabundance of qualified labor can choose a lag policy.

Some firms also may use one form of pay policy at one point but may be forced to switch to another at some future point. One example of this occurred at Public Service Company of New Mexico, a utility company. In the early 1980s, Public Service faced economic prosperity, a positive regulatory environment, high growth, and an increase in available workers. During this time, Public Service prided itself on paying employees better than the going rate. In other words, it followed a lead pay policy. This policy served the company well until the end of the 1980s. At this time, a general downturn in the overall economy occurred. Further, deregulation and diversification entered the picture. Public Service was forced to cut 20 percent of its workforce to remain competitive and now pays its remaining employees well below market rates.[13]

PAY STRUCTURE POLICY

PAY RANGES
The range of wages allowed by a specific wage classification and the amount of overlap between the ranges.

A company must also make a decision about **pay ranges,** the range of wages allowed by a specific wage classification and the amount of overlap between the ranges. The government puts an absolute minimum on any pay range, but, in practice, an organization must decide on the maximum and minimum pay for any job or set of jobs in the pay structure. This maximum and minimum are based on external market wages and the internal job structure.

The results from a salary survey of 338 human resource professionals produced the following statistics with respect to pay range policies. First, 74 percent of the respondents reported that starting salaries for employees are generally in the first quartile of the pay range. Forty-three percent of the respondents indicated that a goal of the organization is to keep salaries near the midpoint of the pay range. With respect to exceeding the pay range maximum, 52 percent reported that individuals were "seldom" paid more than the maximum allowed; 31 percent reported that individuals were never paid above the maximum allowed in the pay range.[14]

A large spread between the minimum and maximum salary allowed in a pay range is termed a *wide pay range.* The wider the pay range, the longer the employee can stay in the same job and still receive pay increases. Wide pay ranges are common in organizations that have only a few pay grades. A pay grade is a group of jobs that have the same classification with respect to pay. Wide pay ranges are needed so that employees have room for movement in the pay range for a number of years before reaching a maximum. An organization with many pay grades, however, generally has narrower pay ranges, and the maximum paid for any job can be reached more quickly. Companies using this type of pay structure encourage their employees to receive pay raises through promotion and movement through pay grades instead of promotion and movement within the pay grade.

BROADBANDING
The collapsing of job clusters or grades of positions into a few wide bands which creates a flatter organizational structure.

Broadbanding is a relatively new concept that refers to the collapsing of job clusters or grades of positions into a few wide bands, creating a flatter organizational structure. Broadbanding is intended to focus management and employee attention on important matters in the delivery of pay and career development. One goal of broadbanding is to enhance the manager's ability to compensate people for what they contribute to the organization beyond what is called for in their job descriptions. Further, broadbanding can direct employee attention to career growth. A flat structure of pay opportunities makes it salient that only significant increases in job responsibilities merit moving to a higher pay band.[15]

Most organizations that choose to implement broadbanding have done so in the past two years. Managers at General Electric (GE) have used broadbanding extensively and have reported great success. Philip Morris, after investigating this pay practice, decided against implementing it. GE and Philip Morris have different organization strategies and cultures and those of Philip Morris did not meet the necessary requirements for successful broadbanding.[16] Examples of cases in which broadbanding is most likely to be successful follow:

1. The organization experiences a significant precipitous event.
2. The organization is ready for a change in its compensation system.
3. Top management is committed to broadbanding.
4. The organization has a decentralized compensation administration.
5. The managers are empowered.

WAGE COMPRESSION
Pay situation arising when new hires are brought in at about the same or higher salaries than the current employees.

One form of pay grades that has fallen from favor is the two-tier pay system. This system allows existing workers to maintain their wage level while new employees are paid at a lower wage rate. Only a decade ago, two-tier wage scales were an extremely useful tool for dealing with escalating labor costs. However, today those that remain are a thorn in the side of both management and labor. New employees, who worked side by side with the longer-tenured workers, performed the same jobs, and received less pay, began to complain. As the size of the workforce receiving the higher wages began to shrink due to retirement and attrition and the number of the lower paid employees began to increase, the inequities between the two groups became too great. Only a few of the newly negotiated contracts now hold two-tier wage level clauses.[17] Interestingly, the opposite problem—**wage compression**—is even more prevalent. This most often occurs when, due to inflation, new hires are brought in at about the same or higher salaries than the current employees. Organizations argue that to attract qualified employees, they must be willing to pay a premium. Unfortunately, organizations do not always adjust the salary levels of the current employees, which can lead to perceptions of inequity and therefore dissatisfaction among employees.

EXTRINSIC VERSUS INTRINSIC REWARDS

So far our discussion has centered around the financial reward system for the organization. However, financial remuneration is not the only alternative the company has for compensating its employees. Economic downturns in the 1980s and early 1990s have led to increased cost consciousness for many companies. Companies have found it difficult to increase salaries, provide cash bonuses, or otherwise provide tangible rewards to their employees. In the absence of cash, some firms are looking for alternative ways to motivate employees.

Some nonmonetary motivators that managers have reached for during lean times include intellectual challenges, a sense of purpose, more flexibility and responsibility, greater freedom and recognition, and increased input in decision making. To instill a sense of purpose, managers have doubled the praise bestowed on their staff to let their employees know how much their work is appreciated. Other managers have tried to assign extremely challenging projects to employees to increase their mental stimulation. Assigning employees challenging projects can keep them from becoming bored and increase their intrinsic motivation for the job. Offering an employee a change in job title, which includes more prestige, also can be an effective nonmonetary reward. Finally, companies have found that flexibility is important in lean times. Sharper Image relaxed its dress code at headquarters for employees who did not meet the public. Employees are now allowed to wear sweaters and slacks and can even wear jeans on Fridays.[18]

What kinds of benefits do individuals get from the nonmonetary rewards? Some examples are a sense of pride and feeling of accomplishment when a job is done well, pleasure received from doing a task that is interesting and challenging, participation and involvement in decision making, and an opportunity for personal and professional growth. The important point is that the design of the job itself, how it is performed, and what one wears while performing it can be used to reward the individual. These types of rewards can have a powerful effect on motivation.

A STRATEGIC APPROACH TO COMPENSATION

An organization's compensation system should be consistent with the overall strategy of the organization. As discussed earlier, Miles and Snow observed that successful firms displayed a consistent strategy supported by complementary organizational structures, designs, and management processes. They identified three fundamental organizational strategies: the defender strategy (seeks narrow and relatively stable product-market domains), the prospector strategy (continually searches for product and market opportunities and experiments with response to environmental trends), and the analyzer strategy (operates in two types of product-market domains—one relatively stable and the other changing).[19]

In defender organizations, compensation systems are oriented toward an employee's position in the organizational hierarchy. The focus is on internal consistency and equity. Compensation is primarily driven by superior/subordinate differentials. Prospector organizations, on the other hand, are oriented toward employee performance (as opposed to hierarchical position) and focus on external performance (as opposed to hierarchical position) and on external competitiveness and equity. Total compensation packages are oriented toward incentives and are driven by recruitment needs. Finally, analyzer organizations are primarily oriented toward hierarchical positions although performance is sometimes considered. Analyzers try to balance both internal consistency with external competitiveness.

PAY FOR PERFORMANCE

It used to be that hourly workers were paid by the hour, salaried workers were paid by the year, and only upper management received bonuses. Many companies now, however, have decided that this method does not work well enough and are experimenting with a variety of pay concepts to improve employee performance.

If a major goal of compensation is to motivate employees to work at their best level, then pay for performance is an intuitively appealing idea. After all, employees who are more productive are more valuable to the organization and should be rewarded for their superior performance.

The move toward paying employees for their contributions, not simply for their time spent at work, has been driven by the need for U.S. firms to be more productive—to do more with less. The "less" normally extends into pay with pay-for-performance plans, which usually start with reduced base wages and salaries but reward employees with handsome bonuses for hitting targets or meeting goals.[20]

The types of firms that have found ways to incorporate a pay-for-performance reward system vary greatly. For example, in the early 1990s, American Airlines ground personnel, who were represented by the Transport Workers Union, ratified a contract that tied pay hikes to performance. Under this contract, baggage handlers could earn pay increases by getting luggage to passengers more quickly. This type of contract incentive provided a benefit to all involved, including travelers, the airline, and the baggage handlers.[21] Pay for performance systems also have been introduced on Wall Street. Shearson Lehman for example, introduced a plan called BONUS. Each letter in BONUS stands for a specific way in which a stock can perform: buy, outperform, neutral, underperform, and sell. Analysts are expected to rate stocks in terms of these outcomes, and their predictions are checked against what the stocks actually did using computers at the end of the year. Analysts' bonuses are related to how well they predicted over the year.[22]

The two pay-for-performance systems described above have one clear advantage over many other pay-for-performance systems: it is easy to measure performance. With respect to the baggage handlers, there is a specific time at which the plane's cargo doors can be opened. This time can be registered and compared to the time when the luggage from that flight begins to reach the luggage carousel. Similarly, Shearson can compare the actual data about the stocks and ratings made by the analysts and develop a result that can't be questioned.

Quantifying and defining performance standards is often a stumbling block when developing pay-for-performance systems. For such systems to work effectively, distinctions among employees' work must be made. However, because most managers are unwilling to make these distinctions and because few companies force them to do so, most pay raises simply move in a lockstep fashion. Further, frequently it is a struggle to determine what workplace behavior is fair and meaningful to measure and reward. The measures frequently are global measures of safety and quality that, although they may be easier to quantify, may not be the workplace behavior that will actually increase productivity.[23]

The difficulty involved in determining and quantifying performance standards is not the only barrier to implementing a pay-for-performance system. Other problems rest in the traditional mindset of employers with respect to what employee compensation should include. For example, many firms believe that they have an obligation to keep employee pay even with inflation. This is normally accomplished by cost-of-living raises, which are equal across the board. While only 2.3 million workers were covered by a cost-of-living agreement in 1991, down from over 6 million in 1977, many more have enjoyed the benefit of cost-of-living raises.[24] After providing employees with cost-of-living raises, frequently little money is left to reward outstanding performers. Similarly, if firms strive to maintain external equity and tie their pay scales to what the competition is paying, the majority of money earmarked for raises may end up being spread across the board, not to the most productive workers. Finally, companies can inhibit their ability to use a pay-for-performance system by striving to keep all workers at the midpoint of the salary range and by allowing managers to provide inflated performance appraisals, which increase expectations of large and deserved raises.[25]

How the pay-for-performance system is developed and implemented, who decides performance based raises, and who benefits from pay-for-performance systems also affect the success of the programs. Pay-for-performance systems that were implemented via a "slam dunk" approach (someone from the top ordered someone below to implement a pay-for-performance system—pronto) frequently fail. The parameters of successful pay-for-performance systems must be negotiated and agreed to by all involved. In addition, in some environments, pay-for-performance systems are not appropriate, and introducing a system in these environments will result only in failure.[26]

Once implemented, the way the program is managed also can result in problems. For example, in many firms, the immediate supervisor determines the merit increases subordinates will be paid, which allows them an extremely broad level of discretion and a good degree of control over the workers.[27] While middle-level managers may have the ability to determine the merit increases for their subordinates, they are all but forgotten in pay-for-performance reward systems. According to compensation consultants, barely 1 percent of the salary paid to middle-level executives earning from $20,000 to $50,000 will be paid through a pay-for-performance system.[28] Further, middle-level managers are frequently evaluated to satisfy budgetary needs, not to reward performance. If merit raises are provided, they are far too small and not as much, proportionally, as they should be with respect to lower-performing colleagues.[29]

 Pay-for-performance reward systems have been implemented in an unlikely location—Japan. Once noted for paying for amount of time in a particular pay grade and rewarding seniority, Japan has begun to take steps to link employee pay with performance. Much of the change can be traced to the changing demographics in the Japanese workforce. As the age of the workforce increases, more and more employees expect to be promoted, because promotion after a certain time in grade was common in the past. However, with the top-heavy situation being experienced by Japanese firms, these traditions must change. The change has frequently been a push for pay and promotion for performance. Nissan is a good example of a Japanese company looking to change. After dropping the courtesy titles such as *kacho* (section chief) that employees attached to their supervisors' names, Nissan told workers that it would base promotions on ability, rather than tenure. Ryobi, a die cast maker, took pay for performance one step further and now bases middle managers' salaries on performance. This is quite a switch from the tenure-based salary structure that had been in place since the company began. Ryobi hopes that the change in compensation will increase managers' activity and spur initiative.[30]

Ryobi's desire to increase managers' activity and initiative is but one of the positive outcomes that can stem from a well-designed pay-for-performance reward system. Other potential benefits include a movement toward focusing on the results rather than on the methods and focusing on the group or the whole instead of the individual.[31] Pay-for-performance systems also can be used to get employees to learn to think like shareholders. This is the main goal of the pay-for-performance system at General Dynamics. J. R. Mellor, chairman and CEO of General Dynamics, explains that if management can get employees to think and act like shareholders, this partnering of interest will result in financial rewards for both. In addition, these rewards will be tied to the long-term success of the organization.[32]

EXECUTIVE PAY AND PAY FOR PERFORMANCE

Many elements of the total compensation package are offered to top executives. Frequently, an executive's base salary is the lowest form of compensation received. Instead of a high base salary, executives receive a combination of perks that lead to a total compensation package that is well above the average pay of the workers or shareholders of the firm. The perks that are included in a compensation package differ with respect to the industry, the board of directors and the firm. However, Exhibit 11.6 provides a list of some of the more common ones.

Some of the items that have been added to the list of executive compensation perks in the past few years have created some controversy. One such item is pension guarantees to protect executives from hostile takeovers and bankruptcies. Shareholders and employees argue that it is not fair that they risk losing their investments and jobs when the firm is taken over or files for bankruptcy while top executives stand to lose nothing. Companies defend the action, saying that it protects executives from losing the benefits that they have earned. Further, companies that normally offer such a plan are in some trouble in the first place. It is difficult to retain qualified top executives in troubled firms without some type of guarantee.[33]

A second issue that concerns many stakeholders is the increased use of stock options in executive compensation plans. A stock option gives the holder the right to buy a certain number of shares at a set price some time in the future. Because the benefits of stock options depend on the stock price, this option does not necessarily guarantee a large payoff. However, many stock option grants today are so large that even a small increase in the price of the stock could yield a sizable payout.

Such guaranteed gains in executive compensation over the past few years have angered many stakeholders.[34] The tough economic times have made employees, who have been asked to tighten their belts and do more with less by top executives in their firms, ask the executives, "What about you?" For example, when the top management of United Press International (UPI) asked workers for a 90-day, 35 percent wage

EXHIBIT 11.6   **Top Executive Perks Frequently Included in Compensation Packages**

Perk	Percentage of CEO/Presidents who Reported Having this Perk
Company-owned or leased car for business use	70
Entertainment expense account	65
Telephone credit cards	58
Company car for personal use	55
Supplemental life insurance	50
Physical exams	40
Tax preparation assistance	30
Dining/social club memberships	25
Country club memberships	25
Car phone	22

SOURCE: Adapted from T. J. Bergmann, H. Gunderson, W. Weil, and B. R. Baliga, "Rewards Tied to Long-term Success," *HRMagazine,* May 1990, p. 68.

reduction, union officials said yes, but only if managers took an equal cut and no bonuses were awarded to executives.[35]

Another way in which top level executives' pay for performance can be evaluated is with respect to how much their firm gave to shareholders, or shareholder return.[36] These calculations were performed by *Business Week* in its annual Executive Pay issue. The top five CEOs who gave their shareholders the most and the bottom five CEOs who gave their shareholders the least are presented in Exhibit 11.7. The exhibit also shows another set of interesting results from this report: the top and bottom five CEOs whose firms did the best and worst with respect to the CEO's individual pay.[37]

Many people agree that CEO compensation systems may need to be revamped but not on how this revamping should be accomplished.[38] Some groups are suggesting reviving the fixed-ratio theory of executive pay.[39] This theory is based on the idea that the highest-paid executives in the firm should make no more than X times the amount earned by the average worker in the firm (that is, a ratio of X to 1). Agreement with respect to what X should be is not clear. For example, Socrates, the Greek philosopher, suggested 5 to 1 as a solid ratio. However, more recently, Peter Drucker, the renowned management consultant, suggested a 20-to-1 ratio. One firm, Ben and Jerry's, implemented a lowest to highest wage ratio of 7 to 1 along with other benefits and bonuses.[40]

It is thought that firms that exhibit too great a differential between the pay for the CEO and for the average worker are less effective. The higher differential leads to less trust, less teamwork, and overall, a less effective organization. In reality, however, this theory does not appear to be true. Michael Eisner, CEO of Walt Disney, makes over 5,000 times more than the average Walt Disney employee, assuming that the average pay at Disney is $40,000. But Walt Disney is known for its wonderful work environment and continued high overall corporate performance and, therefore, does not fit the theory. On the other hand, U.S. Presidents make a mere 10 times more than the average civil servant. However, their bureaucratic governments are not reflective of teamwork, nor is the "senior management" of the United States government often viewed as trustworthy by the majority of the U.S. public.[41] It appears that the fixed ratio theory is not the answer to executive compensation problems.

An alternative plan to make CEOs more accountable for their pay follows three basic steps:

1. Boards should require CEOs to hold substantial amounts of company stock. This makes them view what is good for the shareholders as good for themselves as well.
2. Salary, bonuses, and stock options should be structured to provide big rewards for superior performance and big penalties for poor performance. This means that the pay-for-performance system has no guaranteed base salary for CEOs. Instead, performance is tied to pay in both directions.
3. The threat of dismissal for poor performance should be made real. Not only is the CEO's compensation tied to firm performance, but the position of CEO should be too.[42]

PAY FOR PERFORMANCE AT INDIVIDUAL AND GROUP LEVELS

Although often considered as a method of payment for CEOs, the concept of pay for performance is being implemented at all levels in the organization in a variety of ways. The methods can be divided into three major types: individual, group, and a combination of the two. For individuals, pay for performance can take the form of merit pay, incentives, and bonuses. At the group level, profit sharing, gain sharing, and stock

EXHIBIT 11.7 CEO Pay-for-Performance Results (1991–93)

EXECUTIVES WHO GAVE SHAREHOLDERS THE MOST FOR THEIR PAY

CEO	Firm	Total Pay In Thousands	Shareholder Return
John P. Morgridge	Cisco Systems	$ 967	1,052%
Warren E. Buffett	Berkshire Hathaway	300	145
Craig O. McCaw	McCaw Cellular Communication	353	80
Raymond J. Noorda	Novell	522	152
Michael D. Rose	Promus	2,754	815

EXECUTIVES WHO GAVE SHAREHOLDERS THE LEAST FOR THEIR PAY

CEO	Firm	Total Pay In Thousands	Shareholder Return
Michael D. Eisner	Walt Disney	$215,911	70%
Anthony J.F. O'Reilly	H.J. Heinz	114,177	13
Roberto C. Goizueta	Coca-Cola	89,914	99
Charles P. Lazarus	Toys "R" Us	77,618	82
Sanford I. Weill	Travelers	137,193	249

EXECUTIVES WHOSE COMPANIES DID THE BEST RELATIVE TO THEIR PAY

CEO	Firm	Total Pay in Thousands	Average Return on Equity
John P. Morgridge	Cisco Systems	$ 967	35.1%
William H. Gates III	Microsoft	979	31.4
Warren E. Buffett	Berkshire Hathaway	300	6.2
Gordon M. Binder	Amgen	2,668	29.6
Lawrence A. Hough	Student Loan Marketing	3,264	45.1

EXECUTIVES WHOSE COMPANIES DID THE WORST RELATIVE TO THEIR PAY

CEO	Firm	Total Pay in Thousands	Average Return on Equity
Leon Hess	Amerada Hess	$ 900	−2.1%
Ronald W. Allen	Delta Air Lines	2,127	−20.2
Philip E. Lippincott	Scott Paper	2,515	−4.6
Thomas H. Cruikshank	Halliburton	2,400	−4.5
James A. Unruh	Unisys	4,654	−99.9

SOURCE: Adapted from John Byrne and Lori Bongiorno, "Special Report," *Businessweek,* April 25, 1994.

ownership are the most prevalent.[43] Each of these options will be discussed in the sections that follow. This discussion begins by examining base pay and then introduces the various types of pay for performance plans most commonly used today.[44]

BASE PAY

However a system is designed, most compensation programs use some form of **base pay,** which is the basic cash received for the work performed, adjusted for the individual's skill, education, experience, or some other attribute. The base pay may be either hourly (paid by the hour) or salaried (paid weekly, biweekly, monthly, or yearly). Base pay can be supplemented by incentives, lump-sum bonus payments, or some other form of extra compensation.

MERIT PAY

Perhaps the most familiar form of pay-for-performance plan is merit pay, which rewards work behaviors that have already occurred. Frequently, merit raises are based on the level of the individual's performance in the past year relative to some standard of performance. Merit pay can be given either as an increase to the base salary or as a lump-sum payment.

A primary issue in merit pay-for-performance systems is whether pay truly is based on performance. Many researchers believe that the majority of merit pay systems simply do not work. Merit pay does not increase productivity because the difference in merit pay between the outstanding and poor performers is so small that the pay increase ends up being no incentive at all. For example, one survey of 459 companies found that top performers received, on average, a 7.7 percent increase while average performers received an average increase of 4.7 percent. Although these figures appear to be significantly different, the difference in pay after taxes is approximately 20 dollars a week for a $40,000 employee. In these terms, the monetary increase is barely enough to cover lunch out for the week and can hardly be a motivating factor for high-quality workers.[45]

Another issue in merit pay-for-performance plans is whether employees perceive the relationship between pay and performance, if it does exist. Because it is often so unclear how a person got a higher or lower raise than another, it takes an enormous leap of faith for an employee to determine that pay and performance are really related. To address these problems, companies are getting rid of subjective appraisals and are setting up bonus plans based on specific performance goals. These plans include a strong positive correlation with performance. If performance increases, so does pay. If, on the other hand, performance goes down, so does pay.[46]

When considering whether a performance-based pay system would work for an organization, the potential benefits and costs must be weighed carefully. Four major considerations are listed below.

1. If an organization employs *mostly* professionals, implementing a merit program is risky. Professional employees often have a marketable skill for which employers are always willing to pay. Thus, if the new merit compensation system does not meet their expectations of what their compensation should be, they will be likely and able to change jobs.
2. Employees who like what they are doing and who are enjoying a good deal of intrinsic motivation from their jobs may not like the extra pressure of external rewards placed on their job when a merit system is implemented. In this case, it is better to let the employees enjoy their job without adding performance pressures.
3. If cooperation, teamwork, and work groups are valued above competition, individual initiative, and superstars, then a merit pay plan is not advisable. Merit plans tend to make individuals work to better themselves, perhaps even at the expense of others in the workplace.
4. For any merit pay system to be effective, management must enforce it. If managers are unable or refuse to take on the tough roles required by a merit pay system, such as providing accurate performance appraisals, the system will not work.[47]

INCENTIVES

Like merit plans, incentive plans tie pay to some standard of performance. This standard can be defined as cost-saving goals, quality standards, or production levels, among others. However, incentives differ from merit pay in that they are future oriented; they are used to induce desired behavior. Their time orientation may be short term, long term, or a combination. They also may be tied to individual and/or group performance.

STRAIGHT PIECEWORK PLAN

A type of individual incentive plan that pays a constant amount for each unit that is produced.

STANDARD HOUR PLAN

A type of individual incentive plan that ties pay to a standard amount of time that it takes to perform a service or complete a task.

Most individual incentive plans are of two types: (1) the **straight piecework plan,** which pays a constant amount for each unit that is produced and (2) the **standard hour plan,** which ties pay to a standard amount of time that it takes to perform a service or complete a task. Under a straight piecework plan, an assembly line worker may receive 25 cents for each fishing tie that is completed. An example of the standard hour plan might be found at an appliance repair shop. Standard rates are determined for doing certain repairs, based on the average length of time it usually takes to do the job. If the standard time for a motor repair job is two hours, the repair person is paid for two hours. If the job is finished in less than two hours, the repair person is still paid the full amount. On the other hand, if the job takes longer than two hours, the repair person still earns the same amount.

Many companies have combined the basic incentive plan with a form of year-end bonus. Lincoln Electric in Cleveland is a shining example of a successful piecework plan instituted in 1934. Lincoln pays each factory worker for each acceptable piece that is produced. In addition, each employee receives a year-end bonus based on a yearly merit rating of the employee's dependability and ideas as well as quality and amount of output. For employees, the payoff has been bonuses averaging almost 98 percent of yearly wages. For Lincoln, the payoff has been operating for 54 years without a losing quarter and 40 years without a layoff.

Group plans are similar to individual plans in that pay is tied to performance, but a major goal is to increase cooperative efforts and coordinate activities. Essentially, incentives are based on an increase in profits or a decrease in costs, relative to a "base year." The size of the group may range from work teams to the entire organization, with unitwide and organizationwide plans growing in popularity over the last 10 years.

The use of both individual and group incentive plans by all sizes of firms continues to increase. In 1993 it was estimated that over half of all companies offered some form of incentive to workers below the top executive level. One reason for the increase in use of incentives is that they seem actually to work. For example, introducing an incentive plan to workers has helped Domino's Pizza to see an increase in sales, Ford Motor Company to improve morale and quality of work, Avis to reduce customer complaints by 35 percent in one year, and Warner Lambert Company to witness an increase in the performance of its managers.[48]

There probably are as many incentive plans existing as there are firms using them. However, there is some agreement on the types of plans that work best. Two of three companies that implemented incentive plans indicated that productivity increased when the plan offered to pay incentives to workers in discrete units for meeting specific targets.[49] One small company, headed by Hugh Aaron, that made color concentrates for the plastics industry capitalized on this formula and was able to increase productivity during even the leanest times.

After witnessing a flat profit line month after month after a period of intense growth, Hugh Aaron decided that something had to be done. To increase sales, he added to the salesforce, increased advertising, and purchased more equipment to enable him to produce more product. Profit continued to remain flat. His strategy did allow him to win some new clients, but he lost an equal number. He decided it was time to take a new approach, and he began focusing on the production line.

An incentive plan was introduced to reward plant workers when each production line produced more than the historical average of items per hour. Because the production line was run by a group of workers, teamwork improved and "slackers" received so much social pressure that most quit. When members of a team quit, the remaining team members requested that those positions not be filled. Because the bonus was split with the entire production line, fewer workers meant bigger rewards for the remaining workers. The new incentive system allowed production that used to take more than 100 employees to be performed with less than 40 employees, and production increased more than 50 percent.

The incentive plan clearly produced a win-win situation. For every dollar in bonus the employees earned, the company earned two. Management met with the workers to express its appreciation for the level of performance it was receiving and was informed that even more could be produced, but only if management would make one promise. The promise was that if the workers did increase productivity even further, the historical average production figures on which the incentive program was based would not be changed. Management quickly agreed, in writing, and production levels increased to a point where the profits and productivity were higher than either side ever dreamed.[50]

Not all incentive programs result in a happy ending. Nearly one-third of the respondents to a survey of over 600 companies using incentive programs stated that their programs were ineffective or needed improvements. One reason that some of the programs did not work is that they were introduced primarily because the competition was doing the same thing. When the goals and conditions surrounding the plan are not clearly thought out and linked to overall firm performance goals, any incentive program is doomed to failure.[51]

SKILL-BASED PAY

A form of incentive-based pay wherein employees are paid for the skills they possess, not just the skills performed.

A form of incentive-based pay that has received a great deal of attention in the past few years is **skill-based pay.** Under a skill-based pay plan, employees are paid for the skills they possess, not just the skills performed. Among the advantages of this type of pay system is reduced competition among workers for higher supervisory ratings. Since an individual's pay is determined by his or her ability, not the supervisor's rating, competition between workers is reduced. Similarly, supervisor costs decrease because the workers' skills increase, they take on the responsibility for functions previously performed by supervisors. Finally, employees begin to have a greater understanding of how each position fits into the overall production process.

While the advantages of a skill-based pay plan seem impressive, some disadvantages are associated with it. First, the training costs are high. Frequently, the skills needed by workers are job or company specific and for the employees to gain these skills, in-house training must occur. The costs of setting up the programs and reduced production during the times employees are attending the training classes make a skill-based pay plan a costly proposal. An additional cost involved in this type of incentive program is the increase in the overall hourly wage costs. As employees complete the training programs, the overall hourly wage costs will increase. While highly trained employees allow the firm more flexibility, the wage costs must still be considered. Finally, even though employees see a skill-based pay plan as fair, compensation problems can still occur. Disagreements about the difficulty of the training, the time required, and the frequency with which the skills are required to be used may arise. Ways with which to deal with these problems must be developed.[52]

STAY BONUSES
A variety of cash bonuses and other inducements that firms offer to keep valued workers on the payroll during corporate reorganizations or closedowns.

The increase in mergers, acquisitions, takeovers, and shutdowns in the past several years has produced a new type of incentive: stay bonuses. **Stay bonuses** include a variety of cash bonuses and other inducements offered by firms to keep valued workers on the payroll during corporate reorganizations or closedowns. Frequently offered only to employees at higher levels in the organization, stay bonuses have begun to trickle down to even the lowest levels of the workforce. For example, an office equipment company paid sales commissions even when there were no sales to maintain "business as usual" while it prepared to close. Often the most likely lower-level employees to benefit from stay bonuses are workers who have skills that are difficult to replace. These skills may be job or company specific, or simply a skill that is currently in demand in the marketplace. Other employees who may be involved in stay bonuses are experienced workers. For example, when Rouge Steel Company was acquired by Marico Acquisition Corporation, experienced workers were offered bonuses of up to $13,000 over three years if they would remain with the firm.[53]

GAIN-SHARING PLANS

Although gain-sharing plans have been around for over 50 years, their recent increase in popularity has made them the fastest-growing type of incentive. Exhibit 11.8 lists several types of gain-sharing plans used by both manufacturing and service firms and indicates their usage. Gain-sharing plans involve a participative management approach. The pay for gains results from a reduction of costs, whether or not the organization is profitable at year end. Gain-sharing plans mold employees' perceptions about what they need to do to improve the organization's results overall and along the way.[54]

One widely used cost-saving plan that was developed in 1937 is the Scanlon plan. The Scanlon plan focuses on decreasing labor costs without decreasing output. The two major components of the plan are (1) the development of a productivity norm and (2) the use of a dual-committee system to encourage companywide participation in decision making. In developing a productivity norm, a base year is chosen that is neither a boom nor a bust year. The base year also must be fairly recent so that it represents current factors in the organizational environment. Worker committees are responsible for evaluating suggestions from employees about how to cut costs or improve productivity. Money is added to a bonus pool created each time that output exceeds the productivity norm. Monthly a portion of the fund is distributed to the employees and a portion is reserved in case of a poor month. Anything remaining in the pool is paid out at the end of the year.[55]

The Rucker plan, a second gain-sharing program, is also based on employee involvement but does not make as extensive use of employee committees as does the Scanlon plan. Instead, a suggestion box may be introduced in place of employee

EXHIBIT 11.8   **Number and Percentage of Firms Using Various Types of Gain-Sharing Programs**

Type of Plan	Number Using	Percentage Using
Customized plans	95	54.000
Improshare	47	27.000
Scanlon plans	34	19.000
Rucker plan	1	00.006

SOURCE: Adapted from E. Ost, "Gain Sharing's Potential," *Personnel Administrator,* July 1989, p. 93.

HR CHALLENGE

Improshare

Programs based on Improshare stress quality and quantity goals derived from engineering standards. The bonus formula used in these types of plans is based on productivity standards that emphasize quality and quantity in relation to total labor hours expended. Improshare plans need not include an employee involvement component, but such an element has been used successfully in conjunction with quality circles and other types of work team situations.

Carrier, a subsidiary of United Technologies, introduced Improshare to its employees in 1988. In its first year, productivity increased 24 percent over its base year (1986), and rejects decreased dramatically.

Savings in labor costs are split 50–50 between the company and its employees, with each employee receiving the same percentage bonus. In 1988, 2,500 employees shared $3 million in bonus pay. Carrier claims that its success is due to employee involvement. Plant productivity is posted daily on the bulletin board; quarterly meetings to discuss the budget, business conditions, and the economy are held with all employees in groups of 70 to 80; and employees are encouraged to talk to plant managers about their ideas.

SOURCE: Adapted from Edward Ost, "Gain Sharing's Potential," *Personnel Administrator,* July 1989, pp. 92–96.

---

committees. The Rucker plan also has a bonus formula that is based on value added. Because it is less radical than the Scanlon plan, the Rucker plan is frequently used by firms attempting to change their traditional management style by slowly adding employee involvement.[56] Unlike the typical Scanlon plan, the Rucker value-added formula allows workers to benefit from savings in production-related materials and supplies. Many of these plans also have a reserve pool set aside for low productivity months. If the money in the reserve pool is not used during the year, it is paid out as an additional bonus to employees at the end of the year.[57] A more recent innovation in gain sharing is Improshare, developed in the 1970s by Mitchell Fein.

Successful gain-sharing plans can produce a number of important results for organizations as noted in the Improshare example. However, when deciding whether to implement a gain-sharing plan to achieve some of these benefits, several factors must be considered. First, it is important to clearly define the eligible employees of a group or unit to be included. Who is selected to be included and excluded may very well determine the success of the plan. Second, a great deal of time should be spent specifying the measures and formula calculations that will be used to determine the rewards. The measures and calculations must be easy enough to implement and explain to those involved, but they must also be accurate and reward only the behavior that helps produce the wanted results. Finally, the proportion of total gains to be allocated to eligible employees and the frequency with which these gains will be paid must be clearly defined. The program should be designed to reward the behavior desired as soon after it occurs as possible.[58]

More is involved in implementing a successful gain-sharing plan than simply delineating its parameters. Management must also be involved and help to make the program work. Most of the items in the following list of common qualities found in over 300 successful gain-sharing programs fall directly on the shoulders of management.

1. *Commitment.* The most critical factor that has been found to make or break a gain-sharing program is the level of commitment to the program by the management of the firm. Gain-sharing plans almost always succeed in organizations where the man-

agement staff works diligently to build a culture in which respect, cooperation, and communication are the norm.

2. *Simplicity.* The overall design of the plan, specifically the formulas, must be simple to use and to explain. When the plans are confusing to explain and interpret, mistrust increases and commitment decreases.

3. *Involvement.* Companies that have implemented successful gain-sharing programs have found ways to involve the workers and the management. Finding ways to get people to work together to achieve goals is one key to producing an accepted and successful gain-sharing program.

4. *Communication.* For employees to understand why the gain-sharing program is important to the company, information that is considered "for top level employees only" must be communicated to them. This information includes good (increased orders) and bad (loss of client) news and often the employees, once they understand the information, can provide feedback to their superiors about innovative ways to fix problems or capitalize on the firm's competitive advantage.[59]

PROFIT-SHARING PLANS

Profit sharing ties employees' bonus pay to the success of the company by focusing on profits. Profit-sharing plans generally reward employees only when a certain profit level is reached. These profits typically are distributed either in cash, deferred until a future time (retirement, severance, or disability), or paid in a combination of the two methods.

Profit sharing has several advantages. Generally, the incentive formula is simple and easy to communicate. Pay is variable because the plan pays only when the firm is profitable. Last, it promotes interest in the overall financial health of the company for both management and line employees.

Many companies have found success with profit-sharing plans. Hewlett-Packard believes profit sharing is a powerful tool for improving productivity.[60] Until recently, H-P used deferred profit sharing only for upper management levels. Now, it pays cash bonuses to middle management and white-collar staff each year that specific profit goals are met.

Another believer in profit sharing is Aluminum Company of America (Alcoa). After suffering from several years of downsizing and reorganization, Alcoa decided to use profit sharing as a way to share its hard-earned success with the employees who helped reach its goals. The plan begins once Alcoa's U.S. aluminum operating profits exceed 6 percent of the company's $5 billion in U.S. assets. Salaried employees received cash bonuses averaging 7 percent of each worker's salary. Alcoa believes that profit sharing, combined with a merit raise system that replaced automatic yearly raises, gives it more flexibility in its compensation system.

As you will see in the ending case of this chapter, National Semiconductor has successfully blended the best of profit sharing and gain sharing. However, profit sharing does have its disadvantages. When payments are made annually, long-term goals may be ignored and short-term goals emphasized. Further, many times profits are beyond the control of company employees. As a result, employees who have made sacrifices or worked harder may feel cheated when their efforts do not pay off.

Profit sharing is not always a success. Profits are influenced by a variety of variables, and many employees fail to see how their performance is tied to organizational performance. When payout is deferred for many years, the connection between performance and reward is further blurred.[61] However, some programs may succeed because they change the culture of the firm, leading employees to develop a broader view of the organization and its goals and inspiring greater commitment to those goals.[62]

For incentives to work, companies need a clear idea of their strategy and goals. Next, they must focus on jobs that can be measured and require peak performance levels. Companies must also allow individual business units to tailor their plans to their specific situations and provide conditions under which the program can be modified or even eliminated. Finally, incentives need to be separated from base pay so that employees can more readily see the link between rewards and performance. These recommendations do not ensure success, but they certainly increase its likelihood.

COMMISSIONS

Commission plans are typically developed for sales employees. They may be either straight commission plans, which pay the employee a percentage of sales that are made or a combination of salary and commission (and/or bonus). The percentages vary by industry, product, and nature of the sales job. For example, real estate commissions paid to the selling agency average around 3 percent, with up to 2 percent going directly to high-performing agents. Plans also vary in the determination of how sales are calculated. Using the point-of-sale figures may encourage a very different set of sales behaviors than using the point of delivery.

Companies are working harder to make their commission plans more effective. Behlen Manufacturing in Columbus, Nebraska, ties its commissions partly to company profits. One-fourth of the commission on selling a preengineered building depends on the company's profit on the deal. A different plan is used by an Indianapolis product distributor, Seal Products, Inc. Seal pays up to four times as much when the sale is harder to make than when the customer walks in the front door and the salesperson only has to show the product for the sale to happen. Seal believes its new plan helped boost sales by 25 percent in 1990.[63]

Major department stores have begun switching employees from salary to commission in an effort to boost sales. The concept of an all commission sales force in department stores is not new. Nordstrom's, a northwest service-oriented department store chain, has been using this type of compensation system successfully for quite some time. As lagging sales continue to force stores to close and squeeze profit margins, retailers are looking to imitate Nordstrom's success.

The change in compensation plans has not been as smooth as some would have liked. For one thing, simply placing a salesperson on a commission-based compensation system does not create a customer-oriented salesperson. Customer service is a part of the culture and must be instilled and communicated throughout the organization. Similarly, some employees who had been working for the firm on a salary basis for many years had to be terminated because they were unable to effectively function on a commission-only basis. New salespeople also were turning over as quickly as old. One firm saw its turnover rate jump from 4 percent before the introduction of commission-based pay to over 18 percent after the introduction.

Some employees were thankful for the change in pay policies. These were the people who have been able to increase their pay under the new system. For example, a clerk at Bloomingdale's in New York City was paid $7 an hour and 0.5 percent commission on sales of up to $500,000 under the old compensation system. The total compensation package for this employee would be $16,150 per year based on a 40-hour work week for 49 weeks of the year ($7 × 1,950 hours + 0.5 percent of $500,000). Under the new plan, an employee who sells $500,000 worth of merchandise would earn $25,000 a year (5 percent of $500,000).[64]

Using commissions offers both advantages and disadvantages. Certainly commissions reward performance, are easy to communicate and administer, and allow fluctuation in pay. On the other hand, a straight commission plan may create a high variability in pay from one period to the next and generates lower organizational commitment. Further, the emphasis on volume of sales may cause employees to pay less attention to nonselling duties. Lastly, using commissions assumes that money is the primary motivator of employee behavior.[65]

For these reasons, the majority of organizations use a combination plan. A survey by the American Compensation Association in 1989 found that over 70 percent of sales compensation plans were of the salary plus commission or bonus type.[66] Aside from offering greater income security, it also motivates employees to perform even those duties that do not have an immediate sales-connected payoff. These advantages seem to outweigh the potential disadvantages of increased complexity and consequently higher administration costs.

STOCK OWNERSHIP PLANS

Stock ownership generally is a form of long-term incentive that traditionally has been available only for middle- to top-level management. In theory, managers who are partially paid with company stock have a higher interest in the long-term profitability of the company. Frequently, employees are required to remain with the firm for a specified time to qualify for ownership. Both the number of firms that require this and the length of employment required have risen in recent years.[67] In general, the success of stock ownership depends on the situation and how it is used. In small organizations, stock ownership decreases the need for other forms of incentive plans; in larger organizations, stock ownership is more successful when used in conjunction with other pay-for-performance systems.[68] Three major forms of stock ownership plans are stock options, stock purchase, and employee stock ownership plans (ESOP). They are discussed in the following sections.

Stock Options   Two types of stock options are the classic stock option and the restricted stock option. A classic stock option gives the employee the right to buy the company's stock during a certain period of time (usually 10 years) for a set price. That price usually is the market value of the share on the day the option was offered. If the price rises above that level, the employee can exercise the option to buy the stock and immediately resell it for a "risk-free" gain. Offering stock options to managers is intended to ensure their personal interest in the future of the firm. Firms hope but do not always require, that managers hold their stock as long as they are with the company. Some companies have no record-keeping procedure to check to see whether managers sell or keep their stock.

In a restricted stock option, the employee is given the shares with the restriction that they may not be resold for a specified period of time, generally five years. During that five years, the employee receives all dividends and voting rights. Even if stock prices fall, the sale of the stock still brings a certain sum of money to the employee.[69]

Stock Purchases   In the same way that stock options can tie executives to the company's fate, workers allowed to purchase stock have a greater interest in the company's success and frequently demonstrate higher morale. Organizations frequently allow employees to purchase stock shares either at regular market value or at a reduced value. Often the offer is for a limited time, commonly 30 days, or ongoing, in which the money needed to purchase the stock is withheld from the worker's paycheck. For small organizations with participative management style, performance frequently improves and productivity increases. For large organizations, the effect is less pronounced unless all employees are allowed to participate in the plan.[70]

Employee Stock Ownership Plans (ESOP)   ESOPs work differently from stock purchase plans. Currently, about one-fourth, or about 10 million, of all corporate employees have enrolled in an ESOP. This type of stock ownership plan, pioneered in the 1950s, allows employees to borrow against corporate assets to purchase stock. In some cases, however, employees accept wage concessions in return for stock. When companies do well, ESOP participants can amass significant nest eggs. PepsiCo implemented a program to encourage employees to take initiative in improving individual and organizational performance.[71] A key to the program was an ESOP that allows long-term employees to accumulate large gains based on annual salary, salary growth, and share price.

In recent years, ESOPs have provided two additional benefits to firms. The first is that they provide tax advantages to companies that give shares of stocks to their employees. Fifty percent of the interest on loans granted companies for use in ESOPs is tax exempt. A second benefit is that ESOPs can be used as a defense against hostile takeovers.

The benefits that ESOPs provide also shed light on factors that must be considered before such plans are devised. Workforce retirement needs, changes in the economy, and market position of the organization are key to the successful development and implementation of an ESOP. In Wall Street terms, individuals involved in ESOPs are holding extremely undiversified portfolios. If the portfolio remains unprofitable, the holders will have nothing left with which to diversify.[72]

DEVELOPMENT OF WELL-ROUNDED COMPENSATION SYSTEMS

Many firms are attempting to develop a well-rounded compensation system. To do this, they are using a variety of compensation options. Exhibit 11.9 is an example of an overall compensation package that includes a variety of options. This package is offered to managers of Toys 'R' Us. Another example, which describes an overall compensation package that has gone through some revisions lately, follows.

General Motors set up a new compensation system designed to push its salaried employees to work harder—and to help push those who don't out the door. The move, affecting 112,000 low-level managers, clerical workers, and other white-collar staffers, is part of a trend to tie compensation more closely to performance to make pay more variable from year to year. Two years earlier, GM had stopped giving annual cost-of-living raises. Temporarily suspended salary increases have been reinstated, but with a new philosophy: "A merit increase is something you have to earn," says Roy Roberts, vice president for personnel. "To treat people fairly, you have to treat people differently." GM's new strategy involves base-pay merit raises, lump-sum payments, and profit sharing. The top 5,000 managers have also seen changes. Their 70-year old bonus plan was scrapped, decreasing annual pay for many executives by 50 percent. Instead of cash and stock right away, these managers receive restricted stock grants that will take years to mature. All of this is to get people to work harder and encourage better cooperation.[73]

PAY SECRECY VERSUS OPENNESS

Organizations differ as to the amount and type of information about pay that they readily communicate to their employees. To be sure, an organization that purports to use a pay-for-performance system increases employee trust and confidence in the system when it communicates to its employees how that system works, what level of raises will be received for different levels of performance, and pay increase schedules. Other in-

EXHIBIT 11.9   **Store Management Benefits at Toys "R" Us**

Benefits package effective as of February 1994. This policy may change over time.

Stock Options	Management personnel receive stock options which are normally exercisable four years and nine months after the date they are granted at the original option price. Options are issued each year, usually in November, at the then current price. The number of options granted is dependent upon your position at the time of grant. (At this time, a manager's stock option is 100 shares.)
Incentive Programs	In addition to regular compensation, a performance-oriented incentive award may be achieved annually. The following table summarizes the current award levels by classification.

Position	Incentive Range
Manager	0–15% of base salary
Assistant Director	0–22.5% of base salary
Store Director	0–30% of base salary

	Unlike some other companies, Toys "R" Us incentive bonus is designed to be paid. Our annual budgets actually provide for funding of all incentive awards at the target amount levels shown.
Profit-Sharing and Savings Plan	An employee shall be eligible to participate in the profit sharing and savings plan as of the first day of the month in which he/she completes one year of service.
	The company contributes a portion of its profits to the profit sharing plan. This contribution is usually equal to 8% of participants compensation for the calendar year. With 5 years or more of service you become 100% vested.
	You can contribute anywhere from 1% to 10% of your pre-tax income into the plan. The Company will make a matching contribution of up to one half of the first 6% that you contribute. For example, if you contribute 6% the Company will add another 3% for a total of 9%.
Stock Purchase Plan	Eligibility: Age 18 years or older and completion of 90 days of continuous service. The employee Stock Purchase Plan enables you to invest in company stock through automatic payroll deductions. The company will add 10% to your contribution and pay all commissions on purchases made through payroll deductions.

SOURCE: Copyright © 1994 Toys "R" Us, Inc.

formation, such as pay maximums and minimums for various job classes or even specific individual salaries, also may be communicated.

Next, Inc., hangs a list of all employees' salaries in its company offices in Redwood City and Fremont, California. Phillip E. Wilson, vice president of human resources, maintains that "anything less than openness doesn't establish the same level of trust."[74] Calfed, Inc., a bank in California, is more in the middle between pay secrecy and openness policies. Vanessa Jorgenson, a branch manager, believes that she is better able to handle pay problems and has a better chance of keeping people she has trained because of the bank's open pay policy. Calfed's performance guide, which she discusses with employees, includes data about how to compute a merit raise and salary brackets for every job.

However, the majority of companies prefer a policy of pay secrecy because they believe it gives them more freedom to make pay decisions and keeps employee pay dissatisfaction lower. Communicating information about a pay system that is not performance-related also can reduce employee motivation. The results from a salary survey of 388 human resource professionals further documents the level of pay secrecy in the workplace. While 81 percent of the respondents reported that some information about pay ranges in the organization is made available to employees, 48 percent allowed employees to see only their own pay ranges and did not reveal pay structures for other positions, and approximately 20 percent indicated that no pay-scale information was provided to employees.[75]

Many employees also believe that pay secrecy is the best policy. For some, pay may be tied to the employee's ego. Others may simply be embarrassed about their pay or not want to know about others' pay for fear that it would just make them angry. At Electronic Data Systems, new hires are required to sign a form that acknowledges certain companywide policies. One of these states that employees are permitted to reveal their salaries but they can be fired if such a disclosure leads to "disruptions."

All of the discussion so far assumes that money is a source of motivation to employees. In the following section, the relationship between motivation and compensation is discussed.

MOTIVATION THEORY

The general topic of motivation was discussed in an earlier chapter. In this section, the relationship of equity theory, expectancy theory, and reinforcement theory to compensation is more fully explained.

EQUITY THEORY

EQUITY THEORY
The belief that employees examine the relationship between their outcomes from the job and their inputs to the job. This ratio is then compared to the ratios of relevant others.

A major goal of all compensation systems is fairness or perceived equity. Employees often determine their own individual perception of compensation equity by using the formula espoused in **equity theory.**[76] Equity theory proposes that employees examine the relationship between their outcomes from the job (such as pay, job satisfaction, recognition, and promotion) and their inputs (such as education, experience, skill, and effort). This ratio is then compared to the ratios of others (for example, other employees or the employees at a previous job). If the ratios are perceived as inequitable, dissatisfaction may result.

Dissatisfaction probably does not occur if positive inequity (the person feels overrewarded) is the result of the comparison. Research has shown that workers have been found to be happy when they believe they are paid more than they are worth. Further, this happiness also occurs when workers believe that their colleagues are overrewarded.[77]

When negative inequity (the person is underrewarded) occurs, employees are generally dissatisfied. This dissatisfaction motivates the employee to reduce that inequity by increasing outcomes or decreasing inputs (either cognitively or physically) or changing the comparison in other ways so that the ratios are more equitable. Employees who want to increase their outcomes could ask for a raise or promotion, seek out greater recognition, or even change the perception of the level of satisfaction received from the job. Alternatively, the employee may choose to decrease inputs by using such mechanisms as cognitively downgrading the skill level or amount of experience or by not working as hard.

Research on equity theory has shown that individuals who believe they are paid too little relative to what others earn or what they think they *should* earn may become dissatisfied. This dissatisfaction may cause them to seek new employment, to become less productive, or to be absent more often. Thus, an individual's perception of equity is an important consideration in both the design and administration of the reward system.

In regard to wages, women often experience inequity in the workplace. Although more women are managers, they are not earning top salaries. Nationwide, 40 percent earn less than $500 a week, or $26,000 a year. Further, less than 10 percent of female managers earn gross annual wages of $52,000 to $78,000—a salary that one might assume a middle- to upper-level manager might make in the United States.[78] Although women have made gains in narrowing the gender pay gap over the last decade, pay inequity still exists.

As a proactive strategy, Canada has been experimenting with pay equity policies. Certain jurisdictions in Canada have moved beyond "equal pay for equal work" to deciding whether employees receive "equal pay for work of equal value."[79] For example, the purpose of Ontario's Pay Equity Act is to redress systematic discrimination in compensation. The government stated that the act was necessary because work traditionally performed by women had been undervalued. Ontario's Act is not complaint based, but rather puts the burden on employers to review all jobs to ensure that female-dominated and male-dominated jobs of comparable value receive equal pay. The hope is that fair pay for women will eventually help Ontario employers attract and retain the skilled workers they need.

A Canadian firm must follow several steps in order to be in compliance with the law. First, employers must define job classes or groups of jobs that have similar duties and qualification, must recruit men and women in a similar fashion, and must pay them according to the same compensation schedules. If a class or group is dominated by women, it must be noted. A class is dominated by women if (1) more than 60 percent of the incumbents are female, (2) less than 70 percent of the incumbents are male, (3) historical precedent views the position as female, or (4) popular perception views the job as female.

Next, the jobs are ranked with respect to skill, effort, responsibility, and working conditions. For each female-dominated class, the employer must locate a comparable male-dominated class, and if the salaries, including benefits, are lower for females, the company must raise them. If no comparable male class can be found at the same level, a male class at a lower level is used. Again, women's salaries, if they are lower, must be raised to meet that level of pay.

Finally, the employer must post a pay equity "plan" showing the job classifications for each job and how the pay will be adjusted. Male wages may not be cut to meet the wages paid females—only upward adjustments are allowed.[80] In the United States, at least 20 states have implemented similar programs in an effort to equalize salaries.

EXPECTANCY THEORY

In *Work and Motivation,* Victor Vroom's expectancy theory suggests that employee behavior is a function of the outcomes that are received for the work and the value of those outcomes to the individual.[81] Essentially, the theory has three key concepts: (1) performance-outcome expectancy, (2) value (or attractiveness), and (3) effort-performance expectancy.

The performance-outcome expectancy simply means that an individual believes that every behavior is connected to an outcome, and different levels of that behavior may be connected to different levels of that outcome. The attractiveness of that outcome differs from one individual to the next. For some, the outcome may be a highly valued reward; for another, the same outcome may be perceived as a punishment. For example, the individual who is afraid of the water or is terrified to get in front of a group will not be motivated to work hard enough to "win" an ocean cruise or receive recognition as "Employee of the Month" at an organizationwide meeting. These outcomes are not attractive to that employee.

Last, individuals evaluate the effort-performance expectancy relationship. In essence, the employee asks whether or not he or she is capable of performing successfully at certain levels and then translates those perceptions into probabilities of success. He or she then chooses those behaviors that have the highest likelihood of success for obtaining valued outcomes.

When designing compensation systems, then, expectancy theory suggests that employers must follow several guidelines.

1. Make a clear connection between performance and outcome.
2. Develop flexible reward systems that provide a variety of potentially attractive outcomes.
3. Determine what rewards are valued by employees.
4. Make sure that employees have the appropriate training and ability to perform the job successfully.

REINFORCEMENT THEORY

Reinforcement theories explain an individual's behavior as a response to a stimulus in the environment. Edward Thorndike's law of effect is the basis for many contemporary models of reinforcement and explains how a person's own actions in a situation interact with the environment to influence future reactions in that environment.[82] In essence, this law maintains that behavior that is positively reinforced (rewarded) tends to be repeated in that situation; behavior that is punished tends not to be repeated in similar situations. Rewards, then, are positive reinforcers that strengthen the relationship between the situation and the behavior. They can be as subtle as a pat on the back or a smile or as obvious as a bonus or company car.

The important point, again, is that rewards that are connected to a behavior encourage that behavior to be repeated. As in expectancy theory, then, the manager must make sure that rewards are applied in a timely fashion so that employees (1) make the connection between behavior and outcome and (2) repeat the desired behavior in the future. Whether the behavior is short term or long term in focus and whether quality or quantity issues are relevant, management should understand the relationship between outcomes, their value to employees, and the impact that they have on employee behavior.

MANAGEMENT GUIDELINES

1. Designing a reward system that reinforces the organization's business strategy can make the organization more competitive, increase its effectiveness, and help management focus on both short-term and long-term goals.

Continued

2. The goals of the compensation system can include
   A. Attraction and retention of employees.
   B. Cost efficiency.
   C. Legal compliance.
   D. Equitable salaries for all employees.
   E. Motivation of employee performance.
3. An organization's external environment interacts with its internal environment to influence the choice of compensation systems.
4. Effective reward systems include both intrinsic rewards (those that result from the job itself) and extrinsic rewards (those that are provided by others in the organization) to increase employee motivation.
5. Pay-for-performance plans are becoming increasingly popular because of their ability to tie pay to individual employee or group performance.
6. Three critical factors involved in pay for performance plans include the ability to
   A. Tie pay to performance.
   B. Accurately measure performance.
   C. Provide appropriate incentives.
7. Individual incentive plans tend to encourage competition among workers; group plans are more likely to encourage cooperative efforts and teamwork.
8. Three motivation theories (equity, expectancy, and reinforcement theory) provide important insights into the role that rewards play in influencing employee behavior.
9. Internal and external equity, or perceived fairness, both in the design and implementation of the compensation system, increases employee acceptance of the system and lowers pay dissatisfaction.
10. All rewards are not relevant to all employees. Managers must identify what employees value and then try to match rewards with employees.

QUESTIONS FOR REVIEW

1. What are the important external and internal environmental variables affecting compensation plans? Which are most important? Why?
2. In what way does the competition in the labor market affect the wages a company has to pay?
3. What is one important objective for a compensation system? Why?
4. Define the term *pay-level policy* and discuss the three types of policies. Under what conditions might a company select each strategy?
5. Do you agree or disagree with the following statement? Defend your answer:
   "Money is the most important tool that a manager has for motivating employees."
6. How does the expectancy theory relate to employee compensation?
7. Why have pay-for-performance plans increased in popularity recently? What are some problems associated with them?
8. What is the difference between gain sharing and profit sharing?
9. Why would a manager choose to use an individual incentive plan rather than a group plan?
10. If you were to design a pay system for sales employees at a large men's clothing store, how would you set it up and why?

NATIONAL SEMICONDUCTOR'S HYBRID INCENTIVE PLAN[83]

Moving to a team environment has many advantages. However, as National Semiconductor found, it also has some drawbacks. For example, if individuals are asked to work in teams, solve problems in teams, and think like a team player, why are they rewarded as individual contributors? The goal of a team environment is virtually undermined by the system set up to reward a team member's individual behavior.

To overcome this problem, National Semiconductor set out to redesign its incentive plan. Its goal was to develop a plan that rewarded performance that helped to reach operational goals. In other words, it aligned its strategic business plan with its incentive plan.

The first step in redesigning its incentive plan was to establish a companywide task force. The task force included 20 members from all levels in the organization as well as all pay grades (i.e., exempt, nonexempt, and managerial). The task force was charged with designing an incentive plan that would be perceived as fair companywide while being flexible enough to meet the unique needs of each business unit.

Task force subcommittees were formed. Each subcommittee had a specific area to research including benchmarking, communication, fit and integration, assessment of readiness for incentives, and incentive plan design.

BENCHMARKING

The benchmarking subcommittee contacted 11 different companies to determine why their incentive plans were or were not working. From this research, they learned that many companies were struggling to make their plans work. Common problems included goals that were too complex to understand; goals that were in conflict among departments or areas; lack of input by the employees in the development of the incentive plan; lack of communication about the plan; incentives that were actually part of an individual's salary, not above and beyond it; and lack of support from top management.

To avoid making these same mistakes, the task force developed six guiding principles for the development of the incentive plan. These included (1) linking incentive plan goals with strategic business plans, (2) ensuring alignment between a business unit's goals and management's goals, (3) having easily understandable goals that employees are able to understand, (4) making sure that the plan included monetarily quantifiable goals, (5) guaranteeing that the level of payout opportunity be appropriate for the degree of goal difficulty, and (6) involving employees in the design, goal-setting, implementation, and evaluation of the plan.

COMMUNICATION

To avoid the problems other companies experienced when implementing an incentive system, the task force decided to communicate, up front, that its goal was to develop corporate guidelines for incentive pay plans. It was determined that frequent communication would help to manage expectations of the employees and keep them informed as well. Monthly updates were provided via newsletters and videos.

FIT AND INTEGRATION

It soon became apparent that the current performance appraisal process did not fit well with the team environment or the goal of the new incentive system. After gathering information from employees and managers through focus groups, one major change was implemented. Specifically, feedback on an individual's performance from peers and internal customers was integrated into the assessment system to better reflect the focus of the new team environment.

ASSESSMENT OF READINESS

Within each business unit, a committee for readiness was appointed. This committee determined whether the business unit it represented was ready to implement the incentive program. These committees asked questions such as, "Are management and supervisors supportive of the incentive pay plan changes?" "Is there already an established team environment?"

DESIGN OF THE SYSTEM

The subcommittee assigned to design the incentive plan had the largest task. To accomplish it, members began by evaluating the two most frequently used team incentive plans; profit sharing and gain sharing. Recognizing that each had positive and negative elements, they decided that a combined plan would be the best. They proposed a plan that had the financial focus of profit-sharing plans and the operational focus of gain-sharing plans. Specifically, their incentive formula provided an increased amount of sharing with employees as the business unit performed better on both its profits and a few identified operational goals. Further, increased sharing was awarded for reaching more difficult goals.

SETTING GOALS

As the benchmarking group found, conflicting goals among groups can undermine the effectiveness of a team incentive system. Hence, to avoid this, goals were tied to the unit's preapproved annual business plan with gains defined as performance above the baseline goal set by the business plan. Baseline goals were defined as the easiest goals to achieve. That is, there was an 80% chance that the goal would be achieved. Challenging goals, which received a higher reward when met, were deemed to be achievable 50 percent of the time. Hence, these goals were challenging and achievable.

The highest goal level was called a *stretch goal,* which was expected to be reached only 20 percent of the time. Significant breakthroughs would be needed to accomplish this goal level.

EMPLOYEE INVOLVEMENT

To gain wider acceptance of the goals set, individual business units selected a design team that was charged with collecting the data needed to determine the financial and operational goals for the business unit. This type of employee involvement is crucial for the acceptance of the plan.

HOW MUCH IS ENOUGH?

Once the goals were set, employees needed to know how much they could expect to receive if they reached each level of goal. A range of 3 to 10 percent of one's base salary seemed to be what other companies were paying, based on data collected. However, payment plans of this type were still based on individual salary levels and did not conform to the goals of the new system. Instead, National Semiconductor decided to base the pay on the business unit's total payroll. Specifically, 2 to 5 percent could be expected for reaching challenging goals; 4 to 10 percent could be expected for reaching stretch goals.

DISBURSING THE FUNDS

The final issue that the task force grappled with was how the money should be paid. Payouts are commonly made in two ways: as a percentage of salary or as an equal dollar amount. After a lengthy debate, it was agreed that the equal dollar amount, although favoring the lower-paid individuals in the unit, was more in line with the overall team goal of the incentive system and was selected as the disbursement method.

THIS IS ONLY A TEST

Instead of immediately implementing the new incentive system, several pilot tests were performed. These test cases had positive results, and several gain-sharing opportunities resulted. As long as the business strategies remain aligned with the performance goals, the plan has an excellent chance to succeed.

QUESTIONS

1. The task force itself may have had competing goals. Where might this have happened?
2. How motivating do you think the stretch goals are? Why?
3. Discuss the payout percentages implemented. Do you see these figures as motivational? Why?
4. What are some of the pros and cons for percentage-based and equal-dollar disbursement systems? Which method do you think should have been used? Why?

ADDITIONAL READINGS

Aaron, Hugh. "Making Incentives Pay During a Recession." *The Wall Street Journal,* October 29, 1990, p. A14.

Balkin, David, and Luis Gomez-Mejia. "Matching Compensation and Organizational Strategies." *Strategic Management Journal* 11 (1990), pp. 153–169.

Belcher, David, W., and Thomas J. Atchison. *Compensation Administration.* Englewood Cliffs, NJ: Prentice-Hall, 1987.

Bergmann, Thomas, Harvey Gunderson, D. Weil, and B. Baliga. "Rewards Tied to Long-Term Success." *HRMagazine,* May 1990, pp. 67–72.

Bunning, Richard. "Skill-Based Pay." *Personnel Administrator,* June 1989, pp. 65–70.

Commerce Clearing House. *Executive Compensation.* Chicago, IL: Commerce Clearing House, Inc., 1989.

Drazin, Robert, and Ellen R. Auster. "Wage Differences between Men and Women: Performance Appraisal Ratings vs. Salary Allocation as Locus of Bias." *Human Resource Management* 26 (1987), pp. 157–168.

Ellig, B. "Pay Policies While Downsizing the Organization: A Systematic Approach." *Personnel* 60 (1983), pp. 26–35.

England, John. "Developing a Total Compensation Policy Statement." *Personnel,* May 1988, pp. 71–73.

Finkelstein, Sidney, and Donald Hambrick. "Chief Executive Compensation: A Synthesis and Reconciliation." *Strategic Management Journal* 9 (1988), pp. 543–558.

Foulkes, Fred. *Executive Compensation: A Strategic Guide for the 1990s.* Boston: Harvard Business School Press, 1990.

Gomez-Mejia, Luis. *Compensation and Benefits.* Washington, DC: BNA Books, 1989.

Gomez-Mejia, Luis, David Balkin, and George Milkovich. "Rethinking Rewards for Technical Employees." *Organizational Dynamics* 18 (1990), pp. 62–75.

Graham-Moore, Brian and Timothy Ross. *Gainsharing Plans for Improving Performance.* Washington, DC: BNA Books, 1990.

Hufnagel, Ellen. "Developing Strategic Compensation Plans." *Human Resource Management* 26 (1987), pp. 93–108.

Kerr, Steven. "On the Folly of Rewarding A, While Hoping for B." *Academy of Management Journal* 18, December 1975, pp. 769–783.

Kerr, Steven, and John Slocum. "Managing Corporate Culture through Reward Systems." *Academy of Management Executive* 1 (1987), pp. 99–108.

Kotlikoff, Laurence, and David Wise. *The Wage Carrot and the Pension Stick.* Kalamazoo, MI: W.E. Upjohn Institute, 1989.

Lawler, Edward. *Strategic Pay.* San Francisco: Jossey-Bass, 1990.

Leader, Laurie. *Wages and Hours: Law and Practice.* Albany, NY: Matthew Bender, 1990.

McCaffrey, Robert. *Employee Benefit Programs: A Total Compensation Perspective.* Boston: Kent Publishing, 1988.

Martin, James, and Thomas Heetderks. *Two-Tier Compensation Structures,* Kalamazoo, MI: W.E. Upjohn Institute, 1990.

Michael, Robert, Heidi Hartmann, and Brigid O'Farrell. *Pay Equity: Empirical Inquiries.* Washington DC: National Academic Press, 1989.

Ost, Edward. "Gain Sharing's Potential." *Personnel Administrator,* July 1989, pp. 92–96.

Patton, Thomas. *Fair Pay.* San Francisco: Jossey-Bass, 1988.

Rock, Milton, and Lance Berger. *The Compensation Handbook.* New York: McGraw-Hill, 1991.

Roth, William. *Work and Rewards: Redefining Our Work-Life Reality.* Westport, CT: Greenwood Press, 1989.

Schneier, G. "Implementing Performance Management and Recognition and Rewards (PMRR) Systems at the Strategic Level: A Line Management Driven Effort." *Human Resource Planning* 12 (1989), pp. 205–220.

Tomasko, R. "Focusing Company Reward Systems to Help Achieve Business Objectives." *Management Review* 71 (1982), pp. 8–18.

VonGlinow, Mary Ann. "Reward Strategies for Attracting, Evaluating, and Retraining Professionals." *Human Resource Management* 24 (1985), pp. 191–206.

Wallace, Marc, and Charles Fay. *Compensation Theory and Practice.* Boston: Kent Publishing, 1988.

NOTES

1. Jaclyn Fierman, "The Perilous New World of Fair Pay," *Fortune,* June 13, 1994, pp. 57–64.

2. Christopher Knowlton, "11 Men's Million-Dollar Motivator," *Fortune,* April 1990, pp. 65–67.

3. L. L. Cummings, "Compensation, Culture, and Motivation: A Systems Perspective," *Organizational Dynamics,* Winter 1984, pp. 33–34.

4. W. H. Mobley, *Employee Turnover: Causes, Consequences, and Control* (Reading, MA: Addison-Wesley, 1982).

5. Edward Lawler, *Pay and Organizational Development* (Reading, MA: Addison-Wesley, 1981).

6. Edward Lawler, "The Strategic Design of Reward Systems," in *Strategic Human Resource Management,* eds. C. J. Fombrun, N. Tichy, and M. Devanna, (New York: Wiley, 1984), pp. 127–147.

7. Joel Walters, "Employment Tax Issues," *HRMagazine,* April 1990, pp. 72–76.

8. Jeffrey Tannenbaum, and Udayan Gupta, "Timing of New Basic Wage Hurts Firms," *The Wall Street Journal,* April 9, 1991, p. B1.

9. Albert Karr, "Compromise on Minimum Wage Reached," *The Wall Street Journal,* November 1, 1989, p. A3.

10. C. Conte, "U.S. Hard Hats and Managers Rank High in International Pay Comparisons," *The Wall Street Journal,* March 3, 1992, p. A1; and D. Lohse, "For Foreign Postings, the Accent Is on Frugality," *The Wall Street Journal,* June 23, 1995, p. C1.

11. The group may include (1) all jobs in the company, (2) all jobs in a specific department(s), or whatever combination of jobs that the company wishes to analyze.

12. Much of this discussion relies on D. Belcher and T. Atchison, *Compensation Administration,* 2nd ed. (Englewood Cliffs, NJ: Prentice-Hall, 1987); and G. Milkovich and J. Newman, *Compensation* (Homewood, IL: BPI/Irwin, 1990).

13. Amanda Bennett, "When Money is Tight, Bosses Scramble for Other Ways to Motivate the Troops," *The Wall Street Journal,* October 31, 1990, p. B1.

14. "Most New Hires Start at Low End," *HRNews,* April 1991, p. 2.

15. Kenan S. Abosch, Dan Gilbert, and Susan M. Dempsey, "Broadbanding: Approaches of Two Organizations," *ACA Journal: Perspectives in Compensation and Benefits,* Spring 1994, pp. 46–53.

16. Ibid.

17. Arthur Berkeley, "Companies Drop Tiered Pay Systems," *HRMagazine,* August 1990, p. 69.

18. Bennett, "When Money Is Tight."

19. R. Miles, and C. Snow, "Designing Strategic Human Resources Systems," *Organizational Dynamics,* 13, 1984, pp. 36–52.

20. John Greenwald, "Workers: Risks and Rewards," *Time,* April 15, 1991, pp. 42–43; Shawn Tully, "Your Paycheck Gets Exciting," *Fortune,* November 1, 1993, pp. 83–98.

21. Harris Collingwood, "Pay for Performance at American Airlines," *Business Week,* June 19, 1989, p. 41.

22. William Power, "Wall Street Firms Link Analysts' Pay to Performance," *The Wall Street Journal,* September 19, 1989, p. B1.

23. Amanda Bennett, "Paying Workers to Meet Goals Spreads, but Gauging Performance Proves Tough," *The Wall Street Journal,* September 10, 1991, pp. B1 + .

24. Christopher Cont, "The Checkoff," *The Wall Street Journal,* April 16, 1991, p. A1.

25. Selwyn Feinstein, "Pay for Performance Means Redefining What's Right," *The Wall Street Journal,* February 20, 1991, p. A1.

26. Jerry McAdams, "Performance-Based Reward Systems: Toward a Common-Fate Environment," *Personnel Journal,* June 1988, pp. 103–113.

27. Selwyn Feinstein, "Pay for Performance Hangs Mostly on Boss's Subjective View," *The Wall Street Journal,* October 24, 1989, p. A1.

28. Albert Karr, "Middle Managers Are Ignored in Accelerating Switch to Pay for Performance," *The Wall Street Journal,* January 9, 1990, p. A1.

29. Selwyn Feinstein, "In Federal Government, Pay for Performance Doesn't Seem Very Effective, *The Wall Street Journal,* December 12, 1989, p. A1.

30. Yumiko Ono, and Marcus Brauchli, "Japan Cuts the Middle-Management Fat," *The Wall Street Journal,* August 8, 1989, p. B1.

31. Stephenie Overman, "Compensation Responds to New Marketplace," *HRNews,* June 1990, p. 7

32. William Anders, "Hefty Bonuses for Hefty Gains," *The Wall Street Journal,* May 20, 1991, p. A18.

33. Ron Suskind, "More Executives Get Pension Guarantees to Protect against Takeovers, Failures," *The Wall Street Journal,* July 5, 1991, pp. B1+; and Julia Flynn, "Continental Divide over Executive Pay," *Business Week,* July 3, 1995, pp. 40–41.

34. Kevin Salwen, "Shareholder Proposals on Pay Must Be Aired, SEC to Tell 10 Firms," *The Wall Street Journal,* February 13, 1992, p. A1.

35. Carol Hymowitz, "More Employees, Shareholders Demand That Sacrifices in Pay Begin at the Top," *The Wall Street Journal,* November 8, 1990, pp. B1+.

36. Joann S. Lublin, "Executive Pay: Looking Good," *The Wall Street Journal,* April 13, 1994, pp. R1–R2.

37. John A. Byrne, Lori Bongiorno, and Ronald Grover, "That Eye-Popping Executive Pay," *Business Week,* April 25, 1994, pp. 52–60.

38. Ira T. Kay, Gary M. Lawson, and Diane Lerner, "Executive Pay under Attack," *HRMagazine,* June 1994, pp. 93–97.

39. Jacqueline Mitchell, "Herman Miller Links Worker-CEO Pay," *The Wall Street Journal,* May 7, 1992, p. B1.

40. Jennifer J. Laabs, "Ben & Jerry's Caring Capitalism," *Personnel Journal,* November 1992, p. 50.

41. A. Farnham, "The Trust Gap," *Fortune,* December 4, 1989, pp. 56–78.

42. Lindley Clark, "It's Not How Much You Pay CEOs—But How," *The Wall Street Journal,* May 17, 1990, p. A18; and Bill Leonard, "CEO Compensation Packages Tied to Performance," *HRMagazine,* April 1994, pp. 51–52.

43. See Edward Lawler, "Pay for Performance: A Strategic Analysis," in *Compensation and Benefits,* ed. Luis R. Gomez-Mejia, (Washington, DC: Bureau of National Affairs Books, 1989), for a thorough discussion of the strategic implications of individual and group pay-for-performance plans.

44. This section borrows from Milkovich and Newman, *Compensation,* and Gomez-Mejia, *Compensation and Benefits.*

45. Ira Kay, "Do Your Workers Really Merit a Raise?" *The Wall Street Journal,* March 26, 1990, p. A8.

46. Ibid.

47. Barry Wisdom, "Before Implementing a Merit System . . . ," *Personnel Administrator,* October 1989, pp. 46–50; and Bill Leonard, "New Ways to Pay Employees," *HRMagazine,* February 1994, pp. 61–62.

48. Selwyn Feinstein, "Worker Incentives Proliferate," *The Wall Street Journal,* December 12, 1989, p. A1; and Shawn Tully, "Your Paycheck Gets Exciting," *Fortune,* November 1, 1993, pp. 83–98.

49. Selwyn Feinstein, "Labor Letter," *The Wall Street Journal,* December 5, 1989, p. A1.

50. Hugh Aaron, "Making Incentives Pay during a Recession," *The Wall Street Journal,* October 29, 1990, p. A4.

51. Selwyn Feinstein, "Incentive Plans Keep Spreading beyond Executive Suites. But Do They Work?" *The Wall Street Journal,* November 6, 1990, p. A1.

52. Richard Bunning, "Skill-Based Pay," *Personnel Administrator,* June 1989, pp. 65–69.

53. Selwyn Feinstein, "Labor Letter," p. A1; and "Labor Letter," *The Wall Street Journal,* March 12, 1991, p. A1.

54. Judy Huret, "Paying for Team Results," *HRMagazine,* May 1991, pp. 39–41.

55. Gary Florkowski, "Analyzing Group Incentive Plans," *HRMagazine,* January 1990, pp. 36–39.

56. Edward Ost, "Gain Sharing's Potential," *Personnel Administrator,* July 1989, pp. 92–96.

57. Florkowski, "Analyzing Group Incentive Plans," p. 37.

58. John Dantico and Sandra Sipari, "Gainsharing: Consider a Plan for All Reasons," *HRNews,* February 1991, p. 12.

59. Kevin Paulsen, "Lessons Learned from Gainsharing," *HRMagazine,* April 1991, pp. 70–74.

60. Michael Shroeder, "Watching the Bottom Line Instead of the Clock," *Business Week,* November 7, 1988, p. 64.

61. Pinhaus Schwinger, *Wage Incentive Systems* (New York: Halsted, 1975).

62. R. Bullock and E. Lawler, "Gainsharing: A Few Questions and Fewer Answers," *Human Resource Management* 23, 1984, pp. 23–40.

63. Roger Ricklets, "Whither the Payoff on Sales Commissions," *The Wall Street Journal,* March 6, 1990, p. B1.

64. "Now Salespeople Really Must Sell for Their Supper," *Business Week,* July 31, 1989, p. 50.

65. Several excellent articles and books provide details for designing sales compensation plans. For example, see Bruce Ellig, "Sales Compensation: A Systematic Approach," *Compensation Review,* 1982, pp. 21–45; and J. Barry and P. Henry, *Effective Sales Incentive Compensation* (New York: McGraw-Hill, 1981).

66. Gomez-Mejia, *Compensation and Benefits.*

67. Selwyn Feinstein, "Stay or No Pay," *The Wall Street Journal,* February 27, 1990, p. A1.

68. Gomez-Mejia, *Compensation and Benefits.*

69. Graef Crystal, "Incentive Pay That Doesn't Work," *Fortune,* August 28, 1989, pp. 101–104.

70. John McMillan, Ken Allen, and Robert Salwen, "Private Companies Offer Long-Term Incentives," *HRMagazine,* June 1991, pp. 63–66; and John McMilliam, and Chris Young, "Sweetening the Compensation Package," *HRMagazine,* October 1990, pp. 36–39.

71. Dawn Anfuso, "PepsiCo Shares Power and Stock with Workers," *Personnel Journal,* January 1995, p. 79.

72. James White, "As ESOPs Become Victims of '90s Bankruptcies, Workers Are Watching Their Nest Eggs Vanish," *The Wall Street Journal,* January 25, 1991, p. C1.

73. Jacob Schlesinger, "GM's New Compensation Plan Reflects General Trend Tying Pay to Performance," *The Wall Street Journal,* January 3, 1989, p. B1.

74. Julie Solomon, "Hush Money," *The Wall Street Journal,* April 25, 1990, pp. R22–R24.

75. "Most New Hires Start at the Low End," *HRNews,* April 1991, p. 2.

76. For two classic articles regarding equity theory, see J. Stacey Adams, "Toward an Understanding of Inequity," *Journal of Abnormal and Social Psychology* 67, 1963, pp. 422–436; and George Homans, *Social Behavior: Its Elementary Forms* (New York: Harcourt Brace Jovanovich, 1961).

77. Selwyn Feinstein, "Pay Satisfaction Runs High, Especially at Companies That Street Teamwork," *The Wall Street Journal,* October 9, 1990, p. A1.

78. M. Mahar, "More Women are Calling the Shots, but They're Still Making Less than the Guys," *Working Woman,* June 1994, p. 18.

79. Brian P. Smeenk, "Canada's Pay Equity Experiments," *HRMagazine,* September 1993, pp. 58-61.

80. Julie Solomon, "Pay Equity Gets a Tryout in Canada and U.S. Firms Are Watching Closely," *The Wall Street Journal,* December 28, 1988, p. B1; and Brian P. Smeenk, "Canada's Pay Equity Experiments," *HRMagazine,* September 1993, pp. 58–61.

81. Victor Vroom, *Work and Motivation* (New York: John Wiley & Sons, 1964).

82. Edward L. Thorndike, *Animal Intelligence* (New York: Macmillan, 1911), p. 244.

83. Darlene O'Neill, "Blending the Best of Profit Sharing and Gainsharing," *HRMagazine,* March 1994, pp. 66–70.

CHAPTER 12

IMPROVING PRODUCTIVITY

A main goal of any organization is to be productive. Some organizations successfully reach this goal, while others fail. The dilemma for businesses in the 1990s and beyond is to determine how to do more work with fewer people while improving quality and customer service. Although each successful organization follows a different formula, some common productivity principles are found in all successful organizations, such as training and development, companywide communication, and trust in employees. These and other productivity principles are examined in this chapter.

CHAPTER OBJECTIVES

After reading this chapter, you should be able to
1. Understand the concept of productivity.
2. Recognize ways to increase productivity through organizational restructuring.
3. Understand how to increase productivity through individuals.
4. Recognize ways to increase productivity through leadership.
5. Define *involvement* and explain the benefits of having an involved staff.
6. Be familiar with techniques available to help increase employee involvement.

MOTIVATING MOTOROLA[1]

In recent years, U.S. managers have taken a closer look at the effectiveness of Japanese management and have questioned why workers in the United States seem to lack motivation and why U.S. productivity has declined. What is it about Japanese management style that motivates Japanese workers and increases productivity? In short, corporate America continues to struggle with how to motivate workers.

MOTOROLA—NUMBER 1 IN THE UNITED STATES

Motorola, one of the world's leading high-tech companies, set out to resolve the motivation problem with its workers. Rather than merely mimic Japanese management style, Motorola adopted a strategic approach that adds a U.S. twist to the Japanese style of management. Although Motorola has embraced such Japanese tactics as driving relentlessly for market share, sharply upgrading quality, and constantly honing manufacturing processes to pare costs, it has exploited "Yankee know-how" in areas where Japanese companies have been notoriously weak, such as in marketing and software development. "U.S.–style" Japanese management has put Motorola in the driver's seat in telecommunications. Worldwide, Motorola is recognized as a leader in productivity.

STRATEGIC APPROACH

Robert W. Galvin, the son of the founder of Motorola, and his "handpicked" CEO successor, George Fisher, have engaged in a top-to-bottom overhaul of Motorola's market share both at home and abroad. Motorola has committed itself to a more participative management style and prepares its workers to participate *effectively* by emphasizing education and training for all employees. The company has also emphasized research and development, high quality and low cost, and interdepartmental collaboration.

EDUCATION AND TRAINING

To instill the workforce with the new corporate goals, Motorola launched a massive education drive for all 105,000 employees, both workers and managers. The company spends roughly $100 million a year on educating its employees by offering courses in global competitiveness and risk taking, for example. The courses also teach workers practical skills in statistical process control and ways of reducing product cycle times. After considering work time lost while employees are attending classes, these training cost estimates increase to nearly $200 million. Motorola's dedication to training is apparent by these past expenditures as well as by Motorola's on-going requirement that each manager spend at least 1.5 percent of his or her payroll budget on training.

Training programs help workers to develop new skills and problem-solving techniques. Motorola offers executive programs to discuss real-world topics and problems that do not necessarily have clearcut answers. Such programs enable managers to more effectively deal with a changing environment. For example, Darlene Gerster, a training and development manager at Motorola, states that the company's Manager of Managers' Program helps employees learn the process of thinking through an idea, developing it, and championing it through the organization. Motorola's programs emphasize that managers must be willing to take certain risks in order to adapt to dynamic, changing environments.

By investing in training and development, Motorola is helping its employees to gain confidence in their ability to participate effectively in the decision-making process. Like Motorola, other leading corporations have incorporated case studies into their training and development programs that utilize their own real-life strategic and business issues. Thus, participants in the programs are gaining more practical and applicable experience from which to draw on in the future.

RESEARCH AND DEVELOPMENT

Motorola continues to correct the myopic vision that seems to be intrinsic to other U.S. organizations. The company has distanced itself from the "short-term fix," opting instead for a more long-term focus. It has pumped $100 million into research and development to be spent over a 10-year-period. Such an investment is expected to yield long-term benefits rather than short-run, immediate returns. Motorola's commitment to research and development has resulted in "miniaturized" telecommunications products that, according to John J. Egidio, president of Metromedia Paging Services, Inc., seem to have "scooped the world by a year or two." When Motorola introduced its MicroTac cellular phone and wristwatch pager to the market, for example, it basically "knocked the wind out of the sails of Japanese rival products."

HIGH QUALITY AND LOW COST

Fisher believes that Americans used to fall into the trap of assuming that high quality costs more. But high quality and low cost go hand in hand. His "find it and fix it" quality control philosophy has been saving Motorola approximately $250 million annually. The director of quality estimates that companywide defects have been reduced from nearly 3,000 per million products in 1983 to less than 200 per million. Motorola's ability to improve quality efficiency while reducing costs has been nothing short of spectacular and was a major reason why the company was awarded a Malcolm Baldrige National Quality Award.

COLLABORATION

In an effort to create unified team spirit, Motorola is tearing down the traditional walls that isolate various departments, such as design, manufacturing, and marketing. Motorola is attempting to establish a new tradition of collaboration among disciplines. Representatives from each discipline are now encouraged to get involved in new projects from the start. New-product venture teams composed of five or six employees from different departments are formed to discuss and develop new product ideas, and interdepartmental functional teams rally to ensure that new ideas are successfully developed.

As can be seen in the Motorola case, the company has chosen to break away from the traditional "American way" of doing business. The change in Motorola's attitude toward spending money on programs whose benefits are not immediate is a nontraditional strategic approach. Money spent on training and education is viewed as more of an investment than a cost. Motorola has realized that an investment in its workforce ensures the company a greater sense of enthusiasm and commitment among its employees. This point of view is distinct from other business strategies; it notes the way that employment policies and practices create resources and competencies that achieve competitive advantages. Human resource professionals are a key ingredient in developing firm-specific, valuable resources that impact long-term profits earned by the firm.[2] However, there are other possible strategic choices businesses can make. Some of these choices are outlined in the next section.

STRATEGIC CHOICES

Choosing to include employee involvement in the management of the organization as a means of increasing productivity is a strategic decision in itself. Included in this decision, however, are several other considerations:

1. Top management must decide how much faith it has in its employees. Should managers simply ask for input about how to improve the organization or should they instill in their employees the power necessary to implement these changes? The level of involvement that employees are allowed in an organization is a strategic choice that upper-level management must make, and it ultimately will be based on how much trust management has in its employees.

2. To enable a staff to be productive, the organization must provide the tools needed to perform effectively. These tools can take on a variety of forms, such as education, equipment, or information. Whatever form they take, providing these tools is expensive. Managers must make a strategic choice concerning how much the firm is willing to invest in equipping the employees.

3. Another strategic choice that managers must make is whether or not the organization's culture is supportive of an involved work environment. Because it is difficult to change or adapt an organization's culture, top management must be behind a decision of this nature. Opening up lines of communication and sharing responsibility and power with subordinates may be difficult for some managers to do. However, if the managers see their bosses openly communicating and sharing responsibilities, they may be more open to trying these techniques with their subordinates too.

PRODUCTIVITY

WHAT IS PRODUCTIVITY?

In simple terms, productivity can be defined as output per hour.[3] But this is far too simple. Productivity comes in various forms. For example, some define productivity as the change in unit labor costs, or how much each item costs to produce. Others suggest that productivity is the value of production over paid hours. This ratio determines profitability as well as productivity. Whichever way productivity is defined, it is used to determine whether the firm has been successful.

Recent reports comparing U.S. manufacturing productivity rates to those of other countries present mixed findings. Some suggest that the United States is leading the way. Exhibit 12.1 compares the United States and six other countries on two productivity measures: annual change in manufacturing unit labor costs from 1985 to 1990 and manufacturer increases in output per hour from 1988 to 1989. On one chart, the United States is number one; on the other, it is last. Which figures are correct? They both are. But how can that be?

The numbers in Exhibit 12.1 do not tell the whole story. While it is true that the productivity growth rate has fallen over 60 percent since the 1950s and 1960s, those periods reflected abnormal productivity. The United States was recovering from World War II and the Great Depression and was using untapped accumulations of innovation and savings. Once recovery was complete, productivity slowed. But in comparison to previous years, it appeared to fall. In absolute terms, the productivity level of U.S. manufacturing continues to be the highest in the world.[4]

By some measures Americans have never worked harder. The percentage of Americans in the workforce has risen steadily since 1948 and has risen over 75 percent for women. Sixty-five percent of married households have two or more people working, and over 6 percent of Americans hold two jobs. Not only do we work more at work, but also we work more at home. American men average 44 hours a week for pay and an additional 14 hours of work at home. Their Japanese counterparts average 52 hours of

---

EXHIBIT 12.1   **Manufacturer Productivity Ratings**

ANNUAL PERCENTAGE CHANGE IN MANUFACTURING UNIT LABOR COSTS

Country	Percentage Change
United States	−0.1
Canada	+7.9
Italy	+14.3
Germany	+15.6
France	+11.0
Britain	+10.8
Japan	+10.3

MANUFACTURER PRODUCTIVITY INCREASES IN OUTPUT PER HOUR

Country	1988	1989	Percentage Change
United States	2.2%	1.8%	−4
Canada	1.6%	2.1%	+5
Italy	2.6%	2.7%	+1
Germany	4.3%	4.3%	0
France	4.7%	4.4%	−3
Britain	5.0%	4.7%	−3
Japan	4.4%	5.3%	+9

SOURCE: *The Wall Street Journal,* © 1992 Dow Jones & Company; and *Business Week,* October 8, 1991, © 1991 by McGraw-Hill, Inc.

work for pay, but only 3.5 hours at home. In total, American men work harder than Japanese men.[5]

Defining productivity in service organizations is not easy. While output per hour could be measured by the number of customers serviced, other factors come into play. Two of the recurring factors are quality and service.[6] In practice, the goal of most service organizations is to provide the fastest, most efficient, and friendliest service possible to any and all customers. In terms of productivity, this may mean that minimizing errors or eliminating reworking is stressed. Or it may mean that smiling and offering to go the extra mile for a customer is stressed. In any case, the idea is to make the service industry more productive by having better serviced customers.

MEASURING PRODUCTIVITY

The techniques for measuring productivity are as varied as the industries in which the measurements are taking place. Traditional techniques were developed to measure assembly line productivity. These measures are based on tracking output in units or dollars per inputs usually in the form of human hours spent working on the relevant tasks. These figures are still used in many production-oriented firms today. For example, the average number of human hours required to produce one car in a European plant is 35.5 hours; in a U.S. plant, it is 24.9 hours; and in a Japanese plant it is 16.8 hours.[7] But what do these figures actually mean? Researchers at MIT suggest that each worker in these car plants can be viewed in terms of his or her "value added." In the car plants in Japan, it is difficult to find any worker who cannot be defined as adding value. However, in the European plants, these researchers found that many people add no value, but instead correct mistakes that should have never been made in the first place.[8]

In the service and professional areas, traditional productivity measures have fallen. It is difficult, if not impossible, to measure some types of activities with respect to output per input. When the traditional measures are used in nonproduction areas, great productivity numbers may not result in good outcomes. One example of this was found at Motorola. Recruiters for Motorola were assigned the goal of spending less per hire each year as a measure of productivity. Each year productivity rose. Things should have been good, but they were not. The quality of the new hires began to decrease. Obviously, if you spend only a few dollars to select employees, the new hires selected may not be qualified or effective workers. By cutting costs in this way, the thoroughness of the screening process will deteriorate. To solve this problem, Motorola changed its policy. It now measures recruitment productivity by how well its recruits do at Motorola after being hired. For example, recruiters are measured on items such as how well qualified the person was for the job and whether the salary was determined correctly by whether the new hire leaves soon after employment for a higher paying job. Under the new productivity measures, price per recruit has risen, but so has the quality of the recruits.[9]

Other industries also have developed unique ways to measure productivity in nonproduction areas. Olsten, a temporary help agency, and Avis, a car rental agency, routinely survey customers to help determine employee productivity. Results of the survey can be used in a variety of ways. For example, one travel company uses them to help show employees how to be more aware of customers' individual needs and desires. They have found that by treating each customer like an individual, return business (one measure of productivity) has improved. In the hotel business, similar techniques are used. It is almost impossible to stay overnight in a hotel or motel and not see some type of customer response card asking for a rating of it at some point in a stay. Many of the large chains ask guests upon checkout whether they completed a response card. Other chains leave them in rooms, and many are personalized with the name of the person who cleaned the room that day. In addition to customer input, Quality Inns tracks the number of minutes it takes to clean a room, how many meals are served in an hour, and how frequently a booking agent can turn a call into a reservation.[10]

Whatever method is used, it is important that the results are used to do what they are intended to do—improve productivity. After realizing that other productivity measures, besides the recruitment area, were causing problems down the line, Motorola revamped its entire productivity measurement scheme. Motorola now defines productivity in terms of the opportunity to make mistakes. Most mistakes made are not made due to poor quality of employees but are made because of the way people are told to do their job. Over the years, procedures and policies have become antiquated, complicated, and redundant. Managers at Motorola strive to locate poor procedures and replace them with more efficient ones. This new perspective has saved Motorola both time and money. For example, due to changes in the finance department, the company can now close its books at the end of a month in four days instead of eight. This provides a savings of 576,000 worker-hours, worth about $20 million.[11]

WAYS TO INCREASE PRODUCTIVITY

Increasing organizational productivity can be initiated from the organizational level, the individual level, and the group level. The following sections examine how to increase organizational productivity through restructuring, individual approaches, and leadership. Employee involvement and total quality management are discussed later but also relate to increasing productivity.

ORGANIZATIONAL RESTRUCTURING

Many firms have tried to become more productive through organizational restructuring.[12] Between 1977 and 1992, the Fortune 500 companies have slashed 2.8 million employees from their payrolls. Millions of other employees have taken pay cuts or surrendered their jobs. All of these changes were made in an effort to streamline and restructure corporations.[13] Organizational restructuring can take on a variety of forms: downsizing, mergers and acquisitions, joint ventures, and globalization. We will look at each of these in turn.

DOWNSIZING

Companies that faced a decrease in sales, market share, or profits over the past 10 years began to realize that their human resources were expensive and underutilized. To be more competitive, companies made a strategic decision to gradually lower their payroll numbers. The first step was to use attrition. By not replacing employees who retired or quit, substantial gains were made with respect to overall costs. Employees who were asked to take on the work done by others at first were disgruntled but accepted the change after realizing that it was helping them to keep their jobs.

However, during the 1980s, the economy continued to degrade. Older workers began to postpone retirement indefinitely once mandatory retirement was abolished. Some realized that the pension they would receive would not be enough to support them in the manner in which they were accustomed with the current economy; others decided they were not ready to face the golf course on a daily basis. Similarly, voluntary turnover decreased as well. The poor job market, fueled by the weak economy, made

DOWNSIZING
Reducing the size of the workforce.

any job better than the unemployment line. Attrition was no longer a suitable tool for **downsizing** the workforce.

The next step was budget cutting. In this stage, managers were given mandates to decrease their budgets anywhere from 5 to 50 percent. The easiest way to do this was to reduce the size of the workforce. Often automation could be introduced to make a job that once took as many as a dozen people to complete manageable by only one or two. The other 10 employees were dismissed. Another technique was to reduce the number of people all performing the same job by doubling the work load for half of them and dismissing the other half. Creative ways to cut staff was the focus of most managers during this time. The person with the ax became a very unfriendly sight, even after the cuts were completed. Morale dipped extremely low, even for the survivors. It was difficult for the manager who rearranged the workforce to lead it again after the dust settled.

Some companies fought to keep the morale of the firm up during even the worst times. Firms that communicated the changes early and provided the employees who were to be released with the opportunity to retrain or develop new skills before termination increased the morale for both the leavers and stayers. Additionally, the survivors who were asked to take on more responsibility and work were asked what they needed to make their jobs easier. Training, equipment, and more control were provided as a means of keeping the remaining workers satisfied.[14] However, the quality of the product or service often takes a beating due to downsizing.

Downsizing and budget cutting are only reactions to the problem. They cannot even be considered strategies.[15] These techniques may have helped to save several large companies, such as Caterpillar and Ford Motor Company, but they do not provide a lasting solution to the problem. Human resource professionals should be aware that the negative effects of downsizing are felt not only by those who leave but also by those who stay. Significant adjustments must be made by workers, especially older workers, who may have believed that they would be employed for life. Some firms are finding that acquiring or merging with another company may be a more long-term strategic approach to increase productivity.

MERGERS AND ACQUISITIONS

MERGERS AND ACQUISITIONS
The union of two or more corporate interests or organizations.

During 1985, over 3,000 **mergers and acquisitions** were completed with a total value of over $18 billion.[16] While the financial value of these deals is easily calculated, what is not clear is the human value. Often in mergers and acquisitions, the human resource division is completely left out of the picture. Likewise, the people who are being acquired are frequently given scant attention. In a survey, only 37 percent of the acquirers indicated that they audited the management and personnel prior to buying the firm. Further, the majority of these audits were to examine human resource policies that may limit the buyers' freedom to act, not to examine the personnel themselves.[17]

As mergers and acquisitions become increasingly common, it is important for human resource managers to become involved in the acquisition or merger process early on. To do this successfully, we suggest the following:

1. Get to know the members of the acquisition/merger team. If they speak a different language, either literally or figuratively, learn it. They will be more open to your human resource concerns if you are more aware of theirs.
2. Bring something with you. Show them that you have training programs that could be beneficial to both sides of the merger. Explain how you can help to merge the two cultures. Show them that you are willing to help in any way.

3. Be realistic about what information they will provide you and how much interest they will have in your offers.

4. Be timely. Show them that you are willing to work under their time frame.

5. Maintain a balanced viewpoint. Try not to get bogged down in trivial issues but continue to focus on the bigger picture.[18]

Other issues that human resource managers should be aware of during a merger or acquisition include the fact that personnel uncertainty will be extremely high. The only way to manage this is through accurate and frequent communication about the process. As employees try to manage the uncertainty in their lives, they will continually flip-flop between supporting the change and hating it. Realizing that this behavior is common can help to avoid confusion for human resource managers. Employees will go through culture shock as the two cultures collide, and they will tend to pull out their support and patience if they anticipate more changes to the culture than they can handle. Communication, again, is one way to avoid this problem.[19] Finally, it is important to note that not all mergers and acquisitions will be positive events. Research has shown that about 50 percent of the acquisitions examined were clear failures.[20] Many of these ventures failed because the acquirers did not realize the effectiveness of the current management and structure of the acquired firm and altered it on arrival. Inevitably, the acquired staff was demoted or misplaced and eventually turned over. Ironically, the reason the acquirers wanted the acquired firm in the first place—the management team—may all have vanished.[21]

JOINT VENTURES

JOINT VENTURE
Method of implementing a growth strategy in which two or more companies join forces for a common purpose.

Joint ventures are another way in which organizations can become more productive. By using the strongest skills of each partner in the joint venture, the outcomes can be better than they would have been with each side working alone. One of the industries in which joint ventures frequently occur is the automobile industry. There are so many, in fact, that one automobile trade journal gives subscribers a free wall chart that outlines the current joint ventures in the auto industry. One of the first was between General Motors and Toyota, which combined forces to build the Chevy Nova in Fremont, California. Their 50–50 joint venture, frequently called Nummi (New United Motor Manufacturing, Inc.), began producing Novas in 1984. The sales were slow, mainly due to the number of cars in the Chevy lineup that were so much like the Nova.[22]

Another car industry joint venture, the one between Mazda and Ford, produced what has been termed the first global car, the 1991 Ford Escort. The idea behind the global car is that it can be produced and sold in countries all over the world. The development of the Escort took over eight years. Its history is outlined in Exhibit 12.2. Throughout the planning process, Ford and Mazda had conflicts. One bone of contention was the fact that Mazda didn't believe that the U.S. supplier could provide quality materials and Ford didn't think it could keep up with the grueling pace of the Japanese manufacturing process. The successful, on-schedule prototypes made with over 50 percent U.S. parts in a Japanese plant helped to overcome those fears. Other debates ended in compromise. Engine noise, which Mazda wanted to reduce by retuning the engine and Ford wanted to quiet through other adjustments, was taken care of by retuning the engine, adding more insulation, and installing the motor on softer rubber mounts. While Ford didn't expect to make money on the Escort, the company believes it has saved over $1 billion and has learned what it will take for Ford to be competitive in a world marketplace.[23]

Whenever two parties join forces, they both have a stake in the claim, and what is good for one side may not necessarily be good for the other. GM faced that dilemma when Toyota asked if it could build Toyota trucks in the Nummi factory. There were

▌ EXHIBIT 12.2 ▬▬▬▬▬   **The History of the Ford Escort**

November 1981

Ford begins planning a 1991 replacement for its one-year-old Escort, its best-selling car. Initially, Ford plans to build a "world car" for the United States, Japanese, and European markets.

May 1983

Ford decides to scale back the program and cover only North America and Asia. Ford asks Mazda to take the lead development role and gives Mazda final say over the engineering decisions.

March 1985

Ford belatedly decides that it will need the fuel-efficient Escort to help its domestic fleet meet U.S. fuel-economy regulations, but too many Japanese parts disqualify it from being classified as a domestic model. The decision is made to put a Ford engine in the new car.

Late 1986

Due to the increasing value of the yen against the dollar, the project goes badly over budget. Ford decides it has to use more U.S. suppliers for the Escort.

October 1987

The first prototypes of the Escort are built in a Mazda plant in Hiroshima, Japan. More than 50 percent of the car's parts are from Ford suppliers.

September 1988

Ford and the United Auto Workers agree on a new labor pact covering the production of the Escort at Ford's Wayne, Michigan, stamping and body plant. The new agreement reduces the unskilled job classifications from 24 to 1.

February 1990

First production cars roll off the retooled Wayne assembly line.

April 1990

Escorts go on sale in the United States.

SOURCE: Adapted from J. B. Treece and A. Borrus, "How Ford and Mazda Shared the Driver's Seat," *Business Week,* March 26, 1990, pp. 94–95.

large and certain payoffs for Toyota if GM said yes. If Toyota could build trucks in the United States, it could avoid the 25 percent tariff placed on imported trucks. The payoffs for GM were not so clear. Certainly, the profits at the plant would increase, which would be good for GM. However, GM still competed with Toyota in the marketplace, and allowing Toyota to have an even less expensive truck available to the U.S. consumers was not good business for GM.[24]

Japan is not the only country with which joint ventures have been popular. In 1989, there were 900 joint ventures deals with Hungary. This was up from 1 in 1981. Some of the biggest were with GE, which paid $150 million for 50.1 percent of Tungsram, a Hungarian light bulb manufacturer, and Guardian Industries spent $110 million in a joint venture to convert an obsolete glass plant. Hungary is selected frequently due to a lower wage base and availability of labor. For example, Schwinn Bicycle Company

FOCUS ON INTERNATIONAL ISSUES

Can U.S. Managers Work for a Japanese Company?

In a global marketplace, U.S. managers will be placed in foreign offices and asked to manage foreign workers. A global marketplace also means that foreign managers will be placed in U.S. companies and asked to manage U.S. workers. While many say U.S. managers are not ready for the challenge of an overseas assignment, just as many believe that the U.S. workers, especially managers, may not be ready for the challenge of working for a non–U.S. manager.

Nationwide, more than 350,000 Americans work for Japanese companies. These workers, who hold positions from assembly line worker to executive, see many differences in working for a Japanese company rather than a U.S. one. The line workers, now called associates or team members, work in extremely clean, well-maintained, nonunion plants. They participate in morning exercises and wear company uniforms. They also participate in *kaizen,* a philosophy aimed at continually improving products and production. While these changes may seem drastic at first, they are understandable and acceptable, and workers are highly rewarded for doing so.

Managers who report to Japanese bosses face different changes. Stripped of their decision-making authority and much of their individual responsibility, American managers now must embrace concepts such as *nemawashi* (consensus building) and *ringi* (shared decision making). Often these managers complain of a lack of feedback and of limited communication from their bosses. They also believe they must fight to be heard by their Japanese colleagues. Some suggest that the problem is one of discrimination. Others suggest that it is simply an adjustment problem that will soon fade away. Whichever way the situation is viewed, American managers working for Japanese firms face some rough roads ahead.

SOURCE: Adapted from Thomas O'Boyle, "Under Japanese Bosses, Americans Find Work Both Better and Worse," *The Wall Street Journal,* November 26, 1991, p. A1 +.

is making bikes in a joint venture with Csepel, a heavy-industry complex near Budapest. Schwinn-Csepel workers must wear badges that have both the U.S. and the Hungarian flags and follow different work procedures than the over ten thousand state workers all around them. The benefit to the worker is 25 percent more pay. It is difficult to even begin to imagine the problems human resource managers would face if the same production techniques were used on U.S. soil.[25]

GLOBALIZATION

The term *globalization* raises many questions in the minds of U.S. business people. What exactly is globalization? Does it mean that a certain percent of sales, say 25 percent, must take place overseas? Does it mean that top management must have experience in a variety of countries? Or is it more of a global perspective, in which top officials scan the entire world before making decisions?[26] It is all of these, and more.

Globalization requires having global standards for quality, pricing, service, and design.[27] For instance, if a firm manufactures products for the European market or if it sells machinery, electronics, food products, pharmaceuticals, or other goods in Europe, it will soon need to address the ISO 9000 quality program, which is a blueprint for international standards of manufacturing excellence.[28] Ford's Escort was one of the first U.S. products to be built on a global scale. But globalization takes more than just setting and adhering to standards; it also requires global leadership. This means that Americans will have to live and work overseas. Managers without international management experience will not climb high in the ranks in a true global economy. However, in past years, an overseas stint meant a slow-down in a manager's career path, so many avoided it. For this reason, many U.S. firms may not be ready for a global economy.[29]

One company that is ready is General Electric. GE sold its consumer electronics business in Europe to Thompson SA of France and then bought Thompson's medical equipment business, Thompson CGR, in an effort to strengthen its own medical unit. CGR and GE Medical Systems Asia give GE a global organization that can effectively compete with Siemens, Phillips, and Toshiba in the world market for X-ray, CAT scan, magnetic resonance, and other medical equipment. Sales outside the United States for GE Medical Systems rose from just 13 percent in 1985 to over 45 percent in 1988. John Trani, the GE executive who runs the organization is also using a global leadership style. He has developed a loose and flexible organization with no rigid chain of command. He also has formed leadership groups with managers from three continents to work toward shortening the product development cycle and other major global issues.[30]

Like GE, other firms have decided that globalization is the way to go. However, not all firms are so quick to follow. Some firms foresee several problems. First, executives are not sure exactly how to go about the business of globalization, and, second, they are not truly sure of the benefits of globalization. Exhibit 12.3 presents the results of a

EXHIBIT 12.3   **Results of a CEO Survey on Globalization**

WHY GO GLOBAL?

	United States	Europe	Japan	Pacific Rim
Increase revenue	39%	52%	58%	46%
Increase profitability	27	53	53	40
Achieve technological leadership	20	30	44	34
Diversify into new business	23	35	53	27
Lower business costs	19	39	55	34
Improve product quality	19	35	34	37

HOW DO YOU PLAN TO DO IT?

	United States	Europe	Japan	Pacific Rim
Open a new plant abroad	20%	36%	42%	25%
Launch new products abroad	49	50	42	38
Expand into new foreign markets	60	60	58	65
Roll out new technology abroad	28	23	37	20
Form new strategic alliances	44	48	60	43

HOW MUCH GLOBAL (WORLDLY) EXPERIENCE DO YOUR CEOs HAVE?

	United States	Europe	Japan	Pacific Rim
No foreign experience	14%	3.1%	1.1%	2.6%
Travel abroad only once or twice a year	23	1.0	15	18
Travel abroad more than twice a year	56	80	78	75
Studied abroad	16	28	13	54
Worked abroad	32	47	19	46
Managed a business abroad for current company	16	37	5.3	21
Firm has foreign directors	21	34	3.1	41

SOURCE: *The Wall Street Journal.* © 1989 Dow Jones & Company, Inc.

survey of 433 CEOs in the United States, Europe, Japan, and the Pacific Rim about their views on globalization. Among some of the more interesting findings, these figures indicate that Pacific Rim CEOs are the most worldly, having had many managers work and study abroad. Also of interest in these figures is the rather obvious closed nature of Japan with respect to foreign directors. Only 3.1 percent of those surveyed indicated that there were foreign directors of their firms. The United States, which placed second lowest, had 21 percent.

Globalization is definitely a strategic business decision, one that can and will be made by more and more companies as entry into other areas of the world becomes increasingly easier. What does it mean to the human resource department if an organization decides to go global? The ramifications seem endless. For one thing, training will be affected. Not only will it be important to train American employees who plan to go overseas in the language of the country in which they will be placed, but also it will be just as important to inform them of the culture of the country. Being literate in both word and deed will make the transition easier and more positive. What are the training needs of overseas employees coming to the United States to work? The organizational culture and jargon must be taught to the new employees in a way that they will understand but that is not demeaning. Further, socialization programs must be in place to ensure a smooth transition for these new employees.

Aside from training issues, human resource professionals will face many other problems. What performance appraisals, reward programs, and compensation are needed? Many of these functions have been so Americanized that they will not be effective with foreign workers. In Japan, telling one worker that she or he is doing better than the rest and rewarding that worker for doing so is not appropriate. Japanese workers want to fit in and be like the rest. They do not want to be recognized. Recognizing one worker in a group may cause work group problems, resulting in the need for conflict resolution techniques. Would it be wise to use the American models such as confronting one another and working out the problem? Probably not. This is not appropriate behavior in many foreign cultures. What about wages? Do you pay these new workers what their counterparts in the country from which they came would make, or do you pay them American wages? What if they are transferred back? Do they go back to their home country's pay base? The list of problems goes on and on. Suffice it to say that globalization will have a significant impact on the human resource function of any organization that selects a globalization strategy.

INDIVIDUAL APPROACH

Two major components influence whether or not an employee is productive: ability and attitude. Ability is simply whether or not the person is able to perform the job. It is influenced by whether the person has the training, education, skills, and tools and works in an environment necessary to perform the job. Attitude, on the other hand, refers to whether the person *wants* to perform the job. Attitude is influenced by the employee's level of motivation, about satisfaction with, and commitment to the job to be performed. Organizations have a great deal of control over both of these areas. Organizations that provide well-developed training and development programs, educational reimbursement plans, and state-of-the-art equipment can expect employees with extremely high ability. Likewise, organizations with strong personnel policies with respect to compensation, rewards, promotions, and career development usually have employees with positive attitudes toward their job and the company. The following sections examine more closely the options organizations have with respect to increasing employees' abilities and attitudes.

ABILITY

To have employees who are able to perform their jobs effectively, organizations must hire people with the knowledge, skills, and abilities needed to perform the job or provide training that will develop these qualities. They must also be sure to provide a work environment that is conducive to performing well. This means that the tools and equipment that employees must have to succeed are provided. Furthermore, the organization's environment or culture also must be designed to promote high-quality performance. To achieve these goals, many organizations use a variety of techniques. Let's look first at training, development, and education of the workforce.

The type of training and development required by lower- and higher-level employees differs. At the lower level, employees generally are provided with specific training designed to make them more productive on the job immediately. Higher-level employees receive this type of training, but they also receive more developmental types of training. Developmental training is designed to help the employee now, as well as in the future, by readying them for assignments with more and more responsibility. However, in recent years, it has become more and more obvious that firms that have a large number of lower-level employees, such as the hospitality and fast-food industries, may need to begin developing them as well as training them.

In the past, employees in the fast-food and hospitality industries were treated in the same manner that equipment was treated. They were replaceable. The jobs were designed to be "idiot-proof" so that they could be performed by any person who walked in off the street. However, due to the demographical changes in the marketplace, the increasing costs of turnover, and the ever-increasing demand for quality service, this is no longer feasible. Organizations are quickly realizing that the management techniques used in the higher levels may be applicable at the lower levels as well.[31]

MMI Hotel Group, which owns Holiday Inns and Embassy Suites, has begun sending housekeepers and desk clerks to seminars around the country. Often, the employee is exposed to his or her first airplane flight and hotel stay. This may also be the first time that the employee attends a large evening dinner party at which he or she is not serving. The company believes that this type of training is essential for its employees because it is difficult for employees to understand quality service if they have never been on the receiving end.[32]

Vermont Heating and Ventilation, a winner of the Labor Department's LIFT (Labor Investing for Tomorrow) program, has embraced the idea of training and developing its people at all levels. The firm of only 250 people spends 10 percent of its gross revenue on training and educational programs. It is not unusual to see employees rise through the ranks at VHV. The vice president of administration is one example. She began at the company as a journeyperson sheetmetal worker and credits the educational focus of the organization with developing her abilities so that she could rise through the ranks.[33]

Not all training and educational programs need to be sponsored by the firm. Some innovative firms are finding ways to support education opportunities already available to the employees. For example, a Sonic drive-in manager in Tucson, Arizona, provides high-school-aged employees a retroactive bonus of 15 cents an hour if they maintain a 2.5 grade-point average for a semester. If the employee maintains a 3.0 grade-point average or better, the bonus is increased to 25 cents an hour.[34]

Training and development for managers is also on the rise. The American Society for Training and Development (ASTD) has estimated that 60 percent of the nation's largest companies offer leadership training. ASTD also noted that one-third of the companies include nonsupervisors in their programs. For example, Eastman Kodak trains shop-level workers to develop supportive and coaching skills, middle-level managers learn how to empower their workers, and high-level managers engage in "adventure learning," taking on tough outdoor activities to explore how to perform under pressure or as part of a team.[35]

Organizations are also responsible for developing an environment that is conducive to high performance. Recent reports indicate that organizations may not be doing such a good job at this. Results from a two-year study of over 250 organizations revealed that 7 of every 10 employees are hesitant to speak up at work because they fear the repercussions. This means that many good ideas are dying because of fear. This can only hurt a firm's productivity. While there is no easy solution to solving this problem, the researcher suggested that companies emphasize empowering the workforce by providing it with responsibility for tasks and giving it the authority to carry them out.[36] Organizations must look to new ways to redesign their environments so that high performance and continuous improvement efforts are encouraged and rewarded.[37] One firm uses a Monopoly-type board game as an incentive program to reward excellent performance. The players receive "money" to buy "real estate" on the Monopoly board, and individuals who build up assets can later trade them in for prizes such as time off or vacations.[38]

Another aspect of the work environment is the job itself. Many of the elements of job design that were covered in Chapter 8 are crucial to developing a quality-based work environment. Offering flextime to employees who have obligations before or after work may help them to relax and concentrate on their work instead of having to worry about how they will meet their commitments. Sometimes it takes an act of nature to make organizations realize that flexible schedules are necessary. For example, after the 1989 earthquake in San Francisco, many firms *had* to go to a flextime schedule because the major commuting thoroughfares were closed. Some firms allowed employees to work at branch offices outside of San Francisco, and other firms allowed employees to work from computers in their homes.[39]

Working at home via computer, or telecommuting, is beginning to catch on as another way in which employers can provide a productivity-oriented work environment for employees. Some companies that are beginning to explore this technological opportunity are finding that telecommuting workers who used to have long commutes are becoming much more productive employees. Commuting a long distance is an emotional and mental drain. A worker who has been sitting behind a steering wheel and fighting the traffic for over an hour simply cannot be in the same frame of mind as the person who only has to walk to the den. In the future, technological advances may provide other opportunities for organizations to provide a better working environment for their employees.

ATTITUDE

Employee attitudes have a crucial effect on any firm's bottom line. An employee's attitude determines whether a defective part is placed into a product, whether the customer continues to patronize the firm, and whether the firm is productive. Employees who are burned out, turned off, cynical, demoralized, or any combination of these fail to buy into the spirit of the firm. And their bad attitudes are infectious.

Recent surveys have found that cynicism is running high in the U.S. workplace. Cynical employees distrust their bosses, which is reflected in their work. Cynical employees are less productive, less efficient, and less willing to accept change. The problem lies not only with the worker, however. Cynical bosses who treat employees without dignity are also to blame.[40]

Companies that have realized the impact that employee cynicism and other negative attitudes have on the bottom line have taken steps to combat it. The most useful strategy is information. Anita Roddick, founder and managing director of The Body Shop, believes that the best way to combat cynicism is with information. She bombards her staff with newsletters, videos, brochures, posters, and training programs. The goal is to teach employees that business does not have to be boring. She spends much of her time developing stories and articles for the newsletters, which are not just ordinary newsletters. Many of them are devoted to information about projects to save the environment or anthropological tidbits. Nor are the training programs ordinary. For example, clerks who sell the products participate in sessions that explain how to use the product, not how to sell it. The idea behind this type of training is that if the employees understand the products' benefits and are informed about them, they will be better salespeople.[41]

Other companies have decided to combat poor attitudes in workers with humor. Kodak recently established a humor task force that was charged with building a humor room at corporate headquarters when it was decided that the company needed to lighten up. It seems to be working. When Kodak's downsizing announcement coincided with the release of the movie "Honey, I Shrunk the Kids," ingenious Kodak employees circulated a spoof memo entitled "Honey, I Shrunk the Company." Humor can also be big business. Consulting firms that specialize in humor have been doing a brisk business by teaching firms to give up the old notion that humor is dependent upon putting someone else down. Instead, the focus is on teaching the firm to laugh at itself.[42] Exhibit 12.4 outlines some helpful hints for how one can go about having fun at work.

EXHIBIT 12.4   **How to Start Having Fun at Work**

1. Get to know your people. Then you'll understand what will be fun for them.
2. Acknowledge people's help. Write someone a personal letter of thanks for exceptional work performance. Then go by and shake his or her hand.
3. Think of someone you really respect but who may not know it. Tell the person.
4. Make a joke about yourself. Tell someone one of the most embarrassing things that ever happened to you.
5. Pull a practical joke on someone who can take it.
6. Send someone a gift when he or she has done something exceptional for you or your organization.
7. Pick one or two people to "grow." Make them your special projects and help them in any way you can. (You do not need to tell them you are doing this.)
8. Create a social committee to organize events. Get actively involved in this committee.
9. Tell everyone coming to your next meeting to bring their best joke or work-related story with them to tell everyone at the meeting. (If you want, you could judge the best one and give the person a prize.)
10. Try this for a prize: When someone does a particularly great job of something, do his or her job for a day.
11. Throw a party for the people you work with, or throw a party for your customers and clients.
12. Get everyone involved in skits they make up about their strengths and their weaknesses at work.
13. Ask a customer, co-worker, or supervisor to help you learn something new.
14. Make a list of three things you will do tomorrow to make your work more fun. Do them.
15. Start a new contest at work that is tied to people's performance. You could even create a contest just for yourself. If you are successful at meeting your goal, do something special for yourself.

SOURCE: D. Abramis, "Fun at Work," *Personnel Administrator,* November 1989, p. 63.

Some employees find that laughter in the workplace is motivating. Monsanto researchers, who were taught to press a nickel to their foreheads and then drop it in a cup, reported a 50 percent surge in creativity after taking part in the exercise.[43] Other firms have found different ways to motivate employees. Jan Carlzon, president and CEO of Scandinavian Airlines, frequently tells his staff that there are two factors that motivate people: fear and love. He believes that managers who manage by fear have employees who are unable to work up to their potential. However, managers who manage by love, trust, respect, and faith manage people who behave up to their capabilities.[44]

Carlzon is not alone. Other managers in the service business also reported that management cannot provide quality customer service unless it first truly respects the employees.[45] The problem is that workers don't believe that managers are treating them with respect. Results from a survey that asked workers how well they were treated by their employers revealed that workers were not happy with the lack of respect they received from their supervisors. They felt that the communication they received from their boss was not honest, and they felt as though the company was hiding things from them.[46] In a separate study, 95 percent of the workers polled reported that they could be more productive, but they were not pushed or rewarded to do so. Nearly two-thirds of the workers indicated that their employers who requested their ideas failed to use them at least half of the time.[47]

One company that is truly proving that respected employees can be productive and motivated, even when given little else, is Harbor Sweets. It pays $5 an hour, does not pay for medical or any other type of insurance, provides no pension plan, no 401(k) plan, and no sick days. It also lays off about 60 percent of the workforce after the Christmas rush is over. How can a company with so little to offer find a qualified workforce to support its business? The answer is to hire well-educated and responsible women who don't demand benefits because they are covered by their husbands' benefits packages, who don't require supervision because their work ethic takes care of that, and who don't care if there is no work for months. It turns out that Harbor Sweets offers something that was more important to the workers than anything money could buy: it offered a substitute family for all of the women in the area whose real family had grown up and moved away. It offered a sense of purpose. Obviously, Harbor Sweets is in a unique position and has capitalized upon it.[48]

Providing rewards to employees is often used as a motivation technique. Some of the more commonly used methods include one-time monetary rewards, pay raises, appreciation awards, stock options, or promotions. Because each person is different, what motivates one employee may not be an effective carrot to dangle in front of another. For example, pay is a strong motivating factor for some employees, especially when performance is tied to pay. Even Japanese firms that have traditionally tied pay to seniority and tenure have begun tying it to productivity in an effort to further increase employee performance. Their reasoning for the change was simple: problems arise when there is no difference in the raises and salaries for those people who work hard and those who don't.[49] Merck, a pharmaceutical company, provides another example of a pay-for-performance policy. Merck rewards creativity by giving top performers monetary and non-monetary bonuses.[50]

Recognition is also used as a motivational tool and can be very effective for some employees. For example, the Colgate-Palmolive Company sponsors a "You Can Make a Difference Award" whose winning employees receive $3,500 in stock, a gold medal, an embroidered blazer, and an introduction at the annual meeting. One employee was rewarded for boosting toothpaste output by 50 percent, saving the company $160,000 on equipment. Similar programs are in effect at American Express where 43 employees,

HR CHALLENGE

Union Enforced Quality

On October 4, 1991, United Auto Workers in the Saturn plant in Spring Hill, Tennessee, donned black and orange arm bands and participated in a work slow down. While it may look like yet another labor problem, it really isn't. It is a management problem. What were the employees after? They wanted management to stop increasing output because the speedup was causing quality to decrease. The union leader explained that the workers were not going to sacrifice quality to increase productivity because the workers knew, and management temporarily forgot, that their future depended on making a high-quality product. Management conceded that the union was absolutely right. The workers' concern for quality reinforced the urgency of getting the quality problems fixed, and fixed fast.

The reason that management bumped up the total cars produced from 700 to 900 cars a day is simple: Consumers consider Saturns to be good cars and want to buy them. Saturn generates extraordinary customer satisfaction, as indicated by numerous customer testimonials and a 1994 Customer Satisfaction Index in which Saturn ranked third, just behind luxury cars

Lexus and Infiniti. A recent four-day event for Saturn owners brought 38,000 people to a small town to partake in plant tours and other festivities. Saturn owners recommend their cars to more people than owners of any other make. However, it was difficult to get a Saturn. In 1991, only 50,000 Saturns were built, one-third of the projected 240,000 cars.

As the workers realized, just turning up the speed is not the answer. Saturn had to make some changes, and by 1994, sales increased to 24.7 percent. The Saturn plant is so well tuned that problems in production will lead to a complete shut down in the assembly area in just six minutes. The faster the lines go, the greater chance of a problem. The greater chance of a problem, fewer cars are actually produced. However, with GM's car sales slumping and Saturn being one of the few bright spots on the horizon, the pressure is on the workers in Spring Hill, Tennessee.

SOURCE: David Woodruff, "At Saturn, What Workers Want Is . . . Fewer Defects," *Business Week,* December 2, 1991, pp. 117–118; and R. Serafin, "Saturn Bounces Back with Its Basic Appeal," *Advertising Age,* January 30, 1995, p. 4.

who are named "Great Performers," can receive up to $4,800 worth of travelers checks, a platinum pin, or other awards.[51]

The total cash outlay for firms who used monetary incentives are adding up. In 1988, it was estimated that firms spent over $2.1 billion on recognition programs. This is more than triple the figure reported in 1987.[52] Some firms are responsible for more than their share of these figures. For example, Union National Bank of Little Rock, Arkansas, paid employees $1 million in incentives in 1985. The payroll at that time was only $9 million. The incentives were used to increase productivity from 200 to 300 percent.[53]

Not all recognition awards have to be monetary. Harry Seifert, CEO of Winter Gardens Salad Company, uses a rubber stamp and makes notes in the margins of reports he receives from his employees to let them know that their work was appreciated. Since he has begun using the stamp, he has noticed that the quality of the reports has increased.[54] Other nonmonetary incentives include refrigerators, projection television sets, beach headrests, steak knives, levitating globes, talking crystal balls, chocolate bars with corporate logos, and relaxation tapes with sounds of birds and tropical rain forests. One of the most unique incentives a company can provide their employees is a "congratulator." A congratulator is a device that is placed on an employee's shoulder and when an attached string is pulled, a wooden hand pats him or her on the back. This way the employee can get recognition anytime he or she desires.[55] Some firms have even combined incentives with a corporate message by using T-shirts and mugs to advertise a new procedure the employees should follow. Drawing attention to the new policy through rewards and perks is less threatening to the employee than having the boss keep reminding the employees about it.[56]

Even though incentives seem to be a useful technique for motivating workers, they can sometimes backfire. As long as companies have prizes to give to workers, they will play along and be productive. However, when the prizes run out, so does the motivation. Some managers argue that incentive plans are short range and even confusing to employees. For example, companies that want to place service first have a difficult time convincing employees of their goal when they reward them for working faster and quicker. A California unit of GTE ran into this problem. After conducting a survey of service representatives, they found that employees thought speed came before service. To change this attitude, GTE sent all of the service representatives who wanted to attend to a weekend seminar. Employees who participated received overtime pay. The seminar was designed to show employees that when they pick up the phone, they "own the problem" and should do everything in their power to fix it, regardless of the time it takes to do so. However, when the employees returned to work, the message from the seminar got muddied. While they realized that they owned the problem, they were confused by GTE's continual emphasis on speed, which included timing how long workers talk to each caller. Speed and "owning the problem" were incompatible.[57]

One final technique that some companies use to motivate employees is career path planning. This concept is becoming increasingly important as the available number of paths up the corporate management ladder begin to decrease due to downsizing and an abundance of middle-aged employees jockeying for one or two positions held by people very similar to themselves in age. National Semiconductor found an innovative way to address its decreasing number of management career paths. It designed career paths for individual contributors that are comparable to management paths and are just as rewarding in terms of such factors as decision making, influence, compensation, and responsibility. The design of these paths is good for both the employee and the company because it allows an individual to move from an individual contributor role to a management role and back to an individual contributor role as the qualifications of the employee and needs of the firm change. Because the requirements for movement are clearly explained, employees take control over their own career development. As the individual needs of an employee change, he or she can decide to move into a new position to remain motivated and productive.[58]

Brooklyn Union Gas is another company that is finding creative ways to use career paths to keep its employees motivated. This company has found that many strong salespeople would be content to stay in sales throughout their careers but that to advance, they must move into management. To keep experienced salespeople in the sales area where they can be the most productive, Brooklyn Union Gas has developed account manager positions. In these positions, salespeople are placed in charge of up to 100 of the company's 2,000 largest clients. These clients, who before had to deal with several different sales representatives, now deal exclusively with the account manager. Besides having more prestige, the new positions allow the account managers to command a higher salary base and commissions, depending on how business expands with their clients.[59]

What does this all mean? Why should human resource professionals be concerned with employee attitudes? One clue can be taken from a survey of Baldrige award winners.[60] They suggest that effective human resource policies can significantly influence the attitudes of workers toward their companies. These positive attitudes often translate to less absenteeism and turnover, greater satisfaction and commitment, and, ultimately, more productivity in the workplace for companies that successfully motivate their employees. The previous examples show some of the ways human resource managers are contributing to increased productivity and, in some ways, not only reinforce business strategy but also create new strategies to gain competitive advantage.[61]

As previously mentioned, no one technique improves employees' attitudes across the board. Instead, a combination of motivational tools should be used. Also, it is important to remember that the tools must be consistent with the corporation's culture for them to be effective. Exhibit 12.5 outlines a list of suggestions for human resource managers who are trying to find out what it takes to motivate employees to be productive.

LEADERSHIP AND PRODUCTIVITY

LEADERS
People who do the right things.

An areas's productivity, or lack thereof, can frequently be traced to the **leaders** provided that area. In a recent study of 12 major companies, workers believed that they and the people with whom they worked were committed to providing a quality product. The problem in doing this, they reported, arose at the management level, specifically top management. Two-thirds of the workers surveyed indicated that quality of the work completed was not an important measure of performance in their organization. This belief was frequently supported by top **managers** who verbally stressed the importance of quality workship but offered incentives based only on the number of units produced.[62]

MANAGERS
People who do things right.

One of the first people to even discuss the idea of enhancing quality productivity through leadership was the statistician Dr. W. Edwards Deming. Although he was virtually given saint status in Japan, Deming's philosophy, which helped to rebuild Japan after World War II, was virtually ignored in the United States. He died in December 1993 at the age of 93, but his ideas will continue to have an impact on U.S. firms as they strive to become more productive in the 21st century.[63] A tireless teacher, Deming was concerned whether management's interest in quality was deep enough to ensure lasting improvement. Deming's management philosophy is stated in the form of 14 principles. These principles are listed in Exhibit 12.6. As you read them, notice how closely they reflect the ideas currently being accepted and used in U.S. firms.

EXHIBIT 12.5   **Motivation Tips for Human Resource Managers**

1. Select the best. Motivation comes from within an individual. Therefore, if you hire only the people who have the potential to be motivated, half of the battle is won.

2. Use the Pygmalion effect. If you truly believe in your employees, they will believe in themselves. Take the time to psychologically invest in your employees.

3. Track success. Provide challenging goals with which employees agree and compare their performance regularly to these goals. Make sure to do this in a manner that is not critical or demeaning.

4. Recognize contributions. Provide public recognition for employees who have performed well. Be sure to be consistent about when the rewards are provided. For example, select an employee of the week and announce his or her name at a weekly meeting.

5. Provide incentives and rewards. Remember that the psychological reward of the incentive is often greater than the monetary reward. Also, incentives can be a useful motivatior in the short term.

6. Empower employees. Make employees responsible for the company's product or service. Listen to what they have to say and use their ideas.

7. Enhance career development. Use training and development as a tool to ready employees for the next step in their career paths. Invest in your employees just as you would invest in new equipment.

Source: Adapted from K. Dawson and S. Dawson, "How to Motivate Your Employees," *HRMagazine,* April 1990, pp. 78–80.

EXHIBIT 12.6 **Deming's Fourteen Principles for Managers**

1. Create constancy of purpose toward improvement of product and service with the aim to become competitive, to stay in business, and to provide jobs.
2. Adopt a new philosophy. We are in a new economic age created by Japan. We can no longer live with commonly accepted styles of U.S. management, nor with commonly accepted levels of delays, mistakes, or defective products.
3. Cease dependence on inspection to achieve quality. Eliminate the need for inspection on a mass basis by building quality into the product in the first place.
4. End the practice of awarding business on the basis of the price tag. Instead, minimize the total cost.
5. Improve constantly and forever the system of production and service to improve quality and productivity and thus constantly decrease costs.
6. Institute training on the job.
7. Institute supervision. The aim of supervision should be to help people, machines, and gadgets do a better job. Supervision of management is in need of overhaul, as well as supervision of production workers.
8. Drive out fear so that everyone may work effectively for the company.
9. Break down the barriers between departments. People in research, design, sales, and production must work as a team to foresee problems of production.
10. Eliminate slogans, exhortations, and targets for the workforce that ask for zero defects and new levels of productivity. Such exhortations create only adversarial relationships. The bulk of the causes of low productivity belong to the system and thus lie beyond the power of the workforce.
11. Eliminate work standards that prescribe numerical quotas for the day. Substitute aids and helpful supervision.
12. Remove the barriers that rob the hourly worker of his [or her] right to pride of workmanship. The responsibility of supervisors must be changed from sheer numbers to quality. Remove the barriers that rob people in management and engineering of their right to pride of workmanship. This means abolish the annual rating, or merit rating, and management by objective.
13. Institute a vigorous program of education and retraining.
14. Put everyone in the company to work to accomplish the transformation.

SOURCE: W. Edwards Deming, *Out of Crisis.* Cambridge, MA: Cambridge University Press, 1986.

One of Deming's suggestions was to change the management style that has been used in U.S. business for decades. This is a very difficult task. For managers to support quality production, they must abandon many of the techniques they have used for years in favor of more open and sharing techniques. Delegating the power, prestige, and control that took managers years to build is a bitter pill to swallow, even if it is for the good of the company. However, some managers have been able to successfully mold their leadership styles to promote the new quality-minded workplace. Let's examine a few of these cases.

SUCCESS STORIES

Xerox Corporation, which won the prestigious Malcolm Baldrige National Quality Award that is explained in Exhibit 12.7, has found a way to remold the corporate culture to one that supports and emphasizes quality. The focus at Xerox is on the individual person. If each person who works for Xerox becomes a quality advocate and is extremely knowledgeable about the techniques used to perform his or her job, the result

EXHIBIT 12.7   **The Malcolm Baldrige National Quality Award**

This award was established in 1987 to promote quality awareness, to recognize the quality achievement of U.S. companies, and to publicize successful quality programs and strategies. The criteria are expressed fairly broadly so that they may be applied to both manufacturing and service firms. The seven categories that are viewed as important to quality are listed with the maximum number of points that evaluators may award, depending on their assessment of a company's programs and performance.

1992 EXAMINATION ITEMS AND POINT VALUES

1992 Examination Categories/Items	Point Values
1.0 Leadership	**90**
1.1 Senior Executive Leadership	45
1.2 Management for Quality	25
1.3 Public Responsibility	20
2.0 Information and Analysis	**80**
2.1 Scope and Management of Quality and Performance Data and Information	15
2.2 Competitive Comparisons and Benchmarks	25
2.3 Analysis and Uses of Company-Level Data	40
3.0 Strategic Quality Planning	**60**
3.1 Strategic Quality and Company Performance Planning Process	35
3.2 Quality and Performance Plans	25
4.0 Human Resource Development and Management	**150**
4.1 Human Resource Management	20
4.2 Employee Involvement	40
4.3 Employee Education and Training	40
4.4 Employee Performance and Recognition	25
4.5 Employee Well-Being and Morale	25
5.0 Management of Process Quality	**140**
5.1 Design and Introduction of Quality Products and Services	40
5.2 Process Management—Product and Service Production and Delivery Process	35
5.3 Process Management—Business Processes and Support Services	30
5.4 Supplier Quality	20
5.5 Quality Assessment	15
6.0 Quality and Operational Results	**180**
6.1 Product and Service Quality Results	75
6.2 Company Operational Results	45
6.3 Business Process and Support Service Results	25
6.4 Supplier Quality Results	35
7.0 Consumer Focus and Satisfaction	**300**
7.1 Customer Relationship Management	65
7.2 Commitment to Customers	15
7.3 Customer Satisfaction Determination	35
7.4 Customer Satisfaction Results	75
7.5 Customer Satisfaction Comparison	75
7.6 Future Requirements and Expectations of Customers	35
Total Points	**1,000**

Exactly Who Is W. Edwards Deming?

William Edwards Deming was born on October 14, 1900. After growing up in Iowa and Wyoming, he obtained his first degree in electrical engineering in 1921 from the University of Wyoming. He continued his education at the University of Colorado, earning a master's degree in mathematics and physics, and he received his Ph.D from Yale in mathematical physics in 1928. He began working for the United States Department of Agriculture where considerable attention was being placed on statistical experimental design. Deming enjoyed this work and wanted to continue it. To do this, he moved to London to study under the "father of statistics," Sir Ronald Fisher.

During summer jobs while in school, Deming had learned of the work of Walter Shewhart. Shewhart focused on the statistical control of processes and charting these controls. He believed that there were two variables in the output process; controlled and uncontrolled. While Shewhart focused his attention on improving production processes, Deming realized that these ideas were applicable to all aspects of business. He proved his assumption was correct by applying the concepts to the administrative processes used to prepare the 1940 census, on which he worked.

After this success, he began to teach people involved with the war effort about his 14 principles of quality management. While they listened and implemented some, they never internalized his ideas.

After the war, businesses were not interested in becoming more efficient because the United States was the only country producing anything. There was virtually no competition.

General Douglas MacArthur asked Deming to join him on two trips to Japan to help advise the Japanese in how to reconstruct their country. The contacts he made while on these trips made Deming famous in Japan. He gave the same speech to Japanese managers that he had given to U.S. managers, but the Japanese listened and implemented his 14 principles. His teachings helped Japan become what it is today.

Deming was "introduced" to the United States in a 1980 documentary called "If Japan Can, Why Can't We" produced by Clare Crawford-Mason. She interviewed Deming and marveled at the fact that he was living only minutes from the White House yet *no one* would listen to his remedy for the stagnation in U.S. business. However, after her story aired, Americans began to listen. Deming traveled throughout the United States, giving his seminars to U.S. managers, and some even began to implement his ideas. Two of the most well-known converts are Nashua and Ford. Both of these companies have benefitted greatly from Deming's advice.

SOURCE: Adapted from Henry Neave, *The Deming Dimension,* (Knoxville: SPC Press, 1990).

is a quality product. To achieve this goal, Xerox developed a Leadership through Quality program that focuses on skills training, customer satisfaction, strong union support, and community involvement. By making each employee responsible for Xerox's success, providing the skills and tools necessary to perform the job, and reinforcing the goals, Xerox has reached its goal of creating a total quality organization.[64]

Another successfully managed company is McDonald's. The founder, Ray Kroc, purchased the franchise rights from Dick and Mac McDonald, who ran a small fast-food take-out kitchen in San Bernadino, California. He realized that the formula they used—quick, good food at reasonable prices—was worth his investment, and he knew that the brothers had no intention of expanding. Kroc, who died in 1981 at age 84, has been described as short tempered, politically conservative, tireless, perpetually optimistic, and a fanatic for cleanliness. He motivated workers through maxims that continue to adorn bulletin boards in today's McDonald's. Some of the all-time favorites include "Free enterprise will work if you will" and "If you've got time to lean, you've got time to clean."[65]

Sam Walton, or Mr. Sam as he was known by his employees, was another interesting success case. Beginning in 1962, Walton developed his single store into a 1,300-

store retail chain known as Wal-Mart. Walton followed a savvy, innovative, and carefully mapped strategy to build his chain, which was masked by the cheerleading front that was Walton's style. He avoided putting stores in cities, instead focusing on the heartland of America. His employees are called *associates* and work more like teammates than employees. Each store is in healthy competition with other Wal-Mart stores for recognition as the "best of the area." The rewards are shared by the entire store and doing so builds a more teamlike environment.[66]

Not all leaders have been successful. One example of a leader who failed was Shearson Lehman Hutton, Inc.'s, former CEO, Peter Cohen. Cohen's reputation in the industry prior to taking the CEO position was one of a disciplined and thorough executive. While the securities business is known for inept management, Cohen was found to be an exception to the rule. What forced him to resign as CEO after just two short years? Plenty. Instead of using the managerial style that made him a good choice for the job, he changed, and in a big way. His own personal ambitions began to overshadow the company's goals, and he lost control of the company and of himself. In the weeks preceding his resignation, he gained weight, looked like he was losing sleep, and argued with everyone. After asking for, but not receiving, a confidence vote from his boss, James Robinson, chairman of American Express, he resigned.[67]

The success stories presented above have several commonalities. All of the companies discussed are in the service business, and all have CEOs who believe in their employees. The companies are also a "nice" place to work. Management treats the employees fairly and with dignity. This type of leader can be considered a servant leader. Servant leaders share the following characteristics:

- They take people and their work very seriously.
- They listen and take their leads from the workers.
- They heal the wounds of their workers.
- They are sure of themselves but humble.
- They are stewards for their companies.[68]

Not all CEOs behave this way. Some prefer to be tough as nails and brutal to their staff. Edwin Artzt, chairman of Procter & Gamble, is one such boss. Artzt's aim is to build a tougher, faster, more global P&G. To do this, he is stressing individual accountability, not the team approach used in recent years. He demands that managers consistently beat the competition to market with the latest detergents, face creams, and diapers. He views lightning quick reflexes as the only way to succeed in the new global marketplace and will do anything necessary to get his organization to that point.[69]

Fortune magazine selected America's toughest bosses in 1980, 1984, and again in 1989. Five of those who made the list in 1989 are presented in Exhibit 12.8 with a description of how their staffs view them and how they view themselves. Note as you read through the thoughts in Exhibit 12.8 that they are dramatically different. It is wise to remember that the way a person wants to be viewed may not be the way others actually view them.

The number of tough bosses may be on the rise. Hard times seem to be pushing managers back into the Stone Age of management. Many organizations are taking back the power they gave employees, closing their open doors, and stopping the communication flows. The workplace is becoming a perform or die environment. Gone are the long-term commitments companies used to make to workers and the loyalty employees once had for their companies.[70] Most experts blame this situation on the restructuring and downsizing that is forcing managers to make cuts in human resources. Often these

EXHIBIT 12.8   **America's Toughest Bosses of 1989**

FRANCISCO A. LORENZO, CHAIRMAN, TEXAS AIR

How others see him: He thinks he's a great manager, but he's not. He's incredibly impulsive. He is not trusted inside or outside the organization. He is a good dealmaker.

How he sees himself: I have to be tough, but fair. We built this company from businesses that were failing. We didn't just take over a big company and blow out the cobwebs.

HARRY E. FIGGIE, JR., CHAIRMAN, FIGGIE INTERNATIONAL

How others see him: From horrendous to delightful, from idiotic to brilliant. Working for him was a nightmare. He is really abusive. He is the Steinbrenner of industry.

How he sees himself: You don't build a company like this with lace on your underwear. We bought small companies with no management depth. There's no room for error.

CARL E. REICHARDT, CHAIRMAN, WELLS FARGO & COMPANY

How others see him: Carl's bag is execution, not talk. He's blunt, and you don't want to make mistakes around him. His narrow focus may be limiting middle management, and a lot are leaving.

How he sees himself: Good operations succeed with a minimum of foolishness and glitter. Maybe I am tough. But my 80-year-old mother will be shocked to learn of it.

RICHARD J. MAHONEY, CHAIRMAN, MONSANTO

How others see him: He has a big ego and subordinates have to stroke him a lot. He listens, but he doesn't understand. He has little empathy with subordinates. He can't believe he's wrong.

How he sees himself: I am demanding, not mean. Forgiveness is out of style, shoulder shrugs are out of fashion. Hit the targets on time without excuses.

JIM MANZI, CHAIRMAN, LOTUS DEVELOPMENT

How others see him: You had better have all the answers before you go in; he doesn't suffer comments like, "I'll get back to you on that."

How he sees himself: Real tough guys rely on positional authority. I think that's disgusting. I shy away from it. I rely on trust. And no one is penalized for thinking slowly. That would be stupid.

SOURCE: Adapted from P. Nulty, "America's Toughest Bosses," *Fortune*, February 27, 1989, pp. 40–54.

painful decisions must be based on productivity, and memories tend to be short. If a manager cannot remember what a person has done for him or her lately, then it may mean that the person walks out the door.[71]

WHAT DOES IT TAKE TO BE A GOOD LEADER?

One thing it takes to be a good leader is to have good followers. All of us may not be managers in our lives but each of us fulfills the role of follower. It seems no matter how high a person climbs up the corporate ladder, he or she always has a boss. A boss can make a job easier by hiring good followers. But what exactly is a good follower? Good followers manage themselves well. They are committed to the organization, its purpose, its mission, and to others. They focus their efforts for maximum impact. Finally, they are courageous, honest, and credible.[72]

According to Warren Bennis, one of the foremost authorities on the subject of leadership, good leaders must have certain qualities. The most indispensable quality is a guiding vision and a clear idea of what he or she wants to accomplish; a good leader needs a strongly defined sense of purpose.[73] Bennis differentiates between leaders and managers. He says that leaders are people who do the right things; managers are people who do things right. The major difference is that leaders think about dreams, missions, visions, strategic intent, and purpose. Managers, however, think more about control mechanisms. Leaders ask the what and why questions, not just the how questions. Exhibit 12.9 illustrates the seven characteristics that define a leader, according to Bennis.

WORKPLACE DIVERSITY

Once a person has a qualified staff of effective followers, he or she needs to be a leader who can motivate and challenge each and every one of his or her workers. For example, given the influx of women into the workplace, more attention has been paid to attracting and retaining women. Exhibit 12.10 lists the 10 best companies for working mothers, who represent a large segment of the employee population. Companies are concerned about keeping these employees committed to their work and keeping them productive. Providing on-site child-care facilities, flexible work schedules, parental leave, and tuition reimbursements for children of employees are just some of the ways in which companies are trying to retain their workers.[74] Further, because of the cultural and generational diversity in the workplace, one management style will not be effective with all workers. For example, four distinct generations of workers exist in the current workforce: the swing generation (born 1910–1929), the silent generation (born 1930–1945), the baby-boom generation (born 1946–1964), and the baby-bust generation (born 1965–1976). Each of these generations has a different opinion of work and values different things.

The swing generation was involved in the rebuilding of the United States after World War II. Many of the workers in this generation have retired, but the ones who remain in the workforce often long for the "good old days" and may not be willing to accept change as quickly as the other generations. The silent generation has quietly gathered real estate, boats, and IRAs for their upcoming retirement. Members of this generation currently hold the majority of the power positions in business, and

EXHIBIT 12.9   **Warren Bennis's Seven Characteristics of a Leader**

- **Business literacy:** Does he or she know the business? Does he or she know the real feel of it?
- **People skills:** Does he or she have the capacity to motivate, to bring out the best in people?
- **Conceptual skills:** Does he or she have the capacity to think systematically, creatively, and inventively?
- **Track record:** Has he or she done it before and done it well?
- **Taste:** Does he or she have the ability to pick the right people—not clones of himself or herself but people who can make up for his or her deficiencies?
- **Judgment:** Does he or she have the ability to make quick decisions with imperfect data?
- **Character:** The core competency of leadership is character, but character and judgment are the qualities that we know least about when trying to teach them to others.

SOURCE: Adapted from M. Loeb, "Where Leaders Come From," *Fortune,* September 19, 1994, pp. 241–242.

| **EXHIBIT 12.10** | **The Best Companies for Working Mothers** |

The following 10 companies were identified as exceptionally progressive on *Working Mother* magazine's list of 100 best companies for working mothers, published in the October issue:

- AT&T, New York
- Barnett Banks, Inc., Jacksonville
- Fel-Pro, Inc., Skokie, Ill.
- Glaxo, Inc., Research Triangle Park, NC
- John Hancock Mutual Life Insurance Co., Boston
- International Business Machines Corp., Armonk, N.Y.
- Johnson & Johnson, New Brunswick, N.J.
- Lancaster Laboratories, Inc., Lancaster, Pa.
- NationsBank Corp., Charlotte, N.C.
- Xerox Corp., Stamford, Conn.

SOURCE: R. Naylor, Jr., "The Best Companies for Working Mothers," *Tallahassee Democrat,* September 14, 1994, p. 70.

they view the world with a lack of true interest and no desire to make it better for those who come after. The baby-boom generation believes in the rights of the individual worker, that no one should be dismissed without cause, and that each employee should be rewarded on a merit basis, regardless of race, creed, color, or age. Over the next 10 years, the baby boomers will begin to take on more roles of responsibility as the silent generation begins to retire. Finally, the baby-bust generation has no real sense of oneness. This generation believes that there is a true difference between the haves and the have-nots with respect to economic status and skills. For these workers, managers must be aware of the potential variation in the quality of the workers from this generation.[75] This may explain, in part, the profusion of leadership training courses available to firms seeking to upgrade their managers' leadership skills. Offerings range from a $29 book to a $65,000 speech. Teaching leadership in its many forms has become an industry in itself.[76]

Obviously, workers from each of these generations will not respond favorably to the same leadership techniques. Members of the silent generation are looking for security in their golden years; the baby boomers, who are looking for self-fulfillment, are realizing that it may not be found in the job; and the baby busters are looking for short-term gratification in the form of challenging jobs that take no more than 37.5 hours a week.[77] How does one manager make all these workers happy and productive? The key may be in the organization's culture. If top management can develop the goals for the organization and then find a way to incorporate the needs and rights of each generation into these goals, everyone will be a winner. Let's take a closer look at the blending of leadership and culture.

LEADERSHIP AND CULTURE

CULTURE
The overall organizational environment.

What makes one company able to attract and retain quality leadership? One answer to this question is the overall organizational environment, or **culture.** Organizations that have better-than-average management also have been found to have the following qualities:

1. Strong human resource policies for compensation, promotion, development, and training.
2. Clear communication of job possibilities in the firm.

═══ HR CHALLENGE ═══

Ensuring Productivity at Mars

One company that has been able to implement a companywide corporate culture that supports the organization's goals is Mars, Inc., best known for its candy bars. The best way to understand Mars' culture is to see it in action. All Mars subsidiaries worldwide look the same. There are no walls. Instead, the employees' desks are placed in concentric circles. The president and his or her staff are at the center of the circle and each ring after that is made up of the subordinate staffs. This makes all senior staffers totally accessible; information flows freely.

Quality is an obsession at Mars. The company refuses to allow "incremental degradation" (using lesser quality ingredients to lower costs) to occur. To avoid this, each and every employee is responsible for quality control. Line workers can ditch an entire run of candy bars if the chocolate covering is not perfect. Salespeople can discard entire showcases of products in stores if the expiration date is approaching.

One reason Mars' employees are so willing to take such risks is that they have a great deal of job security and are very well paid. Mars' pay schedule ranks in the 90th percentile when compared to other premier companies worldwide. The pay is high, but it is not diverse. The company has only six pay levels. All vice presidents make approximately the same salary regardless of the function they lead. This allows Mars

to transfer people from one business unit to another and one function to another without much difficulty. And transfer it does. It is rare to find a general manager who has not done at least two tours in different business units.

As is reflected in the organization's salary structure, the owners of Mars believe in treating everyone the same. This aspect of the culture has caused some problems for managers who disagree. For example, one vice president who purchased fancy desks for himself and his immediate staff was dressed down by one of the owners for buying a desk more expensive than his immediate supervisor. While one might think that this type of public reprimand may have a negative effect on the workers and the firm, the opposite is true. The owners have an aura about them, and their outbursts are quickly turned into stories and legends that are circulated around the company to reinforce the culture even more.

Obviously, not all companies can be like Mars and not everyone would want to work for Mars. However, this organization seems to have found a culture that fits its strategies, its goals, its leadership style, and its workers.

SOURCE: Adapted from Craig Cantoni, "Quality Control from Mars," *The Wall Street Journal,* January 27, 1992, p. A12.

3. High-quality career planning.
4. An overall quality work environment.[78]

An organization's choice and use of culture are strategic decisions. Various types of cultures are available for organizations to use; however, the leadership style of the firm must closely mesh with its chosen culture. Researchers have argued that an organization's cultural values influence its human resource strategies, including selection and placement policies, promotion and development procedures, and reward systems.[79] Human resource managers must be aware of the strong links between the strategies of managers with regard to organizational culture and the resulting impact on psychological climates that foster varying levels of commitment to increases in productivity. When an organization's culture is not in sync with the management or with the rapidly changing times, that organization may decide to change its image and develop a new corporate culture. One company to choose this route is Mobile Oil.

In the early 1980s, Mobil realized that the strong centralized controls that it used in the 1960s and 1970s were no longer appropriate and needed to be changed. In the past, Mobil was described as a paternal, traditional organization that had a great deal of loyal, long-tenured employees. To change its culture, Mobil brought in outside consultants who looked at the current management style used and suggested changes to bring it in line with the 1980s style of management. The old management style included heavy layers of people checking up on other people, which interfered with effective performance. To update its culture, Mobil changed the performance evaluations and compensation of the entire organization. Gone were the guaranteed raises every 12 or 15 months. Instead, a pay increase would come for "giving Mobile something extra." Managers were no longer "better than the rest." Instead, they were told to manage people but not try to be smarter than anyone else in the room. Mobil focused on a skills approach. Valued employees were ones who held the skills needed to perform the job effectively, and Mobil began to work closely with its people to ensure that they had the skills needed to succeed. One final change in the culture was an increase in communication. Even the CEO, L. A. Noto, holds annual straight-talk meetings with a handful of employees to discuss the company's future.

All of the changes made at Mobil did not come easy, and some did not work. However, Mobil made a strategic decision to alter its culture to be more in step with the times, and it followed through on this decision. To be successful at changing a corporate culture, other companies that make this strategic decision should be aware of several things. First, corporate culture can never be imposed. A company cannot force employees to change their values simply because it is in the best interests of the organization. However, it can change someone's behavior. By changing an employee's behavior, the company can hope that his or her attitudes will change in the process. Management must be aware of this subtlety and attempt to help guide the change.

Another concern a corporation must keep in mind when developing or changing its culture is that certain cultures work best in specific environments. To determine what culture is right for a company, the goals, mission, and direction of the organization must be taken into consideration. The culture should be developed to support the organization's goal. By focusing on what the organization wants to accomplish, how to do this and what environment is needed become apparent. A culture that supports the organization's goals and environment can then be developed. Employee involvement is critical to the success of a changing corporate culture and overall productivity. The following sections examine employee involvement in detail.

INVOLVEMENT

Until recently, employee involvement (EI) was largely a utopian ideal shared by only a few believers. However, today it is a bona fide movement with an extremely large following. Strangely enough, EI has drawn unlikely bedfellows from camps that are usually diametrically opposed to one another's views: management and unions. EI has been openly welcomed by manufacturing and service industry employees and managers alike as a way to improve commitment, quality, and productivity in the workplace. Exhibit 12.11 shows a symbol that is now found in all Ford warranty packets in the glove compartments of new cars.

WHAT IS EMPLOYEE INVOLVEMENT?

EMPLOYEE INVOLVEMENT
Strategy that allows workers more responsibility and accountability.

Employee involvement is a series of strategies that firms can adopt to allow workers more responsibility and accountability for preparing a product or offering a service. The term itself can refer to a wide range of practices, from simply soliciting employees' work-improvement ideas in small group meetings with front-line workers to forming self-managed work teams of workers who are given total control over their jobs and working environment. Also included in the concept of EI is the idea that unions or other

EXHIBIT 12.11   **Evidence of Employee Involvement at Ford**

SOURCE: Mercury Sable 1990 *Owner's Manual.*

worker-represented groups should have the power to participate in the plant-and company-level decision-making process.[80]

EI is based on two principles that managers have been familiar with for many years. The first is that people tend to support what they helped to create. For example, someone who is actively involved in developing new policy for handling the return procedures for a product is more likely to help ensure that it is carried out correctly, to make sure that it really does work, and to sell it to their friends and co-workers. The second principle underlying EI is the idea that people who know most about the inner functioning of an operation are those who actually perform the work. Asking for information and participation of the people actually performing the job can provide insights not available from managers or consultants.[81]

BENEFITS OF EMPLOYEE INVOLVEMENT

As more and more firms have begun to implement EI techniques, the benefits of doing so have begun to surface. The following is a list of just some of the possible positive repercussions of using EI in an organization.

1. EI provides subordinates a greater understanding of decisions because they are more likely to be involved in making those decisions.
2. Similarly, employees who have a say in the decision are more committed to implementing it.
3. Involving employees in the decision-making and planning practices of the organization provides a greater understanding of the organization's objectives and improves their commitment to achieving these objectives. In addition, employee commitment and loyalty have been associated with higher productivity.[82]

4. EI provides greater fulfillment of psychological needs, and therefore it provides greater employee satisfaction.

5. EI can capitalize on the increased social pressure other members will place on fellow workers to comply with the decisions the group made as a whole.

6. EI provides a greater team and organizational identity, which is shown through greater cooperation and coordination among members at all levels.

7. When conflict does arise under EI situations, the people involved are better able to constructively deal with it.

8. EI produces better decisions.[83]

COMMUNICATION AND INVOLVEMENT

One of the key components of successfully implementing EI is open and truthful communication among and between employees at all levels in the organization. Various techniques can be used to open the lines of communication in an organization; some are more appropriate for service firms, and others are more useful in manufacturing situations. Further, the usefulness of some techniques depends on the level in the organization from which the employees are drawn.

For example, James Orr, CEO of UNUM Corporation, invites his 5,500 employees at corporate headquarters and any other offices in the United States or England who have terminals to "talk" with him via electronic mail. Every night he sits down and "reads" his mail. He has been known to respond to a letter with a personal phone call the following day. Some major changes have resulted from communications with employees. For example, he has begun a company program to subsidize employee child-care expenses because he became aware of the needs of his employees espoused through the e-mail connection.[84]

Managers have tried other ways to reach employees and to be reached by them. One of the most easily installed, yet frequently beneficial, way to reach employees is through an open-door policy. Top managers, who normally have no time in a day to see the average worker, schedule time specifically for conversations with employees. Some managers prefer to hold the meetings in their offices; others select more neutral locations. Palmer Reynolds, CEO of Phoenix Textile Corporation, began hosting monthly "breakfasts with the president." She invites five different employees, one from each department, to join her each month at a local restaurant. She learned that her assumption that employees were communicating well was not correct. For example, at a recent breakfast, sales and production realized that they were both under quota systems. This realization, which came from a breakfast discussion, ended a long-time tug-of-war relationship and started a cooperative one.[85]

Advancements in technology have presented managers with a variety of communication tools from which to choose. Techniques such as voice mail and videoconferencing, which have only been available in recent years, have begun to revolutionize the business of communicating in the workplace.[86] Mike Walsh of Union Pacific uses both videotapes and videoconferencing to reach his employees. Important videoconferences are videotaped, and edited copies of the five-and-a-half-hour meetings are sent directly to employees' homes.[87]

Less technical ways to communicate with employees exist as well. One frequently used method for getting a pulse on the workplace is simply by asking. Employees can be polled in several ways. Many firms use attitude surveys, which request employee opinions on topics such as benefits and compensation and the cafeteria menu. Another way to gather employee input is to interview them. Firms can either hire consultants to perform the interviews or use employees who have been trained in interviewing techniques to collect the information. Although this is more formal, it has been found to be one way to generate a great deal of information in a limited amount of time.[88]

When managers are asked by their supervisors to communicate with lower-level employees, the response is generally, "But I *already* do that." The problem is that managers who think they may be talking with and listening to their employees in reality are not. Managers who fall into this category are often referred to as "deaf, dumb, and blind." It's not that deaf managers cannot hear; they don't take the time to listen. It's not that dumb managers cannot speak; they have been taught to read from scripts and teleprompters and not to talk to employees. It's not that blind managers cannot see; they limit their reading to electronic mail and spreadsheets.

Many of these problems are due to the environment in which the managers work. For example, if a manager's schedule is planned for him or her and booked three weeks in advance, he or she literally doesn't have the time to talk with employees, unless it is scheduled on the calendar.[89] However, some managers have personalities that make them poor communicators.

Employees report that the message they receive from their managers is, "I want to hear what you have to say, but give it to me and let's get on with things." This rushed or hurried approach does not make employees feel that what they have to say is important. It makes them feel that they are simply being listened to because their supervisors were *told* to listen to them. The only way communication is effective is if the employees feel that the managers care about what they have to say and if managers care about the employees as people, not just as employees.[90]

TECHNIQUES FOR EMPLOYEE INVOLVEMENT

Because communication is at the heart of all employee involvement efforts, managers can employ various ways to talk with and listen to their employees. Several different EI techniques, which are becoming increasingly popular in the U.S. workplace, are described in the following sections.

EMPOWERMENT

EMPLOYEE EMPOWERMENT
Strategy of pushing the decision-making level down to the lowest level of qualified employees.

Whether the concept of **employee empowerment** is real or rhetoric has been a hot topic for debate. People on one side of the argument suggest that many employers are simply talking about empowering their employees and doing very little to make it happen. Other people are actually taking steps to empower their employees. These steps generally include pushing decision making down to the lowest level in the organization to the most qualified people who can make the decision. Organizations that employ empowering techniques also try to applaud both the successful and unsuccessful risk-taking behavior of employees. These firms take the attitude that each failure is a learning experience and more is learned by failing then by not doing anything at all. Managers in empowered organizations urge employees to find their own ways to boost productivity.[91] These managers ask employees to question silly rules and find better ways to do things, and then they allow the employee to use the resulting new procedures.[92]

Essentially, empowerment means that management vests decision-making or approval authority in employees instead of keeping it for themselves. Empowerment has become important for several reasons. First, globalization and competition have increased, requiring more and more innovation, which requires more freedom for the innovators. Finally, the increased competition has forced U.S. businesses to be more productive than ever before.[93]

For the managers who have empowered employees, the payoffs have been great. For example, Federal Express, which was the first service category recipient of the Malcolm Baldrige Award for Quality, felt it owed the award to empowered employees. James Perkins, senior vice-president of personnel, said that empowering employees was essential in the company's quest for 100 percent customer satisfaction.[94]

Jack Stack, CEO of Springfield Remanufacturing Corporation (SRC), used empowering techniques before the word was even coined. He called it "the great game of business." Stack found when people were put in charge of reaching a goal, they generally reached it. He decided that he would tell the lowest level workers *everything* about the business. By providing them information about where the company was and where it was headed, employees would realize that they were an important part of whether the company stayed in business. Stack explained to the workers the corporation's goals and mission and how he wanted to achieve them. Then, he asked his employees not to tell anyone. In other words, he trusted them. The trust he placed in his employees paid off well. He saw workers coming in after working hours crawling over tractors to determine what parts were needed and when, and to make sure that enough parts, but only enough parts, were ready for use. The level of productivity in the plant increased greatly. As a team, the plant reached its goals. Stack believes that providing information is the key to productivity, and information is a key to empowering employees.[95]

When Viking Glass wanted to make the change from its top-down approach to one in which employees were empowered, it followed the advice of leadership experts Warren Bennis and Stephen Covey. Essentially, the strategy contains three major components: promises, people, and persistence. The promise component is the most active part of the strategy. Employee trust of management has to be earned, and Viking Glass managers realize their responsibility. The promise component of the strategy is to make several promises for positive change and then make sure that these promises are kept.

The second component of their strategy is people. Empowerment gives the employee "position" in an organization a new perspective. Traditionally, the lower the position in the hierarchy, the lower the status and significance. Viking Glass works to counter this by (1) stressing leadership over management or supervision, (2) having employees do a performance review of their supervisors, and (3) turning the organization chart on its side, making no position more important than any other.

The final component in the strategy is persistence. Viking Glass is committed to persist in trying to build the trust level of the company. Stephen Covey said it best: "You can buy a person's hand but you can't buy his heart. You can buy his back, but you can't buy his brain. His heart is where his enthusiasm is; his brain is where his creativity is, his ingenuity, his resourcefulness."[96]

SUGGESTION BOXES

The suggestion box was the forerunner of quality circles, discussed in an earlier chapter. The reasoning underlying each of these concepts is the same: employees who do the work should have good ideas of how to do it better. Unlike quality circles, which involve only a few people, suggestion boxes encourage all employees to participate. Frequently, the suggestor's identity is kept anonymous until the suggestion is implemented and then an award is presented. This helps people feel more secure about participating.

Sometimes the suggestion box format can be turned into a formal program. For example, Consolidated Edison Company of New York implemented a Front-Line Feedback program. The program requested that employees who work directly with the customer suggest ways in which service could be improved. Employees whose ideas were accepted earned $50 and they and their suggestions were written about in the company newsletter. Many of the recipients felt that the money was nice, but the recognition was better.[97]

The outcome of this program highlights one of the most beneficial reasons for implementing a suggestion box. The public recognition employees receive for submitting winning ideas boosts their self-esteem. Employees have an increased sense of their true abilities when their ideas are deemed good enough to be implemented by a firm. Every time a fellow worker uses the new method, the employee can say, "that's *my* idea."[98]

Japanese firms are strong believers in employee suggestions. A 1988 tally of suggestions made by employees in Japanese firms indicated that 59.2 million suggestions were provided. The average number of suggestions made by a Japanese employee was 31.5. Some of these suggestions were really good ones too. One suggestion saved Canon Oita $123,000 while the combined benefit of the suggestions at Kawasaki Steel saved that company $370 million.[99]

One reason for the high level of suggestions found in Japanese firms is that new employees are expected to submit four daily suggestions in the first few months on the job. Further, Japanese companies use more of the suggestions given by employees than U.S. firms do, encouraging Japanese workers to continue making suggestions. On average, Japanese firms use four of every five suggestions made by their employees while U.S. firms use only one of every four suggestions.[100] The main reason given for the different usage rate between Japanese and U.S. firms is the quality of the suggestions. Quite simply, Japanese workers provide better suggestions than U.S. workers do because Japanese workers have the luxury of lifetime job security. Lifetime commitment leads to a stronger bond with the firm, and more of a willingness to improve things for all. U.S. workers who, in current times, are assured a job only until the following pay period, are less willing to provide ideas that may help the company to eliminate their jobs.[101]

However, this may be changing. A report that surveyed 300 companies about their suggestion programs found that the firms saved $2.2 billion from employee suggestions in one year. Also, the number of suggestions provided was up by 60 percent from just three years earlier. This success may make some firms rethink their use of suggestions programs.[102]

OWNERSHIP

One piece of information a stock buyer can use when deciding which company to invest in is the degree of ownership that top management has in the firm. If top managers are paid a salary that does not depend on the success of the company, then the investor should pass on the stock. If, however, the management's salary is tied to the productivity of the firm—that is, a large portion of the salary is in the form of stocks—then the investor should buy it. The investor wants someone who is running the firm to have the same interests the investor does—profitability. Managers who have a strong ownership in the organization will think in terms of profitability.[103]

The concpet also can be pushed further down into the firm. Workers who have an ownership in the firm also want the firm to be more productive. Armed with this philosophy, many firms are considering employee ownership. Exhibit 12.12 provides an example of this concept in action. A recent survey indicates that this idea has a great deal of support. Two-thirds of the personnel officers at 415 large companies indicated that they want more employees to own stock so that the employees will act like owners.[104] A recent presidential commission engaged to study labor-management relations in the airline industry gave a boost to employee ownership plans. The commission recommended that Internal Revenue Service regulations be changed to encourage broader use of employee stock ownership plans. The belief is that employees who have more say in the direction of their

■ EXHIBIT 12.12   Involvement through Ownership

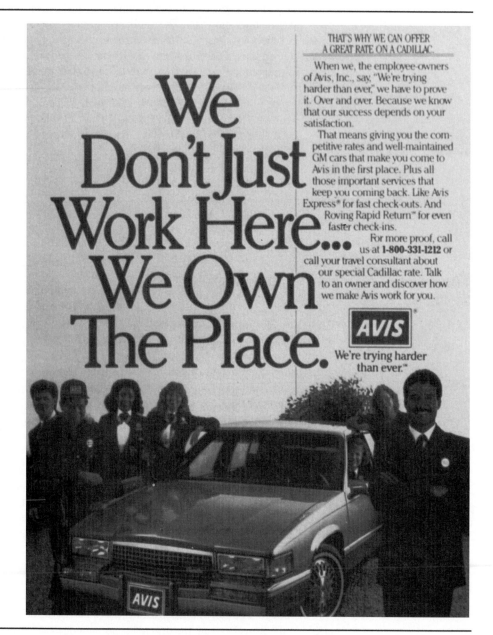

SOURCE: Courtesy of Avis, Inc.

workplace become more productive and more competitive globally.[105] However, some firms have rejected proposals to allow more employee ownership. Some GM managers believed that one way to get the workers to be more productive was to give them more of a stake in the company. However, not all of the voting membership agreed.[106]

Other ways to induce the feeling of ownership besides increasing stock purchases also have been tried. At Dominos, there are no employees, only team members, team leaders, and a coaching staff. DuPont also has no employees; it has people and team members. Replacing the term *employee* has proven beneficial for these firms. By eliminating the words *manager* and *employee,* they have also eliminated the "we-they" mindset. However, it takes more than just simple semantics to make this concept work. Not only does the vocabulary have to change but also the way in which employees turned teammates are treated must reflect the feeling of ownership and importance the company wants to portray.[107] There is no doubt that Wal-Mart "associates" believe that they are valued and important members of the team.

TOTAL QUALITY MANAGEMENT

One concept that seems to incorporate all or many of the topics discussed in these past few sections is **total quality management (TQM).** TQM is an entirely new way of doing things. It asks employees to challenge old rules and find new and better ways to get things done. This can be accomplished in a group, individually, at the bottom of the organization, or at the top. The key is that everyone is involved.

TQM is a strategic, integrated management system for achieving customer satisfaction that involves all managers and employees and uses quantitative methods to continuously improve an organization's processes. TQM is designed to achieve customer satisfaction, make continuous improvements, and give responsibility to everyone. To achieve this goal, the organization must develop performance standards and valid ways to measure these standards. It must strive to focus on the customer, on communication, and on employee involvement. Top management must support and direct the TQM effort by showing a commitment to training and by rewarding and recognizing quality work.

The process of implementing TQM in an organization can be viewed in three phases. To begin, the firm must have an awareness of the need to change. This vision must be supported by the knowledge that workers need to be trained and educated and that the tools they use to do their jobs may need to change. Once the organization recognizes these things, it then becomes committed to implementing TQM, which is the second phase. During this stage, the firm must develop support structures that include steering committees and TQM boards. These groups are responsible for determining the standards and capabilities of the firm. They also must be sure that the resources needed are provided and that the training required is available. Finally, performance improvement teams are established. At this point, the organization is ready to implement TQM. The performance teams begin to analyze the processes in the workplace with an eye toward improving them. During this analysis, seven basic quality tools can be used. They include

1. Process flow analysis—provides a step-by-step chart of the steps involved in the process under investigation.
2. Cause-effect diagram—examines the root cause of painful symptoms.
3. Run chart—illustrates the trends and results over a specified period of time for a particular situation.
4. Control chart—indicates the variation from normal in the situation over time.
5. Scattergram—indicates whether or not a linear relationship exists between variables.
6. Histogram—depicts the distribution from the mean and how close to normal it is.
7. Pareto chart—prioritizes categories from most to least important.[108]

TQM groups initiate changes and are recognized for their accomplishments. Once in place, TQM continues to provide the organization with a way to constantly push itself to be more and more productive.

TOTAL QUALITY MANAGEMENT (TQM)
An integrated management system designed to achieve an extremely high level of customer satisfaction.

Because TQM is completely different from the traditional way in which organizations have been run, it is frequently difficult to use in existing workplaces. Instead, TQM has been more successfully implemented in a new plant or branch of a company that is separate from the parent organization. For example, General Dynamics is implementing a variety of TQM concepts that are used only in its Tallahassee plant. Responsibility and decision making are being pushed to the lower levels of the organization. Self-managed teams are relied on to set their own production agendas, help to hire new employees, and certify members in the group before they are eligible for raises. Frequent meetings at General Dynamics provide the teams with access to the information they may need to manage themselves. Exhibit 12.13 is a list of the guiding principles of TQM at General Dynamics.[109]

Another company that decided to implement TQM at an off-site location was General Motors. GM used the ideas of TQM as the foundation for building its Saturn plant. To begin, the company set up a relocation policy task force composed of United Auto Workers; GM sales, service, marketing, human resources, engineering, and finance people; and representatives from Argonaut Realty, a relocation specialist. These members started with a blank sheet of paper and no rules or infrastructure. But they did have a common goal: work satisfaction.[110]

Throughout the entire development of the plant and the products offered by the plant, the team worked together. The United Auto Workers and GM engineers flew around the world together to investigate technologies and procedures that could be used by Saturn. The relocation team worked with every employee who was eventually relocated to Spring Hill, Tennessee. Even spouses who did not work for GM participated in workshops designed to help them understand the job possibilities and salary expectations in rural Tennessee. Saturn even worked closely with the people who would be maintaining and repairing the Saturn products. The company reasoned that it would not be wise to produce a top-quality product if the same level of quality service was not available for the vehicles. The project seems to be a success, as evidenced by the 1994 Customer Satisfaction Index in which Saturn ranked third following Lexis and Infiniti.[111]

The pursuit of quality appears to be contagious, or at least it is at Hutchinson Technology, Inc. (HTI), a manufacturer of precision computer components. HTI hired consultants in 1983 to fix their problems. HTI was skeptical at first but it implemented the

EXHIBIT 12.13   **Guiding Principles of TQM at General Dynamics**

1. Quality comes first.
2. Our goal is never-ending improvement in customer satisfaction.
3. Teamwork is the way we make decisions.
4. Suppliers are part of our team.
5. Every activity and every process are integral parts of the operation of our company.
6. Mistakes are not "someone's fault."
7. We manage our work by facts.
8. Decisions are made by the lowest appropriate organizational level.
9. We can never be satisfied with "good enough."
10. Employees have the right to as much information as possible about their jobs and the company.

SOURCE: Adapted from F. Schneyer, "Team Management Takes Hold in Tallahassee," *Tallahassee Democrat,* August 7, 1991, pp. B1 +.

programs in the manufacturing processes. It saw great improvements in as little as 18 months. By the end of the fifth year, HTI had saved over $30 million dollars. It was then that HTI decided to develop and implement a quality program in the nonmanufacturing parts of the firm as well. The process worked so well that HTI called its consultants back in and offered to show them how to implement quality programs.[112] In this case, it appears that the student can teach the teacher, too.

Until recently, TQM was seen as the cure for the ills of U.S. business, one that would rescue business from shoddy management practices and inferior quality products. Some firms continue to practice TQM; others have begun to move on, believing that TQM was just another management trend whose time had come and gone.[113] Faced with hard times lately, businesses have soured on TQM.[114] Florida Power & Light, winner of Japan's Deming Prize for quality management, has reduced its TQM program because of worker complaints of excessive paperwork. The Wallace Co., a Houston-based oil supply company and winner of a Baldrige Award, filed for bankruptcy.[115] Reasons for the growing disappointment with TQM include the focus on internal processes instead of external results, the increased bureaucracy associated with many programs, and the emphasis on complicated, standardized practices, which often are of little use to small firms or firms in rapidly changing environments.[116] Proponents of TQM argue that many firms' TQM efforts do not succeed because of a lack of support from top management or because of the mistaken view that results should be immediate.[117] Only time will tell whether total quality management will continue to be a successful tool for continuous process improvement or a management fad relegated to the deep recesses of old college textbooks.

MANAGEMENT GUIDELINES

The productivity and involvement of employees should be major priorities for managers. However, no one set of steps can be followed to make all employees productive and involved. Nor are all companies more productive by simply involving their employees. With these two warnings in mind, let's review some suggestions for managers who want to build a more productive and involved workforce.

1. Almost all of the concepts discussed in this chapter rest on one principle: management must trust its employees. For example, to provide employees with the knowledge necessary for them to set their own goals, they must understand what output is expected overall. For employees to know if the new technique they are suggesting is feasible, they have to know how much the old method costs. For employees to make the sound business decisions that they were empowered to make, they must have the information that they need. If management is not willing to trust its employees, it cannot have an involved organization. An unwillingness to trust employees may imply that quality employees were not selected in the first place and the company's hiring policies need to be reworked. However, if a company hires only competent, qualified employees, then trusting them with organizational information should not be a problem.

Continued

2. Productivity can also be stifled by inappropriate or out-of-date equipment. Managers must remain knowledgeable about current machines and techniques available in the field to help employees do their jobs. Investing in equipment to help increase productivity is one good way for firms that cannot use involvement techniques to increase productivity.

3. Before any steps can be made toward encouraging employees to become involved in the organization, a serious study of the overall corporate culture must be made. Will the current corporate culture allow management to initiate involvement programs? Which techniques, if any, are appropriate for the organization? Implementing a new policy that runs counter to the culture will not be effective.

4. Start small. Once management decides to use involvement techniques, it should select one small project to begin with and see how it goes. Making too many changes all at once, even if they are all good ideas, may be too much for employees to handle.

5. Do not overlook the advantages of training employees. By providing training to employees, a manager can build a smarter, more loyal workforce. The payoff from training is frequently increased productivity and lower turnover.

6. Remember that employee attitudes can be shaped. Monetary rewards coupled with strong promotional and career path planning can increase morale, productivity, and commitment to the organization's goals.

QUESTIONS FOR REVIEW

1. What is productivity? Discuss three ways in which productivity can be impacted.

2. How can training and development help to increase productivity?

3. How can managers influence employee attitudes? Why would they want to?

4. What is employee involvement? What are some of the benefits of involving employees in the organization?

5. How can communication be used to help involve employees in their jobs?

6. In what ways are two of the techniques for increasing employee involvement similar? Different?

7. How would you go about increasing involvement in a plant that assembled toys? In a plant that plucked and cut chickens? In a law firm? In a mail-order catalog organization?

CASE

BRUEGGER'S BAGEL BAKERY[118]

It's the fourth quarter, your team is down by seven points, and the ball is at midfield with less than one minute left to play in the game. What strategy do you put into action to move your team down the field? Do you tighten up and get conservative or do you loosen up and call the unexpected play? Further, do you, as the coach, call the play, or do you let the quarterback call it? Mike Dressell, Nordahl Brue, and Jim

Briggs (who has since left the business), founders of Bruegger's Bagel Bakery, would probably opt for the latter. When the trio first considered the idea of opening a bagel bakery, they knew they had to develop a decentralized approach; that is, they knew they wanted to let the individual managers call the plays. Since each of them was busy in another occupation (Dressell had a construction company; Brue was an attorney, and Briggs was an accountant), they didn't have the time or knowledge to get involved in operating decisions.

PASSING THE BALL, NOT THE BUCK

Basically, Dressell, Brue, and Briggs adopted the attitude that if you wanted something done right, you didn't necessarily have to do it yourself. Rather than getting involved directly in operating decisions, the founders made a strategic decision to hire local managers to run their bagel shops. Local managers were offered a partnership that gave them a 20 percent ownership of the individual shops they supervised. The managers were empowered with the responsibility and authority to make decisions that affected their "cluster" of units. Offering the managers financial incentives beyond their salaries, the owners wanted the managers to have a higher stake in the survival of their shops and therefore more incentive to make things work.

Initially, the playing field was left wide open for local managers in terms of developing their own techniques for managing their shops, watching costs, and creating their own menu items. The principal partners took a sideline approach to overseeing each manager's game plan but would occasionally visit some of the units. Overall, they liked what they saw, as was evident in Brue's comment that "managers took lots of initiative." Bruegger's created an environment that encouraged ingenuity and innovativeness. Each cluster manager was in the driver's seat; and all of them knew who buttered their bagels, so to speak—it was none other than themselves! Various clusters of stores offered different styles of bagels (some lighter, some darker) and different lines of beverages. Some had paper goods with the company logo; others didn't. Some offered creative bagel delights, such as pizza bagels; others offered more traditional bagels. Again, the decisions were made by the individual managers of each cluster of stores, thereby adding an element of uniqueness to each.

SMELL OF VICTORY

Since the principal partners first considered the idea of Bruegger's Bagel Bakery in 1983, the company has grown rapidly. The first market was in Albany, New York, and in less than three years, they added four other markets in Cedar Rapids, Iowa; Minneapolis; Boston; and Raleigh-Durham, North Carolina. Currently, Bruegger's is a $20-million "plus" company with cluster managers operating over 100 stores. Obviously, Dressell and Brue's strategic business plan has worked well. Despite their success, however, the principal partners have not closed their eyes to the possibility that change is needed.

A SLIGHT SHIFT IN THE GAME PLAN

As the company continued to grow, Bruegger reached a point where the decision to set some companywide standards became evident. Although the partners wanted to continue giving managers the freedom to make decisions affecting their individual clusters, they believed there was a need to coordinate the activities of the various stores. For example, until a few years ago, the cluster managers had five different contracts with Coca Cola. The decision was made to combine forces and negotiate a single deal, which resulted in savings to each of the clusters. Such fine-tuning and coordination of activities needed to occur without restricting the responsibility and authority of the local managers.

Bruegger's strategic philosophy had always been in line with the idea of empowerment. The partners wanted their managers to have "bragging rights" for the success of their individual stores. After all, Bruegger's success reflected the individual management techniques and decision making. Although the principal partners did not want to interfere with the manager's decisions to offer particular products, they did persuade the managers to rely on market research to ascertain the viability of keeping certain items on the menu. Cluster managers are still encouraged to develop new ideas; however, before ideas are adopted, they go through extensive market testing.

CONCLUSION

Bruegger's Bagel Bakery has demonstrated that setting standards can be done without "robbing" managers of the motivation to run their shops the way they choose. By empowering people with responsibility and authority and by giving them a stake in their business, Bruegger's has the benefit of many minds working on the same problems and working to ensure the survival of the company.

QUESTIONS

1. The strategic philosophy behind Bruegger's Bagel Bakery is based on at least one of the strategic choices mentioned at the beginning of the chapter. How has Bruegger's been able to implement this strategic choice to develop a successful organization?

2. Various concepts discussed in this chapter have been implemented at Bruegger's. What are two? Discuss how they have been effectively utilized by Bruegger's.

3. What strategic choices described in this chapter has Bruegger's failed to take advantage of? What suggestions do you have for implementing these strategies?

4. If you were asked to measure Bruegger's productivity levels, how would you do it?

ADDITIONAL READINGS

Bass, Bernard M., and Ralph M. Stodgill. *Bass & Stodgill's Handbook of Leadership.* New York: Free Press.

Bastien, David. "Common Patterns of Behavior and Communication in Corporate Mergers and Acquisitions." *Human Resource Management* 26. Spring 1987, pp. 17–33.

Beckhard, Richard, and Wendy Pritchard. *Changing the Essence: The Art of Leading Fundamental Change in Organizations.* San Francisco: Jossey-Bass, 1992.

Bell, Robert R., and John M. Burnham. *Managing Productivity and Change.* Cincinnati: South-Western, 1991.

Bennis, Warren. *Why Leaders Can't Lead.* San Francisco: Jossey-Bass, 1989.

Block, Peter. *The Empowered Manager.* San Francisco: Jossey-Bass, 1987.

Bolman, Lee, and Terrence Deal. *Reframing Organizations.* San Francisco: Jossey-Bass, 1991.

Boyett, Joseph H., and Harry P. Conn. *Workplace 2000: The Revolution Reshaping American Business.* New York: Dutton, 1991.

Brinkerhoff, Robert, and Dennis Dressler. *Productivity Measurement.* Newbury Park, CA: Sage, 1989.

Brown, Stephen, Evert Gummesson, Bo Edvardsson, and BengtOve Gustavsson. *Service Quality.* New York: Lexington Books, 1990.

Buono, Anthony, and James Bowditch. *The Human Side of Mergers and Acquisitions.* San Francisco: Jossey-Bass, 1989.

Campbell, John P., Richard J. Campbell, and Associates. *Productivity in Organizations.* San Francisco: Jossey-Bass, 1988.

Carkhuff, Robert. *Empowering—The Creative Leader in the Age of New Capitalism.* Amherst, MA: HRD Press, 1989.

Carnevale, Anthony Patrick. *America and the New Economy.* San Francisco: Jossey-Bass, 1991.

Casson, Mark. *Enterprise and Competitiveness.* New York: Oxford Press, 1990.

Crosby, Phil. *Let's Talk Quality.* New York: McGraw-Hill, 1989.

Deming, W. Edwards. *Out of Crisis.* Cambridge, MA: Cambridge University Press, 1986.

Denton, D. Keith. *Horizontal Management: Beyond Total Customer Satisfaction.* New York: Lexington Books, 1991.

Ernst and Young Quality Improvement Consulting Group. *Total Quality: An Executive Guide for the 1990s.* Homewood, IL.: Dow Jones-Irwin, 1990.

Gaddis, Paul. "Taken Over, Turned Out." *Harvard Business Review* (1987), pp. 8–22.

Gardner, John W. *On Leadership.* New York: Free Press, 1989.

Goldhaber, Gerald M., and George A. Barnett. *Handbook of Organizational Communication.* Norwood, NJ: Ablex, 1988.

Gomez-Meija, Luis R. *Compensation and Benefits.* Edison, NJ: Bureau of National Affairs, 1989.

Graham-Moore, Brian, and Timothy L. Ross. *Gainsharing for Improving Performance.* Washington, DC: BNA Books, 1990.

Hackman, J. Richard. *Groups That Work (and Those That Don't).* San Francisco: Jossey-Bass, 1989.

Helfgott, Roy B. *Computerized Manufacturing and Human Resources.* Lexington, MA: Lexington Books, 1988.

Hickman, Craig R., and Michael A. Silva. *Creating Excellence.* New York: Plume, 1984.

Holoviak, Stephen J., and Susan S. Sipkoff. *Managing Human Productivity: People Are Your Best Investment.* Westport, CT: Greenwood Press, Inc., 1987.

Hunt, James G., B. Rajaram Baliga, H. Peter Dachler, and Chester A. Schriesheim. *Emerging Leadership Vistas.* Lexington, MA: D.C. Heath, 1988.

Hunt, John. "Hidden Extras: How People Get Overlooked in Takeovers." *Personnel Management* 19 (July 1987), pp. 24–28.

Isen, Alice M. *Motivation and Emotion.* New York: Plenum Press, 1989.

Ivancevich, John, David Schweiger, and Frank Power. "Strategies for Managing Human Resources during Mergers and Acquisition." *Human Resource Planning* 10 (1988), pp. 19–35.

Jablin, Frederic M., Linda L. Putnam, Karlene H. Roberts, and Lyman W. Porter. *Handbook of Organizational Communication.* Newbury Park, CA: Sage, 1987.

Janis, Irving L. *Crucial Decisions: Leadership in Policymaking and Crisis Management.* New York: The Free Press, 1989.

Juran, J. M. *Juran on Quality by Design.* New York: Free Press, 1992.

Kanter, Donald L., and Philip H. Mirvis. *The Cynical American.* San Francisco: Jossey-Bass, 1989.

Ketchum, Lyman, and Eric Trist. *All Teams Are Not Created Equal.* Newbury Park, CA: Sage, 1992.

Kinlaw, Dennis. *Developing Superior Work Teams.* New York: Lexington Books, 1990.

Koestenbaum, Peter. *Leadership: The Inner Side of Greatness.* San Francisco: Jossey-Bass, 1991.

Kotter, John P. *The Leadership Factor.* New York: Free Press, 1988.

——— *Power and Influence.* New York: Free Press, 1985.

——— and James Heskett. *The Corporate Culture Connection.* New York: Free Press, 1992.

Kouzes, James M., and Barry Z. Posner. *The Leadership Challenge.* San Francisco: Jossey-Bass, 1987.

Larson, Carl, and Frank Lafasto. *Teamwork.* Newbury Park, CA: Sage, 1989.

Lawler, Edward E. *High Involvement Management.* San Francisco: Jossey-Bass, 1986.

Lawler, Edward E. "Pay for Performance: Making It Work." *Personnel.* October 1988, pp. 68–71.

Lax, David A., and James Sebenius. *The Manager As Negotiator.* New York: Free Press, 1986.

Lewis, Jordan D. *Partnerships for Profit.* New York: Free Press, 1990.

McIntosh, Stephen. "Buying Time by Delegating." *HRMagazine.* October 1991, p. 47.

McPhee, Robert D., and Phillip K. Tompkins. *Organizational Communication.* Newbury Park, CA: Sage, 1985.

Maidani, Ebrahaim. "Comparative Study of Herzberg's Two-Factor Theory of Job Satisfaction among Public and Private Sectors." *Public Personnel Management* 20 (1991), pp. 441–448.

Malick, Sidney, Solomon Hoberman, and Stephen J. Wall. *The Practice of Management Development.* Lexington, MA: Praeger Publishers, 1988.

Meyer, M. W., and L. G. Zucker. *Permanently Failing Organizations.* Newbury Park, CA: Sage, 1989.

Miller, Danny. *The Icarus Paradox: How Exceptional Companies Bring about Their Own Downfall.* Scarborough, Ontario: HarperCollins Canada, 1990.

Miller, Richard. *Participative Management Quality of Worklife and Job Enrichment.* Park Ridge, NJ: Noyes Data Corporation, 1977.

Morgan, Gareth. *Creative Organization Theory.* Newbury Park, CA: Sage, 1989.

Morgan, Gareth. *Images of Organizations.* Newbury Park, CA: Sage, 1990.

Nadler, Leonard, and Zeace Nadler. *Developing Human Resources.* San Francisco: Jossey-Bass, 1987.

Orsburn, Jack, Linda Moran, Ed Musselwhite, and John Zenger. *Self-Directed Work Teams: The New American Challenge.* Homewood, IL: BusinessOne Irwin, 1990.

Pierce, Jon L., Jon W. Newstrom, Randall B. Dunham, and Alison E. Barber. *Alternative Work Schedules.* Needham Heights, MA: Allyn and Bacon, 1989.

Putnam, Linda L., and Michael E. Pacanowsky. *Communication and Organizations.* Newbury Park, CA: Sage, 1983.

Quinn, Robert. *Beyond Rational Management.* San Francisco: Jossey-Bass, 1991.

Robson, George. *Continuous Process Improvement: Simplifying Work Systems.* New York: Free Press, 1991.

Rosen, Corey M., Katherine J. Klein, and Karen M. Young. *Employee Ownership in America.* Lexington, MA: Lexington Books, 1988.

Rummler, Geary A., and Alan P. Brache. *Improving Performance.* San Francisco: Jossey-Bass, 1990.

Ryan, Kathleen D., and Daniel K. Oestreich. *Driving Fear out of the Workplace: How to Overcome Barriers to Quality, Productivity and Innovation.* San Francisco: Jossey-Bass, 1991.

Sandy, William. *Forging the Productivity Partnership.* New York: McGraw-Hill, 1990.

Schein, Edgar. *Organizational Culture and Leadership.* San Francisco: Jossey-Bass, 1991.

Schoorman, F. David, and Benjamin Schneider. *Facilitating Work Effectiveness.* Lexington, MA: Lexington Books, 1988.

Shapero, Albert. *Managing Precessional People.* New York: Free Press, 1989.

Shetty, Y. K., and Vernon M. Buehler. *Productivity and Quality through Science and Technology.* Westport, CT: Greenwood Press, 1988.

Thibodeaux, Mary, and Dale Yeatts. "Leadership: The Perceptions of Leaders by Followers in Self-Managed Work Teams." Paper presented at the 1991 International Conference on Self-Managed Work Teams. Dallas, 1991.

Thornburg, Linda. "The Push to Improve." *HRMagazine,* December 1990, pp. 36–39.

Tjosvold, Dean, and Mary Tjosvold. *Leading the Team Organization.* New York: Lexington Books, 1992.

Tomer, John F. *Organizational Capital.* Westport, CT: Greenwood Press, 1987.

Varney, Glenn H. *Building Productive Teams.* San Francisco: Jossey-Bass, 1989.

Weisbord, Marvin. *Productive Workplaces.* San Francisco: Jossey-Bass, 1987.

Wellins, Richard, William Byham, and Jeanne Wilson. *Empowered Teams.* San Francisco: Jossey-Bass, 1991.

Womack, James, Daniel Jones, and Daniel Noos. *The Machine That Changed the World.* Boston: MIT, 1990.

Yeatts, Dale. "Self-Managed Work Teams: Innovation in Progress." *Business and Economic Quarterly,* Fall/Winter, 1990/1991, pp. 2–6.

Yasuda, Yuzo. *40 Years, 20 Million Ideas: The Toyota Suggestion System.* Cambridge, MA: Productivity Press, 1991.

Zeithaml, Valarie A. *Delivering Quality Service.* New York: Free Press, 1990.

NOTES

1. L. Therrien, "The Rival Japan Respects," *Business Week,* November 13, 1989, pp. 108–118; G. McManis and M. Liebman, "Management Development: A Lifetime Commitment," *Personnel Administrator,* September 1988, pp. 53–58; E. B. Baatz, "Motorola's Secret Weapon," *Electronic Business,* April 1993, pp. 51–54; and A. K. Gupta and A. Singhal, "Managing Human Resources for Innovation and Creativity," *Research-Technology Management,* May–June 1993, pp. 41–48.

2. P. Cappelli and H. Singh, "Integrating Strategic Human Resources and Strategic Management," in *Research Frontiers in Industrial Relations and Human Resources,* ed. D. Lewin, O. S. Mitchell, and P. D. Sheres (Madison, WI: IPRA, 1992); and M. Huselid, "The Impact of Human Resource Management Practices on Turnover, Pro-

ductivity, and Corporate Financial Performance," *Academy of Management Journal* (forthcoming).

3. G. Koretz, "The Surge in Factory Productivity Looks Like History Now," *Business Week,* October 8, 1990, p. 24.

4. William Baumol, "U.S. Industry's Lead Gets Bigger," *The Wall Street Journal,* March 21, 1990, p. A14; and Joseph Spiers, "Productivity Looks Promising," *Fortune,* March 9, 1992, pp. 21–22.

5. Bob Davis and Dana Milbank, "Job Blues," *The Wall Street Journal,* February 7, 1992, pp. A1 +; Myron Magnet, "The Truth about the American Worker," *Fortune,* May 4, 1992, pp. 48–65; and "Why Japan Must Change," *Fortune,* March 9, 1992, pp. 66–67.

6. R. Henkoff, "Make Your Office More Productive," *Fortune,* February 25, 1991, p. 72.

7. A. Taylor, "New Lessons from Japan's Carmakers," *Fortune,* October 22, 1990, p. 166.

8. Vic Heylen, "Europeans Keep Progress off Assembly Line," *The Wall Street Journal,* June 3, 1991, p. A10.

9. Henkoff, "Make Your Office More Productive," p. 76.

10. A. Karr, "A Special News Report on People and Their Jobs in Offices, Fields, and Factories," *The Wall Street Journal,* April 10, 1990, p. A1.

11. Henkoff, "Make Your Office More Productive," p. 76.

12. Robert Tomasko, "Restructuring: Getting It Right," *Management Review,* April 1992, pp. 10–15.

13. J. McCormick and B. Powell, "Management for the 1990s," *Newsweek,* April 25, 1988, pp. 47–48.

14. B. Reilly, "The New Deal: What Companies and Employees Owe One Another," *Fortune,* June 13, 1994, pp. 44–52.

15. McCormick and Powell, "Management for the 1990s."

16. L. Baytos, "The Human Side of Acquisitions and Divestitures," *Human Resource Planning* 9, no. 4, 1987, pp. 167–175.

17. J. Hunt, "Hidden Extras: How People Get Overlooked in Takeovers," *Personnel Management,* July 1987, pp. 24–28.

18. Baytos, "The Human Side of Acquisitions and Divestitures," p. 170.

19. R. Ford and P. Perrewé, "After the Layoff: Closing the Barn Door Before All the Horses Are Gone," *Business Horizons,* July–August 1993, pp. 1–7.

20. D. T. Bastien, "Common Patterns of Behavior and Communication in Corporate Mergers and Acquisitions," *Human Resource Management* 26, no. 1, Spring 1987, p. 28.

21. P. O. Gaddis, "Taken Over, Turned Out," *Harvard Business Review,* July–August 1987, p. 9.

22. P. Ingrassia and J. White, "GM Mulls Tough Call in Toyota Venture," *The Wall Street Journal,* June 10, 1988, p. A2.

23. J. B. Treece and A. Borrus, "How Ford and Mazda Shared the Driver's Seat," *Business Week,* March 26, 1990, pp. 94–95.

24. Ingrassia and White, "GM Mulls Tough Call in Toyota Venture."

25. P. Revzin, "Ventures in Hungary Test Theory That West Can Uplift East Bloc," *The Wall Street Journal,* April 5, 1990, pp. A1 +.

26. G. Anders, "Going Global: Vision vs. Reality," *The Wall Street Journal,* September 22, 1989, pp. R20–21.

27. J. Main, "The Winning Organization," *Fortune,* September 26, 1988, pp. 50–60.

28. T. P. Pare, "Rebuilding a Lost Reputation," *Fortune,* May 30, 1994, p. 176; and L. S. Richman, "Reengineering under Fire," *Fortune,* April 18, 1994, p. 186.

29. J. Main, "The Winning Organization."

30. Ibid.

31. J. Solomon, "Managers Focus on Low-Wage Workers," *The Wall Street Journal,* May 9, 1989, p. B1.

32. Ibid.

33. C. Trost, "Labor Department Announces Winners of Its Work-Force Quality Competition," *The Wall Street Journal,* September 21, 1991, p. B8.

34. A. Karr, "A Special News Report on People and Their Jobs in Offices, Fields, and Factories," *The Wall Street Journal,* July 25, 1989, p. A1.

35. C. Conte, "Leaders Are Born, But Many Companies Believe They Can Be Nurtured Too," *The Wall Street Journal,* May 21, 1991, p. A1.

36. B. Leonard, "Does Your Office Suffer from Workplacephobia?" *Society for Human Resources Management HRNews,* August 1991, p. 15.

37. J. C. Poole, W. F. Rathgeber, and S. W. Silverman, "Paying for Performance in a TQM Environment," *HRMagazine,* October 1993, pp. 68–73.

38. K. L. Webb and S. L. O'Neil, "Creative Game Rewards Managers," *HRMagazine,* November 1993, pp. 55–56.

39. C. Hymowitz, "Earthquake Prompts Greater Work Flexibility," *The Wall Street Journal,* November 7, 1989, p. B1.

40. S. Feinstein, "Cynicism Runs High in the American Workplace, Two Researchers Conclude," *The Wall Street Journal,* May 30, 1989, p. A1.

41. B. Burlingham, "This Woman Has Changed Business Forever," *Inc.,* June 1990, pp. 34–47.

42. D. Milbank, "In These Gloomy Times, Some Companies Provide Employees with Comic Relief," *The Wall Street Journal,* February 19, 1991, pp. B1 +.

43. Ibid.

44. A. Bennett, "SAS's Nice Guy Is Aiming to Finish First," *The Wall Street Journal,* March 2, 1989, p. B12.

45. J. A. Oliver and E. J. Johnson, "People Motive Redefines Customer Service," *HRMagazine,* June 1990, pp. 119–121.

46. "Workers Want What You'd Expect, But Don't Often Think They are Getting It," *The Wall Street Journal,* June 6, 1989, p. A1.

47. C. Hymowitz, "Many Middle Managers Find Bosses Uninspiring," *The Wall Street Journal,* November 6, 1989, p. B1.

48. M. E. Mangelsdorf, "Managing the New Workforce," *Inc.,* January 1990, pp. 78–83.

49. M. Kanabayashi, "Competence Ousts Seniority in Deciding Who Gets Paid What," *The Wall Street Journal,* March 14, 1989, p. A1.

50. Gupta and Singhal, "Managing Human Resources for Innovation and Creativity."

51. S. Feinstein, "We Love You: More Companies Reward Workers Who Go the Extra Mile," *The Wall Street Journal,* May 2, 1989, p. A1.

52. Ibid.

53. R. Bunning, "Rewarding a Job Well Done," *Personnel Administrator,* January 1989, p. 61.

54. L. Brokaw, P. Brown, T. Lammers, M. Mangelsdorf, and B. Posner, "Stamp of Approval," *Inc.,* January 1990, p. 105.

55. G. Fuchsberg and A. Bennett, "Need a Motivator for a Weary Worker? Try a 'Congratulator,'" *The Wall Street Journal,* May 4, 1990, pp. A1 +.

56. C. Ronald Schwisow, "Tools for Your Motivational Campaign," *HRMagazine,* November 1991, pp. 63–64.

57. J. Rigdon, "More Firms Try to Reward Good Service, but Incentives May Backfire in Long Run," *The Wall Street Journal,* December 5, 1990, pp. B1 +.

58. M. Hawkins and M. Moravec, "Career Paths Discourage Innovation and Deflate Motivation," *Personnel Administrator,* October 1989, pp. 111–112.

59. T. Schellhardt, "Creating Career Ladders to Keep Stellar Sellers," *The Wall Street Journal,* March 22, 1990, p. B1.

60. M. A. Barton, "Baldrige Winners Stress HR Practices," *HRNews,* November 1993, p. 7.

61. Cappelli and Singh, "Integrating Strategic Human Resources and Strategic Management."

62. S. Feinstein, "Blame Bosses If Quality Is Poor," *The Wall Street Journal,* July 10, 1990, p. A1; and Jerry Bowles, "Is American Management Really Committed to Quality?" *Management Review,* April 1992, pp. 42–46.

63. J. A. Byrne, "Remembering Deming, the Godfather of Quality," *Business Week,* January 10, 1994, p. 44.

64. S. Overman, "Leader Helps Improve Competitiveness," *HRMagazine,* May 1990, pp. 58–60.

65. E. Carlson, "McDonald's Kroc Bloomed Late, but Brilliantly," *The Wall Street Journal,* May 23, 1989, p. B2.

66. P. E. Steiger, "Ten for the Textbooks," *The Wall Street Journal,* Centennial Edition, p. B1; and Von Johnston and Herff Moore, "Pride Drives Wal-Mart to Service Excellence," *HRMagazine,* October 1991, pp. 79–80.

67. R. E. Rustin, "How Grand Ambitions Proved the Undoing of Shearson's CEO," *The Wall Street Journal,* January 31, 1990, pp. A1 +.

68. Walter Kiechel, "The Leader as Servant," *Fortune,* May 4, 1992, pp. 121–122.

69. Z. Schiller, "No More Mr. Nice Guy at P&G—Not by a Long Shot," *Business Week,* February 3, 1992, pp. 54–56.

70. R. Kuttner, "Talking Marriage and Thinking One-Night Stand," *Business Week,* October 18, 1993, p. 16; and O'Reilly, "The New Deal: What Companies and Employees Owe One Another."

71. Walter Kiechel, "When Management Regresses," *Fortune,* March 9, 1992, pp. 157–158.

72. R. E. Kelley, "In Praise of Followers," *Harvard Business Review,* November–December 1988, pp. 142–147.

73. M. Loeb, "Where Leaders Come From," *Fortune,* September 19, 1994, pp. 241–242.

74. R. Naylor, Jr., "The Best Companies for Working Mothers," *Tallahassee Democrat,* September 14, 1994.

75. "Managing Generational Diversity," *HRMagazine,* April 1991, pp. 91–92.

76. J. Huey, "The Leadership Industry," *Fortune,* February 21, 1994, pp. 54–56; and B. O'Reilly, "How Execs Learn Now," *Fortune,* April 5, 1993, pp. 52–58.

77. "Managing Generational Diversity."

78. J. P. Kotter, "How Leaders Grow Leaders," *Across the Board* 25, no. 3, March 1988, pp. 38–42; and O'Reilly, "How Execs Learn Now."

79. J. E. Sheridan, "Organizational Culture and Employee Retention," *Academy of Management Journal* 35, no. 5, 1992, pp. 1036–1056.

80. J. Hoerr, "The Strange Bedfellows Backing Workplace Reform," *Business Week,* April 30, 1990, p. 57.

81. S. Bicos, "Employee Participation without Pain," *HRMagazine,* April 1990, p. 89.

82. R. Jacob, "Why Some Customers Are More Equal Than Others," *Fortune,* September 19, 1994, pp. 215–224.

83. N. Margulies and S. Black, "Perspectives on the Implementation of Participative Approaches," *Human Resources Management* 26, no. 3, Fall 1987, p. 386.

84. F. Rice, "Champions of Communication," *Fortune,* June 3, 1991, pp. 111–120.

85. "Sunny Side Up," *Inc.,* January 1990, p. 104.

86. Susan Antilla, "What's on TV? Our 10 A.M. Meeting," *Working Woman,* February 1992, pp. 42–43.

87. Rice, "Champions of Communication," p. 120.

88. B. Shimko, "All Managers Are HR Managers," *HRMagazine,* January 1990, p. 67.

89. M. Falvey, "Deaf, Dumb, and Blind at the Helm," *The Wall Street Journal,* April 10, 1989, p. A14.

90. P. Farish, "HR Update," *Personnel Administrator,* May 1989, p. 19.

91. A. Karr, "Empowering Workers: Is It Real or Overplayed?" *The Wall Street Journal,* June 18, 1991, p. A1; and A. Markels, "Team Approach: A Power Producer Is Intent on Giving Power to Its People," *The Wall Street Journal,* July 3, 1995, p. A1.

92. T. Peters, "Another Bright Idea Squashed by Congress," *The Wall Street Journal,* November 22, 1989, p. A12.

93. Jeffrey Gandz, "The Employee Empowerment Era," *Business Quarterly,* Autumn 1990, pp. 74–79; and Peter Fleming, "Empowerment Strengthens the Rock," *Management Review,* December 1991, pp. 34–37.

94. B. Leonard, "Baldrige Award Winners Empower Workers," *Society for Human Resources Management HRNews,* November 1990, p. 13.

95. "Being the Boss," *Inc.,* October 1989, p. 50.

96. G. Andrews, "Mistrust, the Hidden Obstacle to Empowerment," *HRMagazine,* September 1994, pp. 66–70.

97. "The Power of Suggestions at ConEd," *Personnel Journal,* January 1988, p. 11.

98. R. Meehan, "Programs that Foster Creativity and Innovation," *Personnel,* February 1986, p. 32; and B. Miller, "Not All It's Cracked Up to Be?" *Across the Board,* November 1991, pp. 24–28.

99. "Suggestion Boxes Overflowing at Japanese Firms," *Productivity in Japan,* Autumn 1989, p. 3.

100. T. Schellhardt, "Power of Suggestion Stronger in Japan," *The Wall Street Journal,* October 19, 1989, p. B1.

101. P. Ingrassia, "Wheel Deals: Who's in the Driver's Seat?" *The Wall Street Journal,* November 23, 1990, p. A7.

102. Wendy Chamblee, "Suggestion Programs Empower Employee, Reap Profits," *HRNews,* December 1991, p. A9.

103. K. Fisher, "Ownership Counts," *Forbes,* November 14, 1988, p. 362.

104. A. Karr, "Labor Letter," *The Wall Street Journal,* May 14, 1991, p. A1.

105. M. J. McCarthy, "Administration Looks Favorably on Idea of Employee Ownership," *The Wall Street Journal,* December 23, 1993, p. A6.

106. J. White, "GM Workers Float Plan to Life Stock Prices, Including Boosting Employees' Holdings," *The Wall Street Journal,* January 19, 1990, p. A3.

107. J. Solomon, "When Are Employees Not Employees? When They're Associates, Stakeholders . . . ," *The Wall Street Journal,* November 9, 1989, p. B1.

108. Carla C. Cater, "Seven Basic Quality Tools," *HRMagazine,* January 1992, pp. 81–83.

109. F. Schneyer, "Team Management Takes Hold in Tallahassee," *Tallahassee Democrat,* August 7, 1991, pp. D1 +.

110. L. Thornburg, "Teamwork, Early Start Key to GM Relocation," *HRNews,* June 1990, p. 11.

111. R. Serafin, "Saturn Bounces Back with Its Basic Appeal," *Advertising Age,* January 30, 1995, p. 4.

112. John Butman, "Quality Comes Full Circle," *Management Review,* February 1992, pp. 49–51.

113. J. Steele, "Implementing Total Quality Management for Long- and Short-Term Bottom-Line Results," *National Productivity Review,* Summer 1993, pp. 425–442.

114. O. Harari, "Ten Reasons Why TQM Doesn't Work," *Management Review,* January 1993, pp. 33–38.

115. J. Mathews and P. Katel, "The Cost of Quality," *Newsweek,* September 7, 1992, pp. 48–49.

116. Harari, "Ten Reasons Why TQM Doesn't Work."

117. G. Guchsberg, "'Total Quality' Is Termed Only Partial Success," *The Wall Street Journal,* October 1, 1992, p. B1.

118. Adapted from B. G. Posner, "Raising the Stakes," *Inc.,* March 1990, pp. 100–103; and telephone conversation with company official at home office in Albany, New York, October 3, 1994.

PART FOUR
STRATEGIES FOR MAINTAINING HUMAN RESOURCES

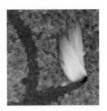

CHAPTER 13

BENEFIT PLANS

Due to major changes in benefit plans over the past years, many employees have difficulty understanding a firm's benefit program, let alone comparing it to those of other firms.[1] In the past, employers provided a fixed set of benefits to all employees, but this practice is changing. In the midst of today's competition, employers are becoming partners with their employees. By communicating with employees to learn more and, in some cases, to discover their needs, employers are offering flexible plans to accommodate a wide array of needs. Flexible benefits and more employee involvement are the keystones of this age, according to more than 300 human resource managers at the Conference Board's Employee Benefits Conference.[2]

CHAPTER OBJECTIVES

As a result of studying this chapter, you should be able to
1. Explain the strategic choices available to a firm in the area of benefits.
2. Explain how benefit plans tie into the overall human resource strategy.
3. List and define various forms of benefits.
4. Distinguish between traditional benefit plans and "cafeteria" or choice plans.
5. Explain the effects of health-care reforms on benefit plans.

C A S E

MANOR CARE[3]

Manor Care, Inc., is a company in the lodging and health-care industries headquartered in Silver Springs, Maryland. In an effort to be the employer of choice, the company is offering a new employee benefits package, Benefits of Choice. The highlights of the new plan include the following:

- A cash accumulation retirement plan that, at retirement, provides lower-paid employees a higher percentage of their salary than it gives more highly paid employees.
- A medical program that provides greater flexibility by accommodating small families.
- A decrease in coinsurance family rates of about 50 percent for long-term employees.
- A decrease in employee contributions to the group insurance plan.
- An increase in the employer match to the 401(k) savings plan, which rewards length of service.

COMMUNICATING THE BENEFITS

Realizing that effective communication is critical to the success of any new program, Manor Care conducted extensive educational activities during a three-week open enrollment period. Forty-nine Manor Care human resource professionals were trained for two days on the intricacies of the new plan. Then, during the 3-week open enrollment period, the human resource professionals made presentations to groups of 5 to 10 employees in sessions given around the clock every hour to accommodate all three shifts. Sessions began with a 10-minute video followed by a 30- to 45-minute period that consisted of overhead slides illustrating the mechanics and meaning of the plan to each employee. At the end of the presentation, employees were given take-home packets to help them gain a better understanding of the new benefits package. In addition, the company implemented a national toll-free number for employees who needed more counseling.

GIVING EMPLOYEES A CHOICE

Manor Care's goal with the training was not to guide the employee's decisions but to provide the information needed for them to make the best choice, depending on each individual's circumstances. As an additional aid, the terminology was explained to help employees understand it. For example, *flex dollar credits* were referred to as *cash out options.* It should be noted that there was no two-tiered communication effort to address upper-level management.

GETTING IMMEDIATE RESULTS

The communication effort had an amazing effect. Almost at the same time the plan was introduced and communicated, "voluntary turnover across the corporation dropped almost 15 percent in all classifications. The turnover of front-line service employees decreased almost 20 percent," according to Chuck Shields, president of human resources for Manor Care, Inc.

PROVIDING COST-EFFECTIVE EDUCATION

Shields also noted that the educational effort proved to be quite cost effective. The 20 percent decrease in turnover of nursing assistants (2,000 fewer recruits each year) experienced by Manor Care has resulted in a savings of $2,000 to $2,500 per employee. The savings more than paid for the investment (which consisted of costs of the video, staffing the hotline, training instructors, sending presenters to locations, and printed literature) of $5.00 to $7.50 per employee.

In short, Manor Care is very pleased with the success of its new effort. The plan has helped to retain employees and recruit new ones. If you were interviewing with Manor Care for a job, would its benefits package be a major factor in your deliberations? How would you know exactly how competitive the Manor Care package is? Do you think a benefits program, such as Manor Care's, actually helps the company keep good employees from leaving?

STRATEGIC CHOICES

You may have some difficulty answering these questions. But so do human resource managers who must develop benefits packages for employees. When faced with a multitude of choices available, how does one decide which to offer?

Frequently, the decisions boil down to three fundamental strategic choices managers must make. Each of these is outlined here.

1. How much of the money that is used to cover employee benefits should be paid by the employer, and how much of it should be covered by the employee? When making this decision, concepts such as corporate culture, corporate strategy, employee rights, and employer responsibilities must be kept in mind. If the firm wants to boast that it offers a comprehensive benefits package, it must not require that the employee pay the majority of the costs. Likewise, if the firm is following a cost containment strategy, it will not want to pick up the total cost of the benefit package.

2. Second, managers must decide how comprehensive their plans should be. Some firms pride themselves on covering any possible need the employee might have. Other firms may decide that only health insurance is important and offer only that to their employees. It may be difficult for some to believe that an employee would select to work for a firm that offers only health insurance, but many workers do. As we have seen in past chapters, not everyone is motivated by money, or, in this case, benefits.

3. Finally, managers must make a fundamental choice as to how flexible the benefits program will be. The changes occurring in today's workforce make some of the traditional benefit packages obsolete. For example, if both husband and wife work, it may be to their benefit to have one spouse cover dental and the other cover major medical because the plans are more comprehensive or less expensive. What they really do not need is for both of them to be covered under both plans. To allow these types of variations in benefit plans, flexibility is a must.

Let's look at each of these choices in more detail.

WHO PAYS FOR THE BENEFITS?

In the past, the employer has been responsible for paying most of the cost of a benefit program. This included premiums and deductibles for insurance as well as premium contributions. This began during World War II when employers were prevented from giving wage increases. Instead, they substituted benefit programs which were not under wage-price controls. However, the trend is being reversed, especially in health insurance.[4] The U.S. health-care system is the world's most expensive. In 1993, health care absorbed 14 percent of the gross national product, far more than in any other industrialized country. By the end of the decade, it is expected to represent 19 percent of the economy.[5] Total health benefit costs averaged $3,781 per employee in 1993, up 8 percent from 1992's average cost of $3,502. Employers also experienced increases. Total health benefit costs for small employers increased 5.9 percent compared to 9.1 percent increases for large companies. The average cost per employee was $3,240 for small employers versus $4,117 for large employers.[6]

Benefits are a labor cost, as are wages and salaries. With the pressure to keep labor costs under control, caused in part by the increased competitiveness discussed in Chapter 2, in the 1990s employers will be forced to make a strategic decision regarding benefits: How much will we ask the employee to pay?

HOW COMPREHENSIVE A LIST OF BENEFITS SHALL BE OFFERED?

COMPULSORY BENEFITS
A range of benefits that all employers must offer, as mandated by law.

A second strategic choice faced by employers involves the breadth and depth of coverage. All employers must offer a certain range of benefits. These are called **compulsory benefits,** such as workers' compensation and unemployment insurance, which are mandated by law.

Beyond these compulsory benefits, employers have a wide choice of benefit packages. Most major employers offer a comprehensive list of benefits, and this list will likely continue to grow. Exhibit 13.1 shows the results of a research study of 1,034 major U.S. companies. Ninety-two percent of the Fortune 100 companies, 56 percent of the Fortune 500 industrials, and 43 percent of the Fortune 500 service companies participated in the survey. Note that the surveyed companies offer a broad mix of benefits. All of the companies offer medical coverage, but only 31 percent offer any type of resource and referral services.[7] As employees become more family oriented, the benefit mix will likely change. For example, as employers seek to expand the work week, employees may expect additional family benefits, such as child care, to compensate for the lost time at home. If other companies begin to offer these benefits, will most employers in the geographic area begin to offer them? The extent of benefit offerings is a strategic question for each employer.

HOW FLEXIBLE SHALL THE BENEFIT OFFERING BE?

The third strategic choice involves the flexibility of benefit offerings. The employer needs to decide whether a standard list of benefits shall be offered to all employees or whether employees will be allowed to pick and choose among benefit offerings in a "cafeteria" style plan. Flexible benefits and employee responsibility are the

EXHIBIT 13.1   **The Changing Benefit Mix of the 1990s**

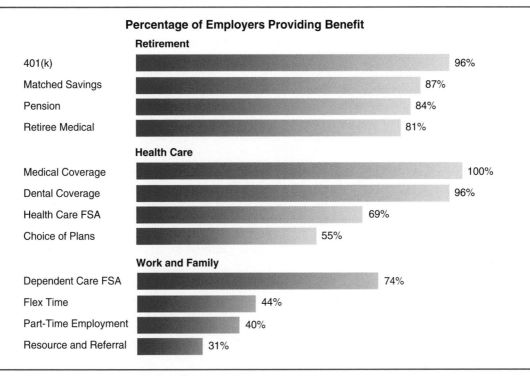

Percentage of Employers Providing Benefit

Retirement

401(k)	96%
Matched Savings	87%
Pension	84%
Retiree Medical	81%

Health Care

Medical Coverage	100%
Dental Coverage	96%
Health Care FSA	69%
Choice of Plans	55%

Work and Family

Dependent Care FSA	74%
Flex Time	44%
Part-Time Employment	40%
Resource and Referral	31%

SOURCE: Hewitt Associates, *Salaried Employee Benefits Provided by Major U.S. Employers in 1993,* Reprinted in Carl Crawford, ed., *People Trends,* April 1994, p. 1.

keystones of this age. No longer do employers provide a fixed set of benefits. A 1987 survey by the Administrative Management Society showed that 20 percent of the 309 companies surveyed offered cafeteria plans. This was up from 17 percent in 1986 and from just 12 companies in 1983.[8] An additional 12 percent were considering such plans for 1988. Thus, the trend seems to be toward cafeteria-style plans to allow increased flexibility to meet the needs of a varied workforce. Despite this trend, each employer must decide whether a flexible program is desired. Cafeteria plans are discussed in more depth later in the chapter.

In an effort to improve the current benefits package, Pitney Bowes, Quaker Oats, Nike, Salomon Brothers, and many others have solicited employee involvement. The starting points are usually surveys and focus groups in which employees are given an opportunity to express their concerns and fears about various issues. Some common concerns include not being able to purchase a home, to send children to college, and to care for elderly parents. After gathering the information, companies then ask employee teams to design a new benefits package offering more choices without raising costs. As a result, companies have broadened the benefits mix and increased employee morale. Employer-provided matching funds for college tuition, offering subsidies for child care or elder care, paid time off for family leave, group discounts on auto or home insurance, discounted mortgages, legal services, and financial planning advice, as well as extending paid vacation time, are among the newest benefits offerings.[9]

THE QUESTION OF COMPETITIVENESS

COMPETITIVE ADVANTAGE
A combination of the ends (goals) for which the firm is striving and the means (policies) by which it is seeking to reach those ends that gives it an advantage over its competitors.

DIFFERENTIAL ADVANTAGE
An edge on competitors achieved by distinguishing or creating a product or service that is unique within the industry.

As you no doubt have determined by now, one key underlining strategy that prevails in benefit offerings is *competitiveness.* Employers want to offer a benefit package that allows them to compete successfully in the labor market for employees but not one that is so costly that labor costs are raised above those of the competition. Exhibit 13.2 provides a list of the reasons given by employers for offering employee benefits. Essentially, employers face the same dilemma with benefit costs as they do with wage costs: they need to offer a high enough wage to attract and hold good employees but not one so high that labor costs exceed those of competitors. Of course, a higher wage rate can be offset by higher productivity, thus resulting in *lower unit labor costs* as we discussed in Chapter 12.

The question becomes: Can benefits be used to achieve a **competitive advantage?** In "Using Employee Benefits," H. W. Hennessey argues that they cannot.[10] Citing various studies showing that employees know little of their own benefit program, let alone those of competing firms, he argues that benefits cannot be used to achieve a competitive differential in hiring. Furthermore, the complexity of current benefit offerings with varying coverages and costs makes it difficult for all but the most diligent employees to understand the package.

The implication is that if a firm wishes to achieve a **differential advantage** in its benefit offering, it must know what is being offered by competitive employers in the labor market and then must design a program that is better. Next it must very clearly

▌ EXHIBIT 13.2

Reasons Given by Employers for Offering Employee Benefits

Company Size in Number of Employees					
Reason	1-10	10-49	50-99	100-499	500+
Attract good employees					
Salaried	10%	38%	44%	57%	53%
Hourly	33%	48%	27%	46%	47%
Reduce turnover					
Salaried	30%	19%	32%	19%	11%
Hourly	33%	22%	42%	18%	18%
Motivate employees					
Salaried	10%	22%	4%	10%	32%
Hourly	11%	19%	8%	21%	12%
Tax-free benefits					
Salaried	40%	22%	12%	8%	6%
Hourly	22%	4%	0%	0%	0%
Keep out the union					
Salaried	0%	0%	4%	2%	0%
Hourly	0%	4%	12%	9%	18%
Meet union requirements					
Salaried	0%	0%	0%	0%	0%
Hourly	0%	4%	8%	5%	0%
Other					
Salaried	10%	0%	4%	4%	0%
Hourly	0%	0%	4%	2%	6%

SOURCE: Adapted from N. Sutton-Bell, "Employee Benefits," September 10, 1990, p. 4.

=== **HR CHALLENGE** ===

Importance of Benefits Keeps Growing

In the past, benefits were not so very important, but today their importance is increasing. In a Gallup poll of 1,000 Americans, 75 percent consider health insurance, pensions, vacations, and other benefits to be very important in deciding whether or not to take a job. In contrast, only 70 percent in 1991 and 57 percent in 1990 thought these benefits were very important. These benefits are likely to become even more important in the future.

The majority of the people surveyed said that they would not accept a job that did not provide health insurance. Individuals with health insurance stated that they would need to earn an average of $4,570 more to give up health benefits. In an effort to attract and maintain competent employees, employers will need to have to offer a competitive benefits package. In many cases, the benefits package greatly influences the decision to accept or decline an employment offer.

SOURCE: Albert R. Karr, "Benefits Keep Growing, at Least in Importance to Workers," *The Wall Street Journal,* November 17, 1992, p. A1.

---

communicate this difference to all job applicants and present employees. Unless these two steps are taken, the benefit program will not be a way to gain a competitive advantage.

Some employers do not wish to gain a competitive advantage with their benefit program; rather, they want to remain competitive. That is, they want to offer a package of benefits that compares to, even though it does not surpass, that of their competition. Of course, even with this approach, clear communication of benefits to job applicants and present employees is essential.

COMPOSITION OF BENEFIT PLANS

Most companies today offer a standard list of benefits, and a wide variety of additional benefits is also offered, especially by the larger companies. Some of the standard benefits are compulsory (required by law). Others have been offered for many years. In this section, we explore the various types of benefits offered. Basically, we can classify benefits into seven major categories as follows:

- Required or mandatory security.
- Voluntary security.
- Retirement-related security.
- Time-off–related security.
- Health insurance.
- Financial services.
- Social and recreational services.

Specific examples in each category are shown in Exhibit 13.3.

REQUIRED SECURITY

Federal and state governments require that employers provide a certain minimum level of protection or a security floor for each employee. There are three primary areas of

■ **EXHIBIT 13.3**   **A Typology of Benefits**

Category	Example Benefit Programs
Mandatory Security	*1.* Worker's compensation *2.* Unemployment compensation *3.* Social Security (old age, survivor's and disability insurance) *4.* Medicare hospital benefits
Vountary Security	*1.* Severance pay *2.* Supplemental unemployment benefits
Retirement Related Security	*1.* Pension funds *2.* Early retirement *3.* Retirement annuity *4.* Disability retirement benefits
Time-Off-Related Security	*1.* Vacations *2.* Holidays *3.* Sick leave *4.* Disability leave *5.* Leaves of absence (sabbaticals) *6.* Military reserve time *7.* Pregnancy or parental leaves
Health and Other Insurance	*1.* Medical *2.* Dental *3.* Disability *4.* Life *5.* Group rates *6.* Survivors' benefits *7.* Wellness and fitness programs *8.* Employee Assistance Programs (EAP)
Financial Services	*1.* Profit sharing *2.* Stock plans *3.* Moving assistance *4.* Tuition reimbursements *5.* Legal services *6.* Financial counseling *7.* Company car *8.* Credit union
Social and Recreational Services	*1.* Paid club membership *2.* Recreational sports sponsorship (such as softball, bowling) *3.* Professional and trade association dues and meeting costs *4.* Child care *5.* Cafeteria *6.* Service awards (such as watches, jewelry) *7.* Company-sponsored social events (such as the Christmas party)

SOURCE: Reprinted by permission from p. 389 of *Personnel/Human Resource Management* by Robert L. Mathis and John H. Jackson; copyright © 1988 by West Publishing Company. All rights reserved.

compulsory security: workers' compensation, unemployment compensation, and Social Security benefits.

WORKERS' COMPENSATION

WORKERS' COMPENSATION
Payments for injuries received while on the job.

Workers' compensation protects the employee from costs due to injury on the job. These costs are paid entirely by the employer. Thus, industrial accidents are viewed as a cost of doing business, and, like any other cost, the company is responsible for keeping the costs as low as possible by furnishing a safe workplace and safe work procedures.[11]

Workers' compensation started with the Federal Employee's Compensation Act of 1908 and the state laws of California, Washington, Wisconsin, and New Jersey passed in 1911. All states now have workers' compensation laws.

CONTRIBUTORY NEGLIGENCE
Doctrine whereby an employee is unable to collect on a lawsuit if the employee is at all liable.

Prior to the passage of workers' compensation laws, if an employee was injured on the job, he or she had to prove negligence on the part of the employer. This was very difficult. Under the doctrine of **contributory negligence,** even if the employee was only 1 percent negligent and the employer 99 percent negligent, the employee could not collect in the suit. Because most employers had no health insurance plans for employees at the time, the net effect was that employees injured on the job had to pay for their medical care entirely on their own. Of course, most workers simply did not have funds to do so.

Workers' compensation originally covered only physical injury. However, today it has been expanded to cover emotional consequences resulting from physical injury. In some cases, job stress and strain are covered if they lead to emotional illness. Furthermore, even an accident at a company-sponsored party may be covered if employees are expected to attend.

Employers pay premiums into a state or private insurance fund. Premiums are based on the company's experience with accident and job-related illness rates: the higher the accident rate, the higher the premium. Thus, employers have an incentive to provide a safe workplace and instruction in safe work habits. However, insurers often refuse to set premium prices for small companies to their level of injury. The result is that some small firms that have had no accidents are placed in a pool with all other firms in their industry and end up paying a much higher premium than is warranted.[12]

Employees collect workers' compensation either in the form of cash paid directly to the employee or in the form of reimbursement for medical expenses, pain, and suffering. When work is missed, the employee is paid for lost work time. Although the amount varies from state to state, payment for lost work time due to illness or injury averages about two-thirds of the employee's regular earnings.

All but three states (Texas, New Jersey, and South Carolina) have compulsory workers' compensation plans that every employer must comply with. Under the elective laws in the three exceptional states, employers have the option of accepting or rejecting the act. If the employer rejects it, the employee must sue to initiate compensation.

To control rising costs of workers' compensation, several hospitals in Massachusetts have formed a self-insurance group and are paying a total of $2.5 million into a workers' compensation fund. The administrators of the fund have promised that a nurse will contact the injured employee within a day of when a claim is filed. This early involvement is intended to decrease the number of days missed from work, which will reduce hospital costs.[13]

CRITICISM OF WORKERS' COMPENSATION

Because benefits and plans vary so much from state to state, organized labor and others have lobbied for more federal control and regulation. Of course, employers and business groups have strongly resisted this because they believe their costs will increase. States also prefer to have their own plans, because those with low benefit levels use that fact as a strong inducement when attracting new industry. However, with the costs of workers' compensation rising rapidly, as shown in Exhibit 13.4, some changes are likely to occur.

Today, employers are paying $40 billion a year to compensate and care for injured workers, with medical bills accounting for 40 percent and compensation the other 60 percent. Insurers and companies that self-insure pay $20 billion a year for medical care for injured workers.[14] These rising costs have some managers worried about how they will pay the premiums. For example, Jean Stinson, a railroad contractor in Florida, lost a great deal of business when her company's workers' compensation liability jumped 187 percent in one year. To cover the $250,000 costs, she raised her bids. However, her customers decided to put all but the necessary projects on hold. She faced a similar problem at the beginning of 1992 when Florida's rates again were increased by 25 - percent.[15]

As some employers find ways to pay workers' compensation premiums, others are devising methods to avoid paying them. Stafcor, an employee leasing agency in California, has found a loophole in the law. The company administers its own workers' compensation program by combining it with its health insurance plan. Stafcor asserts that its "24-hour program," which covers employees on and off the job, is perfectly legal under the Employee Retirement Income Security Act of 1974 (ERISA). This loophole in this federal law allows Stafcor to save as much as 40 percent of the average $4 to $5 per $100 of payroll that California companies now pay to cover their workers in the state's program.[16] To deal with higher costs, top management must become

EXHIBIT 13.4	**Growing Workers' Compensation Claims**

Problem

Medical costs for job-related injuries are rising even faster than health-care costs in general.

Cost

Insurers and companies that self-insure pay $20 billion a year for medical care for injured workers.

Possible Solutions

- Beefed-up emphasis on worker safety
- Cost controls for medical services
- Keeping closer tabs on doctors

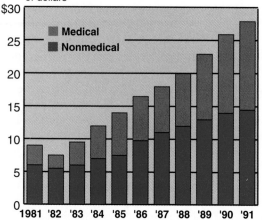

Medical Care Claims
Total medical and nonmedical workers' compensation claims paid by insurers, in billions of dollars

SOURCE: Greg Steinmetz, "States Take on the Job of Holding Down Medical Costs of Workers' Compensation," *The Wall Street Journal,* March 3, 1993, p. B1.

involved. The following are several steps recommended to help managers keep workers' compensation benefits in line.

1. Collect facts about the history of the firm's workers' compensation. Compare these figures to profits, sales, and salaries to see if they are out of proportion.

2. Be sure to understand the current programs in safety and health. Are there areas that can be improved?

3. Invite outside vendors, especially insurance carriers, who often have innovative plans and can propose alternative plans that will help curb rising costs.

4. Become more involved in the workers' compensation reforms in the states in which the company does business. Its voice may help to change the process.

5. Communicate information about workers' compensation benefits to employees—it can keep them from taking an adversarial stance.

6. Show concern in an emergency. The use of in-house clinics that can provide immediate attention to injuries can reduce the need for outside care.

7. Penalize careless managers. Charge claims to the operating unit in which the injury occurs.

8. Get employees back to work fast. The longer the employee stays away from work, the more attitudes toward him or her and work change. The employee may never come back.

9. Find out what's causing injuries. Many injuries can result from common problems that are easily fixed.[17]

UNEMPLOYMENT COMPENSATION
Payment to employees for time missed because of layoff or termination.

UNEMPLOYMENT COMPENSATION

Unemployment compensation pays employees for work time missed due to layoff or termination. This is a state-administered plan, but it was established as part of the Social

Security Act of 1935. The law was passed during the height of the depression to provide income for the millions of people out of work, thus helping to revive the economy. Employers fund this program by paying up to 3.5 percent of an initial amount (often $7,000 of an employee's salary).

Most employees are eligible for benefits unless they are fired for misconduct. They collect 50 to 80 percent of pay, depending on the state, for up to 26 weeks as long as they actively seek employment. During periods of high unemployment, Congress extends the period for collecting benefits up to another 26 weeks. Unemployment compensation has been criticized for encouraging fraud and laziness. Yet it has provided a floor of income for people who leave their jobs usually through no fault of their own. The law requires people receiving unemployment compensation to actively seek work, thus officially encouraging them to go to work as soon as they can.

Some have suggested that the federal law should be changed to eliminate abuse, provide stronger requirements for work search behavior, and provide more funding for the plan, especially during recessions. Standardization among the states also has been advocated.

SOCIAL SECURITY

Virtually everyone who works today is covered by Social Security. Social Security benefits are provided when an employee retires at age 65. It also covers old age, survivors, and disability insurance. Even such programs as Medicare and Medicaid fall under Social Security. In fact, several welfare programs, such as Aid to Families with Dependent Children (AFDC), the program that distributes food stamps, fall under the Social Security Act of 1935. However, our concerns are with those provisions of the program that deal with employment-related issues.

The Social Security program was established by the Social Security Act of 1935. This law was passed during the depression as part of President Franklin D. Roosevelt's New Deal program. The rationale was that government needed to provide a mandatory social insurance program to provide a minimum income for those who retire or are disabled on the job and for their survivors. Although initially limited in coverage, virtually everyone who works today, even farmers who are not included in most programs, is covered by the law.

SOCIAL SECURITY FUNDING

Social Security is funded jointly by the employee and employer through a tax on a set amount of wages. Both the tax and the minimum wage covered have consistently increased throughout the years, as is shown in Exhibit 13.5, but benefits have also increased greatly and are now indexed to inflation.

The Social Security fund is not a strict insurance fund as found in a private insurance company. Rather, the contributions of current employees pay the benefits of current retirees and other eligible recipients. In fact, there is some concern that once the baby boomers begin to retire in the first decade of the next century, there will not be enough people working to cover the massive benefit payments needed to fund such a large number of retirees.

Social Security also provides disability payments to an individual who is disabled on the job for as long as the person lives. These payments are rather modest, however. They are also made to survivors (immediate family) under certain conditions if a person covered by Social Security dies while working or retired.

Finally, Medicaid benefits are funded under the Social Security Act and pay healthcare benefits for the elderly covered under the Social Security Act.

EXHIBIT 13.5   **Social Security Benefits as a Percentage of Social Security Taxes***

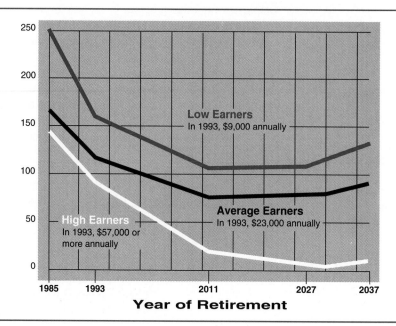

*Lifetime ratio of old age, survivors, and disability benefits to employer and employee payroll taxes, adjusting for interest rates and inflation and not including income taxes paid on benefits.

SOURCE: Social Security Administration

To better fund the program, some changes were made in 1983 in an act passed to amend the basic law. Social Security begins to pay some benefits at age 62, but the normal retirement age is 65. By 2002, the retirement age will increase by two-month increments to age 67 for all employees born in 1960 or later. The age for coverage for widows and widowers will also increase from 60 to 65. Finally, the act was changed so that people with higher incomes pay a tax on their Social Security income.

THE FUTURE CHALLENGES OF SOCIAL SECURITY

Beginning in 1993 for high wage earners and in 2002 for average wage earners, some Americans will be getting less in benefits than the accumulated value of what they and their employers paid in taxes. However, lower income workers will still benefit from the program. As can be seen in Exhibit 13.5, social security is almost guaranteed to be a bad deal for high and average income workers.

A recent survey conducted by the Employment Benefit Research Institute showed that 65 percent of working Americans expect to pay more into Social Security than the amount that they will actually receive. If this persists, it will become more difficult to gain support for Social Security from average and high income individuals.

In addition, meeting the needs of the huge population of aging baby boomers will threaten to bankrupt the Social Security system. Even though Social Security taxes on employees and employers rise annually, there is some doubt that all of the aging baby boomers will be properly cared for under Social Security, especially as life expectancy continues to increase.

HR CHALLENGE

The Need to Fill Empty Retirement Coffers

Many pension plans, both private and public, are underfunded because employers have failed to make the necessary contributions. During economic crises, many employers have postponed contributions, and now problems are beginning to surface.

In the private sector, many corporations do not have enough money to pay benefits to vested employees. In addition, the Pension Benefit Guaranty Corporation, a government agency that insures plans in a manner similar to Federal Deposit Insurance Corporation's insurance of bank deposits, has a $2.8 billion deficit—and it is growing. According to Robert Reich, secretary of labor, "At the present time the problem is not dire, but the trend is disturbing and now is the ideal time to fix it."

It is almost certain that employees and taxpayers will be affected in some way by this problem. What can be done to adequately deal with it before a major crisis emerges?

"Although relatively few people are aware of the problem, state and local pension plans across the country are more than $125 billion short of the money they will need to meet their pension promises." For

example, Dale Barry of Maine always dreamed of retiring from his state job at age 60 and begin enjoying the fruits of his labor. However, well after reaching age 60, Mr. Barry and 21,000 other public employees in Maine are still working as a result of the state's $2.6 billion pension account underfunding. When federal civilian and military employees are included, the gap between the amount saved and the amount required is an astonishing $1.24 trillion. As with the problems facing persons employed in the private sector, employees and taxpayers will have to assist in dealing with the problem.

Americans often are told not to rely solely on Social Security, because it may not be available for their retirement. Should Americans also not rely on the pensions their employers promised? These are very serious issues. What can be done to ensure that our pensions will be available when we reach retirement age?

SOURCES: Richard D. Hylton, "Don't Panic about Pensions—Yet," *Fortune,* April 18, 1994, p. 121+; and Leslie Scism, "Public Pensions Are So Underfunded That Trouble Is Likely," *The Wall Street Journal,* April 6, 1994, p. C1.

VOLUNTARY SECURITY

SEVERANCE PAY
Money given to an employee at termination.

GOLDEN PARACHUTE
Amount paid to executives in the case of a hostile takeover.

SUPPLEMENTAL UNEMPLOYMENT BENEFITS (SUB)
Amount given in excess of unemployment compensation received from the state.

Two of the major security benefit programs used by employers are voluntary: severance pay and supplemental unemployment benefits (SUB). **Severance pay** is pay given to the employee at termination. Its purpose is to provide funds to tie the employee over until he or she finds another job. The amount varies from several weeks of pay for hourly workers to several years' worth of salary for executives. In fact, **golden parachutes,** a form of severance pay, are paid to executives as a form of compensation if they are terminated during a hostile takeover.

Executives who fear hostile takeovers often are able to obtain a golden parachute clause in their contract, which states that they will be paid a large amount—often several years' worth of salary—if they are terminated. Because hostile takeovers usually result in termination of many executives in the acquired company, this protects those executives and is a deterrent to hostile takeovers, since such a large amount of cash is needed to fund the golden parachutes.

The second form of voluntary security is **supplemental unemployment benefits (SUB).** These are payments made by the employer to an employee who is temporarily laid off. They are made in addition to unemployment compensation received from the state. These payments were pioneered by the auto industry (during economic recessions, model changeovers, and so on). In the auto industry, employees receive up to 95 percent of their normal wage through SUB and unemployment compensation.

RETIREMENT

Fully 91 percent of full-time workers at companies with more than 100 employees are covered by retirement plans, according to the Employee Benefits Research Institute. Yet only 43 percent of firms with fewer than 100 employees have pension coverage.[18] About 45 percent of all civilian workers work in firms of 100 or fewer employees, so a large percentage of employees are not covered by pensions. In fact, Congress is considering several bills to encourage more widespread use of pensions by employers; the incentives include reduced paperwork, portability, and tax credits.

Pension plans are considered rewards for long service and are not incentives to work more efficiently or effectively unless the premium is tied to a stock option plan, as Sears' is. Pension plans are used primarily to retain a loyal workforce.

EMPLOYMENT RETIREMENT INCOME SECURITY ACT (ERISA) OF 1974

This law was passed to correct many abuses in pension coverage and to set rules and regulations. It is the major law regulating pensions. It is complex, detailed, and, at least for small firms, costly to follow. Hence, many small fims have terminated their pension coverage to avoid the voluminous paperwork, yet the law has provided increased security to ensure that employees actually receive their pensions when they retire.

The Internal Revenue Service (IRS) also has developed guidelines to try to control discrimination in pensions. Specifically, rules were established so that higher paid employees would not benefit more than lower paid employees.[19] Higher paid employees in 1990 were defined by the IRS as any employee paid more than $85,485 a year or $56,990 if he or she was in the top 20 percent of a company's earners.[20]

FUNDING OF PENSIONS

Funds for paying pension benefits are acquired in two basic ways. An **unfunded plan** pays pensions out of current income generated by the organization. A **funded plan** pays benefits out of money set aside and invested specifically to pay pension benefits; this is the more popular method because a specific fund is set aside to pay benefits. Current income of the firm, which can vary widely from year to year, depending on economic conditions and other factors, is generally viewed as too variable and risky a way to fund pensions.

INSURANCE FOR PENSIONS

Insured pensions are administered through an insurance company that guarantees payment of the benefits. **Uninsured pensions** are administered by the employer and are considered to be less stable and sound than insured pensions. However, some insured pensions are not too safe. For example, Pacific Lumber's retirement payments to its workers were delayed and threatened to be cut completely when the state took over First Executive Corporation's largest insurance units in California and New York. These insurance units, which were responsible for Pacific Lumber's pension plan, invested heavily in junk bonds, and when the bottom fell out of that market, the insurance units had to be taken over. Workers like Bill Hunsaker, who worked for Pacific Lumber for 47 years, were devastated. Hunsaker's medical bills for his wife and himself stacked up, and promises from the company did little to ease his pain.[21]

CONTRIBUTIONS

A **noncontributory pension** is one in which all of the funds for the pensions are paid by the employer. In a **contributory pension,** both the employee and the employer fund the pension.

UNFUNDED PLAN
Plan that pays pensions out of current earnings generated by the company.

FUNDED PLAN
Plan that pays benefits out of money set aside and invested specifically for paying pension benefits.

INSURED PENSIONS
Funds administered through an insurance company that guarantees payment of benefits.

UNINSURED PENSIONS
Plans administered by the employer; considered to be less stable and sound than insured pensions.

NONCONTRIB-UTORY PENSION
Plan in which all pension funds are paid by the employer.

CONTRIBUTORY PENSION
Plan that is funded by the employer as well as the employee.

PENSION BENEFITS

Retirement plans come in two main types: defined-contribution and defined-benefit plans. Exhibit 13.6 illustrates the number of employees involved in both and the assets associated with each. A **defined contribution plan** is one in which the contribution rate paid by the employee is *fixed* and retirement benefits *vary.* Profit sharing, employee stock ownership plans (ESOPs), and thrift plans are defined contribution plans. In a **defined benefit plan,** the benefits paid to employees are *set* as are the methods used to determine them. This allows the use of statistics to determine the employer contribution. Because a defined benefit plan provides a greater assurance of benefits and predictability of benefits available at retirement, older employees generally prefer this type of plan.[22]

Defined benefit plans have become more costly to administer because of new tax and accounting rules. Consequently, more firms have adopted defined-contribution plans, in which salary and service determine annual payments to an employee's account. Heltzel Mortgage began a profit-sharing plan in late 1992. According to owner Robert Heltzel, the continual use of a defined-benefit plan was not in the best interest of the company because the regulations seemed to be changing every day. Moreover, many small companies are switching to defined contribution plans simply because they are cheaper than defined benefit plans.[23]

PORTABILITY

In a **portable pension plan,** employees can move their pension benefits from one employer to another without losing benefits. Portability has become an increasingly important aspect of pensions because the average worker changes jobs every two to three years before age 30 and four to seven years thereafter. To deal with these demographic

DEFINED CONTRIBUTION PLAN

Plan in which the contribution rate paid by the employee is fixed and retirement benefits vary.

DEFINED BENEFIT PLAN

Plan in which the benefits paid to the employees and the method to determine the benefits are set.

PORTABLE PENSION PLAN

Plan that allows employees to move their benefits from one employer to another without incurring a loss.

| **EXHIBIT 13.6** | Retirement Plans by Type |

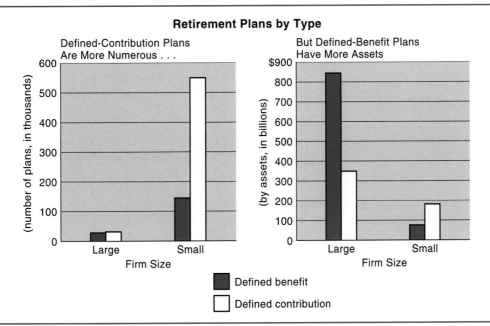

Retirement Plans by Type

SOURCE: Timothy L. O'Brien, "Many Firms Abandon Defined-Benefit Plans," *The Wall Street Journal,* February 12, 1993, p. B1.

changes, in 1978, the Internal Revenue Service addressed the demand for portable pensions by creating 401(k) plans and reducing the number of years needed for vesting. In 1991 the Department of Labor proposed the Pension Opportunities for Workers Expanded Retirement (POWER) to simplify and increase the flexibility of pension systems. As the baby boom generation continues to age, there will be even more demand for portability and security for retirement.[24] If an employee is not in a portable pension, then a lump-sum benefit must be taken at termination, provided the employee is vested.

VESTING RIGHTS

VESTING

The right to receive benefits from a retirement plan.

Vesting is the right to receive benefits from a retirement plan. A person becomes vested after working and contributing for a period of time. Five- and ten-year vesting periods are common. If the employee leaves prior to the vesting requirement, the only funds the employee receives upon employment termination are the funds the employee has contributed. Once vested, however, pension rights are retained and both employee and employer funds are received.

RETIREMENT EQUITY ACT OF 1984

This law liberalized pension regulations that affect women, guaranteed access to benefits, lowered the vesting age, and prohibited employers from discriminating against people who take leaves of absence (such as pregnancy leave). Other provisions of the act lowered the age at which workers can receive pension credits and the age at which they can enroll.

INDIVIDUAL RETIREMENT ACCOUNTS (IRAs)

A popular retirement fund is the individual retirement account. Although IRAs are funded entirely by the employee, they are popular because the salary money contributed, up to $2,000 per year, is not subject to taxes under certain total income limitations. Also, the interest earned on the amount set aside is not taxed regardless of total income.

Money can be set aside until age $70\frac{1}{2}$ and can be withdrawn without penalty beginning at age $59\frac{1}{2}$. Funds drawn prior to that date are subject to income tax plus a 10 percent penalty. The major advantages of an IRA are that the employee can decide how to invest the extra retirement income, and a tax shelter is created because income tax is deferred until retirement when presumably total income is lower and, hence, is taxed at a lower rate.

401(K) PLANS

Named for the section of the IRS code that set them up, 401(k) plans work much like an IRA in that they serve as a tax shelter for a portion of income until retirement. The difference is that the employer deducts the salary, and the money can be invested in only a limited set of employer-approved funds. Also, a larger amount can be set aside in these plans—$7,000 per year or up to $9,000 for educators. These plans are popular with higher paid managers and executives but cannot be limited only to these employees. These types of plans have been used to encourage executives to remain with the company.[25]

KEOGH PLANS

Keogh plans, or self-employment plans (SEPs), are retirement plans that self-employed individuals can use for retirement. These act much like an IRA in that a $2,000 limit is

---

HR CHALLENGE

Using 401(k) Plans at Coors

During 1990, Coors Brewing Company increased 401(k) participation by 16.5 percent and hiked pension benefits by an average of 7.1 percent for all employees. Employees have become involved in their retirement plans. More than one third of Coors employees have requested a computer program to project their retirement benefits. What sparked this dramatic increase? Coors says it's simply communication.

Coors implemented a campaign called the Tax Effective Retirement Account (TERA). This plan was designed to increase employee participation in the company's 401(k) plan. When Coors realized that employees failed to see their retirement income should come from three sources—pensions, Social Security, and personal savings—they decided to do something about it. The TERA promotion focused on helping employees understand the importance of making steady contributions to a retirement savings account to maintain a style of living after retirement to which they have grown accustomed.

One key to the program's success was the TERA turtle, which served as the mascot for the program. The turtle, inspired by the Aesop's fable of the tortoise and the hare, represented that the way to win the retirement race is with steady dependable savings. All employees who enrolled in the 401(k) plan received a turtle lapel pin, and all nonparticipants who requested a personalized computer projection received a pin too. If the nonparticipants joined, they also received a turtle

coffee mug as did those who increased their deferral percentage. To maintain interest in the program, Coors sponsored a weekly drawing for $100. However, the name pulled as the winner could collect only if the person was wearing a turtle pin.

All of these efforts paid off for Coors. In just 10 months, participation in TERA jumped from 73 percent to 84 percent of the workforce. More than 2,200 employees increased their deferral percentage and more than 1,200 employees signed up for first-time participation. Coors believes that its efforts will help to ensure that its employees will be able to retire in style.

Coors is a success story. However, the majority of companies have yet to attain its level of success. The latest evidence from a Gallup survey of defined contribution plans revealed that while 401(k) participants are more familiar with investment terminology than are others surveyed, they lack overall investment knowledge.

Companies are faced with the challenge of educating their employees. IDS helps its employees by issuing GAP statements, which are designed to identify retirement income needs and to demonstrate how to attain the goals. As a human resource manager, what improvements would you make to ensure better understanding of pension plans?

SOURCES: Adapted from Shari Caudron, "Boosting Retirement Benefits," *HRMagazine,* December 1991, pp. 76–79; Richard F. Stolz, "State-of-the-Art in 401(k)," *Advertisement,* 1993.

observed, and the individual directs the plan. Of course, the income and interest are sheltered from taxation until withdrawn.

EARLY RETIREMENT

Most companies offer early retirement whereby a person can retire at a lower age with fewer benefits. This is attractive, especially if a person can supplement company retirement with 401(k), IRA, or Keogh retirement plans. Many companies will "encourage" early retirement when attempting to reduce the number of employees by offering an extra one-time bonus for them to take early retirement. However, they cannot force people to retire against their will. Because of a 1986 amendment to the Age Discrimination in Employment Act, most employees can no longer be forced to retire.[26]

Forcing older workers out the door has not been a problem. Actually, in some cases, the reverse has occurred. For example, a petroleum firm that offered early retirement to its workers was forced to temporarily shut down a refinery because nearly every worker at the power plant that supplied the power for the refinery took early retirement. West Virginia's early retirement plan is costing the state $11 million more than it saved. DuPont was forced to hire back some of the employees it lost through an early retirement offer as consultants because almost twice as many people accepted the offer as the company had anticipated.[27]

Statistics indicate that the number of employees who opt for early retirement offers may continue to increase. For example, in 1955, 65 percent of the men over age 55 were working, but this figure had dropped to only 46 percent by 1980. For the men in the age group of 65 to 69, 57 percent were employed in 1955 as compared to only 29 percent by 1980. The figures are not so dramatic for women, but there has been an increase in their retirement percentages as well.[28] One thing that may make potential retirees think twice about early retirement is a lower standard of living after retirement. For a retiree who earned $40,000 in 1988 to maintain that standard of living, the retiree would need an income of about 68 percent of that amount plus Social Security benefits. By 1992 the amount had risen to 77 percent of that amount. Two of the major culprits for the increase are higher medical costs and lower savings.[29] Exhibit 13.7 shows how employers have raised the cost of retiree medical plans.

As can be seen in Exhibit 13.7, retirees must address another potential problem. For years, employers have promised employees health-care coverage after retiring. However, a new accounting rule requiring companies to show a liability for retirees' health benefits on their financial statements is putting pressure on management to trim costs to improve the bottom line. An easy solution to this is to increase the amount of the premiums paid by retirees. However, some companies have even eliminated the coverage completely. Others, such as Unisys and McDonnell Douglas, are planning to make cuts.[30]

TIME-OFF RELATED BENEFITS

Most companies offer time-off–related benefits in the form of holiday pay, vacation pay, and leaves of absence.

EXHIBIT 13.7   **Retiree Medical Plans Go Under the Knife**

Employer Action*	Percent that Have Done It since 1990	Percent that Planned it by 1994
Raised Premiums	30%	17%
Increased Cost-sharing by Raising Deductible or Out-of-pocket Maximum	26	14
Tightened Eligibility	11	10
Increased Benefits	12	5
Terminated Plan	3	4
*Based on survey of 1,380 companies		

SOURCE: Adapted from Don Dunn, "Retirees, Your Health Plans Look a Bit Peaked," *Personal Business,* November 30, 1992, p. 115.

HOLIDAY PAY

Most employers provide pay for all established holidays such as New Year's Day, Memorial Day, Fourth of July, Thanksgiving, and Christmas. Other firms also provide holiday pay for Christmas Eve, the day after Thanksgiving, and the employee's birthday. Federal employees also receive President's Day, Veteran's Day, Martin Luther King's birthday, and Columbus Day. The average number of holidays given is 10 per year, and many employers offer floating holidays, such as the employee's birthday.[31] Unionized companies negotiate holidays as part of the labor agreement.

VACATIONS

Most employers offer paid vacations that range from one to six weeks per year, depending on length of time (seniority) with the company. In a 1988 poll, employees rated paid vacations and holidays as the third most important benefit behind medical insurance and pensions.[32]

LEAVES OF ABSENCE

SABBATICAL
Extended leave of absence granted to employees for renewal purposes.

Leaves are given for military service, jury duty, elections, disability, funerals (bereavement), sickness, and maternity/paternity. Longer leaves called **sabbaticals** are also given for renewal or special service. For example, IBM and several other large firms offer four- to six-month service leaves that allow managers and executives to perform special service with nonprofit organizations. Several IBM executives have taught at Florida A&M University in Tallahassee over the past several years while on leave from IBM. Most leaves are paid, but some are only partially paid or are unpaid. For example, Florida State University offers a number of fully paid one-semester leaves to qualified faculty members after seven-year periods of service. The number is limited, and faculty members are selected on a competitive basis. However, many more full academic year leaves are available to faculty but at only one-half pay.

MATERNITY LEAVE
Leave of absence associated with child bearing, usually six weeks or more.

The 1978 Pregnancy Discrimination Act requires that **maternity leave** be treated in the same manner as any other medical disability or condition that involves a leave. If an employer has certain guarantees for employees on leave as to rights to certain jobs and pay on return, these also must be made available to women on maternity leave. Companies are finding that with the increase in the number of women in the workforce, an up-to-date maternity leave policy is extremely important. Firms that do not have such a policy may find themselves losing valuable employees.[33]

As a response to employees' need for leaves for fathers of newborn or young children and for other reasons, such as to care for ill or elderly family members, President Clinton signed into law the Family and Medical Leave Act on February 5, 1993, which became effective on August 5, 1993. In the case of a collective bargaining agreement, the act does not apply until the expiration of any existing agreement or one year after enactment, whichever is earlier. All employees who work at least 12 months for employers with 50 or more employees within a 75-mile area of a given workplace are covered. The major elements of the act include 12 weeks of leave during any 12-month period for one or more of the following: birth of a child; placement of a child for adoption or foster care; caring for a spouse, child, or parent with a serious health condition; or the serious health condition of the employee. The 12-week leave can be taken in a variety of ways. For example, the employee could take days as needed or use the leave to reduce the work week or day.[34]

The Family and Medical Leave Act requires that fathers be offered the same child-care leave as mothers. These so-called gender-blind leaves are also mandated by 14 states.[35] However, not many fathers are taking them. While more dads may be changing diapers and helping with child rearing, few can afford to take leave from work, for both financial and career reasons. Normally, after childbirth, the mother cannot work, so the father's paycheck becomes more important. Even with the guarantee that they will return to the same job, men fear taking the leave. Some critics say that the men have watched women who have been "guaranteed" the same position after returning from maternity leave who end up in a less than equal role and do not want to face the same outcome.[36]

DISABILITY LEAVE

Leave of absence granted for employees who get hurt or become ill on the job.

Disability leaves are offered by employers to employees who are hurt or become ill on the job. These leaves are above and beyond those provided under Social Security and Workers' Compensation. While they are usually funded by an insurance program of some sort, they involve absence from the job and are discussed in this section. In a recent Gallup poll, 53 percent to 59 percent of the respondents said that becoming disabled would probably mean the loss of their savings, standard of living, or jobs.[37] Employers as well as employees must develop innovative solutions to this problem.

An increasing number of long-term care policies are being offered through the workplace. Nearly 80,000 people have enrolled in employer-sponsored long-term care plans since 1987, according to a survey by the Health Insurance Association of America. A more recent survey indicates that the number of employer-sponsored plans is increasing by 50 percent per year.[38]

Some organizations are actively seeking ways to minimize disability costs by trying to find ways to keep the employee on the payroll. For example, when an assistant professor at the University of Pittsburgh became disabled with chronic fatigue syndrome, she, her rehabilitation specialist, and her university developed a way in which she could continue her teaching. She videotaped her lectures and held telephone office hours. This unique arrangement not only saved the university $63,000 in disability benefits, but it also kept the position filled with an employee who loves her job.[39]

HEALTH AND INSURANCE-RELATED BENEFITS

Health and insurance benefits are a major benefit expense for most firms. Employers offer various types of insurance coverage, including medical, disability, dental, life, legal, and auto insurance.[40] These health costs and related insurance have increased dramatically in recent years. Maintaining adequate coverage while keeping costs within bounds is a challenge for organizations.

HEALTH BENEFITS

In 1993, health care represented 14 percent of the gross national product, far more than the rate in any other country, and it is projected to increase to an astounding 19 percent by the end of the decade.[41] Thirty-seven million Americans are without insurance coverage, and every month another 2 million lose their insurance for some period of time. In addition, millions of the insured have just bare-bones policies.[42]

Rising health-care costs have driven up premiums for health insurance. In 1989, a single person paid an average $98.94 for coverage compared to $166.00 in 1993. This represents an increase of more than 40 percent. In 1989, families' health-care premiums averaged $292.31 compared to $419.57 in 1993, an increase of more than 30 percent. Exhibit 13.8 illustrates how health-care premiums under the Consolidated Omnibus Budget Reconciliation Act (COBRA) of 1986 have risen over the last several years.[43]

As firms are confronted with rising health-care costs, they must develop plans to curb them. John Deere founded its own health maintenance organization to control

EXHIBIT 13.8   **Average Cost of Health Care under COBRA**

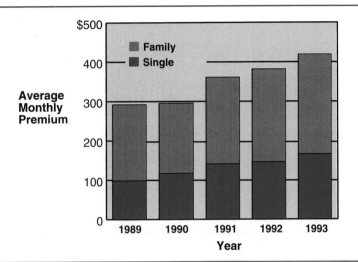

SOURCES: Adapted from Bill Leonard, "Communication Is Key to Employee Benefits Program," *HRMagazine,* January 1994, p. 58; and 1993 Survey by Charles D. Spencer & Associates Inc., Chicago.

spending while providing adequate service to its employees. Deere also opened a primary care clinic in Moline, Illinois, and plans to open others in the near future. As a result of these efforts, the company believes that its health-care costs since 1985 grew by 11 percent per year rather than the anticipated 13 percent.[44]

Corporate medical bills soared 21.6 percent in 1990 after rising 20.4 percent in 1989.[45] In addition, costs of health care for retirees and costs due to high malpractice insurance awards are often cited as contributory to increasing health-care costs.[46]

However, more recent data show that overall benefit costs, while still increasing, are increasing at a slower and slower rate. This is occurring largely because employers are getting health care costs under control. In 1995 employment benefit costs rose a slim 2.8 percent. This increase, along with the overall increase in total employment costs of only 2.9 percent, represents the smallest gains on record. Exhibit 13.9 shows the significant decrease realized since 1990 in this critical strategic cost category. The key strategic tactics used to realize these cost savings were cited to be the broader implementation of HMOs in health care and the use of outsourcing for the firm's benefit management.

Attempts to cut retiree health-care costs have been met by aggressive resistance by retirees.[47] Yet the courts have ruled that retiree medical coverage is no longer a "sacred cow" and that employers have the right to change or terminate health benefits for retirees.[48] And change they will. Sixty-two percent of the firms surveyed indicated that by 1995, they will raise or will definitely consider raising insurance premium contributions for retirees,[49] and 1 in 20 say they will cancel the plan altogether.[50] The Government Accounting Office estimates that annual health-plan costs for retirees will climb to $22 billion in 2008 from about $9 billion in 1988.[51]

In addition to the above mentioned reasons for rising health-care costs, requirements mandated by the **Consolidated Omnibus Budget Reconciliation Act (COBRA)** passed in 1986 have also increased health-care costs.[52] Under the law, employers with 20 or more employees (except the federal government and churches) must provide

COBRA
Law that requires employers to provide extended health-care coverage to employees who leave an organization.

■ **EXHIBIT 13.9**   **Slowing Benefits Costs**

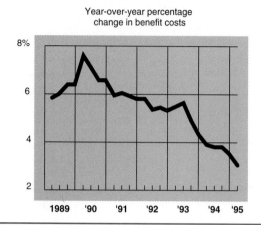

Year-over-year percentage
change in benefit costs

SOURCE: Lucinda Harper, "Company Benefit Costs Rose Only 0.2% in 1st Quarter, Slimmest in Eight Years," *The Wall Street Journal,* April 26, 1995, p. A2.

extended health-care coverage to the following groups, *even when not employed* by the company:

1. Employees who quit.
2. Employees who are terminated but not for "gross misconduct."
3. Widowed or divorced spouses and dependent children of former or current employees.
4. Retirees and their spouses whose health-care coverage ends.

Employees receive coverage for six months after leaving the company and must pay the group rate themselves. Its various requirements on notification, coverage period, and so on have caused COBRA to be a somewhat burdensome and costly law requiring more paperwork for most employers.

COST-CONTAINMENT METHODS

Companies in the 1990s will continue to stress cost containment to achieve competitive advantage. GM recently initiated a significant makeover in its health-care benefits. Through joint efforts with HMOs and traditional health-care providers such as the Mayo Clinic, GM reduced its $3.8 billion annual heath-care bill by 8 percent by using its size to define cost-cutting techniques. Consolidation of its prescription drug business alone saved $100 million in 1994.[53]

Typically, large employers were very generous with health-care coverage during the 1960s, 1970s, and 1980s. Coverages included many services, very few if any employees paid deductibles, and the employer paid all of the premium. In addition, the family of the employee was included in the coverage. This was a legacy left from World War II when employers could not give pay increases and substituted benefits instead. In 1989, approximately 45 percent of employees helped pay for their medical coverage. In 1990, this figure had risen to around 57 percent.[54] By 1991, 9 percent of employees paid all of it.[55] In 1994, only 15 percent of employers paid the full cost of medical coverage for employees, and only 9 percent paid full cost for employees and their families.[56]

HR CHALLENGE

Just Who Should Be Covered?

As the traditional American lifestyle continues to change, some employees are asking that some not-so-traditional dependents be included on their insurance. For example, some employees want their retired parents to be included on their policies. Older workers are sometimes dropped from their own employer's insurance policies after they retire, and it is much too costly to purchase insurance for older citizens, especially if they are in poor health. On the other end of the spectrum, some children get married, have children, and then, for various reasons, move back home. Some employees are requesting insurance help for the children of their dependent children. Also, unmarried live-in domestic partners and their children are frequently asked to be included on the insurance policies employees hold. Sometimes allowing this to happen stirs up quite a controversy.

In September 1991, Lotus Development Company became the nation's first well-known company to offer health insurance to partners of its gay and lesbian employees. To qualify, gay and lesbian couples must sign an affidavit stating that they are each other's "sole spousal equivalent and intend to remain so indefinitely." They must also state that they live together and that they are responsible for each other's welfare. The announcement was expected to raise protests from within and from outside the organization, but not the kind of ruckus that ensued, especially from within. Lotus employees sent so many internal mail messages using the company's electronic mail system that it crashed. Some employees showed up for meetings scheduled by the human resource department to discuss the issues while others simply discussed it in the halls and elevators, and at lunch.

Why all of the commotion? Some employees believe that if other companies don't follow Lotus' lead, the company will become a magnet for gay employees. Others argue that the provision is unfair because single heterosexual employees are being discriminated against. All of the arguments can be traced back to strong opposition to a homosexual lifestyle in the business community.

Following Lotus's lead, more than 70 major companies (including Silicon Graphics, MCA, Microsoft, Viacom, Oracle Systems, Apple, and Time Warner's HBO) offer domestic partner benefits, with most coverage being limited to gay employees.

But organizations must face the fact that the definition of family has changed. Currently, only 25 percent of the households would fall under the 1950s Ozzie and Harriet model in which the husband works and the wife stays home to raise their two children. Some firms, such as Digital Equipment, are rewriting their statement on the definition of family and are requiring each employee to define for himself or herself what his or her "family" includes.

SOURCES: Adapted from William Bulkeley, "Lotus Creates Controversy by Extending Benefits to Partners of Gay Employees," *The Wall Street Journal,* October 25, 1991, pp. B1+; Ceel Pasternak, "Health-Care Coverage for Nontraditional Dependents," *HRMagazine,* November 1990, p. 21; and David Jefferson, "Gay Employees Win Benefits for Partners At More Corporations," *The Wall Street Journal,* March 18, 1994, p. A1+.

Some firms even pay bonuses to employees who volunteer to be covered under a spouse's plan.[57] However, over 60 percent of the 1,000 employees surveyed indicated that they would gladly pay more of their premiums in return for better benefits.[58] Surprisingly, small firms are more likely to continue to pay all of an employee's medical coverage (53 percent) than are large Fortune 500 firms (44 percent).[59]

However, because of the rapid increases in health-care costs, employers are trying a variety of methods and arrangements to cut costs. These are shown in Exhibit 13.10. Let's look at each of these methods.

Health Maintenance Organizations (HMOs)   Although originally established to cut health-care costs, a survey of 163 companies indicated that less than 25 percent said their HMOs actually did cut costs.[60] In fact, in Exhibit 13.9 HMOs are cited as a reason that health-care costs have *increased* because of their tendency to attract

EXHIBIT 13.10   **Ways That Employers Try to Cut Health-Care Costs**

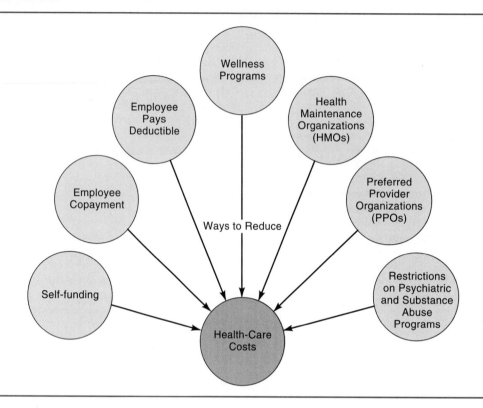

young, healthy workers, leaving the remainder to be covered by other plans offered by the employer.

In theory, HMOs make good sense. Health care is prepaid. Prevention is emphasized. Employers contract with an HMO, which has doctors on its staff. (Hospitalization is usually not covered.) For a fixed fee per enrolled employee, employees can visit the physician as often as necessary for a very small per unit charge. Thus, preventive medicine can be practiced, in an attempt to prevent sickness and illness from escalating. Employees are required to work through their primary physician who refers them to other care or hospitalization. This practice also helps to keep costs down because the primary physician can do screening.

In 1994, more than 41 million Americans were enrolled in HMOs. In 1994, 63 percent of eligible employees signed up for an HMO. The number of employers offering traditional coverage fell to 46 percent in 1994 from 57 percent in 1993.[61] Although some empirical evidence exists suggesting that HMOs actually increase costs, there is evidence that HMOs save money by negotiating lower fees with doctors, hospitals, and other suppliers, by scrutinizing medical decisions, and by discouraging wasteful or unnecessary procedures.[62]

Other evidence suggests that some HMOs have contributed to lower corporate costs, but that others reasons contribute to the high cost of America's health care. To some extent, cost depends on how the HMOs are set up and managed. Some of the early HMOs were not able to control costs and failed. However, most current HMOs have had enough experience to control costs.

Preferred Provider Organizations (PPO)   Another form of contract health service is the Preferred Provider Organization (PPO). This is a group usually organized by a hospital or a group of physicians. It operates much like an HMO, but a larger group of physicians is usually involved and a "looser" organization is provided in that the physicians are still independently operating under the umbrella of an HMO. A PPO allows employees more choice than does an HMO. Costs can still be kept low through prenegotiated fees, rapid claims payment, cost controls, and claims review procedures.

Employee Copayment   As previously stated, the number of organizations requiring employees to pay a part of the annual monthly premium is increasing. For example, the State of Florida government pays about three-fourths of individual health care premiums and one-half of family coverage premiums for its employees. The employee picks up the rest.

As shown in Exhibit 13.11 and previously noted, the percentage of firms paying the total cost of health-care premiums shrank drastically during the 1988–1994 period. Only 34 percent of firms pay all of the premiums for employees, and only 17 percent for dependents. This is about half of the number of firms that paid total costs in 1988.

Employee Payment of Deductible   The deductible system requires that the employee pay an initial fee for each office or hospital procedure. In some cases, the employee pays 20 percent of each visit for an 80 to 20 cost-sharing ratio. This is called a co-payment. In other cases, the employee must pay a certain amount per year before insurance coverage pays. For example, HealthTrust's new health-care plan has a current deductible of $200, but for individuals participating in high-risk activities, it imposes a $1,000 deductible.[63]

In effect, requiring employees to pay a deductible helps to reduce costs and claims for minor illnesses. Of course, it *discourages* employees from obtaining preventive treatment and early diagnosis of illness because the deductible must first be established.

Self-Funded Insurance   Self-funded plans are funded by the employer, not an insurance company.[64] In this instance, the employer sets aside a certain amount of money

EXHIBIT 13.11   **The Number of Employers That Pay All Insurance Premiums Have Dropped**

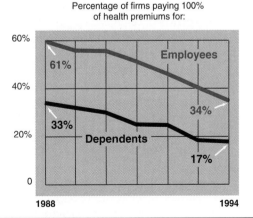

Percentage of firms paying 100% of health premiums for:

SOURCE: *USA Today,* August 29, 1994, p. 1.

to pay claims during the year (for example, $1 million). In addition, a contract often is written with a health insurance company such as Blue Cross/Blue Shield or Aetna to cover claims over the amount set aside and to administer the claims payment process.

Self-funded insurance can cut costs in several ways. First, the employer earns interest on the money set aside for claims, provided it is invested. Second, by paying such a huge deductible (for example, $1 million), the actual policy with the insurance carrier can be very low. Third, the agent (the carrier) is eliminated on the bulk of the claims.

Self-insurance has become very popular as a cost-cutting strategy. For it to work, an employer should have at least 100 or more employees over which to spread the costs.

Wellness/Fitness Programs   Many companies are becoming more aggressive in preventive actions to cut health-care costs. For example, IBM has fitness rooms and jogging tracks in many of its facilities. More and more companies and communities have no-smoking policies in the workplace and encourage employees through contests and awards to give up smoking. Others sponsor weight-loss programs.[65] Some employ health and fitness experts to advise executives and managers. Others, such as Xerox, sponsor employee teams to run in major races like the Boston Marathon. Finally, although done primarily for social reasons, many firms sponsor employee athletic teams and tournaments in bowling, softball, golf, and basketball.

Some firms are even paying employees to get healthy. Bank of Delaware employees receive $6 a month if they agree to wear a seat belt and promise to attend several health seminars. If they agree to take a fitness evaluation and adhere to the prescribed exercise plan, they can earn $9 a month. If they participate in both, they earn $12 a month.[66] U-Haul is taking the reverse approach by fining employees who do not have a healthy lifestyle. Any employee who is overweight, underweight, or who smokes is required to pay up to $10 a paycheck.[67] These companies are not alone. International Paper Corporation, which was hit with seven claims that topped $200,000 in 1989, moved to limit exposure caused by life-style excesses. The company now charges extra insurance or increases the deductibles for workers who smoke, are overweight, do not wear seatbelts, or who drive while intoxicated.[68]

Providing More Information   Companies are providing information and encouraging employees to shop for medical care as they would for any other service. NCR Corporation has provided a schedule showing what the company will pay for 11,000 procedures. This gives employees a starting point to negotiate with their present doctors or to find a new one. Employees who choose not to use the company's managed care networks could end up paying a larger percentage of some doctors' bills.[69]

Other companies, such as International Paper, have a more comprehensive plan. For example, an employee in Greenville, South Carolina, facing gallbladder surgery can use the company's files to learn that International Paper will pay a maximum of $1,219 to the surgeon, $257 per day for a semiprivate room, and $178 a day for nursing care. In addition, the files inform the employee that 19 surgeons in the area perform the procedure with fees ranging from $958 to $1,900. The files also indicate where doctors went to school, completed their residencies, whether they are board certified, at which hospitals they work, and whether they will discuss fees.[70]

Restrictions on Psychiatric and Substance Abuse Programs   Initially, employers attempted to restrict psychiatric and substance abuse programs. However, the trend among large companies that recognize the importance of their employees' mental health is to provide a flexible set of benefits with few, if any, restrictions. Employers are beginning to see that restricting mental health coverage costs more in the long run.[71] Scientific literature shows a strong interrelationship between mental health and medical services. For example, it is more cost effective to treat alcoholics in clinics that help them stop drinking than it is to treat them for gastric disorders.[72]

Other Techniques   One much debated technique that companies have been using to reduce health-care costs is called *managed care*.[73] Essentially, managed-care programs direct employees to a specific doctor, hospital, or treatment center that offers the employer a negotiated low rate. An HMO is a type of managed care program. Additional data such as quality monitoring and dependability are also factored into the equation used to determine where to send the employees. Employees who become patients also can be used to help reduce the cost of health care. By thoroughly informing patients about their medical problems by providing videotapes and other forms of information, patients can make informed decisions about treatment possibilities. Such programs have greatly reduced the number of unnecessary surgeries. For example, in Seattle, surgery rates fell by 60 percent over a three-year period.[74] Managed-care policies also stress second opinions.[75] While many companies have reported that a managed-care program has reduced their costs, others complain that they have had little or no effect.[76]

To reduce the cost of prescription drugs, companies are looking at new ways to deal with pharmacies. Some options include joining discount mail-order drug plans,[77] requiring that prescriptions be filled using generic drugs when they are available and negotiating with local pharmacies to lower prices on drugs. Some firms are even toying with the idea of an in-company pharmacy. The employer would gain control over prescription costs, but the overall price tag may not make it worthwhile.[78] Another in-company trend is employers providing medical care for workers at job locations or in company-run clinics to lower health-care costs and reduce employee downtime due to visits to doctors' offices.[79]

School unions in California have developed trusts to manage health-care costs and to reduce the friction between unions and management. The trust is a board of about 16 members who meet regularly to find ways to cut costs through wellness programs and negotiating new contracts with doctors and pharmacies.[80] Some firms have limited costs by tailoring the insurance programs to their specific needs and by not paying for services not used by their employees.[81] Others have reduced their costs by focusing on the "at-risk" portion of their workforce: those who have terminal diseases such as cancer, heart and respiratory diseases, and childbirth and mental health needs.[82] Recent studies have shown that infant and childbirth-related problems cost businesses over $5 billion a year.[83]

Even cities and states are getting into the action. When Clevelanders found out that they could load their sick employees on a plane and fly them 750 miles to the Mayo Clinic for treatment and still pay less than they would have if their employees checked into the nearby Cleveland hospitals, they knew it was time to do something. They enlisted the help of hospital administrators to obtain costs for hospital procedures and used a computer program to determine what facilities offered the most effective and efficient services. Employees are then directed to the "winning" facility.[84] Approaches like this are being used by other areas as well in an attempt to set up a market approach to health care in which only the most efficient and effective survive.[85]

One alternative to the market approach being used by several cities is a "pay-or-play" proposal.[86] Basically, this approach requires employers to provide medical coverage to all employees (play) or contribute to a government-financed health plan through a new tax (pay).[87] Some firms, such as Chrysler, have announced that they would drop their corporate insurance and pay into the public pool instead if the tax costs were less than the nearly 17 percent of the payroll that now goes to health insurance.[88]

Finally, some firms that have cut their portion of the payment for employees' insurance costs have established "flexible spending accounts" (FSA) to ease the burden on employees. A FSA is an account funded by an employee's pretaxed income that can be used to pay for specified health-care bills, such as deductibles, day care, or medical bills. There are several benefits to this type of account. For example, the money is not taxed. Also, it reduces the employee's taxable income. However, if the employee does not spend the money by the end of the year, it is lost.[89]

Evaluation of Cost-Cutting Measures   A survey by consultant Towers Perrin found that the *rate of increase* in health-care costs dropped in 1994; the increase was only 6 percent. This compares with average annual increases of 20 percent throughout most of the decade of the 1980s and 12 percent in 1993. Three reasons are given for the decline:

1. The severe recession of 1991–1992.
2. Closer control of health-care expenses by employers.
3. Increased use of HMOs by employers.

One year of significantly lower cost increases does not make a trend, but at least there is some indication that the rate of increase in health-care costs may have slowed.[90]

This report by Towers Perrin is consistent with the overall reduction in the growth of benefit costs as shown in Exhibit 13.9 and as previously discussed.

ADDITIONAL ISSUES IN HEALTH INSURANCE

Several additional issues are having a profound effect on the health insurance and medical industries and will, consequently, affect employers.

An Aging Population   The U.S. Census Bureau indicates that the United States will become a gerontocracy as the baby boomers age and the birth rate remains low. By the year 2010, 33.8 percent of the nation will be over age 50.[91] Older people consume vast amounts of health care, which will likely increase as medical advances keep older people alive for longer periods of time. How will the nation adequately fund the care of its elderly in the next millennium?

In his book *The Retirement Myth,* Craig S. Karpel states that the baby-boom generation has virtually no hope of retiring in comfort. He reports that 59 percent of the elderly today depend on the government for more than half their income. He predicts that more Americans will be working past retirement age to offset the impact of lower government subsidies.[92] What must the human resource manager do today to ensure that his or her company is prepared to take competitive advantage through the use of senior employees?

AIDS   Acquired Immune Deficiency Syndrome (AIDS) is a deadly disease for which, at the time of this writing, there is no cure. At the beginning of 1989, 87,188 people were diagnosed with AIDS, producing 49,976 deaths.[93] Once thought to be a disease of male homosexuals, now male heterosexuals, women, and children have it. Costs of finding a cure and treating the disease are likely to place a heavy burden on our medical system. Employers should be aware that placing an exclusion or ceiling for AIDS on insurance benefits may be illegal. As the number of legal remedies available to AIDS patients rises, the risk of employer liability climbs.[94]

Drug Testing   The use of illegal drugs in society has caused many employers to adopt a drug-testing policy. This policy might involve testing at the time of the employee's hire or unannounced tests while employed. There are legal guidelines and prohibitions to follow to have valid tests (chain of custody, invasion of privacy issues, and so on). Drug use on the job and its prevention are critical health issues with which many employers will continue to be concerned.

Expansion of Coverage   Many firms are beginning to offer coverage for dental, chiropractic, and optometric work in addition to mental health coverage. Often this coverage is offered on copayment and fee-share basis. In addition, states are requiring employers to add coverage for such medical services as care by lay midwives, ambulance transport, and breast reconstruction.[95]

NONMEDICAL INSURANCE BENEFITS

Besides health-related insurance, employers also provide other forms of insurance. For example, many employers provide life insurance policies based on a group rate. A typical level is 150 percent of an employee's annual salary, but executives often receive much more than this as part of an executive compensation package. *Long-term* disability coverage is also provided by many employers, which provides a continuation of income in the event of a long-term injury or illness.

Legal insurance is provided by some firms, often in the form of prepaid or negotiated fees between the employer and a group of attorneys. The employee often shares in the premium for this insurance and/or in the fee payment at the time of the service.

Some firms also offer group insurance rates for automobile insurance; these rates are often lower than individual rates.

NATIONAL HEALTH-CARE PLAN

Thirty-seven million Americans have no health insurance, and another 22 million lack adequate coverage. It is estimated that between 1995 and 1997, 63 million Americans will lose coverage for some period of time.[96] As can be seen in Exhibit 13.12, the

EXHIBIT 13.12   **Americans Without Health Insurance**

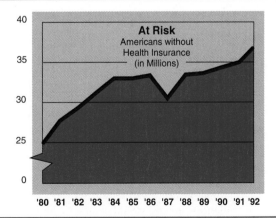

SOURCE: Adapted from Matthew Kopit, "Business is Developing a Resistance to Health Reform," *Business Week,* July 25, 1994, p. 32.

number of uninsured Americans has been increasing since 1988. Unless something is done, these numbers will continue to increase. Concerned with the overall health-care situation in the United States, the Clinton Administration attempted to provide health insurance for all Americans. President Clinton believes that universal coverage will help solve the health-care crisis in this country. While the plan failed to pass Congress, the issue continues to be a top priority of the administration. It is likely that any new plan will contain similar features to the 1994 proposal.

HIGHLIGHTS OF THE CLINTON PLAN SUBMITTED TO CONGRESS IN 1994

Universal Coverage   Every U.S. citizen and legal resident would receive continuous health-care coverage through state-established regional alliances. Coverage would be provided during times of unemployment, sickness, and job changing. Medicare would still be provided for individuals older than 65.

Corporate Alliances   Companies with more than 5,000 workers would be allowed to form corporate alliances. Such alliances would be required to provide the same federally guaranteed benefits package and meet all other government requirements as the regional alliances. In the event that the number of employees dropped below 4,800, the company would have to join one of the regional alliances.

Employer Mandate   Every employer would be required to pay at least 80 percent of the average premium of the benefits package offered in its region. The remainder would be paid by the employee unless the employer chooses to pay all or part of the employee's share. Financial assistance would be provided by the federal government to low-income and unemployed individuals as well as to low-wage businesses.

Benefits   Services covered in the federally guaranteed benefits package would include the following: hospital, emergency, physicians and other health professionals, clinical prevention, mental health and substance abuse, family planning, pregnancy-related care, hospice care, home health care, extended care, ambulance, outpatient laboratory and diagnostic measures, outpatient prescription drugs, outpatient rehabilitation, durable medical equipment, prosthetic and orthotic devices, vision and hearing care, preventive dental care for children, and health education classes.

Workers' Compensation and Auto Injury Insurance   The plan would cover work-related and automobile injuries. Workers' Compensation and automobile insurers would reimburse health plans for services provided.

Antitrust Changes   The plan would clarify antitrust rules so that physicians and other providers could negotiate effectively to form their own health networks as part of the new system. The exemption from antitrust laws currently enjoyed by health insurers would be repealed, eliminating the ability of health plans to collectively determine the rates they charge.

Budgeting and Oversight   A new seven-member, presidentially appointed national health board would set the spending budget for the regional alliances. The alliances, in turn, would contract with health-care plans—be they health maintenance organizations, fee-for-service plans, or hybrids—making sure the average premium price in the region doesn't exceed the specified target.

Long-Term Care A new long-term care program for people with severe disabilities would provide, among other things, expanded home- and community-based services that are funded primarily by the federal government with some input from the states.

Medical Schools The government would direct funding so that after a five-year phase-in period, at least 50 percent of new physicians would be trained in primary care rather than specialty fields.

Underserved Areas Health services would be expanded for rural residents through various incentives, including giving physicians who locate in such underserved areas a personal tax credit of $1,000 a month that can be claimed during the first five years of practice.

Consumer Information The regional alliances would publish information on the cost of health plans and list the doctors and hospitals participating in each one. The alliances would issue annual quality performance reports on each one.

Malpractice Reform Attorneys' fees for malpractice would be limited to a maximum of 33.33 percent of an award. The plan also encourages alternative approaches to resolving disputes between patients and providers. Further, it would provide public access to information in a national data bank, which would track health providers that incur repeated malpractice judgments and settlements. And it would provide federal funds to support state-run enterprise liability demonstration projects, whereby health plans, not physicians, would be held liable.

Consumer Protection Physicians no longer would be able to make self-referrals, that is, to order services from outside entities in which they have a financial interest. Penalties would be stiffer for those who commit health-care fraud.

Standard Forms All health plans would adopt a single, standard claims form. Some of the changes for patients under the original Clinton plan are shown in Exhibit 13.13.

FINANCIAL, SOCIAL, AND RECREATIONAL BENEFITS

Many companies offer a variety of financial benefits to managers and employees. These benefits include **perks** (perquisites), which are special types of additional or added non-cash compensation in the form of benefits or special privileges. Care must be exercised when defining these additional benefits. Employees often perceive programs that benefit only executives as aristocratic, and benefits given only to highly compensated employees can be found to be discriminatory as well as subject to employer and employee taxation. Employers are encouraged to seek employee input in defining benefit package components.[97] Let's examine these additional benefits.

NONFINANCIAL BENEFITS

The use of a company car, company expense accounts, club memberships, help in buying and selling a home, and the use of company-owned resort condominiums are examples of perks available to managers, executives, and some employees. Also, financial planning and counseling, including tax preparation advice, are often offered to managers and executives.

EXHIBIT 13.13   **Points of Change for Patients**

- Everyone will be issued a national health card; this will entitle you to medical coverage offered through your local health alliance.
- You will be encouraged to pick a regular, primary-care doctor, who will be your first point of contact whenever care is needed.
- If you are in a managed-care program, high-priced specialists will be largely off limits unless your primary-care physician refers you to one. Shuttling from specialist to specialist will be discouraged.
- Preventive care will become more common. Healthy people will get cholesterol screenings, Pap tests, smoke-ending classes, and the like—generally with your health plan picking up the tab.
- Data on doctors' past treatment records will become public. Finding out which physicians do especially well—or badly—may be as simple as checking your local newspaper or TV station.
- Highly trained nurses may take over some of the primary-care duties now performed by doctors.

SOURCE: George Anders, "Visits to Doctor's Office Will Be Different," *The Wall Street Journal,* September 13, 1993, p. B1.

Additionally, most medium and large companies offer *credit unions* to employees for lending and saving services. Some firms offer purchase discounts to employees in the form of buying clubs or employee discounts on company merchandise.

THRIFT/STOCK BENEFITS

Employee **thrift, saving, or stock purchase investment plans** are also popular. For example, in a stock option plan, an employee is often guaranteed the right to buy shares of company stock at a discount or at a certain price. Alternatively, the company may purchase the stock for the employee. (This is taxable compensation unless it is in the form of a defined stock plan; then the tax is not levied until the stock is actually taken by the employee.)

EMPLOYEE STOCK OWNERSHIP PLAN (ESOP)
Profit-sharing plan in which employees are offered the opportunity of buying stock in the organization.

ESOP   When stock is provided as a part of a profit-sharing plan, an **employee stock ownership plan (ESOP)** is developed. (ESOPs are also discussed in Chapter 12.) ESOPs receive favorable income tax treatment and have become very popular. They give employees a sense of ownership in the company and allow them to share in the company's success and profits.

ESOPs also have been used in leveraged buyouts (LBOs) of firms by employees.[98] From 1980 to 1987, the number of employee buyouts of firms went from 500 to 1500, a 300 percent increase. However, in 1989 and 1990, things began to slow down. In 1989, 830 new ESOP plans were established and in 1990, only 480 ESOPs were formed. Since then, the rate of growth has steadily declined to about 400 per year. The main reason suggested for the slowdown was that tighter credit restrictions limited borrowing.[99]

In the early 1980s, workers used ESOPs to buy relatively small companies or to become buyers of last resort for large troubled companies. However, by the late 1980s and 1990s, because of favorable tax treatment and as a tactic to thwart hostile takeovers, healthy companies, such as Avis, were purchased by employees through LBOs financed through ESOPs.

As the economy began to worsen in the late 1980s and early 1990s, some ESOPs lost favor with employees. Falling stock prices and rising corporate bankruptcies are rendering some ESOPs null and void. At Thomson McKinnon, where brokers and other employees owned as much as 77 percent of the firm's shares, ESOP employees saw their plan devalued from $140 million to nothing. In 1989, employees received a letter indicating that it was possible that their ESOP would have no value whatsoever.[100]

By 1995, many of the 12,000 ESOPs in the United States denied employees the right to vote on typical "shareholder" issues and often withheld key financial information. For example, morale at Avis in 1995 was very low as a result of declining profits and a 50 percent drop in share value since 1993.[101]

EDUCATIONAL BENEFITS

Many firms offer a tuition reimbursement plan for employees who attend a school, college, or university. Usually the firm requires that the employee take a course related to work, although this is often broadly defined, and that a passing grade be earned in the course.

CHILD-CARE BENEFITS

Working women with small children have become very common in our society, as we previously explained. Although only 6 percent of surveyed employees offered employer-sponsored child care in 1987, one study showed that 66 percent of surveyed benefit directors saw child care as a "major growth" area by 1995.[102] Exhibit 13.14 shows how each region of the country ranks in respect to corporate-sponsored child care.

EXHIBIT 13.14   **Percentage of Companies Offering Child-Care Programs by Region (1993)**

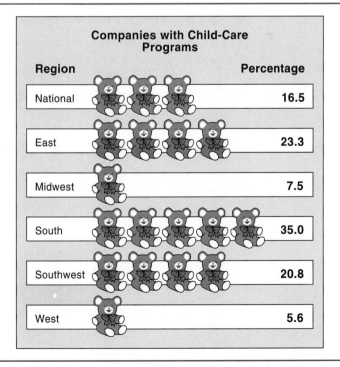

Companies with Child-Care Programs

Region	Percentage
National	16.5
East	23.3
Midwest	7.5
South	35.0
Southwest	20.8
West	5.6

SOURCE: Adapted from C. Pasternak, "HRM Update," *HRMagazine,* December 1990, p. 21.

Costs of day care and the inconvenience of taking and picking up children are stumbling blocks for many working parents. Home care either from relatives or neighbors is often unavailable or simply too expensive. The quality of care is also an issue. All of these factors are increasing the pressure on employers to provide affordable, quality, and convenient child care for employees who desire it as part of the insurance package. Some firms are responding to this need.[103]

St. Joseph's Hospital in Marshfield, Wisconsin, is a 524-bed hospital in a town of 20,000. The hospital employs 2,200 employees, many of whom require child care. Because demand was so great, the hospital opened an on-site day-care center in 1981. In 1989 it expanded its facilities so that it could take care of twice as many children—130. It also extended the hours to midnight and allowed up to 50 children to be there during the evening. Because the center has a waiting list, the hospital can no longer use it as a recruiting tool. However, it can use the benefits offered by the hospital, which are much better than other local facilities, as a recruiting tool for day-care workers.[104]

Some critics argue that child care is being used as a tool to discriminate against employees. For example, Merck & Company opened a day-care facility years ago in Rahway, New Jersey, after one of its top female scientists threatened to resign. However, the monthly cost of using the facility was $680. Professionals can easily afford this service, but secretaries cannot. Merck now has plans to open two other facilities, and it is considering subsidizing the costs for lower-paid employees. The company is anxious not to appear to favor one type of employee over another.[105]

Child care may be one area in which the Japanese can learn something from Americans. Tokyo parents are flocking to the first corporate child-care center, which opened as a result of a joint venture between Bright Horizons Children's Center in Cambridge, Massachusetts, and Temporary Center Corporation, Tokyo's largest temporary placement agency. The center opened January 6, 1992, with all 44 slots taken and a waiting list. Every person who visited the center during its developmental phase enrolled his or her child. With demand so high, two additional facilities have been planned.[106]

ELDER CARE

A study of benefit directors in 1988 indicated that 77 percent of them believed that elder care—care of the elderly—will be a major growth benefit in the 1990s.[107] As the number of elderly citizens increases greatly in the 1990s, and as the baby boomers age, demands will be placed on employers to provide benefit plans to assist with the care of aged parents and aged employees.

One study uses the "dependency ratio" to explain this issue.[108] This ratio compares the number of current workers to the number of dependents. Dependents are defined as those below age 18 and above age 64. Between 1950 and 1982, the ratio of youthful dependents fell from 51.0 per 100 workers to 44.1 and is expected to drop to 36.2 by the year 2080. At the other end, the elderly dependency ratio climbed from 13.3 to 18.8 in the same period, and is expected to soar to 41.9 by the year 2080. Thus, the number of retirees is expected to continue to grow at a much faster pace relative to the number of current workers.

With more and more retirees living longer, a greater number of employees will be supporting their retired parents in addition to their own children. Hence, strong demand will be placed on employers to help with this burden. One study estimated that in 1995, 44 percent of the nation's workforce needed elder care services.[109]

CAFETERIA PLANS

Because of the variety of options in the benefit area, many employers have shifted to or are considering "cafeteria plans." As noted earlier, cafeteria plans allow employees to pick and choose from a variety of benefit options much as a person chooses food at a cafeteria. This allows a person to tailor a benefit program that meets his or her needs. Employees generally purchase benefits with flex credits allocated through their employers or through a salary reduction agreement.[110]

For example, a young, single-parent mother may place greater value on child care, health care, and similar benefits than a 55-year-old male who may be more interested in retirement benefits, long-term health care, and life insurance. Other employees may want to buy extra vacation days; others would like to trade the ones they have in for cash.[111] Cafeteria plans allow for such switches.

Twenty percent of surveyed companies in 1987 offered cafeteria plans and an additional 12 percent were either considering or implementing such a plan.[112] By 1989, 23 percent of employers offered flexible benefits and by 1993 the figure had risen to 35 percent.[113] Half of the companies with such programs say they have been able to demonstrate cost savings as a result. Frequently, the cost savings comes in the form of higher employee contributions.[114] Accurate prediction of employee selections also can help control costs.[115]

Nine of 10 flexible benefit plans surveyed offered major medical and hospital coverage. More than half the plans included life insurance, long-term disability, and dependent care. Flexible plans were most popular in the western part of the country, in medium-sized and large companies, and in the education/government/nonprofit sector. One recent survey indicated that 90 percent of the 1,000 employees surveyed preferred a job that offered flexible benefits over one that did not.[116]

FUTURE BENEFIT CHANGES

While no one can accurately predict the future state of benefits with a high degree of certainty, one analysis suggests the following trends:[117]

1. *More Paid Leave.* Leave will be provided for long-term "refresher" sabbaticals and for social service pursuits.
2. *Education and Training.* Rapidly changing job skill requirements and a shortage of new entrants into the labor force will compel employers to regularly offer education and training programs, leaves, and reimbursement for a wide variety of training to employees.
3. *Career Planning.* Many employers will offer formal career counseling programs to help employees plan careers that adjust to their changing lives.
4. *Housing.* Moving assistance and mortgage aid will become even more common.
5. *Late Retirement.* As baby boomers age and shortages of workers and skills increase, companies will be bending over backwards to help their older employees. TRW's Pat Choate calls these "Platinum Handcuffs"—consisting of company-paid vacation trips, shorter hours, and bonus plans that reward employees for staying on past a certain age or period of service.
6. *Flextime.* Flexible work schedules and job sharing (allowing two or more people to share one 40-hour-a-week job) will become more common as employers adjust to alternative lifestyles and schedules of the elderly and single parents with children to keep enough skilled employees. Many companies have instituted flextime, including DuPont, IBM, Aetna, GE, and Volvo (Saab and Scandia). Flextime has proven to be a form of cost cutting that keeps the best people.[118]

7. *Vacations.* Employees will be able to "buy" extra vacation time if they deserve it by trading it for other available benefits such as sick leave or even a portion of hospital care.

8. *Health Care.* Universal coverage under a national system will be available in some form.

STRATEGIC MANAGEMENT OF BENEFITS

As you can see, benefits have become a costly and complicated area in human resource management. As a reaction, more firms are taking an aggressive strategic approach to benefits; instead of simply "administering" a benefit program, many firms attempt to strategically manage it to obtain the greatest results at the least cost.

COMPETITIVE ADVANTAGE AND BENEFIT COSTS

Many employers develop a benefit program that meets, but does not necessarily exceed, that of competitors. As we pointed out earlier in the chapter, it is unlikely that employers can use a benefit program to achieve a competitive advantage unless they can offer similar benefits at a reduced cost. In fact, Hennessey concludes, "Competitive advantage will be most easily enhanced by controlling benefit costs to the maximum extent possible within constraints imposed by competition."[119] He also concludes that benefit programs do little to attract, motivate, or retain employees.

Yet many employers believe that benefits do, in fact, help to attract and retain, if not motivate, employees and are attempting to verify this through careful study. As was discussed earlier, 75 percent of workers consider employment benefit packages important to making a job decision, up from 57 percent in 1990. Although such studies are often difficult to conduct and are fraught with measurement problems, the next section summarizes some key actions of employers to measure the cost-effectiveness of benefits.

CORPORATE EFFORT TO MEASURE BENEFIT COST-EFFECTIVENESS

Ideally, to determine the cost-effectiveness of a benefits program, controlled experiments comparing the advantages and costs of one type of benefit with the advantages and costs of an alternative benefit need to be conducted. AT&T is conducting a study with its insurers comparing the medical claim data of 1,600 participants in a wellness program with a control group of 1,800 nonparticipants.[120] They expect that wellness program participants will have a lower use of hospitals and doctors, thereby saving medical costs overall.

Some companies attempt to measure problems that would occur if benefits were *not* provided. These costs usually include such negative consequences as turnover, absenteeism, and tardiness. For example, Corning Glass Works decided to measure out-of-pocket expenses associated with turnover, such as interview costs and hiring bonuses. Costs were estimated at $16 million to $18 million annually. This led to a look at the causes of turnover and to the adoption of new policies in flexible work hours and career development to cut turnover.[121]

Some companies are even attempting to measure more complicated linkages among benefits and other factors. One company that has attempted to quantify productivity figures and flexible scheduling is Merck & Company. It interviewed and surveyed a large number of managers and developed a list of 30 cost variables attached to turnover. After developing several methods of cost determination, Merck determined that, depending on the job, turnover costs it 1.5 to 2.5 times the annual salary paid for the job.[122] As a result of this study, the company is attempting to enhance the benefit programs that it believes reduce turnover.

In a study of day care at Union Bank in California, using before day-care and after day-care cost data on absenteeism, turnover, and maternity leave time for both a control group and an experimental group, Union concluded that the day-care center saves the bank $138,000 to $232,000 a year.

MEASUREMENT ISSUES

Quantifying the benefits of any one program is more difficult than estimating its costs. It is also difficult to estimate the costs of failing to implement programs that would reduce absenteeism, turnover, and lost productivity. Yet employers will increasingly devote more time and attention to doing this as benefit options proliferate and as their costs increase.

Human resource managers in all areas are being asked to demonstrate how their programs and actions contribute to the bottom line. Nowhere is this more evident than in the management of benefits. With adequate cost and effectiveness data for various benefit options, human resource managers are in a better position to make strategic decisions as to which benefit programs an organization should have.

MANAGEMENT GUIDELINES

Several key guidelines in the benefits area need to be recognized from a strategic viewpoint:

1. Benefits should be strategically managed, not just "administered."
2. Benefit costs and options are increasing dramatically. Many choices are available, and many ways to reduce costs have been found. Human resource managers need to be aware of the possibilities to provide the best advice to their organizations.
3. The cost-effectiveness of benefits and benefit contributions to the bottom line is and will continue to be emphasized.
4. Benefits can best be used to gain competitive advantage by maintaining or increasing benefit levels while decreasing benefit costs.
5. A changing heterogeneous workforce will require a flexible or cafeteria-style program.
6. Management of benefits must comply with a host of federal and state regulations and requirements, including major changes in national health-care reform.
7. Since present and prospective employees are often unaware of the value of benefits provided them, benefit packages should be clearly and succinctly communicated to employees on a regular basis.
8. Health-care and insurance costs as well as retirement costs for the elderly will likely increase dramatically as baby boomers age and life spans are increased, thereby placing pressure on employee benefit plans.

QUESTIONS FOR REVIEW

1. Why is it that so many potential and present employees are unfamiliar with the benefit plan offered by an organization?

2. What strategic choices does an employer face in managing a benefit program? What factors affect the decision on each choice?

3. Why are health-care costs rising so much? What can organizations do to reduce them?

4. Who should pay the cost of health care: the employee, the employer, or the government? Explain your answer.

5. What are cafeteria-style benefits? Why are they becoming so popular?

6. Critique the state of health-care reform in the United States. What do you think should be done?

7. How should benefit plans tie into an overall human resource strategy?

8. How will the structure of benefits likely change as our population ages?

9. Assume that you were asked to determine the value or worth of a wellness-fitness program for a company. How would you go about this?

10. Although managers believe that benefits aid in attracting, motivating, and retaining employees, studies show little support for this belief. Why do you think that benefits may not be helping to attract, motivate, and retain employees?

CASE

MEDICAL REFORM IN THE TWIN CITIES[123]

Managed competition is radically changing health care in Minneapolis–St. Paul, Minnesota. The current experiences of residents may indicate how the nature of health care may change in the future.

After using virtually every cost-containment device known, 14 major employers in Minneapolis–St. Paul, including Dayton Hudson Corp., Honeywell, Inc., and Ceridan Corp., formed the Business Health Care Action Group in response to rising health-care costs and the current number of uninsured residents. The goal of the group is to use purchasing power to change the way medicine is practiced. Under managed competition, large purchasing groups similar to business coalitions buy care from competing health plans that, in theory at least, thrive only by delivering a high-quality, low-cost product. To achieve this goal, the Twin Cities' firms put their employee health group up for bids and selected a single organization that, among other things, is committed to documenting and improving doctors' performance while encouraging preventive medicine.

Finding a supplier was not an easy task. The coalition invited more than 150 doctors and health-plan administrators to conferences to explain its requirements. In response, about 20 health-care organizations bid for the contract, but only two came close to meeting the coalition's requirements. One was Minnesota Blue Cross and Blue Shield, which argued that it was successfully using six years' worth of accumulated data on physician and hospital performance to encourage cost-effective care. The coalition viewed Blue Cross and Blue Shield as a third party that wanted to set the rules and rejected its bid. Group Care, Inc., a consortium formed

from the marriage of two local HMOs—Group Health, Inc., and Med Centers, Inc.—that joined with the Mayo Clinic in nearby Rochester, Minnesota, was selected. Park Nicollet Medical Center, a 360-doctor group in Minneapolis, is the main physician group in the consortium. Group Care, Inc., was selected because most of its doctors are salaried and thus not compensated according to the number of procedures performed. In addition, Group Care, Park Nicollet, and Mayo have already developed practice guidelines for more than 50 medical conditions. For example, Park Nicollet has new technology that allows a woman with a questionable mammogram to learn whether she has a malignancy without surgery. A new computer-guided machine enables a radiologist instead of a surgeon to perform the biopsy, eliminating the wait for surgery, the surgeon's fee, and hospital costs related to the surgery.

In an effort to develop guidelines for dozens of other medical conditions, the consortium founded a $7 million research institute. One of the first items on the agenda is to create a policy that nearly eliminates all X-rays and physical therapy for back pain patients in the first six weeks of treatment. Through intensive research, doctors have found that 90 percent of all back pain cases resolve themselves in six weeks with proper exercise, heat and ice treatment, and the use of aspirin. The new institute is dealing with many issues that will contribute to changes in health-care provision in Minnesota and other areas.

Demands from the Business Health Care Action Group have pushed the Minnesota health-care community to a frenzy of mergers and acquisitions as it strives to reorganize its jumble of independent doctors and hospitals into streamlined networks that compete on the basis of quality, service, and price. In short, practically every hospital and thousands of doctors in the Twin Cities are competing for patients on the basis of cost as well as quality.

As with most changes, there is some opposition. Opponents of the new system (primarily some doctors) argue that the Twin Cities area is on the "bleeding edge" of medical reform. At any rate, a number of the highly trained specialists have reason to be concerned, for many of them will be replaced by primary-care doctors. To reduce costs, the coalition of employers aims to cut back on the care delivered by expensive cardiologists, orthopedists, and other specialists.

In addition, the fee structure is changing. Instead of the usual itemized hospital bills and separate doctors' fees, health services are offered for a bundled amount.

Employees also face changes. They are expected to attend seminars on how to be better patients. Doctors complain that some patients undermine cost-effective medical practice by demanding costly and unnecessary procedures. For example, a patient may demand unnecessary imaging tests for routine complaints because they assume that insurance picks up most of the tab.

To encourage participation in the new plan, companies are using videos which explain the plan and attest to the quality of care and lower out-of-pocket costs. In February 1993, two months after its inception, 35,000 employees and dependents had joined the plan. In January 1994, the total was expected to reach 90,000, which represents 70 percent of the 125,000 eligible participants.

Whether the changes in the Twin Cities will improve quality and contain costs is unknown at this time. The short-term goal of the coalition is to reduce the cost growth to the overall inflation rate. The goals of the coalition are being criticized by some and adopted by others. Two other employer coalitions are launching similar efforts and a law was passed in 1992 to provide care for the uninsured by requiring that organized networks of doctors and hospitals provide them care.

The recent changes in the Twin Cities may in fact spread throughout the United States and become the basis of a new medical system. The impact of health-care changes is uncertain, but we can be sure that the Twin Cities are well on their way to dealing with the inefficiencies in the current system.

QUESTIONS

1. What is the goal of a business coalition such as the Business Health Care Action Group in Minnesota? How does such a plan work?
2. What is required to make such a plan successful?
3. Would a plan like the Twin Cities' plan work in your geographic region? Why or why not? Cite reasons.

ADDITIONAL READINGS

Brockhart, James, and Robert Reilly. "Employee Stock Ownership Plans after the 1989 Tax Law: Valuation Issues." *Compensation and Benefits Review,* 1990.

Callan, Mary, and David Yeager. *Containing the Health Care Cost Spiral.* New York: McGraw-Hill, 1990.

Cave, Douglas, and Larry Tucker. "10 Facts about Point-of-Service Plans." *HRMagazine.* September 1991, pp. 41–46.

Crawford, Lou Ellen. *Dependent Care and the Employee Benefits Package.* Westport, CT: Quorum Books, 1990.

Denenberg, Tia S., and R. V. Denenberg. *Alcohol and Drugs: Issues in the Workplace.* Washington, DC: BNA Books, 1983.

Driver, R. An Investigation of the Relative Efficacy of Various Techniques for Communicating Benefits to Employees: A Quasi-Experiment in a Field Setting. *Dissertation Abstracts International.* 40, 344A (University Microfilms, No. 7915483), 1979.

Flexible Benefits: Will They Work for You? Chicago: Commerce Clearing House, 1991.

Haar, Jerry, and Sharon Kossack. "Employee Benefit Packages: How Understandable Are They?" *Journal of Business Communication.* 1990, pp. 185–200.

Harrington, Harry, and Nancy Richardson. "Retiree Wellness Plans Cut Health Costs." *Personnel Journal* 69 (1990), pp. 60–62.

Hay/Huggins Benefits Comparison. Philadelphia: The Hay Group, 1987.

Hayes, Cheryl, John Palmer, and Martha Zaslow. *Who Cares for America's Children.* Washington, DC: National Academic Press, 1990.

Huseman, R., J. Hatfield, and R. Robinson. "The MBA and Fringe Benefits." *Personnel Administrator* 23(7) (1978), pp. 57–60.

Iseri, Betty, and Robert Cangemi. "Flexible Benefits: A Growing Option." *Personnel.* 1990, pp. 30–32.

Koenig, R. "Comparison Shopping: Companies Seek New Data on Health-Care Costs to Gain Leverage in Bargaining for Services." *The Wall Street Journal,* April 22, 1988, pp. 19R–20R.

Konrad, W., and G. DeGeorge. "U.S. Companies Go for the Gray." *Business Week.* April 3, 1989, p. 66.

Lee, Alice, and Fred Lee. *A Field Guide to Retirement: 14 Lifestyle Opportunities and Options for Successful Retirement.* New York: Doubleday, 1991.

Lock, E., K. Shaw, L. Saari, and G. Latham. "Goal Setting and Task Performance 1969–1980." *Psychological Bulletin* 90 (1981), pp. 125–152.

McGregor, Eugene. *Strategic Management of Human Knowledge, Skills, and Abilities: Workforce Decision Making in the Post-Industrial Era.* San Francisco: Jossey-Bass, 1991.

Masterson, Joe. "Benefit Plans That Cut Costs and Increase Satisfaction." *Management Review.* April 1990.

Meadows, Anne. *Caring for America's Children.* Washington DC: National Academy Press, 1991.

Mitchell, O. "Fringe Benefits and Labor Mobility." *The Journal of Human Resources* 17(2) (1982), pp. 286–298.

Mitchell, O. "Fringe Benefits and the Cost of Changing Jobs." *Industrial and Labor Relations Review* 37(1) (1983), pp. 70–78.

Mobely, W., R. Griffeth, H. Hand, and B. Meglino. "Review and Conceptual Analysis of the Employee Turnover Process." *Psychological Bulletin* 86 (1979), pp. 493–522.

Mowday, R., L. Porter, and R. Steers. *Employee Organization Linkages: The Psychology of Commitment, Absenteeism, and Turnover.* New York: Academic Press, 1982.

1987 Employee Benefits. Washington, DC: Chamber of Commerce of the United States, 1987.

Phillips, Mary Ellen, Carol Brown, and Norma Nielson. "An Expanding Employee Benefit: Personal Financial Planning with Expert Systems." *Management Accounting.* September 1990, pp. 29–33.

Pillsbury, Dennis. "Nipping Workers' Comp in the Bud." *Risk and Insurance.* October 1991.

Porter, M. *Competitive Advantage: Creating and Sustaining Superior Performance.* New York: Free Press, 1985.

Porter, M. *Competitive Strategy: Techniques for Analyzing Industries and Competitors.* New York: Free Press, 1980.

Roberts, Karen, and Sandra Gleason. "What Employees Want from Workers' Comp." *HRMagazine.* December 1991, pp. 49–54.

Rosenbloom, Jerry S., and G. Victor Hollman. *Employee Benefit Planning,* 2nd ed. Englewood Cliffs, NJ: Prentice-Hall, 1986.

Salancik, G., and J. Pfeffer. "An Examination of Need-Satisfaction Models of Job Attitudes." *Administrative Science Quarterly* 22(3) (1977), pp. 427–456.

———"A Social Information Processing Approach to Job Attitudes and Task Design." *Administrative Science Quarterly* 23(2) (1978), pp. 224–253.

Shanklin, Catherine. "Unemployment Insurance: Survive the System." *Personnel Journal.* March 1990.

Schiller, B., and R. Weiss. "The Impact of Private Pensions on Firm Attachment." *The Review of Economics and Statistics* 62(4) (1979), pp. 369–380.

Schiller, B., and R. Weiss. "Pension and Wages: A Test for Equalizing Differences." *The Review of Economics and Statistics* 62(4) (1980), pp. 529–538.

Smith, Doyle. *Kin Care and the American Corporation: Solving the Work/Family Dilemma.* BusinessOne Irwin, Homewood, IL: 1991.

Spirig, John. "Human Resources Information Systems Can Help Employers Plan and Implement Flexible Benefits Programs." *Employment Relations Today* 16 (1989), pp. 9–17.

Stepina, L., H. Hennessey, and B. Weschler, eds. *Florida's Compensation System: A Comprehensive Study of Career Service Pay and Benefits.* (Final Report, Contract #1986-068). (Available from State of Florida, Department of Administration, Carlton Bldg., Tallahassee, FL), 1987.

Sutton, N. "Are Employers Meeting Their Benefit Objectives?" *Benefits Quarterly* 2(3) (1986), pp. 14–20.

Sutton, N. "Do Employee Benefits Reduce Labor Turnover?" *Benefits Quarterly* 1(2) (1986), pp. 16–22.

Taulbee, Pamela. "What's Ahead for Retiree Health?" *Business & Health.* December 1990, pp. 25–36.

Wilson, M., G. Northcraft, and M. Neale. "The Perceived Value of Fringe Benefits." *Personnel Psychology* 38(2) (1985), pp. 309–320.

NOTES

1. M. Wilson, G. Northcraft, and M. Neale, "The Perceived Value of Fringe Benefits," *Personnel Psychology* 38, no. 2, 1985, pp. 309–320.

2. Bill Leonard, "Experts Hail 'New Age' of Flexible Benefits," *HR News,* April 1994, p. 9.

3. Beth Rogers, "Clarifying the Choices," *HRMagazine,* March 1993, pp. 40–43.

4. Glen Ruffenach, "Health Insurance Premiums to Soar in '89: Workers Likely to Take on More of Costs," *The Wall Street Journal,* October 25, 1988, p. B1.

5. Erik Eckholm, "Introduction," *The President's Health Security Plan* (New York: Random House, 1993), p. 7.

6. Foster Higgins, "National Survey of Employer-Sponsored Plans," *People Trends,* April 1994, p. 9.

7. Rick Wartzman and Hillary Stout, "Clinton Health Plan Would Use Regulation to Spur Competition," *The Wall Street Journal,* September 13, 1993, p. A7.

8. "Cafeteria Plans, Wellness Programs Gaining in Popularity," *Employee Benefit Plan Review,* July 1987, p. 91; and Michael Waldholz, "Cafeteria Benefit Plans Let Employees Fill Their Plates, Then Pay with Tax Free Dollars," *The Wall Street Journal,* May 9, 1983, p. 58.

9. Sue Shellenbarger, "Firms Try to Match People with Benefits," *The Wall Street Journal,* December 17, 1993, p. B1.

10. H. W. Hennessey, Jr., "Using Employee Benefits to Gain Competitive Advantage," *Benefits Quarterly,* Winter 1989, pp. 51–57.

11. James Swanke, "Ways to Tame Workers' Comp Premiums," *HRMagazine,* February 1992, pp. 39–41.

12. Barbara Marsh, "Rising Workers' Compensation Costs Worry Small Firms," *The Wall Street Journal,* December 31, 1991, p. B2.

13. Ron Winslow, "Hospitals Team Up to Trim Workers' Comp," *The Wall Street Journal,* December 8, 1989, p. B1.

14. Greg Steinmetz, "States Take on the Job of Holding Down Medical Costs of Workers' Compensation," *The Wall Street Journal,* March 3, 1993, p. B1.

15. Marsh, "Rising Workers' Compensation Costs Worry Small Firms," p. B2.

16. Ronald Grover, "How Workers' Comp Could Get Mangled," *Business Week,* December 14, 1992, p. 44.

17. Michael Pritula, "Workers' Comp: Tranquilizing a Benefit Gone Mad," *The Wall Street Journal,* January 13, 1992, p. A14; and Mark D. Fefer, "What to Do about Workers' Comp," *Fortune,* June 29, 1992, pp. 80–82.

18. "Labor Letter," *The Wall Street Journal,* September 13, 1988, p. A1.

19. Linda Thornburg, "The Pension Headache," *HRMagazine,* January 1992, pp. 39–46; Wallace Campblee, Jr., "Plans That Upgrade Pensions," *HRMagazine,* November 1991, pp. 71–73; and Selwyn Feinstein, "IRS Regulations on Pension Plans Promise Headaches for Major Employers," *The Wall Street Journal,* May 22, 1990, p. A1.

20. Selwyn Feinstein, "Rules Change for Pensions: Who Gets What," *The Wall Street Journal,* July 3, 1990, pp. B1+.

21. Pauline Yoshihashi, "Junking of Pensions Angers Mill Workers," *The Wall Street Journal,* April 18, 1991, p. A5.

22. Allen Steinberg, "Best Bets for Retirement," *HRMagazine,* January 1992, pp. 47–50.

23. Timothy L. O'Brien, "Many Firms Abandon Defined-Benefit Plans," *The Wall Street Journal,* February 12, 1993, p. B1.

24. Ellen Schultz, "Changing Jobs Means Having to Find a New Home for Cash in Retirement Plan," *The Wall Street Journal,* March 9, 1992, pp. C1 +; and "Pension Portability," *HRMagazine,* February 1992, pp. 99–100.

25. James Herlihy and Jamie Owens, "Methods of Implementing a Nonqualified 401(k) Plan," *HRMagazine,* January 1992, pp. 52–56.

26. Richard Hill and Patricia Dwyer, "Grooming Workers for Early Retirement," *HRMagazine,* September 1990, pp. 59–63.

27. Joann Lubin, "Bosses Alter Early-Retirement Windows to Be Less Coercive—and Less Generous," *The Wall Street Journal,* February 8, 1991, pp. B1 +.

28. Catherine Fyock, "Crafting Secure Retirements," *HRMagazine,* July 1990, pp. 30–33.

29. Christopher Conte, "Falling Behind," *The Wall Street Journal,* March 3, 1992, p. A1.

30. Amy Dunkin, "Retirees, Your Health Plans Look a Bit Peaked," *Business Week,* November 30, 1992, pp. 114 +.

31. *Paid Holidays and/or Vacation Policies,* Personnel Policies Forum no. 130 (Washington, DC: Bureau of National Affairs, November 1980), p. 1.

32. Jolie Solomon, "The Future Look of Employee Benefits," *The Wall Street Journal,* September 7, 1988, p. 29.

33. Gene DeLoux, "Is Your Maternity Policy Ready for the '90s?" *HRMagazine,* November 1990, pp. 57–59.

34. Linda Thornburg, "Family Leave Law Effective August 5," *HR News,* March 1993, p. A1.

35. Albert Karr, "The Daddy Track," *The Wall Street Journal,* April 30, 1991, p. A1.

36. Suzanne Alexander, "Fears for Career Curb Paternity Leave," *The Wall Street Journal,* August 24, 1990, pp. B1 +; and Albert Karr, "Maternity Leave," *The Wall Street Journal,* April 28, 1992, p. A1.

37. Albert R. Karr, "People Worry about Being Disabled and Needing Long-Term Care," *The Wall Street Journal,* November 24, 1992, p. A1.

38. David L. Potter, "Long-Term Care Plans Gain Acceptance," *HRMagazine,* January 1993, p. 63.

39. Jim Mishizen, "In the Eye of the Health-Care Storm," *HRMagazine,* September 1991, pp. 47–50.

40. "Most Employers Offer Disability Leaves," *American Society for Personnel Administration/Resources,* December 1988, p. 4.

41. Eckholm, *The President's Health Security Plan,* p. 7.

42. Walter Zelman, "The Horse's Mouth," *The New Republic,* October 11, 1993, p. 15.

43. Bill Leonard, "Communication Is Key to Employee Benefits Program," *HRMagazine,* January 1994, p. 58.

44. William C. Symonds, "Deere's Surprising Harvest in Health Care," *Business Week,* July 11, 1994, pp. 107–111.

45. Ron Winslow, "Costs of Medical Care Continue to Soar, Defying Corporate Efforts to Find Cures," *The Wall Street Journal,* January 29, 1991, pp. B1 +.

46. Armondo, Bennett, "Firms Stunned by Retiree Health Costs," *The Wall Street Journal,* May 24, 1988, p. 41.

47. Richard Schmidt, "Retirees Fight Cuts in Health Benefits," *The Wall Street Journal,* December 8, 1988, p. B1.

48. Gary Laugharn, "Caught in the FASB Crossfire," *HRMagazine,* July 1990, pp. 38–42.

49. Ceel Pasternak, "HRM Update," *HRMagazine,* August 1991, p. 19.

50. Timothy Schellhardt, "Retirees Benefit Cuts Won't End Soon," *The Wall Street Journal,* September 19, 1990, p. B1.

51. Albert Karr, "Labor Letter," *The Wall Street Journal,* February 7, 1989, p. A1.

52. Gary Kushner and Gina Williams, "COBRA: Answers to the Most-Asked Questions," *Legal Report* (Alexandria, VA: Society for Human Resource Management), 1990.

53. Alex Taylor, "GM: Some Gain, Much Pain," *Fortune,* May 29, 1995, p. 84.

54. Albert Karr, "More Burden Shifting," *The Wall Street Journal,* April 30, 1991, p. A1.

55. Ceel Pasternak, "HRM Update," *HRMagazine,* September 1990, p. 26.

56. Hewitt Associates, *Salaried Employee Benefits Provided by Major U.S. Employers,* February 1994.

57. Selwyn Feinstein, "Heal Thyself," *The Wall Street Journal,* July 10, 1990, p. A1.

58. Albert Karr, "Tough Trade-off," *The Wall Street Journal,* December 17, 1991, p. A1.

59. Michael Selz, "Small Firms Score Well on Health Insurance," *The Wall Street Journal,* August 15, 1991, p. B1.

60. Glenn Ruffenach, "Health Insurance Premiums Soar in 1989," *The Wall Street Journal,* October 25, 1988, p. B1.

61. Ron Winslow, "Employer Costs Slip as Workers Shift to HMOs," *The Wall Street Journal,* February 14, 1995, pp. A1 +.

62. Eckholm, *The President's Health Security Plan,* pp. 13–14.

63. Bill Leonard, "Health-Care Provides Heals Itself," *HRMagazine,* July 1993, p. 51.

64. Karen Munson and David Israel: "Self-Insurance Checkup," *HRMagazine,* February 1992, pp. 83–87.

65. Ceel Pasternak, "Incentives for Wellness," *HRMagazine,* August 1991, p. 19.

66. Hilary Stout, "Paying Workers for Good Health," *The Wall Street Journal,* November 26, 1991, pp. B1 +.

67. Aaron Bernstein, "Health Care Costs: Trying to Cool the Fever," *Business Week,* May 21, 1990, pp. 46–47.

68. Selwyn Feinstein, "Companies Target Catastrophic Illnesses in Bid to Curb Soaring Health Cost," *The Wall Street Journal,* July 30, 1990, p. A1.

69. Glenn Ruffenach, "Firms Use Financial Incentives to Make Employees Set Lower Health-Care Fees," *The Wall Street Journal,* February 9, 1993, p. B1.

70. Ibid., p. B6.

71. Carol Hymowitz and Gabriella Stern, "Cutting Psychotherapy May Trim Productivity," *The Wall Street Journal,* August 10, 1994, pp. B1, B8.

72. Merritt C. Kimball, "The Trend to Give What's Appropriate," *HRMagazine,* January 1994, pp. 49–50.

73. Ron Winslow, "Managed-Care Artworks Show Promise," *The Wall Street Journal,* March 24, 1992, p. B1.

74. Ron Winslow, "Videos, Questionnaires Aim to Expand Role of Patients in Treatment Decisions," *The Wall Street Journal,* February 25, 1992, pp. B1 +.

75. Edward Felsenthal, "Managed Care Helps Curb Costs, Study Says," *The Wall Street Journal,* August 12, 1991, p. B1; Glenn Ruffenach, "Managed-Care Networks Help Rein in Costs," *The Wall Street Journal,* March 27, 1991; Ron Winslow, "Some Companies Try 'Managed Care' in Bid to Curb Health Costs," *The Wall Street Journal,* February 1, 1991, pp. A1 +; and Ron Winslow, "Firms Perform Own Bypass Operations, Purchasing Health Care from the Source," *The Wall Street Journal,* August 19, 1991, pp. B1 +.

76. Ceel Pasternak, "It Doesn't Work," *HRMagazine,* September 1991, p. 24; and Richard Anderson, "Handling Health-Care Costs in the '90s," *HRMagazine,* June 1990, pp. 89–94.

77. Ceel Pasternak, "Dealing in Drugs," *HRMagazine,* March 1992, p. 26.

78. Ceel Pasternak, "In-Company Pharmacy?" *HRMagazine,* September 1991, p. 23.

79. Albert Karr, "Make Workplace Calls?" *The Wall Street Journal,* May 7, 1991, p. A1.

80. Glen Ruffenach, "California School Unions Use Trusts to Cut Costs," *The Wall Street Journal,* March 3, 1992, p. B1.

81. John Sturges, "Examining Your Insurance Carrier," *HRMagazine,* February 1992, pp. 43–46; and William Wymer, George Faulkner, and Joseph Parente, "Achieving Benefit Program Objectives," *HRMagazine,* March 1992, pp. 55–62.

82. Stephenie Overman and Linda Thornburg, "Beating the Odds," *HRMagazine,* March 1992, pp. 42–47.

83. Ron Winslow, "Infant Health Problems Cost Business Billions," *The Wall Street Journal,* May 1, 1992, pp. B1 +.

84. John Morley, "The Cleveland Health-Care Experiment," *The Wall Street Journal,* February 10, 1992, p. A16; and Walt Bogdanich, "Clevelanders Bet Top Health Care Will Be Cheaper," *The Wall Street Journal,* February 2, 1992, pp. B1 +.

85. Ron Winslow, "How Local Business Got Together to Cut Memphis Health Costs," *The Wall Street Journal,* February 4, 1992, pp. A1 +; Alain Enthoven, "How Employers Boost Health Costs," *The Wall Street Journal,* January 24, 1992, p. A14; and David Wessel and Walt Bognadich, " Laws of Economics Often Don't Apply in Health-Care Field," *The Wall Street Journal,* January 22, 1992, pp. A1 +.

86. Edmund Faltermayer, "Let's Really Cure the Health System," *Fortune,* March 23, 1992, pp. 46–58.

87. Stuart Butler, " 'Pay or Play' Health-Care Is Bound to Be a Loser," *The Wall Street Journal,* January 3, 1992, p. A6; Hilary Stout, "Health Care Choices: A Bigger Federal Role or a Market Approach?" *The Wall Street Journal,* January 15, 1992, pp. A1 +; Linda Thornburg, "U.S. Health Care Called a System in Crisis . . . " *HRNews,* January 1992, p. A14; Christine Keen, "National Health-Care Reform: Politics vs. Policy," *HRNews,* February 1992, p. A5; and Linda Thornburg, "Medical Community Proposes National Health-Care Reforms," *HRNews,* February 1992, p. A11.

88. "Pay or Play," *The Wall Street Journal,* January 21, 1992, p. A1.

89. Jill Fraser, "Flexible Spending," *Inc.,* October 1990, pp. 164–167; and Georgette Jason, "Medical Reimbursement Accounts Are a Good Deal for Many Workers," *The Wall Street Journal,* July 26, 1991, p. C1.

90. Bill Leonard, "Cost-Cutting Measures Pay Off," *HRMagazine,* September 1994, p. 50.

91. Walecia Konrad and Gail DeGeorge, "U.S. Companies Go for the Gray," *Business Week,* April 3, 1989, p. 66.

92. James H. Smalhout, "The Not-So-Golden Years," *The Wall Street Journal,* June 29, 1995, p. A14.

93. Marilyn Chase, "Science Edges Closer to Designing Drugs to Defeat AIDS Virus," *The Wall Street Journal,* March 3, 1989, p. A1.

94. David Israel and Debra Scott, "AIDS-Related Insurance Ceilings Are Risky," *HRMagazine,* November 1990, pp. 85–86.

95. David Stipp, "Laws on Health Benefits Raise Firms' Ire," *The Wall Street Journal,* December 28, 1988, p. B1.

96. Wartzman and Stout, "Clinton Health Plan Would Use Regulation to Spur Competition."

97. Bill Leonard, "Perks Give Way to Life-Cycle Benefit Plans," *HRMagazine,* March 1995, pp. 45–46.

98. James P. Miller, "Some Workers Set Up LBOs of Their Own and Benefit Greatly," *The Wall Street Journal,* December 12, 1988, pp. A1, A6.

99. "Employee Stock Ownership Plans Spread More Slowly in 1990," *The Wall Street Journal,* March 12, 1991, p. A1.

100. James White, "As ESOPs Become Victims of '90s Bankruptcies, Workers Are Watching Their Nest Eggs Vanish," *The Wall Street Journal,* January 25, 1991, pp. C1 +.

101. James S. Hirsch, "Avis Employees Find Stock Ownership Is Mixed Blessing," *The Wall Street Journal,* May 2, 1995, pp. B1, B4.

102. "Cafeteria Plans, Wellness Programs Gaining Popularity," *Employee Benefit Plan Review,* July 1987, p. 92; and Jolie Solomon, "The Future Look of Employee Benefits," *The Wall Street Journal,* September 7, 1988, p. 29.

103. Stephenie Overman, "3M Arranges Summer Child Care," *HRMagazine,* March 1991, pp. 46–47.

104. Linda Thornburg, "On-Site Child Care Works for Health-Care Industry," *HRMagazine,* August 1990, pp. 39–40.

105. Janet Guyon, "Inequality in Granting Child-Care Benefits Makes Workers Seethe," *The Wall Street Journal,* October 23, 1991, pp. A1 +.

106. Sue Shellenbarger, "U.S.-Style Child-Care Wins Fans in Japan," *The Wall Street Journal,* February 12, 1992, p. B1.

107. Solomon, "The Future Look of Employee Benefits," p. 29.

108. *America in Transition: Benefits for the Future* (Baltimore: Employee Benefits Research Institution, 1988).

109. "Blue Cross and Blue Shield of New Jersey Announces Pilot Program for Child and Elder Care Services," *PR News Wire* via DowVision, March 28, 1995.

110. Richard Gisonny, "Benefits and Taxes," *HRMagazine,* February 1991, pp. 37–42.

111. Albert Karr, "Vacations for Sale," *The Wall Street Journal,* September 17, 1991, p. A1.

112. "Cafeteria Plans, Wellness Programs Gaining Popularity," p. 91.

113. Kathryn Hoyle, *BLS Report on Employee Benefits in Medium and Large Private Establishments,* 1993 (Washington, D.C., United States Department of Labor, 1994): p. 2.

114. Glenn Ruffenach, "Odds and Ends," *The Wall Street Journal,* March 27, 1991, p. B1.

115. Melissa Barringer, George Milkovich, and Olivia Mitchell, "Predicting Employee Health Insurance Selections in a Flexible Benefits Environment," *On Center* 1, 1992, p. 7.

116. Albert Karr, "Favoring Options," *The Wall Street Journal,* April 30, 1991, p. A1.

117. Solomon, "The Future Look of Employee Benefits," p. 29.

118. Carol Hymowitz, "As Aetna Adds Flextime, Bosses Learn to Cope," *The Wall Street Journal,* June 18, 1990, pp. B1 +; Albert Karr, "IBM Expands Its Flexible-Hours Policy," *The Wall Street Journal,* June 18, 1991, p. A1; Sue Shellenbarger, "GE Unit Sees Advantage in More Family Benefits," *The Wall Street Journal,* February 12, 1992, p. B1; and Cathy Trost, "To Cut Costs and Keep the Best People, More Concerns Offer Flexible Work Plans," *The Wall Street Journal,* February 18, 1992, pp. B1 +.

119. Hennessey, "Using Employee Benefits," p. 57.

120. Jolie Solomon, "Companies Try Measuring Cost Savings from New Types of Corporate Benefits," *The Wall Street Journal,* December 29, 1988, p. B1.

121. Ibid.

122. Ibid.

123. Ron Winslow, "Employers' Attack on Health Bills Spurs Change in Minnesota," *The Wall Street Journal,* February 26, 1993, p. A1.

CHAPTER 14

MANAGING HEALTH, SAFETY, AND STRESS

Employee health and safety represent an area undergoing continual change. Materials that were not considered hazardous in the past have been found to be extremely dangerous as the long-term effects of exposure became known. New ailments caused by acts performed or equipment used on the job are coming to the public's attention more and more frequently.[1] Pressure on employees from both home and work can cause both emotional and physical problems, increased health-care costs, and decreased productivity at work.[2] Because of the flux in this area, it is imperative that organizations remain informed and aware of the changes taking place.

CHAPTER OBJECTIVES

After studying this chapter, you should be able to

1. Outline the strategic choices available to managers with respect to the management of employee safety, health, and stress.
2. Discuss the Occupational Safety and Health Administration (OSHA) and explain its purpose, scope, and procedures.
3. Examine some of the current health and safety problems facing employees, such as repetitive motion problems and AIDS, of which managers need to be aware.
4. Present information regarding fetal protection available in the workplace.
5. Identify types and consequences of workplace stress and present ways to reduce it.
6. Discuss possible organizational strategies available to help improve and maintain the health and safety of workers.

HEALTH AND SAFETY AT GENERAL ELECTRIC[3]

Although problems associated with health and safety problems cost organizations in excess of $33 billion annually in terms of lost wages, medical costs, and indirect costs, few organizations proactively seek opportunities to reduce these losses. One exception is General Electric (GE), which has significantly reduced bottom-line costs by establishing programs aimed at employee health and safety.

HEALTHY EMPLOYEES ARE PRODUCTIVE EMPLOYEES

In 1987, GE developed the General Electric Fitness Center, which consisted of a running track, weight training facilities, and other fitness-related equipment. In addition, the center is staffed by full-time program directors who provide guidance and assistance to employees concerning nutrition and stress management. Also, the General Electric Employee Activity Association (GEEAA) was developed to offer employees additional recreational activities, such as bowling, tennis, and golf, in addition to a host of educational and cultural programs.

When compared to employees who chose to take part in the fitness and recreation programs, it was determined that employees not enrolled in them were absent twice as frequently. In addition, members not enrolled in these programs reported lower levels of job satisfaction and motivation. These findings are similar to those found by Coors Brewery and Johnson & Johnson, which also saw that programs of this nature reduced employee absences while increasing worker motivation.

In terms of bottom-line economic figures, these two programs were shown to save the organization nearly $3 million in terms of absence costs in the first year alone, not to mention the benefits of increased productivity and lower medical claims.

SAFE WORKING CONDITIONS FACILITATE PRODUCTIVITY AND COMMITMENT

General Electric's commitment to the workforce did not end with employee health concerns. The organization has made great strides toward reducing accidents at work. General Electric's self-directed work teams have taken an active role in developing and implementing safety programs and rules recognized across all divisions of the plant. The organization contends that the responsibility for developing safety programs rests with those individuals who are most affected by an unsafe work environment—the firm's employees. Hence, all important programs regarding health and safety are initiated at the worker level with a maximum amount of feedback from workers employed at lower levels of the plant. The participative safety management program reduces accidents and the accident costs absorbed by the firm, and employees participating in the program feel a sense of ownership as their promotion of a safer work environment leads to increased morale and commitment. In addition to the typical pep talks exclaiming the virtues of a safe work site, pocket-size cards are given to each employee to pass on to a co-worker seen working dangerously. Each unit of the plant is responsible for developing a safety work team whose mission is to eliminate work site accidents at its unit. A special unit, Make Accidents Stop Happening (MASH), was developed to focus on the financial implications of having an unsafe work environment. Employees involved in MASH call other GE plants to encourage them to become involved in similar safety programs.

GE has seen great financial savings affecting the bottom line of participating plants. When it was determined that a small GE plant could save $120,000 annually in medical costs alone, management took notice. In addition, a plant in Columbia, Missouri, saved $1.5 million in workers' compensation claims in the first three years alone following the development of the participative safety management system. Finally, visits to the medical department at the plant were significantly reduced following the inception of the program.

A COMMITMENT TO HEALTH AND SAFETY

By developing fitness/activity and participative safety programs, upper management is sending a clear message to its employees: "The organization cares about *your* health and safety while you are an employee at GE." Programs of this nature not only instill a feeling of commitment among its participants but also frequently realize organizational bottom-line objectives. In an era of labor shortages at key positions (that make up a large portion of GE's workforce), GE's active role in the health and safety of its workforce assures employees of the company's good will and allows General Electric to continue to be one of America's most profitable and respected companies.

STRATEGIC CHOICES

The decisions managers make regarding the health and safety of their workers becomes increasingly more important as time passes due to ever-increasing penalties, some aimed directly at the top management,[4] for willfully endangering the lives of employees. Many of the decisions made are based on strategic choices available to the organization. Some of these strategic choices follow:

1. Managers must determine the *level of protection* the organization will provide employees. Some firms, for financial or liability reasons, prefer a minimum level of protection, others prefer a maximum level.

2. Managers can decide whether *safety regulations will be formal or informal.* Formal regulations are written and carefully monitored while informal regulations are enforced through peer pressure or good training.

3. Managers also can be *proactive or reactive in terms of developing procedures or plans* with respect to employee safety and health. Proactive managers seek to improve the safety and health of their employees prior to a need to do so; reactive managers fix safety and health problems after they occur.

4. Managers can decide to use the *safety and health of workers as a marketing tool* for the organization. This type of strategy involves advertising that Company X is a great place to work because of how much it cares about the worker. "Safety before production" could be this company's motto. Other firms take the opposite strategy and stress output over safety.[5]

Keep in mind as you read the chapter that managing health, safety, and stress in the workplace involves making strategic choices in the form of trade-offs. A company may desire a high level of protection but may not always have the resources to achieve its goals with regard to safety. Strategic choices concern fundamental questions about the level of risk a company can afford and the degree of liability it intends to accept. Managers must strike a balance between what is desired and what can be provided. A knowledge of the legal aspects of occupational health and safety can help human resource managers as they work with company managers to formulate strategic plans. The foundation for all safety and health programs in U.S. businesses is the Occupational Safety and Health Act of 1970, discussed in the next section.

OCCUPATIONAL SAFETY AND HEALTH ADMINISTRATION[6]

OCCUPATIONAL SAFETY AND HEALTH ACT OF 1970

Due to the overwhelming number of workers killed on the job (more than 14,000 in 1970 alone), the estimated 300,000 new cases of occupational diseases discovered each year, and the emotional and economic impact these problems caused, Congress passed the Occupational Safety and Health Act of 1970. This act was designed to offer, as far as possible, every working man and woman a safe and healthy work environment.

To include as many employers and employees as possible, Congress passed the Occupational Safety and Health Act under the Commerce Clause of the United States Constitution. By defining the act under this clause, all employers and employees of businesses affecting interstate commerce are included. The few exceptions to this act include federal and state government employees, the self-employed, and domestic servants.

THE BIRTH OF THE OCCUPATIONAL SAFETY AND HEALTH ADMINISTRATION (OSHA)

OCCUPATIONAL SAFETY AND HEALTH ADMINISTRATION (OSHA)
A federal administrative agency that has the authority to set health and safety standards, conduct inspections, and enforce penalties for violations and/or noncompliance with its regulations.

The **Occupational Safety and Health Administration (OSHA)** was created as the primary administrative agency for the Occupational Safety and Health Act of 1970. OSHA is within the Department of Labor and has the authority to set safety and health standards, conduct inspections to ensure compliance with them, and seek enforcement actions for noncompliance. This authority is supervised by the Secretary of Labor.

The act also created two other agencies: the National Institute of Occupational Safety and Health (NIOSH) and the Occupational Safety and Health Review Commission (OSHRC). NIOSH is a research center for occupational safety and health. As such, it studies various health and safety problems occurring in the workplace and provides technical advice and standard recommendations based on its findings. OSHRC is the enforcement arm. OSHA may recommend a penalty for a discovered violation to OSHRC, but only OSHRC may actually impose the penalty.

HOW OSHA WORKS

The Organizational Health and Safety Act provides the secretary of labor with the authority to establish three different types of health and safety standards: interim, permanent, and temporary emergency standards. Interim standards were those established from the date of the act for two years that usually generated from preexisting national consensus standards. Permanent standards are either newly created or revised from interim standards. They often stem from suggestions taken from interested parties (such

---

■ HR CHALLENGE ■

A Matter of Degree

When members of a New Mexico jury learned they had been summoned to determine whether a woman who ordered hot coffee at a McDonald's drive-through should be compensated for the burns she received when it spilled as she was putting cream and sugar in it as she held it between her legs while driving, they were incredulous. It seemed that McDonald's had an open-and-shut case. According to opinion polls and radio talk show callers, the public felt the same way when the jury awarded the woman nearly $3,000,000, finding that McDonald's had served "defective" coffee. The defect? The coffee was too hot and customers should have been warned about the possibility of serious burns. In a seven-day trial, the jury learned (and saw photographs) of the 81-year-old plaintiff's extensive burn-related injuries. It was not sympathy alone, however, that apparently motivated the jury. The jury felt that $160,000 ($200,000 reduced by 20 percent to reflect the degree of fault attributable to the plaintiff for causing her own injuries) was sufficient to compensate her. An additional $2,700,000 was awarded as punitive damages to punish the defendant for intentional, reckless, wanton, or malicious conduct.

It was found that McDonald's coffee (at about 180 degrees) was 20 to 40 degrees hotter than that of most of its competitors in the Albuquerque area. Indeed, McDonald's marketing research showed that its customers preferred its coffee precisely because it was so steaming hot. The company's operations and training manual mandated that coffee be brewed at 195 to 205 degrees and held at 180 to 190 degrees for optimum aroma and taste. So how could a jury find the coffee to be "defective"? In the first place, McDonald's own witnesses acknowledged that the company was aware of previous instances in which customers had been seriously burned by its coffee. However, the company decided against either turning the temperature down or warning customers and took the position that hot coffee burns were statistically insignificant, given that the company sells billions of cups of coffee each year. Moreover, the company failed to consult burn experts. Had such experts been consulted, McDonald's would likely have learned, as the jury heard from the plaintiff's expert witness, that coffee held at 160 degrees would take about 20 seconds to cause third-degree burns; at 180 degrees, it would take 12 to 15 seconds, and at 190 degrees, less than 3 seconds. To the jurors, the company seemed callous and uncaring, and so it punished the corporation by awarding the plaintiff a sum equal to about two days of its companywide coffee sales (about $1.35 million a day).

The lesson for employers? Recognize that some situations and activities in the workplace may be as safe as possible and yet still present risk of harm to employees. In such "unavoidably unsafe" circumstances, a failure to warn of possible dangers may be sufficient to result in liability. Even misuse or carelessness by an employee may result in liability if a sympathetic judge or jury believes that the employer should have foreseen the misuse and warned employees specifically about it.

SOURCE: A Gerlin, " A Matter of Degree: How a Jury Decided that a Coffee Spill Is Worth $2.9 Million," *The Wall Street Journal,* September 1, 1991, p. A1.

---

as unions, employers, or NIOSH) or from an appointed advisory committee. Permanent standards must be published in the Federal Register to provide the public time to respond. If publishing the standard results in a requested public hearing, OSHA must schedule and publicize one. OSHA has 60 days after the close of public comment in which to publish the standard, its effective date, and reasons for its adoption. If the secretary of labor believes that workers are in grave danger from a newly found hazard, he or she has the authority to bypass the permanent standard formalities and establish temporary emergency standards. Once the temporary standard is published, it becomes effective immediately, but for only six months. At the time of publishing, the secretary must also begin the normal procedure for establishing a permanent standard after the temporary emergency status has expired.

EMPLOYER RESPONSIBILITY

The Occupational Safety and Health Act charges employers with three major responsibilities: to furnish and maintain a healthful work environment, to keep records of occupational injuries and illnesses, and to comply with OSHA standards. With respect to the first responsibility, the act specifically states that employers must provide a workplace that is free from recognized hazards that are likely to cause death or other serious physical harm. The recent McDonald's case (see the HR Challenge box) illustrates how a recognized hazard can be a costly mistake. To prove a violation of this general requirement, the secretary of labor must show that the employer failed to produce a hazard-free environment; that a hazard existed that was recognized by either the employer or the industry; that a hazard exists that did or may cause death or serious harm; and there was a means by which the employer could have eliminated or reduced the hazard. If all four elements are not proven, the secretary's case has not been met.

The act also requires that organizations with eight or more employees keep records of any occupational injury or illness if it results in death, loss of consciousness, transfer to another job, medical treatment other than first aid, or one or more lost work days. *Occupational injury* is defined as any injury that results from a work-related accident; *occupational illness* is any condition resulting from exposure to environmental factors at the workplace. The information must be recorded on specific OSHA forms. The organization is required to post this information once a year so that employees are aware of the records and the organization must present these records if requested to do so by an OSHA compliance officer.

INSPECTIONS

To enforce its standards, OSHA conducts workplace inspections in all establishments covered by the act. Obviously, this is a monumental job. With its current budget, OSHA can visit only 2 percent of the 6 million workplaces every year.[7] To concentrate its efforts on the areas most in need of inspections, OSHA has established a four-tier priority system. It gives top priority to cases in which death or serious injury have occurred, followed by cases of valid employee complaints, high-hazard industries, and, finally, general random inspections.

An inspection is unannounced, except for conditions of imminent danger when advance notice is given to allow the employer the opportunity to correct the situation as quickly as possible. The inspector must present proper identification and a warrant to conduct the inspection. A warrant is not needed if the employer consents to the inspection, if the site is open to public view, or if there is an emergency situation in which imminent danger to employees would not allow the time needed to obtain a warrant.

The compliance officer may be escorted on a tour by a representative of the employer or the employees. On this tour, the inspector may question workers and employers in private, take samples, make readings, observe, take photographs, and inspect records. At the end of the inspection tour, the compliance officer holds a closing conference with the employer to review the findings and report any possible violations found. The inspector then reports to the area director, who has six months to decide whether or not to issue a citation and impose a penalty.

Although organizations feared OSHA during the Carter administration, severe budget cuts took the bite out of OSHA during the Reagan administration.[8] Recently, a new OSHA chief, Joseph Dear, has pledged to increase enforcement of violations through better targeting of the most hazardous workplaces.[9] In the past, OSHA made inspections mostly in response to complaints, but OSHA now targets work sites that are particularly susceptible to high-risk operations.

VIOLATIONS, CITATIONS, AND PENALTIES

The Occupational Safety and Health Act delineates the types of violations possible. Exhibit 14.1 provides an overview of these as well as the penalties associated with each violation. The area director, after reviewing the compliance officer's report, sends a certified letter outlining the citations and the proposed penalties. Normally, 30 days are provided as the abatement period during which time the employer must correct the violation or OSHA imposes the penalty. The act allows civil sanctions for each day in which the violation has not been corrected after the abatement period.

Willful violations are the only type that include a prison sentence as well as a fine. Additionally, three states (Illinois, New York, and Michigan) have ruled that the Occupational Health and Safety Act does not preempt states from taking criminal actions against company officials for endangering the safety and health of their employees.[10] While relatively few employers have been criminally prosecuted for workplace hazards,[11] this seems to be changing. In Illinois, five senior executives of Chicago Magnet Wire Company were charged with allowing workers to become ill from exposure to hazardous chemicals and three senior officials of Film Recovery Systems, Inc., were prosecuted on murder and reckless conduct charges after a worker died from inhaling cyanide fumes.[12] In New York, William and Edward Pymm, the former operators of Pymm Thermometer Corporation, were charged with recklessly endangering the lives of several employees by exposing them to mercury during work in an unventilated cellar.

Even without the state's help, OSHA can cause top officials to rue the day they were less than diligent in enforcing OSHA regulations. In one case, Howard Elliott, president of Elliott Plumbing & Heating, was sentenced to six months in jail, of which 45 days must be served, for willfully failing to comply with OSHA trenching standards. Failing to abide by the standards resulted in the death of two of Elliott's company's workers. Elliott was placed on probation for three years and was also fined

---

EXHIBIT 14.1   **Violations of the Occupational Safety and Health Act**

Type	Description	Penalty
Willful	Conscious, intentional, or deliberate decision or a careless disregard for the OSHA standards or indifference to employee safety	Criminal: Up to $10,000 fine or up to 6 months in prison Civil: Up to $10,000 fine
Repeated violations	Prior violation of the same standard	Up to $10,000 fine
Serious	Substantial likelihood that death or serious physical harm could result	Up to $1,000 fine
Nonserious	Causes an unsafe work environment but probably would not cause death or serious physical harm	Up to $1,000 fine, but only if 10 or more nonserious violations are cited
De minimus	Violation has no immediate relationship to job safety	Notice issued

---

━━ HR CHALLENGE ━━

Beware of Salt and Candles!

One unfortunate outgrowth of the recent "right to know" legislation is a distorted sense of proportion and common sense on the part of the makers of caution labels. The purpose of "right to know" legislation is to guarantee the workers' rights to be informed about the hazardous substances they may come into contact with at work.

The following warning appears on a certain laboratory chemical: "WARNING: CAUSES IRRITATION. Avoid contact with eyes, skin or clothing. Avoid breathing dust. Wash thoroughly after handling." The chemical in question is sodium chloride, better known as table salt. A similar warning appears as an advisory against another "hazardous" chemical— paraffin wax, found in ordinary candles.

The problem becomes apparent when one compares the warnings for sodium chloride and paraffin wax to a truly hazardous chemical, such as tetrodotoxin. Tetrodotoxin is thought to be the "magic" behind Haitian voodoo practices intended to paralyze victims and is found in certain species of fish. The warning for tetrodotoxin, although more stringent than that of salt and paraffin wax, is similar enough in impact to cause some to speak out against "crying wolf" over trivial risks. The result of such warnings may be to lower workers' vigilance for real risks, because the intensity of warnings may blur true distinctions between high- and low-risk chemicals.

SOURCE: Adapted from Michael M. Segal, M.D., "Spilled Some Salt? Call OSHA," *The Wall Street Journal*, July 9, 1991, p. A16.

$21,452 in a lump-sum payment, or $544 per month for three years, to cover restitution for funeral expenses and lost earnings.[13] In a more severe case, Phillips Petroleum Company was fined $5.7 million for willful safety violations in connection with a chemical plant explosion near Houston that resulted in 23 deaths and more than 130 injuries.[14]

An OSHA bill was proposed in both the House and the Senate which, if passed, would significantly modify the Occupational Safety and Health Act by creating new standards.[15] Specifically, the new law would require employers to provide immediate notification of all work-related fatalities and 24-hour notification of all accidents requiring hospitalization of two or more workers. Employers would also be required to formulate written health and safety plans, form workplace safety and health committees, and designate a safety and health officer.[16] Finally, the law would require broader training requirements and the establishment of standards for monitoring exposure to toxic or harmful materials.[17]

This bill was backed by labor unions, and for good reason. Research has shown that unionized workers are more likely to complain about unsafe work conditions than are nonunion employees, and union workers dramatically increase the enforcement of existing OSHA standards.[18] Further, this same research found that unionized workplaces face greater scrutiny during a compliance inspection than do nonunion workplaces, and unionized firms are more likely to pay higher fines for violations than their nonunion counterparts.

MANAGING AN OSHA INSPECTION

Workplace inspections by OSHA are conducted for one of three reasons: (1) in response to an accident, injury, or fatality; (2) in response to an employee complaint alleging an OSHA violation; or (3) as part of OSHA's regularly scheduled inspections. Although a company cannot prevent an OSHA inspection, employers should always know how to manage an inspection; employers should expect the following:[19]

1. *Opening Conference*   The employer should hold an opening conference for his or her management team and OSHA representatives. During this initial conference, the employer can explain company policy and procedures regarding OSHA inspections. Employers should explain that any document requests must be in writing and that any documents containing confidential information (e.g., trade secrets) must be kept confidential by OSHA. During this opening conference, the employer should also set up a procedure with OSHA to determine the schedule of employee interviews.
2. *The Walkaround*   During the actual physical inspection of the workplace, the OSHA inspector should be accompanied by a member of the management team. OSHA inspectors should not be allowed to wander off alone into work areas.
3. *Employee Interviews*   Although OSHA may interview employees at the workplace, the employer is entitled not to have business disrupted, but employees should not be discouraged from talking with OSHA inspectors.
4. *Closing Conference*   The employer should insist on a closing conference to correct any misunderstandings or errors. This is also an opportunity to inquire about any citations that are likely to occur.
5. *Postclosing Conference*   The employer may want to bring additional information to the attention of the OSHA inspector. This is also the time to consider a precitation settlement if violations have been found.
6. *Postcitation*   If a citation is issued, the employer may ask for an informal meeting with the OSHA inspector to present any last-minute information. After receiving a citation, an employer's notice of contest must be filed within 15 working days.

"RIGHT TO KNOW" LEGISLATION

"RIGHT TO KNOW" LEGISLATION
State laws that guarantee employees the right to know whether there are harmful substances in the workplace.

In recent years, many states have passed **"right to know" legislation** that guarantees individual workers the right to know of hazardous substances in the workplace, requires employers to inform employee physicians of the chemical composition of workplace substances, and notifies local officials and residents when local employees are working with hazardous substances. The laws vary from state to state, but it is not uncommon for them to require training programs for employees who work with hazardous materials to inform them about the properties of the materials, safe handling procedures, and emergency treatments for overexposure. Also, several states have enacted legislation that requires labels for containers of toxic substances. However, as the HR Challenge box entitled "Beware of Salt and Candles" indicates, efforts to protect employees can sometimes appear to be overdone.

CURRENT SAFETY AND HEALTH PROBLEMS FOR EMPLOYEES

CUMULATIVE TRAUMA DISORDERS
Medical problems caused by repetitive motions using the same muscles.

Although the sweatshop work environment has all but disappeared, employers are still concerned about employee productivity.[20] One way in which increased productivity can be achieved is through automation. Sometimes, however, the introduction of new technology can be responsible for adding safety and health problems.[21] One example is the **cumulative trauma disorder (CTD)** caused by repeated motions of the same muscles hundreds or thousands of times each day. These work-related injuries are also known by other terms, such as *repetitive stress injuries* and *carpal tunnel syndrome*. It is estimated that between 1982 and 1992, reported cases of job-related CTD increased from 20,000 to 280,000 cases.[22] By 1989, CTD accounted for 51.8 percent of all occupational illnesses.[23] CTD injuries have been reported by grocery cashiers, mail sorters, assembly-line workers, violinists, and jackhammer operators, but the most prevalent reports of this disorder come from employees in both the computer and meat-packing industries.[24] By the year 2000, OSHA and National Safety Council experts predict that 50 percent of all workers' compensation cases will be related to CTDs.[25]

CUMULATIVE TRAUMA DISORDERS

COMPUTERS AND CTD

The personal computer has changed the American office. Its introduction into the workplace has enabled typists to move 40 percent faster than when using a typewriter because no manual margin adjustments or paper changes are required with computers.[26] However, this change in the variety of hand motions required to type has caused an increase in the reported cases of CTD in all jobs associated with keyboarding.

The experience of Deborah Tager is a good example of the way that CTD can debilitate a worker. She was a features editor at the *Monitor* in Concord, New Hampshire. One of the requirements of this job was to edit stories on her personal computer 8 to 12 hours a day. At first, Tager assumed that she was fatigued. However, when the tingling and burning in her hands and arms woke her at night, she knew she had a problem. After being diagnosed with CTD, she was no longer able to use her computer. In December of 1988, Tager was fired.[27]

MEAT PACKING AND CTD

The meat industry has faced some hard times since early 1970. Many Americans have given up eating red meat at least once a day in favor of a more healthy diet consisting of more fish and poultry.[28] This change in American diet forced the meat firms to trim staff and run the production lines faster to continue to reach production quotas. This procedural change has caused the meat-packing industry to be dubbed "America's No. 1 disaster area."[29] One extreme example of this was found at Morrell's Sioux Falls plant.

OSHA proposed a record fine of $4.33 million against John Morrell & Company for failure to prevent CTD at the company's Sioux Falls meat-packing plant. OSHA reported that between May 1977 and April 1988, 880 of the 2,000 employees at the Sioux Falls plant sustained injuries, such as tendinitis, elbow and shoulder injuries, and carpal tunnel syndrome, classified under the CTD heading. All of the injuries were traced to the repetitive hand, wrist, and arm motions required for meat packing.[30] Beverly Whaley was one of the Morrell employees stricken with CTD. Her job involved ripping the kidneys from hog carcasses using only her right hand. Before long, she experienced pain in her hand that would wake her at night. She had to run cold water on her hand to get it to open in the morning. Even after two operations, she has not regained full use of her hand and complains that it is difficult even to pick up a coffee cup.[31]

FIGHTING CTD

The objective is to curb the rise of CTDs, such as the well-known *carpal tunnel syndrome*. CTDs, which commonly affect a worker's wrists and hands, are the fastest-growing type of workers' compensation claim. Further, claims of carpal tunnel syndrome and repetitive strain injuries can result in lawsuits for disability discrimination under the Americans with Disabilities Act if management refuses to make reasonable accommodations for the workers.[32]

OshKosh B'Gosh, the Wisconsin-based manufacturer, found that most of its workers' CTD problems arose from small, awkward motions that required force and were highly repetitive. Neither the chairs nor the worktables on the shop floor were adjustable, so workers had to lean over and reach, which put great stress on the hands. After an extensive study, the safety team at OshKosh was authorized to buy a new chair for each person on the production line, 7,000 in all, at $100 each. Among other changes, OshKosh now rotates workers through different jobs within the plants, so that different parts of their bodies can get a rest.[33] Safety precautions, such as those at OshKosh, can prevent injuries due to cumulative trauma disorders.

Other companies also have made a strategic decision to fight CTD in the workplace. Chrysler and the United Auto Workers agreed to begin a program at five assembly plants to control carpal tunnel syndrome and other production-line repetitive motion disorders.[34] IBP, a major meat-packing firm, also introduced a safety program to reduce repetitive motion injuries. This agreement between the union and management has been called a historic agreement that may lead to a redesign of all meat-packing plants in the United States.[35] Other corrective measures management can take include introducing an appropriate **ergonomics** program (ergonomics is the study of job designs that maximize the human–machine interface) that focuses on fitting the job to the worker, not the worker to the job, and training workers to be aware of the possible symptoms of CTD and ways to curtail this disease.[36] A properly positioned terminal and keyboard punctuated with frequent breaks can go a long way to reduce or eliminate CTD.[37]

ERGONOMICS
The study of job designs that match the best human–machine fit.

CHEMICALS IN THE WORKPLACE

Some health problems, such as CTD, are considered new threats to workers while others, such as chemical poisoning and lung disease, have long plagued workers. Chemical poisoning is an old problem, but several new chemical health risks, such as indoor air pollution and passive smoking, have gained attention in recent years. Another reason that chemicals in the workplace have received increased attention is OSHA's issuing of new standards for hazardous materials in May 1988 under the title Hazard Communication Standard. This standard, which once applied only to manufacturers, requires *every* workplace in the country to identify hazardous substances on the premises, list them, and train employees in their use.[38] To comply, employers must observe the following procedures:

1. Identify and list hazardous chemicals in the workplace.
2. Obtain and retain a material safety data sheet (MSDS) for each chemical and make these sheets available to employees.
3. Create and maintain a written chemical communication program.
4. Identify workers who should be trained and provide training that includes instructions in each substance's dangers, safe handling techniques, how to read the MSDS and warning labels, and what to do in case of an emergency.[39]

Due to the complexities of the regulations and the severity of the penalties for noncompliance, OSHA designed and distributed a "Hazard Compliance Kit."[40] It contains looseleaf materials designed to provide employers with simple instructions regarding compliance with OSHA's hazard communication standard. Over the next several years, amendments and updates will be sent to purchasers of the kit, which sells for approximately $20.[41]

INDOOR AIR POLLUTION

The 1976 American Legion convention in Philadelphia will be remembered for many years to come. At this convention, 29 people died from Legionnaire's disease contracted from a bacteria in the hotel's cooling tower that spread through the ventilation system.[42] This was one of the first and most highly publicized cases of "sick building syndrome."

Sick building syndrome is an outgrowth of the energy crisis of the 1970s. Buildings were designed with sealed windows and heavy insulation resulting in inadequate fresh air and poor ventilation systems. The buildup of chemicals from photocopying machines, cleaning liquids, and solvents have caused workers to complain of headaches, dizziness, and bleeding.[43] Four women with such symptoms, who were fired because they refused to work in the building, sued their employer, its parent company, the building's designer, and the contractor.

Only a handful of lawsuits have been filed on the grounds of indoor air pollution, but the Environmental Protection Agency estimates that the economic costs of indoor air pollution totals tens of billions of dollars in such forms as lost productivity, medical care, lost earnings, and sick days. With the increase in both litigation and indirect costs, architects have begun redesigning buildings so that fresh air is available, and engineers are improving air circulation systems for office buildings.[44]

SMOKING IN THE WORKPLACE

The 1990s will likely be referred to as the decade of the smoke-free workplace. The movement toward eliminating smoking in the workplace has been fueled by reports that the 50 largest industrial companies are working to eliminate workplace smoking. Reports indicate that 85 percent of U.S. companies restrict smoking in the workplace, up from 54 percent in 1987. Reasons given for these actions include concern for employee health, worker complaints, the classification of environmental tobacco smoke (ETS) as a human carcinogen by the Environmental Protection Agency (EPA), and the increase in state and local laws.[45]

While not cited, employers may want to see their employees quit smoking for a variety of other reasons. Smokers are 50 percent more likely to be hospitalized than are nonsmoking employees. Smokers lose 80 million work days a year because of their habit and their absenteeism rate is 50 percent higher than that of their nonsmoking counterparts. Employers pay an average of $300 more in insurance claims for smokers than for nonsmokers. Smokers have twice as many job-related accidents as nonsmokers, in part due to loss of attention, hand occupation, eye irritation, and coughing.[46] Smokers also have been found to have more car accidents.[47]

Smokers are not the only victims of the deleterious effects of smoking. A report recently released by the Environmental Protection Agency concluded that "secondhand" smoke has a "serious and substantial public health impact" on nonsmokers.[48] Environmental tobacco smoke comes from two sources: mainstream smoke, which is inhaled directly by the smoker, and sidestream or secondhand smoke, which is emitted by the lighted end of the cigarette. Secondhand smoke, which is unfiltered, has higher concentrations of carbon monoxide, ammonia, and other harmful chemicals than does mainstream smoke and can be inhaled more deeply into the lungs due to its smaller particle size.[49] The EPA report indicates that secondhand smoke kills about 3,000 nonsmokers a year and greatly increases the risk of respiratory illness in children.[50]

A number of companies have made a strategic decision to promote a smoke-free workplace. Merck & Co., a pharmaceutical corporation based in Rahway, New Jersey, has taken somewhat extreme measures; it has severely restricted smoking in all of its 24 sites in the United States. Further, it also has banned smoking at Merck-sponsored off-site events. To help its employees kick the habit, Merck does the following:

1. Reimburses employees and their dependents for successful completion of approved smoking-cessation programs.
2. Encourages smokers to quit through a year-long communications program.
3. Helps fund a smoking clinic at a local hospital.
4. Donates money to the American Cancer Society and the American Lung Association to support public education and no-smoking programs.
5. Produces an antismoking commercial that airs repeatedly on 14 commercial radio stations serving communities surrounding Merck sites nationwide.[51]

Strategies for effective management of smoke-free environments include (1) communicating with employees concerning smoking policies (both smokers and nonsmokers should be consulted); (2) clearly defining a policy and sticking to it; (3) treating the issue with dignity and seriousness; (4) offering incentives and/or help for smokers to quit smoking; (5) working with the union; and, most important, (6) ensuring that top management is seriously committed to the health of all employees.[52]

It is not always easy to get employees to quit smoking. Research has found that only about one-fifth of those attending organized programs did not smoke a year later. However, smokers using less than a pack of cigarettes a day were more than twice as likely to quit as heavy smokers.[53] Reports indicate that married employees are less likely to smoke than are divorced employees, and working women are less likely to smoke than are homemakers or unemployed women.[54]

ASBESTOS IN THE WORKPLACE[55]

ASBESTOS
A fiber used in insulation that has been linked to cancer.

Asbestos is a fiber that was used extensively in insulation for over a century until it was linked to cancer. Workers who were exposed to asbestos contracted a form of cancer called *asbestosis,* which slowly suffocates its victims. The first lawsuit filed by a worker exposed to asbestos was in the 1950s. The lawsuits continued for the next 40 years, with plaintiffs winning big beginning in the 1980s when juries learned that companies knew the risks associated with asbestos but did nothing to protect the workers. Some of the judgments were so high that companies were forced to file Chapter 11 bankruptcy to protect themselves.

As the rewards and the number of suits continued to grow, the asbestos manufacturers' insurance companies grew tired of paying and began to reread the contracts for loopholes. Many filed suit against the asbestos manufacturers, and these cases also ended up in court.

Asbestos suits were becoming so common that lawyers specialized in such cases. It is estimated that more than 1,100 law firms around the country were involved in defending asbestos manufacturers, insurance firms, or victims.

The solution to the escalation of lawsuits came in the form of the Asbestos Claims Facility, a one-stop settlement shop for asbestos claims. The designers saw it as a faster, less costly, and more orderly way to resolve claims. Fifty companies, who included the largest asbestos manufacturers and insurance companies, joined the facility. These companies provided funding for the facility to use in settling claims quickly and without the use of the courts.

Soon after its inception, the flood of claims turned into a deluge. New claims poured in at a rate of 1,300 a month, more than triple the rate from a few years before. With more than 60,000 claims pending, the Asbestos Claims Facility folded. Seven of the biggest participants withdrew their financial support, which accounted for over 60 percent of the funding available. Now companies and plaintiffs alike were forced to return to the overcrowded courts to reach a settlement.

ACCIDENTS AND DEATH ON THE JOB

Occupational accidents seriously injure or kill 1 of every 11 U.S. workers.[56] Some occupations have been found to be more dangerous than others. The most dangerous blue-collar jobs are in the logging and timber industry; airline pilots hold the most dangerous white-collar jobs.[57]

Research has found that when a father holds a hazardous job, the son is more likely to follow in his footsteps.[58] Sons appear to believe that they can control the dangers associated with the job. Another contributing factor is the rate of pay: the higher it is, the higher the chance of the son choosing a hazardous career. However, education level has been found to decrease the rate of occupational following as does race. Research has found that the higher the level of education attained by the son, the less likely he is to perform his father's job. Also, white males are more likely to pursue their fathers' careers than are black males.

One occupation that is extremely hazardous but that is not listed in business industry reports of job-related deaths is farming. The accidental death rate for farm workers is 48 per 100,000 per year. About 1,500 farmers and farmhands are killed each year.[59] Causes for these deaths range from the number one killer, tractor accidents, to angry farm animals and suffocation under tons of grain. Even though farming has proven to be a hazardous occupation, it is not covered by OSHA standards, and farmers fiercely resist any attempts to change this.

Congress has forbidden OSHA to enforce federal safety standards on 97 percent of the nation's farms, those with 10 or fewer employees.[60] Family workers, who are not paid, are not considered employees, nor are neighboring farmers who pitch in to help each other when needed. Farmers believe that farming is one of the last free things a person can do, and they do not want government changing that. Instead, they have decided to change things themselves. The American Farm Bureau Federation (AFBF) has introduced educational programs and redesigned farm implements to improve safety. The AFBF continues to argue that it is doing a good job, even though 341 people died in tractor rollovers in 1987.[61]

Both the type of job one holds and the type of person holding the job influence the accident rate. Research has found that left-handed men are one-third more likely to have accidents on the job than right-handers due to the bias of right-handed equipment.[62] Furthermore, while it was always assumed that blacks, who tend to work in more dangerous occupations, had a higher accident rate than whites, recent reports contradict this assumption. A study by the National Center for Health Statistics reported that whites have slightly higher rates of work-related accidents than blacks, especially in the growing service sector.[63]

Management also has been accused of causing job-related accidents, especially because of the current trend of downsizing and doing more with less. Job-related disabilities jumped 16 percent in 1987, up by 10,000, and labor officials are tying this increase to the effects of mergers and competition. They argue that work crews are becoming smaller but the work load is not. The use of overtime and increased speed on the assembly lines causes fatigued workers to make mistakes that may cost their lives.[64]

Such an incident occurred at Bastian Plating Company in Auburn, Indiana. The company had decided to install a speedier chemical process to increase production, but the changeover was running behind schedule. To speed the changeover, untrained workers at the end of their 12-hour shift were asked to clean the chemical tanks that had been drained. One worker climbed in and was soon overcome by the hydrogen cyanide gases in the tank. Four workers who saw him fall face first into the muddy vat tried to rescue him. Three died in the vat with their colleague; the fourth died later in the hospital. The firm was fined $41,700 for numerous violations, which included the lack of adequate respirators, air monitoring systems, and training for employees.[65]

U.S. firms are not the only ones plagued with the problem of job-related accidents. Exhibit 14.2 compares the fatality rates for workers in various countries, including the United States. As shown, Latin America heads the list.

The total number of job-related accidents for Latin America was an alarming 30,000. However, this figure does not represent the whole picture. The accidents that occurred in rural areas and in small operations are not included in this number. However, accidents that occur on the way to work, which have increased by 150 percent over the past

EXHIBIT 14.2   **Worker Fatality Rates Compared by Country**

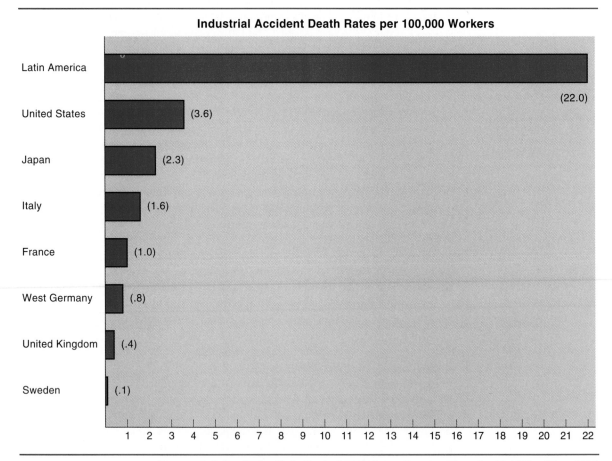

Industrial Accident Death Rates per 100,000 Workers

- Latin America — (22.0)
- United States — (3.6)
- Japan — (2.3)
- Italy — (1.6)
- France — (1.0)
- West Germany — (.8)
- United Kingdom — (.4)
- Sweden — (.1)

SOURCES: S. Cohen, "Pain with the Paycheck," *Tallahassee Democrat,* November 12, 1989, p. D1, and "LA Takes on Safety and Health Challenge," *ILO Information,* October 1989, p. 2.

HR CHALLENGE

Workplace Safety: New Lessons from Japanese Management

Forty years ago Japan had an industrial injury and illness rate five times that of the United States. By 1990, the United States had an injury and illness rate almost six times that of Japan. Today, Japanese employees and managers are working together to promote safety and health. Slogans such as "anzen nakushite seisan nashi"—without safety there can be no production—are spoken frequently by Japanese employees and managers.

The Japanese behavioral approach to promoting workplace safety may be useful for managers in the United States. Specific examples of Japanese strategies for promoting workplace safety and health include the following:

* *Continuous Improvement* Employees and managers are trained to think constantly about changes to the production process that can improve safety and health conditions.
* *Morning Exercise and Safety Check* Stretching exercises are followed by a safety check involving two employees who check each other for any safety or health problem (e.g., jewelry that might get caught in machinery).

* *Articulation of Hazards and Contingencies* Employees learn to identify the hazards involved in their workstation, and they develop a contingency plan should the hazard they study occur.
* *Hazard Prediction Cards* To help employees remember the wide range of possible hazards, cards listing generic hazards are given to workers to carry.

Successful work safety and health programs in Japan and the United States have incorporated employee empowerment and the teamwork concept into the safety processes. In Japan, there is a high degree of cooperation among labor, management, and government. Given that one of the best ways to improve safety and health in an organization is to examine the "best practices" of other successful organizations, managers in the United States may want to examine some of the "best practices" in Japan.

SOURCE: Adapted from W. Neal, "Workplace Health, Safety: A Continuing Process," *HRNews,* September 1994, p. 18; and R. Wokutch, "New Lessons from Japanese Management," *HRMagazine,* September 1994, pp. 72–78.

12 years, are reflected in these numbers. The Latin American Center for Occupational Safety and Health has begun to reverse these numbers through an effort that involves information, prevention, and legislation.[66]

Perhaps lessons from Japanese managers would be helpful in reducing accidents in Latin America and the United States, as discussed in the HR Challenge box on Workplace Safety. Japanese safety and health programs are integrated into the overall production system. Emphasis on promoting safe practices and changing behaviors to avoid injuries and illnesses focus on individuals. Each employee is rigorously trained on the precise motion sequences to follow in each workstation and is required to practice these motions repeatedly before performing them on the job.[67]

An ever-increasing cause of accidents and death on the job is violence in the workplace. A review of litigated cases shows various types of workplace violence. A youth, who was struck by an usher carrying a flashlight, sued the theater operator for damages. A fast-food restaurant employee sued her employer for fraud and bad faith after being injured in a robbery. She charged that the employer promised police protection and other security measures but reneged on his promises. A woman, who was raped and sexually abused by an individual employed by a corporation to prepare bids for construction jobs, sued the employer for negligent retention of the employee and vicarious liability for the employee's violent actions.[68] Homicide has now become the number two work-related cause of death, behind automobile and other machinery accidents.[69] The leading cause of death for women in the workplace is murder.[70] Women often work in retail establishments where the number of homicides is high because of easy entrance by strangers.[71]

The causes of workplace violence are varied; in most cases, employers can be held responsible because they are obligated by law to provide a safe working environment for their employees and a safe place for nonemployees to conduct business.[72] To protect themselves, employers should make a strategic decision to implement policies and practices designed to limit the risk of employing unfit, dangerous, or incompetent employees. In addition, because there is a higher level of awareness and concern about workplace violence, human resource professionals should become familiar with security selection and program design.[73] Prevention and preparation are the keys to minimizing the threat of workplace violence, so human resource professionals should take steps to familiarize themselves with the various options and strategies available to their companies.

ACQUIRED IMMUNE DEFICIENCY SYNDROME (AIDS) ISSUES IN THE WORKPLACE

AIDS, which was known only to a small group of medical personnel a decade ago, has quickly become a serious health threat to Americans. AIDS also has caused significant confusion and disruption in the workforce. Individuals who have AIDS are protected by federal, state, and local legislation. This protection is guaranteed under the Americans with Disabilities Act (ADA) of 1990 because AIDS is considered a disability.[74] This protection generally comes in the form of protection against discrimination and is based on the fact that the virus cannot be spread by casual contact.[75]

The Center for Disease Control (CDC) has concluded that the kind of nonsexual, person-to-person contact that generally occurs among workers and clients or consumers in the workplace does not pose a risk for transmission of HIV, the virus that causes AIDS. Similarly, the United States Surgeon General has indicated that there is no known risk of nonsexual infection in most situations we encounter in our daily lives.[76] However, even with these reassurances, some employees fear working with co-workers who are infected with AIDS. The fear may stem from the fact that employees know little about AIDS, and what they do know is extremely frightening.

Most people know that there is no cure for AIDS. The majority of people who are HIV infected will die as nonlife-threatening diseases attack their bodies that no longer have the ability to fight back. People know that there are no vaccines to prevent AIDS and few drugs available to the general public that help fight the disease once it is contracted. Finally, people know that they do not want to contract AIDS.

This final fact has sometimes caused irrational behavior in some employees. When employees realize that they are working with an infected co-worker, they sometimes issue an ultimatum: "Either that person goes or we go, and if we go, we'll go public." To some employers, this can be an extremely effective scare tactic. Few employers want to be faced with the empty tables, beds, or desks that may appear after the public learns that a chef, chambermaid, or engineer has AIDS.[77] What choice does the employer have? Discharging an employee with AIDS violates the law. If other employees leave and make the situation public, the business could suffer irreparable damage.

The only choice available to employers is to prevent employees from acting irrationally by educating them about AIDS. Several guidelines must be followed if the educational program is effective:

1. One goal of the program is to be certain that employees understand *how* AIDS is contracted. If they understand that the activities required to contract AIDS are not practiced in their workplace, the irrational behavior should disappear.

2. Because the message presented includes sexual references, the presentation should be informed and professional so that the workers do not feel that management is infringing on their personal lives. To achieve this goal, it may be necessary to hire an external expert to present the educational program.

3. Finally, it is imperative that *all* employees attend the sessions.[78]

If these guidelines are followed, employers may not be faced with ultimatums.

Enterprising organizations are taking innovative and proactive approaches to the AIDS crisis in the workplace. First and foremost is the establishment of a responsible AIDS policy that outlines equal treatment for employees, legal responsibilities, education, and confidentiality concerns.[79] The potential for devastation with such a disease is obvious, but those firms that prepare in advance will be able to minimize the impact. Strategies for handling the impact of AIDS are needed, but most organizations continue to ignore the possibilities. Such ignorance will not make the problem disappear, however.

One health problem related to AIDS is the resurgence of tuberculosis in the United States.[80] TB, as it is known, is an infectious disease caused by a bacterium that produces lesions in the lungs. It is curable in most cases; however, drug-resistant strains have complicated public health efforts to treat the disease. TB kills about 3 million people per year worldwide. Since TB is an infectious disease, the rights of contagious people are protected by the Americans with Disabilities Act of 1990.[81] Once again, human resource professionals must be able to formulate strategies for the effective management of the risks and requirements associated with tuberculosis in the workplace.

FETAL PROTECTION IN THE WORKPLACE

In 1982, Johnson Controls, a manufacturer of automobile batteries, established an employment policy forbidding women between the ages of 18 and 70 from holding jobs in any of their 16 battery-producing plants nationwide.[82] The policy was enacted to protect unborn children from the lead that was present at all battery-manufacturing sites. The only way for a woman to gain employment in these units was to provide written medical evidence of infertility.[83]

In 1989, the United Auto Workers brought suit against Johnson Controls, claiming that the fetal protection policy discriminated against women seeking employment in this high-paying unit of the organization. In the court case, called by Judge Frank Easterbrook "the most important sex discrimination case in any court," the courts upheld the employer's decision barring fertile women's employment in this division.[84] The courts found that fetal exposure to high levels of lead resulted in a variety of birth defects including retardation. In addition, the courts concluded that the fetal-protection policy met the requirements of a bona fide occupational qualification (BFOQ) by stating that "Johnson Controls has demonstrated that its fetal protection policy is reasonably necessary to industrial safety."[85] In addition, the courts rejected the claim that the harmful environment would have any impact on the reproductive abilities of males, even though medical reports show that wives of men employed in certain industries have unusually high rates of stillbirths, premature deliveries, underweight pregnancies, and children born with birth defects.[86]

The initial decision was appealed at various courts. The ninth circuit court in Chicago upheld the original decision; the seventh circuit court in California found that lead has an impact on both men and women.[87] Because of the confusion as to the legality of the organizational-based fetal protection policies, this issue was appealed to the Supreme Court of the United States.

In 1991, the Supreme Court ruled that employers may *not* bar women of child-bearing age due to possible fetal dangers.[88] The decision, by a vote of six to three, concluded that this policy represents a sex bias that has been banned by civil rights laws. According to the Court, women as capable of doing their jobs as male counterparts should not be forced to decide between having a job and having a child.

The response of some firms has been to shift the responsibility for a decision to the affected party. Monsanto Co., Olin Corp., and Allied Signal no longer bar women from certain jobs. These companies educate their workers on the potential hazards and provide protective clothing and equipment. General Electric allows workers to transfer out of hazardous areas without a loss of pay.[89] These are some of the strategies available to businesses that deal with hazardous materials.

To many, the controversy over this issue seems misplaced. Those who work with lead, regardless of sex, face a health and safety problem. Companies should focus on this problem and fix it, not the worker. As civil liberties lawyers argue, "If something made your spleen become infected at work, you wouldn't say, 'We'll only take workers who don't have spleens.'"[90]

SAFETY PROGRAMS THAT WORK

For a safety program to be effective, it must be followed. All too often a program is implemented and ignored. There are various reasons that some programs work and others do not. Exhibit 14.3 provides tips for implementing safety programs that work. One of the most important items in this list is that workers must be aware that the program is to their advantage, not just for the company's benefit. This has been referred to as the "What's in it for me?" problem.

EXHIBIT 14.3   **Tips for Implementing a Safety Program That Works**

1. Avoid asking workers to "do as I say, not as I do." Managers and supervisors must serve as role models for the safety program. If workers see their supervisors performing jobs in an unsafe manner, they feel they have every right to do so too. It is the manager's responsibility to perform the job exactly as outlined by the safety program.

2. Avoid having a "participatory facade." Asking for employee suggestions for improving workplace safety will be effective only if the suggestions are implemented in a timely fashion. If the ideas provided by workers are ignored or implementation is postponed, when they are eventually implemented, the workers will not be motivated to support them.

3. Avoid the problem of workers believing that "if I'm not in on it, I'm not up on it," by allowing workers at all levels to participate in the development of the safety program. If workers or managers feel that the program is being pushed down their throats without concern for their feelings, they will not be motivated to abide by the rules.

4. Workers will want to know "what's in it for me." While the company is sure to benefit from increased safety through reduced medical and insurance costs, workers may not see a personal advantage to abiding by the new safety plan. Including an incentive for workers often reverses this trend and increases compliance. However, be sure that the incentive is awarded frequently and as soon after good compliant behavior occurs in order to tie the reward to the behavior you want to see repeated.

SOURCE: Adapted from R. A. Reber, J. A. Walling, and D. L. Dubon, "Safety Programs that Work," *Personnel Administrator,* September 1989, pp. 66–69.

Luitink Manufacturing Company of Menomonee Falls, Wisconsin, implemented a safety program that overcame this problem: a lottery. Workers who have not had accidents in one month receive a ticket. The ticket holders are then eligible for a jackpot, which is awarded every three months. The jackpot starts at $250 and is reduced by $50 for every accident. By the end of the year, employees may be eligible to win jackpots ranging from $1,000 to $250, depending upon the total number of accidents company-wide. If more than 12 accidents occurred during the year, no awards are provided. The program cut the rate of accidents from 20 in 1987 to 4 in 1988. Company officials indicated that if the accident rate continues at the new lower level, the company will save about $40,000 in insurance premiums over a three-year period.[91]

Coca-Cola Company also introduced a successful safety program. Entitled "Back to Work," the program is aimed at the employees who are required to load and lift company products. Before starting the program, employees' backs were examined for strength and overall condition. Employees were then required to attend workshops designed to show how to prevent injury and how to develop a safe exercise routine. Because exercise is one of the best deterrents to back injury, the program incorporated exercise into employees' daily work routine. The first few minutes of each morning are spent doing exercises that prepare them to perform their jobs. Since the start of the program, the company has reduced back injuries by an average of 32 percent and slashed the number of lost work days by 78 percent.[92]

It is apparent that more and more successful safety programs will emerge as companies realize that good safety is good business.[93] Companies such as DuPont, who abandoned safety for productivity and quality a few years ago, are now back to emphasizing both safety and productivity after realizing that the two concepts are actually Siamese twins. Kodak also found that safety fit nicely with its overall theme of quality leadership because safety programs boosted morale and output and strengthened public relations.[94] Employers are realizing that safety programs initiated on the job have positive impacts for off-the-job safety. Defensive driving courses, CPR training, first aid courses, and fire extinguisher training have definite applicability both on the job and off. These hidden benefits of a safe working environment will guide the development of safer workplaces for all.

WORKPLACE STRESS

WHAT IS STRESS?

Stress has been defined as the interaction between the individual and the environment characterized by physiological and psychological changes that cause a deviation from normal performance.[95] This deviation from normal may have a positive or negative outcome. A moderate amount of stress can help to stimulate employees to work longer, harder, and better. However, an extremely low level of stress can leave employees unstimulated, resulting in low productivity. An extremely high level of stress can lead to poor performance due to the diversion of increased energy from production and to dealing with the stress itself.

Stress has both an internal and an external factor. Internal factors are primarily a person's attitudes and expectations. Difficulty living up to these values may cause self-induced stress. External factors can be divided into two categories: physical and psychological. Physical stressors can include poor ventilation or lighting or physically demanding tasks. Examples of psychological stressors include demands of the job or demands from home.[96]

An increase in a person's stress level can result in several physical changes. These changes, often referred to as a *stress response,* include increased blood pressure, heart rate and respiration; an increased output of mental activity and gastric juices; and changes in the blood flow patterns. These changes can result in employee responses such as fatigue or anxiety.[97]

CAUSES OF STRESS

It is difficult to categorize stressors as high level or low level or to even list them because a situation that creates a high level of stress for one person may not cause any stress for another. Further, a person who views a situation as stressful one day may not view it as stressful on another day. However, it is safe to say that every aspect of a person's life is a potential source of stress. Specifically, stress can come from pressures at work or at home, or because of personality traits.

WORK PRESSURES

The type of job a person holds has a significant impact on the degree of stress he or she faces at work. Some occupations have a great deal of stress associated with them; others are less stressful. Exhibit 14.4 is a four-part categorization of occupations based on the tasks associated with the job. Surprisingly, the high-strain jobs listed are the jobs in which the highest levels of stress and stress-related diseases are reported. It appears that the bossed, not the bosses, are the ones who suffer the most from the effects of stress. These individuals have little control but high accountability. Employees who hold active jobs report the lowest levels of stress-related diseases; the passive and low-strain employees fall in between. To determine how healthful your job is, take the quiz in Exhibit 14.5.

Another way in which the workplace can cause an employee stress is by living and working with the constant fear of being replaced. With the downturn in the economy since the late 1980s, companies have been looking for ways to increase productivity and cut costs. Frequently this meant consolidating jobs and laying off employees. Even IBM, which was famous for its policy of lifetime employment, found itself in a position in which it had to lay off workers. Other types of consolidation that have been on the rise since the late 1980s are mergers and acquisitions. These types of activities also led to a reduction in the workforce as the newly merged company found itself with two identical accounting or human resource departments. Yet another worker fear is automation. Workers and managers alike know that one machine can do the jobs of many men and never requires a coffee break. As corporations restructure, managers are finding that they must do more with less. Sales and production quotas keep going up, but operating budgets, salaries, and opportunities keep heading down. The realization that the job has changed and that managers must now find ways to fire people instead of hiring leaves many less than optimistic about their jobs.[98]

The stress from the fear of being replaced or from actually being replaced can cause severe reactions. In one Citibank unit in which 2,000 jobs were eliminated, two employees killed themselves and the number of traffic accidents increased significantly.[99] In 1987, after Westinghouse Electric announced a restructuring and downsizing plan, employees were surveyed. Researchers found a higher than average prevalence of depression among white-collar workers induced by the stress of the impending changes.[100]

The ramifications of downsizing have begun to reach the employers as well. Studies have found that cutting jobs to save money actually increases costs.[101] These costs come in the form of adding stress to the survivors. When the degree of stress felt by an em-

EXHIBIT 14.4 **Categorizations of Occupations**

Active Jobs	These jobs have a heavy pressure to perform but provide leeway in problem solving. Hours may be long but are partly at the worker's discretion. There are chances to advance and to learn new skills. Initiative is a big part of the job. Examples: farmers, doctors, engineers, executives, and other professionals.
Low-Strain Jobs	These are the self-paced occupations. There are low demands from others and a high degree of decision freedom. What is done, in what order, and often at what pace is determined by the employee. Examples: tenured professors, carpenters, repairmen, or artists.
Passive Jobs	These jobs require a low degree of skills and mental-processing ability and have little leeway for learning or for making decisions. This type of job offers almost no latitude for innovation. Some jobs may actually cause workers' skills to decline. Examples: janitors, billing clerks, watchmen, or data-entry operators.
High-Strain Jobs	These jobs have a heavy pressure to perform, but provide no leeway in decision making. Hours and procedures are rigid and the threat of layoffs is present. The jobs provide no opportunities to learn new skills. It is extremely difficult to take an unscheduled break or to take time off for personal reasons. Examples: assembly-line workers, telephone operators, or waiters/waitresses.

Source: Adapted from R. Karasek and T. Theorell, *Healthy Work.* New York: Basic Books, 1991.

EXHIBIT 14.5 **How Healthful Is Your Job?**

Place the number that best agrees with your feelings about each of the following statements with respect to your job in the blank before each statement. Total scores below 14 indicate a job that encourages good health. Total scores over 30 indicate a stress-inducing job.

Strongly Agree	Neither Agree Nor Disagree	Strongly Disagree
1 2	.... 3 4	 5

_____ My job requires me to make maximum use of my skills and offers me a chance to increase them.

_____ I am free from worker-as-child disciplines. I control the machines on which I work, I can participate in long-term planning, and I have flexible work hours.

_____ The demands placed on me are mixed. The changes made are challenging but predictable. I have some input with respect to the magnitude of changes made.

_____ Collaboration on my job is encouraged.

_____ My workplace believes in the democratic process. I have an avenue to air and settle grievances.

_____ I know what it is I produce and why it is necessary. Customers provide me feedback so that I know how well I am performing.

_____ My job allows me time and energy for activities other than work.

Source: Adapted from K. Karasek and T. Theorell, *Healthy Work.* New York: Basic Books, 1991.

ployee reaches a point where he or she believes that it has become debilitating, he or she may file a lawsuit. Over the last 10 years, stress disability cases have doubled, and each case has cost the employer an average of $73,270.[102]

HOME STRESSORS

Americans have seen dramatic changes in the family structure over the last 10 years. Single-parent families, which include fathers raising children, and dual-career couples are becoming commonplace. These changes have made the conflict between parent as parent and parent as paid employee an extremely deep source of stress and anxiety in the American family member today.[103]

Mothers frequently report stress induced by the guilt of not being a good parent when work pressures are high and not being a good employee when home pressures take priority. In a recent survey, 16 percent of the 3,000 working mothers surveyed reported that they felt intense guilt about spending too little time with their children and spouses or not spending enough time on themselves. These mothers reported little support at home and few work rewards.[104]

Fathers, too, have begun to wrestle with the pressures from both career and family. One survey of over 1,600 employees at a large public utility company indicated that almost as many men as women (36 percent versus 37 percent) reported feeling "a lot of stress" in balancing their work and family lives.[105] A separate survey of over 1,200 employees at a Minneapolis company found that more than 70 percent of the fathers under the age of 35 had serious concerns about problems they were having managing work and family conflicts with their spouses. Over 60 percent of the male respondents reported that family concerns were affecting their work goals and plans. Many indicated that they were not seeking promotions or transfers because they needed to spend more time with their families.[106]

Research suggests that women may be better able to handle the stress of both family and career. Researchers had 166 couples in Detroit keep diaries of when they felt extreme pressure from both work and home or when they had arguments. The results indicate that men, not women, reported more incidents. Evidence also showed that men were more likely to have work problems spill over into family time and vice versa than women. Researchers suggested that differences in upbringing and role expectations have made women better able to handle family/work stress.[107]

PERSONALITY

Individuals who have what has been referred to as *Type A personalities* (hard-driving workaholics) have long been thought to be prime candidates for heart problems.[108] The reason behind this is that Type As have a strong bodily reaction to stressful situations. Their heart rate and blood pressure rise, causing increased blood flow to their muscles. This change in their systems, when repeated over and over throughout their lives, can place severe strain on their hearts and eventually cause damage. Recent evidence suggests, however, that not all Type As are prone to coronary heart disease. By looking at the various components of Type A behavior, it has been found that only the anger and hostility components of Type A behavior are associated with heart disease.[109] This means that the chronically angry and hostile person is the one who is most at risk.

Other personality characteristics can lead to increased stress as well. Researchers have found that certain personal characteristics draw certain individuals to specific jobs. These jobs, in turn, tend to cause stress in the people they attract. For example, clergy, who often have a distorted view of "selflessness," tend to have extremely high levels of stress that may eventually lead to burnout because they ignore their own needs and give too much of themselves to others.[110] Other examples of jobs and the people who are attracted to them are presented in Exhibit 14.6. As you read through the lists, see whether your personality has drawn you to a specific career. Although this list highlights the stereotypes often associated with certain professions, research supports the link between personality and job choice.[111]

CONSEQUENCES AND EXPENSES OF JOB STRESS

Stress can cause physical and emotional problems for people who suffer from excess stress. The most frequent disorders range from chronic fatigue to depression brought on by insomnia, anxiety, migraine headaches, emotional upsets, stomach ulcers, allergies, skin disorders, lumbago and rheumatic attacks, high blood pressure, tobacco and

EXHIBIT 14.6   **Jobs to Which Certain Personalities Are Drawn**

Profession	Personality Traits	Stress Comes From
Police	Have courage and a penchant for action	Never admitting fear causes strain
Lawyers	Love to give advice	Fearing to give poor advice
Teachers	Need to have rules and procedures to follow	Confronting authority and placing themselves in jeopardy for following some imposed rules
Dentists	Have exacting personalities	Patients and staff who are not as exact
Government workers	Don't like to cause problems or draw attention to themselves	Having their passive behavior rewarded tends to turn them into lethargic, automated individuals
Computer programmers	Love to play with machines	Finding people difficult to control and predict cause them stress when having to deal with people
Managers	Seek stability	As companies begin to downsize even the once stable ranks of management, the instability causes stress
Actors	Have low self-esteem	After becoming successful, actors, who had hoped for an increase in self-esteem find themselves asking, "Is this all?"
Politicians	Have a lack of reality	Some begin to believe the commercials made about them and are stressed when they realize they are not that image
Physicians	Need to help others and save the world	When doctors lose patients, they face a great deal of stress
Therapists	Want to know what makes people tick	Difficulty to stop analyzing people puts a strain on their interpersonal relations
Air traffic controllers	Are quick thinkers	Ambiguity in human relationships does not allow them to analyze situations and make quick decisions

SOURCE: Adapted from R. Sandroff, "Is Your Job Driving You Crazy?" *Psychology Today,* July/August 1989, pp. 41–45.

HR CHALLENGE

High-Tech Stress Therapy

The Japanese are known for their ability to excel at innovative product development and for the long hours they spend at work, well above our 40-hour standard. It should come as no surprise that the latest solution to the stress created in everyday Japanese life is a high-technology Brain Mind Gym.

Japanese workers go here for a mental massage that helps them relax. Comfortable chairs, soothing music, herbal tea, and pastoral scenes shown on television monitors combine to set the mood for relaxation. Special goggles shoot light patterns through the client's closed eyelids. The environment is thought to allow complete relaxation, something very rare and valued by the hard-working Japanese, who often suffer from high levels of stress and fatigue. In fact, a recent newspaper survey in

Japan found that almost 90 percent of the surveyed workers said they feel chronic fatigue, and most took no more than half of their allowed vacation time.

The Brain Mind Gym boasts more than 1,000 members and has been in business for only seven years. Most clients are men between the ages of 25 and 35, seeking relief from everyday stress. Although more traditional methods of relaxation are still popular in Japan (such as yoga, health clubs, and drinking with friends), this high-technology answer to the stress of a demanding lifestyle is gaining in popularity.

SOURCE: Adapted from "Japanese Are Hard at Work Finding Ways to Relieve Stress," *Tallahassee Democrat,* September 9, 1991, p. 6A.

alcohol abuse, overeating, family abuse, cynicism, distrust, and even colds. In severe cases, the end results can even be death from heart attacks, accidents, or suicide.[112]

All of the medical complications associated with stress are an ever-increasing burden on the medical costs for companies. Some experts have estimated the overall cost for many large corporations at over $200 million a year for employee medical benefits. This figure rises to over $150 billion a year when the costs to the overall economy, caused by repercussions of stress, such as reduced production due to ill, absent, or non-motivated employees, are factored in.[113]

Additional costs in the form of court-awarded settlements also are beginning to increase. Americans filed a record number of stress-related workers' compensation claims in 1993. UNUM Life Insurance, which writes more disability policies than any other U.S. insurer, says that the number of such claims it processed rose from 7.8 percent of its total in 1989 to 10.2 percent in 1993.[114] The cases recorded range from a female deputy sheriff who sued because her personality was not suited for police work and having to perform such work caused her to have a chronic psychiatric disability to a furniture rental manager who claimed her stress was induced by a hostile supervisor who blamed her for everything from a dead cricket on the floor to another store's long-distance phone bill.[115]

STRESS REDUCTION TECHNIQUES

In an effort to reduce their costs, companies have begun implementing stress reduction or control programs for their employees. These programs represent proactive strategies toward stress management and come in a variety of forms, depending on the needs of the employees. Commonly found programs include discussion groups, stress education classes, relaxation techniques, time management programs, physical fitness programs, weight-loss clinics, drug and alcohol rehabilitation clinics, family counseling, hobbies, sports, and goal-setting classes.[116]

Some firms have taken an even more innovative approach. H. J. Heinz Company in Pittsburgh is one of these companies. Overworked and stressed-out employees at Heinz can look forward to a 15-minute massage in the director's lounge. With the lights dimmed and jazz piano music playing softly in the background, Sabina Vidunas, the masseuse, gently kneads the tightly knotted necks and shoulders of fully-dressed employees sitting in a massage chair. A massage chair, a padded easel-looking apparatus, allows employees to lean forward and rest their chest and face on padding, taking the pressure off of their neck and shoulders.[117] The Japanese have taken the idea of a massage one step further and developed the Brain Mind Gym where over-stressed Japanese workers can go for a high-tech mental massage. See the HR Challenge box titled "High-Tech Stress Therapy" for a description of this technological innovation.

Other companies have invested in programs to reduce the source of worker stress. For example, employee fear of quality control slips by overworked or overstressed employees made Boeing step up its training. Before placing its employees on the assembly line, workers at the Everett, Washington, plant take blueprint reading classes and practice riveting and drilling techniques. Boeing also conducts preemployment training for serious job candidates at local vocational and technical schools.[118]

Stress in one's life is virtually unavoidable. For those who are not lucky enough to have a stress reduction program available to them, or for those who are between programs, a few techniques are available to help oneself.

1. List items that cause stress. Isolate the ones you can fix and concentrate your time and effort on them. Avoid the ones that you can do nothing about.
2. We all need to take pride in our accomplishments and receive praise from others. If your job does not provide for these needs, find an activity that does.
3. Experiment with different forms of relaxation, such as exercise, sports, or meditation, until you find one that relieves your anxiety.
4. Remember that a sense of control and a reason to live lead to a healthy and productive life.[119]

STRATEGIES FOR IMPROVING HEALTH AND SAFETY

Managers have the extremely important role of providing a safe and healthy environment for their employees. The opportunities available for doing this have become more and more varied over time. Two of the most important strategic choices regarding health programs currently are fitness, drug testing, and rehabilitation plans.

FITNESS PROGRAMS

The number of health and fitness programs sponsored by corporations has increased over the past few years and continues to climb. A 1986 survey of the 1,500 largest firms in the United States found that more than 32 percent had established health-promotion policies and objectives. Over 40 percent offered or paid for programs to help workers quit smoking, nearly 40 percent sponsored stress management courses, 27 percent provided back care programs, and more than 28 percent provided physical fitness centers either on or off the premises.[120]

Perhaps one reason for these increases is the fact that health promotion has proven to be a cost-effective organizational strategy. Each dollar invested in workplace health education can yield $1.42 over two years in lower absentee costs. Some companies have reported absences from illness dropping by as much as 15 percent.[121] Other studies have found that the difference in the productivity of participants and nonparticipants in organization-sponsored health programs was valued at over $1 million.[122]

The key to building an effective organization fitness program is to follow some basic rules. First, employees must see something in it for themselves or their family. If employees see it as just another cost-cutting ploy, they will not be responsive to it. To make it appeal to employees, a firm should offer incentives and rewards. Second, it must appeal to all employees and so should be varied and fun. Ask employees what they want. Finally, do not have a workplace environment that contradicts the firm's goals. Some examples of fitness programs include banning smoking in the workplace, providing nutritional meal alternatives in the cafeteria, and sponsoring fun runs rather than bake sales.[123]

Companies that have followed these guidelines have reported great success. One of the most impressive was introduced by Mesa Limited Partnership, a holding company in Amarillo, Texas, headed by T. Boone Pickens. The first phase of the program is a computerized health-risk appraisal. All participants are eligible to receive up to $240 annually for participating. They must complete a written test and submit to a glucose, cholesterol, and blood pressure screening. Results from these tests are used in phase 2: goal setting for weight loss or weight control, strength improvement, and general health maintenance. To get employees to participate in phase 2, monetary incentives provide up to $916 a year per employee for participating. For example, an employee may receive $36 for exercising three times a week and an additional $216 if a spouse participates. In total, Mesa has paid $115,000 in bonuses to employees but has more than earned it back in lower health-care costs. Mesa estimates that the health-care costs for employees who did not participate averaged $434 per person as compared to only $173 for participants. The differences in these figures equates to about a $200,000 a year savings companywide.[124]

DRUG TESTING AND REHABILITATION

One area of employee safety and health that continues to evolve is drug testing. Estimates from various government and task force groups indicate that substance (drugs, alcohol) abusers make up from 8 to 17 percent of our workforce. Absenteeism rates for these workers are 16 times greater than for other workers. In addition, substance abusers have been shown to file five times as many workers' compensation claims as nonabusers. However, drug testing remains a controversial issue in the workplace.[125] In 1988, President Reagan issued Executive Order 12564 establishing a drug-free workplace in the federal government. This order established a drug testing program for federal workers. Also in 1988, Congress passed the Drug Free Workplace Act to abolish drug use among employees within an organization that works directly with the federal government.[126]

The Drug Free Workplace Act states that employers must notify their employees of drug-free workplace requirements, outline actions that will be taken against those who violate the requirements, and establish awareness programs that include supervisory staff training in identifying drug abuse.[127] However, as organizations begin to implement these requirements, they must not violate the rights guaranteed their employees under the Fourth Amendment, specifically, the right to be free of illegal search and seizures.

Although only contractors that are awarded government contracts over $25,000 are required to comply with the act, many other businesses have begun implementing drug testing programs. Exhibit 14.7 outlines the industries in which drug testing is prevalent.

EXHIBIT 14.7   **Industries in Which Drug Testing Is Used**

Mining	72.0	12.7
Construction	326.6	11.9
Durable goods manufacturing	767.6	11.2
Nondurable goods manufacturing	1106.5	12.7
Transportation	451.8	9.9
Communications, utilities	143.5	5.5
Wholesale trade	260.5	17.4
Retail trade	169.7	24.4
Finance, insurance, and real estate	308.4	6.7
Other services	306.2	9.9
Total	3913.7	11.9

SOURCE: Adapted from *The Wall Street Journal,* © 1989 Dow Jones & Company, Inc.

A survey by the American Management Association found that 63 percent of the firms surveyed use drug testing. This figure represents an increase from 51.5 percent reported in a survey the previous year. A 1993 survey of drug testing in the workplace revealed that the percentage of organizations using drug testing increased to 84%.[128] Moreover, the same survey indicated that the number of job applicants testing positive for drug use decreased.

One would expect employees to hold a negative view concerning drug testing in the workplace, but at least one survey has found the opposite to be true. An attitude survey of the Anchorage Telephone Utility indicated that employees actually held a more favorable view than expected. Employees indicated that although they felt drug testing was an invasion of their privacy, they did not feel that it was unreasonable. However, they also indicated that all levels in the organization should be required to participate if a drug testing program is enforced.[129]

A recent example of successful drug testing programs involves Motorola Inc. which has implemented a random and universal program with the ultimate goal of improving customer service and productivity.[130] Implementation of the program was not easy. Motorola incurred extensive first year costs of nearly $1.5 million and the program was met with some employee resistance.[131] However, Motorola has seen a decrease in positive drug tests among employees to a low of about 1 percent. Other benefits derived from a successful drug testing program include increased productivity and lower absenteeism. Other companies have reported similar successes. For example, Burlington Northern reduced the rate of employees testing positive for drug use to only .5 percent of the total workforce and has substantially lowered insurance claims costs since the implementation of its drug testing program.[132]

Other people hold a less favorable view of drug testing, especially if it is used as a deterrent for use. Ray Richardson, who held a $3 million contract with the New Jersey Nets, was informed that he would be banished from the National Basketball Association if he tested positive for drugs once more. In 1986, Richardson tested positive once more and was expelled from the NBA. His agent at the time, who went on to become the director of the NBA, indicated that he began to doubt the deterrent power of drug testing in the NBA if a person can say yes to drugs and no to $3 million dollars.[133] The legal aspects of drug testing in the workplace are complicated, especially with regard to the provisions of the Americans with Disabilities Act, which provides protection from discrimination for recovering substance abusers.[134] Before a company engages in any type of drug testing, it must make sure that the testing complies with state and federal laws and guidelines.

One positive outcome of the drug testing issue is the continued development of employee assistance programs (EAPs) to help employees who are found to be using drugs. One of the requirements of the Drug Free Workplace Act is that employees who are convicted of drug usage must be required to satisfactorily complete a rehabilitation program. Many organizations pay for or offer these programs to their employees because firms are finding that EAPs may be more helpful in curbing drug abuse than drug testing.[135]

Company-sponsored EAPs are designed to help employees whose personal problems have an adverse impact on their job performance. These programs may be administered in-house or through outside organizations. EAPs can be designed to help employees with a variety of personal problems, ranging from alcohol and drug abuse to marital problems, financial concerns, and stress.[136] EAPs have been found to save employers $17 for every $1 spent on the program.[137]

These programs are generally designed to help employees, but the employers are helped as well. Early intervention in chemical dependency can save the organization a great deal. Medical care utilization by a drug-using employee can be cut by up to 69 percent, sick days can be reduced by 47 percent, and accident benefits can be reduced by as much as 48 percent if the drug abuse is caught early enough. Alcohol rehabilitation has a better success rate than drug abuse. If one defines success as not having a drink one year after treatment, 40 to 50 percent of those who complete the program would be deemed successful. One way to help the employee ensure a successful recovery is to require follow-up treatment after the initial rehabilitation. IBM requires employees who have completed a drug rehabilitation program to participate in medical monitoring for a minimum of one year as a way to increase their chances of remaining drug free. If they relapse, IBM may terminate them or, if they appear to have a sincere interest in seeking immediate help, they may be retained.[138]

On the surface, EAPs appear to be a win-win solution to a severe problem. They are a cost-effective way for organizations to provide help for employees who really need it. However, the effectiveness of EAPs as a drug intervention are described as only "fairly effective." Research has found that 26.1 percent of the programs rated were only fairly effective, 37 percent were rated as having limited effectiveness, 10.7 percent were rated as not very effective, 17.7 percent had an uncertain rating, and only 8.4 percent had a very effective rating.[139]

Whether or not a program is deemed successful depends on the definition of *success.* Overall, drug rehabilitation success has not been high. Some firms believe that they are very successful if they can keep 20 to 30 percent of their members off drugs.

THE COST OF INSURANCE FOR SMALL AND LARGE BUSINESSES

Health-care insurance has become a nightmare for thousands of small businesses due to soaring premiums. One manager of a welding firm with eight employees was forced to drop the insurance plan for employees when the insurance company raised the premium by 214 percent. Other small businesses are faced with the same problem. One manager was required to pay $105 a month to insure a worker who was paid $5 an hour. The $105 coverage did not include maternity coverage or office visits and required a $500 deductible. Prices like these have caused the number of uninsured workers in companies of less than 25 employees to increase from 23 percent to 24.4 percent in just one year. While the percentage increase may seem small, the actual number of employees who lost their insurance coverage may be as high as 1 million.[140]

While Congress continues to debate the appropriate make-up of health-care legislation, small businesses can take several steps to reduce their insurance costs. First, companies can become involved in insurance pools designed specifically for small businesses. Some states (for example, Connecticut, Maine, Florida, and New Jersey) are creating insurance pools for small companies. This will provide lower premiums for participating firms because the monetary foundation is larger and the risk of an expensive claim is reduced. Some large insurance companies are also providing small-group risk pools designed to cover small business insurance needs. However, to qualify, four low-risk employees must be enrolled for every one high-risk employee.[141]

Another alternative is called *partnering;* it involves direct contracting with health-care providers. The major building blocks of partnering include long-term exclusive contracts between employers and health-care providers, promoting a healthy workplace through maintenance and wellness programs, sharing risks and rewards among the providers, employers, and employees, and communicating among all participants. This alternative is available to small businesses that ban together to form coalitions.[142]

Concerns about health care may be settled, in part, with the passage of a national health-care bill, which is expected to entail increased costs in the form of management expenses for businesses. Certainly, human resource professionals need to become more involved in the employee health-care process. A more detailed knowledge of the benefits and costs of various alternatives provides more strategic choices concerning the long-term health and well-being of employees.

MANAGEMENT GUIDELINES

The following guidelines represent many of the important elements that organizations need to include as part of an effective health and safety program. Management must give employee safety and well-being serious consideration and ensure that these issues never be neglected or ignored. An effective health and safety program can help ensure that the strategic plan, goals, and objectives of the company are realized.

1. Employee health and safety programs should be a major priority for management because they save lives, increase productivity, and reduce costs. These health and safety programs should stress employee involvement, continued monitoring, and an overall wellness component.
2. Jobs that employees currently perform should be examined in an effort to locate the ones that may present a potential health or safety problem for employees. Steps should be taken to eliminate these problems.
3. It is important to be aware of the health risks that production may cause workers. All sources of workplace chemicals or of other health concerns should be recorded and all employees be made aware of these records.
4. Safe-handling procedures for harmful substances should be developed and employees should be trained in these procedures.
5. Employee assistance programs should be developed to help employees deal with emotional, physical, or other problems caused by their employment.

Continued

6. Jobs should be analyzed for potential sources of stress and redesigned to eliminate these pressures.
7. Employers should strive to meet and surpass the health and safety guidelines imposed by OSHA. Frequent and continual updating of procedures may be necessary to remain in compliance.
8. A firm that decides to offer a fitness or wellness program to employees should be sure that it is something they will want to use and should make it easy for them to participate. Offering incentives to participate may also be useful.
9. AIDS informational campaigns in an organization should focus on reducing the workers' fear about AIDS by educating them about the disease.
10. As court decisions continue to change and redefine the rules in the workplace, it is imperative that human resource managers be up to date with respect to the rules and regulations governing their industry. Providing educational incentives for these managers will help them achieve this goal.

QUESTIONS FOR REVIEW

1. When and why was the Occupational Safety and Health Act passed? Describe some of the provisions of this act.
2. What are two of the current safety and health problems facing U.S. businesses today?
3. If asked to design an employee health and safety program that would help to eliminate accidents in the workplace, what would your plan include?
4. What is the relationship between job stress and productivity?
5. How can employers reduce job stress?
6. What are some techniques that employers can use to ensure that employees participate in fitness or wellness programs?

7. Why is it important for organizations to provide informational programs about AIDS?
8. Fetal protection policies have almost always been directed at female workers. Why is this? Why is it not important to protect potential fathers from chemicals that may harm their potential children?
9. What are some of the tips managers should be aware of when developing safety programs that work?
10. If an organization makes a strategic decision to stress employee health and well-being, what are some of the potential advantages of adopting this strategy?

CASE

SAFETY IN THE WORKPLACE— WHOSE RESPONSIBILITY?[143]

"**O**n this site, 146 workers lost their lives in the Triangle Shirtwaist Co. fire on March 26, 1911. Out of their martyrdom came new concepts of social responsibility and labor legislation that have helped make American working conditions the finest in the world."

This quotation appears on a plaque commemorating the 146 people who died in the fires at Triangle Shirtwaist Company. The majority of those who died were low-paid young women who were trapped inside the building. Management at Triangle routinely kept doors locked to prevent employees from stealing. Although Triangle had four major fires in the

nine years prior to the 1911 blaze, they failed to prepare their workers for just such a crisis (for example, no fire drills were conducted).

The Triangle fire was a landmark incident that led to legislation requiring companies to install sprinkler systems, have wider exits, unlock doors, and conduct regular fire drills. This incident, along with other workplace accidents, focused attention on the need for employers to provide a safe and healthful work environment for their workers and eventually led to the creation of the Occupational Safety and Health Administration (OSHA).

However, a recent accident has called into question the effectiveness of health and safety regulations in the workplace. Despite efforts to improve working conditions, has significant improvement been made over the last 80 years?

FIRE AT IMPERIAL FOOD PRODUCTS PLANT

September 3, 1991, started out as a typical work day for workers at the Imperial Foods Products plant in Hamlet, North Carolina. Workers arrived to work on Tuesday morning and began preparing for the day. No one had any reason to suspect that this day would be any different from any other. At 8:30 A.M., however, an event took place that would change the lives of each and every worker at Imperial; a fryer at Imperial's chicken-processing plant caught fire, leaving 25 workers dead, over 40 injured, and countless grieving. Although workers were heard banging on doors screaming "Let me out!" witnesses outside were unable to open the locked doors. Just as at Triangle, management at the Imperial plant also routinely kept doors locked to prevent employees from stealing. In addition to locked doors, one of the exits was blocked by a delivery truck, and workers had to wait for it to be moved.

SAFETY IN THE WORKPLACE

With the exception of those who work under extremely hazardous conditions, most of us rarely think about safety in the workplace. We assume that the company will provide a safe environment and that officials at OSHA will ensure that the company is not in violation of safety regulations. Unfortunate and tragic accidents at the workplace, however, remind us that this idealistic situation is not always in accord with the realistic situation.

In 1970, OSHA began requiring employers to keep exit doors clear so they can serve as escape hatches. Why, then, was Imperial placing its employees at risk by keeping exits locked on a continual basis in an environment where fires have posed a threat in the past? Similar to Triangle, Imperial had had three fires in the previous 11 years, and it also did nothing to prepare workers for such a crisis, such as conducting fire drills. Federal laws allow states to set up their own regulatory agencies, and although OSHA is responsible for monitoring these state programs, they rarely enforce safety regulations in the 23 states that currently have their own programs.

STATE PROGRAMS

North Carolina is among the 23 states responsible for performing their own inspections and fining those in violation. Imperial Foods, however, had never been inspected in its 11 years of operation, which is not surprising considering that North Carolina's state legislature has cut the safety budget by 40 percent over the last decade. North Carolina has only 27 inspectors and trainees to patrol over 180,000 employers.

Whereas not every state program is so lax in enforcment, many have been less than rigorous in their effort to protect workers on the job. It is often the business community itself that pushes for state-run programs in an effort to "keep the monkey off their backs" and to reduce costly fines that may be imposed on them by the federal government. North Carolina, for example, fined Perdue Farms, another poultry-processing plant, $39,000 for exposing workers to repetitive motion injuries in two plants; in contrast, Cargill, Inc., was fined $1 million by OSHA for similar violations at plants in Georgia and Missouri. This is an indication of why companies may prefer to be out from under OSHA's thumb and why they may prefer to keep the control at the state level.

WHAT NOW?

The incident in North Carolina has prompted renewed interest in health and safety in the workplace. Under the Clinton Administration, OSHA's enforcement policy has never been more clear. OSHA intends to use high-cost, high-profile litigation against employers to "encourage" compliance with the law. Although state-run OSHA programs were intended to be as strict or more strict than the federally run OSHA programs, this had not been the case during the 1980s and early 1990s. All state-run OSHA programs are under the federal government and the cost of not following federal guidelines at this time is extremely high.

OSHA fines and the number of penalties assessed are likely to increase and any employer violating OSHA standards could be criminally prosecuted and fined up to $10,000. In fact, fines amounting to $30 million in 1990 are estimated to grow to up to $180 million per year. Although any new legislation will not make restitution for those who lost their lives in the fires at both Triangle and Imperial, it may serve to prevent similar accidents from occurring in the future.

An important footnote to this case came on Monday, March 9, 1992, when three management officials of the Imperial Foods plant were indicted on charges of involuntary manslaughter. Families of those killed in the fire filed criminal charges against the managers who allowed the safety violations to occur. Imperial Food Products' owner Emmett Roe was sentenced to 19 years 11 months in jail. Roe plea bargained so that his son and the plant's operations manager did not serve any jail time. This development raises the costs of willfully violating safety standards to a new level.

QUESTIONS

1. How true is the opening quotation in this case today, given all of the workplace hazards discussed in this chapter? What can be done at any and all levels to make this quotation true?

2. Would a state inspection of the Imperial Foods plant have prevented this accident? Why or why not? What could have been done to prevent it?

3. The case mentions fines imposed by OSHA and the state for exposing workers to CTD. Do you think the differences in the size of the fines caused the companies to react differently to them? Why or why not?

4. How appropriate do you think it is for states to have control over the safety of the workplace? Devise a state plan that would allow for effective policing of workplace safety. Why hasn't your plan been implemented?

ADDITIONAL READINGS

Backer, T. E. *Strategic Planning for Workplace Drug-Abuse Programs.* Rockville, MD: National Institute on Drug Abuse, 1987.

Baker, T. L. "Preventing Drug Abuse at Work." *Personnel Administrator.* July 1989, pp. 56–59.

Cooper, C. L., and R. Payne. *Causes, Coping and Consequences of Stress at Work.* Somerset, NJ: John Wiley & Sons, 1988.

———, and M. Smith. *Job Stress and Blue Collar Work.* Somerset, NJ: John Wiley & Sons, 1986.

Cox, W. N. *Employee Relations, Occupational Safety and Health, and Product Liability: A Handbook for Business.* Holland, MI: CR & Associates, 1988.

DeCarlo, D. T., and D. H. Gruenfeld. *Stress in the American Workplace—Alternatives for the Working Wounded.* Washington, PA: LRP Publications, 1989.

DeCresce, R. P., M. S. Lifshitz, A. C. Mazura, and J. E. Tilson. *Drug Testing in the Workplace.* Chicago, IL: ASCAP Press, 1989.

Denenberg, T. S., and R. V. Denenberg. *Alcohol and Drugs: Issues in the Workplace.* Washington, DC: BNA, 1983.

Fassel, D. *Working Ourselves to Death: The High Cost of Workaholism and the Rewards of Recovery.* San Francisco: Harper, 1990.

Frances, R. J., and J. E. Franklin. *Concise Guide to Treatment of Alcoholism and Addictions.* American Psychiatric Press, Inc., 1989.

Garrett, J., L. Cralley, and L. Cralley. *Industrial Hygiene Management.* Somerset, NJ: John Wiley & Sons, 1988.

Golembiewski, R. T., and R. F. Munzenrider. *Phases of Burnout: Developments in the Concepts and Applications.* New York: Praeger Press, 1988.

Hartstein, B. A. "Drug Testing in the Workplace: A Primer for Employers." *Employee Relations Law Journal,* Spring 1987.

Klarreich, S. H. *Health and Fitness in the Workplace: Health Education in Business Organizations.* New York: Praeger Press, 1987.

Kupfer, A. "Is Drug Testing Good or Bad?" *Fortune,* December 1988, pp. 133–140.

Miletich, J. J. *Work and Alcohol Abuse: An Annotated Bibliography.* Westport, CT: Greenwood Press, 1987.

Mintz, B. M. *OSHA: History, Law, and Policy.* Washington, DC: BNA, 1984.

Murphy, L. R., and T. F. Schoenborn. *Stress Management in Work Settings.* New York: Praeger Publishers, 1989.

Nogay, B. *The New Drug-free Workplace Act: The Complete Guide for Federal Contractors and Grantees.* Washington, DC: BNA, 1989.

Pritchard, R. E., and G. C. Potter. *Fitness Inc: A Guide to Corporate Health and Wellness Programs.* Homewood, IL: Dow Jones-Irwin Books, 1990.

Quick, J. C., R. S. Bhagat, J. E. Dalton, and J. D. Quick. *Work Stress: Health Care Systems in the Workplace.* New York: Praeger Publishers, 1987.

Riley, A. W., and S. J. Zaccaro. *Occupational Stress and Organizational Effectiveness.* New York: Praeger Press, 1987.

Rumpel, D. A. "Motivating Alcoholic Workers to Seek Help." *Management Review,* July 1989, pp. 37–39.

Salvendy, G. *Handbook of Human Factors.* Somerset, NJ: John Wiley & Sons, 1987.

Segal, J. A. "How Reasonable Is Your Suspicion?" *Personnel Administrator,* December 1989, pp. 103–104.

Sethi, A. S., D. Caro, and R. S. Schuler. *Strategic Management of Technostress in an Information Society.* Lewiston, NY: Hogrefe & Huber Publishers, 1987.

Sloan, R. P., J. C. Gruman, and J. P. Allegrante. *Investing in Employee Health: A Guide to Effective Health Promotion in the Workplace.* San Francisco: Jossey-Bass, 1987.

Slothe, L. *Handbook of Occupational Safety and Health.* Somerset, NJ: John Wiley & Sons.

Smith, C. C. *Recovery at Work: A Clean and Sober Career Guide.* San Francisco: Harper Collins Publishers, 1990.

Smits, S. J., L. D. Pace, and W. J. Perryman. "EAPs Are Big Business," *Personnel Journal,* June 1989, pp. 96–106.

Speller, J. L. *Executives in Crisis: Recognizing and Managing the Alcoholic, Drug-Addicted, or Mentally Ill Executive.* San Francisco: Jossey-Bass, 1989.

Timmins, W. M., and C. B. Timmins. *Smoking in the Workplace: Issues and Answers for Human Resource Professional.* Westport, CT: Greenwood Press, 1989.

Wadden, R. A., and P. A. Scheff. *Indoor Air Pollution: Characterization, Prediction, and Control.* Somerset, NJ: John Wiley & Sons, 1982.

Withers, J. *Major Industrial Hazards: Their Appraisal and Control.* Somerset, NJ: John Wiley & Sons, 1988.

NOTES

1. Stanley Kalin, "The Ubiquitous Nip Point: The Booby Trap of Industry," *Experts-at-Law,* September–October 1990, pp. 39–42.

2. S. A. Joure et al., "Stress: The Pressure Cooker of Work," *Personnel Administrator,* March 1989, pp. 92–95.

3. "Labor Letter," *The Wall Street Journal,* April 14, 1987, p. 1; K. Shinew and J. Crossly, "A Comparison of Employee Recreation and Fitness Program Benefits," *Employee Benefit Journal* 4, 1988, pp. 20–23; T. Callahan, "Adolph Coors Company," *Company Fitness and Recreation* 5(4), 1986, pp. 11–12; J. Hoffman and C. Hobson, "Physical Fitness and Employee Effectiveness," *Personnel Administrator* 29(4), 1986, pp. 101–114; and J. Jenkins, "Self-directed Work Force Promote Safety," *HRMagazine* 2, 1990, pp. 54–56.

4. "Contractor Sentenced under OSHA after Two Die," *American Society for Personnel Administration/Resource,* February 1989, p. 15; see also B. D. Platt, "Negligent Retention and Hiring in Florida: Safety of Customers versus Security of Employers," *Florida State University Law Review,* 1993, pp. 697–716.

5. C. Ansberry, "Nucor Steel's Sheen is Marred by Deaths of Workers at Plants," *The Wall Street Journal,* May 10, 1991, pp. A1 +.

6. The following discussion is based on D. P. Twomey, *A Concise Guide to Employment Law EEO & OSHA* (Cincinnati: South-Western, 1986), pp. 109–134.

7. S. B. Garland, "A New Chief Has OSHA Growling Again," *Business Week,* August 20, 1990, p. 57.

8. Ibid.

9. B. Bowers, "OSHA to Mix a Little Mercy with Latest Crackdown," *The Wall Street Journal,* February 1, 1994, p. B2.

10. A. D. Marcus, "Employers Can Face Charges for Endangering Workers," *The Wall Street Journal,* October 17, 1990, p. B5.

11. S. Wermiel, "Justices Let States Prosecute Executives for Work Site Hazards Covered by OSHA, *The Wall Street Journal,* October 3, 1989, p. A5.

12. S. B. Garland, "This Safety Ruling Could Be Hazardous to Employers' Health," *Business Week,* February 20, 1989, p. 34.

13. "Contractor Sentenced Under OSHA after Two Die," p. 20.

14. A. R. Karr, D. D. Medina, and C. Solomon, "OSHA Seeks to Fine Phillips Petroleum $5.7 Million for 'Willful' Safety Breaches," *The Wall Street Journal,* April 20, 1990, p. A4.

15. M. R. Losey, "Comprehensive Occupational Safety and Health Reform Act," *Society for Human Resource Management Memorandum,* March 10, 1994.

16. Ibid.

17. Ibid.

18. "Study Finds Unions Affect OSHA Enforcement," *Society for Human Resource Management/HRNews/Legal Report,* March 1991, p. A11.

19. W. Goldsmith, "Preparing for and Managing an OSHA Inspection," *Society for Human Resource Management/HRNews/Legal Report,* Summer 1994, pp. 1–4.

20. S. Cohen, "Pain with the Paycheck," *Tallahassee Democrat,* November 12, 1989, pp. D1 +.

21. E. Scalia, "OSHA to Business: Slow Down, You Work Too Fast," *The Wall Street Journal,* January 13, 1994, p. A18.

22. E. Felsenthal, "Out of Hand," *The Wall Street Journal,* July 14, 1994, pp. A1 +.

23. "Safety Measures for Users of Computers," *HRMagazine,* July 1991, pp. 77–78.

24. D. Huntly, "Key Injuries Hurt Companies," *HRMagazine,* June 1990, pp. 72–75.

25. S. Overman and L. Thornburg, "Hidden Health Care Costs," *HRMagazine,* March 1992, pp. 48–53.

26. A. Gabor, "On-the-Job Straining," *U.S. News & World Report,* May 21, 1990, pp. 51–53.

27. M. Mallory, "An Invisible Workplace Hazard Gets Harder to Ignore," *Business Week,* January 30, 1989, pp. 92–93.

28. J. S. Hirsch, "U.S. Diet Mixes Indulgence, Health," *The Wall Street Journal,* December 6, 1989, p. B1.

29. Gabor, "On-the-Job Straining," p. 51.

30. "OSHA Hits John Morrell & Co. with Record $4.33 Million Fine," *American Society for Personnel Administration/Resource/Legal Report,* December 1988, p. 16.

31. Gabor, "On-the-Job Straining," p. 51.

32. M. Lotito and F. Alvarez, "Integrate Claims Management with ADA Compliance Strategy," *HRMagazine,* August 1993, pp. 86–92.

33. M. Fefer, "Taking Control of Your Workers' Comp Costs," *Fortune,* October 3, 1994, pp. 131–136.

34. A. R. Karr, "Chrysler, UAW Agree to Fight Motion Injuries," *The Wall Street Journal,* November 3, 1989, p. A4.

35. "Meatpacker Launches Model Safety Program," *The Miami Herald,* November 24, 1988, p. 22A.

36. R. F. Bettendorf, "Curing the New Ills of Technology," *HRMagazine,* March 1990, p. 35.

37. C. Conte, "Fighting Technostress," *The Wall Street Journal,* May 4, 1993, p. A1.

38. S. L. Jacob, "Small Business Slowly Wakes to OSHA Hazard Rule," *The Wall Street Journal,* November 22, 1988, p. B2.

39. Ibid.

40. "OSHA Issues Hazard Compliance Kit," *American Society for Personnel Administration/Resource/Legal Report,* February 1989, p. 20.

41. Ibid.

42. A. D. Marcus, "In Some Workplaces, Ill Winds Blow," *The Wall Street Journal,* October 9, 1989, p. B1.

43. Ibid.

44. Ibid.

45. R. M. Yandrick, "Smoking in the Workplace: More Employers Prohibit Smoking," *HRMagazine,* July 1994, pp. 68–71.

46. "Smoking Employees Post Cost Risks," *Communications,* September–October 1990, p. 1.

47. C. Pasternak, "High-cost Habit," *HRMagazine,* October 1990, p. 23.

48. S. Overman, "New EPA Study," *HRMagazine,* February 1993, p. 73.

49. J. S. Harris, "Clearing the Air," *HRMagazine,* February 1993, pp. 72–79.

50. Overman, "New EPA Study," p. 73.

51. C. Pasternak, "Totally Smoke-free," *HRMagazine,* February 1990, p. 21.

52. R. M. Yandrick, "Smoking in the Workplace: More Employers Prohibit Smoking," *HRMagazine,* July 1994, pp. 68–71; and Harris, "Clearing the Air," pp. 72–79.

53. "It Doesn't Matter Much How You Quit Smoking," *The Wall Street Journal,* November 28, 1989, p. B1.

54. D. Feinstein, "Labor Letter," *The Wall Street Journal,* September 26, 1989, p. A1.

55. The following discussion is based on C. F. Mitchell and P. M. Barrett, "Trial and Error: Novel Effort to Settle Asbestos Claims Fails as Lawsuits Multiply," *The Wall Street Journal,* June 7, 1988, pp. A1 +.

56. Cohen, "Pain with the Paycheck," p. D1.

57. Feinstein, "Labor Letter," p. A1.

58. Ibid.

59. B. Ingersoll, "Perilous Profession: Farming Is Dangerous, but Fatalistic Farmers Oppose Safety Laws," *The Wall Street Journal,* July 20, 1989, pp. A1 +.

60. Ibid.

61. Ibid.

62. G. Feinstein, "Labor Letter," *The Wall Street Journal,* August 8, 1989, p. A1.

63. A. L. Otten, "People Patterns," *The Wall Street Journal,* April 6, 1989, p. B1.

64. C. Ansberry, "Risky Business: Workplace Injuries Proliferate as Concerns Push People to Produce," *The Wall Street Journal,* June 6, 1989, pp. A1 +.

65. Ibid.

66. "LA Takes on Safety and Health Challenge," *ILO Information,* October 1989, p. 2.

67. R. Wokutch, "New Lessons from Japanese Management," *HRMagazine,* September 1994, pp. 72–78.

68. R. P. Hunter, "Workplace Violence: A Growing Trend," *Legal Report for the Society for Human Resource Management,* Summer 1990, p. 1.

69. J. E. Rigdon, "Companies See More Workplace Violence," *The Wall Street Journal,* April 12, 1994, p. B1.

70. D. Harbrecht, "Talk about Murder Inc.," *Business Week,* July 11, 1994, p. 8.

71. L. Thornburg, "When Violence Hits Business," *HRMagazine,* July 1993, pp. 40–45.

72. J. A. Segal, "When Charles Manson Comes to the Workplace," *HRMagazine,* June 1994, pp. 33–40.

73. S. Overman, "Be Prepared Should Be Your Motto," *HRMagazine,* July 1993, pp. 46–49.

74. J. A. Segal, "HIV: How High the Risk?" *HRMagazine,* February 1993, pp. 93–100.

75. T. J. Dilauro, "Relieving the Fear of Contagion," *Personnel Administrator,* February 1989, p. 52.

76. W. F. McHugh, "AIDS in the Workplace: Policy, Practice, and Procedure," *AIDS in the Workplace: Florida and Federal Legal Guidelines 1989,* December 1988, p. 39.

77. J. A. Segal, "AIDS Education Is a Necessary High-Risk Activity," *HRMagazine,* February 1991, p. 82; and V. Alliton, "Financial Realities of AIDS in the Workplace," *HRMagazine,* February 1992, pp. 78–81.

78. Ibid.

79. R. Knotts and J. L. Johnson, "AIDS in the Workplace: The Pandemic Firms Want to Ignore," *Business Horizons,* July–August 1993, pp. 5–9.

80. T. Lassa, "Tuberculosis Threat Returns," *HRMagazine,* June 1994, pp. 86–91.

81. J. Bovard, "Disabilities Law, Health Hazard," *The Wall Street Journal,* March 23, 1994, p. A14.

82. "Fetal Protection Policies," *HRMagazine,* January 1991, pp. 81–82.

83. H. Simon, "Fetal Protection Policies after Johnson Controls: No Easy Answer," *Employee Relations Law Journal* 15, 1990, pp. 491–511.

84. C. Trost, "Busisesses and Women Anxiously Watch Suit on 'Fetal Protection,'" *The Wall Street Journal,* October 8, 1990, pp. A1 +.

85. R. Sand, "Current Developments in Health and Safety," *Employee Relations Law Journal* 16, 1990, pp. 99–106.

86. "Fetal Protection Policies," p. 82.

87. Simon, "Fetal Protection Policies after Johnson Controls," p. 493.

88. "Justices Bar 'Fetal Protection' Policy," *The Wall Street Journal,* March 21, 1991, pp. A1 +.

89. C. Trost, "Labor Letter," *The Wall Street Journal,* October 27, 1992, p. A1.

90. "Fetal Protection Policies," p. 81.

91. "Safety First," *Inc.,* September 1989, p. 114.

92. M. N. Martinez, "Reduce Health Costs with Back-care Programs," *Society for Human Resource Management/HRNews,* September 1991, p. A12.

93. J. Applegate, "Workplaces Play the Safety Game and Win," *Los Angeles Times,* October 14, 1993.

94. "Labor Letter," *The Wall Street Journal,* January 29, 1991, p. A1.

95. J. D. Brodzinski, R. F. Scherer, and K. A. Goyer, "Workplace Stress," *Personnel Administrator,* July 1989, pp. 76–80.

96. Ibid.

97. Ibid.

98. L. Smith, "Burned-Out Bosses," *Fortune,* July 25, 1994, pp. 44–52.

99. T. F. O'Boyle, "Fear and Stress in the Office Take Toll," *The Wall Street Journal,* November 6, 1990, p. B1.

100. R. Winslow, "Workplace Turmoil is Reflected in Depression Among Employees," *The Wall Street Journal,* December 13, 1989, p. B1.

101. R. Waxler and T. Higginson, "Discovering Methods to Reduce Workplace Stress," *Industrial Engineering,* June 1993.

102. "Wrapup," *Washington Report* 13, June 1991, p. 4.

103. "Workplace Stress," *HRMagazine,* August 1991, pp. 75–76.

104. A. R. Karr, "Guilty or Innocent?" *The Wall Street Journal,* May 14, 1991, p. A1.

105. C. Trost, "Men, Too, Wrestle with Career-Family Stress," *The Wall Street Journal,* November 1, 1988, p. B1.

106. Ibid.

107. A. L. Otter, "How Work, Home Stress Affects Working Couples," *The Wall Street Journal,* February 22, 1991, p. B1.

108. S. A. Joure et al., "Stress: The Pressure Cooker of Work," *Personnel Administrator,* March 1989, p. 92.

109. R. Williams, *"The Trusting Heart: Great News about Type A Behavior* (New York: New York Times Books, 1989).

110. R. Sandroff, "Is Your Job Driving You Crazy?" *Psychology Today,* July–August 1989, pp. 41–45.

111. Ibid.

112. A. Bennett, "Is Your Job Making You Sick?" *The Wall Street Journal Reports,* April 22, 1988, p. 1; "Coming to Terms with Stress," *ILO Information,* February 1991, p. 1; M. Snider, "Stress May Be Something to Sneeze About," *USA Today,* August 29, 1991, p. 1A; and R. Winslow, "Study Uncovers New Evidence Linking Strain on the Job and High Blood Pressure," *The Wall Street Journal,* April 11, 1990, p. B4.

113. Waxler and Higginson, "Discovering Methods to Reduce Workplace Stress."

114. Smith, "Burned-Out Bosses."

115. A. Miller et al., "Stress on the Job," *Newsweek,* April 25, 1988, pp. 40–45.

116. G. Smith, "Meditation, the New Balm for Corporate Stress," *Business Week,* May 10, 1993, pp. 86–87.

117. J. S. Hirsch, "Doesn't Everyone Need to be Kneaded Once in a While?" *The Wall Street Journal,* October 17, 1989, p. A23.

118. M. Shao et al., "Trying Times at Boeing," *Business Week,* March 13, 1989, pp. 34–36.

119. D. Robinson, "Stressbusters," *Parade Magazine,* July 22, 1990, pp. 12 +.

120. P. N. Keaton and M. J. Semb, "Shaping Up the Bottom Line," *HRMagazine,* September 1990, pp. 81–86.

121. S. Feinstein, "Health Promotion Brings Dollar-and-Cents Return, a Study Shows," *The Wall Street Journal,* September 18, 1990, p. A1.

122. Keaton and Semb, "Shaping Up the Bottom Line."

123. C. Garzona, "How to Get Employees Behind Your Programs," *Personnel Administrator,* October 1989, pp. 60–62.

124. Keaton and Semb, "Shaping Up the Bottom Line," p. 81.

125. "Drug Testing in the Workplace," *Occutrax,* July–August 1993, p. 1.

126. S. Mazaroff and J. P. Ayres, "Controlling Drug Abuse in the Workplace: The Legal Groundrules," *Human Resources Management Legal Report,* Spring 1989, p. 1.

127. J. Deming, "Drug-free Workplace Is Good Business," *HRMagazine,* April 1990, pp. 61–62.

128. "Fewer People Fail as Workplace Drug Testing Increases," *HR Focus* 70(6), June 1993, p. 24.

129. D. McGlothin and T. Stimson, "Employees Hold Favorable View of Drug Testing," *Society for Human Resource Management/HRNews,* August 1991, p. 14.

130. H. G. DeYoung, "Motorola's Preemptive Strike Against Drug Abuse," *Electronic Business* 48(5), March 1993, pp. 72–74.

131. Ibid.

132. B. Oliver, "Fight Drugs with Knowledge," *Training & Development,* May 1994, pp. 105–109.

133. D. Wessel, "Evidence is Skimpy that Drug Testing Works, but Employers Embrace Practice," *The Wall Street Journal,* September 7, 1989, p. B1.

134. "Drug Testing in the Workplace," p. 1.

135. A. Karr, "Labor Letter," *The Wall Street Journal,* August 21, 1990, p. A1.

136. D. Gold and B. Unger, "Better Pregnancy Benefit Not Discriminating," *Society for Human Resource Management/HRNews,* January 1990, p. 7.

137. Deming, "Drug-free Workplace Is Good Business," p. 62.

138. S. Bergsman, "Help Employees Who Help Themselves," *HRMagazine,* April 1990, p. 48; and J. Castelli, "Employer-Provided Programs Pay Off," *HRMagazine,* April 1990, p. 57.

139. C. Pasternak, "HRM Update," *HRMagazine,* August 1990, p. 24.

140. A. Bernstein, "Small Companies Are in Big Pain Over Health Care," *Business Week,* November 26, 1990, pp. 187–190.

141. Ibid.

142. C. F. Hendricks and G. L. McManis, "Partnering for Employee Health Care," *Personnel Administrator,* November 1989, pp. 32–37.

143. Bill Bishop, "Those Who Died in the Plant Fire Are Waiting for Justice," *Tallahassee Democrat,* September 15, 1991, p. 3B; S. B. Garland, "What a Way to Watch Out for Workers," *Business Week,* September 23, 1991, p. 42; "Three Indicted in Plant Fire," *Tallahassee Democrat,* March 10, 1992, p. 3A; J. E. Roughton, "The OSHA Man Cometh," *Security Management* 39(2), February 1995, pp. 41–46; and "Price of Neglect," *Time,* September 28, 1992, p. 24.

CHAPTER 15

ETHICS, EMPLOYEE RIGHTS, AND EMPLOYER RESPONSIBILITIES

Ethical behavior, employee rights, and employer responsibilities are dynamic segments of the human resource management field. Important related issues are constantly developing, and new issues emerge with startling frequency. Organizations that do not pay attention to the latest developments in the ethics-rights-responsibility field are likely to face large lawsuits and many forms of hostile actions from both employees and the government. We examine these and a number of other related issues in this chapter, including discrimination, employment at will, privacy, and due process, to name only a few.

CHAPTER OBJECTIVES

After studying this chapter, you should be able to
1. Describe the strategic choices managers face with respect to ethical considerations, employee rights, and employer responsibilities.
2. Be familiar with the laws pertaining to employee rights.
3. Understand the ethical and legal responsibilities of employers to both their employees and the community at large.
4. Discuss the way to manage a problem employee.
5. Delineate the characteristics of a good disciplinary climate.

I BELIEVE IN THE SECOND COMING OF CHRIST AND OTHER TEST QUESTIONS[1]

How would you feel if you were asked the following true/false questions as part of a job application test?

- I am very strongly attracted to members of my own sex.
- I believe in the second coming of Christ.
- I have no difficulty starting or holding my urine.

These questions are part of an ongoing battle over employee rights and the employer's need to know. They are just some of the over 700 questions that are part of a test routinely used by many organizations in the hiring process. The test helps evaluate an individual's personality characteristics, including honesty, motivation, and ambition. Sibi Soroka had to answer these questions as a candidate for a job as security guard with Minneapolis-based Target Stores. Soroka got the job but believed that these questions were too intrusive of his private life and did not reflect his qualifications as a security guard. Target countered that the test was necessary to screen applicants for sensitive positions that may involve theft from the company. Sibi Soroka, as well as other plaintiffs, alleged that Target Stores violated his right to privacy. Target reached a settlement of a class-action lawsuit in 1991. Target said it chose to settle the four-year-old case in order to avoid prolonged, costly litigation, and that the settlement was in the best interest of all parties. The company stopped using the tests in 1991 to comply with the Americans with Disabilities Act (ADA), which was also a factor in Target's decision to settle the case.

The controversy over personality testing is part of a larger battle emerging over an employer's right to test current and potential employees. Testing can take many forms, including personality tests, polygraph tests, drug tests, and even genetic tests. On a broader scale, the issue includes the employer's ability to obtain and use other kinds of supposedly confidential employee information such as medical records and credit histories. At stake is the very question of an employee's privacy and an employer's need to know about its employees.

In recent years, organizations have come under increasing pressure to hire employees with escalating amounts of scrutiny. Organizations that hire carelessly or those exhibiting negligent hiring practices are often the targets of massive lawsuits when their employees make errors or commit crimes. Examples include the possibility that Federal Express might be judged liable for an employee who stole merchandise from a client's store if it cannot prove that it was not negligent in the hiring process and the wave of lawsuits filed against Northwest Airlines after two of its pilots were found guilty of flying drunk. To avoid these legal problems, many organizations have begun to test extensively both current and potential employees. But which tests are legal and which are not?

POLYGRAPH TESTS

Polygraph machines were once one of the most commonly used devices for determining employee honesty and truthfulness regarding specific events. It is estimated that approximately 2,000,000 such tests were given in 1987. Of these,

1.3 million were given to job applicants while another 500,000 were given to current employees. Experts guess that 30 percent of America's Fortune 500 firms used polygraph testing.

In general, polygraph tests measure changes in a subject's physiological reactions (through a series of electrodes) as the subject answers a set of questions. Certain kinds of changes indicate that the subject was experiencing stress and possibly lying. Despite its widespread use, it was generally believed to be unreliable in determining whether the subject was telling the truth or a lie. Subjects' individual physiological characteristics and testing conducted by improperly trained examiners all complicated the test's reliability. In addition, many organizations tended to place too much emphasis in the test results without taking into account other circumstances or evidence. All of these factors proved to be insurmountable. Congress and President Reagan outlawed the use of polygraph tests by organizations by passing and signing, respectively, the Employee Polygraph Protection Act of 1988.

PERSONALITY TESTS

Organizations have long used personality tests, and these are being more widely used since polygraphs have been outlawed. Popular tests include the Minnesota Multiphasic Personality Inventory (MMPI), the California Personality Inventory (CPI), and the Inwald Personality Inventory (IPI). In addition to some of the issues related above, personality tests can be used to determine whether a person is introverted or extroverted or self-driven or other-directed and has a host of other personality traits.

Many components of these tests are widely accepted. For example, it is generally agreed that an organization has the right to know whether an applicant for a sales position is introverted or extroverted. The problems arising with these tests stem from some of their predictive components and their probing into what many contend are private areas that are not job related, such as requests for information like that encountered by Sibi Soroka.

Many of these tests were designed for specific purposes but are administered in a wide variety of situations. Like the problems with polygraph testing, the tests often are administered by untrained professionals. As Sibi Soroka's case illustrates, a long line of court cases and government legislation is likely to occur before the hows, whens, and whys of personality testing are resolved.

Changes in employment laws complicate possible resolutions even further. In 1992, the Americans with Disabilities Act (ADA) became law with the aim of protecting disabled individuals from unfair employment practices. In particular, the ADA strictly set forth provisions regarding the use of medical examinations in the hiring process in that a medical examination can be given after a job offer has been extended to an individual but not as an employment screening device. Questions arose among employers about whether or not personality tests were considered a medical examination and, therefore, covered under the ADA provisions. To clarify the ADA, the Equal Employment Opportunity Commission (EEOC) recently published some guidelines stating that personality tests were not considered part of the ADA's definition of medical examinations and therefore could be used at any time during the employment process.

FINANCIAL DATA AND MEDICAL HISTORY OR TESTING

The increasing use of personal credit and medical histories in the hiring process is also a hotly debated subject. This issue includes the right of organizations to demand that potential employees undergo various medical tests, such as the AIDS test, as a condition of employment. Although this information is supposedly confidential, technology has given organizations the ability to gather much of this information. Some concerns that arise given this new technology are test accuracy and the need for employers to know whether an employee has AIDS. The blood test for HIV AIDS is not perfect and shows the existence of the virus, but not whether the AIDS condition is present.[2] Most states have some provision regarding AIDS testing as part of the employment process, either prohibiting testing altogether or allowing tests only when an individual consents to a test.

Two large issues are emerging here. The first is strictly a question of access. Does your future boss have the right to know that your mother had leukemia or that your aunt has a history of chronic depression? Does he or she have the right to demand that you undergo genetic testing? Or how about knowing that you missed a Visa payment in March 1995?

In general, it is important to remember that if a question is illegal in an interview, then surreptitiously obtaining the information is not permitted. However, under some circumstances, an employer would be negligent in missing certain elements of a background check. When it comes to inquiries regarding more complicated issues than simple legal background checks, we enter a new and perhaps dangerous area. For example, genetic traits can also be assessed in some medical testing procedures, and the Congressional Office of Technology Assessment recently indicated that issues of fairness and reliability must be dealt with in genetic testing. If tests are not used and analyzed properly, misleading conclusions can be drawn about a person's susceptibility to certain diseases or environmental exposure. The privacy of the individual and the extent to which employers and society need to know medical and financial histories are still critical issues in the employment process.

Organizations assert that this information is vital for several reasons. First, they argue that the skyrocketing cost of medical coverage makes it necessary for them to know an employee's complete medical history before that person is hired. In many instances, organizations are requiring applicants to undergo certain kinds of medical exams, such as AIDS tests. This can help them plan their medical expenses, employee absenteeism, and turnover, among other things. In addition, the trend for insurance companies not to cover illnesses or diseases for individuals who have "preexisting conditions" is increasing. Many argue against these practices, which they assert to be essentially clever methods by organizations to practice discrimination against perceived undesirables.

Second, organizations argue that this information, especially financial information, can help determine employee reliability. They argue that employees who cannot manage their own finances are viewed as being unlikely to be able to manage a department's budget. Organizations have also used the negligent hiring doctrine as a basis for obtaining employee medical and financial data.

DRUG TESTS

Perhaps some of the most talked about and controversial tests today are drug tests. The most common of these tests are urinalysis and hair sampling. Drug testing is a particularly sensitive issue for several reasons. First, many people believe that drug tests, especially urinalysis, are particularly intrusive of their privacy. Second, organizations that do not screen for drug users are most open to lawsuits concerning the negligent hiring doctrine. A third emerging issue is that of the conflict between the individual's right to privacy and the public's right to safety. The public policy issues are by no means settled and will be debated for some time.

The first issue concerns public safety. The right to perform drug tests on employees who are directly responsible for public safety, such as military personnel, police officers, airline pilots, and bus drivers, is being increasingly supported by both court precedent and public legislation. Another issue relates to the increasing frequency of employees winning court cases against organizations that conduct poorly planned and poorly implemented drug-testing programs. This includes nonrandom testing or testing without justifiable cause, improperly administering tests, or other forms of discriminatory actions. Like the other testing issues, the future of drug testing employees is uncertain. While it is safe to say that drug testing is a permanent part of organization life, it is unwise to predict exactly what form drug testing will be allowed to take in the future.

These issues relating to employee testing represent only one portion of the ethical behavior, employee rights, and employer responsibility segment of human resource management. Many of these issues are emotion packed, and virtually everyone has an opinion or strong feeling about them. While managers have laws, precedents, and corporate policies to guide their behavior, sometimes these may not be enough. The decisions that managers make concerning these issues are difficult and often extremely important to the organization.

STRATEGIC CHOICES

Many factors influence the choices managers make about how they will carry out their responsibilities in recognizing and respecting employee rights. The organization must establish policies to guide managers to consider the appropriate factors when they must make choices. In doing so, organizations should consider the following.

1. How can it ensure that its managers are treating employees with the respect they deserve?
2. What type of ethical standards should the organization set for its managers? How should these standards be disseminated to the managers?
3. Is there ever a time when a manager has the right to violate an employee's right to privacy?
4. How does an organization keep all of its managers up to date with respect to the legal ramifications of their treatment of employees?

STRATEGIC FACTORS

The main factors that directly influence managers' decisions about how they will treat employees include (1) management philosophy, (2) the tightness of the labor market, (3) the law, (4) union and employee power, and (5) organizational culture as it relates to discipline and control.

MANAGEMENT PHILOSOPHY

The main question relating to management philosophy is the extent to which top management and other managers throughout the organization believe in protecting employee rights. If top managers strongly believe in protecting employee rights, they will more likely ensure that company policy and actions respect these rights. They will more likely treat their subordinates with respect and expect them to do likewise with theirs. Furthermore, they will develop and communicate a set of core values that manifest these beliefs.

If, on the other hand, top management holds little regard for the rights of individual employees, very little, if anything, will be communicated about protecting these rights. Employees will more likely be treated as common factors of production without explicit consideration or respect for individual human dignity. In her study of General Motors, Maryann Keller shows how this basic orientation among top management permeated the organization and was a major cause for the decline of GM's competitiveness in the labor market.[3] By creating a stifling bureaucracy that provided little respect or allowance for individual differences, managers were not encouraged to explicitly recognize individual rights. Keller quotes an employee's letter that points out management's failure to recognize him as a human being. She indicates that mutual respect for the rights of each party, management and workers, is the way for GM to pull out of its tailspin.

Sometimes an organization formulates a set of core values that act as a basic guide for the treatment of employees. For example, Exhibit 15.1 is a set of core values for a large hospital in the southeastern United States. These core values appear in the employee manual, the firm's strategic plan, and are posted in the lobby of the hospital. In addition, they have been printed on wallet-sized cards that all managers and employees were encouraged to carry with them. It is certainly possible for an organization to develop such statements of core values for public relations purposes, but the fact that this statement was developed by the CEO and other members of the top management team and was circulated so widely gave the statement real meaning. One of your authors worked with this organization for several months, and it was apparent that management attempted to live by these values.

TIGHTNESS OF THE LABOR MARKET

The second variable that affects the extent to which a firm respects the rights of employees is the tightness of the labor market. If labor is plentiful and readily available at prevailing or below prevailing wage rates, firms are less likely to respect individual rights than if labor markets are tight, everything else being equal. This occurs because management knows that disgruntled and unhappy employees who quit or are fired can easily be replaced when there is an abundant supply of labor.

The United States experienced this most dramatically during both the great immigration waves of the early 20th century and the Great Depression of the 1930s. During

EXHIBIT 15.1   **Statement of a Hospital's Core Values**

1. We will treat each employee with respect.
2. We will observe the Golden Rule when dealing with all employees regardless of rank or job title.
3. We will make every effort to communicate with each employee and will listen to each.
4. We will respect the individual rights of each employee as a human being.
5. We will make every effort to involve each employee fully in his or her work.

these periods, employee rights were frequently abused because of the abundance of labor relative to the demand. Child labor, long hours, unsafe and unhealthy working conditions, low wages, and arbitrary and discriminatory treatment were all too common during these periods. In fact, because of these abuses, both industrial unions were formed and legislation was passed in an attempt to protect the rights of employees. These two factors are discussed below.

LEGISLATION

To the extent that legislation exists and that it is vigorously enforced, employee rights will be protected. If laws and court cases clearly define employee rights and if agencies exist specifically to uphold these laws, employers will more likely respect employee rights by observing the law and fearing sanctions. Initially, much of the law protecting employee rights was passed at the state level. For example, early in this century, Wisconsin had laws regulating child labor and working conditions for women. Such laws varied greatly among states that had them, but many states had no legislation. It was not until federal legislation was passed that comprehensive coverage and enforcement practices occurred.

UNIONS AND EMPLOYEE POWER

The greater the power of employees to protect their rights, especially through collective action (unions), the more likely employers will respect employee rights, all other things being equal. If employers know that employees can take concerted action to enforce rights, the power of employees is heightened. To a large extent, respect for rights depends on a power relationship: those who have power tend to get their way. Their rights are protected because they have the power to enforce their protection.

Unions have played a very strong role in defining and protecting employee rights. By uniting, employees have greatly increased their power in relation to employers. Unions have acted as advocates for employees both in collective bargaining with employers and in lobbying Congress for legislation to protect employee rights.

CULTURE

The final variable we consider is culture. Both the external culture and the organization's internal culture are key variables in terms of how the employer defines employee rights. For example, historically communist countries, such as the former Soviet Union, guaranteed employees jobs, resulting in a very low reported unemployment rate. Western countries traditionally have not actually made this guarantee, although most have a national economic policy of full employment to be achieved through monetary and fiscal policy (government spending, taxation, and central bank actions). Former communist countries experimenting with free enterprise will likely allow some unemployment to exist in the future.

Internal culture—organizational culture—also determines employee rights. A culture that places great value on employees and the worth of the individual will likely define and protect more employee rights than a culture that does not value employees as individuals. Exhibit 15.2 presents the corporate values of Apple Computer and Hewlett-Packard in relation to their employees. Apple and Hewlett-Packard have reputations as two of the most innovative and highest performing firms in the computer industry. Yet, as Exhibit 15.2 shows, their approaches to their employees are completely different.

Hewlett-Packard is known as a company that historically fosters and nurtures its employees. Its pay scale is average for the computer industry, but it is committed to a no-layoff policy.[4] Apple in contrast, is often viewed as a high-stress organization with high levels of employee turnover. In turn, Apple places a great emphasis on financially rewarding high performance. Apple does not even have a formal retirement policy, because, as one Apple executive states, "We don't expect people to last that long." Another Apple executive asserts, "Someone who worries about a retirement plan isn't an Apple type of person."[5] It is obvious that these two organizations take different attitudes toward employee rights. Much of this difference is due to their corporate cultures.

The key factors that affect the strategic choices employers have in defining employee rights and management responsibilities are as follows: management philosophy; the tightness of the labor market; the law, union and employee power; and the outside as well as the organizational culture. These variables are interrelated and work together. Therefore, it is important to try to understand their cumulative effect to understand how rights and responsibilities are viewed in individual organizations.

ETHICS

The focus of this chapter is on the discussion of employee rights and employer responsibilities, however, as important as these topics are to practicing human resource managers, many of the problems facing organizations today arise from the decisions managers make concerning what may or may not be ethical behavior. This "gray area" between what is legal and what is patently illegal is the domain of ethical dispute. For instance, is it ethical to take home pens and pencils from the office? Is it okay to make a short, personal long distance call on the company phone, use the company mail for a few personal items, or take the company car on a trip to the mall? Is it unethical to

EXHIBIT 15.2   **Corporate Values of Apple and Hewlett-Packard Concerning Their Employees**

APPLE'S STATEMENT OF VALUES

Individual Performance—We expect individual commitment and performance above the standard for our industry. Only thus will we make profits that permit us to seek our other corporate objectives. Each employee can and must make a difference in the final analysis. *Individuals* determine the character and strength of Apple.

Individual Reward—We recognize each person's contribution to Apple's success, and we share the financial rewards that flow from high performance. We recognize also that rewards must be psychological as well as financial and strive for an atmosphere where each individual can share the adventure and excitement of working at Apple.

HEWLETT-PACKARD'S STATEMENT OF VALUES

Our People
To help HP people share in the company's success, which they make possible; to provide employment security based on their performance; to ensure them a safe and pleasant work environment; to recognize their individual achievements; and to help them gain a sense of satisfaction and accomplishment from their work.

SOURCE: Apple Computer and Hewlett-Packard.

"pad" an expense account? Should an employee follow company orders that conflict with the teachings of his or her church? Should a family member be hired even if there was a more qualified person available? Should an employee withhold information from a local reporter who is investigating whether or not the company is dumping hazardous waste into a local river?

These are examples of ethical dilemmas that individuals face; there are no absolute right or wrong answers. Some situations are minor and more familiar; some are more serious, but all concern areas in which explicit guidance, in the form of written policy or regulation, may be lacking. There are no agreed upon ethical standards that guide all behavior in organizations because ethical behavior depends on what society considers the norm for such behavior and on who is judging the behavior. No doubt, some of you may find that certain behaviors are more suspect than others; others of you may find that all of the behaviors cited are unethical. And since ethics is such an individual quality, individual interpretations of what is and is not ethical serve to keep the gray area in constant ebb and flow.

Consider the source of an individual's ethical code. Ethics and values are intimately related. Values are learned early in life from parents and family, peers, teachers, and significant others and are either reinforced or altered by subsequent experience. Values consist of those enduring beliefs that specify that a certain mode of conduct or end-state of existence is personally or socially desirable. Values tend to be learned in an all-or-nothing fashion (for example, it is *always* right to tell the truth), but they are subject to modification ("fudging" the numbers on a tax return isn't really lying because everyone does it to a degree). The wide variation in childrearing practices and upbringing contributes in part to the wide variation in how people behave and how they evaluate the behavior of others.

Ethics follow from values and concern an individual's beliefs about what is right or wrong, good or bad. There is always a degree of subjective judgment involved. As such, questions about ethics concern matters well beyond mere compliance with organizational policy and state and federal laws. The Congressional furor over former Assistant Secretary of the Treasury Roger Altman's informal "heads up" to members of the Clinton White House staff concerning government investigations into alleged improprieties regarding the Whitewater Affair is one such example. Although no specific laws were broken, the hint of improper contact, and subsequent statements by Altman to Congress, which were considered misleading at best, resulted in Altman's eventual resignation from his post.

ETHICS AND STRATEGIC CHOICES

An organization that wants to be perceived as ethical cannot simply hope that its members will act ethically; it must take action to ensure that individuals know what appropriate behavior entails.[6] In recent years, courses on business ethics have been added to the curriculum of many major universities. In-house ethics training classes at large corporations have been developed. Orientation programs have begun to include sections on the ethical stance of the organization. Some organizations have even set up formal ethics offices complete with an ethics officer who is responsible for creating and maintaining the company's ethics program. The HR Challenge box describes ethics programs and prompts you to question whether the recent emphasis on ethics in universities and businesses is more smoke than substance. In essence, the discussion questions whether the investment in ethics training (a strategic choice) is worth it.

═══ **HR CHALLENGE** ═══

Ethics—Is It Just Another Fad?

What is behind the rush to install ethics programs in U.S. universities and industries? In the aftermath of the 1980s, have revelations about ethical improprieties such as insider trading scams and the savings and loan fiasco spurred businesses to action? Some believe that ethics training is no more than window dressing construed to give the appearance that businesses have changed their tune. Take, for example, the case of the second largest U.S. defense contractor General Dynamics, which in 1985 set up one of the first corporate ethics offices. By February of that year, Congress was investigating General Dynamics on charges that it billed for services not authorized (including charges for expensive dinners and the services of a dog kennel).

One prominent business school lauded its new ethics program in an alumni newsletter. The newsletter described the program on one page, which included new elective courses on ethics and a student code of ethics; on another page it described in the main feature story a course in Creativity in Business taught by Michael Milken. Milken, you will recall, was the junk bond trader who bilked many people, including many elderly individuals and those on a fixed income, out of millions of dollars. He was later convicted and served a few years in a federal minimum security prison.

Perhaps the drive to install ethics programs is something less than internally motivated. In November 1991, strict federal sentencing guidelines concerning unlawful business practices took effect. In addition, new guidelines were developed to help organizations set up internal mechanisms, including the establishment of ethics offices, for preventing, detecting, and reporting criminal conduct in the workplace. Perhaps the establishment of ethics programs is in response to an increased threat of government sanctions or poor publicity.

Supporters of ethics training argue that teaching ethics allows individuals to experience decision-making opportunities that involve ethical questions, thereby exposing individuals to the consequences associated with their actions. Supporters suggest that values can be learned, and that exposure to ethical dilemmas heightens awareness of appropriate value systems, thereby helping to improve decision-making skills in today's complex business environment. What do you think?

Source: Adapted from N. K. Austin, "The New Corporate Watchdogs," *Working Woman,* January 1994, pp. 19–20; and S. P. Robbins, *Organizational Behavior* (Englewood Cliffs, NJ: Prentice-Hall, 1993), p. 566.

ETHICS AND THE HUMAN RESOURCE MANAGER

This discussion of ethics is applicable to the day-to-day activities of human resource managers. In a recent survey, human resource professionals were asked to report their feelings and observations about the ethical conduct in their organizations. Exhibit 15.3 lists the top 10 most serious ethical problems reported in this survey. As one might expect, most of the issues raised were human resource-related problems because one of the main functions of the human resource staff is to monitor compliance with guidelines established by law or the organization concerning not only what is legal and appropriate but also what is ethical and fair.

The high costs of unethical behavior are increasingly being felt by individuals and organizations alike. The following is a list of reasons that ethics has become such a hot topic in the business literature.

1. There appears to be a widespread breakdown in ethical conduct among senior managers. As the double standard is employed to allow top management to take advantage of the system and is gradually revealed to the American public (such as the savings and loan scandal, or the Wall Street problems), people are growing concerned and are beginning to ask for changes.

The Ten Most Serious Ethical Situations Reported by Human Resource Professionals

1. Hiring, training, or promoting based on favoritism.
2. Allowing differences in pay, discipline, promotion, and so on due to friendships with top management.
3. Allowing sexual harassment.
4. Allowing gender bias to be considered when determining promotion.
5. Using discipline for managerial and nonmanagerial personnel inconsistently.
6. Not maintaining confidentiality.
7. Allowing gender bias to be considered when determining compensation.
8. Using nonperformance factors in appraisals.
9. Making arrangements with vendors or consulting agencies for personal gain.
10. Allowing gender bias to influence recruitment or hiring.

SOURCE: Adapted from "HR Professionals Agree: Workplace Ethics Require People to be Judged Solely on Job Performance," *1991 SHRM/CCH Survey,* June 1991, p. 1.

2. Time and productivity can be stolen more easily than goods and services. Workers who are treated as professionals may take advantage of the freedoms they enjoy. Experts estimate that payroll could be cut by 20 percent without any change in productivity.
3. The family, where the ethical values were conveyed, has all but disappeared. The "family meal," during which family members discuss their problems and learn the "correct" way to solve them, no longer exists.
4. Organizational loyalty is declining sharply as employees adopt a "what's in it for me" attitude. This attitude shift often has been a reaction to selfish acts of management, such as leveraged buyouts and golden parachutes, witnessed by workers.[7]

What can organizations do to ensure that ethical standards are upheld? We suggest a combination approach based on an appropriate management philosophy that is transmitted and reinforced within the culture of the organization. This approach includes at a minimum a set of written ethical guidelines that specify standards for appropriate conduct backed by top management support and visible demonstrations that ethical behaviors are encouraged and rewarded. These guidelines can help to make ethical actions a cornerstone of corporate culture and provide businesses with a source of increased competitive advantage. Such was the case at Johnson & Johnson, the makers of Tylenol, when someone poisoned several bottles of the product. Knowing that Johnson & Johnson viewed ethical treatment of customers as a priority, workers in drug and grocery stores did not hesitate to check with headquarters before removing millions of bottles of Tylenol from store shelves.[8] The threat to customers, in the minds of Johnson & Johnson, far outweighed the costs of destroying great quantities of Tylenol, even though only a few tainted bottles had been found. In the long run, this disaster contributed to the implementation of tamper-proof packages on medicine and food products, and Johnson & Johnson now enjoys an even more prominent position as a trusted supplier of quality pharmaceuticals because of the way it handled the situation.

Defining what constitutes ethical business practices is not easy and becomes increasingly difficult as organizations internationalize. As top organizational managers search for a universal code of ethics, they become increasingly aware of the role of

HR CHALLENGE

Conducting Business "Ethically" in a Global Market

Most managers with global experience believe that there should be a set of shared global ethical values. Rushworth Kidder, from the Institute for Global Ethics, conducted a values survey and found the following common values: love, truth, freedom, fairness, community, tolerance, responsibility, and reverence for life. The problem is that even if there is an underlying agreement on values, these values may be prioritized differently in different cultures.

A general rule of business is that a company doing business in other countries should comply with all of the laws of those countries. A corporation must be responsible to what the society is demanding. Further, a company can use what is called "ethical displacement," which means that ethical dilemmas are displaced upward to a higher level. For example, a company policy might solve a dilemma for a manager who is offered a gift. The manager might explain that it is not his or her decision but that company policy prohibits accepting gifts.

Initiating an ethics program in today's multicultural environment is a complex task for any manager, but the following guidelines may help:

- Make ethics an important and salient issue by developing a clear code of conduct for employees that is value based and addresses cross-cultural issues.
- Provide employees opportunities to learn and understand ethical dilemmas as well as alternatives for resolving these dilemmas. Study the best practices of other multicultural firms.
- Continually review and update the company's ethics policy and communicate this policy to employees frequently.

SOURCE: Adapted from S. Richter and C. Barnum, "When Values Clash," *HRMagazine,* September 1994, pp. 42–45; and B. Rogers, "Serious about Its Code of Ethics," *HRMagazine,* September 1994, pp. 46–48.

---

cultural differences. For example, if a company practices gender equality regarding status and pay, what is the role of the company if a woman from the company, working in a foreign country, is treated by the locals as a second-class citizen, following that country's norms, values, and beliefs? Does the company have an obligation to her? Similarly, if a company has a rule prohibiting the acceptance of gifts, but the country in which you are doing business views *not* accepting a gift as an insult, what should your company do?

THE LAW AND EMPLOYEE RIGHTS

Because many rights have been codified either in legislation or case law, we now examine one key aspect of employee rights—the law. We do not intend to cover each and every aspect of the law; much of this has been done in other chapters of the book. Our intent here is to highlight those aspects of the law that deal with rights and responsibilities. We review three key areas of the law: discrimination, employment at will, and rights. The basic legislation and case law in each area is summarized.

DISCRIMINATION

Employees have the right to employment free from discrimination based on race, color, creed, religious belief, country of national origin, age, sex, or physical or mental handicap. This protection covers all aspects of employment—from hiring to placement, training, promotion, pay, discipline, or termination. The primary laws prohibiting discrimination are Title VII of the 1964 Civil Rights Act and the 1990 Americans with Disabilities Act, as amended and as interpreted by case law. Employees are also protected against sexual harassment because this has been defined as a type of sexual discrimination.

ANTIDISCRIMINA-TION LAWS

Employment laws that say all employment decisions should be based on job-relevant factors such as skill, knowledge, and ability.

The **antidiscrimination laws** are quite complex, but basically they require that employment decisions should be made strictly on factors relevant to the job. This means that the decisions should be based on skill, job knowledge, and abilities—factors that relate to a person's ability to do the job. Even such factors as experience and educational level could be ruled as discriminatory if these factors are not relevant to a particular job. In fact, they could serve as institutional forms of covert (hidden) discrimination if white people consistently have higher levels of education than minority groups and if this educational level is irrelevant to the job. From an employment standpoint, the skills and knowledge that education and experience represent are the desired qualities. In other words, just because a person has a certain formal education level or years of experience does not necessarily mean that the person has the required skill or knowledge to do the job. Employers use education and experience to represent skill and knowledge because it is a screening device easy to use and because so few sophisticated tests exist to test job knowledge and skill and those few are relatively expensive to administer; it is much easier to require a certain education level and use this prerequisite to screen out the mass of applicants.

Discrimination can be overt or covert. The law has essentially eliminated overt discrimination, but covert discrimination is more difficult to identify and therefore eliminate. The major controversial aspects of discrimination, particularly affirmative action, which was adopted as national policy even before the passage of Title VII as a way to eliminate discrimination, was discussed previously.

EMPLOYMENT AT WILL

EMPLOYMENT AT WILL

A policy under which employers are free to discharge their employees for any reason unless the discharge is limited by contract or state or federal statute.

The policy of **employment at will** exists in many states. It means that an employer or an employee is free to break the employment relationship "at will" unless there is a written or implied employment contract. Examples of employment-at-will statements are provided in Exhibit 15.4. The rationale behind this concept is the belief that an employee ought to be free to quit to seek employment elsewhere and that an employer ought to be able to terminate an employee to hire another one.

Five primary factors temper the employment-at-will concept: (1) an employment contract, (2) civil service protection, (3) antidiscrimination laws, (4) unions, and (5) discharges contrary to the public interest.[9]

EMPLOYMENT CONTRACT

In an individual employment contract, a clause specifying reasons for terminations is usually spelled out. This protects the employee from termination for other reasons. The following is an example of such a clause:

> This Agreement shall, at the employer's sole option and without further notice, be terminated upon the occurrence of any one or more of the following events:
> **(a)** the conviction of the employee of a felony;
> **(b)** the conviction of the employee of a misdemeanor involving moral turpitude;
> **(c)** gross negligence by the employee in the performance of his or her duties;
> **(d)** the willful and intentional commission of any act which act or failure to act the employee knew, or should have known, would result in substantial and material harm to the employer's business or goodwill.

EXHIBIT 15.4   **Employment-at-Will Clause Examples**

STRONG FORM

I understand that if I am employed by _____ Company, my employment and compensation can be terminated with or without cause and with or without notice at any time, at the option of either the company or myself. I also understand that neither this application for employment nor any present or future employee handbook or personnel policy manual is an employment agreement, either expressed or implied, and that no employee or manager of _____ Company, except the vice-president of human resources, has any authority to enter into any agreement for employment for any specified period of time or to make any agreement contrary to the foregoing.

MODERATELY STRONG FORM

In the event of employment, I understand that my employment is not for any definite period or succession of periods and is considered an "at-will" arrangement. This means that I am free to terminate my employment at any time for any reason, as is the company, so long as there is no violation of applicable federal or state law.

SOFT FORM

I understand that no representative of the company is authorized to state or imply that a contract for permanent employment shall exist between the company and me.

SOURCE: Adapted from R. Hilgert, "Employers Protected by At-Will Statements," *HRMagazine,* March 1991, pp. 57–60.

These are vague terms and would need to be specifically defined by a court or arbitrator if contested by the employee. Yet if this were in an employment contract, these would be the only reasons that an employee could be terminated.

In the absence of a written contract, courts often infer a contract of employment. For example, if in the employee handbook a statement is made that a new employee moves from probationary to permanent status after a period of time, such as 90 days, courts have held that the word *permanent* implies a contractual relationship. For this reason, employers should use the word *regular* instead of *permanent* in employee manuals, other publications, and policy statements unless they wish to imply permanent status.

An implied contract can also be inferred from oral statements made by superiors in the organization.[10] For example, organizations should be careful about saying things like the following at the time of hire: "We plan to keep you here for your entire career" or "We view our relationship as a long-term, permanent one." Statements similar to these have been ruled in cases as an implied contract of lifetime employment in the supreme courts of New Jersey, New Mexico, and Michigan.[11]

The costs an organization incurs to protect itself from wrongful termination lawsuits are being passed on to employees in the form of fewer jobs. To offset the costs involved, some firms are simply hiring fewer people. However, it appears that the actual court costs are minimal; it is the actions organizations take to prevent litigation that are costly. Many firms are spending more per employee to avoid litigation than they are spending for litigation itself.[12]

To minimize a firm's chances of being sued over an implied contract, it should take the following steps:

1. Establish a written at-will statement and place it on all applications. Make potential employees sign the form.

HR CHALLENGE

Relocation Can Lead to an Implied Contract

Getting employees to transfer to a new location seems to be getting more and more difficult. Issues such as dual careers, children having to change schools, especially high school, and extreme differences in the cost of living or quality of life sometimes make it hard to sell an employee on a transfer.

All too frequently, while managers are trying to convince an employee to make a move, the use of seemingly harmless words to persuade the employee can be interpreted legally as an implied contract. For example, mentioning that the move will "be worth the employee's while over the long haul" or that this move is "simply one more step in the employee's career ladder" may be considered by a court as an implied contract.

A case recently decided on this issue illustrates this problem. After 25 years of service as an accountant at Dresser Industries, Thomas Krause had worked his way up to the highest accounting position in southern Louisiana. During a general cutback, he was demoted and told that he would have to move to Oklahoma City

to keep his job. After being assured by his supervisor that if he moved, his job would be safe because future job cuts would be determined by seniority, he decided to move to Oklahoma City. When he arrived there, he found that the only other accountant was the 27-year-old son of a senior vice-president. Soon the ax fell and he was fired. When the VP's son found a new position at Dresser but Krause didn't, he sued for both age discrimination (he was 52 at the time of the firing) and for wrongful discharge under the implied contract theory. He won on both accounts—$168,000 for the age discrimination claim and an additional $166,000 for the wrongful discharge suit.

As this one example shows, relocation is a gray area. Managers must be made aware that what they say may be used against them later if the transferred employee is terminated.

SOURCE: Adpated from Jack Raisner, "Relocate without Making False Moves," *HRMagazine,* February 1991, pp. 46–50.

---

2. Stipulate the standards of conduct for employees and the kinds of conduct that will lead to termination.
3. Indicate that even though the firm uses progressive discipline, it is by no means a guarantee of employment and the progression can be suspended at any time.
4. Reserve the right to dismiss the employee without following disciplinary procedures.
5. Do not establish a probationary period for new hires. They may expect that if they pass the probationary period they are guaranteed employment.[13]

CIVIL SERVICE PROTECTION

Employees working for government agencies are protected from discharge without justifiable cause through civil service rules and regulations. These specify dischargeable offenses as well as the procedure to be used. Exhibit 15.5 shows an example of a civil service clause and procedure concerning discharge.

DISCRIMINATION LAW

People cannot legally be dismissed from a job if it occurs because of their race, creed, color, religious belief, country of national origin, sex, age, or physical or mental handicap except as provided by the law.

UNIONS

The fourth factor that modifies the employment-at-will doctrine is the presence of a union. Unions, through the collective bargaining process, negotiate and enforce a col-

EXHIBIT 15.5   **Florida's Career Service Discharge Statute**

110.227 SUSPENSIONS, DISMISSALS, REDUCTIONS IN PAY, DEMOTIONS, LAYOFFS, AND TRANSFERS.

(1) Any employee who has permanent status in the career service may only be suspended or dismissed for cause. Cause shall include, but not be limited to, negligence, inefficiency or inability to perform assigned duties, willful violation of the provisions of law or agency rules, conduct unbecoming a public employee, misconduct, habitual drug abuse, or conviction of any crime involving moral turpitude.

(2) The department [Florida Department of Administration] shall establish rules and procedures for the suspension, reduction in pay, transfer, layoff, demotion, and dismissal of employees in the career service. Such rules shall be approved by the Administration Commission prior to their adoption by the department.

(3)(a) When a layoff becomes necessary, such layoff shall be conducted within the competitive area identified by the agency head and approved by the Department of Administration. Such competitive area shall be established taking into consideration the similarity of work; the organizational unit, which may be any agency, department, division, bureau, or other organizational unit; and the commuting area for the work affected.

(b) Layoff procedures shall be developed to establish the relative merit and fitness of employees and shall include a formula for uniform application among all employees in the competitive area, taking into consideration the type of employment, the length of service, and the quality of performance.

(4) Any permanent career service employee subject to reduction in pay, transfer, layoff, or demotion shall be notified in writing by the agency prior to its taking such action. Such notice shall be sent by certified mail with return receipt requested. Such actions shall be appealable to the Public Employees Relations Commission, pursuant to s. 447.208 [Florida Statutes] and rules adopted by the commission.

(5)(a) Any permanent career service employee who is subject to suspension or dismissal shall receive written notice of such action at least 10 days prior to the date such action is to be taken. Subsequent to such notice, and prior to the date the action is to be taken, the affected employee shall be given an opportunity to appear before the agency or official taking the action to answer orally and in writing the charges against him.

SOURCE: Section 110.227, Florida Statutes 1989.   *continued*

lective bargaining agreement called a *contract,* which specifies causes and procedures for discharge. These items, as well as other aspects of unions and collective bargaining, are discussed in the next chapter.

DISCHARGES CONTRARY TO THE PUBLIC INTEREST

The final factor that modifies the employment-at-will doctrine concerns discharges for reasons that involve the public interest. For instance, if an employee is fired for going against his supervisor's orders to dump battery acid down the drain and into the local sewer (an act clearly against the public interest), that employee may sue for wrongful termination. Every employee has the right to disobey orders that violate laws and to feel free to speak when violations occur (commonly referred to as *whistleblowing*). However, not all free speech in the workplace is protected. An employee is not protected if he or she violates the confidentiality of business information or makes unfounded accusations about management.[14] The law does not protect those who "cry wolf."

continued

EXHIBIT 15.5	**Florida's Career Service Discharge Statute**

(b) In extraordinary situations, such as when the retention of a permanent career service employee would result in damage to state property, would be detrimental to the interests of the state, or would result in injury to the employee, a fellow employee, or some other person, such employee may be suspended or dismissed without 10 days prior notice provided that written or oral notice of such action, evidence of the reasons therefore, and an opportunity to rebut the charges are furnished to the employee prior to such dismissal or suspension.

110.233 POLITICAL ACTIVITIES AND UNLAWFUL ACTS PROHIBITED

(1) No person shall be appointed to, demoted, or dismissed from any position in the career service, or in any way favored or discriminated against with respect to employment in the career service, because of race, color, national origin, sex, handicap, religious creed, or political opinion or affiliation.

TYPES OF RIGHTS

Any list of employee rights is likely to be incomplete. No one source lists employee rights just as no one source lists the rights we have as citizens of our country. However, both legislation and case law, as well as certain key documents such as the Constitution, provide a framework to use in listing employee rights. For our purposes, we will look at the following seven rights:[15]

1. Privacy.
2. Fair treatment.
3. Safe and healthful workplace, including freedom from a hostile environment regarding sexual harassment.
4. Collective bargaining.
5. Communication and involvement in the organization.
6. Notice of plant closings and of disciplinary action.
7. Due process.

PRIVACY

The right to privacy is grounded in the U.S. Constitution. The Fourth Amendment prevents unreasonable search and seizure. Most state constitutions provide for some form of protection similar to that of the Fourth Amendment. Ten states even have specific privacy guarantees in their constitution. Beyond this, the law is complex and unclear. Most of the privacy concept has evolved as the result of the decision of hundreds of past court cases. The right to privacy is an ever-changing and evolving concept.

Basically, however, the right to privacy means that employees are free to work without undue interference from their employer and that employee records are protected from examination unless a legitimate interest exists.

Monitoring employee behavior without invading an employee's right to privacy can raise some sensitive issues.[16] For example, does an employer have the right to search an employee's desk? How can drug tests be conducted without violating the right to privacy? How can employers monitor the conversations held by telephone operators with-

HR CHALLENGE

How Far Can the Employer's Arm Reach?

As a manager, do you have the right to know whether an employee has been accused of a crime while in your employ? Is it legal to terminate an employee due to his or her violation of the law, even if the employee is extremely productive and has never missed a day's work? Does the severity of the crime matter? What if the employee was convicted of child molestation, or drunk driving, or armed robbery? Managers who must answer these tough questions are being guided by an every-increasing body of laws.

In general, the case law suggests that misconduct outside the workplace in some cases may not be a lawful justification for employee discipline. As a defense, an employee could argue that what he or she does outside of work is none of the company's business as long as the employee is still productive. This defense is being taken more and more seriously as privacy issues become a significant area for judicial examination.

The employer's best defense is to link the crime to some aspect of the job. For example, Pepsi-Cola was able to terminate a vending-machine serviceman who

was convicted of child molestation because he worked unsupervised in areas where children frequented. Employers could argue that the employee's presence in the workplace is disruptive. In one case, workers were so repulsed by an employee who was accused of sexual misconduct that the peer pressure they exerted upon him made him quit. However, the firm would have chosen to terminate him if he did not quit on his own on the grounds that the employee's misconduct had a disruptive impact on the workplace.

These issues are very controversial. Some states, such as Hawaii, have laws that specifically preclude employers from basing disciplinary actions on the fact that the employee has been arrested for a crime; other states do not have such laws. Further, businesses also enjoy special protection in this area by some laws. Regardless of the laws protecting either side, the employer is frequently placed in a difficult situation that must be handled with extreme care.

SOURCE: Adapted from Steve Bergsman, "Employee Conduct Outside the Workplace," *HRMagazine,* March 1991, pp. 62–64.

out violating privacy rights? Employee monitoring has become one of the most controversial issues in human resource management today. According to corporate lawyer Eric Joss, it is "the hottest employment law topic of the 1990s."[17] These issues will be explored more fully in the case at the end of the chapter.

FAIR TREATMENT

FAIR TREATMENT
Employee freedom from arbitrary and capricious behavior on the part of the employer.

The second right we examine is the right to **fair treatment** by employers. By *fair treatment,* we mean freedom from arbitrary and capricious behavior on the part of the employer. It means that individual employees will not be singled out for discipline when others also deserve it and that overt favoritism on the part of the employer will be minimized. It also means that in the absence of mitigating circumstances, precedence will be followed by the employer. In a recent survey, fair treatment was citied as the most serious ethical problem human resource managers must deal with.[18]

The fair treatment concept applied to Florida Governor Bob Martinez's firing of Florida Department of Corrections classification officer Phillip Adams. Adams recommended, against inmate classification guidelines, that convicted murderer Donald Dillbeck be reclassified from medium security to minimum security. Governor Martinez fired Adams after Dillbeck walked away from a work detail and murdered a woman in a mall parking lot. A hearing officer ruled that Adams had been treated differently than other officers who were not fired after violating the same decision-making guidelines and recommended that he be reinstated.[19]

SAFE AND HEALTHFUL WORKPLACE FREE FROM SEXUAL HARASSMENT

The Occupational Safety and Health Act of 1970, as amended, gives employees the right to a safe and healthful workplace. The law set up the Occupational Safety and Health Administration (OSHA) to enforce the law and to conduct inspections, levy fines, and, in severe cases, shut down operations. Finally, the law gives employees the right to complain to OSHA about safety violations without fear of retribution from employers.

HOSTILE ENVIRONMENT

HOSTILE ENVIRONMENT
An organizational environment or surrounding that promotes or tolerates sexual harassment.

In the landmark case of *Vinson* v. *Meritor Savings Bank, FSB,* the U.S. Supreme Court ruled that Vinson had been subjected to sexual harassment on the job by her employer, Meritor Savings Bank, because the employer had created a **hostile environment** with regard to sexual harassment. A series of activities took place involving off-color jokes, fondling, and even sexual intercourse. The plaintiff, Vinson, did not complain until she was terminated for excessive sick leave, even though the company had a complaint procedure in place. She claimed that she was afraid to complain for fear of losing her job. The court ruled in her favor and stated that the employer had created a hostile environment that prevented Vinson from voicing her complaint.[20] The EEOC guidelines define a hostile environment as one in which sexual harassment interferes with the employee's work behavior or creates an offensive work environment.[21] Since passage of the Civil Rights Act of 1991, which allows victims of sexual harassment to sue for punitive and compensatory damages, companies are taking a harder look at their work environments to ensure that they are not sexually offensive.[22]

COLLECTIVE BARGAINING

Employees have the right to form or to join unions to bargain collectively with their employers with regard to wages, hours, and other terms and conditions of employment. This right is protected by federal law. By bargaining collectively, employees increase their power relative to their employer. This increased power enables them to secure those aspects desired in an employment relationship, such as higher wages and improved hours, working conditions, and terms and conditions of employment.

COMMUNICATION AND INVOLVEMENT IN THE ORGANIZATION

Employees have the right to be informed about all aspects of their jobs and their employment. They also have the right to be fully involved in their employing organization. In some countries, this right is commonly adhered to by employers who communicate with and involve their employees through quality circles, suggestion programs, and consensus decision making. However, U.S. employers have not always believed in this right, although more employers such as Ford, GM, 3M, Motorola, and Florida Power Corp. are embracing this right today.

No doubt, some would argue that although this communication and involvement might be good management practice, it does not constitute an employee right. However, we take the position that for an employee to properly do his or her job, he or she must be kept informed as to what is expected of him or her.[23] Furthermore, as an employee, an individual is entitled to full membership privileges in the employing organization. This includes participation in the benefit programs offered and access to information on organizational operations, at least in so far as they relate to the individual's job duties and responsibilities. Some argue that this right also includes the right to knowledge of organizational missions, goals, and objectives.[24] Finally, an employee has the right to know how he or she will be evaluated, including the criteria and the process used. This right is part and parcel of the right to be communicated with on aspects related to job duties and expectations.

NOTICE OF PLANT CLOSINGS AND OF DISCIPLINARY ACTION

WARN
Worker Adjustment and Retraining Notification Act of 1988, a federal act that requires advance notification to employees of plant closings.

Federal law requires that employers provide notice to employees of planned plant or facilities closings. The Worker Adjustment and Retraining Notification Act of 1988 (WARN) was passed by Congress after nearly 15 years of legislative battling. **WARN** basically requires that all firms employing more than 100 full-time workers give at least 60 days advance notice of any plans to close plants or lay off workers. Firms are required to notify their employees under the law if a plant closing results in the loss of more than 50 jobs at one location. Notice is required in mass layoff situations if the firm lays off more than 500 people for more than six months or if it lays off 50 workers that constitute more than 33 percent of its workforce. Firms that employ fewer than 100 people are exempt from the law. It is estimated that only 2 percent of the companies in the United States are large enough to be affected by the law, but these companies employ approximately 50 percent of the workforce.[25] Exhibit 15.6 presents the number of days a firm is required to give employees before a plant closing.

In addition it is a well established practice in arbitration hearings that an employer must give notice to employees on new rules or regulations or when it intends to enforce a previously existing but unenforced rule or regulation. Employees cannot be expected to adhere to rules and regulations that have not been made public or otherwise communicated to them. Even an existing rule or regulation that the organization has not been enforcing is unenforceable unless the organization first puts employees on notice stating that the rule will be enforced from this day forward.

For example, one of your authors is familiar with a no-smoking rule that existed in a warehouse of a large consumer products manufacturer. This rule had been communicated to employees; in fact, no-smoking signs were clearly posted on walls in the warehouse.

■ EXHIBIT 15.6

A Comparison of Advance Notice on Plant Closing Laws in the United States and Other Nations

Nation	Advance Notice Requirement
United States	60 days
Canada	1–16 weeks, depending on case
Germany	30 days after notifying government
Great Britain	60–90 days, depending on case
France	2–14 weeks, depending on case
Sweden	60 days to 6 months, depending on case
Belgium	60 days
Japan	"Sufficient" advance notice

SOURCE: Adapted from the article "New Plant Closing Law Aids Workers in Transition," by Paul Staudohar, © January 1989. Reprinted with the permission of *Personnel Journal,* Costa Mesa, California. All rights reserved.

The rule was clearly stated in the employee handbook. The penalty for violating the rule was also clearly stated—an immediate three-day suspension without pay on the first offense and termination on the second offense.

However, this rule was enforced neither by the supervisors in the warehouse nor by the warehouse superintendent. When the old superintendent retired and a new one was appointed, he decided to enforce the rule. The morning of his first day on the job, he suspended an employee caught smoking. The employee filed a grievance through the union, which went to third-party arbitration. The arbitrator ruled that the suspension was improper because past practice showed that the rule existed on paper only because the company had not enforced it. He ruled that the employer should have first put all employees on notice that the rule would be enforced, even though it had not been in the past. This ruling is well established in arbitration cases—the arbitrator looks to past practice prior to making the ruling.

DUE PROCESS

DUE PROCESS
Employees' right to tell their side of the story and to have all facts considered in an impartial manner when charged with a rule violation.

The final right we examine here is the right to due process. **Due process** refers to the right to a fair hearing or adjudication that considers all facts in an impartial manner when a person is charged with a rule violation. In most cases, this means the right to file a grievance and have it heard. In a unionized organization, this right is protected by the labor agreement and the grievance process is usually spelled out in the contract. Even in a nonunion organization, a grievance process is often spelled out. A typical grievance starts with the immediate supervisor and ends with arbitration, which is a binding ruling by an outside neutral third party. This process allows both the employee and the employer to state their cases—to have "their day in court," so to speak.

Of course, if arbitration is not present in a grievance process, an employee can sue an employer for damages. This due process procedure is usually more time consuming and costly than a grievance and arbitration.

EMPLOYER RESPONSIBILITIES

To this point, we have discussed the rights of employees. Employers have responsibilities with respect to these rights. This responsibility is not the reverse side of the same coin, although employee rights do suggest corresponding employer responsibilities. However, employers have responsibilities to the community at large as well as to employees. Some concepts concerning the social responsibilities of business are discussed here.

For example, actions of employers often have impact beyond the immediate boundary of the organization. This was the key issue in the U.S. government's loan guarantee to Chrysler in late 1977. It was reasoned that it would be better for the federal government to guarantee the loans to Chrysler in hope of saving the company than to let the company go bankrupt and thereby throw thousands of people out of work. The potential costs in unemployment insurance, food stamps, and other welfare programs were thought to far exceed the costs of guaranteeing the loan. In retrospect, the decision appears to have been the correct one since the company recovered nicely and even paid off the loans ahead of schedule.

Therefore, firms have responsibilities not only to their employees and stockholders but also to other groups and to the community at large. Making charitable donations, supporting the United Way, backing arts groups, supporting colleges and universities, working to reduce or eliminate drugs and crime are but some activities firms can par-

HR CHALLENGE

A Company with a Conscience Meeting the Needs of Socially Conscious Consumers

Working Assets is a tiny, eight-year-old consumer services firm located in San Francisco. A part of its profits is donated to socially responsible causes. Laura Scher, a 1985 Harvard graduate who placed in the top 5 percent of her business school class, is the CEO. Why would a woman who could have gone to work for virtually any other company select to work for Working Assets? Because the company has a conscience.

For example, one of Scher's most recent projects was Working Assets Long Distance. It's a phone company that targets people who want to speak out on political and environmental issues. Along with the usual services offered by a long-distance carrier, WA's long distance program offers Free Speech Days, during which time customers can call Congress for free. She signed up 20,000 customers in three months. She has also developed a WA Visa card. Every time a customer uses the card, WA donates a nickel to a pool that supports 36 nonprofit groups. The 120,000 cardholders have charged enough items to create a pool of almost $1.5 million.

As Scher's work indicates, plenty of socially conscious consumers are out there. The trick is appealing to them. These customers are leery of three-color mailout pamphlets and are suspicious of advertisers' motives. What these people want is simply to support causes they believe in. The top four causes include economic justice, the environment, peace, and human rights.

How does Scher please her audience? She follows three principles in running her business. First, she identifies an opportunity within an existing industry, such as credit cards and long distance calling; then she finds ways to piggyback her services onto these everyday needs. Second, because she knows that her customers are big readers, she explains everything about the program in brochures and advertisements. Finally, she doesn't try to be all things to all people. She is sure to be outspoken only in areas that she really cares about. Obviously, her rules are working for Working Assets.

SOURCE: Adapted from "Making Money While Making a Difference," *Working Woman*, February 1992, pp. 31–34.

ticipate in to improve the quality of life in the communities where they operate. While firms may have selfish motives for doing these things—they want good schools and safe streets for their employees—the community as a whole benefits.

RESPONSIBILITIES TO STAKEHOLDERS

STAKEHOLDER
Any organizational constituency or group that has a vested interest in what an organization does or does not do.

One way to view these responsibilities of companies is from the perspective of a **stakeholder.** This approach holds that organizations serve multiple constituencies and each group has a set of expectations or a vested interest in what the organization does. Consequently, the organization has a responsibility to each of these groups. Exhibit 15.7 lists some of the stakeholder groups for a large corporation. Notice that the corporation has a responsibility to try to fulfill the expectations of each of the stakeholder groups. For example, owners want a return on their investment so the organization strives to earn a profit. Employees want good wages, security, and fair treatment. Customers want a product or service at desired quality, quantity, place, time, and price. Government agencies want taxes and want the organization to obey appropriate laws.

In fulfilling these obligations to these various groups, organizations often face conflicting expectations. For example, employees make a claim to profit in the form of higher wages or other incentive pay, such as profit sharing. They compete with owners who want a share of profit in the form of dividends. The organization must balance these competing interests. Requests for financial support for college and university

EXHIBIT 15.7   **Examples of Organization Stakeholders**

Internal Stakeholders	External Stakeholders
Employees	Suppliers
Management	Distributors
Board of directors	Board of directors
(internally chosen)	(externally chosen)
Owner (sole proprietorship)	Customers
	Government agencies
	Public interest groups
	Stakeholders

programs come from many institutions of higher learning; the corporation must decide which ones it will support and which ones it will not. This requires the organization to practice the art of compromise and to properly assess the power of each stakeholder and the consequences of not fulfilling the expectations of each.

In the next section, we briefly discuss employer responsibilities as they pertain primarily to employees. However, it is important to recognize that these responsibilities are tempered by other responsibilities to other stakeholder groups.

RESPONSIBILITY TO KNOW THE LAW

"Ignorance of the law is no excuse" is an old saying that is especially pertinent to employee rights. The law is so complex and changes so rapidly that it is vital that both human resource managers and other managers try to stay abreast of the law as best they can as well as seek legal assistance on a regular basis. Actively staying current on legal matters is an important responsibility of human resource managers today. Communicating legal requirements to line managers is a very important part of every human resource manager's job. Human resource managers must read extensively, attend workshops on legal matters, and communicate frequently with counsel to keep line managers properly educated and informed as to what they legally can and cannot do.

RESPONSIBILITY TO COMMUNICATE WITH EMPLOYEES

Human resource managers should communicate effectively with employees and should ensure that line managers also communicate effectively with employees. This responsibility is related to the employee right to notice described previously. The right to notice cannot be fulfilled if the employer does not adequately communicate with employees.

Today, companies use many forms of communication. In addition to the standard ways of face-to-face communication through one-on-one encounters and meetings, letters, memoranda, postings, telephoning, and reports, organizations now use the fax machine, videos, and electronic communication (E-mail). For example, IBM, among other organizations, regularly uses videos in the communication process, not only from central headquarters but also within regions. A multimedia approach seems to be more effective in reaching employees than using just one communication medium, and adding visual images enhances the communication process.

RESPONSIBILITY TO TREAT EMPLOYEES WITH HUMAN DIGNITY

A third employer responsibility is to treat employees with human dignity. People are not just another factor of production as is a machine, desk, or factory. They deserve respect and consideration. This is sometimes difficult to achieve, as we saw during the massive restructuring effort in the 1980s when thousands abruptly lost their jobs. Yet ethical values and our system of morals based on the Judeo-Christian ethic as well as our political system give people certain rights to be treated with dignity and respect. The movie *Roger and Me* demonstrated the conflict that can result when a large corporation (GM) takes action to close a plant that the citizens of the town wish to keep open. In situations such as this, individual rights and dignity are sometimes lost in the process and the question becomes who can exercise the most power to assert their rights as they interpret them. Certainly, GM has the right to close a plant, but those involved have the right to be treated with human dignity.

RESPONSIBILITY TO BARGAIN COLLECTIVELY

The law requires that employers bargain collectively with employees if a union has been certified as the bargaining agent. The employer has no choice as to whether to bargain in good faith or not. However, the employer does have a choice in trying to keep a union from forming. An employer can legally take action to keep a union from forming, although strict guidelines as to what can and cannot be done must be followed.

RESPONSIBILITY TO PROVIDE DUE PROCESS

As noted in a previous section of this chapter, the right to a fair treatment and a fair hearing on the part of the employee requires that the employer accept the responsibility to provide due process. When a union is present, due process is usually obtained through the grievance process. Governmental organizations usually provide some type of civil service hearing procedure. Nonunionized employers often have impartial panels of employees and managers to hear an employee complaint or grievance. Many Japanese companies do this. For example, Toyota uses a series of committees made up of elected worker representatives and appointed managers to hear disciplinary cases involving workers. At Northrop Corporation in Los Angeles, a management appeals committee hears complaints from employees who believe they have been treated unfairly.[26] We discuss the right to due process in more depth in a later chapter.

In the next section, we look at a particularly difficult situation that is all too common in organizations today: the problem employee. Employee rights and employer responsibilities come to a head in situations that involve a problem employee. Because this is so difficult a situation and involves rights and legal responsibilities, we devote the remainder of the chapter to the issues involved.

MANAGING THE PROBLEM EMPLOYEE

Suppose you find yourself in this position: One of your employees comes to work acting very strangely. He seems to be in a fog and unable to concentrate, but you do not smell alcohol on his breath. Furthermore, you have noticed this employee acting in this manner several times over the past six weeks. You have talked with him twice in the past about this "spacey" behavior only to be told that everything was all right and that the employee was simply tired and under a lot of stress because of an impending divorce. Yet you suspect drug use and are concerned that the employee's judgment and coordination are severely impaired. What do you do? If you order a drug test, will you violate the employee's right to privacy? If you take no action, will you be held liable for any accident or injury caused by the employee?

This example shows just how difficult it is to handle problem employee situations.[27] The employer must find a way to deal effectively with the problem employee situation while protecting the employee's rights. In this example, the employer would be much better off if the firm has a policy on drug testing that was approved by legal counsel and circulated to all employees prior to the incident. The employer would also be better able to handle this situation if the company has an employee assistance program (EAP). Without a drug policy and an EAP, the employer can still take effective action. That action is the subject of the remainder of this chapter.

THE PROBLEM EMPLOYEE

All employees have problems from time to time. They are usually transitory and clear up with little if any help from the employer. However, if this is not true, the person may be a problem employee, characterized by the following factors:

- Has a major problem.
- Has a chronic problem that recurs.
- Has a problem that requires high costs to resolve.
- Has a problem that will result in high costs if not resolved.

From a strategic standpoint, the organization must decide how much action it can afford to take in resolving the problem: that is, how much can it afford to spend to salvage an employee? The answer to this question is usually not easy to determine and depends on a number of factors:

- The law.
- The importance of the employee to the organization.
- The ease with which the organization can replace the employee.
- The returns that will come to the organization by saving the employee.
- The organization's human resource philosophy.

Of course, these factors are not always easy to determine, especially the costs and potential benefits involved in the process.

TAKING ACTION VERSUS NOT TAKING ACTION

At first, managers typically ignore problem employees for several reasons. They hope the problem is not serious. They believe the problem will go away on its own. They are unsure about what to do. They have other things on their minds that divert their attention from the problem employee situation. Of course, in many cases, the problem does clear up with little, if any, managerial action. This reinforces the inactivity on the manager's part. But if it does not resolve itself, the manager is in a difficult situation because he or she has let the problem go on for some length of time.

From a strategic standpoint, this becomes dangerous because the costs associated with clearing up the problem at this point can become quite high. In addition, if the organization is tolerant of a problem employee's behavior, other employees will notice

HR CHALLENGE

Model Employment Termination Act (META)

The current state of wrongful discharge litigation is more like a lottery than a legal process. Some complainants become rich with awards for damages; others with similar complaints receive nothing. Neither the employers nor the employees benefit from such actions. To correct this problem, the Model Employment Termination Act (META) was introduced.

One reason for the random outcomes in the courts for wrongful discharge cases is the ever-increasing common-law exception being developed on a case-by-case basis as states decide wrongful discharge cases brought on by terminations in employment-at-will situations. The main provision of META supports arbitration instead of court litigation for discharges. The arbitrator will be severely limited in the amount of damages that can be awarded, usually to back pay and up to four years of future pay.

META also provides a universal definition of just and unjust dismissals that could be used by all states. Just discharges would be those based upon performance problems, economic problems, company relocations, and the like.

META favors the employers for several reasons. First, the threat of large settlements are gone; only back and front pay can be offered. Second, because just cause is clearly defined, there is no fear of a poor interpretation of the situation. Finally, an arbitrator, not the court system, decides the case. This is less costly and frequently quicker.

The employee also receives some benefits. First, all employees must be made aware of the process when terminated. In the past, many suffered in silence because they did not know they had any other options. Also, because the termination policy is standardized across states, employees have a clearer idea of why and how the termination process works.

SOURCE: Jeremy Fox and Hugh Hindman, "State to Address Model Termination Law," *HRNews,* January 1992, pp. 1+.

---

this, providing a precedent. Should tolerance for this type of behavior become established in the organization's culture, it will be very difficult and costly to correct.

Consequently, it is recommended that managers take immediate action when a problem employee is initially encountered. Waiting can exacerbate the situation and make it very difficult and expensive to rectify later. Of course, managers need good policy guidance from human resource professionals to help take action that is both effective and legal.

COST ISSUES

The costs involved in resolving a problem employee situation are difficult to predict. At the onset, managers do not know how much it will cost them to resolve the situation. It is difficult to predict just what will work, what will be covered by insurance, and what the costs of lost production are due to the problem employee's behavior. Furthermore, opportunity costs are associated with trying to correct problem employee behavior: the manager could be doing something with his or her time and effort other than trying to deal with the problem employee.

Because of these costs, many managers become frustrated and simply attempt to terminate the employee. Termination is sometimes an effective solution, but it is considered the "capital punishment" in the employment relationship and generally should not be the first action taken. In addition, such termination may cause many liabilities such as wrongful discharge; discharge that could be interpreted to violate a union contract or civil service protection in government; or discharge that might be judged to be discriminatory based on race, sex, age, creed, and so on. For these reasons, termination should be carefully thought out and substantiated with documentation that will stand up in a hearing or court of law.

A final note on the termination of problem employees concerns the provisions of the Americans with Disabilities Act of 1990, which protects recovering alcohol and drug abusers because these illnesses are considered treatable. If termination is carried out without first trying to rehabilitate the employee, a court or hearing officer may order reinstatement based on the fact that the employee was dismissed on the basis of a handicap—a reasonable accommodation was not first attempted (perhaps a rehabilitation program). Options other than termination are discussed below.

THE COUNSELING PROCESS

Managers should counsel problem employees to the extent that they can and should readily refer them to professional counseling as necessary. This is one reason that having an EAP program is so beneficial in dealing with problem employees.[28] We are not suggesting that managers attempt a full-blown counseling program with the employee, but that management constructively confront the employee about the problem and attempt to find out more information about what is going on and how the behavior can be changed.

A few counseling guidelines appropriate for managers follow:

- Talk with the employee to specifically define the problem in terms of the behavior that needs to be changed.
- Focus on behavior that the employee can change and that is within control of the employee.
- Enlist the employee's assistance in determining specific suggestions for changing the behavior in order to create a sense of ownership on the part of the employee for the solution to the problem.
- Jointly establish a means of monitoring and follow up with the employee to verify compliance.
- Emphasize the consequences of not fulfilling the "behavior contract"—specifically deal with the question of what will happen to the employee. Schedule follow-up meetings with a timetable.
- Offer encouragement and indicate that you support the employee and that you want him or her to do better.

Avoid getting involved in personal off-the-job problems with the employee, and certainly avoid telling the employee specific steps he or she should take in his or her personal life.[29] For example, do not ever tell an employee that he or she should divorce his or her spouse. If the problem rests here, suggest marriage counseling.

TYPES OF PROBLEM EMPLOYEES

Managers can encounter a variety of problem employees. We do not list every type here, nor do we go into extensive detail as to how to handle each type. Rather, our purpose is to identify each type and to point out some strategic considerations that must be kept in mind from a rights and responsibilities standpoint.

ALCOHOL/DRUG ABUSER

Unfortunately, this problem is becoming more common in organizations. An estimated 8–17 percent of the nation's workforce suffers from some form of substance abuse today, and the figures are not improving.[30] The primary consideration here is to give the employee the opportunity to rehabilitate without risking injury to self or others and without doing damage to the organization's operations. As indicated earlier in the chapter, it is essential for the organization to have a policy on drug and alcohol use and drug testing and to thoroughly communicate and enforce it. Exhibit 15.8 presents some guidelines that organizations may follow when adopting a drug/alcohol policy. It is also important to have or have access to an EAP.

Approaching alcohol and drug abuse as treatable medical problems is legally safe and usually protects employee rights better by giving the employee the opportunity to correct behavior prior to disciplinary action or termination.

MARGINAL/LOW PERFORMER

This employee is one who is just meeting minimum standards of job accomplishment. From a strategic standpoint, it is better for the organization to create a culture of involvement and leadership to inform the employee of the situation and provide guidance to improve it. A reward system that provides financial and nonfinancial incentives for top performance can work to prevent or alleviate problems of this type.

TARDY/ABSENT EMPLOYEE

A person can be absent or tardy for many reasons, but if a person is gone, regardless of the reason, his or her work is not getting done or must be done by others. To avoid being placed in the position of ruling on the appropriateness of the reason for absence or tardiness, many organizations offer these options:

- Flexible working hours (flextime).
- Accumulation of leave time that can be taken for either vacation or illness.
- Bonuses at the end of the year or at retirement for unused sick leave.

EXHIBIT 15.8   **General Alcohol/Drug Policy Development Guidelines**

- Address the problem of alcohol and drug abuse squarely
- Conduct proper investigations of suspected violations
- Follow appropriate disciplinary guidelines
- Train supervisors and educate employees
- Develop a policy on rehabilitation or employee assistance
- Be sensitive to employees' privacy rights
- Take reasonable steps to protect employees and others from harm caused by substance abusers
- Know the applicable statutes and regulations
- Practice good employee relations

In addition:

- Define the problem in workplace terms while avoiding legal, moral, and medical definitions
- Safeguard privacy, due process, and confidentiality
- Avoid conflict with applicable federal, state, and local statutes and regulations
- Apply substance-abuse policies equitably throughout the organization

SOURCE: Adapted from S. J. Smits and L. Pace, "Workplace Substance Abuse: Establish Policies," *Personnel Journal,* May 1989, p. 88.

- Wellness programs that encourage employees to develop good health and fitness habits, thereby reducing illness.
- Day care for employees with small children.
- The organization should have a clearly stated policy concerning absences; its violations may result in loss of the job.

Whatever policy the organization adopts, it should be effectively communicated to all employees and consistently enforced. With the advent of newer work arrangements, such as telecommuting (working at home via computer link to office), the tardiness and absence problem that sometimes plagues organizations may subside as an issue.

SABOTEUR/THIEF

Our system believes that an individual is innocent until proven guilty. Yet continuing the employment of a person suspected of a criminal act against the organization can be disastrous. How can the organization protect itself from criminal actions while protecting the rights of a suspected employee?

One common action taken by employers is to suspend suspected employees with or without pay until a hearing can be held to determine whether the evidence indicates guilt. Assuming a speedy and fair hearing is held, the organization can either reinstate the employee or take other disciplinary action up to and including termination and prosecution through the courts.[31]

CAUSTIC/SARCASTIC/NEGATIVE ATTITUDE

An employee characterized in this way can be the rotten apple that spoils the barrel in that the poor attitude can become contagious. This situation must be dealt with by focusing on the behavior that results from the negative attitude. For example, if this attitude causes the employee to lose his or her temper when working with customers or other employees, it is appropriate for management to point out that such behavior will not be tolerated in the future. If the attitude results in spreading vicious lies, gossip, or character assassinations, the employee must be confronted with such remarks and told to stop making such statements.

Changing an attitude is very difficult because it is not directly observable and is open to much debate. For example, just what exactly is a "bad attitude"? Unlike a negative attitude a negative behavior is observable and verifiable.

The final section of this chapter addresses the issue of discipline and relates it to the protection of employee rights and the handling of problem employees. Creating the proper disciplinary climate is important for preventing and resolving disciplinary issues while protecting the rights of employees.

BUILDING A GOOD DISCIPLINARY CLIMATE

From a strategic standpoint, management has a responsibility to create the proper disciplinary climate rather than just allow any climate to evolve. This means that management and human resource managers must have in mind a set of desirable criteria. A good disciplinary climate includes the following:

- Self-discipline over externally imposed discipline.
- Positive and future orientation.
- Prevention and correction.

- Progressive nature.
- Proper communication.
- Fair and impartial administration.
- The right of appeal.

We briefly look at each of these characteristics.

SELF-DISCIPLINE

The best discipline is the kind that employees impose on themselves. They do the right thing because they know it is expected and they want to do it. Such discipline is difficult to reach in many organizations. Instead, many external control measures are imposed to ensure that people do the right thing. Some level of external control is always necessary, but the emphasis should be shifted to creating a culture that fosters and rewards self-control and self-discipline. For example, Thomas J. Peters and Robert H. Waterman, in their book *In Search of Excellence,* report on the astounding success of IBM. They attribute this success to IBM's focus on its people:

> Treat people as adults. Treat them as partners; treat them with dignity; treat them with respect. . . . Thomas J. Watson, Jr. [former CEO of IBM], puts it well: "IBM's philosophy is largely contained in three simple beliefs. I want to begin with what I think is the most important: *our respect for the individual.* This is a simple concept, but in IBM it occupies a major portion of management time. We devote more effort to it than anything else."[32]

Peters and Waterman report on dozens of companies that succeed by enabling their employees to control themselves. The advantage of self-control is that the bureaucratic red tape and cumbersome reporting and check-up procedures are greatly reduced. Instead, managers *manage by exception.* People are assumed to be doing the right thing unless they demonstrate otherwise. Managers need only monitor in a general sense and become involved only when performance does not meet standards and is not quickly self-corrected. This approach reflects Theory Y assumptions about people as described earlier in the book. People want to work and want to do a good job, and the manager's role is to create conditions that allow this to happen.

POSITIVE AND FUTURE ORIENTATION

Discipline should focus on positive actions expected in the future rather than on negative ones experienced in the past. This means that the climate should focus on explaining what behaviors are expected and how employees can achieve these behaviors rather than on punishing behaviors of the past.

PREVENTION AND CORRECTION

A good disciplinary climate prevents as well as corrects undesirable behavior. Of course, from a strategic standpoint, it is better to prevent undesirable behavior from occurring in the first place than it is to correct it after the fact. In other words, there must be incentives to do the right thing and anticipated negative sanctions for doing the wrong thing. These negative sanctions can serve as a deterrent provided they are

- Known ahead of time.
- Administered in a timely fashion.

Equally applied to everyone (the "hot stove" rule: the consequence is immediately applied to everyone who touches the hot stove).

Corrective actions should focus just on that: correcting the behavior. This means that managers and human resource managers must clearly spell out in very specific terms what the employee must do and must instruct the employee on how to do it. Incentives for compliance as well as negative sanctions for noncompliance should also be clearly indicated.

PROGRESSIVE NATURE

Progressive discipline means that the severity of the sanction increases with the severity and repeated nature of the offense. Some actions might warrant immediate dismissal, such as theft; others trigger a series of steps. Exhibit 15.9 shows part of the progressive discipline schedule used by a restaurant chain for a series of relatively minor offenses that range from showing up late for one's shift to failing to clean up one's workstation at the end of the shift. Notice that the disciplinary action proceeds from a relatively light sanction of oral warning to a serious one of termination. Of course, this schedule is clearly spelled out to the employees ahead of time so they know what to expect.

PROPER COMMUNICATION

As indicated, proper communication with employees is essential for good discipline. Employees must be absolutely clear as to expectations. They must also know what is required to achieve these expectations and what happens to them if they do not. Further, they need to be properly put on notice if a previously unenforced rule is now going to be enforced.

To ensure good communication, a variety of methods should be used to clearly communicate expectations and desired behavior: face-to-face meetings, written handouts, bulletin board postings, and videos. Sunshine Junior Stores, Inc., a convenience store chain in the southeastern United States, makes extensive use of videos in new employee orientation where expectations, policies, procedures, and rules are clearly covered. The advantage of a video is that the desired and undesired behavior can be very clearly demonstrated visually.

FAIR AND IMPARTIAL ADMINISTRATION

Finally, the disciplinary process should be fairly and impartially administered. This means that individual rights should be protected and that favoritism should largely be

---

EXHIBIT 15.9   **An Example of Progressive Discipline**

DISCIPLINARY PROBLEM: FAILURE TO REPORT TO SHIFT ON TIME

First offense: Oral warning

Second offense: Written warning

Third offense: Loss of one shift's pay

Fourth offense: Three days off without pay

Fifth offense: Dismissal

---

absent from the process. People are treated alike no matter what their relationship to key people, wealth, or other factors. In practice, of course, this is difficult to achieve. But the system must be perceived as fair if it is to be respected and voluntarily followed. In a union situation, the concepts of fairness and equity are often spelled out in the labor agreement. Since the employees have had some say on discipline through their union in collective bargaining negotiations, a union system might have higher perceptions of equity than in a nonunion situation.

THE RIGHT OF APPEAL

Perceptions of fairness and equity also involve the right of appeal. A dissatisfied employee should have the right to appeal a disciplinary decision to a person or board. As we see in the next chapter, this right is clearly spelled out in union agreements. In nonunion situations the right might involve simply appealing the decision to the next higher level of supervision.

These rights and responsibilities are further discussed in Chapter 16, which deals with unions. Unions present a special strategic challenge to organizations because they provide employees with an organized way to make their wishes known and to seek redress for grievances. The unions of the 1990s are far different from unions of the 1930s, 1940s, and 1950s. The next chapter explores these differences and challenges for organizations.

MANAGEMENT GUIDELINES

The following management guidelines are based on the issues addressed in this chapter.

1. Five basic factors influence management's approach to its responsibilities and employee rights: management philosophy, the tightness of the labor market, the law, union and employee power, and organizational culture. Managers must consider the balance these factors create when developing their approach to rights and responsibilities.
2. The law has a large influence on employee rights. Legislation on discrimination, employment at will, and privacy all play major roles in management's creation of employee rights policies.
3. Employee rights policies must include seven basic areas. These areas are privacy, fair treatment, workplace health and safety, organization communication and employee involvement, notice of plant closings and disciplinary action, and due process. Management failure to adequately deal with any of these areas is likely to result in severe organizational problems.
4. Management must seek to reduce the conflict between its responsibilities to its internal and external stakeholders without unduly harming any one group, such as employees. This can usually be accomplished by making ethically correct decisions.
5. Management responsibilities include knowing the law, providing open communication, treating all employees with dignity, bargaining collectively, and providing due process.

Continued

6. Management must treat problem employees according to its own rules and methods.

7. Employee discipline is essential to organizational success. In general, the best policies are those that emphasize employee self-discipline. Good discipline policies are positive and future oriented, emphasize prevention and correction, are progressive and properly communicated, and are fairly and impartially administered. Poor policies are likely to produce organizational turmoil and severely hamper company performance.

QUESTIONS FOR REVIEW

1. What arguments can an employer use to justify having a drug or AIDS testing policy? Why might an applicant or employee be concerned about such a test?

2. What are three examples of how the culture of a society can influence employer treatment of their employees?

3. Many firms that thought they were operating under an employment-at-will doctrine later ended up in court defending themselves. What are two precautions that managers can take to ensure that their organization does not get sued for a wrongful discharge?

4. This chapter lists and describes seven basic employee rights. What are two? Explain them.

5. What is the stakeholder concept with respect to employer responsibilities? What are some of the problems with this approach?

6. What is organizational ethics? How are ethical standards instilled in people? What, if anything, can an organization do to raise or alter the ethical standards of its employees?

7. What can be done to help a problem employee?

8. What are four different types of problem employees? Compare and contrast how a manager should deal with each type.

9. How should one go about developing a good disciplinary climate?

10. At your yearly performance evaluation interview, you are informed by your boss that she has been spying on you periodically throughout the year to gather accurate information to be used in your appraisal. You receive high marks and a large raise. How do you feel about the fact that your boss has been spying on you? What if you receive a poor evaluation and no raise? Would it change your opinion about the boss' spying?

CASE

THE CLASH BETWEEN EMPLOYEE RIGHTS AND EMPLOYER MONITORING[33]

Imagine that you are at work and need to use the phone. How would you feel if you knew that your employer might be listening in on your conversation? Is your employer justified in listening to you in an effort to save expenses and monitor your job performance? Or is this an invasion of your right to privacy? The technology exists today for employers to electronically monitor employees' phone calls, watch what they type at their computer terminals, read their electronic mail, and watch them talk to their co-workers.

The advent of the modern electronics age has made the privacy issue one of the decade's hottest topics in employee rights. Consider the following situations:

• General Electric uses fisheye lenses mounted in wall and ceiling pinholes to watch employees suspected of crimes.

• DuPont uses long-distance cameras to watch employees on its loading docks.

• Delta Airlines monitors booking agent productivity through its computer system.

• Management Recruiters, Inc., monitors computer-based employee schedules to see who interviews the most candidates.

• Holy Cross Hospital in Silver Spring, Maryland, mounted a surveillance camera in the women nurses' locker room to investigate missing narcotics.

- Safeway Stores uses electronic systems in its trucks to monitor employee driving habits.
- Until recently, police departments in Connecticut, Rhode Island, West Virginia, and Utah routinely tapped all incoming and outgoing phone calls to the barracks—including privileged defendant-attorney conversations.

Which of these actions are fair and which represent an invasion of employee privacy? Almost all forms of electronic monitoring have been challenged in court (see for example, *James* v. *Newspaper Agency Corporation* for phone monitoring or *McIntyre* v. *United States* for bugging), but federal, state, and local legislation and court decisions still do not make clear what is acceptable and what is not.

From the employer's perspective, most of these monitoring situations can be attributed to one of two basic causes: (1) the need to increase employee performance and (2) attempts to reduce employee theft. Many firms argue that lost revenues due to theft and poor productivity hamper their ability to compete. Estimates of losses due to employee theft in U.S. companies range between $15 and $25 billion per year. Productivity losses are assumed to be much higher. Employers are turning to electronic monitoring techniques more frequently to combat these problems. A recent survey indicates that 15 percent of the nation's firms use employee phone monitoring. One estimate calculates that 14,000 firms monitored 1.5 million workers' phone calls in 1987—all without worker knowledge. All told, approximately 15 million people work in industries in which some form of electronic monitoring is used.

Most challenges to electronic monitoring are based on the "reasonable expectation of privacy" doctrine. This doctrine generally holds that there are situations in which a person can reasonably expect to be free of any form of monitoring or surveillance. Any invasion of this reasonable expectation of privacy should not be allowed. Unfortunately, what constitutes a reasonable expectation of privacy is not clear. In "Protecting Private Employees," Terry Dworkin suggests that in areas in which employees have high expectations of privacy, such as private offices, changing areas, and bathrooms, the use of electronic monitoring equipment could lead to successful employee suits against the employer unless the employer can show a great need for the surveillance. However, she adds that there are even exceptions to this rule. A recent federal court

case, *Postal Workers Union* v. *United States Postal Service,* held that "relative lack of scrutiny" in these areas did not necessarily create a reasonable expectation of privacy.

Furthermore, violations of privacy rights generally are a combination of civil and criminal offenses. Often, victims must sue in civil court to obtain damages and must prove that the employer's monitoring was done without sufficient cause to do so. In criminal cases, courts have generally held that people give up a great deal of privacy expectations when they become employees of an organization. Even when privacy rights are generally established, organizations can often monitor their employees by informing workers that monitoring is a general policy or by making workers sign privacy waivers as a condition of employment.

Another problem is that it is believed that the use of monitoring techniques generally harms employee morale, strains labor-management relations, and often produces increased stress in employees under surveillance. Managers are strongly cautioned to consider these side effects when developing a monitoring policy.

All of these problems associated with employee monitoring make it one of the most controversial—and litigated and legislated—human resource issues of the 1990s.

QUESTIONS

1. What ways besides electronic monitoring are available to managers to determine how productive employees are?
2. One aspect of the human resource function is to hire employees whom the organization can trust. If managers feel compelled to spy on employees to reduce employee theft, is human resource failing at its job?
3. Telephone operators who are aware that their manager may be listening or watching them have reported high incidents of headaches, back pain, fatigue, shoulder soreness, anxiety, and sore wrists. Obviously, these problems could reduce an employee's effectiveness. Do you think that these managers are hurting productivity by monitoring their employees?
4. Several software packages on the market can be used by managers to spy on their employees by tapping into the employees' computers and viewing what is on their screens. Often these programs can be run without the knowledge of the employee. Should it be illegal for software companies to market this type of product? Why or why not?

ADDITIONAL READINGS

Barrar, Peter, and Cary Cooper. *Managing Organizations in 1992.* New York: Routledge, 1992.

Barrett, Paul. "High Court Upholds Workers' Comp Law in Setback to Employer-Rights Advocates." *The Wall Street Journal,* March 10, 1992, p. A3.

Bellingham, Richard, and Barry Cohen. *Ethical Leadership: A Competitive Edge.* Amherst, MA: HRD Press, 1991.

Bible, Jon. "When Employers Look for Things Other than Drugs: The Legality of AIDS, Genetic, Intelligence, and Honesty Testing in the Workplace." *Labor Law Journal,* April 1990, pp. 195–213.

Brown, Darrel, and George Gray. "A Positive Alternative to Employment at Will." *Advanced Management Journal,* Summer 1988, pp. 13–16.

Carrell, Michael, and Christina Heavrin. "Before You Drug Test." *HRMagazine,* June 1990, pp. 64–68.

Center for Employment Relations and Law, College of Law, Florida

State University. "Wrongful Discharge." *Employment Relations Bulletin,* January 1990.

Cross, Jeffrey. "The Employee Polygraph Protection Act of 1988: Background and Implications." *Labor Law Journal,* October 1989, pp. 663–671.

Daniels, Robert. "Storm is Brewing between Employers, Employees over the Right to Privacy." *The Wall Street Journal,* August 10, 1990, p. B6A.

Dworkin, Terry. "Protecting Private Employees from Enhanced Monitoring: Legislative Approaches." *American Business Law Journal* 28, 1990, pp. 59–85.

Etziono, Amitai. *The Responsive Society.* San Francisco: Jossey-Bass, 1991.

Florida Statutes 1989, Chapter 110.227 and Chapter 447.208.

Goff, J. Larry. "Corporate Responsibilities to the Addicted Employee: A Look at Practical, Legal, and Ethical Issues." *Labor Law Journal,* April 1990, pp. 214–221.

Goldblatt, Michael. "Preserving the Right to Fire." *Small Business Report,* December 1986, p. 87.

Hawkins, Robert. "Diversity and Municipal Openness." *Public Management,* January 1992, pp. 33–35.

Hayes, Arthur. "Layoffs Take Careful Planning to Avoid Losing the Suits that Are Apt to Follow." *The Wall Street Journal,* November 2, 1990, p. B1.

Henry, Sandra. "Can You Recognize the Wrongful Discharge?" *Labor Law Journal,* March 1989, pp. 168–176.

Henshaw, Georgeanne, and Kenwood Youmans. "Employee Privacy in the Workplace and an Employer's Right to Conduct Workplace Searches and Surveillance." *Society for Human Resource Management Legal Report,* Spring 1990, pp. 1–5.

Israel, David, Pamela Sweeny, and Michael Mitchell. "Workplace Surveillance Risky Business for Employers." *HRNews/Society for Human Resource Management,* January 1990, p. 15.

Kelly, Kevin, and Michael Oneal. "This Turnaround Will Be Tougher Than Al Cheechi Thought." *Business Week,* December 24, 1990, pp. 28–30.

Marcus, Amy. "Courts Uphold Oral Pledges of Lifetime Employment." *The Wall Street Journal,* December 12, 1989, p. B1.

Mathis, Robert, and John Jackson. *Personnel/Human Resource Management,* 5th ed. New York: West, 1988.

Miceli, Marcia, and Janet Near. *Blowing the Whistle.* New York: Free Press, 1992.

Oliver, Bill. "Do You Drug Test Your Employees?" *HRMagazine,* October 1990, p. 57.

Pace, Larry, and Stanley Smits. "Workplace Substance Abuse: A Proactive Approach." *Personnel Journal,* April 1989, pp. 84–88.

Peters, Thomas, and Robert Waterman. *In Search of Excellence: Lessons from America's Best-Run Companies.* New York: Warner Books, 1982.

Rosen, Benson, and Catherine Schwoerer. "Balanced Protection Policies." *HRMagazine,* February 1990, pp. 59–64.

Rothfeder, Jeffrey, et al. "Is Nothing Private?" *Business Week,* September 4, 1989, pp. 74–82.

Rothfeder, Jeffrey, Michelle Galen, and Lisa Driscoll. "Is Your Boss Spying on You?" *Business Week,* January 15, 1990, pp. 74–75.

Salaman, Graeme. *Human Resource Strategies.* Newbury Park, CA: Sage, 1992.

Segal, Jonathan. "Follow the Yellow Brick Road." *HRMagazine,* February 1990, pp. 83–86.

_____. "Test Suspected Users Only." *HRMagazine,* November 1990, p. 79.

Sheppard, Blair, Roy Lewicki, and John Minton. *Organizational Justice.* New York: Free Press, 1992.

Smits, Stanley, and Larry Pace. "Workplace Substance Abuse: Establish Policies." *Personnel Journal,* May 1989, pp. 88–93.

Staudohar, Paul. "New Plant Closing Law Aids Workers in Transition." *Personnel Journal,* January 1989, pp. 87–90.

Tompkins, Jonathan, "Legislating the Employment Relationship: Montana's Wrongful-Discharge Law." *Employee Relations Law Journal,* Winter 1988/1989, pp. 387–398.

Willard, Richard. "Drug Test All Employees Randomly." *HRMagazine,* November 1990, p. 78.

Zachary, G. Pascal. "Bruised Apple." *The Wall Street Journal,* February 15, 1990, p. A1.

NOTES

1. Michael Carrell and Christina Heavrin, "Before You Drug Test," *HRMagazine,* June 1990, pp. 64–68; Robert Daniels, "Storm is Brewing between Employers, Employees over the Right to Privacy," *The Wall Street Journal,* August 10, 1990, p. B6; Terry Dworkin, "Protecting Private Employees from Enhanced Monitoring: Legislative Approaches," *American Business Law Journal* 28, 1990, pp. 59–85; Georgeanne Henshaw and Kenwood Youmans, "Employee Privacy in the Workplace and an Employer's Right to Conduct Workplace Searches and Surveillance," *Society for Human Resource Management Legal Report,* Spring 1990, pp. 1–5; David Israel, Pamela Sweeny, and Michael Mitchell, "Workplace Surveillance Risky Business for Employers," *Society for Human Resource Management/ HRNews,* January 1990, p. 15; Benson Rosen and Catherine Schwoerer, "Balanced Protection Policies," *HRMagazine,* February 1990, pp. 59–64; Jeffrey Rothfeder, Michelle Galen, and Lisa Driscoll, "Is Your Boss Spying on You?" *Business Week,* January 15, 1990, pp. 74–75; Kevin Kelly and Michael Oneal, "This Turnaround Will Be Tougher than Al Cheechi Thought," *Business Week,* December 24, 1990, pp. 28–30; Jeffrey L. Cross, "The Employee Polygraph Protection Act of 1988: Background and Implications," *Labor Law Journal,* October 1989, p. 663; Jeffrey Rothfeder et al., "Is Nothing Private?" *Business Week,* September 4, 1989, pp. 74–82; "Division of Workers' Compensation Proposes Changes to Drug Testing Rules," *Florida Employment Lawletter,* October 1991, pp. 1–2; David Gold and Beth Unger, "Weigh Legalities in Formulating AIDS Policy," *HRNews,* August 1991, p. 5; M. K. St. Clair and D. W. Arnold, "Preemployment Screening: No More Test Stress," *Security Management,* February 1995, p. 73; R. E. Smith, "Corporations that Fail the Fair Hiring Test," *Business & Society Review* 88, Winter 1994, pp. 29–33; and G. D. Webster, "Hiring Dos and Don'ts," *Association Management,* November 1992, pp. 100–102.

2. Jon Bible, "When Employers Look for Things Other than Drugs: The Legality of AIDS, Genetic, Intelligence, and Honesty Testing in the Workplace," *Labor Law Journal,* April 1990, pp. 195–213.

3. Maryann Keller, *Rude Awakening: The Rise, Fall, and Struggle for Recovery of General Motors* (New York: William Morrow, 1989).

4. Thomas Peters and Robert Waterman, *In Search of Excellence: Lessons from America's Best-Run Companies* (New York: Warner Books, 1982), pp. 244–245.

5. G. Pascal Zachary, "Bruised Apple," *The Wall Street Journal,* February 15, 1990, p. A1.

6. S. Carlson and P. L. Perrewé, "Institutionalization of Organizational Ethics through Transformational Leadership," *Journal of Business Ethics* 13, 1994, pp. 1–10.

7. Alan Weiss, "Seven Reasons to Examine Workplace Ethics," *HRMagazine,* March 1991, pp. 69–74.

8. "Unfuzzing Ethics for Managers," *Fortune,* November 23, 1987, pp. 229–234.

9. Forty states have enacted some form of legislation that modifies the employment-at-will concept. For more information on employment-at-will legislation, see Michael Goldblatt, "Preserving the Right to Fire," *Small Business Report,* December 1986, p. 87; and Darrel Brown and George Gray, "A Positive Alternative to Employment at Will," *Advanced Management Journal,* Summer 1988, pp. 13–16. In 1987 Montana became the first state to pass a wrongful discharge law, which essentially allows workers to challenge the employment-at-will doctrine in court under several conditions. For more information on the Montana law, see Jonathan Tompkins, "Legislating the Employment Relationship: Montana's Wrongful-Discharge Law," *Employee Relations Law Journal,* Winter 1988/1989, pp. 387–398.

10. "Distribution of Employee Manual Does Not Give Rise to Contract," *Employment Law Report,* November 1991, p. 1; and Ellen J. Pollock, "Ruling Frowns on Employers' False Promises," *The Wall Street Journal,* October 7, 1992, pp. B1 +.

11. See, for example, Amy Dockser Marcus, "Courts Uphold Oral Pledges of Lifetime Employment," *The Wall Street Journal,* December 12, 1989, p. B1.

12. Milo Greyelin and Jonathan Moses, "Rulings on Wrongful Firing Curb Hiring," *The Wall Street Journal,* April 9, 1992, p. B3.

13. Debbie Keary, "Minimize the Risk of Wrongful Discharge, Urges Brown," *HRNews,* June 1990, p. 7.

14. D. Farber, "Free Speech Is Not a Crime, but It Can Still Get You Fired," *Newsday,* February 12, 1990.

15. We recognize that this list is somewhat arbitrary and that other authors might have a different list. However, our list generally conforms to accepted listings. See James Hunt, *The Law of the Workplace: Rights of Employers and Employees* (Edison, NJ: BNA, 1988).

16. Jonathan Segal, "A Need Not to Know," *HRMagazine,* October 1991, pp. 85–90; J. Rothfeder, "Computers May Be Personal, but Are They Private?" *Beyond Computing,* January/February 1994, pp. 50–53; and Ellen E. Schultz, "Employee Beware: The Boss May Be Listening," *The Wall Street Journal,* July 29, 1994, pp. C1 +.

17. Rothfeder, Galen, and Driscoll, "Is Your Boss Spying on You?", p. 74.

18. "Most Serious Ethical Problems Involve Differences in the Way People are Treated Based on Favoritism or Relationship to Top Management," *1991 SHRM/CCH Survey,* June 1991, p. 3.

19. Center for Employment Relations and Law, College of Law, Florida State University, "Wrongful Discharge," *Employment Relations Bulletin,* January 1990, p. 3.

20. See Kenneth L. Sovereign, *Personnel Law,* 2d ed. (Englewood Cliffs, NJ: Prentice-Hall, 1989), pp. 87–93.

21. 29 CFR 16.011 (A).

22. Troy Segal, "Getting Serious about Sexual Harrassment," *Business Week,* November 9, 1992, pp. 78–82.

23. James B. Treece, "Breaking the Chains of Command," *Business Week: The Information Revolution,* 1994, pp. 112–114.

24. See, for example, Peters and Waterman, *In Search of Excellence.*

25. Paul Staudohar, "New Plant Closing Law Aids Workers in Transition," *Personnel Journal,* January 1989, pp. 87–90.

26. David W. Ewing, "Corporate Due Process Lowers Legal Costs," *The Wall Street Journal,* October 23, 1989, p. A14.

27. Cecily A. Waterman and Teresa A. Maginn, "Investigating Suspect Employees," *HRMagazine,* January 1993, pp. 85–87.

28. Ellen E. Schultz, "Be Careful What You Tell Your Firm's Counselors; It May Be Used Against You," *The Wall Street Journal,* May 26, 1994, pp. C1 +.

29. "Employees' Rights, After Hours," *Manager's Legal Bulletin,* 1994, Alexander Hamilton Institute Incorporated.

30. "Drug Testing in the Workplace," *Occutrax,* July–August 1993, p. 1.

31. Michael Allen, "Security Experts Advise Firms to Avoid Panic, Excess Zeal in Probing Data Leaks," *The Wall Street Journal,* September 20, 1991, pp. B1 +.

32. Peters and Waterman, *In Search of Excellence,* p. 238.

33. Israel, Sweeny, and Mitchell, "Workplace Surveillance Risky Business for Employers," p. 15; Daniels, "Storm is Brewing between Employers, Employees," p. B6; Rothfeder, Galen, and Driscoll, "Is Your Boss Spying on You?" pp. 74–75; Henshaw and Youmans, "Employee Privacy in the Workplace," pp. 1–5; Gene Bylinsky, "How Companies Spy on Employees," *Fortune,* November 4, 1991, pp. 130–140; and L. Harper, "Concern about Privacy," *The Wall Street Journal,* May 17, 1994, p. A1.

CHAPTER 16

UNIONS AND STRATEGIC COLLECTIVE BARGAINING

One of the most significant issues facing managers in the mid-1990s is the changing role that unions are playing in the economy. Important economic shifts have impacted not only companies and unions but also the very essence of their relationship. World-wide markets, changing demographics, and attitude changes make it necessary for managers, particularly human resource managers, to understand the strategic role of unions.

This chapter examines how and why unions came into existence in the country, their legal basis, some of the driving forces that are causing their roles to shift, the current state of union–employer relationships, innovative solutions to some old labor–management problems, and the outlook for labor relations in the mid-1990s.

The chapter also looks at international competition, attitudes toward unions, and legislative solutions that have dramatically affected the role of unions and management. The impact of these and other important concerns on the collective bargaining process is also discussed.

CHAPTER OBJECTIVES

As a result of studying this chapter, you should be able to
1. Identify strategic issues that affect labor unions today.
2. Describe the current state of union growth and decline.
3. Discuss the role and objectives of unions in society today.
4. Explain the laws that regulate relations between union and management.
5. Identify strategic variables and choices regarding the collective bargaining process.
6. Distinguish between adversarial and cooperative problem-solving union roles.
7. Debate the pros, cons, and legalities of "union-busting" tactics and union avoidance techniques.
8. Outline the formal bargaining process, including preparation, negotiations, settlement, and mediation and arbitration.

CATERPILLAR—MOVING FORWARD INTO THE FUTURE OR TURNING THE CLOCK BACK?[1]

"Quality People Working Together"
>—Banner in late 1980s that union member Bob Thorpien convinced the company to erect.

"Cat Treats Workers Like Dogs"
>—Sign displayed by Mr. Thorpien in June 1994. When he was suspended by the company for his actions, the United Auto Workers staged the ninth wildcat strike since the fall of 1993.

The name *Big Blue* is synonymous with IBM, and Bright Yellow represents the Big Cat to tens of thousands of farmers, construction workers, and owners. Caterpillar Company, maker of Big Cats, is based in the heart of middle America in Peoria, Illinois. Over the last half of the century, Caterpillar has become the largest worldwide producer of construction and earth-moving equipment and of large powerplants (engines) that are used in farm equipment, trucks, and construction equipment. Like the auto industry, the construction and earth-moving equipment industry grew dramatically after World War II. Times were good and profits high, which led to the growth and strengthening of the major labor union the United Auto Workers. During the 1960s and early to mid-1970s negotiations between the company and the union were difficult, but the ultimate settlements were generous, and profits remained high. Between 1955 and 1982, 10 strikes occurred during 10 contracts.

During these prosperous years, efficiency often was of little concern; the shop floor was described by one union member as being like a "playground." Workers came in drunk or stoned on drugs, and union stewards spent a great deal of time trying to keep them from being fired. Given the overall economic prosperity, however, such inefficiencies were tolerated and the large wage and benefit packages could be passed along in the form of higher prices to the customer.

THE BEST OF TIMES BECOME THE WORST OF TIMES

In the late 1970s, the economic bubble burst. A grain embargo against the Soviets, issued by then President Carter, led to a precipitous decline in farm incomes and land prices. Interest rates climbed to dizzying heights, in some cases in excess of 20 percent. Caterpillar, which had enjoyed market domination in a number of countries most affected by the economic crisis, had planned massive expansion of its facilities. When the market for construction equipment dried up, Cat had to stop construction of two new plants in Burlington, Iowa, and Morton, Illinois, after the structural steel had been erected. Both were ultimately torn down.

Rather than needing new capacity, Caterpillar could not keep existing capacity busy. Costs were spiraling out of control and demand was down. Workers were laid off and, in many cases, permanently furloughed. The number of United Auto Workers (UAW) working for Caterpillar in 1979 declined from approximately 23,000 in the Peoria area alone to fewer than 12,000 in 1984, and has declined since (see Exhibit 16.1). The situation was grim for both the union and the company. No longer were layoffs limited to the blue-collar workforce; managerial ranks were being reduced as well. In 1982 the UAW conducted a 205-day strike that led many to believe that the old adversarial relationship had to be changed.

Cat's Tale

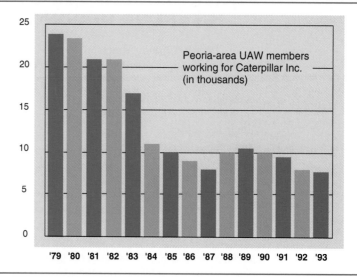

Peoria-area UAW members working for Caterpillar Inc. (in thousands)

SOURCE: Dennis Farley, "To End Impasse: Workers at Caterpillar Hope against Hope Clinton Will Be True," *The Wall Street Journal* July 26, 1993, p. A7.

NEW IDEAS AND NEW APPROACHES: WILL THEY PLAY IN PEORIA?

Once both the company and union realized that the 1980s were not a repeat of the temporary layoff–hire back cycle of the past, there was a very strong incentive to work together. New management concepts such as quality circles, just-in-time inventory, and total quality management were becoming popular in the mid-1980s. Companies such as Deere, General Motors, and other UAW shops were experimenting with new cooperative arrangements. This was difficult often for both management and union. Their long-term adversarial relationship was more comfortable and the rules more certain and predictable than these new arrangements. Managers frequently believed that they did not want to give control to the "workers." Union officials who sought too much cooperation were accused of "selling out." Nevertheless, over time many of the deeply held suspicions were put aside to save as many jobs as possible.

In the spring of 1986, Caterpillar managers and UAW representatives met in Michigan to try to develop a more cooperative spirit. The meetings went so well that one union official remarked, "I'm getting worried; I'm agreeing too much with you guys." An outflow of this session was the employee satisfaction process (ESP). In Aurora, Illinois, plant workers helped plan everything, including the purchase of machinery and reorganizing the assembly line. Rich Clausel, one of the workers, summed up the new positive attitude of many of the union members: "For the first time, I felt when I went to work, I made a difference." Even doubtful employees like Bob Thorpien were won over. He suggested that training classes be held to help new workers in his area; he ended up teaching the classes himself.

Clausel took the challenge seriously. At home he read about employee involvement programs and freely shared his knowledge and ideas with other workers. He moved from his line job and became one of the facilitators. New alliances and friendships formed between old rivals, and problems were approached creatively. The UAW workers enjoyed an increased sense of value. Furthermore, Caterpillar's costs went down and productivity up. It saved almost $5 million from 241 team-generated ideas in the Aurora plant. Downtime and product defects declined. Clausel and a company official even went so far as to conduct workshops for hourly, salaried, and managerial employees, demonstrating that bad attitudes hurt product quality. Was this the beginning of a new era of good feelings that many had wanted for years?

CHAIRMAN FITES ARRIVES: A KNIGHT ON A WHITE HORSE OR A BLACK CAT?

PATTERN BARGAINING
A type of contract bargaining in which one settlement is used as a model for other settlements in a given industry.

Meanwhile the Peoria headquarters applauded such efforts, but the company continued to suffer through the recession of the early 1990s. Economic performance was lackluster. In an effort to reverse the decline, Caterpillar named Donald Fites chairman. He wanted to embark on a *radically different strategy.* He reorganized the company into profit centers and engaged in an effort to hold down costs as he attempted to make the company competitive in the world market. To him, holding costs meant taking on the UAW. The auto industry, farm equipment industry, and construction industry had a tradition of **pattern bargaining,** whereby a settlement between one company and a union is used as a model for the other companies in the industry. For example, the UAW might target Ford in a given contract cycle for negotiation. Whatever agreement the UAW is able to get with Ford would be accepted later by GM and Chrysler. In 1991, Deere & Company was the targeted company in the construction/farm equipment business. Deere agreed to a very lucrative package of wages and benefits. In addition, it agreed to other concessions and provided increased job security. Caterpillar determined that a similar package based on the pattern bargaining concept would involve an approximate 26 percent increase in costs. Fites refused to go along with the pattern bargaining and offered a package worth 17 percent. He argued that Deere served a different market and did not face the same worldwide competitive battles that Caterpillar did.

The UAW was outraged and launched a strike on November 4, 1991. On November 5, the UAW suspended the ESP. Clausel was caught between the company and his union. He initially crossed the picket line to jeering union members. After two days, he joined the strikers, but the damage had been done. The ESP was dead and Clausel was censured from ever running for a union office. Fites took an extremely tough line. Bolstered by the antiunion sentiment of the 1980s and growth of management power, he threatened to hire permanent replacement workers. The union ended the strike, and Fites imposed a mandated agreement. Many saw this as a major embarrassment for the union and the end of a promising new era in labor–management relations. Production was slowed, grievances increased significantly, and new ESP buttons were issued by the union that read "Employees Stop Participating."

From a bottom-line standpoint, the company may have come out ahead. The mandated contract, as opposed to the UAW demands, saved about $80 million over three years as opposed to the estimated $50 million savings from the employee involvement plans. Many wondered, however, whether the long-term damage to morale and productivity could ever be undone.

COMPANY PERSPECTIVE: THE PROOF IS IN THE PROFITS

By 1994, Caterpillar's sales and profits had risen dramatically, recovering from the recession-plagued years 1991 and 1992 (see Exhibit 16.2). The 1994 earnings were

█ **EXHIBIT 16.2**   **Caterpillar by the Numbers**

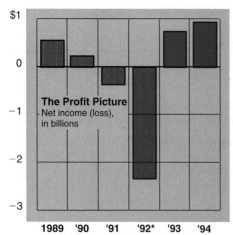

The Profit Picture
Net income (loss), in billions

1989 '90 '91 '92* '93 '94

* Includes $2.22 billion charge from accounting changes

The Fundamentals

	1994	1993	1992
Sales (billions)	$14.33	$11.62	$10.19
Net Income (Loss) (millions)	$955	$652	($2,435)*
Earnings (Loss) Per Share	$4.70	$3.36	($24.12)*

*1992 loss includes loss of $2,217 million, or $21.96 a share, from accounting changes

MAJOR PRODUCTS

Earth-moving, construction and materials-handling equipment; diesel engines; and financial services to customers

MAJOR COMPETITORS

Deere & Co.; the Case Corp. unit of Tenneco Inc.; Komatsu Ltd. and Hitachi Ltd. of Japan; and Fiat SpA of Italy

Source: Robert L. Rose, "Labor Strife Threatens Caterpillar's Booming Business," *The Wall Street Journal,* June 10, 1994, p. B4.

$942 million on sales of $14 billion worldwide, finishing Caterpillar's fifth consecutive quarter of record profits in March 1995. This trend is expected to continue through 1996. Caterpillar maintains that the imposed settlement of 1992 was necessary and that labor relations are really pretty good. It blames much of the current discord on "peer pressure." Even with threatened strikes and work slowdowns, productivity has increased. Management clearly believes that it won the battle and the war. The lean, efficient organization is poised to take advantage of the growing market for its products worldwide.

UNION PERSPECTIVE: TIME DOES NOT HEAL ALL WOUNDS

RANK AND FILE
Regular union members, not union leaders.

The UAW sees the situation very differently. The discord in the plants is growing, and a series of wildcat strikes has occurred since 1993. Grassroots rebellion may be building as exemplified by Thorpien's sign, "Cat treats its workers like dogs." During the 1991–1992 labor dispute, the company had severe financial problems and the union believed that it had very few options. With increasing demand and increasing profits, as well as a backlog on several of the products, the UAW perceived that the balance of power might be shifting. The humiliating defeat in 1992 weighed heavily on not only union officials but on the **rank-and-file** members. Most of the walkouts were not led from the top down but by line workers, who complained about harassment and gratuitous suspensions. Over 80 complaints were filed with the National Labor Relations Board.

THE FUTURE: CAT AND MOUSE, OR WILL THE UNION COME ROARING BACK?

The outlook for Caterpillar and the UAW is unclear as of mid-1995. The company is prospering, but the UAW membership is restless. Much of what happens may be beyond the direct control of both the company and union. The economic conditions both in this country and worldwide impact demand and profits. Ironically, the better the outlook for Caterpillar, the more likely the UAW is to press its claims. The Clinton administration, which organized labor strongly supports, recently intiated federal legislation via executive order to prohibit the permanent replacement of striking union members. This legislation, discussed later in this chapter, is very controversial, and if it remains federal law, the strategy employed by Caterpillar in the 1991–1992 strike would be rendered useless.

Caterpillar's experience should cause concern in company managers and union officials alike. It raises several significant questions that must be dealt with in the 1990s, including the following:

1. Can managers and union members work in cooperative team efforts without violating collective bargaining agreements? What do management and labor have to gain or lose by these arrangements?
2. Are cooperative efforts such as those discussed at Caterpillar merely a short-term departure from the long-term animosity between labor and management, or are they the beginning of a new era?
3. When a new corporate strategy such as that installed by Donald Fites is deemed necessary, what role, if any, should the unions have in determining the creation and implementation of that strategy? What are the perils of inclusion and exclusion?
4. To what degree do outside environmental issues such as economic conditions and political conditions impact the relationships between management and labor?
5. Does the election of the Clinton administration represent a significant shift in the balance of power between labor and management, reversing the decline of union power during the 1980s?

STRATEGIC CHOICES

Managers have a number of strategic choices to make regarding the role of unions in the organization. Some of the most important choices follow:

1. Managers who work for unionized organizations must decide what type of union–management relationship they want. Once determined, they must take appropriate steps to make this type of relationship a reality. Many additional strategic choices will arise as these steps are determined and taken.
2. Managers who work for organizations without a union must decide how important it is to keep the union out of the company. If it is determined important to remain nonunion, management must determine the necessary steps to keep unions out.
3. Management must also choose the type of bargaining tactics to use during contract negotiations with unions.
4. Managers who wish to decertify an existing union must be aware of laws concerning this.

THE HISTORICAL DEVELOPMENT OF UNIONS

To fully understand today's trends in the labor movement, managers should appreciate the historical basis and development of unions over the last 150 years. Much of the current policy debate and the future direction of the labor movement is rooted in the uniquely U.S. experience with unions, which has developed within the context of democratic institutions.

THE EARLY LABOR MOVEMENT

UNION HIRING HALL
Office that maintains a list of qualified union members available for work.

Early attempts at organization go back to around the time of the American Revolution. The earliest movements involved mostly craft organizations and were local in nature.[2] These unions had a common bond of common skill. They sought to protect their chosen occupation through entrance requirements, apprenticeship training, and a form of certification using the "journeyman" and "master" designations. This practice assured employers that they could depend on the quality of work provided by a union member. These same concepts of controlled entrance, apprenticeship training, and quality assurance serve as the basis of craft unions even today. In fact, craft unions often operate a **union hiring hall** that maintains a list of qualified individuals for work. This actually helps employers with the recruiting, screening, hiring, and training functions. The American Federation of Labor (AFL) eventually grew as the group or federation of allied craft unions.

HISTORY OF INDUSTRIAL UNIONS

INDUSTRIAL UNIONS
Unions whose members work in "industrial" professions such as manufacturing or mining.

Prior to the 1930s, organizing industrial (factory, mining, and so on) workers met with little success. In the 1930s, however, **industrial unions** began to grow in both numbers and power. Some would argue that the powerful emergence of the unions in the 1930s was a result of excesses and the unchecked power of large emerging corporate entities.[3]

The AFL was against industrial unions because it viewed the workers as unskilled. The unwillingness of the AFL to pursue industrial unionism eventually resulted in the formation of the Congress of Industrial Organization (CIO), which served as the federation for the developing industrial unions. During the 1950s, the AFL and the CIO merged, and now most, but not all, unions are members of the AFL-CIO union federation in the United States (the most notable nonmembers include the West Coast Longshoremen and, until 1987, the Teamsters).

Because members of industrial unions typically are not highly skilled, industrial unions do not perform the same screening, training, and placement functions performed by craft unions. Unions' strength lies in numbers; they seek to get as many employees into the union as possible.

LEGAL FRAMEWORK

COLLECTIVE BARGAINING
The contract negotiation process between union and management representatives.

As unions began to grow, many bloody, violent battles erupted between unions and management. The courts and the federal government played a role in trying to stem this violence and to provide a web of rules to govern unionization and **collective bargaining,** the process of contract negotiation between union and management representatives about issues such as wages, hours, and working conditions. Each of these rules is described and summarized in Exhibit 16.3.

CHANGES FOR UNIONS IN THE LATTER PART OF THE TWENTIETH CENTURY

In the early 1990s, approximately 16 to 17 million workers in the United States belonged to a union of some type. Membership in the public and education sectors

EXHIBIT 16.3   **Major Legislation and Legal Cases Affecting Unions**

GENERAL COURT INJUNCTION

A court order is used to control the actions of another party. These were used by employers to stop strikes, boycotts, picketing, and organizing activity but are rarely used today.

SHERMAN ACT (1914)

Originally passed to break up monopolies and trusts, it was used against unions because they were viewed as monopolies in restraint of trade.

CLAYTON ACT (1914)

Sought to exclude unions from provisions of the Sherman Act.

DUPLEX CASE (1921)

Supreme Court affirmed earlier right to prosecute unions under antitrust legislation.

RAILWAY-LABOR ACT (1926)

First favorable legislation for unions. Gave railway workers the right to organize and bargain collectively.

NORRIS-LAGUARDIA ACT (1932)

Made it much more difficult for employers to obtain a court injunction and eliminated yellow-dog contracts under which an employee had to sign a pledge never to join a union to gain employment.

WAGNER ACT (1935)

Guaranteed the right of employees to form, join, assist, and bargain collectively. Formulated procedures for establishing a union and limited employers' actions. Created the National Labor Relations Board (NLRB).

JONES AND LAUGHLIN STEEL CASE (1937)

Supreme Court upheld the Wagner Act as a valid regulation of interstate commerce.

TAFT-HARTLEY ACT (1947)

Prohibited unions from refusing to bargain in good faith, using secondary boycotts, and featherbedding (paying for time not worked), among other things. Set the stage for "right to work" laws.

LANDRUM-GRIFFIN ACT (1959)

Regulated the internal working of unions and set standards for union treatment of members.

has begun to increase; in fact, more than 40 percent of public sector employees are unionized.

Although the *number* of union workers remains moderately stable, the increase in membership does not reflect the increase in the overall labor market. Since 1983, union membership has fallen 6 percent to about 16.7 million. This represents only about 15.5 percent of the labor force, which is the lowest percentage since the Great Depression (see Exhibit 16.4).[4] In the period 1983–1994, union membership in the private non-agricultural industries declined from 17 percent to 11 percent. The percentage had been

EXHIBIT 16.4   **Percentage of Union Membership**

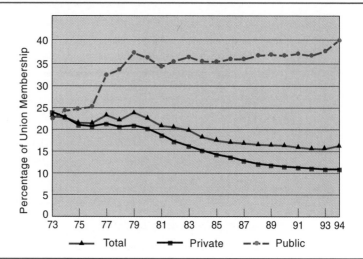

SOURCE: Data from Barry T. Hirsch and David A. Macpherson, *Union Membership and Earnings Data Book 1993: Compilations from the Current Population Survey* (Washington: Bureau of National Affairs, 1994), Table 1, p. 8. Figures represent the percentage of wage and salary workers who are union members among all workers, private sector workers, and public sector workers. Public sector percentage increased in 1977 owing to a definition change in union membership, which for the first time included members of "employee associations similar to a union."

as high as 40 percent in the mid-1950s.[5] A major reason for this decline is global competition, which has drawn millions of low-skill U.S. jobs to Asia and other third-world countries. For example, 500,000 U.S. jobs in the apparel and textiles industries were lost in the 1980s. Of course, many of these jobs were nonunion, but the downward pressure on wages has weakened the power of existing unions and discourages the formation of new locals. The fear that the North American Free Trade Agreement would encourage even more relocation of jobs to Mexico was the reason that organized labor in general opposed it.

There is some evidence, however, that the steep decline in union membership experienced during the 1980s may be leveling off. As mentioned, the membership in the public sector has increased rapidly. The National Education Association (NEA) is now recognized as one of the largest and most powerful unions in the country. Among potential union organizing targets during the remainder of the twentieth century are the following:

- Service sector employees
- Professional associations (such as the NEA)
- Sunbelt state workers
- Small businesses

No one expects labor unions to regain the power they had in the decades of the 1940s and 1950s, but the total destruction of unions would be considered detrimental to the economy.

According to the 1994 *Economic Report of the President,* the decline of union power results in a drop in pay for millions of people and could threaten the American social fabric.[6] Indeed, the pay increases for union members actually lagged behind those of their nonunion counterparts during the 1980s.

Of increasing concern for U.S. workers is the erosion of benefit packages such as health-care and pension benefits. In 1980, 63 percent of workers in companies with more than 1,000 employees had employer-provided health care. By 1991, that percentage had dropped to 56 percent.

Interestingly, a 1994 survey from Roper Starch Worldwide, Inc., reports that employee job satisfaction was at its lowest in 21 years. Could this be signalling an opportunity for unions to strengthen membership and bargaining power?[7]

Some managers argue that unions have been their own worst enemy and caused their own decline in the 1980s. To remain competitive on a worldwide basis, these managers say, unions must become more realistic and cooperative.[8] New attitudes are beginning to emerge in some quarters. In these cases, both unions and companies are exhibiting a willingness to try new cooperative arrangements. In a landmark report in February 1994, the AFL-CIO encouraged its members to become partners with management to increase productivity. Efforts such as those between Xerox and Amalgamated Clothing & Textile Workers and LTV and unionized steel workers are becoming more common. The Caterpillar case at the beginning of this chapter, however, demonstrates how fragile these agreements can be given the background of the traditional adversarial role between labor and management. This was critical in 1995 as the Bureau of Labor and Statistics estimated that 42 percent of the nation's union contracts expired, the largest percentage in 11 years.

UNIONS IN THE EARLY TWENTY-FIRST CENTURY

The future of unions is uncertain. The success of unions in the next 10 to 15 years clearly will be based on how well they match their objectives and strategies with the opportunities and threats in the environment. Unions must establish a strategic fit as must other organizations. This means that unions must reevaluate their role in society given the major changes in the workplace over the last 20 years. A 1994 AFL-CIO report recognized that change was needed.[9] Let's look at some of these potential roles and discuss how they are changing or might change.

ADVANTAGES OF UNIONIZATION

MEMBERS' PERSPECTIVE

Union membership provides a number of advantages to workers. Unions negotiate wages and benefits for their members and seek to provide them job security, social affiliation, training and development, and the opportunity to exert political influence.

Larry Reynolds, in "Labor's Leaders Changing to Meet the Times," states that union leaders are no longer billing themselves just as the guardians of organized labor, but also as employee rights advocates. They seek cooperation instead of confrontation and participation in both decision making and profits.[10] As unions seek to diversify their membership, issues such as health benefits for part-time employees, child care, flexible hours, and pension security have become important.[11]

WAGES AND BENEFITS

Unions act as a collective bargaining agent for the rank and file with a company. In recent years, the success of these negotiations has been somewhat limited. Union leaders contend, however, that in an age of givebacks and concessions, they have prevented deeper erosion and unfair singling out of workers for cuts. Increasingly, unions have turned their attention to issues such as job security in exchange for lower raises or, perhaps, actual reduced wage rates.

Health-care benefits have become an area of contention between labor and management. With an aging workforce at one end and young families or single-parent families at the other end, basic health care is a high priority. The premiums have risen far more sharply than the general inflation rate, as we saw in Chapter 14. Many workers expect the employer to pay a full 100 percent of a health-care premium, but, as previously discussed, employers are seeking to share the costs, reduce benefits, and raise deductibles.[12] From 1979 to 1988, the share of workers aged 25 to 64 with employer-paid health care actually decreased from 63 percent to 56 percent. Some of this was due to deunionization, and some due to a shift to small companies. Smaller companies are particularly hard pressed to provide benefits. Attempts to reform the nation's health-care system in 1994 focused on this particular issue.[13]

JOB SECURITY

Provision of job security continues to be an important issue for union members. In the era of the "go-go" 1960s, when jobs were plentiful and employment was steady, the job security issue was often one of providing protection against what the union considered unfair retribution and arbitrariness on the part of management or protection against cyclical layoffs, such as those that occurred in the steel and auto industries. Work rules and rigid job classifications also were developed to keep a certain number of jobs intact. When a company had considerable financial resources and slack, having extra positions was not a problem. Unions, such as the United Automobile Workers (UAW), negotiated contracts with pay clauses to cover layoffs (supplemental unemployment benefits) and other clauses, such as the "30 and out provision" whereby a worker could "retire" after 30 years of service, regardless of age, with a very attractive financial package. Today, in the age of cutbacks, buyouts, and global competition, unions have difficulty maintaining these clauses.

Due to the economic turbulence since the 1970s, long-term employment is no longer assumed. When the slack disappeared, layoffs and givebacks became pervasive. Akio Morita, former chairman of Sony, espouses the Japanese philosophy of lifetime employment. He severely criticized the layoff practice of U.S. businesses: "American management treats workers as just a tool to make money. You know, when the economy is booming, they hire more workers, and [when] the recession comes, they lay off the workers. But, you know, recession is not caused by the workers."[14] Some large U.S. companies have no-layoff policies, but several of them have discontinued this policy under increasing financial pressures; these companies include Bank of America, Eastman Kodak, Morgan Guaranty, R.J. Reynolds Tobacco, and IBM.

TWO-TIERED WAGE SYSTEM

A wage system in which newer employees are paid less than more experienced employees for performing the same job.

Union leadership has increasingly turned to the issue of guaranteed job security in exchange for reduced wages, **two-tiered wage systems** (new workers are paid a lower wage scale than existing employees), easing of work rules, and so forth. Companies such as Maxwell House are making the distinction between job security and employment security. Employees with at least five years of seniority may be guaranteed no layoffs (except in the event of extreme economic conditions), but they are not necessarily guaranteed their present job duties.

A relatively new approach to the job security issue has been for unions to become more actively involved in mergers and buyouts through union-sponsored employee stock ownership plans, discussed in Chapter 14. Some labor leaders believe workers can bring a different investment perspective to the company. Public stockholders want the highest rate of return, and union members-owners may be more interested in good wages or job-saving capital investment programs.

Union ownership poses interesting questions. What will happen if the union is forced to impose wage cuts on its members? The process of ownership, some argue, will change the union's very outlook and operation.[15] The employee buyout of United Airlines in July 1994 will test whether this type of reconfiguration can work. The UAL purchase represents the nation's second largest employee-owned company ever. One factor complicating this buyout is the fact that multiple unions are involved. See the United case at the end of this chapter. Just how this will affect the human resource function is a serious, unresolved question at this time.

SOCIAL AFFILIATION

SOCIAL AFFILIATION
Community and social support and services offered by a union to its members.

Unions offer important **social affiliation** for their members to provide a sense of community and help to avoid alienation caused by the work routine. Unions may sponsor social events and involve members in the community. During hard economic times, the union can help ease the problems associated with shutdowns and reduction in income by providing a sense of social and psychological support.

TRAINING AND DEVELOPMENT

Many unions are instrumental in the training of their membership. As we discussed earlier, this is particularly true of craft unions. They often provide apprenticeship programs to develop highly skilled workers. As plant closedowns continue, industrial unions will need to be more involved with the company in helping their members to be retrained for new jobs requiring new skills. When International Harvester was preparing to shut down its Rock Island, Illinois, plant permanently, the union and management negotiated significant funds for retraining and basic job search programs in cooperation with state and local officials.

POLITICAL INFLUENCE

Unions often support political issues or causes. A great deal of legislation protecting workers (union and nonunion as well) has been passed as a result of direct lobbying or union support.

MANDATED BENEFITS
Benefits required by the federal government to be given workers.

In recent years, labor has advocated more **mandated benefits,** such as guaranteed medical insurance, higher minimum wages, and time off for family emergencies as provided for by the Family Leave Bill passed in 1993. It is certainly more efficient to seek these on a national scale than to resort to local union, state legislature, or even industrywide efforts. With organized labor's shrinking percentage of the workforce, these national efforts allow labor to build coalitions with other political and social advocacy groups that may share some or all of their views on certain issues. These coalitions may be one way to maintain past union political clout.

Involvement in politics can be a double-edged sword, however. One of the difficulties with political action is that union members may hold a wide diversity of views. When union leaders take an official position or support a certain candidate, they risk the estrangement of rank-and-file members.

MANAGEMENT'S PERSPECTIVE

UNION SUPPRESSION
Management tactics, legal and/or illegal, to keep a union out of a company.

As noted previously, management seeks to protect the company's interests. Issues of importance to management are discussed in the following section. As a general rule, management has resisted unionization and has viewed it as a severe limitation of management's power and discretion. Management resistance can be classified into two types of strategies: (1) union suppression and (2) union substitution. **Union suppression** includes a variety of active legal (or perhaps illegal) opposition tactics during the

UNION SUBSTITUTION
Management's creation of positive work conditions so that employees will not want to unionize.

organizing campaign. **Union substitution** entails progressive and proactive human resource policies designed to reduce the desire for a union. Such tactics may include high wages, complaint-resolution systems, and participation plans such as profit sharing. In *Labor Relations,* Sloane and Whitney have defined the following five different management philosophies toward labor:

1. Conflict involves open hostility and direct action opposing the objectives of labor. It was widespread before World War II and led to bitter strikes, union militancy, and even sometimes physical violence. Today open conflict is rare because of laws protecting the rights of both employers and employees.
2. An armed truce philosophy consists of a letter-of-the-law approach. The company believes that the interests of the union and the company are far apart. The company will stay inside the law but be very rigid in bargaining and insist on strict adherence by the union of even the smallest details of the contract.
3. A power bargaining approach recognizes the reality of a union but focuses on maximizing the power and posture of the company at the bargaining table.
4. The accommodation philosophy recognizes the rights of union members. The company adjusts to the reality of the union and tries to minimize conflict and disputes. There still is, however, a clear distinction between management and union roles.
5. A cooperative approach means accepting the union as an active partner in the decision-making process.[16]

HIGH COMMITMENT POLICY
A company's policy to develop highly motivated and well-trained employees.

In "Toward the Study of Human Resources Policy," George Strauss states that a **high commitment policy** is a viable alternative to the traditional practices of the past. According to Strauss, high commitment policies are designed to develop broadly trained, highly motivated employees who are prepared to exercise high orders of discretion. The organization commits itself to provide job security and a career, not just a job. Specific high commitment policies may include the following:

1. Broad job classifications, team-oriented decision making, quality of work life programs.
2. Lifetime employment or efforts at least to moderate dislocation during economic downturns.
3. Training in both skills and attitudes along with orientation programs that stress corporate values.
4. New compensation plans, including profit sharing and pay for knowledge.[17]

A variety of attitudes exists today in the employer–union area. Many companies and unions are experimenting with a more cooperative role or the high commitment policy.[18] On the other hand, labor disputes such as the one at Caterpillar seem to be moving in the opposite direction. Regardless of the philosophy of the company, unions can play several key roles that can actually be helpful. These include reducing the number of individual negotiations, specification of work rules, procedures for disagreements and grievances, and easier communications. Each of these is discussed below and is listed in Exhibit 16.5.

REDUCED NUMBER OF NEGOTIATIONS

Once a contract is negotiated with the union, managers need not worry about being approached by individual workers for raises or special benefit considerations. The manager merely needs to refer to the contract. From a planning perspective, this provides

HR CHALLENGE

Working With a Union to Save Jobs *and* Increase Profits

In February 1993, General Electric was on the verge of closing its Appliance Park near Louisville, Kentucky. Over 2,500 workers were employed in this aging facility, which manufactured a rather outdated line of washing machines, refrigerators, and other appliances. A dramatic turnaround has occurred thanks, in part, to a pioneering 43-point agreement between Local 761 of the International Union of Electronic Workers and General Electric. The plan to eliminate piecework and narrow job definitions has raised productivity significantly. The company in turn has cut the number of supervisors and organized most of the workers into teams. Given the new flexibility of the union, GE has decided to invest more than $1 billion in capital equipment and product development over a three-year period. This investment is 50 percent higher than in the past. The results have been very promising so far. Profits in 1993 and 1994 totaled $91 million, reversing the $47 million loss of 1992.

SOURCE: Adapted from Zachary Schiller and Tim Smart, "If You Can't Stand the Heat, Upgrade the Kitchen," *Business Week,* April 25, 1994, p. 35; and General Electric 1994 *Annual Report.*

greater accuracy in forecasting costs. Multiple-year contracts can greatly reduce the time that must be spent on the compensation issue. Of course, the preparation for the negotiations and the actual sessions put a heavy load on managers, particularly human resource managers, once every contract cycle.

If a dispute over wage and benefit issues arises, the company deals with the representative of the union, not with the individual worker. While union representatives may be more skillful in negotiations than individual workers, the negotiation process with them is more predictable, and procedures are usually outlined in the contract.

SPECIFICATION OF WORK RULES AND PROCEDURES FOR DISAGREEMENT AND GRIEVANCES

A union contract can clearly define work rules and guidelines for settling disagreements and grievances. If an individual worker disagrees with an action taken by his or her supervisor, but the supervisor is acting within the rules agreed to by the union, the problem is

EXHIBIT 16.5   **Advantages of Unionization**

UNION MEMBERS' PERSPECTIVE

Negotiation of wages and benefits

Job security protection

Social affiliation

Training and development opportunities

Social/political influence

COMPANY MANAGEMENT PERSPECTIVE

Reduced number of negotiations

Specification of work rules, disagreements, and grievances

Efficient communication and enforcement of predictable standards

==

HR CHALLENGE

Using Teams Could be Hazardous to Your Company's Health

Using employee teams to solve problems can be a tricky and difficult issue in light of a controversial 1992 NLRB ruling against Electromation, Inc., of Elkhart, Indiana. Suppose that several employees approach a company's human relations manager, asking that smoking be banned in the plant. Other employees object to this outright ban and prefer that the current policy of designated smoking areas be maintained. The manager decides that the best way to resolve this conflict is to form an employee committee. This sounds like a good idea, but it may violate the law, according to the NLRB ruling.

In the case of Electromation, the Teamsters Union objected to committees that had been formed to deal with issues ranging from absenteeism to smoking policies; communication networks; attendance bonuses; and pay progression for premium positions. The Teamsters contended that such committees violate a prohibition against company unions. The NLRB agreed. Compounding the problem, the NLRB confused the difference between what constitutes a company union and a team. The NLRB ruling bans employer domination of the team or any attempt to interfere with ongoing company and labor relationships. A *team* is defined very broadly as any group of two or more employees who discuss workplace problems with management members in an attempt to resolve them.

U.S. Representative Steve Gunderson (R.–Wisconsin) argues that the effect of this ruling may be very chilling to even the most successful employee involvement teams. He contends that "the effect is that management refinements in the workplace to create a more comfortable environment, to improve product quality or to meet employee concerns—including health and safety concerns—may be illegal if they result from dialogue between management and an employee group . . . how can any committee talk about any issue in the workplace without crossing the fine line into conditions of work?"

For now, the issue is murky for human resource managers in a union environment as they attempt to balance the benefits of using teams with the possible repercussions of the ruling. Representative Gunderson has urged Congress to clarify the issues related to this ruling.

SOURCE: Adapted from Steve Gunderson, "NLRB Muddies Regulatory Waters," *The Wall Street Journal,* February 1, 1993, p. A10.

==

not between the supervisor and the employee but is an issue that the union steward must work out with the worker. This may reduce the information-processing load on the supervisors and the human resource department. Dr. Richard Lyles contends that for financial reasons, companies may prefer keeping a union intact. He uses the example of a company not giving an employee a wage increase. If the employee is represented by a union, the dispute goes through a grievance process. If the company cannot resolve the issue and has to go to arbitration, it may spend $2,500. On the other hand, without a union, the dispute may end up in court and the same complaint may cost the company $250,000.[19]

EFFICIENT COMMUNICATION AND ENFORCEMENT OF PREDICTABLE STANDARDS

Communication can be facilitated by a union contract. In many cases, the company communicates with the union and the union in turn with its members. Because the contract often spells out in some detail the various procedures, work rules, and ways of handling disputes, the total number of channels may be reduced as compared with the situation for a union-free environment. This may eventually benefit management as well. If participative management is introduced into a plant, the communication channels that already exist can be used to help disseminate the required information.[20] A 1993 National Labor Relations Board ruling prohibits communication with teams regarding work rules and working conditions if they are seen as going around union agreements. Managers in union shops need to be clear about the NLRB ruling when working with teams.[21]

Unions can be the source of highly qualified, well-trained, and disciplined workers, which can help to maintain productivity and high standards. This is especially true for craft unions, such as carpenters, electricians, steamfitters, millwrights, tool and die makers, and the like. They may have long apprentice programs, certification examinations, and high levels of craft pride. Building contractors often hire from union halls rather than maintain their own employee rolls. One advantage to the employer is the ability to hire only for the duration of the project. The company, while being assured of adequately trained employees, does not have to permanently employ workers in slack demand phases.

Exhibit 16.5 summarizes this section from the perspective of both the members and the management of the company. As discussed, unionization holds advantages for *both* members and management. Management can reap certain benefits from a carefully and skillfully managed union relationship. Of course, management also pays a price for these benefits. In "Avoiding Labor Management Conflict," Alexander Trowbridge has identified several new approaches that unions and companies are exploring. These include the following:

1. Gainsharing, that is, paying workers exceeding base productivity levels.
2. Employee participation in decision making, also known as *jointness programs.*
3. Employment security and productivity agreements.
4. Corporate acceptance of the union in a partnership role.[22]

The point here is that, once a company has been unionized, managers need to make the best of the situation and exploit potential new areas of productive relationships.

THE ROLE OF LABOR UNIONS IN SOCIETY TODAY

As the Caterpillar case indicates, the role, power, and relative influence of unions changed dramatically in the 1980s. Human resource managers need to be well aware of these changes. Several strategic variables must be considered to understand the labor situation in the mid-1990s. Let us consider them one at a time.

STRATEGIC VARIABLES

COMPETITION

When high-quality, price-competitive foreign products started making inroads in the 1970s and 1980s, many previously insulated U.S. corporations had to compete with the manufacturing facilities of countries such as Japan, China, Poland, and Mexico that had significantly lower wage rates. Often higher-quality products could be sold at a significantly lower rate than products made in the United States.

Fluctuating currency exchange rates, along with what many economists and politicians considered unfair trade barriers for our products, made the strong export industry decline. During the 1980s, for example, the United States went from the status of being the largest creditor nation to that of being the largest debtor nation. This foreign competition limits the ability of the U.S. companies to pass along higher labor costs in the form of increased prices.

FOCUS ON INTERNATIONAL ISSUES

International Labor Markets Are a Two-Way Street

The Exit Route

Organized labor fought hard against the passage of the North American Free Trade Agreement (NAFTA). Labor has argued such agreements result either in loss of U.S. jobs to offshore facilities, including Mexico, or in suppressing U.S. wage rates under threat of reallocation. This indeed may be true in certain low-wage factories that employ unskilled workers. Monroe Manufacturing Company of Monroe, Louisiana, provides a case in point. Monroe, which produces a variety of baby products, pays many of its workers the $4.25 minimum wage. President Edward Hankin bluntly tells his workers: "You know what the job paid when you applied for it . . . if I can't compete in America with American jobs, I'll take your jobs overseas where we can be competitive." The workers face a dilemma. Many of them find that the wage is not enough to support a family, but the company has argued that it can take the jobs out of the country, paying hourly rates of 70 cents in Mexico and 8 cents in China.

Ironically, the low wage rate and low skill levels make this labor force difficult to organize. Union organizers can argue that the employees are not receiving a fair rate, but the company can counter that it will move work out of the country if it has to pay higher rates. Workers do not consider these to be idle threats because more than 1.2 million manufacturing jobs have been moved to other countries during the 1980s.

The Entry Route

On the other hand, two recent announcements by European car manufacturers indicate that worldwide competition can actually benefit U.S. skilled workers. In an attempt to expand its North American sales and given the relatively high expense of producing automobiles in Europe, Mercedes Benz has decided to build a new plant in Alabama. BMW likewise opened a South Carolina facility in 1995. A partnership of government, private sector, and labor leaders worked very closely with these companies to convince them to locate in these southern states. These plants join an already long list of foreign auto plants in the United States, including Honda's in Marysville, Ohio, Toyota's in Georgetown, Kentucky, and Mazda's in Flat Rock, Michigan.

It may be said that in the long run, both the interests of management and labor can be served by growing international trade. Loss of some low-skill jobs seems likely, but these may be offset by higher-paying, higher-skill jobs. The key to increasing pay for both high- and low-wage jobs is productivity. Improving productivity must be a key strategic goal of the human resource department. Managing labor relations effectively, whether in a union or union-free environment, helps to remain internationally competitive.

SOURCE: Ron Suskind, "Tough Vote: Threat of Cheap Labor Abroad Complicates Decisions to Unionize," *The Wall Street Journal,* July 28, 1992, pp. A1, A8.

Foreign competition seems to be increasing. The growth of sophistication among third-world nations such as Korea, Malaysia, and the People's Republic of China promises to keep pressure on U.S. companies. The growing power of Europe, particularly of Germany, offers competition to many U.S. core industries. Political and economic changes in Eastern Europe and the dissolution of the Soviet Union promise additional sources of competition as well as opportunity. To summarize, the industrial corporations that have been the stronghold of labor unions must now truly compete in a worldwide market.

Domestic competition by nonunion workers can radically affect a labor union's ability to negotiate. Consider, for example, the long and bitter dispute between Local P-9 of the United Food and Commercial Workers and the George A. Hormel Company in Minnesota. For years, the company and union prospered together and there was relative labor peace. Then the Iowa Beef Processors (IBP) became more aggressive. IBP set out to be a low-cost, price-leading firm by holding labor costs to a minimum. Riding the antiunion sentiment of the late 1970s and early 1980s, IBP was successful in setting up

NONUNION COMPETITION
Competition from a company that does not employ a unionized workforce.

nonunion shops. In the process, it created significant price competition for established union firms such as Oscar Meyer, Wilson Foods, and Hormel. To remain competitive, Hormel sought major concessions from its unionized workforce. The result was a long and bitter strike. An interesting feature of this labor dispute was that the national union was opposed to it and ordered the strike ended, but the P-9 defied the national union and continued the walkout.[23] This **nonunion competition** has become a major concern for large national unions. In many cases, the choice is between a crippling strike seeking wage and benefit concessions and forcing the company into bankruptcy.

ANTIUNION SENTIMENT

Clearly, the 1980s saw a dramatic shift in the sentiment toward unions. According to a Gallup poll, labor's approval rating dropped from 76 percent in 1957 to about 55 percent by 1987–1988.[24] A number of factors contributed to that change, including well-publicized union corruption cases, such as that of Jackie Presser, the Teamsters president;[25] the disruption of the public conveniences via airline, train, or bus strikes, such as the public transit workers' strike in Los Angeles in the summer of 1994; a public perception that high union wage settlements led to inflationary cycles; and a generation more dedicated to personal goals than to group action. Also, strikes by public employees, such as teachers, produced very mixed reactions. Many Americans believed that the unions epitomized parochial greed over the public good.

ILLEGAL STRIKE
A strike by a union that is prohibited by law or statute from conducting a work stoppage.

President Reagan's firing of the air traffic controllers in 1981 may have served as a watershed that demonstrated the change in the public's attitude toward labor. Even though such **illegal strikes** by public employees happened on occasion, it was unthinkable that the employees would actually be fired. While there may have been some protests over these firings, there certainly was not a mass public outcry. In fact, the action was perceived by many as a bold, courageous step by the president. Exhibit 16.6 illustrates several factors that may lead to antiunion sentiment.

As mentioned earlier in the chapter, there is some evidence that the antiunion sentiment may have moderated some during the first few years of the 1990s. Some of the tactics employed by management during the 1980s such as firing pro-union employees with impunity have moderated antiunion sentiments. Successful examples of cooperative efforts to improve productivity at companies such as Deere, Xerox, and General Electric have led many managers and the general public to look at unions in a more positive way. Also, many white-collar workers and nonunion workers have found that their own annual salaries and benefit packages have decreased as contract settlements for union members have been less favorable. Perhaps the pendulum has started to swing

■ **EXHIBIT 16.6**   **Factors Leading to Antiunion Sentiment**

Well-publicized union corruption cases

Personal inconvenience of public from strike or slowdown

Perception of inflationary wages caused by unions

"Me" generation unwilling to join communal group

Strikes by professionals, such as teachers, viewed as "unprofessional"

View that unions have narrow, parochial interests and are antithetical to the common good

Political rhetoric of Reagan administration during the 1980s back toward a positive perception of unions. Yet, according to the Bureau of Labor Statistics, 1994 contract settlements were lower on average than 1993 settlements, continuing the trend for nine consecutive quarters.

It is critical for human resource managers to be aware of public sentiment in this area as well as their particular organizational climate because such trends ultimately affect most organizations. In what may be a move favoring unions, the Clinton administration agreed to rehire the fired air traffic controllers whom the Reagan administration had fired in 1981. This appears to have been a symbolic gesture because most former air traffic controllers had secured other jobs or had permanently retired.

DISPERSION OF LABOR

Much of the successful labor-organizing activity earlier in the century was based in the Northeast or Midwest, where there were large concentrations of industrial installations. For example, the auto industry was concentrated in states like Michigan and Ohio, the farm implement industry in Iowa and Illinois, steel making in Pennsylvania, and apparel in the Northeast. Since the factories were large and geographically concentrated, it was easier to organize and to control the labor supply in these areas.

RIGHT-TO-WORK LEGISLATION
State laws that give workers the right to refuse to join a union and yet be able to work in a unionized shop.

SMOKESTACK INDUSTRIES
Traditional, heavy industries such as steel, coal, chemical making, and auto making.

Several important changes have occurred during the last 10 to 20 years. More factories and facilities are moving into smaller, rural communities, often in the Sunbelt states. One reason for the shift is the **right-to-work legislation** that is more common in the Sunbelt region. In addition, many new specialized companies are small. James Medoff, a Harvard economist, maintains that unions cannot survive unless they learn to represent workers in small units. He estimates that about one-half of all nonunion workers are employed in companies that hire fewer than 100 workers.[26] Large corporations may prefer to set up a more decentralized system with smaller plants. Service organizations, because of their need to be near the customer, also result in small units. The change in economy away from the **smokestack industries** toward a service and information-based economy may have profound effects on the ability of labor organizers who try and use traditional approaches to implement collective bargaining agreements.

ECONOMIC CONDITIONS AND EMPLOYMENT

From 1982 to the early 1990s, the U.S. economy experienced the longest sustained economic expansion in history. Overall job growth was occurring, despite the decline of employment in industries such as steel and autos. During relatively prosperous times, when jobs are plentiful and wages are rising, unions have difficulty attracting new members. It is hard to organize new unions around the issues of unemployment and poor wage and working conditions. In *Megatrends 2000,* Naisbitt and Aburdeen forecast an ever-increasing shortage of skilled labor in the 1990s.[27] According to a Hudson Institute study sponsored by the Department of Labor, the manufacturing sector will generate almost no new jobs by the year 2000 and will shrink to only 17 percent of the gross domestic product contribution.[28] Many of the remaining manufacturing jobs will be seriously impacted by computer-integrated manufacturing, robotics, and JIT (just-in-time—see Chapter 4) systems.

An interesting and new phenomenon occurring during the economic recovery of 1993–1995 has potentially negative consequences for union membership. Even though the economy was growing at a rapid rate in excess of 4 percent, companies such as IBM, AT&T, and Kodak were making large cutbacks.[29] Part-time employment, which usually increases during a recession, did so during the recovery. Companies were filling positions with not only part-timers but also temporary workers, both of whom are

FOCUS ON ETHICS

Unionizing Health-Care Professionals

Historically, society in general has perceived health-care professionals as choosing that profession because they are altruistic and primarily motivated by compassion and caring. As in many professions, union organization in the health field has been slow. In the last 15 to 20 years, however, profound changes have occurred. Dramatic technological breakthroughs, shifting demographics, increased government regulation and participation, an increase in for-profit facilities, and the rapidly increasing costs have led health-care workers to become more aggressive in seeking job security and in becoming a voice in health-care reform.

Hospital workers filed 158 petitions for union elections in 1993, an increase from 19 petitions in 1989. Unions won 58 percent of those elections, compared with only 48 percent of all union elections in the United States in 1993. In 1993, health-care professionals were involved in 43 strikes, an increase of 11 strikes over 1992. Such dramatic increases are the result of cost-cutting measures implemented by hospital managers due to proposed federal mandates and health-care reform bills. Administrators are attempting to cut operating costs, reduce overtime hours, close facilities, and reduce benefit packages. These actions are making nurses, medical technicians, and maintenance workers

more open to unionization. Nurses in a Syracuse, New York, hospital were told that they would no longer be paid for their half-hour meal breaks, resulting in a 6 percent pay cut. Those nurses, who had earlier overwhelmingly rejected a unionization attempt, agreed to join the Service Employees Union.

Another issue attracting new members to unions of health-care professionals concerns the ratio of staff to patients. Health-care workers contend that fewer staff caring for more patients will reduce the quality of service. As society wrestles with issues of health-care rights, universal coverage, cost control, and access to services, it must also deal with the fact that these issues impact the relationship between health-care managers, their employees, and their patients. Whether a growing union presence in the health-care industry is helpful or harmful to the nation's health-care goals is unclear. In the zeal to save money, a manager may inadvertently thwart many of his or her goals if the result is the installation of a union that, perhaps, neither the manager nor staff really wanted to begin with.

SOURCE: Robert Tomsho, "Mounting Sense of Job Malaise Prompts More Health-Care Workers to Join Unions," *The Wall Street Journal,* June 9, 1994, pp. B1, B8.

less costly, especially because they typically are not paid benefits and present few problems when their employment is terminated.

In this situation, unemployed or underemployed workers might again turn to labor unions for help in difficult times. Human resource managers need to study the trends in their business to be able to predict the likely effect of such economic changes on the company's labor relations environment.

LAW

As we saw in Chapter 15, more and more employee rights have been codified into the law through court decisions and the legislative process. This trend has the potential to "forge revolutionary changes in the workplace and the way companies manage people."[30] Broad legislation has been written to protect employees in the areas of privacy, severance pay, plant shutdowns, and discrimination based on age, sex, and race. Health and safety issues have been addressed at both the state and federal levels. It is clear that many times large labor groups such as the AFL-CIO led these actions. Unions recently lobbied for the Family Leave Bill, which was signed into law in 1993, the prohibition of striker replacement through legislation introduced in Congress in 1994, and health-care reform.

The passage of legislation may be a mixed blessing for the unions, however. Support of issues provided the unions a platform on which to attract new members. However, once legislation has been passed and court cases have been completed, the public may no longer be aware of the efforts unions make on behalf of their members.[31]

Legal solutions usually apply to a much broader segment of the labor force than do those gained in collective bargaining; therefore, the differential advantage of belonging to a union may narrow. Given the costs associated with belonging to a union, such as dues, limitation of individual action, and the requirement to participate in strikes, membership may be unattractive to potential members. In "Unions' Future Is Bleak," Audrey Freedman argues that labor failed to recognize several potential issues that later became legislative priorities. She argues that unions might have moved directly toward a strong equal-opportunity agenda at the end of World War II, but they did not. Instead, unions fought to preserve privilege, seniority, and preference of the past. As Freedman points out, the unions have been lukewarm toward legislation to correct past discriminatory practices, and in many cases have led the fight against such reforms.[32] Often the public has suspected that unions are basically special-interest groups representing a privileged elite, a campaign issue in the 1984 election.[33]

The trend toward legally based employee rights protection is likely to increase despite the decline of unions. Nonunionized members can bring potential pressure to bear that may, over time, result in significantly more benefits than organized labor can produce. The human resource manager must carefully monitor the legislative and court actions at the national, state, and local levels.

ENLIGHTENED MANAGEMENT

It is often argued that the management of many companies has taken a more progressive view toward the human resources of the organization. Unions have long maintained that they would have little reason to exist if it were not for poor and self-serving management. Whether for humane reasons or economic self-interest, many companies have begun to understand that either avoiding unionization altogether or working in harmony with its union makes sense. After six years of trying to organize workers at the Nissan plant in Smyrna, Tennessee, the United Auto Workers acknowledged defeat. The results of the 1989 election were convincing: 1,622 workers voted against the union; 711 were in favor of it. Bucky Kahl, the director of human resources at the plant, stated, "We pride ourselves in being a company that functions in a participatory way. The vote was a statement of support for the strongly participatory management."[34]

Management can take an openly hard-line or a more subtle approach in avoiding unionization. In *The Transformation of American Industrial Relations,* Kochan, Katz, and McKersie argued that during the late 1950s and early 1960s, managers in nonunion plants started introducing "innovative, new systems of human resource management" into their shops.[35] A number of union companies, such as Motorola, General Motors, Ford, Honeywell, Mead, Xerox, and GTE among others, have publicly committed to changes in the way they manage their employees.[36] An important question for both unions and management in the 1990s is whether unions have a reason to exist in their present form and with their present objectives if management improves.

"GRAYING" OF THE WORKFORCE

The increase in the average age of workers because of the "baby boom" of the 1940s and 1950s and the "birth dearth" of the 1960s.

CHANGING DEMOGRAPHICS

The changing demographics of the United States labor force can have a significant effect on the union movement. The **"graying" of the workforce** can potentially pit one segment against the other. For instance, older workers may be much more interested in pension and retirement benefits; younger workers may desire current high wages.

| EXHIBIT 16.7 | **Strategic Variables Affecting Unions** |

COMPETITION

Foreign and domestic competition poses a threat to the unions' power base.

ANTIUNION SENTIMENT

The 1980s reflected growing suspicion and disfavor toward unions, but that may be changing in the mid-1990s.

DISPERSION OF LABOR

Many companies are relocating or building new plants in the South and/or rural areas, or in foreign countries, to escape the stronghold area of unions, particularly unions in the northeastern and midwestern United States.

ECONOMIC CONDITIONS AND EMPLOYMENT

Strong growth in jobs and nonunion wages have dampened the incentive to join organized labor. Use of more part-time and temporary workers has also reduced union bargaining power.

LAW

Many basic employee rights are now legislated or decreed by court decisions, thereby removing many issues from bargaining and negotiation.

ENLIGHTENED MANAGEMENT

Management tends to be better trained and more effective in dealing with human relation issues without being forced to by contracts.

CHANGING DEMOGRAPHICS/JOB SECTOR CHANGES

More older workers, part-time employees, women, and minorities are entering the workforce. Unions have been the stronghold of white male workers for the past 50 years or so. More jobs in service sector and information sector, relative decrease in manufacturing sector.

The entry into the workforce of more minorities and women may make union growth unlikely. The demographic shifts will be dramatic. Today's workforce is approximately 47 percent native white males. Many of the current core workers are middle-aged and will be retiring from the workforce in the next few years. By the year 2000, the percentage of white males in the workforce is expected to drop to about 15 percent. The Hudson Institute study forecasts that five-sixths of the new workers entering the labor force between 1988 and 2000 are likely to be minorities and women.[37] Unions that protect the seniority system will find it difficult to support the demands of the new type of worker. These workers will be concerned with different economic, cultural, and sociological issues.

Exhibit 16.7 summarizes the critical variables discussed in the previous sections.

STRATEGIC CHOICES FACING UNIONS

Several strategic choices are open to unions as they fight for their survival and position in society. Each of these is discussed below and is summarized in Exhibit 16.8.

■ **EXHIBIT 16.8**   **Examples of the Economic and Political Objectives of Unions**

ECONOMIC ISSUES—BREAD AND BUTTER

Category	Example
Wages	United Auto Workers bargaining with Ford for a 6 percent annual increase for 3 years
Benefits	Teamsters asking for full family health coverage to be paid by employer
Seniority	Steelworkers negotiating with USX to give priority to longer tenured employees in awarding overtime hours
Working Conditions	Airline Pilots Association working out an agreement with United Airlines on maximum number of nights away from home
Security	UAW agreeing to two-tiered wage structure in return for non-layoff clauses

POLITICAL ISSUES

Category	Example
Political Endorsements	AFL-CIO endorsement of Bill Clinton in the 1992 presidential election
Political Action Committees (PACs)	Contribution of campaign funds to local, state, and national elections
Endorsement or Opposition to Government Policies	During the Vietnam War era, certain unions supported, while others opposed, the war
Endorsement of Certain Political Stances	The American Federation of Teachers encouraged defense cuts and more money for education

BREAD-AND-BUTTER VERSUS POLITICAL OBJECTIVES

BREAD AND BUTTER ISSUES
Bargaining objectives based on economic rather than social or political concerns.

Unions differ, of course, as to their particular objectives and goals, but the goals of unions in the United States can be separated in two broad classes. **Bread and butter issues** include economic concerns of members, such as wage rates, life and health insurance, paid vacations, and job security. Historically, unions have emphasized these issues. When Samuel Gompers was asked what unions wanted, he boldly declared, "More!" The late Jimmy Hoffa said the success of the unions depended on their ability to deliver "the highest buck."[38]

The second goal of unions involves political issues. Unions have supported or opposed the country's foreign policy objectives or allocation of government spending programs, such as increasing spending for education, over the years. The political influence of U.S. unions is usually indirect.

Generally, U.S. unions have done best with the economic issues, although as the environment has changed, the economic paradigm may no longer be in the forefront.[39] As noted previously, when unions have become involved in political issues, they frequently

HR CHALLENGE

Union Membership Has Its Privileges

The AFL-CIO has begun offering the Union Privilege program. The program is designed to help union members off the job. Eventually, the AFL-CIO hopes to offer over 60 different programs to its members. John Ross, the communications director for the program, states that he wants the membership to begin turning to the union for any need.

The goal is to attract people who are not part of any collective bargaining unit as associate union members. Offering associates program benefits will tie them to the union and the union movement. More than 325,000 associates have signed up for the program.

Several benefits are currently offered by the program:

- A credit card with no annual fee and a variable rate of only 5 percent above the prime rate. The credit card has no cash advance fees or check fees.

- Money market deposit accounts available that paid an average of 6.26 percent in 1990.
- Mortgages with rates at or below the national average and low down payments and closing costs with special deals for first-time home buyers.
- Life insurance plans that Union Privilege says are up to 25 percent lower than comparable plans.
- Prescription discounts for union members and their families. The mail service prescription plan allows members to save up to 30 percent on most brand name medications and more on generic drugs.
- Legal services including a free 30-minute consultation and a 30 percent discount on services.

SOURCE: Adapted from Stephanie Overman, "The Union Pitch Has Changed," *HRMagazine,* December 1991, pp. 44-46.

have stirred up hostility not only among the general population but also among their members. For example, even though the AFL-CIO endorsed Jimmy Carter in 1980 and Walter Mondale in 1984, the rank and file voted for Ronald Reagan in both elections. Since 1964, only two union-endorsed presidential candidates have won election.

A CHANGE IN ROLE?

ADVERSARIAL RELATIONSHIP
A management-union relationship in which each side is in competition with or seeks different objectives from the other.

Over the past century or so, the union–employer relationship has basically been an **adversarial relationship** with each side having different objectives or interests. Unions have defined their role as challenging management rather than cooperating with it. Unions believed this was the best way to advocate their members' interests, a philosophy consistent with the U.S. pluralistic political and economic system. However, many union members and company managers are now questioning whether the relationship is necessarily adversarial or a closer cooperation might be needed in this era of global competition.

Cooperative efforts between companies and unions are increasing, including those by Xerox and the Amalgamated Clothing and Textile Workers Union, and National Steel Corporation and United Steel Workers of America. Frequently, the driving force behind these efforts is the threat to close a local plant or facility or a major cutback of the labor force.

JOINTNESS PROGRAMS
Cooperative efforts by both unions and management.

Unions have responded to, talked about, and/or actually implemented workplace innovations, such as **jointness programs,** in a variety of ways. Many unions have offered their wholehearted cooperation and collaboration with the innovations. They follow this path because they believe that the adversarial relationship is hurting their members and that a change may help everyone involved. Finally, unions can use the innovations to assert their own interests. For example, the innovations may improve the quality of work life for their members, and bargaining units will be sure to include the improvement in the next negotiated contract.[40]

From a strategic human resource management perspective, these cooperative experiments are important. If they are to yield beneficial results, the human resource professionals and line managers must rethink their positions just as the labor movement is doing. It may be as difficult for the managers of the company to reorient their stance toward cooperation as it is for the union leadership to put aside a long history of confrontation. Substantial training efforts can facilitate these changes. In "Union–Management Cooperation," Cohen-Rosenthal and Burton indicate that any joint union–management training effort needs to include the following:

- An explanation of what the program is and how it will work.
- The basic principles, process, and procedures of the program.
- Skills training in the specific areas necessary to meet the goals and objectives of the program.
- A component on commitment and motivation.[41]

DOMAIN CONSIDERATIONS

Exhibit 16.9 is an illustrative presentation of several environmental factors that affect the unions' strategic choices. Earlier we mentioned the changes in the economy that have affected the traditional strength of the unions, for example, the decline of smokestack industries, the increase of service sector jobs, the movement of jobs to the Sunbelt, a more global economy with worldwide competition now a reality, and the increase of jobs in small companies.

Several additional factors also need to be considered. High-technology jobs are often filled by well-trained, often college-educated individuals. This presents a new type of worker who has to be communicated with differently. Professionals such as accoun-

EXHIBIT 16.9   **Factors Affecting Strategic Choices of Unions**

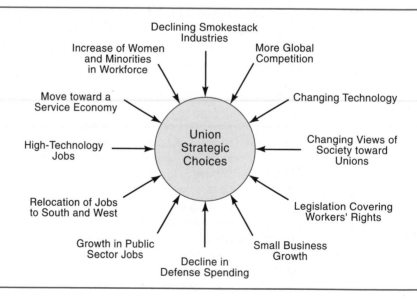

tants, nurses, doctors, and market researchers may consider themselves more closely aligned with management than with the unions. Yet the growth of professional positions has been significant, and unions must consider such groups for inclusion as the number of unskilled or semiskilled jobs declines in other sectors. Exhibit 16.10 dramatically demonstrates the decline in the traditional industrial unions and the increased membership in the government, service, and professional unions. Notice the steep decline of membership in the auto, electrical, machinists, and steelworkers unions. In contrast, membership in public, service, and education unions has increased.

The entry of more women into the labor force has expanded the issues that unions must support. For example, although women now hold more than 53 million jobs, representing 45 percent of the labor force, they earn only about 64 cents for each dollar earned by men. Unions must therefore support equality in wages between genders. Another concern of many women, as well as some men, is the need for child care support.

Only 13 percent of women in the workforce belong to unions. One reason for this may be explained by the fact that 30 percent of women employees hold low-pay positions, which have been difficult to organize.[42] While seeking to attract women to membership, unions also need to look at inequalities in their own "houses." In "Profiles of Local Union Officers," Chaison and Andiappan have found that women are not represented in union leadership positions to the degree that they should be based on their numbers in the workforce.[43]

One of the most significant trends in the labor movement in the last 25 years or so has been the growth in public sector unionization. Employees at the federal, state, and local levels have participated in this phenomenon. John F. Kennedy's 1960 campaign promise and his 1962 Executive Order 10988 were regarded by the postal workers and federal workers as their **magna carta,** or statement of rights and privileges.[44] This order provided postal workers with the ability to bargain collectively in all aspects of their job except wages. However, later legislation (Postal Reorganization Act of 1970) granted them the right to bargain for wages, too. The continued growth in public sector

MAGNA CARTA
A statement of rights and privileges.

EXHIBIT 16.10   **Where America's Biggest Unions Are Heading**

Name	Membership		
	1991	**1981**	
National Education Association	2,095,474	1,717,483	+22%
International Brotherhood of Teamsters, Chauffeurs, Warehousemen, and Helpers of America	1,510,985	1,832,247	−18%
United Food and Commercial Workers International	1,300,000	1,200,000	+8%
American Federation of State, County, and Municipal Employees	1,250,000	970,000	+29%
Service Employees International	1,000,000	600,000	+67%
International Union of Automobile, Aerospace, and Agricultural Implement Workers of America	900,000	1,335,387	−33%
American Federation of Teachers	790,000	575,000	+37%
International Brotherhood of Electrical Workers	788,769	1,034,961	−24%
International Association of Machinists and Aerospace Workers	729,000	950,000	−23%
United Steelworkers of America	570,362	1,037,075	−45%

Source: Peter Nulty, "Look What the Unions Want Now," *Fortune*, February 18, 1993, pp. 128–135.

employment and the relatively high percentage of union membership is changing the balance of the private/public influence in the overall labor movement.

The union movement must make strategic choices in the last few years of the century regarding where it will position itself. Should it double its effort at organizing what is left of the basic manufacturing industries? Should it change its approach and try and organize more white-collar workers? Should it change its outlook toward women and minorities and move more of them into union leadership positions?

These are more than minor considerations; they determine whether the labor movement will remain a viable force in society. In 1985, the AFL-CIO issued a landmark report on "The Changing Situation of Workers and Their Unions." It recognized these questions and the shifting environment and suggested more cooperative and productive relationships with management. This was confirmed by the AFL-CIO in 1994.

CONSOLIDATION

A final strategic choice facing unions is the extent to which they should consolidate. Should unions merge with one another to increase power and reduce costs? This tactic of merger and consolidation has been popular with businesses for many years. Unions are now considering and taking such action. For example, in July 1995, the United Auto Workers, United Steel Workers of America, and International Association of Machinists signed an agreement to merge into one union. Their agreement calls for the gradual integration of such key union departments as organizing and lobbying, with completion of the integration by the year 2000. The combined union is estimated to have nearly two million members. This consolidation will not only reduce overhead but also inter-union rivalry in competing for organization of the same workers.[45]

STRATEGIC VARIABLES FACING MANAGEMENT

Managers many times must work with a union. The union may be a long-standing fixture that was organized in response to problems and abuses of past decades, or it may have recently been organized at the particular company in response to current management or economic conditions. Regardless of how and why the company became unionized, the managers must consider several key strategic variables in the collective bargaining process. Five of these variables are discussed in the following sections and are presented in Exhibit 16.11.

HARMONY

Probably the biggest change that occurred during the 1980s from a strategic standpoint is the reduction in the confrontational approach between union and management and an increase in the more collaborative approach. It has been noted, however, that in the mid-1990s, a return to more adversarial relationships may be occurring. Most managers recognize the value of harmony in creating a work climate that can lead to high productivity. Harmony involves working together on common goals without conflict or discord. At the same time, experienced managers would also agree that harmony may be a necessary but not sufficient condition for productivity. For example, harmony could almost always be achieved in the short run by simply agreeing to every union demand. However, in most cases, short-term harmony would result in financial bankruptcy and business failure.

Discord between a company's management and its union can have a direct negative impact on customers. For example, the strike by the Teamsters Union against United

| **EXHIBIT 16.11** | **Key Strategic Variables in the Collective Bargaining Process** |

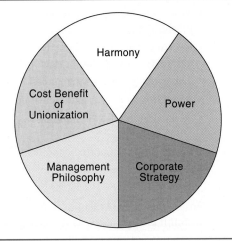

Parcel Service (UPS) over the weight of packages to be handled by UPS delivery personnel could have been devastating on businesses relying on UPS for short delivery schedules. Fortunately, the strike was settled quickly.

Managers must examine their history with the union and keep in touch with the current attitudes of supervisors and union members to increase the commitment to harmony whenever possible. With the fast-changing environment, managers and union officials may find that past bitter disputes color the present attitudes, which may be highly detrimental to the *current* interest of both sides.

Management generally recognizes the importance of harmony to the work climate. However, as noted above, the potential return to an adversarial relationship is a trend that very well could continue and that managers in general, human resource managers in particular, should monitor.[46]

POWER

Unions exist to advance their members with respect to wages, benefits, and working conditions. Unions are seen to have power when they are able to deliver these for their members; when they are not able to do so, they are perceived as losing their power. Members may consider the union to have lost power if it has accomplished its agenda, leaving little, if anything, to negotiate with management. At the other extreme, members may become concerned that the union has lost power when it must make concessions or accept givebacks during negotiations as a way to save jobs.

When enlightened management commits to work with unions to solve disputes, the rank and file may question whether union leaders have become too cozy with managers, a situation discussed in the Caterpillar case. In such instances, union officials may find it necessary to provoke a dispute to reassert their power or at least create the perception of a power play. It has even been suggested that managers sometimes "let" the union win these relative **nonissues** to avoid more serious problems. Exhibit 16.12 lists conditions that can lead to the perception of union power loss.

Power is also an issue for management. Managers may feel compelled to demonstrate that they are in charge. Many traditional managers see cooperation as unwisely giving away management rights and responsibilities. The board of directors should

NONISSUE
An objective that is insignificant and that may be given up for a symbolic purpose.

■ EXHIBIT 16.12   **Conditions that Can Lead to the Perception of Union Power Loss**

- More enlightened management committed to working out issues rather than disputing them.
- Recent cooperative efforts by union officials that contrast sharply with their past aggressive confrontation approach.
- Necessary givebacks demanded by the company.
- Reduction in overall number of employees and union membership.
- Reduction in union campaigns, strike benefits, and so on caused by decreasing union budgets.
- Fewer union-supported candidates being elected to political office.

POWER TACTICS

Negotiating tactics based on a side's perception of its power rather than on a willingness to bargain based on rightness or fairness.

UNION BUSTING

Management's removing a union or rendering a union ineffective.

GRAND STRATEGY

A company's long-term plan and direction.

ensure that management exercises power only to achieve the company's objectives, not to fulfill the ego needs of the managers.

The use of **power tactics** in negotiations has a long-standing historical precedent. Use of such tactics in bargaining may be an attempt to intimidate the union into making concessions that management might not otherwise be able to obtain. For example, management might suggest that plant closings or cutbacks might be necessary if the union will not concede to its demands. Likewise, a union might threaten to strike at an inopportune time over long-standing disagreements. For example, the union might make strike threats at a time it knows the company is in a high-demand situation and is making substantial profits. A strike at such a time could cause the company to lose business (and profits) to its competitors.

The relative balance of power has shifted in the last few years to favor management. Unions have accused management of deliberately resorting to power and making totally unreasonable demands that will force strikes, allowing the company to hire permanent replacement workers, which the unions call disguised **union busting.** During the summer of 1994, a group of labor lobbyists continued to work on a striker replacement bill that would force companies to rehire striking workers and fire replacement workers if necessary. *The Wall Street Journal* reporter Robert Thompson argues that "the simple, underlying motivation of the Striker Replacement legislation is power—union power."[47] He goes on to say that often the only defense a company has is to let the union strike rather than yield to unreasonable demands. If the union had no risk of permanent replacement, the number of strikes would increase significantly.

Early in 1995, President Clinton supported the shift back to labor's power by initiating Executive Order 12954 to discourage companies doing more than $100,000 worth of business with the federal government from hiring replacement workers during a strike. Companies found in violation of the order could lose contracts or become ineligible for future contracts. As of this writing, Congress was continuing its efforts to challenge this order.[48]

Clearly, power bargaining by either management or unions can have unintended and destructive consequences.

THE RELATIONSHIP OF CORPORATE STRATEGY TO THE COLLECTIVE BARGAINING PROCESS

A company's **grand strategy,** or long-term plan, must be considered in determining its position in the collective bargaining process. Exhibit 16.13 lists several corporate

FOCUS ON ETHICS

Leadership Has a Price

In the summer of 1993, Northwest Airlines, the nation's fourth largest, was on the verge of bankruptcy. To avoid this dismal scenario, employees agreed to take an $886 million cut in wages. Top managers took an approximate 20 percent pay cut. Employees, including managers, received 34.2 percent ownership in the airline. CEO John J. Dasburg's agreement included a base salary of $463,906 plus an incentive-based bonus of $450,705. Finally, Dasburg was paid a special $750,000 for restructuring Northwest's finances. The company justified these bonuses, saying it had to keep good people. The Machinists Union, though, objected to the annual bonuses and especially to the special $750,000. In an unusual move, Dasburg agreed to give it back.

Commenting on the move, he said, "It's more important to this airline to accomplish its goal than it is for me to have another $750,000. Leadership sometimes has a price, and sometimes it includes my pocketbook."

Management has generally maintained that executive compensation is solely an issue between the company, the board of directors, and its management team. Employees could make no legal claim on this issue, but CEO Dasburg's action may have been determined by both pragmatic and ethical considerations.

SOURCE: Adapted from "Northwest Air Chief Agrees to Give Back $750,000 Bonus under Union Pressure," *The Wall Street Journal,* March 28, 1994.

strategies and their impact on collective bargaining. For example, a company pursuing a low-cost price strategy may have to take a very tough stance in negotiating any significant increases in wages and benefit costs that would negate its competitive advantage. The company may be more agreeable to quality-of-work-life issues or sharing decision making so long as costs are not forced up as a result. Another company may choose to pursue a product differentiation strategy that relies on a special, highly trained labor force. If the company can easily pass along these costs, it may yield on wages but seek concessions that require a reduction in the number of labor classifications, which would allow more flexibility in scheduling skilled craftspeople for a variety of tasks.

Companies that have been involved in mergers and acquisitions present special strategic problems for managers. One salient problem is bringing together two differing **cultures.**[49] When unions are involved, the problems may be intensified. Entirely different unions, with different goals and expectations, may be inherited, or different locals of the same international union may be involved. USAir's merger with Piedmont, generally hailed as a model of success, caused significant headaches in combining

CULTURE
A company's or union's accepted way of doing things.

EXHIBIT 16.13   **Corporate Strategy and Collective Bargaining Impact**

Strategy	Collective Bargaining Impact
Low-cost producer	Tough negotiations over wages
High-quality/high-price goods	More flexibility in work rules to utilize skilled workers
Lower costs by cutting expenses	Seek wage concessions; reduce benefits
Downsizing—reducing overcapacity and inefficient plants	Layoff clauses, earlier retirements, seniority revisions, improved productivity
Merger and acquisitions	Common contract provisions; change in pension language

existing contracts with various unions. Journalist James Fraze, referring to the merger, argued, "The thorniest problem for company officials has been the merger of existing contracts among the various employee unions."[50] Particularly difficult was the issue of pilot seniority, which determined who would sit in which seat and the resulting salary. The pay difference between the pilot and copilot is significant. USAir decided to let a committee of pilots work out the differences.[51]

In "Strategic Human Resources Management," Lengnick-Hall and Lengnick-Hall advocate the need to tie together human resource planning and strategy.[52] This proactive stance provides an organization with the proper mix of personnel for its present as well as future needs. A significant change in strategic direction may very well require different human skills than companies currently possess. In the collective bargaining process, constraints and opportunities need to be carefully examined in terms of current and future strategic thrusts and whether the contract allows enough flexibility for training, relocating, promoting, hiring, or laying off personnel as needed.

MANAGEMENT POSITION TOWARD UNIONS

Managers have historically held different views toward unions. Some have been opposed to them at any cost and have even engaged in intimidation to avoid the entry by a union or to get rid of an existing one. Although this extreme position is usually rare today, management's philosophy toward unions in the 1980s reflected an increasing hostility, or at least a high level of opposition, toward unions. Managers may believe that the 1990s provided an opportunity to correct the negative view they had toward labor in the 1940s, 1950s, 1960s, and 1970s. Many believe that the firing of the air traffic controllers (PATCO) by then President Reagan set the stage for the decline of the unions during the 1980s.

NATIONAL LABOR RELATIONS BOARD (NLRB)
The federal agency that concerns itself with labor issues.

Regardless of the shift, the collective bargaining process often indicates the company's level of power vis-à-vis organized labor. In the late 1980s and early 1990s, union leaders sometimes accused management of deliberately provoking labor problems by negotiating in bad faith. Clear guidelines have been set by the **National Labor Relations Board (NLRB)** regarding good faith negotiations, but labor would argue that the NLRB has not enforced these provisions as closely as it may once have.

UNION REMOVAL/DECERTIFICATION VERSUS UNION BUSTING

During the 1980s and early 1990s, attempts were made to remove unions from companies. From the perspective of the unions, this union-busting activity has been perceived as a sinister attempt to take away the rights that workers have gained through hard-fought battles with companies for over a century. Many times managers have argued that unions have become excessively powerful, are out of touch with the needs of their members, and are unwilling to recognize that U.S. companies are engaged in worldwide competition. These managers see the removal of the union or the reduction of its power as beneficial to everyone concerned, except perhaps union leadership.

DECERTIFICATION
The removal of a union as the official legal representative of a company's workforce.

A union *can* be removed through the formal process of **decertification.** Until the Taft-Hartley Law of 1947, it was generally assumed that once a union was certified, it was forever.[53] Decertification is more or less the reversal of the certification process. It must be initiated by the union members. The timing of the filing is important. The petition must be signed by at least 30 percent of the bargaining unit members and must be filed within 60 to 90 days. If all procedures are followed, the NLRB schedules an election. A majority of votes to decertify is required. Unions have been decertified in approximately 75 percent of such elections.[54] Over 600 bargaining units per year have decertified their unions over the past several years.[55] Management cannot initiate decertification, but it can legally support the decertification *after* the petition is filed by using the following strategies:

1. Meeting with union members to discuss the merits of becoming a union-free shop.
2. Providing legal assistance in preparing for decertification.
3. Changing the corporate culture and atmosphere so that workers feel they no longer need a union as an intermediary.

An alternative to a formal decertification election process has been used in recent years. Employees can oust the union by collecting 50 percent or more of the bargaining unit's employees' signatures and then demanding that the management stop any further bargaining with the union's representatives.[56]

If a company desires to remove a union, it must remember the following:

1. To be very careful in following the rules laid down by the NLRB to prevent the decertification election from being voided. At the same time, it cannot be timid in voicing its position within the legal guidelines.
2. To be prepared to change its corporate environment to the extent that employees no longer need a union.
3. To prepare the human resource function to change its emphasis after a union is removed from that of grievance handling and contract negotiation to creating an atmosphere in which productive cooperative arrangement can be facilitated.

AVOIDING UNIONIZATION

MOVING TO ANOTHER REGION OF THE COUNTRY

In an expanding market, a company may leave its union facilities intact and seek to open new facilities in a union-free environment. What has been more typical, however, has been the closing of labor union-dominated facilities in the north and opening new plants elsewhere without a union. This strategy has been especially offensive to unions and is seen as one of the many antiunion and union-busting strategies that labor considers unfair and even immoral. It is illegal to close or move a plant solely to avoid a union, but a firm can often make a case that the move is based on cost savings brought about by lower taxes, a newer plant, or lower wages. As a result of this type of action, unions are seeking to bring more security issues to the bargaining table. Communities that stand to lose a major tax base are supporting unions on these issues.

During the 1970s and 1980s, a number of communities, states, and localities provided a variety of subsidies in forms of training dollars, wage subsidies, and tax abatements to lure new business into a community, provide funds for an expansion, or at least avoid major shutdowns. In return for those incentives, cities have often joined union lawsuits when companies decide to move to a more attractive location.[57] While companies may argue persuasively that economic conditions do not allow them to compete effectively using high-priced labor, and in some cases outdated equipment, the argument often falls on unsympathetic ears. Community leaders counter that companies lose a measure of freedom if they accept public money. Dan Boroff, city manager of Clarksburg, West Virginia, states that companies "have the freedom to come and go . . ." but they should not "accept taxpayer dollars to subsidize these moves."[58] The implication is that the strategic flexibility of a company may be greatly impaired by these agreements.

Often local and state legal action is taken to prohibit or restrict plant closing. In addition, action can be taken at the federal level under the 1988 Worker Adjustment and Retraining Notification Act, which took effect February 4, 1989. It requires companies that hire over 100 workers to notify their employees at least 60 days in advance of a plant closing.[59] This allows workers and communities to better prepare for the impending closure. This legislation was heavily supported and lobbied for by organized labor in an attempt to slow its eroding power base.

MOVING TO FOREIGN COUNTRIES

OFFSHORE
Outside the United States, as in Mexico, Canada, or overseas countries.

Another manifestation of the attempt to escape unionization involves going **offshore,** that is, transferring jobs from the United States to countries that are predominantly nonunion. These are often third world or developing countries that desire and welcome industrial jobs. While the workers may be paid anywhere from one-half to less than one-tenth of what their U.S. counterparts would receive, in many countries this wage puts the worker in a much higher economic class than most other workers in the same country. When the wages are low enough and productivity rates are similar to those in the United States, increased shipping costs and other costs associated with doing business in a foreign land are not considered serious limitations to competitiveness.

In other situations, however, companies choosing to move jobs to foreign countries to reduce labor costs experience problems that at least partially offset the advantages of doing so. Many critics, particularly organized labor, are quick to point out these problems, including the following:

1. Lower productivity per worker due to inadequate education, training, and incentives.
2. Lower quality of goods because workers are less skilled.
3. High costs of doing business in a foreign country.
4. The perception of a lack of loyalty to the United States, causing backlash by the U.S. public.

Some analysts maintain that these criticisms are basically the self-serving propaganda of unions and believe that U.S. companies cannot compete in world markets unless they produce for markets in a variety of countries. Locations can range from technologically advanced to third world countries, depending on a variety of factors such as labor costs and proximity to markets.

These issues will not be resolved soon but will directly affect the collective bargaining process. Whether a given company is selling in global markets today or not will not insulate the company or its unions from opportunities to avoid unionization by moving to foreign countries. Very likely, more and more domestic and foreign competitors in almost all industries will consider using a mixed U.S. and foreign labor force as a competitive strategic weapon. Union officials and company management need to be concerned because this type of international workforce will likely become more important as a bargaining issue.

The fight over the passage of the North American Free Trade Agreement (NAFTA) illustrates the strong differences of opinion over the issue of jobs and competitiveness. For the most part, organized labor fought the bill and was supported by a majority of the Democratic members of Congress. They feared that the passage of NAFTA would continue to erode union strength and cost U.S. jobs. Nevertheless, a coalition of business groups, Republicans in Congress, and President Clinton prevailed in passing the agreement. They argued that a few jobs might be lost in the short term, but in the long term, NAFTA would open new markets and result in a net creation of jobs in the United States. At the time of this writing, job loss caused by NAFTA was thought to be very small. Only time will tell whether it is a good piece of legislation from labor's perspective.

OUTSOURCING

OUTSOURCING
Buying parts or services externally rather than producing them internally.

A relatively recent trend that has become a major point of contention in contract bargaining is the issue of outsourcing. **Outsourcing** occurs when a company subcontracts work to other companies that had previously been done in-house. Consider, for example, a machined component for a large truck transmission that costs $150 for materials and uses six hours of labor. At a labor rate of $33 per hour (including benefits), the total cost of the part is $348. The company may seek a small job shop that has a nonunion workforce and an average wage rate of $21 per hour. If the outsourcing subcontractor takes a $32 per piece margin, the total cost comes to $314. The company may decide to reduce its union labor force and buy externally.

The company can accrue other benefits by specifying that it will pay for only "perfect" parts, thereby eliminating scrap. If demand falls, the company can eliminate its contract and not be saddled with long-term unemployment compensation liabilities. Of course, outsourcing has some liabilities as well, but it has led unions to accuse companies of using it as just one more union-busting tactic. It is likely that outsourcing will become a more important collective bargaining issue in the 1990s. Unions often try to negotiate a say in which parts or services can be subcontracted.

Managers and union leaders do need to recognize, however, that outsourcing can work to the benefit of both parties in certain situations. It provides more flexibility for the company in adjusting to varying demands and can provide a more stable core of unionized workers. When a downturn occurs, these external contracts can be eliminated before well-trained, experienced union members are laid off.

MAKING A UNION UNNECESSARY

UNION-FREE SHOP
A company that has no union representation of workers.

Many companies have never had a union or have had one that has been decertified. If a company wants to remain a **union-free shop,** it must take care to develop and maintain policies that will balance the needs of the company to make a fair profit with the legitimate needs of the workers. Managers must remember that economic issues are not the only issues that concern workers. Exhibit 16.14 lists a variety of issues that should be addressed.

It is not uncommon for companies to clearly state their commitment to remain union free and try to persuade employees that the company has their best interests at heart. A formal policy statement is frequently made to indicate that the success of the company is based on the skill and efforts of its employees and that in the opinion of the management, unionization would interfere with the respect that the company has for its employees. The statement might go on to say that a union-free environment is in the best interest of the employees, the customers, and the company itself.[60] Such a statement may be included in an employee handbook and emphasized during new employee orientation sessions.

EXHIBIT 16.14   **Some Worker Concerns That Management Must Address to Maintain Good Industrial Relations**

ECONOMIC-RELATED ISSUES

- Wages and benefits
- Secure pension and retirement benefits
- Assignment of hours and overtime
- Layoff provisions and protection
- Profit sharing
- Promotions
- Subcontracting limitations

QUALITY OF WORK LIFE ISSUES

- Clean, safe work environment
- Recreational facilities
- Day care subsidies and/or on-site day care
- Work team involvement, such as quality teams
- Grievance procedures
- Recognition for work accomplishment
- Training and development programs that can lead to advancements
- Internal hiring policies when possible

The company should be very careful in its policy considerations to consider all effects a given policy will have on the union-free environment. In some situations, a company may have paid a substantial price to maintain its nonunion status. For example, a company fearing a union may be very generous in granting wage increases in an attempt to discourage union organizers. But the company may find that the cost increases cannot be fully supported by the market price of its product, thereby decreasing the company's bottom line. Having made such sacrifices to remain union free, the company must not risk its union-free status over some minor disagreement with the workforce. These issues cannot be left to chance but need to be a part of a comprehensive human resource management strategy that is linked with corporate and business unit strategies.

VIOLENCE AND SABOTAGE AS A RESULT OF NEGOTIATION BREAKDOWNS

Sabotage and violence are not common today, but they still happen. Managers need to develop contingency plans to deal with outbreaks of violence should they occur. But first and foremost, careful planning should prevent this from happening. Today, most union officials and company managers realize that bargaining disagreements should be discussed only at the bargaining table. Discussing these issues with people other than the bargaining teams can cause very real danger to lives and property.

In summary, company management should seek an ironclad commitment from its union leaders to avoid, prevent, and denounce the use and advocacy of violence and/or sabotage. In especially bitter disputes, management should have a plan to protect the lives and property of those involved.

HR CHALLENGE

Management Can Deunionize a Workforce

Using only the most positive tactics available, Kenneth Barr, president of Cypress Mineral Company, convinced his workers that they no longer needed a union to protect themselves.

Cypress is a copper mine located in Miami, Arizona. The mine had been a part of the Teamsters Union and United Steelworkers Union for nearly 50 years. Even though the workers were loyal union members and stood by the union in strikes and hard times, Barr was able to convince them to decertify the union by a convincing margin of 2 to 1.

To orchestrate this turnaround, Barr used a psychological—not physical—game plan. He provided "charm school" seminars, called "I'm OK, You're OK" to encourage the workers and managers to talk about the 50-year chasm that stood between them. Barr instituted changes in the workplace, providing raises, changing work rules, offering cross-training, and

pushing for a safer workplace. All these tactics helped to convince most of the workers that there was a better way than "us versus them."

Without the union contract to guide their behavior, managers decided to make even more changes. They give extra days off when they believe it is justified, allow truck drivers to get out and walk around when they feel tired without fear of being yelled at by a supervisor, and most important, they listen when their workers tell them something is or is not working.

As with all changes, some people are not content. Older workers point to the new policies that favor youth over seniority as favoritism. Some workers complain about having to learn new tasks.

SOURCE: Adapted from Marj Charlier, "How a Mine in Arizona Wooed Workers Away from Union Loyalties," *The Wall Street Journal,* August 8, 1989, pp. A1 +.

THE COLLECTIVE BARGAINING PROCESS

The collective bargaining process consists of seven stages: (1) preparing for negotiations, (2) reaching a settlement through contract negotiation, (3) reaching a settlement through mediation and arbitration, (4) reaching a settlement through last-resort options, (5) ratifying the settlement, (6) implementing the settlement, and (7) administering the contract. These phases are illustrated in Exhibit 16.15.

EXHIBIT 16.15   **The Collective Bargaining Process**

Preparing for negotiations
Settlement (negotiations, mediation, arbitration, last-resort options)
Ratifying settlement
Implementing settlement
Contract administration

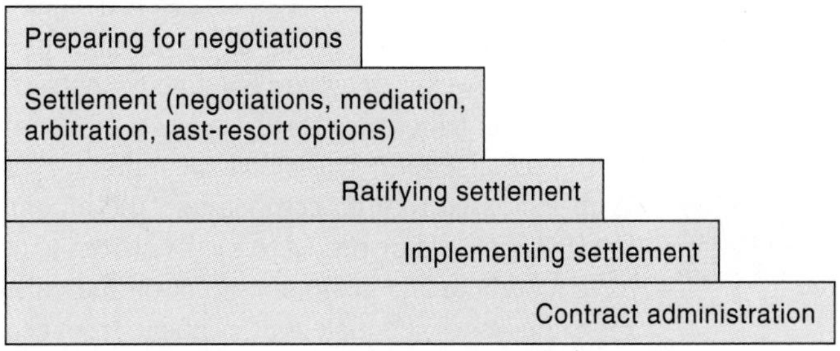

MANDATORY, PERMISSIVE, AND PROHIBITED NEGOTIATING ISSUES

It is important in designing a strategic negotiating approach that management and the negotiating team understand the types of issues that can be negotiated as well as those prohibited. The 1947 Taft-Hartley law defines three types of negotiating issues:

MANDATORY ISSUE
An issue that is required by law to be bargained for.

PERMISSIVE ISSUE
An issue that can be bargained on but that is not required by law to be bargained on.

PROHIBITED OR ILLEGAL ISSUE
An issue that cannot be bargained on by law, even if both sides wanted to bargain on it.

1. **Mandatory issues** must be negotiated by law. They include such items as wages, hours, benefits, and other terms and conditions of employment. These have the most direct impact on workers' day-to-day functioning. Refusal to bargain on these issues can result in charges of unfair labor practices and an NLRB investigation. These issues are mandatory for both sides, not only the employer.

2. **Permissive issues** may be discussed only if both parties agree to do so. Permissive issues often include items that are of mutual interest, including a company's pricing policy, the pensions and benefits of retired workers, or safety rules. Neither the union nor the employer can refuse to sign a contract based on failure to reach agreement on a permissive issue.

3. **Prohibited or illegal issues** are strictly forbidden by law. They cannot be subject to negotiation even if both parties want to negotiate them. Included are closed-shop agreements, discrimination against protected classes of individuals, featherbedding, and hot-cargo agreements.

Additional examples of the three types of issues are listed in Exhibit 16.16.

In most contracts, a special section called a *managerial prerogative clause* reserves certain rights for management that are not specifically enumerated in the contract. It might read like this:

> It is herewith recognized that all management functions shall be retained by the company. These functions include, but are not limited to, the full, complete, and exclusive control of direction of the workforce, scheduling of production, operation of the plant, acquisition of materials, production of products, the location of such production, and the methods or sale and distribution of its products; the right to change or establish job classifications and descriptions; the right to introduce new or improved procedures; the right to abolish any job or department; the right to make and enforce reasonable shop rules; and the right to hire, fire, suspend, train, discipline, discharge, advance, transfer, lay off, and recall employees. These rights shall all be the function of management unless expressly stated otherwise within this agreement.[61]

Basically, managerial prerogative clauses allow management a great deal of discretion in the day-to-day and strategic management of the company. Traditionally, unions have taken the attitude that management can make decisions, which the union will challenge if it perceives them to be unfair. Management has sought maximum flexibility and has been reluctant to give up any more control than is absolutely necessary. These past attitudes, however, may be changing on both sides. For a variety of reasons, more cooperative–collaborative relationships may be in the offing.

 In exchange for concessions, the union may ask for a larger role in decision making. With increased foreign competition, the union and management may decide to work jointly on increasing productivity. Decisions to develop a collaborative environment will have a definite and profound effect on the collective bargaining process in two ways. First, the issues negotiated may change from economic issues to those related to quality of work, decision control, and jointly determined investment decisions. Second, such collaboration can take both management and unions into uncharted waters. Roles may not be as clear as before. Human resource managers must think through the implications

EXHIBIT 16.16   **Examples of Mandatory, Permissive, and Prohibited Bargaining Issues**

MANDATORY ISSUES

Wages
Benefits, including insurance, vacation, holidays
Overtime rules and compensation
Subcontracting work
Posting procedures of job openings
Layoff plan
Shift differentials
Safety
Promotions
Stock purchase plans
Seniority
Management rights clause
Retirement age

PERMISSIVE ISSUES

Pricing policy of firm
Pensions and benefit level and rights of retired personnel
Supervisory compensation
Supervisory discipline

PROHIBITED ISSUES

Featherbedding
Hot-cargo agreements
Discrimination against protected classes
Closed-shop agreements
Union or agency shop clauses in right-to-work states
Secondary boycott agreements

of these changes *before* they get to the bargaining table. Many benefits are to be gained from cooperative efforts, but there is a price to be paid in terms of control on the part of management and increased responsibility and accountability on the part of unions.

PREPARING FOR THE NEGOTIATING PROCESS

Each side should be prepared for negotiating by understanding its own strategic position, analyzing its strengths and weaknesses as well as those of the other side, and selecting the team for negotiating. Preparations should include a high level of planning and research.

UNDERSTANDING THE STRATEGIC POSITION

Each side in the negotiating process should understand its overall mission. The company must understand its corporate mission and how the negotiated issues will affect it. The union must identify its objectives. Each side may identify certain "non-negotiable" issues on which it will not bargain.

ANALYZING STRENGTHS AND WEAKNESSES

Labor negotiators for both the company and the union should be as informed as possible of the strengths and weaknesses of both their own side and of the opposing side.

Each is likely, therefore, to investigate the other's position; information concerning the company's finances, inventory levels, sales forecast, and market share is important. Information about the union, such as the level of its strike funds, should also be considered. These data must be accurate so that each side can evaluate its position and that of the other side. Sometimes the best way to identify current issues is by obtaining a clear understanding of the history between the company and the union and of the past negotiation behavior of each side.

Both the company and the union use the information obtained to create realistic negotiation scenarios. For example, a company with strong sales and low inventory could see this as a vulnerable position. To prevent this from hampering its negotiations, the company might choose the defensive—and expensive—strategy of increasing production for several months prior to negotiations. A union that has a large amount of strike funds is likely to come to the bargaining table with a different position than one with low funds. Such strengths and weaknesses should be evaluated carefully in planning negotiation objectives and tactics.

The human resource factor is an important element that each side should consider. For example, if a firm has workers who are so highly skilled that it could not operate in the event of a work stoppage, the union might use this fact to its advantage. If operations are automated to the extent that a certain level of service can be maintained, as has happened during recent labor disputes in the telephone industry, management might use this to its advantage.

SELECTING THE NEGOTIATION TEAM

Each side must exercise great care in choosing its negotiators. Such factors as age and educational level should be considered. Union negotiators are usually less well educated and younger than management representatives, but union representatives are often more "street smart."

Within the limits of propriety, it is highly recommended that each side analyze the personalities of members of the negotiating teams and try to predict how the different people will behave in the negotiating session. The following questions may help in this preparation:

1. Who is the most influential person on both sides?
2. What sort of emotional tactics are team members likely to employ?
3. Can some negotiators be "read" more easily than others?
4. Based on past negotiations, what are the tactics that each side should be prepared for, and how can one react to these tactics to gain an advantage?

REACHING A SETTLEMENT THROUGH CONTRACT NEGOTIATIONS

Contract negotiation is the actual bargaining between the two parties to reach agreement as to a contract. It is one specific aspect of the entire collective bargaining process, which is an ongoing procedure as both sides work under the terms of the existing contract. Collective bargaining sets the tone for contract negotiations. For example, if the union and the firm have experienced constant disagreements and grievances during the current three-year contract, this confrontational atmosphere is almost sure to affect negotiations for the next contract.

The result of successful negotiations is a written contract, signed by each party, that will govern the employment relationship for the period covered by the contract. Both parties must be willing to compromise on issues until a reasonable accommodation is reached.

Negotiation between the union and management is the give-and-take process between them to reach a mutually acceptable agreement. Each party tries to maximize its position relative to that of the other party. In doing so, it may use a variety of tactics.

TACTICS USED IN NEGOTIATIONS

Each party may use one or more different tactics while negotiating. For example, **bluffing and/or posturing** involves appearing to be interested in obtaining a concession that can later be traded away for a different concession. **Window dressing** refers to making a list of extraneous, unimportant demands that can be easily traded away if obtained. **Timing** is another tactical device that saves important issues until late in the negotiation process. **Misrepresentation** refers to the use of false data or facts to use as bargaining leverage. It borders on lying, perhaps, and involves using fabricated data, withholding data, or actually stating a position that the party does not believe. Careful preparations by the negotiators should ameliorate the vulnerability of each side to these tactics.

IMPORTANCE OF POWER IN NEGOTIATIONS

The success of negotiations depends on the relative *power* of each party to get the other side to do something it would normally not do or to refrain from doing something it would normally do. The 1992 contract imposed by Caterpillar's Fites was the result of a pure power play; union members grudgingly gave in to his demands because they felt powerless to do anything about it.

For one party to have power over another in the bargaining relationship, it must have something the other wants. A car sale provides a good example of this. It is much easier to sell a car at the price wanted if the other person *really* wants it. In the employment relationship, the union wants higher pay, better hours, and job security. The employer has these things. It needs a stable, skilled workforce that it can employ in a flexible manner to produce a sufficient quantity of quality good at competitive prices and a reasonable level of profitability. The union controls the labor factor of production, and the employer provides the materials and equipment to produce the goods. The two parties then negotiate with each other over what each one can give up relative to what the other wants. Thus, negotiating involves making a trade-off. Exhibit 16.17 is a simplified negotiating model. The model in Exhibit 16.18 is more realistic, although it still

BLUFFING/ POSTURING

Feigning interest in winning a concession when that concession will actually be traded away later in the interests of a true issue.

WINDOW DRESSING

A group of unimportant demands that can easily be traded away if needed.

TIMING

Saving arbitration of important issues until late in the negotiation process.

MISREPRESENTA- TION

Using false data or inaccuracies in advocating a position.

EXHIBIT 16.17   **A Simplified Model of the Negotiating Process**

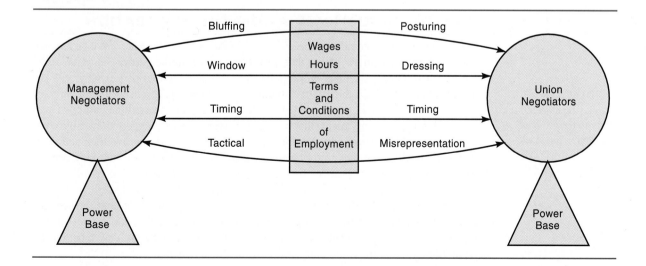

EXHIBIT 16.18   **An Extended Model of the Negotiating Process**

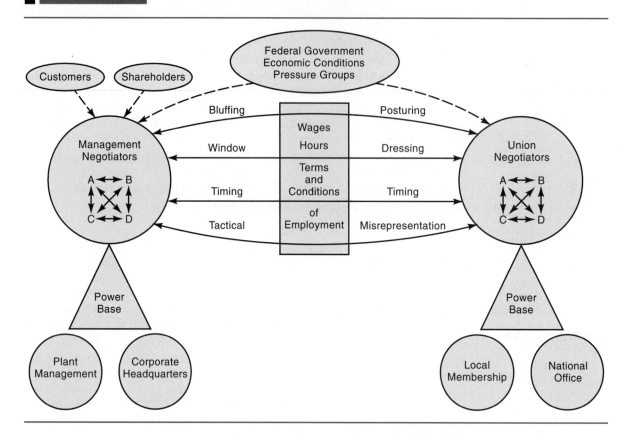

simplifies the highly complex negotiation process. As illustrated in Exhibit 16.18, the two parties bargain not only with each other but also among themselves to please their constituencies, who do not always agree on what their positions as a group should be. Plant management and the company's board of directors are among its constituencies. Those of the union include local membership and the national union office.

REACHING A SETTLEMENT THROUGH MEDIATION AND ARBITRATION

MEDIATION
Employing a neutral third party to try and break a bargaining impasse.

In some cases, the negotiation process breaks down and a settlement cannot be reached through normal channels. Rather than resort to a strike on the part of the union and a lockout or hiring replacement workers by the company, the two parties may seek the outside intervention of a third party. **Mediation** involves having a neutral third party try to break a bargaining impasse. Mediators may be called upon to get the parties to start negotiating again, clarify points that have been misunderstood, suggest alternative compromises that have not occurred to the bargaining parties, and improve trust and communication. Mediators have no power to enforce a settlement, but they may bring a fresh viewpoint into the process that can reopen the negotiations.

The Federal Mediation and Conciliation Service (FMCS) was created as an independent agency by the 1947 Taft-Hartley Act. Labor, management, or both can seek the assistance of FMCS or they can seek some other third party to mediate the negotiating process. Since these mediators have no power to force a settlement, they must have a reputation of being impartial, fair, well informed, and patient.

ARBITRATION
Employing a neutral third party to break a bargaining impasse via a recommendation that binds both sides to agreement.

CONTRACT RIGHTS ARBITRATION
Settlement of an impasse regarding the actual administration of a contract.

INTEREST ARBITRATION
Settlement of an impasse regarding the content of a contract.

Arbitration, on the other hand, involves a neutral third party listening to both sides, evaluating the evidence, and making a binding recommendation. Arbitration is of two basic types: contract rights arbitration and interest arbitration. **Contract rights arbitration** consists of settling impasses in the actual administration of the contract and is usually the outcome of a grievance procedure that cannot be settled by the parties. **Interest arbitration** involves the terms of the contract itself. While interest arbitration is used in the public sector, where strikes are illegal, it is rarely used in the private sector.[62] Normally, neither of the bargaining parties is willing to give up control of such basic issues as wages, benefits, working conditions, and so forth. They generally would rather rely on the negotiation process and the threat of economic pressure. In *The Labor Relations Process,* Holley and Jennings point out that relying on interest arbitration has some additional drawbacks: delays and extra costs may occur; the arbitration may put a damper on the working environment; arbitrators may be inconsistent from case to case; arbitrators may end up splitting the difference, causing the parties to take extreme positions; and reliance on the arbitration process may lead to over-reliance on arbitration rather than working out differences through negotiations.[63]

Contract rights arbitrators generally come from two sources: either the FMCS or the American Arbitration Association (AAA). The AAA is a nonprofit organization that acts as a clearinghouse for qualified arbitrators. To be considered, potential arbitrators must be able to present their credentials and must be recommended by a representative of labor, management, and a neutral third party. A fairly large number of arbitrators and mediators tend to be members of the legal profession and may specialize in labor law.

Sometimes the parties cannot conclude a workable agreement. They may have not sought mediation, or the mediation efforts were not successful. With binding arbitration, both parties must agree to accept the outcome. If either party or both parties refuse to agree to arbitration, then a labor stoppage is almost assured.

The FMCS requires unions to file a 30-day notice of all contract expirations. It estimates that about 2 to 3 percent of these expirations involve a strike. Cynthia Gramm, however, asserts that this may be misleading because of the number of small companies in the FMCS sample. Her research indicates that between 1971 and 1980, companies with more than 1,000 employees had a strike rate of 13.8 percent.[64]

REACHING A SETTLEMENT—LAST RESORT OPTIONS FOR THE UNION

A STRIKE

STRIKE
A refusal by labor to work.

A union frequently takes a strike authorization vote to give its negotiating team a bargaining lever. A **strike** is a refusal by labor to work. It is not casually used. The union measures carefully the cost/benefit factor in considering a strike. Timing is crucial. For instance, if the demand for the company's product is high and in a growth phase, the company may not want to bear the opportunity cost of lost sales or alienated customers. On the other hand, if demand is slack and inventory is high, labor's threat of a strike may ring hollow. As noted previously, companies sometimes work overtime to build up inventories in anticipation of tough bargaining and a potential strike; this is common in both the steel and auto industries, among others.

REPLACEMENT WORKERS
Workers hired either temporarily or permanently to perform the jobs of striking employees.

A strike may force the company to give in on key union demands, but it is a high-risk strategy for the union. A 1989 Supreme Court ruling determined that if a company hires **replacement workers** during a labor walkout, it does not have to fire its replacement workers once the strike is over *(TWA* v. *Independent Federation of Flight Attendants).* This can effectively eliminate or greatly reduce the size of the union. Even if replacement workers are not hired, it can take a significant amount of time to make up for losses incurred in a strike situation.

For example, imagine the workers of a canning factory striking over a dispute of a 3 percent company-offered raise versus an 8 percent union-demanded raise. If the average worker would make $8.50 under the company's offer, Exhibit 16.19 demonstrates how long it would take to make up the lost wages under different strike lengths, assuming that the company finally gives in. Of course, there is the risk that the company may (1) hire replacement workers, (2) agree only to the previous 3 percent raise, or (3) lower the raise to 1 percent or even ask for a decrease. This example presumes that the worker receives a $150 per week strike benefit package from the union fund and/or unemployment. Some union members might receive more; some might receive less. Even with a relatively short strike, union members may take up to two-thirds of a year to make up for the losses. In the case of a prolonged 20-week strike, it could take several years to make up for the losses. The company correspondingly has to weigh the long-term cost of increasing pay and benefits against the potential of lost revenue and profits.

Both the company and the union have to evaluate carefully not only the possibility of lost profits and wages but also intangibles such as reputation, competitiveness, discord, and various other social and psychological factors. Human resource managers and union leaders have come to realize that other avenues are generally more attractive to settle even wide differences. Yet unions sometimes strike on a small wage difference as a matter of principle, although this is not as common today as it was during the 1960s and 1970s. In fact, work stoppages fell to a near-record low in 1991. There were only 40 work stoppages affecting 392,000 workers in 1991. This averages to workers being idle 2 of every 10,000 available work days.[65] More recently, the Bureau of Labor Statistics reported that all measures of work stoppage increased slightly in 1994. However, this was after a record low number of stoppages was recorded in 1993.

A BOYCOTT

BOYCOTT

An agreement by union members not to buy or use a targeted company's goods or services.

A **boycott** can be defined as an agreement of union members not to buy or use the goods or services of a company targeted for a strike. Secondary boycotts, in which the union openly encourages suppliers and customers to not sell to or purchase from the targeted company, were made illegal by the Taft-Hartley Act. Boycotts are difficult to use effectively because in most cases the share of a company's sales made to union members and their families is a small proportion of the total sales volume.

EXHIBIT 16.19

What a Strike Could Cost Union Members*

WEEKS OF STRIKE	HOURS LOST	WAGES LOST	UNION BENEFITS	NET LOSS	HOURS TO MAKE UP	WEEKS TO MAKE UP
1	40	$ 340	$ 150	$ 190	447.1	11.2
2	80	680	300	380	894.1	22.4
3	120	1,020	450	570	1341.2	33.5
4	160	1,360	600	760	1788.2	44.7
5	200	1,700	750	950	2235.3	55.9
10	400	3,400	1,500	1,900	4470.6	111.8
15	600	5,100	2,250	2,850	6705.9	167.6
20	800	6,800	3,000	3,800	8941.2	223.5

*Example assumes a company offer of $8.50 per hour (3 percent over previous rate) versus a union demand of $8.925 per hour (8 percent).

Table illustrates the point that even if the company finally meets the union's 8 percent demand, it will take a long time for the union members to make up their losses due to the strike.

■ HR CHALLENGE ■

Negotiation Rules to Follow to Reach an Agreement

Robert J. Harding, a veteran labor negotiator, offers seven rules to follow in negotiations to enhance the chances of reaching agreement.

1. Use the preliminary meetings to set the ground rules for future sessions. For example, the negotiators might agree that negotiations will take place during normal business hours, not in all-night marathon sessions.
2. Document carefully all meetings. Include who was there, what was said, what the intent was behind contract language, and what proposals and counterproposals were made. At the end of each day's session, the note taker can dictate the outlines of the sessions and have typewritten documents prepared for review. Missing information or disagreement can be filled in. This documentation will help not only in the negotiation process but also in interpreting the contract once it is signed.
3. If the company CEO is well regarded by the employees, consider using him or her in certain negotiating sessions, particularly the early ones. This helps the CEO understand the position of the union.
4. Within the bounds of what is legal, establish a comprehensive file on the in-plant union negotiating committee. This can be a basis for better

participation and drawing out the union members who are perhaps the most qualified to speak on a given issue. For instance, if a worker has been with the company 20 years and a management representative believes that the current proposal might not benefit her, the representative might post a question such as, "Janet, are you aware that the current proposal will give workers with 20 years' seniority only about half the benefits as those who have been with the company from 5 to 10 years?"
5. Accept union negotiators as equal peers. Never underestimate their abilities. A condescending attitude can hurt the process and may result in winning an ego battle but losing the contract war. Many of the union people are street smart and savvy when it comes to negotiations.
6. Sustain strong communication links with managers and first-line supervisors after the contract is settled. They are the ones who actually administer the contract on a day-to-day basis.
7. If an impasse is reached, consider federal mediation. This demonstrates good faith and a commitment to avoid a bitter labor dispute.

SOURCE: Adapted from Robert J. Harding, "Seven Tips for Successful Collective Bargaining," pp. 220–221.

A local business that operates in a strong pro-union community may be the most vulnerable. An example would be a grocery store that has a union contract with its checkout clerks. In the event of a labor dispute, the workers' families and friends may stop shopping at that grocery. While that may not be enough of an economic lever, other union members from unrelated industries as well as other community members may join in the boycott in sympathy. According to the law, the union that is in dispute with the chain could not openly solicit a secondary boycott. However, it may happen through word of mouth and/or media attention to the issue. Even these quasi-secondary boycotts rarely meet the objectives of the unions. The boycott against California lettuce, led by labor leader Cesar Chavez during the 1980s, was eventually dropped without forcing the growers to concede to Chavez's demands.

REACHING A SETTLEMENT—LAST RESORT OPTIONS FOR THE COMPANY

THE LOCKOUT

LOCKOUT
A management prohibition of union members' entering the company facility.

A management tactic somewhat akin to a strike is a **lockout**. Management may prohibit union members from entering the facility and instead run the company with management employees and temporary replacement workers. As industries become more automated and less reliant on highly skilled employees, lockouts are more feasible. The communications business is becoming much more automated. As noted earlier, telephone companies, for instance, increasingly depend on computer hardware and software that minimizes the need for human intervention. Think about what happens when you make a long-distance call with a credit card. By using a touch-tone phone, you can complete the call without any direct human intervention. Such technology made it possible for NYNEX managers during a labor dispute in 1989 to continue all the company's basic services with management employees.

Other industries that are becoming increasingly automated are banking, continuous-process operations such as oil refining and chemical manufacturing, and even retailing with an increased emphasis on self-service and phone-based orders.

REPLACEMENT WORKERS

The lockout tactic often utilizes temporary workers to get the union back to the negotiating table and move toward a settlement that will allow the resumption of normal operations. In recent years, replacement workers have been hired not just to temporarily fill the gap but also to permanently replace the striking union members. The 1981 firing of the air traffic controllers (PATCO union members) by the Reagan administration and subsequent hiring of replacement controllers actually paved the way for a more widespread use of this tactic. As mentioned earlier, a controversial 1989 Supreme Court decision confirmed the employers' right to keep the replacement workers after a strike is over. From the union's perspective, this is a powerful counter to a strike, and it can result in the effective end of a union's influence in a company, as demonstrated by the UAW's return to work at Caterpillar when its CEO threatened to hire replacement workers. Union leaders have accused management of deliberately provoking strikes to allow management the opportunity to hire replacement workers who will decertify the union.

National labor leaders have been pressing Congress to pass a restrictive law to prohibit the hiring of permanent replacement workers. National labor policy has tended to recognize two parallel but competing rights. Unions have been given the clear right to strike, but businesses have been given an equal right to stay open.[66] During the remainder of the 1990s, these competing rights will certainly be at the center of attention in legislative and court decision.[67]

RATIFYING A SETTLEMENT

RATIFICATION PROCESS
A vote of the rank-and-file union members on whether to accept or reject a negotiated contract.

In large organizations, the final settlement is the result of a complex procedure over an extended period of time. Settlements in smaller companies are frequently more straightforward.

In large organizations, the immediate union bargaining team typically submits the settlement to a representative council. If the council approves the agreement, the rank and file vote on it. This is called the **ratification process.** If the rank and file do not accept the settlement, their negotiators go back to the table. In recent years, approximately 10 percent of the negotiated contracts were not ratified on the first vote. This should not happen if union leadership is in close contact with the desires and needs of its membership.

IMPLEMENTING A SETTLEMENT

Assuming that ratification does take place, the following steps should be taken to implement it:

1. The contract provisions should be submitted to lawyers on both sides to determine that the agreed-upon provisions are transferred into appropriate language that is both understandable and enforceable.

2. Appropriate news releases and a joint union–company news conference may be appropriate. Whatever the outcome of negotiations, it is better for the parties involved to explain the facts rather than let them be disseminated by rumor or innuendo. The union may focus on the shutdown of a production line at a plant, but to the company, the fact that it is giving workers the chance to be retrained, retired, or relocated is just as important.

3. Internal publications from the union and company should communicate the most important aspects of the agreement.

4. If the settlement involves major changes in work rules, compensation packages, or benefit allowances, human resource managers should prepare and offer appropriate training and development programs for both managers and workers. For example, if a new quality improvement program and related compensation rules are included in a new contract, management cannot assume that everyone will understand them; specific technical training may be needed. If the company–union relationship is poor, it may be important for the first-line supervisory staff to attend sessions on appropriate human relations topics.

5. Both the union leadership and company management need to clearly state their commitment to make the agreement work, recognizing that whether the process was smooth or rough, all the parties must now work together to abide by the settlement.

ADMINISTERING THE CONTRACT

Once the contract is ratified, its day-to-day implementation is critical. If a contract is well written and clearly specifies the responsibilities of both sides, administering the contract becomes relatively easy. The tone of the negotiations can affect the contract administration process. If the contract is settled without a strike or lockout, the agreement is less likely to lead to grievances. If the negotiations were tough and resulted in a prolonged walkout, the day-to-day administration may develop into a version of the cold war.

The administration of a settlement that is less than satisfactory to one or both sides can be difficult. One or each party may try to obtain concessions not obtained by the negotiations by what is called *grievance bargaining* as the contract is implemented and interpreted. Suppose, for example, that the contract stipulates that a worker be paid for at least four hours when he or she is called in by a department head for unscheduled work, perhaps on a weekend. Suppose also that a supervisor calls the worker in for unscheduled duties that take two hours to perform. The company might justify paying the worker for only two hours, not four as the contract requires, because a supervisor, not a department head, called in the worker.

The union obviously would support the employee, stating that it does not matter who called the employee in; the fact is that the employee came in and worked two hours and should be paid for four. Such a case would likely go to arbitration, especially if the company is trying to find a means to do away with this call-in provision and has not been able to eliminate it in actual contract negotiations. The company is attempting to win something through arbitration that it could not win at the bargaining table.

LETTER OF THE LAW
The strict, inflexible interpretation of a contract.

It is not uncommon for companies to try to circumvent strict **letter-of-the-law** interpretation of the contract. Managers will argue that during a three-year contract, economic and competitive conditions can change so radically that they need some flexibility. Depending on the union's strength and/or goals, it may agree to this flexibility. It is very possible that both parties may benefit from some flexibility. If this is so, it should be built into the contract during the negotiation process rather than relying on the grievance and arbitration process, which can be extremely costly and disruptive.

It should be obvious that the negotiations process cannot be taken lightly, nor can the consequences of the signed contract be ignored. From a strategic viewpoint, long-term implementation should always be kept in mind during the negotiation process. Frequently, the management team involved in the bargaining process is not as involved in the day-to-day administration as are the first-line supervisors. Therefore, the management team should carefully review the feasibility of the provisions, anticipate potential areas of conflict, and try to preempt as many of these situations as possible. Management should establish an effective channel of communication between these supervisors to ensure that ongoing problem areas are properly dealt with in any subsequent negotiations.

GRIEVANCES

Even when a satisfactory agreement is negotiated, inevitable disagreements occur regarding contract language. Management has the primary responsibility of administering the contract. The union watches carefully to be sure that the contract language is observed. In most contracts, a specific procedure is spelled out about how complaints and concerns over contract administration will be handled. Grievances have several causes.

The grievance process usually involves submitting a complaint to the first-line supervisor. It can be settled at that level, or it can be submitted to as many as three or four more levels. If it cannot be settled in this way, it may go to arbitration.

MISUNDERSTANDING OR MISINTERPRETATION

A contract may vary from a few pages to over 50 pages, but every eventuality cannot be anticipated, so the language is written in general terms. The worker and supervisor might interpret the language differently. For a variety of legal reasons, the contract may be full of legal terms. The average supervisor or worker may interpret these provisions in his or her own particular way. Long-term employees may think they understand the agreement and not bother to read the actual contract, assuming that the new contract is just about the same as the old one. This can lead to a contract violation due to neglect.

PREMEDITATED CONTRACT VIOLATION

PREMEDITATED CONTRACT VIOLATION
A deliberate attempt to violate the terms of a labor agreement by either a union or management.

Occasionally, one side or the other will intentionally commit a **premeditated contract violation** to draw attention to an issue that could not be resolved in the negotiations process. For instance, a union might be unhappy about a work rule that allows a supervisor to change a worker's assignment to a different machining operation more than three times in a shift. The union worker may complain and deliberately slow down after being transferred the third time to test management's intent to enforce the contract. Management may choose to ignore the worker's behavior and in the future assign a worker to a maximum of two machines, leading to a *de facto* drop of the provision. Or the management may discipline the worker, the worker subsequently may file a grievance, and the union may force the grievance to binding arbitration, where it hopes to get a change in the contract provision.

Management, likewise, sometimes forces an issue for economic reasons. Changes in economic conditions might make a work rule too restrictive to allow the company to remain competitive; thus, the management may disregard the rule. The union may ignore the violation if it serves union interest to do so, or it may immediately file a grievance. The outcome of these willful violations is often a function of the relative power of the management and the union, which could change dramatically during the course of a contract. Some provisions in contracts that run from two to five years are usually open to negotiation every year.

"SMOKE SCREEN" VIOLATIONS

It is possible that a grievance may be filed for a less-than-obvious reason. If the union leadership seems to be losing control, or if the members are starting to wonder whether the union officials are too cozy in their relationship with the company, the union may provoke a grievance to prove to the membership that it is in control and is serving the needs of the members after all.

Management as well may provoke a problem in an attempt to embarrass the union or test its power. If the management of the company is working to move to a union-free environment, a series of violations may serve as a means to divide the union into factions.

Such **smoke screen violations** can be very risky and dangerous because the other party may misinterpret the intent and take retaliatory action. It is recommended that disagreements be dealt with whether during the contract negotiations or through a formal grievance process rather than by covert political moves.

SMOKE SCREEN VIOLATION
An obvious contract violation that disguises an underlying problem or disagreement.

MANAGEMENT GUIDELINES

Some of the managerial implications from this chapter include the following:

1. It is important for managers to understand that the nature of union activity has changed dramatically in the last 20 years due to a variety of circumstances encompassing economic shifts within the United States and global economy, demographic changes, and political and social attitudes. As a percentage of the workforce, union representation has declined significantly. Managers of facilities both with and without unions need to be aware of these changes.
2. Unions must determine the degree to which they should concentrate on "bread-and-butter" issues, working conditions, job security, or affinity services. Human resource managers need to understand what their unions want and what they are willing to give in return.
3. The 1970s and 1980s became a time of conflict, concession bargaining, and some notable bitter struggles, but the 1990s have offered signs of new cooperative efforts. Managers must try to explore and develop these areas, which is not easy.
4. A variety of laws, including the Sherman-Clayton Act, Taft-Hartley Act, Wagner Act, and Landrum-Griffin Act, clearly spell out the legal rights and responsibilities of labor and management. In addition, a plethora of court decisions impact the general legal framework. Managers need the advice of legal experts when dealing with unions.
5. Management needs to be clear about its strategic goals and then align its labor policy with those goals. For example, if a company wants to serve a high-quality-high-price niche, it may be more flexible in negotiating wages but more stringent on flexible work assignments that will allow it to take advantage of highly skilled craftspeople without cumbersome job classifications.
6. The negotiating team must be very well prepared before it goes into the negotiating sessions. Preparations should include the following:
   A. A thorough review of past contracts.

Continued

> **B.** A listing of disagreements, disputes, and grievances since the last contract.
> **C.** An analysis of what the union will ask for and a careful assessment of the personalities of the negotiators on each side as well as the issues that are likely to arise.
> **D.** A list of objectives that the team wants to accomplish.
>
> **7.** Once an agreement is worked out, the manager should ensure that supervisors understand the provisions of the contract with particular focus on how it is different from the last contract. The human resource department should ensure that the contract is distributed to all management personnel. It is also wise to hold workshops or briefing sessions to be sure that everyone understands the precise language.

QUESTIONS FOR REVIEW

1. What, if anything, could the management and labor unions have done at Caterpillar to avoid the bitter struggle?

2. How will the changing demographics of the workforce affect union attempts at organizing?

3. In your opinion, should management resist the formation of a union? Why or why not? What are the advantages for the company? Are there any disadvantages to having a union?

4. Suppose you were attempting to organize a union in a large restaurant of 150 employees. How would you convince fellow employees they should vote for a union? Now reverse the role. How would you as a manager respond?

5. What are the most important roles that unions play today? Are they the same as they were 20 years ago? Why or why not?

6. What is meant by jointness efforts? Provide an example of where a jointness effort is being tried.

7. Have unions outlived their usefulness? Make a case for and against this issue.

8. What is your forecast for union–management relations for the year 2005?

9. What are the most important reasons that some unions and managers now believe that a more collaborative relationship is in their best interest?

10. How does the relative power of the company and union affect the negotiating process?

11. What connection is there between a company's strategy and its approach to negotiating? How would the issues differ for a low-cost producer strategy versus a company that produces high-quality, high-priced luxury items focused on a special market niche?

12. What are some ways in which companies that have unions try to eliminate them? What are some methods that companies without unions use to remain union free? What are the legal and ethical issues involved in each case?

13. Regarding the collective bargaining process, what is the difference between mandatory, permissible, and prohibited issues? Give an example of each.

14. When negotiations break down, what are some tactics employed by unions to try to force a settlement? What tactics might a company use?

15. "The next 10 years are likely to be a period of increasing labor/management strife based on the resurgence of militant union power." Do you agree or disagree with this statement? Explain your answer.

CASE

UNITED AIRLINES[68]

UNITED WE FLY; DIVIDED WE CRASH

In recent years, the skies have been stormy and turbulent for the airline that touts the motto "Fly the Friendly Skies of United." The nation's largest air carrier, with 76,000 employees and 550 aircraft, has been plagued with chronic financial losses and increasing competition. Particularly troubling for United has been the entry of the low-cost and profitable Southwest Airlines into United's prime Midwest-based operations (see Chapter 3). United achieved its number 1 carrier status before deregulation. At that time, territories were protected and costs were easily passed on to the traveling public. Labor unions demanded and got premium wage rates that to this day are still 49 percent higher than manufacturing wages. Labor rules created at that time hamper productivity today. The 1980s proved to be tempestuous and dynamic for the airlines. There were new start-up airlines without unions and their attendant restrictions. At the same time, some airlines experienced bankruptcies and consolidations that resulted in even more of the new breed of low-cost competitors.

United's shareholders and employees alike had been unhappy with the results and perceived sacrifices over the 1984-1995 period. The company has tried to hold down costs but has had little success in competing with the low-cost, higher productivity airlines. Starting in 1987, several attempts were made to engineer an employee buyout. In fact, between 1987 and 1994, five separate buyout plans were advanced. During 1993, the situation became more serious, and United's management proposed either a buyout/concessions deal *or* the real threat of asset sales and massive employee layoffs. With so many *stakeholders* pressing their individual interests, including management, stockholders, several unions—including machinists, pilots, and flight attendants—and even nonunion employees, an historic agreement was reached in July 1994.

THE FIFTH TIME IS A CHARM

The precedent-setting $4.8 billion buyout involved workers' investment of 55 percent in the company in exchange for wage cuts and other concessions designed to make United a sleeker airline. The stockholders voted acceptance by an overwhelming 70 percent majority. Support by union members was certainly not unanimous. The pilots' union, which was leading the buyout, faced significant objections from many members of the machinists' union, which believed that double-digit wage cuts were a steep price to pay. Nevertheless, enough members went along to seal the deal. Under the agreement, the unions were given three seats on the board of directors and therefore had input into the selection of the new

CEO Gerald Greenwald, the former Chrysler executive who helped to engineer the automaker's turnaround.

With the new wage rates and work rule concessions, United launched its "Shuttle by United" service in 1994 to compete with the low-cost carriers such as Southwest and Continental.

CAN IT WORK?

This agreement has many positive supporters. Labor Secretary Robert Reich sees the United agreement as a prototype for U.S. companies to restructure themselves without massive layoffs and dislocations. Union representatives, while a bit skeptical, see this as the best option when compared with the bleak future United faced before the agreement. Not everyone, of course, is so positive. Lee Iacocca, Greenwald's former boss at Chrysler, raised a red flag. He says, "Somebody's crazy. It can't work. What do you think will happen when it's a choice between employee benefits and capital investment?"

Managing an employee-owned company certainly involves challenges. An encounter between the well-liked Greenwald and a rank and file worker at United's San Francisco maintenance center sums up the challenge ahead. The worker demanded to know of Greenwald, "So what are you going to do for me?" Greenwald's response: "I was just going to ask you the same question."

QUESTIONS

1. Do you think that employee buyouts that are made during a financial crisis can succeed in the long run?

2. What complications for an HR manager are inherent in an employee-owned company? What might be some advantages for an HR manager in this type of situation?

3. Does Lee Iacocca have a point when he says this arrangement is crazy and can't work? What argument would you make against his assessment?

4. Is Robert Reich correct in seeing this as a prototype of future management–labor relations? Why or why not?

ADDITIONAL READINGS

Aaron, Benjamin, Joyce M. Najita, and James L. Stern, eds. *Public Sector Bargaining,* 2d ed. Washington, DC: The Bureau of National Affairs, Inc., 1988.

Adams, Roy. "Industrial Relations Systems: Canada in Comparative Perspective." In *Union-Management Relations in Canada,* 2d ed., ed. by John C. Anderson, Morley Gunderson, and Allen Ponak. Ontario: Addison-Wesley, 1989.

Arthur, Jeffrey, and James Dworkin. "Current Topics in Industrial and Labor Relations Research and Practice." *Journal of Management* 17 (1991), pp. 515–551.

Ballott, Michael. *Labor-Management Relations in a Changing Environment.* New York: Wiley, 1992.

Barbush, Jack. "Do We Really Want Labor on the Ropes? We're Entering a New Era of Industrial Relations and That's Cause for Concern." *Harvard Business Review* 63. July–August 1985, pp. 10–16.

Barling, Julian, E. Kevin Kelloway, and Eric Bremermann. "Preemployment Predictors of Union Attitudes: The Role of Family Socialization and Work Beliefs." *Journal of Applied Psychology* 76 (1991), pp. 725–731.

Barney, Jay B., and William G. Ouichi. *Organizational Economics: Toward a New Paradigm for Understanding and Studying Organizations.* San Francisco: Jossey-Bass, 1986.

Blake, Robert R., and Jane S. Mouton. *Solving Costly Organizational Conflicts.* San Francisco: Jossey-Bass, 1984.

Chelius, James, and James Dworkin, eds. *Reflections on the Transformation of Industrial Relations.* Metuchen, NJ: IMLR Press/ Rutgers University, 1990.

Cimini, Michael. "Union Members in 1989." *News: United States Department of Labor.* Washington, DC: Bureau of Labor Statistics, February 7, 1990.

Clark, Paul F. *The Miners' Fight for Democracy: Arnold Miller and the Reform of the United Mine Workers.* Ithaca, NY: IRL Press, 1986.

Coleman, Charles J. *Managing Labor Relations in the Public Sector.* San Francisco: Jossey-Bass, 1990.

Cooke, W. N. *Union Organizing and Public Policy.* Kalamazoo, MI: Upjohn Institute, 1985.

Doherty, Robert E. *Labor Relations Premier: An Introduction to Collective Bargaining through Documents.* ILR Bulletin, No. 54. Ithaca, NY: ILR Press, 1984.

Dunlop, John T. *Industrial Relations Systems.* New York: Henry Holt, 1958.

———.*The Management of Labor Unions.* New York: Lexington Books, 1989.

Evans, Martin G., and Daniel A. Ondrack. "The Role of Job Outcomes and Values in Understanding the Union's Impact of Job Satisfaction: A Replication." *Human Relations,* May 1990.

Freeman, Richard, and James Medoff. *What Do Unions Do?* New York: Basic Books, 1984.

Fulmer, William E., and Ann C. Casey. "Employment at Will: Options for Managers." *Academy of Management Executive* 4(2) (1990), pp. 102–107.

Gerhart, Paul F. *Saving Plants and Jobs: Union–Management Negotiations in the Context of Threatened Plant Closing.* Kalamazoo, MI: Upjohn Institute, 1987.

Gilbert, Beth. "The Impact of Union Involvement on the Design and Introduction of Quality of Work Life." *Human Relations,* December 1989.

Gold, Charlotte. *Labor–Management Committees: Confrontation, Cooptation, or Cooperation?* Ithaca, NY: ILR Press, 1986.

Heckscher, Charles C. *The New Unionism.* New York: Basic Books, 1988.

Helfgott, Roy. *Computerized Manufacturing and Human Resources.* Lexington, MA: Lexington Books, 1986.

Herrick, Neal Q. *Joint Management and Employee Participation— Labor and Management at the Crossroads.* San Francisco: Jossey-Bass, 1990.

Hill, Marvin, Jr., and Anthony Sinicropi. *Management Rights.* Washington, DC: Bureau of National Affairs, 1986.

Huang, Wei-Chiao, ed. *Organized Labor at the Crossroads.* Kalamazoo, MI: Upjohn Institute, 1989.

Hurd, Richard W. "Big Labor Regains Its Muscle." *Business & Society Review* 68, Winter 1989, pp. 4–8.

Hutchens, Robert M., and David B. Lipsky. *Strikers and Subsidies— The Influence of Government Transfer Programs on Strike Activity.* Ithaca, NY: ILR Press, 1989.

Ichniowski, Casey, and Anne E. Preston. *The Competitive Edge: Managing Human Resources in Non-Union and Union Firms.* Glenview, IL: Scott-Foresman, 1988.

Ichniowski, Casey, and Jeffrey Zax. "Today's Associations, Tomorrow's Unions." *Industrial and Labor Relations Review* 43 (1990), pp. 191–208.

Kalish, Doug. "The New-Collar Workers and Unions' Changing Roles." *Personnel Journal* 55(12), December 1986, pp. 16–21.

Kerr, Clark, and Paul Straudor, eds. *Industrial Relations in a New Age.* San Francisco: Jossey-Bass, 1986.

Kleiner, Morris M., Robert A. McLean, and George F. Dreher. *Labor Markets and Human Resource Management.* Glenview, IL: Scott-Foresman, 1988.

Kochan, Thomas A., and Harry C. Katz. *Collective Bargaining and Industrial Relations,* 2d ed. New York: McGraw-Hill, 1988.

Kochan, Thomas A., Harry C. Katz, and Robert B. McKersie. *The Transformation of American Industrial Relations.* New York: Basic Books, 1986.

Kochan, Thomas A., Harry C. Katz, and Nancy R. Mower. *Worker Participation and American Unions—Threat or Opportunity?* Kalamazoo, MI: Upjohn Institute, 1984.

Lareau, N. Peter. *Drafting the Union Contract.* Albany, NY: Matthew Bender, 1988.

Lawler, John J. *Unionization and Deunionization: Strategy, Tactics, and Outcomes.* Columbia, SC: University of South Carolina Press, 1990.

Lewin, David, Peter Fruille, Thomas Kochan, and John Delaney. *Public Sector Labor Relations.* Lexington, MA: Lexington Books, 1988.

Lipset, Seymour M. *Unions in Transition: Entering the Second Century.* San Francisco: ICS Press, 1986.

Lipsky, David, and Clifford Donn. *Collective Bargaining in American Industry.* Lexington, MA: Lexington Books, 1981.

Martin, James E. *Two-Tier Compensation Structures—Their Impact on Unions, Employers, and Employees.* Kalamazoo, MI: Upjohn Institute, 1990.

Meier, Gretl S. *Job Sharing—A New Pattern for Quality of Work and Life.* Kalamazoo, MI: Upjohn Institute, 1979.

Mills, Daniel Quinn. *Labor Management Relations,* 4th ed. New York: McGraw-Hill, 1989.

Moore, Christopher W. *The Mediation Process—Practical Strategies for Resolving Conflict.* San Francisco: Jossey-Bass, 1986.

Quaglieri, Philip. *America's Labor Leaders.* Lexington, MA: Lexington Books, 1989.

Rosenbloom, David H., and Jay M. Shafritz. *Essentials of Labor Relations.* Reston, VA: Reston Publishing Company, 1985.

Rosow, Jerome M., ed. *Teamwork: Joint Labor–Management Programs in America.* Elmsford, NY: Work in America Institute, Inc., 1986.

Rothstein, Lawrence E. *Plant Closings: Power, Politics, and Workers.* Dover, MA: Auburn House Press, 1986.

Schuster, M. H. *Union–Management Cooperation.* Kalamazoo, MI: Upjohn Institute, 1985.

Siegel, Irving H., and Edgar Weinburg. *Labor–Management Cooperation—The American Experience.* Kalamazoo, MI: Upjohn Institute, 1982.

Slichter, Sumner, James Healy, and E. Robert Livernash. *The Impact of Collective Bargaining on Management.* Washington, DC: The Brookings Institute, 1960.

Stern, Robert N., K. H. Wood, and Tove H. Hammer. *Employer Ownership in Plant Shutdowns—Prospects for Employment Stability.* Kalamazoo, MI: Upjohn Institute, 1979.

Strauss, George, David Gallagher, and Jack Fiorito, eds. *The State of the Unions.* Madison, WI: Industrial Relations Research Association, 1991.

Taylor, Benjamin J. *Cases in Labor Relations Law, 1987.* Englewood Cliffs, NJ: Prentice-Hall, 1987.

Uly, William L., Jeanne M. Brett, and Stephen B. Goldberg. *Getting Disputes Resolved: Designing Systems to Cut the Costs of Conflict.* San Francisco: Jossey-Bass, 1988.

Wendling, Wayne R. *The Plant Closure Policy Dilemma—Labor, Law, and Bargaining.* Kalamazoo, MI: Upjohn Institute, 1984.

Whyte, William F., et al. *Worker Participation and Ownership: Cooperative Strategies for Strengthening Local Economies.* Ithaca, NY: ILR Press, 1983.

Zack, Arnold M. *Grievance Arbitration.* New York: American Arbitration Association, 1989.

NOTES

1. "UAW Blasts New Caterpillar Takeaways," *UAW Washington Report,* December 11, 1992, p. 2; Bill Casstevens, "UAW vs. Caterpillar—The Battle Continues," *The Wall Street Journal,* April 22, 1993, p. A15; Dennis Farley, "Workers at Caterpillar Hope against Hope Clinton Will Be True," *The Wall Street Journal,* July 26, 1993, p. A1; Kevin Kelly, "Cat Is Purring, But They're Hissing on the Floor," *Business Week,* May 16, 1994, p. 33; Robert L. Rose and Alex Kotlowitz, "Strife between UAW and Caterpillar Blights Promising Labor Idea," *The Wall Street Journal,* pp. A1 +; and Robert L. Rose, "Caterpillar, Aided by Economy's Gains, Posts Profit Surge, But Stock Falls 4.5%," *The Wall Street Journal,* April 21, 1994, p. A2, "UAW Rejects Caterpillar Bid for Negotiations," *The Wall Street Journal,* May 16, 1994, p. A9, "Labor Strife Threatens Caterpillar's Booming Business," *The Wall Street Journal,* June 10, 1994, p. B4, and "Caterpillar Refuses to Let Strikers Resume Their Jobs," *The Wall Street Journal,* June 14, 1994, p. B11.

2. *Brief History of the American Labor Movement* (Washington, DC: U.S. Department of Labor Statistics, 1970), Bulletin 1000, p. 1.

3. Arthur A. Sloane and Fred Whitney, *Labor Relations* 4th ed. (Englewood Cliffs, NJ: Prentice-Hall, 1981), pp. 69–76.

4. Aaron Bernstein, "Why America Needs Unions, But Not the Kind It Has Now," *Business Week,* May 23, 1994, pp. 70–82.

5. Ron Suskind, "Where Have All the Unions Gone?" *The Wall Street Journal,* July 28, 1992, pp. A1 +.

6. Bernstein, "Why America Needs Unions, But Not the Kind It Has Now."

7. Raju Narisetti, "Labor Letter," *The Wall Street Journal,* November 29, 1994, p. A1.

8. *Economic Report of the President* (Washington, DC: U.S. Government Printing Office, 1994).

9. Bernstein, "Why America Needs Unions, But Not the Kind It Has Now."

10. Larry Reynolds, "Labor's Leaders Changing to Meet the Times," *Management Review,* February 1988, pp. 57–58.

11. Peggy Connerton, "Union's Future Is Bright," *Personnel Administrator,* December 1989, pp. 99–100.

12. Stephanie Overman, "Commission to Tackle Pittston Strike Issues," *HRM News,* February 1990, pp. A1, A4.

13. Bernstein, "Why America Needs Unions, But Not the Kind It Has Now."

14. John Hoerr and Wendy Zellner, "A Japanese Import That's Not Selling," *Business Week,* February 26, 1990, pp. 86–87.

15. Aaron Bernstein, "Move Over Boone, Carl and Irv—Here Comes Labor," *Business Week,* December 14, 1987, pp. 124–125.

16. Sloane and Whitney, *Labor Relations,* pp. 69–76.

17. George Strauss, "Toward the Study of Human Resources Policy," in *Reflections on the Transformation of Industrial Relations,* ed. by James Chelius and James Dworkin (Metuchen, NJ: IMLR Press–Rutgers University, 1990), pp. 73–106.

18. Dana Milbank, "National Steel Claims Strength in Its Labor-Management Alloy," *The Wall Street Journal,* April 30, 1992, pp. B1 +.

19. Don Nichols, "The Management Revolution and Loss of Union Clout," (an inverview with Dr. Richard I. Lyles), *Management Review,* February 1988, pp. 25–26.

20. Ben Fisher, "Union Busting or Empowerment?" *Across the Board,* April 1990, pp. 11–12.

21. Steve Gunderson, "NLRB Muddies Regulatory Water," *The Wall Street Journal,* February 1, 1993, p. A10.

22. Alexander B. Trowbridge, "Avoiding Labor–Management Conflict," *Management Review,* February 1988, pp. 47–49.

23. Jeremy Main, "The Labor Rebel Leading the Hormel Strike," *Fortune,* June 9, 1986, pp. 105–110.

24. Rod Willis, "Can American Unions Transform Themselves?" *Management Review,* February 1988, pp. 14–21.

25. James Neff, *Mobbed Up: Jackie Presser's High-Wire Life in the Teamsters, the Mafia, and the FBI* (New York: Atlantic Monthly Press, 1989).

26. Willis, "Can American Unions Transform Themselves?"

27. John Naisbitt and Patricia Aburdeen, *Megatrends 2000—Ten New Directions for the 1990's* (New York: Morrow, 1990), p. 42.

28. Willis, "Can American Unions Transform Themselves?"

29. Robert Kuttner, "The Fed's Thermostat Is on the Fritz," *Business Week,* April 11, 1994, p. 18.

30. John Hoerr et al., "Beyond Unions," *Business Week,* July 8, 1985, p. 72.

31. Peter Drucker, "Reinventing Unions," *Across the Board,* September 1989, pp. 12–13.

32. Audrey Freedman, "Unions' Future Is Bleak," *Personnel Administrator,* December 1989, p. 98.

33. Ibid.

34. Stephie Overman, "Nissan Sees Union's Loss as Management Style's Win," *Resource,* September 1989, p. 1.

35. Thomas A. Kochan, Harry C. Katz, and Robert B. McKersie, *The Transformation of American Industrial Relations* (New York: Basic Books, 1986).

36. Edward E. Lawler III and Susan A. Mohrman, "Unions and the New Management," *Academy of Management Executive* 1(3), 1987.

37. Willis, "Can American Unions Transform Themselves?"

38. Lawler and Mohrman, "Unions and the New Management."

39. Alan I. Murray and Yonatan Reshef, "American Manufacturing Unions' Stasis: A Paradigmatic Perspective," *Academy of Management Review* 13(4), 1988, pp. 639–652.

40. Adrienne Eaton and Paula Voos, "The Ability of Unions to Adapt to Innovative Workplace Arrangements," *AEA Papers and Proceedings* 79, May 1989, pp. 172–176.

41. Edward Cohen-Rosenthal and Cynthia Burton, "Union–Management Cooperation," *Training and Development Journal,* May 1986, pp. 96–98.

42. Constance Gustke, "Unions Move to Recruit Women," *Management Review,* February 1988, p. 52.

43. Gary N. Chaison and P. Andiappan, "Profiles of Local Union Officers: Females v. Males," *Industrial Relations* 26(3), 1987, pp. 281–283.

44. Benjamin Aaron, Joyce M. Najita, and James L. Stern, eds. *Public Sector Bargaining,* 2d ed. (Washington, DC: The Bureau of National Affairs, 1988).

45. R. L. Rose, N. M. Christian, and A. Q. Nomani, "Union Merger Sounds Painless, But It Won't Be," *The Wall Street Journal,* July 28, 1995, p. B1.

46. Robert Frank, "UPS, Teamsters Reach Accord, Ending Strike," *The Wall Street Journal,* February 8, 1994, p. A2.

47. Robert T. Thompson, "An Anti-Worker Labor Bill," *The Wall Street Journal,* August 31, 1990, p. A10.

48. Leon Rubis, "Striker Order Argued in Congress, Court," *HRNews,* May 1995, p. 14.

49. Robert Blake and Jane S. Mouton, "How to Achieve the Integration on the Human Side of the Merger," *Organizational Dynamics* 13(3), 1985, pp. 41–56.

50. James Fraze, "After Model Merger Taking Two Years, USAir Growing Pilot Seniority Issue Unresolved," *Resource,* September 1989, p. 11.

51. Ibid.

52. Cynthia A. Lengnick-Hall and Mark L. Lengnick-Hall, "Strategic Human Resources Management: A Review of the Literature and a Proposed Typology," *Academy of Management Review* 13(3), 1982, pp. 454–470.

53. Daily Congressional Record 3954 (April 23, 1947).

54. Francis T. Coleman, "Once a Union Not Always a Union," *Personnel Journal,* March 1985, pp. 42–45.

55. R. Wayne Mondy and Robert M. Noe III, *Human Resource Management,* 4th ed. (Boston: Allyn & Bacon, 1990), p. 650.

56. Marc Singer, *Human Resource Management* (Boston: PWS-Kent, 1990), p. 414.

57. Joseph B. White, "Worker's Revenge: Factory Towns Start to Fight Back Angrily When Firms Pull Out," *The Wall Street Journal,* March 8, 1988, pp. A1 +.

58. Ibid.

59. Paul D. Staudohar, "New Plant Closing Law Aids Workers in Transition," *Personnel Journal,* January 1989, pp. 87–90.

60. James F. Rand, "Preventive-Maintenance Techniques for Staying Union-Free," *Personnel Journal* 59, June 1980, p. 497.

61. Singer, *Human Resource Management,* p. 437.

62. Richard Johnson, "Interest Arbitration Examined," *Personnel Administrator,* January 1983, pp. 53–57.

63. William H. Holley and Kenneth M. Jennings, *The Labor Relations Process,* 3d ed. (Chicago: The Dryden Press, 1988), p. 246.

64. Cynthia T. Gramm, "The Determinants of Strike Incidence and Severity: A Micro-Level Study," *Industrial and Labor Relations Review* 39, April 1986, pp. 361–376.

65. Christopher Conte, "Work Stoppages," *The Wall Street Journal,* March 3, 1992, p. A1.

66. Thompson, "An Anti-Worker, Labor Bill."

67. Andrew Kupfis, "Caterpillar's Union Fallout," *Fortune,* May 18, 1992, p. 16.

68. Kevin Kelly and Aaron Bernstein, "United Unions Would Rather Buy than Strike," *Business Week,* August 23, 1993, p. 71; Frank J. Dooley, "Why Airlines Crash," *The Wall Street Journal,* March 30, 1994, p. A16; Susan Chandler, "A United United Is Still a Way Off," *Business Week,* May 23, 1994, p. 32; and Michael J. McCarthy, "Holders of UAL Approve Bold $4.8 Billion Buyout," *The Wall Street Journal,* July 13, 1994, pp. A3 +.

CHAPTER 17
Strategic Restructuring and the Virtual
Organization

CHAPTER 7

BANKRUPTCY
A bankruptcy filing in which a firm ceases to operate.

COMPETITIVE STRATEGY
The combination of the ends (goals) for which a firm is striving and the means (policies) by which it seeks to achieve those goals.

OVERALL COST LEADERSHIP
A competitive strategy in which a firm seeks to sell products that are less expensive than its competitors' products.

DIFFERENTIATION
A competitive strategy in which a firm seeks to create a product or service that is unique within the industry.

FOCUS
A competitive strategy in which a firm seeks to concentrate on a narrow industry segment that matches its skills.

STUCK IN THE MIDDLE
A situation in which a firm essentially lacks a competitive strategy.

strategy as "a combination of the ends (goals) for which the firm is striving and the means (policies) by which it is seeking to get there."[9] Porter identifies 3 generic types of strategies that an organization may pursue: an overall cost leadership, a differentiation, or a focus strategy in relation to its competitors.[10]

Firms pursuing an **overall cost leadership** strategy seek to sell products that are less expensive in price than their competitors' products. This strategy involves vigorous pursuit of organizational efficiency. Managers emphasize efficient and large-scale assembly line and manufacturing techniques and strict control of operating and overhead costs. In addition, they reduce spending on perceived nonessential areas such as research and development, maintenance, and sales. Often when an organization adopts a cost leadership strategy, it seeks to reduce what it views as nonessential workers by cutting levels of bureaucracy, reducing redundant functions within the organization, and trimming staffing in nonessential departments. It also tries to reduce the number of workers on the assembly line by investing heavily in automation, robotics, and other related techniques. Air South, ValueJet, and Mark Air are examples of airlines that pursued this strategy in the 1990s.

Firms pursuing a **differentiation** strategy seek to create a product or service that is unique within the industry and, thus, gain a competitive advantage. Firms using this strategy try to build a brand loyalty in their customers. Increased brand loyalty reduces the customer's sensitivity to price and substitute products. Product design, quality, customer service, dealer networks, technology, features, or a combination of these factors serves to increase brand loyalty. A differentiation strategy does not allow firms to ignore costs but many of its parts are costly. Organizations that adopt a differentiation strategy must build some form of strength. This strength may be in marketing, research and development, manufacturing skill, or other related capabilities. This strategy requires personnel who are highly skilled, creative, and talented. Critical areas include R&D labs, marketing departments, and product design/engineering shops. Quality people in these areas are always in high demand. As a result, getting the necessary skills to be a strong competitor using the differentiation strategy is time consuming and expensive. This strategy is often costlier to adopt than other strategies because success is more difficult to measure. The basis of employee performance ratings is subjective, not quantitative, because output is difficult to measure. Mercedes Benz, BMW, and other luxury car makers use this strategy.

A third option is the **focus** strategy. Firms adopting a focus strategy seek to "get back to the basics." Instead of trying to compete in many markets with a wide range of products, they concentrate on a narrow segment that matches their skills.[11] Firms cut nonessential functions and personnel not directly serving the direct aim of the organization's focus. Many focused firms are smaller than those using a low-cost or differentiation strategy. Management often organizes focused firms functionally to avoid waste and duplication. It puts its resources into doing one or two jobs well. Segmentation may occur by focusing on certain buyers, products, or geographic locations. A firm with a focus orientation may be the low-cost producer or have high differentiation in the market segment it serves. Kentucky Fried Chicken is a good example of a firm that has successfully pursued a focus strategy: "We do chicken right."

A final strategy is essentially a lack of strategy. Porter calls this the **stuck in the middle** strategy. Firms stuck in the middle are unable to adopt successfully a generic strategy due to a lack of capital, market share, products, or managerial skill. They wander from one strategy to another and do poorly in each. This results in declining profits and market share. Decisive action may be the only solution to this problem if the firm wishes to remain a real competitor. This action almost always includes some form of restructuring. Exhibit 17.4 summarizes the common organizational requirements necessary for each of Porter's three generic strategies. Continental Airlines was an example of this strategy when, in the mid-1990s, it instituted a low-cost strategy called "Continental Lite" only to abandon it after a number of months in Chapter 11 bankruptcy.

MANAGEMENT PHILOSOPHY CONCERNING EMPLOYEES AND TECHNOLOGY

The philosophy of the firm's managers concerning its employees and technology may also influence restructuring. Some firms, such as Japanese automobile producers, commit themselves to no-layoff policies, although during the early 1990s this policy was modified somewhat during Japan's severest post-World War II recession. Honda in Marysville, Ohio, employs 12,000 workers and is the region's largest employer. By mid-1995, it had not laid off one worker.[12] Other organizations view personnel as easily replaced assets. Many organizations that require skilled people, such as those in the electronics industry, believe that it is cheaper to keep employees than to let them go during a restructuring and then have to rehire and train new people later.

Firms in some industries can easily replace employees due to the low level of skills needed to perform many of the jobs. This is particularly true of service industries, such as fast-food restaurants. Many firms in these industries have relatively low training costs for new employees. If not, they are willing to pay for the increased training costs due to high employee turnover because alternatives are less appealing. These alternatives may include automation or increased salaries for employees. Exhibit 17.5 highlights some of the jobs that are easy and not so easy to refill.

AUTOMATION
Replacing people with machines and equipment.

Management philosophy toward **automation** may also affect a firm's restructuring decision. Some firms believe that high levels of automation are necessary to compete effectively in the market. As a result, employees in these organizations become more expendable during times of restructuring. Other firms place an emphasis on the flexibility of humans over robots. In these cases, capital investment may suffer during times of restructuring compared to employment levels. In any situation, management's philosophy toward its employees and its technology plays a significant role in determining the form of the restructuring.

EXHIBIT 17.4

Common Organizational Requirements of Porter's Three Generic Strategies

GENERIC STRATEGY	COMMON ORGANIZATIONAL REQUIREMENTS
Overall Cost Leadership	Tight cost control
	Frequent, detailed control reports
	Structured organization and responsibilities
	Incentives based on meeting strict quantitative targets
Differentiation	Strong coordination among functions in R&D, product development, and marketing
	Subjective measurement and incentives instead of quantitative measures
	Amenities to attract highly skilled labor, scientists, or creative people
Focus	Combination of the above policies directed at the particular strategic target

SOURCE: Michael Porter, *Competitive Strategy*. New York: Free Press, 1980, pp. 40–41.

EXHIBIT 17.5   **Easy- and Hard-to-Fill Jobs**

HARD-TO-FILL JOBS: TRY TO AVOID LAYING OFF WORKERS IN THESE AREAS

Physical Therapists	Electrical Engineers
Veterinarians	Computer Scientists
Computer Systems Analysts	Dietitians
Physicians	Chemical Engineers
Pharmacists	Dentists
Biological Scientists	Lawyers
Vocational Counselors	Actuaries
Registered Nurses	

EASY-TO-FILL JOBS: LAYOFFS IN THIS AREA SHOULD NOT RESULT IN PROBLEMS

Telephone Operators	Butchers/Meat Cutters
Rail Transport Workers	Telephone Installers
Machine Operators	Typists
Water Transport Workers	Statistical Clerks
Barbers	Data Processors
Photographers	Stenographers
Metalworkers	Firefighters
Plumbers	

SOURCE: Adapted from G. Fuchsberg, "Despite Layoffs, Firms Find Some Jobs Hard to Fill," *The Wall Street Journal,* January 22, 1991, p. B1.

BUSINESS CYCLES

Business cycle stages may also influence a firm's restructuring decision. Each stage of the business cycle—prosperity, recession, depression, and recovery—has a unique effect on an organization. Weak economic conditions often force restructuring decisions on firms. In other instances, restructuring can arise from the opportunities to make changes in times of prosperity. Restructuring during these times is often less painful to carry out than during slowdowns.

PROSPERITY AND RECOVERY
A period of the business cycle characterized by strong economic times and increasing sales.

Characteristics of **prosperity** and **recovery** in economic terms are strong and increasing sales. Organizations have extra resources and capital as a result of the prosperous times, and restructuring often causes little disruption to the organization. Firms typically add extra employees to meet the strong demand from the market. Other firms may choose to restructure by putting a freeze on hiring or filling only critical positions, thus limiting the size of the organization. Still other firms may restructure by reassigning personnel from noncritical to critical positions. This enables organizations to emphasize areas that are essential to their success. Many firms transfer employees out of corporate headquarters or support roles into sales and marketing positions.

Restructuring often occurs during times of recession or depression. **Recessions** are periods of general economic slowdowns. Rising unemployment, lack of market demand for goods and services, and excess productive capacity characterize recessions. **Depressions** are severe forms of recessions. Unemployment may reach 25 percent of the

RECESSION
A period of the business cycle characterized by economic slowdowns, rising unemployment, lack of market demand for goods and services, and excess productive capacity.

DEPRESSION
A severe recession characterized by prolonged economic slowdowns, extremely high unemployment levels, severely declining market demand for goods and services, and high levels of excess productive capacity.

total workforce and firm bankruptcies increase significantly. Fortunately, business cycles do not always pass through all four stages. The last general depression in the United States coincided with the start of World War II.

Not all segments of the economy are at the same stage of the business cycle. Thus, the electronics industry may be in a period of prosperity while the steel industry is in a recession. Recessions and depressions often force firms to restructure to survive. Restructuring during these times is often more radical as a result. In times of prosperity, firms consider the optimal number of employees they need to succeed. During recessions and depressions, they consider how many employees they can cut and still function. However, recessions and depressions allow organizations to make changes that they would not have been able to make during prosperous times.

Many union contracts forbid layoffs or worker reassignments during strong economic periods, but allow them during downturns. Resistance to restructuring may be high during periods of prosperity since it is difficult to justify cutbacks when the latest quarter just produced record profits. Resistance is often much lower if the organization's members are convinced that a restructuring is necessary to ensure the organization's continued existence. As a result, restructuring is often easier to accomplish during periods of recession or depression, and greater changes are possible than in stable economic times.[13] However, once workers are laid off during poor economic times, they may not be rehired when the economy turns around. More and more companies are deciding to remain lean and make the job cuts permanent.[14]

COST RESTRUCTURE

The 1980s saw great changes in U.S. business practices. Many organizations underwent radical changes in their operating methods. These changes were largely due to the increase in international competition. Many U.S. firms discovered that their decades-old methods of operating were unsuitable to match the increase in foreign competition. Many foreign firms began to sell products that were both less expensive and higher in quality than those produced by their American counterparts. Peter Reid, in the book *Well Made in America,* described the reaction of a group of Harley-Davidson managers and employees who toured the Honda motorcycle plant in Marysville, Ohio, in 1982. He remembers that Honda's total overhead staff at Marysville (president, secretaries, personnel department, accounting, material planning, and so on) numbered 30 of 500 employees. Harley's managers were surprised that they could find no squadrons of engineers and planners stashed in the back room. Further, Harley managers couldn't even conceive of how to do such a thing. This episode was a sobering lesson in the basic difference between Honda's costs and Harley's: overhead staff.[15]

COST RESTRUCTURING
The process by which a firm seeks to change certain costs within the organization, usually with the goal of reducing costs to a lower level.

Harley-Davidson's reaction to this problem was typical of many U.S. firms facing similar situations in the 1980s and 1990s. It began a process of **cost restructuring,** a process in which a firm seeks to change certain costs within the organization, usually with the goal of reducing them. Cost restructuring is usually a common goal of any organization restructuring strategy. In Harley-Davidson's case, one of its main cost restructuring goals was to reduce its overhead costs. A 1989 joint survey of 1,837 firms undertaken by the American Society for Personnel Administration and the Commerce Clearing House reported that the main goal of almost 50 percent of all restructuring efforts is labor cost reduction. The survey also found that over two-thirds of the firms that had restructured experienced a decrease in the size of their workforce.[16] Exhibit 17.6 shows that cost control is the most common reason firms undertake a restructuring program.

Other common cost restructuring goals include reducing production costs, inventory costs, and capital spending costs. Firms such as Oryx, a Texas oil and gas producer,

EXHIBIT 17.6   **Reasons Companies Restructure**

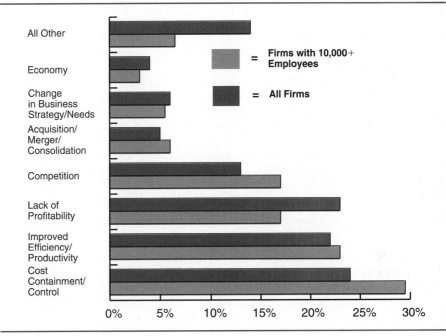

SOURCE: *People Trends,* September 1993, p. 2.

have achieved significant cost restructuring by cutting or reducing bureaucratic red tape. This red tape may include rules, procedures, reviews, reports, and approval processes.[17] Kodak has restructured four times since 1982 to make it more efficient and allow it to post better earnings. Kodak also wanted the restructuring to put it on the growth track again. But in 1991, it had a 5.7 percent drop in profit after adjusting for inflation. Even Kodak conceded that some of the restructuring attempts have not achieved their goals.[18]

Another major cause of cost restructuring that began in the 1980s is the widespread use of the **leveraged buyout (LBO).** An LBO is the takeover of a company, usually using borrowed funds, either in the form of bank loans or low-rated "junk bonds." Collateral for the buyout is usually the target company's own assets. The acquirer generally pledges to repay the loans out of the cash flow of the acquired company.[19] As LBO mania peaked in the middle to late 1980s, financing methods often became poorly thought out or unsound. **Junk bonds,** which are high-yielding, low-grade bonds, formed the basis of many LBO financing plans. In short, junk-bond buyers were paid high rates of interest to offset the inherent risk.

Many LBOs gave firms the unique opportunity to restructure their costs. This is true because LBOs often involve the arrival of a new management team not tied to old ways. As a result, the new management team may sell off operations that are not part of the organization's core business, thereby shifting the organization's emphasis from one business to another and achieving a cost restructuring in the process. Other LBOs are successful because they force firms to be aware of their cost structures. This may occur because the debt convenant has strict rules about the organization's cost structure. Management may also seek to control costs that would cause the organization to default on its debt payments. Payment defaults often force the firm into bankruptcy.

LEVERAGED BUYOUT (LBO)
The takeover of a company, usually using borrowed funds, using the acquired company's assets as collaterai.

JUNK BONDS
High-yield, low-grade bonds often used as the basis for LBO financing plans.

FOCUS ON ETHICS AND SOCIAL RESPONSIBILITY

Honesty Is the Best Cost-Cutting Strategy

Against the better judgment of everyone he knew, Hugh Aaron, CEO of a small plastics firm, decided that the best way to make his workers understand why he had to make major cost-cutting changes was to let them see the books. He decided that his hourly workers should be made privy to the profit and loss statement. By showing them the facts and figures, they would surely agree with his plans.

So one day Aaron closed the plant for an hour and a half and with the use of a chalkboard, he explained the financial picture of the firm to all of his workers. As he began to explain the situation, he was asked many questions. Some, such as "What is gross profit?" made him realize that just explaining the situation would not be enough. He would first have to educate the workers about the business of being in business.

One of his managers volunteered to hold daily work sessions with the employees to explain business concepts to them. He was also given the task of explaining the profit and loss statement to the workers at the next organizationwide meeting.

At that meeting, the workers began to accuse the management of having two sets of books: the ones it was sharing with the workers to show how bad things were to garner wage cuts and the real set the accountants and lawyers used.

To combat these fears, the lawyers and accountants were present at the next meeting to reassure the workers that the figures they saw were the figures that the firm actually reported. Once the workers began to believe that the numbers were accurate, things started to change.

Some of the changes were small; others were not. For example, the workers noticed that there was a $4,000 entry on the books for renting and laundering uniforms. They suggested that the firm purchase an industrial washing machine to use at the end of the shift to save the laundering costs. This one change saved the firm $12,000 a year, approximately the same amount of money as one worker's yearly salary.

The only workers who did not seem to enjoy the new open information format were the managers. They seemed to thrive under the old traditional style of closed shops, which is exactly where Aaron asked them to go.

SOURCE: Adapted from Hugh Aaron, "In Troubled Times, Run an Open Company," *The Wall Street Journal,* December 10, 1990, p. A10.

The main problem with less successful LBOs is the inability to meet the debt payments. Many organizations are unable to reduce costs enough to generate the extra cash necessary to make the debt payments. These payments are large because the interest rate on the debt is usually high. Other organizations run into problems when economic conditions change. Both of these situations occurred during Robert Campeau's $6.5 billion acquisition of Federated Department Stores in April 1988, which ultimately failed, even though the stores recovered and were still operating in the 1990s.

LBOs have been accused of causing a decrease in R&D expenditures. Some have suggested that an acquisition can be used as a substitute for innovation and that managers absorbed in LBOs will lose sight of the importance of R&D. To avoid this pitfall, firms should consider the following:

1. LBOs should be focused to complement the firm's R&D.
2. R&D should be woven into the organization's new mission after the LBO.
3. Top management should keep interest in R&D high.
4. R&D projects should be linked directly to key executives.[20]

Finally, LBOs can lead to failures on the part of recently placed executives. With LBOs come new management teams who may not be familiar with current procedures and cultures. The entrance of new management can be advantageous to the firm from a cost-cutting perspective, but it can be detrimental to the manager's career. LBOs often do not provide sufficient time for managers to become familiar with key players and understand what is expected of them before they must make major decisions that can cause the LBO to succeed or fail.[21]

THE IMPACT OF RESTRUCTURING ON HUMAN RESOURCES

Once an organization decides to restructure, its managers must make several broad choices to determine the type of human resource restructuring it will use. These choices are based on the answers to four basic questions:

1. Should the firm use a no-layoff strategy?
2. If the firm does not use a no-layoff strategy, should it use wage cuts?
3. If the firm uses layoffs, should they be temporary layoffs or permanent plant closings?
4. Should the organization cushion its terminations or use "harsh" terminations?

These issues represent the increasing severity of the impact of restructuring on employees. No-layoff strategies usually represent the least severe impact on employees as a whole in the organization. They are, however, often the most difficult for the firm to control and implement. Terminations, at the other end, are often the easiest form of restructuring for the organization to control and implement. Terminations hurt because they usually have the greatest negative impact on the employees. The time frame of each type of strategy also creates problems. No-layoff strategies usually take the longest to implement but often have the greatest long-term benefits to the organization if they are successful. Layoff and termination strategies, on the other hand, can take effect almost immediately after management has chosen them.

Layoffs may have unintended long-term side effects that are difficult to control, however. These side effects include losing valuable employees and long-term employee morale problems. Of course, a firm that is facing imminent bankruptcy may need the immediate benefits of massive layoffs to survive. For other firms, the shock of large-scale layoffs may be the solution for revitalizing a lethargic and unresponsive organization.[22] Each strategy has its own unique characteristics and advantages and disadvantages. These issues will be discussed in the remainder of this chapter.

Exhibit 17.7 illustrates some of the negative effects companies have reported experiencing as a result of implementing restructuring programs. Exhibit 17.8 lists practices most helpful in helping businesses' restructuring goals.

NO-LAYOFF STRATEGIES

NO-LAYOFF RESTRUCTURING
An organizational strategy that seeks to reduce the size of a firm's workforce without having to lay off or terminate employees.

Many firms view their employees as their most valuable assets. They recognize that employees have unique skills gained over years of service to the organization. Other employees have skills that are rare in the marketplace, thus increasing their value to the firm. In other cases, groups of employees have unique combinations of skills that make them valuable to the organization. The need to reduce the number of active employees on the payroll conflicts with their need of the employees' special skills. If the organization terminates employees, they may never return, or the unique combination of skills that made particular work teams valuable may be lost forever. On the other hand, if the organization does not reduce the size of its workforce, its operating costs may be too high. Many firms in this position choose to use a **no-layoff restructuring** policy.

EXHIBIT 17.7

The Results of Restructuring

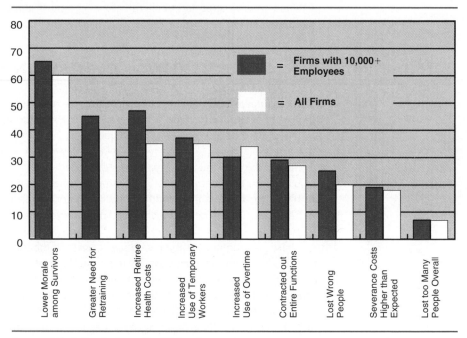

SOURCE: *People Trends,* September 1993, p. 3.

EXHIBIT 17.8

Effective Practices Used to Attain Restructuring Goals

PRACTICE	PERCENTAGE TERMING IT "VERY EFFECTIVE"	PERCENTAGE WHO USED IT
Creating restructuring project teams	64%	56%
Small-group meetings with employees	63	65
Involving employees on task forces	60	60
One-on-one counseling on early retirement	52	63
Briefings for managers and supervisors	51	74
Eliminating low-value work	51	58
Conducting team-building activities	45	61
Total-quality-management initiatives	41	68
Developing a restructuring communications strategy	41	63

SOURCE: Gilbert Fuchsberg, "Why Shakeups Work for Some, Not for Others," *The Wall Street Journal,* October 1, 1993, p. B1.

No-layoff strategies are organization actions that seek to reduce the size of an organization's workforce without having to lay off or terminate anyone. No-layoff policies usually involve some combination of three alternatives: (1) reduce the workforce through attrition, (2) provide for worker reassignment/retraining, or (3) loan employees to other firms.

WORKFORCE REDUCTION THROUGH ATTRITION

REDUCTION THROUGH ATTRITION

A no-layoff strategy in which a firm tries to stop the growth in the total number of its employees and reduce the total number without laying off employees.

Reduction through attrition is perhaps the most common method of no-layoff restructuring. Firms that use this method try to reduce the total number of people employed by the firm without laying off anyone. This is a popular method in government organizations. There are three basic types of attrition: hiring freezes in new and planned jobs, nonreplacement of current job vacancies, and nonreplacement of fired workers. The three methods are different from one another, but they share some similarities. Most firms use all three to some extent when carrying out a workforce attrition strategy.

HIRING FREEZE

A workforce attrition method in which a firm forgoes all new, planned hirings.

Perhaps the most common method that firms use for workforce attrition is the **hiring freeze.** Firms operating under hiring freezes forgo all new planned hirings. In many instances, hiring freezes are organizationwide. In other instances, firms selectively implement hiring freezes. In these situations, firms stop hiring in most departments while continuing to hire in areas critical to the success of the organization. Both methods are used in practice; the remainder of this discussion concentrates on total, or organizationwide, hiring freezes.

Hiring freezes have several advantages and disadvantages. One advantage is that firms can immediately control and predict their wage and benefit expenses. Because no new employees are being hired, the firm can easily calculate how much it is spending and decide how to control these costs in the future. Another advantage lies in controlling costs related to recruitment and training of new employees. These costs include advertising funds, the time and money spent by managers interviewing potential employees, the internal costs related to new hires such as placement on payroll, the assignment of office supplies and equipment, and the funds allocated to train and orient new employees. Other costs saved include state and federal taxes paid on employees' wages and benefits. For example, if a firm chooses not to fill a $30,000-a-year position in the engineering department, the actual savings could be much higher:

Salary saved	$30,000
Benefits saved (such as insurance and vacation)	10,000
Taxes saved	7,000
Training costs saved (such as orientation, familiarization with rules and procedures, and job education)	2,000
Office supplies and equipment (desk, chair, computer, supplies)	5,000
Hiring costs saved (such as entering in payroll, establishing employee file, and insurance policy paperwork)	1,000
Recruitment costs saved (such as campus interviews, advertising, manager's interviewing time, and committee decision time)	5,000
Total savings	$60,000

This example shows that the actual savings from not hiring new employees are much higher than just an employee's salary. Savings may be higher or lower, depending on the nature of the job and the company, but either way, the savings can be significant.

Using such a strategy has several possible disadvantages, however. First, not hiring new employees may overburden current employees. This may result in decreased productivity and lower morale. Hiring freezes may also have additional effects on employees who are seeking promotion within the organization because the freezes either explicitly or accidentally result in promotion freezes because current workers become more necessary in the positions that they now hold. As a result, many employees in line for promotions may become frustrated at a perceived lack of advancement potential. This, coupled with the additional work load that accompanies hiring freezes, may cause these employees to seek other employment opportunities.

In addition, firms that compete in technology-based industries may find themselves falling behind the competition as they fail to hire employees with new and valuable skills. For example, let's return to the example of the firm that did not hire the new engineer. If the firm needed a civil engineer, it probably would not experience too many competitive problems in the future because the supply of civil engineers is relatively good compared to the demand. If the position was for a computer engineer, however, the firm may soon experience severe problems because the average computer technology lasts for less than three years before it becomes obsolete and well-trained computer engineers are, therefore, relatively scarce. Firms that choose to use selective hiring freezes can often escape this problem, as mentioned earlier.

In summary, hiring freezes have two main advantages and disadvantages. They can help a firm immediately control costs and can save other related costs in hiring new employees. On the other hand, hiring freezes can have a negative impact on current employees and can result in the loss of competitive advantage from failing to gain new and valuable skills.

Another attrition method that firms use is *not to replace those people who naturally leave the organization.* Unlike hiring freezes, which try to stop growth by halting the creation of new jobs, this method seeks to reduce total employment by not filling current positions as they become vacant. People who quit, retire, die, or leave at the end of a contract are considered to have naturally left the organization. Organizations often offer some form of incentive to employees to accelerate this process. These incentives include cash bonuses to people who leave during a specified period, accelerated or early retirement benefits, and free outplacement services (discussed in more depth later in the chapter).[23] This method has several advantages. First, organizations can save a considerable amount of money in the recruitment, hiring, and training of new employees. This is the same type of advantage gained by organizations that use the no-new-hire strategy discussed earlier.

Another advantage of the attrition method is the ability to cut positions that have become unneeded or inefficient within the organization. A position that was important in the past may become obsolete as the organization changes. Positions created to fit certain needs during periods of success with little forethought or planning may have outlived their benefits. These positions may become redundant or unnecessary during periods of retrenchment.

EMPIRE BUILDING
Actions by individuals to entrench themselves in positions through a combination of politics, length of time on the job, and the ability to project a perceived value to the firm, thus making it more difficult for the firm to eliminate their jobs or lay them off.

When a firm decides to downsize, it may be difficult to cut positions due to several factors. These factors include the building of an "empire" by the individuals holding the positions. **Empire building** occurs when individuals entrench themselves in positions through a combination of politics, length of time in the job, and the ability to project a perceived value to the firm. Management may also be reluctant to fire or lay off an individual who is close to retirement. Finally, struggles by individual managers to protect the size of their departments may affect downsizing. These struggles often serve as a surrogate measure of the individual power and prestige of each manager. Firms that choose not to replace people who naturally leave the organization are often able to avoid most of these problems.

A main disadvantage of using an attrition strategy is that the organization is unable to control exactly who leaves and who stays. It may seek to reduce its overhead positions, but it may also lose a significant number of people in marketing and research and development in the process. Another disadvantage is that this method may take a long time to carry out. Unlike other strategies, such as worker layoffs, which take only days or weeks, a nonreplacement strategy may take months or even years to reach its full potential. Because the organization is not forcing employees to leave, it must wait for individuals to decide to leave. The incentives mentioned earlier can help to speed the process, but even they do not guarantee that the firm will reach its goals in the time desired. Finally, the nonreplacement of workers who naturally leave can be problematic in the short term. Many of the incentives designed to encourage workers to leave require the organization to spend large sums of money up front. This is often contrary to the immediate goals of a restructuring.

Another major type of no-layoff restructuring is **worker reassignment and retraining.** Firms that use this strategy often do not want to reduce the size of their workforce but want instead to move workers from one job and into another that may be more important to the organization. For example, a common reassignment involves transferring workers to sales and manufacturing jobs and out of support and overhead positions. This is typical because sales and manufacturing jobs often create real value for the organization because they both directly generate revenues. A larger sales force can generate more sales for the company, and a larger manufacturing force can produce more items and become more specialized. Because support and overhead positions such as clerical staff, maintenance workers, and corporate headquarters staff do not directly produce real value for the organization, they may be treated as a "necessary evil." In fact, some firms use **value chain analysis,** which attempts to determine the amount of added value produced by each position and unit in the organization. Those positions and units not producing sufficient added value are the first to go.

In addition, worker productivity is more easily measured in sales and manufacturing jobs. Sales employees' productivity measures are based on sales volume. The productivity of manufacturing employees is based on the number of units produced and the percentage of defective units produced. The productivity of support and overhead positions is not as easily measured as it is in sales and manufacturing. For example, how can the value of a raw materials price forecast prepared by a corporate analyst be determined? Is one good forecast equivalent to three average forecasts produced by another analyst? Could the money spent by the organization in preparing the forecast (employee salaries, purchasing or development of economic information, use of computer resources, and so on) be better used in other areas, such as purchasing a more efficient milling machine for the assembly line? How can one tell today if the forecast for the future is good or poor? How would the organization's performance be affected if the forecast was not produced? Clearly, it is difficult to determine how helpful these positions are to the organization. Many of these questions can be answered, but often only after a long time and at a great expense. Thus, many firms are willing to move workers into sales and manufacturing because it is much easier to measure their contribution in terms of how well the organization is operating.

Organizations often use worker reassignments as a prelude to or with other types of restructuring. The transfer of workers into sales and manufacturing, in addition to directly impacting the firm's performance, enables the organization to begin the process of cutting workers. The productivity measures in sales and manufacturing jobs make it easier to determine which employees are worthwhile to the organization and which are not. Hence, it is easier to document and release poor performers in these areas. In addition, these transfers can either be voluntary programs or mandated by the organization. If the

WORKER REASSIGNMENT AND RETRAINING
Moving workers out of one job and into another job that may be more important to the organization, often accompanied by the teaching of new and previously unrelated job skills.

VALUE CHAIN ANAYSIS
Determining the amount of value added to the organization by each job and unit.

transfers are voluntary, the organization is often able to keep good employees who may have been getting stale in their previous positions. In these situations, the transfers often result in improved employee morale and performance.

Voluntary transfers present problems to organizations seeking to lay off workers, however. Many poorer performing employees will choose to stay in their current jobs out of a fear of failing in a new job. Again, it may be difficult to lay off or replace these workers since productivity measures are difficult to determine in these positions. Employees who are valuable in these support and overhead positions may also transfer into manufacturing and sales. This can hurt the organization because they may be more valuable in their original positions. For example, a purchasing agent may have spent years learning the dynamics of the firm's industry and may have built strong relationships with many suppliers. The loss of these intangible benefits to the organization may be far greater than the immediate additional revenues generated by transferring the purchasing agent to sales. The chance also exists that a good performer in one position may transfer into a new position and become a poor performer because individual skills, interests, and abilities may not be transferrable.

Mandatory transfers also have specific advantages and disadvantages. Unlike voluntary transfers, the results of mandatory transfers are more certain. Firms using mandatory transfers can target areas they consider to be less important and reduce them while emphasizing other areas with a virtual certainty of achieving their goals. Mandatory transfer programs often permit firms to target specific employees for transfer. This can produce a better match of job skills and can essentially force unwanted employees to leave the organization. This method is not without its problems, however. Mandatory transfers can hurt employee morale as the organization moves people into positions they do not want. They can also disrupt synergies that have developed in various work groups over the years.

Union contracts often prohibit organizations from implementing these policies, and they may meet fierce resistance from unions with contracts that do not prohibit such strategies. Unions have recently begun to accept contracts that allow firms to transfer employees to remain competitive. In recognizing this need in contracts, unions are, in turn, having more say in determining the nature of these transfers. Members of nonunion firms may also fight the transfers. Their fights may range from subtle resistance to open hostility or even to legal challenges. Finally, mandatory transfers may also result in valued employees leaving the organization.

WORKER RETRAINING
An upgrade or improvement of an employee's existing job skills.

Another complementary method to worker reassignment is organizational incentives to employees to undergo **worker retraining,** or career development. While worker reassignment often involves some form of skills retraining, retraining here refers to an upgrading or improvement of jobs skills, not the learning of new and unrelated ones. Organization incentives to retrain include unpaid sabbaticals, financing of education, a partial release from duties, and possible future promotions.

Such a policy has many advantages. First, the strategy can help to reduce employee anxiety caused by the restructuring. With the organization sponsoring or encouraging retraining, employees often feel more secure about their futures with the organization. If retraining programs are offered on a large scale, the resistance to the restructuring may decrease dramatically or at least help the employees accept what is happening.[24] Another advantage is that retraining programs during restructuring are often complementary to the new work systems and new directions that the organization seeks to achieve with the restructuring. Finally, the organization is often able to reduce the immediate direct and indirect labor costs that would result if the employee were working full-time during the restructuring.

Of course, some disadvantages do exist. Some employees who may benefit the most from retraining may be the employees who are most needed to help the organization successfully complete the restructuring. Furthermore, without a specific contract binding the employee to the company after the retraining period is over, the employee may take his or her additional skills to a new job. Despite these potential disadvantages, the case for further training during restructuring is strong. It is important that firms understand that career development training should still be used under these conditions, but designing it within such an environment may be challenging.

A final no-layoff restructuring strategy that has emerged within the past few years is the **worker loan-out program.** Although this strategy is somewhat rare, it might become more common during the 1990s. Worker loan-out programs involve one organization lending workers to another for a specified period, such as to government or charitable organizations. For example, IBM and Polaroid support programs that allow their employees to work as teachers in public schools and universities for up to two years while still drawing a salary from their companies.[25] Motorola has begun training workers to pass on their knowledge to students through an advisement program, and Sears has assigned officials to work with schools to build stronger curriculums.[26] Exhibit 17.9 provides an example of an employer loaning employees to another noncompetitive firm.

Lockheed's loan-out of employees to Boeing is a recent example of the loan strategy. Lockheed's aircraft division derives most of its business from military orders. Cutbacks in U.S. military budgets resulted in a work slowdown for Lockheed. In contrast, Boeing is the world's leading manufacturer of commercial aircraft. Some of its planes have order backlogs as long as 10 years. Rather than having to lay off, and possibly lose highly skilled employees, Lockheed has agreed to lend 670 of its workers to Boeing, which due to its recent success, needs more employees than it can recruit. Boeing agreed to use Lockheed's workers and pay their salaries for the loan-out period.[27] Hewlett-Packard used an internal employee loan program, among other plans, to deal with more than 400 employees who were displaced when it made the strategic decision to exit the fabrication business. Employees were loaned to other divisions where short-term hiring needs existed. Some of the loans were for as short a duration as one day; others lasted up to a year. H-P provided housing and transportation costs if the loan crossed regional boundaries.[28]

There are several advantages to both organizations involved in these situations. The organization loaning out its employees can keep them as its employees, often without having to incur the expenses of paying their salaries or to lay them off, during the loan-out period. Consequently, the organization can gain many of the advantages of a layoff and restructuring without incurring all of the related expenses, such as severance pay, outplacement services, and the recruitment and training costs of new employees in the

WORKER LOAN-OUT PROGRAM
Lending of workers from one organization to another for a specified period, such as lending employees to government or to charitable organizations.

EXHIBIT 17.9   **Saved by the Boss**

Brooks Beverage Management of Holland, Michigan, lent 20 workers to Haworth, Inc., an office furniture maker, rather than lay them off after an unexpectedly sharp seasonal decline. Brooks pays the employees' insurance benefits and compensates them for salary cuts so that when business picks up, the company can avoid the expense of recruiting and training new workers.

SOURCE: Rochelle Sharpe, "Labor Letter," *The Wall Street Journal,* September 13, 1994, p. A1.

future. These programs also enable the loaning companies' employees to keep their skills up to date or to learn new skills without incurring the retraining expenses. Another advantage for the loaning organization is that its employees often return with new ideas and new outlooks as a result of their experiences. This may result in significant improvements in the organization's operations. These programs often generate large amounts of goodwill within the organization's home community, especially if the organization receiving the employees is a local government agency or charity. This goodwill can result in positive press and publicity and favorable attitudes toward the organization by the receiving organization.

These programs also can generate goodwill with the organization's employees, who may interpret the move in several different ways. Employees may perceive that the organization is willing to let them become involved in activities that are personally important without hurting their careers in the organization. In addition, employee loyalty to an organization that is not willing to let its employees join the unemployment line is likely to increase.

There are a number of advantages for the organization receiving the loaned-out employees. One advantage is the training expenses saved by borrowing workers who are already skilled. Another is the saving of recruiting costs. Because the length of the worker loan-out is usually fixed, the receiving firm saves money by having workers for only as long as they are needed. The receiving firm also avoids having to incur layoff and separation expenses. Receiving organizations can also gain the same type of benefit from the fresh outlook of the loaned-out employees. Finally, charities and government organizations obtain employees and skills that they would not be able to afford under normal circumstances.

Of course, this type of strategy has some disadvantages. If there is a sudden change in the circumstances of the loan out, for example, the loaning company's business suddenly picks up, the workers cannot return until the end of the agreed loan-out period. Hence, a firm may be unable to recover workers that it needs. There is also the chance that the loaning firm may permanently lose its employees, possibly even to competitors. Some loan-out agreements may specifically forbid a receiving firm from hiring loaned-out employees after the expiration of the loan-out period, but nothing prevents individuals from deciding not to return to their first organization. Finally, an organization may inadvertently give up some of its skills or secrets in loaning out its employees.

LAYOFF STRATEGIES

LAYOFF

A restructuring strategy in which an organization seeks to temporarily reduce the size of its workforce, usually through the release of employees from work for a specified time.

Layoffs are among the most common strategies used in restructuring (see Exhibit 17.10). **Layoffs** usually involve some form of temporary reduction in the organization's workforce and are particularly common in cyclical industries. Under this strategy, the organization releases employees from work for a specific time, but they remain employees of the organization and continue to receive benefits. Under an **indefinite layoff,** the organization may release the employees from the company after a fixed period, such as six months or a year. An indefinite layoff strategy is typical in situations in which the workforce is highly skilled and the costs of recruiting and training new employees may be high. Thus, the organization tries to keep its employees as long as possible without terminating them. Firms primarily use layoffs to reduce labor costs temporarily without losing valuable employees. Layoffs are commonly found in industries in which union contracts may prohibit the firing of employees due to changes in business conditions. Layoffs are common in automobile manufacturing, agriculture, steel making, and tourism.

EXHIBIT 17.10   **Strategies Used to Downsize**

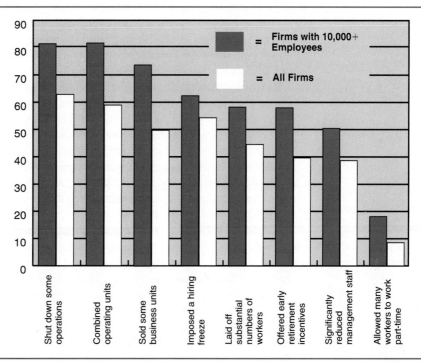

SOURCE: *People Trends,* September 1993, p. 2.

INDEFINITE LAYOFF
A layoff strategy in which the organization permanently releases an employee from the company after a fixed layoff period, such as six months or a year.

SUPPLEMENTAL UNEMPLOYMENT BENEFIT (SUB)
A layoff strategy in which employees receive a fixed percentage of their wages through a combination of state and federal unemployment benefits and organizational payments for periods of up to one year.

Several layoff methods are available. One popular method within the automobile and steel industries is the use of **supplemental unemployment benefits,** or **SUBs.** They provide a fixed percentage (up to 95 percent in some instances) of a laid-off employee's wages through a combination of state and federal unemployment benefits and additional organization payments for periods up to one year. SUBs are common in these industries because they are cyclical or they involve periods of major plant shutdowns for renovations. For example, most U.S. automobile plants shut down for a period each summer to allow the company to change or "gear up" assembly lines for the new automobile model year that begins in October. Steel plants often close for routine maintenance or major upgrades in equipment.

A major advantage of SUBs is that they allow firms to lay off their skilled employees for up to one year with little risk of losing them to other firms. Critics of SUBs, however, point out that the high level of benefits often discourages employees from seeking other jobs. This may hurt the laid-off workers more than it helped when the benefits expire at the end of the year and the firm chooses not to bring the employees back to work. Another disadvantage of SUBs is their high cost to the firm, but these costs must be weighed against the costs of hiring and training new employees.

Another common lay-off strategy is the use of the **reduced work week** for employees. The reduced work week allows organizations to reduce their payroll costs while still holding employees and providing work for them. The size of the reduction varies from firm to firm, but most reduced work weeks are between 20 and 30 hours for full-time employees.[29] Like SUBs, the reduced work week enables firms to keep their valuable employees, but it also enables employees to keep their skills up-to-date. Many

REDUCED WORK WEEK
A layoff strategy in which a firm lowers its payroll costs by reducing the number of hours worked every week by each employee.

firms also try to lessen the impact of the reduced work week by scheduling special work that would not be done during normal company operations. Examples include repair and maintenance of plant and equipment to reorganizing plants and warehouses or taking special inventories. Some states even make up the difference in the workers' pay if the firm keeps them on at least part-time. The money spent by the state is less than the firms would spend for unemployment benefits, and the workers have the chance to go back full time if the company's business picks up.[30]

Reduced work weeks have several disadvantages. A main disadvantage involves predicting the number of hours that employees are needed each week. Reduced work weeks may also require that many staff members continue to work full-time to support those employees working reduced weeks because it is difficult to cut back support functions only partially. An example of this includes the need to keep a fully staffed payroll department, where the volume of work does not depend on the number of hours worked by line employees. Finally, reduced work weeks may prevent employees from seeking other jobs because they cannot predict when they will be available for work due to the unpredictable hours of the first job.

REDUCED SHIFT
A layoff strategy in which an organization cuts back on the total number of hours it operates, either by cutting back on the total number of employees per shift or eliminating one or more shifts entirely.

A third lay-off strategy includes the use of **reduced shifts,** which involves cutting the total number of hours that the organization operates. Reduced shift layoffs can take one of two forms. One type cuts back on the total number of employees per shift. For example, a firm may usually operate three 8-hour shifts per day during normal conditions with 300 employees per shift. The first type of reduced shift strategy may be to reduce the total number of employees to 200 per shift. This approach affects all shifts equally. Another form of reduced shifts is to eliminate one or more shifts from the schedule entirely. In this example, the firm may choose to cut the midnight to 8:00 A.M. shift entirely while maintaining the other two shifts at full capacity.

Organizations may, of course, take a middle ground between these two extremes. They may decide to drop one shift and partially cut back on other shifts or use some other combination of cutbacks. Several factors usually determine the type of reduced shift approach used. The first factor is the nature of the work being done on each shift and the skills of the employees. If each shift performs essentially the same job, many organizations consider cutting entire shifts, especially the late-evening/early morning shifts that have some form of salary differential. If a job takes several shifts to complete, with each shift performing a specialized function, the organization may consider laying off some employees on each shift but maintaining all shifts to some extent.

Other factors may also affect the choice of reduced shift. A major factor in many decisions is the type of production process that the organization uses. If the organization's equipment is geared toward long continuous runs that would be expensive to interrupt, such as would be the case in the glass, steel, or paper-making industries, it may choose to reduce the number of employees per shift. This is typical of the paper-making industry in which it is expensive to start up and shut down machinery and the process of paper making is a round-the-clock effort.[31]

If the organization employs a batch production process, with each shift capable of producing a complete job, the decision may be to close down an entire shift instead of reducing all shifts. This is typical of clothing manufacturers.[32] A similar situation exists in the automobile industry, where the production process is a machine-paced line flow. Because the production process is standardized over each shift and the cost of shutting down and starting up machinery is not prohibitively expensive, reduced shift layoffs are often an entire shift approach.

Another common layoff strategy is the use of plant or office closings. Unlike reduced shifts, which affect only a portion of the employees of the work unit, plant and office

PLANT AND OFFICE CLOSINGS
A layoff strategy in which an organization either temporarily or permanently shuts down independent work units as part of a restructuring.

closings affect all employees of the unit. **Plant and office closings** are the temporary or permanent shutdown of independent work units as part of an organization's restructuring. Plants may be entire production facilities, such as when General Motors closed seven car plants in the first half of 1990.[33] An example of an office closing is the closing of a district sales office by a national organization. Of course, other closings also qualify under this definition, even though they are not offices or plants. Burger King closed some of its older stores and Ames closed many of its retail stores as part of their bankruptcy reorganizations.

Closings may occur for a variety of reasons. They may be part of a focus strategy discussed earlier in the chapter. The closings may be the result of a downsizing due to bankruptcy, as is the case with Ames. Or, as is the case with GM, they may result from the modernization of facilities or the conversion of facilities to meet a change in strategic orientation.[34] Closings are often the only practical means of conversion or modernization since an attempt to undertake such an operation while still operating may be prohibitively expensive and time consuming.

Management must consider several human resource side effects of plant and office closings. First, closings affect all employees of the unit. Unlike other layoff strategies, closings affect everyone from the plant's part-time personnel to its upper level management. Thus, a firm may inadvertently lose some of its best people if it does not plan the closing carefully. This means that the organization will lose its 30-year veterans as well as its recent hires. The advantage of this strategy, however, is that the firm may be able to keep its best employees by offering to move them to other parts of the organization. Of course, the organization may find itself in the position of having nowhere to send its skilled individuals, even though it does not want to lose them. Plant closings may be expensive because they often involve some form of lay-off pay, such as the supplemental unemployment benefits used by the automobile and steel industries mentioned earlier.

Plant closings can often have serious effects on morale in other parts of the organization. This is particularly true if the organization is undertaking a large restructuring and is not completely communicating its plans to its employees; that is, closings are not announced and explained in advance. In such situations, employees begin to wonder if their plant or office will be the next one closed. In addition to damaging morale organizationwide, plant closings often affect worker productivity and may result in higher employee turnover in other parts of the organization as employees begin to seek what they perceive to be safer employment.

WORKER ADJUSTMENT AND RETRAINING NOTIFICATION ACT (WARN)
A federal law that requires employers of 50 or more to give 60 days' written notice to employees of large-scale layoffs and plant closings.

Recent federal legislation, the federal **Worker Adjustment and Retraining Notification Act (WARN),** makes it mandatory that organizations with at least 50 employees announce the decision to close plants or engage in massive layoffs at least 60 days in advance of the action.[35] Critics argue that it is unnecessary because it will hurt productivity in the plant as employees seek new jobs and take time off to do so. They also argue that early announcements of plant closings hurt the competitiveness of U.S. firms since they are, in effect, forced prematurely to reveal valuable information about their strategies in a tough marketplace. Finally, critics of the legislation assert that because many decisions to close plants are made less than 60 days before an actual closing, the law puts management in a bind of having to make crucial decisions earlier than they would normally have been made. Supporters of the law argue that productivity losses are minimal. They also assert that management has an obligation to inform its employees of decisions affecting their future employment as soon as they are made. Finally, supporters argue that management should plan ahead in situations that have as broad an impact on employees as plant and office closings.

EMPLOYEE SENIORITY LAYOFF CRITERION
A layoff method in which employees are laid off according to the length of time each employee has worked with the firm.

EMPLOYEE ABILITY LAYOFF CRITERION
A layoff method in which employees are laid off according to each employee's skill level and productivity.

A final issue in using a layoff strategy is how organizations determine whom to lay off and whom it gets to keep. In plant closings the issue is rather clear: everyone is laid off. In other situations, such as reduced shifts, the task is not so easy. Two of the most common methods for determining layoffs are the use of employee seniority layoff criterion and the use of employee ability criterion. Firms that use **employee seniority layoff criterion** lay off workers according to the length of time that each employee has been with the firm. This is common in unionized firms. Most systems based on this method give greater protection to the employees with the most tenure or seniority, all other things being equal. If a firm has to lay off one of two welders, with each performing the same job, the welder who has been with the organization the longest will be kept.

Organizations that use an **employee ability layoff criterion** take a different approach. These firms lay off workers according to the skill level and productivity of each employee. Using the example of the two welders, the firm would keep the better of the two welders and lay off the other one. The United States Air Force is cutting back its total troop levels by as much as 25 percent as a result of budget cuts in the Department of Defense. It is trying to use attrition methods but is prepared to make cutbacks if necessary. It is using a standard proficiency test as a measure of ability to determine which pilots and aircraft mechanics to retain and which ones to let go.[36]

Each layoff approach has a number of advantages and disadvantages. Perhaps the greatest advantage of using a seniority-based layoff strategy is the objective manner in which it can be applied. Layoffs using this type of strategy are based on length of service to the organization, so workers know what their position is in a layoff program. It is also very hard to accuse management of "playing favorites" with employees using a seniority-based system because the layoff order is well known in advance. Any deviation from this system is likely to be noticed immediately by the workforce. The appearance of fairness and the ease of checking deviations from policy have made seniority-based layoff systems particularly popular in unionized organizations.

A main rationale behind a seniority-based layoff strategy is that employees who have been with the organization a long time have earned the right to be insulated from temporary changes in the firm's environment. Another belief behind a seniority-based layoff system is that it is easier for younger employees to find work and adapt their lives to layoffs than it is for older workers.

There are two disadvantages to a seniority-based system. The first is that it ignores worker talent and effort. Critics of the system argue that adherence to such rules are arbitrary and without merit. The long-standing ethic of "reward good work" often loses its value in organizations that adhere to seniority-based layoff systems. If workers know in advance that layoffs will be based on seniority, the incentive for them to operate at their peak levels is reduced. Instead, they may do only the minimal work necessary to ensure that they keep their jobs. In short, critics argue that this system shifts the focus from rewarding good work to job survival. If this is the case, the organization should experience higher labor costs, lower productivity, and lower work quality compared to its competitors who use other types of layoff strategies. Critics also argue that this system may keep the organization's payroll bloated because more experienced workers tend to earn higher wages. Hence, a seniority-based layoff system tends to cut back on the lower-paid employees while keeping the higher-paid ones. Of course, the counterargument is that the more experienced employee has a greater familiarity with the organization and how it operates. Ideally, this should make him or her more valuable to the organization because it has already sunk a great deal of money into training and developing the employee over the years. Either way, this can be a particularly problematic decision when the main goal is some form of cost restructuring.

Ability-based layoff systems seek to address some of the problems of seniority-based systems. Perhaps the greatest advantage of ability-based systems is that they keep the best workers during layoffs, often enabling the firm to maintain or increase productivity and quality levels during a restructuring. Firms using ability-based layoff systems should also realize a greater cost savings than firms using seniority-based layoffs. Further, ability-based systems appeal to the ethics of rewarding good work and should give workers incentives to seek to improve their performance. This approach may run into problems in reality, however, The most serious problem of such a system is defining ability. In many instances, this is not a problem, especially when the work is standardized. For example, in the textile industry, where productivity is based on the volume of material produced, determining the best workers is usually a straightforward process. The problem becomes more complex in other situations, however, especially in white-collar and skilled craft positions. As we discussed earlier, how does one place a quality figure on a raw materials price forecast prepared by a corporate analyst? The situation can even be complex in assembly-line situations where one worker's productivity depends on the output of another worker. Management must devise a system for determining how much one employee's work affects another. This is often a complicated and expensive process. Even when a fair system is in place, it is often difficult to communicate all of its aspects to employees in a clear and understandable manner.

In addition, ability-based systems encourage political behavior by workers. These systems sometimes generate the impression that it is the manager's favorite workers, not the best workers, who are kept during layoffs. Many workers oppose such a system as a result of the difficulty in understanding the rules of the system and the perception of managerial favoritism. Consequently, ability-based systems are more likely to generate hostility with unions and possibly lead to lawsuits against the organization than are seniority-based systems.[37]

TERMINATION STRATEGIES

EMPLOYEE TERMINATIONS
Actions initiated by an organization to permanently separate employees from the organization.

PROTECTION AND COMPENSATION PLANS
Organizational policies relating to the handling of employees during termination situations.

TENURE
A measure of the time an employee has worked in an organization and the rights and benefits the person has accrued as a result.

Finally, organizations may choose to use **employee terminations** as part of a restructuring strategy. These are actions initiated by the organization to permanently separate employees from the organization, and they may come in many forms. Terminations may be the end result of an indefinite layoff or plant closing. They may also be the first action taken by a firm in a restructuring. Unlike firings, where employees are released from the organization for causes such as poor performance or high absenteeism, terminations are initiated with the purpose of reducing the size of the workforce. Massive terminations have become a particularly popular method of downsizing in the 1990s as companies have struggled to reduce costs and increase productivity. Exhibit 17.11 illustrates the 25 largest workforce reductions by U.S. corporations in the 1990s.

TERMINATION ISSUES

Organizations that pursue termination strategies must consider a number of issues. For example, all termination decisions must consider the organization's employee **protection and compensation plans,** which are its policies relating to the handling of employees during termination situations. Many organizations have clearly defined plans for their employees. Others have no formal policies in place. Either way, the organization must deal with these issues. They typically include tenure, golden parachutes, severance pay, outplacement services, and career counseling.

Tenure relates to the length of time that an employee has worked in an organization and the rights that the person accrues as a result. It is similar to seniority. In many

EXHIBIT 17.11   **Major Corporate Downsizings, 1992–April 1994**

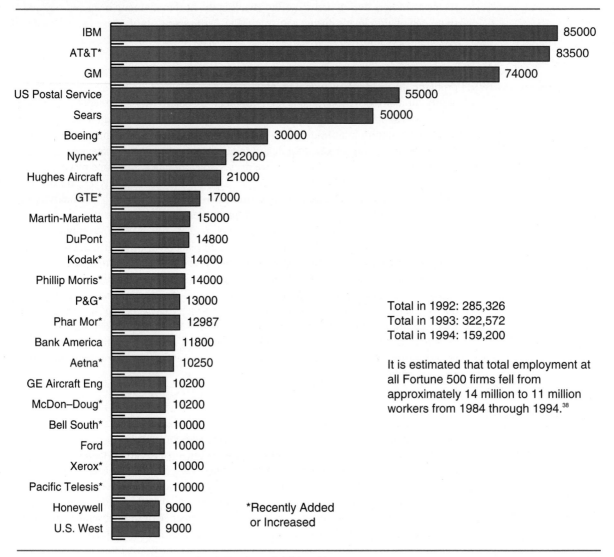

IBM	85000
AT&T*	83500
GM	74000
US Postal Service	55000
Sears	50000
Boeing*	30000
Nynex*	22000
Hughes Aircraft	21000
GTE*	17000
Martin-Marietta	15000
DuPont	14800
Kodak*	14000
Phillip Morris*	14000
P&G*	13000
Phar Mor*	12987
Bank America	11800
Aetna*	10250
GE Aircraft Eng	10200
McDon–Doug*	10200
Bell South*	10000
Ford	10000
Xerox*	10000
Pacific Telesis*	10000
Honeywell	9000
U.S. West	9000

Total in 1992: 285,326
Total in 1993: 322,572
Total in 1994: 159,200

It is estimated that total employment at all Fortune 500 firms fell from approximately 14 million to 11 million workers from 1984 through 1994.[38]

*Recently Added or Increased

SOURCE: *People Trends,* April 1994, p. 12.

instances, employees with longer tenure, or length of service (seniority), have more rights and benefits than less tenured or nontenured employees. These rights may include added benefits such as increased vacation time, sick leave, and insurance benefits, office and parking space privileges, stock options, and company cars. Many organizations also offer greater job protection to tenured employees. In universities and colleges, tenure for professors means guaranteed employment for life, as long as the professor continues to do his or her job. Even if the professor becomes incompetent or fails to do his or her job, tenure results in a long and formal termination process.

===== HR CHALLENGE =====

Developing a Strong Outplacement Program

Traditionally, outplacement programs have been established by organizations to minimize the negative experiences associated with the loss of a job and to avoid the possibility of litigation by dismissed employees. However, companies are now realizing that it is important that employees who are joining or leaving the organization have a positive experience. Developing an effective and cost-efficient outplacement progam is one way to ensure departing employees a positive experience.

Developing an effective outplacement program should be done as soon as possible. If brought in early, an outplacement company can help managers to more effectively handle the termination interview. Often if the interview is inappropriately handled, employees do not understand why they have been terminated and spend a great deal of time pondering the reason. This takes away from the time they could be preparing for a new job.

Companies should introduce the employee to the outplacement program early in the week of termination so that they can begin immediately to prepare themselves for the job market. By focusing the terminated employee's attention on the outplacement process rather than on the termination, more positive outcomes occur. Further, by introducing the employee to the outplacement program immediately after termination, the outplacement company can be ready to offer crisis interventions if necessary.

A company should be prepared to pay for a good outplacement program. In general, the base cost for a full-service outplacement program is 15 percent of the outplaced worker's W-2 earnings for the previous year plus an administrative fee that averages about $1,000. Some firms set a minimum fee of between $6,000 and $7,000 per program. Group programs can also be arranged. Costs for these services include a per diem charge of $1,000 to $1,500 plus an additional charge of $40 to $50 for each participant. Programs that are significantly lower than these ranges may not be of a high quality.

SOURCE: Adapted from Virginia Gibson, "The Ins and Outs of Outplacement," *Management Review,* October 1991, pp. 59–61.

Consequently, organizations that use terminations as part of a restructuring must examine their tenure policies. Many of these tenure benefits are given as rewards for service, and many represent a long-term commitment by the organization to the employee. For example, an organization may guarantee stock options worth 20 percent of an executive's pay over 10 years as part of his or her promotion to upper management. Suppose, however, that the organization decides to close the executive's division and terminate all employees in the division (including the manager) three years after the manager has taken over the division. The organization must consider how to handle the stock options. The manager has been guaranteed the options due to performance, but a change in the organization's strategy—a variable beyond the manager's control—eliminates the firm's need for the manager's services. This issue is complicated further by the fact that the manager is not being released for incompetence but as a change in organization strategy.

Such scenarios are becoming more and more frequent as the rate of terminations at the white-collar level continue to increase. From January 1990 to May 1991, managerial unemployment rose by over 60 percent. Many of the managers terminated were well-known figures such as John Sununu, President Bush's chief of staff; William Powe, head of Westinghouse's credit union; and George Conrades, senior vice-president at IBM.[39] Further, many of these managers were terminated from more than one job within a year. As the length of time they are out of work increases, it becomes harder and harder for them to find jobs. They become paralyzed by depression and numbed by the economic pain they are inflicting on their families.[40]

EMPLOYMENT AT WILL
A doctrine stating that workers are employed at the will of the organization and the organization is free to end this employment at any time it chooses and for any reason it chooses.

In previous years, U.S. law has given precedence to the **employment-at-will** doctrine. It states that workers are employed at the will of the organization and that the organization is free to end this employment at any time it chooses and for any reason it chooses. This doctrine also applies in reverse; employees are free to choose the organizations that they work for and can leave the organization at any time they wish for whatever reason they wish. As we saw in Chapter 15, this concept has been challenged in recent years, and its validity is no longer guaranteed, especially when applied to employees who may have built up tenure within an organization. Courts have been increasingly sensitive to instances that are deemed wrongful or abusive discharges on the part of the employer.[41] Wrongful or abusive discharge situations involve firing without cause, discrimination of almost any kind, failure to properly document the cause of the firing, or situations in which the procedure for firing is not standardized. Even if the organization is sure that it is in a situation in which the employment-at-will doctrine is valid, tenure-related issues often ensure that terminated employees may bring legal action against the organization to recover or be compensated for lost benefits and privileges.[42] The average jury verdict in wrongful discharge cases is over $500,000. To avoid such litigation, companies are retraining poor performers, using overtime or temporary workers, offering generous severance payments, and adopting elaborate screening and performance review processes.[43]

GOLDEN PARACHUTES
Guarantees by organizations to employees (usually top managers) detailing the types of benefits they will receive in termination situations.

Many organizations are responding to these problems by offering **golden parachutes** to their employees, especially top managers. Golden parachutes are guarantees by organizations to employees detailing the type of benefits they will receive in termination situations. Golden parachutes are offered as enticements to convince managers to take on the responsibility of joining a struggling firm for the purpose of turning it around. They are popular in organizations that are targets of LBOs or hostile takeovers. As we mentioned earlier, many LBOs end with the replacement of the old management team by a new one. In these situations the board of directors may vote to offer golden parachutes to key managers as a reward for their performance with the organization and because it makes it prohibitively expensive for new management to replace the old management. Finally, golden parachutes are also popular since they represent a contractual agreement between the firm and the employee. Hence, if the employee is terminated, there is less chance of a legal challenge by the employee.

A main problem with golden parachutes is that they tend to be rather expensive to the organization. It is not uncommon to find golden parachutes containing provisions that range from one to two years salary and other substantial cash payments. As a result, golden parachutes are mainly used for key managers. They are rarely offered to rank-and-file employees. Golden parachutes, if their existence is made known in the organization, may cause a great deal of hostility among members who are not protected in a similar manner. For example, in the bankruptcy of Drexel Burnham Lambert, top managers of the organization received $260 million in bonuses just weeks before the firm was forced into bankruptcy. When the organization filed for bankruptcy, all of its employees were terminated without any form of compensation, even though the organization owed them approximately $40 million in severance payments, which it appears that they will never receive. Many employees are upset that such bonus payments were made because the nature of their timing resembled that of a golden parachute to upper management. Even though the bonuses were, in reality, regularly scheduled payments to management, their perceived appearance as golden parachutes alienated many former organization members.[44]

Even with their negative connotations, golden parachutes can serve broader organization purposes. Eastman Kodak has added a unique twist to golden parachutes to protect itself from the threat of a hostile takeover. Kodak's plan, nicknamed "tin-parachutes," guarantees all 80,000 of its employees severance pay, health and life insurance benefits, and outplacement assistance if they lose their jobs in the wake of a takeover. Such a plan means that any organization that took over Kodak (which has a stock value of approximately $25 billion) could also face another $12 billion in debt if it started releasing Kodak employees.[45] Of course, the main advantages of golden parachutes is that they can convince key individuals to join or remain in particularly risky situations for the organization, and they reduce the chances of legal action against the organization by terminated employees. Kodak's case illustrates that parachutes, whether made of gold or tin, can be highly effective weapons against unwanted takeover attempts.

SEVERANCE PAY
A payment to terminated workers based on their years of service to the organization and on their salary.

A related and more common approach to terminations than golden parachutes is the use of **severance pay.** It is a payment to terminated workers based on their years of service to the organization and their salary. A typical severance pay might be four weeks of full pay for each year the employee has worked for the organization. For example, an employee who has worked for an organization for seven years and earned $400 per week would receive 7 years × 4 weeks per year = 28 weeks × $400 per week = $11,200 in severance pay. Severance pay may also include other payments such as accrued vacation and sick leave and possibly some medical coverage. How the pay is provided varies by organization. Some firms offer a lump-sum payment. Others offer the money over a specified period of time, like a weekly paycheck. Other firms use a combination of these tactics or let the employee decide how he or she wants the money.[46] Like golden parachutes, a clearly defined severance pay policy may reduce the chances of legal action against the organization if widespread terminations occur. But where golden parachutes are designed as incentives and rewards to top management, severance pay is usually a hardship compensation to all employees. A main advantage of a severance package is that it immediately clears most of the organization's obligations to its former employees.

Severance packages are also used by organizations to help them improve employee relations. Many organizations use the existence of the severance programs as a recruiting tool for new employees. Firms that terminate employees with the possible intention of rehiring them at a later date face a much better chance of getting them back if there is some form of severance pay involved in the termination.

The main disadvantage of severance pay is that it requires the organization to spend large sums of money almost immediately. This may be particularly difficult for the organization, especially if the terminations are a result of a restructuring or bankruptcy. In LBOs or consolidations, severance pay may be an ideal solution. Because both LBOs and consolidations often involve the acquisition of one organization by another, severance pay is a convenient way to accelerate the transition process. This is because many restructuring costs are tax deductible, and the organization may write off the severance expense and realize a tax savings or reduction as a result.

The cost of firing a manager differs by country. In the United States, it costs about $19,000 to fire a $50,000 manager. Only Ireland has a lower termination cost, $13,000. Italy and Spain spend more than $100,000 when terminating the same $50,000 manager, while Greece falls somewhere between at $67,000.[47]

Another issue that an organization must consider before it begins terminating employees is its outplacement policy. Outplacement programs are corporate programs whose purpose is to help terminated employees adjust to their terminations and to assist them in finding other jobs.[48] Most outplacement programs assist terminated employees in three areas: financial support, psychological support, and job search support. Financial support functions typically include wage/salary continuation, health insurance,

---

■ HR CHALLENGE ■

Disgruntled Customers—A Big Disadvantage of Downsizing

The story of former AT&T customer Gary Russell, telecommunications chief at KeyCorp in Albany, New York, is not all uncommon. Russell complained that AT&T circuits were constantly out of service. Whenever he called for help, he received no response. Finally, he offered his business to a competitor of AT&T. The competition gladly accepted the challenge and things have run smoothly ever since. Russell believes that AT&T is continuing to treat its customers as if it were the only game in town when that is no longer true.

In actuality, AT&T is having trouble managing its downsizing. Take for example, Al Caron, who was a technician at AT&T for over seven years. He said the pressure of trying to keep his family intact after three moves in one year was more than he could take. It appears that the determination of AT&T to become efficient and flexible through restructuring, may come at the expense of its reputation for reliability, which is central to its success.

Losing qualified employees such as Caron has forced AT&T to subcontract work. One angry AT&T customer who is paying a great deal of money for an AT&T maintenance contract feels cheated when a non-AT&T employee shows up to work on the system, especially when the subcontractor has been shown how to get into the system and how it works. More

significant problems have also been traced to AT&T. In September 1991, a voice communications outage in the Northeast crippled Wall Street and closed down the air traffic control system on the East Coast.

Major problems, such as a loss of service quality due to downsized staffing levels, can create a positive outcome—for competitors. For example, in the long distance market, AT&T's market share fell from 80 percent in 1989 to 61 percent in 1991. Competitors MCI and Sprint are eagerly picking up disgruntled AT&T customers.

It appears that AT&T realized that its reputation was on the line. One advertising campaign simply asked for old AT&T customers to come back. The company also offered to waive the switchover fee for its returning customers and to pay to switch the customers back if they were not satisfied with the service they receive.

Despite these and other more recent highly focused marketing campaigns, AT&T's market share remained at 60 percent in 1995, indicating that downsizing losses in market share may be difficult to regain.

SOURCE: Adapted from John Keller, "Some AT&T Clients Gripe That Cost Cuts Are Hurting Service," *The Wall Street Journal*, January 24, 1992, pp. A1 +; and Subrata N. Chakravarty, "Nimble Upstart," *Forbes*, May 8, 1995, pp. 96–99.

---

unemployment compensation, and credit management. Psychological support functions usually include self-esteem counseling, stress management, spouse and family counseling, and counseling for retained employees. Job search support includes secretarial services, office space, telephones, self-assessment, job search skills, resume writing, interviewing, follow-up and evaluation, and other forms of career-counseling.[49]

Well-run outplacement programs can greatly ease the former employee's transition into a new job or career while maintaining the organization's image both internally and within its community.[50] On the other hand, outplacement programs can quickly become expensive if they are not managed properly. Most organizations cannot afford to offer all of these services and consequently they are placed in the position of having to decide the level of outplacement services to offer. Because an outplacement program can have such a large impact on the outcome of a termination strategy, its design should be carefully tailored to meet the most critical needs of the organization's overall termination strategy.

TYPES OF TERMINATIONS

An organization may pursue three basic types of termination strategies. The first is a **leave 'em naked termination** strategy. Firms that pursue this strategy essentially

LEAVE 'EM NAKED TERMINATION
A termination strategy in which a firm releases employees from the organization without providing any protection or compensation benefits or outplacement services.

HR CHALLENGE

Preparing Managers to Terminate Employees

Handling the termination process effectively can go a long way to ease tensions and reduce the chances of employee retaliation. The following suggestions may help managers to be better prepared for terminating employees.

1. Plan the termination for early in the week so that the employee does not get the weekend to mull it over.
2. Do not let the termination interview last longer than 15 minutes. Long meetings allow time for debate. Simply state your case and move on.
3. Meet in the worker's office so that he or she does not have to leave the meeting and explain it to workers on the way back to his or her office. Make sure that the location is private.
4. Do not plan the meeting on important dates such as birthdays or holidays or when the employee has just returned from a vacation.
5. Don't leave room for confusion. Tell the employee in the first sentence that he or she is terminated. Make it clear that the decision is final.

6. Clearly communicate all aspects of the severance package offered to the employee.
7. Be prepared for a terminated employee to be emotional and hostile.
8. Outline the remaining steps in the termination process, such as the last day, key return policies, and so on.
9. Provide the employee with the name of an individual at the outplacement service if one is being offered. If possible, personally introduce the employee to the counselor.
10. Discuss the transfer of the employee's responsibilities and work to other employees.
11. Wish the employee luck and express confidence in his or her ability to find a new job.

SOURCES: Adapted from Phyllis Macklin and Lester Minsuk, "10 Ways to Ease Dismissal Dread," *HRMagazine,* November 1991, pp. 104–105; and Susan Alexander, "Firms Get Plenty of Practice at Layoffs, but They Often Bungle the Firing Process," *The Wall Street Journal,* October 14, 1991, p. B1.

EARLY RETIREMENT TERMINATION
A termination strategy in which an organization provides some form of inducements for employees to retire from the organization before they reach normal retirement age.

release employees from the organization without providing any protection or compensation benefits or outplacement services. Such a strategy has two main advantages. First, it involves relatively little up-front cash investment on the part of the organization since it provides no severance pay, outplacement, or counseling benefits. Second, the firm can decide exactly whom it wishes to release from the organization and whom it wishes to keep. These advantages can also be its main liabilities, however, because they often expose the organization to lawsuits by terminated employees with wrongful or abusive discharge claims. Other disadvantages include the likely adverse reactions from the remaining employees, the terminated employees, and the community at large. This is due to the fact that leave 'em-naked strategies can easily be perceived as the action of a firm with only its own concerns in mind. Even with these disadvantages, many firms still choose to pursue this type of strategy, especially if immediate cash-flow problems are the main concern of the organization.

Two other common strategies are forced resignation and early retirement incentives before proceeding with terminations. **Early retirement termination** usually provides some form of inducements for employees to retire from the organization before they reach the normal retirement age. Typical inducements are called "5-5-4" packages. These packages add five years of service to the employees' record with the company and five years to the employee's age when calculating early retirement benefits. The "4" part of the package is typically the number of weeks of full pay that the employee will receive for each year he or she has worked for the organization. Other common packages include "3-3-2" or "2-2-1" plans.

Telecommunications giant AT&T is one of several firms that operates with a 5-5-4 early retirement plan as a part of its restructuring strategy. In late 1989, the firm expanded the scope of its program. Approximately 34,000 AT&T managers qualified for the program and the company expected as many as one-third of all eligible managers to take advantage of it in 1990. The total savings from the program reached $450 million in 1990.[51] AT&T also extended a similar program to at least some of its 173,500 non-management workers. Once this second plan was adopted, AT&T's total savings reached $1 billion annually.[52] Added benefits are in the form of lower health-care costs when firms select to implement an early retirement plan. As health-care costs soar, companies have responded by cutting the number of the most expensive employees to cover: older workers.[53]

FORCED RESIGNATION TERMINATION

A termination strategy in which employees are offered the option of either resigning or being terminated outright.

Forced resignation termination is much more direct in nature. It is usually offered as alternatives to outright terminations. Each of these strategies has its own unique comparative restructuring advantages and disadvantages. The two types of strategies (early retirement and forced resignation) differ in cash outlays, legal issues, risks of losing valued employees, the impact on organization climate and culture, and the impact on the organization's public image. Exhibit 17.12 compares these two methods of downsizing.[54]

The organization must consider the impact of these types of terminations. It should determine the cash outlays involved in deciding whether to use an early retirement or a forced resignation termination strategy. It must make early retirement financially attractive enough to employees that they will accept it. Consequently, an organization that chooses to use an early retirement program should be prepared to spend large sums of money early on to induce employees to retire. In addition, the costs of the program may increase rapidly as the size of the program grows. In contrast, forced resignation programs require relatively little up-front cash investment on the part of the organization. Usually, forced resignations offer little to employees. At best, they offer a small severance package.

The organization must also consider the legal aspects of each program. Because early retirement programs are strictly voluntary on the part of the employees, there is relatively little chance of legal action against organizations using them. Forced resignations, on the other hand, incur a great risk of legal action, especially when issues such as tenure are involved or wrongful discharge can be proven.

The type of strategy that the organization undertakes also determines whether it loses valuable employees. Because voluntary retirements must generally be offered to

EXHIBIT 17.12   **Comparison of Two Methods of Downsizing and Their Impact on Critical Organizational Variables**

METHOD OF DOWNSIZING

Variable	Early Retirement	Forced Resignations
Cash outlays	Relatively high	Relatively low
Possible litigation	Relatively low risk	Relatively high risk
Losing valued employees	Relatively high risk	Relatively low risk
Impact on organization climate and culture	Minimal	Relatively high likelihood of negative impact
Impact on public image	Relatively low risk of negative impact	Relatively high risk of negative impact

SOURCE: Frank E. Kuzmits and Lyle Sussman, "Early Retirement or Forced Resignation: Policy Issues for Downsizing Human Resources," *SAM Advanced Management Journal,* Winter 1988, p. 32.

all eligible employees, organizations run the risk of losing valuable employees as well as less valuable ones. In addition, valuable employees usually have skills that enable them to continue working with another organization. By taking early retirement from one organization and going to work for another, they are often able to increase their incomes dramatically as they receive funds from both organizations. As a result, the organization may wind up losing its most valuable employees to competitors during voluntary retirement programs. Forced resignations generally do not suffer from these problems. Again, the organization essentially decides who is going to resign and who is going to be kept, and it is natural to assume that the organization is not going to ask its key members to resign.

Finally, the organization must consider the impact of each strategy on its culture, climate, and public image. Because forced resignations are involuntary in nature, they tend to have a large negative impact both internally and externally. The public is likely to interpret such actions as cold and uncaring on the part of the organization, especially if the program affects members with long tenure in the organization, which does not fully explain the rationale behind its actions. Internally, forced resignations are likely to foster hostility toward and resentment of upper management by employees. Even generous severance packages, which are usually rare in these situations, generally cannot overcome the resentment generated by making employees leave the organization. The level of resentment felt may differ by employee, but research has found that women executives cope better with forced resignations than do men. It appears that men take the firing personally. They view it as age discrimination or a conflict in personalities. Women, on the other hand, more readily accept the fact that the change is due to downsizing or economic conditions rather than a problem with them.[55] Early retirement terminations, on the other hand, do not suffer from such a stigma. Many organizations make employee retirement an occasion for celebration, and the community is likely to react positively to an organization that offers generous incentives to those employees who wish to retire early.[56]

Whatever method of termination is selected, human resource managers generally offer an exit interview so that terminated employees can have the opportunity to candidly discuss their work experience. Topics covered during this interview include the worker's impressions of the supervisor's performance, the adequacy of the training and development received, company policies, advancement opportunities, and overall job satisfaction. Managers can learn much about how employees feel during these interviews and should endeavor to hold one whenever an employee leaves.[57]

Organizations that consider a termination strategy as part of a restructuring plan must contend with many issues. Each strategy has its own advantages and shortcomings. In many instances, termination strategies can help the organization achieve its restructuring more quickly than either layoff or no-layoff strategies. The risks and costs may be greater, however, depending on the type of strategy used. About the only absolute in determining the type of strategy to use is that management should carefully consider all alternatives and the likely impact of each. Often the best solution is not a single restructuring approach but a combination of methods. Rarely can one organization's experiences be directly applied to those of another organization.

DOES DOWNSIZING WORK?

Hamel and Prahalad argue that downsizing is a form of **"corporate anorexia"** in that it can make a company thinner but not necessarily healthier. They argue that downsizing is merely an inefficient attempt to overcome bad management. In this view, it results from a firm's failure to recognize its core competencies—the firm's key skills and

CORPORATE ANOREXIA
The effect of too much downsizing that results in a very "thin" but very unhealthy orgainzation.

resources—and to leverage them to the greatest extent possible. Downsizing is a meat cleaver way to cut costs and often results in throwing out the baby with the bath water. It takes great management insight to go beyond these quick fixes.[58]

To bolster their argument, Hamel and Prahalad provide data to show that downsized companies have not performed any better than other firms. Downsizing results in immediate labor savings as well as skill shortages and increased workloads for the employees left to do the work. While employees are happy to have a job, they are also *unhappy* because of the increased workload and uncertainty surrounding their jobs.

Despite the Hamel and Prahalad study, it is still too early to adequately assess the effects of downsizing. More time is needed to determine whether corporate performance is better in downsized firms compared to similar firms.

THE VIRTUAL ORGANIZATION, CONTINGENT WORKERS, AND OUTSOURCING

VIRTUAL ORGANIZATION
Fungible modules built around information networks, flexible workforces, outsourcing, and webs of strategic partnerships.

To cope with these changes organizations are experiencing, they are experimenting with new forms of employment. One form is the emergence of the **virtual organization,** also known as the *virtual corporation. Fortune* magazine calls the virtual corporation "fungible modules built around information networks, flexible workforces, outsourcing, and webs of strategic partnerships."[59] Unlike typical images of organizations where all workers show up for work at the plant at 9 A.M. and leave at 5 P.M., the virtual organization is something very different. Employees may indeed begin work at 9, but "the office" might mean the old spare bedroom down the hall from the kids' room that has been converted into an office. Workers may never have to leave their homes thanks to computers, telephones, fax machines, video conferencing, and modems, which enable them to be just as productive as they would be at corporate headquarters. Other workers may not start work until after 3:30 when the kids get home from school. In addition, some workers may work for the organization only on a temporary or part-time basis. Finally, the organization's payroll might be issued by another company specializing in payroll management. The following are six trends that are helping to create the virtual organization.

1. The average company will become smaller, employing fewer people.
2. The traditional hierarchical organization will give way to a variety of organizational forms, the network of specialists foremost among these.
3. Technicians, ranging from computer repairers to radiation therapists, will replace manufacturing operatives as the worker elite.
4. The vertical division of labor will be replaced by a horizontal division.
5. The paradigm of doing business will shift from making a product to providing a service.
6. Work itself will be redefined, emphasizing constant learning and high-order thinking and deemphasizing set work hours.[60]

The basic tenant of the virtual organization is that traditional organizations, characterized by hierarchical management and rigid 9 to 5 work schedules are being made obsolete by global competition, advances in information and communication technologies, changes in workers' skills and expectations, and the switch from manufacturing to services as the basis of capital creation.

The impact of global competition cannot be understated. The quality challenge provided by Asian and European manufacturers, the need to sell in international markets, and the need to conduct business with organizations that are literally oceans and continents away has forced U.S. businesses to adapt to global competition. Simple logistical problems such as cultural differences and how to communicate with employees in separate time zones and who may speak one of 100 different languages have forced companies to change if they wish to remain competitive. Some of these problems have been alleviated by computer and communications technologies. Instead of having to work an extra hour at the end of the day to telephone the United States to get permission from the headquarters to undertake a new project, a European employee can send the request via E-mail and have it waiting for his boss when she arrives for work at 8:00 A.M. in Los Angeles. When the European employee arrives at work the next day, he can quickly check his E-mail to see what the boss' answer is.

Domestically, computer and communication technologies can provide the same advantages they can internationally. With a computer, a fax machine, a telephone, and a modem at home, a book editor may have all the tools she needs to do her job—and the company doesn't have to worry about costs associated with office assignments, parking spaces, and other work amenities for the employee. Computer networks can even allow for employees who may be spread across huge distances, such as continents and oceans, to work together on projects.

Further, many U.S. companies and workers have undergone a change in attitude about what they expect from a job. The Family-Leave Act, enacted in 1993, enables workers to take unpaid leave time for pregnancy or family illness. It is still too early to tell what impact the act will have on organizations, but analysts have predicted that many workers will take advantage of it to start families or take care of ill or older family members. It does appear that the career orientation of the baby boomer generation of the 1980s has changed to a greater desire to spend time with the family. Postbaby-boomers, often referred to as *Generation X,* have displayed a tendency to hold many part-time or temporary jobs before settling down with a permanent full-time position. In addition, many of the fastest-growing jobs require highly specialized skills (see Exhibit 17.5). Employees with these skills often have strong bargaining leverage with potential employers.

A final component of the virtual corporation is the switch from value creation through manufacturing to value creation through service creation. Traditional businesses depended on the factory floor for the creation of wealth. A key component of the factory floor was immobility: workers came to the factory, not the other way around. Today, many of the fast-growing industries, such as computer software, are based on the creation of a service. These service-based industries do not depend on the production of physical products for their wealth. Instead, they rely on the creation of knowledge by workers. A computer programmer can just as easily do her job at home as she can in the office if she has a computer to work on. Ernst & Young's information technology consulting division is typical of this type of knowledge creation. It estimates that its consultants and auditors spend from 50 percent to 80 percent of their time in the field.[61]

For our discussion, two components of the virtual corporation have a direct impact on how firms strategically manage their human resources. The first component is the increased use of contingent workers by organizations. The second is the trend of firms to contract, or outsource, components of their operations to outside firms.

The number of contingent workers in the workforce has increased dramatically in recent years. In essence, a **contingent worker** is any person who works for an

CONTINGENT WORKER
Any person who works for an organization, but not on a permanent or full-time basis.

organization but not on a permanent or full-time basis. Temporary employees, part-time workers, contract laborers, and leased employees are examples. *The Wall Street Journal* estimates that temporary, contract, and part-time workers now account for approximately 25 percent of the U.S. workforce.[62] Other studies indicate that this is only the beginning. It is estimated that nearly one-half of the U.S. workforce will be contingent workers by the year 2000.[63] Exhibit 17.13 reports the results of a poll of CEOs regarding their use of contingent workers.

The use of contingent workers by corporations provides a number of advantages and disadvantages. The advantages include reduced payroll and benefit costs and increased flexibility in operations. The disadvantages include increased costs in training employees, failure to develop in-house skills, potential morale problems, difficulties in scheduling work, and lower levels of employee loyalty.

Perhaps the main reason that most companies are increasingly using contingency workers is to *save money*. Firms that shift a position from being full-time to contingent can save money in a number of areas including benefit packages such as health insurance, vacation salaries, and sick days. And, depending on the type of contingency worker the company uses, it may be able to shift most of the employee's tax burden to the employee or the outside contractor providing the employee. It is estimated that the average contingent worker costs an organization 20 percent to 40 percent less than the average full-time worker.[64]

The other reason that companies use contingent workers is to increase their *flexibility* in responding to changing conditions. By using contingent workers, companies can easily increase or decrease the sizes of their staffs to meet increases or decreases in consumer demand. A typical use of contingent workers in this situation is the annual hiring of temporary workers by retail stores to meet the demands of the holiday buying rush each year. Further, companies can hire contingent workers to complete special one-time tasks or projects. Many people are familiar with agencies that provide temporary secretarial services, but they may not be aware of other organizations that exist to temporarily provide firms with highly skilled workers such as engineers, computer programmers, and even top managers. Prior to the advent of these specialized contingent workers, an organization was forced to hire the workers permanently, even if it needed them only for a single project. Once the organization has completed its project, it no longer has to worry about what to do with the contingent worker.

There can be several *disadvantages* associated with contingent workers, however. One disadvantage is that companies that indiscriminately use contingency workers may actually wind up *increasing their training costs*. This situation often arises when com-

EXHIBIT 17.13   **CEOs' Use of Contingent Workers**

	Compared to 1988, My Company's Use of Contingent Workers Has	Five Years from Now, My Company's Use of Them Will Have
Increased	44%	44%
Decreased	13	9
Remained the same	43	44
Not sure	—	3

SOURCE: Joclyn Fierman, "The Contingency Workforce," *Fortune*, January 24, 1994, p. 31.

panies have unique or nonstandard methods of doing business. For example, most secretaries from temporary services are usually trained in the use of three of four specific word processors. If a company uses an uncommon one, it may find that it has to train its temporary workers how to use it before they can be productive. Temporary secretary Jillian Perlberger relates this experience: "One lawyer told me if he has to use a temp, he considers it a lost day."[65] The chances are that the more unique or specialized the requirements are for a job, the higher the probability that the organization will have to invest in the training of the contingent worker.

Related to the first disadvantage is that companies could *potentially fail to adequately develop their own knowledge base,* or even worse, allow that knowledge to be copied by competitors if they rely too heavily on contingent workers. Like people, most organizations learn through trial and error. Over time, the organization builds a pool of experiences that it relies upon to accomplish its goals efficiently. If the organization relies too heavily on contingent workers, especially those in key positions, it may fail to develop that knowledge necessary for competitive success. Since contingent workers often by design are not meant to be permanent or long-term workers with the organization, they frequently do not take part in organization rituals designed to pass along the organization's accumulated knowledge. Consequently, whatever skills or knowledge the contingent worker has may never be passed along to the organization. An even worse scenario for many organizations is that a contingent worker does learn valuable knowledge or skills from the organization—and then goes to work for its competitor. Therefore, organizations that use an unusually high number of contingent workers or use them in positions directly related to the organization's key skills may find themselves in the situation where the process of creating organizational knowledge is stunted. If this problem is not corrected in time, the organization may find that it has lost its key competitive skills or has become a "hollow corporation."

Another key problem associated with contingent workers is *low morale.* Many employees voluntarily choose to become contingent workers. Contingency status often provides workers with flexible schedules that enable them to work second jobs, spend more time with their families, provide additional family income for special occasions such as vacations, or pursue additional education. Many employees, however, become contingency workers because it is forced upon them by their employers or because they are unable to find permanent full-time work. Permanent employees who are forced into contingency status by their employers often resent the loss of wages and benefits that are usually associated with contingent status. Further, they resent the organization's expectation of them to perform the same job at the same level as permanent employees but at the reduced rate. Organizations that make shifts to contingency work without clearly communicating their plan may incur morale problems from employees who are worried about their jobs. Another problem occurs when employees join a firm on a contingency status and seek to become permanent members. If the firm indicates that permanent status may be an option in the future, employees will gear their work and attitudes toward the achievement of permanent status. If the organization does not come through with what the employee perceives as a promise of a reward for good work his or her morale and productivity are likely to suffer. Exhibit 17.14 relays the experiences of two contingent workers.

Another problem with contingent workers may occur with *scheduling work.* Because contingent workers often work part-time schedules or on fixed schedules, many organizations find it difficult to get all of their employees involved in a project together at the same time for important meetings. Further, organizations must take into account that the schedule of contingent workers may often impact the schedule of permanent

■ **EXHIBIT 17.14** **Contingent Work: Two Views**

Some people thrive on temporary employment. Karen Cerrone says working in Pancoast Temporary Services in Pittsburgh gives her flexibility to travel to summer training and World Series games with her husband, vice president of public relations for the Pittsburgh Pirates.

On the other hand, Beverly Garner finds temporary work disheartening. She started work in October 1991 as a temporary doing quality control work at Schmid Laboratories, which makes condoms in Anderson, S.C. Eager to land a full-time slot, she came in early and worked through breaks earning $5 an hour, while full-timers earned $8.

When no full-time job materialized by July 1992, she became frustrated and on occasion showed up late. A day after she told supervisors about having attended a meeting on the rights of temporary workers, she was fired for coming into work a few minutes late on 11 occasions and being sick on more than three days. She doesn't deny it.

"It got to the point where I hated to work. I hated who I worked for because I wasn't being paid or treated fairly. And I know I was less productive because I was so disheartened," she says.

SOURCE: Clare Ansberry, "Hired Out," *The Wall Street Journal,* March 11, 1994, p. A9.

workers, especially when both types of workers are involved in a task together. Failure to anticipate these needs may bring chaos to an organization's scheduling and result in severe productivity declines.

As noted, contingent workers seldom develop loyalty to the organization. Their temporary status allows them to develop a "here today, gone tomorrow" attitude. While certainly all do not develop this attitude, the job situation they face is less stable than that of regular employees. Exhibit 17.16 summarizes the big issues involved in using contingent or temporary employees.

OUTSOURCING

Firms have three basic options in deciding how to achieve a specific task or goal. First, they can rely on full-time workers who are permanently assigned to performing the duties that the goal requires. Second, they can rely on contingent workers to fulfill the goal. Finally, they can strike a balance between the two and *contract out,* or *outsource,* their operations to another organization. Most organizations today use at least two, if not all three, options. An example of this is Digital Equipment's decision to outsource responsibility for sales and support for 7,000 of its customers while still continuing to provide sales and support for its 1,000 biggest customers.

Like the use of contingent workers, firms that outsource are frequently able to achieve cost savings by contracting small or inefficient operations to outside organizations. Outsourcing activities range from manufacturing machined parts to job recruitment function. Exhibit 17.15 shows human resource functions that are commonly outsourced by organizations. For example, among the most commonly outsourced activities are those related to payroll processing, especially in small organizations. Instead of maintaining a staff dedicated to processing the organization's payroll each week or taking the time away from persons with other duties, the organization can contract the work to firms that specialize in payroll processing. The firm immediately saves money by being able to free up employees for other tasks or by eliminating the department dedicated to payroll processing. Further, much outsourced work can be done less expensively by specialty

EXHIBIT 17.15   **Human Resource Services Most* Frequently Outsourced**

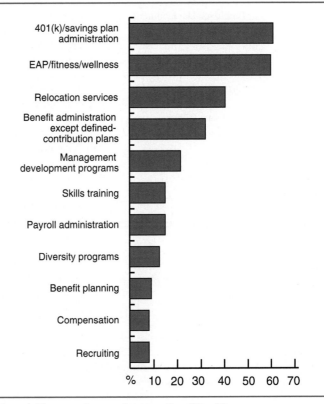

*Based on employers with outsourcing experiences or plans (N = 67)

SOURCE: *HRM Magazine,* July 1994, p. 53.

organizations than it can be done in-house. By outsourcing small or inefficient activities, the organization is free to focus on those activities it does well.

Another advantage of outsourcing is that it gives the organization flexibility to change its mind if it chooses to do so. The organization is free to shop around to various organizations for the services or jobs it needs done, and it can specify the criteria it needs to have met—whether those criteria are cost, quality, delivery time, quantity, or so on. Also, if at a later date, the organization chooses to bring the activities in-house, it is free to do so.

Outsourcing shares many of the same disadvantages of using contingent workers. These include a loss of skills, which could lead to a possible "hollowing" of the corporation and possible morale problems associated with the inevitable downsizing of the organization that comes with the outsourcing. Like the problems associated with contingent workers, management must pay careful attention to the course of action it takes. Finally, the organization must make sure that it dedicates adequate resources to coordinating its activities with the activities of the organization or organizations that it has outsourced its work to. Like the problems associated with scheduling contingent workers, failure to provide adequate coordination between the organization and its outsources may result in lost productivity, increased costs, lowered quality, and depressed morale.

EXHIBIT 17.16   **Some Cautions in Using Temporary Workers**

Employee Development	Using temporary workers can decimate employers' reservoir of knowledge, skills, and abilities (KSAs) since training investment in temporary workers is not made.
Loyalty	Temporary employees show little commitment or loyalty to the organization and its vision and long-term goals.
Customer Service	Temporaries may be unlikely to build relationships with customers based on a commitment to the organization.
Corporate Culture	Temporary employees may not buy into or reenforce the corporate culture.
Safety	Temporary employees may not be fully trained and educated on unique employee safety requirements and hazards.
Discrimination	Since temporaries are usually paid lower wages and no benefits compared to regular employees, they may feel discriminated against and may not perform adequately.
Social Responsibility	Since temporaries work intermittently, employers who use them extensively may be relying on supplements by federal, state, and local unemployment and welfare benefits during gaps between work engagements.
Impact on Human Resource Professionals	Extensive use of temporaries may hurt the professional image of human resource professionals since they became primarily work schedulers, running people in and out of the organization rather than a builder of an organization's human resource assets.

SOURCE: Adapted from Earnest R. Archer, "Words of Caution on the Temporary Workforce," *HRMagazine,* September 1994, pp. 164–168.

EXHIBIT 17.17   **Some Sample Outsourced Products**

PRODUCT	MANUFACTURER
Rayovac's battery recharger	Avex Electronics
Apple's PowerPC	Solectron
General Mills' Granola Bars	Coosa Baking
Snapple	Various local bottlers
Cytogen's Oncscint	Celltech

SOURCE: Thomas Martin, "You'll Never Guess Who Really Makes . . . ," *Fortune,* October 3, 1994, p. 125.

MANAGEMENT GUIDELINES

Based on the information presented in this chapter, several guidelines for managers who face an organizational restructuring can be offered.

1. Any organization restructuring involves a trade-off between the impact on the employees and the immediate benefits to the organization. It is the manager's responsibility to balance the impact against the benefits.

Continued

2. Each type of restructuring strategy has its own time horizon for implementation. The manager must match the strategy to the timeframe needed for the restructuring.
3. Each type of restructuring strategy has a different basic cost structure. The manager must consider the costs involved in each type of restructuring and the organization's ability to pay for it.
4. A critical determinant of a successful reorganization is the amount of managerial communication about the reasons for and goals of the restructuring. Poor communication between managers and employees may ruin the best planned restructuring.[66]
5. There are several laws and doctrines concerning organization restructuring. Managers should make sure that they are in compliance with these laws and doctrines before they begin a restructuring.
6. All types of restructuring involve organizational trauma. To reduce trauma and ensure a successful restructuring, managers should attempt to plan the elements of a restructuring before they begin the restructuring.
7. The strategic variables and choices facing an organization are often strong determinants of the type of restructuring that the organization undertakes. Managers should carefully examine these variables and choices before embarking on a restructuring.
8. The three types of restructuring strategies are not mutually exclusive. Managers should always consider using elements of all three types of restructuring strategies before making a final decision on the way to organize the restructuring.
9. Investigating the use of outsourcing, contingent workers, and the "virtual organization" may allow the organization to better cut costs and meet the variable changes in demand for the firm's goods and services.

QUESTIONS FOR REVIEW

1. What is organization restructuring? What does it usually involve?
2. Identify and briefly discuss the three general types of restructuring. How are they alike? How do they differ?
3. What is the role of the human resource professional in a restructuring?
4. Briefly identify and discuss the strategic variables involved in a restructuring decision. Describe the elements of each variable.
5. What is an LBO? How is it usually related to a restructuring decision?
6. Identify the four broad strategic choices that an organization must make in deciding to restructure. Discuss the general impact on both the employees and the organization in each type of restructuring decision.
7. What are no-layoff strategies? Briefly compare and contrast the different types of no-layoff strategies.
8. What are layoff strategies? List the various types of layoff strategies and discuss the advantages and disadvantages of each.
9. What are termination strategies? How do they differ from other restructuring strategies?
10. What roles do tenure and protection and compensation plans have in a termination strategy?
11. What is the employment-at-will doctrine? How does it relate to termination strategies?
12. Briefly describe the role of golden parachutes in termination strategies.
13. How is severance pay used in a termination strategy? What are its main advantages and disadvantages?
14. Discuss an organization's outplacement policy in relation to termination strategies. What are the three elements of a typical outplacement policy?
15. Identify and discuss the three basic types of termination strategies that an organization may pursue. How are they alike? How do they differ?
16. What is the virtual organization? Why is it being considered by many organizations? How is it related to the contingent workforce and outsourcing?

THE SAFEWAY LBO—NEED OR GREED?[67]

James White had worked for Safeway supermarkets as a trucker for nearly 30 years. One year after Safeway had taken itself private in a 1986 leveraged buyout (LBO) worth $5.65 billion, White was laid off in a massive restructuring. In 1988 White marked the one year anniversary of his layoff by locking himself in his bathroom and killing himself with his .22 caliber hunting rifle.

White was one of the 63,000 people who have lost their jobs with the world's largest supermarket chain since the LBO, and he was not the only one to have died from the experience. Patricia Vasquez, a 14-year Safeway veteran and recipient of numerous company awards, was found dead on her bathroom floor from a heart attack the day after she was laid off. Richard Quigley, a transportation manager, lost his wife less than a week after he was laid off. He claims that the trauma of his layoff caused her to have a diabetic relapse for the first time in several years. Phil Anich died of a heart attack a week after filing for unemployment. Friends attribute his heart attack to the stress created by his layoff.

Other former employees have also paid the price. Mikhail Vaynberg, a refrigeration engineer who has saved Safeway $1.6 million per year with an improvement to its cooling systems, has been unable to find work since he has been laid off. Bill Mayfield, Jr., a 15-year Safeway mechanic, slashed his wrists and shot himself in the stomach after he was laid off. He survived. In spite of claims to the contrary by upper management, the LBO has crippled employee morale in a company that was once noted for its loyal and hardworking employees. All of this happened in a company whose pre-LBO employee motto was "Safeway Offers Security."

GREED OR STRUGGLE

Is the Safeway LBO another example of greed run wild or a company's struggle to survive in an ever-increasingly competitive world? It all depends on who you talk to. Critics of the LBO point out that the company had earned a record $231.1 million in profits on $19.6 billion in sales in 1985, the last year before the buyout. These results represented a doubling of earnings in less than four years. During that time, Safeway's stock price had tripled in value and dividends had just posted their fourth straight yearly increase. The buyout netted $25 million for the company's management. Shareholders saw the value of their stock increase 82 percent as a result of the buyout. The Hafts, father and son Wall Street takeover specialists, made $100 million on the deal. Kolberg Kravis Roberts, the LBO specialists, charged $60 million just to arrange the deal. Lawyers, accountants, and investment banks associated with the buyout made another $90 million.

In 1989, the company's profit was a meager $2.5 million on sales of $14.3 billion. This was down from $31 million in 1988. The company recently had to settle for a $11.25 per share initial stock offering instead of its anticipated $20 per share due to a lack of market confidence in the success of the LBO. One prime reason was the fact that Safeway lacks the ability to generate the approximate $3.2 billion in capital it needs to renovate and open new stores over the next five years.

The company has sold off 1,100 of its 2,325 stores and has closed numerous other operations. In 1987 Safeway closed its entire Dallas-area division. Over 9,000 employees, with an average tenure of 17 years, were laid off. The action had a ripple effect in the already-depressed Dallas economy. Numerous food and beverage suppliers, construction firms, and even the local food bank have fallen on even harder times as a result of the closings. More than 300 people were laid off in corporate headquarters almost immediately after the takeover was completed.

The company has not been particularly generous to its former employees. Many of the layoffs have come without warning, and employees claim that they had to sign waivers agreeing not to sue the company later to get their severance package—one-half to one week's worth of pay for every year with the company up to a maximum of eight weeks of pay. The unions representing the former Safeway employees have even had to go to arbitration to get these benefits. There are complaints that some employees had to wait up to eight months to receive their severance pay and as long as a year and a half for their accrued vacation time. Many former Safeway employees have attempted to get jobs with the organizations that have bought the old Safeway stores, but so far their luck has been minimal. Even those who have gotten their old jobs back have had to take substantial cuts in salary.

LOW MORALE

The 110,000 employees who still work with Safeway are not much happier. Worker morale is at an all-time low, and many employees complain of being overworked—even to the point of being dangerous. Many Safeway truckers report having to work 16-hour days, and one company joke advises "if you see a Safeway truck, get out of the way," since the drivers may be asleep at the wheel from overwork. Many accuse the company of trying to lower costs by forcing out older workers or using arcane job classifications with lower pay scales to bring in newer workers. Employees say it is not untypical for store managers to cut employee pay, or in the case of older workers, drop them from full-time status to part-time. This drop in hours not only reduces salaries (needed hours are made up by other new, lower paid part-time employees), it also results in employees losing medical and other benefits.

Another aspect of the restructuring that is strongly opposed by workers is Safeway's new Return on Market Value (ROMV) productivity quota system. Many store managers complain that if they do not meet weekly quotas determined by the ROMV system, they are penalized by actions like being forced to work a seven-day week and twelve-hour days. Many managers report that they have worked entire months without a day off. Managers also complain that in some areas less than 10 percent of the managers have ever actually qualified to receive incentive pay as a result of having met the quotas. Safeway executives claim the figure is more like 50 percent.

Rank-and-file employees complain that the incentive system does not trickle down to them, but they must make sacrifices to make it work. Reportedly, the incentive plan is linked to the number of employee grievances and work-related medical claims. Charles Mercer, president of the Denver local of the United Food and Commercial workers union, reports that many of his employees have been actively discouraged from filing workmans' compensation claims because it will hurt the store's bonus.

PRODUCTIVITY UP

Supporters of the Safeway LBO paint another picture of the situation. Peter Magowan, son of the founders of Safeway and the current CEO, points out that worker productivity is up since the restructuring began and that Safeway is now number one or number two in every market in which it competes. He argues that the wage reductions were necessary to compete with other firms that have a less expensive salary structure. He defends the closings and the selling off of units as necessary actions to trim organization fat. One sale of the company's 132 stores in Britain netted Safeway $929 million, or 40 percent more than had initially been predicted. In addition, the operating profit per employee has risen more than 62 percent since 1985, the last year before the buyout.

Since the buyout, Safeway has also been able to install in some of its stores "boutique style" departments to cater to the yuppie crowd. Even though the company has turned in disappointing operating profits over the past few years, it has been able to significantly increase its cash flows, which are now about twice the level needed to cover the interest payments on its debt. The company has even begun to pay off some of its debt earlier than expected.

Magowan strongly disagrees with the supposed employee morale problems, too. He agrees that there have been problems in the past, but he states, "I am convinced that today's typical Safeway employee feels better about the company than he or she has at any point since the buyout." He even refers to a recent survey sponsored by the company that finds 80 percent of Safeway's employees feel that the organization offers advancement opportunity and other advantages.

So far, the jury is out on the results of the Safeway LBO. Was it really needed? Were the actions of top management justified and are the employees just reacting to changes that were necessary to keep the chain competitive in the market? Or, is Safeway's experience typical of the LBO binge of the 1980s in which management prospers at the expense of its employees?

QUESTIONS

1. What advantages and disadvantages were there for each of the constituencies involved in Safeway's LBO? Who stands to gain the most? Who stands to lose the most?
2. Do you think that any of the horrible consequences, such as death and attempted suicide of released workers, were preventable? If so, how?
3. As a human resource manager for Safeway, what are some of the challenges you would face before, during, and after the LBO?
4. What, if anything, does Safeway owe to the employees whose jobs were lost or changed due to the LBO?
5. If you were asked to fix the morale problems reported in this case, what would you do?

ADDITIONAL READINGS

Beer, Michael, Russell Eisenstat, and Bert Spector. *The Critical Path.* Boston: Harvard Business School Press, 1991.

Bolman, Lee, and Terrence Deal. *Reframing Organizations.* San Francisco, CA: Jossey-Bass, 1991.

Boyette, Joseph, and Henry Conn. *Workplace 2000: The Revolution Reshaping American Business.* New York: Dutton, 1991.

Bridges, William. *Managing Transitions.* Reading, MA: Addison-Wesley, 1991.

Cameron, Kim, Sarah Freeman, and Aneil Mishra. "Best Practices in White-collar Downsizing: Managing Contradictions." *Academy of Management Executive* 5 (1991), pp. 57–73.

Carrier, Leana, and Daniel Feldman. "Layoffs: How Employees and Companies Cope." *Personnel Journal.* September 1988, p. 31.

Carroll, Paul. "Hurt by a Pricing War, IBM Plans a Writeoff and Cut of 10,000 Jobs." *The Wall Street Journal.* December 6, 1989, p. A6.

Carroll Paul. "IBM Launches Retirement Plan to Cut Outlays." *The Wall Street Journal.* October 2, 1989, p. A4.

Cohen, Laurie. "AT&T Expands Early-Retirement Plan; Earnings Climbed 19% in Third Period." *The Wall Street Journal.* October 20, 1989, p. A4.

"Corporate Restructuring." *1989 ASPA/CCH Survey.* June 27, 1989.

Coulson, Robert. *Empowered at Forty: How to Negotiate the Best Time and Terms of Your Retirement.* New York: Harper-Business, 1992.

Dorn, Phillip. "Change and Change Again at IBM." *Computer World.* October 31, 1988, p. 19.

Downes, John, and Jordan Goodman. *Dictionary of Finance and Investment Terms.* 2nd ed. New York: Barron's, 1987.

Faludi, Susan. "The Reckoning: Safeway LBO Yields Vast Profits but Exacts a Heavy Human Toll." *The Wall Street Journal.* May 16, 1990, pp. A1; 6.

Farrell, Christopher. "LBOs: The Stars, the Strugglers, the Flops." *Business Week.* January 15, 1990, pp. 58–62.

Ford, Robert, and Pamela Perrewe. "After the Layoff: Closing the Barn Door before All the Horses Are Gone." 1992, paper under review at *Academy of Management Executive.*

Fox, Isaac, and Alfred Marcus. "The Causes and Consequences of Leveraged Buyouts." *Academy of Management Journal* 17, (1992), pp. 62–85.

Hartley, Jean, Dan Jacobson, Bert Klandermans, and Tinka Van Vuren. *Job Insecurity.* Newbury Park, CA: Sage, 1991.

Heery, William. "Outplacement through Specialization." *Personnel Administrator.* June 1989, p. 151.

Henkoff, Ronald. "Cost Cutting: How to Do It Right." *Fortune.* April 9, 1990, p. 41.

Hogan, Mike, "Hayes Reduces." *PC World.* June 1990, p. 11.

Hymowitz, Carol. "Kodak Passes Out 'Tin Parachutes' to All Its Employees." *The Wall Street Journal.* January 12, 1990, p. B1.

IBM. *1988 Annual Report,* p. 40.

Karr, Albert. "As the Army Shrinks, the Civilian Market Will Tighten for Job Seekers." *The Wall Street Journal.* June 19, 1990, p. A1.

Keller, John. "AT&T Weighs Early Retirement Plan that May Slash Non-Management Staff." *The Wall Street Journal.* March 15, 1990, p. A3.

Kissler, Gary. *Change Riders.* Reading, MA: Addison-Wesley, 1991.

Kuhn, Susan. "How Business Helps Schools." *Fortune.* Education 1990 Issue, pp. 91–106.

Kuzmits, Frank, and Lyle Sussman. "Early Retirement or Forced Resignation: Policy Issues for Downsizing Human Resources." *SAM Advanced Management Journal.* Winter 1988, p. 28.

Leana, Carrie, and Daniel Feldman. "Layoffs: How Employees and Companies Cope." *Personnel Journal.* September 1988, p. 31.

Loomis, Carol. "The Biggest Looniest Deal Ever." *Fortune.* June 18, 1990, pp. 48–72.

Mainiero, Lisa, and Paul Upham. "Beating a Stacked Deck—Restructuring vs. Career Development." *Personnel Journal.* June 1987, p. 126.

Messmer, Max. "Right-Sizing Reshapes Staffing Strategies." *HRMagazine.* October 1991, pp. 60–62.

Meyer, Alan. "Adapting to Environmental Jolts." *Administrative Science Quarterly,* 27. December 1982, pp. 515–537.

Milkovich, George, and John Boudreau. *Personnel/Human Resource Management: A Diagnostic Approach.* Plano, TX: Business Publications, 1988.

Petras, Kathryn, and Ross Petras. *The Only Retirement Guide You'll Ever Need.* New York: Poseidon, 1992.

"Plant-Closing Law Affects Casino." *HRM News/Society for Human Resource Management.* February 1990, p. A11.

Porter, Michael. *Competitive Strategy.* New York: Free Press, 1980.

Reid, Peter. *Well Made in America: Lessons from Harley-Davidson on Being the Best.* New York: McGraw-Hill, 1990.

Schmenner, Roger. *Production/Operations Management.* 3rd ed. Chicago: SRA, 1988.

Shao, Maria. "Boeing: A Backlog Strains Its Assembly Line." *Business Week.* May 8, 1989, pp. 35–36.

Siconolfi, Michael. "Drexel Owes Its Former Employees About $40 Million in Severance Fees." *The Wall Street Journal.* February 26, 1990, pp. A4;1.

Siehl, C., and D. Smith. "Avoiding the Loss of a Gain: Retraining Top Managers in an Acquisition." *Human Resource Management* 29 (1991), pp. 167–185.

Soukup, William, Miriam Rothman, and Dennis Brisco. "Outplacement Services: A Vital Component of Personnel Policy." *SAM Advanced Management Journal.* Autumn 1987, pp. 19–23.

Starbuck, William, and Bo Hedberg. "Saving an Organization from a Stagnating Environment," in H. Thorelli, ed. *Strategy + Structure = Performance.* Bloomington: Indiana University Press, 1977, pp. 249–258.

Sweet, Donald. *A Manager's Guide to Conducting Terminations.* Lexington, MA: Lexington Books, 1990.

Walsh, J., and J. Ellwood. "Mergers, Acquisitions, and the Pruning of Managerial Deadwood." *Strategic Management Journal* 12 (1991), pp. 210–217.

White, Joseph. "GM's Plant Closings Help It Win Wall Street Applause." *The Wall Street Journal.* May 25, 1990, p. C1.

Wilke, John. "At Digital Equipment, Slowdown Reflects Industry's Big Changes." *The Wall Street Journal.* September 15, 1989, p. A1.

NOTES

1. Carrie Leana and Daniel Feldman, "Layoffs: How Employees and Companies Cope," *Personnel Journal,* September 1988, p. 31.

2. "Corporate Restructuring," 1989 ASPA/CCH Survey, June 27, 1989, p. 2.

3. Aaron Bernstein and Wendy Zeller, "Outsourced—and Out of Luck," *Business Week,* July 17, 1995, p. 61.

4. Brian Dumaine, "The Bureaucracy Busters," *Fortune,* June 17, 1991, pp. 36–50.

5. Ibid; and Frank Kuzmits and Lyle Sussman, "Early Retirement or Forced Resignation: Policy Issues for Downsizing Human Resources," *SAM Advanced Management Journal,* Winter 1988, p. 28.

6. Leana and Feldman, "Layoffs: How Employees and Companies Cope," p. 31.

7. John Wilke, "At Digital Equipment, Slowdown Reflects Industry's Big Changes," *The Wall Street Journal,* September 15, 1989, pp. A1 +; John R. Wilke, "Digital Plans at Least 20,000 More Job Cuts," *The Wall Street Journal,* May 6, 1994, p. A3; Joseph Weber, "Desperate Hours at DEC," *Business Week,* May 9, 1994, pp. 26–30; William M. Bulkeley, "Digital Equipment to Slash 14,000 Jobs in Core Computer Lines by Restructuring," *The Wall Street Journal,* July 19, 1994, p. B3; and Carrie Dolan, "Quantum Set to Pay about $400 Million for Digital Line," *The Wall Street Journal,* July 20, 1994, p. B6.

8. Dean Tjosvold, "Foolproof Your Restructuring Plan," *HRMagazine,* November 1991, pp. 79–84.

9. Michael Porter, *Competitive Strategy* (New York: Free Press, 1980), p. xvi.

10. Ibid., pp. 34–46.

11. Harold Weinstein and Michael Liebman, "Corporate Sales Down, What Comes Next?" *HRMagazine,* April 1991, pp. 33–36.

12. Zachary Schiller and Robert Neff, "The Backlash Isn't Just Against Japan," *Business Week,* February 10, 1992, p. 30; and Krystal

Miller, "Honda, Seeking to Avert Output Cuts, Stores 2,000 Cars at Ohio Parking Lot," *The Wall Street Journal,* March 5, 1991, p. A5.

13. Alan Meyer, "Adapting to Environmental Jolts," *Administrative Science Quarterly,* 1982, pp. 515–537.

14. Albert Karr, "Staying Lean," *The Wall Street Journal,* July 16, 1991, p. A1.

15. Peter C. Reid, *Well Made in America: Lessons from Harley-Davidson on Being the Best* (New York: McGraw-Hill, 1990), p. 14.

16. 1989 ASPA/CCH Survey, pp. 2–3.

17. Ronald Henkoff, "Cost Cutting: How to Do It Right," *Fortune,* April 9, 1990, p. 41.

18. Joan Rigdon, "Kodak's Changes Produce Plenty of Heat, Little Light," *The Wall Street Journal,* April 8, 1992, p. B4.

19. John Downes and Jordan Goodman, *Dictionary of Finance and Investment Terms,* 2nd ed. (New York: Barron's, 1987), p. 209.

20. Shaker Zahra and Michael Fescina, "Will Leveraged Buyouts Kill U.S. Corporate Research & Development?" *Academy of Management Executive* 5, 1991, pp. 7–21; and Michael Hitt, Robert Hoskisson, Duane Ireland, and Jeffrey Harrison, "Are Acquisitions a Poison for Innovation?" *Academy of Management Executive* 5, 1991, pp. 23–34.

21. Halya Duda, "The Honeymoon Is Over for Corporate America," *HRMagazine,* February 1992, pp. 66–70.

22. William Starbuck and Bo Hedberg, "Saving an Organization from a Stagnating Environment," in H. Thorelli, ed., *Strategy + Structure = Performance* (Bloomington: Indiana University Press, 1977), pp. 249–258.

23. Stephanie Overman, "The Layoff Legacy," *HRMagazine,* August 1991, pp. 29–32.

24. Lisa Mainiero and Paul Upham, "Beating a Stacked Deck—Restructuring vs. Career Development," *Personnel Journal,* June 1987, p. 126.

25. Susan Kuhn, "How Business Helps Schools," *Fortune,* Education 1990 Issue, pp. 91–106.

26. "Job-Based Learning: Some Firms Build Closer Ties between School and Work," *The Wall Street Journal,* September 10, 1991, p. A1.

27. Maria Shao, "Boeing: A Backlog Strains Its Assembly Line," *Business Week,* May 8, 1989, p. 36.

28. James Francis, John Mohr, and Kelly Anderson, "HR Balancing: Alternative Downsizing," *Personnel Journal,* January 1992, pp. 71–78.

29. "The Axeman Cometh," *The Economist,* December 1990, pp. 15–16.

30. Udayan Gupta, "Cutting Payrolls Without Axing Any Employees," *The Wall Street Journal,* March 26, 1991, pp. B1 +.

31. For more information, see Roger W. Schmenner, *Production/Operations Management,* 3rd ed. (Chicago: SRA, 1987), pp. 5–23.

32. Ibid., pp. 52–85.

33. Joseph White, "GM's Plant Closings Help It Win Wall Street Applause," *The Wall Street Journal,* May 25, 1990, p. C1.

34. Ibid.

35. "Plant-Closing Law Affects Casino," *HRM News/Society for Human Resource Management,* February 1990, p. A11.

36. Albert Karr, "As the Army Shrinks, the Civilian Market Will Tighten for Job Seekers," *The Wall Street Journal,* June 19, 1990, pp. A1 +.

37. Kim Cameron, "Downsizing Can Be Hazardous to Your Future," *HRMagazine,* July 1991, pp. 96 +.

38. Bernstein and Zeller, "Outsourced—and Out of Luck," p. 61.

39. Gabriella Stren, Paul Carroll, and Michel McQueen, "In a Weak Economy, Some Top-Level Aides Are Bound to Topple," *The Wall Street Journal,* December 13, 1991, pp. A1 +.

40. Joann Lublin, "Executives Find Unemployment Takes a Heavier Toll the Second Time Around," *The Wall Street Journal,* July 9, 1991, pp. B1 +.

41. "Wrongful Discharge: Legal Experts Propose a New Approach," *The Wall Street Journal,* September 10, 1991, p. A1.

42. George Milkovich and John Boudreau, *Personnel/Human Resource Management: A Diagnostic Approach* (Plano, TX: Business Publications, 1988), pp. 465–467.

43. Christopher Conte, "Litigation Losses," *The Wall Street Journal,* May 12, 1992, p. A1.

44. Michael Siconolfi, "Drexel Owes Its Former Employees About $40 Million in Severance Fees," *The Wall Street Journal,* February 26, 1990, p. A4.

45. Carol Hymowitz, "Kodak Passes Out 'Tin Parachutes' to All Its Employees," *The Wall Street Journal,* January 12, 1990, pp. B1 +.

46. "Severance: The Corporate Response," *The Right Research Report* (Fort Lauderdale: Right Associates).

47. "Goodbyes Can Cost Plenty in Europe," *Fortune,* April 6, 1992, p. 16; and Christopher Conte, "Terminating Workers," *The Wall Street Journal,* May 12, 1992, p. A1.

48. William Heery, "Outplacement through Specialization," *Personnel Administrator,* June 1989, p. 151.

49. William Soukup, Miriam Rothman, and Dennis Brisco, "Outplacement Services: A Vital Component of Personnel Policy," *SAM Advanced Management Journal,* Autumn 1987, pp. 19–23.

50. A. B. Karr, "There Is Life After Outplacement, but Career Views Change," *The Wall Street Journal,* December 24, 1991, p. A1.

51. Laurie P. Cohen, "AT&T Expands Early-Retirement Plan; Earnings Climbed 19% in Third Period," *The Wall Street Journal,* October 20, 1989, p. A4.

52. John Keller, "AT&T Weighs Early Retirement Plan That May Slash Non-Management Staff," *The Wall Street Journal,* March 15, 1990, p. A3.

53. Lenore Schiff, "Is Health Care a Job Killer?" *Fortune,* April 6, 1992, p. 30.

54. The following discussion is based on the article "Early Retirement or Forced Resignation: Policy Issues for Downsizing Human Resources," by Frank E. Kuzmits and Lyle Sussman, in *SAM Advanced Management Journal,* Winter 1988, pp. 28–32.

55. J. E. Rigdon, "Women Appear to Take Firings Less Personally," *The Wall Street Journal,* December 6, 1991, p. B1.

56. Gregory Patterson, "More Employers Offer Early Retirement to Help Shrink Blue-Collar Work Force," *The Wall Street Journal,* August 30, 1991, p. B1.

CASE 1

FEDEX CORPORATION

FedEx, formerly Federal Express, became a leader in the air transport industry in only a few years.[1] The company founded the small-package/document express market in 1973, and it constantly adds products and services and extends its service areas. Its main air freight forwarding competitors, most notably United Parcel Service (UPS) and Emery Air Freight, have been around for twenty-five years and were content with the market positions they occupied. FedEx "changed the rules of the game" and took the market by storm.[2]

INDUSTRY

Firms involved in cargo movement include all-cargo air carriers, traditional freight forwarders, passenger airlines, ground transportation companies, and air couriers. Competitors directly involved in the small-package/document express market include Federal Express, Purolator, UPS, and the United States Postal Service.

Regulation for this industry falls under the Federal Aviation Act of 1958 and is enforced by the Federal Aviation Administration (FAA). The FAA's regulatory authority relates primarily to the safety aspects of air transportation, which includes aircraft standard and maintenance. Federal Express operations are also subject to regulation by the Federal Communications Act of 1934 because of the use of radio and communication equipment in ground and air units. In addition, the Department of Transportation exercises regulatory authority over the company.

COMPANY BACKGROUND

Frederick W. Smith, founder of FedEx, earned his pilot's license before entering college. His experience as an aviator and his observation of material shipments out of airports while a student majoring in political science and economics at Yale University in the 1960s were the impetus for developing his firm in 1973. His initial conceptualization of FedEx was that of an air cargo firm that specialized in overnight package delivery on a door-to-door basis using its own planes.

The idea for FedEx was first laid out in an overdue economics paper. To cut cost and time, packages from all over the country would be flown to a central point, or hub, late at night when the traffic lanes were comparatively empty. At the hub the packages would be sorted, redistributed, and flown out again to their ultimate locations. Airports

NOTE: This case was prepared by Mark Dawkins and Erich Brockmann.

681

in sizable cities would be used, and trucks would carry the packages to their final destinations. The destinations served would include the airport locations and smaller communities in the vicinity. The goal was to deliver equipment and documents shipped from any location in the United States to any other location within the United States the next day.[3]

FedEx received its original name because of Smith's ambition to serve the Federal Reserve and to create a name with a broad geographic connotation. He wanted to assist the Federal Reserve in its float management efforts by selling them a delivery system that would cut down on float time (the period between receipt of a check and collection of funds). Unfortunately, Fred Smith's contract bid was turned down by the Federal Reserve.

After college, Smith served two tours of duty in Vietnam. He decided to give his air express idea a try after returning home. A study showed that Memphis, Tennessee, was near the center of business shipping in the continental United States. Its airport offered long runways, a large abandoned ramp, and a pair of inexpensive hangars from World War II, and it was closed only an average of ten hours per year due to adverse weather conditions.[4] Thus, Smith chose Memphis as a home base and started his firm with $4 million he had inherited.

FINANCING

Since $4 million was not enough for an entire fleet of planes, Smith went to New York and Chicago in search of additional funds. With his impressive knowledge of the air freight industry and his ability to impress investors, Smith raised $72 million in loans and equity investment within one year.

With fresh capital, FedEx expanded its focus from operating a charter service to its present business. It began transporting packages weighing less than 70 pounds from thirteen airports in April 1973. Volume increased rapidly, resulting in extended service. FedEx appeared to be an overnight success. The success, however, did not last long as the Organization of Petroleum Exporting Countries' inflation of fuel prices increased expenses faster than revenues were growing. By mid-1974 the company was losing more than $1 million per month.[5]

Bankruptcy became a real possibility, forcing Smith to return to his disappointed investors for more money to keep the company growing until revenues could catch up with expenses. He raised $11 million in additional funds. Having lost $27 million during its first two years, FedEx posted profits of $3.6 million in 1976 and revenues of $75 million. Profits increased annually throughout 1986 and continued strong through 1994, the time of this writing.

MANAGEMENT/PERSONNEL

Fred Smith's charisma enabled him to motivate investors and employees to share his vision for FedEx. A man of great integrity, Smith attributed his drive to scars from his military service tours. He stated that he would not have the same perspective if not for his Vietnam experiences.[6]

Despite many challenges, Smith never relinquished his entrepreneurial vision. He courted investors for more money when the Arab oil embargo resulted in skyrocketing fuel costs. He went to Washington and lobbied for airline deregulation when the Civil

Aeronautics Board (CAB) regulations made it impossible for FedEx to use the larger aircraft it needed. He jumped at the opportunity to deliver overnight letter service when the postal service relaxed its regulations against private delivery of extremely urgent mail.[7]

Smith's colleagues had the same entrepreneurial attitude toward FedEx. All were former pilots and entrepreneurs. Although most thought his idea very strange, the camaraderie and loyalty exhibited by employees of FedEx was strong from day one. This camaraderie and loyalty strengthened FedEx. By the late 1970s, however, FedEx had grown too large for the entrepreneurial approach to management used by Smith and his colleagues.

Company president Art Bass, one of the initial team members, decided to leave in 1979. He took five vice-presidents with him, all but one of whom had been with FedEx from the start. Bass and his colleagues felt that FedEx had matured, and that they lacked the ability to adapt their entrepreneurial perspectives to managing this mature operation. Smith replaced his former colleagues with managers who were comfortable with the traditional corporate organization, including several new key executives in 1990.[8]

FedEx's backbone from the beginning had been its employees. The dedication of its more than 100,000 employees to professional, faultless service has kept FedEx at the forefront of the air cargo industry.

Each employee hired is viewed as a long-term investment. Part-time employees are scheduled to permit operations to expand or contract according to traffic levels, thereby avoiding the need to furlough full-time employees.[9] In addition, by employing part-time college students who come and go as they complete their education, FedEx has created a buffer between its operations and the entrance of unions to the hub.[10] This has allowed FedEx to keep its labor costs lower than any other company in the industry.[11]

However, they have not been totally successful. The flight-crew members decided to form a collective bargaining unit. Therefore, on August 26, 1993, the company began interim negotiations with the Airline Pilot's Association (ALPA), a powerful and active organization. Negotiations toward a comprehensive collective bargaining agreement began in May 1994. Other labor organizations are also attempting to organize certain other groups of employees without success. FedEx's management is doing everything legal to prevent the introduction of organized labor.[12]

OPERATIONS

FedEx provides overnight express delivery service for high-priority packages and documents on a door-to-door basis. Services are available Monday through Saturday in 187 countries—the majority of the industrial world.[13] These services are provided through FedEx's hub-and-spoke system, an intricate ground/air network.

FedEx's central sorting facility in Memphis made its service operation unique in the field. Every package and letter handled by FedEx passes through the center in Memphis to be sorted and dispatched to its delivery destination. FedEx now has five U.S. sorting facilities, or hubs: Indianapolis, Memphis, Newark, Oakland, and Anchorage. Regional metroplexes in Chicago and Los Angeles support these five facilities as additional sites for sorting and distribution.[14] In addition, three overseas hubs operate similarly: Narita in Japan, Charles de Gaulle Airport in France, and Stansted Airport in England. A fourth in Subie Bay, Phillipines, is scheduled to open in 1995.[15]

Hub operations are fine tuned for maximum efficiency. Packages are collected in sorting facilities and offices during the day in hundreds of cities. Packages are then transported to the local airport and flown to the nearest hub. The planes are unloaded, and the packages are then sorted and loaded back onto the planes headed for their intended destinations. Couriers then transport the packages from sorting facilities at local airports to local offices, where they are routed to the receiver.

Contact with couriers is maintained through the use of digitally assisted dispatch units (DADs). Dispatch information can be left in couriers' vans, even when unoccupied.[16] FedEx also uses a computer network for dispatch entry and tracking. The satellite and telephone network, called COSMOS, uses a satellite and telephone network to locate a package as it passes through numerous electronic gates during transit. Each parcel is bar-coded for monitoring and recording each step of the journey.[17]

As of year-end 1994, FedEx operated 458 aircraft and over 31,000 delivery vehicles. Other vehicles owned by the company include ground support equipment, cargo loaders, transports, and aircraft tugs.

PRODUCT LINES[18]

On a domestic level, FedEx offers six basic services: priority overnight service (POS), standard overnight service (SOS), international priority service (IPS), economy two-day service (ES), heavyweight service (HS), and deferred heavyweight service (DHS). Products are grouped into three weight classifications: documents and light parcels, boxes, and air freight.

Documents and light parcels are items shipped primarily in FedEx packaging. Boxes are unlimited weight shipments, provided no single piece weighs more than 150 pounds. Air freight shipments have no size or weight limitations. The products offered by weight class are identified below:

Documents and light parcels—POS, SOS, and IPS

Boxes—POS, and ES

Air freight—HS, and DHS

POS guarantees delivery by 10:30 A.M. the next business morning. SOS guarantees delivery by 3:00 P.M. the next business day. IPS guarantees door-to-door delivery, including customs clearance, within 1 to 3 business days. ES guarantees delivery on the second business afternoon by 4:30 P.M. HS guarantees delivery the second business morning by 10:30 A.M. DHS guarantees delivery the second business afternoon by 4:30 P.M.

On an international level, FedEx offers three basic services: international priority service (IPS), international distribution service (IDS), and airport-to-airport service (AAS). Products are grouped into the three weight classifications identified earlier. The products offered by weight class are identified below:

Documents and light parcels—IPS

Boxes—IPS, IDS, and AAS

Air freight—IDS, and AAS

IPS guarantees door-to-door delivery, including customs clearance, within 1 to 3 business days. IDS guarantees 1 to 3 day airport-to-airport service, excluding customs clearance. AAS is a committed or space-available, international, airport-to-airport service, and delivery is guaranteed within 2 to 4 days excluding customs clearance.

MARKETING/ADVERTISING

FedEx was an innovator. Having founded the small-package/document express market, FedEx hoped to dominate it. Fred Smith stated that FedEx was selling time, thereby allowing people to be more effective in their day-to-day activities.[19] Smith went all out to get the message across. Initial emphasis was on building the public's trust by convincing customers that FedEx would do what it claimed to do—"get it there overnight." Price was and is seen as a distant factor, becoming important to customers after they are assured that the package will be delivered on time.

In 1994 FedEx made the most drastic change in its image yet. It decided to update its identity in an effort to set it apart from its competition. By adopting the ubiquitous "FedEx" in lieu of the previous "Federal Express," it established itself as responsive and global. The intent of the new, user-friendly logo is to increase the likelihood that the worldwide customer will think of FedEx first for express delivery. Furthermore, dropping the "Federal" eliminates the mistaken assumption of a government connection.

ACQUISITIONS

In 1987, FedEx purchased the assets of the Island Courier Companies and acquired Cansica, Inc. In 1989, the company acquired Tiger International for $895,000,000, a major strategic acquisition. In 1989, it also acquired East-West Couriers, Ltd., Yuill Courier Services, Ltd., and Bluejay Courier Services in Canada; Winchmore Developments, Ltd., and Home Delivery Services, Ltd., in the United Kingdom; Transport Group Alvarcht in Holland; Elbe-Klaus in Germany; Saimex in Italy; Rainer's in Australia; the Daisei Companies in Japan; and the Binghalib Express in the United Arab Emirates. In 1990, the company acquired Transports Transvendeens Chronoservice in France and Aeroenvios in Mexico.[20]

COMPETITION

In 1994, FedEx's major competitors were United Parcel Service, the United States Postal Service, and Emery Air Freight Corporation.

United Parcel Service provides transportation services, primarily through the delivery of small packages. The company is the giant in package delivery and occupies a strong position in the transportation industry. Only the Postal Service can rival its package volume. Service is offered throughout the United States, Western Europe, and Canada. Service is also provided to many locations in the Soviet Union, Eastern Europe, Asia, the Middle East, Africa, and Central and South America.

UPS has long enjoyed a reputation of dependability, productivity, and efficiency. As of late 1989, the company owned and operated a fleet of more than 112,000 vehicles, utilized 347 aircraft (101 owned and the remainder leased), and employed a work force of over 230,000.[21] The company entered the overnight package delivery market late in 1982 with their rate substantially lower than those charged by FedEx.[22] Reported revenue was $12.3 billion in 1989, $11.0 billion in 1988, and $9.7 billion in 1987. Net income was $693 million in 1989, $759 million in 1988, and $784 million in 1987.[23]

The U.S. Postal Service competes in the overnight package delivery business with its Express Mail next-day service, which guarantees delivery to the addressee the following day by 3:00 P.M. The addressee, at his or her option, can pick up the package as early as 10:00 A.M. on the delivery day. Customers can obtain full refunds for shipments not arriving on time. Postal Service statistics show that 95 percent of all shipments do arrive on time.[24] Regularly scheduled package pickup is also available for a flat charge, regardless of the number of packages.

The U.S. Postal Service employed over 760,000 people as of late 1988.[25] Service areas include most major metropolitan areas in the United States, with international service to major cities in the United Kingdom, Australia, Brazil, Japan, Belgium, France, Hong Kong, and the Netherlands.[26] Reported revenue was $35.6 billion in 1988 and $32.2 billion in 1987. Net losses of $597.0 million and $22.7 million were reported in 1988 and 1987, respectively.[27]

Emery is also a major competitor in the domestic and international markets. The company provides worldwide air courier/air cargo service through an integrated courier/cargo system. Overnight door-to-door delivery service for packages of any size and weight, and 24- to 72-hour door-to-door service to cities throughout the world are provided. Emery's overnight delivery services include Same Day (A.M. or P.M.), Day 2, and the Emery Urgent Letter.[28] Emery also has several subsidiaries engaged in closely related activities.

During the 1980s, the company made major capital investments in state-of-the-art technology, as well as expanded and modernized existing facilities and aircraft for purposes of fostering future business growth. Emery also purchased Purolator Courier Corporation in 1987.[29]

FINANCIAL

FedEx was not an immediate financial success. It took four years, $70 million in venture capital, and several perches on the edge of bankruptcy before the company reported its first profitable period in late 1975. The initial offering in 1974–1975 raised only $32 million, and new capital for 1975 was $10 million. The company constantly asked banks, other corporations, and venture capitalists for additional loans and equity participation arrangements. The company survived because a dozen or more equity groups participated in three rounds of critical financing. During this difficult period Smith gave up virtually all his equity in FedEx, but earned true loyalty from his employees for his determination and steadfast belief in the company. (Smith recaptured a substantial portion of his equity in later refinancings.)

Exhibit 1 contains selected financial information about FedEx and its operations. In addition to the financial and operating data, FedEx's commitment to geographic growth and expansion of service is evidenced by its capital outlay expenditures. Average expenditure was $1.1 billion per year. The bulk of these outlays were for aircraft and to expand and improve sorting facilities. These expenditures have been necessitated by volume growth and the company's efforts to reduce costs through the continued automation of package handling and routing systems. FedEx expects significant capital expenditures to continue into the future.[30]

In 1994, international operations contributed 27 percent of the company's revenue, a $153 million year-over-year improvement. That follows the previous $177 million improvement in 1993. The growing international contribution is attributed to the 1992 restructuring. This reduced the scope of European operations to match demand. Furthermore, the intercontinental aircraft fleet was modernized to the highly efficient MD-

EXHIBIT 1 **Selected Consolidated Financial Data**

Years ended May 31 In thousands, except per share data and Other Operating Data	1994	1993	1992
Operating Results			
Revenues	$8,479,456	$7,808,043	$7,550,060
Operating income	530,632	377,173	22,967
Income (loss) before income taxes	378,462	203,576	(146,828)
Income (loss) from continuing operations	204,370	109,809	(113,782)
Net income (loss)	$ 204,370	$ 53,866	$(113,782)
Per Share Data			
Earnings (loss) per share:			
Continuing operations	$ 3.65	$ 2.01	$ (2.11)
Discontinued operations	—	—	—
Cumulative effects of changes in accounting principles	—	(1.03)	—
Net earnings (loss) per share	$ 3.65	$ .98	$ (2.11)
Average shares outstanding	56,012	54,719	53,961
Cash dividends	—	—	—
Financial Position			
Property and equipment, net	$3,449,093	$3,476,268	$3,411,297
Total assets	5,992,498	5,793,064	5,463,186
Long-term debt	1,632,202	1,882,279	1,797,844
Common stockholders' investment	1,924,705	1,671,381	1,579,722
Other Operating Data			
Express package:			
Average daily package volume	1,925,105	1,710,561	1,472,642
Average pounds per package	6.0	5.8	5.7
Average revenue per pound	$ 2.48	$ 2.60	$ 2.87
Average revenue per package	$ 14.95	$ 15.17	$ 16.25
Airfreight:			
Average daily pounds	1,844,270	2,050,033	2,258,303
Average revenue per pound	$ 1.06	$ 1.09	$ 1.22
Operating weekdays	257	255	254
Aircraft fleet:			
Airbus A300-600	2	—	—
Boeing 747-100	—	—	4
Boeing 747-200	6	8	9
McDonnell Douglas MD-11	13	8	4
McDonnell Douglas DC-10-10	11	11	11
McDonnell Douglas DC-10-30	19	19	17
McDonnell Douglas DC-8	—	—	—
Boeing 727-100	69	80	85
Boeing 727-200	90	87	66
Cessna 208A	10	10	10
Cessna 208B	206	206	206
Fokker F-27	32	32	32
Vehicle fleet	30,900	28,100	30,400
Average number of employees (based on a standard full-time workweek)	88,502	84,104	84,162

11 and DC-10 aircraft. Express freight and express packages now account for two-thirds of the $2.3 billion international revenue, up from one-half in 1992.

The domestic market has shown a similar volume improvement. However, since 1991, the average revenue received for each package shipped has been declining. Low-yield, higher-discount, and general market trends were the main causes of the decline. The bright side is that service is now affordable to more people, which contributes to the increased volume. FedEx is concentrating efforts to reduce the average per-package cost by one-third in six years. State-of-the-art technology and more fuel-efficient aircraft should provide the savings. Fuel cost as a percentage of total operating expenses has dropped from a high of 7.5 percent in 1991 to a low of 4.7 percent in 1994.

HUMAN RESOURCE POLICIES AND PROGRAMS

FedEx management believes that the company's most important component is the human one: employees whose commitment and dedication to the company results in continuing prosperity.[31] The company is equally committed to its employees. Over the past decade, the company has routinely been cited for its no-layoff policy, minority recruitment efforts, and guaranteed fair treatment practice (GFTP). It has frequently been referred to as having a premier human resources program. It won the 1987 Strategic Human Resource Management Award for Excellence, had a manager selected as a Fellow of the National Academy of Human Resource (NAHR), won a Personnel Journal Optima Award, is treated as a benchmark by other companies (the truest measure of success, being recognized by its peers), and won the 1990 Malcolm Baldrige National Quality Award.

Human resource practices at FedEx epitomize the popular views. The corporate philosophy is "People-Service-Profit," it has executive and upper management support, its PRISM Human Resource Information System (HRIS) makes the best use of technology, the Survey-Feedback-Action (SFA) system and GFTP generate empowered employees, and the company makes good use of Total Quality Management (TQM) practices. Other examples exist in the areas of communications, training, recruiting/retention, and recognition/incentives.

EXECUTIVE SUPPORT

The emphasis on human resources begins at the top. Corporate philosophy of People-Service-Profit places people first by no accident. The company has remained virtually non-union since its inception in 1973. Fred Smith, CEO, spends 25 percent of his time on personnel issues—nearly five times that of the average CEO.[32] Fred Smith implements his philosophy by having programs that answer three basic questions. First, "What is expected of me, and what do you want me to do?" This is answered by extensive orientation programs that pervade an employee's career. Second is "What's in it for me?" This is addressed by the promotion from within policy, the career progression policy, and incentives such as tuition reimbursement. The third question is "Where do I go to resolve a problem?" This is answered in the open door and guaranteed fair treatment practices. All encompassing is the personal philosophy of Fred Smith that training is one of the most important events at the company to meet the goal of 100 percent customer satisfaction.[33]

Independent organizations likewise have recognized the support by senior management. James A. Perkins, Senior Vice-President and Chief Personnel Officer, has been awarded the highest honor of the human resource profession. He was selected as a Fellow of the NAHR for the individual who has led the development of the human resource profession. Previous recognition occurred in 1987 with his receipt of the Strategic Human Resource Management Award for Excellence.[34] Other awards include Stephen Rutherford's, Human Resource Analysis Manager, and receipt of the First Annual Human Resource Award of Excellence sponsored by the Olsten Staffing Services and the American Management Association in 1993. He is responsible for FedEx's SFA program. FedEx also won the Second Annual Personnel Journal Optima Award in 1992. It was one of ten companies recognized as having a human resource department that participates in corporate decision making, has human resource policies and strategies that are integrated so that a decision in one area considers the others, has human resource programs that are consistent with overall business goals, and is cost effective. In particular, FedEx was singled out from the other nine winners because of its commitment to training.[35] All these people, and other senior managers, routinely participate in interactive discussion and question-and-answer programs.[36]

TECHNOLOGY

To help administer the human resource programs, FedEx uses its PRISM HRIS.[37] This is virtually a paperless system that affects all areas of the company. It maintains a job applicant database and processes new hires. When someone is hired, PRISM automatically creates an employee record and transfers it to the employee database after adding all applicable information. The employee database is updated by employees who are empowered and expected to maintain their own personal data. Typically, 25,000 such transactions occur daily. PRISM also supports job posting and bidding. Any interested employee can apply on-line for a position anywhere in the company's worldwide net. It provides the necessary data to hiring managers so that they can select those to interview. It then automatically updates the organizational chart when staff changes occur. Routinely, 1,700 positions are posted and 7,000 applications are processed each month. Job training and testing, one of the CEO's three most important events, is coordinated through PRISM. It controls all aspects of enrollment, training, and testing on 1,200 personal computers and 25,000 on-line terminals. More than 4,000 different courses are available with 5,000 job knowledge tests administered and scored monthly. The results are often available the next day. The Managing-By-Objective (MBO) point system and reward program is tracked by PRISM. Here, employees can monitor their individual progress at any time. The system automatically forwards information to the payroll department so that bonus checks can be cut. PRISM has vastly improved FedEx's compliance with equal employment and affirmative action programs. It tracks employment data and provides a daily report comparing minority- or gender-based availability versus employment level by each group.

Another widely used tool is FedEx's Survey-Feedback-Action (SFA) program. This is the foundation for many of the human resource initiatives as well as other initiatives (for example, safety). It is often used as a benchmark by other companies and has been cited as the key human resource system strength by the Baldrige Award examiners when FedEx won in 1990. The SFA complements the GFTP and other communication tools. It is an annual survey of employee attitude toward both specific departments and the company in general. Management never sees the individual responses, which are anonymous. The applicable area manager is required to meet and discuss employee concerns within six weeks after group results have been tallied—a process requiring about a month.[38] The manager must then develop and implement corrective action if his or her department was identified as having problems.[39] Another indicator of employee importance is the drive to minimize safety risks. Through feedback received by front-line employees via the SFA, safety improvement teams are replacing safety managers.[40]

TOTAL QUALITY MANAGEMENT

The Baldrige Award confirms incorporation of many TQM principles in FedEx's human resource policies. Employee action teams permeate FedEx. They have improved the safety results,[41] saved $3.5 million in one year through reduced training time,[42] and eased implementation of the new on-line system for SFA. Quality Action teams are likewise used to reach the goal of 100 percent customer satisfaction—4,000 such teams are used at FedEx.[43] Everyone attends two programs: "Quality Advantage," which covers the basics of quality management, and "Quality Action Teams," where team development is learned. Through these programs, employees are empowered and learn that they can make a difference. Company policy allows all 92,000 employees to do whatever is necessary to ensure customer satisfaction, a fairly broad statement. Employees are allowed to take appropriate risks and are not penalized for occasional errors.[44] Well-intentioned efforts are considered as important as successes. Furthermore, the SFA is an excellent example of continuous improvement.

COMMUNICATIONS

Timely communication, another tool to empower employees, is used to keep everyone informed, boost morale, and make employees feel important. Three examples are FedEx Television (FXTV), the internal television network; the Open Door policy, an internal employee response program; and the GFTP, a practice similar to formal grievance procedures in union plants. FXTV reaches people in the United States, Canada, and overseas. The program "FedEx Overnight" is a daily broadcast of nightly progress. It allows daytime employees to get a recap of operations worldwide so that they can prevent errors and respond to customer problems either before or as they occur.[45] The network is also used as an interactive call-in program.[46] It allows key managers to respond immediately to questions and concerns. The open door policy is an extension of this program. It allows employees to find answers to situations they regard as disagreeable, controversial, or contrary to existing policy. No time limit is placed on the employee; however, management must respond to concerns within 14 days. To keep the program robust, the CEO receives a print-out of every concern submitted and how and when it was answered. The more formal GFTP is available automatically whenever an employee is disciplined and gives the employee the right to have any eligible issue go through a systematic review by progressively higher levels of management without fear of retribution.[47] Three basic steps are used. First, a management review is conducted. A written complaint is submitted within seven days of the questionable occurrence. A response is required within ten days of receipt of the complaint. If the employee is still dissatisfied, the complaint is forwarded within seven days to the Officer Review, where a vice-president or senior vice-president can uphold, modify, or overturn any previous decision. If the employee is still dissatisfied, the complaint can go to the Executive Review, where an appeals board makes a final determination within fourteen days. As with most of these processes, the time requirements can be relaxed if agreed upon by both parties. FedEx's policy is to answer these complaints as soon as possible so that problems do not fester.[48]

TRAINING

Training is obviously important to any company that implements 1,500 changes in any year.[49] FedEx has 650 full-time trainers in quality alone. The tie between human resource and corporate goals is best expressed by Larry W. McMahan, Vice-President of Human Resource:

> Because we expect our employees to keep up with a lot of changes, we have to equip them with enough tools to give them a good running chance at satisfying customers. Therefore, we can't support a customer-oriented objective without having a strong emphasis on training.[50]

For FedEx, training is a continuous process. Every six months, employees are required to pass a job knowledge test. In 1986, an interactive video training system was incorporated, allowing employees to work at their own pace, repeat necessary sections, and take advantage of slack periods to train themselves. Anyone failing a test is removed from customer-related duties until able to pass the test. Job training is not the only program available. FedEx offers the Leadership Evaluation and Awareness Program (LEAP) that qualifies non-management employees for management positions; the Management Applied Personnel Skills (MAPS) program, a three-day in-depth program of background information and practical application of personnel and legal issues normally encountered in the workplace; and the Leadership Institute, a full week of required management training for all new managers covering quality management, leadership concepts, and company philosophy.

RETENTION

Good employee relations, following good recruiting, translate into good retention.[51] FedEx has the benefit of a turnover rate of less than 1 percent. They accomplish this with 25 centers nationwide using a peer recruiter program. In this way recruits receive a more realistic idea of what is expected of them and what their potential positions entail. Retention is also aided by FedEx's excellent use and support of its part-time employees, who represent 23 to 35 percent of the workforce. And although not required, they receive full medical coverage, a guaranteed work week, and wage parity. Furthermore, they are given credit toward seniority for local full-time positions—a change adopted because of the SFA process. Previously, more senior full-time employees from outside the local area were cutting off local part-time employees' opportunities to advance.

Incentives and recognition, in addition to career advancement, provide another means of retaining employees. Nearly 85 percent of the employees at FedEx participate in some type of incentive program. Key executives can earn up to 40 percent of their salary in performance-based bonuses.[52] Awards programs reinforce desired behavior such as quality work and customer focus. Acknowledging effort is essential for a motivated and satisfied workforce. It stimulates new ideas and encourages better performance and team spirit.[53] FedEx has a wide range of incentive and recognition programs. The Bravo Zulu (BZ) Voucher Program recognizes individual performance that surpasses normal job responsibilities. It is based on the U.S. Navy code flags "B-Z," which decode into "Well done." Awards range from nonfinancial BZ letters of recognition to cash or noncash awards presented by management. The Suggestion Awards Program encourages employees to submit ideas to improve company performance. These are usually in the areas of lowering cost, increasing productivity, increasing revenues, or promoting safer working conditions. Awards range from $100 to $25,000 for ideas that are implemented. The Golden Falcon Award is for any full-time employee who has demonstrated service to the customer that goes above and beyond the call of duty. It is based on unsolicited internal as well as external letters citing outstanding performance. Winners are announced monthly through company publications and video programs, with winners receiving an award and shares of stock. The ultimate Five-Star Award is for individuals who materially helped the company enhance service, profitability, and teamwork. These awards demonstrate the empowerment, senior management support, and company philosophies. Similarly, performance evaluations routinely include peer evaluations. Evaluations use internal and external customers and suppliers and cover such areas as quality of work and customer service dimensions.[54]

CHALLENGES

Even though FedEx has enjoyed the position of having good employee relations, it still has some challenges. Some issues that face FedEx are how to respond to the encroachment of organized labor and determining the impacts that an emphasis on improved productivity will have. FedEx's human relations programs have kept the desire and need for union representation low. Now that the ALPA is a part of the picture, will it affect other employees? Even though volume is up, per-package revenue is still declining. The need to increase productivity without increasing pay is known as a "Speed-up" in industry. How will this affect employee relations? Also, UPS has enhanced the pay of its employees. How will this affect the competitive position of FedEx? Finally, some believe that the electronic revolution will make FedEx's services obsolete (except for package delivery). Meeting this new "threat" is believed by some analysts to be FedEx's biggest challenge.

NOTES

1. Standard & Poors *Industry Surveys,* December 6, 1984, p. A 36.

2. Geoffrey Colvin, "Federal Express Dives into Air Mail," *Fortune,* June 15, 1981, pp. 106–108.

3. Henry Altman, "A Business Visionary Who Really Delivered," *Nation's Business,* November, 1981, p. 50.

4. Geoffrey Colvin, "Federal Express Dives," p. 107.

5. Altman, "Business," p. 54.

6. "Creativity with Bill Moyers: Fred Smith and the Federal Express," *PBS Video,* 1981.

7. "The Memphis Connection," *Marketing and Media Decisions,* May 1982, p. 62.

8. *Federal Express 1994 Annual Report,* pp. 20, 21.

9. *Federal Express 1982 Annual Report,* p. 14.

10. Colvin, "Federal Express Dives," p. 107.

11. Ibid, p. 108.

12. *Federal Express 1994 Form 10-K,* Securities and Exchange Commission, p. 8.

13. *Federal Express 1994 Annual Report,* p. 6.

14. Ibid., p. 6.

15. *Federal Express 1994 Form 10-K,* Securities and Exchange Commission, p. 8.

16. Colvin, "Federal Express Dives," pp. 6, 7.

17. Ibid, p. 9.

18. Information in this section contained in the *Federal Express 1994 Annual Report,* pp. 17, 18.

19. Sean Milmo, "British Air Couriers Welcome U.S. Entrant," *Business Marketing,* April 1984, p. 9.

20. Moody's *Transportation Manual,* 1990, p. 1173.

21. Ibid., 1990, pp. 1216, 1217.

22. "Behind the UPS Mystique: Puritanism and Productivity," *Business Week,* June 6, 1983, p. 66.

23. Moody's *Transportation Manual,* 1990, pp. 1216, 1217.

24. "Express Mail Next Day Service," *U.S. Postal Service Pamphlet Notice #43,* July 1977, p. 2.

25. Moody's *Municipal & Government Manual,* 1990, p. 41.

26. "Express Mail Next Day Service," *U.S. Postal Service Pamphlet Notice #43,* July 1977, p. 6.

27. Moody's *Municipal & Government Manual,* 1990, p. 41.

28. *Emery Air Freight 1983 Annual Report,* Introduction.

29. *Moody's Transportation Manual,* 1990, p. 1171.

30. *Federal Express 1994 Annual Report,* p. 27.

31. *Federal Express Annual Report,* 1994, p. 24.

32. D. Keith Denton, "Keeping Employees: The Federal Express Approach," *Advanced Management Journal,* 3(3), Summer 1992, pp. 10–13.

33. "1992 Optimas Awards," *Personnel Journal* 71(1), January 1992, pp. 51–61.

34. "National Academy of Human Resources Installs 1992 Class," *HRMagazine* 38(1), January 1993, pp. 52–53.

35. "1992 Optimas Awards."

36. Stephen Stapleton, "Reducing Customer Irritation," *Across the Board* 30(9), November/December 1993, p. 48.

37. Prashant Palvia, Sherry Sullivan, and Steven Zeltman, "PRISM Profile: An Employee-Oriented System," *HR Focus* 70(6), June 1993, p. 19.

38. Bob Smith, "Award Honors Excellence in Human Resources." *HR Focus* 70(7), July 1993, p. 9.

39. Denton, "Keeping Employees: The Federal Express Approach."

40. Rosa Lindahl and Stacey Leary, "A Joint Effort Strengthens Safety Policies," *HR Focus* 69(10), October 1992, p. 13.

41. Ibid.

42. "1992 Optimas Awards."

43. Richard Blackburn and Benson Rosen, "Total Quality and Human Resources Management: Lessons Learned from Baldrige Award-Winning Companies," *Executive* 7(3), August 1993, pp. 49–66.

44. Stapleton, "Reducing Customer Irritation."

45. Ibid.

46. Blackburn and Rosen, "Total Quality and Human Resources Management: Lessons Learned from Baldrige Award-Winning Companies."

47. Denton, "Keeping Employees: The Federal Express Approach."

48. Ibid.

49. "1992 Optimas Awards."

50. Ibid.

51. Denton, "Keeping Employees: The Federal Express Approach."

52. Blackburn and Rosen, "Total Quality and Human Resources Management: Lessons Learned from Baldrige Award-Winning Companies."

53. Denton, "Keeping Employees: The Federal Express Approach."

54. Blackburn and Rosen, "Total Quality and Human Resources Management: Lessons Learned from Baldrige Award-Winning Companies."

CASE 2

DELTA AIR LINES, INC.

Delta Air Lines is a certified trunk air carrier providing scheduled air transportation for passengers, freight, and mail over a network of routes throughout the United States and abroad.[1] These routes connect the Northeast and Midwest with the southern states; the Southeast to the Midwest, West, Northwest, and California; and the East Coast to Florida.[2] The company also operates flights to Canada, Bermuda, the Bahamas, France, Ireland, Japan, South Korea, Mexico, Taiwan, Puerto Rico, England, the Netherlands, Thailand, and Germany.[3] As of June 30, 1993, the company provided air transportation to 161 domestic cities in 44 states, Washington, D.C., Puerto Rico and the U.S Virgin Islands, and 55 cities in 33 foreign countries.[4]

In these challenging times for the airline industry, Delta's strategic plan places a high priority on steady and cost effective growth.[5] This strategy is designed to maintain Delta's financial strength and flexibility, while keeping service to its passengers as its number one objective.[6] The following is an overview of Delta Air Lines from a strategic human resource perspective, since the key to Delta's success is the dedication of its more than 60,000 employees. These employees are committed to the highest standards of excellence in every area of Delta's operations.

HISTORY[7]

Delta Air Lines is one of the most successful air carriers in the United States. Before 1991, with the exception of 1983, the company had not lost money since 1947. The company was originally founded as a crop-dusting service in 1924. This start resulted from a conversation between Collet Everman Woolman, an associate, and some Louisiana farmers concerned about the threat to their crops from boll weevils.

Woolman, an agricultural scientist and pilot, knew that calcium arsenate would kill boll weevils. The problem he faced was devising a way to apply the chemical effectively to crops. Woolman wanted to drop the chemical from an airplane and engineered a "hooper" for the chemical. After perfecting the system he began selling his services to farmers throughout the region, thus forming the world's first crop-dusting service.

Woolman left the agricultural extension service in 1925 to take charge of the duster's entomological work. The crop-dusting operation was separated from its parent company in 1928 to form a new company named Delta Air Service. Woolman expanded his crop-dusting business into Mexico, South America, and throughout the South. The

NOTE: This case was prepared by Mark Dawkins and revised by Patricia Duffy, Daniel Griffin, Kris Inchcombe, and Patty Pinholster.

company also diversified by securing airmail contracts. Passenger service was inaugurated in 1929, with initial service to Jackson, Dallas, Atlanta, and Charleston.

Delta Air Service began its climb to prominence when it received a U.S. government airmail contract in 1930. The company, now called Delta Air Corporation, received three more airmail contracts in 1941. During World War II, the company, under contract to the War Department, devoted itself to the allied war effort by transporting troops and supplies. Delta returned to civilian service in 1945, entering an age of growth and competition never seen before in the airline industry.

Delta prospered as a major regional trunk carrier through the 1950s and 1960s. Several mergers were consummated during these two decades. On May 1, 1953, Delta merged with Chicago and Southern Airlines. In June of 1967, Delta merged with Delaware Airlines and officially adopted the name of Delta Air Lines.

Delta's exposure to the Northeast increased with the acquisition of Northeast Airlines on August 1, 1972. Delta also purchased Storer Leasing in July of 1976, a move that added several jets to the existing fleet of about 200. Delta formed two computerized marketing subsidiaries in the early 1980s to coordinate and sell more passenger seats on all Delta flights. These subsidiaries are named Epsilon Trading Corporation and Datas Incorporated. In March 1988, Delta acquired 20 percent of the voting securities of SkyWest Incorporated. In 1991, Delta completed its asset acquisitions under the Asset Purchase Agreement dated July 27, 1991, with Pan Am Corporation and certain subsidiaries of Pan Am. This was done to expand Delta's international operations, which were already inferior to those of many other airlines.[8]

Delta's consistent growth can be partially attributed to its successful transition of leadership. In the early days of commercial air transport, airlines were run by individual men who would be better described as aviation pioneers first and businessmen second. For example, Woolman led Delta until his death in 1966, a period covering 40 years. His influence at Delta is similar to the influence of his counterparts at Delta's three major competitors: Eddie Rickenbacker at Eastern, Juan Trippe at Pan Am, and Howard Hughes at TWA.

At Eastern, Pan Am, TWA, and Delta, these pioneers established almost dictatorial operations. They retained their posts as long as they possibly could. Many of these men were majority stockholders who refused to share their power or prepare a successor to operate the company after they died. As a result, many airline companies faced a difficult period of adjustment to new management after the chairman died.

Woolman's departure at Delta was not surrounded by difficulties. After suffering a heart attack, he was forced to relinquish some of his duties to other Delta board members. The board members gradually assumed more of his duties as his health deteriorated. Woolman died at the age of 76, and the airline was able to make a smooth transition to a more modern, corporate style of collective management.

Delta has adhered to the principles of its founder, C. E. Woolman, by placing a high value on people, both its customers and its personnel. Woolman used to ride on flights and mingle with passengers in an effort to gauge the public opinion concerning his airline. He was once quoted as saying, "We have a responsibility over and above the price of a ticket, let's put ourselves on the other side of the counter."

MANAGEMENT

Delta is recognized for having one of the best planning and management teams in the airline industry. Specifically, Delta's management is agile and responsive to problems that arise. Delta's sound financial policy allows greater flexibility in decision making, even at the highest levels. Also, its consensus-style of management affords Delta cohesiveness and enduring stability.

Delta's productivity in the "trunk," or domestic, airline business is the highest among major carriers. The company's employees are nonunionized, with the exception of pilots and dispatchers. The machinist union, for example, reports that it is difficult to organize Delta employees because the company maintains pay and benefits above its unionized competition. Clearly, workers have little incentive to unionize as long as the company outperforms union contracts.

Overall, management–employee relations are generally on very good terms. In the absence of union rules and constraints, employees regularly move to other positions in order to fill temporary labor shortages. The employees' willingness to adjust to the needs of the company gives Delta the unique ability to weather hardships in the airline industry and is a major reason that the company remains competitive.

The company's willingness to adjust to the needs of the employees has also not gone unnoticed. Delta is known for treating all its employees as "family" and has gone a long way to avoid layoffs. For example, the airline refused to release workers during the 1973 oil crisis and the 1981 PATCO strike. Company profitability suffered as a result. However, employee commitment and loyalty is high as a result of Delta's willingness to support its workforce in difficult times.

Delta Air Lines has long been considered an industry leader in terms of employee morale, customer service, and profitability. However, operating losses for fiscal years 1991, 1992, and 1993 have put a major strain on Delta's management–employee relations.[9] For the first time in 35 years, Delta is furloughing pilots and planning on eliminating 15,000 jobs (20 percent of its workforce) by 1997. Delta is struggling to maintain its amiable relationship with its employees by emphasizing attrition and early retirement incentives.[10] The airline is also eliminating seven vice-president and six assistant vice-president positions.[11] Delta's plan has been labeled as one of the most aggressive and sweeping restructuring plans in the embattled airline industry.[12]

OPERATIONS

Delta was the first airline to employ the "hub-and-spoke" system. Under this system, a number of flights are scheduled to land at a hub airport within a 30-minute timespan. Passengers can then make connections for final destinations conveniently and quickly, thus avoiding long layovers. This process is known as the "big push" and is regarded by management as an effective marketing tool. The process, however, is not immune to problems caused by inclement weather or maintenance delays. Delta has hub operations in Atlanta, Dallas/Fort Worth, Boston, Memphis, and Cincinnati.

Delta's jetliner fleet is among the most modern fleets in domestic service. The company's policy is not to purchase new models until they have been proven, often in a costly way, at other airlines. This "wait-and-see" policy has saved the company large amounts of money. It is typical of Delta that a 20-year strategy for flight equipment and support facility planning is used. Former vice-chairman and chief financial officer Robert Oppenlander once said that "success is based on the long-term maintenance of a technical edge, which is cost efficiency."

In 1990, Delta invested $1.42 billion in flight equipment, $265 million in ground property and equipment, $267 million to acquire equity interests in two international carriers, and $48 million to purchase an additional interest in a new computer reserva-

8888888888

tion system partnership called WORLDSPAN.[13] This partnership (with Northwest Airlines and TWA) offers computerized reservations system (CRS) services to travel agents around the world, and it has begun to form links with other international CRS organizations.

Delta Air Lines announced a consolidation of its reservations offices that resulted in closures of eight of the airline's 19 U.S. reservations facilities. Company reservations centers in Detroit, Houston, Jacksonville, Knoxville, Memphis, New Orleans, San Francisco, and Seattle were to be closed between June 1993 and fall 1994. The reservations office closures represent part of the company's ongoing comprehensive program to return to sustained profitability. This consolidation was in an effort to improve customer service through the implementation of improved telecommunications technology in larger full-service offices while cutting operating costs significantly. The approximately 1,500 permanent personnel affected by this action were guaranteed positions in other Delta reservations centers and relocated at company expense.[14] The company also purchased 23 acres of land adjacent to its general office complex for future growth. Construction of a hangar in which three airplanes at a time can be stripped and painted within a controlled environment began at the Technical Operations Center in Atlanta during 1990.[15] Other construction projects at this site include a wide-body hangar bay, a ground support equipment maintenance building, and expansion and renovation of certain shops and support facilities.

INDUSTRY EXPANSION

Delta has taken on a more aggressive corporate personality in recent years. The company's commitment to internal growth has been threatened by the general trend in the industry toward external growth. As a result, Delta is becoming relatively smaller as companies such as TWA, Texas Air, and Northwest expand through mergers.

Mergers and acquisitions are not foreign to Delta, however. David Garrett, Delta's retired chairman of the board and chief executive officer, once explained that "for a merger to be worthwhile, two plus two has to equal seven." A case in point is the 1986 purchase of Western Air Lines, another air carrier based in Los Angeles, for $680 million. This purchase added Western's hubs in Los Angeles and Salt Lake City to Delta's existing network.

On November 1, 1991, Delta Air Lines completed its asset acquisitions under the Asset Purchase Agreement with Pan Am Corporation and certain subsidiaries of Pan Am. The assets acquired include, among other things, several route authorities between the United States and Frankfurt and Europe, Asia, and Africa; certain take-off and landing authorizations and slots; equity interests in three used A310-200 aircraft as well as certain aircraft spare engines and spare parts, and leasehold interests in certain airport facilities. Delta's purchase of Pan Am was $416,000,000, subject to certain adjustments.[16] For the next two years, Delta would incur its first and second net loss in nearly 50 years. According to Helane Becker, an analyst at Lehman Brothers, "60 percent of Delta's losses could be attributed to the carrier's international routes."[17] The airline, which had virtually no visibility in Europe before acquiring Pan Am routes, has struggled to make an identity for itself among the well-known and highly competitive international airlines. Trying to combat this problem, Delta has begun making arrangements with European carriers, such as Virgin Atlantic Airways. This agreement would give Delta access to London's Heathrow Airport and increase Delta's market share of British travellers.[18] Delta has also begun to advertise more aggressively and structure the agent compensation for all basic international bookings to a flat 10 percent.[19] Three years after storming into the trans-Atlantic market, Delta is finally heading toward success. In the first quarter of 1994, Delta announced that its traffic across the North Atlantic was up 13 percent with operating revenues up 9 percent and costs per seat-mile down 3 percent.[20] Delta has corrected many of its problems, but one central problem remains: the vicious competition that exists in trans-Atlantic bookings.

MARKETING

Delta continued to implement aggressive marketing programs in 1990. The company's major initiatives included strengthening its route system, solidifying its relationship with Swissair, Aeromexico, and Singapore Airlines via a cross-purchase arrangement, and enhancing its position in the computer reservations system market via WORLDSPAN.[21]

Cooperative marketing programs planned with Swissair, Aeromexico, and Singapore Airlines include code sharing, schedule coordination, possible joint services on certain routes, around-the-world-fares, joint advertising and promotional activities, and Frequent Flyer programs.[22] Delta's Frequent Flyer program currently has more than 6.8 million members.[23]

Advertising and promotional programs for the year supported Delta's marketing efforts for business and leisure travel, military and government travel, and package tours. Delta's Fantastic Flyer program for children, a natural tie-in with the company's official airline relationships with Walt Disney World in Florida and Disneyland in California, continues to be successful.[24] Other continuing official airline relationships include those with the Atlanta Braves, the Los Angeles Dodgers, The Professional Golf Association of America (PGA) and the PGA Tour, the Kentucky Derby, the Breeders Cup, the Portland Rose Festival, and the Tournament of Roses.[25]

Delta's cargo marketing efforts resulted in its being the second largest passenger/cargo combination carrier in terms of U.S. domestic mail ton miles (a measure of cargo volume).[26] Delta also led U.S. airlines in market share for both domestic and overseas military traffic.[27]

To continue efforts of improving its financial performance, Delta reallocated aircraft on 58 domestic flight segments in 1993. The aircraft were redeployed to markets that provided greater revenue potential, including the Atlanta, Cincinnati, and Dallas/Fort Worth hubs. In addition, Delta added 37 daily flights and five new destinations from Atlanta. On June 30, 1993, Delta's Atlanta hub had 518 daily departures to 113 destinations, constituting the largest hub operation in the world. The Cincinnati hub has expanded to include five additional daily departures and three new destinations. The Delta Connection partners—Atlantic Southeast Airlines (ASA), Business Express, Comair, and SkyWest—have continued to expand, and Delta announced that ASA and SkyWest would replace the company's service in particular short-haul markets from Dallas/Fort Worth and Salt Lake City. This enables the affected markets to be accommodated more efficiently by ASA's and SkyWest's smaller aircraft and, consequently, permits Delta to reallocate aircraft to long-haul routes with better revenue potential.

Delta's international capacity has grown 33 percent during fiscal year 1993, compared with the 1992 figures. This is in large part due to an entire year's operation of the route authorities acquired from Pan Am on November 1, 1991, and the new international markets added during the year.

Delta's international efforts during 1993 included strengthening its trans-Atlantic operation by increasing service to its Frankfurt hub and other European destinations, introducing seasonal services, discounting service on some unprofitable routes, and implementing code-sharing agreements with international airlines. The company increased services from San Francisco to Frankfurt, and from Cincinnati to Munich in 1993. Additionally, Delta began seasonal service from New York-Kennedy to Athens, Greece, and Atlanta to Nice, France.

During fiscal year 1993, Delta also cancelled service from Orlando to Paris, from New York-Kennedy to Hamburg, and from Newark to Frankfurt. On June 1, 1993, under a code-sharing arrangement with Sabena, Delta started service from Atlanta to Brussels. Delta also began a code-sharing agreement with Swissair on Swissair's flights from New York-Kennedy to Geneva and Zurich, to replace the company's scheduled service in these markets and from Delta's Atlanta and Cincinnati to Zurich service. Finally, Delta increased its Pacific operation in 1993 by including nonstop service from Portland, Oregon to Taipei and from Los Angeles to Hong Kong.[28]

FINANCIAL CONDITION

Delta was once known for having the most conservative balance sheet in the airline industry. For 1991–1993, the company's debt-to-equity ratio was above one-to-one and steadily rising. Financial results for Delta Air Lines are presented in Exhibits 1 through 3 showing that over the past four years the company has lost money, which, excluding 1983, had not occurred in any year since 1947.

In 1991, Delta Air Lines reported a net loss for only the second time in 50 years. This loss was a result of several factors: the increase in fuel prices due to the Middle East crisis, increased fare competition, and massive expenses related to the company's expanded route system through purchase agreements with Pan Am.[29]

In 1992, for the first time in Delta's history, a net loss was recorded in two consecutive years. Continuing poor economic conditions, both domestic and international, and expansion costs were found as causes for this half-billion dollar loss.[30] As a result of this, Ronald Allen, chairman and chief executive officer of Delta announced that "cost-cutting steps" would be implemented, including a reduction of $900,000,000 in planned aircraft expenditures and $600,000,000 in facilities and ground equipment expenditures through fiscal year 1995. Mr. Allen also announced that Delta's directors voluntary cut their own compensations by 20 percent.[31] Delta also decided to consolidate its reservation offices, which resulted in the closure of eight of the airline's 19 U.S. reservations facilities. These consolidations were completed between June 1993 and fall 1994.[32]

Also in 1993, new accounting standards added to Delta's financial worries. On July 15, 1993, Delta announced that retroactive to July 1, 1992, it would adopt two accounting standards required by the Financial Accounting Standards Board and retroactive to April 1, 1993, would implement the two changes in its accounting estimates. The adoption of these two policies resulted in a net after-tax charge of about $668,000,000, or $13.41 per share for fiscal 1993. Delta also announced that it was revising its depreciation policy for flight equipment by increasing the depreciable lives to 20 years from 15 and decreasing residual values to 5 percent from 10 percent. This change was estimated to reduce fiscal 1994 pretax operating expenses by $126,000,000. As of April 1, 1993, Delta increased the expected return on plan assets associated with defined benefit pension plans to 10 percent from 9 percent annually. This change reduced fiscal 1994 pretax operating expenses by an estimated $48,000,000. The changes in accounting estimates offset the effects of the new accounting standards and provided a net after-tax improvement of about $9,000,000, or $0.18 per share in June 1993 alone.[33] Chief

| EXHIBIT 1 | | Summary Operating and Nonoperating Results | | | |

	1994	1993	1992	1991	1990
Operating Revenues	$12,359,000	11,996,650	10,836,785	9,170,613	8,582,231
Operating Expenses	12,806,000	12,572,089	11,511,691	9,620,595	8,162,719
Operating Income (Loss)	(447,000)	(575,439)	(674,905)	(449,982)	419,512
Loss Before Cumulative Effect of Accounting Changes	(409,000)	(414,748)	(506,318)	(324,380)	—
Cumulative Effect of Accounting Changes	—	(587,144)	—	—	—
Net Income (Loss)	(409,000)	(1,001,892)	(506,318)	(324,380)	302,783
Net Income (Loss) Per Primary and Fully Diluted Common Share Before Accounting Changes	(10.32)	(10.54)	(10.60)	(7.73)	5.28
Net Income (Loss) Per Primary and Fully Diluted Common Share After Accounting Changes	(10.32)	(22.32)	(10.60)	(7.73)	5.28
Dividends Paid	10,000	34.815	59,405	53,844	84,550
Dividends Per Share	.20	.70	1.20	1.20	1.20
Average Shares Outstanding	50,453,272	50,063,841	49,699,098	49,401,779	46,086,110
Debt to Equity	70%/30%	66%/34%	60%/40%	46%/54%	34%/66%
Flyers Enplaned	87,399,000	85,084,733	77,030,029	69,127,249	67,240,233
Flyer Miles (000)	85,206,000	82,405,893	72,692,734	62,086,304	58,986,912
Available Miles (000)	131,780,000	132,282,319	123,101,743	104,327,918	76,463,052
Flyer Mile Yield	13.28¢	13.44¢	13.91¢	13.80¢	13.63¢
Flyer Load Factor	64.66%	62.30%	59.05%	59.51%	61.15%
Break-Even Load Factor	67.21%	65.53%	62.99%	62.64%	57.96%
Cargo Ton Miles (000)	1,384,000	1,257,223	1,086,949	887,054	790,697
Cargo Yield/Ton Mile	55.59¢	55.47¢	54.06¢	53.61¢	52.63¢
Fuel Gallons (000)	2,550,000	2,528,692	2,383,608	2,059,902	1,965,602
Price Per Gallon	55.34¢	62.95¢	62.19¢	77.63¢	62.71¢
Available Miles/Gallon	51.7	52.3	51.6	50.6	49.1
Available Seats/Mile	178	178.0	174.6	170.5	168.9
Cost Per Seat Mile	9.32¢	9.44¢	9.35¢	9.22¢	8.46¢
Average Flyer Trip (Miles)	975	969	944	898	877
Average Flight (Miles)	756	742	711	679	665
Plane Utilization (Hours Per Day)	8.27	8.32	8.47	8.68	8.82

Executive Officer Allen announced that Delta planned to defer approximately $1.8 billion in aircraft capital expenditures that would have been made through June 20, 1995. This action reduced Delta's planned aircraft acquisitions by 35, including aircraft manufactured by both Boeing and McDonnell Douglas Corporation. These reductions were in addition to changes announced in 1992 in which Delta estimated that it would reduce its planned aircraft acquisitions by greater than 100 through the year 2001.[34]

These plans were part of Delta's commitment to returning to profitability while maintaining its high standards of quality, both to the consumer as well as to its employees.

HUMAN RESOURCE ISSUES

As previously stated, Delta is largely nonunion. Despite being nonunion, however, the company does not exploit its workers. In fact, Delta's employees are some of the high-

EXHIBIT 2   **Earnings and Dividends**

	1994	1993	1992	1991	1990
Operation Income	$(447,000)	(575,439)	(674,906)	(449,982)	419,512
Other Income (Expense): Interest Expense	(304,000)	(238,829)	(220,815)	(162,828)	(83,937)
Less: Interest Capital	33,000	61,948	69,445	65,287	57,226
	(271,000)	(176,881)	(151,430)	(97,541)	(26,711)
Gain (Loss) on Flight Equipment	2,000	64,843	34,563	10,843	17,906
Miscellaneous Income, Net	56,000	36,193	5,400	30,496	57,205
	(213,000)	(75,845)	(111,467)	(50,202)	48,400
Income (Loss) Before Taxes	(660,000)	(651,284)	(786,373)	(500,184)	467,912
Income Taxes	250,000	233,609	271,005	162,646	(186,722)
Amortization of ITCs	1,000	2,927	9,050	13,158	21,593
Net Income (Loss)	(409,000)	(414,748)	(506,318)	(324,380)	302,783
Preferred Dividends (Net)	(110,000)	(110,392)	(18,567)	(18,592)	(18,144)
Net Income (Loss), Common	(519,000)	(525,140)	(524,885)	(342,972)	284,639
Net Income Per Share	(10.32)	(10.54)	(10.60)	(7.73)	5.28
Average Shares Outstanding	50,453,272	50,063,841	49,699,098	49,401,779	46,086,110

EXHIBIT 3   **Operating Expenses and Statistics**

	1994	1993	1992	1991	1990
Salaries and Related Costs	$4,589,000	4,797,910	4,436,402	3,752,398	3,425,865
Aircraft Fuel	1,411,000	1,591,722	1,482,372	1,599,165	1,232,561
Maintenance and Repairs	418,000	465,128	445,947	326,218	281,024
Aircraft Rent	732,000	728,566	641,914	413,106	325,781
Facilities and Other Rent	380,000	355,628	355,412	255,742	219,761
Landing Fees	261,000	262,534	224,351	168,307	137,278
Passenger Service	530,000	548,650	524,223	409,420	367,504
Passenger Commissions	1,318,000	1,250,488	1,153,184	923,122	768,140
Depreciation/Amortization	678,000	734,920	634,528	521,457	459,162
Other	1,963,000	1,754,043	1,613,358	1,251,660	985,643
Total	12,280,000	12,512,089	11,511,691	9,620,595	8,162,719
Plane Miles		743,050	705,142	611,752	571,265
Available Seat Miles	131,780,000	132,282,319	123,101,743	104,327,918	96,463,052
Available Ton Miles	18,302,000	18,182,484	16,625,472	13,825,313	12,499,745
Fuel Gallons Consumed	2,550,000	2,528,692	2,383,608	2,059,902	1,965,602
Average Fuel Price/Gallon	55.34¢	62.95¢	62.19¢	77.63¢	62.71¢
Passenger Load Factor	64.66%	62.30%	59.05%	59.51%	61.15%
Break-Even Load Factor	67.21%	65.53%	62.99%	62.64%	57.96%
Cost Per Available Seat Mile	9.32¢	9.44¢	9.35¢	9.22¢	8.46¢

est paid among the major carriers. They earn approximately 21 percent more than the industry average.[35] This favorable pay rate and absence of restrictive union rules results in good employee morale, which leads to high productivity and good service.[36] The good service rendered by employees has resulted in Delta having the fewest number of consumer complaints of any major carrier for the past 20 years.[37]

As Russell Heil, Delta's executive vice-president of operations and personnel, puts it, "Passenger airlines are a tough industry, because you have to provide the best possible service or you lose your customers. And it's the individual employee who is the key in that process. The company expects performance from employees, and in turn Delta provides the best possible work situation and compensation for its employees."[38]

Delta Air Lines' former no-layoff policy was a huge part of the company's commitment to its employees. However, due to the increasing losses the airline has suffered over the past few years, the policy is no longer feasible. Yet even when faced with making huge employee cutbacks, Delta seems to be handling it with as much concern as possible. It offers attrition and early retirement incentives and releases temporary positions before full-time positions.[39] Delta chairman Ronald W. Allen recognizes that the cutbacks will be painful, yet declares that it would be "an injustice to employees to do otherwise."[40] He expresses a genuine regard for Delta and especially its employees.

Heil takes great pride in the people of Delta Airlines. He believes that the company's employees have made the airline one of the most successful in the history of aviation.[41] His experience with Delta during the early 1970s oil embargo, during which pilots and flight attendants had to be reassigned but no jobs were lost, helped him realize how much Delta cared about its staff. "I learned then that when people know you really care and are willing to do everything to save their jobs, they are willing to work that much harder for you."[42]

Heil landed his first job with Delta as an aircraft performance engineer after an eight-month tour of duty in Vietnam.[43] After completing his MBA he became an administrative assistant at Delta. He was asked to help with the personnel function on a temporary basis after the company merged with Northeast Airlines in 1972.[44] The arrangement was so satisfactory to both parties that the job became permanent. Heil became senior vice-president of personnel for Delta after the then senior vice-president of personnel, Ron Allen, was named president and chief operating officer for Delta.[45] Allen later became chairman and chief executive officer for Delta.

"Ron Allen's appointment as president and then chairman of the board proves Delta's commitment to human resources," says Heil. "It is very rare in any industry, especially airlines, that the chief executive officer comes from the personnel function."[46] In fact, two of the company's last three chief executive officers came from the airline's personnel function. Heil attributes this fact to the company's philosophy and personnel policy, the essence of which is that airlines are basically alike and people make them different.[47] Delta strives to ensure that it has the best people on the job.

Heil demonstrates a genuine concern for Delta's employees. According to Maurice Worth, Delta's vice-president of personnel, "Russ is extremely sensitive to the concerns of our people and I think most of our employees here realize and appreciate that. . . . You can't be around him and not feel good about Delta and the way the airline handles its employees."[48] Worth adds that Heil is "always willing to go that extra mile for the employees. He wouldn't ask his staff to do anything that he wouldn't do himself."[49] This trait, combined with his excellent communication skills, makes Heil an effective leader. "He will always let you know what's happening and why it's happening," Worth said.[50]

Heil feels that communication is the most important part of his job because he serves as the fundamental link between Delta's employees and upper management.[51] Heil says that the most important lesson he has learned while working at Delta is that communication is essential.[52] ". . . Most of the problems between management and employees are just a lack of communication. . . . If you can identify the problems and communicate why certain decisions were made, you can avoid bigger and more costly problems later. . . . It is most important we continue communicating with our employees."[53]

Heil has also helped develop several programs and policies at Delta. These include an open-door policy through which an employee can speak with anyone in management concerning questions or problems.[54] Delta also holds personnel/employee meetings about every six weeks. These meetings, which are run by department heads, update employees on the company's financial picture and other topics of interest, such as new equipment and aircraft.[55] A question-and-answer period is conducted after each meeting. Questions that cannot be answered during the meeting are directed to the appropriate department, and the response is relayed to the employees as quickly as possible.[56]

CONCLUSION

Delta's biggest challenge is to find a way to continue providing friendly, customer-oriented service in the face of massive employee cutbacks. Will the remaining employees continue to be well trained and customer friendly, or will they be "stressed out" from overwork as they take on the added duties of the released employees? Will this cause increased union activity at the airline? These and other issues occupied management's attention as 1995 drew to a close.

NOTES

1. *Moody's Transportation Manual,* 1990.
2. Standard and Poor's Corporate Record.
3. Ibid.
4. *Annual Report 1993,* Delta Air Lines, Inc.
5. *Annual Report 1990,* Delta Air Lines, Inc., p. 3
6. Ibid.
7. This section is principally a reproduction of Delta's corporate history as compiled by the *International Directory of Company Histories,* 1988, Vol. 1, pp. 99–100.
8. *Moody's Transportation Manual,* 1993.
9. Joan M. Feldman, "Straining the Family Ties," *Air Transport World* 30(6), p. 32.
10. Marc Rice, "Delta to Cut as Many as 15,000 Jobs," *Tallahassee Democrat,* April 29, 1994, p. 10A.
11. *Moody's Transportation Manual,* 1993.
12. Bridget O'Brian, "Delta Air to Pare Up to 15,000 Jobs, or 20% of Staff, in Big Restructuring," *The Wall Street Journal,* April 29, 1994, p. A3.
13. *Annual Report 1990,* Delta Air Lines, Inc., p. 2.
14. *Moody's Transportation Manual,* 1992, p. 1,954.
15. *Annual Report 1990,* Delta Air Lines, Inc., p. 16.
16. *Moody's Transportation Manual,* 1993.
17. Edward A. Gargan, "Jump into Europe Leaves Delta with Some Aches," *The New York Times,* May 5, 1994, p. D6.
18. Rik Fairlie, "Delta Would Get Heathrow Access with Virgin Deal," *Travel Weekly,* April 18, 1994, p. 3.
19. Isae Wada, "Delta to Offer 10% Agent Pay on International Routes," *Travel Weekly,* December 20, 1993, p. 1.
20. Gargan, "Jump into Europe Leaves Delta with Some Aches."
21. *Annual Report 1990,* Delta Air Lines, Inc., p. 13.
22. Ibid., p. 14.
23. Ibid.
24. Ibid.
25. Ibid.
26. Ibid.
27. Ibid.
28. *Annual Report 1993,* Delta Air Lines, Inc.
29. Ibid.
30. Ibid.
31. *Moody's Transportation Manual,* 1993.
32. Ibid.
33. Ibid.
34. Ibid.
35. Seth Lubove, "Full Speed Ahead—but Cautiously," *Forbes,* October 29, 1990, pp. 36–38.
36. Ibid.
37. Ibid.

38. Bill Leonard, "Making the Message Clear," *Personnel Administrator,* November 1989, pp. 47–49.

39. "Delta to Offer Early Retirement to 3,000 Employees," *The New York Times,* August 24, 1993, p. D4.

40. Rice, "Delta to Cut as Many as 15,000 Jobs."

41. Leonard, "Making the Message Clear," p. 47.

42. Ibid., p. 48.

43. Ibid., p. 47.

44. Ibid., p. 48.

45. Ibid.

46. Ibid.

47. Ibid.

48. Ibid.

49. Ibid., p. 49.

50. Ibid.

51. Ibid.

52. Ibid.

53. Ibid.

54. Ibid.

55. Ibid.

56. Ibid.

CASE 3

McDONALD'S CORPORATION

INTRODUCTION

HISTORY

McDonald's is the largest fast-food chain in the world. It has become a leading institution and symbol of American culture since it burst onto the scene in the mid-1950s. Its computerized, standardized operations and premeasured servings have been labeled "quintessentially American,"[1] and its restaurants have been hailed as "monuments to our culture!"[2] The company philosophy of Q.S.C. & V. (Quality food; fast, friendly service; restaurant cleanliness; and a menu that provides value) and its family-oriented image are the product of a Mr. Ray Kroc.

The first McDonald's was a drive-in restaurant started in San Bernardino, California, by two brothers, Dick and Mac McDonald, in 1948. Ray Kroc, the man who made McDonald's the household name it is today, became a franchising agent for the McDonald brothers in 1954 and opened his first McDonald's in Illinois in 1955. The McDonald brothers sold the company to Ray Kroc in 1961 for $2.7 million. In 1993 alone McDonald's generated over $7.5 billion in total revenues.[3] The company menu, which originally consisted of only hamburgers, cheeseburgers, french fries, sodas, milkshakes, milk, and coffee, has grown considerably since.

A more technical definition of McDonald's would be "an organization that develops, operates, franchises, and services a worldwide system of restaurants that prepare, assemble, package, and sell a limited menu of quickly prepared, moderately priced foods."[4] The McDonald's system is the largest food service organization in the world. The company franchises joint-venture partners, and restaurant managers operate about 14,000 restaurants in 70 countries, each offering a limited menu of high-quality food that can be part of a well-balanced meal plan. McDonald's has pioneered food quality specifications, equipment technology, marketing and training programs, and operational and supply systems, all of which are considered the standards of the industry throughout the world.[5] Q.S.C. & V.—Quality, Service, Cleanliness, and Value—are the standards upon which McDonald's was built and are the reasons McDonald's continues to operate so successfully today.[6]

NOTE: This case was prepared by Alexandra Orsin, Mike Martin, Ken Nielson, and Robert Graves and revised by Paola Belfranin, Jennifer Frazier, Todd Griffith, and Steve Roach.

EXHIBIT 1	McDonald's Corporation Consolidated Statement of Income

(In millions of dollars, except per common share data)	Years ended December 31, 1993	1992	1991
Revenues			
Sales by company-operated restaurants	$5,157.2	$5,102.5	$4,908.5
Revenues from franchised restaurants	2,250.9	2,030.8	1,786.5
Total revenues	7,408.1	7,133.3	6,695.0
Operating costs and expenses			
Company-operated restaurants			
Food and packaging	1,735.1	1,688.8	1,627.5
Payroll and other employee benefits	1,291.2	1,281.4	1,259.2
Occupancy and other operating expenses	1,138.3	1,156.3	1,142.4
	4,164.6	4,126.5	4,029.1
Franchised restaurants—occupancy expenses	380.4	348.6	306.5
General, administrative and selling expenses	941.1	860.6	794.7
Other operating (income) expense—net	(62.0)	(64.0)	(113.8)
Total operating costs and expenses	5,424.1	5,271.7	5,016.5
Operating income	1,984.0	1,861.6	1,678.5
Interest expense—net of capitalized interest of $20.0, $19.5 and $26.2	316.1	373.6	391.4
Nonoperating income (expense)—net	7.8	(39.9)	12.3
Income before provision for income taxes	1,675.7	1,448.1	1,299.4
Provision for income taxes	593.2	489.5	439.8
Net income	$1,082.5	$ 958.6	$ 859.6
Net income per common share	$2.91	$2.60	$2.35
Dividends per common share	$.42	$.39	$.36

SOURCE: *McDonald's 1993 Annual Report,* p. 37.

FINANCIAL INFORMATION

Most aspects of McDonald's consolidated balance sheet (see Exhibit 1) and consolidated statement of income (see Exhibit 2) reflect the company's growth. Current assets in 1993 decreased 23 percent over the previous year, with total revenues increasing 3.9 percent and net income increasing 13 percent.

Average sales by restaurants open at least one year were $1,768,000 in 1993, which was $35,000 higher than in 1992. Average sales both in and outside the United States improved due to the value program and various promotional efforts. Expansion has continued at an accelerated pace as 900 restaurants were added in 1993, compared with 675 in 1992 and 615 in 1991. McDonald's planned to add between 900 and 1,200 restaurants around the world in 1994 and in each of the next several years.[7]

The 1993 and 1992 revenue and operating income increases reflected accelerated expansion and better performance despite weak economies in several major markets. Changing foreign currencies had a negative effect in 1993 and a positive one in 1992 on these increases. Company-operated franchised dollar margins were negatively impacted by weaker foreign currencies. Company-operated margins increased $6 million, or 1 percent, in 1993. There margins improved to 20.1 percent of sales in 1993, compared with 19.8 percent in 1992 and 18.8 percent in 1991. The 1993 and 1992 increases in general, administrative, and selling expenses were caused primarily by higher employee costs associated with expansion, partially offset by weaker foreign currencies in 1993.[8]

EXHIBIT 2	McDonald's Corporation Consolidated Balance Sheet

(In millions of dollars)	December 31, 1993	1992
Assets		
Current assets		
Cash and equivalents	$185.8	$436.5
Accounts receivable	287.0	245.9
Notes receivable	27.6	33.7
Inventories, at cost, not in excess of market	43.5	43.5
Prepaid expenses and other current assets	118.9	105.1
Total current assets	662.8	864.7
Other assets and deferred charges		
Notes receivable due after one year	90.0	99.0
Investments in and advances to affiliates	446.7	399.7
Miscellaneous	338.6	330.7
Total other assets and deferred charges	875.3	829.4
Property and equipment		
Property and equipment, at cost	13,459.0	12,658.0
Accumulated depreciation and amortization	(3.377.6)	(3,060.6)
Net property and equipment	10,081.4	9,597.4
Intangible assets—net	415.7	389.7
Total assets	$12,035.2	$11,681.2
Liabilities and shareholders' equity		
Current liabilities		
Notes payable	$193.3	$411.0
Accounts payable	395.7	434.3
Income taxes	56.0	109.7
Other taxes	90.2	74.8
Accrued interest	132.9	133.3
Other accrued liabilities	203.9	203.1
Current maturities of long-term debt	30.0	269.2
Total current liabilities	1,102.0	1,544.6
Long-term debt	3,489.4	3,176.4
Other long-term liabilities and minority interests	334.4	225.2
Deferred income taxes	835.3	748.6
Common equity put options		94.0
Shareholders' equity		
Preferred stock, no par value; authorizes—	677.3	680.2
165.0 million shares; issues—5.7 and 5.8 million		
Common stock, no par value; authorizes—	46.2	46.2
1.25 billion shares; issued—415.2 million		
Additional paid-in capital	302.8	260.2
Guarantee of ESOP notes	(253.6)	(271.3)
Retained Earnings	7,612.6	6,727.3
Foreign currency translation adjustment	(192.2)	(127.4)
	8,193.1	7,315.2
Common stock in treasury, at cost;	(1,919.0)	(1,422.8)
61.5 and 51.6 million shares		
Total shareholders' equity	6,274.1	5,892.4
Total liabilities and shareholders' equity	$12,035.2	$11,681.2

SOURCE: *McDonald's 1993 Annual Report,* p. 38.

HISTORICAL GROWTH

McDonald's strategy for growth focuses on three key elements: adding restaurants, maximizing sales and profits at existing restaurants, and improving international profitability.

Adding restaurants can be achieved with our people and capital resources. Maximizing sales and profits at existing restaurants can be accomplished through better operations, reinvestment, product development, effective marketing, and lower development costs. Improving international profitability can be realized as economies of scale are achieved in individual markets.[9]

In 1967 McDonald's moved into Canada and Puerto Rico, the first countries outside the United States to have a McDonald's franchise. McDonald's operated 9,283 restaurants in the United States in 1993, a growth of 17.4 percent in the past five years. In the same time frame, restaurants in the international market increased 80.7 percent to number 4,710.

FRANCHISE

The unprecedented growth of the McDonald's Corporation is due largely to its successful use of franchisee entrepreneurs to promote the McDonald's product. McDonald's is highly selective in choosing its franchisees—it sends 13,000 brochures each year to interested parties and receives 5,000 applications for 100 new placements. Before franchisees open their restaurant, they generally spend more than two years in training and work about 2,000 uncompensated hours in a McDonald's restaurant.

A franchise arrangement is generally for a term of 20 years and requires an investment of approximately $520,000, 60 percent of which may be financed. In addition, a business facilities lease arrangement enables individuals who do not have sufficient capital, but who meet all other criteria, to become franchisees. Candidates for this program generally must have liquid assets of approximately $75,000.

With limited exceptions, McDonald's does not supply food, paper, or equipment to any of its restaurants, but approves suppliers from which franchised and company-operated restaurants can purchase these items. Franchisees are required to pay related occupancy costs, which include property taxes, insurance, maintenance, and a refundable, noninterest-bearing security deposit.[10]

Revenues from franchised restaurants are based on fees paid as a percent of sales, with specified minimum payments. Expenses associated with these restaurants are rent and depreciation, which are relatively fixed. Accordingly, the franchise margins are positively impacted by increases in sales, yet protected from rises in operating costs. Fees from franchises to McDonald's typically include rent and service fees. A monthly fee based on the restaurant's sales performance (currently a service fee of 3.5 percent of monthly sales) plus the greater of (a) monthly base rent, or (b) percentage rent that is at least 8.5 percent of monthly sales.[11]

PRODUCT

McDonald's restaurants offer a substantially uniform menu consisting of hamburgers and cheeseburgers, including the Big Mac and Quarter Pounder with Cheese sandwiches, the Filet-O-Fish, McGrilled Chicken and McChicken sandwiches, french fries, Chicken McNuggets, salads, low-fat shakes, sundaes and cones made with low-fat frozen yogurt, pies, cookies, and a limited number of soft drinks and other beverages.

In addition, the restaurants sell a variety of products during limited promotional time periods. McDonald's restaurants operating in the United States are open during breakfast hours and offer a full breakfast menu including the Egg McMuffin and the Sausage McMuffin with Egg sandwiches; hotcakes and sausage; three varieties of biscuit sandwiches; apple-bran muffins; and cereals. McDonald's restaurants in countries around the world offer many of these same products as well as other products and limited breakfast menus. The company tests new products on an ongoing basis.[12]

COMPETITION

McDonald's restaurants compete with international, national, regional, and local retailers. McDonald's competes on the basis of price and service—two key components of value—and by offering quality food products. McDonald's views its competition in the broadest perspectives: quick-service eating establishments, mom and pops, take-outs, pizza parlors, coffee shops, street vendors, convenience food store chains, delis, supermarket freezers, and microwave ovens.

In the United States about 372,000 restaurants generate nearly $213 billion in annual sales. McDonald's accounts for about 2.5 percent of those restaurants and 6.7 percent of those sales. That leaves 93.3 percent, or nearly $200 billion. Competitors include, but are not limited to, Kentucky Fried Chicken, Burger King, Wendy's, Hardees, and Taco Bell.[13]

EMPLOYEES

Employees of eating and drinking establishments are paid considerably less than are employees of any other nonagricultural industry. Most of the employees are students and other young people working for the first time with an average work week of less than 26 hours.[14] Wages in the fast food industry in the United States are largely unaffected by collective bargaining or the threat of unionization with the exception of one Burger King in Detroit.[15]

The typical McDonald's restaurant has sixty employees and a $350,000 payroll with $1.6 million in sales. In 1993, when minimum wage was $4.35 an hour, McDonald's average hourly wage was $5.60 an hour.[16]

Managers in company-owned stores in 1993 average $34,000 a year. A profit-sharing plan contributed an additional 14 to 14.5 percent to the manager's compensation. Managers were also entitled to stock options in some cases.[17]

McDonald's employee strategy hinges on its ability to infuse every store with its gung-ho culture and standardized procedures. Every job is broken down into the smallest of steps, and the whole process is automated. So rule bound is McDonald's that one sociologist recently claimed jobs in its restaurants are unfit for young people. "These are breeding grounds for robots working for yesterday's assembly lines, not tomorrow's high-tech posts," contends Professor Anitai Ezioni of George Washington University.[18]

AGENCY COSTS

One relevant market parameter that can make agency costs high is the physical dispersion of operations. Franchising avoids the monitoring costs of specialization because the local manager is now an investor whose wealth is strongly dependent on the performance of her or his local unit, thus making franchising more common with physically dispersed operations, as in rural areas. Also, for a given level of output, monitoring costs will rise with an increasing labor/output ratio. Using local managers who

EXHIBIT 3   **(a) Number of McDonald's Restaurants in the United States**

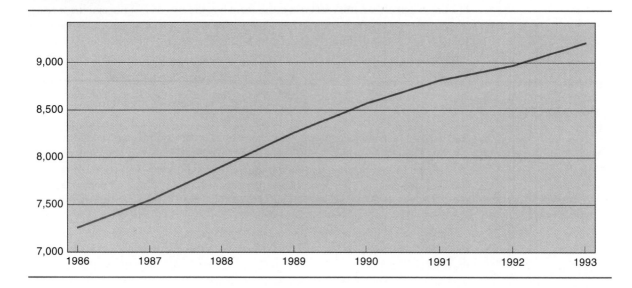

make heavy site-specific investments and post a large bond in the form of a franchise fee makes quality debasing less likely, because a franchisee has much more to lose upon termination than a local employee-manager.[19]

TURNOVER

McDonald's finds a strong link between the quality of its labor force at the store level and the sales of a given restaurant. Michael Quinlan, chief executive officer for McDonald's, has indicated that reducing turnover is a key priority for the chain. In 1989, turnover was 130 percent, down from 180 percent five years prior. More recent figures have not been released by the company, which probably indicates that turnover is still a significant problem. In fact, periodically placemats used on trays are employment applications—every customer a potential employee!

OVERALL CORPORATE STRATEGY

McDonald's is the largest food service organization in the world, with nearly 14,000 stores. Its goal has been to provide the highest quality products and friendly service in clean restaurants at good values (Q.S.C. & V.). In 1994 McDonald's plans on adding 900–1,200 restaurants in 94 countries, which comes out to about one restaurant every seven to nine hours.[20] To meet this goal, McDonald's current strategies have focused on the following factors.

CUSTOMER SATISFACTION

McDonald's was founded on the principle of uniformity. An operations manual of 600 pages ensured the consistency and quality of products served by McDonald's. While this strategy worked well in the past, customers are now demanding more than consis-

EXHIBIT 3

(b) Domestic and International Change in Number of Restaurants
continued

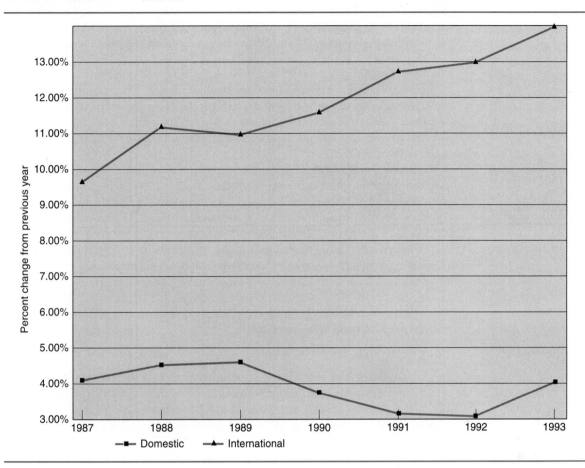

tency. In response to the changing market, McDonald's has taken a "do whatever it takes to make a customer happy"[21] strategy and has given its employees, managers, and stores the flexibility to carry out this new strategy.

HEALTHIER FOODS

Customers are demanding that restaurants provide healthier foods. McDonald's has heard their cry, and it has changed the way foods are prepared: hamburgers are made with lean ground beef and enriched sandwich buns, french fries and hash browns are fried in 100 percent vegetable oil, milkshakes are made with 1% lowfat milk, and the amount of sodium used has been decreased. It has also added more nutritious foods to the menu: whole-grain breakfast cereals, apple bran muffins, fresh fruit and vegetables, and lowfat frozen yogurt. As one advertisement states, "McDonald's is committed to making sure that when you've got an appetite for healthy food, [McDonald's will] always have the choices to satisfy you."[22]

FOOD QUALITY AND NUTRITION

The safety and quality of McDonald's food is maintained through a combination of stringent product standards, strict enforcement of operating procedures, and close working relationships with suppliers. Specifications for both raw and cooked product quality are established and enforced by the quality assurance labs in the United States, Europe, and Asia/Pacific. This quality assurance process involves ongoing testing and thorough on-site inspections of suppliers' facilities. Food preparation is also closely monitored, as well as cooking and equipment maintenance and procedures.[23]

The introduction of new frying baskets has also proved to increase the quality and nutrition of McDonald's food. These baskets optimize the separation and provide a "chimney effect" for maximum steam-driven oil circulation. This faster frying shortens the time that customers have to wait and reduces the amount of oil used. Therefore, an order that would have previously taken 3 minutes to cook can now be cooked 30 to 40 seconds quicker. This benefits not only the customer's health, but also the overall profits of McDonald's.[24]

McDonald's has nutrition information on products available to customers so that they can make informed decisions about how McDonald's can be part of a healthy, well-balanced diet. Posters are displayed with complete nutritional and ingredient information, in the United States and international restaurants, and a brochure entitled "McDonald's Food Facts" is also available upon request.

McDonald's also takes it upon itself to educate health-care professionals about the menu through advertising, convention exhibits, and patient educational materials. Efforts like these have lead to partnership programs with leading health associations, including the American Dietetic Association for the Food FUNdamentals Happy Meal, and "What's on your Plate?", a nutrition education program for children established through the Society for Nutrition Education.[25]

LARGER MENUS

In addition to healthy foods, customers want more choices. In response, McDonald's added a breakfast menu that included eggs, sausage, biscuits, Canadian ham, rolls, pancakes, and cereals. Other items, such as chicken fajitas, Chicken McNuggets and McRibs, have also been added. The latest menu items to be added include a grilled chicken sandwich and McPizza.

RESTAURANT DIVERSITY

When Ray Kroc was CEO of McDonald's, each restaurant looked the same and served the same food. He wanted products to look and taste the same no matter where the customer was. In the 1990s, the customer wants more than fast food. Michael Quinlan, the current CEO, has recognized these changes and is allowing individual stores to experiment with their formats. The new store formats that are being tested include self-service stores, drive-thru only stores, cafes, and customized outlets. More than 100 other sites known as satellite locations are currently in Wal-Marts, Home Depots, service stations, and other unusual locations.[26] Flexibility also exists in selecting menu items. Stores no longer have to carry a standard menu. Franchisees can experiment with new items and alter the menu to conform to regional and ethnic tastes.

DIVERSIFICATION

According to projections, the U.S. population in the 5- to 14-year old age group is expected to grow at over 14 percent through the year 2000. Since children help make 36.6 percent of the family dining decisions,[27] McDonald's has targeted them with nonfood-related products. It has installed playlands at its stores, marketed McDonald's clothes and toys, and started a new venture called Leaps and Bounds that allows parents and children to play together. McDonald's hopes that this strategy of diversification will make children think of McDonald's when it is time to eat.

UNTAPPED MARKETS

The dinner and international markets have remained virtually untapped by McDonald's and new strategies are focusing on penetrating these markets. These strategies include a wider dinner menu that focuses on items such as meatloaf, ham, and mashed potatoes. Internationally, there are still 121 countries without a McDonald's.[28]

DINNER

Currently, McDonald's dinner sales are only 20 percent of daily sales.[29] In order to boost this figure, McDonald's has plans to offer a separate dinner menu that will include roast chicken and spaghetti with meatballs. More than a dinner menu is needed, however. The proper atmosphere needs to be created. "People's expectations at dinner are totally different than at lunch."[30] "Evidence suggests that diners often want full course meals with table service, and maybe even a cocktail or two."[31] McDonald's is currently considering a "test concept" of a sit-down restaurant. Now being built in a Chicago suburb is Hearth Express, a cafe-style restaurant with a focus on home-style cooking.[32]

INTERNATIONAL

The domestic operations have been expanding. Operating income has increased, while expenditures have decreased.[33]

In 1993, international systemwide sales posted a gain, while operating income increased 7.4 percent.[34] 1993 was a strong year for McDonald's internationally, despite weak foreign currency, especially in the European market.[35] This growth should continue since McDonald's, which currently operates in 68 countries, plans to penetrate new markets around the world.[36] McDonald's added 576 new restaurants internationally in 1993 alone.[37]

SOCIAL RESPONSIBILITY

McDonald's annual report states that "being a good corporate citizen means treating people with fairness and integrity, and sharing success with the communities in which we do business."[38] Because of this, McDonald's overall corporate strategy includes many charitable programs:

> *Plan to Get Out Alive*—McDonald's home fire safety program is designed to extend the proven effectiveness of school fire drills into the home.[39]

> *Book Some Time Together*—McDonald's partnered with the American Library Association to encourage families to read.[40]

> *Cartoon All-Stars to the Rescue*—McDonald's sponsored this animated, anti-substance abuse television special, which was broadcasted on every major network in North America.[41]

EDUCATION

Supporting and providing education is one way McDonald's helps society. McDonald's is committed to making the work in the restaurant part of the learning process by teaching self-confidence, self-esteem, responsibility, people skills, and time and money

| **EXHIBIT 4** | **Fast-Food Market Share, 1985 and 1990** |

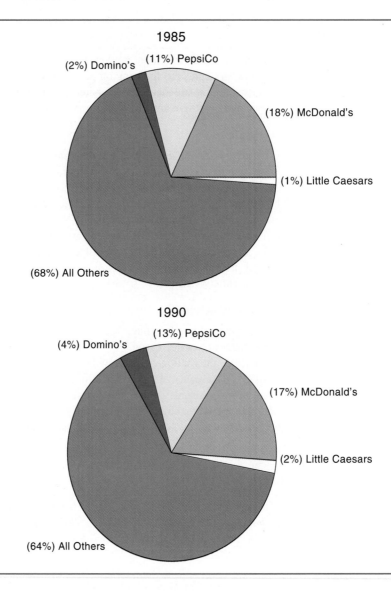

management. McDonald's Education Department also works with educators, schools, and its franchises and employees to coordinate the company's diverse educational initiatives. McDonald's has developed a comprehensive variety of educational curriculum and programs for students at all levels. The topics range from environmental awareness, nutrition, and fitness to stay-in-school and drug prevention programs. National programs that educators and students participate in include McDonald's All-American High School Basketball Team, the Ray A. Kroc Youth Achievement Award, and McDonald's National Association of Secondary School Principals' Assistant Principals recognition program. McDonald's commitment to the responsible student employee consists of balancing part-time work with school by providing flexible working hours to accommodate classes, homework responsibilities, and extracurricular activities, overcomplying with minor labor laws, recognizing scholastic achievement, and also as-

EXHIBIT 5   **Domestic Systemwide Sales**

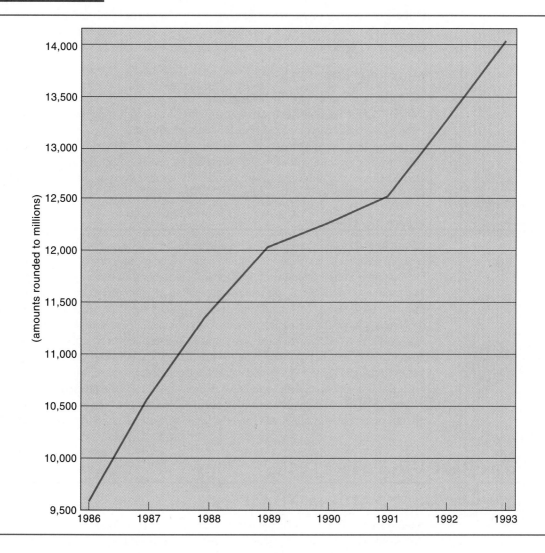

sisting employees in pursuing their education through book/tuition reimbursement pro-grams and local scholarships.[42] In addition to sponsoring events that encourage and rec-ognize achievement, it has created five programs designed to further education. Two of the programs, "When I Grow Up" and "Stay in School," focus on the importance of ed-ucation, while the "It's Our Business" program teaches economic principles to students in grades 7 through 10 and the "Hispanic American Commitment to Education Re-sources" program provides college scholarships. McDonald's Crew College Education program also provides financial aid grants through an agreement with the United Negro College Fund to promote higher education.[43]

EQUAL OPPORTUNITY

Equal opportunity is also an ideal supported by McDonald's. McJobs, McMasters, and affirmative action programs are aimed at ensuring full and equal participation by all members in society.[44]

Equal opportunity is a major issue in today's business world. McDonald's has made it a point to attract and retain a diversified workforce.[45] McDonald's was recently listed in the 1993 edition of *The Top Companies for Minorities to Work.*[46] McDonald's also received the 1993 Catalyst award for fostering leadership development of women.[47] Currently 60 percent of franchisees in training are minorities or women.[48]

CHILDREN'S CHARITIES

McDonald's is "dedicated to helping children achieve their fullest potential."[49] The Ronald McDonald Charities provide grants to programs that support education, drug awareness, health care, medical research, and rehabilitation.

To help families of seriously ill children, the Ronald McDonald House program provides a place for the families to stay while their child is hospitalized. The Ronald McDonald House program serves more than 2,400 families every night. At year-end 1993, there were 157 houses in 10 countries.

ENVIRONMENT

Environmental issues have taken a prominent place in today's society and McDonald's is doing what it can to make the world a better place to live. In its "commitment to the Environment Policy Statement," McDonald's is striving to reduce packaging, recycle and use recycled materials, promote conservation of natural resources, and protect the tropical rain forests. McDonald's has recently joined the Paper Task Force to develop recommendations for increasing the use of environmentally preferable paperboard products. It is also working with local communities and teachers in schools by providing educational materials to promote sound environmental practices and values.[50] McDonald's has even established the McDonald's All-Star Green Teens award, which recognizes and rewards high-school students who have demonstrated exceptional environmental leadership.[51] McDonald's environmental concerns also extend to the preservation of clean air, humane treatment of animals, and the pioneering of a smoke-free atmosphere.[52]

HUMAN RESOURCE STRATEGY

MANAGING DIVERSITY/LABOR SHORTAGE

According to the Bureau of Labor Statistics, annual workforce growth in the United States will slow dramatically, from 2 percent a year in 1988 to 1.2 percent until the year 2000. Another prediction is that 73 percent of the new entrants to the workforce will be minorities, elderly, and women. The buzz word for recruiting, training, and retaining this new rainbow coalition of human resources is "managing diversity." In recognition of the changing demographics and the shrinking labor force, McDonald's has created programs to deal with employee diversity.

In addition to billions of hamburgers every year, McDonald's is serving up employment opportunities to two growing segments of the workforce: the disabled and the elderly. The McDonald's corporate identification is strategically named in these employment programs, which are known as McJobs and McMasters.

At sites across the country, more than 9,000 mentally and physically disabled people between the ages of 16 and 60 have graduated from the McJobs program and have begun work at McDonald's restaurants.[53] Specially trained and selected managers serve as job coaches, who work closely with local vocational rehabilitation agencies to monitor each candidate's progress. Job coaches work one-on-one with four or five candidates at a time. Each receives standard McDonald's training—classroom instruction, demonstration, and supervised practice at various job stations.[54]

McMasters is a nationwide program that identifies, recruits, trains, and retains workers who are 55 years of age and older. It also features job coaches, who function in much the same capacity as the coaches in McJobs, as well as a referral program that works through a vast network of agencies that alert older workers to the opportunities at McDonald's. Workers hired through McDonald's referral program are immediately teamed up with a "partner"—an experienced worker who helps the team member through the initial training.

The corporation offers its managers solid diversity training, including a workshop designed to help managers deal with older workers, minorities, and the mentally and physically handicapped. "We believe that management must understand what diversity is, and how it works to the company's and the individual's advantage," said Monica Boyles, past director of McDonald's Changing Workforce program. She adds,

> Not only do we want a representative work force, but we want to clearly empower cultural differences so that we have full advantage of what everybody brings; we want to ensure that people at all levels of McDonald's are free to be themselves and to bring their energy and creativity into the work environment.[55]

In addition, McDonald's offers career-development programs designed for various minority groups and training for managers that identifies diversity from a value-added perspective. As a result of their programs, 56 percent of the top managers at restaurants owned by McDonald's are women and minorities.[56]

TRAINING

Each year, more than 3,000 franchisers and McDonald's managers graduate with a degree in hamburgerology from Hamburger University, Oak Brook, Illinois.[57] Hamburger U. is an 80-acre campus that all the company's managers and franchise holders must attend. Formal classroom sessions are provided in which participants learn management skills, market evaluation, financial budgets, and the reinforcement of Ray Kroc's philosophy of Q.S.C. & V. A two-week curriculum covers four major areas: equipment, operations, human relations skills, and interpersonal/communication skills.[58]

Training for employees begins with in-store videotapes and one-on-one instruction "even before the crew member cooks their first french fry."[59] "The book" at McDonald's—the company's policies and procedures manual—spells out the precise details at each station in the restaurant. "Cooks must turn, never flip, hamburgers one, never two, at a time." Or, "If they haven't been purchased, Big Macs must be discarded ten minutes after being cooked and french fries in seven."

Training programs are always being refined and updated to provide the crew with the tools needed to handle the challenges of operating a McDonald's restaurant.[60] Recently, McDonald's has added a class to its career-development program designed to build leadership and communication skills. Training competencies extends to McDonald's Quality Management (MQM) programs, whereby quality tools such as long-range planning, process reengineering, benchmarking, and continuous improvement are taught.[61]

CAREERS: THE GOLDEN OPPORTUNITY UNDER THE ARCHES

McDonald's is not only the biggest fast-food restaurant in America, it's also the nation's largest youth employer. About half of the more than 550,000 employees are under the

EXHIBIT 6 **International Sales**

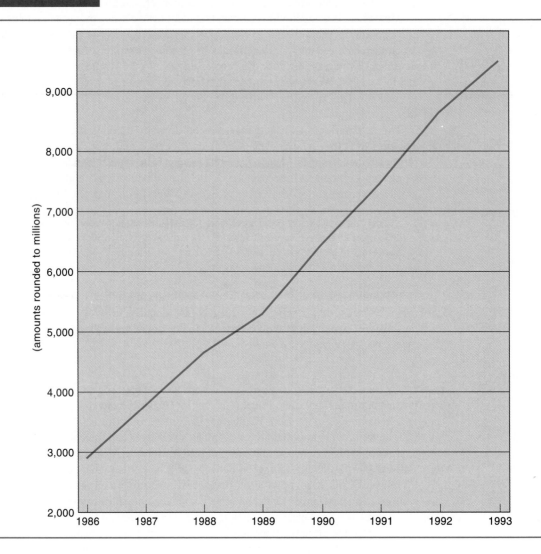

(amounts rounded to millions)

age of 20. "Its impact on the U.S. work force greatly exceeds its current employment, because it trains so many high school students for their first jobs."[62]

Every new employee begins as a trainee on the easiest of jobs—cooking french fries. Once that station is perfected, an employee moves to the next designated station, and so on. McDonald's functions as a de facto job-training program by teaching youth discipline and the basics of how to work.[63] For workers who show initiative, McDonald's offers opportunities for quick advancement. An employee can work his or her way up to "crew chief" where he or she can manage an entire operation and its crew.

The youth will continue to work as crew chief—given that the annual turnover rate is more than 100 percent—until promotion to a manager. McDonald's has a long tradition of promoting from within on the basis of skill and hustle, not academic credentials.[64] More than half of its corporate executives never graduated from college. This fits right into the philosophy of Ray Kroc on what education should be:

Career education, that's what this country needs. Many young people emerge from college unprepared to hold down a steady job or to cook or do housework and it makes them depressed. No wonder! They should train for a career, learn how to support themselves and how to enjoy work first. Then if they have a thirst for advanced learning, they can go to night school.[65]

The possibilities for advancing to corporate headquarters are also attainable. More than half of McDonald's top corporate management started out as crew members. However, the organizational chart is "flat" for being one of the nation's biggest employers. As Kroc states, "I believe that *less is more* in the case of corporate management; for its size, McDonald's is the most unstructured corporation I know and I don't think you could find a happier, more secure, harder working group of executives anywhere."[66]

BENEFITS

One of the increasing concerns of McDonald's is its growing, increasingly diverse workforce and matching and effectively communicating the benefits to all segments of that workforce. The main emphasis on the benefits approach is good communication about the benefits plan itself. According to Robert Witcloff, Director of Employee Benefits at the Chicago headquarters, proper communication "lets employees know more, value more, appreciate it more." Furthermore, "the effectiveness of the plan operation will go better."[67]

McDonald's, which self-insures its benefits programs, provides health insurance to 15,000 full-time employees in the United States. These include the employees of company-owned restaurants, regional offices, and the corporate headquarters.

Benefit Communication Planning Teams are established to reflect the employment demographics: an exceptionally young workforce with the average age being in the low thirties, very few employees above the age of 65, large employments of minorities, and a domination of women in management. The teams are also designed to include a variety of people from various corporate departments to ensure a diverse representation. These teams simplify and streamline materials to improve communication with the diverse workforce.

The accomplishments of the Benefit Communication Planning Team include:

- Plastic insurance cards with a magnetic strip to automatically bill for prescriptions.
- Co-worker communication programs, which allow a group of trained employees to explain the program to other workers.

The McDonald's benefit plan also emphasizes the concept of simplicity. Mike Quinlan, McDonald's chairman and chief executive officer, simplified health plan enrollment by including a chart in the package that outlines which of the three medical plans would be most cost effective for an individual or a family based on anticipated future medical costs. The three comprehensive medical plans are as follows:

- Plan 1 requires a $200 deductible, 90 percent coinsurance, and a $2,000 out-of-pocket cap.
- Plan 2 requires a $250 deductible, 80 percent coinsurance, and a $2,000 out-of-pocket cap.
- Plan 3 requires a $750 deductible and 100 percent coinsurance.

These plans differ only in deductible and coinsurance requirements. McDonald's pays 80 percent of the premium.

Simplicity has also affected written benefit materials. McDonald's provides Spanish-speaking language materials, Spanish-speaking representatives to answer questions about the plan, and interactive communication including telephone enrollment, slide shows, and videos.

In February 1993, McDonald's also continued the tradition of simplicity by eliminating the claims form entirely and providing instructive, pre-addressed envelopes. This improved turnaround time for payment of claims from 23 to 6 days.[68]

PROFIT SHARING

The company's program for U.S. employees includes profit sharing, 401(k) (McDESOP—McDonald's Employee Stock Ownership Plan), and leveraged employee stock ownership features.[69] McDESOP allows employees to invest in McDonald's common stock by making contributions that are partially matched by the company. Certain foreign subsidiaries also offer profit sharing, stock purchase, or other similar benefit plans. The company does not provide any other postretirement benefits.

PREFERRED PROVIDER ORGANIZATION (PPO)[70]

PPO applies to all full-time staff and store management selecting McDonald's medical coverage. PPO is a network of hospitals across the United States that provides quality care and a discount to McDonald's employees who use these facilities for either inpatient or outpatient services.

EDUCATIONAL ASSISTANCE PROGRAM[71]

McDonald's supports the educational objectives of its employees and offers a job-related Education Assistance Program (EAP). Eligible employees (store management and its assistants with at least 6 months of service) will be reimbursed for 75 percent of their course fees to a maximum of $400 per course (two courses per semester). Home office approval is required.

SABBATICALS[72]

McDonald's believes that sabbaticals are the best way to replenish its employees' energy. After 10 years of service, you are eligible for a sabbatical leave program acknowledging "the need to nurture individuals within a corporate culture dedicated, in part, to mass-producing an identical, high-quality product and service."[73]

CHILD CARE[74]

McDonald's makes available to all employees, through Kinder Care and La Petite Academy, a tuition discount for child care.

ACCOMPLISHMENTS

DOMINATION OF THE INDUSTRY

McDonald's Corporation operates, licenses, and services the world's largest chain of fast-food restaurants and competes with virtually all restaurants (as well as with food stores on certain items). McDonald's Corporation has broadened its menu over the years to compete, to some extent, in virtually all areas. While McDonald's sales of food service or fast-food restaurants in the United States totaled 24 percent in 1993,[75] its market share of all restaurants, including convenience stores, cafeterias, and caterers,

EXHIBIT 7   **Profits and Assets**

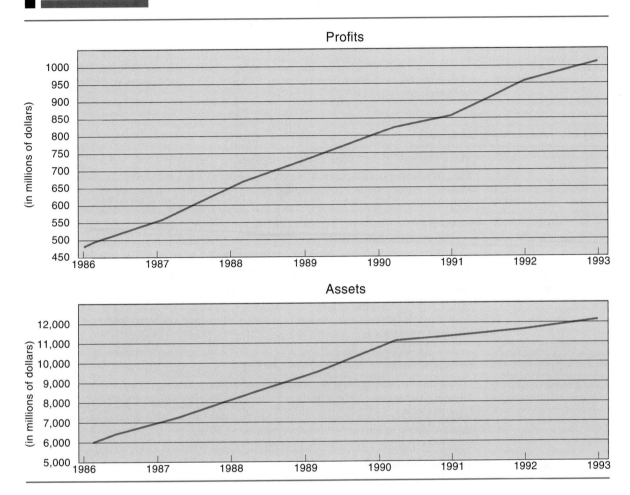

was 6.7 percent of the $213 billion market.[76] Hence, it appears that the company has room to grow from its current base.[77]

GROWTH

In recent years, domestic growth has slowed as a result of market saturation. Transactions and sales are best described as flat year over year, even though there has been a slight increase in U.S. sales from 6 percent to 7 percent from 1992 to 1993. This is not enough to signal a turnaround if compared with the 14 percent growth of 1985–89.[78] As a result, overall profit has grown at a slower rate from 11 percent between 1991 and 1992 to 7 percent between 1992 and 1993. From a qualitative point of view, the company's domestic profit mix is becoming more and more tied to franchise fee income. In 1993, earnings from company-owned stores represented 21 percent of total U.S. sales, down from 24 percent only 2 years ago.[79] McDonald's Corporation appears to be restructuring its domestic operations somewhat to receive more profits from franchise fees and less from store operations.

The 1993 sales increases were due to higher sales and transaction counts at existing restaurants and expansions, although sales outside the United States were negatively impacted by weaker foreign currencies.[80] This is a significant reason why the growth of sales outside the United States went from 17 percent between 1991 and 1992 to 9 percent between 1992 and 1993.[81] Estimates of stronger foreign currencies will bring McDonald's growth levels back up. McDonald's is a U.S. business with a growing excess cash flow that is being wisely reinvested outside the United States (a high-growth investment vehicle).

INTERNATIONAL SECTOR

Since the first international restaurant opened in Canada in 1967, McDonald's restaurants have expanded throughout the globe. Between 1985 and 1990, the number of McDonald's international restaurants has almost doubled. By December 31, 1993,[82] there were 9,283 units in the United States and 4,710 units in foreign countries, mostly in Japan, Canada, Germany, the United Kingdom, and Australia.[83]

The international sector's operating income growth fell to 9 percent between 1992 and 1993, from 21 percent between 1991 and 1992.[84] Improvements were achieved despite the effects of increasing capital expenditures and weak economies in several countries (including Canada and the United Kingdom, where McDonald's has a large percentage of its restaurants).

Because it presents the most growth potential, the international market is being emphasized to address the sluggish sales problem. McDonald's expects to boost expansion outside the United States in 1994 and in each of the next several years by adding 600 to 800 restaurants to the already existing 4,710.[85] Record first-day sales are common for restaurants located outside the United States. Thirty thousand customers visited McDonald's in Moscow on its first day of operation, and even more waited to try their first taste of McDonald's when it opened in Shenzhen, China.[86] By the end of 1993, more than $9 billion in international sales represented 40 percent of McDonald's systemwide sales.[87] McDonald's has considerable profit growth potential in the international sector because, although it has units in 68 countries, the majority of foreign profits are derived from only six countries: Canada, the United Kingdom, Germany, Japan, Australia, and France.

REFERENCES

"Big Mac Attacks with Pizza." *Fortune.* February 26, 1990, pp. 87–89.

Bowie, Norman. "New Directions in Corporate Responsibility." *Business Horizons.* July–August 1991, pp. 56–65.

Brown, Miriam. "Burger, Fries, Coke and a Career: Tallahassee's Fast-Food Managers Feel Good about Their Job Choice but Admit That Sometimes the Going Can Get Tough." *Tallahassee Democrat.* October 13, 1991, p. E1.

"Company Profile, McDonald's Corporation." *Fortune Business Reports.* October 9, 1991.

Curtis, James R. "McDonald's Abroad: Outpost of American Culture." *Journal of Geography.* January–February 1982, pp. 14–19.

Deveny, Kathleen. "McWorld?" *Business Week.* October 13, 1986, pp. 78–86.

"The Economics of the Golden Arches: A Case Study of McDonald's." *American Economist* 34. Fall 1990, pp. 60–64.

Emerson, Robert L. *The New Economics of Fast Food.* New York: Van Nostrand Reinhold, 1990, pp. 98–104.

Gerber, Beverly. "The Disabled: Ready, Willing and Able." *Training.* December 1990, pp. 29–36.

"Getting In on the Ground Floor." *Fortune.* Fall 1990, pp. 61–67.

Gibson, Richard. "Discount Menu Is Coming to McDonald's." *The Wall Street Journal.* November 30, 1990, p. B1.

Hassell, Greg. "Making Change." *Houston Chronicle.* January 6, 1991.

Hesselberg, George. "McDonald's in Moscow: A New Culture." *The Wall Street Journal.* February 25, 1990, p. G1.

Keeler, Bill. "Of Famous Arches, Beeg Meks and Rubles." *The New York Times.* January 28, 1990, pp. 1, 7.

King, Margaret J. "McDonald's and the New American Landscape." *USA Today.* January 1980, p. 46.

Krueger, Alan B. "Ownership, Agency, and Wages: An Examination of Franchising in the Fast Food Industry." *Quarterly Journal of Economics.* February 1991, pp. 75–101.

Laabs, Jennifer J. "The Golden Arches Provide Golden Opportunities." *Personnel Journal.* July 1991, pp. 52–57.

Love, John F. *McDonald's: Behind the Arches.* Toronto, New York: Bantam Books, 1986.

Mabry, Marcus. "Inside the Golden Arches." *Newsweek*. December 18, 1989, pp. 46–47.

McDonalds 1990 Company Report.

"McDonald's Corporation." Securities and Exchange Commission Form 10-K for Year Ended December 31, 1990.

"McD's Sizzles with New Ideas." *Advertising Age* 61. September 3, 1990, pp. 1, 53.

"The McDonald's Mystique." *Fortune*. July 4, 1988, pp. 112–116.

Melloan, George. "Global View." *The Wall Street Journal*. February 5, 1991, p. A15.

Noren, D. L. "The Economics of the Golden Arches." *American Economist*. Fall 1990, pp. 60–64.

Norton, Seth. "An Empirical Look at Franchising as an Organizational Form." *Journal of Business* 61, no 2 (1988), pp. 197–214.

"Nostalgia's Free at Golden Arch: New McDonald's Restaurant Concept." *Advertising Age* 61. September 10, 1990, p. 28.

Raiter, Gregory. "Inside Intelligence on Soviet Ventures." *HRMagazine*. January 1991, pp. 46–49.

"Reduced-fat Burgers and an Environmental Sense Help McDonald's Change Its Image." *Tallahassee Democrat*. June 12, 1991, p. D5.

"Slow Food: McDonald's in Moscow." *The Economist*. February 3, 1990, p. 25.

"Strategy." *Business Month* 136. October 1, 1990, pp. 38–42.

Therrien, Lois. "McRisky." *Business Week*. October 21, 1991, pp. 114–122.

Therrien, Lois. "Michael Quinlan." *Business Week 1000*, (1991). p. 62.

Therrien, Lois. "Restaurants: Doing Well by Being Big." *Business Week*. January 14, 1991, p. 92.

Upchurch, Jenny. "Burger, Fries, Coke, and a Career: Managers of Fast-Food Restaurants Are Finding Plenty of Opportunities." *Tallahassee Democrat*. October 13, 1991, p. E1.

"'Value' Trend Nibbles at Fast-Food Profits." *Advertising Age* 62. May 6, 1991, p. 20.

Waldrop, Judith. "Meet the New Boss." *American Demographics*. June 1991, pp. 26–38.

"Wanna Make a Deal in Moscow?" *Fortune*. October 22, 1990, pp. 113–115.

Wilcox, John. "A Campus Tour of Corporate Colleges." *Training & Development Journal*. May 1987, pp. 51–56.

Wildavsky, Ben. "McJobs." *Reader's Digest*. January 1990, pp. 126–130.

Willis, Clint. "Starting Out Right." *Money*. June 1991, pp. 85–96.

NOTES

1. "The Burger That Conquered the Country," *Time*, September 17, 1983, p. 84.

2. Margaret J. King, "McDonald's and the New American Landscape," *USA Today*, January 1980, p. 46.

3. *McDonald's 1993 Annual Report*, p. 37.

4. "The McDonald's Franchise" Brochure, June 10, 1994.

5. Ibid.

6. "McDonald's Franchising," The McDonald's Corporation 65-1555/McD 19373 2/94, p. 2.

7. *McDonald's 1993 Annual Report*, p. 15.

8. McDonald's Form 10-K, p. 16.

9. *McDonald's 1990 Annual Report*.

10. *McDonald's 1993 Annual Report*, p. 46.

11. "McDonald's Franchising" Brochure, June 10, 1994.

12. McDonald's Form 10-K, p. 2.

13. *McDonald's 1993 Annual Report*, pp. 10–11.

14. Robert L. Emerson, *The New Economics of Fast Food* (New York: Van Nostrand Reinhold, 1990), p. 102.

15. Alan B. Krueger, "Ownership, Agency, and Wages: An Examination of Franchising in the Fast Food Industry," *Quarterly Journal of Economics*, February 1991, p. 81.

16. *McDonald's 1993 Annual Report*, p. 15.

17. *McDonald's 1993 Annual Report*, pp. 16–17.

18. Kathleen Deveney, "McWorld?" *Business Week*, October 13, 1986, pp. 78–86.

19. Seth W. Norton, "Empirical Look at Franchising as an Organization Form," *Journal of Business* 61, April 1988, pp. 197–218.

20. Richard Gibson, "Dividend Boost, Stock Split Set at McDonald's," *The Wall Street Journal*, May 31, 1994. p. A4.

21. Lois Therrien, "McRisky," *Business Week*, October 19, 1991, p. 117.

22. *Time*, September 9, 1991, pp. 38–39.

23. *McDonald's 1993 Annual Report*, pp. 8–9.

24. "Out of the Frying Pan, Into the Fryer," *Science and Technology*, January 15, 1994, p. 89.

25. *McDonald's 1993 Annual Report*, pp. 8–9.

26. Gibson, "Dividend Boost, Stock Split Set at McDonald's," p. A4.

27. Denise Brennan, "The Name of the Game: Kidding Around," *Restaurant Business*, June 10, 1991, pp. 98–106.

28. Gibson, "Dividend Boost, Stock Split Set at McDonald's," p. A4.

29. Sales after 4:00 P.M. are considered dinner sales.

30. Therrien, "McRisky," p. 120.

31. Therrien, "McRisky," p. 120.

32. "McDonald's Mulls Idea of a Sit-Down Restaurant," *The Wall Street Journal*, March 7, 1994, p. B6.

33. *McDonald's 1993 Annual Report*, p. 18.

34. *McDonald's 1993 Annual Report*, p. 21.

35. Ibid.

36. Ibid.

37. Ibid.

38. *McDonald's 1990 Annual Report*.

39. McDonald Student Packet 1993, Vol. MCD1-1274, pp. 9–10.

40. Ibid.

41. Ibid.

42. "McDonald's Commitment to Education" Pamphlet, McD1-1332.

43. Ibid.

44. These programs are discussed in further detail in the "Human Resources" section of the case.

45. *McDonald's 1993 Annual Report*, p. 13.

46. Ibid.

47. Ibid.

48. Ibid.

49. *McDonald's 1990 Annual Report,* p. 18.

50. "McDonald's Commitment to the Environment" Pamphlet, 1994, McDonald's Corporation, McD-4/94.

51. *McDonald's Student Packet,* 1994 McDonald's Corporation, McD1-1274.

52. *McDonald's 1993 Annual Report,* p. 13.

53. *McDonald's Student Packet,* 1994, McDonald's Corporation, McD 19169-4/94.

54. Jennifer J. Laabs, "The Golden Arches Provide Golden Opportunities," *Personnel Journal,* July 1991, pp. 52–57.

55. Telephone interview with Monica Boyles, past director of McDonald's Changing World Force Program.

56. Laabs, "The Golden Arches Provide Golden Opportunities," pp. 52–57.

57. John Wilcox, "A Campus Tour of Corporate Colleges," *Training & Development Journal,* May 1987, pp. 51–56.

58. *McDonald's 1993 Annual Report,* p. 9.

59. *McDonald's 1990 Annual Report.*

60. Ray Kroc, *Grinding It Out: The Making of McDonald's* (Chicago: Contemporary Books, 1977).

61. *McDonald's 1993 Annual Report,* p. 9.

62. John F. Love, *McDonald's Behind the Arches* (Toronto: Bantam Books, 1986).

63. Marcus Mabry, "Inside the Golden Arches," *Newsweek,* December 18, 1989, pp. 46–47.

64. Ibid.

65. Kroc, *Grinding It Out: The Making of McDonald's.*

66. Ibid.

67. Deborah Shalowitz-Cowans, "Expanding the Menu: Broadened Efforts Helps McDonald's Explain Benefits," *Business Insurance,* May 9, 1994, p. 3.

68. Ibid.

69. *McDonald's 1990 Annual Report.*

70. McDonald's Brochure on Benefits and Compensation, January 1991.

71. Ibid.

72. Ibid.

73. Kroc, *Grinding It Out: The Making of McDonald's.*

74. Ibid.

75. Reddy Darnay, *Market Share Reporter 1993,* p. 1,631.

76. *McDonald's 1993 Annual Report,* p. 11.

77. J. C. Frazzano, "McDonald's Corporation—Company Report," Oppenheimer & Co., Inc., 1991, Thomson Financial Network, Inc., May 2, 1991.

78. *McDonald's 1993 Annual Report,* pp. 15–20.

79. Ibid.

80. Ibid.

81. Ibid.

82. *McDonald's 1993 Annual Report,* p. 17.

83. "Company Profile, McDonald's Corporation," *Fortune Reports.*

84. *McDonald's 1993 Annual Report,* pp. 20–21.

85. Ibid.

86. McDonald's Student Packet 1993, Vol. MCD1-1274, p. 33.

87. *McDonald's 1993 Annual Report,* p. 20.

CASE 4

THE WALT DISNEY COMPANY

INTRODUCTION

OVERVIEW OF THE COMPANY

The Walt Disney Company has become one of the most recognized organizations in the world. The company is spirited by the success of its theme parks, resort hotels, consumer goods, and movies. Even those who have not visited one of Disney's many theme parks and/or resorts or seen a Disney movie have certainly seen or heard about the likes of one of the most notable characters of all time: Mickey Mouse. He has been a key to Disney's success. From the creation of Mickey Mouse to the exciting play of the National Hockey League's Anaheim Mighty Ducks, the Disney Company has grown in its diversification without neglecting its success. Disney currently operates many different businesses while continuing its strong alliances with licensees, manufacturers, and retail outlets. This diverse and successful company has spawned from the success of a mouse and the talents of Walter E. Disney.

As shown in Exhibit 1, Disney's income for 1994 is expected to be more than $800 million, up sharply from $300 million in 1993, as the drag on earnings from EuroDisney lessens. Exhibit 1 also shows that filmed entertainment and theme parks/resorts contribute the bulk of the revenue. Note also that Disney's box office share has increased dramatically from 4 percent in 1984 to 20 percent in 1994. No question about it—Disney is a very successful company.

By mid-1995, Disney has embarked on an entirely new venture. In one of the largest acquisitions of all time, Disney acquired Capital Cities/ABC. This was done to leverage Disney's name and products throughout network broadcasting.

COMPANY HISTORY

Since Walt Disney's personality, dreams, and attitudes still influence the company, a look at both his and his company's history until his death offers insights into the Disney of today. His successes and battles with distributors, strikers, merchandisers, and even friends left an indelible mark on the man and the realization of his dream.

NOTE: This case was prepared by Kathleen Peterson, Jennifer Bowers, Troy Smith, and Warren Saunders and revised by Tina Daly, Beth Roper, Dennis Solo, and Steve Waters.

■ EXHIBIT 1   Disney's Success

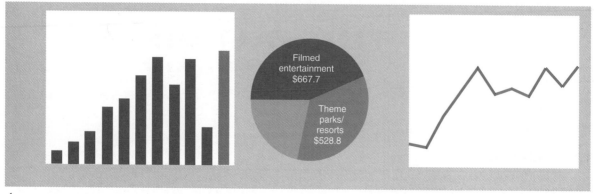

Profits	**Business Lines**	**Market Share**
Net Income, in millions	Based on 1994 revenue[2], in millions	Disney's box-office share based on ticket sales in the U.S. and Canada

[1] Includes $350 million fourth-quarter charge related to investment in EuroDisney
[2] First nine months
[3] Through Aug. 23

Source: Richard Tarner, "Walt Disney Presents: Forward to the Future," *The Wall Street Journal*, August 26, 1994, p. B1.

THE BEGINNING

Walter Elias Disney was born in 1901 in Chicago, but his family moved to a farm near Marcilene, Missouri, in 1906. It was this place that proved to be the inspiration for things to come and also the place where four-year-old Walter first learned to draw. The story goes that Walt and his sister Ruth discovered a barrel of tar on the farm and proceeded to draw on the newly whitewashed fence with sticks dipped in the black liquid. Since his father Elias was rather a strict disciplinarian, Walt and Ruth were appropriately punished. Despite this, Walt's Aunt Margaret encouraged him by bringing paper and crayons from Kansas City, where she lived.[1]

Walt was an avid reader, but in grammar school his first love remained drawing. His unusual style sometimes got him in trouble, though. Once, when he was asked to draw a pot of flowers, he added faces to the blooms and arms instead of leaves. He attended children's art classes at the Kansas City Art Institute and persuaded his father to pay for a correspondence course in art, which he did. As Walt grew older, it seemed that he was either in school (McKinley High), washing bottles at this father's jelly factory, or drawing.[2]

Walt was eager to play his part in the war effort and in 1918 enlisted in the American Ambulance Corps. He convinced his mother to sign his passport application, which showed Walt to be of age, and he was sent to France. He kept up with his drawing, and when he returned to the United States he applied for jobs as a cartoonist at several papers. He failed to find an opening but soon signed on at the Pesmin-Rubin Commercial Art Studio for the sum of $50 per week.[3]

WALT'S EARLY EFFORTS

Walt didn't realize that he was taken on to meet a seasonal increase in work, and he was laid off after the Christmas rush. He and a friend, Ub Iwerks, created a company called

Iwerks-Disney Commercial Artists, which quickly failed. This trend continued at a slightly less disastrous company called Laugh-O-Grams, which Walt and other investors formed in 1920. Following his brother Roy's advice to "get out of there," Walt traveled to Hollywood in 1923, after the firm went bankrupt.[4]

Hollywood met all of Walt's expectations, and he set up shop in a small office and got some stationary printed that boldly said "Walt Disney—Cartoonist." He contacted a distributor in New York that he had sent information to while with Laugh-O-Gram and explained an idea for a cartoon/live action series called "Alice Comedies." He prevailed upon the creditors of Laugh-O-Gram to allow him to release the only existing cartoon to the distributor. With a few changes, a deal was struck, and Walt hired a lot on Hollywood Boulevard for live-action filming. He rented a shop adjoining the premises, called the signwriters in, and emblazoned the words "Disney Bros. Studio," with his brother Roy as partner.[5]

TEMPORARY SUCCESS

Roy had more of a talent for managing the money than for animation, and Walt had quite a talent for spending what little money they had. This was characteristic of the quest for quality that obsessed Walt, and the early days were a preamble of what was to come. Walt and Roy begged loans from anyone they could, and the company was in a perilous situation in 1924. Walt had no choice but continue on with the relationship.[6]

About this time, Universal Pictures was looking for a new cartoon series featuring a rabbit, and it was suggested that Walt be given the project, with the Alice Series' company as the distributor. Walt gladly accepted, and created "Oswald, the lucky rabbit." The series was a critical and financial success, and all seemed to be going well for the studios. The frequent checks were now being delivered by Walt's distributors.[7]

During this time, Walt married Lillian Bounds, who was employed as an ink-and-paint girl at the studios. She and Walt took a trip to New York to negotiate a deal for the next series of Oswald cartoons with his distributor. Walt had intended to ask the distributor for an increase in the fee per picture, but they offered Walt a reduced price. Walt angrily refused and was informed that if he chose to refuse the offer, the distributor would take his whole firm away from him (they had signed up all his animators). A quick phone call to Roy revealed that what the distributor said was true, and Walt started to look frantically for an alternative distributor. However, Walt's distributor informed him that even if he did find another distributor, Universal held all the rights to the character he had created. Walt and Lillian took the train back to Hollywood, and Walt vowed never to lose control over his interests again.[8]

THE MOUSE

"DON'T WORRY EVERYTHING OK GIVE DETAILS WHEN I ARRIVE." This was the cable that Walt sent Roy before leaving for home from New York, and it is definitely an example of the incredible optimism that so characterized Walt Disney. The truth was, however, that things were not okay, but Walt viewed the situation as an opportunity to create a character that could be even more successful than Oswald, the not-so-lucky rabbit.

No one really knows how the idea of the character came about. So much of the tale is shrouded in myth, to the delight of Walt Disney, that we may never know exactly what happened. What we do know is that out of the turmoil of that visit to New York came a character that would become perhaps the best-known icon of our time and the key to the success of Disney Studios. As Walt would later remark to his employees, "I hope we never lose sight of one fact . . . that this was all started by a mouse. . . ."[9]

When he arrived back in Hollywood, Walt had to break the news about the loss to his brother Roy and the only other loyal animator, Ub Iwerks. He was able to temper it with news about the new cartoon series he had envisioned. The mouse, originally to be named Mortimer, would be called Mickey (at the insistence of Lillian). The defecting animators would not be leaving for another three months, so Walt and Ub had to labor in secret and very quickly to boot. The cartoon, called *Plane Crazy,* was churned out in only two weeks, with Ub averaging an amazing seven hundred drawings per day—one per minute! The plot revolved around a rickety plane built by Mickey and his barnyard friends after Mickey reads about Charles Lindbergh. Mickey then sets off with his girlfriend Minnie, and the two characters became symbols of youth, optimism, and adventure.[10]

The cartoon was received warmly, but no distributor could be found. It seemed that the mouse was likable enough, but he didn't have a unique hook to set him apart from the other cartoon characters. After *The Jazz Singer,* the first movie with synchronized sound, was released, Walt decided that this would be what made Mickey different—sound. He authorized Roy to hock everything, including his car. With the company teetering on the edge of bankruptcy, Walt made the first cartoon to incorporate sound, *Steamboat Willie.*[11]

The film was held over two weeks at the Roxy Theater and was no less than a triumph. The next three Mickey Mouse cartoons had sound added, and "the mouse" was soon so popular that more animators had to be added to the staff. More films came, including the *Silly Symphony* series, and soon Mickey and Minnie were as popular as any flesh-and-blood movie actors. In 1929, Walt was approached by a man offering him $300 to put the image of Mickey and Minnie on children's notebooks. As usual, the money was needed, and Walt agreed. Within a year, hundreds of manufacturers were producing officially licensed products, and the fortunes of the company seemed safe at last.[12]

THE COMPANY TAKES OFF

Mickey's place among the public was secure, and the offshots of the cartoons were bringing in substantial revenues. Consumer products, such as the Mickey Mouse watch, sold like hotcakes, and the Mickey Mouse Clubs that cinema owners across the country put together boasted a million members. In 1930, one of the most well-regarded promoters in the country, Herman Kamen, offered to manage the licensing of Disney characters, and the brothers jumped at the opportunity.[13]

The cartoons were the core business of the studios, after all, and they were turned out one after another. In addition to the *Silly Symphonies* and Mickey Mouse cartoons, the studios put out *The Ugly Duckling, Three Blind Mouseketeers,* and *The Three Little Pigs.* In the 1930s, Mickey got such sidekicks as Clara Cluck, Pluto, Goofy, and the irrepressible Donald Duck. These characters were successful, but Walt had a more ambitious project in mind—a full length animated film.

SNOW WHITE—A NEW ERA

No one else had dared to make a full-length animated feature previously. The task was daunting, and the amount of drawings alone would be enormous. But Walt was positive that not only could it be done, but that it would be successful. He began preparation for this full-length cartoon as a general would prepare for battle. By the time it was over, the *Snow White* team would include eighty-five animators, story and gag writers, inkers, painters, and several departments of technicians. Not only did *Snow White* have to be produced, but the regular quota of short films had to be continued. Both tasks were accomplished, but the financial and personal pressures were great. Production took five years.[14]

What had been called "Disney's folly" was an absolute success, both nationally and internationally with its release on February 4, 1938. The studio's place in history had been assured, and the genius of Disney and his artists was without question. Adding to the success of the film were the revenues from various consumer products, including seeds, shampoos, and even diapers.[15]

"THE GOLDEN YEARS"

It was clear to Walt that the current studio was not adequate to meet the needs of an ambitious schedule as the company grew, so a suitable site was located in Burbank and construction began. During this time, Walt also felt it necessary to reorganize the company. In 1938, a huge document detailing organizational structure and job descriptions was drawn up, a far cry from the ad hoc type of arrangement that had been operating for years.

DISNEY GOES PUBLIC

Germany invaded Poland on September 1, 1939. As the war consumed more and more of Europe, the 45 percent in revenues that Disney enjoyed from that part of the world quickly dried up. As income diminished, costs escalated, particularly on the production of *Fantasia*. Disney had over 1,000 people working for him, and despite *Pinocchio's* critical success, the film did not do well at the box office. The new studios were just being completed and payment was due. Roy Disney confronted his brother in the spring of 1940 with the news—the company was $4.5 million in debt.[16]

Walt's first response was to laugh, because he remembered a time in the not-so-distant past when the studio could not borrow a thousand dollars, much less a million. But the situation was serious, so the Disney brothers opted for an issue of stock on the public market. In April of 1940, the company offered 155,000 shares of 6 percent cumulative convertible preferred stock at $25 par value and 600,000 shares of common stock at $5 per share. The offering raised $3,500,000 in much-needed capital.[17]

An ominous threat was brewing, however, and it would prove to be more trying to Walt than merely funding the company.

THE STRIKE

It seemed that ever since the move from the old studios, the atmosphere of camaraderie and creativity had been on the wane. The artists felt cut off from the creative process and, worst of all, from Walt himself. Rumors about the staff and management began to circulate, ranging from the cost of the number of waitresses in the cafeteria to a fictitious "inner ring" of Walt's employees who enjoyed privileges that others did not. The legalistic job descriptions and organizational charts did nothing to help, and it wasn't long before there was unrest in the Disney organization.

The disharmony was evident, and when the price of Disney stock began to fall, many employees chose to cash in. Walt demonstrated his belief in the company by buying the shares of anyone who wanted to sell. The stage was set for some type of union organization, and the Disney animators became the prime target for activists.

Disney had always operated a closed shop with various other trades, but the animators were not organized. Two separate unions canvassed the animators: the independent Federation of Screen Cartoonists and the Screen Cartoonists Guild, led by Herbert Sorrell and affiliated with the Brotherhood of Painters, Paperhangers, and Decorators of America. Many animators, being a bit naive, joined both unions, and some joined neither. Sorrell tried to get Walt Disney to join his union, claiming that a majority of his animators already had. Walt told Sorrell that he wanted the matter put to a ballot organized by the National Labor Relations Board, but Sorrell refused.[18]

Walt tried to calm the rumors and increase communication with his staff by issuing a recorded speech addressing the concerns of the animators. He stressed that he had never been interested in a personal gain or profit, and said that instead of complaining, the employees of the company should count their blessings. Despite this plea, the tensions came to a head when Goofy's chief animator, Art Babbit, was dismissed. He had long been a supporter of the Guild and Herb Sorrell maintained that the dismissal was in reprisal for union activities. The long-threatened strike was called in May of 1941. Walt said, "to me, the entire situation is a catastrophe."[19]

The strike was settled in October of 1941, with Sorrell claiming victory for the unions. Walt said that the strike was settled in the simplest way—"the negotiators gave Sorrell everything he wanted."[20] The animosities and confrontations were not easily forgotten, and within two years many of the strikers had left the company, including Art Babbit. A noticeable change came over Walt, and, wary of further trouble, he insisted that every employee join the proper union, down to the gardeners. He became more cautious and remote in his relationships.

THE YEARS 1940–1966

A NEW OUTLOOK ON COSTS

The financial problems that had always plagued the company did not vanish, however, and Walt announced a new policy regarding costs. Staff were urged to adopt "a constructive attitude toward every dollar that went into developing, producing, and selling the scheduled pictures."[21] From now on, there would be a production schedule that would be adhered to, movies would come in within budgets, stories would be more thoroughly prepared to eliminate costly changes, and all departments would be policed in order to prevent unnecessary expenses. Selling and exploiting the pictures to the fullest would also be of utmost importance.

Under the new rules, the studio continued to produce hits. *Cinderella* was released in 1950, followed by *Alice in Wonderland* in 1951. *Peter Pan* arrived in 1953, along with the Disney signature fairy, Tinkerbell. Also in the 1950s, Disney turned to films with live characters, such as *Treasure Island* (1950), *20,000 Leagues Under the Sea* (1954), and the musical fantasy, *Mary Poppins* (1964). Disney also turned to the filmed entertainment area for nature films, whose fine photography was marred for some critics by the sentimentality of approach. Disney also produced many films for television audiences: the "Davy Crockett" series and the "Mickey Mouse Club" helped revive the old cartoon figures for several new generations of children. The Disney Channel today offers "Disneyfied" entertainment to subscribed cable television viewers. But in the early 1950s, the greatest production of all, however, was just beginning to brew in the mind of its creator.

DISNEYLAND

The original concept for Disneyland came to Walt's mind in early 1939, but the details were not thought out until 1951. Walt formed WED Enterprises so that stockholders would not object to the new venture, and attempted to persuade investors to fund the project. This proved difficult, so Walt backed his idea with his own money. A site was selected in 1953—160 acres in Anaheim, California, just 25 miles from Los Angeles. As Walt put it:

> There's nothing like it in the whole world—I know, because I've looked. That's why it can be great; because it will be unique. A new concept in entertainment, and I think—I *know*—it can be a success.[22]

Disneyland opened on July 17, 1955. That morning traffic was jammed for over seven miles on the roads leading to the park, and by midday over 30,000 people had passed through the turnstiles. It was the beginning of what Walt was later to term "Black Sunday." The staff had been hired from agencies and treated the guests with the same belligerence they used for dealing with crowds at racetracks and ballparks. Several rides broke down, while others were dangerously overcrowded. The food and drinks ran out, water fountains were inadequate, and the park became littered with trash.

To make the changes necessary, Walt built an apartment over the Main Street Fire Station and spent 24 hours a day at the park for two weeks. An army of young men was employed to clean up the litter, standards for staff courtesy and efficiency were established, and ways of speeding up the waiting times for rides were found. It was a headache, but this experience afforded an opportunity not found in the movies—a chance for continual improvement. Disneyland, as it turned out, was a turning point in the fortunes of the company. After 16 months, net profits were the highest in the company's history.[23]

FROM DISNEYLAND UNTIL WALT'S DEATH

For the World's Fair in 1964, Walt approached a number of corporations and asked to design their attractions. It was a decision that would have far-reaching consequences. The Ford Motor Company bought Walt's design for a car ride through history from caveman to spaceman, and Pepsi helped develop the idea that would eventually become the boat ride known as "It's a Small World." The president of the World's Fair commissioned what would become one of the fair's major attractions, a three-dimensional, talking and moving Abraham Lincoln. Audiences experienced a sensation of being in the crowd listening to a Lincoln speech. The Disney-designed exhibits drew over 46 million visitors.

During this time, Walt also began to acquire land for "Disneyland East," another theme park to be located in Orlando, Florida. The idea of a prototype community, later to be known as EPCOT, was also taking shape, and Walt began sharing his dream with the world—after the land was purchased, however. The cost of the two projects was estimated at $500 million.[24]

Unbeknownst to anyone but his closest aides, Walt Disney was very ill. He was admitted to the hospital on November 2, 1966, and X-rays showed a spot on his left lung. It was found to be cancerous and was removed, and Walt seemed to be recovering. He went back to work but soon fell ill again. After two more weeks in the hospital, he rallied somewhat, and even spoke with his brother Roy about details of the Disneyland project on December

14. The next morning, Walt Disney died of acute circulatory collapse. As Richard Zanuck said, "No eulogy will be read or monument built to equal the memorial Walt Disney has left in the hearts and minds and imaginations of the world's peoples."[25]

LIFE AFTER WALT

The years after Walt Disney's death were marked by feuds between "Roy men," the financial types, and "Walt men," the creative types. Nearly everything, including film making, was undertaken only after a discussion over what Walt would have done. This philosophy worked for a while but eventually led to the deterioration of the film segment of the company. This was marked by Disney's refusal to produce *Raiders of the Lost Ark* and *E.T.* simply because of the creator's desire to have a share of the profits. The dismal decisions led to a devaluation of Disney's stock and a takeover effort in 1984 by Roy Disney, Jr., among others.[26]

Sid Bass and Stanley Gold were the "white knights" that helped stave off the raiders. On the inside, they insisted upon a shakeup in management. This resulted in the hiring of Michael Eisner, Frank Wells, and Jeffry Katzenberg. These individuals engineered a remarkable turnaround in the film division as well as other divisions within the company, and Disney has shown record earnings and growth for the past few years. It was a choice that Walt would have approved. In 1995, after Frank Wells's death, Disney hired Michael Ovitz, Hollywood's premier powerbroker from Creative Artists Agency, as its president. His contacts with celebrities are expected to help Disney in movies and films.[27]

WHAT DISNEY SELLS?

Disney "sells" family entertainment through its theme parks, resorts, filmed entertainment, and consumer products. Future developments include two 2,400-passenger cruise ships and a theatrical touring company à la Andrew Lloyd Webber, one that might, ultimately, have a repertoire of two or three plays. And the company continues to invest in other units such as television, music, publishing, video games, professional sports, a new movie label, and interactive video. Near-term, television is Disney's most promising growth area. When Disney's television hit "Home Improvement" goes into syndication in 1995, it is estimated to bring in $100 million during the first year of its running and approximately $50 million in each of the following three years.[28] These entertainment products can be found throughout the world.

Due to the growing affection for Mickey Mouse and friends, Disney theme parks are scattered across the globe. Park attractions now include Walt Disney World, EPCOT, and Disney-MGM Studios in Orlando, Florida; Disneyland in Anaheim, California; Tokyo Disneyland in Japan; and EuroDisney in Marne-La-Valle'e, France, with plans for Disney's America theme park in Manassas, Virginia, scheduled to open in 1998. Disney has used the public's growing affection to venture into different markets.

ACQUISITIONS AND DEVELOPMENTS

Disney has begun to sell its products outside of the normal settings of its theme parks. Currently, Disney products can be found in department stores on clothing, in grocery stores on food products, and in toy stores. Also, the Disney name can now be found on Mattel products, since the two companies joined forces in the toy industry. From this alliance will come "Mattel-sponsored attractions at Disney theme parks, the development of park-related toys, and the expansion of Disney's lucrative toy-licensing pacts with Mattel."

Disney continues to maintain, develop, and improve its current theme parks, resorts, and entertainment productions while expanding into different ventures to improve its company image. Some recent developments include Disney's expansion into the ownership and marketing of professional sports. The company's 1992 purchase of the NHL's Anaheim Mighty Ducks has proved successful, as they are leading in sales of licensed merchandise. This Disney success has the company exploring the option to purchase the NBA franchise, The Los Angeles Clippers, hoping to open new avenues in sports programming. With today's increasing computer technology, Disney plans to educate the youth of America with its publication *Family PC,* released in March 1995. Disney's attempt to establish a strong corporate and artistic presence has led to its funding of the restoration of The New Amsterdam Theatre on W. 42nd Street in New York.[29] This enables Disney to bring a new crowd to Broadway, with its recent release of the musical "Beauty and the Beast," currently playing to standing-room-only audiences.[30] Finally, Disney's acquisition of Capital Cities/ABC is expected to provide new opportunities and synergies to leverage Disney assets.

GLOBALIZATION

On April 2, 1992, The Walt Disney Company expanded to Marne-la-Valle'e, France, in an effort to further diversify within the theme park segment of the industry. However, this investment, EuroDisney, bombed because attendance was much weaker than Disney had anticipated; and those that did attend the park left their hands out of their pockets. Other dismal results of EuroDisney's expectations include a prolonged labor dispute that could further threaten the financial stability of the theme park. The best news about the theme park is that Disney may own less of it. If all goes well with EuroDisney's new stock offering, Disney's share will be reduced to 36 percent from 46 percent, thanks to His Royal Highness Prince Al-Waleed Bin Talai Bin Abdulaziz Al Saud, the Saudi billionaire who has become EuroDisney's new "White Knight." Under the terms of the agreement, if the prince cannot buy a sufficient amount of stock from the shareholders, Disney is required to sell him up to $178 million worth of its own shares. Disney still insists that, in the end, EuroDisney will prove a profitable investment.[31]

Disney films have been in the global market for quite some time. Disney blockbusters have also been very popular overseas. For example, *Dead Poets Society* did 25 percent more business in foreign countries than in the United States.[32] Disney home videos and consumer products are faring well in foreign lands. Even though only seven of Disney's twenty-two animated movies have been released overseas, the response for this market has been overwhelming.

THEME PARKS AND RESORTS

Theme parks and resorts are the largest segment of Disney, accounting for more than 40 percent of Disney profits.[33] However, with the weak economic picture, park admissions have been stagnant, with sales and operating income increasing by approximately 2 percent per year for the 1991–93 period. In hopes of achieving a turnaround, Disney is planning to revamp its current park system. EPCOT's new "Innoventions" exhibit, a tomorrowland of technology, will feature products created by General Motors Corporation and Apple Computer, Inc. Disney hopes this will spark a dwindling fire of outdated technology that the park currently offers. Disney also plans expansions on its Disneyland theme park in California and new attractions at MGM studios in Florida, including the Tower of Terror Hotel attraction opened in summer 1994. More ideas on the horizon include the Disney Institute, which Disney calls "a new generation of vacation experiences combining enrichment and entertainment" and "Celebration," a new city that ultimately will house 20,000 residents.

Disney had planned to build a theme park called "Disney America" on a Civil War battlefield in Manassas, Virginia, that is designated as a national park. This project has stirred much controversy among preservationists and others, who oppose the 3,000-acre development. Disney America, however, has received a standing ovation by government officials in Virginia, who say the park would bring 19,000 new jobs to the area. Disney plans to depict American heritage in a theme park setting while trying to bring history and patriotism alive. However, at the time of this writing, the plans for this theme park had been put on hold.

FILMED ENTERTAINMENT

The Disney popularity has carried over from the theme parks into its other product lines. For example, Disney movies have always been known as major players in the field of family entertainment. Disney Studios has produced such recent blockbusters as *Pretty Woman, Aladdin, The Little Mermaid, Beauty and the Beast,* and *The Lion King.* These complement long-standing hits such as *Bambi, Snow White,* and *Dumbo.* These movies, along with others from Disney's Touchstone and Hollywood Pictures, have lead to Disney's continued success in film entertainment.

Currently, Disney films are at the height of their success. Disney has been relying on its animated films for continued increasing profits. Disney Studios has produced some of the biggest profiting blockbusters of all time. Its list of such hits includes *The Little Mermaid* (1991), *Beauty and the Beast* (1992), *Aladdin* (1993), and *The Lion King* (1994). Disney continues its one-hit-per-year approach with the release of *Pocahontas* in 1995. Disney's vision of success in the filmed entertainment business has overlapped into large profits from the home video arena. Home video allows the Disney Studios to benefit from the returns from its re-released classics (i.e., *Dumbo, Snow White,* and *Bambi*). Filmed entertainment has quickly risen as one of Disney's most successful and profitable areas. (See Exhibit 2.)

CONSUMER PRODUCTS

In 1987, the people who brought us everything from Mickey Mouse to *Pretty Woman* decided to open their first retail store outside of their theme parks. The first store was opened in the Glendale Galleria, near Disney company headquarters in Anaheim, California. By 1991, the Disney Store had become one of the most sought-after chains in the shopping center industry.[34] Disney consumer products are doing well in both the domestic and foreign markets. These products range from watches and clothing to toys and food products. Disney consumer product lines are carried in Disney theme parks, department stores, specialty stores, and supermarkets. As of May 1994, there were 263 Disney Stores. This segment of Disney is growing rapidly and depends on the success of other Disney products, such as the theme parks and movie characters. The stores expertly combine retailing and entertainment while promoting Disney's films and theme parks at the same time. Disney has several joint ventures or alliances with companies in related businesses. For example, Disney has a 10-year contract with Nestlé that allows Nestlé to produce food products using Disney characters. These ventures and others will help Disney to make a strong stand in the consumer products market.

EXHIBIT 2   **Disney Operating Income by Product Group**

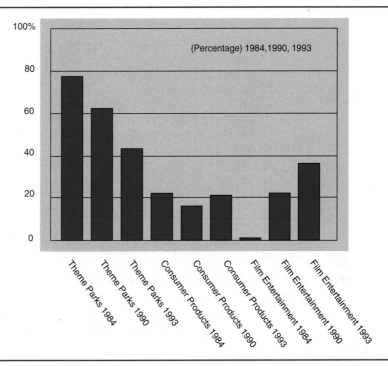

SOURCE: Michael K. Ozanian, "Mouse Trap?" *Financial World,* March 15, 1994, pp. 28–31.

HUMAN RESOURCES

Walt Disney once said, "You can dream, create, design, and build the most wonderful place in the world, but it requires people to make that dream a reality" ("The Disney Approach to People Management"). The success of the entire Disney empire is built on the excellent customer service that Disney provides for its guests. Disney calls this customer service "Disney Courtesy." The key for getting all 39,000-plus Disney cast members to live, eat, breathe, and sleep Disney courtesy is the Disney Orientation process, part of Disney's well-organized, structured approach to human relations.

ORIENTATION

Disney's orientation process is ongoing for all Disney cast members beginning from the recruitment stage. It continuously reinforces the values, philosophies, and guest service standards that Disney has prided itself on for so many years. Exhibit 3 shows Disney's comprehensive approach to employee relations. It is reinforced with activities, management style, and language. Employees at Disney are called "cast members" and they do not work at a job, they are "cast in a role for the show." Disney uses this terminology to immerse its employees in an environment that constantly reinforces the image Disney wants to project to the public. Also, cast members work either on-stage or back-stage, and they wear costumes instead of uniforms. Since they could interact with guests at any time, all Disney employees, whether they are on-stage cast members or back-stage cast members, are required to learn and use Disney courtesy at all times. (See Exhibit 4.)

| **EXHIBIT 3** | **Employee Relations Philosophy** |

We believe in

1. Being fair and impartial in our relations with all employees without regard to race, religion, color, national origin, age, sex, marital status, and handicaps.
2. Providing an opportunity for all employees to reach their personal goals while accomplishing the goals of the organization.
3. Providing a safe and meaningful working environment that contributes to a feeling of worth and individual dignity for each member of our "family."
4. Providing opportunities for growth and development on the job through comprehensive training programs.
5. Providing competitive pay and benefits which recognize employee loyalty, dedication, and individual contribution.
6. Promoting from within our organization when and where feasible.
7. An informal, friendly management style, encouraging open lines of communications at all levels.
8. Teamwork—each of us working together toward common, understood goals.

| **EXHIBIT 4** | **The Disney Product: Guest Service** |

In providing the Disney brand of GUEST SERVICE, our cast members are . . .

I. COURTEOUS
  - Tone of Voice
  - Smile
  - Considerate
  - Hospitable
II. IMAGE-CONSCIOUS
  - Appearance
  - Demeanor
  - Attitude
  - Eye Contact
III. HIGH PERFORMERS
  - Knowledgeable
  - Accurate
  - Thorough
  - Helpful
  - Creative

RECRUITMENT

Disney has a clean-cut image and conservative approach that helps potential employees self-select; thus, Disney usually attracts the type of applicants it wants. The Disney "casting" department (known as the human resource department in most businesses) is responsible for hiring qualified applicants that will be cast for a role in Disney's show. This department hires for general employment and college, international, and professional staffing. Hiring for general employment can come from both internal and external sources. Approximately 85 percent of Disney's middle- and executive-level management is hired from within; therefore, the majority of new general employment applicants come from internal sources.

All new-to-Disney applicants go through the same recruitment process. First, there is an eight-to-ten minute preliminary interview that contains a great number of applicants. The main emphasis of this initial interview is to give a realistic view of employment at Disney, to eliminate those who are not interested or are not qualified, and to reschedule a full interview for those applicants who are still interested in becoming a Disney cast member. Would-be cast members need to understand that a job at Disney is not all glamour and that it takes a lot of hard work. For example, Disney theme parks, resorts, and hotels are open 365 days a year and cast members work early mornings, days, evenings, weekends, holidays, and vacations. Additionally, all cast members must adhere to strict grooming standards. All would-be employees are shown a film that details the discipline, grooming, and dress codes that Disney expects all cast members to adhere to at all times. People with extreme styles will know at this point of the interview process if they will be able to adapt in order to be a part of Disney's show. The next step, the full interview, is conducted with three prospective candidates for forty-five minutes. These peer interviews allow the interviewer to get a closer look at the applicant by observing how each interacts with the others. One Disney manager stated, "This is a good indication of how they'll work with fellow cast members and guests. We're looking for human relations and communications skills. We can train them in the technical skills."[35]

DISNEY UNIVERSITY

Disney University is the corporate structure that teaches "Disney courtesy," translates company policy, and trains employees.[36] In other words, it is the framework that keeps all those things together. The concept of the Disney University started in Disneyland in 1955, along with Walt Disney's vision of an amusement park unlike any other. Disney dreamed of a family park that would be safe and friendly, and to which people would return. Thus, he decided that Disneyland (the only theme park at that time) needed a training facility to introduce new employees to the business of entertainment as he imagined it. Sharon Haywood, manager of the Disney Studio Disney University stated, "I doubt that (Walt Disney) called it the 'Disney Culture' but he had his finger on the pulse of what was necessary. He knew that you need to treat employees in the same way you want them to treat the guests."[37] What started as a one-hour program called "You Create Happiness" grew as Disneyland grew. In the 1960s, the Disney University was officially established.

Today, since each Disney facility has unique challenges and varying employee needs, each Disney facility has its own Disney University. Each university is responsible for training and development, employee activities, employee communications (such as ongoing written and audiovisual communications), researching and analyzing the organization's people needs, proposing plans to meet those needs, and, lastly, continually researching the effectiveness of the orientation and training programs.

TRADITIONS I & II AT DISNEY UNIVERSITY

All new cast members at any Disney facility begin their Disney careers with a two-day orientation seminar called "Traditions" that is conducted at the Disney University. (See Exhibit 5.) The role of the Disney University and the Traditions seminar is to provide cast members with a sound understanding of Disney's corporate tradition and values, provide skills essential to job performance, and provide accredited continuing professional growth and development for all cast members. (See Exhibit 6.) The Traditions two-day seminar is carefully scripted and conducted in a comfortable, specially

EXHIBIT 5   **Orientation and Development Process**

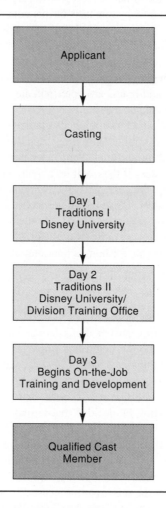

EXHIBIT 6   **Why Extensive Orientation?**

Disney provides extensive orientation:

- To establish the corporate culture and overall company knowledge
- To strengthen the self-image of cast members
- To communicate employee benefits, activities, and services
- To communicate the why and wherefore of company policies and procedures
- To transmit to cast members the people skills and attitudes prerequisite to the job skills needed to perform their roles in the show
- To create a team spirit among new members of the Disney cast
- To answer the initial questions of new cast members
- To review safety procedures, right-to-know regulations, and other required regulations

designed training room. The first day of orientation, Traditions I, cast members learn the history, traditions, and milestones of the worldwide Disney team, Walt Disney's philosophy and the standards of guest service, and where they fit into the corporate structure (their role in the show), and they receive a tour of the Disney property where they will work. Cast members are also introduced to the intangible product, happiness, and their role in creating it. The second day of orientation, Traditions II, is devoted to the Disney policies and practices cast members must know to perform their jobs, an overview of what the company provides the cast members in terms of social, recreational, and personal services, and a four-hour orientation of their specific work area that includes meeting with their supervisors, learning what costumes they will wear, and reviewing general policies and procedures.

When the two-day Traditions orientation is completed, cast members begin a series of learning experiences at on-site practice sessions and classes at the university. This training may run from 8 to 16 hours before cast members are allowed to go to their specific work area after closing and practice.

The next step, paired training, allows exceptional cast members to act as role models. The benefits of paired training include (1) the new cast member rehearses with a respected member of the troupes and (2) the veteran cast member is recognized by management, as well as by peers, and held in esteem. These new cast members are required to have between 16 to 48 hours of paired training and are not allowed to interact solo with guests until they have successfully completed paired training and have successfully answered questions on the training checklist.

REINFORCEMENT KEEPS CAST MEMBERS COMMITTED TO DISNEY PRINCIPLES

Many of Disney's hourly jobs can be routine and repetitive, but Disney still expects "energy, enthusiasm, commitment and pride" from its cast members at all times. Recognition, communications, and social relations programs are especially important at Disney. Disney's goal is to constantly look for a variety of ways to tell workers how much they are valued. Cast member appreciation from Disney management comes in the form of service recognition awards, peer recognition programs, attendance awards, informal recognition parties, and milestone banquets for 10, 15, and 20 years of service.

Each year the centralized Disney University gives special recognition to several outstanding cast members who are called University Leaders. Four to six hourly, costumed cast members are interviewed and selected for a year-long assignment at the Disney University. The entire Disney University orientation is conducted by these University Leaders. These cast members help bring the philosophical Disney ideals to reality by a person who is currently fulfilling that role. This program allows Disney to recognize outstanding cast members while better utilizing their talents.

Another expression of gratitude and appreciation from Disney management comes during the Christmas holidays. All Disney theme parks reopen one evening for cast members and their families. The management team says "Happy Holidays" by dressing in costume and operating the parks.[38]

DEVELOPMENT: AN ONGOING PROCESS

Training does not stop when cast members learn their roles. Hourly cast members are offered career development, goal setting, and interviewing technique classes. Clerical staff are offered courtesy and clerical stress management classes. Disney's Leaders (hourly workers who have been given a leadership role for their job classification) and trainers receive special development including performance appraisals and how to train and lead development, all of which strengthen their human resource skills. Salaried cast members can attend classes such as counseling and listening, understanding people as individuals, Disney's courtesy, stress and time management, and an array of specific skill-related programs.

Since Disney promotes 85 percent of its middle- and executive-level management from within, Disney has developed the Disney Intern Program to meet these needs. Cast members from different divisions of the company who have management potential go through six months of on-the-job training. Halfway through the program, these students are given an assignment to develop an idea or modification to implement at Disney. Small groups work together to develop a presentation for top management. The six-month program ends with an exam and graduation. Unfortunately, completion of the internship is no guarantee of a job, but at least, cast members know this going into the program. Rather than promote and then train them for the job, Disney trains them in advance. Division managers project how many salaried people they think they will need and the company tries to make sure that there will be enough interns to meet those needs.

CONCLUSION

The Disney Company has proved to be as successful as its creator, Walter E. Disney, would have imagined it. The company continues to grow at an astronomical rate. Disney has expanded into many diverse avenues to the current day. After overcoming difficulties during its expansion processes, Disney has still proved to be one of the largest and most recognizable organizations known. As each day passes, Disney supplies its magic and continues its successful growth. The company stands at the forefront and serves as a mecca to the hearts of people worldwide. Disney, with assistance from Mickey and friends, put smiles on the faces of individuals everywhere, young and old, including its creator, the late Walt Disney.

NOTES

1. Richard Holliss and Brian Sibley, *The Disney Studio Story,* London: Octopus Books Ltd., 1988.

2. Ibid.

3. Adrian Bailey, *Walt Disney's World of Fantasy,* Secaucus, NJ: Chartwell Books, 1982.

4. Hollis and Sibley, *The Disney Studio Story.*

5. Ibid.

6. Ibid.

7. Ibid.

8. Ibid.

9. Bailey, *Walt Disney's World of Fantasy.*

10. Hollis and Sibley, *The Disney Studio Story.*

11. Ibid.

12. Ibid.

13. Ibid.

14. Bailey, *Walt Disney's World of Fantasy.*

15. Hollis and Sibley, *The Disney Studio Story.*

16. Ibid.

17. Ibid.

18. Ibid.

19. Ibid.

20. Ibid.

21. Ibid.

22. Ibid.

23. Ibid.

24. Ibid.

25. Ibid.

26. Roy Grover, *The Disney Touch,* Homewood, IL: Business One Irwin, 1991.

27. Ronald Grover and Michael Oneal, "Disney: Room for Two Lion Kings," *Business Week,* August 28, 1995, pp. 28–29.

28. Company news provided by Dow Jones/News Retrieval; copyright © 1994, Dow Jones & Company.

29. Jeremy Gerard, "Disney's New Dream: 42nd Street Fantasia," *Variety,* February 7, 1994, pp. 57–59.

30. "Disney Gives New Life to Amsterdam," *Variety,* February 7, 1994, p. 59.

31. Michael Ozanian, "Mouse Trap?" *Financial World,* March 15, 1994, pp. 28–31.

32. Maggie Mahar, "No Mickey Mouse Company: Wall Street's Losing Sight of Disney's Bright Prospects," *Barron's,* June 24, 1991, pp. 8–25.

33. Ibid.

34. "Mice, Magic, and Malls," *Shopping Centers Today,* May 1991, pp. 27–43.

35. Charlene Marmer Solomon, "How Does Disney Do It?" *Personnel Journal,* December 1989, pp. 50–57.

36. Ibid.

37. Ibid.

38. Ibid.

CASE 5

WAL-MART STORES INC.

When J.C. Penney let Samuel Moore Walton slip away from its management trainee program in 1942, the company had no warning of the resounding impact that resignation would have on its industry in the coming decades. After three years in the Army, Sam Walton opened the first Walton's Ben Franklin store in Newport, Arkansas, in September 1945.

In 1950, Mr. Sam (as he was to be known to his associates) relocated in Bentonville, Arkansas, after losing the lease on his Newport store. During the 1950s, Mr. Sam increased the number of Walton-owned Ben Franklin stores to nine. In 1962, Mr. Sam and his brother, Bud, opened the first Wal-Mart Discount City in Rogers, Arkansas. Growth was anything but exponential during that period: The second Wal-Mart store didn't open for two more years. David Glass, now president, attended that grand opening in Harrison:

> It was the worst retail store I had ever seen. Sam had brought a couple of trucks of watermelons and stacked them on the sidewalk. He also had donkey rides out in the parking lot. It was 115 degrees, and the watermelons began to pop, and the donkeys began to do what donkeys do, and it got all mixed together and ran all over the parking lot. And when you went inside the store, the mess continued. He was a nice fellow, but I wrote him off. It was just terrible.[1]

From that dubious beginning, Wal-Mart Corporation has surprised Wall Street as well as its competitors by becoming America's largest retailer by 1990.[2] Late in 1969, the company was incorporated: 12 months later, its stock was publicly traded over the counter. In another two years the stock was approved and listed on the New York Stock Exchange. Sales for 1970 were $44 million and by 1979 had reached $1.248 billion. By 1994 Wal-Mart's sales would be 67 billion dollars and annual growth in revenue would average at 34 percent.[3]

A unique feature of this type of retailing is that it is virtually recession-proof. In times of economic downturn, consumers flock to discount retailers. During the recession of 1974–1975, sales expanded 42 percent, and in the 1981–1982 recession, sales grew 44 percent annually and also grew by 30 percent in the 1990s recession. As such, Wal-Mart is not affected by economic downturn as other retailers are.[4]

Wal-Mart has obtained a distinct competitive advantage by targeting small, rural communities, which results in lower operating costs. These result from lower rents, moderate wages, and the absence of unionization. Real estate is significantly cheaper, and smaller communities have a more loyal and productive workforce.

NOTE: This case was prepared by Steve R. Avera, Elizabeth D. Ellis, Don W. Reinhard, Andrew M. Thomas, and Tammy Wilkerson and revised by Jeff Sesterhenn, Joe Shawfield, Brad Rogers, and Suzy Kennah.

Although the store location strategy was innovative, several other factors have played a strong role in vaulting Wal-Mart to the top of the discount mountain. For instance, Mr. Sam's management practices were even more trend setting than his store location strategy. A strong advocate of participatory management practices, Wal-Mart has been a prototype in employee relations. Employees are not employees but "associates," a term coined by Mr. Sam at the very first Wal-Mart store. Other factors that have contributed to Wal-Mart's success include rigorous cost control, an excellent distribution network, and a technological advantage.

EFFICIENT OPERATIONS

Wal-Mart is proud of its efficient operations, which have been a decisive factor in Wal-Mart's ascension to become America's top discount store. With its stated goal to be the low-cost leader,[5] Wal-Mart has built a network of store/offices that serve two important functions: they avoid the cost of building separate administrative offices, and they create a close feeling between store management and customers while promoting a better working bond between coworkers. This design allows managers to interact with the customers during business hours. It also has the added feature of allowing managers close contact with associates.

The low-overhead style of management Wal-Mart has developed has allowed the company to keep its operating expenses under control. Since 1988, sales have risen from $15 billion to $55 billion in 1994. During this same period, 913 Wal-Marts, 212 Sams Clubs, 51 Bud's Warehouses, 40 Supercenters and 6 distribution centers were placed into operation. Wal-Mart's management style is so efficient that operating expenses, expressed as a percentage of sales, have actually decreased from 16 percent of sales in 1988 to 14.9 in 1993. These figures show how successful Wal-Mart has been in controlling its operating expenses during a period of rapid growth.[6]

Support systems such as excellent distribution, a state-of-the-art communications network, and certainly the associates have given management the ability to manage this large-scale growth while controlling operating costs.

Another measure of efficiency of which Wal-Mart is particularly proud is inventory shrinkage. Shrinkage occurs as a result of shoplifting, inventory shortages, and employee theft. While the discount retail industry's average shrinkage per store is 2 percent, Wal-Mart employees pride themselves on a per-store shrinkage that is around 1 percent.[7] With this low shrinkage rate comes clear rewards: Stores that achieve target shrinkage rates earn bonuses of several hundred dollars each.

Clearly, operating efficiencies have played a critical role in the success of Wal-Mart. These operating efficiencies have allowed Wal-Mart to offer services that customers notice, such as keeping extra checkout lines open and posting a "greeter" at the entrance to each Wal-Mart store. This results in what Stephen F. Mandel, Jr., an analyst with Tiger Management Corporation, calls the "productivity loop," in which Wal-Mart's ability to offer lower prices and better service will inevitably attract more shoppers. This prompts more sales, making the company more efficient and able to lower prices even more.

DISTRIBUTION NETWORK

Wal-Mart's distribution system is another key component of Wal-Mart's efficiency strategy. Its 25 distribution centers strategically blanket Wal-Mart's market areas. Most

Wal-Mart stores are located within one day's drive of a distribution center. Deliveries are made daily to each Wal-Mart store.

Between 70 and 80 percent of all purchasing is done centrally, taking advantage of Wal-Mart's state-of-the-art satellite network (see the discussion of computer technology that follows). Similarly, 77 percent of the purchases made by Wal-Mart stores were shipped from the distribution centers in 1993. The remaining 23 percent were shipped directly to the stores from suppliers.[8] All but one of the distribution centers are automated, utilizing a complex conveyor system that involves up to 11 *miles* of belts. Laser scanners route the goods (up to 190,000 cases per day), which are also strategically tied to the satellite network core in Bentonville.

COMPUTER TECHNOLOGY

Wal-Mart boasts the world's largest private, fully integrated satellite network.[9] This satellite network connects the Wal-Mart management information system (MIS) to every Wal-Mart store and distribution center in 45 states. By using audio, video, and data signals via more than 1,400 earth stations, it maintains constant communication between the organization's communications center and all its operations and suppliers. As a result, every store is connected in real time to the corporate information center in Bentonville so that each and every transaction is made on-line. The network not only monitors inventory and orders replacement stock, it also electronically approves credit transactions. Authorization is sent back to the remote store from the network in less than six seconds.

The operational goal of this network is to provide better customer service and improve business efficiency. For instance, if a credit authorization transaction can be completed in 25 percent less time, one checker can handle four customers in the time it took to handle three using the manual system. Hence, a checker can process more customers in the same amount of time. Customers spend less time in the checkout line and leave with positive feelings toward the store.

Other business efficiencies that result from the network include the monitoring of inventory and movement, the ability to track trends by item, and the assurance of a smooth product flow from supplier to distribution center to retail stores to consumers. Products that are in demand flow into the stores at the desired rate. This rapid response time has allowed Wal-Mart to maintain an enviable in-stock rate, a high asset utilization rate, and industry leadership in holding waste and costs down while keeping productivity and profits high.[10]

BUY AMERICAN PROGRAM

As a result of Mr. Sam's concern for the economy's high balance of trade deficits and the subsequent loss of jobs (and American dollars flowing out of the country), in 1985, Mr. Sam sent a message to his merchandise managers: "Find products that American manufacturers have stopped producing because they couldn't compete with foreign imports." This was the foundation for the "Buy American Program," begun that year. It was not an anti-import campaign or an effort to organize grassroots support of trade regulation legislation, tariffs, or other controls on import items. It was not a mandate by the company to buy domestic goods that are inferior just because they are domestic. The program, as defined by Mr. Sam, "is a cooperative effort between retailers and domestic manufacturers to re-establish a competitive position in price and quality of American made goods to the market place."

The cooperative nature of the program requires that both Wal-Mart and its suppliers employ flexibility and creativity in the production of their products. American producers are forced to be more "market-driven," and Wal-Mart extends many of the terms and cooperation formerly given only foreign suppliers. Payment for products is made on a more timely basis, allowing the producers to decrease their cost of financing inventories. Wal-Mart suppliers have a commitment to improve facilities where necessary, remain financially conservative, and work with Wal-Mart to meet the needs of their customers. The key to the program is improving employee efficiency, which reduces costs and allows the supplier to be more competitive with the foreign competition.

One example of this cooperative is Farris Fashions, which in 1984 was a struggling shirt manufacturer in eastern Arkansas. After Van Heusen, the men's shirt and clothing manufacturer, pulled its contract to manufacture shirts, 90 employees faced permanent layoff. Mr. Sam and David Glass contacted President Farris Burroughs. A few weeks later, Farris Fashions had a contract to make 240,000 flannel shirts, a product that Wal-Mart had been buying in the Far East. By 1988, Wal-Mart's order from Farris Fashions had leaped to 1.5 million garments, and employment has exploded to 325 workers. The company has invested over $1 million in new production equipment, which has increased productivity and further lowered costs. Another cost-lowering mechanism is Wal-Mart's cooperation with Farris Fashions' suppliers. Wal-Mart buys the material for the shirts and gives Farris the benefit of the lower prices it can command.

THE WAL-MART EFFECT

With Wal-Mart growing and continuing to expand, what effect does this have on the small towns that Wal-Mart descends upon? Wal-Mart has all but turned the clocks back to represent itself as having good, old-fashioned family values, and the image is working. Your typical Wal-Mart seems to be nothing more than a collection of down-home folks, working in a store with reasonable prices. Even Wal-Mart's advertising uses actual store employees as opposed to models. "Real folks," that's the image that Wal-Mart has successfully perpetrated through the years. But these same down-home, real folks are the people Wal-Mart drives out of business when opening a store in their town.

At least three predator pricing suits were filed against the giant retailer in the 1980s. All were settled out of court, with fierce nondisclosure agreements. In the 1990s, however, a man named Dwayne Goode took on Wal-Mart and won. A judge in the Arkansas state court ruled on October 11, 1993, that the world's biggest retailer deliberately set out between 1987 and 1991 to squeeze out three tiny businesses run by Mr. Goode and two other pharmacists in Conway, a small Arkansas town. Citing an obscure 1937 state law, the judge found Wal-Mart guilty of predator pricing at its local superstore. Mr. Goode said he used to buy bulk products himself from Wal-Mart because its prices were cheaper than the wholesaler, but after watching Wal-Mart undercut him for four years, his patience snapped.

One of the important factors for the judge was the evidence suggesting that Wal-Mart would lift its prices as, and when, competitors disappeared. Nearer to Little Rock, where there are plenty of pharmacies, Wal-Mart's drug prices are lower; in more remote towns, they are higher. The local law firm, acting for Mr. Goode, received more than 100 inquiries about the case within four days of the Conway verdict. Half of them, says the firm, were specifically linked to possible future actions against Wal-Mart.[11]

OPERATING SEGMENTS

Wal-Mart's chief operating unit is the Wal-Mart Discount City. These stores offer a wide variety of name-brand merchandise including clothing, books, and auto and home accessories. The main emphasis for these stores is the variety of goods available at the lowest price. Wal-Mart stores would not come to be known for sale items but rather "everyday low prices," which would become the company's slogan. The everyday low price theme would be implemented by another Wal-Mart slogan called "Rollback America."

Wal-Mart has averaged 150 new stores per year for the 1991–1993 period and opened an additional 103 in 1994.[12] The tremendous success of this segment, along with new entrants such as Target, have motivated Wal-Mart to seek growth in other areas of retailing.

Wal-Mart Stores, Inc., has made a conscious strategic decision to focus on retailing; therefore, it has focused its resources on businesses that help it achieve its stated retail strategies. Expansion into other areas has been through market penetration: Sam's Clubs cater to small businesses; Supercenters incorporate both food and general merchandise in a simple, massive store; and Hypermart USA is a European experimental retail concept.

SAM'S CLUBS

Sam's Clubs has become the front-runner among the discount wholesale clubs that emerged during the 1980s. These large, no-frills warehouses handle a limited number of fast-selling products (approximately 3,000 stock keeping units [SKUs], compared with Wal-Mart's typical 65,000 SKUs). Inventory turnover and minimal operating costs are the keys to profitability. An established Sam's Club will turn over its inventory about every 20 to 22 days, more than three times faster than the typical Wal-Mart store. With vendor terms of net/30 days, inventory is sold before the company must pay for it. Cannibalization (losing business at one company owned store to another company owned store) between Sam's Clubs and Wal-Mart stores is minimal due to limited merchandise overlap, which is less than several hundred SKUs.[13]

SUPERCENTERS

In 1993 Wal-Mart finalized a deal with its closest competitor, Kmart, to buy 95 out of 113 Pace Warehouses, which were to be converted to Sam's Clubs. Since 1988, sales at the 321 Sam's Clubs have risen to $12.3 billion by 1993. Wal-Mart also opened 51 Bud's Warehouses in 1993.[14]

A variation on the Supercenters, the Hypermart USA, offers a combination discount store and supermarket as well as 15 to 20 free-standing, fast-food, and specialized service providers, such as photo finishing, dry cleaners, optical shops, shoe repair, and hair salons. The Supercenter and the Hypermart USA formats have been refined somewhat by Wal-Mart; this new hybrid retail format is called Supercenters.[15]

The refinement of the Supercenter retailer will provide the convenience-minded consumer with "one-stop shopping": both food items and general merchandise can be found under one roof, both at discount prices. Like Wal-Mart Stores and Sam's Clubs, this retail concept is anticipated to be recession-proof. There are currently four Hypermart USAs and 30 Supercenters. The company opened 38 new Supercenters in 1994.

Two recent additions to the Wal-Mart segments were the acquisitions of McLane Distribution and a 50 percent interest in CIFRA, Mexico's largest retailer. McLane Distribution is a segment of Wal-Mart, Inc., that predominantly sells goods to the convenience-store industry. McLane also sells goods to the Wal-Mart and Sam's stores. These goods include tobacco, candy, toys, and a wide variety of grocery items. Before the joining of these companies, Wal-Mart accounted for 20 percent of McLane's business. With McLane under Wal-Mart control, the company can ensure the timely delivery of the products it needs, where it needs them, in the correct quantities, and still at everyday low prices.

In late 1992, Wal-Mart, Inc. acquired a 50 percent interest in CIFRA, seemingly the company's only effort in the international market thus far. As of January 1, 1994, the venture operated eight stores throughout Mexico.

HUMAN RESOURCES

CORPORATE CULTURE/GENERAL PHILOSOPHY

Our philosophy is that management's role is simply to get the right people in the right places to do a job and then encourage them to use their own inventiveness to accomplish the task at hand.[16]

Sam Walton

We have no superstars at Wal-Mart; we have average people operating in an environment that encourages everyone to perform way above average.[17]

David Glass

Most of us wear a button that says, "Our People Make the Difference." That is not a slogan at Wal-Mart, it is a way of life. Our people really do make a difference.[18]

David Glass

In the late 1960s when Sam and his brother, Bud, owned about 20 Wal-Marts, a union tried to organize two stores in Missouri, and Sam hired labor lawyer John Tate, now an executive vice-president of Wal-Mart, to help. Tate told Walton, "You can approach this one of two ways. Hold people down, and pay me or some other lawyer to make it work. Or devote time and attention to proving to people that you care." Sam chose the latter and subsequently held his first management seminar, entitled "We care."

Sam insisted upon calling all employees "associates," since it implies a partnership. Department managers see figures that many companies never show general managers. Profit goals are set for each store, and if exceeded, hourly associates share part of the additional profit. This "partnership" goes past monetary participation to open-door policies and an atmosphere that says, "Hey, if you've got a problem, talk to somebody. Don't talk about it in the lounge or the parking lot; come to management." This is ingrained in Wal-Mart's culture.

Wal-Mart's culture is its most fearsome weapon. The company gospel is "Be an agent for consumers, find out what they want, and sell it to them for the lowest possible price."[19] One source described Wal-Mart as follows:

The key to Wal-Mart's success is the quality of their management, its style and its recognition of the importance of the individual player in the overall team effort. Other companies are striving to achieve the same cultural level, but no other retail company is close. Wal-Mart people work harder than most, probably because they have more fun. They are constantly being challenged by one another and forced to laugh at themselves. They take pride in working for perhaps the finest company in the world and their individual contributions are recognized.[20]

It is Wal-Mart's familylike environment that emphasizes teamwork and encourages employee ideas and participation. The work atmosphere is a down-home "concern for the individual." Individual contributions to the team effort are welcomed and rewarded. Participatory management from top to bottom is stressed, and listening is an important part of a manager's job.

According to Mr. Sam, "99 percent of the best ideas we ever had came from our employees."[21] His explanation was simplistic but to the point: "If people believe in themselves, it's truly amazing what they can accomplish."[22]

Sam Walton "managed by walking around" and expected the same from his managers. Glass, along with other top executives, spends several days a week visiting the stores. To heighten associates' sense of mission, they are given plenty of responsibility. Managers for each of the 34 departments within a typical Wal-Mart are expected to run their operations as if they were running their own businesses.[23] According to one manager, 90 percent of his day is spent walking around stores communicating with associates—he praises them for well-done jobs, discusses how improvements could be made, and listens to comments and solicits suggestions. This management style also encourages the steady stream of ideas that Wal-Mart receives from its associates.

Low threshold of change (LTC) is a highly valued concept at Wal-Mart. The planning process begins with store management asking each associate what he or she could do individually or how store operations could improve. Associates are encouraged to challenge and change any policies perceived to detract from operations.

STORE MEETINGS

Every morning before stores open and every evening after stores close, associates and managers meet for ten minutes to discuss overall operations, expectations, how things went, and so on. Every Friday morning, each store has a general store meeting during which associates at every level can ask questions and expect to get straightforward answers from management. These meetings communicate to associates information on new company initiatives and policy change announcements. Video training films are also shown from time to time. As part of these meetings, corporate management, via satellite, emphasizes the company's five most important priorities, which gives employees goals and keeps them focused.[24]

Each week department and store figures are posted on the back wall of each store so associates can see how they rank. If the figures are better than average, associates are praised. Associates in departments that regularly outperform averages can expect annual bonuses and raises. Performances lower than average are discussed so solutions can be found.[25]

SATURDAY MORNING MEETINGS AT HEADQUARTERS

Since 1961, every Saturday morning in Bentonville, Arkansas, at 7:30 A.M., Wal-Mart conducts a very informal and relaxed meeting. Employees dress casually, some in hunting or tennis clothes for after-meeting fun. Employees attending include top officers, merchandising staff, regional managers who oversee store districts, and the Bentonville headquarters staff (over 100 people). They meet to discuss Wal-Mart issues, such as the week's sales, payroll percentages, special promotional items, unusual problems, and reports on transportation, loss prevention, and information systems.[26]

PEOPLE DIVISION

Instead of a personnel department, Wal-Mart has a people division. According to Von Johnston, director of the people division, "We deal with people; people are our job. One of our board members last year suggested that we change our name to reflect our job and we did."[27]

This division is divided into five functions: store operations, warehouse personnel, training and development, general office personnel staff, and the Walton Life Fitness Center staff. A primary focus of this division has been the recruitment of new associates.

"THE WAL-MART WAY"

"The Wal-Mart Way" summarizes the company's unconventional approach to business and the determination of the associates. This commitment to "total quality" is essential to the company's future success; it proliferates the very best things the company does, while incorporating the new ideas of company employees.[28] "Quality the Wal-Mart Way" is an ongoing focus, with the emphasis on doing everything right the first time, since that is the most efficient way. Key elements are productivity, teamwork, the "elimination of dumb things," innovation that calls for "breaking the frame," and an effort to continuously improve. This mindset has also been adopted by Sam's Clubs, which has adopted HEATKTE—"high expectations are the key to everything"—as its strategic rallying cry.[29]

Wal-Mart's senior management is able to keep on top of all that is happening because management believes in delegating authority, sharing decisions, and trusting the people charged with specific responsibilities. "The esprit de corps and the desire of the individuals to excel are so engendered as to assure that the best possible job is performed in practically every sector of Wal-Mart."[30] Wal-Mart's people are focused, responsive, willing to change, and willing to execute their jobs in a superior fashion. The company has grown tremendously without losing sight of the basic principles that made it great in the first place. Wal-Mart's corporate culture is very much ingrained in all of its associates since they have had the benefit of working in such a positive environment over nearly 30 years.

THE DATING GAME

With Wal-Mart's corporate culture consisting of high interaction between associates, it is bound to create personal bonds among them. Most of the time the relationships that occur do not affect employment status, except in the case of Laural Allen and Samuel Johnson. They were dismissed from their jobs because they dated while working at Wal-Mart in Johnstown, New York.

At issue in the case is a section in the 1989 company handbook entitled "Fraternization." In it the company cautions its sales associates to maintain "sound business relationships" with their co-workers. Wal-Mart strongly believes and supports the "family unit," and the handbook states, "A dating relationship between a married associate and another associate, other than his or her own spouse, is not consistent with this belief and is prohibited."

The relationship between Ms. Allen and Mr. Johnson began when her husband, David, a 27-year-old machinist, moved out of their house in December. Ms. Allen said she had met Mr. Johnson a few weeks before her husband had left, and they became friends, getting to know each other in informal gatherings with other co-workers over a frame of bowling or a meal. At no time, she said, did the two show any affection in the store. The relationship came to the attention of the Wal-Mart managers when Laural's estranged husband's lawyer served her with custody papers at the store. Distraught, she said she shared the papers, which included a reference to Mr. Johnson, with a supervisor. After management confirmed the relationship with the two, they were both promptly dismissed.

With a new law passed in July, 1993, which makes it unlawful for a business to terminate employment based on "an individual's legal recreational activities outside of work hours and off of the employers premises," the couple sued Wal-Mart for $2 million under wrongful discharge. New York Attorney General Robert Abrams says, "What's problematic about it is the fact that the employer is terminating the employee not on the basis of job performance, but on what they're doing in their private lives outside the work place. When they were dismissed, there was no allegation of this relationship interfering with their job performance."

Allen's work now consists of folding sheets at a laundromat, and Johnson works as a stock clerk in a lumberyard. As of mid-1994, their case had not been decided by the courts.[31]

STAFFING

Wal-Mart has been the number one creator of new jobs in the United States since 1984.[32] As of January 31, 1994, Wal-Mart employed 528,000 full-time and part-time employees.[33]

Employees at Wal-Mart consist of two categories: managers (salaried) and associates (hourly). Every retail outlet is managed by a store manager and one or more assistants. Managers are hired in one of three ways:

1. Hourly associates move up through the ranks from sales to department manager of check lanes to store management training.
2. People from other retail companies with outstanding merchandising skills are recruited.
3. College graduates are hired.

Approximately 50 percent of all managers began in hourly positions, 35 percent are recent college graduates, and 15 percent are from other retailers. Wal-Mart hires over 1,500 management people per year, just to maintain management staffing levels in its stores and corporate headquarters.

Each time a new store opens, corporate headquarters selects a store manager, who is brought to company headquarters for a one-week orientation, during which one day is devoted to hiring practices. Store managers are either transferred from another store or are assistant managers who have been promoted. Assistant managers transferred from stores in the community or at least the same state are also selected by corporate headquarters. The store manager and the assistant manager(s) are totally responsible for hiring all of the store's associates.

Wal-Mart's recruitment process is highly structured, yet decentralized. Established stores have a rotating employee screening committee responsible for hiring new associates. This committee consists of five associates. Before being hired, candidates are interviewed by the committee a minimum of two times.

Wal-Mart views drug screening, initiated in 1987, as an important part of its hiring process. According to Von Johnston, director of the people division, "If you don't have plans for drug screening, then you will be hiring our rejects." Drug screening is done subsequent to a candidate passing the second interview.[34]

Wal-Mart does not try to hire a large ratio of part-time employees to avoid paying benefits. In 1985 Wal-Mart claimed its ratio of full-time employees to part-time employees was approximately 5 to 1. Part-time employees are primarily sales personnel. This statistic, however, is irrelevant in 1994. In a pending battle over health-care reform, Wal-Mart, Inc. will be organized labor's retailing symbol of why employers should be required to help pay for a universal health-care system.[35]

According to the United Food and Commercial Workers Union, the employer mandate in health-care reform is essential. The union believes everyone has to do the same thing so that no one can seek a competitive advantage through lower health-care costs. The union is singling out non-union retailers, in part, because they are large, visible employers, particularly in the case of Wal-Mart.

Wal-Mart officials failed to respond to UFCW claims of its insufficient health-care plan. Internal Revenue Service records show that roughly 43 percent of Wal-Mart's 490,000 workers are insured. Eligibility in the plan begins after 90 days for those working 20 hours a week or more. Workers pick up 36 percent of their premium costs.[36]

The union argues that bottom-line businesses such as Wal-Mart save money on health care by making insurance eligibility for part-time workers difficult and otherwise paying inadequate employee health-care benefits. The union calculates that the health-care costs shifted to other employers by Wal-Mart was $480 million in 1993. This shift is the burden of the employer's spouse providing health-care coverage. By not covering a worker, someone else is picking up the health-care costs. The union maintains that this simply allows Wal-Mart to fatten its profits at someone else's expense.[37]

Wal-Mart has created a unique atmosphere by positioning associates with whom shoppers interact at various points in the store. For example, greeters placed at the front door add warmth to the customers' shopping experience. "The addition of more people to the stores comes at a time when other retailers are trying to reduce their expense ratios and are firmly limiting the number of payroll hours budgeted for the stores."[38] Wal-Mart's financial strength has allowed it the opportunity to offer value-added services such as this, which has changed the "rules of the game."

TRAINING AND DEVELOPMENT

Wal-Mart considers people development its number one priority. Developing people allows the company to push decision making down to lower levels. Extensive training is provided to managers at the corporate level; managers, in turn, are expected to train hourly associates.

MANAGEMENT TRAINING

In order to assure well-trained future store managers, Wal-Mart is committed to an ongoing training program for store managers, assistant managers, and department managers. All managers complete a structured management training program that consists of on-the-job training and book work.[39] Areas studied include management topics such as internal/external theft, scheduling, store staffing, retail math, merchandise replenishment, and the Wal-Mart "keys to supervision" series dealing with interpersonal skills and personnel responsibilities. After completing the training program, trainees are made responsible for an area in a store. The length of time they are in this position varies according to how the trainee progresses. Subsequent to this training, the trainee is promoted to assistant manager.

As an assistant manager, training continues with the one-week Retail Management Training Seminar.[40] According to Suzanne Allford, vice-president of the people division,

> We believe our store and club managers are our best teachers and instructors; corporately, it's our job to provide them with the very best tools and facilities; our belief that this can only be done using practical hands-on methods led us to move our retail management seminars from our home office out to ten of our distribution centers, near to the store and clubs, to expose our management team to the heart of our distribution network.

In 1985, Wal-Mart created the Walton Institute of Retailing, which was opened in affiliation with the University of Arkansas. Currently, every Wal-Mart corporate and store manager is expected to participate in the Institute's special programs to strengthen and develop the company's managerial capabilities.[41]

Wal-Mart believes that good people need new challenges. Therefore, with respect to senior management, Wal-Mart offers cross training to enable them to master new areas.

ASSOCIATE TRAINING

"If you are not looking at those people who are at the bottom of the line and looking to train and develop them, you're going to continue having employment problems," according to Von Johnston.[42]

Upon hiring, employees are immediately placed in positions for on-the-job training (OJT). No formal training is provided from Wal-Mart headquarters for hourly associates. OJT is Wal-Mart's philosophy regarding associate training. Store managers and department managers train and supervise employees. The use of video films is a popular training technique, shown from time to time in the Friday morning meetings.[43]

PERFORMANCE EVALUATIONS AND REWARD SYSTEMS/BENEFITS

PERFORMANCE EVALUATIONS

Wal-Mart calls the process of performance appraisals "evaluations."[44] All managers and associates are evaluated annually.

Associates are hired at higher than minimum wage ($5.25 per hour in Tallahassee, Florida.) and can expect a raise within the first year at two of the three performance evaluations. New associates receive three evaluations during their first year—the first at 90 days, the second at six months, and the third on their anniversary date. Assuming performance is satisfactory, the employee receives raises at the 90-day evaluation and at the annual evaluation. Employees who are performing at outstanding levels may receive merit raises any time during the year. After successfully completing the first year, associates receive annual evaluations. Exceptions to this include promotions or ratings other than "marginal progress."[45]

REWARD SYSTEMS

As previously indicated, management positions are salaried. Store managers receive additional compensation based on their store's profits. Assistant store managers receive additional compensation based on the company's profitability. All other personnel are compensated on an hourly basis with the opportunity of receiving additional incentive bonuses based on the company's productivity and profitability.[46]

Relatively speaking, Wal-Mart's people are highly motivated, well trained, and very productive. Ideas for productivity and efficiency are quickly disseminated. For example, each week, an average of about 1,200 stores submit approximately 5,000 suggestions. The best of these ideas are adopted, leading to substantial sales gains, cost reductions, and improved productivity. Successful ideas receive companywide recognition, such as a mention in Saturday morning meetings at headquarters, or even the personal praise of the chairperson. This reward system motivates employees to think of ways to improve operations, such as how to decrease shoplifting or improve merchandising.

Shrinkage bonuses were implemented in 1980 to control losses from theft and damage. If a store holds shrinkage below the corporate goal, every associate in that store receives up to $300.[47] In the second quarter of 1991, Wal-Mart paid $6.3 million in bonuses to stores for improving their shrinkage problem.[48]

A very successful incentive program is its Volume Producing Item contests, whereby departments within a store do special promotions and pricing on items they want to feature. This program helped boost sales and sell slow-moving items. It also encouraged employees to be innovative.

PROFIT SHARING AND STOCK OPTIONS PLANS

Wal-Mart believes that each of its associates is a partner in the company and encourages stock ownership. Profit sharing is available to every associate. Eighty percent of Wal-Mart's full time associates own stock.[49]

The company maintains a profit-sharing plan under which most full and many part-time employees become participants. They are eligible to participate in the plan one month following one year of employment with the company. Annual contributions, based on the profitability of the company, are made at the sole discretion of the company. Participants are fully vested after seven years of service. For fiscal years ended January 31, 1987, through January 31, 1993, the following contributions were made:[50]

1987	$51,772,000
1988	$59,466,000
1989	$77,067,000
1990	$90,447,000
1991	$98,327,000
1992	$129,635,000
1993	$166,035,000

Wal-Mart's stock purchase plan allows eligible associates a means of purchasing shares of common stock at market prices through regular payroll deductions of no more than $75 per biweekly pay period, or $1,800 per year. The company will contribute 15 percent of each participant's contribution under the stock plan. As of January 31, 1994, 30 percent of its 490,000 employees were participating in the plan.[51]

NOTES

1. John Huey, "America's Most Successful Merchant," *Fortune,* September 23, 1991, pp. 46–59.

2. "Facts About Wal-Mart Stores, Inc.," Wal-Mart Stores, Inc., 1991.

3. Subrata N. Chakravarty, "A Tale of Two Companies," *Forbes,* May 27, 1991, pp. 86–96.

4. *Annual Report,* Wal-Mart Stores, Inc., 1993.

5. *Annual Report,* Wal-Mart Stores, Inc., 1991.

6. "Wal-Mart Future Is Supercenters," *Chain Store Age Executive,* September 1993, p. 26.

7. Huey, "America's Most Successful Merchant."

8. Wal-Mart Stores, Inc. *1991 Form 10-K,* Securities and Exchange Commission, 1991.

9. Jamal Munshi, *MIS: Cases in Action,* New York: McGraw-Hill, 1990.

10. Ibid.

11. Blant Hurt, "The Irrational Antitrust Case Against Wal-Mart," *The Wall Street Journal,* October 20, 1993, p. A15; and "Slinging Pebbles at Wal-Mart," *The Economist,* October 23, 1993, p. 76.

12. *Annual Report,* Wal-Mart Stores, Inc., 1994.

13. D. T. Spindel, "Wal-Mart Stores, Inc.—Company Report," A. G. Edwards & Sons, Inc., July 9, 1991.

14. Wendy Zellner, "Why Sams Wants Businesses to Join the Club," *Business Week,* June 27, 1994, p. 48.

15. Spindel, "Wal-Mart Stores, Inc.—Company Report."

16. Kem A. King, "Wal-Mart Stores, Inc.," *Strategic Management,* Homewood, IL: Richard D. Irwin, 1985.

17. "Quality of Management," *Fortune,* January 29, 1990.

18. King, "Wal-Mart Stores, Inc."

19. Bill Saporito, "Is Wal-Mart Unstoppable?" *Fortune,* May 6, 1991, pp. 50–59.

20. First Boston, *Wal-Mart Stores, Inc., Equity Research Report,* Number RT2697, December 3, 1990.

21. Saporito, "Is Wal-Mart Unstoppable?"

22. John Huey, "Wal-Mart: Will It Take Over the World?" *Fortune,* January 30, 1989, pp. 52–61.

23. "Quality of Management."

24. Joan Bergmann, "Saga of Sam Walton," *Stores,* January 1988, pp. 129–142.

25. King, "Wal-Mart Stores, Inc."

26. Ibid.

27. Allan Halcrow, "Voices of HR Experience—Part II," *Personnel Journal* 68(5), May 1989, pp. 38–53.

28. *Annual Report,* Wal-Mart Stores, Inc., 1991.

29. Ibid.

30. First Boston, *Wal-Mart Stores, Inc., Equity Research Report.*

31. Jacques Steinberg, "Fraternization and Friction in the Store Aisles," *The New York Times,* July 14, 1993, p. B1.

32. Halcrow, "Voices of HR Experience—Part II."

33. *Annual Report,* Wal-Mart Stores, Inc., 1994.

34. Halcrow, "Voices of HR Experience—Part II."

35. Joanna Ramey, "Union Disputes Wal-Mart, Kmart over Who Pays Costs," *HFD Weekly Home Furnishings* 68(6), February 7, 1994, p. 13.

36. Ibid.

37. Ibid.

38. Oppenheimer & Co., Inc., "Wal-Mart Stores Bigger and Better," Report Number 91-698, May 31, 1991.

39. Sandy Brummett, personal interview with public relations assistant of Wal-Mart Stores, Inc., Bentonville, Arkansas. Interview conducted by telephone on November 19, 1991.

40. Ibid.

41. Ibid.

42. Halcrow, "Voices of HR Experience—Part II."

43. George Wilkins, Personal Interview with Assistant Manager of Wal-Mart Store (Capital Circle Southeast, Tallahassee, Florida). Interview conducted by telephone on November 18, 1991.

44. Halcrow, "Voices of HR Experience—Part II."

45. Wilkins, personal interview.

46. Wal-Mart Stores, Inc., *1991 Form 10-K.*

47. Wilkins, personal interview.

48. M. A. Gilliam, "Wal-Mart Stores, Inc.—Company Report," The First Boston Corp. July 8, 1991.

49. Ibid.

50. Wal-Mart Stores, Inc., *1991 Form 10-K.*

51. Ibid.

TEXT AND EXHIBIT CREDITS

CHAPTER 2: definitions of societal environment and task environment, © 1992 by Addison-Wesley Publishing Company, Inc. Reprinted by permission of Addison-Wesley Publishing Company, Inc.; Exhibit 2.2, ©1992 by Addison Wesley Publishing Company, Inc. Reprinted by permission of Addison-Wesley Publishing Company, Inc.; Exhibit 2.6, FORTUNE, © 1994 Time Inc. All rights reserved; Exhibit 2.10, reprinted by permission of The Wall Street Journal, ©1992 Dow Jones & Company Inc. All Rights Reserved Worldwide; Exhibit 2.16, reprinted by permission of The Wall Street Journal, ©1993 Dow Jones & Company, Inc. All Rights Reserved Worldwide; Exhibit 2.17, FORTUNE, ©1994 Time Inc. All rights reserved; chapter-ending case, some text reprinted by permission of The Wall Street Journal, © 1992 Dow Jones & Company, Inc. All Rights Reserved Worldwide, and reprinted by permission of The Wall Street Journal, © 1993 Dow Jones & Company, Inc. All Rights Reserved Worldwide.

CHAPTER 3: chapter-opening case, some text reprinted by permission of The Wall Street Journal, © 1994 Dow Jones & Company, Inc. All Rights Reserved Worldwide and FORTUNE, © 1994 Time Inc. All rights reserved; discussion of megatrends, copyright © 1990 by Megatrends Ltd. By permission of William Morrow & Company, Inc.; discussion of generic corporate- and business-level strategies, © 1988, adapted by permission of Prentice-Hall, Upper Saddle River, NJ; Exhibit 3.7, reprinted by permission from Cynthia A. Lengneck-Hall and Mark L. Lengneck-Hall, 'Strategic Human Resources Management: A Review of the Literature and a Proposed Typology,' Academy of Management Review, Vol. 13, No. 3 (July 1988), p. 467.

CHAPTER 4: example of company policy on sexual harassment, based on General Motors' Corporate policy on sexual harassment. Used with permission of General Motors; Focus on International Issues box (Danish Women Begin to Sing "I've Been Working on the Railroad"), reprinted by permission of The Wall Street Journal, © 1994 Dow Jones & Company, Inc. All Rights Reserved Worldwide; Exhibit 4.10, FORTUNE, © 1991 Time Inc. All rights reserved; Exhibit 4.11, reprinted with the permission of PERSONNEL JOURNAL, ACC Communications, Inc., Costa Mesa, California, all rights reserved; Exhibit 4.12, reprinted with permission of Olsten Corporation.

CHAPTER 7: Exhibit 7.3, reprinted with their permission of HR Magazine published by the Society for Human Resource Management, Alexandria, VA; Exhibit 7.5a, reprinted with the permission of HR Magazine published by the society for Human Resource Management, Alexandria, VA; Exhibit 7.5b, reprinted by permission of The Wall Street Journal, © 1994 Dow Jones & Company, Inc. All Rights Reserved Worldwide; Exhibit 7.8, reprinted by permission from the National Business Employment Weekly, © Dow Jones & Company, Inc. All Rights Reserved Worldwide; HR Challenge box ("Exactly What Is a Personality Inventory?"), adaptation reprinted with their permission of HR Magazine published by the Society for Human Resource Management, Alexandria, VA; end-of-chapter case, some text reprinted by permission of The Wall Street Journal, © 1994 Dow Jones & Company, Inc. All Rights Reserved Worldwide.

CHAPTER 8: Exhibit 8.4, reprinted by permission of The Wall Street Journal, © 1990 Dow Jones & Company, Inc. All Rights Reserved Worldwide.

CHAPTER 9: chapter-opening case, some text from 'Journey Toward a More Inclusive Culture,' by Linda Thornburg, HR Magazine (February 1994); Exhibit 9.5, reprinted by permission from Quaker Oats Company; copyright © Quaker Oats Company. All Rights Reserved; Exhibit 9.8, from Training in Organizations by I. L. Goldstein, (2nd edition), p. 16. Copyright © 1993, 1986, 1974 Brooks/Cole Publishing Company, a division of International Thomson Publishing Inc., Pacific Grove, CA 93950. By permission of the publisher; Exhibit 9.10, reprinted with the permission of HR Magazine published by the Society for Human Resource Management, Alexandria, VA.

CHAPTER 11: Exhibit 11.3, George Milkovich and Jerry Newman, Compensation, second edition, Irwin © 1987, p. 16; Exhibit 11.10, © Toys "R" Us, Inc., 1994.

CHAPTER 12: Exhibit 12.1, reprinted by permission of The Wall Street Journal, © 1992 Dow Jones & Company, Inc. All Rights Reserved Worldwide; and reprinted from October 8, 1991 issue of Business Week by special permission, copyright © 91 by McGraw-Hill, Inc.; Exhibit 12.2, FORTUNE, © 1991 Time Inc. All rights reserved; Exhibit 12.4, reprinted by permission of The Wall Street Journal, © 1989 Dow Jones & Company, Inc. All Rights Reserved Worldwide; Exhibit 12.7, reprinted from OUT OF CRISIS by W. Edwards Deming by permission of MIT and The W. Edwards Deming Institute. Published by MIT, Center for Advanced Engineering Study, Cambridge, MA 02139. Copyright 1986 by The W. Edwards Deming Institute; Exhibit 12.10, FORTUNE, © 1994 Time Inc. All rights reserved; Exhibit 12.11, © 1994 Associated Press; Exhibit 12.13, © Ford Motor Company. Reprinted with permission.

CHAPTER 13: chapter-opening case, based on 'Clarifying the Choices,' by Beth Rogers, HR Magazine (March 1993); Exhibit 13.1, from Salaried Employee Benefits Provided by Major U.S. Employers in 1994, Hewitt Associates; Exhibit 13.3, reprinted by permission from p. 401 of PERSONNEL/HUMAN RESOURCE MANAGEMENT, fifth edition, by Mathis & Jackson; copyright © 1988 by West Publishing Company. All rights reserved; Exhibit 13.4, reprinted by permission of The Wall Street Journal, © 1993 Dow Jones & Company, Inc. All Rights Reserved Worldwide; Exhibit 13.6, reprinted by permission of The Wall Street Journal, © 1991 Dow Jones & Company, Inc. All Rights Reserved Worldwide; Exhibit 13.7, reprinted from November 30, 1992 issue of BUSINESS WEEK by special permission, copyright © 1992 by McGraw-Hill, Inc.; Exhibit 13.8, © 1994 Associated Press; Exhibit 13.9, reprinted by permission of The

Wall Street Journal, © 1995 Dow Jones & Company, Inc. All Rights Reserved Worldwide; Exhibit 13.12, copyright 1994, USA TODAY. Reprinted with permission; Exhibit 13.15, reprinted by permission of The Wall Street Journal, © 1993 Dow Jones & Company, Inc. All Rights Reserved Worldwide; chapter-ending case, reprinted by permission of The Wall Street Journal, © 1993 Dow Jones & Company, Inc. All Rights Reserved Worldwide.

CHAPTER 14: HR Challenge box ("A Matter of Degree") reprinted by permission of The Wall Street Journal, © 1994 Dow Jones & Company, Inc. All Rights Reserved Worldwide; Exhibit 14.6, reprinted by permission of The Wall Street Journal, © 1989 Dow Jones & Company, Inc. All Rights Reserved Worldwide.

CHAPTER 15: Adapted from the article 'New Plant Closing Law Aids Workers in Transition,' by Paul Staudohar, copyright 1989. Reprinted with permission of PERSONNEL JOURNAL, ACC Communications, Inc., Costa Mesa, California, all rights reserved.

CHAPTER 16: Exhibit 16.1, reprinted by permission of The Wall Street Journal, © 1993 Dow Jones & Company, Inc. All Rights Reserved Worldwide; Exhibit 16.2, reprinted by permission of The Wall Street Journal, © 1994 Dow Jones & Company, Inc. All Rights Reserved Worldwide; Exhibit 16.4, data from Richard Freeman, National Bureau of Economic Research, and Leo Troy, Rutgers University; HR Challenge ("Working with a Union to Save Jobs and Increase Profits"), reprinted from April 25, 1994 issue of BUSINESS WEEK by special permission, copyright © 1994 by McGraw-Hill, Inc.; HR Challenge ("Using Teams Could Be Hazardous to Your Company's Health"), adapted by permission of The Wall Street Journal, © 1993 Dow Jones & Company, Inc. All Rights Reserved Worldwide; Exhibit 16.10, FORTUNE, © 1993 Time Inc. All rights reserved.

CHAPTER 17: Exhibits 17.5, 17.6, and 17.9, People Trends (September 1993), p. 2. Reprinted with permission; Exhibit 17.7, reprinted by permission of The Wall Street Journal, © 1993 Dow Jones & Company, Inc. All Rights Reserved Worldwide; Exhibits 17.8 and 17.14, reprinted by permission of The Wall Street Journal, © 1994 Dow Jones & Company, Inc. All Rights Reserved Worldwide; Exhibit 17.10, People Trends (April 1994), p. 12. Reprinted with permission; Exhibit 17.12, FORTUNE, © 1993 Time Inc. All rights reserved; Exhibit 17.15, from 'HR Services Most Frequently Outsourced,' by Bill Leonard (July 1994). Reprinted with the permission of HR Magazine published by the Society for Human Resource Management, Alexandria, VA; Exhibit 17.16, from 'Word of Caution on the Temporary Workforce,' by Earnest R. Archer (September 1994). Reprinted with the permission of HR Magazine published by the Society for Human Resource Management, Alexandria, VA; Exhibit 17.17, FORTUNE, © 1994 Time Inc. All rights reserved.